THE COMPLETE WORKS OF

WILLIAM
SHAKESPEARE

THE COMPLETE WORKS OF

WILLIAM SHAKESPEARE

ARRANGED IN THEIR CHRONOLOGICAL ORDER

Edited by

W. G. CLARK AND W. ALDIS WRIGHT

WITH AN INTRODUCTION TO EACH PLAY,
ADAPTED FROM THE SHAKESPEAREAN
PRIMER OF PROFESSOR DOWDEN

Volume One

NELSON DOUBLEDAY, INC.
Garden City   *New York*

CONTENTS.

Volume One.

Volume Two.

TITUS ANDRONICUS.

(WRITTEN ABOUT 1588-90.)

INTRODUCTION.

The great majority of English critics either reject this play altogether, upon the ground that in style and subject it is unlike any other work of Shakespeare, or accept as true the tradition of *Ravenscroft*, who altered the play in 1687, that " it was not his [Shakespeare's]," but that he only gave " some master-touches to one or two of the principal parts or characters." Says one critic : " Shakespeare's tragedy is never bloodily sensual ; . . . . this play is a perfect slaughter-house, and the blood makes appeal to all the senses. . . . . It reeks blood, it smells of blood, we almost feel that we have handled blood—it is so gross." Besides the tradition of *Ravenscroft*, the external evidence with reference to the authorship of *Titus* is the following : (1) It is mentioned by Meres (1598) among other undoubted plays of Shakespeare. (2) It is printed in the First Folio. A play called *Titus and Vespasian* was acted in 1592, and though itself lost, a translation into German, acted early in the 17th century by English comedians in Germany, remains in existence. It is not the play attributed to Shakespeare. Henslowe also mentions a *Titus and Andronicus* as a new play, acted January 23, 1594 : it is doubtful whether this was the Shakespearean play. If it be, and it was then written, the tragedy is certainly not by Shakespeare. It is impossible to believe that in 1594, when Shakespeare had written his *Venus and Adonis* and his *Lucrece*, he could have dealt so coarsely with details of outrage and unnatural cruelty as does the author of this tragedy. Ben Jonson, in the introduction to *Bartholomew Fair* (1614), speaks of *Titus Andronicus*, with *Jeronimo*, as belonging to " twenty-five or thirty years " previously : this would carry back the date of the play (if it be of this *Titus Andronicus* that Jonson speaks) to 1589, or earlier. That it was a play of that period, and was re-touched by Shakespeare, we may accept as the opinion best supported by internal evidence and by the weight of critical authority. The importance of the tragedy lies in the fact that, if Shakespeare wrote it, we find him as a young man carried away by the influence of a " storm and stress " movement similar to that which urged Schiller to write his *Robbers*. *Titus Andronicus* belongs essentially to the pre-Shakespearean group of bloody tragedies, of which Kyd's *Spanish Tragedy* is the most conspicuous example. If it is of Shakespearean authorship, it may be regarded as representing the years of crude and violent youth before he had found his true self ; his second tragedy, *Romeo and Juliet,* as representing the years of transition ; and *Hamlet,* the period of maturity and adult power.

DRAMATIS PERSONÆ.

SATURNINUS, son to the late Emperor of Rome, and afterwards declared Emperor.
BASSIANUS, brother to Saturninus ; in love with Lavinia.
TITUS ANDRONICUS, a noble Roman, general against the Goths.
MARCUS ANDRONICUS, tribune of the people, and brother to Titus.
LUCIUS,
QUINTUS,
MARTIUS, } sons to Titus Andronicus.
MUTIUS,
YOUNG LUCIUS, a boy, son to Lucius.
PUBLIUS, son to Marcus the Tribune.
SEMPRONIUS,
CAIUS, } kinsmen to Titus.
VALENTINE,

ÆMILIUS, a noble Roman.
ALARBUS,
DEMETRIUS, } sons to Tamora.
CHIRON,
AARON, a Moor, beloved by Tamora.
A Captain, Tribune, Messenger, and Clown ; Romans.
Goths and Romans.

TAMORA, Queen of the Goths.
LAVINIA, daughter of Titus Andronicus.
A Nurse.

Senators, Tribunes, Officers, Soldiers, and Attendants.

SCENE : *Rome, and the country near it.*

ACT I.

SCENE I. *Rome. Before the Capitol.*

The Tomb of the ANDRONICI *appearing; the* Tribunes *and* Senators *aloft. Enter, below, from one side,* SATURNINUS *and his* Followers; *and, from the other side,* BASSIANUS *and his* Followers; *with drum and colors.*

Sat. Noble patricians, patrons of my right,
Defend the justice of my cause with arms,
And, countrymen, my loving followers,
Plead my successive title with your swords :
I am his first-born son, that was the last
That wore the imperial diadem of Rome ;
Then let my father's honors live in me,
Nor wrong mine age with this indignity.

Bas. Romans, friends, followers, favorers
    of my right,
If ever Bassianus, Cæsar's son,   10
Were gracious in the eyes of royal Rome,
Keep then this passage to the Capitol
And suffer not dishonor to approach
The imperial seat, to virtue consecrate,
To justice, continence and nobility ;
But let desert in pure election shine,
And, Romans, fight for freedom in your choice.

Enter MARCUS ANDRONICUS, *aloft, with the crown.*

Marc. Princes, that strive by factions and
    by friends
Ambitiously for rule and empery,
Know that the people of Rome, for whom we
    stand   20
A special party, have, by common voice,
In election for the Roman empery,
Chosen Andronicus, surnamed Pius
For many good and great deserts to Rome :
A nobler man, a braver warrior,
Lives not this day within the city walls :
He by the senate is accited home
From weary wars against the barbarous Goths ;
That, with his sons, a terror to our foes,
Hath yoked a nation strong, train'd up in
    arms.   30
Ten years are spent since first he undertook
This cause of Rome and chastised with arms
Our enemies' pride : five times he hath re-
    turn'd
Bleeding to Rome, bearing his valiant sons
In coffins from the field ;
And now at last, laden with honor's spoils,
Returns the good Andronicus to Rome,
Renowned Titus, flourishing in arms.
Let us entreat, by honor of his name,
Whom worthily you would have now succeed.
And in the Capitol and senate's right,   41
Whom you pretend to honor and adore,
That you withdraw you and abate your
    strength ;
Dismiss your followers and, as suitors should,
Plead your deserts in peace and humbleness.

Sat. How fair the tribune speaks to calm
    my thoughts !

Bas. Marcus Andronicus, so I do affy
In thy uprightness and integrity,
And so I love and honor thee and thine,
Thy noble brother Titus and his sons,   50
And her to whom my thoughts are humbled
    all,

Gracious Lavinia, Rome's rich ornament,
That I will here dismiss my loving friends,
And to my fortunes and the people's favor
Commit my cause in balance to be weigh'd.
        [*Exeunt the followers of Bassianus.*

Sat. Friends, that have been thus forward
    in my right,
I thank you all and here dismiss you all,
And to the love and favor of my country
Commit myself, my person and the cause.
        [*Exeunt the followers of Saturninus.*
Rome, be as just and gracious unto me   60
As I am confident and kind to thee.
Open the gates, and let me in.

Bas. Tribunes, and me, a poor competitor.
        [*Flourish. Saturninus and Bassianus*
                 go up into the Capitol.

Enter a Captain.

Cap. Romans, make way : the good An-
    dronicus,
Patron of virtue, Rome's best champion,
Successful in the battles that he fights,
With honor and with fortune is return'd
From where he circumscribed with his sword,
And brought to yoke, the enemies of Rome.
    Drums and trumpets sounded. Enter MARTIUS
    and MUTIUS ; *after them, two* Men *bearing*
    a coffin covered with black ; then LUCIUS *and*
    QUINTUS. *After them,* TITUS ANDRONICUS ;
    and then TAMORA, *with* ALARBUS, DEME-
    TRIUS, CHIRON, AARON, *and other* Goths,
    prisoners ; Soldiers *and* people *following.*
    The Bearers *set down the coffin, and* TITUS
    speaks.

Tit. Hail, Rome, victorious in thy mourning
    weeds !   70
Lo, as the bark, that hath discharged her
    fraught,
Returns with precious lading to the bay
From whence at first she weigh'd her anchor-
    age,
Cometh Andronicus, bound with laurel boughs,
To re-salute his country with his tears,
Tears of true joy for his return to Rome.
Thou great defender of this Capitol,
Stand gracious to the rites that we intend !
Romans, of five and twenty valiant sons,
Half of the number that King Priam had,   80
Behold the poor remains, alive and dead !
These that survive let Rome reward with love ;
These that I bring unto their latest home,
With burial amongst their ancestors :
Here Goths have given me leave to sheathe my
    sword.
Titus, unkind and careless of thine own,
Why suffer'st thou thy sons, unburied yet,
To hover on the dreadful shore of Styx ?
Make way to lay them by their brethren.
        [*The tomb is opened.*
There greet in silence, as the dead are wont, 90
And sleep in peace, slain in your country's
    wars !
O sacred receptacle of my joys,
Sweet cell of virtue and nobility,
How many sons of mine hast thou in store,
That thou wilt never render to me more !

Luc. Give us the proudest prisoner of the
    Goths,
That we may hew his limbs, and on a pile
Ad manes fratrum sacrifice his flesh,
Before this earthy prison of their bones ;

That so the shadows be not unappeased, 100
Nor we disturb'd with prodigies on earth.
  Tit. I give him you, the noblest that survives,
The eldest son of this distressed queen.
  Tam. Stay, Roman brethren! Gracious conqueror,
Victorious Titus, rue the tears I shed,
A mother's tears in passion for her son :
And if thy sons were ever dear to thee,
O, think my son to be as dear to me!
Sufficeth not that we are brought to Rome,
To beautify thy triumphs and return, 110
Captive to thee and to thy Roman yoke,
But must my sons be slaughter'd in the streets,
For valiant doings in their country's cause ?
O, if to fight for king and commonweal
Were piety in thine, it is in these.
Andronicus, stain not thy tomb with blood :
Wilt thou draw near the nature of the gods ?
Draw near them then in being merciful :
Sweet mercy is nobility's true badge :
Thrice noble Titus, spare my first-born son.
  Tit. Patient yourself, madam, and pardon me. 121
These are their brethren, whom you Goths beheld
Alive and dead, and for their brethren slain
Religiously they ask a sacrifice :
To this your son is mark'd, and die he must,
To appease their groaning shadows that are gone.
  Luc. Away with him! and make a fire straight ;
And with our swords, upon a pile of wood,
Let's hew his limbs till they be clean consumed.
  [*Exeunt Lucius, Quintus, Martius, and Mutius, with Alarbus.*
  Tam. O cruel, irreligious piety! 130
  Chi. Was ever Scythia half so barbarous ?
  Dem. Oppose not Scythia to ambitious Rome.
Alarbus goes to rest ; and we survive
To tremble under Titus' threatening looks.
Then, madam, stand resolved, but hope withal
The self-same gods that arm'd the Queen of Troy
With opportunity of sharp revenge
Upon the Thracian tyrant in his tent,
May favor Tamora, the Queen of Goths—
When Goths were Goths and Tamora was queen— 140
To quit the bloody wrongs upon her foes.

  Re-enter LUCIUS, QUINTUS, MARTIUS, *and* MUTIUS, *with their swords bloody.*

  Luc. See, lord and father, how we have perform'd
Our Roman rites : Alarbus' limbs are lopp'd,
And entrails feed the sacrificing fire,
Whose smoke, like incense, doth perfume the sky.
Remaineth nought, but to inter our brethren,
And with loud 'larums welcome them to Rome.
  Tit. Let it be so ; and let Andronicus
Make this his latest farewell to their souls.
  [*Trumpets sounded, and the coffin laid in the tomb.*
In peace and honor rest you here, my sons ;
Rome's readiest champions, repose you here in rest, 151

Secure from worldly chances and mishaps!
Here lurks no treason, here no envy swells,
Here grow no damned grudges ; here are no storms,
No noise, but silence and eternal sleep :
In peace and honor rest you here, my sons!

           Enter LAVINIA

  Lav. In peace and honor live Lord Titus long ;
My noble lord and father, live in fame!
Lo, at this tomb my tributary tears
I render, for my brethren's obsequies ; 160
And at thy feet I kneel, with tears of joy,
Shed on the earth, for thy return to Rome :
O, bless me here with thy victorious hand,
Whose fortunes Rome's best citizens applaud!
  Tit. Kind Rome, that hast thus lovingly reserved
The cordial of mine age to glad my heart!
Lavinia, live ; outlive thy father's days,
And fame's eternal date, for virtue's praise!

  Enter, below, MARCUS ANDRONICUS *and* Tribunes ; *re-enter* SATURNINUS *and* BASSIANUS, *attended.*

  Marc. Long live Lord Titus, my beloved brother,
Gracious triumpher in the eyes of Rome! 170
  Tit. Thanks, gentle tribune, noble brother Marcus.
  Marc. And welcome, nephews, from successful wars,
You that survive, and you that sleep in fame!
Fair lords, your fortunes are alike in all,
That in your country's service drew your swords :
But safer triumph is this funeral pomp,
That hath aspired to Solon's happiness
And triumphs over chance in honor's bed.
Titus Andronicus, the people of Rome, 179
Whose friend in justice thou hast ever been,
Send thee by me, their tribune and their trust,
This palliament of white and spotless hue ;
And name thee in election for the empire,
With these our late-deceased emperor's sons :
Be candidatus then, and put it on,
And help to set a head on headless Rome.
  Tit. A better head her glorious body fits
Than his that shakes for age and feebleness :
What should I don this robe, and trouble you ?
Be chosen with proclamations to-day, 190
To-morrow yield up rule, resign my life,
And set abroad new business for you all ?
Rome, I have been thy soldier forty years,
And led my country's strength successfully,
And buried one and twenty valiant sons,
Knighted in field, slain manfully in arms,
In right and service of their noble country
Give me a staff of honor for mine age,
But not a sceptre to control the world :
Upright he held it, lords, that held it last. 200
  Marc. Titus, thou shalt obtain and ask the empery.
  Sat. Proud and ambitious tribune, canst thou tell ?
  Tit. Patience, Prince Saturninus.
  Sat.   Romans, do me right :
Patricians, draw your swords, and sheathe them not
Till Saturninus be Rome's emperor.

Andronicus, would thou wert shipp'd to hell,
Rather than rob me of the people's hearts!
    Luc. Proud Saturnine, interrupter of the
        good
That noble-minded Titus means to thee!
    Tit. Content thee, prince; I will restore to
        thee   210
The people's hearts, and wean them from
        themselves.
    Bas. Andronicus, I do not flatter thee,
But honor thee, and will do till I die:
My faction if thou strengthen with thy friends,
I will most thankful be; and thanks to men
Of noble minds is honorable meed.
    Tit. People of Rome, and people's tribunes
        here,
I ask your voices and your suffrages:
Will you bestow them friendly on Andro-
        nicus?
    Tribunes. To gratify the good Andronicus,
And gratulate his safe return to Rome,   221
The people will accept whom he admits.
    Tit. Tribunes, I thank you: and this suit I
        make,
That you create your emperor's eldest son,
Lord Saturnine; whose virtues will, I hope,
Reflect on Rome as Titan's rays on earth,
And ripen justice in this commonweal:
Then, if you will elect by my advice,
Crown him, and say 'Long live our emperor!'
    Marc. With voices and applause of every
        sort,   230
Patricians and plebeians, we create
Lord Saturninus Rome's great emperor,
And say 'Long live our Emperor Saturnine!'
        [*A long flourish till they come down.*
    Sat. Titus Andronicus, for thy favors done
To us in our election this day,
I give thee thanks in part of thy deserts,
And will with deeds requite thy gentleness:
And, for an onset, Titus, to advance
Thy name and honorable family,
Lavinia will I make my empress,   240
Rome's royal mistress, mistress of my heart,
And in the sacred Pantheon her espouse:
Tell me, Andronicus, doth this motion please
        thee?
    Tit. It doth, my worthy lord; and in this
        match
I hold me highly honor'd of your grace:
And here in sight of Rome to Saturnine,
King and commander of our commonweal,
The wide world's emperor, do I consecrate
My sword, my chariot and my prisoners;
Presents well worthy Rome's imperial lord:
Receive them then, the tribute that I owe, 251
Mine honor's ensigns humbled at thy feet.
    Sat. Thanks, noble Titus, father of my
        life!
How proud I am of thee and of thy gifts
Rome shall record, and when I do forget
The least of these unspeakable deserts,
Romans, forget your fealty to me.
    Tit. [*To Tamora*] Now, madam, are you
        prisoner to an emperor;
To him that, for your honor and your state,
Will use you nobly and your followers.   260
    Sat. A goodly lady, trust me; of the hue
That I would choose, were I to choose anew.
Clear up, fair queen, that cloudy counte-
        nance:

Though chance of war hath wrought this
        change of cheer,
Thou comest not to be made a scorn in
        Rome:
Princely shall be thy usage every way.
Rest on my word, and let not discontent
Daunt all your hopes: madam, he comforts
        you
Can make you greater than the Queen of
        Goths.
Lavinia, you are not displeased with this? 270
    Lav. Not I, my lord; sith true nobility
Warrants these words in princely courtesy.
    Sat. Thanks, sweet Lavinia. Romans, let
        us go;
Ransomless here we set our prisoners free:
Proclaim our honors, lords, with trump and
        drum.
        [*Flourish. Saturninus courts Tamora
                in dumb show.*
    Bas. Lord Titus, by your leave, this maid
        is mine.   [*Seizing Lavinia.*
    Tit. How, sir! are you in earnest then, my
        lord?
    Bas. Ay, noble Titus; and resolved withal
To do myself this reason and this right.
    Marc. 'Suum cuique' is our Roman jus-
        tice: 280
This prince in justice seizeth but his own.
    Luc. And that he will, and shall, if Lucius
        live.
    Tit. Traitors, avaunt! Where is the em-
        peror's guard?
Treason, my lord! Lavinia is surprised!
    Sat. Surprised! by whom?
    Bas.   By him that justly may
Bear his betroth'd from all the world away.
        [*Exeunt Bassianus and Marcus with Lavinia.*
    Mut. Brothers, help to convey her hence
        away,
And with my sword I'll keep this door safe.
        [*Exeunt Lucius, Quintus, and Martius.*
    Tit. Follow, my lord, and I'll soon bring
        her back.
    Mut. My lord, you pass not here.   289
    Tit.   What, villain boy!
Barr'st me my way in Rome?   [*Stabbing
                                        Mutius.*
    Mut.   Help, Lucius, help! [*Dies.*
[*During the fray, Saturninus, Tamora, Deme-
    trius, Chiron and Aaron go out and re-enter,
    above.*

                Re-enter LUCIUS.

    Luc. My lord, you are unjust, and, more
        than so,
In wrongful quarrel you have slain your son.
    Tit. Nor thou, nor he, are any sons of
        mine;
My sons would never so dishonor me:
Traitor, restore Lavinia to the emperor.
    Luc. Dead, if you will; but not to be his
        wife,
That is another's lawful promised love. [*Exit.*
    Sat. No, Titus, no; the emperor needs
        her not,
Nor her, nor thee, nor any of thy stock: 300
I'll trust, by leisure, him that mocks me
        once;
Thee ever, nor thy traitorous haughty sons,
Confederates all thus to dishonor me.
Was there none else in Rome to make a stale,

But Saturnine ? Full well, Andronicus,
Agree these deeds with that proud brag of
thine,
That said'st I begg'd the empire at thy hands.
   Tit. O monstrous ! what reproachful words
are these ?
   Sat. But go thy ways ; go, give that chang-
ing piece
To him that flourish'd for her with his sword :
A valiant son-in-law thou shalt enjoy ;   311
One fit to bandy with thy lawless sons,
To ruffle in the commonwealth of Rome.
   Tit. These words are razors to my wounded
heart.
   Sat. And therefore, lovely Tamora, queen
of Goths,
That like the stately Phœbe 'mongst her
nymphs
Dost overshine the gallant'st dames of Rome,
If thou be pleased with this my sudden choice,
Behold, I choose thee, Tamora, for my bride,
And will create thee empress of Rome,   320
Speak, Queen of Goths, dost thou applaud my
choice ?
And here I swear by all the Roman gods,
Sith priest and holy water are so near
And tapers burn so bright and every thing
In readiness for Hymenæus stand,
I will not re-salute the streets of Rome,
Or climb my palace, till from forth this place
I lead espoused my bride along with me.
   Tam. And here, in sight of heaven, to
Rome I swear,
If Saturnine advance the Queen of Goths, 330
She will a handmaid be to his desires,
A loving nurse, a mother to his youth.
   Sat. Ascend, fair queen, Pantheon. Lords,
accompany
Your noble emperor and his lovely bride,
Sent by the heavens for Prince Saturnine,
Whose wisdom hath her fortune conquered :
There shall we consummate our spousal rites.
              [Exeunt all but Titus.
   Tit. I am not bid to wait upon this bride.
Titus, when wert thou wont to walk alone, 339
Dishonor'd thus, and challenged of wrongs ?

Re-enter Marcus, Lucius, Quintus, *and*
Martius.

   Marc. O Titus, see, O, see what thou hast
done !
In a bad quarrel slain a virtuous son.
   Tit. No, foolish tribune, no ; no son of
mine,
Nor thou, nor these, confederates in the deed
That hath dishonor'd all our family ;
Unworthy brother, and unworthy sons !
   Luc. But let us give him burial, as be-
comes ;
Give Mutius burial with our brethren.
   Tit. Traitors, away ! he rests not in this
tomb :
This monument five hundred years hath stood,
Which I have sumptuously re-edified :   351
Here none but soldiers and Rome's servitors
Repose in fame ; none basely slain in brawls :
Bury him where you can ; he comes not here.
   Marc. My lord, this is impiety in you :
My nephew Mutius' deeds do plead for him ;
He must be buried with his brethren.
   Quin. } And shall, or him we will accom-
   Mart. }   pany.

   Tit. ' And shall ! ' what villain was it spake
that word ?
   Quin. He that would vouch it in any place
but here.   360
   Tit. What, would you bury him in my
despite ?
   Marc. No, noble Titus, but entreat of thee
To pardon Mutius and to bury him.
   Tit. Marcus, even thou hast struck upon
my crest,
And, with these boys, mine honor thou hast
wounded :
My foes I do repute you every one ;
So, trouble me no more, but get you gone.
   Mart. He is not with himself ; let us with-
draw.
   Quin. Not I, till Mutius' bones be buried.
       [Marcus and the Sons of Titus kneel.
   Marc. Brother, for in that name doth
nature plead,—   370
   Quin. Father, and in that name doth na-
ture speak,—
   Tit. Speak thou no more, if all the rest will
speed.
   Marc. Renowned Titus, more than half my
soul,—
   Luc. Dear father, soul and substance of
us all,—
   Marc. Suffer thy brother Marcus to inter
His noble nephew here in virtue's nest,
That died in honor and Lavinia's cause.
Thou art a Roman ; be not barbarous :
The Greeks upon advice did bury Ajax
That slew himself ; and wise Laertes' son 380
Did graciously plead for his funerals :
Let not young Mutius, then, that was thy joy
Be barr'd his entrance here.
   Tit.   Rise, Marcus, rise.
The dismall'st day is this that e'er I saw,
To be dishonor'd by my sons in Rome !
Well, bury him, and bury me the next.
           [Mutius is put into the tomb.
   Luc. There lie thy bones, sweet Mutius,
with thy friends,
Till we with trophies do adorn thy tomb.
   All. [*Kneeling*] No man shed tears for
noble Mutius ;
He lives in fame that died in virtue's cause.
   Marc. My lord, to step out of these dreary
dumps,   391
How comes it that the subtle Queen of Goths
Is of a sudden thus advanced in Rome ?
   Tit. I know not, Marcus ; but I know it is,
Whether by device or no, the heavens can
tell :
Is she not then beholding to the man
That brought her for this high good turn so
far ?
Yes, and will nobly him remunerate.

Flourish. Re-enter, from one side, Saturninus *attended,* Tamora, Demetrius, Chiron, *and* Aaron ; *from the other,* Bassianus, Lavinia, *and others.*

   Sat. So, Bassianus, you have play'd your
prize :
God give you joy, sir, of your gallant bride !
   Bas. And you of yours, my lord ! I say
no more,   401
Nor wish no less ; and so, I take my leave.
   Sat. Traitor, if Rome have law or we have
power,

Thou and thy faction shall repent this rape.
   Bas. Rape, call you it, my lord, to seize
      my own,
My truth-betrothed love and now my wife ?
But let the laws of Rome determine all ;
Meanwhile I am possess'd of that is mine.
   Sat. 'Tis good, sir : you are very short
      with us ;
But, if we live, we'll be as sharp with you. 410
   Bas. My lord, what I have done, as best I
      may,
Answer I must and shall do with my life.
Only thus much I give your grace to know :
By all the duties that I owe to Rome,
This noble gentleman, Lord Titus here,
Is in opinion and in honor wrong'd ;
That in the rescue of Lavinia
With his own hand did slay his youngest son,
In zeal to you and highly moved to wrath
To be controll'd in that he frankly gave : 420
Receive him, then, to favor, Saturnine,
That hath express'd himself in all his deeds
A father and a friend to thee and Rome.
   Tit. Prince Bassianus, leave to plead my
      deeds :
'Tis thou and those that have dishonor'd me.
Rome and the righteous heavens be my judge,
How I have loved and honor'd Saturnine !
   Tam. My worthy lord, if ever Tamora
Were gracious in those princely eyes of thine,
Then hear me speak indifferently for all ; 430
And at my suit, sweet, pardon what is past.
   Sat. What, madam ! be dishonor'd openly,
And basely put it up without revenge ?
   Tam. Not so, my lord ; the gods of Rome
      forfend
I should be author to dishonor you !
But on mine honor dare I undertake
For good Lord Titus' innocence in all ;
Whose fury not dissembled speaks his griefs :
Then, at my suit, look graciously on him ;
Lose not so noble a friend on vain suppose,
Nor with sour looks afflict his gentle heart.
[*Aside to Sat.*] My lord, be ruled by me, be
      won at last ;
Dissemble all your griefs and discontents :
You are but newly planted in your throne ;
Lest, then, the people, and patricians too,
Upon a just survey, take Titus' part,
And so supplant you for ingratitude,
Which Rome reputes to be a heinous sin,
Yield at entreats ; and then let me alone :
I'll find a day to massacre them all   450
And raze their faction and their family,
The cruel father and his traitorous sons,
To whom I sued for my dear son's life,
And make them know what 'tis to let a queen
Kneel in the streets and beg for grace in vain.
[*Aloud.*] Come, come, sweet emperor ; come,
      Andronicus ;
Take up this good old man, and cheer the
      heart
That dies in tempest of thy angry frown.
   Sat. Rise, Titus, rise ; my empress hath
      prevail'd.
   Tit. I thank your majesty, and her, my
      lord :   460
These words, these looks, infuse new life in
      me.
   Tam. Titus, I am incorporate in Rome,
A Roman now adopted happily,
And must advise the emperor for his good.

This day all quarrels die, Andronicus ;
And let it be mine honor, good my lord,
That I have reconciled your friends and you.
For you, Prince Bassianus, I have pass'd
My word and promise to the emperor,
That you will be more mild and tractable. 470
And fear not, lords, and you, Lavinia ;
By my advice, all humbled on your knees,
You shall ask pardon of his majesty.
   Luc. We do, and vow to heaven and to his
      highness,
That what we did was mildly as we might,
Tendering our sister's honor and our own.
   Marc. That, on mine honor, here I do pro-
      test.
   Sat. Away, and talk not ; trouble us no
      more.
   Tam. Nay, nay, sweet emperor, we must
      all be friends :   479
The tribune and his nephews kneel for grace ;
I will not be denied : sweet heart, look back.
   Sat. Marcus, for thy sake and thy brother's
      here,
And at my lovely Tamora's entreats,
I do remit these young men's heinous faults :
Stand up.
Lavinia, though you left me like a churl,
I found a friend, and sure as death I swore
I would not part a bachelor from the priest.
Come, if the emperor's court can feast two
      brides,
You are my guest, Lavinia, and your friends.
This day shall be a love-day, Tamora.   491
   Tit. To-morrow, an it please your majesty
To hunt the panther and the hart with me,
With horn and hound we'll give your grace
      bonjour.
   Sat. Be it so, Titus, and gramercy too.
               [*Flourish. Exeunt.*

ACT II.

SCENE I. *Rome. Before the Palace.*

Enter AARON.

   Aar. Now climbeth Tamora Olympus' top,
Safe out of fortune's shot ; and sits aloft,
Secure of thunder's crack or lightning flash ;
Advanced above pale envy's threatening reach.
As when the golden sun salutes the morn,
And, having gilt the ocean with his beams,
Gallops the zodiac in his glistering coach,
And overlooks the highest-peering hills ;
So Tamora :
Upon her wit doth earthly honor wait,   10
And virtue stoops and trembles at her frown.
Then, Aaron, arm thy heart, and fit thy
      thoughts,
To mount aloft with thy imperial mistress,
And mount her pitch, whom thou in triumph
      long
Hast prisoner held, fetter'd in amorous chains
And faster bound to Aaron's charming eyes
Than is Prometheus tied to Caucasus.
Away with slavish weeds and servile thoughts !
I will be bright, and shine in pearl and gold,
To wait upon this new-made empress.   20
To wait, said I ? to wanton with this queen,
This goddess, this Semiramis, this nymph,
This siren, that will charm Rome's Saturnine,

And see his shipwreck and his commonweal's.
Holloa ! what storm is this ?

Enter Demetrius *and* Chiron, *braving.*

Dem. Chiron, thy years want wit, thy wit
    wants edge,
And manners, to intrude where I am graced ;
And may, for aught thou know'st, affected be.
Chi. Demetrius, thou dost over-ween in
    all ;
And so in this, to bear me down with
    braves.   30
'Tis not the difference of a year or two
Makes me less gracious or thee more fortu-
    nate :
I am as able and as fit as thou
To serve, and to deserve my mistress' grace ;
And that my sword upon thee shall approve,
And plead my passions for Lavinia's love.
Aar. [*Aside*] Clubs, clubs ! these lovers will
    not keep the peace.
Dem. Why, boy, although our mother, un-
    advised,
Gave you a dancing-rapier by your side,
Are you so desperate grown, to threat your
    friends ?   40
Go to ; have your lath glued within your
    sheath
Till you know better how to handle it.
Chi. Meanwhile, sir, with the little skill I
    have,
Full well shalt thou perceive how much I dare.
Dem. Ay, boy, grow ye so brave ?
                     [*They draw.*
Aar. [*Coming forward*] Why, how now,
    lords !
So near the emperor's palace dare you draw,
And maintain such a quarrel openly ?
Full well I wot the ground of all this grudge :
I would not for a million of gold
The cause were known to them it most con-
    cerns ;   50
Nor would your noble mother for much more
Be so dishonour'd in the court of Rome.
For shame, put up.
Dem.   Not I, till I have sheathed
My rapier in his bosom and withal
Thrust these reproachful speeches down his
    throat
That he hath breathed in my dishonor here.
Chi. For that I am prepared and full re-
    solved.
Foul-spoken coward, that thunder'st with thy
    tongue,
And with thy weapon nothing darest perform !
Aar. Away, I say !   60
Now, by the gods that warlike Goths adore,
This petty brabble will undo us all.
Why, lords, and think you not how dangerous
It is to jet upon a prince's right ?
What, is Lavinia then become so loose,
Or Bassianus so degenerate,
That for her love such quarrels may be
    broach'd
Without controlment, justice, or revenge ?
Young lords, beware ! and should the em-
    press know
This discord's ground, the music would not
    please.   70
Chi. I care not, I, knew she and all the
    world :
I love Lavinia more than all the world.

Dem. Youngling, learn thou to make some
    meaner choice :
Lavinia is thine elder brother's hope.
Aar. Why, are ye mad ? or know ye not,
    in Rome
How furious and impatient they be,
And cannot brook competitors in love ?
I tell you, lords, you do but plot your deaths
By this device.
Chi.   Aaron, a thousand deaths
Would I propose to achieve her whom I
    love.   80
Aar. To achieve her ! how ?
Dem.   Why makest thou it so strange ?
She is a woman, therefore may be woo'd ;
She is a woman, therefore may be won ;
She is Lavinia, therefore must be loved.
What, man ! more water glideth by the mill
Than wots the miller of ; and easy it is
Of a cut loaf to steal a shive, we know :
Though Bassianus be the emperor's brother,
Better than he have worn Vulcan's badge.
Aar. [*Aside*] Ay, and as good as Satur-
    ninus may.   90
Dem. Then why should he despair that
    knows to court it
With words, fair looks and liberality ?
What, hast not thou full often struck a doe,
And borne her cleanly by the keeper's nose ?
Aar. Why, then, it seems, some certain
    snatch or so
Would serve your turns.
Chi.   Ay, so the turn were served.
Dem. Aaron, thou hast hit it.
Aar.   Would you had hit it
    too !
Then should not we be tired with this ado.
Why, hark ye, hark ye ! and are you such
    fools
To square for this ? would it offend you,
    then,   100
That both should speed ?
Chi. Faith, not me.
Dem.   Nor me, so I were
    one.
Aar. For shame, be friends, and join for
    that you jar :
'Tis policy and stratagem must do
That you affect ; and so must you resolve,
That what you cannot as you would achieve,
You must perforce accomplish as you may.
Take this of me : Lucrece was not more chaste
Than this Lavinia, Bassianus' love.
A speedier course than lingering languishment
Must we pursue, and I have found the path.
My lords, a solemn hunting is in hand ;
There will the lovely Roman ladies troop :
The forest walks are wide and spacious ;
And many unfrequented plots there are
Fitted by kind for rape and villany :
Single you thither then this dainty doe,
And strike her home by force, if not by
    words :
This way, or not at all, stand you in hope.
Come, come, our empress, with her sacred wit
To villany and vengeance consecrate,   121
Will we acquaint with all that we intend ;
And she shall file our engines with advice,
That will not suffer you to square yourselves,
But to your wishes' height advance you both.
The emperor's court is like the house of Fame,
The palace full of tongues, of eyes, and ears :

The woods are ruthless, dreadful, deaf, and
  dull ;
There speak, and strike, brave boys, and take
  your turns ;
There serve your lusts, shadow'd from heav-
  en's eye, 130
And revel in Lavinia's treasury.
  Chi. Thy counsel, lad, smells of no cow-
    ardice,
  Dem. Sit fas aut nefas, till I find the
    stream
To cool this heat, a charm to calm these fits,
Per Styga, per manes vehor.   [*Exeunt.*

SCENE II. *A forest near Rome. Horns and
    cry of hounds heard.*

Enter TITUS ANDRONICUS, *with* Hunters, &c.,
  MARCUS, LUCIUS, QUINTUS, *and* MARTIUS.

  Tit. The hunt is up, the morn is bright and
    grey,
The fields are fragrant and the woods are
  green :
Uncouple here and let us make a bay
And wake the emperor and his lovely bride
And rouse the prince and ring a hunter's peal,
That all the court may echo with the noise.
Sons, let it be your charge, as it is ours,
To attend the emperor's person carefully :
I have been troubled in my sleep this night,
But dawning day new comfort hath inspired.

*A cry of hounds and horns, winded in a peal.
  Enter* SATURNINUS, TAMORA, BASSIANUS,
  LAVINIA, DEMETRIUS, CHIRON, *and* At-
  tendants.

Many good morrows to your majesty ;   11
Madam, to you as many and as good :
I promised your grace a hunter's peal.
  Sat. And you have rung it lustily, my lord ;
Somewhat too early for new-married ladies.
  Bas. Lavinia, how say you ?
  Lav.   I say, no ;
I have been broad awake two hours and more.
  Sat. Come on, then ; horse and chariots let
    us have,
And to our sport. [*To Tamora*] Madam, now
  shall ye see
Our Roman hunting.
  Marc.   I have dogs, my lord, 20
Will rouse the proudest panther in the chase,
And climb the highest promontory top.
  Tit. And I have horse will follow where
    the game
Makes way, and run like swallows o'er the
  plain.
  Dem. Chiron, we hunt not, we, with horse
    nor hound,
But hope to pluck a dainty doe to ground.
                      [*Exeunt.*

SCENE III. *A lonely part of the forest.*
  Enter AARON, *with a bag of gold.*

  Aar. He that had wit would think that I
    had none,
To bury so much gold under a tree,
And never after to inherit it.
Let him that thinks of me so abjectly
Know that this gold must coin a stratagem,
Which, cunningly effected, will beget
A very excellent piece of villany :

And so repose, sweet gold, for their unrest
                   [*Hides the gold.*
That have their alms out of the empress' chest.

Enter TAMORA.

  Tam. My lovely Aaron, wherefore look'st
    thou sad,   10
When every thing doth make a gleeful boast ?
The birds chant melody on every bush,
The snake lies rolled in the cheerful sun,
The green leaves quiver with the cooling wind
And make a chequer'd shadow on the ground :
Under their sweet shade, Aaron, let us sit,
And, whilst the babbling echo mocks the
  hounds,
Replying shrilly to the well-tuned horns,
As if a double hunt were heard at once,   19
Let us sit down and mark their yelping noise ;
And, after conflict such as was supposed
The wandering prince and Dido once enjoy'd,
When with a happy storm they were surprised
And curtain'd with a counsel-keeping cave,
We may, each wreathed in the other's arms,
Our pastimes done, possess a golden slumber ;
Whiles hounds and horns and sweet melodious
  birds
Be unto us as is a nurse's song
Of lullaby to bring her babe asleep.
  Aar. Madam, though Venus govern your
    desires,   30
Saturn is dominator over mine :
What signifies my deadly-standing eye,
My silence and my cloudy melancholy,
My fleece of woolly hair that now uncurls
Even as an adder when she doth unroll
To do some fatal execution ?
No, madam, these are no venereal signs :
Vengeance is in my heart, death in my hand,
Blood and revenge are hammering in my head.
Hark, Tamora, the empress of my soul,   40
Which never hopes more heaven than rests in
  thee,
This is the day of doom for Bassianus :
His Philomel must lose her tongue to-day,
Thy sons make pillage of her chastity
And wash their hands in Bassianus' blood.
Seest thou this letter ? take it up, I pray thee,
And give the king this fatal plotted scroll.
Now question me no more ; we are espied ;
Here comes a parcel of our hopeful booty,
Which dreads not yet their lives' destruc-
  tion.   50
  Tam. Ah, my sweet Moor, sweeter to me
    than life !
  Aar. No more, great empress ; Bassianus
    comes :
Be cross with him ; and I'll go fetch thy sons
To back thy quarrels, whatsoe'er they be.
                      [*Exit.*

Enter BASSIANUS *and* LAVINIA.

  Bas. Who have we here ? Rome's royal
    empress,
Unfurnish'd of her well-beseeming troop ?
Or is it Dian, habited like her,
Who hath abandoned her holy groves
To see the general hunting in this forest ?
  Tam. Saucy controller of our private
    steps !
Had I the power that some say Dian had,   61
Thy temples should be planted presently
With horns, as was Actæon's ; and the hounds

Should drive upon thy new-transformed limbs,
Unmannerly intruder as thou art!
  Lav. Under your patience, gentle empress,
'Tis thought you have a goodly gift in horn-
  ing;
And to be doubted that your Moor and you
Are singled forth to try experiments:
Jove shield your husband from his hounds
  to-day!   70
'Tis pity they should take him for a stag.
  Bas. Believe me, queen, your swarth Cim-
    merian
Doth make your honor of his body's hue,
Spotted, detested, and abominable.
Why are you sequester'd from all your train,
Dismounted from your snow-white goodly
  steed,
And wander'd hither to an obscure plot,
Accompanied but with a barbarous Moor,
If foul desire had not conducted you?
  Lav. And, being intercepted in your sport,
Great reason that my noble lord be rated 81
For sauciness. I pray you, let us hence,
And let her joy her raven-color'd love;
This valley fits the purpose passing well.
  Bas. The king my brother shall have note
    of this.
  Lav. Ay, for these slips have made him
    noted long:
Good king, to be so mightily abused!
  Tam. Why have I patience to endure all
    this?

    Enter Demetrius *and* Chiron.

  Dem. How now, dear sovereign, and our
    gracious mother!
Why doth your highness look so pale and
    wan?
  Tam. Have I not reason, think you, to
    look pale?   91
These two have 'ticed me hither to this place:
A barren detested vale, you see it is;
The trees, though summer, yet forlorn and
  lean,
O'ercome with moss and baleful mistletoe:
Here never shines the sun; here nothing
  breeds,
Unless the nightly owl or fatal raven:
And when they show'd me this abhorred pit,
They told me, here, at dead time of the night,
A thousand fiends, a thousand hissing snakes,
Ten thousand swelling toads, as many urchins,
Would make such fearful and confused cries
As any mortal body hearing it
Should straight fall mad, or else die suddenly.
No sooner had they told this hellish tale,
But straight they told me they would bind me
  here
Unto the body of a dismal yew,
And leave me to this miserable death:
And then they call'd me foul adulteress,
Lascivious Goth, and all the bitterest terms
That ever ear did hear to such effect: 111
And, had you not by wondrous fortune come,
This vengeance on me had they executed.
Revenge it, as you love your mother's life,
Or be ye not henceforth call'd my children.
  Dem. This is a witness that I am thy son.
    [*Stabs Bassianus.*
  Chi. And this for me, struck home to show
    my strength.
    [*Also stabs Bassianus, who dies.*

  Lav. Ay, come, Semiramis, nay, barbarous
    Tamora,
For no name fits thy nature but thy own!
  Tam. Give me thy poniard; you shall
    know, my boys,   120
Your mother's hand shall right your mother's
  wrong.
  Dem. Stay, madam; here is more belongs
    to her;
First thrash the corn, then after burn the
    straw:
This minion stood upon her chastity,
Upon her nuptial vow, her loyalty,
And with that painted hope braves your
    mightiness:
And shall she carry this unto her grave?
  Chi. An if she do, I would I were an eu-
    nuch.
Drag hence her husband to some secret hole,
And make his dead trunk pillow to our lust.
  Tam. But when ye have the honey ye de-
    sire,   131
Let not this wasp outlive, us both to sting.
  Chi. I warrant you, madam, we will make
    that sure.
Come, mistress, now perforce we will enjoy
That nice-preserved honesty of yours.
  Lav. O Tamora! thou bear'st a woman's
    face,—
  Tam. I will not hear her speak; away with
    her!
  Lav. Sweet lords, entreat her hear me but
    a word.
  Dem. Listen, fair madam: let it be your
    glory
To see her tears; but be your heart to them
As unrelenting flint to drops of rain.   141
  Lav. When did the tiger's young ones
    teach the dam?
O, do not learn her wrath; she taught it thee;
The milk thou suck'dst from her did turn to
    marble;
Even at thy teat thou hadst thy tyranny.
Yet every mother breeds not sons alike:
[*To Chiron*] Do thou entreat her show a
    woman pity.
  Chi. What, wouldst thou have me prove
    myself a bastard?
  Lav. 'Tis true; the raven doth not hatch a
    lark:
Yet have I heard,—O, could I find it now!—
The lion moved with pity did endure   151
To have his princely paws pared all away:
Some say that ravens foster forlorn children,
The whilst their own birds famish in their
    nests:
O, be to me, though thy hard heart say no,
Nothing so kind, but something pitiful!
  Tam. I know not what it means; away
    with her!
  Lav. O, let me teach thee! for my father's
    sake,
That gave thee life, when well he might have
    slain thee,
Be not obdurate, open thy deaf ears.   160
  Tam. Hadst thou in person ne'er offended
    me,
Even for his sake am I pitiless.
Remember, boys, I pour'd forth tears in vain,
To save your brother from the sacrifice;
But fierce Andronicus would not relent;

Therefore, away with her, and use her as you
  will,
The worse to her, the better loved of me.
  Lav. O Tamora, be call'd a gentle queen,
And with thine own hands kill me in this
  place !
For 'tis not life that I have begg'd so long ;170
Poor I was slain when Bassianus died.
  Tam. What begg'st thou, then ? fond
  woman, let me go.
  Lav. 'Tis present death I beg ; and one
  thing more
That womanhood denies my tongue to tell :
O, keep me from their worse than killing lust,
And tumble me into some loathsome pit,
Where never man's eye may behold my body :
Do this, and be a charitable murderer.
  Tam. So should I rob my sweet sons of
  their fee :
No, let them satisfy their lust on thee.   180
  Dem. Away ! for thou hast stay'd us here
  too long.
  Lav. No grace ? no womanhood ? Ah,
  beastly creature !
The blot and enemy to our general name !
Confusion fall—
  Chi. Nay, then I'll stop your mouth. Bring
  thou her husband :
This is the hole where Aaron bid us hide him.
  [*Demetrius throws the body of Bassianus
  into the pit ; then exeunt Demetrius and
  Chiron, dragging off Lavinia.*
  Tam. Farewell, my sons : see that you
  make her sure.
Ne'er let my heart know merry cheer indeed,
Till all the Andronici be made away.
Now will I hence to seek my lovely Moor, 190
And let my spleenful sons this trull deflour.
  [*Exit.*

Re-enter AARON, *with* QUINTUS *and* MARTIUS.

  Aar. Come on, my lords, the better foot
  before :
Straight will I bring you to the loathsome pit
Where I espied the panther fast asleep.
  Quin. My sight is very dull, whate'er it
  bodes.
  Mart. And mine, I promise you ; were't
  not for shame,
Well could I leave our sport to sleep awhile.
  [*Falls into the pit.*
  Quin. What, art thou fall'n ? What subtle
  hole is this,
Whose mouth is cover'd with rude-growing
  briers,
Upon whose leaves are drops of new-shed
  blood   200
As fresh as morning dew distill'd on flowers ?
A very fatal place it seems to me.
Speak, brother, hast thou hurt thee with the
  fall ?
  Mart. O brother, with the dismall'st ob-
  ject hurt
That ever eye with sight made heart lament !
  Aar. [*Aside*] Now will I fetch the king to
  find them here,
That he thereby may give a likely guess
How these were they that made away his
  brother.   [*Exit.*
  Mart. Why dost not comfort me, and help
  me out   209

From this unhallowed and blood-stained
  hole ?
  Quin. I am surprised with an uncouth
  fear ;
A chilling sweat o'er-runs my trembling
  joints :
My heart suspects more than mine eye can
  see.
  Mart. To prove thou hast a true-divining
  heart,
Aaron and thou look down into this den,
And see a fearful sight of blood and death.
  Quin. Aaron is gone ; and my compassion-
  ate heart
Will not permit mine eyes once to behold
The thing whereat it trembles by surmise ;
O, tell me how it is ; for ne'er till now   220
Was I a child to fear I know not what.
  Mart. Lord Bassianus lies embrewed here,
All on a heap, like to a slaughter'd lamb,
In this detested, dark, blood-drinking pit.
  Quin. If it be dark, how dost thou know
  'tis he ?
  Mart. Upon his bloody finger he doth
  wear
A precious ring, that lightens all the hole,
Which, like a taper in some monument,
Doth shine upon the dead man's earthy
  cheeks,
And shows the ragged entrails of the pit : 230
So pale did shine the moon on Pyramus
When he by night lay bathed in maiden blood.
O brother, help me with thy fainting hand—
If fear hath made thee faint, as me it hath—
Out of this fell devouring receptacle,
As hateful as Cocytus' misty mouth.
  Quin. Reach me thy hand, that I may help
  thee out ;
Or, wanting strength to do thee so much good,
I may be pluck'd into the swallowing womb
Of this deep pit, poor Bassianus' grave.   240
I have no strength to pluck thee to the brink.
  Mart. Nor I no strength to climb without
  thy help.
  Quin. Thy hand once more ; I will not
  loose again,
Till thou art here aloft, or I below :
Thou canst not come to me : I come to thee.
  [*Falls in.*

Enter SATURNINUS *with* AARON.

  Sat. Along with me : I'll see what hole is
  here,
And what he is that now is leap'd into it.
Say who art thou that lately didst descend
Into this gaping hollow of the earth ?
  Mart. The unhappy son of old Andro-
  nicus :
Brought hither in a most unlucky hour,   251
To find thy brother Bassianus dead.
  Sat. My brother dead ! I know thou dost
  but jest :
He and his lady both are at the lodge
Upon the north side of this pleasant chase ;
'Tis not an hour since I left him there.
  Mart. We know not where you left him all
  alive ;
But, out, alas ! here have we found him dead.

Re-enter TAMORA, *with* Attendants ; TITUS
  ANDRONICUS, *and* LUCIUS.

  Tam. Where is my lord the king ?

Sat. Here, Tamora, though grieved with
　　killing grief. 260
Tam. Where is thy brother Bassianus ?
Sat. Now to the bottom dost thou search
　　my wound :
Poor Bassianus here lies murdered.
Tam. Then all too late I bring this fatal
　　writ,
The complot of this timeless tragedy ;
And wonder greatly that man's face can fold
In pleasing smiles such murderous tyranny.
　　　　　[*She giveth Saturnine a letter.*
Sat. [*Reads*] ' An if we miss to meet him
　　handsomely—
Sweet huntsman, Bassianus 'tis we mean—
Do thou so much as dig the grave for
　　him : 270
Thou know'st our meaning. Look for thy re-
　　ward
Among the nettles at the elder-tree
Which overshades the mouth of that same pit
Where we decreed to bury Bassianus.
Do this, and purchase us thy lasting friends.'
O Tamora ! was ever heard the like ?
This is the pit, and this the elder-tree.
Look, sirs, if you can find the huntsman out
That should have murdered Bassianus here.
Aar. My gracious lord, here is the bag of
　　gold. 280
Sat. [*To Titus*] Two of thy whelps, fell curs
　　of bloody kind,
Have here bereft my brother of his life.
Sirs, drag them from the pit unto the prison :
There let them bide until we have devised
Some never-heard-of torturing pain for them.
Tam. What, are they in this pit ? O won-
　　drous thing !
How easily murder is discovered !
Tit. High emperor, upon my feeble knee
I beg this boon, with tears not lightly shed,
That this fell fault of my accursed sons, 290
Accursed, if the fault be proved in them,—
Sat. If it be proved ! you see it is apparent.
Who found this letter ? Tamora, was it you ?
Tam. Andronicus himself did take it up.
Tit. I did, my lord : yet let me be their
　　bail ;
For, by my father's reverend tomb, I vow
They shall be ready at your highness' will
To answer their suspicion with their lives.
Sat. Thou shalt not bail them : see thou
　　follow me.
Some bring the murder'd body, some the mur-
　　derers : 300
Let them not speak a word ; the guilt is plain ;
For, by my soul, were there worse end than
　　death,
That end upon them should be executed.
Tam. Andronicus, I will entreat the king ;
Fear not thy sons ; they shall do well enough.
Tit. Come, Lucius, come ; stay not to talk
　　with them. [*Exeunt.*

SCENE IV. *Another part of the forest.*

Enter DEMETRIUS *and* CHIRON *with* LAVINIA,
*ravished ; her hands cut off, and her tongue
cut out.*

Dem. So, now go tell, an if thy tongue can
　　speak,
Who 'twas that cut thy tongue and ravish'd
　　thee.

Chi. Write down thy mind, bewray thy
　　meaning so,
An if thy stumps will let thee play the scribe.
Dem. See, how with signs and tokens she
　　can scrowl.
Chi. Go home, call for sweet water, wash
　　thy hands.
Dem. She hath no tongue to call, nor
　　hands to wash ;
And so let's leave her to her silent walks.
Chi. An 'twere my case, I should go hang
　　myself.
Dem. If thou hadst hands to help thee
　　knit the cord. 10
　　　　　[*Exeunt Demetrius and Chiron.*

Enter MARCUS.

Mar. Who is this ? my niece, that flies
　　away so fast !
Cousin, a word ; where is your husband ?
If I do dream, would all my wealth would
　　wake me !
If I do wake, some planet strike me down,
That I may slumber in eternal sleep !
Speak, gentle niece, what stern ungentle hands
Have lopp'd and hew'd and made thy body
　　bare
Of her two branches, those sweet ornaments,
Whose circling shadows kings have sought to
　　sleep in,
And might not gain so great a happiness 20
As have thy love ? Why dost not speak to me ?
Alas, a crimson river of warm blood,
Like to a bubbling fountain stirr'd with wind,
Doth rise and fall between thy rosed lips,
Coming and going with thy honey breath.
But, sure, some Tereus hath deflowered thee,
And, lest thou shouldst detect him, cut thy
　　tongue.
Ah, now thou turn'st away thy face for
　　shame !
And, notwithstanding all this loss of blood,
As from a conduit with three issuing spouts,
Yet do thy cheeks look red as Titan's face 31
Blushing to be encountered with a cloud.
Shall I speak for thee ? shall I say 'tis so ?
O, that I knew thy heart ; and knew the beast,
That I might rail at him, to ease my mind !
Sorrow concealed, like an oven stopp'd,
Doth burn the heart to cinders where it is.
Fair Philomela, she but lost her tongue,
And in a tedious sampler sew'd her mind :
But, lovely niece, that mean is cut from thee ;
A craftier Tereus, cousin, hast thou met, 41
And he hath cut those pretty fingers off,
That could have better sew'd than Philomel.
O, had the monster seen those lily hands
Tremble, like aspen-leaves, upon a lute,
And make the silken strings delight to kiss
　　them,
He would not then have touch'd them for his
　　life !
Or, had he heard the heavenly harmony
Which that sweet tongue hath made,
He would have dropp'd his knife, and fell
　　asleep 50
As Cerberus at the Thracian poet's feet.
Come, let us go, and make thy father blind ;
For such a sight will blind a father's eye :
One hour's storm will drown the fragrant
　　meads ;

What will whole months of tears thy father's
  eyes ?
Do not draw back, for we will mourn with
  thee
O, could our mourning ease thy misery !
                                  [Exeunt.

ACT III.

SCENE I. *Rome. A street.*

Enter Judges, Senators *and* Tribunes, *with*
MARTIUS *and* QUINTUS, *bound, passing on
to the place of execution;* TITUS *going before, pleading.*

Tit. Hear me, grave fathers ! noble trib-
  unes, stay !
For pity of mine age, whose youth was spent
In dangerous wars, whilst you securely slept ;
For all my blood in Rome's great quarrel
  shed ;
For all the frosty nights that I have watch'd ;
And for these bitter tears, which now you see
Filling the aged wrinkles in my cheeks ;
Be pitiful to my condemned sons,
Whose souls are not corrupted as 'tis thought.
For two and twenty sons I never wept,   10
Because they died in honor's lofty bed.
    *[Lieth down ; the Judges, &c., pass by
            him, and Exeunt.*
For these, these, tribunes, in the dust I write
My heart's deep languor and my soul's sad
  tears :
Let my tears stanch the earth's dry appetite ;
My sons' sweet blood will make it shame and
  blush.
O earth, I will befriend thee more with rain,
That shall distil from these two ancient urns,
Than youthful April shall with all his
  showers :
In summer's drought I'll drop upon thee still ;
In winter with warm tears I'll melt the
  snow,   20
And keep eternal spring-time on thy face,
So thou refuse to drink my dear sons' blood.

Enter LUCIUS, *with his sword drawn.*

O reverend tribunes ! O gentle, aged men !
Unbind my sons, reverse the doom of death ;
And let me say, that never wept before,
My tears are now prevailing orators.
  Luc. O noble father, you lament in vain :
The tribunes hear you not ; no man is by ;
And you recount your sorrows to a stone.
  Tit. Ah, Lucius, for thy brothers let me
  plead.   30
Grave tribunes, once more I entreat of you,—
  Luc. My gracious lord, no tribune hears
  you speak.
  Tit. Why, 'tis no matter, man ; if they did
  hear,
They would not mark me, or if they did mark,
They would not pity me, yet plead I must ;
And bootless unto them . . . .
Therefore I tell my sorrows to the stones ;
Who, though they cannot answer my distress,
Yet in some sort they are better than the
  tribunes,
For that they will not intercept my tale :   40
When I do weep, they humbly at my feet
Receive my tears and seem to weep with me ;

And, were they but attired in grave weeds,
Rome could afford no tribune like to these.
A stone is soft as wax,—tribunes more hard
  than stones ;
A stone is silent, and offendeth not,
And tribunes with their tongues doom men
  to death.   *[Rises.*
But wherefore stand'st thou with thy weapon
  drawn ?
  Luc. To rescue my two brothers from
  their death :
For which attempt the judges have pro-
  nounced   50
My everlasting doom of banishment.
  Tit. O happy man ! they have befriended
  thee.
Why, foolish Lucius, dost thou not perceive
That Rome is but a wilderness of tigers ?
Tigers must prey, and Rome affords no prey
But me and mine : how happy art thou, then,
From these devourers to be banished !
But who comes with our brother Marcus
  here ?

Enter MARCUS *and* LAVINIA.

  Marc. Titus, prepare thy aged eyes to
  weep ;
Or, if not so, thy noble heart to break :   60
I bring consuming sorrow to thine age.
  Tit. Will it consume me ? let me see it,
  then.
  Marc. This was thy daughter.
  Tit.   Why, Marcus, so she is.
  Luc. Ay me, this object kills me !
  Tit. Faint-hearted boy, arise, and look
  upon her.
Speak, Lavinia, what accursed hand
Hath made thee handless in thy father's sight ?
What fool hath added water to the sea,
Or brought a faggot to bright-burning Troy ?
My grief was at the height before thou camest,
And now, like Nilus, it disdaineth bounds. 71
Give me a sword, I'll chop off my hands too ;
For they have fought for Rome, and all in
  vain ;
And they have nursed this woe, in feeding life ;
In bootless prayer have they been held up,
And they have served me to effectless use :
Now all the service I require of them
Is that the one will help to cut the other.
'Tis well, Lavinia, that thou hast no hands ;
For hands, to do Rome service, are but vain.
  Luc. Speak, gentle sister, who hath mar-
  tyr'd thee ?   81
  Marc. O, that delightful engine of her
  thoughts,
That blabb'd them with such pleasing elo-
  quence,
Is torn from forth that pretty hollow cage,
Where, like a sweet melodious bird, it sung
Sweet varied notes, enchanting every ear !
  Luc. O, say thou for her, who hath done
  this deed ?
  Marc. O, thus I found her, straying in the
  park,
Seeking to hide herself, as doth the deer
That hath received some unrecuring wound.
  Tit. It was my deer ; and he that wounded
  her   91
Hath hurt me more than had he killed me
  dead :
For now I stand as one upon a rock

Environed with a wilderness of sea,
Who marks the waxing tide grow wave by
    wave,
Expecting ever when some envious surge
Will in his brinish bowels swallow him.
This way to death my wretched sons are gone ;
Here stands my other son, a banished man,
And here my brother, weeping at my woes.
But that which gives my soul the greatest
    spurn,   101
Is dear Lavinia, dearer than my soul.
Had I but seen thy picture in this plight,
It would have madded me : what shall I do
Now I behold thy lively body so ?
Thou hast no hands, to wipe away thy tears ;
Nor tongue, to tell me who hath martyr'd
    thee :
Thy husband he is dead : and for his death
Thy brothers are condemn'd, and dead by
    this.   109
Look, Marcus ! ah, son Lucius, look on her !
When I did name her brothers, then fresh
    tears
Stood on her cheeks, as doth the honey-dew
Upon a gather'd lily almost wither'd.
    Marc. Perchance she weeps because they
    kill'd her husband ;
Perchance because she knows them innocent.
    Tit. If they did kill thy husband, then be
    joyful,
Because the law hath ta'en revenge on them.
No, no, they would not do so foul a deed ;
Witness the sorrow that their sister makes.
Gentle Lavinia, let me kiss thy lips.   120
Or make some sign how I may do thee ease :
Shall thy good uncle, and thy brother Lucius,
And thou, and I, sit round about some
    fountain,
Looking all downwards, to behold our cheeks
How they are stain'd, as meadows, yet not
    dry,
With miry slime left on them by a flood ?
And in the fountain shall we gaze so long
Till the fresh taste be taken from that clear-
    ness,
And made a brine-pit with our bitter tears ?
Or shall we cut away our hands, like thine ?
Or shall we bite our tongues, and in dumb
    shows   131
Pass the remainder of our hateful days ?
What shall we do ? let us, that have our
    tongues,
Plot some device of further misery,
To make us wonder'd at in time to come.
    Luc. Sweet father, cease your tears ; for,
    at your grief,
See how my wretched sister sobs and weeps.
    Marc. Patience, dear niece. Good Titus,
    dry thine eyes.
    Tit. Ah, Marcus, Marcus ! brother, well I
    wot
Thy napkin cannot drink a tear of mine,   140
For thou, poor man, hast drown'd it with
    thine own.
    Luc. Ah, my Lavinia, I will wipe thy
    cheeks.
    Tit. Mark, Marcus, mark ! I understand
    her signs :
Had she a tongue to speak, now would she say
That to her brother which I said to thee :
His napkin, with his true tears all bewet,
Can do no service on her sorrowful cheeks.

O, what a sympathy of woe is this,
As far from help as Limbo is from bliss !

Enter AARON.

    Aar. Titus Andronicus, my lord the em-
    peror   150
Sends thee this word,—that, if thou love thy
    sons,
Let Marcus, Lucius, or thyself, old Titus,
Or any one of you, chop off your hand,
And send it to the king : he for the same
Will send thee hither both thy sons alive ;
And that shall be the ransom for their fault.
    Tit. O gracious emperor ! O gentle Aaron !
Did ever raven sing so like a lark,
That gives sweet tidings of the sun's uprise ?
With all my heart, I'll send the emperor   160
My hand :
Good Aaron, wilt thou help to chop it off ?
    Luc. Stay, father ! for that noble hand of
    thine,
That hath thrown down so many enemies,
Shall not be sent : my hand will serve the
    turn :
My youth can better spare my blood than
    you ;
And therefore mine shall save my brothers'
    lives.
    Marc. Which of your hands hath not de-
    fended Rome,
And rear'd aloft the bloody battle-axe,
Writing destruction on the enemy's castle ?170
O, none of both but are of high desert :
My hand hath been but idle ; let it serve
To ransom my two nephews from their death ;
Then have I kept it to a worthy end.
    Aar. Nay, come, agree whose hand shall
    go along,
For fear they die before their pardon come.
    Marc. My hand shall go.
    Luc.   By heaven, it shall not go !
    Tit. Sirs, strive no more : such wither'd
    herbs as these
Are meet for plucking up, and therefore mine.
    Luc. Sweet father, if I shall be thought
    thy son,   180
Let me redeem my brothers both from death.
    Marc. And, for our father's sake and
    mother's care,
Now let me show a brother's love to thee.
    Tit. Agree between you ; I will spare my
    hand.
    Luc. Then I'll go fetch an axe.
    Marc. But I will use the axe.
                    [*Exeunt Lucius and Marcus.*
    Tit. Come hither, Aaron ; I'll deceive them
    both :
Lend me thy hand, and I will give thee mine.
    Aar. [*Aside*] If that be call'd deceit, I will
    be honest,
And never, whilst I live, deceive men so :   190
But I'll deceive you in another sort,
And that you'll say, ere half an hour pass.
                    [*Cuts off Titus's hand.*

Re-enter LUCIUS *and* MARCUS.

    Tit. Now stay your strife : what shall be
    is dispatch'd.
Good Aaron, give his majesty my hand :
Tell him it was a hand that warded him
From thousand dangers ; bid him bury it
More hath it merited ; that let it have.

As for my sons, say I account of them
As jewels purchased at an easy price;
And yet dear too, because I bought mine
    own.   200
    Aar. I go, Andronicus : and for thy hand
Look by and by to have thy sons with thee.
[*Aside*] Their heads, I mean. O, how this
    villany
Doth fat me with the very thoughts of it!
Let fools do good, and fair men call for grace,
Aaron will have his soul black like his face.
                                      [*Exit.*
    Tit. O, here I lift this one hand up to
    heaven,
And bow this feeble ruin to the earth :
If any power pities wretched tears,
To that I call! [*To Lav.*] What, wilt thou
    kneel with me?   210
Do, then, dear heart ; for heaven shall hear
    our prayers ;
Or with our sighs we'll breathe the welkin dim,
And stain the sun with fog, as sometime
    clouds
When they do hug him in their melting
    bosoms.
    Marc. O brother, speak with possibilities,
And do not break into these deep extremes.
    Tit. Is not my sorrow deep, having no
    bottom?
Then be my passions bottomless with them.
    Marc. But yet let reason govern thy la-
    ment.
    Tit. If there were reason for these miseries,
Then into limits could I bind my woes :   221
When heaven doth weep, doth not the earth
    o'erflow?
If the winds rage, doth not the sea wax mad,
Threatening the welkin with his big-swoln
    face?
And wilt thou have a reason for this coil?
I am the sea ; hark, how her sighs do blow!
She is the weeping welkin, I the earth :
Then must my sea be moved with her sighs ;
Then must my earth with her continual tears
Become a deluge, overflow'd and drown'd ; 231
For why my bowels cannot hide her woes,
But like a drunkard must I vomit them.
Then give me leave, for losers will have leave
To ease their stomachs with their bitter
    tongues.

Enter a Messenger, *with two heads and a
    hand.*

    Mess. Worthy Andronicus, ill art thou re-
    paid
For that good hand thou sent'st the emperor.
Here are the heads of thy two noble sons ;
And here's thy hand, in scorn to thee sent
    back ;
Thy griefs their sports, thy resolution mock'd ;
That woe is me to think upon thy woes   240
More than remembrance of my father's death.
                                      [*Exit.*
    Marc. Now let hot Ætna cool in Sicily,
And be my heart an ever-burning hell!
These miseries are more than may be borne.
To weep with them that weep doth ease some
    deal ;
But sorrow flouted at is double death.
    Luc. Ah, that this sight should make so
    deep a wound,
And yet detested life not shrink thereat!

That ever death should let life bear his name,
Where life hath no more interest but to
    breathe!   [*Lavinia kisses Titus.*
    Marc. Alas, poor heart, that kiss is com-
    fortless   251
As frozen water to a starved snake.
    Tit. When will this fearful slumber have
    an end?
    Marc. Now, farewell, flattery : die, An-
    dronicus ;
Thou dost not slumber : see, thy two sons'
    heads,
Thy warlike hand, thy mangled daughter here :
Thy other banish'd son, with this dear sight
Struck pale and bloodless ; and thy brother, I,
Even like a stony image, cold and numb.
Ah, now no more will I control thy griefs : 260
Rend off thy silver hair, thy other hand
Gnawing with thy teeth ; and be this dismal
    sight
The closing up of our most wretched eyes ;
Now is a time to storm ; why art thou still?
    Tit. Ha, ha, ha!
    Marc. Why dost thou laugh? it fits not
    with this hour.
    Tit. Why, I have not another tear to shed :
Besides, this sorrow is an enemy,
And would usurp upon my watery eyes,   269
And make them blind with tributary tears :
Then which way shall I find Revenge's cave?
For these two heads do seem to speak to me,
And threat me I shall never come to bliss
Till all these mischiefs be return'd again
Even in their throats that have committed
    them.
Come, let me see what task I have to do.
You heavy people, circle me about,
That I may turn me to each one of you,
And swear unto my soul to right your wrongs.
The vow is made. Come, brother, take a head ;
And in this hand the other will I bear.   281
Lavinia, thou shalt be employ'd : these arms!
Bear thou my hand, sweet wench, between thy
    teeth.
As for thee, boy, go get thee from my sight ;
Thou art an exile, and thou must not stay :
Hie to the Goths, and raise an army there :
And, if you love me, as I think you do,
Let's kiss and part, for we have much to do.
          [*Exeunt Titus, Marcus, and Lavinia.*
    Luc. Farewell, Andronicus, my noble
    father,   289
The wofull'st man that ever lived in Rome :
Farewell, proud Rome ; till Lucius come
    again,
He leaves his pledges dearer than his life :
Farewell, Lavinia, my noble sister ;
O, would thou wert as thou tofore hast been!
But now nor Lucius nor Lavinia lives
But in oblivion and hateful griefs.
If Lucius live, he will requite your wrongs ;
And make proud Saturnine and his empress
Beg at the gates, like Tarquin and his queen.
Now will I to the Goths, and raise a power,
To be revenged on Rome and Saturnine. [*Exit.*

SCENE II. *A room in Titus's house.
    A banquet set out.*

Enter TITUS, MARCUS, LAVINIA, *and young*
    LUCIUS, *a* Boy.

    Tit. So, so ; now sit : and look you eat no
    more

Than will preserve just so much strength in us
As will revenge these bitter woes of ours.
Marcus, unknit that sorrow-wreathen knot :
Thy niece and I, poor creatures, want our
  hands,
And cannot passionate our tenfold grief
With folded arms. This poor right hand of
  mine
Is left to tyrannize upon my breast ;
Who, when my heart, all mad with misery,
Beats in this hollow prison of my flesh,   10
Then thus I thump it down.
[*To Lavinia.*] Thou map of woe, that thus dost
  talk in signs !
When thy poor heart beats with outrageous
  beating,
Thou canst not strike it thus to make it still.
Wound it with sighing, girl, kill it with
  groans ;
Or get some little knife between thy teeth,
And just against thy heart make thou a hole ;
That all the tears that thy poor eyes let fall
May run into that sink, and soaking in
Drown the lamenting fool in sea-salt tears. 20
  Marc. Fie, brother, fie ! teach her not thus
    to lay
Such violent hands upon her tender life.
  Tit. How now ! has sorrow made thee dote
    already ?
Why, Marcus, no man should be mad but I.
What violent hands can she lay on her life ?
Ah, wherefore dost thou urge the name of
  hands ;
To bid Æneas tell the tale twice o'er,
How Troy was burnt and he made miserable ?
O, handle not the theme, to talk of hands,
Lest we remember still that we have none. 30
Fie, fie, how franticly I square my talk,
As if we should forget we had no hands,
If Marcus did not name the word of hands !
Come, let's fall to ; and, gentle girl, eat this :
Here is no drink ! Hark, Marcus, what she
  says ;
I can interpret all her martyr'd signs ;
She says she drinks no other drink but tears,
Brew'd with her sorrow, mesh'd upon her
  cheeks :
Speechless complainer, I will learn thy
  thought ;
In thy dumb action will I be as perfect   40
As begging hermits in their holy prayers :
Thou shalt not sigh, nor hold thy stumps to
  heaven,
Nor wink, nor nod, nor kneel, nor make a
  sign,
But I of these will wrest an alphabet
And by still practice learn to know thy mean-
  ing.
  Boy. Good grandsire, leave these bitter
    deep laments :
Make my aunt merry with some pleasing tale.
  Marc. Alas, the tender boy, in passion
    moved,
Doth weep to see his grandsire's heaviness.
  Tit. Peace, tender sapling ; thou art made
    of tears,   50
And tears will quickly melt thy life away.
    [*Marcus strikes the dish with a knife.*
What dost thou strike at, Marcus, with thy
  knife ?
  Marc. At that that I have kill'd, my lord ;
    a fly.

  Tit. Out on thee, murderer ! thou kill'st
    my heart ;
Mine eyes are cloy'd with view of tyranny :
A deed of death done on the innocent
Becomes not Titus' brother : get thee gone ;
I see thou art not for my company.
  Marc. Alas, my lord, I have but kill'd a
    fly.
  Tit. But how, if that fly had a father and
    mother ?   60
How would he hang his slender gilded wings,
And buzz lamenting doings in the air !
Poor harmless fly,
That, with his pretty buzzing melody,
Came here to make us merry ! and thou hast
  kill'd him.
  Marc. Pardon me, sir ; it was a black ill-
    favor'd fly,
Like to the empress' Moor ; therefore I kill'd
  him.
  Tit. O, O, O,
Then pardon me for reprehending thee,
For thou hast done a charitable deed.   70
Give me thy knife, I will insult on him ;
Flattering myself, as if it were the Moor
Come hither purposely to poison me.—
There's for thyself, and that's for Tamora.
Ah, sirrah !
Yet, I think, we are not brought so low,
But that between us we can kill a fly
That comes in likeness of a coal-black Moor.
  Marc. Alas, poor man ! grief has so
    wrought on him,
He takes false shadows for true substances. 80
  Tit. Come, take away. Lavinia, go with
    me :
I'll to thy closet ; and go read with thee
Sad stories chanced in the times of old.
Come, boy, and go with me : thy sight is
  young,
And thou shalt read when mine begin to
  dazzle.   [*Exeunt.*

ACT IV.

Scene I. *Rome. Titus's garden.*

Enter young Lucius, *and* Lavinia *running
  after him, and the boy flies from her, with
  books under his arm. Then enter* Titus
  and Marcus.

  Young Luc. Help, grandsire, help ! my
    aunt Lavinia
Follows me every where, I know not why :
Good uncle Marcus, see how swift she comes.
Alas, sweet aunt, I know not what you mean.
  Marc. Stand by me, Lucius ; do not fear
    thine aunt.
  Tit. She loves thee, boy, too well to do
    thee harm.
  Young Luc. Ay, when my father was in
    Rome she did.
  Marc. What means my niece Lavinia by
    these signs ?
  Tit. Fear her not, Lucius : somewhat doth
    she mean :
See, Lucius, see how much she makes of
  thee :   10
Somewhither would she have thee go with her.
Ah, boy, Cornelia never with more care
Read to her sons than she hath read to thee

Sweet poetry and Tully's Orator.

Marc. Canst thou not guess wherefore she
　　plies thee thus?

Young Luc. My lord, I know not, I, nor
　　can I guess,
Unless some fit or frenzy do possess her:
For I have heard my grandsire say full oft,
Extremity of griefs would make men mad;
And I have read that Hecuba of Troy　　20
Ran mad through sorrow: that made me to
　　fear;
Although, my lord, I know my noble aunt
Loves me as dear as e'er my mother did,
And would not, but in fury, fright my youth:
Which made me down to throw my books,
　　and fly,
Causeless, perhaps. But pardon me, sweet
　　aunt:
And, madam, if my uncle Marcus go,
I will most willingly attend your ladyship.

Marc. Lucius, I will.
　　[*Lavinia turns over with her stumps
　　　the books which Lucius has let fall.*

Tit. How now, Lavinia! Marcus, what
　　means this?　　30
Some book there is that she desires to see.
Which is it, girl, of these? Open them, boy.
But thou art deeper read, and better skill'd:
Come, and take choice of all my library,
And so beguile thy sorrow, till the heavens
Reveal the damn'd contriver of this deed.
Why lifts she up her arms in sequence thus?

Marc. I think she means that there was
　　more than one
Confederate in the fact: ay, more there was;
Or else to heaven she heaves them for re-
　　venge.　　40

Tit. Lucius, what book is that she tosseth
　　so?

Young Luc. Grandsire, 'tis Ovid's Meta-
　　morphoses;
My mother gave it me.

Marc. 　　For love of her that's gone,
Perhaps she cull'd it from among the rest.

Tit. Soft! see how busily she turns the
　　leaves!　　[*Helping her.*
What would she find? Lavinia, shall I read?
This is the tragic tale of Philomel,
And treats of Tereus' treason and his rape;
And rape, I fear, was root of thine annoy.

Marc. See, brother, see; note how she
　　quotes the leaves.　　50

Tit. Lavinia, wert thou thus surprised,
　　sweet girl,
Ravish'd and wrong'd, as Philomela was,
Forced in the ruthless, vast, and gloomy
　　woods?
See, see!
Ay, such a place there is, where we did hunt—
O, had we never, never hunted there!—
Pattern'd by that the poet here describes,
By nature made for murders and for rapes.

Marc. O, why should nature build so foul
　　a den,
Unless the gods delight in tragedies?　　60

Tit. Give signs, sweet girl, for here are
　　none but friends,
What Roman lord it was durst do the deed:
Or slunk not Saturnine, as Tarquin erst,
That left the camp to sin in Lucrece' bed?

Marc. Sit down, sweet niece: brother, sit
　　down by me.

Apollo, Pallas, Jove, or Mercury,
Inspire me, that I may this treason find!
My lord, look here: look here, Lavinia:
This sandy plot is plain; guide, if thou canst,
This after me, when I have writ my name　70
Without the help of any hand at all.
　　[*He writes his name with his staff, and
　　　guides it with feet and mouth.*
Cursed be that heart that forced us to this
　　shift!
Write thou, good niece; and here display, at
　　last,
What God will have discover'd for revenge:
Heaven guide thy pen to print thy sorrows
　　plain,
That we may know the traitors and the truth!
　　[*She takes the staff in her mouth, and
　　　guides it with her stumps, and writes.*

Tit. O, do ye read, my lord, what she hath
　　writ?
'Stuprum. Chiron. Demetrius.'

Marc. What, what! the lustful sons of
　　Tamora
Performers of this heinous, bloody deed?　80

Tit. Magni Dominator poli,
Tam lentus audis scelera? tam lentus vides?

Marc. O, calm thee, gentle lord; although
　　I know
There is enough written upon this earth
To stir a mutiny in the mildest thoughts
And arm the minds of infants to exclaims.
My lord, kneel down with me; Lavinia, kneel;
And kneel, sweet boy, the Roman Hector's
　　hope;
And swear with me, as, with the woful fere
And father of that chaste dishonor'd dame, 90
Lord Junius Brutus sware for Lucrece' rape,
That we will prosecute by good advice
Mortal revenge upon these traitorous Goths,
And see their blood, or die with this reproach.

Tit. 'Tis sure enough, an you knew how.
But if you hunt these bear-whelps, then be-
　　ware:
The dam will wake; and, if she wind you once,
She's with the lion deeply still in league,
And lulls him whilst she playeth on her back,
And when he sleeps will she do what she list.
You are a young huntsman, Marcus; let it
　　alone;　　101
And, come, I will go get a leaf of brass,
And with a gad of steel will write these words,
And lay it by: the angry northern wind
Will blow these sands, like Sibyl's leaves,
　　abroad,
And where's your lesson, then? Boy, what say
　　you?

Young Luc. I say, my lord, that if I were
　　a man,
Their mother's bed-chamber should not be safe
For these bad bondmen to the yoke of Rome.

Marc. Ay, that's my boy! thy father hath
　　full oft　　110
For his ungrateful country done the like.

Young Luc. And, uncle, so will I, an if I
　　live.

Tit. Come, go with me into mine armory;
Lucius, I'll fit thee; and withal, my boy,
Shalt carry from me to the empress' sons
Presents that I intend to send them both:
Come, come; thou'lt do thy message, wilt
　　thou not?

Young Luc. Ay, with my dagger in their
    bosoms, grandsire.
Tit. No, boy, not so ; I'll teach thee an-
    other course.
Lavinia, come. Marcus, look to my house :
Lucius and I'll go brave it at the court : 121
Ay, marry, will we, sir ; and we'll be waited
    on.
    [Exeunt Titus, Lavinia, and Young Luc.
Marc. O heavens, can you hear a good man
    groan,
And not relent, or not compassion him ?
Marcus, attend him in his ecstasy,
That hath more scars of sorrow in his heart
Than foemen's marks upon his batter'd
    shield ;
But yet so just that he will not revenge.
Revenge, ye heavens, for old Andronicus !
    [Exit.

SCENE II. *The same. A room in the palace.*

Enter, from one side, AARON, DEMETRIUS,
and CHIRON ; *from the other side, young*
LUCIUS, *and an* Attendant, *with a bundle
of weapons, and verses writ upon them.*

Chi. Demetrius, here's the son of Lucius ;
He hath some message to deliver us.
Aar. Ay, some mad message from his mad
    grandfather.
Young Luc. My lords, with all the hum-
    bleness I may,
I greet your honors from Andronicus.
  [Aside] And pray the Roman gods confound
    you both !
Dem. Gramercy, lovely Lucius : what's the
    news ?
Young Luc. *[Aside]* That you are both de-
    cipher'd, that's the news,
For villains mark'd with rape.—May it please
    you,
My grandsire, well advised, hath sent by me
The goodliest weapons of his armory   11
To gratify your honorable youth,
The hope of Rome ; for so he bade me say ;
And so I do, and with his gifts present
Your lordships, that, whenever you have need,
You may be armed and appointed well :
And so I leave you both : *[Aside]* like bloody
    villains.
    [Exeunt young Lucius, and Attendant.
Dem. What's here ? A scroll ; and written
    round about ?
Let's see :
  [Reads] ' Integer vitæ, scelerisque purus, 20
      Non eget Mauri jaculis, nec arcu.'
Chi. O, 'tis a verse in Horace ; I know it
    well :
I read it in the grammar long ago.
Aar. Ay, just ; a verse in Horace ; right,
    you have it.
  [Aside] Now, what a thing it is to be an ass !
Here's no sound jest ! the old man hath found
    their guilt ;
And sends them weapons wrapped about with
    lines,
That wound, beyond their feeling, to the quick.
But were our witty empress well afoot,
She would applaud Andronicus' conceit : 30
But let her rest in her unrest awhile.

And now, young lords, was't not a happy star
Led us to Rome, strangers, and more than so,

Captives, to be advanced to this height ?
It did me good, before the palace gate
To brave the tribune in his brother's hearing.
Dem. But me more good, to see so great a
    lord
Basely insinuate and send us gifts.
  Aar. Had he not reason, Lord Demetrius ?
Did you not use his daughter very friendly ? 40
Dem. I would we had a thousand Roman
    dames
At such a bay, by turn to serve our lust.
Chi. A charitable wish and full of love.
Aar. Here lacks but your mother for to
    say amen.
Chi. And that would she for twenty thou-
    sand more.
Dem. Come, let us go ; and pray to all the
    gods
For our beloved mother in her pains.
  Aar. *[Aside]* Pray to the devils ; the gods
    have given us over.
          [Trumpets sound within.
Dem. Why do the emperor's trumpets
    flourish thus ?
Chi. Belike, for joy the emperor hath a
    son.
Dem. Soft ! who comes here ?   51

Enter a Nurse, *with a blackamoor* Child *in
her arms.*

Nur.   Good morrow, lords :
O, tell me, did you see Aaron the Moor ?
Aar. Well, more or less, or ne'er a whit at
    all,
Here Aaron is ; and what with Aaron now ?
Nur. O gentle Aaron, we are all undone !
Now help, or woe betide thee evermore !
Aar. Why, what a caterwauling dost thou
    keep !
What dost thou wrap and fumble in thine
    arms ?
Nur. O, that which I would hide from
    heaven's eye,
Our empress' shame, and stately Rome's dis-
    grace !   60
She is deliver'd, lords ; she is deliver'd.
Aar. To whom ?
Nur.   I mean, she is brought a-bed.
Aar. Well, God give her good rest ! What
    hath he sent her ?
Nur. A devil.
Aar. Why, then she is the devil's dam ; a
    joyful issue.
Nur. A joyless, dismal, black, and sorrow-
    ful issue !
Here is the babe, as loathsome as a toad
Amongst the fairest breeders of our clime :
The empress sends it thee, thy stamp, thy seal,
And bids thee christen it with thy dagger's
    point.   71
Aar. 'Zounds, ye whore ! is black so base
    a hue ?
Sweet blowse, you are a beauteous blossom,
    sure.
Dem. Villain, what hast thou done ?
Aar. That which thou canst not undo.
Chi. Thou hast undone our mother.
Aar. Villain, I have done thy mother.
Dem. And therein, hellish dog, thou hast
    undone.
Woe to her chance, and damn'd her loathed
    choice !

Accursed the offspring of so foul a fiend!
Chi. It shall not live.　　　　　　　　81
Aar. It shall not die.
Nur. Aaron, it must; the mother wills it
　so.
Aar. What, must it, nurse? then let no
　man but I
Do execution on my flesh and blood.
Dem. I'll broach the tadpole on my rapier's
　point:
Nurse, give it me; my sword shall soon dis-
　patch it.
Aar. Sooner this sword shall plough thy
　bowels up.
　　　　*[Takes the Child from the Nurse,
　　　　　　　　　and draws.*
Stay, murderous villains! will you kill your
　brother?
Now, by the burning tapers of the sky,
That shone so brightly when this boy was got,
He dies upon my scimitar's sharp point　91
That touches this my first-born son and heir!
I tell you, younglings, not Enceladus,
With all his threatening band of Typhon's
　brood,
Nor great Alcides, nor the god of war,
Shall seize this prey out of his father's hands.
What, what, ye sanguine, shallow-hearted
　boys!
Ye white-limed walls! ye alehouse painted
　signs!
Coal-black is better than another hue,
In that it scorns to bear another hue;　100
For all the water in the ocean
Can never turn the swan's black legs to white,
Although she lave them hourly in the flood.
Tell the empress from me, I am of age
To keep mine own, excuse it how she can.
Dem. Wilt thou betray thy noble mistress
　thus?
Aar. My mistress is my mistress; this my-
　self,
The vigor and the picture of my youth:
This before all the world do I prefer;
This maugre all the world will I keep safe, 110
Or some of you shall smoke for it in Rome.
Dem. By this our mother is forever
　shamed.
Chi. Rome will despise her for this foul
　escape.
Nur. The emperor, in his rage, will doom
　her death.
Chi. I blush to think upon this ignomy.
Aar. Why, there's the privilege your
　beauty bears:
Fie, treacherous hue, that will betray with
　blushing
The close enacts and counsels of the heart!
Here's a young lad framed of another leer:
Look, how the black slave smiles upon the
　father,　　　　　　　　　　　　120
As who should say 'Old lad, I am thine own.'
He is your brother, lords, sensibly fed
Of that self-blood that first gave life to you,
And from that womb where you imprison'd
　were
He is enfranchised and come to light:
Nay, he is your brother by the surer side,
Although my seal be stamped in his face.
Nur. Aaron, what shall I say unto the
　empress?

Dem. Advise thee, Aaron, what is to be
　done,
And we will all subscribe to thy advice:　130
Save thou the child, so we may all be safe.
Aar. Then sit we down, and let us all
　consult.
My son and I will have the wind of you:
Keep there: now talk at pleasure of your
　safety.　　　　　　　　　*[They sit.*
Dem. How many women saw this child of
　his?
Aar. Why, so, brave lords! when we join
　in league,
I am a lamb: but if you brave the Moor,
The chafed boar, the mountain lioness,
The ocean swells not so as Aaron storms.
But say, again, how many saw the child?　140
Nur. Cornelia the midwife and myself;
And no one else but the deliver'd empress.
Aar. The empress, the midwife, and your-
　self:
Two may keep counsel when the third's away:
Go to the empress, tell her this I said.
　　　　　　　　　[He kills the nurse.
Weke, weke! so cries a pig prepared to the
　spit.
Dem. What mean'st thou, Aaron? where-
　fore didst thou this?
Aar. O Lord, sir, 'tis a deed of policy:
Shall she live to betray this guilt of ours,
A long-tongued babbling gossip? no, lords,
　no:　　　　　　　　　　　　150
And now be it known to you my full intent.
Not far, one Muli lives, my countryman;
His wife but yesternight was brought to bed;
His child is like to her, fair as you are:
Go pack with him, and give the mother gold,
And tell them both the circumstance of all;
And how by this their child shall be advanced,
And be received for the emperor's heir,
And substituted in the place of mine,
To calm this tempest whirling in the court;160
And let the emperor dandle him for his own.
Hark ye, lords; ye see I have given her physic,
　　　　　　　[Pointing to the nurse.
And you must needs bestow her funeral;
The fields are near, and you are gallant
　grooms:
This done, see that you take no longer days,
But send the midwife presently to me.
The midwife and the nurse well made away,
Then let the ladies tattle what they please.
Chi. Aaron, I see thou wilt not trust the
　air
With secrets.
Dem.　For this care of Tamora,　170
Herself and hers are highly bound to thee.
　　*[Exeunt Dem. and Chi. bearing off the
　　　　　　　　　Nurse's body.*
Aar. Now to the Goths, as swift as swal-
　low flies;
There to dispose this treasure in mine arms,
And secretly to greet the empress' friends.
Come on, you thick-lipp'd slave, I'll bear you
　hence;
For it is you that puts us to our shifts:
I'll make you feed on berries and on roots,
And feed on curds and whey, and suck the
　goat,
And cabin in a cave, and bring you up
To be a warrior, and command a camp.　180
　　　　　　　　　　　　　[Exit.

SCENE III. *The same. A public place.*

Enter TITUS, *bearing arrows with letters at
the ends of them; with him,* MARCUS, *Young*
LUCIUS, PUBLIUS, SEMPRONIUS, CAIUS, *and
other Gentlemen, with bows.*

Tit. Come, Marcus; come, kinsmen; this
  is the way.
Sir boy, now let me see your archery;
Look ye draw home enough, and 'tis there
  straight.
Terras Astræa reliquit :
Be you remember'd, Marcus, she's gone, she's
  fled.
Sirs, take you to your tools. You, cousins,
  shall
Go sound the ocean, and cast your nets;
Happily you may catch her in the sea;
Yet there's as little justice as at land :
No; Publius and Sempronius, you must do
  it;   10
'Tis you must dig with mattock and with
  spade,
And pierce the inmost centre of the earth :
Then, when you come to Pluto's region,
I pray you, deliver him this petition;
Tell him, it is for justice and for aid,
And that it comes from old Andronicus,
Shaken with sorrows in ungrateful Rome.
Ah, Rome! Well, well; I made thee miserable
What time I threw the people's suffrages
On him that thus doth tyrannize o'er me. 20
Go, get you gone; and pray be careful all,
And leave you not a man-of-war unsearch'd :
This wicked emperor may have shipp'd her
  hence;
And, kinsmen, then we may go pipe for justice.
Marc. O Publius, is not this a heavy case,
To see thy noble uncle thus distract?
Pub. Therefore, my lord, it highly us con-
  cerns
By day and night to attend him carefully,
And feed his humor kindly as we may,
Till time beget some careful remedy. 30
Marc. Kinsmen, his sorrows are past
  remedy.
Join with the Goths; and with revengeful war
Take wreak on Rome for this ingratitude,
And vengeance on the traitor Saturnine.
Tit. Publius, how now! how now, my
  masters!
What, have you met with her?
Pub. No, my good lord; but Pluto sends
  you word,
If you will have Revenge from hell, you shall :
Marry, for Justice, she is so employ'd,
He thinks, with Jove in heaven, or somewhere
  else,   40
So that perforce you must needs stay a time.
Tit. He doth me wrong to feed me with
  delays.
I'll dive into the burning lake below,
And pull her out of Acheron by the heels.
Marcus, we are but shrubs, no cedars we,
No big-boned men framed of the Cyclops'
  size;
But metal, Marcus, steel to the very back,
Yet wrung with wrongs more than our backs
  can bear :
And, sith there's no justice in earth nor hell,
We will solicit heaven and move the gods 50
To send down Justice for to wreak our wrongs.

Come, to this gear. You are a good archer,
  Marcus;   *[He gives them the arrows.*
'Ad Jovem,' that's for you : here, 'Ad Apol-
  linem : '
'Ad Martem,' that's for myself :
Here, boy, to Pallas : here, to Mercury :
To Saturn, Caius, not to Saturnine;
You were as good to shoot against the wind.
To it, boy! Marcus, loose when I bid.
Of my word, I have written to effect;
There's not a god left unsolicited.   60
  Marc. Kinsmen, shoot all your shafts into
  the court :
We will afflict the emperor in his pride.
Tit. Now, masters, draw. [*They shoot.*] O,
  well said, Lucius!
Good boy, in Virgo's lap; give it Pallas.
  Marc. My lord, I aim a mile beyond the
  moon;
Your letter is with Jupiter by this.
Tit. Ha, ha!
Publius, Publius, what hast thou done?
See, see, thou hast shot off one of Taurus'
  horns.
  Marc. This was the sport, my lord : when
  Publius shot,   70
The Bull, being gall'd, gave Aries such a knock
That down fell both the Ram's horns in the
  court;
And who should find them but the empress'
  villain?
She laugh'd, and told the Moor he should
  not choose
But give them to his master for a present.
  Tit. Why, there it goes : God give his lord-
  ship joy!

Enter a Clown, *with a basket, and two pigeons
in it.*

News, news from heaven! Marcus, the post
  is come.
Sirrah, what tidings? have you any letters?
Shall I have justice? what says Jupiter? 79
  Clo. O, the gibbet-maker! he says that he
hath taken them down again, for the man
must not be hanged till the next week.
  Tit. But what says Jupiter, I ask thee?
  Clo. Alas, sir, I know not Jupiter; I never
drank with him in all my life.
  Tit. Why, villain, art not thou the carrier?
  Clo. Ay, of my pigeons, sir; nothing else.
  Tit. Why, didst thou not come from
  heaven?
  Clo. From heaven! alas, sir, I never came
there : God forbid I should be so bold to
press to heaven in my young days. Why, I am
going with my pigeons to the tribunal plebs,
to take up a matter of brawl betwixt my uncle
and one of the emperial's men.
  Marc. Why, sir, that is as fit as can be to
serve for your oration; and let him deliver the
pigeons to the emperor from you.
  Tit. Tell me, can you deliver an oration to
the emperor with a grace?
  Clo. Nay, truly, sir, I could never say
grace in all my life.   101
  Tit. Sirrah, come hither : make no more
  ado,
But give your pigeons to the emperor :
By me thou shalt have justice at his hands.
Hold, hold; meanwhile here's money for thy
  charges.

Give me pen and ink, Sirrah, can you with a
grace deliver a supplication ?
Clo. Ay, sir.
Tit. Then here is a supplication for you.
And when you come to him, at the first ap-
proach you must kneel, then kiss his foot,
then deliver up your pigeons, and then look
for your reward. I'll be at hand, sir ; see you
do it bravely.
Clo. I warrant you, sir, let me alone.
Tit. Sirrah, hast thou a knife ? come, let
me see it.
Here, Marcus, fold it in the oration ;
For thou hast made it like an humble sup-
pliant.
And when thou hast given it the emperor,
Knock at my door, and tell me what he says.
Clo. God be with you, sir ; I will.   120
Tit. Come, Marcus, let us go. Publius, fol-
low me.   [*Exeunt.*

SCENE IV. *The same. Before the palace.*

Enter SATURNINUS, TAMORA, DEMETRIUS,
CHIRON, Lords, *and others;* SATURNINUS
with the arrows in his hand that TITUS *shot.*

Sat. Why, lords, what wrongs are these !
was ever seen
An emperor in Rome thus overborne,
Troubled, confronted thus ; and, for the ex-
tent
Of egal justice, used in such contempt ?
My lords, you know, as know the mightful
gods,
However these disturbers of our peace
Buz in the people's ears, there nought hath
pass'd,
But even with law, against the wilful sons
Of old Andronicus. And what an if
His sorrows have so overwhelm'd his wits, 10
Shall we be thus afflicted in his wreaks,
His fits, his frenzy, and his bitterness ?
And now he writes to heaven for his redress :
See, here's to Jove, and this to Mercury ;
This to Apollo ; this to the god of war ;
Sweet scrolls to fly about the streets of Rome !
What's this but libelling against the senate,
And blazoning our injustice every where ?
A goodly humor, is it not, my lords ?
As who would say, in Rome no justice were. 20
But if I live, his feigned ecstasies
Shall be no shelter to these outrages :
But he and his shall know that justice lives
In Saturninus' health, whom, if she sleep,
He'll so awake as she in fury shall
Cut off the proud'st conspirator that lives.
Tam. My gracious lord, my lovely Satur-
nine,
Lord of my life, commander of my thoughts,
Calm thee, and bear the faults of Titus' age,
The effects of sorrow for his valiant sons, 30
Whose loss hath pierced him deep and scarr'd
his heart ;
And rather comfort his distressed plight
Than prosecute the meanest or the best
For these contempts. [*Aside*] Why, thus it
shall become
High-witted Tamora to gloze with all :
But, Titus, I have touched thee to the quick,
Thy life-blood out : if Aaron now be wise,
Then is all safe, the anchor's in the port.

Enter Clown.

How now, good fellow ! wouldst thou speak
with us ?
Clo. Yea, forsooth, an your mistership be
emperial.   40
Tam. Empress I am, but yonder sits the
emperor.
Clo. 'Tis he. God and Saint Stephen give
you good den : I have brought you a letter and
a couple of pigeons here.
                    [*Saturninus reads the letter.*
Sat. Go, take him away, and hang him
presently.
Clo. How much money must I have ?
Tam. Come, sirrah, you must be hanged.
Clo. Hanged ! by'r lady, then I have
brought up a neck to a fair end.
                              [*Exit, guarded.*
Sat. Despiteful and intolerable wrongs ! 50
Shall I endure this monstrous villany ?
I know from whence this same device pro-
ceeds :
May this be borne ?—as if his traitorous sons,
That died by law for murder of our brother,
Have by my means been butcher'd wrong-
fully !
Go, drag the villain hither by the hair ;
Nor age nor honor shall shape privilege :
For this proud mock I'll be thy slaughter-
man ;
Sly frantic wretch, that holp'st to make me
great,
In hope thyself should govern Rome and me.

Enter ÆMILIUS.

What news with thee, Æmilius ?   61
Æmil. Arm, arm, my lord ;—Rome never
had more cause.
The Goths have gather'd head ; and with a
power
Of high-resolved men, bent to the spoil,
They hither march amain, under conduct
Of Lucius, son to old Andronicus ;
Who threats, in course of this revenge, to do
As much as ever Coriolanus did.
Sat. Is warlike Lucius general of the
Goths ?
These tidings nip me, and I hang the head 70
As flowers with frost or grass beat down with
storms :
Ay, now begin our sorrows to approach :
'Tis he the common people love so much ;
Myself hath often over-heard them say,
When I have walked like a private man,
That Lucius' banishment was wrongfully,
And they have wish'd that Lucius were their
emperor.
Tam. Why should you fear ? is not your
city strong ?
Sat. Ay, but the citizens favor Lucius,
And will revolt from me to succor him. 80
Tam. King, be thy thoughts imperious, like
thy name.
Is the sun dimm'd, that gnats do fly in it ?
The eagle suffers little birds to sing,
And is not careful what they mean thereby,
Knowing that with the shadow of his wings
He can at pleasure stint their melody :
Even so mayst thou the giddy men of Rome.
Then cheer thy spirit : for know, thou em-
peror,

I will enchant the old Andronicus
With words more sweet, and yet more dan-
    gerous,   90
Than baits to fish, or honey-stalks to sheep,
When as the one is wounded with the bait,
The other rotted with delicious feed.
  Sat. But he will not entreat his son for us.
  Tam. If Tamora entreat him, then he will :
For I can smooth and fill his aged ear
With golden promises ; that, were his heart
Almost impregnable, his old ears deaf,
Yet should both ear and heart obey my
    tongue.
[*To Æmilius*] Go thou before, be our am-
    bassador :   100
Say that the emperor requests a parley
Of warlike Lucius, and appoint the meeting
Even at his father's house, the old Andro-
    nicus.
  Sat. Æmilius, do this message honorably :
And if he stand on hostage for his safety,
Bid him demand what pledge will please him
    best.
  Æmil. Your bidding shall I do effectually.
                                                [*Exit.*
  Tam. Now will I to that old Andronicus,
And temper him with all the art I have,
To pluck proud Lucius from the warlike
    Goths.
And now, sweet emperor, be blithe again, 111
And bury all thy fear in my devices.
  Sat. Then go successantly, and plead to
    him.   [*Exeunt.*

ACT V.

Scene I. *Plains near Rome.*

Enter Lucius *with an army of* Goths, *with
    drum and colors.*

  Luc. Approved warriors, and my faithful
    friends,
I have received letters from great Rome,
Which signify what hate they bear their em-
    peror
And how desirous of our sight they are.
Therefore, great lords, be, as your titles wit-
    ness,
Imperious and impatient of your wrongs,
And wherein Rome hath done you any scath,
Let him make treble satisfaction.
  First Goth. Brave slip, sprung from the
    great Andronicus,
Whose name was once our terror, now our
    comfort ;   10
Whose high exploits and honorable deeds
Ingrateful Rome requites with foul contempt,
Be bold in us : we'll follow where thou lead'st,
Like stinging bees in hottest summer's day
Led by their master to the flowered fields,
And be avenged on cursed Tamora.
  All the Goths. And as he saith, so say we
    all with him.
  Luc. I humbly thank him, and I thank you
    all.
But who comes here, led by a lusty Goth ?

Enter a Goth, *leading* Aaron *with his Child in
    his arms.*

  Sec. Goth. Renowned Lucius, from our
    troops I stray'd   20

To gaze upon a ruinous monastery ;
And, as I earnestly did fix mine eye
Upon the wasted building, suddenly
I heard a child cry underneath a wall.
I made unto the noise ; when soon I heard
The crying babe controll'd with this discourse :
'Peace, tawny slave, half me and half thy
    dam !
Did not thy hue bewray whose brat thou art,
Had nature lent thee but thy mother's look,
Villain, thou mightst have been an emperor :
But where the bull and cow are both milk-
    white,   31
They never do beget a coal-black calf.
Peace, villain, peace ! '—even thus he rates the
    babe,—
'For I must bear thee to a trusty Goth ;
Who, when he knows thou art the empress'
    babe,
Will hold thee dearly for thy mother's sake.'
With this, my weapon drawn, I rush'd upon
    him,
Surprised him suddenly, and brought him
    hither,
To use as you think needful of the man.
  Luc. O worthy Goth, this is the incarnate
    devil   40
That robb'd Andronicus of his good hand ;
This is the pearl that pleased your empress'
    eye,
And here's the base fruit of his burning lust.
Say, wall-eyed slave, whither wouldst thou
    convey
This growing image of thy fiend-like face ?
Why dost not speak ? what, deaf ? not a word ?
A halter, soldiers ! hang him on this tree.
And by his side his fruit of bastardy.
  Aar. Touch not the boy ; he is of royal
    blood.   49
  Luc. Too like the sire for ever being good.
First hang the child, that he may see it sprawl ;
A sight to vex the father's soul withal.
Get me a ladder.
                    [*A ladder brought, which Aaron is
                        made to ascend.*
  Aar.   Lucius, save the child,
And bear it from me to the empress.
If thou do this, I'll show thee wondrous things,
That highly may advantage thee to hear :
If thou wilt not, befall what may befall,
I'll speak no more but 'Vengeance rot you
    all ! '
  Luc. Say on : an if it please me which thou
    speak'st,
Thy child shall live, and I will see it nour-
    ish'd.   60
  Aar. An if it please thee ! why, assure thee,
    Lucius,
'Twill vex thy soul to hear what I shall speak ;
For I must talk of murders, rapes and mas-
    sacres,
Acts of black night, abominable deeds,
Complots of mischief, treason, villanies
Ruthful to hear, yet piteously perform'd :
And this shall all be buried by my death,
Unless thou swear to me my child shall live.
  Luc. Tell on thy mind ; I say thy child
    shall live.
  Aar. Swear that he shall, and then I will
    begin.   70
  Luc. Who should I swear by ? thou be-
    lievest no god :

That granted, how canst thou believe an oath?

Aar. What if I do not? as, indeed, I do not;
Yet, for I know thou art religious
And hast a thing within thee called conscience,
With twenty popish tricks and ceremonies,
Which I have seen thee careful to observe,
Therefore I urge thy oath; for that I know
An idiot holds his bauble for a god
And keeps the oath which by that god he swears, 80
To that I'll urge him: therefore thou shalt vow
By that same god, what god soe'er it be,
That thou adorest and hast in reverence,
To save my boy, to nourish and bring him up;
Or else I will discover nought to thee.

Luc. Even by my god I swear to thee I will.

Aar. First know thou, I begot him on the empress.

Luc. O most insatiate and luxurious woman!

Aar. Tut, Lucius, this was but a deed of charity
To that which thou shalt hear of me anon. 90
'Twas her two sons that murder'd Bassianus;
They cut thy sister's tongue and ravish'd her
And cut her hands and trimm'd her as thou saw'st.

Luc. O detestable villain! call'st thou that trimming?

Aar. Why, she was wash'd and cut and trimm'd, and 'twas
Trim sport for them that had the doing of it.

Luc. O barbarous, beastly villains, like thyself!

Aar. Indeed, I was their tutor to instruct them:
That codding spirit had they from their mother,
As sure a card as ever won the set; 100
That bloody mind, I think, they learn'd of me,
As true a dog as ever fought at head.
Well, let my deeds be witness of my worth.
I train'd thy brethren to that guileful hole
Where the dead corpse of Bassianus lay:
I wrote the letter that thy father found
And hid the gold within the letter mention'd,
Confederate with the queen and her two sons:
And what not done, that thou hast cause to rue,
Wherein I had no stroke of mischief in it? 110
I play'd the cheater for thy father's hand,
And, when I had it, drew myself apart
And almost broke my heart with extreme laughter:
I pry'd me through the crevice of a wall
When, for his hand, he had his two sons' heads;
Beheld his tears, and laugh'd so heartily,
That both mine eyes were rainy like to his:
And when I told the empress of this sport,
She swooned almost at my pleasing tale,
And for my tidings gave me twenty kisses.

First Goth. What, canst thou say all this, and never blush? 121

Aar. Ay, like a black dog, as the saying is.

Luc. Art thou not sorry for these heinous deeds?

Aar. Ay, that I had not done a thousand more.
Even now I curse the day—and yet, I think,

Few come within the compass of my curse—
Wherein I did not some notorious ill,
As kill a man, or else devise his death,
Ravish a maid, or plot the way to do it,
Accuse some innocent and forswear myself,
Set deadly enmity between two friends, 131
Make poor men's cattle break their necks;
Set fire on barns and hay-stacks in the night,
And bid the owners quench them with their tears.
Oft have I digg'd up dead men from their graves,
And set them upright at their dear friends' doors,
Even when their sorrows almost were forgot;
And on their skins, as on the bark of trees,
Have with my knife carved in Roman letters,
'Let not your sorrow die, though I am dead.'
Tut, I have done a thousand dreadful things
As willingly as one would kill a fly,
And nothing grieves me heartily indeed
But that I cannot do ten thousand more.

Luc. Bring down the devil; for he must not die
So sweet a death as hanging presently.

Aar. If there be devils, would I were a devil,
To live and burn in everlasting fire,
So I might have your company in hell,
But to torment you with my bitter tongue! 150

Luc. Sirs, stop his mouth, and let him speak no more.

Enter a Goth.

Third Goth. My lord, there is a messenger from Rome
Desires to be admitted to your presence.

Luc. Let him come near.

Enter ÆMILIUS.

Welcome, Æmilius: what's the news from Rome?

Æmil. Lord Lucius, and you princes of the Goths,
The Roman emperor greets you all by me;
And, for he understands you are in arms,
He craves a parley at your father's house,
Willing you to demand your hostages, 160
And they shall be immediately deliver'd.

First Goth. What says our general?

Luc. Æmilius, let the emperor give his pledges
Unto my father and my uncle Marcus,
And we will come. March away. [*Exeunt.*

SCENE II. *Rome. Before Titus's house.*

Enter TAMORA, DEMETRIUS, *and* CHIRON, *disguised.*

Tam. Thus, in this strange and sad habiliment,
I will encounter with Andronicus,
And say I am Revenge, sent from below
To join with him and right his heinous wrongs.
Knock at his study, where, they say, he keeps,
To ruminate strange plots of dire revenge;
Tell him Revenge is come to join with him,
And work confusion on his enemies.
[*They knock.*

Enter TITUS, *above.*

Tit. Who doth molest my contemplation?
Is it your trick to make me ope the door, 10

That so my sad decrees may fly away,
And all my study be to no effect?
You are deceived : for what I mean to do
See here in bloody lines I have set down ;
And what is written shall be executed.
Tam. Titus, I am come to talk with thee.
Tit. No, not a word ; how can I grace my
    talk,
Wanting a hand to give it action ?
Thou hast the odds of me ; therefore no more.
Tam. If thou didst know me, thou would-
    est talk with me.   20
Tit. I am not mad ; I know thee well
    enough :
Witness this wretched stump, witness these
    crimson lines ;
Witness these trenches made by grief and
    care ;
Witness the tiring day and heavy night ;
Witness all sorrow, that I know thee well
For our proud empress, mighty Tamora :
Is not thy coming for my other hand ?
Tam. Know, thou sad man, I am not Ta-
    mora ;
She is thy enemy, and I thy friend :
I am Revenge : sent from the infernal king-
    dom,   30
To ease the gnawing vulture of thy mind,
By working wreakful vengeance on thy foes.
Come down, and welcome me to this world's
    light ;
Confer with me of murder and of death :
There's not a hollow cave or lurking-place,
No vast obscurity or misty vale,
Where bloody murder or detested rape
Can couch for fear, but I will find them out ;
And in their ears tell them my dreadful name,
Revenge, which makes the foul offender quake.
Tit. Art thou Revenge ? and art thou sent
    to me,   41
To be a torment to mine enemies ?
Tam. I am ; therefore come down, and
    welcome me.
Tit. Do me some service, ere I come to
    thee.
Lo, by thy side where Rape and Murder
    stands ;
Now give me some surance that thou art Re-
    venge,
Stab them, or tear them on thy chariot-
    wheels ;
And then I'll come and be thy waggoner,
And whirl along with thee about the globe.
Provide thee two proper palfreys, black as jet,
To hale thy vengeful waggon swift away,   51
And find out murderers in their guilty caves :
And when thy car is loaden with their heads,
I will dismount, and by the waggon-wheel
Trot, like a servile footman, all day long,
Even from Hyperion's rising in the east
Until his very downfall in the sea :
And day by day I'll do this heavy task,
So thou destroy Rapine and Murder there.
Tam. These are my ministers, and come
    with me.   60
Tit. Are these thy ministers ? what are they
    call'd ?
Tam. Rapine and Murder ; therefore called
    so,
Cause they take vengeance of such kind of
    men.

Tit. Good Lord, how like the empress'
    sons they are !
And you, the empress ! but we worldly men
Have miserable, mad, mistaking eyes.
O sweet Revenge, now do I come to thee ;
And, if one arm's embracement will content
    thee,
I will embrace thee in it by and by.
                    [Exit above.
Tam. This closing with him fits his lunacy
Whate'er I forge to feed his brain-sick fits, 71
Do you uphold and maintain in your speeches,
For now he firmly takes me for Revenge ;
And, being credulous in this mad thought,
I'll make him send for Lucius his son ;
And, whilst I at a banquet hold him sure,
I'll find some cunning practice out of hand,
To scatter and disperse the giddy Goths,
Or, at the least, make them his enemies.
See, here he comes, and I must ply my
    theme.   80

    Enter Titus *below.*

Tit. Long have I been forlorn, and all for
    thee :
Welcome, dread Fury, to my woful house :
Rapine and Murder, you are welcome too.
How like the empress and her sons you are !
Well are you fitted, had you but a Moor :
Could not all hell afford you such a devil ?
For well I wot the empress never wags
But in her company there is a Moor ;
And, would you represent our queen aright,
It were convenient you had such a devil : 90
But welcome, as you are. What shall we do ?
Tam. What wouldst thou have us do,
    Andronicus ?
Dem. Show me a murderer, I'll deal with
    him.
Chi. Show me a villain that hath done a
    rape,
And I am sent to be revenged on him.
Tam. Show me a thousand that have done
    thee wrong,
And I will be revenged on them all.
Tit. Look round about the wicked streets
    of Rome ;
And when thou find'st a man that's like thyself,
Good Murder, stab him ; he's a murderer. 100
Go thou with him ; and when it is thy hap
To find another that is like to thee,
Good Rapine, stab him ; he's a ravisher.
Go thou with them ; and in the emperor's
    court
There is a queen, attended by a Moor ;
Well mayst thou know her by thy own pro-
    portion,
For up and down she doth resemble thee :
I pray thee, do on them some violent death ;
They have been violent to me and mine.
Tam. Well hast thou lesson'd us ; this shall
    we do.   110
But would it please thee, good Andronicus,
To send for Lucius, thy thrice-valiant son,
Who leads towards Rome a band of warlike
    Goths,
And bid him come and banquet at thy house ;
When he is here, even at thy solemn feast,
I will bring in the empress and her sons,
The emperor himself and all thy foes ;
And at thy mercy shalt they stoop and kneel,
And on them shalt thou ease thy angry heart.

What says Andronicus to this device ?　120
　Tit. Marcus, my brother ! 'tis sad Titus
　　calls.

Enter MARCUS.

Go, gentle Marcus, to thy nephew Lucius ;
Thou shalt inquire him out among the Goths :
Bid him repair to me, and bring with him
Some of the chiefest princes of the Goths ;
Bid him encamp his soldiers where they are :
Tell him the emperor and the empress too
Feast at my house, and he shall feast with
　　them.
This do thou for my love ; and so let him,
As he regards his aged father's life.　　130
　Marc. This will I do, and soon return
　　again.　　　　　　　　　　　　　[*Exit.*
　Tam. Now will I hence about thy business,
And take my ministers along with me.
　Tit. Nay, nay, let Rape and Murder stay
　　with me ;
Or else I'll call my brother back again,
And cleave to no revenge but Lucius.
　Tam. [*Aside to her sons*] What say you,
　　boys ? will you bide with him,
Whiles I go tell my lord the emperor
How I have govern'd our determined jest ?
Yield to his humor, smooth and speak him
　　fair,　　　　　　　　　　　　　　140
And tarry with him till I turn again.
　Tit. [*Aside*] I know them all, though they
　　suppose me mad,
And will o'erreach them in their own devices :
A pair of cursed hell-hounds and their dam !
　Dem. Madam, depart at pleasure ; leave us
　　here.
　Tam. Farewell, Andronicus : Revenge now
　　goes
To lay a complot to betray thy foes.
　Tit. I know thou dost ; and, sweet Revenge,
　　farewell　　　　　　　　　[*Exit Tamora.*
　Chi. Tell us, old man, how shall we be em-
　　ploy'd ?　　　　　　　　　　　　149
　Tit. Tut, I have work enough for you to
　　do.
Publius, come hither, Caius, and Valentine !

Enter PUBLIUS and others.

　Pub. What is your will ?
　Tit. Know you these two ?
　Pub. The empress' sons, I take them,
　　Chiron and Demetrius.
　Tit. Fie, Publius, fie ! thou art too much
　　deceiv'd ;
The one is Murder, Rape is the other's name ;
And therefore bind them, gentle Publius.
Caius and Valentine, lay hands on them.
Oft have you heard me wish for such an
　　hour,　　　　　　　　　　　　　160
And now I find it ; therefore bind them sure,
And stop their mouths, if they begin to cry.
　　　　　　　　　　　　　　　　　[*Exit.*
[*Publius, &c. lay hold on Chiron and
　　Demetrius.*
　Chi. Villains, forbear ! we are the em-
　　press' sons.
　Pub. And therefore do we what we are
　　commanded.
Stop close their mouths, let them not speak a
　　word.
Is he sure bound ? look that you bind them
　　fast.

Re-enter TITUS, *with* LAVINIA ; *he bearing a
　　knife, and she a basin.*

　Tit. Come, come, Lavinia ; look, thy foes
　　are bound.
Sirs, stop their mouths, let them not speak to
　　me ;
But let them hear what fearful words I utter.
O villains, Chiron and Demetrius !　　170
Here stands the spring whom you have stain'd
　　with mud,
This goodly summer with your winter mix'd.
You kill'd her husband, and for that vile fault
Two of her brothers were condemn'd to death,
My hand cut off and made a merry jest ;
Both her sweet hands, her tongue, and that
　　more dear
Than hands or tongue, her spotless chastity,
Inhuman traitors, you constrain'd and forced.
What would you say, if I should let you
　　speak ?　　　　　　　　　　　　179
Villains, for shame you could not beg for
　　grace.
Hark, wretches ! how I mean to martyr you.
This one hand yet is left to cut your throats,
Whilst that Lavinia 'tween her stumps doth
　　hold
The basin that receives your guilty blood.
You know your mother means to feast with
　　me,
And calls herself Revenge, and thinks me
　　mad :
Hark, villains ! I will grind your bones to dust
And with your blood and it I'll make a paste,
And of the paste a coffin I will rear
And make two pasties of your shameful
　　heads,　　　　　　　　　　　　190
And bid that strumpet, your unhallow'd dam,
Like to the earth swallow her own increase.
This is the feast that I have bid her to,
And this the banquet she shall surfeit on ;
For worse than Philomel you used my
　　daughter,
And worse than Progne I will be revenged :
And now prepare your throats. Lavinia,
　　come,　　　　　　　[*He cuts their throats.*
Receive the blood : and when that they are
　　dead,
Let me go grind their bones to powder small
And with this hateful liquor temper it ;　200
And in that paste let their vile heads be baked.
Come, come, be every one officious
To make this banquet ; which I wish may
　　prove
More stern and bloody than the Centaurs'
　　feast.
So, now bring them in, for I'll play the cook,
And see them ready 'gainst their mother
　　comes.
　　　　　[*Exeunt, bearing the dead bodies.*

SCENE III. *Court of Titus's house. A
　　banquet set out.*

Enter LUCIUS, MARCUS, *and* Goths, *with*
　　AARON *prisoner.*

　Luc. Uncle Marcus, since it is my father's
　　mind
That I repair to Rome, I am content.
　First Goth. And ours with thine, befall
　　what fortune will.
　Luc. Good uncle, take you in this barba-
　　rous Moor,

This ravenous tiger, this accursed devil ;
Let him receive no sustenance, fetter him,
Till he be brought unto the empress' face,
For testimony of her foul proceedings :
And see the ambush of our friends be strong ;
I fear the emperor means no good to us.   10

Aar. Some devil whisper curses in mine
    ear,
And prompt me, that my tongue may utter
    forth
The venomous malice of my swelling heart !

Luc. Away, inhuman dog ! unhallow'd
    slave !
Sirs, help our uncle to convey him in.
        [*Exeunt Goths, with Aaron.
        Flourish within.*
The trumpets show the emperor is at hand.

Enter SATURNINUS *and* TAMORA, *with* ÆMIL-
IUS, *Tribunes, Senators, and others.*

Sat. What, hath the firmament more suns
    than one ?

Luc. What boots it thee to call thyself a
    sun ?

Marc. Rome's emperor, and nephew, break
    the parle ;
These quarrels must be quietly debated.   20
The feast is ready, which the careful Titus
Hath ordain'd to an honorable end,
For peace, for love, for league, and good to
    Rome :
Please you, therefore, draw nigh, and take
    your places.

Sat. Marcus, we will.
    [*Hautboys sound. The Company sit down
    at table.*

Enter TITUS *dressed like a Cook,* LAVINIA
veiled, young LUCIUS, *and others.* TITUS
places the dishes on the table.

Tit. Welcome, my gracious lord ; welcome,
    dread queen ;
Welcome, ye warlike Goths ; welcome, Lucius ;
And welcome, all : although the cheer be poor,
'Twill fill your stomachs ; please you eat of it.

Sat. Why art thou thus attired, Andro-
    nicus ?   30

Tit. Because I would be sure to have all
    well,
To entertain your highness and your empress.

Tam. We are beholding to you, good An-
    dronicus.

Tit. An if your highness knew my heart,
    you were.
My lord the emperor, resolve me this :
Was it well done of rash Virginius
To slay his daughter with his own right hand,
Because she was enforced, stain'd, and de-
    flower'd ?

Sat. It was, Andronicus.

Tit. Your reason, mighty lord ?   40

Sat. Because the girl should not survive her
    shame,
And by her presence still renew his sorrows.

Tit. A reason mighty, strong, and effec-
    tual ;
A pattern, precedent, and lively warrant,
For me, most wretched, to perform the like.
Die, die, Lavinia, and thy shame with thee ;
    [*Kills Lavinia.*
And, with thy shame, thy father's sorrow die !

Sat. What hast thou done, unnatural and
    unkind ?

Tit. Kill'd her, for whom my tears have
    made me blind.
I am as woful as Virginius was,   50
And have a thousand times more cause than he
To do this outrage : and it now is done.

Sat. What, was she ravish'd ? tell who did
    the deed.

Tit. Will't please you eat ? will't please
    your highness feed ?

Tam. Why hast thou slain thine only
    daughter thus ?

Tit. Not I ; 'twas Chiron and Demetrius :
They ravish'd her, and cut away her tongue ;
And they, 'twas they, that did her all this
    wrong.

Sat. Go fetch them hither to us presently.

Tit. Why, there they are both, baked in
    that pie ;   60
Whereof their mother daintily hath fed,
Eating the flesh that she herself hath bred.
'Tis true, 'tis true ; witness my knife's sharp
    point.   [*Kills Tamora.*

Sat. Die, frantic wretch, for this accursed
    deed !   [*Kills Titus.*

Luc. Can the son's eye behold his father
    bleed ?
There's meed for meed, death for a deadly
    deed !
    [*Kills Saturninus. A great tumult.
    Lucius, Marcus, and others go
    up into the balcony.*

Marc. You sad-faced men, people and sons
    of Rome,
By uproar sever'd, like a flight of fowl
Scatter'd by winds and high tempestuous gusts,
O, let me teach you how to knit again   70
This scatter'd corn into one mutual sheaf,
These broken limbs again into one body ;
Lest Rome herself be bane unto herself,
And she whom mighty kingdoms court'sy to,
Like a forlorn and desperate castaway,
Do shameful execution on herself.
But if my frosty signs and chaps of age,
Grave witnesses of true experience,
Cannot induce you to attend my words,
[*To Lucius*] Speak, Rome's dear friend, as
    erst our ancestor,   80
When with his solemn tongue he did discourse
To love-sick Dido's sad attending ear
The story of that baleful burning night
When subtle Greeks surprised King Priam's
    Troy,
Tell us what Sinon hath bewitch'd our ears,
Or who hath brought the fatal engine in
That gives our Troy, our Rome, the civil
    wound.
My heart is not compact of flint nor steel ;
Nor can I utter all our bitter grief,
But floods of tears will drown my oratory,   90
And break my utterance, even in the time
When it should move you to attend me most,
Lending your kind commiseration.
Here is a captain, let him tell the tale ;
Your hearts will throb and weep to hear him
    speak.

Luc. Then, noble auditory, be it known to
    you,
That cursed Chiron and Demetrius
Were they that murdered our emperor's
    brother ;

And they it were that ravished our sister :
For their fell faults our brothers were be-
	headed ;			100
Our father's tears despised, and basely cozen'd
Of that true hand that fought Rome's quarrel
	out,
And sent her enemies unto the grave.
Lastly, myself unkindly banished,
The gates shut on me, and turn'd weeping out,
To beg relief among Rome's enemies :
Who drown'd their enmity in my true tears,
And oped their arms to embrace me as a
	friend.
I am the turned forth, be it known to you,
That have preserved her welfare in my blood ;
And from her bosom took the enemy's point,
Sheathing the steel in my adventurous body.
Alas, you know I am no vaunter, I ;
My scars can witness, dumb although they are,
That my report is just and full of truth.
But, soft ! methinks I do digress too much,
Citing my worthless praise : O, pardon me ;
For when no friends are by, men praise them-
	selves.
	Marc. Now is my turn to speak. Behold
		this child :
	[*Pointing to the Child in the arms of
			an Attendant.*
Of this was Tamora delivered ;		120
The issue of an irreligious Moor,
Chief architect and plotter of these woes :
The villain is alive in Titus' house,
And as he is, to witness this is true.
Now judge what cause had Titus to revenge
These wrongs, unspeakable, past patience,
Or more than any living man could bear.
Now you have heard the truth, what say you,
	Romans ?
Have we done aught amiss,—show us wherein,
And, from the place where you behold us
	now,					130
The poor remainder of Andronici
Will, hand in hand, all headlong cast us down,
And on the ragged stones beat forth our
	brains,
And make a mutual closure of our house.
Speak, Romans, speak ; and if you say we
	shall,
Lo, hand in hand, Lucius and I will fall.
	Æmil. Come, come, thou reverend man of
		Rome,
And bring our emperor gently in thy hand,
Lucius our emperor ; for well I know
The common voice do cry it shall be so.	140
	All. Lucius, all hail, Rome's royal em-
		peror !
	Marc. Go, go into old Titus' sorrowful
		house,			[*To Attendants.*
And hither hale that misbelieving Moor,
To be adjudged some direful slaughtering
	death,
As punishment for his most wicked life.
				[*Exeunt Attendants.*

	Lucius, Marcus, *and the others descend.*

	All. Lucius, all hail, Rome's gracious gov-
		ernor !
	Luc. Thanks, gentle Romans : may I gov-
		ern so,
To heal Rome's harms, and wipe away her
	woe !

But, gentle people, give me aim awhile,
For nature puts me to a heavy task :	150
Stand all aloof : but, uncle, draw you near,
To shed obsequious tears upon this trunk.
O, take this warm kiss on thy pale cold lips,
				[*Kissing Titus.*
These sorrowful drops upon thy blood-stain'd
	face,
The last true duties of thy noble son !
	Marc. Tear for tear, and loving kiss for
		kiss,
Thy brother Marcus tenders on thy lips :
O, were the sum of these that I should pay
Countless and infinite, yet would I pay them !
	Luc. Come hither, boy ; come, come, and
		learn of us			160
To melt in showers : thy grandsire loved thee
	well :
Many a time he danced thee on his knee,
Sung thee asleep, his loving breast thy pillow :
Many a matter hath he told to thee,
Meet and agreeing with thine infancy ;
In that respect, then, like a loving child,
Shed yet some small drops from thy tender
	spring,
Because kind nature doth require it so :
Friends should associate friends in grief and
	woe :					169
Bid him farewell ; commit him to the grave ;
Do him that kindness, and take leave of him.
	Young Luc. O grandsire, grandsire ! even
		with all my heart
Would I were dead, so you did live again !
O Lord, I cannot speak to him for weeping ;
My tears will choke me, if I ope my mouth.

	Re-enter Attendants *with* Aaron.

	Æm. You sad Andronici, have done with
		woes :
Give sentence on this execrable wretch,
That hath been breeder of these dire events.
	Luc. Set him breast-deep in earth, and
		famish him ;
There let him stand, and rave, and cry for
	food ;					180
If any one relieves or pities him,
For the offence he dies. This is our doom :
Some stay to see him fasten'd in the earth.
	Aar. O, why should wrath be mute, and
		fury dumb ?
I am no baby, I, that with base prayers
I should repent the evils I have done :
Ten thousand worse than ever yet I did
Would I perform, if I might have my will ;
If one good deed in all my life I did,
I do repent it from my very soul.		190
	Luc. Some loving friends convey the em-
		peror hence,
And give him burial in his father's grave :
My father and Lavinia shall forthwith
Be closed in our household's monument.
As for that heinous tiger, Tamora,
No funeral rite, nor man in mourning weeds,
No mournful bell shall ring her burial ;
But throw her forth to beasts and birds of
	prey :
Her life was beast-like, and devoid of pity ;
And, being so, shall have like want of pity.
See justice done on Aaron, that damn'd Moor,
By whom our heavy haps had their beginning :
Then, afterwards, to order well the state,
That like events may ne'er it ruinate. [*Exeunt.*

KING HENRY VI. PART I.

(WRITTEN ABOUT 1590–91.)

INTRODUCTION.

This is almost certainly an old play, by one or more authors, which, as we find it in the First Folio, had received touches from the hand of Shakespeare. In Henslowe's diary a *Henry VI.* is said to have been acted March 3, 1591–92. It was extremely popular. Nash, in his *Pierce Pennilesse* (1592), alludes to the triumph on the stage of "brave Talbot" over the French. But we have no reason for assuming that the play which we possess was that mentioned by Henslowe, or alluded to by Nash. Greene had, perhaps, a chief hand in the play, and he may have been assisted by Peele and Marlowe. There is a general agreement among critics in attributing to Shakespeare the scene (Act II. Sc. IV.) in which the white and red roses are plucked as emblems of the rival parties in the state ; perhaps the scene of the wooing of Margaret by Suffolk (Act V., Sc. III., L. 45, and onwards), if not written by Shakespeare was touched by him. The general spirit of the drama belongs to an older school than the Shakespearean, "and it is a happiness," says Prof. Dowden, " not to have to ascribe to our greatest poet the crude and hateful handling of the character of Joan of Arc, excused though to some extent it may be by the concurrence of view in our old English chronicles."

DRAMATIS PERSONÆ.

KING HENRY the Sixth.
DUKE OF GLOUCESTER, uncle to the King, and Protector.
DUKE OF BEDFORD, uncle to the King, and Regent of France.
THOMAS BEAUFORT, Duke of Exeter, great-uncle to the King.
HENRY BEAUFORT, great-uncle to the King, Bishop of Winchester, and afterwards Cardinal.
JOHN BEAUFORT, Earl, afterwards Duke, of Somerset.
RICHARD PLANTAGENET, son of Richard late Earl of Cambridge, afterwards Duke of York.
EARL OF WARWICK.
EARL OF SALISBURY.
EARL OF SUFFOLK.
LORD TALBOT, afterwards Earl of Shrewsbury.
JOHN TALBOT, his son.
EDMUND MORTIMER, Earl of March.
SIR JOHN FASTOLFE.
SIR WILLIAM LUCY.
SIR WILLIAM GLANSDALE.
SIR THOMAS GARGRAVE.
Mayor of London.
WOODVILE, Lieutenant of the Tower.

VERNON, of the White-Rose or York faction.
BASSET, of the Red-Rose or Lancaster faction.
A Lawyer. Mortimer's Keepers.
CHARLES, Dauphin, and afterwards King, of France.
REIGNIER, Duke of Anjou, and titular King of Naples.
DUKE OF BURGUNDY.
DUKE OF ALENÇON.
BASTARD OF ORLEANS.
Governor of Paris.
Master-Gunner of Orleans, and his Son.
General of the French forces in Bourdeaux.
A French Sergeant. A Porter.
An old Shepherd, father to Joan la Pucelle.

MARGARET, daughter to Reignier, afterwards married to King Henry.
COUNTESS OF AUVERGNE.
JOAN LA PUCELLE, commonly called Joan of Arc.

Lords, Warders of the Tower, Heralds, Officers, Soldiers, Messengers, and Attendants.
Fiends appearing to La Pucelle.

SCENE : *Partly in England, and partly in France.*

ACT I.

SCENE I. *Westminster Abbey.*

Dead March. Enter the Funeral of KING
HENRY *the Fifth, attended on by the* DUKE
OF BEDFORD, *Regent of France; the* DUKE
OF GLOUCESTER, *Protector; the* DUKE OF
EXETER, *the* EARL OF WARWICK, *the*
BISHOP OF WINCHESTER, *Heralds, &c.*

Bed. Hung be the heavens with black,
    yield day to night!
Comets, importing change of times and states,
Brandish your crystal tresses in the sky,
And with them scourge the bad revolting stars
That have consented unto Henry's death!
King Henry the Fifth, too famous to live long!
England ne'er lost a king of so much worth.
    Glou. England ne'er had a king until his
    time.
Virtue he had, deserving to command:
His brandish'd sword did blind men with his
    beams: 10
His arms spread wider than a dragon's wings;
His sparking eyes, replete with wrathful fire,
More dazzled and drove back his enemies
Than mid-day sun fierce bent against their
    faces.
What should I say? his deeds exceed all
    speech:
He ne'er lift up his hand but conquered.
    Exe. We mourn in black: why mourn we
    not in blood?
Henry is dead and never shall revive:
Upon a wooden coffin we attend,
And death's dishonorable victory   20
We with our stately presence glorify,
Like captives bound to a triumphant car.
What! shall we curse the planets of mishap
That plotted thus our glory's overthrow?
Or shall we think the subtle-witted French
Conjurers and sorcerers, that afraid of him
By magic verses have contrived his end?
    Win. He was a king bless'd of the King
    of kings.
Unto the French the dreadful judgement-day
So dreadful will not be as was his sight.   30
The battles of the Lord of hosts he fought:
The church's prayers made him so prosperous.
    Glou. The church! where is it? Had
    not churchmen pray'd,
His thread of life had not so soon decay'd:
None do you like but an effeminate prince,
Whom, like a school-boy, you may over-awe.
    Win. Gloucester, whate'er we like, thou
    art protector
And lookest to command the prince and
    realm.
Thy wife is proud; she holdeth thee in awe,
More than God or religious churchmen
    may.   40
    Glou. Name not religion, for thou lovest
    the flesh,
And ne'er throughout the year to church thou
    go'st
Except it be to pray against thy foes.
    Bed. Cease, cease these jars and rest your
    minds in peace:
Let's to the altar: heralds, wait on us:
Instead of gold, we'll offer up our arms:
Since arms avail not now that Henry's dead.

Posterity, await for wretched years,
When at their mothers' moist eyes babes shall
    suck,
Our isle be made a nourish of salt tears,   50
And none but women left to wail the dead.
Henry the Fifth, thy ghost I invocate:
Prosper this realm, keep it from civil broils,
Combat with adverse planets in the heavens!
A far more glorious star thy soul will make
Than Julius Cæsar or bright ——

Enter a Messenger.

    Mess. My honorable lords, health to you
    all!
Sad tidings bring I to you out of France,
Of loss, of slaughter and discomfiture:
Guienne, Champagne, Rheims, Orleans,   60
Paris, Guysors, Poictiers, are all quite lost.
    Bed. What say'st thou, man, before dead
    Henry's corse?
Speak softly, or the loss of those great towns
Will make him burst his lead and rise from
    death.
    Glou. Is Paris lost? is Rouen yielded up?
If Henry were recall'd to life again,
These news would cause him once more yield
    the ghost.
    Exe. How were they lost? what treachery
    was used?
    Mess. No treachery; but want of men and
    money.
Amongst the soldiers this is muttered,   70
That here you maintain several factions,
And whilst a field should be dispatch'd and
    fought,
You are disputing of your generals:
One would have lingering wars with little cost;
Another would fly swift, but wanteth wings;
A third thinks, without expense at all,
By guileful fair words peace may be obtain'd.
Awake, awake, English nobility!
Let not sloth dim your honors new-begot:
Cropp'd are the flower-de-luces in your arms;
Of England's coat one half is cut away.   81
    Exe. Were our tears wanting to this
    funeral,
These tidings would call forth their flowing
    tides.
    Bed. Me they concern; Regent I am of
    France.
Give me my steeled coat. I'll fight for France.
Away with these disgraceful wailing robes!
Wounds will I lend the French instead of
    eyes,
To weep their intermissive miseries.

Enter to them another Messenger.

    Mess. Lords, view these letters full of bad
    mischance.
France is revolted from the English quite,   90
Except some petty towns of no import:
The Dauphin Charles is crowned king of
    Rheims;
The Bastard of Orleans with him is join'd;
Reignier, Duke of Anjou, doth take his part;
The Duke of Alençon flieth to his side.
    Exe. The Dauphin crowned king! all fly
    to him!
O, whither shall we fly from this reproach?
    Glou. We will not fly, but to our enemies'
    throats.
Bedford, if thou be slack, I'll fight it out.

Bed. Gloucester, why doubt'st thou of my
    forwardness ?   100
An army have I muster'd in my thoughts,
Wherewith already France is overrun.

        Enter another Messenger.

Mess. My gracious lords, to add to your
    laments,
Wherewith you now bedew King Henry's
    hearse,
I must inform you of a dismal fight
Betwixt the stout Lord Talbot and the French.
Win. What ! wherein Talbot overcame ?
    is't so ?
Mess. O, no ; wherein Lord Talbot was
    o'erthrown :
The circumstance I'll tell you more at large.
The tenth of August last this dreadful lord,
Retiring from the siege of Orleans,   111
Having full scarce six thousand in his troop,
By three and twenty thousand of the French
Was round encompassed and set upon.
No leisure had he to enrank his men ;
He wanted pikes to set before his archers ;
Instead whereof sharp stakes pluck'd out of
    hedges
They pitched in the ground confusedly,
To keep the horsemen off from breaking in.
More than three hours the fight continued ;
Where valiant Talbot above human thought
Enacted wonders with his sword and lance :
Hundreds he sent to hell, and none durst
    stand him ;
Here, there, and every where, enraged he flew :
The French exclaim'd, the devil was in arms ;
All the whole army stood agazed on him :
His soldiers spying his undaunted spirit
A Talbot ! a Talbot ! cried out amain
And rush'd into the bowels of the battle.
Here had the conquest fully been seal'd up,
If Sir John Fastolfe had not play'd the cow-
    ard :   131
He, being in the vaward, placed behind
With purpose to relieve and follow them,
Cowardly fled, not having struck one stroke.
Hence grew the general wreck and massacre ;
Enclosed were they with their enemies :
A base Walloon, to win the Dauphin's grace,
Thrust Talbot with a spear into the back,
Whom all France with their chief assembled
    strength
Durst not presume to look once in the face.
Bed. Is Talbot slain ? then I will slay my-
    self,   141
For living idly here in pomp and ease,
Whilst such a worthy leader, wanting aid,
Unto his dastard foemen is betray'd.
Mess. O no, he lives ; but is took prisoner,
And Lord Scales with him and Lord Hunger-
    ford :
Most of the rest slaughter'd or took likewise.
Bed. His ransom there is none but I shall
    pay :
I'll hale the Dauphin headlong from his
    throne :   149
His crown shall be the ransom of my friend ;
Four of their lords I'll change for one of ours.
Farewell, my masters ; to my task will I ;
Bonfires in France forthwith I am to make,
To keep our great Saint George's feast withal :
Ten thousand soldiers with me I will take,

Whose bloody deeds shall make all Europe
    quake.
Mess. So you had need ; for Orleans is be-
    sieged :
The English army is grown weak and faint :
The Earl of Salisbury craveth supply,
And hardly keeps his men from mutiny,   160
Since they, so few, watch such a multitude.
Exe. Remember, lords, your oaths to
    Henry sworn,
Either to quell the Dauphin utterly,
Or bring him in obedience to your yoke.
Bed. I do remember it ; and here take my
    leave,
To go about my preparation.   [*Exit.*
Glou. I'll to the Tower with all the haste I
    can,
To view the artillery and munition ;
And then I will proclaim young Henry king.
                                        [*Exit.*
Exe. To Eltham will I, where the young
    king is,   170
Being ordain'd his special governor,
And for his safety there I'll best devise. [*Exit.*
Win. Each hath his place and function to
    attend :
I am left out ; for me nothing remains.
But long I will not be Jack out of office :
The king from Eltham I intend to steal
And sit at chiefest stern of public weal.
                                        [*Exeunt.*

        SCENE II. *France. Before Orleans.*

Sound a flourish. Enter CHARLES, ALEN-
    ÇON, *and* REIGNIER, *marching with drum
    and Soldiers.*

Char. Mars his true moving, even as in the
    heavens
So in the earth, to this day is not known :
Late did he shine upon the English side ;
Now we are victors ; upon us he smiles.
What towns of any moment but we have ?
At pleasure here we lie near Orleans ;
Otherwhiles the famish'd English, like pale
    ghosts,
Faintly besiege us one hour in a month.
Alen. They want their porridge and their
    fat bull-beeves :
Either they must be dieted like mules   10
And have their provender tied to their mouths
Or piteous they will look, like drowned mice.
Reig. Let's raise the siege : why live we idly
    here ?
Talbot is taken, whom we wont to fear :
Remaineth none but mad-brain'd Salisbury ;
And he may well in fretting spend his gall,
Nor men nor money hath he to make war.
Char. Sound, sound alarum ! we will rush
    on them.
Now for the honor of the forlorn French !
Him I forgive my death that killeth me   20
When he sees me go back one foot or fly.
                                        [*Exeunt.*

*Here alarum ; they are beaten back by the
    English with great loss. Re-enter* CHARLES,
    ALENÇON, *and* REIGNIER.

Char. Who ever saw the like ? what men
    have I !
Dogs ! cowards ! dastards ! I would ne'er have
    fled,
But that they left me 'midst my enemies.

Reig. Salisbury is a desperate homicide ;
He fighteth as one weary of his life.
The other lords, like lions wanting food,
Do rush upon us as their hungry prey.
    Alen. Froissart, a countryman of ours, re-
        cords,
England all Olivers and Rowlands bred,   30
During the time Edward the Third did reign.
More truly now may this be verified ;
For none but Samsons and Goliases
It sendeth forth to skirmish. One to ten !
Lean, raw-boned rascals ! who would e'er sup-
        pose
They had such courage and audacity ?
    Char. Let's leave this town ; for they are
        hare-brain'd slaves,
And hunger will enforce them to be more
        eager :
Of old I know them ; rather with their teeth
The walls they'll tear down than forsake the
        siege.   40
    Reig. I think, by some odd gimmors or
        device
Their arms are set like clocks, still to strike
        on ;
Else ne'er could they hold out so as they do.
By my consent, we'll even let them alone.
    Alen. Be it so.

        Enter the BASTARD *of Orleans.*

    Bast. Where's the Prince Dauphin ? I have
        news for him.
    Char. Bastard of Orleans, thrice welcome
        to us.
    Bast. Methinks your looks are sad, your
        cheer appall'd :
Hath the late overthrow wrought this offence ?
Be not dismay'd, for succor is at hand :   50
A holy maid hither with me I bring,
Which by a vision sent to her from heaven
Ordained is to raise this tedious siege
And drive the English forth the bounds of
        France.
The spirit of deep prophecy she hath,
Exceeding the nine sibyls of old Rome :
What's past and what's to come she can
        descry.
Speak, shall I call her in ? Believe my words,
For they are certain and unfallible.
    Char. Go, call her in. [*Exit Bastard.*] But
        first, to try her skill,   60
Reignier, stand thou as Dauphin in my place :
Question her proudly ; let thy looks be stern :
By this means shall we sound what skill she
        hath.

Re-enter the BASTARD *of Orleans, with* JOAN
        LA PUCELLE.

    Reig. Fair maid, is't thou wilt do these
        wondrous feats ?
    Puc. Reignier, is't thou that thinkest to
        beguile me ?
Where is the Dauphin ? Come, come from
        behind ;
I know thee well, though never seen before.
Be not amazed, there's nothing hid from me :
In private will I talk with thee apart.
Stand back, you lords, and give us leave
        awhile.   70
    Reig. She takes upon her bravely at first
        dash.

    Puc. Dauphin, I am by birth a shepherd's
        daughter,
My wit untrain'd in any kind of art.
Heaven and our Lady gracious hath it pleased
To shine on my contemptible estate :
Lo, whilst I waited on my tender lambs,
And to sun's parching heat display'd my
        cheeks,
God's mother deigned to appear to me
And in a vision full of majesty
Will'd me to leave my base vocation   80
And free my country from calamity :
Her aid she promised and assured success :
In complete glory she reveal'd herself ;
And, whereas I was black and swart before,
With those clear rays which she infused on me
That beauty am I bless'd with which you see.
Ask me what question thou canst possible,
And I will answer unpremeditated :
My courage try by combat, if thou darest,
And thou shalt find that I exceed my sex.   90
Resolve on this, thou shalt be fortunate,
If thou receive me for thy warlike mate.
    Char. Thou hast astonish'd me with thy
        high terms :
Only this proof I'll of thy valor make,
In single combat thou shalt buckle with me,
And if thou vanquishest, thy words are true ;
Otherwise I renounce all confidence.
    Puc. I am prepared : here is my keen-
        edged sword,
Deck'd with five flower-de-luces on each side ;
The which at Touraine, in Saint Katharine's
        churchyard,   100
Out of a great deal of old iron I chose forth.
    Char. Then come, o' God's name ; I fear
        no woman.
    Puc. And while I live, I'll ne'er fly from a
        man.
    [*Here they fight, and Joan la Pucelle
        overcomes.*
    Char. Stay, stay thy hands ! thou art an
        Amazon
And fightest with the sword of Deborah.
    Puc. Christ's mother helps me, else I were
        too weak.
    Char. Whoe'er helps thee, 'tis thou that
        must help me :
Impatiently I burn with thy desire ;
My heart and hands thou hast at once sub-
        dued.
Excellent Pucelle, if thy name be so,   110
Let me thy servant and not sovereign be :
'Tis the French Dauphin sueth to thee thus.
    Puc. I must not yield to any rites of love,
For my profession's sacred from above :
When I have chased all thy foes from hence,
Then will I think upon a recompense.
    Char. Meantime look gracious on thy
        prostrate thrall.
    Reig. My lord, methinks, is very long in
        talk.
    Alen. Doubtless he shrives this woman to
        her smock ;
Else ne'er could he so long protract his speech.
    Reig. Shall we disturb him, since he keeps
        no mean ?   121
    Alen. He may mean more than we poor
        men do know :
These women are shrewd tempters with their
        tongues.

Reig. My lord, where are you ? what devise
   you on ?
Shall we give over Orleans, or no ?
Puc. Why, no, I say, distrustful recreants !
Fight till the last gasp ; I will be your guard.
Char. What she says I'll confirm : we'll
   fight it out.
Puc. Assign'd am I to be the English
   scourge.
This night the siege assuredly I'll raise :   130
Expect Saint Martin's summer, halcyon days,
Since I have entered into these wars.
Glory is like a circle in the water,
Which never ceaseth to enlarge itself
Till by broad spreading it disperse to nought.
With Henry's death the English circle ends ;
Dispersed are the glories it included.
Now am I like that proud insulting ship
Which Cæsar and his fortune bare at once.
Char. Was Mahomet inspired with a
   dove ?
Thou with an eagle art inspired then.   141
Helen, the mother of great Constantine,
Nor yet Saint Philip's daughters, were like
   thee.
Bright star of Venus, fall'n down on the earth,
How may I reverently worship thee enough ?
Alen. Leave off delays, and let us raise the
   siege.
Reig. Woman, do what thou canst to save
   our honors ;
Drive them from Orleans and be immortal-
   ized.
Char. Presently we'll try : come, let's away
   about it :
No prophet will I trust, if she prove false. 150
                                [Exeunt.

Scene III. *London. Before the Tower.*
Enter the Duke of Gloucester, *with his*
   Serving-men *in blue coats.*
Glou. I am come to survey the Tower this
   day :
Since Henry's death, I fear, there is convey-
   ance.
Where be these warders, that they wait not
   here ?
Open the gates ; 'tis Gloucester that calls.
First Warder. [*Within*] Who's there that
   knocks so imperiously ?
First Serv. It is the noble Duke of Glouces-
   ter.
Second Warder. [*Within*] Whoe'er he be,
   you may not be let in.
First Serv. Villains, answer you so the
   lord protector ?
First Warder. [*Within*] The Lord protect
   him ! so we answer him :
We do no otherwise than we are will'd.   10
Glou. Who willed you ? or whose will
   stands but mine ?
There's none protector of the realm but I.
Break up the gates, I'll be your warrantize.
Shall I be flouted thus by dunghill grooms ?
[*Gloucester's men rush at the Tower Gates,
and Woodvile the Lieutenant speaks within.*
Woodv. What noise is this ? what traitors
   have we here ?
Glou. Lieutenant, is it you whose voice I
   hear ?
Open the gates ; here's Gloucester that would
   enter.

Woodv. Have patience, noble duke ; I may
   not open ;
The Cardinal of Winchester forbids :
From him I have express commandment   20
That thou nor none of thine shall be let in.
Glou. Faint-hearted Woodvile, prizest him
   'fore me ?
Arrogant Winchester, that haughty prelate,
Whom Henry, our late sovereign, ne'er could
   brook ?
Thou art no friend to God or to the king :
Open the gates, or I'll shut thee out shortly.
Serving-men. Open the gates unto the lord
   protector,
Or we'll burst them open, if that you come
   not quickly.

Enter to the Protector at the Tower Gates
Winchester *and his men in tawny coats.*
Win. How now, ambitious Humphry !
   what means this ?
Glou. Peel'd priest, dost thou command
   me to be shut out ?   30
Win. I do, thou most usurping proditor,
And not protector, of the king or realm.
Glou. Stand back, thou manifest conspir-
   ator,
Thou that contrivedst to murder our dead
   lord ;
Thou that givest whores indulgences to sin :
I'll canvass thee in thy broad cardinal's hat,
If thou proceed in this thy insolence.
Win. Nay, stand thou back, I will not
   budge a foot :
This be Damascus, be thou cursed Cain,
To slay thy brother Abel, if thou wilt.   40
Glou. I will not slay thee, but I'll drive
   thee back :
Thy scarlet robes as a child's bearing-cloth
I'll use to carry thee out of this place.
Win. Do what thou darest ; I beard thee
   to thy face.
Glou. What ! am I dared and bearded to
   my face ?
Draw, men, for all this privileged place ;
Blue coats to tawny coats. Priest, beware your
   beard,
I mean to tug it and to cuff you soundly :
Under my feet I stamp thy cardinal's hat :
In spite of pope or dignities of church,   50
Here by the cheeks I'll drag thee up and down.
Win. Gloucester, thou wilt answer this be-
   fore the pope.
Glou. Winchester goose, I cry, a rope ! a
   rope !
Now beat them hence ; why do you let them
   stay ?
Thee I'll chase hence, thou wolf in sheep's
   array.
Out, tawny coats ! out, scarlet hypocrite !

*Here Gloucester's men beat out the Cardinal's
men, and enter in the hurly-burly the* Mayor
of London *and his* Officers.
May. Fie, lords ! that you, being supreme
   magistrates,
Thus contumeliously should break the peace !
Glou. Peace, mayor ! thou know'st little of
   my wrongs :
Here's Beaufort, that regards nor God nor
   king,   60
Hath here distrain'd the Tower to his use.

Win. Here's Gloucester, a foe to citizens,
One that still motions war and never peace,
O'ercharging your free purses with large fines,
That seeks to overthrow religion,
Because he is protector of the realm,
And would have armor here out of the Tower,
To crown himself king and suppress the
  prince.
  Glou. I will not answer thee with words,
  but blows. [*Here they skirmish again.*
  May. Naught rests for me in this tumul-
  tuous strife   70
But to make open proclamation:
Come, officer; as loud as e'er thou canst,
Cry.
  Off. All manner of men assembled here
in arms this day against God's peace and
the king's, we charge and command you, in his
highness' name, to repair to your several
dwelling-places; and not to wear, handle, or
use any sword, weapon, or dagger, henceforward, upon pain of death.
  Glou. Cardinal, I'll be no breaker of the
  law:
But we shall meet, and break our minds at
  large.
  Win. Gloucester, we will meet; to thy
  cost, be sure:
Thy heart-blood I will have for this day's
  work.
  May. I'll call for clubs, if you will not
  away.
This cardinal's more haughty than the devil.
  Glou. Mayor, farewell: thou dost but
  what thou mayst.
  Win. Abominable Gloucester, guard thy
  head;
For I intend to have it ere long.
  [*Exeunt, severally, Gloucester and Win-
  chester with their Serving-men.*
  May. See the coast clear'd, and then we
  will depart.
Good God, these nobles should such stomachs
  bear!   90
I myself fight not once in forty year.
  [*Exeunt.*

SCENE IV. *Orleans.*

Enter, on the walls, a MASTER GUNNER *and
his Boy.*

  M. Gun. Sirrah, thou know'st how Orleans
  is besieged,
And how the English have the suburbs won.
  Boy. Father, I know; and oft have shot at
  them,
Howe'er unfortunate I miss'd my aim.
  M. Gun. But now thou shalt not. Be thou
  ruled by me:
Chief master-gunner am I of this town;
Something I must do to procure me grace.
The prince's espials have informed me
How the English, in the suburbs close in-
  trench'd,
Wont, through a secret grate of iron bars   10
In yonder tower, to overpeer the city,
And thence discover how with most advantage
They may vex us with shot, or with assault.
To intercept this inconvenience,
A piece of ordnance 'gainst it I have placed;
And even these three days have I watch'd,
If I could see them.
Now do thou watch, for I can stay no longer.

If thou spy'st any, run and bring me word;
And thou shalt find me at the governor's.
                                            [*Exit.*
  Boy. Father, I warrant you; take you no
  care;
I'll never trouble you, if I may spy them.
                                            [*Exit.*

Enter, on the turrets, the LORDS SALISBURY
and TALBOT, SIR WILLIAM GLANSDALE, SIR
THOMAS GARGRAVE, *and others.*

  Sal. Talbot, my life, my joy, again re-
  turn'd!
How wert thou handled being prisoner?
Or by what means got'st thou to be released?
Discourse, I prithee, on this turret's top.
  Tal. The Duke of Bedford had a prisoner
Call'd the brave Lord Ponton de Santrailles;
For him was I exchanged and ransomed.
But with a baser man of arms by far   30
Once in contempt they would have barter'd
  me:
Which I, disdaining, scorn'd; and craved
  death,
Rather than I would be so vile esteem'd.
In fine, redeem'd I was as I desired.
But, O! the treacherous Fastolfe wounds my
  heart,
Whom with my bare fists I would execute,
If I now had him brought into my power.
  Sal. Yet tell'st thou not how thou wert en-
  tertain'd.
  Tal. With scoffs and scorns and contume-
  lious taunts.
In open market-place produced they me,   40
To be a public spectacle to all:
Here, said they, is the terror of the French,
The scarecrow that affrights our children so.
Then broke I from the officers that led me,
And with my nails digg'd stones out of the
  ground,
To hurl at the beholders of my shame:
My grisly countenance made others fly;
None durst come near for fear of sudden
  death.
In iron walls they deem'd me not secure;
So great fear of my name 'mongst them was
  spread,   50
That they supposed I could rend bars of steel,
And spurn in pieces posts of adamant:
Wherefore a guard of chosen shot I had,
That walked about me every minute-while;
And if I did but stir out of my bed,
Ready they were to shoot me to the heart.

Enter the Boy *with a linstock.*

  Sal. I grieve to hear what torments you
  endured,
But we will be revenged sufficiently.
Now it is supper-time in Orleans:
Here, through this grate, I count each one   60
And view the Frenchmen how they fortify:
Let us look in; the sight will much delight
  thee.
Sir Thomas Gargrave, and Sir William Glans-
  dale,
Let me have your express opinions
Where is best place to make our battery next.
  Gar. I think, at the north gate; for there
  stand lords.
  Glan. And I, here, at the bulwark of
  the bridge.

Tal. For aught I see, this city must be
  famish'd,
Or with light skirmishes enfeebled.
  [*Here they shoot. Salisbury and Gargrave*
                        fall.
Sal. O Lord, have mercy on us, wretched
  sinners!   70
Gar. O Lord, have mercy on me, woful
  man!
Tal. What chance is this that suddenly
  hath cross'd us?
Speak, Salisbury; at least, if thou canst speak:
How farest thou, mirror of all martial men?
One of thy eyes and thy cheek's side struck
  off!
Accursed tower! accursed fatal hand
That hath contrived this woful tragedy!
In thirteen battles Salisbury o'ercame;
Henry the Fifth he first train'd to the wars;
Whilst any trump did sound, or drum struck
  up,   80
His sword did ne'er leave striking in the field.
Yet livest thou, Salisbury? though thy speech
  doth fail,
One eye thou hast, to look to heaven for
  grace:
The sun with one eye vieweth all the world.
Heaven, be thou gracious to none alive,
If Salisbury wants mercy at thy hands!
Bear hence his body; I will help to bury it.
Sir Thomas Gargrave, hast thou any life?
Speak unto Talbot; nay, look up to him.
Salisbury, cheer thy spirit with this comfort;
Thou shalt not die whiles—   91
He beckons with his hand and smiles on me,
As who should say 'When I am dead and
  gone,
Remember to avenge me on the French.'
Plantagenet, I will; and like thee, Nero,
Play on the lute, beholding the towns burn:
Wretched shall France be only in my name.
[*Here an alarum, and it thunders and lightens.*
What stir is this? what tumult's in the heav-
  ens?
Whence cometh this alarum and the noise?

        Enter a Messenger.

Mess. My lord, my lord, the French have
  gathered head: 100
The Dauphin, with one Joan la Pucelle join'd,
A holy prophetess new risen up,
Is come with a great power to raise the siege.
[*Here Salisbury lifteth himself up and groans.*
Tal. Hear, hear how dying Salisbury doth
  groan!
It irks his heart he cannot be revenged.
Frenchmen, I'll be a Salisbury to you:
Pucelle or puzzel, dolphin or dogfish,
Your hearts I'll stamp out with my horse's
  heels,
And make a quagmire of your mingled brains.
Convey me Salisbury into his tent,   110
And then we'll try what these dastard French-
  men dare.   [*Alarum. Exeunt.*

        SCENE V. *The same.*

Here an alarum again: and TALBOT *pursu-
eth the* DAUPHIN, *and driveth him: then
enter* JOAN LA PUCELLE, *driving Englishmen before her, and exit after them: then
re-enter* TALBOT.

Tal. Where is my strength, my valor, and
  my force?
Our English troops retire, I cannot stay them:
A woman clad in armor chaseth them.

      Re-enter LA PUCELLE.

Here, here she comes. I'll have a bout with
  thee;
Devil or devil's dam, I'll conjure thee:
Blood will I draw on thee, thou art a witch,
And straightway give thy soul to him thou
  servest.
Puc. Come, come, 'tis only I that must dis-
  grace thee.   [*Here they fight.*
Tal. Heavens, can you suffer hell so to
  prevail?
My breast I'll burst with straining of my cour-
  age   10
And from my shoulders crack my arms asun-
  der,
But I will chastise this high-minded strumpet.
             [*They fight again.*
Puc. Talbot, farewell; thy hour is not yet
  come:
I must go victual Orleans forthwith.
  [*A short alarum; then enter the town with
                      soldiers.*
O'ertake me, if thou canst; I scorn thy
  strength.
Go, go, cheer up thy hungry-starved men;
Help Salisbury to make his testament:
This day is ours, as many more shall be.
                      [*Exit.*
Tal. My thoughts are whirled like a pot-
  ter's wheel;
I know not where I am, nor what I do; 20
A witch, by fear, not force, like Hannibal,
Drives back our troops and conquers as she
  lists:
So bees with smoke and doves with noisome
  stench
Are from their hives and houses driven away.
They call'd us for our fierceness English
  dogs;
Now, like to whelps, we crying run away.
               [*A short alarum.*
Hark, countrymen! either renew the fight,
Or tear the lions out of England's coat;
Renounce your soil, give sheep in lions' stead:
Sheep run not half so treacherous from the
  wolf,   30
Or horse or oxen from the leopard,
As you fly from your oft-subdued slaves.
      [*Alarum. Here another skirmish.*
It will not be: retire into your trenches:
You all consented unto Salisbury's death,
For none would strike a stroke in his revenge.
Pucelle is enter'd into Orleans,
In spite of us or aught that we could do.
O, would I were to die with Salisbury!
The shame hereof will make me hide my head.
  [*Exit Talbot. Alarum; retreat; flourish.*

        SCENE VI. *The same.*

Enter, on the walls, LA PUCELLE, CHARLES,
  REIGNIER, ALENÇON, *and Soldiers.*

Puc. Advance our waving colors on the
  walls;
Rescued is Orleans from the English:
Thus Joan la Pucelle hath perform'd her
  word.

Char. Divinest creature, Astræa's daugh-
    ter,
How shall I honor thee for this success ?
Thy promises are like Adonis' gardens
That one day bloom'd and fruitful were the
    next.
France, triumph in thy glorious prophetess !
Recover'd is the town of Orleans :
More blessed hap did ne'er befall our state.10
  Reig. Why ring not out the bells aloud
    throughout the town ?
Dauphin, command the citizens make bon-
    fires
And feast and banquet in the open streets,
To celebrate the joy that God hath given us.
  Alen. All France will be replete with
    mirth and joy,
When they shall hear how we have play'd the
    men.
  Char. 'Tis Joan, not we, by whom the day
    is won ;
For which I will divide my crown with her,
And all the priests and friars in my realm
Shall in procession sing her endless praise. 20
A statelier pyramis to her I'll rear
Than Rhodope's or Memphis' ever was :
In memory of her when she is dead,
Her ashes, in an urn more precious
Than the rich-jewel'd coffer of Darius,
Transported shall be at high festivals
Before the kings and queens of France.
No longer on Saint Denis will we cry,
But Joan la Pucelle shall be France's saint.
Come in, and let us banquet royally,   30
After this golden day of victory.
                            [*Flourish. Exeunt.*

ACT II.

SCENE I. *Before Orleans.*

Enter a Sergeant *of a band with two* Sentinels.
  Serg. Sirs, take your places and be vigi-
    lant :
If any noise or soldier you perceive
Near to the walls, by some apparent sign
Let us have knowledge at the court of guard.
  First Sent. Sergeant, you shall. [*Exit Ser-
    geant.*] Thus are poor servitors,
When others sleep upon their quiet beds,
Constrain'd to watch in darkness, rain and
    cold.

Enter TALBOT, BEDFORD, BURGUNDY, *and*
    forces, with scaling-ladders, their drums
    beating a dead march.

  Tal. Lord Regent, and redoubted Bur-
    gundy,
By whose approach the regions of Artois,
Wallon and Picardy are friends to us,   10
This happy night the Frenchmen are secure,
Having all day caroused and banqueted :
Embrace we then this opportunity
As fitting best to quittance their deceit
Contrived by art and baleful sorcery.
  Bed. Coward of France ! how much he
    wrongs his fame,
Despairing of his own arm's fortitude,
To join with witches and the help of hell !
  Bur. Traitors have never other company.

But what's that Pucelle whom they term so
    pure ?   20
  Tal. A maid, they say.
  Bed.   A maid ! and be so martial !
  Bur. Pray God she prove not masculine
    ere long,
If underneath the standard of the French
She carry armor as she hath begun.
  Tal. Well, let them practise and converse
    with spirits :
God is our fortress, in whose conquering
    name
Let us resolve to scale their flinty bulwarks.
  Bed. Ascend, brave Talbot ; we will follow
    thee.
  Tal. Not all together : better far, I guess,
That we do make our entrance several ways;30
That, if it chance the one of us do fail,
The other yet may rise against their force.
  Bed. Agreed : I'll to yond corner.
  Bur.   And I to this.
  Tal. And here will Talbot mount, or make
    his grave.
Now, Salisbury, for thee, and for the right
Of English Henry, shall this night appear
How much in duty I am bound to both.
  Sent. Arm ! arm ! the enemy doth make as-
    sault !

        [*Cry : ' St. George,' ' A Talbot.'*

The French leap over the walls in their shirts.
Enter, several ways, the BASTARD *of Orleans,*
ALENÇON, *and* REIGNIER, *half ready, and*
half unready.

  Alen. How now, my lords ! what, all un-
    ready so ?
  Bast. Unready ! ay, and glad we 'scaped so
    well.   40
  Reig. 'Twas time, I trow, to wake and
    leave our beds,
Hearing alarums at our chamber-doors.
  Alen. Of all exploits since first I follow'd
    arms,
Ne'er heard I of a warlike enterprise
More venturous or desperate than this.
  Bast. I think this Talbot be a fiend of hell.
  Reig. If not of hell, the heavens, sure, fa-
    vor him.
  Alen. Here cometh Charles : I marvel how
    he sped.
  Bast. Tut, holy Joan was his defensive
    guard.

Enter CHARLES *and* LA PUCELLE.

  Char. Is this thy cunning, thou deceitful
    dame ?   50
Didst thou at first, to flatter us withal,
Make us partakers of a little gain,
That now our loss might be ten times so
    much ?
  Puc. Wherefore is Charles impatient with
    his friend !
At all times will you have my power alike ?
Sleeping or waking must I still prevail,
Or will you blame and lay the fault on me ?
Improvident soldiers ! had your watch been
    good,
This sudden mischief never could have fall'n.
  Char. Duke of Alençon, this was your de-
    fault,   60
That, being captain of the watch to-night,
Did look no better to that weighty charge.

Alen. Had all your quarters been as safely
    kept
As that whereof I had the government,
We had not been thus shamefully surprised.
  Bast. Mine was secure.
  Reig.   And so was mine, my lord.
  Char. And, for myself, most part of all
    this night,
Within her quarter and mine own precinct
I was employ'd in passing to and fro,
About relieving of the sentinels :   70
Then how or which way should they first break
    in ?
  Puc. Question, my lords, no further of the
    case,
How or which way : 'tis sure they found some
    place
But weakly guarded, where the breach was
    made.
And now there rests no other shift but this ;
To gather our soldiers, scatter'd and dis-
    persed,
And lay new platforms to endamage them.

  Alarum. Enter an English Soldier, *crying ' A
    Talbot ! a Talbot !' They fly, leaving their
    clothes behind.*

  Sold. I'll be so bold to take what they have
    left.
The cry of Talbot serves me for a sword ;
For I have loaden me with many spoils,   80
Using no other weapon but his name.   [*Exit.*

  SCENE II. *Orleans. Within the town.*

Enter TALBOT, BEDFORD, BURGUNDY, *a* Cap-
    tain, *and others.*

  Bed. The day begins to break, and night
    is fled,
Whose pitchy mantle over-veil'd the earth.
Here sound retreat, and cease our hot pursuit.
                        [*Retreat sounded.*
  Tal. Bring forth the body of old Salisbury,
And here advance it in the market-place,
The middle centre of this cursed town.
Now have I paid my vow unto his soul ;
For every drop of blood was drawn from him,
There hath at least five Frenchmen died to-
    night.
And that hereafter ages may behold   10
What ruin happen'd in revenge of him,
Within their chiefest temple I'll erect
A tomb, wherein his corpse shall be interr'd :
Upon the which, that every one may read,
Shall be engraved the sack of Orleans,
The treacherous manner of his mournful death
And what a terror he had been to France.
But, lords, in all our bloody massacre,
I muse we met not with the Dauphin's grace,
His new-come champion, virtuous Joan of
    Arc,
Nor any of his false confederates.   21
  Bed. 'Tis thought, Lord Talbot, when the
    fight began,
Roused on the sudden from their drowsy beds,
They did amongst the troops of armed men
Leap o'er the walls for refuge in the field.
  Bur. Myself, as far as I could well discern
For smoke and dusky vapors of the night,
Am sure I scared the Dauphin and his trull,
When arm in arm they both came swiftly
    running,
Like to a pair of loving turtle-doves   30

That could not live asunder day or night.
After that things are set in order here,
We'll follow them with all the power we have.

              Enter a Messenger.

  Mess. All hail, my lords ! Which of this
    princely train
Call ye the warlike Talbot, for his acts
So much applauded through the realm of
    France ?
  Tal. Here is the Talbot : who would speak
    with him ?
  Mess. The virtuous lady, Countess of
    Auvergne,
With modesty admiring thy renown,
By me entreats, great lord, thou wouldst
    vouchsafe   40
To visit her poor castle where she lies,
That she may boast she hath beheld the man
Whose glory fills the world with loud report.
  Bur. Is it even so ? Nay, then, I see our
    wars
Will turn unto a peaceful comic sport,
When ladies crave to be encounter'd with.
You may not, my lord, despise her gentle suit.
  Tal. Ne'er trust me then ; for when a
    world of men
Could not prevail with all their oratory,
Yet hath a woman's kindness over-ruled :   50
And therefore tell her I return great thanks,
And in submission will attend on her.
Will not your honors bear me company ?
  Bed. No, truly ; it is more than manners
    will :
And I have heard it said, unbidden guests
Are often welcomest when they are gone.
  Tal. Well then, alone, since there's no
    remedy,
I mean to prove this lady's courtesy.
Come hither, captain. [*Whispers.*] You
    perceive my mind ?
  Capt. I do, my lord, and mean accord-
    ingly.   [*Exeunt.* 60

  SCENE III. *Auvergne. The* COUNTESS'S
                    castle.

  Enter the COUNTESS *and her* Porter.

  Count. Porter, remember what I gave in
    charge ;
And when you have done so, bring the keys
    to me.
  Port. Madam, I will.   [*Exit.*
  Count. The plot is laid : if all things fall
    out right,
I shall as famous be by this exploit
As Scythian Tomyris by Cyrus' death.
Great is the rumor of this dreadful knight,
And his achievements of no less account :
Fain would mine eyes be witness with mine
    ears,
To give their censure of these rare reports. 10

          Enter Messenger *and* TALBOT.

  Mess. Madam,
According as your ladyship desired,
By message craved, so is Lord Talbot come.
  Count. And he is welcome. What ! is this
    the man ?
  Mess. Madam, it is.
  Count.   Is this the scourge of France ?
Is this the Talbot, so much fear'd abroad

That with his name the mothers still their
    babes ?
I see report is fabulous and false :
I thought I should have seen some Hercules,
A second Hector, for his grim aspect,   20
And large proportion of his strong-knit limbs.
Alas, this is a child, a silly dwarf !
It cannot be this weak and writhled shrimp
Should strike such terror to his enemies.
    Tal. Madam, I have been bold to trouble
    you ;
But since your ladyship is not at leisure,
I'll sort some other time to visit you.
    Count. What means he now ? Go ask him
    whither he goes.
    Mess. Stay, my Lord Talbot ; for my lady
    craves
To know the cause of your abrupt departure.
    Tal. Marry, for that she's in a wrong be-
    lief,   31
I go to certify her Talbot's here.

            Re-enter Porter *with keys.*

    Count. If thou be he, then art thou pris-
    oner.
    Tal. Prisoner ! to whom ?
    Count.   To me, blood-thirsty lord ;
And for that cause I trained thee to my house.
Long time thy shadow hath been thrall to me,
For in my gallery thy picture hangs :
But now the substance shall endure the like,
And I will chain these legs and arms of thine,
That hast by tyranny these many years   40
Wasted our country, slain our citizens
And sent our sons and husbands captivate.
    Tal. Ha, ha, ha !
    Count. Laughest thou, wretch ? thy mirth
    shall turn to moan.
    Tal. I laugh to see your ladyship so fond
To think that you have aught but Talbot's
    shadow
Whereon to practise your severity.
    Count. Why, art not thou the man ?
    Tal.   I am indeed.
    Count. Then have I substance too.
    Tal. No, no, I am but shadow of my-
    self :   50
You are deceived, my substance is not here ;
For what you see is but the smallest part
And least proportion of humanity :
I tell you, madam, were the whole frame here,
It is of such a spacious lofty pitch,
Your roof were not sufficient to contain't.
    Count. This is a riddling merchant for the
    nonce ;
He will be here, and yet he is not here :
How can these contrarieties agree ?
    Tal. That will I show you presently.   60
        [*Winds his horn. Drums strike up : a
            peal of ordnance. Enter soldiers.*
How say you, madam ? are you now per-
    suaded
That Talbot is but shadow of himself ?
These are his substance, sinews, arms and
    strength,
With which he yoketh your rebellious necks,
Razeth your cities and subverts your towns
And in a moment makes them desolate.
    Count. Victorious Talbot ! pardon my
    abuse :
I find thou art no less than fame hath bruited
And more than may be gather'd by thy shape.

Let my presumption not provoke thy wrath ;70
For I am sorry that with reverence
I did not entertain thee as thou art.
    Tal. Be not dismay'd, fair lady ; nor mis-
    construe
The mind of Talbot, as you did mistake
The outward composition of his body.
What you have done hath not offended me ;
Nor other satisfaction do I crave,
But only, with your patience, that we may
Taste of your wine and see what cates you
    have ;
For soldiers' stomachs always serve them well.
    Count. With all my heart, and think me
    honored   81
To feast so great a warrior in my house.
                                        [*Exeunt.*

SCENE IV. *London. The Temple-garden.*

Enter the EARLS OF SOMERSET, SUFFOLK, *and*
    WARWICK ; RICHARD PLANTAGENET, VER-
    NON, *and another* Lawyer.

    Plan. Great lords and gentlemen, what
    means this silence ?
Dare no man answer in a case of truth ?
    Suf. Within the Temple-hall we were too
    loud ;
The garden here is more convenient.
    Plan. Then say at once if I maintain'd the
    truth ;
Or else was wrangling Somerset in the error ?
    Suf. Faith, I have been a truant in the law,
And never yet could frame my will to it ;
And therefore frame the law unto my will.
    Som. Judge you, my Lord of Warwick,
    then, between us.   10
    War. Between two hawks, which flies the
    higher pitch ;
Between two dogs, which hath the deeper
    mouth ;
Between two blades, which bears the better
    temper :
Between two horses, which doth bear him
    best ;
Between two girls, which hath the merriest
    eye ;
I have perhaps some shallow spirit of judge-
    ment ;
But in these nice sharp quillets of the law,
Good faith, I am no wiser than a daw.
    Plan. Tut, tut, here is a mannerly forbear-
    ance :
The truth appears so naked on my side   20
That any purblind eye may find it out.
    Som. And on my side it is so well ap-
    parell'd,
So clear, so shining and so evident
That it will glimmer through a blind man's
    eye.
    Plan. Since you are tongue-tied and so
    loath to speak,
In dumb significants proclaim your thoughts :
Let him that is a true-born gentleman
And stands upon the honor of his birth,
If he suppose that I have pleaded truth,
From off this brier pluck a white rose with
    me.
    Som. Let him that is no coward nor no
    flatterer,   31
But dare maintain the party of the truth,
Pluck a red rose from off this thorn with me.

War. I love no colors, and without all
	color
Of base insinuating flattery
I pluck this white rose with Plantagenet.
	Suf. I pluck this red rose with young Som-
	erset
And say withal I think he held the right.
	Ver. Stay, lords and gentlemen, and pluck
	no more,
Till you conclude that he upon whose side   40
The fewest roses are cropp'd from the tree
Shall yield the other in the right opinion.
	Som. Good Master Vernon, it is well ob-
	jected :
If I have fewest, I subscribe in silence.
	Plan. And I.
	Ver. Then for the truth and plainness of
	the case,
I pluck this pale and maiden blossom here,
Giving my verdict on the white rose side.
	Som. Prick not your finger as you pluck
	it off,
Lest bleeding you do paint the white rose red
And fall on my side so, against your will.   51
	Ver. If I, my lord, for my opinion bleed,
Opinion shall be surgeon to my hurt
And keep me on the side where still I am.
	Som. Well, well, come on : who else ?
	Law. Unless my study and my books be
	false,
The argument you held was wrong in you :
				[*To Somerset.*
In sign whereof I pluck a white rose too.
	Plan. Now, Somerset, where is your argu-
	ment ?
	Som. Here in my scabbard, meditating that
Shall dye your white rose in a bloody red.   61
	Plan. Meantime your cheeks do counter-
	feit our roses ;
For pale they look with fear, as witnessing
The truth on our side.
	Som.			No, Plantagenet,
'Tis not for fear but anger that thy cheeks
Blush for pure shame to counterfeit our roses,
And yet thy tongue will not confess thy error.
	Plan. Hath not thy rose a canker, Som-
	erset ?
	Som. Hath not thy rose a thorn, Plantag-
	enet ?
	Plan. Ay, sharp and piercing, to maintain
	his truth ;				70
Whiles thy consuming canker eats his false-
	hood.
	Som. Well, I'll find friends to wear my
	bleeding roses,
That shall maintain what I have said is true,
Where false Plantagenet dare not be seen.
	Plan. Now, by this maiden blossom in my
	hand,
I scorn thee and thy fashion, peevish boy.
	Suf. Turn not thy scorns this way, Plan-
	tagenet.
	Plan. Proud Pole, I will, and scorn both
	him and thee.
	Suf. I'll turn my part thereof into thy
	throat.				79
	Som. Away, away, good William de la
	Pole !
We grace the yeoman by conversing with him.
	War. Now, by God's will, thou wrong'st
	him, Somerset ;

His grandfather was Lionel Duke of Clarence,
Third son to the third Edward King of Eng-
	land :
Spring crestless yeomen from so deep a root ?
	Plan. He bears him on the place's privi-
	lege,
Or durst not, for his craven heart, say thus.
	Som. By him that made me, I'll maintain
	my words
On any plot of ground in Christendom.
Was not thy father, Richard Earl of Cam-
	bridge,				90
For treason executed in our late king's days ?
And, by his treason, stand'st not thou at-
	tainted,
Corrupted, and exempt from ancient gentry ?
His trespass yet lives guilty in thy blood ;
And, till thou be restored, thou art a yeoman.
	Plan. My father was attached, not at-
	tainted,
Condemn'd to die for treason, but no traitor ;
And that I'll prove on better men than Som-
	erset,
Were growing time once ripen'd to my will.
For your partaker Pole and you yourself,   100
I'll note you in my book of memory,
To scourge you for this apprehension :
Look to it well and say you are well warn'd.
	Som. Ah, thou shalt find us ready for thee
	still ;
And know us by these colors for thy foes,
For these my friends in spite of thee shall
	wear.
	Plan. And, by my soul, this pale and an-
	gry rose,
As cognizance of my blood-drinking hate,
Will I for ever and my faction wear,
Until it wither with me to my grave   110
Or flourish to the height of my degree.
	Suf. Go forward and be choked with thy
	ambition !
And so farewell until I meet thee next.   [*Exit.*
	Som. Have with thee, Pole. Farewell, am-
	bitious Richard.			[*Exit.*
	Plan. How I am braved and must perforce
	endure it !
	War. This blot that they object against
	your house
Shall be wiped out in the next parliament
Call'd for the truce of Winchester and
	Gloucester ;
And if thou be not then created York,
I will not live to be accounted Warwick.   120
Meantime, in signal of my love to thee,
Against proud Somerset and William Pole,
Will I upon thy party wear this rose :
And here I prophesy : this brawl to-day,
Grown to this faction in the Temple-garden,
Shall send between the red rose and the white
A thousand souls to death and deadly night.
	Plan. Good Master Vernon, I am bound
	to you,
That you on my behalf would pluck a flower.
	Ver. In your behalf still will I wear the
	same.				130
	Law. And so will I.
	Plan. Thanks, gentle sir.
Come, let us four to dinner : I dare say
This quarrel will drink blood another day.
				[*Exeunt.*

SCENE V. *The Tower of London.*

Enter MORTIMER, *brought in a chair, and Gaolers.*

Mor. Kind keepers of my weak decaying age,
Let dying Mortimer here rest himself.
Even like a man new haled from the rack,
So fare my limbs with long imprisonment;
And these grey locks, the pursuivants of death,
Nestor-like aged in an age of care,
Argue the end of Edmund Mortimer.
These eyes, like lamps whose wasting oil is spent,
Wax dim, as drawing to their exigent;
Weak shoulders, overborne with burthening grief,   10
And pithless arms, like to a wither'd vine
That droops his sapless branches to the ground;
Yet are these feet, whose strengthless stay is numb,
Unable to support this lump of clay,
Swift-winged with desire to get a grave,
As witting I no other comfort have.
But tell me, keeper, will my nephew come?
First Gaol. Richard Plantagenet, my lord, will come:
We sent unto the Temple, unto his chamber;
And answer was return'd that he will come. 20
Mor. Enough: my soul shall then be satisfied.
Poor gentleman! his wrong doth equal mine.
Since Henry Monmouth first began to reign,
Before whose glory I was great in arms,
This loathsome sequestration have I had:
And even since then hath Richard been obscured,
Deprived of honor and inheritance.
But now the arbitrator of despairs,
Just death, kind umpire of men's miseries,
With sweet enlargement doth dismiss me hence: 30
I would his troubles likewise were expired,
That so he might recover what was lost.

Enter RICHARD PLANTAGENET.

First Gaol. My lord, your loving nephew now is come.
Mor. Richard Plantagenet, my friend, is he come?
Plan. Ay, noble uncle, thus ignobly used,
Your nephew, late despised Richard, comes.
Mor. Direct mine arms I may embrace his neck,
And in his bosom spend my latter gasp:
O, tell me when my lips do touch his cheeks,
That I may kindly give one fainting kiss.   40
And now declare, sweet stem from York's great stock,
Why didst thou say, of late thou wert despised?
Plan. First, lean thine aged back against mine arm;
And, in that ease, I'll tell thee my disease.
This day, in argument upon a case,
Some words there grew 'twixt Somerset and me:
Among which terms he used his lavish tongue
And did upbraid me with my father's death:
Which obloquy set bars before my tongue,
Else with the like I had requited him.   50

Therefore, good uncle, for my father's sake,
In honor of a true Plantagenet
And for alliance sake, declare the cause
My father, Earl of Cambridge, lost his head.
Mor. That cause, fair nephew, that imprison'd me
And hath detain'd me all my flowering youth
Within a loathsome dungeon, there to pine,
Was cursed instrument of his decease.
Plan. Discover more at large what cause that was,
For I am ignorant and cannot guess.   60
Mor. I will, if that my fading breath permit
And death approach not ere my tale be done.
Henry the Fourth, grandfather to this king,
Deposed his nephew Richard, Edward's son,
The first-begotten and the lawful heir
Of Edward king, the third of that descent:
During whose reign the Percies of the north,
Finding his usurpation most unjust,
Endeavor'd my advancement to the throne:
The reason moved these warlike lords to this   70
Was, for that—young King Richard thus removed,
Leaving no heir begotten of his body—
I was the next by birth and parentage;
For by my mother I derived am
From Lionel Duke of Clarence, the third son
To King Edward the Third; whereas he
From John of Gaunt doth bring his pedigree,
Being but fourth of that heroic line.
But mark: as in this haughty great attempt
They labored to plant the rightful heir,   80
I lost my liberty and they their lives.
Long after this, when Henry the Fifth,
Succeeding his father Bolingbroke, did reign,
Thy father, Earl of Cambridge, then derived
From famous Edmund Langley, Duke of York,
Marrying my sister that thy mother was,
Again in pity of my hard distress
Levied an army, weening to redeem
And have install'd me in the diadem:
But, as the rest, so fell that noble earl   90
And was beheaded. Thus the Mortimers,
In whom the title rested, were suppress'd.
Plan. Of which, my lord, your honor is the last.
Mor. True; and thou seest that I no issue have
And that my fainting words do warrant death;
Thou art my heir; the rest I wish thee gather:
But yet be wary in thy studious care.
Plan. Thy grave admonishments prevail with me:
But yet, methinks, my father's execution
Was nothing less than bloody tyranny.   100
Mor. With silence, nephew, be thou politic:
Strong-fixed is the house of Lancaster,
And like a mountain, not to be removed.
But now thy uncle is removing hence:
As princes do their courts, when they are cloy'd
With long continuance in a settled place.
Plan. O, uncle, would some part of my young years
Might but redeem the passage of your age!
Mor. Thou dost then wrong me, as that slaughterer doth   109

Which giveth many wounds when one will kill.
Mourn not, except thou sorrow for my good ;
Only give order for my funeral :
And so farewell, and fair be all thy hopes
And prosperous be thy life in peace and war !
                                   [*Dies.*
  Plan. And peace, no war, befall thy part-
    ing soul !
In prison hast thou spent a pilgrimage
And like a hermit overpass'd thy days.
Well, I will lock his counsel in my breast ;
And what I do imagine let that rest.
Keepers, convey him hence, and I myself 120
Will see his burial better than his life.
    [*Exeunt Gaolers, bearing out the body
                          of Mortimer.*
Here dies the dusky torch of Mortimer ;
Choked with ambition of the meaner sort :
And for those wrongs, those bitter injuries,
Which Somerset hath offer'd to my house,
I doubt not but with honor to redress ;
And therefore haste I to the parliament,
Either to be restored to my blood,
Or make my ill the advantage of my good.
                                   [*Exit.*

ACT III.

SCENE I. *London. The Parliament-house.*

Flourish. Enter KING, EXETER, GLOUCESTER,
  WARWICK, SOMERSET, *and* SUFFOLK ; *the*
  BISHOP OF WINCHESTER, RICHARD PLAN-
  TAGENET, *and others.* GLOUCESTER *offers to
  put up a bill ;* WINCHESTER *snatches it, and
  tears it.*

  Win. Comest thou with deep premeditated
    lines,
With written pamphlets studiously devised,
Humphrey of Gloucester ? If thou canst ac-
    cuse,
Or aught intend'st to lay unto my charge,
Do it without invention, suddenly ;
As I with sudden and extemporal speech
Purpose to answer what thou canst object.
  Glou. Presumptuous priest ! this place
    commands my patience,
Or thou shouldst find thou hast dishonor'd me.
Think not, although in writing I preferr'd 10
The manner of thy vile outrageous crimes,
That therefore I have forged, or am not able
Verbatim to rehearse the method of my pen :
No, prelate ; such is thy audacious wickedness,
Thy lewd, pestiferous and dissentious pranks,
As very infants prattle of thy pride.
Thou art a most pernicious usurer,
Forward by nature, enemy to peace ;
Lascivious, wanton, more than well beseems
A man of thy profession and degree ; 20
And for thy treachery, what's more manifest ?
In that thou laid'st a trap to take my life,
As well at London bridge as at the Tower,
Beside, I fear me, if thy thoughts were sifted,
The king, thy sovereign, is not quite exempt
From envious malice of thy swelling heart.
  Win. Gloucester, I do defy thee. Lords,
    vouchsafe
To give me hearing what I shall reply.
If I were covetous, ambitious or perverse,
As he will have me, how am I so poor ? 30
Or how haps it I seek not to advance

Or raise myself, but keep my wonted calling ?
And for dissension, who preferreth peace
More than I do ?—except I be provoked.
No, my good lords, it is not that offends ;
It is not that that hath incensed the duke :
It is, because no one should sway but he ;
No one but he should be about the king ;
And that engenders thunder in his breast
And makes him roar these accusations
    forth.   40
But he shall know I am as good—
  Glou.   As good !
Thou bastard of my grandfather !
  Win. Ay, lordly sir ; for what are you, I
    pray,
But one imperious in another's throne ?
  Glou. Am I not protector, saucy priest ?
  Win. And am not I a prelate of the
    church ?
  Glou. Yes, as an outlaw in a castle keeps
And useth it to patronage his theft.
  Win. Unreverent Gloster !
  Glou.   Thou art reverent
Touching thy spiritual function, not thy life. 50
  Win. Rome shall remedy this.
  War.   Roam thither, then.
  Som. My lord, it were your duty to for-
    bear.
  War. Ay, see the bishop be not overborne.
  Som. Methinks my lord should be religious
And know the office that belongs to such.
  War. Methinks his lordship should be
    humbler ;
It fitteth not a prelate so to plead.
  Som. Yes, when his holy state is touch'd
    so near.
  War. State holy or unhallow'd, what of
    that ?
Is not his grace protector to the king ? 60
  Plan. [*Aside*] Plantagenet, I see, must hold
    his tongue,
Lest it be said 'Speak, sirrah, when you
    should ;
Must your bold verdict enter talk with lords ?'
Else would I have a fling at Winchester.
  King. Uncles of Gloucester and of Win-
    chester,
The special watchmen of our English weal,
I would prevail, if prayers might prevail,
To join your hearts in love and amity.
O, what a scandal is it to our crown, 69
That two such noble peers as ye should jar !
Believe me, lords, my tender years can tell
Civil dissension is a viperous worm
That gnaws the bowels of the commonwealth.
    [*A noise within,* 'Down with the tawny-
                                   coats ! '
What tumult's this ?
  War.   An uproar, I dare warrant,
Begun through malice of the bishop's men.
    [*A noise again,* 'Stones ! stones ! '

Enter Mayor.

  May. O, my good lords, and virtuous
    Henry,
Pity the city of London, pity us !
The bishop and the Duke of Gloucester's men,
Forbidden late to carry any weapon,
Have fill'd their pockets full of pebble stones 80
And banding themselves in contrary parts
Do pelt so fast at one another's pate

That many have their giddy brains knock'd
out :
Our windows are broke down in every street
And we for fear compell'd to shut our shops.

Enter Serving-men, *in skirmish, with bloody
pates.*

King. We charge you, on allegiance to
ourself,
To hold your slaughtering hands and keep the
peace.
Pray, uncle Gloucester, mitigate this strife.
First Serv. Nay, if we be forbidden stones,
We'll fall to it with our teeth.   90
Sec. Serv. Do what ye dare, we are as
resolute.   [*Skirmish again.*
Glou. You of my household, leave this
peevish broil
And set this unaccustom'd fight aside.
Third Serv. My lord, we know your grace
to be a man
Just and upright ; and, for your royal birth,
Inferior to none but to his majesty :
And ere that we will suffer such a prince,
So kind a father of the commonweal,
To be disgraced by an inkhorn mate,   99
We and our wives and children all will fight
And have our bodies slaughtered by thy foes.
First Serv. Ay, and the very parings of our
nails
Shall pitch a field when we are dead.
          [*Begin again.*
Glou.   Stay, stay, I say !
And if you love me, as you say you do,
Let me persuade you to forbear awhile.
King. O, how this discord doth afflict my
soul !
Can you, my Lord of Winchester, behold
My sighs and tears and will not once relent ?
Who should be pitiful, if you be not ?
Or who should study to prefer a peace.   110
If holy churchmen take delight in broils ?
War. Yield, my lord protector ; yield,
Winchester ;
Except you mean with obstinate repulse
To slay your sovereign and destroy the realm.
You see what mischief and what murder too
Hath been enacted through your enmity,
Then be at peace, except ye thirst for blood.
Win. He shall submit, or I will never yield.
Glou. Compassion on the king commands
me stoop ;   119
Or I would see his heart out, ere the priest
Should ever get that privilege of me.
War. Behold, my Lord of Winchester, the
duke
Hath banish'd moody discontented fury,
As by his smoothed brows it doth appear :
Why look you still so stern and tragical ?
Glou. Here, Winchester, I offer thee my
hand.
King. Fie, uncle Beaufort ! I have heard
you preach
That malice was a great and grievous sin ;
And will not you maintain the thing you teach,
But prove a chief offender in the same ?   130
War. Sweet king ! the bishop hath a kindly
gird.
For shame, my lord of Winchester, relent !
What, shall a child instruct you what to do ?
Win. Well, Duke of Gloucester, I will
yield to thee ;

Love for thy love and hand for hand I give.
Glou. [*Aside*] Ay, but, I fear me, with a
hollow heart.—
See here, my friends and loving countrymen,
This token serveth for a flag of truce
Betwixt ourselves and all our followers :
So help me God, as I dissemble not !   140
Win. [*Aside*] So help me God, as I intend
it not !
King. O loving uncle, kind Duke of
Gloucester,
How joyful am I made by this contract !
Away, my masters ! trouble us no more ;
But join in friendship, as your lords have
done.
First Serv. Content : I'll to the surgeon's.
Sec. Serv.   And so will I.
Third Serv. And I will see what physic the
tavern affords.
          [*Exeunt Serving-men, Mayor, &c.*
War. Accept this scroll, most gracious
sovereign,
Which in the right of Richard Plantage-
net   150
We do exhibit to your majesty.
Glou. Well urged, my Lord of Warwick :
for, sweet prince,
An if your grace mark every circumstance,
You have great reason to do Richard right ;
Especially for those occasions
At Eltham Place I told your majesty.
King. And those occasions, uncle, were of
force :
Therefore, my loving lords, our pleasure is
That Richard be restored to his blood.   159
War. Let Richard be restored to his
blood ;
So shall his father's wrongs be recompensed.
Win. As will the rest, so willeth Win-
chester.
King. If Richard will be true, not that
alone
But all the whole inheritance I give
That doth belong unto the house of York,
From whence you spring by lineal descent.
Plan. Thy humble servant vows obedience
And humble service till the point of death.
King. Stoop then and set your knee against
my foot ;
And, in reguerdon of that duty done,   170
I gird thee with the valiant sword of York :
Rise, Richard, like a true Plantagenet,
And rise created princely Duke of York.
Plan. And so thrive Richard as thy foes
may fall !
And as my duty springs, so perish they
That grudge one thought against your maj-
esty !
All. Welcome, high prince, the mighty
Duke of York !
Som. [*Aside*] Perish, base prince, ignoble
Duke of York !
Glou. Now will it best avail your majesty
To cross the seas and to be crown'd in
France :
The presence of a king engenders love   181
Amongst his subjects and his loyal friends,
As it disanimates his enemies.
King. When Gloucester says the word,
King Henry goes ;
For friendly counsel cuts off many foes.

Glou. Your ships already are in readiness.

[*Sennet. Flourish. Exeunt all but Exeter.*

Exe. Ay, we may march in England or in France,
Not seeing what is likely to ensue.
This late dissension grown betwixt the peers
Burns under feigned ashes of forged love   190
And will at last break out into a flame :
As fester'd members rot but by degree,
Till bones and flesh and sinews fall away,
So will this base and envious discord breed.
And now I fear that fatal prophecy
Which in the time of Henry named the Fifth
Was in the mouth of every sucking babe ;
That Henry born at Monmouth should win all
And Henry born at Windsor lose all :
Which is so plain that Exeter doth wish   200
His days may finish ere that hapless time.
[*Exit.*

SCENE II.   *France. Before Rouen.*

Enter LA PUCELLE *disguised, with four Soldiers with sacks upon their backs.*

Puc. These are the city gates, the gates of Rouen,
Through which our policy must make a breach :
Take heed, be wary how you place your words ;
Talk like the vulgar sort of market men
That come to gather money for their corn.
If we have entrance, as I hope we shall,
And that we find the slothful watch but weak,
I'll by a sign give notice to our friends,
That Charles the Dauphin may encounter them.

First Sol. Our sacks shall be a mean to sack the city,   10
And we be lords and rulers over Rouen ;
Therefore we'll knock.   [*Knocks.*

Watch. [*Within*] Qui est là ?

Puc. Paysans, pauvres gens de France ;
Poor market folks that come to sell their corn.

Watch. Enter, go in ; the market bell is rung.

Puc. Now, Rouen, I'll shake thy bulwarks to the ground.   [*Exeunt.*

Enter CHARLES, *the* BASTARD *of Orleans,* ALENÇON, REIGNIER, *and forces.*

Char. Saint Denis bless this happy stratagem !
And once again we'll sleep secure in Rouen.

Bast. Here enter'd Pucelle and her practisants ;   20
Now she is there, how will she specify
Where is the best and safest passage in ?

Reign. By thrusting out a torch from yonder tower ;
Which, once discern'd, shows that her meaning is,
No way to that, for weakness, which she enter'd.

Enter LA PUCELLE *on the top, thrusting out a torch burning.*

Puc. Behold, this is the happy wedding torch
That joineth Rouen unto her countrymen,
But burning fatal to the Talbotites !   [*Exit.*

Bast. See, noble Charles, the beacon of our friend ;
The burning torch in yonder turret stands.   30

Char. Now shine it like a comet of revenge,
A prophet to the fall of all our foes !

Reign. Defer no time, delays have dangerous ends ;
Enter, and cry ' The Dauphin ! ' presently,
And then do execution on the watch.
[*Alarum. Exeunt.*

An alarum. Enter TALBOT *in an excursion.*

Tal. France, thou shalt rue this treason with thy tears,
If Talbot but survive thy treachery.
Pucelle, that witch, that damned sorceress,
Hath wrought this hellish mischief unawares,
That hardly we escaped the pride of France.
[*Exit.*

An alarum : excursions. BEDFORD, *brought in sick in a chair. Enter* TALBOT *and* BURGUNDY *without : within* LA PUCELLE, CHARLES, BASTARD, ALENÇON, *and* REIGNIER, *on the walls.*

Puc. Good morrow, gallants ! want ye corn for bread ?
I think the Duke of Burgundy will fast
Before he'll buy again at such a rate :
'Twas full of darnel ; do you like the taste ?

Bur. Scoff on, vile fiend and shameless courtezan !
I trust ere long to choke thee with thine own
And make thee curse the harvest of that corn.

Char. Your grace may starve perhaps before that time.

Bed. O, let no words, but deeds, revenge this treason !

Puc. What will you do, good grey-beard ? break a lance,   50
And run a tilt at death within a chair ?

Tal. Foul fiend of France, and hag of all despite,
Encompass'd with thy lustful paramours !
Becomes it thee to taunt his valiant age
And twit with cowardice a man half dead ?
Damsel, I'll have a bout with you again,
Or else let Talbot perish with this shame.

Puc. Are ye so hot, sir ? yet, Pucelle, hold thy peace ;
If Talbot do but thunder, rain will follow.
[*The English whisper together in council.*
God speed the parliament ! who shall be the speaker ?   60

Tal. Dare ye come forth and meet us in the field ?

Puc. Belike your lordship takes us then for fools,
To try if that our own be ours or no.

Tal. I speak not to that railing Hecate,
But unto thee, Alençon, and the rest ;
Will ye, like soldiers, come and fight it out ?

Alen. Signior, no.

Tal. Signior, hang ! base muleters of France !
Like peasant foot-boys do they keep the walls
And dare not take up arms like gentlemen.   70

Puc. Away, captains ! let's get us from the walls ;
For Talbot means no goodness by his looks.
God be wi' you, my lord ! we came but to tell you

That we are here.   [*Exeunt from the walls*
  Tal. And there will we be too, ere it be
    long,
Or else reproach be Talbot's greatest fame !
Vow, Burgundy, by honor of thy house,
Prick'd on by public wrongs sustain'd in
    France,
Either to get the town again or die :
And I, as sure as English Henry lives   80
And as his father here was conqueror,
As sure as in this late-betrayed town
Great Cœur-de-lion's heart was buried,
So sure I swear to get the town or die.
  Bur. My vows are equal partners with thy
    vows.
  Tal. But, ere we go, regard this dying
    prince,
The valiant Duke of Bedford. Come, my lord,
We will bestow you in some better place,
Fitter for sickness and for crazy age.
  Bed. Lord Talbot, do not so dishonor me :
Here will I sit before the walls of Rouen 91
And will be partner of your weal or woe.
  Bur. Courageous Bedford, let us now per-
    suade you.
  Bed. Not to be gone from hence ; for
    once I read
That stout Pendragon in his litter sick
Came to the field and vanquished his foes :
Methinks I should revive the soldiers' hearts,
Because I ever found them as myself.
  Tal. Undaunted spirit in a dying breast !
Then be it so : heavens keep old Bedford safe !
And now no more ado, brave Burgundy,   101
But gather we our forces out of hand
And set upon our boasting enemy.
    [*Exeunt all but Bedford and Attendants.*

  An alarum : excursions. Enter SIR JOHN
    FASTOLFE *and a* Captain.

  Cap. Whither away, Sir John Fastolfe, in
    such haste ?
  Fast. Whither away ! to save myself by
    flight :
We are like to have the overthrow again.
  Cap. What ! will you fly, and leave Lord
    Talbot ?
  Fast.   Ay,
All the Talbots in the world, to save my life.
    [*Exit.*
  Cap. Cowardly knight ! ill fortune follow
    thee !   [*Exit.*

Retreat : excursions. LA PUCELLE, ALENÇON,
    and CHARLES *fly.*

  Bed. Now, quiet soul, depart when heaven
    please,   110
For I have seen our enemies' overthrow.
What is the trust or strength of foolish man ?
They that of late were daring with their scoffs
Are glad and fain by flight to save themselves.
    [*Bedford dies, and is carried in by two
        in his chair.*

  An alarum. Re-enter TALBOT, BURGUNDY, *and
    the rest.*

  Tal. Lost, and recover'd in a day again !
This is a double honor, Burgundy :
Yet heavens have glory for this victory !
  Bur. Warlike and martial Talbot, Bur-
    gundy
Enshrines thee in his heart and there erects

Thy noble deeds as valor's monuments.   120
  Tal. Thanks, gentle duke. But where is
    Pucelle now ?
I think her old familiar is asleep :
Now where's the Bastard's braves, and
    Charles his gleeks ?
What, all amort ? Rouen hangs her head for
    grief
That such a valiant company are fled.
Now will we take some order in the town,
Placing therein some expert officers,
And then depart to Paris to the king,
For there young Henry with his nobles lie.
  Bur. What wills Lord Talbot pleaseth Bur-
    gundy.   130
  Tal. But yet, before we go, let's not for-
    get
The noble Duke of Bedford late deceased,
But see his exequies fulfill'd in Rouen :
A braver soldier never couched lance,
A gentler heart did never sway in court ;
But kings and mightiest potentates must die,
For that's the end of human misery. [*Exeunt.*

    SCENE III.   *The plains near Rouen.*

Enter CHARLES, *the* BASTARD *of Orleans,* ALEN-
    ÇON, LA PUCELLE, *and forces.*

  Puc. Dismay not, princes, at this accident,
Nor grieve that Rouen is so recovered :
Care is no cure, but rather corrosive,
For things that are not to be remedied.
Let frantic Talbot triumph for a while
And like a peacock sweep along his tail ;
We'll pull his plumes and take away his train,
If Dauphin and the rest will be but ruled.
  Char. We have been guided by thee hith-
    erto,
And of thy cunning had no diffidence :   10
One sudden foil shall never breed distrust.
  Bast. Search out thy wit for secret poli-
    cies,
And we will make thee famous through the
    world.
  Alen. We'll set thy statue in some holy
    place,
And have thee reverenced like a blessed saint :
Employ thee then, sweet virgin, for our good.
  Puc. Then thus it must be ; this doth Joan
    devise :
By fair persuasions mix'd with sugar'd words
We will entice the Duke of Burgundy
To leave the Talbot and to follow us.   20
  Char. Ay, marry, sweeting, if we could do
    that,
France were no place for Henry's warriors ;
Nor should that nation boast it so with us,
But be extirped from our provinces.
  Alen. For ever should they be expulsed
    from France
And not have title of an earldom here.
  Puc. Your honors shall perceive how I will
    work
To bring this matter to the wished end.
    [*Drum sounds afar off.*
Hark ! by the sound of drum you may per-
    ceive
Their powers are marching unto Paris-
    ward.   30

*Here sound an English march. Enter, and
    pass over at a distance,* TALBOT *and his
    forces.*

There goes the Talbot, with his colors spread,
And all the troops of English after him.

French march. Enter the DUKE OF BURGUNDY
and forces.

Now in the rearward comes the duke and his :
Fortune in favor makes him lag behind.
Summon a parley ; we will talk with him.
                    [*Trumpets sound a parley.*
  Char. A parley with the Duke of Bur-
      gundy !
  Bur. Who craves a parley with the Bur-
      gundy ?
  Puc. The princely Charles of France, thy
      countryman.
  Bur. What say'st thou, Charles ? for I am
      marching hence.
  Char. Speak, Pucelle, and enchant him
      with thy words.   40
  Puc. Brave Burgundy, undoubted hope of
      France !
Stay, let thy humble handmaid speak to thee.
  Bur. Speak on ; but be not over-tedious.
  Puc. Look on thy country, look on fertile
      France,
And see the cities and the towns defaced
By wasting ruin of the cruel foe.
As looks the mother on her lowly babe
When death doth close his tender dying eyes,
See, see the pining malady of France ;
Behold the wounds, the most unnatural
      wounds,   50
Which thou thyself hast given her woful
      breast.
O, turn thy edged sword another way ;
Strike those that hurt, and hurt not those
      that help.
One drop of blood drawn from thy country's
      bosom
Should grieve thee more than streams of for-
      eign gore :
Return thee therefore with a flood of tears,
And wash away thy country's stained spots.
  Bur. Either she hath bewitch'd me with
      her words,
Or nature makes me suddenly relent.
  Puc. Besides, all French and France ex-
      claims on thee,   60
Doubting thy birth and lawful progeny.
Who joint'st thou with but with a lordly na-
      tion
That will not trust thee but for profit's sake ?
When Talbot hath set footing once in France
And fashion'd thee that instrument of ill,
Who then but English Henry will be lord
And thou be thrust out like a fugitive ?
Call we to mind, and mark but this for proof,
Was not the Duke of Orleans thy foe ?
And was he not in England prisoner ?   70
But when they heard he was thine enemy,
They set him free without his ransom paid,
In spite of Burgundy and all his friends.
See, then, thou fight'st against thy country-
      men
And joint'st with them will be thy slaughter-
      men.
Come, come, return ; return, thou wandering
      lord :
Charles and the rest will take thee in their
      arms.
  Bur. I am vanquished ; these haughty
      words of hers

Have batter'd me like roaring cannon-shot,
And made me almost yield upon my knees. 80
Forgive me, country, and sweet countrymen,
And, lords, accept this hearty kind embrace :
My forces and my power of men are yours :
So farewell, Talbot ; I'll no longer trust thee.
  Puc. [*Aside*] Done like a Frenchman :
      turn, and turn again !
  Char. Welcome, brave duke ! thy friend-
      ship makes us fresh.
  Bast. And doth beget new courage in our
      breasts.
  Alen. Pucelle hath bravely play'd her part
      in this,
And doth deserve a coronet of gold.
  Char. Now let us on, my lords, and join
      our powers,   90
And seek how we may prejudice the foe.
                                   [*Exeunt.*

SCENE IV. *Paris. The palace.*

Enter the KING, GLOUCESTER, BISHOP OF
WINCHESTER, YORK, SUFFOLK, SOMERSET,
WARWICK, EXETER : VERNON, BASSET, *and
others. To them with his* SOLDIERS, TALBOT.

  Tal. My gracious prince, and honorable
      peers,
Hearing of your arrival in this realm,
I have awhile given truce unto my wars,
To do my duty to my sovereign :
In sign whereof, this arm, that hath reclaim'd
To your obedience fifty fortresses,
Twelve cities and seven walled towns of
      strength,
Beside five hundred prisoners of esteem,
Lets fall his sword before your highness' feet,
And with submissive loyalty of heart   10
Ascribes the glory of his conquest got
First to my God and next unto your grace.
                                   [*Kneels.*
  King. Is this the Lord Talbot, uncle
      Gloucester,
That hath so long been resident in France ?
  Glou. Yes, if it please your majesty, my
      liege.
  King. Welcome, brave captain and victo-
      rious lord !
When I was young, as yet I am not old,
I do remember how my father said
A stouter champion never handled sword.
Long since we were resolved of your truth, 20
Your faithful service and your toil in war ;
Yet never have you tasted our reward,
Or been reguerdon'd with so much as thanks,
Because till now we never saw your face :
Therefore, stand up ; and, for these good
      deserts,
We here create you Earl of Shrewsbury ;
And in our coronation take your place.
     [*Sennet. Flourish. Exeunt all but Vernon
                                and Basset.*
  Ver. Now, sir, to you, that were so hot at
      sea,
Disgracing of these colors that I wear
In honor of my noble Lord of York :   30
Darest thou maintain the former words thou
      spakest ?
  Bas. Yes, sir ; as well as you dare patron-
      age
The envious barking of your saucy tongue
Against my lord the Duke of Somerset.
  Ver. Sirrah, thy lord I honor as he is.

Bas. Why, what is he ? as good a man as
  York.
Ver. Hark ye ; not so : in witness, take ye
  that.   [*Strikes him.*
Bas. Villain, thou know'st the law of arms
  is such
That whoso draws a sword, 'tis present death,
Or else this blow should broach thy dearest
  blood.   40
But I'll unto his majesty, and crave
I may have liberty to venge this wrong ;
When thou shalt see I'll meet thee to thy cost.
Ver. Well, miscreant, I'll be there as soon
  as you ;
And, after, meet you sooner than you would.
                                      [*Exeunt.*

ACT IV.

SCENE I. *Paris. A hall of state.*

Enter the KING, GLOUCESTER, BISHOP OF
WINCHESTER, YORK, SUFFOLK, SOMERSET,
WARWICK, TALBOT, EXETER, *the* Governor
of Paris, *and others.*

Glou. Lord bishop, set the crown upon
  his head.
Win. God save King Henry, of that name
  the sixth !
Glou. Now, governor of Paris, take your
  oath,
That you elect no other king but him ;
Esteem none friends but such as are his
  friends,
And none your foes but such as shall pretend
Malicious practices against his state :
This shall ye do, so help you righteous God !

Enter SIR JOHN FASTOLFE.

Fast. My gracious sovereign, as I rode
  from Calais,
To haste unto your coronation,   10
A letter was deliver'd to my hands,
Writ to your grace from the Duke of Bur-
  gundy.
Tal. Shame to the Duke of Burgundy and
  thee !
I vow'd, base knight, when I did meet thee
  next,
To tear the garter from thy craven's leg,
                                [*Plucking it off.*
Which I have done, because unworthily
Thou wast installed in that high degree.
Pardon me, princely Henry, and the rest
This dastard, at the battle of Patay,
When but in all I was six thousand strong 20
And that the French were almost ten to one,
Before we met or that a stroke was given,
Like to a trusty squire did run away :
In which assault we lost twelve hundred men ;
Myself and divers gentlemen beside
Were there surprised and taken prisoners.
Then judge, great lords, if I have done amiss ;
Or whether that such cowards ought to wear
This ornament of knighthood, yea or no.
Glou. To say the truth, this fact was in-
  famous   30
And ill beseeming any common man,
Much more a knight, a captain and a leader.
Tal. When first this order was ordain'd,
  my lords,

Knights of the garter were of noble birth,
Valiant and virtuous, full of haughty cour-
  age,
Such as were grown to credit by the wars ;
Not fearing death, nor shrinking for distress,
But always resolute in most extremes.
He then that is not furnish'd in this sort
Doth but usurp the sacred name of knight,
Profaning this most honorable order,   41
And should, if I were worthy to be judge,
Be quite degraded, like a hedge-born swain
That doth presume to boast of gentle blood.
King. Stain to thy countrymen, thou hear'st
  thy doom !
Be packing, therefore, thou that wast a
  knight :
Henceforth we banish thee, on pain of death.
                                [*Exit Fastolfe.*
And now, my lord protector, view the letter
Sent from our uncle Duke of Burgundy.
Glou. What means his grace, that he hath
  changed his style ?   50
No more but, plain and bluntly, ' To the
  king ! '
Hath he forgot he is his sovereign ?
Or doth this churlish superscription
Pretend some alteration in good will ?
What's here ? [*Reads*] ' I have, upon especial
  cause,
Moved with compassion of my country's
  wreck,
Together with the pitiful complaints
Of such as your oppression feeds upon,
Forsaken your pernicious faction
And join'd with Charles, the rightful King of
  France. '   60
O monstrous treachery ! can this be so,
That in alliance, amity and oaths,
There should be found such false dissembling
  guile ?
King. What ! doth my uncle Burgundy re-
  volt ?
Glou. He doth, my lord, and is become
  your foe.
King. Is that the worst this letter doth con-
  tain ?
Glou. It is the worst, and all, my lord, he
  writes.
King. Why, then, Lord Talbot there shall
  talk with him
And give him chastisement for this abuse.
How say you, my lord ? are you not content ?
Tal. Content, my liege ! yes, but that I am
  prevented,   71
I should have begg'd I might have been em-
  ploy'd.
King. Then gather strength and march
  unto him straight :
Let him perceive how ill we brook his trea-
  son
And what offence it is to flout his friends.
Tal. I go, my lord, in heart desiring still
You may behold confusion of your foes.
                                        [*Exit.*

Enter VERNON *and* BASSET.

Ver. Grant me the combat, gracious sovereign.
Bas. And me, my lord, grant me the combat too.
York. This is my servant : hear him,
  noble prince.   80

Som. And this is mine : sweet Henry, fa-
   vor him.
K. Hen. Be patient, lords ; and give them
   leave to speak.
Say, gentlemen, what makes you thus ex-
   claim ?
And wherefore crave you combat ? or with
   whom ?
Ver. With him, my lord ; for he hath done
   me wrong.
Bas. And I with him ; for he hath done
   me wrong.
K. Hen. What is that wrong whereof you
   both complain ?
First let me know, and then I'll answer you.
Bas. Crossing the sea from England into
   France,
This fellow here, with envious carping tongue,
Upbraided me about the rose I wear ;   91
Saying, the sanguine color of the leaves
Did represent my master's blushing cheeks,
When stubbornly he did repugn the truth
About a certain question in the law
Argued betwixt the Duke of York and him ;
With other vile and ignominious terms :
In confutation of which rude reproach
And in defence of my lord's worthiness,
I crave the benefit of law of arms.   100
Ver. And that is my petition, noble lord :
For though he seem with forged quaint con-
   ceit
To set a gloss upon his bold intent,
Yet know, my lord, I was provoked by him ;
And he first took exceptions at this badge,
Pronouncing that the paleness of this flower
Bewray'd the faintness of my master's heart.
York. Will not this malice, Somerset, be
   left ?
Som. Your private grudge, my Lord of
   York, will out,
Though ne'er so cunningly you smother it. 110
K. Hen. Good Lord, what madness rules
   in brainsick men,
When for so slight and frivolous a cause
Such factious emulations shall arise !
Good cousins both, of York and Somerset,
Quiet yourselves, I pray, and be at peace.
York. Let this dissension first be tried by
   fight,
And then your highness shall command a
   peace.
Som. The quarrel toucheth none but us
   alone ;
Betwixt ourselves let us decide it then.
York. There is my pledge ; accept it,
   Somerset.   120
Ver. Nay, let it rest where it began at first.
Bas. Confirm it so, mine honorable lord.
Glou. Confirm it so ! Confounded be your
   strife !
And perish ye, with your audacious prate !
Presumptuous vassals, are you not ashamed
With this immodest clamorous outrage
To trouble and disturb the king and us ?
And you, my lords, methinks you do not well
To bear with their perverse objections ;
Much less to take occasion from their mouths
To raise a mutiny betwixt yourselves :   131
Let me persuade you take a better course.
Exe. It grieves his highness : good my
   lords, be friends.

K. Hen. Come hither, you that would be
   combatants :
Henceforth I charge you, as you love our
   favor,
Quite to forget this quarrel and the cause.
And you, my lords, remember where we are,
In France, amongst a fickle wavering nation :
If they perceive dissension in our looks
And that within ourselves we disagree,   140
How will their grudging stomachs be provoked
To wilful disobedience, and rebel !
Beside, what infamy will there arise,
When foreign princes shall be certified
That for a toy, a thing of no regard,
King Henry's peers and chief nobility
Destroy'd themselves, and lost the realm of
   France !
O, think upon the conquest of my father,
My tender years, and let us not forego
That for a trifle that was bought with blood
Let me be umpire in this doubtful strife.   151
I see no reason, if I wear this rose,
                 [*Putting on a red rose.*
That any one should therefore be suspicious
I more incline to Somerset than York :
Both are my kinsmen, and I love them both :
As well they may upbraid me with my crown,
Because, forsooth, the king of Scots is
   crown'd.
But your discretions better can persuade
Than I am able to instruct or teach :
And therefore, as we hither came in peace,
So let us still continue peace and love.   161
Cousin of York, we institute your grace
To be our regent in these parts of France :
And, good my Lord of Somerset, unite
Your troops of horsemen with his bands of
   foot ;
And, like true subjects, sons of your progen-
   itors,
Go cheerfully together and digest
Your angry choler on your enemies.
Ourself, my lord protector and the rest
After some respite will return to Calais ;   170
From thence to England ; where I hope ere
   long
To be presented, by your victories,
With Charles, Alençon and that traitorous
   rout.
   [*Flourish. Exeunt all but York, Warwick,*
                    Exeter and Vernon.
War. My Lord of York, I promise you,
   the king
Prettily, methought, did play the orator.
York. And so he did ; but yet I like it not,
In that he wears the badge of Somerset.
War. Tush, that was but his fancy, blame
   him not ;
I dare presume, sweet prince, he thought no
   harm.
York. An if I wist he did,—but let it rest ;
Other affairs must now be managed.   181
                 [*Exeunt all but Exeter.*
Exe. Well didst thou, Richard, to suppress
   thy voice ;
For, had the passions of thy heart burst out,
I fear we should have seen decipher'd there
More rancorous spite, more furious raging
   broils,
Than yet can be imagined or supposed.
But howsoe'er, no simple man that sees
This jarring discord of nobility,

This shoulderilig of each other in the court,
This factious bandying of their favorites,   190
But that it doth presage some ill event.
'Tis much when sceptres are in children's hands ;
But more when envy breeds unkind division ;
There comes the ruin, there begins confusion.   [*Exit.*

SCENE II.   *Before Bourdeaux.*

Enter TALBOT, *with trump and drum.*

Tal. Go to the gates of Bourdeaux, trumpeter :
Summon their general unto the wall.

Trumpet sounds. Enter General *and others, aloft.*

English John Talbot, captains, calls you forth,
Servant in arms to Harry King of England ;
And thus he would : Open your city gates ;
Be humble to us ; call my sovereign yours,
And do him homage as obedient subjects ;
And I'll withdraw me and my bloody power :
But, if you frown upon this proffer'd peace,
You tempt the fury of my three attendants, 10
Lean famine, quartering steel, and climbing fire ;
Who in a moment even with the earth
Shall lay your stately and air-braving towers,
If you forsake the offer of their love.

Gen. Thou ominous and fearful owl of death,
Our nation's terror and their bloody scourge !
The period of thy tyranny approacheth.
On us thou canst not enter but by death ;
For, I protest, we are well fortified
And strong enough to issue out and fight : 20
If thou retire, the Dauphin, well appointed,
Stands with the snares of war to tangle thee :
On either hand thee there are squadrons pitch'd,
To wall thee from the liberty of flight ;
And no way canst thou turn thee for redress,
But death doth front thee with apparent spoil
And pale destruction meets thee in the face.
Ten thousand French have ta'en the sacrament
To rive their dangerous artillery
Upon no Christian soul but English Talbot. 30
Lo, there thou stand'st, a breathing valiant man,
Of an invincible unconquer'd spirit !
This is the latest glory of thy praise
That I, thy enemy, due thee withal ;
For ere the glass, that now begins to run,
Finish the process of his sandy hour,
These eyes, that see thee now well colored,
Shall see thee wither'd, bloody, pale and dead.
                                    [*Drum afar off.*
Hark ! hark ! the Dauphin's drum, a warning bell,
Sings heavy music to thy timorous soul ; 40
And mine shall ring thy dire departure out.
                                    [*Exeunt General, &c.*

Tal. He fables not ; I hear the enemy :
Out, some light horsemen, and peruse their wings.
O, negligent and heedless discipline !
How are we park'd and bounded in a pale,
A little herd of England's timorous deer,
Mazed with a yelping kennel of French curs !
If we be English deer, be then in blood ;

Not rascal-like, to fall down with a pinch,
But rather, moody-mad and desperate stags,
Turn on the bloody hounds with heads of steel   51
And make the cowards stand aloof at bay :
Sell every man his life as dear as mine,
And they shall find dear deer of us, my friends.
God and Saint George, Talbot and England's right,
Prosper our colors in this dangerous fight !
                                    [*Exeunt.*

SCENE III.   *Plains in Gascony.*

Enter a Messenger *that meets* YORK. *Enter* YORK *with trumpet and many* Soldiers.

York. Are not the speedy scouts return'd again,
That dogg'd the mighty army of the Dauphin ?

Mess. They are return'd, my lord, and give it out
That he is march'd to Bourdeaux with his power,
To fight with Talbot : as he march'd along,
By your espials were discovered
Two mightier troops than that the Dauphin led,
Which join'd with him and made their march for Bourdeaux.

York. A plague upon that villain Somerset,
That thus delays my promised supply   10
Of horsemen, that were levied for this siege !
Renowned Talbot doth expect my aid,
And I am lowted by a traitor villain
And cannot help the noble chevalier :
God comfort him in this necessity !
If he miscarry, farewell wars in France.

Enter SIR WALTER LUCY.

Lucy. Thou princely leader of our English strength,
Never so needful on the earth of France,
Spur to the rescue of the noble Talbot,
Who now is girdled with a waist of iron   20
And hemm'd about with grim destruction :
To Bourdeaux, warlike duke ! to Bourdeaux, York !
Else, farewell Talbot, France, and England's honor.

York. O God, that Somerset, who in proud heart
Doth stop my cornets, were in Talbot's place !
So should we save a valiant gentleman
By forfeiting a traitor and a coward.
Mad ire and wrathful fury makes me weep,
That thus we die, while remiss traitors sleep.

Lucy. O, send some succor to the distress'd lord !   30

York. He dies, we lose ; I break my warlike word ;
We mourn, France smiles ; we lose, they daily get ;
All 'long of this vile traitor Somerset.

Lucy. Then God take mercy on brave Talbot's soul ;
And on his son young John, who two hours since
I met in travel toward his warlike father !
This seven years did not Talbot see his son ;
And now they meet where both their lives are done.

York. Alas, what joy shall noble Talbot
    have
To bid his young son welcome to his grave ?
Away ! vexation almost stops my breath,   41
That sunder'd friends greet in the hour of
    death.
Lucy, farewell ; no more my fortune can,
But curse the cause I cannot aid the man.
Maine, Blois, Poictiers, and Tours, are won
    away,
'Long all of Somerset and his delay.
                    [*Exit, with his soldiers.*
Lucy. Thus, while the vulture of sedition
Feeds in the bosom of such great commanders,
Sleeping neglection doth betray to loss
The conquest of our scarce cold conqueror,
That ever living man of memory,   51
Henry the Fifth : whiles they each other cross,
Lives, honors, lands and all hurry to loss.
                    [*Exit.*

SCENE IV.   *Other plains in Gascony.*

Enter SOMERSET, *with his army ; a* Captain *of*
TALBOT'S *with him.*

Som. It is too late ; I cannot send them
    now :
This expedition was by York and Talbot
Too rashly plotted : all our general force
Might with a sally of the very town
Be buckled with : the over-daring Talbot
Hath sullied all his gloss of former honor
By this unheedful, desperate, wild adventure :
York set him on to fight and die in shame,
That, Talbot dead, great York might bear the
    name.
Cap. Here is Sir William Lucy, who with
    me   10
Set from our o'ermatch'd forces forth for aid.

Enter SIR WILLIAM LUCY.

Som. How now, Sir William ! whither
    were you sent ?
Lucy. Whither, my lord ? from bought
    and sold Lord Talbot ;
Who, ring'd about with bold adversity,
Cries out for noble York and Somerset,
To beat assailing death from his weak legions :
And whiles the honorable captain there
Drops bloody sweat from his war-wearied
    limbs,
And, in advantage lingering, looks for rescue,
You, his false hopes, the trust of England's
    honor,   20
Keep off aloof with worthless emulation.
Let not your private discord keep away
The levied succors that should lend him aid,
While he, renowned noble gentleman,
Yields up his life unto a world of odds :
Orleans the Bastard, Charles, Burgundy,
Alençon, Reignier, compass him about,
And Talbot perisheth by your default.
Som. York set him on ; York should have
    sent him aid.
Lucy. And York as fast upon your grace
    exclaims ;   30
Swearing that you withhold his levied host,
Collected for this expedition.
Som. York lies ; he might have sent and
    had the horse :
I owe him little duty, and less love ;
And take foul scorn to fawn on him by send-
    ing.

Lucy. The fraud of England, not the force
    of France,
Hath now entrapp'd the noble-minded Talbot :
Never to England shall he bear his life ;
But dies, betray'd to fortune by your strife.
Som. Come, go ; I will dispatch the horse-
    men straight :   40
Within six hours they will be at his aid.
Lucy. Too late comes rescue : he is ta'en
    or slain ;
For fly he could not, if he would have fled ;
And fly would Talbot never, though he might.
Som. If he be dead, brave Talbot, then
    adieu !
Lucy. His fame lives in the world, his
    shame in you.   [*Exeunt.*

SCENE V.   *The English camp near Bourdeaux.*

Enter TALBOT *and* JOHN *his son.*

Tal. O young John Talbot ! I did send for
    thee
To tutor thee in stratagems of war,
That Talbot's name might be in thee revived
When sapless age and weak unable limbs
Should bring thy father to his drooping chair.
But, O malignant and ill-boding stars !
Now thou art come unto a feast of death,
A terrible and unavoided danger :
Therefore, dear boy, mount on my swiftest
    horse ;
And I'll direct thee how thou shalt escape   10
By sudden flight : come, dally not, be gone.
John. Is my name Talbot ? and am I your
    son ?
And shall I fly ? O, if you love my mother,
Dishonor not her honorable name,
To make a bastard and a slave of me !
The world will say, he is not Talbot's blood,
That basely fled when noble Talbot stood.
Tal. Fly, to revenge my death, if I be slain.
John. He that flies so will ne'er return
    again.
Tal. If we both stay, we both are sure to
    die.   20
John. Then let me stay ; and, father, do
    you fly :
Your loss is great, so your regard should be ;
My worth unknown, no loss is known in me.
Upon my death the French can little boast ;
In yours they will, in you all hopes are lost.
Flight cannot stain the honor you have won ;
But mine it will, that no exploit have done :
You fled for vantage, every one will swear ;
But, if I bow, they'll say it was for fear.
There is no hope that ever I will stay,   30
If the first hour I shrink and run away.
Here on my knee I beg mortality,
Rather than life preserved with infamy.
Tal. Shall all thy mother's hopes lie in one
    tomb ?
John. Ay, rather than I'll shame my
    mother's womb.
Tal. Upon my blessing, I command thee
    go.
John. To fight I will, but not to fly the foe.
Tal. Part of thy father may be saved in
    thee.
John. No part of him but will be shame in
    me.
Tal. Thou never hadst renown, nor canst
    not lose it.   40

John. Yes, your renowned name : shall
     flight abuse it ?
Tal. Thy father's charge shall clear thee
     from that stain.
John. You cannot witness for me, being
     slain.
If death be so apparent, then both fly.
Tal. And leave my followers here to fight
     and die ?
My age was never tainted with such shame.
John. And shall my youth be guilty of such
     blame ?
No more can I be sever'd from your side,
Than can yourself yourself in twain divide :
Stay, go, do what you will, the like do I ;   50
For live I will not, if my father die.
Tal. Then here I take my leave of thee,
     fair son,
Born to eclipse thy life this afternoon.
Come, side by side together live and die ;
And soul with soul from France to heaven fly.
                         [*Exeunt.*

SCENE VI. *A field of battle.*

Alarum : excursions, wherein TALBOT'S Son *is
hemmed about, and* TALBOT *rescues him.*

Tal. Saint George and victory ! fight, sol-
     diers, fight.
The regent hath with Talbot broke his word
And left us to the rage of France his sword.
Where is John Talbot ? Pause, and take thy
     breath ;
I gave thee life and rescued thee from death.
John. O, twice my father, twice am I thy
     son !
The life thou gavest me first was lost and done,
Till with thy warlike sword, despite of fate,
To my determined time thou gavest new date.
Tal. When from the Dauphin's crest thy
     sword struck fire,   10
It warm'd thy father's heart with proud desire
Of bold-faced victory. Then leaden age,
Quicken'd with youthful spleen and warlike
     rage,
Beat down Alençon, Orleans, Burgundy,
And from the pride of Gallia rescued thee.
The ireful bastard Orleans, that drew blood
From thee, my boy, and had the maidenhood
Of thy first fight, I soon encountered,
And interchanging blows I quickly shed
Some of his bastard blood ; and in disgrace 20
Bespoke him thus ; ' Contaminated, base
And misbegotten blood I spill of thine,
Mean and right poor, for that pure blood of
     mine
Which thou didst force from Talbot, my brave
     boy : '
Here, purposing the Bastard to destroy,
Came in strong rescue. Speak, thy father's
     care,
Art thou not weary, John ? how dost thou
     fare ?
Wilt thou yet leave the battle, boy, and fly,
Now thou art seal'd the son of chivalry ?
Fly, to revenge my death when I am dead : 30
The help of one stands me in little stead.
O, too much folly is it, well I wot,
To hazard all our lives in one small boat !
If I to-day die not with Frenchmen's rage,
To-morrow I shall die with mickle age :
By me they nothing gain an if I stay ;
'Tis but the shortening of my life one day :

In thee thy mother dies, our household's name,
My death's revenge, thy youth, and England's
     fame :
All these and more we hazard by thy stay ;   40
All these are saved if thou wilt fly away.
John. The sword of Orleans hath not made
     me smart ;
These words of yours draw life-blood from my
     heart :
On that advantage, bought with such a shame,
To save a paltry life and slay bright fame,
Before young Talbot from old Talbot fly,
The coward horse that bears me fall and die !
And like me to the peasant boys of France,
To be shame's scorn and subject of mis-
     chance !
Surely, by all the glory you have won,   50
An if I fly, I am not Talbot's son :
Then talk no more of flight, it is no boot ;
If son to Talbot, die at Talbot's foot.
Tal. Then follow thou thy desperate sire of
     Crete,
Thou Icarus ; thy life to me is sweet :
If thou wilt fight, fight by thy father's side ;
And, commendable proved, let's die in pride.
                         [*Exeunt.*

SCENE VII. *Another part of the field.*

Alarum : excursions. Enter old TALBOT *led
by a* Servant.

Tal. Where is my other life ? mine own is
     gone ;
O, where's young Talbot ? where is valiant
     John ?
Triumphant death, smear'd with captivity,
Young Talbot's valor makes me smile at thee :
When he perceived me shrink and on my knee,
His bloody sword he brandish'd over me,
And, like a hungry lion, did commence
Rough deeds of rage and stern impatience ;
But when my angry guardant stood alone,
Tendering my ruin and assail'd of none,   10
Dizzy-eyed fury and great rage of heart
Suddenly made him from my side to start
Into the clustering battle of the French ;
And in that sea of blood my boy did drench
His over-mounting spirit, and there died,
My Icarus, my blossom, in his pride.
Serv. O my dear lord, lo, where your son
     is borne !

Enter Soldiers, *with the body of young*
TALBOT.

Tal. Thou antic death, which laugh'st us
     here to scorn,
Anon, from thy insulting tyranny,
Coupled in bonds of perpetuity,   20
Two Talbots, winged through the lither sky,
In thy despite shall 'scape mortality.
O thou, whose wounds become hard-favor'd
     death,
Speak to thy father ere thou yield thy breath !
Brave death by speaking, whether he will or
     no ;
Imagine him a Frenchman and thy foe.
Poor boy ! he smiles, methinks, as who should
     say,
Had death been French, then death had died
     to-day.
Come, come and lay him in his father's arms :
My spirit can no longer bear these harms. 30
Soldiers, adieu ! I have what I would have,

Now my old arms are young John Talbot's
  grave.   [*Dies.*

Enter CHARLES, ALENÇON, BURGUNDY, BAS-
  TARD, LA PUCELLE, *and forces.*

  Char. Had York and Somerset brought
    rescue in,
We should have found a bloody day of this.
  Bast. How the young whelp of Talbot's,
    raging-wood,
Did flesh his puny sword in Frenchmen's
  blood !
  Puc. Once I encounter'd him, and thus I
    said :
' Thou maiden youth, be vanquish'd by a
  maid : '
But, with a proud majestical high scorn,
He answer'd thus : ' Young Talbot was not
  born   40
To be the pillage of a giglot wench : '
So, rushing in the bowels of the French,
He left me proudly, as unworthy fight.
  Bur. Doubtless he would have made a no-
    ble knight ;
See, where he lies inhearsed in the arms
Of the most bloody nurser of his harms !
  Bast. Hew them to pieces, hack their bones
    asunder
Whose life was England's glory, Gallia's
  wonder.
  Char. O, no, forbear ! for that which we
    have fled
During the life, let us not wrong it dead.   50

Enter SIR WILLIAM LUCY, *attended ;* Herald
  of the French *preceding.*

  Lucy. Herald, conduct me to the Dau-
    phin's tent,
To know who hath obtained the glory of the
  day.
  Char. On what submissive message art
    thou sent ?
  Lucy. Submission, Dauphin ! 'tis a mere
    French vaunt ;
We English warriors wot not what it means.
I come to know what prisoners thou hast ta'en
And to survey the bodies of the dead.
  Char. For prisoners ask'st thou ? hell our
    prison is.
But tell me whom thou seek'st.
  Lucy. But where's the great Alcides of the
    field,   60
Valiant Lord Talbot, Earl of Shrewsbury,
Created, for his rare success in arms,
Great Earl of Washford, Waterford and Val-
  ence ;
Lord Talbot of Goodrig and Urchinfield,
Lord Strange of Blackmere, Lord Verdun of
  Alton,
Lord Cromwell of Wingfield, Lord Furnival of
  Sheffield,
The thrice-victorious Lord of Falconbridge ;
Knight of the noble order of Saint George,
Worthy Saint Michael and the Golden Fleece ;
Great marshal to Henry the Sixth   70
Of all his wars within the realm of France ?
  Puc. Here is a silly stately style indeed !
The Turk, that two and fifty kingdoms hath,
Writes not so tedious a style as this.
Him that thou magnifiest with all these titles
Stinking and fly-blown lies here at our feet.

  Lucy. Is Talbot slain, the Frenchmen's
    only scourge,
Your kingdom's terror and black Nemesis ?
O, were mine eyeballs into bullets turn'd,
That I in rage might shoot them at your
  faces !
O, that I could but call these dead to life ! 81
It were enough to fright the realm of France :
Were but his picture left amongst you here,
It would amaze the proudest of you all.
Give me their bodies, that I may bear them
  hence
And give them burial as beseems their worth.
  Puc. I think this upstart is old Talbot's
    ghost,
He speaks with such a proud commanding
  spirit.
For God's sake let him have 'em ; to keep
  them here,
They would but stink, and putrefy the air. 90
  Char. Go, take their bodies hence.
  Lucy. I'll bear them hence ; but from their
    ashes shall be rear'd
A phœnix that shall make all France afeard.
  Char. So we be rid of them, do with 'em
    what thou wilt.
And now to Paris, in this conquering vein :
All will be ours, now bloody Talbot's slain.
                          [*Exeunt.*

ACT V.

SCENE I. *London. The palace.*

Sennet. Enter KING, GLOUCESTER, *and*
  EXETER.

  King. Have you perused the letters from
    the pope,
The emperor and the Earl of Armagnac ?
  Glou. I have, my lord : and their intent is
    this :
They humbly sue unto your excellence
To have a godly peace concluded of
Between the realms of England and of France.
  King. How doth your grace affect their
    motion ?
  Glou. Well, my good lord ; and as the only
    means
To stop effusion of our Christian blood
And 'stablish quietness on every side.   10
  King. Ay, marry, uncle ; for I always
    thought
It was both impious and unnatural
That such immanity and bloody strife
Should reign among professors of one faith.
  Glou. Beside, my lord, the sooner to effect
And surer bind this knot of amity,
The Earl of Armagnac, near knit to Charles,
A man of great authority in France,
Proffers his only daughter to your grace
In marriage, with a large and sumptuous
  dowry.   20
  King. Marriage, uncle ! alas, my years are
    young !
And fitter is my study and my books
Than wanton dalliance with a paramour.
Yet call the ambassador ; and, as you please,
So let them have their answers every one :
I shall be well content with any choice
Tends to God's glory and my country's weal.

Enter WINCHESTER *in Cardinal's habit, a*
Legate *and two* Ambassadors.

Exe. What ! is my Lord of Winchester in-
stall'd,
And call'd unto a cardinal's degree ?
Then I perceive that will be verified   30
Henry the Fifth did sometime prophesy,
' If once he come to be a cardinal,
He'll make his cap co-equal with the crown.'
King. My lords ambassadors, your several
suits
Have been consider'd and debated on.
Your purpose is both good and reasonable ;
And therefore are we certainly resolved
To draw conditions of a friendly peace ;
Which by my Lord of Winchester we mean
Shall be transported presently to France.   40
Glou. And for the proffer of my lord your
master,
I have inform'd his highness so at large
As liking of the lady's virtuous gifts,
Her beauty and the value of her dower,
He doth intend she shall be England's queen.
King. In argument and proof of which
contract,
Bear her this jewel, pledge of my affection.
And so, my lord protector, see them guarded
And safely brought to Dover ; where inshipp'd
Commit them to the fortune of the sea.   50
      [*Exeunt all but Winchester and Legate.*
Win. Stay, my lord legate : you shall first
receive
The sum of money which I promised
Should be deliver'd to his holiness
For clothing me in these grave ornaments.
Leg. I will attend upon your lordship's
leisure.
Win. [*Aside*] Now Winchester will not
submit, I trow,
Or be inferior to the proudest peer.
Humphrey of Gloucester, thou shalt well per-
ceive
That, neither in birth or for authority,
The bishop will be overborne by thee :   60
I'll either make thee stoop and bend thy knee,
Or sack this country with a mutiny. [*Exeunt.*

SCENE II. *France. Plains in Anjou.*

Enter CHARLES, BURGUNDY, ALENÇON, BAS-
TARD, REIGNIER, LA PUCELLE, *and forces.*

Char. These news, my lord, may cheer our
drooping spirits :
'Tis said the stout Parisians do revolt
And turn again unto the warlike French.
Alen. Then march to Paris, royal Charles
of France,
And keep not back your powers in dalliance.
Puc. Peace be amongst them, if they turn
to us ;
Else, ruin combat with their palaces !

Enter Scout.

Scout. Success unto our valiant general,
And happiness to his accomplices !
Char. What tidings send our scouts ? I
prithee, speak.   10
Scout. The English army, that divided was
Into two parties, is now conjoined in one,
And means to give you battle presently.
Char. Somewhat too sudden, sirs, the
warning is ;

But we will presently provide for them.
Bur. I trust the ghost of Talbot is not
there :
Now he is gone, my lord, you need not fear.
Puc. Of all base passions, fear is most ac-
cursed.
Command the conquest, Charles, it shall be
thine,
Let Henry fret and all the world repine.   20
Char. Then on, my lords ; and France be
fortunate !   [*Exeunt.*

SCENE III. *Before Angiers.*

Alarum. Excursions. Enter LA PUCELLE.

Puc. The regent conquers, and the French-
men fly.
Now help, ye charming spells and periapts ;
And ye choice spirits that admonish me
And give me signs of future accidents.
            [*Thunder*
You speedy helpers, that are substitutes
Under the lordly monarch of the north,
Appear and aid me in this enterprise.

Enter Fiends.

This speedy and quick appearance argues
proof
Of your accustom'd diligence to me.
Now, ye familiar spirits, that are cull'd   10
Out of the powerful regions under earth,
Help me this once, that France may get the
field.   [*They walk, and speak not.*
O, hold me not with silence over-long !
Where I was wont to feed you with my blood,
I'll lop a member off and give it you
In earnest of a further benefit,
So you do condescend to help me now.
            [*They hang their heads.*
No hope to have redress ? My body shall
Pay recompense, if you will grant my suit.
            [*They shake their heads.*
Cannot my body nor blood-sacrifice   20
Entreat you to your wonted furtherance ?
Then take my soul, my body, soul and all,
Before that England give the French the foil.
            [*They depart.*
See, they forsake me ! Now the time is come
That France must vail her lofty-plumed crest
And let her head fall into England's lap.
My ancient incantations are too weak,
And hell too strong for me to buckle with :
Now, France, thy glory droopeth to the dust.
            [*Exit.*

Excursions. Re-enter LA PUCELLE *fighting
hand to hand with* YORK : LA PUCELLE *is
taken. The French fly.*

York. Damsel of France, I think I have
you fast :   30
Unchain your spirits now with spelling charms
And try if they can gain your liberty.
A goodly prize, fit for the devil's grace !
See, how the ugly wench doth bend her brows,
As if with Circe she would change my shape !
Puc. Changed to a worser shape thou canst
not be.
York. O, Charles the Dauphin is a proper
man ;
No shape but his can please your dainty eye.
Puc. A plaguing mischief light on Charles
and thee !
And may ye both be suddenly surprised   40

By bloody hands, in sleeping on your beds !
York. Fell banning hag, enchantress, hold
    thy tongue !
Puc. I prithee, give me leave to curse
    awhile.
York. Curse, miscreant, when thou comest
    to the stake.   [*Exeunt.*

Alarum. Enter SUFFOLK *with* MARGARET
    in his hand.

Suf. Be what thou wilt, thou art my pris-
    oner.   [*Gazes on her.*
O fairest beauty, do not fear nor fly !
For I will touch thee but with reverent hands ;
I kiss these fingers for eternal peace,
And lay them gently on thy tender side.
Who art thou ? say, that I may honor thee.
Mar. Margaret my name, and daughter to
    a king,   51
The King of Naples, whosoe'er thou art.
Suf. An earl I am, and Suffolk am I call'd.
Be not offended, nature's miracle,
Thou art allotted to be ta'en by me :
So doth the swan her downy cygnets save,
Keeping them prisoner underneath her wings.
Yet, if this servile usage once offend,
Go, and be free again, as Suffolk's friend.
                    [*She is going.*
O, stay ! I have no power to let her pass ; 60
My hand would free her, but my heart says no
As plays the sun upon the glassy streams,
Twinkling another counterfeited beam,
So seems this gorgeous beauty to mine eyes.
Fain would I woo her, yet I dare not speak :
I'll call for pen and ink, and write my mind.
Fie, de la Pole ! disable not thyself ;
Hast not a tongue ? is she not here ?
Wilt thou be daunted at a woman's sight ?
Ay, beauty's princely majesty is such, 70
Confounds the tongue and makes the senses
    rough.
Mar. Say, Earl of Suffolk—if thy name be
    so—
What ransom must I pay before I pass ?
For I perceive I am thy prisoner.
Suf. How canst thou tell she will deny thy
    suit,
Before thou make a trial of her love ?
Mar. Why speak'st thou not ? what ransom
    must I pay ?
Suf. She's beautiful, and therefore to be
    woo'd ;
She is a woman, therefore to be won.
Mar. Wilt thou accept of ransom ? yea, or
    no.
Suf. Fond man, remember that thou hast
    a wife ; 80
Then how can Margaret be thy paramour ?
Mar. I were best to leave him, for he will
    not hear.
Suf. There all is marr'd ; there lies a cool-
    ing card.
Mar. He talks at random ; sure, the man is
    mad.
Suf. And yet a dispensation may be had.
Mar. And yet I would that you would an-
    swer me.
Suf. I'll win this Lady Margaret. For
    whom ?
Why, for my king : tush, that's a wooden
    thing !

Mar. He talks of wood : it is some carpen-
    ter.   90
Suf. Yet so my fancy may be satisfied,
And peace established between these realms
But there remains a scruple in that too ;
For though her father be the King of Naples,
Duke of Anjou and Maine, yet is he poor,
And our nobility will scorn the match.
Mar. Hear ye, captain, are you not at lei-
    sure ?
Suf. It shall be so, disdain they ne'er so
    much.
Henry is youthful and will quickly yield.
Madam, I have a secret to reveal. 100
Mar. What though I be enthrall'd ? he
    seems a knight,
And will not any way dishonor me.
Suf. Lady, vouchsafe to listen what I say.
Mar. Perhaps I shall be rescued by the
    French ;
And then I need not crave his courtesy.
Suf. Sweet madam, give me a hearing in
    a cause—
Mar. Tush, women have been captivate ere
    now.
Suf. Lady, wherefore talk you so ?
Mar. I cry you mercy, 'tis but Quid for
    Quo.
Suf. Say, gentle princess, would you not
    suppose 110
Your bondage happy, to be made a queen ?
Mar. To be a queen in bondage is more vile
Than is a slave in base servility ;
For princes should be free.
Suf.   And so shall you,
If happy England's royal king be free.
Mar. Why, what concerns his freedom
    unto me ?
Suf. I'll undertake to make thee Henry's
    queen,
To put a golden sceptre in thy hand
And set a precious crown upon thy head,
If thou wilt condescend to be my—
Mar.   What ? 120
Suf. His love.
Mar. I am unworthy to be Henry's wife.
Suf. No, gentle madam ; I unworthy am
To woo so fair a dame to be his wife,
And have no portion in the choice myself.
How say you, madam, are ye so content ?
Mar. An if my father please, I am content.
Suf. Then call our captains and our col-
    ors forth.
And, madam, at your father's castle walls
We'll crave a parley, to confer with him. 130

A parley sounded. Enter REIGNIER *on the*
    walls.

See, Reignier, see, thy daughter prisoner !
Reig. To whom ?
Suf.   To me.
Reig.   Suffolk, what remedy ?
I am a soldier, and unapt to weep,
Or to exclaim on fortune's fickleness.
Suf. Yes, there is remedy enough, my
    lord :
Consent, and for thy honor give consent,
Thy daughter shall be wedded to my king ;
Whom I with pain have woo'd and won
    thereto ;
And this her easy-held imprisonment
Hath gained thy daughter princely liberty. 140

Reig. Speaks Suffolk as he thinks ?
Suf.   Fair Margaret knows
That Suffolk doth not flatter, face, or feign.
Reig. Upon thy princely warrant, I descend
To give thee answer of thy just demand.
               [*Exit from the walls.*
Suf. And here I will expect thy coming.

Trumpets sound. Enter REIGNIER, *below.*

Reig. Welcome, brave earl, into our terri-
tories :
Command in Anjou what your honor pleases.
Suf. Thanks, Reignier, happy for so sweet
a child,
Fit to be made companion with a king :
What answer makes your grace unto my suit ?
Reig. Since thou dost deign to woo her lit-
tle worth   151
To be the princely bride of such a lord ;
Upon condition I may quietly
Enjoy mine own, the country Maine and An-
jou,
Free from oppression or the stroke of war,
My daughter shall be Henry's, if he please.
Suf. That is her ransom ; I deliver her ;
And those two counties I will undertake
Your grace shall well and quietly enjoy.
Reig. And I again, in Henry's royal name,
As deputy unto that gracious king,   161
Give thee her hand, for sign of plighted faith.
Suf. Reignier of France, I give thee kingly
thanks,
Because this is in traffic of a king.
[*Aside*] And yet, methinks, I could be well
content
To be mine own attorney in this case.
I'll over then to England with this news,
And make this marriage to be solemnized.
So farewell, Reignier : set this diamond safe
In golden palaces, as it becomes.   170
Reig. I do embrace thee, as I would em-
brace
The Christian prince, King Henry, were he
here.
Mar. Farewell, my lord : good wishes,
praise and prayers
Shall Suffolk ever have of Margaret. [*Going.*
Suf. Farewell, sweet madam : but hark
you, Margaret ;
No princely commendations to my king ?
Mar. Such commendations as becomes a
maid,
A virgin and his servant, say to him.
Suf. Words sweetly placed and modestly
directed.
But, madam, I must trouble you again ;   180
No loving token to his majesty ?
Mar. Yes, my good lord, a pure unspotted
heart,
Never yet taint with love, I send the king.
Suf. And this withal.   [*Kisses her.*
Mar. That for thyself : I will not so pre-
sume
To send such peevish tokens to a king.
         [*Exeunt Reignier and Margaret.*
Suf. O, wert thou for myself ! But, Suffolk,
stay ;
Thou mayst not wander in that labyrinth ;
There Minotaurs and ugly treasons lurk.
Solicit Henry with her wondrous praise :   190
Bethink thee on her virtues that surmount,
And natural graces that extinguish art ;

Repeat their semblance often on the seas,
That, when thou comest to kneel at Henry's
feet,
Thou mayst bereave him of his wits with wonder.   [*Exit.*

SCENE IV. *Camp of the* DUKE OF YORK
in Anjou.

Enter YORK, WARWICK, *and others.*

York. Bring forth that sorceress condemn'd to burn.

Enter LA PUCELLE, *guarded, and a* Shepherd.

Shep. Ah, Joan, this kills thy father's heart
outright !
Have I sought every country far and near,
And, now it is my chance to find thee out,
Must I behold thy timeless cruel death ?
Ah, Joan, sweet daughter Joan, I'll die with
thee !
Puc. Decrepit miser ! base ignoble wretch !
I am descended of a gentler blood :
Thou art no father nor no friend of mine.
Shep. Out, out ! My lords, an please you,
'tis not so ;   10
I did beget her, all the parish knows :
Her mother liveth yet, can testify
She was the first fruit of my bachelorship.
War. Graceless ! wilt thou deny thy par-
entage ?
York. This argues what her kind of life
hath been,
Wicked and vile ; and so her death concludes.
Shep. Fie, Joan, that thou wilt be so ob-
stacle !
God knows thou art a collop of my flesh ;
And for thy sake have I shed many a tear :
Deny me not, I prithee, gentle Joan.   20
Puc. Peasant, avaunt ! You have suborn'd
this man,
Of purpose to obscure my noble birth.
Shep. 'Tis true, I gave a noble to the priest
The morn that I was wedded to her mother.
Kneel down and take my blessing, good my
girl.
Wilt thou not stoop ? Now cursed be the time
Of thy nativity ! I would the milk
Thy mother gave thee when thou suck'dst her
breast,
Had been a little ratsbane for thy sake !
Or else, when thou didst keep my lambs
a-field,   30
I wish some ravenous wolf had eaten thee !
Dost thou deny thy father, cursed drab ?
O, burn her, burn her ! hanging is too good.
                     [*Exit.*
York. Take her away ; for she hath lived
too long,
To fill the world with vicious qualities.
Puc. First, let me tell you whom you have
condemn'd :
Not me begotten of a shepherd swain,
But issued from the progeny of kings ;
Virtuous and holy ; chosen from above,
By inspiration of celestial grace,
To work exceeding miracles on earth.
I never had to do with wicked spirits :
But you, that are polluted with your lusts,
Stain'd with the guiltless blood of innocents,
Corrupt and tainted with a thousand vices,
Because you want the grace that others have,
You judge it straight a thing impossible

To compass wonders but by help of devils.
No, misconceived! Joan of Arc hath been   50
A virgin from her tender infancy,
Chaste and immaculate in very thought;
Whose maiden blood, thus rigorously effused,
Will cry for vengeance at the gates of heaven.
   York. Ay, ay : away with her to execu-
     tion !
   War. And hark ye, sirs ; because she is a
     maid,
Spare for no faggots, let there be enow :
Place barrels of pitch upon the fatal stake,
That so her torture may be shortened.
   Puc. Will nothing turn your unrelenting
     hearts ?
Then, Joan, discover thine infirmity,   60
That warranteth by law to be thy privilege.
I am with child, ye bloody homicides :
Murder not then the fruit within my womb,
Although ye hale me to a violent death.
   York. Now heaven forfend ! the holy maid
     with child !
   War. The greatest miracle that e'er ye
     wrought !
Is all your strict preciseness come to this ?
   York. She and the Dauphin have been jug-
     gling :
I did imagine what would be her refuge.
   War. Well, go to ; we'll have no bastards
     live ;   70
Especially since Charles must father it.
   Puc. You are deceived ; my child is none
     of his :
It was Alençon that enjoy'd my love.
   York. Alençon ! that notorious Machia-
     vel !
It dies, an if it had a thousand lives.
   Puc. O, give me leave, I have deluded
     you :
'Twas neither Charles nor yet the duke I
     named,
But Reignier, king of Naples, that prevail'd.
   War. A married man ! that's most intoler-
     able.
   York. Why, here's a girl ! I think she
     knows not well,   80
There were so many, whom she may accuse.
   War. It's sign she hath been liberal and
     free.
   York. And yet, forsooth, she is a virgin
     pure.
Strumpet, thy words condemn thy brat and
     thee :
Use no entreaty, for it is in vain.
   Puc. Then lead me hence ; with whom I
     leave my curse :
May never glorious sun reflex his beams
Upon the country where you make abode ;
But darkness and the gloomy shade of death
Environ you, till mischief and despair   90
Drive you to break your necks or hang your-
     selves !   [*Exit, guarded.*
   York. Break thou in pieces and consume
     to ashes,
Thou foul accursed minister of hell !

   Enter Cardinal Beaufort, *Bishop of*
     Winchester, attended.

   Car. Lord regent, I do greet your excel-
     lence
With letters of commission from the king.
For know, my lords, the states of Christendom,

Moved with remorse of these outrageous
     broils,
Have earnestly implored a general peace
Betwixt our nation and the aspiring French ;
And here at hand the Dauphin and his train
Approacheth, to confer about some matter.
   York. Is all our travail turn'd to this ef-
     fect ?
After the slaughter of so many peers,
So many captains, gentlemen and soldiers,
That in this quarrel have been overthrown
And sold their bodies for their country's bene-
     fit,
Shall we at last conclude effeminate peace ?
Have we not lost most part of all the towns,
By treason, falsehood and by treachery,
Our great progenitors had conquered ?   110
O, Warwick, Warwick ! I foresee with grief
The utter loss of all the realm of France.
   War. Be patient, York : if we conclude a
     peace,
It shall be with such strict and severe cove-
     nants
As little shall the Frenchmen gain thereby.

   Enter Charles, Alençon, Bastard, Reignier,
     and others.

   Char. Since, lords of England, it is thus
     agreed
That peaceful truce shall be proclaim'd in
     France,
We come to be informed by yourselves
What the conditions of that league must be.
   York. Speak, Winchester ; for boiling
     choler chokes   120
The hollow passage of my poison'd voice,
By sight of these our baleful enemies.
   Car. Charles, and the rest, it is enacted
     thus :
That, in regard King Henry gives consent,
Of mere compassion and of lenity,
To ease your country of distressful war,
And suffer you to breathe in fruitful peace,
You shall become true liegemen to his crown :
And, Charles, upon condition thou wilt swear
To pay him tribute, and submit thyself,   130
Thou shalt be placed as viceroy under him,
And still enjoy thy regal dignity.
   Alen. Must he be then as shadow of him-
     self ?
Adorn his temples with a coronet,
And yet, in substance and authority,
Retain but privilege of a private man ?
This proffer is absurd and reasonless.
   Char. 'Tis known already that I am pos-
     sess'd
With more than half the Gallian territories,
And therein reverenced for their lawful king :
Shall I, for lucre of the rest unvanquish'd,   141
Detract so much from that prerogative,
As to be call'd but viceroy of the whole ?
No, lord ambassador, I'll rather keep
That which I have than, coveting for more,
Be cast from possibility of all.
   York. Insulting Charles ! hast thou by se-
     cret means
Used intercession to obtain a league,
And, now the matter grows to compromise,
Stand'st thou aloof upon comparison ?   150
Either accept the title thou usurp'st,
Of benefit proceeding from our king
And not of any challenge of desert,

Or we will plague thee with incessant wars.
Reig. My lord, you do not well in obstinacy
To cavil in the course of this contract :
If once it be neglected, ten to one
We shall not find like opportunity.
Alen. To say the truth, it is your policy
To save your subjects from such massacre 160
And ruthless slaughters as are daily seen
By our proceeding in hostility ;
And therefore take this compact of a truce,
Although you break it when your pleasure serves.
War. How say'st thou, Charles ? shall our condition stand ?
Char. It shall ;
Only reserved, you claim no interest
In any of our towns of garrison.
York. Then swear allegiance to his majesty,
As thou art knight, never to disobey   170
Nor be rebellious to the crown of England,
Thou, nor thy nobles, to the crown of England.
So, now dismiss your army when ye please :
Hang up your ensign, let your drums be still,
For here we entertain a solemn peace.
[*Exeunt.*

SCENE V. *London. The palace.*

Enter SUFFOLK *in conference with the* KING,
GLOUCESTER *and* EXETER.

King. Your wondrous rare description, noble earl,
Of beauteous Margaret hath astonish'd me :
Her virtues graced with external gifts
Do breed love's settled passions in my heart :
And like as rigor of tempestuous gusts
Provokes the mightiest hulk against the tide,
So am I driven by breath of her renown
Either to suffer shipwreck or arrive
Where I may have fruition of her love.
Suf. Tush, my good lord, this superficial tale   10
Is but a preface of her worthy praise ;
The chief perfections of that lovely dame
Had I sufficient skill to utter them,
Would make a volume of enticing lines,
Able to ravish any dull conceit :
And, which is more, she is not so divine,
So full-replete with choice of all delights,
But with as humble lowliness of mind
She is content to be at your command ;
Command, I mean, of virtuous chaste intents,
To love and honor Henry as her lord.   21
King. And otherwise will Henry ne'er presume.
Therefore, my lord protector, give consent
That Margaret may be England's royal queen.
Glou. So should I give consent to flatter sin.
You know, my lord, your highness is betroth'd
Unto another lady of esteem :
How shall we then dispense with that contract,
And not deface your honor with reproach ?
Suf. As doth a ruler with unlawful oaths ;
Or one that, at a triumph having vow'd   31
To try his strength, forsaketh yet the lists
By reason of his adversary's odds :
A poor earl's daughter is unequal odds,
And therefore may be broke without offence.
Glou. Why, what, I pray, is Margaret more than that ?

Her father is no better than an earl,
Although in glorious titles he excel.
Suf. Yes, my lord, her father is a king,
The King of Naples and Jerusalem ;   40
And of such great authority in France
As his alliance will confirm our peace
And keep the Frenchmen in allegiance.
Glou. And so the Earl of Armagnac may do,
Because he is near kinsman unto Charles.
Exe. Beside, his wealth doth warrant a liberal dower,
Where Reignier sooner will receive than give.
Suf. A dower, my lords ! disgrace not so your king,
That he should be so abject, base and poor,
To choose for wealth and not for perfect love.
Henry is able to enrich his queen
And not to seek a queen to make him rich :
So worthless peasants bargain for their wives,
As market-men for oxen, sheep, or horse.
Marriage is a matter of more worth
Than to be dealt in by attorneyship ;
Not whom we will, but whom his grace affects,
Must be companion of his nuptial bed :
And therefore, lords, since he affects her most,
It most of all these reasons bindeth us,   60
In our opinions she should be preferr'd.
For what is wedlock forced but a hell,
An age of discord and continual strife ?
Whereas the contrary bringeth bliss,
And is a pattern of celestial peace.
Whom should we match with Henry, being a king,
But Margaret, that is daughter to a king ?
Her peerless feature, joined with her birth,
Approves her fit for none but for a king :
Her valiant courage and undaunted spirit,   70
More than in women commonly is seen,
Will answer our hope in issue of a king ;
For Henry, son unto a conqueror,
Is likely to beget more conquerors,
If with a lady of so high resolve
As is fair Margaret he be link'd in love.
Then yield, my lords ; and here conclude with me
That Margaret shall be queen, and none but she.
King. Whether it be through force of your report,
My noble Lord of Suffolk, or for that   80
My tender youth was never yet attaint
With any passion of inflaming love,
I cannot tell ; but this I am assured,
I feel such sharp dissension in my breast,
Such fierce alarums both of hope and fear,
As I am sick with working of my thoughts.
Take, therefore, shipping ; post, my lord, to France ;
Agree to any covenants, and procure
That Lady Margaret do vouchsafe to come
To cross the seas to England and be crown'd
King Henry's faithful and anointed queen :
For your expenses and sufficient charge,
Among the people gather up a tenth.
Be gone, I say ; for, till you do return,
I rest perplexed with a thousand cares.
And you, good uncle, banish all offence :
If you do censure me by what you were,
Not what you are, I know it will excuse
This sudden execution of my will.   99
And so, conduct me where, from company,

I may revolve and ruminate my grief.   [*Exit.*
  Glou. Ay, grief, I fear me, both at first and
     last.   [*Exeunt Gloucester and Exeter.*
  Suf. Thus Suffolk hath prevail'd; and thus
     he goes,
As did the youthful Paris once to Greece,
With hope to find the like event in love,
But prosper better than the Trojan did.
Margaret shall now be queen, and rule the
     king;
But I will rule both her, the king and realm.
     [*Exit.*

LOVE'S LABOUR'S LOST.

(WRITTEN ABOUT 1590.)

INTRODUCTION.

This play is supposed to be wholly of Shakespeare's own invention, no source of the plot having been discovered. It is precisely such a one as a clever young man might imagine, who had come lately from the country—with its " daisies pied and violets blue," its " merry larks," its maidens who " bleach their summer smocks," its pompous parish schoolmaster, and its dull constable (a great public official in his own eyes)—to the town, where he was surrounded by more brilliant unrealities, and affectation of dress, of manner, of language, and of ideas. *Love's Labour's Lost* is a dramatic plea on behalf of nature and common sense against all that is unreal and affected. It maintains, in a gay and witty fashion, the superiority of life, as a means of education, over books; the superiority of the large world into which we are born over any little world we can construct for ourselves, and into which we may hedge ourselves by rule ; and, while maintaining this, it also asserts that we must not educate ourselves only by what is mirthful and pleasant in the world, but must recognize its sorrow, and that we cannot be rightly glad without being grave and earnest. Thus, with its apparent lightness, there is a serious spirit underlying the play ; but the surface is all jest, and stir, and sparkle. It is a comedy of dialogue rather than of incident, and in the persons of Don Adriano de Armado, a fantastical Spaniard, of Sir Nathaniel the curate, and of Holofernes the schoolmaster, are caricatured various Elizabethan absurdities of speech, pseudo-refinement, and pseudo-learning. The braggart soldier and the pedant are characters well known in Italian comedy, and perhaps it was from that quarter that the hint came to Shakespeare, which stirred his imagination to create these ridiculous figures. Holofernes, some persons have supposed to be a satirical sketch of John Florio, author of an Italian dictionary ; but Shakespeare did not in any ascertained instances satirize individual persons, and there is little evidence in this case to warrant the supposition. The play contains nothing which serves to indicate its precise date, but it certainly belongs to Shakespeare's earliest dramatic period. The first quarto edition was published in 1598, " as it was presented before her Highness [Queen Elizabeth] this last Christmas [probably the Christmas of 1598], Newly corrected and augmented." Two traces of the alterations from the original play may still be observed. In Act V. Sc. II., the lines 827–832 ought not to appear, being almost certainly the fragment of the play in its first form which was afterwards marked out in the lines 833–879. Similarly, in Biron's great speech, Act IV. Sc. III., the lines 296–317 contain passages which are repeated or altered in the lines which follow (318–354), and obviously some of the lines in the original version have here been retained through a mistake.

DRAMATIS PERSONÆ.

FERDINAND, king of Navarre.
BIRON,
LONGAVILLE, }lords attending on the King.
DUMAIN,
BOYET, } lords attending on the Princess
MERCADE, } of France.
DON ADRIANO DE ARMADO, a fantastical
    Spaniard.
SIR NATHANIEL, a curate.
HOLOFERNES, a schoolmaster.
DULL, a constable.

COSTARD, a clown.
MOTH, page to Armado.
A Forester.
The PRINCESS of France.
ROSALINE, } ladies attending on the
MARIA, } Princess.
KATHARINE,
JAQUENETTA, a country wench.

Lords, Attendants, &c.

SCENE: *Navarre.*

ACT I.

SCENE I. *The king of Navarre's park.*

Enter FERDINAND, *king of* NAVARRE, BIRON,
LONGAVILLE *and* DUMAIN.

King. Let fame, that all hunt after in their
lives,
Live register'd upon our brazen tombs
And then grace us in the disgrace of death ;
When, spite of cormorant devouring Time,
The endeavor of this present breath may buy
That honor which shall bate his scythe's keen
edge
And make us heirs of all eternity.
Therefore, brave conquerors,—for so you are,
That war against your own affections
And the huge army of the world's desires,—10
Our late edict shall strongly stand in force :
Navarre shall be the wonder of the world ;
Our court shall be a little Academe,
Still and contemplative in living art.
You three, Biron, Dumain, and Longaville,
Have sworn for three years' term to live with
me
My fellow-scholars, and to keep those statutes
That are recorded in this schedule here :
Your oaths are pass'd ; and now subscribe
your names,
That his own hand may strike his honor down
That violates the smallest branch herein :   21
If you are arm'd to do as sworn to do,
Subscribe to your deep oaths, and keep it too.
Long. I am resolved ; 'tis but a three
years' fast :
The mind shall banquet, though the body
pine :
Fat paunches have lean pates, and dainty bits
Make rich the ribs, but bankrupt quite the
wits.
Dum. My loving lord, Dumain is morti-
fied :
The grosser manner of these world's delights
He throws upon the gross world's baser
slaves :   30
To love, to wealth, to pomp, I pine and die ;
With all these living in philosophy.
Biron. I can but say their protestation
over ;
So much, dear liege, I have already sworn,
That is, to live and study here three years.
But there are other strict observances ;
As, not to see a woman in that term,
Which I hope well is not enrolled there ;
And one day in a week to touch no food
And but one meal on every day beside,   40
The which I hope is not enrolled there ;
And then, to sleep but three hours in the
night,
And not be seen to wink of all the day—
When I was wont to think no harm all night
And make a dark night too of half the day—
Which I hope well is not enrolled there :
O, these are barren tasks, too hard to keep,
Not to see ladies, study, fast, not sleep !
King. Your oath is pass'd to pass away
from these.
Biron. Let me say no, my liege, an if you
please :   50

I only swore to study with your grace
And stay here in your court for three years'
space.
Long. You swore to that, Biron, and to
the rest.
Biron. By yea and nay, sir, then I swore
in jest.
What is the end of study ? let me know.
King. Why, that to know, which else we
should not know.
Biron. Things hid and barr'd, you mean,
from common sense ?
King. Ay, that is study's god-like recom-
pense.
Biron. Come on, then ; I will swear to
study so,
To know the thing I am forbid to know :   60
As thus,—to study where I well may dine,
When I to feast expressly am forbid ;
Or study where to meet some mistress fine,
When mistresses from common sense are
hid ;
Or, having sworn too hard a keeping oath,
Study to break it and not break my troth.
If study's gain be thus and this be so,
Study knows that which yet it doth not know :
Swear me to this, and I will ne'er say no.
King. These be the stops that hinder study
quite   70
And train our intellects to vain delight.
Biron. Why, all delights are vain ; but
that most vain,
Which with pain purchased doth inherit pain :
As, painfully to pore upon a book
To seek the light of truth ; while truth the
while
Doth falsely blind the eyesight of his look :
Light seeking light doth light of light be-
guile :
So, ere you find where light in darkness lies,
Your light grows dark by losing of your eyes.
Study me how to please the eye indeed   80
By fixing it upon a fairer eye,
Who dazzling so, that eye shall be his heed
And give him light that it was blinded by.
Study is like the heaven's glorious sun
That will not be deep-search'd with saucy
looks :
Small have continual plodders ever won
Save base authority from others' books
These earthly godfathers of heaven's lights
That give a name to every fixed star
Have no more profit of their shining nights 90
Than those that walk and wot not what
they are.
Too much to know is to know nought but
fame ;
And every godfather can give a name.
King. How well he's read, to reason
against reading !
Dum. Proceeded well, to stop all good
proceeding !
Long. He weeds the corn and still lets
grow the weeding.
Biron. The spring is near when green
geese are a-breeding.
Dum. How follows that ?
Biron.   Fit in his place and time.
Dum. In reason nothing.
Biron.   Something then in rhyme.

King. Biron is like an envious sneaping
          frost,
    That bites the first-born infants of
          the spring.   101
Biron. Well, say I am; why should proud
          summer boast
    Before the birds have any cause
          to sing?
Why should I joy in any abortive birth?
At Christmas I no more desire a rose
Than wish a snow in May's new-fangled
          mirth;
But like of each thing that in season grows.
So you, to study now it is too late,
Climb o'er the house to unlock the little gate.
King. Well, sit you out: go home, Biron:
          adieu.   110
Biron. No, my good lord; I have sworn to
          stay with you:
And though I have for barbarism spoke more
    Than for that angel knowledge you can say,
Yet confident I'll keep what I have swore
And bide the penance of each three years'
          day.
Give me the paper; let me read the same;
And to the strict'st decrees I'll write my name.
King. How well this yielding rescues thee
          from shame!
Biron [*reads*]. 'Item, That no woman
shall come within a mile of my court:' Hath
this been proclaimed?   121
Long. Four days ago.
Biron. Let's see the penalty. [*Reads*] 'On
pain of losing her tongue.' Who devised this
penalty?
Long. Marry, that did I.
Biron. Sweet lord, and why?
Long. To fright them hence with that
          dread penalty.
Biron. A dangerous law against gentility!
[*Reads*] 'Item, If any man be seen to talk
with a woman within the term of three years,
he shall endure such public shame as the rest
of the court can possibly devise.'
This article, my liege, yourself must break;
    For well you know here comes in embassy
The French king's daughter with yourself to
          speak—
A maid of grace and complete majesty—
About surrender up of Aquitaine
To her decrepit, sick and bedrid father:
Therefore this article is made in vain,   140
    Or vainly comes the admired princess
          hither.
King. What say you, lords? why, this was
          quite forgot.
Biron. So study evermore is overshot:
While it doth study to have what it would
It doth forget to do the thing it should,
And when it hath the thing it hunteth most,
'Tis won as towns with fire, so won, so lost.
King. We must of force dispense with this
          decree;
She must lie here on mere necessity.
Biron. Necessity will make us all forsworn
Three thousand times within this three
          years' space;   151
For every man with his affects is born,
    Not by might master'd but by special grace:
If I break faith, this word shall speak for me;
I am forsworn on 'mere necessity.'

So to the laws at large I write my name:
                              [*Subscribes.*
    And he that breaks them in the least degree
Stands in attainder of eternal shame:
    Suggestions are to other as to me;
But I believe, although I seem so loath,   160
I am the last that will last keep his oath.
But is there no quick recreation granted?
King. Ay, that there is. Our court, you
          know, is haunted
With a refined traveller of Spain;
A man in all the world's new fashion planted,
That hath a mint of phrases in his brain;
One whom the music of his own vain tongue
    Doth ravish like enchanting harmony;
A man of complements, whom right and
          wrong
Have chose as umpire of their mutiny: 170
This child of fancy, that Armado hight,
    For interim to our studies shall relate
In high-born words the worth of many a
          knight
    From tawny Spain lost in the world's de-
          bate.
How you delight, my lords, I know not, I;
But, I protest, I love to hear him lie
And I will use him for my minstrelsy.
Biron. Armado is a most illustrious wight,
A man of fire-new words, fashion's own
          knight.
Long. Costard the swain and he shall be
          our sport;   180
And so to study, three years is but short.

    Enter DULL *with a letter, and* COSTARD.

Dull. Which is the duke's own person?
Biron. This, fellow: what wouldst?
Dull. I myself reprehend his own person,
for I am his grace's tharborough: but I would
see his own person in flesh and blood.
Biron. This is he.
Dull. Signior Arme — Arme — commends
you. There's villany abroad: this letter will
tell you more.   190
Cost. Sir, the contempts thereof are as
touching me.
King. A letter from the magnificent Ar-
mado.
Biron. How low soever the matter, I hope
in God for high words.
Long. A high hope for a low heaven: God
grant us patience!
Biron. To hear? or forbear laughing?
Long. To hear meekly, sir, and to laugh
moderately; or to forbear both.   200
Biron. Well, sir, be it as the style shall
give us cause to climb in the merriness.
Cost. The matter is to me, sir, as concerning Jaquenetta. The manner of it is, I was
taken with the manner.
Biron. In what manner?
Cost. In manner and form following, sir;
all those three: I was seen with her in the
manor-house, sitting with her upon the form,
and taken following her into the park; which,
put together, is in manner and form following.
Now, sir, for the manner,—it is the manner of
a man to speak to a woman: for the form,—
in some form.
Biron. For the following, sir?
Cost. As it shall follow in my correction:
and God defend the right!

King. Will you hear this letter with attention ?
Biron. As we would hear an oracle.
Cost. Such is the simplicity of man to hearken after the flesh. 220
King [*reads*]. ' Great deputy, the welkin's vicegerent and sole dominator of Navarre, my soul's earth's god, and body's fostering patron.'
Cost. Not a word of Costard yet.
King [*reads*]. ' So it is,'—
Cost. It may be so : but if he say it is so, he is, in telling true, but so.
King. Peace !
Cost. Be to me and every man that dares not fight ! 230
King. No words !
Cost. Of other men's secrets, I beseech you.
King [*reads*]. ' So it is, besieged with sable-colored melancholy, I did commend the black-oppressing humor to the most wholesome physic of thy health-giving air ; and, as I am a gentleman, betook myself to walk. The time when. About the sixth hour ; when beasts most graze, birds best peck, and men sit down to that nourishment which is called supper : so much for the time when. Now for the ground which ; which, I mean, I walked upon : it is ycleped thy park. Then for the place where ; where, I mean, I did encounter that obscene and preposterous event, that draweth from my snow-white pen the ebon-colored ink, which here thou viewest, beholdest, surveyest, or seest ; but to the place where ; it standeth north-north-east and by east from the west corner of thy curious-knotted garden : there did I see that low-spirited swain, that base minnow of thy mirth,'—
Cost. Me ?
King [*reads*]. ' that unlettered small-knowing soul,'—
Cost. Me ?
King [*reads*]. ' that shallow vassal,'—
Cost. Still me ?
King [*reads*]. ' which, as I remember, hight Costard,'—
Cost. O, me ! 260
King [*reads*]. ' sorted and consorted, contrary to thy established proclaimed edict and continent canon, which with,—O, with—but with this I passion to say wherewith,—
Cost. With a wench.
King [*reads*]. ' with a child of our grandmother Eve, a female ; or, for thy more sweet understanding, a woman. Him I, as my ever-esteemed duty pricks me on, have sent to thee, to receive the meed of punishment, by thy sweet grace's officer, Anthony Dull ; a man of good repute, carriage, bearing, and estimation.'
Dull. Me, an't shall please you ; I am Anthony Dull.
King [*reads*]. ' For Jaquenetta,—so is the weaker vessel called which I apprehended with the aforesaid swain,—I keep her as a vessel of the law's fury ; and shall, at the least of thy sweet notice, bring her to trial. Thine, in all compliments of devoted and heart-burning heat of duty.
DON . ADRIANO . DE . ARMADO.'
Biron. This is not so well as I looked for, but the best that ever I heard.

King. Ay, the best for the worst. But, sirrah, what say you to this ?
Cost. Sir, I confess the wench.
King. Did you hear the proclamation ?
Cost. I do confess much of the hearing it but little of the marking of it.
King. It was proclaimed a year's imprisonment, to be taken with a wench. 290
Cost. I was taken with none, sir : I was taken with a damsel.
King. Well, it was proclaimed ' damsel.'
Cost. This was no damsel, neither, sir ; she was a virgin.
King. It is so varied, too ; for it was proclaimed ' virgin.'
Cost. If it were, I deny her virginity : I was taken with a maid.
King. This maid will not serve your turn, sir.
Cost. This maid will serve my turn, sir.
King. Sir, I will pronounce your sentence : you shall fast a week with bran and water.
Cost. I had rather pray a month with mutton and porridge.
King. And Don Armado shall be your keeper.
My Lord Biron, see him deliver'd o'er :
And go we, lords, to put in practice that
Which each to other hath so strongly sworn.
[*Exeunt King, Longaville, and Dumain.*
Biron. I'll lay my head to any good man's hat,
These oaths and laws will prove an idle scorn.
Sirrah, come on.
Cost. I suffer for the truth, sir ; for true it is, I was taken with Jaquenetta, and Jaquenetta is a true girl ; and therefore welcome the sour cup of prosperity ! Affliction may one day smile again ; and till then, sit thee down, sorrow ! [*Exeunt.*

Scene II. *The same.*

Enter ARMADO *and* MOTH.

Arm. Boy, what sign is it when a man of great spirit grows melancholy ?
Moth. A great sign, sir, that he will look sad.
Arm. Why, sadness is one and the self-same thing, dear imp.
Moth. No, no ; O Lord, sir, no.
Arm. How canst thou part sadness and melancholy, my tender juvenal ?
Moth. By a familiar demonstration of the working, my tough senior. 10
Arm. Why tough senior ? why tough senior ?
Moth. Why tender juvenal ? why tender juvenal ?
Arm. I spoke it, tender juvenal, as a congruent epitheton appertaining to thy young days, which we may nominate tender.
Moth. And I, tough senior, as an appertinent title to your old time, which we may name tough.
Arm. Pretty and apt.
Moth. How mean you, sir ? I pretty, and my saying apt ? or I apt, and my saying pretty ?
Arm. Thou pretty, because little.
Moth. Little pretty, because little. Wherefore apt ?

Arm. And therefore apt, because quick.

Moth. Speak you this in my praise, master?

Arm. In thy condign praise.

Moth. I will praise an eel with the same praise.

Arm. What, that an eel is ingenious?

Moth. That an eel is quick.　30

Arm. I do say thou art quick in answers: thou heatest my blood.

Moth. I am answered, sir.

Arm. I love not to be crossed.

Moth. [*Aside*] He speaks the mere contrary; crosses love not him.

Arm. I have promised to study three years with the duke.

Moth. You may do it in an hour, sir.

Arm. Impossible.　40

Moth. How many is one thrice told?

Arm. I am ill at reckoning; it fitteth the spirit of a tapster.

Moth. You are a gentleman and a gamester, sir.

Arm. I confess both: they are both the varnish of a complete man.

Moth. Then, I am sure, you know how much the gross sum of deuce-ace amounts to.

Arm. It doth amount to one more than two.

Moth. Which the base vulgar do call three.

Arm. True.

Moth. Why, sir, is this such a piece of study? Now here is three studied, ere ye'll thrice wink: and how easy it is to put 'years' to the word 'three,' and study three years in two words, the dancing horse will tell you.

Arm. A most fine figure!

Moth. To prove you a cipher.　59

Arm. I will hereupon confess I am in love: and as it is base for a soldier to love, so am I in love with a base wench. If drawing my sword against the humor of affection would deliver me from the reprobate thought of it, I would take Desire prisoner, and ransom him to any French courtier for a new-devised courtesy. I think scorn to sigh: methinks I should outswear Cupid. Comfort, me, boy: what great men have been in love?

Moth. Hercules, master.

Arm. Most sweet Hercules! More authority, dear boy, name more; and, sweet my child, let them be men of good repute and carriage.

Moth. Samson, master: he was a man of good carriage, great carriage, for he carried the town-gates on his back like a porter: and he was in love.

Arm. O well-knit Samson! strong-jointed Samson! I do excel thee in my rapier as much as thou didst me in carrying gates. I am in love too. Who was Samson's love, my dear Moth?　80

Moth. A woman, master.

Arm. Of what complexion?

Moth. Of all the four, or the three, or the two, or one of the four.

Arm. Tell me precisely of what complexion.

Moth. Of the sea-water green, sir.

Arm. Is that one of the four complexions?

Moth. As I have read, sir; and the best of them too.

Arm. Green indeed is the color of lovers; but to have a love of that color, methinks Samson had small reason for it. He surely affected her for her wit.

Moth. It was so, sir; for she had a green wit.

Arm. My love is most immaculate white and red.

Moth. Most maculate thoughts, master, are masked under such colors.

Arm. Define, define, well-educated infant.

Moth. My father's wit and my mother's tongue, assist me!　101

Arm. Sweet invocation of a child; most pretty and pathetical!

Moth. If she be made of white and red,
　　Her faults will ne'er be known,
　For blushing cheeks by faults are bred
　　And fears by pale white shown:
　Then if she fear, or be to blame,
　　By this you shall not know,
　For still her cheeks possess the same　110
　　Which native she doth owe.
A dangerous rhyme, master, against the reason of white and red.

Arm. Is there not a ballad, boy, of the King and the Beggar?

Moth. The world was very guilty of such a ballad some three ages since: but I think now 'tis not to be found; or, if it were, it would neither serve for the writing nor the tune.

Arm. I will have that subject newly writ o'er, that I may example my digression by some mighty precedent. Boy, I do love that country girl that I took in the park with the rational hind Costard: she deserves well.

Moth. [*Aside*] To be whipped; and yet a better love than my master.

Arm. Sing, boy; my spirit grows heavy in love.

Moth. And that's great marvel, loving a light wench.

Arm. I say, sing.　130

Moth. Forbear till this company be past.

Enter DULL, COSTARD, *and* JAQUENETTA.

Dull. Sir, the duke's pleasure is, that you keep Costard safe: and you must suffer him to take no delight nor no penance; but a' must fast three days a week. For this damsel, I must keep her at the park: she is allowed for the day-woman. Fare you well.

Arm. I do betray myself with blushing. Maid!

Jaq. Man?

Arm. I will visit thee at the lodge.　140

Jaq. That's hereby.

Arm. I know where it is situate.

Jaq. Lord, how wise you are!

Arm. I will tell thee wonders.

Jaq. With that face?

Arm. I love thee.

Jaq. So I heard you say.

Arm. And so, farewell.

Jaq. Fair weather after you!

Dull. Come, Jaquenetta, away!　150
　　　　　[*Exeunt Dull and Jaquenetta.*

Arm. Villain, thou shalt fast for thy offences ere thou be pardoned.

Cost. Well, sir, I hope, when I do it, I shall do it on a full stomach.

Arm. Thou shalt be heavily punished.

Cost. I am more bound to you than your fellows, for they are but lightly rewarded.

Arm. Take away this villain ; shut him up.

Moth. Come, you transgressing slave ; away !   160

Cost. Let me not be pent up, sir : I will fast, being loose.

Moth. No, sir ; that were fast and loose : thou shalt to prison.

Cost. Well, if ever I do see the merry days of desolation that I have seen, some shall see.

Moth. What shall some see ?

Cost. Nay, nothing, Master Moth, but what they look upon. It is not for prisoners to be too silent in their words ; and therefore I will say nothing : I thank God I have as little patience as another man ; and therefore I can be quiet.   171

              [Exeunt Moth and Costard.

Arm. I do affect the very ground, which is base, where her shoe, which is baser, guided by her foot, which is basest, doth tread. I shall be forsworn, which is a great argument of falsehood, if I love. And how can that be true love which is falsely attempted ? Love is a familiar ; Love is a devil : there is no evil angel but Love. Yet was Samson so tempted, and he had an excellent strength ; yet was Solomon so seduced, and he had a very good wit. Cupid's butt-shaft is too hard for Hercules' club ; and therefore too much odds for a Spaniard's rapier. The first and second cause will not serve my turn ; the passado he respects not, the duello he regards not : his disgrace is to be called boy ; but his glory is to subdue men. Adieu, valor ! rust, rapier ! be still, drum ! for your manager is in love ; yea, he loveth. Assist me, some extemporal god of rhyme, for I am sure I shall turn sonnet. Devise, wit ; write, pen ; for I am for whole volumes in folio.   *[Exit.*

ACT II.

SCENE I. *The same.*

Enter the Princess of France, ROSALINE, MARIA, KATHARINE, BOYET, Lords, *and other* Attendants.

Boyet. Now, madam, summon up your dearest spirits :
Consider who the king your father sends,
To whom he sends, and what's his embassy :
Yourself, held precious in the world's esteem,
To parley with the sole inheritor
Of all perfections that a man may owe,
Matchless Navarre ; the plea of no less weight
Than Aquitaine, a dowry for a queen.
Be now as prodigal of all dear grace
As Nature was in making graces dear   10
When she did starve the general world beside
And prodigally gave them all to you.

Prin. Good Lord Boyet, my beauty, though but mean,
Needs not the painted flourish of your praise :
Beauty is bought by judgement of the eye,
Not utter'd by base sale of chapmen's tongues :
I am less proud to hear you tell my worth
Than you much willing to be counted wise
In spending your wit in the praise of mine.

But now to task the tasker : good Boyet,   20
You are not ignorant, all-telling fame
Doth noise abroad, Navarre hath made a vow,
Till painful study shall outwear three years,
No woman may approach his silent court :
Therefore to's seemeth it a needful course,
Before we enter his forbidden gates,
To know his pleasure ; and in that behalf,
Bold of your worthiness, we single you
As our best-moving fair solicitor.   29
Tell him, the daughter of the King of France,
On serious business, craving quick dispatch,
Importunes personal conference with his grace :
Haste, signify so much ; while we attend,
Like humble-visaged suitors, his high will.

Boyet. Proud of employment, willingly I go.

Prin. All pride is willing pride, and yours is so.   *[Exit Boyet.*
Who are the votaries, my loving lords,
That are vow-fellows with this virtuous duke ?

First Lord. Lord Longaville is one.

Prin.   Know you the man?

Mar. I know him, madam : at a marriage-feast,   40
Between Lord Perigort and the beauteous heir
Of Jaques Falconbridge, solemnized
In Normandy, saw I this Longaville :
A man of sovereign parts he is esteem'd ;
Well fitted in arts, glorious in arms :
Nothing becomes him ill that he would well.
The only soil of his fair virtue's gloss,
If virtue's gloss will stain with any soil,
Is a sharp wit match'd with too blunt a will ;
Whose edge hath power to cut, whose will still wills   50
It should none spare that come within his power.

Prin. Some merry mocking lord, belike ; is't so ?

Mar. They say so most that most his humors know.

Prin. Such short-lived wits do wither as they grow.
Who are the rest ?

Kath. The young Dumain, a well-accomplished youth,
Of all that virtue love for virtue loved :
Most power to do most harm, least knowing ill ;
For he hath wit to make an ill shape good,
And shape to win grace though he had no wit.
I saw him at the Duke Alençon's once ;   61
And much too little of that good I saw
Is my report to his great worthiness.

Ros. Another of these students at that time
Was there with him, if I have heard a truth.
Biron they call him ; but a merrier man,
Within the limit of becoming mirth,
I never spent an hour's talk withal :
His eye begets occasion for his wit ;
For every object that the one doth catch   70
The other turns to a mirth-moving jest,
Which his fair tongue, conceit's expositor,
Delivers in such apt and gracious words
That aged ears play truant at his tales
And younger hearings are quite ravished ;
So sweet and voluble is his discourse.

Prin. God bless my ladies ! are they all in love,
That every one her own hath garnished

With such bedecking ornaments of praise?
First Lord. Here comes Boyet.

Re-enter BOYET.

Prin. Now, what admittance, lord?   80
Boyet. Navarre had notice of your fair approach;
And he and his competitors in oath
Were all address'd to meet you, gentle lady,
Before I came. Marry, thus much I have learnt:
He rather means to lodge you in the field,
Like one that comes here to besiege his court,
Than seek a dispensation for his oath,
To let you enter his unpeopled house.
Here comes Navarre.

Enter King, LONGAVILLE, DUMAIN, BIRON,
        and Attendants.

King. Fair princess, welcome to the court
    of Navarre.   90
Prin. 'Fair' I give you back again; and
'welcome' I have not yet: the roof of this
court is too high to be yours; and welcome
to the wide fields too base to be mine.
King. You shall be welcome, madam, to
my court.
Prin. I will be welcome, then: conduct me
    thither.
King. Hear me, dear lady; I have sworn
    an oath.
Prin. Our Lady help my lord! he'll be forsworn.
King. Not for the world, fair madam, by
    my will.
Prin. Why, will shall break it; will and
    nothing else.   100
King. Your ladyship is ignorant what it is.
Prin. Were my lord so, his ignorance were
    wise,
Where now his knowledge must prove ignorance.
I hear your grace hath sworn out house-keeping:
'Tis deadly sin to keep that oath, my lord,
And sin to break it.
But pardon me, I am too sudden-bold:
To teach a teacher ill beseemeth me.
Vouchsafe to read the purpose of my coming,
And suddenly resolve me in my suit.   110
King. Madam, I will, if suddenly I may.
Prin. You will the sooner, that I were
    away;
For you'll prove perjured if you make me
    stay.
Biron. Did not I dance with you in Brabant once?
Ros. Did not I dance with you in Brabant once?
Biron. I know you did.
Ros. How needless was it then to ask the
    question!
Biron. You must not be so quick.
Ros. 'Tis 'long of you that spur me with
    such questions.
Biron. Your wit's too hot, it speeds too
    fast, 'twill tire.   120
Ros. Not till it leave the rider in the mire.
Biron. What time o' day?
Ros. The hour that fools should ask.
Biron. Now fair befall your mask!
Ros. Fair fall the face it covers!

Biron. And send you many lovers!
Ros. Amen, so you be none.
Biron. Nay, then will I be gone.
King. Madam, your father here doth intimate
The payment of a hundred thousand crowns;
Being but the one half of an entire sum   131
Disbursed by my father in his wars.
But say that he or we, as neither have,
Received that sum, yet there remains unpaid
A hundred thousand more; in surety of the
    which,
One part of Aquitaine is bound to us,
Although not valued to the money's worth.
If then the king your father will restore
But that one half which is unsatisfied,
We will give up our right in Aquitaine,   140
And hold fair friendship with his majesty.
But that, it seems, he little purposeth,
For here he doth demand to have repaid
A hundred thousand crowns; and not demands,
On payment of a hundred thousand crowns,
To have his title live in Aquitaine;
Which we much rather had depart withal
And have the money by our father lent
Than Aquitaine so gelded as it is.   149
Dear Princess, were not his requests so far
From reason's yielding, your fair self should
    make
A yielding 'gainst some reason in my breast
And go well satisfied to France again.
Prin. You do the king my father too much
    wrong
And wrong the reputation of your name,
In so unseeming to confess receipt
Of that which hath so faithfully been paid.
King. I do protest I never heard of it;
And if you prove it, I'll repay it back
Or yield up Aquitaine.
Prin.   We arrest your word.   160
Boyet, you can produce acquittances
For such a sum from special officers
Of Charles his father.
King.   Satisfy me so.
Boyet. So please your grace, the packet is
    not come
Where that and other specialties are bound:
To-morrow you shall have a sight of them.
King. It shall suffice me: at which interview
All liberal reason I will yield unto.
Meantime receive such welcome at my hand
As honor without breach of honor may   170
Make tender of to thy true worthiness:
You may not come, fair princess, in my gates;
But here without you shall be so received
As you shall deem yourself lodged in my heart,
Though so denied fair harbor in my house.
Your own good thoughts excuse me, and farewell:
To-morrow shall we visit you again.
Prin. Sweet health and fair desires consort your grace!
King. Thy own wish wish I thee in every
    place!   [*Exit.*
Biron. Lady, I will commend you to mine
    own heart.   180
Ros. Pray you, do my commendations; I
    would be glad to see it.
Biron. I would you heard it groan.
Ros. Is the fool sick?

Biron. Sick at the heart.
Ros. Alack, let it blood.
Biron. Would that do it good ?
Ros. My physic says ' ay.'
Biron. Will you prick't with your eye ?
Ros. No point, with my knife.   190
Biron. Now, God save thy life !
Ros. And yours from long living !
Biron. I cannot stay thanksgiving.
                                   [*Retiring.*
Dum. Sir, I pray you, a word : what lady
    is that same ?
Boyet. The heir of Alençon, Katharine her
    name.
Dum. A gallant lady. Monsieur, fare you
    well.   [*Exit.*
Long. I beseech you a word : what is she
    in the white ?
Boyet. A woman sometimes, an you saw
    her in the light.
Long. Perchance light in the light. I de-
    sire her name.
Boyet. She hath but one for herself ; to
    desire that were a shame.   200
Long. Pray you, sir, whose daughter ?
Boyet. Her mother's, I have heard.
Long. God's blessing on your beard !
Boyet. Good sir, be not offended.
She is an heir of Falconbridge.
Long. Nay, my choler is ended.
She is a most sweet lady.
Boyet. Not unlike, sir, that may be.
                              [*Exit Long.*
Biron. What's her name in the cap ?
Boyet. Rosaline, by good hap.   210
Biron. Is she wedded or no ?
Boyet. To her will, sir, or so.
Biron. You are welcome, sir : adieu.
Boyet. Farewell to me, sir, and welcome
    to you.   [*Exit Biron.*
Mar. That last is Biron, the merry mad-
    cap lord :
Not a word with him but a jest.
Boyet.   And every jest but a word.
Prin. It was well done of you to take him
    at his word.
Boyet. I was as willing to grapple as he
    was to board.
Mar. Two hot sheeps, marry.
Boyet.   And wherefore not ships ?
No sheep, sweet lamb, unless we feed on your
    lips.   220
Mar. You sheep, and I pasture : shall that
    finish the jest ?
Boyet. So you grant pasture for me.
                         [*Offering to kiss her.*
Mar.   Not so, gentle beast :
My lips are no common, though several they
    be.
Boyet. Belonging to whom ?
Mar.   To my fortunes and me.
Prin. Good wits will be jangling ; but,
    gentles, agree :
This civil war of wits were much better used
On Navarre and his book-men ; for here 'tis
    abused.
Boyet. If my observation, which very sel-
    dom lies,
By the heart's still rhetoric disclosed with
    eyes,
Deceive me not now, Navarre is infected. 230
Prin. With what ?

Boyet. With that which we lovers entitle
    affected.
Prin. Your reason ?
Boyet. Why, all his behaviors did make
    their retire
To the court of his eye, peeping thorough de-
    sire :
His heart, like an agate, with your print im-
    press'd,
Proud with his form, in his eye pride ex-
    press'd :
His tongue, all impatient to speak and not see,
Did stumble with haste in his eyesight to be ;
All senses to that sense did make their repair,
To feel only looking on fairest of fair :   241
Methought all his senses were lock'd in his
    eye,
As jewels in crystal for some prince to buy ;
Who, tendering their own worth from where
    they were glass'd,
Did point you to buy them, along as you
    pass'd :
His face's own margent did quote such amazes
That all eyes saw his eyes enchanted with
    gazes.
I'll give you Aquitaine and all that is his,
An you give him for my sake but one loving
    kiss.
Prin. Come to our pavilion : Boyet is dis-
    posed.
Boyet. But to speak that in words which
    his eye hath disclosed.   250
I only have made a mouth of his eye,
By adding a tongue which I know will not lie.
Ros. Thou art an old love-monger and
    speakest skilfully.
Mar. He is Cupid's grandfather and learns
    news of him.
Ros. Then was Venus like her mother, for
    her father is but grim.
Boyet. Do you hear, my mad wenches ?
Mar.   No.
Boyet.   What then, do you see ?
Ros. Ay, our way to be gone.
Boyet.   You are too hard for me.
                                [*Exeunt.*

ACT III.

Scene I. *The same.*

Enter Armado *and* Moth.

Arm. Warble, child ; make passionate my
sense of hearing.
Moth. Concolinel.   [*Singing.*
Arm. Sweet air ! Go, tenderness of years ;
take this key, give enlargement to the swain,
bring him festinately hither : I must employ
him in a letter to my love.
Moth. Master, will you win your love with
a French brawl ?
Arm. How meanest thou ? brawling in
French ?
Moth. No, my complete master : but to jig
off a tune at the tongue's end, canary it with
your feet, humor it with turning up your
eyelids, sigh a note and sing a note, sometime
through the throat, as if you swallowed love
with singing love, sometime through the nose,
as if you snuffed up love by smelling love ;
with your hat penthouse-like o'er the shop of
your eyes ; with your arms crossed on your

thin-belly doublet like a rabbit on a spit; or your hands in your pocket like a man after the old painting; and keep not too long in one tune, but a snip and away. These are complements, these are humors; these betray nice wenches, that would be betrayed without these; and make them men of note—do you note me?—that most are affected to these.

Arm. How hast thou purchased this experience?

Moth. By my penny of observation.

Arm. But O,—but O,—

Moth. 'The hobby-horse is forgot.'　　30

Arm. Callest thou my love 'hobby-horse'?

Moth. No, master; the hobby-horse is but a colt, and your love perhaps a hackney. But have you forgot your love?

Arm. Almost I had.

Moth. Negligent student! learn her by heart.

Arm. By heart and in heart, boy.

Moth. And out of heart, master: all those three I will prove.

Arm. What wilt thou prove?　　40

Moth. A man, if I live; and this, by, in, and without, upon the instant: by heart you love her, because your heart cannot come by her; in heart you love her, because your heart is in love with her; and out of heart you love her, being out of heart that you cannot enjoy her.

Arm. I am all these three.

Moth. And three times as much more, and yet nothing at all.　　50

Arm. Fetch hither the swain: he must carry me a letter.

Moth. A message well sympathized; a horse to be ambassador for an ass.

Arm. Ha, ha! what sayest thou?

Moth. Marry, sir, you must send the ass upon the horse, for he is very slow-gaited. But I go.

Arm. The way is but short: away!

Moth. As swift as lead, sir.

Arm. The meaning, pretty ingenious? Is not lead a metal heavy, dull, and slow?　60

Moth. Minimè, honest master; or rather, master, no.

Arm. I say lead is slow.

Moth. You are too swift, sir, to say so: Is that lead slow which is fired from a gun?

Arm. Sweet smoke of rhetoric! He reputes me a cannon; and the bullet, that's he: I shoot thee at the swain.

Moth. 　　　　Thump then and I flee. [*Exit.*

Arm. A most acute juvenal; voluble and free of grace! By thy favor, sweet welkin, I must sigh in thy face: Most rude melancholy, valor gives thee place. My herald is return'd.　　70

Re-enter MOTH *with* COSTARD.

Moth. A wonder, master! here's a costard broken in a shin.

Arm. Some enigma, some riddle: come, thy l'envoy; begin.

Cost. No egma, no riddle, no l'envoy; no salve in the mail, sir: O, sir, plantain, a plain plantain! no l'envoy, no l'envoy; no salve, sir, but a plantain!

Arm. By virtue, thou enforcest laughter; thy silly thought my spleen; the heaving of my lungs provokes me to ridiculous smiling. O, pardon me, my stars! Doth the inconsiderate take salve for l'envoy, and the word l'envoy for a salve?　　80

Moth. Do the wise think them other? is not l'envoy a salve?

Arm. No, page: it is an epilogue or discourse, to make plain Some obscure precedence that hath tofore been sain. I will example it: The fox, the ape, and the humble-bee, Were still at odds, being but three. There's the moral. Now the l'envoy.

Moth. I will add the l'envoy. Say the moral again.　　89

Arm. The fox, the ape, the humble-bee, Were still at odds, being but three.

Moth. Until the goose came out of door, And stay'd the odds by adding four. Now will I begin your moral, and do you follow with my l'envoy. The fox, the ape, and the humble-bee, Were still at odds, being but three.

Arm. Until the goose came out of door, Staying the odds by adding four.100

Moth. A good l'envoy, ending in the goose: would you desire more?

Cost. The boy hath sold him a bargain, a goose, that's flat. Sir, your pennyworth is good, an your goose be fat. To sell a bargain well is as cunning as fast and loose: Let me see; a fat l'envoy; ay, that's a fat goose.

Arm. Come hither, come hither. How did this argument begin?

Moth. By saying that a costard was broken in a shin. Then call'd you for the l'envoy.

Cost. True, and I for a plantain: thus came your argument in; Then the boy's fat l'envoy, the goose that you bought;　　110 And he ended the market.

Arm. But tell me; how was there a costard broken in a shin?

Moth. I will tell you sensibly.

Cost. Thou hast no feeling of it, Moth: I will speak that l'envoy: I Costard, running out, that was safely within, Fell over the threshold and broke my shin.

Arm. We will talk no more of this matter.

Cost. Till there be more matter in the shin.

Arm. Sirrah Costard, I will enfranchise thee.

Cost. O, marry me to one Frances: I smell some l'envoy, some goose, in this.

Arm. By my sweet soul, I mean setting thee at liberty, enfreedoming thy person; thou wert immured, restrained, captivated, bound.

Cost. True, true; and now you will be my purgation and let me loose.

Arm. I give thee thy liberty, set thee from durance; and, in lieu thereof, impose on thee nothing but this: bear this significant [*giving a letter*] to the country maid Jaquenetta: there

is remuneration; for the best ward of mine honor is rewarding my dependents. Moth, follow. [*Exit.*
Moth. Like the sequel, I. Signior Costard, adieu.
Cost. My sweet ounce of man's flesh! my incony Jew! [*Exit Moth.*
Now will I look to his remuneration. Remuneration! O, that's the Latin word for three farthings: three farthings—remuneration.—'What's the price of this inkle?'—'One penny.'—'No, I'll give you a remuneration:' why, it carries it. Remuneration! why, it is a fairer name than French crown. I will never buy and sell out of this word.

Enter BIRON.

Biron. O, my good knave Costard! exceedingly well met.
Cost. Pray you, sir, how much carnation ribbon may a man buy for a remuneration?
Biron. What is a remuneration?
Cost. Marry, sir, halfpenny farthing.
Biron. Why, then, three-farthing worth of silk. 150
Cost. I thank your worship: God be wi' you!
Biron. Stay, slave; I must employ thee:
As thou wilt win my favor, good my knave,
Do one thing for me that I shall entreat.
Cost. When would you have it done, sir?
Biron. This afternoon.
Cost. Well, I will do it, sir: fare you well.
Biron. Thou knowest not what it is.
Cost. I shall know, sir, when I have done it.
Biron. Why, villain, thou must know first.
Cost. I will come to your worship to-morrow morning. 161
Biron. It must be done this afternoon.
Hark, slave, it is but this:
The princess comes to hunt here in the park,
And in her train there is a gentle lady;
When tongues speak sweetly, then they name her name,
And Rosaline they call her: ask for her;
And to her white hand see thou do commend
This seal'd-up counsel. There's thy guerdon; go. 170
[*Giving him a shilling.*
Cost. Gardon, O sweet gardon! better than remuneration, a'leven-pence farthing better: most sweet gardon! I will do it, sir, in print. Gardon! Remuneration! [*Exit.*
Biron. And I, forsooth, in love! I, that have been love's whip;
A very beadle to a humorous sigh;
A critic, nay, a night-watch constable;
A domineering pedant o'er the boy;
Than whom no mortal so magnificent! 180
This whimpled, whining, purblind, wayward boy;
This senior-junior, giant-dwarf, Dan Cupid;
Regent of love-rhymes, lord of folded arms,
The anointed sovereign of sighs and groans,
Liege of all loiterers and malcontents,
Dread prince of plackets, king of codpieces,
Sole imperator and great general
Of trotting 'paritors:—O my little heart:—
And I to be a corporal of his field, 189
And wear his colors like a tumbler's hoop!
What, I! I love! I sue! I seek a wife!

A woman, that is like a German clock,
Still a-repairing, ever out of frame,
And never going aright, being a watch,
But being watch'd that it may still go right!
Nay, to be perjured, which is worst of all;
And, among three, to love the worst of all;
A wightly wanton with a velvet brow,
With two pitch-balls stuck in her face for eyes;
Ay, and, by heaven, one that will do the deed
Though Argus were her eunuch and her guard:
And I to sigh for her! to watch for her!
To pray for her! Go to; it is a plague
That Cupid will impose for my neglect
Of his almighty dreadful little might.
Well, I will love, write, sigh, pray, sue and groan:
Some men must love my lady and some Joan.
[*Exit.*

ACT IV.

SCENE I. *The same.*

Enter the Princess, *and her train, a* Forester, BOYET, ROSALINE, MARIA, *and* KATHARINE.

Prin. Was that the king, that spurred his horse so hard
Against the steep uprising of the hill?
Boyet. I know not; but I think it was not he.
Prin. Whoe'er a' was, a' show'd a mounting mind.
Well, lords, to-day we shall have our dispatch:
On Saturday we will return to France.
Then, forester, my friend, where is the bush
That we must stand and play the murderer in?
For. Hereby, upon the edge of yonder coppice;
A stand where you may make the fairest shoot.
Prin. I thank my beauty, I am fair that shoot, 11
And thereupon thou speak'st the fairest shoot.
For. Pardon me, madam, for I meant not so.
Prin. What, what? first praise me and again say no?
O short-lived pride! Not fair? alack for woe!
For. Yes, madam, fair.
Prin. Nay, never paint me now:
Where fair is not, praise cannot mend the brow.
Here, good my glass, take this for telling true:
Fair payment for foul words is more than due.
For. Nothing but fair is that which you inherit. 20
Prin. See, see, my beauty will be saved by merit!
O heresy in fair, fit for these days!
A giving hand, though foul, shall have fair praise.
But come, the bow: now mercy goes to kill,
And shooting well is then accounted ill.
Thus will I save my credit in the shoot:
Not wounding, pity would not let me do't;
If wounding, then it was to show my skill,
That more for praise than purpose meant to kill.
And out of question so it is sometimes, 30
Glory grows guilty of detested crimes,

When, for fame's sake, for praise, an outward
   part,
We bend to that the working of the heart;
As I for praise alone now seek to spill
The poor deer's blood, that my heart means
   no ill.
  Boyet. Do not curst wives hold that self-
   sovereignty
Only for praise sake, when they strive to be
Lords o'er their lords?
  Prin. Only for praise: and praise we may
   afford
To any lady that subdues a lord.   40
  Boyet. Here comes a member of the com-
   monwealth.

Enter COSTARD.

  Cost. God dig-you-den all! Pray you,
which is the head lady?
  Prin. Thou shalt know her, fellow, by the
rest that have no heads.
  Cost. Which is the greatest lady, the high-
est?
  Prin. The thickest and the tallest.
  Cost. The thickest and the tallest! it is so;
truth is truth.
An your waist, mistress, were as slender as my
   wit,
One o' these maids' girdles for your waist
   should be fit.   50
Are not you the chief woman? you are the
   thickest here.
  Prin. What's your will, sir? what's your
   will?
  Cost. I have a letter from Monsieur Biron
to one Lady Rosaline.
  Prin. O, thy letter, thy letter! he's a good
friend of mine:
Stand aside, good bearer. Boyet, you can
   carve;
Break up this capon.
  Boyet.   I am bound to serve.
This letter is mistook, it importeth none here;
It is writ to Jaquenetta.
  Prin.   We will read it, I swear.
Break the neck of the wax, and every one give
   ear.   59
  Boyet [*reads*]. 'By heaven, that thou art
fair, is most infallible; true, that thou art
beauteous; truth itself, that thou art lovely.
More fairer than fair, beautiful than beauteous, truer than truth itself, have commiseration
on thy heroical vassal! The magnanimous and
most illustrate king Cophetua set eye upon the
pernicious and indubitate beggar Zenelophon;
and he it was that might rightly say, Veni,
vidi, vici; which to annothanize in the vulgar,
—O base and obscure vulgar!—videlicet, He
came, saw, and overcame: he came, one; saw
two; overcame, three. Who came? the king:
why did he come? to see: why did he see?
to overcome: to whom came he? to the beggar: what saw he? the beggar: who overcame he? the beggar. The conclusion is victory: on whose side? the king's. The captive
is enriched: on whose side? the beggar's. The
catastrophe is a nuptial: on whose side? the
king's: no, on both in one, or one in both.
I am the king; for so stands the comparison:
thou the beggar; for so witnesseth thy lowliness. Shall I command thy love? I may: shall
I enforce thy love? I could: shall I entreat
thy love? I will. What shalt thou exchange
for rags? robes; for tittles? titles; for thyself? me. Thus, expecting thy reply, I profane
my lips on thy foot, my eyes on thy picture,
and my heart on thy every part. Thine, in the
dearest design of industry,
               DON ADRIANO DE ARMADO.'
Thus dost thou hear the Nemean lion roar 90
  'Gainst thee, thou lamb, that standest as his
   prey.
Submissive fall his princely feet before,
  And he from forage will incline to play:
But if thou strive, poor soul, what art thou
   then?
Food for his rage, repasture for his den.
  Prin. What plume of feathers is he that
   indited this letter?
What vane? what weathercock? did you ever
   hear better?
  Boyet. I am much deceived but I remem-
   ber the style.
  Prin. Else your memory is bad, going o'er
   it erewhile.
  Boyet. This Armado is a Spaniard, that
   keeps here in court;   100
A phantasime, a Monarcho, and one that
   makes sport
To the prince and his bookmates.
  Prin.   Thou fellow, a word:
Who gave thee this letter?
  Cost.   I told you; my lord.
  Prin. To whom shouldst thou give it?
  Cost.   From my lord to my lady.
  Prin. From which lord to which lady?
  Cost. From my lord Biron, a good master
   of mine,
To a lady of France that he call'd Rosaline.
  Prin. Thou hast mistaken his letter. Come,
   lords, away.
[*To Ros.*] Here, sweet, put up this: 'twill be
   thine another day.
             [*Exeunt Princess and train.*
  Boyet. Who is the suitor? who is the
   suitor?
  Ros.   Shall I teach you to know? 110
  Boyet. Ay, my continent of beauty.
  Ros.   Why, she that bears the bow.
Finely put off!
  Boyet. My lady goes to kill horns; but, if
   thou marry,
Hang me by the neck, if horns that year mis-
   carry.
Finely put on!
  Ros. Well, then, I am the shooter.
  Boyet.   And who is your deer?
  Ros. If we choose by the horns, yourself
   come not near.
Finely put on, indeed!
  Mar. You still wrangle with her, Boyet,
   and she strikes at the brow.
  Boyet. But she herself is hit lower: have
   I hit her now?   120
  Ros. Shall I come upon thee with an old
saying, that was a man when King Pepin of
France was a little boy, as touching the hit it?
  Boyet. So I may answer thee with one as
old, that was a woman when Queen Guinover
of Britain was a little wench, as touching the
hit it.
  Ros. Thou canst not hit it, hit it, hit it,
   Thou canst not hit it, my good man.

Boyet. An I cannot, cannot, cannot,
　　An I cannot, another can.　　130
　　　　　[*Exeunt Ros. and Kath.*
Cost. By my troth, most pleasant : how
　both did fit it !
Mar. A mark marvellous well shot, for
　they both did hit it.
Boyet. A mark ! O, mark but that mark !
　A mark, says my lady !
Let the mark have a prick in't, to mete at, if
　it may be.
Mar. Wide o' the bow hand ! i' faith, your
　hand is out.
Cost. Indeed, a' must shoot nearer, or he'll
　ne'er hit the clout.
Boyet. An if my hand be out, then belike
　your hand is in.
Cost. Then will she get the upshoot by
　cleaving the pin.
Mar. Come, come, you talk greasily ; your
　lips grow foul.
Cost. She's too hard for you at pricks, sir :
　challenge her to bowl.　　140
Boyet. I fear too much rubbing. Good
　night, my good owl.
　　　　　[*Exeunt Boyet and Maria.*
Cost. By my soul, a swain ! a most simple
　clown !
Lord, Lord, how the ladies and I have put him
　down !
O' my troth, most sweet jests ! most incony
　vulgar wit !
When it comes so smoothly off, so obscenely,
　as it were, so fit.
Armado o' th' one side,—O, a most dainty
　man !
To see him walk before a lady and to bear her
　fan !
To see him kiss his hand ! and how most
　sweetly a' will swear !
And his page o' t' other side, that handful of
　wit !
Ah, heavens, it is a most pathetical nit !　　150
Sola, sola !　　　　　[*Shout within.*
　　　　　[*Exit Costard, running.*

Scene II. *The same.*

Enter Holofernes, Sir Nathaniel, *and* Dull.

Nath. Very reverend sport, truly ; and
done in the testimony of a good conscience.
Hol. The deer was, as you know, sanguis,
in blood ; ripe as the pomewater, who now
hangeth like a jewel in the ear of caelo, the
sky, the welkin, the heaven ; and anon falleth
like a crab on the face of terra, the soil, the
land, the earth.
Nath. Truly, Master Holofernes, the epi-
thets are sweetly varied, like a scholar at the
least : but, sir, I assure ye, it was a buck of
the first head.　　10
Hol. Sir Nathaniel, haud credo.
Dull. 'Twas not a haud credo ; 'twas a
pricket.
Hol. Most barbarous intimation ! yet a
kind of insinuation, as it were, in via, in way,
of explication ; facere, as it were, replication,
or rather, ostentare, to show, as it were, his inclination, after his undressed, unpolished, un-
educated, unpruned, untrained, or rather, unlettered, or ratherest, unconfirmed fashion, to
insert again my haud credo for a deer.　　20

Dull. I said the deer was not a haud
credo ; 'twas a pricket.
Hol. Twice-sod simplicity, bis coctus !
O thou monster Ignorance, how deformed dost
thou look !
Nath. Sir, he hath never fed of the dainties
that are bred in a book ; he hath not eat paper, as it were ; he hath not drunk ink : his
intellect is not replenished ; he is only an animal, only sensible in the duller parts :
And such barren plants are set before us, that
　we thankful should be,
Which we of taste and feeling are, for those
　parts that do fructify in us more than
　he.　　30
For as it would ill become me to be vain, in-
　discreet, or a fool,
So were there a patch set on learning, to see
　him in a school :
But omne bene, say I ; being of an old father's
　mind,
Many can brook the weather that love not the
　wind.
Dull. You two are book-men : can you tell
　me by your wit
What was a month old at Cain's birth, that's
　not five weeks old as yet ?
Hol. Dictynna, goodman Dull ; Dictynna,
　goodman Dull.
Dull. What is Dictynna ?
Nath. A title to Phœbe, to Luna, to the
　moon.
Hol. The moon was a month old when
　Adam was no more,　　40
And raught not to five weeks when he came to
　five-score.
The allusion holds in the exchange.
Dull. 'Tis true indeed ; the collusion holds
　in the exchange.
Hol. God comfort thy capacity ! I say, the
allusion holds in the exchange.
Dull. And I say, the pollusion holds in the
exchange ; for the moon is never but a month
old : and I say beside that, 'twas a pricket
that the princess killed.
Hol. Sir Nathaniel, will you hear an extemporal epitaph on the death of the deer ? And,
to humor the ignorant, call I the deer the princess killed a pricket.
Nath. Perge, good Master Holofernes,
perge ; so it shall please you to abrogate scurrility.
Hol. I will something affect the letter, for
it argues facility.
The preyful princess pierced and prick'd a
　pretty pleasing pricket ;
　Some say a sore ; but not a sore, till now
　　made sore with shooting.
The dogs did yell : put L to sore, then sorel
　jumps from thicket ;　　60
　Or pricket sore, or else sorel ; the people
　　fall a-hooting.
If sore be sore, then L to sore makes fifty sores
　one sorel.
Of one sore I an hundred make by adding but
　one more L.
Nath. A rare talent !
Dull. [*Aside*] If a talent be a claw, look
how he claws him with a talent.
Hol. This is a gift that I have, simple, simple ; a foolish extravagant spirit, full of forms,
figures, shapes, objects, ideas, apprehensions,

motions, revolutions : these are begot in the ventricle of memory, nourished in the womb of pia mater, and delivered upon the mellowing of occasion. But the gift is good in those in whom it is acute, and I am thankful for it.

Nath. Sir, I praise the Lord for you ; and so may my parishioners ; for their sons are well tutored by you, and their daughters profit very greatly under you : you are a good member of the commonwealth.

Hol. Mehercle, if their sons be ingenuous, they shall want no instruction ; if their daughters be capable, I will put it to them : but vir sapit qui pauca loquitur ; a soul feminine saluteth us.

Enter JAQUENETTA *and* COSTARD.

Jaq. God give you good morrow, master Parson.

Hol. Master Parson, quasi pers-on. An if one should be pierced, which is the one ?

Cost. Marry, master schoolmaster, he that is likest to a hogshead.

Hol. Piercing a hogshead ! a good lustre of conceit in a tuft of earth ; fire enough for a flint, pearl enough for a swine : 'tis pretty ; it is well.

Jaq. Good master Parson, be so good as read me this letter : it was given me by Costard, and sent me from Don Armado : I beseech you, read it.

Hol. Fauste, precor gelida quando pecus omne sub umbra Ruminat,—and so forth. Ah, good old Mantuan ! I may speak of thee as the traveller doth of Venice ;
    Venetia, Venetia,
    Chi non ti vede non ti pretia.   100
Old Mantuan, old Mantuan ! who understandeth thee not, loves thee not. Ut, re, sol, la, mi, fa. Under pardon, sir, what are the contents ? or rather, as Horace says in his—What, my soul, verses ?

Nath. Ay, sir, and very learned.

Hol. Let me hear a staff, a stanze, a verse ; lege, domine.

Nath. [*reads*]
If love make me forsworn, how shall I swear to love ?
Ah, never faith could hold, if not to beauty vow'd !   110
Though to myself forsworn, to thee I'll faithful prove :
Those thoughts to me were oaks, to thee like osiers bow'd.
Study his bias leaves and makes his book thine eyes,
Where all those pleasures live that art would comprehend :
If knowledge be the mark, to know thee shall suffice ;
Well learned is that tongue that well can thee commend,
All ignorant that soul that sees thee without wonder ;
Which is to me some praise that I thy parts admire ;
Thy eye Jove's lightning bears, thy voice his dreadful thunder,
Which, not to anger bent, is music and sweet fire.   120
Celestial as thou art, O, pardon, love, this wrong,

That sings heaven's praise with such an earthly tongue.

Hol. You find not the apostraphas, and so miss the accent : let me supervise the canzonet. Here are only numbers ratified ; but, for the elegancy, facility, and golden cadence of poesy, caret. Ovidius Naso was the man : and why, indeed, Naso, but for smelling out the odoriferous flowers of fancy, the jerks of invention ? Imitari is nothing : so doth the hound his master, the ape his keeper, the tired horse his rider. But, damosella virgin, was this directed to you ?

Jaq. Ay, sir, from one Monsieur Biron, one of the strange queen's lords.

Hol. I will overglance the superscript : ' To the snow-white hand of the most beauteous Lady Rosaline.' I will look again on the intellect of the letter, for the nomination of the party writing to the person written unto : ' Your ladyship's in all desired employment, BIRON.' Sir Nathaniel, this Biron is one of the votaries with the king ; and here he hath framed a letter to a sequent of the stranger queen's, which accidentally, or by the way of progression, hath miscarried. Trip and go, my sweet ; deliver this paper into the royal hand of the king : it may concern much. Stay not thy compliment ; I forgive thy duty : adieu.

Jaq. Good Costard, go with me. Sir, God save your life !   150

Cost. Have with thee, my girl.

[*Exeunt Cost. and Jaq.*

Nath. Sir, you have done this in the fear of God, very religiously ; and, as a certain father saith,—

Hol. Sir, tell not me of the father ; I do fear colorable colors. But to return to the verses : did they please you, Sir Nathaniel ?

Nath. Marvellous well for the pen.

Hol. I do dine to-day at the father's of a certain pupil of mine ; where, if, before repast, it shall please you to gratify the table with a grace, I will, on my privilege I have with the parents of the foresaid child or pupil, undertake your ben venuto ; where I will prove those verses to be very unlearned, neither savoring of poetry, wit, nor invention : I beseech your society.

Nath. And thank you too ; for society, saith the text, is the happiness of life.

Hol. And, certes, the text most infallibly concludes it. [*To* DULL] Sir, I do invite you too ; you shall not say me nay : pauca verba. Away ! the gentles are at their game, and we will to our recreation.   [*Exeunt.*

SCENE III. *The same.*

Enter BIRON, *with a paper.*

Biron. The king he is hunting the deer ; I am coursing myself : they have pitched a toil ; I am toiling in a pitch,—pitch that defiles : defile ! a foul word. Well, set thee down, sorrow ! for so they say the fool said, and so say I, and I the fool : well proved, wit ! By the Lord, this love is as mad as Ajax : it kills sheep ; it kills me, I a sheep : well proved again o' my side ! I will not love : if I do, hang me ; i' faith, I will not. O, but her eye,—by this light, but for her eye, I would not love her ; yes, for her two eyes. Well, I do nothing in the world but lie, and lie in my throat. By

heaven, I do love : and it hath taught me to
rhyme and to be melancholy ; and here is part
of my rhyme, and here my melancholy. Well,
she hath one o' my sonnets already : the clown
bore it, the fool sent it, and the lady hath it :
sweet clown, sweeter fool, sweetest lady ! By
the world, I would not care a pin, if the other
three were in. Here comes one with a paper :
God give him grace to groan ! [*Stands aside.*

Enter the King, *with a paper.*

King. Ay me !
Biron. [*Aside*] Shot, by heaven ! Proceed,
sweet Cupid : thou hast thumped him with thy
bird-bolt under the left pap. In faith, secrets !
King [*reads*].
So sweet a kiss the golden sun gives not
    To those fresh morning drops upon the rose,
As thy eye-beams, when their fresh rays have
    smote
The night of dew that on my cheeks down
    flows :   29
Nor shines the silver moon one half so bright
    Through the transparent bosom of the deep,
As doth thy face through tears of mine give
    light ;
Thou shinest in every tear that I do weep :
No drop but as a coach doth carry thee ;
So ridest thou triumphing in my woe.
Do but behold the tears that swell in me,
    And they thy glory through my grief will
    show :
But do not love thyself ; then thou wilt keep
My tears for glasses, and still make me weep.
O queen of queens ! how far dost thou excel,
No thought can think, nor tongue of mortal
    tell.
How shall she know my griefs ? I'll drop the
    paper :
Sweet leaves, shade folly. Who is he comes
    here ?   [*Steps aside.*
What, Longaville ! and reading ! listen, ear.
    Biron. Now, in thy likeness, one more fool
    appear !

Enter LONGAVILLE, *with a paper.*

Long. Ay me, I am forsworn !
Biron. Why, he comes in like a perjure,
    wearing papers.
King. In love, I hope : sweet fellowship in
    shame !
Biron. One drunkard loves another of the
    name.   50
Long. Am I the first that have been per-
    jured so ?
Biron. I could put thee in comfort. Not
    by two that I know :
Thou makest the triumviry, the corner-cap of
    society,
The shape of Love's Tyburn that hangs up
    simplicity.
Long. I fear these stubborn lines lack
    power to move :
O sweet Maria, empress of my love !
These numbers will I tear, and write in prose.
    Biron. O, rhymes are guards on wanton
    Cupid's hose :
Disfigure not his slop.
    Long.   This same shall go. [*Reads.*
Did not the heavenly rhetoric of thine eye, 60
'Gainst whom the world cannot hold argu-
    ment,

Persuade my heart to this false perjury ?
Vows for thee broke deserve not punish-
    ment.
A woman I forswore ; but I will prove,
    Thou being a goddess, I forswore not thee :
My vow was earthly, thou a heavenly love ;
    Thy grace being gain'd cures all disgrace
    in me.
Vows are but breath, and breath a vapor is :
    Then thou, fair sun, which on my earth dost
    shine,
Exhalest this vapor-vow ; in thee it is :   70
    If broken then, it is no fault of mine :
If by me broke, what fool is not so wise
To lose an oath to win a paradise ?
    Biron. This is the liver-vein, which makes
    flesh a deity,
A green goose a goddess : pure, pure idolatry.
God amend us, God amend ! we are much
    out o' the way.
Long. By whom shall I send this ?—Com-
    pany ! stay.   [*Steps aside.*
Biron. All hid, all hid ; an old infant play.
Like a demigod here sit I in the sky,
And wretched fools' secrets heedfully o'er-
    eye.   80
More sacks to the mill ! O heavens, I have
    my wish !

Enter DUMAIN, *with a paper.*

Dumain transform'd ! four woodcocks in a
    dish !
    Dum. O most divine Kate !
    Biron. O most profane coxcomb !
    Dum. By heaven, the wonder in a mortal
    eye !
    Biron. By earth, she is not, corporal, there
    you lie.
    Dum. Her amber hair for foul hath amber
    quoted.
    Biron. An amber-color'd raven was well
    noted.
    Dum. As upright as the cedar.
    Biron.   Stoop, I say ;
Her shoulder is with child.
    Dum.   As fair as day.   90
    Biron. Ay, as some days ; but then no sun
    must shine.
    Dum. O that I had my wish !
    Long.   And I had mine !
    King. And I mine too, good Lord !
    Biron. Amen, so I had mine : is not that a
    good word ?
    Dum. I would forget her ; but a fever she
Reigns in my blood and will remember'd be.
    Biron. A fever in your blood ! why, then
    incision
Would let her out in saucers : sweet mis-
    prision !
    Dum. Once more I'll read the ode that I
    have writ.
    Biron. Once more I'll mark how love can
    vary wit.   100
    Dum. [*reads*]
On a day—alack the day !—
    Love, whose month is ever May,
Spied a blossom passing fair
    Playing in the wanton air :
Through the velvet leaves the wind,
    All unseen, can passage find ;
That the lover, sick to death,
    Wish himself the heaven's breath.

Air, quoth he, thy cheeks may blow;
Air, would I might triumph so!   110
But, alack, my hand is sworn
Ne'er to pluck thee from thy thorn;
Vow, alack, for youth unmeet,
Youth so apt to pluck a sweet!
Do not call it sin in me,
That I am forsworn for thee;
Thou for whom Jove would swear
Juno but an Ethiope were;
And deny himself for Jove,
Turning mortal for thy love.   120
This will I send, and something else more
     plain,
That shall express my true love's fasting pain.
O, would the king, Biron, and Longaville,
Were lovers too! Ill, to example ill,
Would from my forehead wipe a perjured
     note;
For none offend where all alike do dote.
     Long. [*advancing.*] Dumain, thy love is
          far from charity.
That in love's grief desirest society:
You may look pale, but I should blush, I
     know,
To be o'erheard and taken napping so.   130
     King [*advancing*]. Come, sir, you blush;
          as his your case is such;
You chide at him, offending twice as much;
You do not love Maria; Longaville
Did never sonnet for her sake compile,
Nor never lay his wreathed arms athwart
His loving bosom to keep down his heart.
I have been closely shrouded in this bush
And mark'd you both and for you both did
     blush:
I heard your guilty rhymes, observed your
     fashion,
Saw sighs reek from you, noted well your
     passion: 140
Ay me! says one; O Jove! the other cries;
One, her hairs were gold, crystal the other's
     eyes:
[*To Long.*] You would for paradise break
     faith and troth;
[*To Dum.*] And Jove, for your love, would
     infringe an oath.
What will Biron say when that he shall hear
Faith so infringed, which such zeal did swear?
How will he scorn! how will he spend his wit!
How will he triumph, leap and laugh at it!
For all the wealth that ever I did see,   149
I would not have him know so much by me.
     Biron. Now step I forth to whip hypocrisy.
                                   [*Advancing.*
Ah, good my liege, I pray thee, pardon me!
Good heart, what grace hast thou, thus to re-
     prove
These worms for loving, that art most in
     love?
Your eyes do make no coaches; in your tears
There is no certain princess that appears;
You'll not be perjured, 'tis a hateful thing;
Tush, none but minstrels like of sonneting!
But are you not ashamed? nay, are you not,
All three of you, to be thus much o'ershot?
You found his mote; the king your mote did
     see;   161
But I a beam do find in each of three.
O, what a scene of foolery have I seen,
Of sighs, of groans, of sorrow and of teen!
O me, with what strict patience have I sat,

To see a king transformed to a gnat!
To see great Hercules whipping a gig,
And profound Solomon to tune a jig,
And Nestor play at push-pin with the boys,
And critic Timon laugh at idle toys!   170
Where lies thy grief, O, tell me, good Dumain?
And, gentle Longaville, where lies thy pain?
And where my liege's? all about the breast:
A caudle, ho!
     King.   Too bitter is thy jest.
Are we betray'd thus to thy over-view?
     Biron. Not you to me, but I betray'd by
          you:
I, that am honest; I, that hold it sin
To break the vow I am engaged in;
I am betray'd, by keeping company
With men like men of inconstancy.   180
When shall you see me write a thing in
     rhyme?
Or groan for love? or spend a minute's time
In pruning me? When shall you hear that I
Will praise a hand, a foot, a face, an eye,
A gait, a state, a brow, a breast, a waist,
A leg, a limb?
     King.   Soft! whither away so fast?
A true man or a thief that gallops so?
     Biron. I post from love: good lover, let
          me go.

          Enter JAQUENETTA *and* COSTARD.

     Jaq. God bless the king!
     King.   What present hast thou there?
     Cost. Some certain treason.
     King.   What makes treason here?   190
     Cost. Nay, it makes nothing, sir.
     King.   If it mar nothing neither,
The treason and you go in peace away to-
     gether.
     Jaq. I beseech your grace, let this letter
          be read:
Our parson misdoubts it; 'twas treason, he
     said.
     King. Biron, read it over.
                         [*Giving him the paper.*
Where hadst thou it?
     Jaq. Of Costard.
     King. Where hadst thou it?
     Cost. Of Dun Adramadio, Dun Adrama-
          dio.   [*Biron tears the letter.*
     King. How now! what is in you? why
          dost thou tear it?   200
     Biron. A toy, my liege, a toy: your grace
          needs not fear it.
     Long. It did move him to passion, and
          therefore let's hear it.
     Dum. It is Biron's writing, and here is his
          name.   [*Gathering up the pieces.*
     Biron. [*To Costard*] Ah, you whoreson
          loggerhead! you were born to do me
          shame.
Guilty, my lord, guilty! I confess, I confess.
     King. What?
     Biron. That you three fools lack'd me fool
          to make up the mess:
He, he, and you, and you, my liege, and I,
Are pick-purses in love, and we deserve to die.
O, dismiss this audience, and I shall tell you
     more.
     Dum. Now the number is even.
     Biron.   True, true; we are four.
Will these turtles be gone?
     King.   Hence, sirs; away!

Cost. Walk aside the true folk, and let the
traitors stay.
   [*Exeunt Costard and Jaquenetta.*
Biron. Sweet lords, sweet lovers, O, let us
embrace !
As true we are as flesh and blood can be :
The sea will ebb and flow, heaven show his
face ;
Young blood doth not obey an old decree :
We cannot cross the cause why we were born ;
Therefore of all hands must we be forsworn.
King. What, did these rent lines show
  some love of thine ?   220
Biron. Did they, quoth you ? Who sees the
  heavenly Rosaline,
That, like a rude and savage man of Inde,
At the first opening of the gorgeous east,
Bows not his vassal head and strucken blind
Kisses the base ground with obedient
  breast ?
What peremptory eagle-sighted eye
Dares look upon the heaven of her brow,
That is not blinded by her majesty ?
King. What zeal, what fury hath inspired
  thee now ?   229
My love, her mistress, is a gracious moon ;
  She an attending star, scarce seen a light.
Biron. My eyes are then no eyes, nor I
  Biron :
O, but for my love, day would turn to
  night !
Of all complexions the cull'd sovereignty
  Do meet, as at a fair, in her fair cheek,
Where several worthies make one dignity,
  Where nothing wants that want itself doth
  seek.
Lend me the flourish of all gentle tongues,—
  Fie, painted rhetoric ! O, she needs it not :
To things of sale a seller's praise belongs, 240
  She passes praise ; then praise too short
  doth blot.
A wither'd hermit, five-score winters worn,
  Might shake off fifty, looking in her eye :
Beauty doth varnish age, as if new-born,
  And gives the crutch the cradle's infancy :
O, 'tis the sun that maketh all things shine.
King. By heaven, thy love is black as
  ebony.
Biron. Is ebony like her ? O wood divine !
  A wife of such wood were felicity. 249
O, who can give an oath ? where is a book ?
  That I may swear beauty doth beauty lack,
If that she learn not of her eye to look :
  No face is fair that is not full so black.
King. O paradox ! Black is the badge of
  hell,
The hue of dungeons and the suit of night ;
  And beauty's crest becomes the heavens well.
Biron. Devils soonest tempt, resembling
  spirits of light.
O, if in black my lady's brows be deck'd,
  It mourns that painting and usurping hair
Should ravish doters with a false aspect ; 260
  And therefore is she born to make black
  fair.
Her favor turns the fashion of the days,
  For native blood is counted painting now ;
And therefore red, that would avoid disprase,
  Paints itself black, to imitate her brow.
Dum. To look like her are chimney-sweep-
  ers black.

Long. And since her time are colliers
  counted bright.
King. And Ethiopes of their sweet com-
  plexion crack.
Dum. Dark needs no candles now, for
  dark is light.
Biron. Your mistresses dare never come
  in rain,   270
For fear their colors should be wash'd away.
King. 'Twere good, yours did ; for, sir, to
  tell you plain,
I'll find a fairer face not wash'd to-day.
Biron. I'll prove her fair, or talk till
  doomsday here.
King. No devil will fright thee then so
  much as she.
Dum. I never knew man hold vile stuff so
  dear.
Long. Look, here's thy love : my foot and
  her face see.
Biron. O, if the streets were paved with
  thine eyes,
Her feet were much too dainty for such
  tread !
Dum. O vile ! then, as she goes, what up-
  ward lies   280
The street should see as she walk'd overhead.
King. But what of this ? are we not all in
  love ?
Biron. Nothing so sure ; and thereby all
  forsworn.
King. Then leave this chat ; and, good Bi-
  ron, now prove
Our loving lawful, and our faith not torn.
Dum. Ay, marry, there ; some flattery for
  this evil.
Long. O, some authority how to proceed ;
Some tricks, some quillets, how to cheat the
  devil.
Dum. Some salve for perjury.
Biron.   'Tis more than need. 289
Have at you, then, affection's men at arms.
Consider what you first did swear unto,
To fast, to study, and to see no woman ;
Flat treason 'gainst the kingly state of youth.
Say, can you fast ? your stomachs are too
  young ;
And abstinence engenders maladies.
And where that you have vow'd to study,
  lords,
In that each of you have forsworn his book,
Can you still dream and pore and thereon
  look ?
For when would you, my lord, or you, or you,
Have found the ground of study's excellence
Without the beauty of a woman's face ?
[From women's eyes this doctrine I derive ;
They are the ground, the books, the academes
From whence doth spring the true Promethean
  fire.]
Why, universal plodding poisons up
The nimble spirits in the arteries,
As motion and long-during action tires
The sinewy vigor of the traveller.
Now, for not looking on a woman's face,
You have in that forsworn the use of eyes
And study too, the causer of your vow ; 311
For where is any author in the world
Teaches such beauty as a woman's eye ?
Learning is but an adjunct to ourself
And where we are our learning likewise is :
Then when ourselves we see in ladies' eyes,

Do we not likewise see our learning there ?
O, we have made a vow to study, lords,
And in that vow we have forsworn our books.
For when would you, my liege, or you, or you,
In leaden contemplation have found out 321
Such fiery numbers as the prompting eyes
Of beauty's tutors have enrich'd you with ?
Other slow arts entirely keep the brain ;
And therefore, finding barren practisers,
Scarce show a harvest of their heavy toil :
But love, first learned in a lady's eyes,
Lives not alone immured in the brain ;
But, with the motion of all elements,   329
Courses as swift as thought in every power,
And gives to every power a double power,
Above their functions and their offices.
It adds a precious seeing to the eye ;
A lover's eyes will gaze an eagle blind ;
A lover's ear will hear the lowest sound,
When the suspicious head of theft is stopp'd :
Love's feeling is more soft and sensible
Than are the tender horns of cockled snails ;
Love's tongue proves dainty Bacchus gross in
    taste :
For valor, is not Love a Hercules,   340
Still climbing trees in the Hesperides ?
Subtle as Sphinx ; as sweet and musical
As bright Apollo's lute, strung with his hair :
And when Love speaks, the voice of all the
    gods
Makes heaven drowsy with the harmony.
Never durst poet touch a pen to write
Until his ink were temper'd with Love's sighs ;
O, then his lines would ravish savage ears
And plant in tyrants mild humility.   349
From women's eyes this doctrine I derive :
They sparkle still the right Promethean fire ;
They are the books, the arts, the academes,
That show, contain and nourish all the world :
Else none at all in ought proves excellent.
Then fools you were these women to forswear,
Or keeping what is sworn, you will prove
    fools.
For wisdom's sake, a word that all men love,
Or for love's sake, a word that loves all men,
Or for men's sake, the authors of these
    women,
Or women's sake, by whom we men are men,
Let us once lose our oaths to find ourselves,
Or else we lose ourselves to keep our oaths.
It is religion to be thus forsworn,
For charity itself fulfils the law,
And who can sever love from charity ?
  King. Saint Cupid, then ! and, soldiers, to
    the field !
  Biron. Advance your standards, and upon
    them, lords ;
Pell-mell, down with them ! but be first ad-
    vised,
In conflict that you get the sun of them.
  Long. Now to plain-dealing ; lay these
    glozes by :
Shall we resolve to woo these girls of France ?
  King. And win them too : therefore let us
    devise
Some entertainment for them in their tents.
  Biron. First, from the park let us conduct
    them thither ;
Then homeward every man attach the hand
Of his fair mistress : in the afternoon
We will with some strange pastime solace
    them,

Such as the shortness of the time can shape ;
For revels, dances, masks and merry hours
Forerun fair Love, strewing her way with
    flowers.
  King. Away, away ! no time shall be
    omitted
That will betime, and may by us be fitted.
  Biron. Allons ! allons ! Sow'd cockle reap'd
    no corn ;
And justice always whirls in equal measure :
Light wenches may prove plagues to men for-
    sworn ;
If so, our copper buys no better treasure.
                                    [*Exeunt.*

ACT V.

SCENE I. *The same.*

Enter HOLOFERNES, SIR NATHANIEL, *and*
    DULL.

  Hol. Satis quod sufficit.
  Nath. I praise God for you, sir : your reasons at dinner have been sharp and sententious ; pleasant without scurrility, witty without affection, audacious without impudency,
learned without opinion, and strange without
heresy. I did converse this quondam day with
a companion of the king's, who is intituled,
nominated, or called, Don Adriano de Armado.
  Hol. Novi hominem tanquam te : his
humor is lofty, his discourse peremptory, his
tongue filed, his eye ambitious, his gait majestical, and his general behavior vain, ridiculous, and thrasonical. He is too picked, too
spruce, too affected, too odd, as it were, too
peregrinate, as I may call it.
  Nath. A most singular and choice epithet.
                        [*Draws out his table-book.*
  Hol. He draweth out the thread of his verbosity finer than the staple of his argument. I
abhor such fanatical phantasimes, such insociable and point-devise companions ; such
rackers of orthography, as to speak dout, fine,
when he should say doubt ; det, when he should
pronounce debt,—d, e, b, t, not d, e, t : he
clepeth a calf, cauf ; half, hauf ; neighbor vo-
catur nebor ; neigh abbreviated ne. This is
abhominable,—which he would call abbom-
inable : it insinuateth me of insanie : anne in-
telligis, domine ? to make frantic, lunatic.
  Nath. Laus Deo, bene intelligo.   30
  Hol. Bon, bon, fort bon, Priscian ! a little
scratch'd, 'twill serve.
  Nath. Videsne quis venit ?
  Hol. Video, et gaudeo.

Enter ARMADO, MOTH, *and* COSTARD.

  Arm. Chirrah !   [*To Moth.*
  Hol. Quare chirrah, not sirrah ?
  Arm. Men of peace, well encountered.
  Hol. Most military sir, salutation.
  Moth. [*Aside to Costard*] They have been
at a great feast of languages, and stolen the
scraps.
  Cost. O, they have lived long on the alms-
basket of words. I marvel thy master hath
not eaten thee for a word ; for thou art not so
long by the head as honorificabilitudinitati-
bus : thou art easier swallowed than a flap-
dragon.

Moth. Peace! the peal begins.

Arm. [*To Hol.*] Monsieur, are you not lettered?

Moth. Yes, yes; he teaches boys the horn-book. What is a, b, spelt backward, with the horn on his head? 51

Hol. Ba, *pueritia*, with a horn added.

Moth. Ba, most silly sheep with a horn. You hear his learning.

Hol. Quis, quis, thou consonant?

Moth. The third of the five vowels, if you repeat them; or the fifth, if I.

Hol. I will repeat them,—a, e, i,—

Moth. The sheep: the other two concludes it,—o, u. 60

Arm. Now, by the salt wave of the Mediterranean, a sweet touch, a quick venue of wit! snip, snap, quick and home! it rejoiceth my intellect: true wit!

Moth. Offered by a child to an old man; which is wit-old.

Hol. What is the figure? what is the figure?

Moth. Horns.

Hol. Thou disputest like an infant: go, whip thy gig. 70

Moth. Lend me your horn to make one, and I will whip about your infamy *circum circa*,—a gig of a cuckold's horn.

Cost. An I had but one penny in the world, thou shouldst have it to buy gingerbread: hold, there is the very remuneration I had of thy master, thou halfpenny purse of wit, thou pigeon-egg of discretion. O, an the heavens were so pleased that thou wert but my bastard, what a joyful father wouldst thou make me! Go to; thou hast it *ad dunghill*, at the fingers' ends, as they say.

Hol. O, I smell false Latin; dunghill for *unguem*.

Arm. Arts-man, preambulate, we will be singuled from the barbarous. Do you not educate youth at the charge-house on the top of the mountain?

Hol. Or *mons*, the hill.

Arm. At your sweet pleasure, for the mountain.

Hol. I do, sans question. 91

Arm. Sir, it is the king's most sweet pleasure and affection to congratulate the princess at her pavilion in the posteriors of this day, which the rude multitude call the afternoon.

Hol. The posterior of the day, most generous sir, is liable, congruent and measurable for the afternoon: the word is well culled, chose, sweet and apt, I do assure you, sir, I do assure.

Arm. Sir, the king is a noble gentleman, and my familiar, I do assure ye, very good friend: for what is inward between us, let it pass. I do beseech thee, remember thy courtesy; I beseech thee, apparel thy head: and among other important and most serious designs, and of great import indeed, too, but let that pass: for I must tell thee, it will please his grace, by the world, sometime to lean upon my poor shoulder, and with his royal finger, thus, dally with my excrement, with my mustachio; but, sweet heart, let that pass. By the world, I recount no fable: some certain special honors it pleaseth his greatness to impart to Armado, a soldier, a man of travel,

that hath seen the world; but let that pass. The very all of all is,—but, sweet heart, I do implore secrecy,—that the king would have me present the princess, sweet chuck, with some delightful ostentation, or show, or pageant, or antique, or firework. Now, understanding that the curate and your sweet self are good at such eruptions and sudden breaking out of mirth, as it were, I have acquainted you withal, to the end to crave your assistance.

Hol. Sir, you shall present before her the Nine Worthies. Sir, as concerning some entertainment of time, some show in the posterior of this day, to be rendered by our assistants, at the king's command, and this most gallant, illustrate, and learned gentleman, before the princess; I say none so fit as to present the Nine Worthies. 130

Nath. Where will you find men worthy enough to present them?

Hol. Joshua, yourself; myself and this gallant gentleman, Judas Maccabæus; this swain, because of his great limb or joint, shall pass Pompey the Great; the page, Hercules,—

Arm. Pardon, sir; error: he is not quantity enough for that Worthy's thumb: he is not so big as the end of his club.

Hol. Shall I have audience? he shall present Hercules in minority: his enter and exit shall be strangling a snake; and I will have an apology for that purpose.

Moth. An excellent device! so, if any of the audience hiss, you may cry 'Well done, Hercules! now thou crushest the snake!' that is the way to make an offence gracious, though few have the grace to do it.

Arm. For the rest of the Worthies?—

Hol. I will play three myself. 150

Moth. Thrice-worthy gentleman!

Arm. Shall I tell you a thing?

Hol. We attend.

Arm. We will have, if this fadge not, an antique. I beseech you, follow.

Hol. Via, goodman Dull! thou hast spoken no word all this while.

Dull. Nor understood none neither, sir.

Hol. Allons! we will employ thee.

Dull. I'll make one in a dance, or so; or I will play 160

On the tabor to the Worthies, and let them dance the hay.

Hol. Most dull, honest Dull! To our sport, away! [*Exeunt.*

SCENE II. *The same.*

Enter the Princess, KATHARINE, ROSALINE *and* MARIA.

Prin. Sweet hearts, we shall be rich ere we depart,

If fairings come thus plentifully in:

A lady wall'd about with diamonds!

Look you what I have from the loving king.

Ros. Madame, came nothing else along with that?

Prin. Nothing but this! yes, as much love in rhyme

As would be cramm'd up in a sheet of paper,

Writ o' both sides the leaf, margent and all,

That he was fain to seal on Cupid's name.

Ros. That was the way to make his godhead wax, 10

For he hath been five thousand years a boy.

Kath. Ay, and a shrewd unhappy gallows
too.

Ros. You'll ne'er be friends with him; a'
kill'd your sister.

Kath. He made her melancholy, sad, and
heavy;

And so she died : had she been light, like you,
Of such a merry, nimble, stirring spirit,
She might ha' been a grandam ere she died :
And so may you; for a light heart lives long.

Ros. What's your dark meaning, mouse,
of this light word?

Kath. A light condition in a beauty dark.

Ros. We need more light to find your
meaning out. 21

Kath. You'll mar the light by taking it in
snuff;

Therefore I'll darkly end the argument.

Ros. Look, what you do, you do it still i'
the dark.

Kath. So do not you, for you are a light
wench.

Ros. Indeed I weigh not you, and therefore light.

Kath. You weigh me not? O, that's you
care not for me.

Ros. Great reason; for 'past cure is still
past care.'

Prin. Well bandied both; a set of wit well
play'd.

But, Rosaline, you have a favor too : 30
Who sent it? and what is it?

Ros. I would you knew :
An if my face were but as fair as yours,
My favor were as great; be witness this.
Nay, I have verses too, I thank Biron :
The numbers true; and, were the numbering
too,

I were the fairest goddess on the ground :
I am compared to twenty thousand fairs.
O, he hath drawn my picture in his letter!

Prin. Any thing like?

Ros. Much in the letters; nothing in the
praise. 40

Prin. Beauteous as ink; a good conclusion.

Kath. Fair as a text B in a copy-book.

Ros. 'Ware pencils, ho! let me not die
your debtor,

My red dominical, my golden letter :
O that your face were not so full of O's!

Kath. A pox of that jest! and I beshrew
all shrows.

Prin. But, Katharine, what was sent to you
from fair Dumain?

Kath. Madam, this glove.

Prin. Did he not send you twain?

Kath. Yes, madam, and moreover
Some thousand verses of a faithful lover, 50
A huge translation of hypocrisy,
Vilely compiled, profound simplicity.

Mar. This and these pearls to me sent
Longaville :
The letter is too long by half a mile.

Prin. I think no less. Dost thou not wish
in heart
The chain were longer and the letter short?

Mar. Ay, or I would these hands might
never part.

Prin. We are wise girls to mock our lovers so.

Ros. They are worse fools to purchase
mocking so.

That same Biron I'll torture ere I go : 60
O that I knew he were but in by the week!
How I would make him fawn and beg and
seek
And wait the season and observe the times
And spend his prodigal wits in bootless rhymes
And shape his service wholly to my hests
And make him proud to make me proud that
jests !
So perttaunt-like would I o'ersway his state
That he should be my fool and I his fate.

Prin. None are so surely caught, when they
are catch'd, 69
As wit turn'd fool : folly, in wisdom hatch'd,
Hath wisdom's warrant and the help of school
And wit's own grace to grace a learned fool.

Ros. The blood of youth burns not with
such excess
As gravity's revolt to wantonness.

Mar. Folly in fools bears not so strong a
note
As foolery in the wise, when wit doth dote;
Since all the power thereof it doth apply
To prove, by wit, worth in simplicity.

Prin. Here comes Boyet, and mirth is in
his face.

Enter BOYET.

Boyet. O, I am stabb'd with laughter!
Where's her grace? 80

Prin. Thy news, Boyet?

Boyet. Prepare, madam, prepare !
Arm, wenches, arm! encounters mounted are
Against your peace : Love doth approach dis-
guised,
Armed in arguments; you'll be surprised :
Muster your wits; stand in your own defence ;
Or hide your heads like cowards, and fly
hence.

Prin. Saint Denis to Saint Cupid! What
are they
That charge their breath against us? say,
scout, say.

Boyet. Under the cool shade of a syca-
more
I thought to close mine eyes some half an
hour;
When, lo! to interrupt my purposed rest, 91
Toward that shade I might behold address
The king and his companions : warily
I stole into a neighbor thicket by,
And overheard what you shall overhear,
That, by and by, disguised they will be here.
Their herald is a pretty knavish page,
That well by heart hath conn'd his embassage:
Action and accent did they teach him there;
'Thus must thou speak,' and 'thus thy body
bear : ' 100
And ever and anon they made a doubt
Presence majestical would put him out,
'For,' quoth the king, 'an angel shalt thou
see;'
Yet fear not thou, but speak audaciously.'
The boy replied, 'An angel is not evil;
I should have fear'd her had she been a devil.'
With that, all laugh'd and clapp'd him on the
shoulder,
Making the bold wag by their praises bolder :
One rubb'd his elbow thus, and fleer'd and
swore

A better speech was never spoke before ; 110
Another, with his finger and his thumb,
Cried, ' Via ! we will do't, come what will
  come ; '
The third he caper'd, and cried, 'All goes
  well ; '
The fourth turn'd on the toe, and down he
  fell.
With that, they all did tumble on the ground,
With such a zealous laughter, so profound,
That in this spleen ridiculous appears,
To check their folly, passion's solemn tears.
 Prin. But what, but what, come they to
  visit us ?
 Boyet. They do, they do : and are ap-
  parell'd thus,   120
Like Muscovites or Russians, as I guess.
Their purpose is to parle, to court and dance ;
And every one his love-feat will advance
Unto his several mistress, which they'll know
By favors several which they did bestow.
 Prin. And will they so ? the gallants shall
  be task'd ;
For, ladies, we will every one be mask'd ;
And not a man of them shall have the grace,
Despite of suit, to see a lady's face.
Hold, Rosaline, this favor thou shalt wear,130
And then the king will court thee for his dear ;
Hold, take thou this, my sweet, and give me
  thine,
So shall Biron take me for Rosaline.
And change your favors too ; so shall your
  loves
Woo contrary, deceived by these removes.
 Ros. Come on, then ; wear the favors most
  in sight.
 Kath. But in this changing what is your
  intent ?
 Prin. The effect of my intent is to cross
  theirs :
They do it but in mocking merriment ;
And mock for mock is only my intent. 140
Their several counsels they unbosom shall
To loves mistook, and so be mock'd withal
Upon the next occasion that we meet,
With visages display'd, to talk and greet.
 Ros. But shall we dance, if they desire us
  to't ?
 Prin. No, to the death, we will not move a
  foot ;
Nor to their penn'd speech render we no
  grace,
But while 'tis spoke each turn away her face.
 Boyet. Why, that contempt will kill the
  speaker's heart,
And quite divorce his memory from his part.
 Prin. Therefore I do it ; and I make no
  doubt   151
The rest will ne'er come in, if he be out
There's no such sport as sport by sport o'er-
  thrown,
To make theirs ours and ours none but our
  own :
So shall we stay, mocking intended game,
And they, well mock'd, depart away with
  shame.   [*Trumpets sound within.*
 Boyet. The trumpet sounds : be mask'd ;
  the maskers come. [*The Ladies mask.*

Enter Blackamoors with music ; Moth ; *the*
 King, Baron, Longaville, *and* Dumain, *in*
 Russian habits, and masked.

 Moth. All hail, the richest beauties on the
  earth !—
 Boyet. Beauties no richer than rich taffeta.
 Moth. A holy parcel of the fairest dames.
  [*The Ladies turn their backs to him.*
That ever turn'd their — backs — to mortal
  views !
 Biron. [*Aside to Moth*] Their eyes, vil-
  lain, their eyes.
 Moth. That ever turn'd their eyes to mor-
  tal views !—
Out—
 Boyet. True ; out indeed.
 Moth. Out of your favors, heavenly spir-
  its, vouchsafe
Not to behold—
 Biron. [*Aside to Moth*] Once to behold,
  rogue.
 Moth. Once to behold with your sun-
  beamed eyes,
  —with your sun-beamed eyes—
 Boyet. They will not answer to that epi-
  thet ;
You were best call it ' daughter-beamed eyes.'
 Moth. They do not mark me, and that
  brings me out.
 Biron. Is this your perfectness ? be gone,
  you rogue !   [*Exit Moth.*
 Ros. What would these strangers ? know
  their minds, Boyet ;
If they do speak our language, 'tis our will
That some plain man recount their purposes :
Know what they would.
 Boyet. What would you with the princess?
 Biron. Nothing but peace and gentle visi-
  tation.
 Ros. What would they, say they ? 180
 Boyet. Nothing but peace and gentle visi-
  tation.
 Ros. Why, that they have ; and bid them
  so be gone.
 Boyet. She says, you have it, and you may
  be gone.
 King. Say to her, we have measured many
  miles
To tread a measure with her on this grass.
 Boyet. They say, that they have measured
  many a mile
To tread a measure with you on this grass.
 Ros. It is not so. Ask them how many
  inches
Is in one mile : if they have measured many,
The measure then of one is easily told. 190
 Boyet. If to come hither you have meas-
  ured miles,
And many miles, the princess bids you tell
How many inches doth fill up one mile.
 Biron. Tell her, we measure them by
  weary steps.
 Boyet. She hears herself.
 Ros.   How many weary steps,
Of many weary miles you have o'ergone,
Are number'd in the travel of one mile ?
 Biron. We number nothing that we spend
  for you :
Our duty is so rich, so infinite,
That we may do it still without accompt. 200
Vouchsafe to show the sunshine of your face,
That we, like savages, may worship it.
 Ros. My face is but a moon, and clouded
  too.

King. Blessed are clouds, to do as such
        clouds do!
Vouchsafe, bright moon, and these thy stars,
        to shine,
Those clouds removed, upon our watery eyne.
Ros. O vain petitioner! beg a greater
        matter;
Thou now request'st but moonshine in the
        water.
King. Then, in our measure do but vouch-
        safe one change.
Thou bid'st me beg: this begging is not
        strange.   210
Ros. Play, music, then! Nay, you must do
        it soon.   [*Music plays.*
Not yet! no dance! Thus change I like the
        moon.
King. Will you not dance? How come
        you thus estranged?
Ros. You took the moon at full, but now
        she's changed.
King. Yet still she is the moon, and I the
        man.
The music plays; vouchsafe some motion to
        it.
Ros. Our ears vouchsafe it.
King.   But your legs should do it.
Ros. Since you are strangers and come
        here by chance,
We'll not be nice: take hands. We will not
        dance.
King. Why take we hands, then?
Ros.   Only to part friends: 220
Curtsy, sweet hearts; and so the measure
        ends.
King. More measure of this measure; be
        not nice.
Ros. We can afford no more at such a
        price.
King. Prize you yourselves: what buys
        your company?
Ros. Your absence only.
King.   That can never be.
Ros. Then cannot we be bought: and so,
        adieu;
Twice to your visor, and half once to you.
King. If you deny to dance, let's hold
        more chat.
Ros. In private, then.
King.   I am best pleased with that.
                        [*They converse apart.*
Biron. White-handed mistress, one sweet
        word with thee.   230
Prin. Honey, and milk, and sugar; there
        is three.
Biron. Nay then, two treys, and if you
        grow so nice,
Metheglin, wort, and malmsey: well run, dice!
There's half-a-dozen sweets.
Prin.   Seventh sweet, adieu:
Since you can cog, I'll play no more with you.
Biron. One word in secret.
Prin.   Let it not be sweet.
Biron. Thou grievest my gall.
Prin.   Gall! bitter.
Biron.   Therefore meet.
                        [*They converse apart.*
Dum. Will you vouchsafe with me to
        change a word?
Mar. Name it.
Dum.   Fair lady,—
Mar.   Say you so? Fair lord,—

Take that for your fair lady.
Dum.   Please it you, 240
As much in private, and I'll bid adieu.
                        [*They converse apart.*
Kath. What, was your vizard made with-
        out a tongue?
Long. I know the reason, lady, why you
        ask.
Kath. O for your reason! quickly, sir; I
        long.
Long. You have a double tongue within
        your mask,
And would afford my speechless vizard half.
Kath. Veal, quoth the Dutchman. Is not
        'veal' a calf?
Long. A calf, fair lady!
Kath.   No, a fair lord calf.
Long. Let's part the word.
Kath.   No, I'll not be your half:
Take all, and wean it; it may prove an ox.
Long. Look, how you butt yourself in
        these sharp mocks!   251
Will you give horns, chaste lady? do not so.
Kath. Then die a calf, before your horns
        do grow.
Long. One word in private with you, ere I
        die.
Kath. Bleat softly then; the butcher hears
        you cry.   [*They converse apart.*
Boyet. The tongues of mocking wenches
        are as keen
As is the razor's edge invisible,
Cutting a smaller hair than may be seen,
Above the sense of sense; so sensible
Seemeth their conference; their conceits have
        wings   260
Fleeter than arrows, bullets, wind, thought,
        swifter things.
Ros. Not one word more, my maids;
        break off, break off.
Biron. By heaven, all dry-beaten with pure
        scoff!
King. Farewell, mad wenches; you have
        simple wits.
Prin. Twenty adieus, my frozen Muscovits.
        [*Exeunt King, Lords, and Blackamoors.*
Are these the breed of wits so wonder'd at?
Boyet. Tapers they are, with your sweet
        breaths puff'd out.
Ros. Well-liking wits they have; gross,
        gross; fat, fat.
Prin. O poverty in wit, kingly-poor flout!
Will they not, think you, hang themselves to-
        night?   270
Or ever, but in vizards, show their faces?
This pert Biron was out of countenance quite.
Ros. O, they were all in lamentable cases!
The king was weeping-ripe for a good word.
Prin. Biron did swear himself out of all
        suit.
Mar. Dumain was at my service, and his
        sword:
No point, quoth I; my servant straight was
        mute.
Kath. Lord Longaville said, I came o'er his
        heart;
And trow you what he called me?
Prin.   Qualm, perhaps.
Kath. Yes, in good faith.
Prin.   Go, sickness as thou art! 280
Ros. Well, better wits have worn plain stat-
        ute-caps.

But will you hear ? the king is my love sworn.
Prin. And quick Biron hath plighted faith
to me.
Kath. And Longaville was for my service
born.
Mar. Dumain is mine, as sure as bark on
tree.
Boyet. Madam, and pretty mistresses, give
ear :
Immediately they will again be here
In their own shapes ; for it can never be
They will digest this harsh indignity.
Prin. Will they return ?
Boyet. They will, they will, God knows,
And leap for joy, though they are lame with
blows :   291
Therefore change favors ; and, when they re-
pair,
Blow like sweet roses in this summer air.
Prin. How blow ? how blow ? speak to be
understood.
Boyet. Fair ladies mask'd are roses in their
bud ;
Dismask'd, their damask sweet commixture
shown,
Are angels vailing clouds, or roses blown.
Prin. Avaunt, perplexity ! What shall we
do,
If they return in their own shapes to woo ?
Ros. Good madam, if by me you'll be ad-
vised,
Let's mock them still, as well known as dis-
guised :
Let us complain to them what fools were here,
Disguised like Muscovites, in shapeless gear ;
And wonder what they were and to what end
Their shallow shows and prologue vilely
penn'd
And their rough carriage so ridiculous,
Should be presented at our tent to us.
Boyet. Ladies, withdraw : the gallants are
at hand.
Prin. Whip to our tents, as roes run o'er
land.
[*Exeunt Princess, Rosaline, Katharine, and
Maria.*

Re-enter the King, BIRON, LONGAVILLE, *and*
DUMAIN, *in their proper habits.*

King. Fair sir, God save you ! Where's the
princess ?   310
Boyet. Gone to her tent. Please it your
majesty
Command me any service to her thither ?
King. That she vouchsafe me audience for
one word.
Boyet. I will ; and so will she, I know, my
lord.   [*Exit.*
Biron. This fellow pecks up wit as pigeons
pease,
And utters it again when God doth please :
He is wit's pedler, and retails his wares
At wakes and wassails, meetings, markets,
fairs ;
And we that sell by gross, the Lord doth
know,
Have not the grace to grace it with such show.
This gallant pins the wenches on his sleeve ;
Had he been Adam, he had tempted Eve ;
A' can carve too, and lisp : why, this is he
That kiss'd his hand away in courtesy ;
This is the ape of form, monsieur the nice,

That, when he plays at tables, chides the dice
In honorable terms : nay, he can sing
A mean most meanly ; and in ushering
Mend him who can : the ladies call him sweet ;
The stairs, as he treads on them, kiss his feet :
This is the flower that smiles on every one,
To show his teeth as white as whale's bone ;
And consciences, that will not die in debt,
Pay him the due of honey-tongued Boyet.
King. A blister on his sweet tongue, with
my heart,
That put Armado's page out of his part !
Biron. See where it comes ! Behavior, what
wert thou
Till this madman show'd thee ? and what art
thou now ?

Re-enter the Princess, *ushered by* BOYET ;
ROSALINE, MARIA, *and* KATHARINE.

King. All hail, sweet madam, and fair time
of day !
Prin. 'Fair' in 'all hail' is foul, as I con-
ceive.
King. Construe my speeches better, if you
may.
Prin. Then wish me better ; I will give you
leave.
King. We came to visit you, and purpose
now
To lead you to our court ; vouchsafe it then.
Prin. This field shall hold me ; and so hold
your vow :
Nor God, nor I, delights in perjured men.
King. Rebuke me not for that which you
provoke :
The virtue of your eye must break my oath.
Prin. You nickname virtue ; vice you
should have spoke ;
For virtue's office never breaks men's troth.
Now by my maiden honor, yet as pure   351
As the unsullied lily, I protest,
A world of torments though I should endure,
I would not yield to be your house's guest ;
So much I hate a breaking cause to be
Of heavenly oaths, vow'd with integrity.
King. O, you have lived in desolation here,
Unseen, unvisited, much to our shame.
Prin. Not so, my lord ; it is not so, I
swear ;
We have had pastimes here and pleasant
game :   360
A mess of Russians left us but of late.
King. How, madam ! Russians !
Prin.   Ay, in truth, my lord ;
Trim gallants, full of courtship and of state.
Ros. Madam, speak true. It is not so, my
lord :
My lady, to the manner of the days,
In courtesy gives undeserving praise.
We four indeed confronted were with four
In Russian habit : here they stay'd an hour,
And talk'd apace ; and in that hour, my lord,
They did not bless us with one happy word.
I dare not call them fools ; but this I think,
When they are thirsty, fools would fain have
drink.
Biron. This jest is dry to me. Fair gentle
sweet,
Your wit makes wise things foolish : when we
greet,
With eyes best seeing, heaven's fiery eye,
By light we lose light : your capacity

Is of that nature that to your huge store
Wise things seem foolish and rich things but
    poor.
Ros. This proves you wise and rich, for in
    my eye,—
Biron. I am a fool, and full of poverty.
Ros. But that you take what doth to you
    belong,   381
It were a fault to snatch words from my
    tongue.
Biron. O, I am yours, and all that I pos-
    sess !
Ros. All the fool mine ?
Biron.   I cannot give you less.
Ros. Which of the vizards was it that you
    wore ?
Biron. Where ? when ? what vizard ? why
    demand you this ?
Ros. There, then, that vizard ; that super-
    fluous case
That hid the worse and show'd the better face.
King. We are descried ; they'll mock us
    now downright.
Dum. Let us confess and turn it to a jest.
Prin. Amazed, my lord ? why looks your
    highness sad ?   391
Ros. Help, hold his brows ! he'll swoon !
    Why look you pale ?
Sea-sick, I think, coming from Muscovy.
Biron. Thus pour the stars down plagues
    for perjury.
Can any face of brass hold longer out ?
Here stand I : lady, dart thy skill at me ;
    Bruise me with scorn, confound me with a
    flout ;
Thrust thy sharp wit quite through my igno-
    rance ;
Cut me to pieces with thy keen conceit ;
And I will wish thee never more to dance, 400
    Nor never more in Russian habit wait.
O, never will I trust to speeches penn'd,
    Nor to the motion of a schoolboy's tongue,
Nor never come in vizard to my friend,
    Nor woo in rhyme, like a blind harper's
    song !
Taffeta phrases, silken terms precise,
    Three-piled hyperboles, spruce affectation,
Figures pedantical ; these summer-flies
    Have blown me full of maggot ostentation :
I do forswear them ; and I here protest,   410
    By this white glove,—how white the hand,
    God knows !—
Henceforth my wooing mind shall be ex-
    press'd
In russet yeas and honest kersey noes :
And, to begin, wench,—so God help me, la !—
My love to thee is sound, sans crack or flaw.
Ros. Sans sans, I pray you.
Biron.   Yet I have a trick
Of the old rage : bear with me, I am sick ;
I'll leave it by degrees. Soft, let us see :
Write, 'Lord have mercy on us' on those
    three ;
They are infected ; in their hearts it lies ; 420
They have the plague, and caught it of your
    eyes ;
These lords are visited ; you are not free,
For the Lord's tokens on you do I see.
Prin. No, they are free that gave these
    tokens to us.
Biron. Our states are forfeit : seek not to
    undo us.

Ros. It is not so ; for how can this be true,
That you stand forfeit, being those that sue ?
Biron. Peace ! for I will not have to do
    with you.
Ros. Nor shall not, if I do as I intend.
Biron. Speak for yourselves ; my wit is at
    an end.
King. Teach us, sweet madam, for our
    rude transgression
Some fair excuse.
Prin.   The fairest is confession.
Were not you here but even now disguised ?
King. Madam, I was.
Prin.   And were you well advised ?
King. I was, fair madam.
Prin.   When you then were here,
What did you whisper in your lady's ear ?
King. That more than all the world I did
    respect her.
Prin. When she shall challenge this, you
    will reject her.
King. Upon mine honor, no.
Prin.   Peace, peace ! forbear :
Your oath once broke, you force not to for-
    swear.   440
King. Despise me, when I break this oath
    of mine.
Prin. I will : and therefore keep it. Rosa-
    line,
What did the Russian whisper in your ear ?
Ros. Madam, he swore that he did hold
    me dear
As precious eyesight, and did value me
Above this world ; adding thereto moreover
That he would wed me, or else die my lover.
Prin. God give thee joy of him ! the noble
    lord
Most honorably doth unhold his word.
King. What mean you, madam ? by my
    life, my troth,   450
I never swore this lady such an oath.
Ros. By heaven, you did ; and to confirm
    it plain,
You gave me this : but take it, sir, again.
King. My faith and this the princess I did
    give :
I knew her by this jewel on her sleeve.
Prin. Pardon me, sir, this jewel did she
    wear ;
And Lord Biron, I thank him, is my dear.
What, will you have me, or your pearl again ?
Biron. Neither of either ; I remit both
    twain.
I see the trick on't : here was a consent, 460
Knowing aforehand of our merriment,
To dash it like a Christmas comedy :
Some carry-tale, some please-man, some slight
    zany,
Some mumble-news, some trencher-knight,
    some Dick,
That smiles his cheek in years and knows the
    trick
To make my lady laugh when she's disposed,
Told our intents before ; which once disclosed,
The ladies did change favors : and then we,
Following the signs, woo'd but the sign of she.
Now, to our perjury to add more terror,   470
We are again forsworn, in will and error.
Much upon this it is : and might not you
                                        [*To Boyet.*
Forestall our sport, to make us thus untrue ?
Do not you know my lady's foot by the squier,

And laugh upon the apple of her eye?
And stand between her back, sir, and the fire,
Holding a trencher, jesting merrily?
You put our page out : go, you are allow'd ;
Die when you will, a smock shall be
your shroud.
You leer upon me, do you? there's an eye
Wounds like a leaden sword. 481
Boyet. Full merrily
Hath this brave manage, this career, been run.
Biron. Lo, he is tilting straight ! Peace !
I have done.

Enter COSTARD.

Welcome, pure wit ! thou partest a fair fray.
Cost. O Lord, sir, they would know
Whether the three Worthies shall come in or
no.
Biron. What, are there but three?
Cost. No, sir ; but it is vara fine,
For every one pursents three.
Biron. And three times thrice is nine.
Cost. Not so, sir ; under correction, sir ; I
hope it is not so.
You cannot beg us, sir, I can assure you, sir ;
we know what we know : 490
I hope, sir, three times thrice, sir,—
Biron. Is not nine.
Cost. Under correction, sir, we know
whereuntil it doth amount.
Biron. By Jove, I always took three threes
for nine.
Cost. O Lord, sir, it were pity you should
get your living by reckoning, sir.
Biron. How much is it ?
Cost. O Lord, sir, the parties themselves,
the actors, sir, will show whereuntil it doth
amount : for mine own part, I am, as they say,
but to parfect one man in one poor man, Pompion the Great, sir.
Biron. Art thou one of the Worthies?
Cost. It pleased them to think me worthy
of Pompion the Great : for mine own part, I
know not the degree of the Worthy, but I am
to stand for him.
Biron. Go, bid them prepare. 510
Cost. We will turn it finely off, sir ; we will
take some care. [*Exit.*
King. Biron, they will shame us : let them
not approach.
Biron. We are shame-proof, my lord : and
'tis some policy
To have one show worse than the king's and
his company.
King. I say they shall not come.
Prin. Nay, my good lord, let me o'errule
you now :
That sport best pleases that doth least know
how :
Where zeal strives to content, and the con-
tents
Dies in the zeal of that which it presents :
Their form confounded makes most form in
mirth,
When great things laboring perish in their
birth.
Biron. A right description of our sport, my
lord.

Enter ARMADO.

Arm. Anointed, I implore so much expense

of thy royal sweet breath as will utter a brace
of words.
[*Converses apart with the King, and
delivers him a paper.*
Prin. Doth this man serve God?
Biron. Why ask you?
Prin. He speaks not like a man of God's
making.
Arm. That is all one, my fair, sweet,
honey monarch ; for, I protest, the schoolmaster is exceeding fantastical ; too too vain, too
too vain : but we will put it, as they say, to
fortuna de la guerra. I wish you the peace of
mind, most royal couplement ! [*Exit.*
King. Here is like to be a good presence
of Worthies. He presents Hector of Troy ; the
swain, Pompey the Great ; the parish curate,
Alexander ; Armado's page, Hercules ; the
pedant, Judas Maccabæus : 540
And if these four Worthies in their first show
thrive,
These four will change habits, and present the
other five.
Biron. There is five in the first show.
King. You are deceived ; 'tis not so.
Biron. The pedant, the braggart, the hedge-
priest, the fool and the boy :—
Abate throw at novum, and the whole world
again
Cannot pick out five such, take each one in
his vein.
King. The ship is under sail, and here she
comes amain.

Enter COSTARD, *for Pompey.*

Cost. I Pompey am,—
Boyet. You lie, you are not he. 550
Cost. I Pompey am,—
Boyet. With libbard's head on knee.
Biron. Well said, old mocker : I must
needs be friends with thee.
Cost. I Pompey am, Pompey surnamed the
Big,—
Dum. The Great.
Cost. It is, ' Great,' sir :—
Pompey surnamed the Great ;
That oft in field, with targe and shield, did
make my foe to sweat :
And travelling along this coast, I here am
come by chance,
And lay my arms before the legs of this sweet
lass of France,
If your ladyship would say, ' Thanks, Pompey,'
I had done.
Prin. Great thanks, great Pompey. 560
Cost. 'Tis not so much worth ; but I hope
I was perfect : I made a little fault in ' Great.'
Biron. My hat to a halfpenny, Pompey
proves the best Worthy.

Enter SIR NATHANIEL, *for Alexander.*

Nath. When in the world I lived, I was the
world's commander ;
By east, west, north, and south, I spread my
conquering might :
My scutcheon plain declares that I am Alisander,—
Boyet. Your nose says, no, you are not ;
for it stands too right.
Biron. Your nose smells ' no ' in this, most
tender-smelling knight.

Prin. The conqueror is dismay'd. Proceed, good Alexander.   570
Nath. When in the world I lived, I was the world's commander,—
Boyet. Most true, 'tis right; you were so, Alisander.
Biron. Pompey the Great,—
Cost. Your servant, and Costard.
Biron. Take away the conqueror, take away Alisander.
Cost. [*To Sir Nath.*] O, sir, you have overthrown Alisander the conqueror! You will be scraped out of the painted cloth for this: your lion, that holds his poll-axe sitting on a close-stool, will be given to Ajax: he will be the ninth Worthy. A conqueror, and afeard to speak! run away for shame, Alisander. [*Nath. retires.*] There, an't shall please you; a foolish mild man; an honest man, look you, and soon dashed. He is a marvellous good neighbor, faith, and a very good bowler: but, for Alisander,—alas, you see how 'tis,—a little o'erparted. But there are Worthies a-coming will speak their mind in some other sort.   590
Prin. Stand aside, good Pompey.

Enter HOLOFERNES, *for Judas; and* MOTH, *for Hercules.*

Hol. Great Hercules is presented by this imp,
Whose club kill'd Cerberus, that three-headed canis;
And when he was a babe, a child, a shrimp,
    Thus did he strangle serpents in his manus.
Quoniam he seemeth in minority,
Ergo I come with this apology.
Keep some state in thy exit, and vanish.
        [*Moth retires.*
Judas I am,—
Dum. A Judas!   600
Hol. Not Iscariot, sir.
    Judas I am, ycliped Maccabæus.
Dum. Judas Maccabæus clipt is plain Judas.
Biron. A kissing traitor. How art thou proved Judas?
Hol. Judas I am,—
Dum. The more shame for you, Judas.
Hol. What mean you, sir?
Boyet. To make Judas hang himself.
Hol. Begin, sir; you are my elder.
Biron. Well followed: Judas was hanged on an elder.   610
Hol. I will not be put out of countenance.
Biron. Because thou hast no face.
Hol. What is this?
Boyet. A cittern-head.
Dum. The head of a bodkin.
Biron. A Death's face in a ring.
Long. The face of an old Roman coin, scarce seen.
Boyet. The pommel of Cæsar's falchion.
Dum. The carved-bone face on a flask.
Biron. Saint George's half-cheek in a brooch.   620
Dum. Ay, and in a brooch of lead.
Biron. Ay, and worn in the cap of a tooth-drawer.
And now forward; for we have put thee in countenance.
Hol. You have put me out of countenance.

Biron. False; we have given thee faces.
Hol. But you have out-faced them all.
Biron. An thou wert a lion, we would do so.
Boyet. Therefore, as he is an ass, let him go.
And so adieu, sweet Jude! nay, why dost thou stay?
Dum. For the latter end of his name.   630
Biron. For the ass to the Jude; give it him:—Jud-as, away!
Hol. This is not generous, not gentle, not humble.
Boyet. A light for Monsieur Judas! it grows dark, he may stumble.
        [*Hol. retires.*
Prin. Alas, poor Maccabæus, how hath he been baited!

Enter ARMADO, *for Hector.*

Biron. Hide thy head, Achilles: here comes Hector in arms.
Dum. Though my mocks come home by me, I will now be merry.
King. Hector was but a Troyan in respect of this.   640
Boyet. But is this Hector?
King. I think Hector was not so clean-timbered.
Long. His leg is too big for Hector's.
Dum. More calf, certain.
Boyet. No; he is best indued in the small.
Biron. This cannot be Hector.
Dum. He's a god or a painter; for he makes faces.
Arm. The armipotent Mars, of lances the almighty,   650
Gave Hector a gift,—
Dum. A gilt nutmeg.
Biron. A lemon.
Long. Stuck with cloves.
Dum. No, cloven.
Arm. Peace!—
The armipotent Mars, of lances the almighty,
    Gave Hector a gift, the heir of Ilion;
A man so breathed, that certain he would fight; yea
    From morn till night, out of his pavilion.
I am that flower,—   661
Dum.   That mint.
Long.   That columbine.
Arm. Sweet Lord Longaville, rein thy tongue.
Long. I must rather give it the rein, for it runs against Hector.
Dum. Ay, and Hector's a greyhound.
Arm. The sweet war-man is dead and rotten; sweet chucks, beat not the bones of the buried: when he breathed, he was a man. But I will forward with my device. [*To the Princess*] Sweet royalty, bestow on me the sense of hearing.   670
Prin. Speak, brave Hector: we are much delighted.
Arm. I do adore thy sweet grace's slipper.
Boyet. [*Aside to Dum.*] Loves her by the foot.
Dum. [*Aside to Boyet*] He may not by the yard.
Arm. This Hector far surmounted Hanni-bal,—

Cost. The party is gone, fellow Hector, she is gone; she is two months on her way.
Arm. What meanest thou ? 680
Cost. Faith, unless you play the honest Troyan, the poor wench is cast away : she's quick ; the child brags in her belly already : 'tis yours.
Arm. Dost thou infamonize me among potentates ? thou shalt die.
Cost. Then shall Hector be whipped for Jaquenetta that is quick by him and hanged for Pompey that is dead by him.
Dum. Most rare Pompey !
Boyet. Renowned Pompey ! 690
Biron. Greater than great, great, great Pompey ! Pompey the Huge !
Dum. Hector trembles.
Biron. Pompey is moved. More Ates, more Ates ! stir them on ! stir them on !
Dum. Hector will challenge him.
Biron. Ay, if a' have no more man's blood in's belly than will sup a flea.
Arm. By the north pole, I do challenge thee.
Cost. I will not fight with a pole, like a northern man : I'll slash ; I'll do it by the sword. I bepray you, let me borrow my arms again.
Dum. Room for the incensed Worthies !
Cost. I'll do it in my shirt.
Dum. Most resolute Pompey !
Moth. Master, let me take you a buttonhole lower. Do you not see Pompey is uncasing for the combat ? What mean you ? You will lose your reputation.
Arm. Gentlemen and soldiers, pardon me ; I will not combat in my shirt. 710
Dum. You may not deny it : Pompey hath made the challenge.
Arm. Sweet bloods, I both may and will.
Biron. What reason have you for't ?
Arm. The naked truth of it is, I have no shirt ; I go woolward for penance.
Boyet. True, and it was enjoined him in Rome for want of linen : since when, I'll be sworn, he wore none but a dishclout of Jaquenetta's, and that a' wears next his heart for a favor.

Enter MERCADE.

Mer. God save you, madam !
Prin. Welcome, Mercade ;
But that thou interrupt'st our merriment.
Mer. I am sorry, madam ; for the news I bring
Is heavy in my tongue. The king your father—
Prin. Dead, for my life !
Mer. Even so ; my tale is told. 730
Biron. Worthies, away ! the scene begins to cloud.
Arm. For mine own part, I breathe free breath. I have seen the day of wrong through the little hole of discretion, and I will right myself like a soldier. [*Exeunt Worthies.*
King. How fares your majesty ?
Prin. Boyet, prepare ; I will away tonight.
King. Madam, not so ; I do beseech you, stay.
Prin. Prepare, I say. I thank you, gracious lords,
For all your fair endeavors ; and entreat, 740
Out of a new-sad soul, that you vouchsafe

In your rich wisdom to excuse or hide
The liberal opposition of our spirits,
If over-boldly we have borne ourselves
In the converse of breath : your gentleness
Was guilty of it. Farewell, worthy lord !
A heavy heart bears not a nimble tongue :
Excuse me so, coming too short of thanks
For my great suit so easily obtain'd.
King. The extreme parts of time extremely forms 750
All causes to the purpose of his speed,
And often at his very loose decides
That which long process could not arbitrate :
And though the mourning brow of progeny
Forbid the smiling courtesy of love
The holy suit which fain it would convince,
Yet, since love's argument was first on foot,
Let not the cloud of sorrow justle it
From what it purposed ; since, to wail friends lost
Is not by much so wholesome-profitable 760
As to rejoice at friends but newly found.
Prin. I understand you not : my griefs are double.
Biron. Honest plain words best pierce the ear of grief ;
And by these badges understand the king.
For your fair sakes have we neglected time,
Play'd foul play with our oaths : your beauty, ladies,
Hath much deform'd us, fashioning our humors
Even to the opposed end of our intents :
And what in us hath seem'd ridiculous,—
As love is full of unbefitting strains, 770
All wanton as a child, skipping and vain,
Form'd by the eye and therefore, like the eye,
Full of strange shapes, of habits and of forms,
Varying in subjects as the eye doth roll
To every varied object in his glance :
Which parti-coated presence of loose love
Put on by us, if, in your heavenly eyes,
Have misbecomed our oaths and gravities,
Those heavenly eyes, that look into these faults,
Suggested us to make. Therefore, ladies, 780
Our love being yours, the error that love makes
Is likewise yours : we to ourselves prove false,
By being once false for ever to be true
To those that make us both,—fair ladies, you :
And even that falsehood, in itself a sin,
Thus purifies itself and turns to grace.
Prin. We have received your letters full of love ;
Your favors, the ambassadors of love ;
And, in our maiden council, rated them
At courtship, pleasant jest and courtesy, 790
As bombast and as lining to the time :
But more devout than this in our respects
Have we not been ; and therefore met your loves
In their own fashion, like a merriment.
Dum. Our letters, madam, show'd much more than jest.
Long. So did our looks.
Ros. We did not quote them so.
King. Now, at the latest minute of the hour,
Grant us your loves.
Prin. A time, methinks, too short
To make a world-without-end bargain in.
No, no, my lord, your grace is perjured much,
Full of dear guiltiness ; and therefore this :

If for my love, as there is no such cause,
You will do aught, this shall you do for me :
Your oath I will not trust ; but go with speed
To some forlorn and naked hermitage,
Remote from all the pleasures of the world ;
There stay until the twelve celestial signs
Have brought about the annual reckoning.
If this austere insociable life
Change not your offer made in heat of blood ;
If frosts and fasts, hard lodging and thin weeds
Nip not the gaudy blossoms of your love,
But that it bear this trial and last love ;
Then, at the expiration of the year,
Come challenge me, challenge me by these
     deserts,
And, by this virgin palm now kissing thine
I will be thine ; and till that instant shut
My woeful self up in a mourning house,
Raining the tears of lamentation   819
For the remembrance of my father's death.
If this thou do deny, let our hands part,
Neither intitled in the other's heart.
     King. If this, or more than this, I would
          deny,
To flatter up these powers of mine with rest,
The sudden hand of death close up mine eye !
Hence ever then my heart is in thy breast.
[*Biron.* And what to me, my love ? and what
     to me ?
     Ros. You must be purged too, your sins
          are rack'd,
You are attaint with faults and perjury :
Therefore if you my favor mean to get,   830
A twelvemonth shall you spend, and never rest,
But seek the weary beds of people sick.]
     Dum. But what to me, my love ? but what
     to me ?
A wife ?
     Kath. A beard, fair health, and honesty ;
With three-fold love I wish you all these three.
     Dum. O, shall I say, I thank you, gentle
     wife ?
     Kath. Not so, my lord ; a twelvemonth and
     a day
I'll mark no words that smooth-faced woo-
     ers say :
Come when the king doth to my lady come ;
Then, if I have much love, I'll give you some.
     Dum. I'll serve thee true and faithfully till
     then.   841
     Kath. Yet swear not, lest ye be forsworn
     again.
     Long. What says Maria ?
     Mar.   At the twelvemonth's end
I'll change my black gown for a faithful friend.
     Long. I'll stay with patience ; but the time
     is long.
     Mar. The liker you ; few taller are so
     young.
     Biron. Studies my lady ? mistress, look on
     me ;
Behold the window of my heart, mine eye,
What humble suit attends thy answer there :
Impose some service on me for thy love.   850
     Ros. Oft have I heard of you, my Lord
     Biron,
Before I saw you ; and the world's large tongue
Proclaims you for a man replete with mocks,
Full of comparisons and wounding flouts,
Which you on all estates will execute
That lie within the mercy of your wit.

To weed this wormwood from your fruitful
     brain,
And therewithal to win me, if you please,
Without the which I am not to be won,
You shall this twelvemonth term from day to
     day   860
Visit the speechless sick and still converse
With groaning wretches ; and your task shall
     be,
With all the fierce endeavor of your wit
To enforce the pained impotent to smile.
     Biron. To move wild laughter in the throat
     of death ?
It cannot be ; it is impossible :
Mirth cannot move a soul in agony.
     Ros. Why, that's the way to choke a gibing
     spirit,
Whose influence is begot of that loose grace
Which shallow laughing hearers give to fools :
A jest's prosperity lies in the ear   871
Of him that hears it, never in the tongue
Of him that makes it : then, if sickly ears,
Deaf'd with the clamors of their own dear
     groans,
Will hear your idle scorns, continue then,
And I will have you and that fault withal ;
But if they will not, throw away that spirit,
And I shall find you empty of that fault,
Right joyful of your reformation.
     Biron. A twelvemonth ! well ; befall what
     will befall,   880
I'll jest a twelvemonth in an hospital.
     Prin. [*To the King*] Ay, sweet my lord ;
     and so I take my leave.
     King. No, madam ; we will bring you on
     your way.
     Biron. Our wooing doth not end like an old
     play ;
Jack hath not Jill : these ladies' courtesy
Might well have made our sport a comedy.
     King. Come, sir, it wants a twelvemonth
     and a day,
And then 'twill end.
     Biron.   That's too long for a play.

Re-enter ARMADO.

     Arm. Sweet majesty, vouchsafe me,—
     Prin. Was not that Hector ?
     Dum. The worthy knight of Troy.   890
     Arm. I will kiss thy royal finger, and take
leave. I am a votary ; I have vowed to Jaquenetta to hold the plough for her sweet love
three years. But, most esteemed greatness, will
you hear the dialogue that the two learned men
have compiled in praise of the owl and the
cuckoo ? it should have followed in the end of
our show.
     King. Call them forth quickly ; we will do
     so.
     Arm. Holla ! approach.   900

Re-enter HOLOFERNES, NATHANIEL, MOTH,
     COSTARD, *and others.*

This side is Hiems, Winter, this Ver, the
Spring ; the one maintained by the owl, the
other by the cuckoo. Ver, begin.

THE SONG.

SPRING.

When daisies pied and violets blue
     And lady-smocks all silver-white
And cuckoo-buds of yellow hue
     Do paint the meadows with delight,

The cuckoo then, on every tree,
Mocks married men; for thus sings he,
        Cuckoo;   910
Cuckoo, cuckoo : O word of fear,
Unpleasing to a married ear !

When shepherds pipe on oaten straws
  And merry larks are ploughmen's clocks,
When turtles tread, and rooks, and daws,
  And maidens bleach their summer smocks
The cuckoo then, on every tree,
Mocks married men; for thus sings he,
        Cuckoo;
Cuckoo, cuckoo : O word of fear,   920
Unpleasing to a married ear !

        WINTER.
When icicles hang by the wall
  And Dick the shepherd blows his nail
And Tom bears logs into the hall
  And milk comes frozen home in pail,

When blood is nipp'd and ways be foul,
Then nightly sings the staring owl,
        Tu-whit ;
Tu-who, a merry note,
While greasy Joan doth keel the pot.   930

When all aloud the wind doth blow
  And coughing drowns the parson's saw
And birds sit brooding in the snow
  And Marian's nose looks red and raw,
When roasted crabs hiss in the bowl,
Then nightly sings the staring owl,
        Tu-whit ;
Tu-who, a merry note,
While greasy Joan doth keel the pot.

  Arm. The words of Mercury are harsh after the songs of Apollo. You that way : we this way.   [*Exeunt.*

THE COMEDY OF ERRORS.

(WRITTEN ABOUT 1591.)

INTRODUCTION.

This is Shakespeare's one farcical play. Its sources of laughter lie almost wholly in the situations and incidents, hardly at all in the characters. The spectator of the play is called upon to accept much that is improbable and all but impossible; not, as in *A Midsummer Night's Dream*, for the sake of freer play of imagination, and because the world pictured by the poet is a fairy-world of romantic beauty and grotesqueness, but for the sake of mere fun and laughter-stirring surprises. So cleverly, however, are the incidents and persons entangled and disentangled, so rapidly does surprise follow surprise, that we are given no time to raise difficulties or offer objections. The subject of the comedy is the same as that of the *Menaechmi* of Plautus —mistakes of identity arising from the likeness of twin-born children. How Shakespeare made acquaintance with Plautus has not been ascertained; possibly through William Warner's translation of the *Menaechmi*, seen in manuscript before its publication in 1595 : more probably through an earlier play, not now extant. To the twins of the *Menaechmi*, Shakespeare has added a second pair of brothers, the twins Dromio. This does not make the improbability of the whole seem greater, but rather the reverse; for the fun is doubled, and where so much is incredible we are carried away and have no wish but to yield ourselves up to belief in the incredible for the time being, so as to enter thoroughly into the jest. Shakespeare added other characters— the Duke Solinus (when he can he always introduces a duke), Ægeon, Balthazar, Angelo, the Abbess, and Luciana ; and he alters the character of the married brother, Antipholus, from the repulsive Menaechmus of Plautus, with whom we can have little sympathy, into a person who at least is not base and vicious. The scene he transfers from Epidamnum to Ephesus, that city which had an evil repute for its roguery, licentiousness, and magical practices, a city in which such *errors* might be supposed to be the result of sorcery and witchcraft. (See Act I., Sc. II., L. 97–102.) To Shakespeare belongs wholly the serious background, from which the farcical incidents stand out in relief—the story of the Syracusan merchant who almost forfeits his life in the search for his lost children, and finally recovers both the lost ones and his own liberty. The date of the play cannot be exactly determined, but it is certainly one of the very earliest. " In what part of her body stands . . . . France ? " asks Antipholus of Syracuse, questioning Dromio about the kitchen-wench, who is so large and round that she has been compared to a globe ; and Dromio answers : " In her forehead, armed and reverted, making war against her *heir*." (Act III., Sc. II., L. 125–127). France was in a state of civil war, fighting for and against her heir, Henri IV., from August, 1589, until shortly before his coronation in February, 1594. In 1591, Henri received the assistance of troops from England, commanded by the Earl of Essex.

DRAMATIS PERSONÆ.

SOLINUS, duke of Ephesus.
ÆGEON, a merchant of Syracuse.

ANTIPHOLUS of Ephesus, ⎰ twin brothers,
ANTIPHOLUS of Syracuse, ⎱ and sons to Ægeon and Æmilia.

DROMIO of Ephesus, ⎰ twin brothers, and
DROMIO of Syracuse, ⎱ attendants on the two Antipholuses.

BALTHAZAR, a merchant
ANGELO, a goldsmith.
First Merchant, friend to Antipholus of Syracuse.

Second Merchant, to whom Angelo is a debtor.
PINCH, a schoolmaster.

ÆMILIA, wife to Ægeon, an abbess at Ephesus.
ADRIANA, wife to Antipholus of Ephesus.
LUCIANA, her sister.
LUCE, servant to Adriana.
A Courtezan.

Gaoler, Officers, and other Attendants

SCENE : *Ephesus.*

ACT I.

Scene I. *A hall in the* Duke's *palace.*

Enter Duke, Ægeon, Gaoler, Officers, *and other* Attendants.

Æge. Proceed, Solinus, to procure my fall
And by the doom of death end woes and all.
Duke. Merchant of Syracuse, plead no
    more;
I am not partial to infringe our laws:
The enmity and discord which of late
Sprung from the rancorous outrage of your
    duke
To merchants, our well-dealing countrymen,
Who wanting guilders to redeem their lives
Have seal'd his rigorous statutes with their
    bloods,
Excludes all pity from our threatening looks.
For, since the mortal and intestine jars   11
'Twixt thy seditious countrymen and us,
It hath in solemn synods been decreed,
Both by the Syracusians and ourselves,
To admit no traffic to our adverse towns
Nay, more,
If any born at Ephesus be seen
At any Syracusian marts and fairs;
Again: if any Syracusian born
Come to the bay of Ephesus, he dies,   20
His goods confiscate to the duke's dispose,
Unless a thousand marks be levied,
To quit the penalty and to ransom him.
Thy substance, valued at the highest rate,
Cannot amount unto a hundred marks;
Therefore by law thou art condemned to die.
Æge. Yet this my comfort: when your
    words are done,
My woes end likewise with the evening sun.
Duke. Well, Syracusian, say in brief the
    cause   29
Why thou departed'st from thy native home
And for what cause thou camest to Ephesus.
Æge. A heavier task could not have been
    imposed
Than I to speak my griefs unspeakable:
Yet, that the world may witness that my end
Was wrought by nature, not by vile offence,
I'll utter what my sorrows give me leave.
In Syracusa was I born, and wed
Unto a woman, happy but for me,
And by me, had not our hap been bad.
With her I lived in joy; our wealth increased
By prosperous voyages I often made   41
To Epidamnum; till my factor's death
And the great care of goods at random left
Drew me from kind embracements of my
    spouse:
From whom my absence was not six months
    old
Before herself, almost at fainting under
The pleasing punishment that women bear,
Had made provision for her following me,
And soon and safe arrived where I was.
There had she not been long, but she became
A joyful mother of two goodly sons;   51
And, which was strange, the one so like the
    other,
As could not be distinguish'd but by names.
That very hour, and in the self-same inn,
A meaner woman was delivered
Of such a burden, male twins, both alike:

Those,—for their parents were exceeding
    poor,—
I bought and brought up to attend my sons.
My wife, not meanly proud of two such boys,
Made daily motions for our home return: 60
Unwilling I agreed. Alas! too soon,
We came aboard.
A league from Epidamnum had we sail'd,
Before the always wind-obeying deep
Gave any tragic instance of our harm:
But longer did we not retain much hope;
For what obscured light the heavens did grant
Did but convey unto our fearful minds
A doubtful warrant of immediate death;
Which though myself would gladly have em-
    braced,   70
Yet the incessant weepings of my wife,
Weeping before for what she saw must come,
And piteous plainings of the pretty babes,
That mourn'd for fashion, ignorant what to
    fear,
Forced me to seek delays for them and me.
And this it was, for other means was none:
The sailors sought for safety by our boat,
And left the ship, then sinking-ripe, to us:
My wife, more careful for the latter-born,
Had fasten'd him unto a small spare mast,   80
Such as seafaring men provide for storms;
To him one of the other twins was bound,
Whilst I had been like heedful of the other:
The children thus disposed, my wife and I,
Fixing our eyes on whom our care was fix'd,
Fasten'd ourselves at either end the mast;
And floating straight, obedient to the stream,
Was carried towards Corinth, as we thought.
At length the sun, gazing upon the earth,
Dispersed those vapors that offended us;   90
And, by the benefit of his wished light,
The seas wax'd calm, and we discovered
Two ships from far making amain to us,
Of Corinth that, of Epidaurus this:
But ere they came,—O, let me say no more!
Gather the sequel by that went before.
Duke. Nay, forward, old man; do not
    break off so;
For we may pity, though not pardon thee.
Æge. O, had the gods done so, I had not
    now
Worthily term'd them merciless to us!   100
For, ere the ships could meet by twice five
    leagues,
We were encounter'd by a mighty rock;
Which being violently borne upon,
Our helpful ship was splitted in the midst;
So that, in this unjust divorce of us,
Fortune had left to both of us alike
What to delight in, what to sorrow for.
Her part, poor soul! seeming as burdened
With lesser weight but not with lesser woe,
Was carried with more speed before the wind;
And in our sight they three were taken up   111
By fishermen of Corinth, as we thought.
At length, another ship had seized on us;
And, knowing whom it was their hap to save,
Gave healthful welcome to their shipwreck'd
    guests;
And would have reft the fishers of their prey,
Had not their bark been very slow of sail;
And therefore homeward did they bend their
    course.
Thus have you heard me sever'd from my
    bliss;

That by misfortunes was my life prolong'd,
To tell sad stories of my own mishaps.   121
    Duke. And for the sake of them thou sorrowest for,
Do me the favor to dilate at full
What hath befall'n of them and thee till now.
    Æge. My youngest boy, and yet my eldest care,
At eighteen years became inquisitive
After his brother : and importuned me
That his attendant—so his case was like,
Reft of his brother, but retain'd his name—
Might bear him company in the quest of him :
Whom whilst I labor'd of a love to see,   131
I hazarded the loss of whom I loved.
Five summers have I spent in furthest Greece,
Roaming clean through the bounds of Asia,
And, coasting homeward, came to Ephesus ;
Hopeless to find, yet loath to leave unsought
Or that or any place that harbors men.
But here must end the story of my life ;
And happy were I in my timely death,
Could all my travels warrant me they live.
    Duke. Hapless Ægeon, whom the fates have mark'd   141
To bear the extremity of dire mishap !
Now, trust me, were it not against our laws,
Against my crown, my oath, my dignity,
Which princes, would they, may not disannul,
My soul should sue as advocate for thee.
But, though thou art adjudged to the death
And passed sentence may not be recall'd
But to our honor's great disparagement,
Yet I will favor thee in what I can.   150
Therefore, merchant, I'll limit thee this day
To seek thy life by beneficial help :
Try all the friends thou hast in Ephesus ;
Beg thou, or borrow, to make up the sum,
And live ; if no, then thou art doom'd to die.
Gaoler, take him to thy custody.
    Gaol. I will, my lord.
    Æge. Hopeless and helpless doth Ægeon wend,
But to procrastinate his lifeless end. [*Exeunt.*

SCENE II. *The Mart.*

Enter ANTIPHOLUS *of Syracuse,* DROMIO *of Syracuse, and* First Merchant.

    First Mer. Therefore give out you are of Epidamnum,
Lest that your goods too soon be confiscate.
This very day a Syracusian merchant
Is apprehended for arrival here ;
And not being able to buy out his life
According to the statute of the town,
Dies ere the weary sun set in the west.
There is your money that I had to keep.
    Ant. S. Go bear it to the Centaur, where we host,
And stay there, Dromio, till I come to thee. 10
Within this hour it will be dinner-time :
Till that, I'll view the manners of the town,
Peruse the traders, gaze upon the buildings,
And then return and sleep within mine inn,
For with long travel I am stiff and weary.
Get thee away.
    Dro. S. Many a man would take you at your word,
And go indeed, having so good a mean. [*Exit.*
    Ant. S. A trusty villain, sir, that very oft,
When I am dull with care and melancholy, 20
Lightens my humor with his merry jests.

What, will you walk with me about the town,
And then go to my inn and dine with me ?
    First Mer. I am invited, sir, to certain merchants,
Of whom I hope to make much benefit ;
I crave your pardon. Soon at five o'clock,
Please you, I'll meet with you upon the mart
And afterward consort you till bed-time :
My present business calls me from you now.
    Ant. S. Farewell till then : I will go lose myself   30
And wander up and down to view the city.
    First Mer. Sir, I commend you to your own content.   [*Exit.*
    Ant. S. He that commends me to mine own content
Commends me to the thing I cannot get.
I to the world am like a drop of water
That in the ocean seeks another drop,
Who, falling there to find his fellow forth,
Unseen, inquisitive, confounds himself :
So I, to find a mother and a brother,
In quest of them, unhappy, lose myself.   40

Enter DROMIO *of Ephesus.*

Here comes the almanac of my true date.
What now ? how chance thou art return'd so soon ?
    Dro. E. Return'd so soon ! rather approach'd too late :
The capon burns, the pig falls from the spit,
The clock hath strucken twelve upon the bell ;
My mistress made it one upon my cheek :
She is so hot because the meat is cold ;
The meat is cold because you come not home ;
You come not home because you have no stomach ;
You have no stomach having broke your fast ;
But we that know what 'tis to fast and pray 51
Are penitent for your default to-day.
    Ant. S. Stop in your wind, sir : tell me this, I pray :
Where have you left the money that I gave you ?
    Dro. E. O,—sixpence, that I had o' Wednesday last
To pay the saddler for my mistress' crupper ?
The saddler had it, sir ; I kept it not.
    Ant. S. I am not in a sportive humor now :
Tell me, and dally not, where is the money ?
We being strangers here, how darest thou trust
So great a charge from thine own custody ? 61
    Dro. E. I pray you, jest, sir, as you sit at dinner :
I from my mistress come to you in post ;
If I return, I shall be post indeed,
For she will score your fault upon my pate.
Methinks your maw, like mine, should be your clock,
And strike you home without a messenger.
    Ant. S. Come, Dromio, come, these jests are out of season ;
Reserve them till a merrier hour than this.
Where is the gold I gave in charge to thee ? 70
    Dro. E. To me, sir ? why, you gave no gold to me.
    Ant. S. Come on, sir knave, have done your foolishness,
And tell me how thou hast disposed thy charge.
    Dro. E. My charge was but to fetch you from the mart

Home to your house, the Phœnix, sir, to
  dinner :
My mistress and her sister stays for you.
  Ant. S. Now, as I am a Christian, answer
  me
In what safe place you have bestow'd my
  money,
Or I shall break that merry sconce of yours
That stands on tricks when I am undis-
  posed :   80
Where is the thousand marks thou hadst of
  me ?
  Dro. E. I have some marks of yours upon
  my pate,
Some of my mistress' marks upon my shoulders,
But not a thousand marks between you both.
If I should pay your worship those again,
Perchance you will not bear them patiently.
  Ant. S. Thy mistress' marks ? what mis-
  tress, slave, hast thou ?
  Dro. E. Your worship's wife, my mistress
  at the Phœnix ;
She that doth fast till you come home to
  dinner,
And prays that you will hie you home to
  dinner.
  Ant. S. What, wilt thou flout me thus unto
  my face,   91
Being forbid ? There, take you that, sir knave.
  Dro. E. What mean you, sir ? for God's
  sake, hold your hands !
Nay, and you will not, sir, I'll take my heels.
                         [*Exit.*
  Ant. S. Upon my life, by some device or
  other
The villain is o'er-raught of all my money.
They say this town is full of cozenage,
As, nimble jugglers that deceive the eye,
Dark-working sorcerers that change the mind,
Soul-killing witches that deform the body, 100
Disguised cheaters, prating mountebanks,
And many such-like liberties of sin :
If it prove so, I will be gone the sooner.
I'll to the Centaur, to go seek this slave :
I greatly fear my money is not safe. [*Exit.*

ACT II.

Scene I. *The house of* Antipholus *of*
Ephesus.

Enter Adriana *and* Luciana.

  Adr. Neither my husband nor the slave re-
  turn'd,
That in such haste I sent to seek his master !
Sure, Luciana, it is two o'clock.
  Luc. Perhaps some merchant hath invited
  him,
And from the mart he's somewhere gone to
  dinner.
Good sister, let us dine and never fret :
A man is master of his liberty :
Time is their master, and, when they see time,
They'll go or come : if so, be patient, sister.
  Adr. Why should their liberty than ours be
  more ?   10
  Luc. Because their business still lies out o'
  door.
  Adr. Look, when I serve him so, he takes
  it ill.
  Luc. O, know he is the bridle of your will.

  Adr. There's none but asses will be bridled
  so.
  Luc. Why, headstrong liberty is lash'd with
  woe.
There's nothing situate under heaven's eye
But hath his bound, in earth, in sea, in sky :
The beasts, the fishes, and the winged fowls,
Are their males' subjects and at their controls:
Men, more divine, the masters of all these, 20
Lords of the wide world and wild watery seas,
Indued with intellectual sense and souls,
Of more pre-eminence than fish and fowls,
Are masters to their females, and their lords :
Then let your will attend on their accords.
  Adr. This servitude makes you to keep
  unwed.
  Luc. Not this, but troubles of the marriage-
  bed.
  Adr. But, were you wedded, you would
  bear some sway.
  Luc. Ere I learn love, I'll practise to obey.
  Adr. How if your husband start some other
  where ?   30
  Luc. Till he come home again, I would
  forbear.
  Adr. Patience unmoved ! no marvel though
  she pause ;
They can be meek that have no other cause.
A wretched soul, bruised with adversity,
We bid be quiet when we hear it cry ;
But were we burden'd with like weight of pain,
As much or more we should ourselves com-
  plain :
So thou, that hast no unkind mate to grieve
  thee,
With urging helpless patience wouldst relieve
  me ;
But, if thou live to see like right bereft, 40
This fool-begg'd patience in thee will be left.
  Luc. Well, I will marry one day, but to try.
Here comes your man ; now is your husband
  nigh.

Enter Dromio *of Ephesus.*

  Adr. Say, is your tardy master now at
  hand ?
  Dro. E. Nay, he's at two hands with me,
and that my two ears can witness.
  Adr. Say, didst thou speak with him ?
  know'st thou his mind ?
  Dro. E. Ay, ay, he told his mind upon
  mine ear :
Beshrew his hand, I scarce could understand it.
  Luc. Spake he so doubtfully, thou couldst
not feel his meaning ?   51
  Dro. E. Nay, he struck so plainly, I could
too well feel his blows ; and withal so doubt-
fully that I could scarce understand them.
  Adr. But say, I prithee, is he coming
home ? It seems he hath great care to please
his wife.
  Dro. E. Why, mistress, sure my master is
horn-mad.
  Adr. Horn-mad, thou villain !
  Dro. E.   I mean not cuckold-mad ;
But, sure, he is stark mad.
When I desired him to come home to dinner,
He ask'd me for a thousand marks in gold :
' 'Tis dinner-time,' quoth I ; ' My gold ! ' quoth
  he :
' Your meat doth burn,' quoth I ; ' My gold ! '
  quoth he :

'Will you come home?' quoth I; 'My gold!'
    quoth he.
'Where is the thousand marks I gave thee,
    villain?'
'The pig,' quoth I, 'is burn'd;' 'My gold!'
    quoth he:
'My mistress, sir,' quoth I; 'Hang up thy
    mistress!
I know not thy mistress; out on thy mistress!'
  Luc. Quoth who?
  Dro. E. Quoth my master: 70
'I know,' quoth he, 'no house, no wife, no
    mistress.'
So that my errand, due unto my tongue,
I thank him, I bare home upon my shoulders;
For, in conclusion, he did beat me there.
  Adr. Go back again, thou slave, and fetch
    him home.
  Dro. E. Go back again, and be new beaten
    home?
For God's sake, send some other messenger.
  Adr. Back, slave, or I will break thy pate
    across.
  Dro. E. And he will bless that cross with
    other beating:
Between you I shall have a holy head.   80
  Adr. Hence, prating peasant! fetch thy
    master home.
  Dro. E. Am I so round with you as you
    with me,
That like a football you do spurn me thus?
You spurn me hence, and he will spurn me
    hither:
If I last in this service, you must case me in
    leather.   [*Exit.*
  Luc. Fie, how impatience loureth in your
    face!
  Adr. His company must do his minions
    grace,
Whilst I at home starve for a merry look.
Hath homely age the alluring beauty took
From my poor cheek? then he hath wasted it:
Are my discourses dull? barren my wit?   91
If voluble and sharp discourse be marr'd,
Unkindness blunts it more than marble hard:
Do their gay vestments his affections bait?
That's not my fault: he's master of my state:
What ruins are in me that can be found,
By him not ruin'd? then is he the ground
Of my defeatures. My decayed fair
A sunny look of his would soon repair:
But, too unruly deer, he breaks the pale   100
And feeds from home; poor I am but his stale.
  Luc. Self-harming jealousy! fie, beat it
    hence!
  Adr. Unfeeling fools can with such wrongs
    dispense.
I know his eye doth homage otherwhere;
Or else what lets it but he would be here?
Sister, you know he promised me a chain;
Would that alone, alone he would detain,
So he would keep fair quarter with his bed!
I see the jewel best enamelled
Will lose his beauty; yet the gold bides still,
That others touch, and often touching will   111
Wear gold: and no man that hath a name,
By falsehood and corruption doth it shame.
Since that my beauty cannot please his eye,
I'll weep what's left away, and weeping die.
  Luc. How many fond fools serve mad jeal-
    ousy!   [*Exeunt.*

SCENE II. *A public place.*

Enter ANTIPHOLUS *of Syracuse.*

  Ant. S. The gold I gave to Dromio is laid
    up
Safe at the Centaur; and the heedful slave
Is wander'd forth, in care to seek me out
By computation and mine host's report.
I could not speak with Dromio since at first
I sent him from the mart. See, here he comes.

Enter DROMIO *of Syracuse.*

How now, sir! is your merry humor alter'd?
As you love strokes, so jest with me again.
You know no Centaur? you received no gold?
Your mistress sent to have me home to dinner?
My house was at the Phœnix? Wast thou
    mad,   11
That thus so madly thou didst answer me?
  Dro. S. What answer, sir? when spake I
    such a word?
  Ant. S. Even now, even here, not half an
    hour since.
  Dro. S. I did not see you since you sent
    me hence,
Home to the Centaur, with the gold you gave
    me.
  Ant. S. Villain, thou didst deny the gold's
    receipt,
And told'st me of a mistress and a dinner;
For which, I hope, thou felt'st I was displeased.
  Dro. S. I am glad to see you in this merry
    vein: 20
What means this jest? I pray you, master, tell
    me.
  Ant. S. Yea, dost thou jeer and flout me in
    the teeth?
Think'st thou I jest? Hold, take thou that, and
    that.   [*Beating him.*
  Dro. S. Hold, sir, for God's sake! now
    your jest is earnest:
Upon what bargain do you give it me?
  Ant. S. Because that I familiarly sometimes
Do use you for my fool and chat with you,
Your sauciness will jest upon my love
And make a common of my serious hours.
When the sun shines let foolish gnats make
    sport,   30
But creep in crannies when he hides his beams.
If you will jest with me, know my aspect,
And fashion your demeanor to my looks,
Or I will beat this method in your sconce.
  Dro. S. Sconce call you it? so you would
leave battering, I had rather have it a head:
an you use these blows long, I must get a
sconce for my head and insconce it too; or
else I shall seek my wit in my shoulders. But,
I pray, sir, why am I beaten?   40
  Ant. S. Dost thou not know?
  Dro. S. Nothing, sir, but that I am beaten.
  Ant. S. Shall I tell you why?
  Dro. S. Ay, sir, and wherefore; for they
say every why hath a wherefore.
  Ant. S. Why, first,—for flouting me; and
    then, wherefore,—
For urging it the second time to me.
  Dro. S. Was there ever any man thus
    beaten out of season,
When in the why and the wherefore is neither
    rhyme nor reason?
Well, sir, I thank you.   50
  Ant. S. Thank me, sir, for what?

Dro. S. Marry, sir, for this something that
you gave me for nothing.
Ant. S. I'll make you amends next, to give
you nothing for something. But say, sir, is it
dinner-time ?
Dro. S. No, sir ; I think the meat wants
that I have.
Ant. S. In good time, sir ; what's that ?
Dro. S. Basting.
Ant. S. Well, sir, then 'twill be dry.   60
Dro. S. If it be, sir, I pray you, eat none
of it.
Ant. S. Your reason ?
Dro. S. Lest it make you choleric and pur-
chase me another dry basting.
Ant. S. Well, sir, learn to jest in good time:
there's a time for all things.
Dro. S. I durst have denied that, before
you were so choleric.
Ant. S. By what rule, sir ?
Dro. S. Marry, sir, by a rule as plain as
the plain bald pate of father Time himself.   71
Ant. S. Let's hear it.
Dro. S. There's no time for a man to re-
cover his hair that grows bald by nature.
Ant. S. May he not do it by fine and recovery ?
Dro. S. Yes, to pay a fine for a periwig and
recover the lost hair of another man.
Ant. S. Why is Time such a niggard of
hair, being, as it is, so plentiful an excrement ?
Dro. S. Because it is a blessing that he be-
stows on beasts ; and what he hath scanted
men in hair he hath given them in wit.   80
Ant. S. Why, but there's many a man hath
more hair than wit.
Dro. S. Not a man of those but he hath
the wit to lose his hair.
Ant. S. Why, thou didst conclude hairy
men plain dealers without wit.
Dro. S. The plainer dealer, the sooner lost:
yet he loseth it in a kind of jollity.   90
Ant. S. For what reason ?
Dro. S. For two ; and sound ones too.
Ant. S. Nay, not sound, I pray you.
Dro. S. Sure ones, then.
Ant. S. Nay, not sure, in a thing falsing.
Dro. S. Certain ones then.
Ant. S. Name them.
Dro. S. The one, to save the money that
he spends in trimming ; the other, that at din-
ner they should not drop in his porridge.
Ant. S. You would all this time have
proved there is no time for all things.   101
Dro. S. Marry, and did, sir ; namely, no
time to recover hair lost by nature.
Ant. S. But your reason was not substan-
tial, why there is no time to recover.
Dro. S. Thus I mend it : Time himself is
bald and therefore to the world's end will have
bald followers.
Ant. S. I knew 'twould be a bald conclusion :   110
But, soft ! who wafts us yonder ?

Enter ADRIANA *and* LUCIANA.

Adr. Ay, ay, Antipholus, look strange and
frown :
Some other mistress hath thy sweet aspects ;
I am not Adriana nor thy wife.
The time was once when thou unurged wouldst
vow

That never words were music to thine ear,
That never object pleasing in thine eye,
That never touch well welcome to thy hand,
That never meat sweet-savor'd in thy taste,
Unless I spake, or look'd, or touch'd, or carved
to thee.   120
How comes it now, my husband, O, how comes
it,
That thou art thus estranged from thyself ?
Thyself I call it, being strange to me,
That, undividable, incorporate,
Am better than thy dear self's better part.
Ah, do not tear away thyself from me !
For know, my love, as easy mayst thou fall
A drop of water in the breaking gulf,
And take unmingled thence that drop again,
Without addition or diminishing,   130
As take from me thyself and not me too.
How dearly would it touch thee to the quick,
Shouldst thou but hear I were licentious
And that this body, consecrate to thee,
By ruffian lust should be contaminate !
Wouldst thou not spit at me and spurn at me
And hurl the name of husband in my face
And tear the stain'd skin off my harlot-brow
And from my false hand cut the wedding-ring
And break it with a deep-divorcing vow ?   140
I know thou canst ; and therefore see thou do
it.
I am possess'd with an adulterate blot ;
My blood is mingled with the crime of lust :
For if we two be one and thou play false,
I do digest the poison of thy flesh,
Being strumpeted by thy contagion.
Keep then fair league and truce with thy true
bed ;
I live unstain'd, thou undishonored.
Ant. S. Plead you to me, fair dame ? I
know you not :
In Ephesus I am but two hours old,   150
As strange unto your town as to your talk ;
Who, every word by all my wit being scann'd,
Want wit in all one word to understand.
Luc. Fie, brother! how the world is
changed with you !
When were you wont to use my sister thus ?
She sent for you by Dromio home to dinner.
Ant. S. By Dromio ?
Dro. S. By me ?
Adr. By thee ; and this thou didst return
from him,   160
That he did buffet thee, and, in his blows,
Denied my house for his, me for his wife.
Ant. S. Did you converse, sir, with this
gentlewoman ?
What is the course and drift of your compact?
Dro. S. I, sir ? I never saw her till this
time.
Ant. S. Villain, thou liest ; for even her
very words
Didst thou deliver to me on the mart.
Dro. S. I never spake with her in all my
life.
Ant. S. How can she thus then call us by
our names,
Unless it be by inspiration.   169
Adr. How ill agrees it with your gravity
To counterfeit thus grossly with your slave,
Abetting him to thwart me in my mood !
Be it my wrong you are from me exempt,
But wrong not that wrong with a more con-
tempt.

Come, I will fasten on this sleeve of thine :
Thou art an elm, my husband, I a vine,
Whose weakness, married to thy stronger state,
Makes me with thy strength to communicate :
If aught possess thee from me, it is dross,
Usurping ivy, brier, or idle moss ;   180
Who, all for want of pruning, with intrusion
Infect thy sap and live on thy confusion.

   Ant. S. To me she speaks ; she moves me
     for her theme :
What, was I married to her in my dream ?
Or sleep I now and think I hear all this ?
What error drives our eyes and ears amiss ?
Until I know this sure uncertainty,
I'll entertain the offer'd fallacy.

   Luc. Dromio, go bid the servants spread
     for dinner.

   Dro. S. O, for my beads ! I cross me for a
     sinner.   190
This is the fairy land : O spite of spites !
We talk with goblins, owls and sprites :
If we obey them not, this will ensue,
They'll suck our breath, or pinch us black and
     blue.

   Luc. Why pratest thou to thyself and an-
     swer'st not ?
Dromio, thou drone, thou snail, thou slug,
     thou sot !

   Dro. S. I am transformed, master, am I
     not ?

   Ant. S. I think thou art in mind, and so
     am I.

   Dro. S. Nay, master, both in mind and in
     my shape.

   Ant. S. Thou hast thine own form.

   Dro. S.   No, I am an ape. 200

   Luc. If thou art changed to aught, 'tis to
     an ass.

   Dro. S. 'Tis true ; she rides me and I long
     for grass.
'Tis so, I am an ass ; else it could never be
But I should know her as well as she knows
     me.

   Adr. Come, come, no longer will I be a
     fool,
To put the finger in the eye and weep,
Whilst man and master laugh my woes to
     scorn.
Come, sir, to dinner. Dromio, keep the gate.
Husband, I'll dine above with you to-day
And shrive you of a thousand idle pranks. 210
Sirrah, if any ask you for your master,
Say he dines forth, and let no creature enter.
Come, sister. Dromio, play the porter well.

   Ant. S. Am I in earth, in heaven, or in
     hell ?
Sleeping or waking ? mad or well-advised ?
Known unto these, and to myself disguised !
I'll say as they say and persever so,
And in this mist at all adventures go.

   Dro. S. Master, shall I be porter at the
     gate ?

   Adr. Ay; and let none enter, lest I break
     your pate.   220

   Luc. Come, come, Antipholus, we dine too
     late.   [*Exeunt.*

ACT III.

SCENE I. *Before the house of* ANTIPHOLUS
of Ephesus.

Enter ANTIPHOLUS *of* Ephesus, DROMIO *of*
Ephesus, ANGELO, *and* BALTHAZAR.

   Ant. E. Good Signior Angelo, you must ex
     cuse us all ;
My wife is shrewish when I keep not hours :
Say that I linger'd with you at your shop
To see the making of her carcanet,
And that to-morrow you will bring it home.
But here's a villain that would face me down
He met me on the mart, and that I beat him,
And charged him with a thousand marks in
     gold,
And that I did deny my wife and house.
Thou drunkard, thou, what didst thou mean
     by this ?   10

   Dro. E. Say what you will, sir, but I know
     what I know ;
That you beat me at the mart, I have your
     hand to show :
If the skin were parchment, and the blows you
     gave were ink,
Your own handwriting would tell you what I
     think.

   Ant. E. I think thou art an ass.

   Dro. E.   Marry, so it doth appear
By the wrongs I suffer and the blows I bear.
I should kick, being kick'd ; and, being at that
     pass,
You would keep from my heels and beware of
     an ass.

   Ant. E. You're sad, Signior Balthazar :
     pray God our cheer
May answer my good will and your good wel-
     come here.   20

   Bal. I hold your dainties cheap, sir, and
     your welcome dear.

   Ant. E. O, Signior Balthazar, either at flesh
     or fish,
A table full of welcome make scarce one
     dainty dish.

   Bal. Good meat, sir, is common ; that
     every churl affords.

   Ant. E. And welcome more common ; for
     that's nothing but words.

   Bal. Small cheer and great welcome makes
     a merry feast.

   Ant. E. Ay, to a niggardly host, and more
     sparing guest :
But though my cates be mean, take them in
     good part ;
Better cheer may you have, but not with better
     heart.
But, soft ! my door is lock'd. Go bid them let
     us in.   30

   Dro. E. Maud, Bridget, Marian, Cicel,
     Gillian, Ginn !

   Dro. S. [*Within*] Mome, malt-horse, ca-
     pon, coxcomb, idiot, patch !
Either get thee from the door, or sit down at
     the hatch.
Dost thou conjure for wenches, that thou
     call'st for such store,
When one is one too many ? Go, get thee from
     the door.

   Dro. E. What patch is made our porter ?
     My master stays in the street.

   Dro. S. [*Within*] Let him walk from
     whence he came, lest he catch cold
     on's feet.

   Ant. E. Who talks within there ? ho, open
     the door !

Dro. S. [*Within*] Right, sir ; I'll tell you
    when, an you'll tell me wherefore.
Ant. E. Wherefore ? for my dinner : I have
    not dined to-day.   40
Dro. S. [*Within*] Nor to-day here you must
    not ; come again when you may.
Ant. E. What art thou that keepest me out
    from the house I owe ?
Dro. S. [*Within*] The porter for this time,
    sir, and my name is Dromio.
Dro. E. O villain ! thou hast stolen both
    mine office and my name.
The one ne'er got me credit, the other mickle
    blame.
If thou hadst been Dromio to-day in my place,
Thou wouldst have changed thy face for a
    name or thy name for an ass.
Luce. [*Within*] What a coil is there, Dro-
    mio ? who are those at the gate ?
Dro. E. Let my master in, Luce.
Luce. [*Within*] Faith, no ; he comes too
    late ;
And so tell your master.
Dro. E.   O Lord, I must laugh !
Have at you with a proverb—Shall I set in my
    staff ?
Luce. [*Within*] Have at you with another ;
    that's—When ? can you tell ?
Dro. S. [*Within*] If thy name be call'd
    Luce,—Luce, thou hast answered him
    well.
Ant. E. Do you hear, you minion ? you'll
    let us in, I hope ?
Luce. [*Within*] I thought to have asked
    you.
Dro. S. [*Within*] And you said no.
Dro. E. So, come, help : well struck ! there
    was blow for blow.
Ant. E. Thou baggage, let me in.
Luce. [*Within*] Can you tell for whose
    sake ?
Dro. E. Master, knock the door hard.
Luce. [*Within*] Let him knock till it ache.
Ant. E. You'll cry for this, minion, if I
    beat the door down.
Luce. [*Within*] What needs all that, and a
    pair of stocks in the town ?   60
Adr. [*Within*] Who is that at the door
    that keeps all this noise ?
Dro. S. [*Within*] By my troth, your town
    is troubled with unruly boys.
Ant. E. Are you there, wife ? you might
    have come before.
Adr. [*Within*] Your wife, sir knave ! go
    get you from the door.
Dro. E. If you went in pain, master, this
    ' knave ' would go sore.
Ang. Here is neither cheer, sir, nor wel-
    come : we would fain have either.
Bal. In debating which was best, we shall
    part with neither.
Dro. E. They stand at the door, master ;
    bid them welcome hither.
Ant. E. There is something in the wind,
    that we cannot get in.
Dro. E. You would say so, master, if your
    garments were thin.   70
Our cake there is warm within ; you stand
    here in the cold :
would make a man mad as a buck, to be so
    bought and sold.

Ant. E. Go fetch me something : I'll break
    ope the gate.
Dro. S. [*Within*] Break any breaking here,
    and I'll break your knave's pate.
Dro. E. A man may break a word with
    you, sir, and words are but wind,
Ay, and break it in your face, so he break it
    not behind.
Dro. S. [*Within*] It seems thou want'st
    breaking : out upon thee, hind !
Dro. E. Here's too much ' out upon thee ! '
    I pray thee, let me in.
Dro. S. [*Within*] Ay, when fowls have no
    feathers and fish have no fin.
Ant. E. Well, I'll break in : go borrow me
    a crow.   80
Dro. S. A crow without feather ? Master,
    mean you so ?
For a fish without a fin, there's a fowl without
    a feather :
If a crow help us in, sirrah, we'll pluck a crow
    together.
Ant. E. Go get thee gone ; fetch me an
    iron crow.
Bal. Have patience, sir ; O, let it not be
    so !
Herein you war against your reputation
And draw within the compass of suspect
The unviolated honor of your wife.
Once this,—your long experience of her wis-
    dom,
Her sober virtue, years and modesty,   90
Plead on her part some cause to you un-
    known ;
And doubt not, sir, but she will well excuse
Why at this time the doors are made against
    you.
Be ruled by me : depart in patience,
And let us to the Tiger all to dinner,
And about evening come yourself alone
To know the reason of this strange restraint.
If by strong hand you offer to break in
Now in the stirring passage of the day,
A vulgar comment will be made of it,   100
And that supposed by the common rout
Against your yet ungalled estimation
That may with foul intrusion enter in
And dwell upon your grave when you are
    dead ;
For slander lives upon succession,
For ever housed where it gets possession.
Ant. E. You have prevail'd : I will depart
    in quiet,
And, in despite of mirth, mean to be merry.
I know a wench of excellent discourse,   109
Pretty and witty ; wild, and yet, too, gentle :
There will we dine. This woman that I mean,
My wife—but, I protest, without desert—
Hath oftentimes upbraided me withal :
To her will we to dinner. [*To Ang.*] Get
    you home
And fetch the chain ; by this I know 'tis
    made :
Bring it, I pray you, to the Porpentine ;
For there's the house : that chain will I be-
    stow—
Be it for nothing but to spite my wife—
Upon mine hostess there : good sir, make
    haste.
Since mine own doors refuse to entertain me,
I'll knock elsewhere, to see if they'll disdain
    me.   121

Ang. I'll meet you at that place some hour hence.

Ant. E. Do so. This jest shall cost me some expense. [*Exeunt.*

SCENE II. *The same.*

Enter LUCIANA *and* ANTIPHOLUS *of Syracuse.*

Luc. And may it be that you have quite forgot
A husband's office? shall, Antipholus.
Even in the spring of love, thy love-springs rot?
Shall love, in building, grow so ruinous?
If you did wed my sister for her wealth,
Then for her wealth's sake use her with more kindness:
Or if you like elsewhere, do it by stealth;
Muffle your false love with some show of blindness:
Let not my sister read it in your eye;
Be not thy tongue thy own shame's orator;
Look sweet, speak fair, become disloyalty; 11
Apparel vice like virtue's harbinger;
Bear a fair presence, though your heart be tainted;
Teach sin the carriage of a holy saint;
Be secret-false: what need she be acquainted?
What simple thief brags of his own attaint?
'Tis double wrong, to truant with your bed
And let her read it in thy looks at board:
Shame hath a bastard fame, well managed;
Ill deeds are doubled with an evil word. 20
Alas, poor women! make us but believe,
Being compact of credit, that you love us;
Though others have the arm, show us the sleeve;
We in your motion turn and you may move us.
Then, gentle brother, get you in again;
Comfort my sister, cheer her, call her wife:
'Tis holy sport to be a little vain,
When the sweet breath of flattery conquers strife.

Ant. S. Sweet mistress,—what your name is else, I know not,
Nor by what wonder you do hit of mine,—
Less in your knowledge and your grace you show not 31
Than our earth's wonder, more than earth divine.
Teach me, dear creature, how to think and speak;
Lay open to my earthy-gross conceit,
Smother'd in errors, feeble, shallow, weak,
The folded meaning of your words' deceit.
Against my soul's pure truth why labor you
To make it wander in an unknown field?
Are you a god? would you create me new?
Transform me then, and to your power I'll yield. 40
But if that I am I, then well I know
Your weeping sister is no wife of mine,
Nor to her bed no homage do I owe:
Far more, far more to you do I decline.
O, train me not, sweet mermaid, with thy note,
To drown me in thy sister's flood of tears:
Sing, siren, for thyself and I will dote:
Spread o'er the silver waves thy golden hairs,
And as a bed I'll take them and there lie,
And in that glorious supposition think 50

He gains by death that hath such means to dio:
Let Love, being light, be drowned if she sink!

Luc. What, are you mad, that you do reason so?

Ant. S. Not mad, but mated; how, I do not know.

Luc. It is a fault that springeth from your eye.

Ant. S. For gazing on your beams, fair sun, being by.

Luc. Gaze where you should, and that will clear your sight.

Ant. S. As good to wink, sweet love, as look on night.

Luc. Why call you me love? call my sister so.

Ant. S. Thy sister's sister.

Luc. That's my sister.

Ant. S. No; 60
It is thyself, mine own self's better part,
Mine eye's clear eye, my dear heart's dearer heart,
My food, my fortune and my sweet hope's aim,
My sole earth's heaven and my heaven's claim.

Luc. All this my sister is, or else should be.

Ant. S. Call thyself sister, sweet, for I am thee.
Thee will I love and with thee lead my life:
Thou hast no husband yet nor I no wife.
Give me thy hand.

Luc. O, soft, sir! hold you still: 69
I'll fetch my sister, to get her good will. [*Exit.*

Enter DROMIO *of Syracuse.*

Ant. S. Why, how now, Dromio! where runn'st thou so fast?

Dro. S. Do you know me, sir? am I Dromio? am I your man? am I myself?

Ant. S. Thou art Dromio, thou art my man, thou art thyself.

Dro. S. I am an ass, I am a woman's man and besides myself.

Ant. S. What woman's man? and how besides thyself? 80

Dro. S. Marry, sir, besides myself, I am due to a woman; one that claims me, one that haunts me, one that will have me.

Ant. S. What claim lays she to thee?

Dro. S. Marry, sir, such claim as you would lay to your horse; and she would have me as a beast: not that, I being a beast, she would have me; but that she, being a very beastly creature, lays claim to me.

Ant. S. What is she? 90

Dro. S. A very reverent body; ay, such a one as a man may not speak of without he say 'Sir-reverence.' I have but lean luck in the match, and yet is she a wondrous fat marriage.

Ant. S. How dost thou mean a fat marriage?

Dro. S. Marry, sir, she's the kitchen wench and all grease; and I know not what use to put her to but to make a lamp of her and run from her by her own light. I warrant, her rags and the tallow in them will burn a Poland winter: if she lives till doomsday, she'll burn a week longer than the whole world.

Ant. S. What complexion is she of?

Dro. S. Swart, like my shoe, but her face

nothing like so clean kept : for why, she
sweats ; a man may go over shoes in the grime
of it.

Ant. S.   That's a fault that water will mend.

Dro. S.   No, sir, 'tis in grain ; Noah's flood
could not do it.

Ant. S.   What's her name ?   110

Dro. S.   Nell, sir ; but her name and three
quarters, that's an ell and three quarters, will
not measure her from hip to hip.

Ant. S.   Then she bears some breadth ?

Dro. S.   No longer from head to foot than
from hip to hip : she is spherical, like a globe ;
I could find out countries in her.

Ant. S.   In what part of her body stands
Ireland ?   120

Dro. S.   Marry, sir, in her buttocks : I
found it out by the bogs.

Ant. S.   Where Scotland ?

Dro. S.   I found it by the barrenness ; hard
in the palm of the hand.

Ant. S.   Where France ?

Dro. S.   In her forehead ; armed and reverted, making war against her heir.

Ant. S.   Where England ?

Dro. S.   I looked for the chalky cliffs, but I
could find no whiteness in them ; but I guess
it stood in her chin, by the salt rheum that
ran between France and it.

Ant. S.   Where Spain ?

Dro. S.   Faith, I saw it not ; but I felt it
hot in her breath.

Ant. S.   Where America, the Indies ?

Dro. S.   Oh, sir, upon her nose, all o'er
embellished with rubies, carbuncles, sapphires,
declining their rich aspect to the hot breath of
Spain ; who sent whole armadoes of caracks
to be ballast at her nose.   141

Ant. S.   Where stood Belgia, the Nether-
lands ?

Dro. S.   Oh, sir, I did not look so low. To
conclude, this drudge, or diviner, laid claim to
me ; called me Dromio ; swore I was assured
to her ; told me what privy marks I had about
me, as, the mark of my shoulder, the mole in
my neck, the great wart on my left arm, that
I amazed ran from her as a witch :
And, I think, if my breast had not been made
of faith and my heart of steel,   150
she had transform'd me to a curtal dog and
made me turn i' the wheel.

Ant. S.   Go hie thee presently, post to the
road :
An if the wind blow any way from shore,
will not harbor in this town to-night :
If any bark put forth, come to the mart,
Where I will walk till thou return to me.
If every one knows us and we know none,
'Tis time, I think, to trudge, pack and be gone.

Dro. S.   As from a bear a man would run
for life,
So fly I from her that would be my wife. [*Exit.*

Ant. S.   There's none but witches do in-
habit here ;   161
And therefore 'tis high time that I were hence.
She that doth call me husband, even my soul
Doth for a wife abhor. But her fair sister,
Possess'd with such a gentle sovereign grace,
Of such enchanting presence and discourse,
Hath almost made me traitor to myself :
But, lest myself be guilty to self-wrong,
I'll stop mine ears against the mermaid's song.

Enter ANGELO *with the chain.*

Ang.   Master Antipholus,—

Ant. S.   Ay, that's my name.   170

Ang.   I know it well, sir, lo, here is the
chain.
I thought to have ta'en you at the Porpentine :
The chain unfinish'd made me stay thus long.

Ant. S.   What is your will that I shall do
with this ?

Ang.   What please yourself, sir : I have
made it for you.

Ant. S.   Made it for me, sir ! I bespoke it
not.

Ang.   Not once, nor twice, but twenty times
you have.
Go home with it and please your wife withal ;
And soon at supper-time I'll visit you
Ant then receive my money for the chain.   180

Ant. S.   I pray you, sir, receive the money
now,
For fear you ne'er see chain nor money more.

Ang.   You are a merry man, sir : fare you
well.   [*Exit.*

Ant. S.   What I should think of this, I can-
not tell :
But this I think, there's no man is so vain
That would refuse so fair an offer'd chain.
I see a man here needs not live by shifts,
When in the streets he meets such golden gifts.
I'll to the mart, and there for Dromio stay :
If any ship put out, then straight away. [*Exit.*

ACT IV.

SCENE I. *A public place.*

Enter Second Merchant, ANGELO, *and an*
Officer.

Sec. Mer.   You know since Pentecost the
sum is due,
And since I have not much importuned you ;
Nor now I had not, but that I am bound
To Persia, and want guilders for my voyage :
Therefore make present satisfaction,
Or I'll attach you by this officer.

Ang.   Even just the sum that I do owe to
you
Is growing to me by Antipholus,
And in the instant that I met with you
He had of me a chain : at five o'clock   10
I shall receive the money for the same.
Pleaseth you walk with me down to his house,
I will discharge my bond and thank you too.

Enter ANTIPHOLUS *of Ephesus and* DROMIO
of Ephesus from the courtezan's.

Off.   That labor may you save : see where
he comes.

Ant. E.   While I go to the goldsmith's
house, go thou
And buy a rope's end : that will I bestow
Among my wife and her confederates,
For locking me out of my doors by day.
But, soft ! I see the goldsmith. Get thee gone ;
Buy thou a rope and bring it home to me.   20

Dro. E.   I buy a thousand pound a year : I
buy a rope.   [*Exit.*

Ant. E.   A man is well holp up that trusts
to you :
I promised your presence and the chain ;

But neither chain nor goldsmith came to me.
Belike you thought our love would last too
 long,
If it were chain'd together, and therefore came
 not.

Ang. Saving your merry humor, here's the
 note
How much your chain weighs to the utmost
 carat,
The fineness of the gold and chargeful fashion.
Which doth amount to three odd ducats more
Than I stand debted to this gentleman : 31
I pray you, see him presently discharged,
For he is bound to sea and stays but for it.

Ant. E. I am not furnish'd with the present
 money ;
Besides, I have some business in the town.
Good signior, take the stranger to my house
And with you take the chain and bid my wife
Disburse the sum on the receipt thereof :
Perchance I will be there as soon as you.

Ang. Then you will bring the chain to her
 yourself ? 40

Ant. E. No ; bear it with you, lest I come
 not time enough.

Ang. Well, sir, I will. Have you the chain
 about you ?

Ant. E. An if I have not, sir, I hope you
 have ;
Or else you may return without your money.

Ang. Nay, come, I pray you, sir, give me
 the chain :
Both wind and tide stays for this gentleman,
And I, to blame, have held him here too long.

Ant. E. Good Lord ! you use this dalliance
 to excuse
Your breach of promise to the Porpentine.
I should have chid you for not bringing it, 50
But, like a shrew, you first begin to brawl.

Sec. Mer. The hour steals on ; I pray you,
 sir, dispatch.

Ang. You hear how he importunes me ;—
 the chain !

Ant. E. Why, give it to my wife and fetch
 your money.

Ang. Come, come, you know I gave it you
 even now.
Either send the chain or send me by some
 token.

Ant. E. Fie, now you run this humor out
 of breath,
Come, where's the chain ? I pray you, let me
 see it.

Sec. Mer. My business cannot brook this
 dalliance.
Good sir, say whether you'll answer me or
 no : 60
If not, I'll leave him to the officer.

Ant. E. I answer you ! what should I answer you ?

Ang. The money that you owe me for the
 chain.

Ant. E. I owe you none till I receive the
 chain.

Ang. You know I gave it you half an hour
 since.

Ant. E. You gave me none : you wrong
 me much to say so.

Ang. You wrong me more, sir, in denying
 it :
Consider how it stands upon my credit.

Sec. Mer. Well, officer, arrest him at my
 suit.

Off. I do ; and charge you in the duke's
 name to obey me. 70

Ang. This touches me in reputation.
Either consent to pay this sum for me
Or I attach you by this officer.

Ant. E. Consent to pay thee that I never
 had !
Arrest me, foolish fellow, if thou darest.

Ang. Here is thy fee ; arrest him, officer,
I would not spare my brother in this case,
If he should scorn me so apparently.

Off. I do arrest you, sir : you hear the suit.

Ant. E. I do obey thee till I give thee bail.
But, sirrah, you shall buy this sport as dear 81
As all the metal in your shop will answer.

Ang. Sir, sir, I shall have law in Ephesus,
To your notorious shame ; I doubt it not.

Enter DROMIO *of Syracuse, from the bay.*

Dro. S. Master, there is a bark of Epi-
 damnum
That stays but till her owner comes aboard,
And then, sir, she bears away. Our fraughtage,
 sir,
I have convey'd aboard ; and I have bought
The oil, the balsamum and aqua-vitæ.
The ship is in her trim ; the merry wind 90
Blows fair from land : they stay for nought at
 all
But for their owner, master, and yourself.

Ant. E. How now ! a madman ! Why,
 thou peevish sheep,
What ship of Epidamnum stays for me ?

Dro. S. A ship you sent me to, to hire
 waftage.

Ant. E. Thou drunken slave, I sent thee
 for a rope ;
And told thee to what purpose and what end.

Dro. S. You sent me for a rope's end as
 soon :
You sent me to the bay, sir, for a bark.

Ant. E. I will debate this matter at more
 leisure 100
And teach your ears to list me with more
 heed.
To Adriana, villain, hie thee straight :
Give her this key, and tell her, in the desk
That's cover'd o'er with Turkish tapestry,
There is a purse of ducats ; let her send it :
Tell her I am arrested in the street
And that shall bail me ; hie thee, slave, be
 gone !
On, officer, to prison till it come.

 [*Exeunt Sec. Merchant, Angelo, Officer,
        and Ant. E.*

Dro. S. To Adriana ! that is where we
 dined,
Where Dowsabel did claim me for her hus-
 band : 110
She is too big, I hope, for me to compass.
Thither I must, although against my will,
For servants must their masters' minds fulfil

            [*Exit.*

SCENE II. *The house of* ANTIPHOLUS *of*
      Ephesus.

Enter ADRIANA *and* LUCIANA.

Adr. Ah, Luciana, did he tempt thee so ?
Mightst thou perceive austerely in his eye
That he did plead in earnest ? yea or no ?

Look'd he or red or pale, or sad or merrily ?
What observation madest thou in this case
Of his heart's meteors tilting in his face ?
  Luc. First he denied you had in him no right.
  Adr. He meant he did me none ; the more my spite.
  Luc. Then swore he that he was a stranger here.
  Adr. And true he swore, though yet forsworn he were. 10
  Luc. Then pleaded I for you.
  Adr.   And what said he ?
  Luc. That love I begg'd for you he begg'd of me.
  Adr. With what persuasion did he tempt thy love ?
  Luc. With words that in an honest suit might move.
First he did praise my beauty, then my speech.
  Adr. Didst speak him fair ?
  Luc.   Have patience, I beseech.
  Adr. I cannot, nor I will not, hold me still ;
My tongue, though not my heart, shall have his will.
He is deformed, crooked, old and sere,
Ill-faced, worse bodied, shapeless everywhere ;
Vicious, ungentle, foolish, blunt, unkind, 21
Stigmatical in making, worse in mind.
  Luc. Who would be jealous then of such a one ?
No evil lost is wail'd when it is gone.
  Adr. Ah, but I think him better than I say,
And yet would herein others' eyes were worse.
Far from her nest the lapwing cries away :
My heart prays for him, though my tongue do curse.

      Enter DROMIO *of Syracuse.*

  Dro. S. Here ! go ; the desk, the purse ! sweet, now, make haste.
  Luc. How hast thou lost thy breath ?
  Dro. S.   By running fast. 30
  Adr. Where is thy master, Dromio ? is he well ?
  Dro. S. No, he's in Tartar limbo, worse than hell.
A devil in an everlasting garment hath him ;
One whose hard heart is button'd up with steel ;
A fiend, a fury, pitiless and rough ;
A wolf, nay, worse, a fellow all in buff ;
A back-friend, a shoulder-clapper, one that countermands
The passages of alleys, creeks and narrow lands ;
A hound that runs counter and yet draws dryfoot well ;
One that before the judgement carries poor souls to hell. 40
  Adr. Why, man, what is the matter ?
  Dro. S. I do not know the matter : he is 'rested on the case.
  Adr. What, is he arrested ? Tell me at whose suit.
  Dro. S. I know not at whose suit he is arrested well ;
But he's in a suit of buff which 'rested him, that can I tell.

Will you send him, mistress, redemption, the money in his desk ?
  Adr. Go fetch it, sister.   [*Exit Luciana.*]
This I wonder at,
That he, unknown to me, should be in debt.
Tell me, was he arrested on a band ?
  Dro. S. Not on a band, but on a stronger thing ; 50
A chain, a chain ! Do you not hear it ring ?
  Adr. What, the chain ?
  Dro. S. No, no, the bell : 'tis time that I were gone :
It was two ere I left him, and now the clock strikes one.
  Adr. The hours come back ! that did I never hear.
  Dro. S. O, yes ; if any hour meet a sergeant, a' turns back for very fear.
  Adr. As if Time were in debt ! how fondly dost thou reason !
  Dro. S. Time is a very bankrupt, and owes more than he's worth, to season.
Nay, he's a thief too : have you not heard men say,
That Time comes stealing on by night and day ? 60
If Time be in debt and theft, and a sergeant in the way,
Hath he not reason to turn back an hour in a day ?

      Re-enter LUCIANA *with a purse.*

  Adr. Go, Dromio ; there's the money, bear it straight,
And bring thy master home immediately.
Come, sister : I am press'd down with conceit—
Conceit, my comfort and my injury.
                              [*Exeunt.*

      SCENE III. *A public place.*
      Enter ANTIPHOLUS *of Syracuse.*

  Ant. S. There's not a man I meet but doth salute me
As if I were their well-acquainted friend ;
And every one doth call me by my name.
Some tender money to me ; some invite me ;
Some other give me thanks for kindnesses ;
Some offer me commodities to buy ;
Even now a tailor call'd me in his shop
And show'd me silks that he had bought for me,
And therewithal took measure of my body.
Sure, these are but imaginary wiles 10
And Lapland sorcerers inhabit here.

      Enter DROMIO *of Syracuse.*

  Dro. S. Master, here's the gold you sent me for. What, have you got the picture of old Adam new-apparelled ?
  Ant. S. What gold is this ? what Adam dost thou mean ?
  Dro. S. Not that Adam that kept the Paradise, but that Adam that keeps the prison : he that goes in the calf's skin that was killed for the Prodigal ; he that came behind you, sir, like an evil angel, and bid you forsake your liberty. 20
  Ant. S. I understand thee not.
  Dro. S. No ? why, 'tis a plain case : he that went, like a bass-viol, in a case of leather ; the man, sir, that, when gentlemen are tired,

gives them a sob and 'rests them ; he, sir, that
takes pity on decayed men and gives them suits
of durance ; he that sets up his rest to do more
exploits with his mace than a morris-pike.

Ant. S. What, thou meanest an officer ?

Dro. S. Ay, sir, the sergeant of the band ;
he that brings any man to answer it that
breaks his band ; one that thinks a man always
going to bed, and says, ' God give you good
rest ! '

Ant. S. Well, sir, there rest in your foolery.
Is there any ship puts forth to-night ? may we
be gone ?

Dro. S. Why, sir, I brought you word an
hour since that the bark Expedition put forth
to-night ; and then were you hindered by the
sergeant, to tarry for the hoy Delay. Here are
the angels that you sent for to deliver you.

Ant. S. The fellow is distract, and so am
I ;
And here we wander in illusions :
Some blessed power deliver us from hence !

Enter a Courtezan.

Cour. Well met, well met, Master Antiph-
olus.
I see, sir, you have found the goldsmith now :
Is that the chain you promised me to-day ?

Ant. S. Satan, avoid ! I charge thee, tempt
me not.

Dro. S. Master, is this Mistress Satan ?

Ant. S. It is the devil.   50

Dro. S. Nay, she is worse, she is the devil's
dam ; and here she comes in the habit of a
light wench : and thereof comes that the
wenches say ' God damn me ; ' that's as much
to say ' God make me a light wench.' It is
written, they appear to men like angels of
light : light is an effect of fire, and fire will
burn ; ergo, light wenches will burn. Come not
near her.

Cour. Your man and you are marvellous
merry, sir.
Will you go with me ? We'll mend our dinner
here ?   60

Dro. S. Master, if you do, expect spoon-
meat ; or bespeak a long spoon.

Ant. S. Why, Dromio ?

Dro. S. Marry, he must have a long spoon
that must eat with the devil.

Ant. S. Avoid then, fiend ! what tell'st
thou me of supping ?
Thou art, as you are all, a sorceress :
I conjure thee to leave me and be gone.

Cour. Give me the ring of mine you had
at dinner,
Or, for my diamond, the chain you promised,
And I'll be gone, sir, and not trouble you.   71

Dro. S. Some devils ask but the parings of
one's nail,
A rush, a hair, a drop of blood, a pin,
A nut, a cherry-stone ;
But she, more covetous, would have a chain.
Master, be wise : an if you give it her,
The devil will shake her chain and fright us
with it.

Cour. I pray you, sir, my ring, or else the
chain :
I hope you do not mean to cheat me so.

Ant. S. Avaunt, thou witch ! Come,
Dromio, let us go.   80

Dro. S. ' Fly pride,' says the peacock :
mistress, that you know.
              [*Exeunt Ant. S. and Dro. S.*

Cour. Now, out of doubt Antipholus is
mad,
Else would he never so demean himself.
A ring he hath of mine worth forty ducats,
And for the same he promised me a chain :
Both one and other he denies me now.
The reason that I gather he is mad,
Besides this present instance of his rage,
Is a mad tale he told to-day at dinner,
Of his own doors being shut against his en-
trance.   90
Belike his wife, acquainted with his fits,
On purpose shut the doors against his way.
My way is now to hie home to his house,
And tell his wife that, being lunatic,
He rush'd into my house and took perforce
My ring away. This course I fittest choose ;
For forty ducats is too much to lose.   [*Exit.*

SCENE IV. *A street.*

Enter ANTIPHOLUS *of Ephesus and the* Officer.

Ant. E. Fear me not, man ; I will not
break away :
I'll give thee, ere I leave thee, so much money,
To warrant thee, as I am 'rested for.
My wife is in a wayward mood to-day,
And will not lightly trust the messenger
That I should be attach'd in Ephesus,
I tell you, 'twill sound harshly in her ears.

Enter DROMIO *of Ephesus with a rope's-end.*

Here comes my man ; I think he brings the
money.
How now, sir ! have you that I sent you for ?

Dro. E. Here's that, I warrant you, will
pay them all.   10

Ant. E. But where's the money ?

Dro. E. Why, sir, I gave the money for the
rope.

Ant. E. Five hundred ducats, villain, for a
rope ?

Dro. E. I'll serve you, sir, five hundred at
the rate.

Ant. E. To what end did I bid thee hie
thee home ?

Dro. E. To a rope's-end, sir ; and to that
end am I returned.

Ant. E. And to that end, sir, I will welcome you.   [*Beating him.*

Off. Good sir, be patient.   20

Dro. E. Nay, 'tis for me to be patient ; I
am in adversity.

Off. Good, now, hold thy tongue.

Dro. E. Nay, rather persuade him to hold
his hands.

Ant. E. Thou whoreson, senseless villain !

Dro. E. I would I were senseless, sir, that
I might not feel your blows.

Ant. E. Thou art sensible in nothing but
blows, and so is an ass.

Dro. E. I am an ass, indeed ; you may
prove it by my long ears. I have served him
from the hour of my nativity to this instant
and have nothing at his hands for my service
but blows. When I am cold, he heats me with
beating ; when I am warm, he cools me with
beating ; I am waked with it when I sleep
raised with it when I sit ; driven out of doors
with it when I go from home ; welcomes

home with it when I return ; nay, I bear it on
my shoulders, as a beggar wont her brat ; and,
I think, when he hath lamed me, I shall beg
with it from door to door.

Ant. E. Come, go along ; my wife is coming yonder.

Enter ADRIANA, LUCIANA, *the* Courtezan, *and*
PINCH.

Dro. E. Mistress, ' respice finem,' respect
your end ; or rather, the prophecy like the
parrot, ' beware the rope's-end.'

Ant. E. Wilt thou still talk ? [*Beating him.*

Cour. How say you now ? is not your husband mad ?

Adr. His incivility confirms no less.
Good Doctor Pinch, you are a conjurer ;   50
Establish him in his true sense again,
And I will please you what you will demand.

Luc. Alas, how fiery and how sharp he
looks !

Cour. Mark how he trembles in his
ecstasy !

Pinch. Give me your hand and let me feel
your pulse.

Ant. E. There is my hand, and let it feel
your ear.   [*Striking him.*

Pinch. I charge thee, Satan, housed within
this man,
To yield possession to my holy prayers
And to thy state of darkness hie thee straight:
I conjure thee by all the saints in heaven !   60

Ant. E. Peace, doting wizard, peace ! I am
not mad.

Adr. O, that thou wert not, poor distressed soul !

Ant. E. You minion, you, are these your
customers ?
Did this companion with the saffron face
Revel and feast it at my house to-day,
Whilst upon me the guilty doors were shut
And I denied to enter in my house ?

Adr. O husband, God doth know you
dined at home ;
Where would you had remain'd until this
time,
Free from these slanders and this open
shame !

Ant. E. Dined at home ! Thou villain, what
sayest thou ?   71

Dro. E. Sir, sooth to say, you did not dine
at home.

Ant. E. Were not my doors lock'd up and
I shut out ?

Dro. E. Perdie, your doors were lock'd
and you shut out.

Ant. E. And did not she herself revile me
there ?

Dro. E. Sans fable, she herself reviled you
there.

Ant. E. Did not her kitchen-maid rail,
taunt, and scorn me ?

Dro. E. Certes, she did ; the kitchen-vestal
scorn'd you.

Ant. E. And did not I in rage depart
from thence ?

Dro. E. In verity you did ; my bones bear
witness,   80
That since have felt the vigor of his rage.

Adr. Is't good to soothe him in these con-
traries ?

Pinch. It is no shame : the fellow finds his
vein,
And yielding to him humors well his frenzy.

Ant. E. Thou hast suborn'd the goldsmith
to arrest me.

Adr. Alas, I sent you money to redeem
you,
By Dromio here, who came in haste for it.

Dro. E. Money by me ! heart and good-
will you might ;
But surely, master, not a rag of money.

Ant. E. Went'st not thou to her for a
purse of ducats ?   90

Adr. He came to me and I deliver'd it.

Luc. And I am witness with her that she
did.

Dro. E. God and the rope-maker bear me
witness
That I was sent for nothing but a rope !

Pinch. Mistress, both man and master is
possess'd ;
I know it by their pale and deadly looks :
They must be bound and laid in some dark
room.

Ant. E. Say, wherefore didst thou lock me
forth to-day ?
And why dost thou deny the bag of gold ?

Adr. I did not, gentle husband, lock thee
forth.   100

Dro. E. And, gentle master, I received no
gold ;
But I confess, sir, that we were lock'd out.

Adr. Dissembling villain, thou speak'st
false in both.

Ant. E. Dissembling harlot, thou art false
in all ;
And art confederate with a damned pack
To make a loathsome abject scorn of me :
But with these nails I'll pluck out these false
eyes
That would behold in me this shameful sport.

Enter three or four, and offer to bind him.
He strives.

Adr. O, bind him, bind him ! let him not
come near me.

Pinch. More company ! The fiend is strong
within him.   110

Luc. Ay me, poor man, how pale and wan
he looks !

Ant. E. What, will you murder me ? Thou
gaoler, thou,
I am thy prisoner : wilt thou suffer them
To make a rescue ?

Off.   Masters, let him go :
He is my prisoner, and you shall not have
him.

Pinch. Go bind this man, for he is frantic
too.   [*They offer to bind Dro. E.*

Adr. What wilt thou do, thou peevish offi-
cer ?
Hast thou delight to see a wretched man
Do outrage and displeasure to himself ?   119

Off. He is my prisoner : if I let him go,
The debt he owes will be required of me.

Adr. I will discharge thee ere I go from
thee :
Bear me forthwith unto his creditor,
And, knowing how the debt grows, I will pay
it.
Good master doctor, see him safe convey'd
Home to my house. O most unhappy day !

Ant. E. O most unhappy strumpet!
Dro. E. Master, I am here entered in bond
  for you.
Ant. E. Out on thee, villain! wherefore
  dost thou mad me?   130
Dro. E. Will you be bound for nothing?
  be mad, good master: cry 'The devil!'
Luc. God help, poor souls, how idly do
  they talk!
Adr. Go bear him hence. Sister, go you
  with me.
    [*Exeunt all but Adriana, Luciana,
      Officer and Courtezan.*
Say now, whose suit is he arrested at?
Off. One Angelo, a goldsmith: do you
  know him?
Adr. I know the man. What is the sum he
  owes?
Off. Two hundred ducats.
Adr.   Say, how grows it due?
Off. Due for a chain your husband had of
  him.
Adr. He did bespeak a chain for me, but
  had it not.
Cour. When as your husband all in rage
  to-day   140
Came to my house and took away my ring—
The ring I saw upon his finger now—
Straight after did I meet him with a chain.
Adr. It may be so, but I did never see it.
Come, gaoler, bring me where the goldsmith
  is:
I long to know the truth hereof at large.

Enter ANTIPHOLUS of Syracuse *with his rapier
  drawn, and* DROMIO *of Syracuse.*

Luc. God, for thy mercy! they are loose
  again.
Adr. And come with naked swords.
Let's call more help to have them bound
  again.
Off. Away! they'll kill us.   150
    [*Exeunt all but Ant. S. and Dro. S.*
Ant. S. I see these witches are afraid of
  swords.
Dro. S. She that would be your wife now
  ran from you.
Ant. S. Come to the Centaur; fetch our
  stuff from thence:
I long that we were safe and sound aboard.
Dro. S. Faith, stay here this night; they
will surely do us no harm: you saw they
speak us fair, give us gold: methinks they are
such a gentle nation that, but for the mountain
of mad flesh that claims marriage of me, I
could find in my heart to stay here still and
turn witch.   160
Ant. S. I will not stay to-night for all the
  town;
Therefore away, to get our stuff aboard.
                              [*Exeunt.*

ACT V.

SCENE I. *A street before a Priory.*

Enter Second Merchant *and* ANGELO.

Ang. I am sorry, sir, that I have hinder'd
  you;
But, I protest, he had the chain of me,
Though most dishonestly he doth deny it.

Sec. Mer. How is the man esteemed here
  in the city?
Ang. Of very reverend reputation, sir,
Of credit infinite, highly beloved,
Second to none that lives here in the city:
His word might bear my wealth at any time.
Sec. Mer. Speak softly; yonder, as I think,
  he walks.

Enter ANTIPHOLUS of Syracuse *and* DROMIO
  of Syracuse.

Ang. 'Tis so; and that self chain about
  his neck   10
Which he forswore most monstrously to have.
Good sir, draw near to me, I'll speak to him.
Signior Antipholus, I wonder much
That you would put me to this shame and
  trouble;
And, not without some scandal to yourself,
With circumstance and oaths so to deny
This chain which now you wear so openly:
Beside the charge, the shame, imprisonment,
You have done wrong to this my honest
  friend,
Who, but for staying on our controversy, 20
Had hoisted sail and put to sea to-day:
This chain you had of me; can you deny it?
Ant. S. I think I had; I never did deny it.
Sec. Mer. Yes, that you did, sir, and for-
  swore it too.
Ant. S. Who heard me to deny it or for-
  swear it?
Sec. Mer. These ears of mine, thou know'st
  did hear thee.
Fie on thee, wretch! 'tis pity that thou livest
To walk where any honest man resort.
Ant. S. Thou art a villain to impeach me
  thus:
I'll prove mine honor and mine honesty 30
Against thee presently, if thou darest stand.
Sec. Mer. I dare, and do defy thee for a
  villain.   [*They draw.*

Enter ADRIANA, LUCIANA, *the* Courtezan, *and
  others.*

Adr. Hold, hurt him not, for God's sake!
  he is mad.
Some get within him, take his sword away:
Bind Dromio too, and bear them to my house.
Dro. S. Run, master, run; for God's sake,
  take a house!
This is some priory. In, or we are spoil'd!
[*Exeunt Ant. S. and Dro. S. to the Priory.*

Enter the Lady Abbess.

Abb. Be quiet, people. Wherefore throng
  you hither?
Adr. To fetch my poor distracted husband
  hence.
Let us come in, that we may bind him fast 40
And bear him home for his recovery.
Ang. I knew he was not in his perfect wits.
Sec. Mer. I am sorry now that I did draw
  on him.
Abb. How long hath this possession held
  the man?
Adr. This week he hath been heavy, sour,
  sad,
And much different from the man he was;
But till this afternoon his passion
Ne'er brake into extremity of rage.

Abb. Hath he not lost much wealth by
    wreck of sea?
Buried some dear friend? Hath not else his
    eye   50
Stray'd his affection in unlawful love?
A sin prevailing much in youthful men,
Who give their eyes the liberty of gazing.
Which of these sorrows is he subject to?
Adr. To none of these, except it be the
    last;
Namely, some love that drew him oft from
    home.
Abb. You should for that have repre-
    hended him.
Adr. Why, so I did.
Abb.   Ay, but not rough enough.
Adr. As roughly as my modesty would let
    me.
Abb. Haply, in private.
Adr.   And in assemblies too.
Abb. Ay, but not enough.   61
Adr. It was the copy of our conference:
In bed he slept not for my urging it;
At board he fed not for my urging it;
Alone, it was the subject of my theme;
In company I often glanced it;
Still did I tell him it was vile and bad.
Abb. And thereof came it that the man
    was mad.
The venom clamors of a jealous woman
Poisons more deadly than a mad dog's tooth.
It seems his sleeps were hinder'd by thy rail-
    ing,   71
And therefore comes it that his head is light.
Thou say'st his meat was sauced with thy up-
    braidings;
Unquiet meals make ill digestions;
Thereof the raging fire of fever bred;
And what's a fever but a fit of madness?
Thou say'st his sports were hinder'd by thy
    brawls:
Sweet recreation barr'd, what doth ensue
But moody and dull melancholy,
Kinsman to grim and comfortless despair,   80
And at her heels a huge infectious troop
Of pale distemperatures and foes to life?
In food, in sport and life-preserving rest
To be disturb'd, would mad or man or beast:
The consequence is then thy jealous fits
Have scared thy husband from the use of wits.
Luc. She never reprehended him but
    mildly,
When he demean'd himself rough, rude and
    wildly,
Why bear you these rebukes and answer not?
Adr. She did betray me to my own re-
    proof.
Good people enter and lay hold on him.   91
Abb. No, not a creature enters in my
    house.
Adr. Then let your servants bring my hus-
    band forth.
Abb. Neither: he took this place for sanc-
    tuary,
And it shall privilege him from your hands
Till I have brought him to his wits again,
Or lose my labor in assaying it.
Adr. I will attend my husband, be his
    nurse,
Diet his sickness, for it is my office,
And will have no attorney but myself;   100
And therefore let me have him home with me.

Abb. Be patient; for I will not let him
    stir
Till I have used the approved means I have,
With wholesome syrups, drugs and holy
    prayers,
To make of him a formal man again:
It is a branch and parcel of mine oath,
A charitable duty of my order.
Therefore depart and leave him here with me.
Adr. I will not hence and leave my hus-
    band here:
And ill it doth beseem your holiness   110
To separate the husband and the wife.
Abb. Be quiet and depart: thou shalt not
    have him.   [*Exit.*
Luc. Complain unto the duke of this indig-
    nity.
Adr. Come, go: I will fall prostrate at his
    feet
And never rise until my tears and prayers
Have won his grace to come in person hither
And take perforce my husband from the ab-
    bess.
Sec. Mer. By this, I think, the dial points
    at five:
Anon, I'm sure, the duke himself in person
Comes this way to the melancholy vale,   120
The place of death and sorry execution,
Behind the ditches of the abbey here.
Ang. Upon what cause?
Sec. Mer. To see a reverend Syracusian
    merchant,
Who put unluckily into this bay
Against the laws and statutes of this town,
Beheaded publicly for his offence.
Ang. See where they come: we will be-
    hold his death.
Luc. Kneel to the duke before he pass the
    abbey.

Enter Duke, *attended;* Ægeon *bareheaded;*
    with the Headsman *and other* Officers.

Duke. Yet once again proclaim it publicly,
If any friend will pay the sum for him,   131
He shall not die; so much we tender him.
Adr. Justice, most sacred duke, against the
    abbess!
Duke. She is a virtuous and a reverend
    lady:
It cannot be that she hath done thee wrong.
Adr. May it please your grace, Antipholus,
    my husband,
Whom I made lord of me and all I had,
At your important letters,—this ill day
A most outrageous fit of madness took him;
That desperately he hurried through the street,
With him his bondman, all as mad as he,—141
Doing displeasure to the citizens
By rushing in their houses, bearing thence
Rings, jewels, any thing his rage did like.
Once did I get him bound and sent him home,
Whilst to take order for the wrongs I went,
That here and there his fury had committed.
Anon, I wot not by what strong escape,
He broke from those that had the guard of
    him;
And with his mad attendant and himself,   150
Each one with ireful passion, with drawn
    swords,
Met us again and madly bent on us,
Chased us away; till, raising of more aid,
We came again to bind them. Then they fled

Into this abbey, whither we pursued them :
And here the abbess shuts the gates on us
And will not suffer us to fetch him out,
Nor send him forth that we may bear him
    hence.
Therefore, most gracious duke, with thy com-
    mand
Let him be brought forth and borne hence
    for help.
  Duke. Long since thy husband served me
    in my wars,   161
And I to thee engaged a prince's word,
When thou didst make him master of thy bed,
To do him all the grace and good I could.
Go, some of you, knock at the abbey-gate
And bid the lady abbess come to me.
I will determine this before I stir.

        Enter a Servant.

  Serv. O mistress, mistress, shift and save
    yourself !
My master and his man are both broke loose,
Beaten the maids a-row and bound the doctor,
Whose beard they have singed off with brands
    of fire ;   171
And ever, as it blazed, they threw on him
Great pails of puddled mire to quench the
    hair :
My master preaches patience to him and the
    while
His man with scissors nicks him like a fool,
And sure, unless you send some present help,
Between them they will kill the conjurer.
  Adr. Peace, fool ! thy master and his man
    are here,
And that is false thou dost report to us.
  Serv. Mistress, upon my life, I tell you
    true ;
I have not breathed almost since I did see it.
He cries for you, and vows, if he can take you,
To scorch your face and to disfigure you.
                    [Cry within.
Hark, hark ! I hear him, mistress : fly, be
    gone !
  Duke. Come, stand by me ; fear nothing.
    Guard with halberds !
  Adr. Ay me, it is my husband ! Witness
    you,
That he is borne about invisible :
Even now we housed him in the abbey here ;
And now he's there, past thought of human
    reason.

Enter ANTIPHOLUS *of* Ephesus *and* DROMIO *of*
                Ephesus.

  Ant. E. Justice, most gracious duke, O,
    grant me justice !   190
Even for the service that long since I did thee,
When I bestrid thee in the wars and took
Deep scars to save thy life ; even for the blood
That then I lost for thee, now grant me justice.
  Æge. Unless the fear of death doth make
    me dote,
I see my son Antipholus and Dromio.
  Ant. E. Justice, sweet prince, against that
    woman there !
She whom thou gavest to me to be my wife,
That hath abused and dishonor'd me
Even in the strength and height of injury ! 200
Beyond imagination is the wrong
That she this day hath shameless thrown on
    me.

  Duke. Discover how, and thou shalt find
    me just,
  Ant. E. This day, great duke, she shut the
    doors upon me,
While she with harlots feasted in my house.
  Duke. A grievous fault ! Say, woman, didst
    thou so ?
  Adr. No, my good lord : myself, he and
    my sister
To-day did dine together. So befall my soul
As this is false he burdens me withal !
  Luc. Ne'er may I look on day, nor sleep
    on night,   210
But she tells to your highness simple truth !
  Ang. O perjured woman ! They are both
    forsworn :
In this the madman justly chargeth them.
  Ant. E. My liege, I am advised what I say,
Neither disturbed with the effect of wine,
Nor heady-rash, provoked with raging ire,
Albeit my wrongs might make one wiser mad.
This woman lock'd me out this day from din-
    ner :
That goldsmith there, were he not pack'd with
    her,   219
Could witness it, for he was with me then ;
Who parted with me to go fetch a chain,
Promising to bring it to the Porpentine,
Where Balthazar and I did dine together.
Our dinner done, and he not coming thither,
I went to seek him : in the street I met him
And in his company that gentleman.
There did this perjured goldsmith swear me
    down
That I this day of him received the chain,
Which, God he knows, I saw not : for the
    which
He did arrest me with an officer.   230
I did obey, and sent my peasant home
For certain ducats : he with none return'd
Then fairly I bespoke the officer
To go in person with me to my house.
By the way we met
My wife, her sister, and a rabble more
Of vile confederates. Along with them
They brought one Pinch, a hungry lean-faced
    villain,
A mere anatomy, a mountebank,
A threadbare juggler and a fortune-teller,
A needy, hollow-eyed, sharp-looking wretch
A living-dead man : this pernicious slave, 241
Forsooth, took on him as a conjurer,
And, gazing in mine eyes, feeling my pulse,
And with no face, as 'twere, outfacing me
Cries out, I was possess'd. Then all togethe
They fell upon me, bound me, bore me thenc
And in a dark and dankish vault at home
There left me and my man, both bound to-
    gether ;
Till, gnawing with my teeth my bonds in sun
    der,
I gain'd my freedom, and immediately   25
Ran hither to your grace ; whom I beseech
To give me ample satisfaction
For these deep shames and great indignities
  Ang. My lord, in truth, thus far I witnes
    with him,
That he dined not at home, but was lock'
    out.
  Duke. But had he such a chain of thee o
    no ?

Ang. He had, my lord : and when he ran
    in here,
These people saw the chain about his neck.
Sec. Mer. Besides, I will be sworn these
    ears of mine
Heard you confess you had the chain of him
After you first forswore it on the mart :   261
And thereupon I drew my sword on you ;
And then you fled into this abbey here,
From whence, I think, you are come by
    miracle.
Ant. E. I never came within these abbey-
    walls,
Nor ever didst thou draw thy sword on me :
I never saw the chain, so help me Heaven !
And this is false you burden me withal.
Duke. Why, what an intricate impeach is
    this !
I think you all have drunk of Circe's cup.   270
If here you housed him, here he would have
    been ;
If he were mad, he would not plead so coldly :
You say he dined at home ; the goldsmith here
Denies that saying. Sirrah, what say you ?
Dro. E. Sir, he dined with her there, at the
    Porpentine.
Cour. He did, and from my finger snatch'd
    that ring.
Ant. E. 'Tis true, my liege ; this ring I had
    of her.
Duke. Saw'st thou him enter at the abbey
    here ?
Cour. As sure, my liege, as I do see your
    grace.
Duke. Why, this is strange. Go call the
    abbess hither.   280
I think you are all mated or stark mad.
    [*Exit one to the Abbess.*
Æge. Most mighty duke, vouchsafe me
    speak a word :
Haply I see a friend will save my life
And pay the sum that may deliver me.
Duke. Speak freely, Syracusian, what thou
    wilt.
Æge. Is not your name, sir, call'd Antiph-
    olus ?
And is not that your bondman, Dromio ?
Dro. E. Within this hour I was his bond-
    man sir,
But he, I thank him, gnaw'd in two my cords :
Now am I Dromio and his man unbound.   290
Æge. I am sure you both of you remem-
    ber me.
Dro. E. Ourselves we do remember, sir, by
    you ;
For lately we were bound, as you are now
You are not Pinch's patient, are you, sir ?
Æge. Why look you strange on me ? you
    know me well.
Ant. E. I never saw you in my life till
    now.
Æge. O, grief hath changed me since
    you saw me last,
And careful hours with time's deformed hand
Have written strange defeatures in my face :
But tell me yet, dost thou not know my voice ?
Ant. E. Neither.   301
Æge. Dromio, nor thou ?
Dro. E.   No, trust me, sir, nor I.
Æge. I am sure thou dost.
Dro. E. Ay, sir, but I am sure I do not ;

and whatsoever a man denies, you are now
bound to believe him.
Æge. Not know my voice ! O time's ex-
    tremity,
Hast thou so crack'd and splitted my poor
    tongue
In seven short years, that here my only son
Knows not my feeble key of untuned cares ?
Though now this grained face of mine be hid
In sap-consuming winter's drizzled snow,
And all the conduits of my blood froze up,
Yet hath my night of life some memory,
My wasting lamps some fading glimmer left,
My dull deaf ears a little use to hear :
All these old witnesses—I cannot err—
Tell me thou art my son Antipholus.
Ant. E. I never saw my father in my life.
Æge. But seven years since, in Syracuse,
    boy,   320
Thou know'st we parted : but perhaps, my
    son,
Thou shamest to acknowledge me in misery.
Ant. E. The duke and all that know me in
    the city
Can witness with me that it is not so :
I ne'er saw Syracusa in my life.
Duke. I tell thee, Syracusian, twenty years
Have I been patron to Antipholus,
During which time he ne'er saw Syracusa :
I see thy age and dangers make thee dote.
Re-enter Abbess, *with* Antipholus *of Syra-*
    cuse and Dromio *of Syracuse.*
Abb. Most mighty duke, behold a man
    much wrong'd.   330
    [*All gather to see them.*
Adr. I see two husbands, or mine eyes de-
    ceive me.
Duke. One of these men is Genius to the
    other ;
And so of these. Which is the natural man,
And which the spirit ? who deciphers them ?
Dro. S. I, sir, am Dromio ; command him
    away.
Dro. E. I, sir, am Dromio ; pray, let me
    stay.
Ant. S. Ægeon art thou not ? or else his
    ghost ?
Dro. S. O, my old master ! who hath
    bound him here ?
Abb. Whoever bound him, I will loose his
    bonds
And gain a husband by his liberty.   340
Speak, old Ægeon, if thou be'st the man
That hadst a wife once call'd Æmilia
That bore thee at a burden two fair sons :
O, if thou be'st the same Ægeon, speak,
And speak unto the same Æmilia !
Æge. If I dream not, thou art Æmilia :
If thou art she, tell me where is that son
That floated with thee on the fatal raft ?
Abb. By men of Epidamnum he and I
And the twin Dromio all were taken up ;   350
But by and by rude fishermen of Corinth
By force took Dromio and my son from them
And me they left with those of Epidamnum.
What then became of them I cannot tell ;
I to this fortune that you see me in.
Duke. Why, here begins his morning story
    right ;
These two Antipholuses, these two so like,
And these two Dromios, one in semblance,—

Besides her urging of her wreck at sea,—
These are the parents to these children,   360
Which accidentally are met together.
Antipholus, thou camest from Corinth first?

Ant. S. No, sir, not I; I came from Syracuse.

Duke. Stay, stand apart; I know not which is which.

Ant E. I came from Corinth, my most gracious lord,—

Dro. E. And I with him.

Ant. E. Brought to this town by that most famous warrior,

Duke Menaphon, your most renowned uncle.

Adr. Which of you two did dine with me to-day?

Ant. S. I, gentle mistress.

Adr.   And are not you my husband?

Ant. E. No; I say nay to that.   371

Ant. S. And so do I; yet did she call me so:
And this fair gentlewoman, her sister here,
Did call me brother. [*To Luc.*] What I told you then,
I hope I shall have leisure to make good;
If this be not a dream I see and hear.

Ang. That is the chain, sir, which you had of me.

Ant. S. I think it be, sir; I deny it not.

Ant. E. And you, sir, for this chain arrested me.   380

Ang. I think I did, sir; I deny it not.

Adr. I sent you money, sir, to be your bail,
By Dromio; but I think he brought it not.

Dro. E. No, none by me.

Ant. S. This purse of ducats I received from you,
And Dromio, my man, did bring them me.
I see we still did meet each other's man,
And I was ta'en for him, and he for me,
And thereupon these ERRORS are arose.

Ant. E. These ducats pawn I for my father here.

Duke. It shall not need; thy father hath his life.

Cour. Sir, I must have that diamond from you.   391

Ant. E. There, take it; and much thanks for my good cheer.

Abb. Renowned Duke, vouchsafe to take the pains
To go with us into the abbey here
And hear at large discoursed all our fortunes:
And all that are assembled in this place,
That by this sympathized one day's error
Have suffer'd wrong, go keep us company,
And we shall make full satisfaction.   399
Thirty-three years have I but gone in travail
Of you, my sons; and till this present hour
My heavy burthen ne'er delivered.
The duke, my husband and my children both,
And you the calendars of their nativity,
Go to a gossips' feast, and go with me;
After so long grief, such festivity!

Duke. With all my heart, I'll gossip at this feast. [*Exeunt all but Ant. S., Ant. E., Dro. S., and Dro. E.*

Dro. S. Master, shall I fetch your stuff from shipboard?

Ant. E. Dromio, what stuff of mine hast thou embark'd?

Dro. S. Your goods that lay at host, sir, in the Centaur.   410

Ant. S. He speaks to me. I am your master, Dromio:
Come, go with us; we'll look to that anon:
Embrace thy brother there; rejoice with him. [*Exeunt Ant. S. and Ant. E.*

Dro. S. There is a fat friend at your master's house,
That kitchen'd me for you to-day at dinner:
She now shall be my sister, not my wife.

Dro. E. Methinks you are my glass, and not my brother:
I see by you I am a sweet-faced youth.
Will you walk in to see their gossiping?

Dro. S. Not I, sir; you are my elder.   420

Dro. E. That's a question: how shall we try it?

Dro. S. We'll draw cuts for the senior: till then lead thou first.

Dro. E. Nay, then, thus:
We came into the world like brother and brother;
And now let's go hand in hand, not one before another.   [*Exeunt.*

THE
TWO GENTLEMEN OF VERONA.

(WRITTEN ABOUT 1592–93.)

INTRODUCTION.

This play, though slightly worked out in parts, exhibits an advance on the preceding comedies. The *Errors* was a clever tangle of diverting incidents, with a few passages of lyric beauty, and one of almost tragic pathos ; *Love's Labour's Lost* was a play of glittering and elaborate dialogue. In *The Two Gentlemen of Verona* Shakespeare struck into a new path, which he was to pursue with admirable results ; it is his earliest comedy in which a romantic love-story is told in dramatic form. Here first he records the tender and passionate history of a woman's heart, and the adventures to which love may prompt her. Julia is the first of that charming group of children of Shakespeare's imagination which includes Viola, Portia, Rosalind, and Imogen—women who assume, under some constraint of fortune, the disguise of male attire, and who, while submitting to their transformation, forfeit none of the grace, the modesty, the sensitive delicacy, or the pretty wilfulness of their sex. Launce, accompanied by his immortal dog, leads the train of Shakespeare's humorous clowns : his rich, grotesque humanity is "worth all the light, fantastic interludes of Boyet and Adriano, Costard and Holofernes," worth all the "dancing doggerel or broad-witted prose of either Dromio." The characters of the play are clearly conceived, and contrasted with almost too obvious a design : the faithful Valentine is set over against the faithless Proteus ; the bright and clever Sylvia is set over against the tender and ardent Julia ; the clown Speed, notable as a verbal wit and quibbler, is set over against the humorous Launce. The general theme of the play may be defined as love and friendship, with their mutual relations. The date of the play cannot be definitely fixed ; but its place among the comedies is probably after *Love's Labour's Lost* and before *A Midsummer Night's Dream*. The language and verse are characterized by an even sweetness ; rhymed lines and doggerel verses are lessening in number ; the blank verse is written with careful regularity. It is as if Shakespeare were giving up his early licences of versification, were aiming at a more refined style (which occasionally became a little tame), but being still a novice in the art of writing blank verse, were timid and failed to write it with the freedom and "happy valiancy" which distinguish his later manner. The story of the play is identical in many particulars with *The Story of the Shepherdess Felismena* in the Spanish pastoral romance, *Diana*, by George of Montemayor ; but though manuscript translations of the *Diana* existed at an earlier date, no translation was published before that of Yonge, in 1598. Valentine's consenting to become captain of the robbers' band has been compared with a somewhat similar incident in Sidney's *Arcadia*, but the coincidences are slight, and it may be doubted that Shakespeare had then any thought of the *Arcadia*.

DRAMATIS PERSONÆ.

DUKE OF MILAN, Father to Silvia.
VALENTINE, }
PROTEUS, } the two Gentlemen.
ANTONIO, Father to Proteus.
THURIO, a foolish rival to Valentine.
EGLAMOUR, Agent for Silvia in her escape.
HOST, where Julia lodges.
OUTLAWS, with Valentine.
SPEED, a clownish servant to Valentine.

LAUNCE, the like to Proteus.
PANTHINO, Servant to Antonio.
JULIA, beloved of Proteus.
SILVIA, beloved of Valentine.
LUCETTA, waiting-woman to Julia.

Servants, Musicians.

SCENE, *Verona ; Milan ; the frontiers of Mantua.*

ACT I.

SCENE I. *Verona. An open place.*

Enter VALENTINE *and* PROTEUS.

Val. Cease to persuade, my loving Proteus :

Home-keeping youth have ever homely wits.
Were't not affection chains thy tender days
To the sweet glances of thy honor'd love,
I rather would entreat thy company
To see the wonders of the world abroad,
Than, living dully sluggardized at home,
Wear out thy youth with shapeless idleness.

But since thou lovest, love still and thrive
  therein,
Even as I would when I to love begin.   10
  Pro. Wilt thou be gone? Sweet Valen-
  tine, adieu!
Think on thy Proteus, when thou haply seest
Some rare note-worthy object in thy travel:
Wish me partaker in thy happiness
When thou dost meet good hap; and in thy
  danger,
If ever danger do environ thee,
Commend thy grievance to my holy prayers,
For I will be thy beadsman, Valentine.
  Val. And on a love-book pray for my suc-
  cess?
  Pro. Upon some book I love I'll pray for
  thee.   20
  Val. That's on some shallow story of deep
  love:
How young Leander cross'd the Hellespont.
  Pro. That's a deep story of a deeper love:
For he was more than over shoes in love.
  Val. 'Tis true; for you are over boots in
  love,
And yet you never swum the Hellespont.
  Pro. Over the boots? nay, give me not
  the boots.
  Val. No, I will not, for it boots thee not.
  Pro.   What?
  Val. To be in love, where scorn is bought
  with groans;
Coy looks with heart-sore sighs; one fading
  moment's mirth   30
With twenty watchful, weary, tedious nights:
If haply won, perhaps a hapless gain;
If lost, why then a grievous labor won;
However, but a folly bought with wit,
Or else a wit by folly vanquished.
  Pro. So, by your circumstance, you call
  me fool.
  Val. So, by your circumstance, I fear
  you'll prove.
  Pro. 'Tis love you cavil at: I am not Love.
  Val. Love is your master, for he masters
  you:
And he that is so yoked by a fool,   40
Methinks, should not be chronicled for wise.
  Pro. Yet writers say, as in the sweetest
  bud
The eating canker dwells, so eating love
Inhabits in the finest wits of all.
  Val. And writers say, as the most forward
  bud
Is eaten by the canker ere it blow,
Even so by love the young and tender wit
Is turn'd to folly, blasting in the bud,
Losing his verdure even in the prime
And all the fair effects of future hopes. 50
But wherefore waste I time to counsel thee,
That art a votary to fond desire?
Once more adieu! my father at the road
Expects my coming, there to see me shipp'd.
  Pro. And thither will I bring thee, Valen-
  tine.
  Val. Sweet Proteus, no; now let us take
  our leave.
To Milan let me hear from thee by letters
Of thy success in love, and what news else
Betideth here in absence of thy friend;
And I likewise will visit thee with mine. 60
  Pro. All happiness bechance to thee in
  Milan!

  Val. As much to you at home! and so,
  farewell.   [*Exit.*
  Pro. He after honor hunts, I after love:
He leaves his friends to dignify them more,
I leave myself, my friends and all, for love.
Thou, Julia, thou hast metamorphosed me,
Made me neglect my studies, lose my time,
War with good counsel, set the world at
  nought;
Made wit with musing weak, heart sick with
  thought.

Enter SPEED.

  Speed. Sir Proteus, save you! Saw you
  my master?   70
  Pro. But now he parted hence, to embark
  for Milan.
  Speed. Twenty to one then he is shipp'd
  already,
And I have play'd the sheep in losing him.
  Pro. Indeed, a sheep doth very often stray,
An if the shepherd be a while away.
  Speed. You conclude that my master is a
  shepherd, then, and I a sheep?
  Pro. I do.
  Speed. Why then, my horns are his horns,
  whether I wake or sleep.   80
  Pro. A silly answer and fitting well a
  sheep.
  Speed. This proves me still a sheep.
  Pro. True; and thy master a shepherd.
  Speed. Nay, that I can deny by a circum-
  stance.
  Pro. It shall go hard but I'll prove it by
  another.
  Speed. The shepherd seeks the sheep, and
  not the sheep the shepherd; but I seek my
  master, and my master seeks not me: therefore I am no sheep.   91
  Pro. The sheep for fodder follow the shepherd; the shepherd for food follows not the
  sheep: thou for wages followest thy master;
  thy master for wages follows not thee: therefore thou art a sheep.
  Speed. Such another proof will make me
  cry 'baa.'
  Pro. But, dost thou hear? gavest thou my
  letter to Julia?
  Speed. Ay, sir: I, a lost mutton, gave
  your letter to her, a laced mutton, and she, a
  laced mutton, gave me, a lost mutton, nothing
  for my labor.
  Pro. Here's too small a pasture for such
  store of muttons.
  Speed. If the ground be overcharged, you
  were best stick her.
  Pro. Nay: in that you are astray, 'twere
  best pound you.   110
  Speed. Nay, sir, less than a pound shall
  serve me for carrying your letter.
  Pro. You mistake; I mean the pound,—a
  pinfold.
  Speed. From a pound to a pin? fold it over
  and over,
'Tis threefold too little for carrying a letter to
  your lover.
  Pro. But what said she?
  Speed. [*First nodding*] Ay.
  Pro. Nod—Ay—why, that's noddy.
  Speed. You mistook, sir; I say, she did
  nod: and you ask me if she did nod; and I
  say, 'Ay.'   121

Pro. And that set together is noddy.
Speed. Now you have taken the pains to set it together, take it for your pains.
Pro. No, no; you shall have it for bearing the letter.
Speed. Well, I perceive I must be fain to bear with you.
Pro. Why, sir, how do you bear with me?
Speed. Marry, sir, the letter, very orderly; having nothing but the word 'noddy' for my pains.
Pro. Beshrew me, but you have a quick wit.
Speed. And yet it cannot overtake your slow purse.
Pro. Come, come, open the matter in brief: what said she?
Speed. Open your purse, that the money and the matter may be both at once delivered.
Pro. Well, sir, here is for your pains. What said she?   140
Speed. Truly, sir, I think you'll hardly win her.
Pro. Why, couldst thou perceive so much from her?
Speed. Sir, I could perceive nothing at all from her; no, not so much as a ducat for delivering your letter: and being so hard to me that brought your mind, I fear she'll prove as hard to you in telling your mind. Give her no token but stones; for she's as hard as steel.
Pro. What said she?   150
Speed. No, not so much as 'Take this for thy pains.' To testify your bounty, I thank you, you have testerned me; in requital whereof, henceforth carry your letters yourself: and so, sir, I'll commend you to my master.
Pro. Go, go, be gone, to save your ship from wreck,
Which cannot perish having thee aboard,
Being destined to a drier death on shore.
                                                 [*Exit Speed.*
I must go send some better messenger:
I fear my Julia would not deign my lines,   160
Receiving them from such a worthless post.
                                                 [*Exit.*

SCENE II. *The same. Garden of* JULIA'S *house.*

Enter JULIA *and* LUCETTA.

Jul. But say, Lucetta, now we are alone,
Wouldst thou then counsel me to fall in love?
Luc. Ay, madam, so you stumble not unheedfully.
Jul. Of all the fair resort of gentlemen
That every day with parle encounter me,
In thy opinion which is worthiest love?
Luc. Please you repeat their names, I'll show my mind
According to my shallow simple skill.
Jul. What think'st thou of the fair Sir Eglamour?
Luc. As of a knight well-spoken, neat and fine;   10
But, were I you, he never should be mine.
Jul. What think'st thou of the rich Mercatio?
Luc. Well of his wealth; but of himself, so so.
Jul. What think'st thou of the gentle Proteus?

Luc. Lord, Lord! to see what folly reigns in us!
Jul. How now! what means this passion at his name?
Luc. Pardon, dear madam: 'tis a passing shame
That I, unworthy body as I am,
Should censure thus on lovely gentlemen.
Jul. Why not on Proteus, as of all the rest?
Luc. Then thus: of many good I think him best.
Jul. Your reason?
Luc. I have no other, but a woman's reason;
I think him so because I think him so.
Jul. And wouldst thou have me cast my love on him?
Luc. Ay, if you thought your love not cast away.
Jul. Why he, of all the rest, hath never moved me.
Luc. Yet he, of all the rest, I think, best loves ye.
Jul. His little speaking shows his love but small.
Luc. Fire that's closest kept burns most of all.   30
Jul. They do not love that do not show their love.
Luc. O, they love least that let men know their love.
Jul. I would I knew his mind.
Luc. Peruse this paper, madam.
Jul. 'To Julia.' Say, from whom?
Luc. That the contents will show.
Jul. Say, say, who gave it thee?
Luc. Sir Valentine's page; and sent, I think, from Proteus.
He would have given it you; but I, being in the way,
Did in your name receive it: pardon the fault I pray.   40
Jul. Now, by my modesty, a goodly broker!
Dare you presume to harbor wanton lines?
To whisper and conspire against my youth?
Now, trust me, 'tis an office of great worth
And you an officer fit for the place.
There, take the paper: see it be return'd;
Or else return no more into my sight.
Luc. To plead for love deserves more fee than hate.
Jul. Will ye be gone?
Luc.   That you may ruminate.
                                                 [*Exit.*
Jul. And yet I would I had o'erlooked the letter: 50
It were a shame to call her back again
And pray her to a fault for which I chid her.
What a fool is she, that knows I am a maid,
And would not force the letter to my view!
Since maids, in modesty, say 'no' to that
Which they would have the profferer construe 'ay.'
Fie, fie, how wayward is this foolish love
That, like a testy babe, will scratch the nurse
And presently all humbled kiss the rod!
How churlishly I chid Lucetta hence,   60
When willingly I would have had her here!
How angerly I taught my brow to frown,

When inward joy enforced my heart to
  smile !
My penance is to call Lucetta back
And ask remission for my folly past.
What ho ! Lucetta !

Re-enter LUCETTA.

Luc.   What would your ladyship ?
Jul. Is't near dinner-time ?
Luc.   I would it were,
That you might kill your stomach on your
  meat
And not upon your maid.   70
Jul. What is't that you took up so gin-
  gerly ?
Luc. Nothing.
Jul. Why didst thou stoop, then ?
Luc. To take a paper up that I let fall.
Jul. And is that paper nothing ?
Luc. Nothing concerning me.
Jul. Then let it lie for those that it con-
  cerns.
Luc. Madam, it will not lie where it con-
  cerns,
Unless it have a false interpreter.
Jul. Some love of yours hath writ to you
  in rhyme.
Luc. That I might sing it, madam, to a
  tune.   80
Give me a note : your ladyship can set.
Jul. As little by such toys as may be pos-
  sible.
Best sing it to the tune of ' Light o' love.'
Luc. It is too heavy for so light a tune.
Jul. Heavy ! belike it hath some burden
  then ?
Luc. Ay, and melodious were it, would
  you sing it.
Jul. And why not you ?
Luc.   I cannot reach so high.
Jul. Let's see your song. How now, min-
  ion !
Luc. Keep tune there still, so you will sing
  it out :
And yet methinks I do not like this tune. 90
Jul. You do not ?
Luc.   No, madam ; it is too sharp.
Jul. You, minion, are too saucy.
Luc. Nay, now you are too flat
And mar the concord with too harsh a des-
  cant :
There wanteth but a mean to fill your song.
Jul. The mean is drown'd with your un-
  ruly bass.
Luc. Indeed, I bid the base for Proteus.
Jul. This babble shall not henceforth trou-
  ble me.
Here is a coil with protestation !
          [*Tears the letter.*
Go get you gone, and let the papers lie : 100
You would be fingering them, to anger me.
Luc. She makes it strange ; but she would
  be best pleased
To be so anger'd with another letter. [*Exit.*
Jul. Nay, would I were so anger'd with
  the same !
O hateful hands, to tear such loving words !
Injurious wasps, to feed on such sweet honey
And kill the bees that yield it with your
  stings !
I'll kiss each several paper for amends.

Look, here is writ ' kind Julia.' Unkind
  Julia !
As in revenge of thy ingratitude,   110
I throw thy name against the bruising stones,
Trampling contemptuously on thy disdain.
And here is writ ' love-wounded Proteus.'
Poor wounded name ! my bosom as a bed
Shall lodge thee till thy wound be thoroughly
  heal'd ;
And thus I search it with a sovereign kiss.
But twice or thrice was ' Proteus ' written
  down.
Be calm, good wind, blow not a word away
Till I have found each letter in the letter,
Except mine own name : that some whirlwind
  bear   120
Unto a ragged fearful-hanging rock
And throw it thence into the raging sea !
Lo, here in one line is his name twice writ,
' Poor forlorn Proteus, passionate Proteus,
To the sweet Julia : ' that I'll tear away.
And yet I will not, sith so prettily
He couples it to his complaining names.
Thus will I fold them one upon another :
Now kiss, embrace, contend, do what you will.

Re-enter LUCETTA.

Luc. Madam,   130
Dinner is ready, and your father stays.
Jul. Well, let us go.
Luc. What, shall these papers lie like tell-
  tales here ?
Jul. If you respect them, best to take them
  up.
Luc. Nay, I was taken up for laying them
  down :
Yet here they shall not lie, for catching cold.
Jul. I see you have a month's mind to
  them.
Luc. Ay, madam, you may say what sights
  you see ;
I see things too, although you judge I wink.
Jul. Come, come ; will't please you go ?
          [*Exeunt.*

SCENE III. *The same.* ANTONIO'S *house.*

Enter ANTONIO *and* PANTHINO.

Ant. Tell me, Panthino, what sad talk was
  that
Wherewith my brother held you in the clois-
  ter ?
Pan. 'Twas of his nephew Proteus, your
  son.
Ant. Why, what of him ?
Pan.   He wonder'd that your lordship
Would suffer him to spend his youth at home,
While other men, of slender reputation,
Put forth their sons to seek preferment out :
Some to the wars, to try their fortune there ;
Some to discover islands far away ;
Some to the studious universities.   10
For any or for all these exercises,
He said that Proteus your son was meet,
And did request me to importune you
To let him spend his time no more at home,
Which would be great impeachment to his age,
In having known no travel in his youth.
Ant. Nor need'st thou much importune
  me to that
Whereon this month I have been hammering.
I have consider'd well his loss of time
And how he cannot be a perfect man,   20

Not being tried and tutor'd in the world :
Experience is by industry achieved
And perfected by the swift course of time.
Then tell me, whither were I best to send
  him ?
  Pan. I think your lordship is not ignorant
How his companion, youthful Valentine,
Attends the emperor in his royal court.
  Ant. I know it well.
  Pan. 'Twere good, I think, your lordship
    sent him thither :
There shall he practise tilts and tournaments,
Hear sweet discourse, converse with noble-
  men,   31
And be in eye of every exercise
Worthy his youth and nobleness of birth.
  Ant. I like thy counsel ; well hast thou
    advised :
And that thou mayst perceive how well I like
  it,
The execution of it shall make known.
Even with the speediest expedition
I will dispatch him to the emperor's court.
  Pan. To-morrow, may it please you, Don
    Alphonso,
With other gentlemen of good esteem,   40
Are journeying to salute the emperor
And to commend their service to his will.
  Ant. Good company ; with them shall Pro-
    teus go :
And, in good time ! now will we break with
  him.

                Enter Proteus.

  Pro. Sweet love ! sweet lines ! sweet life !
Here is her hand, the agent of her heart ;
Here is her oath for love, her honor's pawn.
O, that our fathers would applaud our loves,
To seal our happiness with their consents !
O heavenly Julia !   50
  Ant. How now ! what letter are you read-
    ing there ?
  Pro. May't please your lordship, 'tis a word
    or two
Of commendations sent from Valentine,
Deliver'd by a friend that came from him.
  Ant. Lend me the letter ; let me see what
    news.
  Pro. There is no news, my lord, but that
    he writes
How happily he lives, how well beloved
And daily graced by the emperor ;
Wishing me with him, partner of his fortune.
  Ant. And how stand you affected to his
    wish ?   60
  Pro. As one relying on your lordship's
    will
And not depending on his friendly wish.
  Ant. My will is something sorted with his
    wish.
Muse not that I thus suddenly proceed ;
For what I will, I will, and there an end.
I am resolved that thou shalt spend some time
With Valentinus in the emperor's court :
What maintenance he from his friends re-
  ceives,
Like exhibition thou shalt have from me.
To-morrow be in readiness to go :   70
Excuse it not, for I am peremptory.
  Pro. My lord, I cannot be so soon pro-
    vided :
Please you, deliberate a day or two.

  Ant. Look, what thou want'st shall be sent
    after thee :
No more of stay ! to-morrow thou must go.
Come on, Panthino : you shall be employ'd
To hasten on his expedition.
              [*Exeunt Ant. and Pan.*
  Pro. Thus have I shunn'd the fire for fear
    of burning,
And drench'd me in the sea, where I am
    drown'd.
I fear'd to show my father Julia's letter,   80
Lest he should take exceptions to my love ;
And with the vantage of mine own excuse
Hath he excepted most against my love.
O, how this spring of love resembleth
The uncertain glory of an April day,
Which now shows all the beauty of the sun,
And by and by a cloud takes all away !

              Re-enter Panthino.

  Pan. Sir Proteus, your father calls for
    you :
He is in haste ; therefore, I pray you, go.
  Pro. Why, this it is : my heart accords
    thereto,   90
And yet a thousand times it answers 'no.'
                            [*Exeunt.*

                —————

                 ACT II.

  Scene I. *Milan. The* Duke's *palace.*

       Enter Valentine *and* Speed.

  Speed. Sir, your glove.
  Val.   Not mine ; my gloves are on.
  Speed. Why, then, this may be yours, for
    this is but one.
  Val. Ha ! let me see : ay, give it me, it's
    mine :
Sweet ornament that decks a thing divine !
Ah, Silvia, Silvia !
  Speed. Madam Silvia ! Madam Silvia !
  Val. How now, sirrah ?
  Speed. She is not within hearing, sir.
  Val. Why, sir, who bade you call her ?
  Speed. Your worship, sir ; or else I mis-
    took.   10
  Val. Well, you'll still be too forward.
  Speed. And yet I was last chidden for be-
ing too slow.
  Val. Go to, sir : tell me, do you know
Madam Silvia ?
  Speed. She that your worship loves ?
  Val. Why, how know you that I am in
    love ?
  Speed. Marry, by these special marks :
first, you have learned, like Sir Proteus, to
wreathe your arms, like a malecontent ; to
relish a love-song, like a robin-redbreast ; to
walk alone, like one that had the pestilence ;
to sigh, like a school-boy that had lost his
A B C ; to weep, like a young wench that had
buried her grandam ; to fast, like one that
takes diet ; to watch, like one that fears robbing ; to speak puling, like a beggar at Hallowmas. You were wont, when you laughed,
to crow like a cock ; when you walked, to
walk like one of the lions ; when you fasted,
it was presently after dinner ; when you looked
sadly, it was for want of money : and now
you are metamorphosed with a mistress, that,

when I look on you, I can hardly think you
my master.

Val. Are all these things perceived in me ?

Speed. They are all perceived without ye.

Val. Without me ? they cannot.

Speed. Without you ? nay, that's certain,
for, without you were so simple, none else
would : but you are so without these follies,
that these follies are within you and shine
through you like the water in an urinal, that
not an eye that sees you but is a physician to
comment on your malady.

Val. But tell me, dost thou know my lady
Silvia ?

Speed. She that you gaze on so as she sits
at supper ?

Val. Hast thou observed that ? even she,
I mean.

Speed. Why, sir, I know her not.   50

Val. Dost thou know her by my gazing on
her, and yet knowest her not ?

Speed. Is she not hard-favored, sir ?

Val. Not so fair, boy, as well-favored.

Speed. Sir, I know that well enough.

Val. What dost thou know ?

Speed. That she is not so fair as, of you,
well-favored.

Val. I mean that her beauty is exquisite,
but her favor infinite.   60

Speed. That's because the one is painted
and the other out of all count.

Val. How painted ? and how out of
count ?

Speed. Marry, sir, so painted, to make her
fair, that no man counts of her beauty.

Val. How esteemest thou me ? I account
of her beauty.

Speed. You never saw her since she was
deformed.

Val. How long hath she been deformed ?

Speed. Ever since you loved her.   71

Val. I have loved her ever since I saw
her ; and still I see her beautiful.

Speed. If you love her, you cannot see
her.

Val. Why ?

Speed. Because Love is blind. O, that you
had mine eyes ; or your own eyes had the
lights they were wont to have when you chid
at Sir Proteus for going ungartered !

Val. What should I see then ?   80

Speed. Your own present folly and her
passing deformity : for he, being in love,
could not see to garter his hose, and you, being in love, cannot see to put on your hose.

Val. Belike, boy, then, you are in love ;
for last morning you could not see to wipe
my shoes.

Speed. True, sir ; I was in love with my
bed : I thank you, you swinged me for my
love, which makes me the bolder to chide
you for yours.

Val. In conclusion, I stand affected to
her.

Speed. I would you were set, so your affection would cease.   91

Val. Last night she enjoined me to write
some lines to one she loves.

Speed. And have you ?

Val. I have.

Speed. Are they not lamely writ ?

Val. No, boy, but as well as I can do
them. Peace ! here she comes.

Speed. [*Aside*] O excellent motion ! O exceeding puppet ! Now will he interpret to her.

Enter SILVIA.

Val. Madam and mistress, a thousand
good-morrows.

Speed. [*Aside*] O, give ye good even !
here's a million of manners.

Sil. Sir Valentine and servant, to you
two thousand.

Speed. [*Aside*] He should give her interest, and she gives it him.

Val. As you enjoin'd me, I have writ your
letter

Unto the secret nameless friend of yours ;
Which I was much unwilling to proceed in
But for my duty to your ladyship.

Sil. I thank you, gentle servant : 'tis very
clerkly done.

Val. Now trust me, madam, it came hardly
off ;
For being ignorant to whom it goes
I writ at random, very doubtfully.

Sil. Perchance you think too much of so
much pains ?

Val. No, madam ; so it stead you, I will
write,
Please you command, a thousand times as
much ;
And yet—

Sil. A pretty period ! Well, I guess the
sequel ;
And yet I will not name it ; and yet I care
not ;
And yet take this again ; and yet I thank you,
Meaning henceforth to trouble you no more.

Speed. [*Aside*] And yet you will ; and yet
another ' yet.'

Val. What means your ladyship ? do you
not like it ?

Sil. Yes, yes ; the lines are very quaintly
writ ;
But since unwillingly, take them again.
Nay, take them.   130

Val. Madam, they are for you.

Sil. Ay, ay : you writ them, sir, at my re-
quest ;
But I will none of them ; they are for you ;
I would have had them writ more movingly.

Val. Please you, I'll write your ladyship
another.

Sil. And when it's writ, for my sake read
it over,
And if it please you, so ; if not, why, so.

Val. If it please me, madam, what then ?

Sil. Why, if it please you, take it for your
labor :
And so, good morrow, servant.   [*Exit.* 140

Speed. O jest unseen, inscrutable, invisible,
As a nose on a man's face, or a weathercock
on a steeple !
My master sues to her, and she hath taught
her suitor,
He being her pupil, to become her tutor.
O excellent device ! was there ever heard a
better,
That my master, being scribe, to himself
should write the letter ?

Val. How now, sir ? what are you reasoning with yourself ?

Speed. Nay, I was rhyming : 'tis you that have the reason.   150

Val. To do what ?

Speed. To be a spokesman for Madam Silvia.

Val. To whom ?

Speed. To yourself : why, she wooes you by a figure.

Val. What figure ?

Speed. By a letter, I should say.

Val. Why, she hath not writ to me ?

Speed. What need she, when she hath made you write to yourself ? Why, do you not perceive the jest ?   160

Val. No, believe me.

Speed. No believing you, indeed, sir. But did you perceive her earnest ?

Val. She gave me none, except an angry word.

Speed. Why, she hath given you a letter.

Val. That's the letter I writ to her friend.

Speed. And that letter hath she delivered, and there an end.

Val. I would it were no worse.

Speed. I'll warrant you, 'tis as well :   170
For often have you writ to her, and she, in modesty,
Or else for want of idle time, could not again reply ;
Or fearing else some messenger that might her mind discover,
Herself hath taught her love himself to write unto her lover.
All this I speak in print, for in print I found it.
Why muse you, sir ? 'tis dinner-time.

Val. I have dined.

Speed. Ay, but hearken, sir ; though the chameleon Love can feed on the air, I am one that am nourished by my victuals, and would fain have meat. O, be not like your mistress ; be moved, be moved.   [*Exeunt.*

Scene II.   *Verona.*   Julia's *house.*

Enter Proteus *and* Julia.

Pro. Have patience, gentle Julia.

Jul. I must, where is no remedy.

Pro. When possibly I can, I will return.

Jul. If you turn not, you will return the sooner.
Keep this remembrance for thy Julia's sake.
     [*Giving a ring.*

Pro. Why, then, we'll make exchange ; here, take you this.

Jul. And seal the bargain with a holy kiss.

Pro. Here is my hand for my true constancy ;
And when that hour o'erslips me in the day   10
Wherein I sigh not, Julia, for thy sake,
The next ensuing hour some foul mischance
Torment me for my love's forgetfulness !
My father stays my coming ; answer not ;
The tide is now : nay, not thy tide of tears ;
That tide will stay me longer than I should.
Julia, farewell !   [*Exit Julia.*
     What, gone without a word ?
Ay, so true love should do : it cannot speak ;
For truth hath better deeds than words to grace it.

Enter Panthino.

Pan. Sir Proteus, you are stay'd for.

Pro. Go ; I come, I come.   20
Alas ! this parting strikes poor lovers dumb.
     [*Exeunt.*

Scene III.   *The same.   A street.*

Enter Launce, *leading a dog.*

Launce. Nay, 'twill be this hour ere I have done weeping ; all the kind of the Launces have this very fault. I have received my proportion, like the prodigious son, and am going with Sir Proteus to the Imperial's court. I think Crab, my dog, be the sourest-natured dog that lives : my mother weeping, my father wailing, my sister crying, our maid howling, our cat wringing her hands, and all our house in a great perplexity, yet did not this cruel-hearted cur shed one tear : he is a stone, a very pebble stone, and has no more pity in him than a dog : a Jew would have wept to have seen our parting ; why, my grandam, having no eyes, look you, wept herself blind at my parting. Nay, I'll show you the manner of it. This shoe is my father : no, this left shoe is my father : no, no, this left shoe is my mother : nay, that cannot be so neither : yes, it is so, it is so, it hath the worser sole. This shoe, with the hole in it, is my mother, and this my father ; a vengeance on't ! there 'tis : now, sit, this staff is my sister, for, look you, she is as white as a lily and as small as a wand : this hat is Nan, our maid : I am the dog : no, the dog is himself, and I am the dog —Oh ! the dog is me, and I am myself ; ay, so, so. Now come I to my father ; Father, your blessing : now should not the shoe speak a word for weeping : now should I kiss my father ; well, he weeps on. Now come I to my mother : O, that she could speak now like a wood woman ! Well, I kiss her ; why, there 'tis ; here's my mother's breath up and down. Now come I to my sister ; mark the moan she makes. Now the dog all this while sheds not a tear nor speaks a word ; but see how I lay the dust with my tears.

Enter Panthino.

Pan. Launce, away, away, aboard ! thy master is shipped and thou art to post after with oars. What's the matter ? why weepest thou, man ? Away, ass ! you'll lose the tide, if you tarry any longer.

Launce. It is no matter if the tied were lost ; for it is the unkindest tied that ever any man tied.

Pan. What's the unkindest tide ?

Launce. Why, he that's tied here, Crab, my dog.

Pan. Tut, man, I mean thou'lt lose the flood, and, in losing the flood, lose thy voyage, and, in losing thy voyage, lose thy master, and, in losing thy master, lose thy service, and, in losing thy service,—Why dost thou stop my mouth ?   51

Launce. For fear thou shouldst lose thy tongue.

Pan. Where should I lose my tongue ?

Launce. In thy tale.

Pan. In thy tail !

Launce. Lose the tide, and the voyage, and

the master, and the service, and the tied!
Why, man, if the river were dry, I am able to
fill it with my tears ; if the wind were down, I
could drive the boat with my sighs.   60
Pan. Come, come away, man ; I was sent
to call thee.
Launce. Sir, call me what thou darest.
Pan. Wilt thou go ?
Launce. Well, I will go.   [*Exeunt.*

SCENE IV. *Milan. The* DUKE's *palace.*

Enter SILVIA, VALENTINE, THURIO, *and*
SPEED.

Sil. Servant !
Val. Mistress ?
Speed. Master, Sir Thurio frowns on you.
Val. Ay, boy, it's for love.
Speed. Not of you.
Val. Of my mistress, then.
Speed. 'Twere good you knocked him.
    [*Exit.*
Sil. Servant, you are sad.
Val. Indeed, madam, I seem so.
Thu. Seem you that you are not ?   10
Val. Haply I do.
Thu. So do counterfeits.
Val. So do you.
Thu. What seem I that I am not ?
Val. Wise.
Thu. What instance of the contrary ?
Val. Your folly.
Thu. And how quote you my folly ?
Val. I quote it in your jerkin.
Thu. My jerkin is a doublet.   20
Val. Well, then, I'll double your folly.
Thu. How ?
Sil. What, angry, Sir Thurio ! do you
change color ?
Val. Give him leave, madam ; he is a kind
of chameleon.
Thu. That hath more mind to feed on
your blood than live in your air.
Val. You have said, sir.
Thu. Ay, sir, and done too, for this
time.   30
Val. I know it well, sir ; you always end
ere you begin.
Sil. A fine volley of words, gentlemen, and
quickly shot off.
Val. 'Tis indeed, madam ; we thank the
giver.
Sil. Who is that, servant ?
Val. Yourself, sweet lady ; for you gave
the fire. Sir Thurio borrows his wit from your
ladyship's looks, and spends what he borrows
kindly in your company.   40
Thu. Sir, if you spend word for word with
me, I shall make your wit bankrupt.
Val. I know it well, sir ; you have an exchequer of words, and, I think, no other treasure to give your followers, for it appears by
their bare liveries, that they live by your bare
words.
Sil. No more, gentlemen, no more : here
comes my father.

Enter DUKE.

Duke. Now, daughter Silvia, you are hard
beset.   49
Sir Valentine, your father's in good health :
What say you to a letter from your friends
Of much good news ?

Val.   My lord, I will be thankful.
To any happy messenger from thence.
Duke. Know ye Don Antonio, your coun-
tryman ?
Val. Ay, my good lord, I know the gentle-
man
To be of worth and worthy estimation
And not without desert so well reputed.
Duke. Hath he not a son ?
Val. Ay, my good lord ; a son that well
deserves
The honor and regard of such a father.   60
Duke. You know him well ?
Val. I know him as myself ; for from our
infancy
We have conversed and spent our hours to-
gether :
And though myself have been an idle truant,
Omitting the sweet benefit of time
To clothe mine age with angel-like perfection,
Yet hath Sir Proteus, for that's his name,
Made use and fair advantage of his days ;
His years but young, but his experience old ;
His head unmellow'd, but his judgment ripe ;
And, in a word, for far behind his worth   71
Comes all the praises that I now bestow,
He is complete in feature and in mind
With all good grace to grace a gentleman.
Duke. Beshrew me, sir, but if he make
this good,
He is as worthy for an empress' love
As meet to be an emperor's counsellor.
Well, sir, this gentleman is come to me,
With commendation from great potentates ;
And here he means to spend his time awhile :
I think 'tis no unwelcome news to you.   81
Val. Should I have wish'd a thing, it had
been he.
Duke. Welcome him then according to
his worth.
Silvia, I speak to you, and you, Sir Thurio ;
For Valentine, I need not cite him to it :
I will send him hither to you presently. [*Exit.*
Val. This is the gentleman I told your
ladyship
Had come along with me, but that his mis-
tress
Did hold his eyes lock'd in her crystal looks.
Sil. Belike that now she hath enfranchised
them   90
Upon some other pawn for fealty.
Val. Nay, sure, I think she holds them
prisoners still.
Sil. Nay, then he should be blind ; and,
being blind,
How could he see his way to seek out you ?
Val. Why, lady, Love hath twenty pair of
eyes.
Thu. They say that Love hath not an eye
at all.
Val. To see such lovers, Thurio, as your-
self :
Upon a homely object Love can wink.
Sil. Have done, have done ; here comes
the gentleman.   [*Exit* THURIO.

Enter PROTEUS.

Val. Welcome, dear Proteus ! Mistress, I
beseech you,   100
Confirm his welcome with some special favor.
Sil. His worth is warrant for his welcome
hither,

If this be he you oft have wish'd to hear from.
Val. Mistress, it is : sweet lady, entertain
him
To be my fellow-servant to your ladyship.
Sil. Too low a mistress for so high a
servant.
Pro. Not so, sweet lady : but too mean a
servant
To have a look of such a worthy mistress.
Val. Leave off discourse of disability : 109
Sweet lady, entertain him for your servant.
Pro. My duty will I boast of ; nothing else.
Sil. And duty never yet did want his
meed :
Servant, you are welcome to a worthless mis-
tress.
Pro. I'll die on him that says so but your-
self.
Sil. That you are welcome ?
Pro.   That you are worthless.

Re-enter THURIO.

Thu. Madam, my lord your father would
speak with you.
Sil. I wait upon his pleasure. Come, Sir
Thurio,
Go with me. Once more, new servant, wel-
come :
I'll leave you to confer of home affairs ;
When you have done, we look to hear from
you.
Pro. We'll both attend upon your ladyship.
                    [*Exeunt Silvia and Thurio.*
Val. Now, tell me, how do all from
whence you came ?
Pro. Your friends are well and have them
much commended.
Val. And how do yours ?
Pro.   I left them all in health.
Val. How does your lady ? and how
thrives your love ?
Pro. My tales of love were wont to weary
you ;
I know you joy not in a love-discourse.
Val. Ay, Proteus, but that life is alter'd
now :
I have done penance for contemning Love,
Whose high imperious thoughts have punish'd
me
With bitter fasts, with penitential groans,
With nightly tears and daily heart-sore sighs ;
For in revenge of my contempt of love,
Love hath chased sleep from my enthralled
eyes
And made them watchers of mine own heart's
sorrow.
O gentle Proteus, Love's a mighty lord,
And hath so humbled me, as, I confess,
There is no woe to his correction,
Nor to his service no such joy on earth.
Now no discourse, except it be of love ;   140
Now can I break my fast, dine, sup and sleep,
Upon the very naked name of love.
Pro. Enough ; I read your fortune in your
eye.
Was this the idol that you worship so ?
Val. Even she ; and is she not a heavenly
saint ?
Pro. No ; but she is an earthly paragon.
Val. Call her divine.
Pro.   I will not flatter her.

Val. O, flatter me ; for love delights in
praises.
Pro. When I was sick, you gave me bitter
pills,
And I must minister the like to you.   150
Val. Then speak the truth by her ; if not
divine,
Yet let her be a principality,
Sovereign to all the creatures on the earth.
Pro. Except my mistress.
Val.   Sweet, except not any ;
Except thou wilt except against my love.
Pro. Have I not reason to prefer mine
own ?
Val. And I will help thee to prefer her
too :
She shall be dignified with this high honor—
To bear my lady's train, lest the base earth
Should from her vesture chance to steal a kiss
And, of so great a favor growing proud,   161
Disdain to root the summer-swelling flower
And make rough winter everlastingly.
Pro. Why, Valentine, what braggardism is
this ?
Val. Pardon me, Proteus : all I can is
nothing
To her whose worth makes other worthies
nothing ;
She is alone.
Pro.   Then let her alone.
Val. Not for the world : why, man, she is
mine own,
And I as rich in having such a jewel
As twenty seas, if all their sand were pearl,
The water nectar and the rocks pure gold. 171
Forgive me that I do not dream on thee,
Because thou see'st me dote upon my love.
My foolish rival, that her father likes
Only for his possessions are so huge,
Is gone with her along, and I must after,
For love, thou know'st, is full of jealousy.
Pro. But she loves you ?
Val. Ay, and we are betroth'd : nay, more,
our marriage-hour,
With all the cunning manner of our flight, 180
Determined of ; how I must climb her win-
dow,
The ladder made of cords, and all the means
Plotted and 'greed on for my happiness.
Good Proteus, go with me to my chamber,
In these affairs to aid me with thy counsel.
Pro. Go on before ; I shall inquire
you forth :
I must unto the road, to disembark
Some necessaries that I needs must use,
And then I'll presently attend you.
Val. Will you make haste ?   190
Pro. I will.   [*Exit Valentine.*
Even as one heat another heat expels,
Or as one nail by strength drives out another,
So the remembrance of my former love
Is by a newer object quite forgotten.
Is it mine, or Valentine's praise,
Her true perfection, or my false transgression,
That makes me reasonless to reason thus ?
She is fair ; and so is Julia that I love—
That I did love, for now my love is thaw'd ;
Which, like a waxen image, 'gainst a fire,   201
Bears no impression of the thing it was.
Methinks my zeal to Valentine is cold,
And that I love him not as I was wont.
O, but I love his lady too too much,

And that's the reason I love him so little.
How shall I dote on her with more advice,
That thus without advice begin to love her!
'Tis but her picture I have yet beheld,
And that hath dazzled my reason's light;   210
But when I look on her perfections,
There is no reason but I shall be blind.
If I can check my erring love, I will;
If not, to compass her I'll use my skill. [*Exit.*

SCENE V. *The same. A street.*

Enter SPEED *and* LAUNCE *severally.*

Speed. Launce! by mine honesty, welcome
to Milan!

Launce. Forswear not thyself, sweet youth,
for I am not welcome. I reckon this always,
that a man is never undone till he be hanged,
nor never welcome to a place till some certain
shot be paid and the hostess say 'Welcome!'

Speed. Come on, you madcap, I'll to the
alehouse with you presently; where, for one
shot of five pence, thou shalt have five thousand welcomes. But, sirrah, how did thy
master part with Madam Julia?

Launce. Marry, after they closed in earnest, they parted very fairly in jest.

Speed. But shall she marry him?

Launce. No.

Speed. How then? shall he marry her?

Launce. No, neither.

Speed. What, are they broken?

Launce. No, they are both as whole as a
fish.

Speed. Why, then, how stands the matter
with them?

Launce. Marry, thus; when it stands well
with him, it stands well with her.

Speed. What an ass art thou! I understand thee not.

Launce. What a block art thou, that thou
canst not! My staff understands me.

Speed. What thou sayest?

Launce. Ay, and what I do too: look thee,
I'll but lean, and my staff understands me.

Speed. It stands under thee, indeed.

Launce. Why, stand-under and understand is all one.

Speed. But tell me true, will't be a match?

Launce. Ask my dog: if he say ay, it will!
if he say no, it will; if he shake his tail and
say nothing, it will.

Speed. The conclusion is then that it will.

Launce. Thou shalt never get such a secret
from me but by a parable.

Speed. 'Tis well that I get it so. But,
Launce, how sayest thou, that my master is
become a notable lover?

Launce. I never knew him otherwise.

Speed. Than how?

Launce. A notable lubber, as thou report-
est him to be.

Speed. Why, thou whoreson ass, thou mistakest me.   50

Launce. Why, fool, I meant not thee; I
meant thy master.

Speed. I tell thee, my master is become a
hot lover.

Launce. Why, I tell thee, I care not though
he burn himself in love. If thou wilt, go with
me to the alehouse; if not, thou art an Hebrew, a Jew, and not worth the name of a
Christian.

Speed. Why?

Launce. Because thou hast not so much
charity in thee as to go to the ale with a
Christian. Wilt thou go?

Speed. At thy service.   [*Exeunt.*

SCENE VI. *The same. The* DUKE'S *palace.*

Enter PROTEUS.

Pro. To leave my Julia, shall I be for-
      sworn;
To love fair Silvia, shall I be forsworn;
To wrong my friend, I shall be much for-
      sworn;
And even that power which gave me first my
      oath
Provokes me to this threefold perjury;
Love bade me swear and Love bids me for-
      swear.
O sweet-suggesting Love, if thou hast sinn'd,
Teach me, thy tempted subject, to excuse it!
At first I did adore a twinkling star,
But now I worship a celestial sun.   10
Unheedful vows may heedfully be broken,
And he wants wit that wants resolved will
To learn his wit to exchange the bad for
      better.
Fie, fie, unreverend tongue! to call her bad,
Whose sovereignty so oft thou hast preferr'd
With twenty thousand soul-confirming oaths.
I cannot leave to love, and yet I do;
But there I leave to love where I should love.
Julia I lose and Valentine I lose:
If I keep them, I needs must lose myself;   20
If I lose them, thus find I by their loss
For Valentine myself, for Julia Silvia.
I to myself am dearer than a friend,
For love is still most precious in itself;
And Silvia—witness Heaven, that made her
      fair!—
Shows Julia but a swarthy Ethiope.
I will forget that Julia is alive,
Remembering that my love to her is dead;
And Valentine I'll hold an enemy,
Aiming at Silvia as a sweeter friend.   30
I cannot now prove constant to myself,
Without some treachery used to Valentine.
This night he meaneth with a corded ladder
To climb celestial Silvia's chamber-window,
Myself in counsel, his competitor.
Now presently I'll give her father notice
Of their disguising and pretended flight;
Who, all enraged, will banish Valentine;
For Thurio, he intends, shall wed his daugh-
      ter;
But, Valentine being gone, I'll quickly cross
By some sly trick blunt Thurio's dull pro-
      ceeding.
Love, lend me wings to make my purpose
      swift,
As thou hast lent me wit to plot this drift!
                                              [*Exit.*

SCENE VII. *Verona.* JULIA'S *house.*

Enter JULIA *and* LUCETTA.

Jul. Counsel, Lucetta; gentle girl, assist
      me;
And even in kind love I do conjure thee,
Who art the table wherein all my thoughts
Are visibly character'd and engraved,
To lesson me and tell me some good mean
How, with my honor, I may undertake
A journey to my loving Proteus.

Luc. Alas, the way is wearisome and long!
Jul. A true-devoted pilgrim is not weary
To measure kingdoms with his feeble steps;
Much less shall she that hath Love's wings to
　　fly,　　11
And when the flight is made to one so dear,
Of such divine perfection, as Sir Proteus.
Luc. Better forbear till Proteus make re-
　　turn.
Jul. O, know'st thou not his looks are my
　　soul's food?
Pity the dearth that I have pined in,
By longing for that food so long a time.
Didst thou but know the inly touch of love,
Thou wouldst as soon go kindle fire with snow
As seek to quench the fire of love with words.
Luc. I do not seek to quench your love's
　　hot fire,　　21
But qualify the fire's extreme rage,
Lest it should burn above the bounds of rea-
　　son.
Jul. The more thou damm'st it up, the
　　more it burns.
The current that with gentle murmur glides,
Thou know'st, being stopp'd, impatiently doth
　　rage;
But when his fair course is not hindered,
He makes sweet music with the enamell'd
　　stones,
Giving a gentle kiss to every sedge
He overtaketh in his pilgrimage,　　30
And so by many winding nooks he strays
With willing sport to the wild ocean.
Then let me go and hinder not my course
I'll be as patient as a gentle stream
And make a pastime of each weary step,
Till the last step have brought me to my love;
And there I'll rest, as after much turmoil
A blessed soul doth in Elysium.
Luc. But in what habit will you go along?
Jul. Not like a woman; for I would pre-
　　vent　　40
The loose encounters of lascivious men:
Gentle Lucetta, fit me with such weeds
As may beseem some well-reputed page.
Luc. Why, then, your ladyship must cut
　　your hair.
Jul. No, girl, I'll knit it up in silken strings
With twenty odd-conceited true-love knots.
To be fantastic may become a youth
Of greater time than I shall show to be.
Luc. What fashion, madam, shall I make
　　your breeches?
Jul. That fits as well as 'Tell me, good my
　　lord,　　50
What compass will you wear your farthin-
　　gale?'
Why even what fashion thou best likest,
　　Lucetta.
Luc. You must needs have them with a
　　codpiece, madam.
Jul. Out, out, Lucetta! that would be ill-
　　favor'd.
Luc. A round hose, madam, now's not
　　worth a pin,
Unless you have a codpiece to stick pins on.
Jul. Lucetta, as thou lovest me, let me have
What thou thinkest meet and is most man-
　　nerly.
But tell me, wench, how will the world repute
　　me
For undertaking so unstaid a journey?　　60

I fear me, it will make me scandalized.
Luc. If you think so, then stay at home
　　and go not.
Jul. Nay, that I will not.
Luc. Then never dream on infamy, but go.
If Proteus like your journey when you come,
No matter who's displeased when you are
　　gone:
I fear me, he will scarce be pleased withal.
Jul. That is the least, Lucetta, of my fear:
A thousand oaths, an ocean of his tears
And instances of infinite of love　　70
Warrant me welcome to my Proteus.
Luc. All these are servants to deceitful
　　men.
Jul. Base men, that use them to so base
　　effect!
But truer stars did govern Proteus' birth;
His words are bonds, his oaths are oracles,
His love sincere, his thoughts immaculate,
His tears pure messengers sent from his heart,
His heart as far from fraud as heaven from
　　earth.
Luc. Pray heaven he prove so, when you
　　come to him!
Jul. Now, as thou lovest me, do him not
　　that wrong　　80
To bear a hard opinion of his truth:
Only deserve my love by loving him;
And presently go with me to my chamber,
To take a note of what I stand in need of,
To furnish me upon my longing journey.
All that is mine I leave at thy dispose,
My goods, my lands, my reputation;
Only, in lieu thereof, dispatch me hence.
Come, answer not, but to it presently!
I am impatient of my tarriance.　　90
　　　　　　　　　　　　　　[Exeunt.

ACT III.

SCENE I. *Milan. The* DUKE'S *palace.*

Enter DUKE, THURIO, *and* PROTEUS.

Duke. Sir Thurio, give us leave, I pray,
　　awhile;
We have some secrets to confer about.
　　　　　　　　　　　　　　[Exit Thu.
Now, tell me, Proteus, what's your will with
　　me?
Pro. My gracious lord, that which I would
　　discover
The law of friendship bids me to conceal;
But when I call to mind your gracious favors
Done to me, undeserving as I am,
My duty pricks me on to utter that
Which else no worldly good should draw from
　　me.　　9
Know, worthy prince, Sir Valentine, my friend,
This night intends to steal away your daugh-
　　ter:
Myself am one made privy to the plot.
I know you have determined to bestow her
On Thurio, whom your gentle daughter hates;
And should she thus be stol'n away from you,
It would be much vexation to your age,
Thus, for my duty's sake, I rather chose
To cross my friend in his intended drift
Than, by concealing it, heap on your head
A pack of sorrows which would press you
　　down,　　20

Being unprevented, to your timeless grave.
    Duke. Proteus, I thank thee for thine hon-
        est care ;
Which to requite, command me while I live.
This love of theirs myself have often seen,
Haply when they have judged me fast asleep,
And oftentimes have purposed to forbid
Sir Valentine her company and my court :
But fearing lest my jealous aim might err
And so unworthily disgrace the man,
A rashness that I ever yet have shunn'd,   30
I gave him gentle looks, thereby to find
That which thyself hast now disclosed to me.
And, that thou mayst perceive my fear of this,
Knowing that tender youth is soon suggested,
I nightly lodge her in an upper tower,
The key whereof myself have ever kept ;
And thence she cannot be convey'd away.
    Pro. Know, noble lord, they have devised a
        mean
How he her chamber-window will ascend
And with a corded ladder fetch her down ;   40
For which the youthful lover now is gone
And this way comes he with it presently ;
Where, if it please you, you may intercept him.
But, good my Lord, do it so cunningly
That my discovery be not aimed at ;
For love of you, not hate unto my friend,
Hath made me publisher of this pretence.
    Duke. Upon mine honor, he shall never
        know
That I had any light from thee of this.
    Pro. Adieu, my Lord ; Sir Valentine is
        coming.   [*Exit.* 50

              Enter VALENTINE.

    Duke. Sir Valentine, whither away so fast ?
    Val. Please it your grace, there is a mes-
        senger
That stays to bear my letters to my friends,
And I am going to deliver them.
    Duke. Be they of much import ?
    Val. The tenor of them doth but signify
My health and happy being at your court.
    Duke. Nay then, no matter ; stay with me
        awhile ;
I am to break with thee of some affairs
That touch me near, wherein thou must be se-
        cret.   60
'Tis not unknown to thee that I have sought
To match my friend Sir Thurio to my daugh-
        ter.
    Val. I know it well, my Lord ; and, sure,
        the match
Were rich and honorable ; besides, the gentle-
        man
Is full of virtue, bounty, worth and qualities
Beseeming such a wife as your fair daughter :
Cannot your Grace win her to fancy him ?
    Duke. No, trust me ; she is peevish, sullen,
        froward,
Proud, disobedient, stubborn, lacking duty,
Neither regarding that she is my child   70
Nor fearing me as if I were her father ;
And, may I say to thee, this pride of hers,
Upon advice, hath drawn my love from her ;
And, where I thought the remnant of mine
        age
Should have been cherish'd by her child-like
        duty,
I now am full resolved to take a wife
And turn her out to who will take her in :

Then let her beauty be her wedding-dower ;
For me and my possessions she esteems not.
    Val. What would your Grace have me to
        do in this ?   80
    Duke. There is a lady in Verona here
Whom I affect ; but she is nice and coy
And nought esteems my aged eloquence :
Now therefore would I have thee to my
        tutor—
For long agone I have forgot to court ;
Besides, the fashion of the time is changed—
How and which way I may bestow myself
To be regarded in her sun-bright eye.
    Val. Win her with gifts, if she respect not
        words :
Dumb jewels often in their silent kind   90
More than quick words do move a woman's
        mind.
    Duke. But she did scorn a present that I
        sent her.
    Val. A woman sometimes scorns what best
        contents her.
Send her another ; never give her o'er ;
For scorn at first makes after-love the more.
If she do frown, 'tis not in hate of you,
But rather to beget more love in you :
If she do chide, 'tis not to have you gone ;
For why, the fools are mad, if left alone.
Take no repulse, whatever she doth say ;   100
For ' get you gone,' she doth not mean
        ' away ! '
Flatter and praise, commend, extol their
        graces ;
Though ne'er so black, say they have angels'
        faces.
That man that hath a tongue, I say, is no man,
If with his tongue he cannot win a woman.
    Duke. But she I mean is promised by her
        friends
Unto a youthful gentleman of worth,
And kept severely from resort of men,
That no man hath access by day to her.
    Val. Why, then, I would resort to her by
        night.   110
    Duke. Ay, but the doors be lock'd and keys
        kept safe,
That no man hath recourse to her by night.
    Val. What lets but one may enter at her
        window ?
    Duke. Her chamber is aloft, far from the
        ground,
And built so shelving that one cannot climb it
Without apparent hazard of his life.
    Val. Why then, a ladder quaintly made of
        cords,
To cast up, with a pair of anchoring hooks,
Would serve to scale another Hero's tower,
So bold Leander would adventure it.   120
    Duke. Now, as thou art a gentleman of
        blood,
Advise me where I may have such a ladder.
    Val. When would you use it ? pray, sir,
        tell me that.
    Duke. This very night ; for Love is like a
        child,
That longs for every thing that he can come
        by.
    Val. By seven o'clock I'll get you such a
        ladder.
    Duke. But, hark thee ; I will go to her
        alone :
How shall I best convey the ladder thither ?

Val. It will be light, my lord, that you may
 bear it
Under a cloak that is of any length.   130
 Duke. A cloak as long as thine will serve
 the turn?
 Val. Ay, my good lord.
 Duke.   Then let me see thy cloak:
I'll get me one of such another length.
 Val. Why, any cloak will serve the turn,
 my lord.
 Duke. How shall I fashion me to wear a
 cloak?
I pray thee, let me feel thy cloak upon me.
What letter is this same? What's here? ' To
 Silvia'!
And here an engine fit for my proceeding.
I'll be so bold to break the seal for once. 140
          [*Reads.*
' My thoughts do harbor with my Silvia
 nightly,
And slaves they are to me that send them
 flying:
O, could their master come and go as lightly,
 Himself would lodge where senseless they
 are lying!
My herald thoughts in thy pure bosom rest
 them:
 While I, their king, that hither them impor-
 tune,
Do curse the grace that with such grace hath
 bless'd them,
 Because myself do want my servants' for-
 tune:
I curse myself, for they are sent by me,
That they should harbor where their lord
 would be.'
What's here?   150
' Silvia, this night I will enfranchise thee.'
'Tis so; and here's the ladder for the purpose.
Why, Phaeton,—for thou art Merops' son,—
Wilt thou aspire to guide the heavenly car
And with thy daring folly burn the world?
Wilt thou reach stars, because they shine on
 thee?
Go, base intruder! overweening slave!
Bestow thy fawning smiles on equal mates,
And think my patience, more than thy desert,
Is privilege for thy departure hence: 160
Thank me for this more than for all the favors
Which all too much I have bestow'd on thee.
But if thou linger in my territories
Longer than swiftest expedition
Will give thee time to leave our royal court,
By heaven! my wrath shall far exceed the love
I ever bore my daughter or thyself.
Be gone! I will not hear thy vain excuse;
But, as thou lovest thy life, make speed from
 hence.   [*Exit.*
 Val. And why not death rather than living
 torment?   170
To die is to be banish'd from myself;
And Silvia is myself: banish'd from her
Is self from self: a deadly banishment!
What light is light, if Silvia be not seen?
What joy is joy, if Silvia be not by?
Unless it be to think that she is by
And feed upon the shadow of perfection
Except I be by Silvia in the night,
There is no music in the nightingale,
Unless I look on Silvia in the day,   180
There is no day for me to look upon;
She is my essence, and I leave to be,

If I be not by her fair influence
Foster'd, illumined, cherish'd, kept alive.
I fly not death, to fly his deadly doom:
Tarry I here, I but attend on death:
But, fly I hence, I fly away from life.

    Enter PROTEUS *and* LAUNCE.

 Pro. Run, boy, run, run, and seek him out.
 Launce. Soho, soho!
 Pro. What seest thou?   190
 Launce. Him we go to find: there's not a
hair on's head but 'tis a Valentine.
 Pro. Valentine?
 Val. No.
 Pro. Who then? his spirit?
 Val. Neither.
 Pro. What then?
 Val. Nothing.
 Launce. Can nothing speak? Master, shall
 I strike?
 Pro. Who wouldst thou strike?   200
 Launce. Nothing.
 Pro. Villain, forbear.
 Launce. Why, sir, I'll strike nothing: I
 pray you,—
 Pro. Sirrah, I say, forbear. Friend Valen-
 tine, a word.
 Val. My ears are stopt and cannot hear
 good news,
So much of bad already hath possess'd them.
 Pro. Then in dumb silence will I bury
 mine,
For they are harsh, untuneable and bad.
 Val. Is Silvia dead?
 Pro. No, Valentine.   210
 Val. No Valentine, indeed, for sacred Sil-
 via.
Hath she forsworn me?
 Pro. No, Valentine.
 Val. No Valentine, if Silvia have forsworn
 me.
What is your news?
 Launce. Sir, there is a proclamation that
 you are vanished.
 Pro. That thou art banished—O, that's the
 news!—
From hence, from Silvia and from me thy
 friend.
 Val. O, I have fed upon this woe already,
And now excess of it will make me surfeit. 220
Doth Silvia know that I am banished?
 Pro. Ay, ay; and she hath offer'd to the
 doom—
Which, unreversed, stands in effectual force—
A sea of melting pearl, which some call tears:
Those at her father's churlish feet she ten-
 der'd;
With them, upon her knees, her humble self;
Wringing her hands, whose whiteness so be-
 came them
As if but now they waxed pale for woe:
But neither bended knees, pure hands held up,
Sad sighs, deep groans, nor silver-shedding
 tears,   230
Could penetrate her uncompassionate sire;
But Valentine, if he be ta'en, must die.
Besides, her intercession chafed him so,
When she for thy repeal was suppliant,
That to close prison he commanded her,
With many bitter threats of biding there.
 Val. No more; unless the next word that
 thou speak'st

Have some malignant power upon my life :
If so, I pray thee, breathe it in mine ear,
As ending anthem of my endless dolor.   240
   Pro. Cease to lament for that thou canst
        not help,
And study help for that which thou lament'st.
Time is the nurse and breeder of all good.
Here if thou stay, thou canst not see thy love ;
Besides, thy staying will abridge thy life.
Hope is a lover's staff ; walk hence with that
And manage it against despairing thoughts.
Thy letters may be here, though thou art
        hence ;
Which, being writ to me, shall be deliver'd
Even in the milk-white bosom of thy love. 250
The time now serves not to expostulate :
Come, I'll convey thee through the city-gate ;
And, ere I part with thee, confer at large
Of all that may concern thy love-affairs.
As thou lovest Silvia, though not for thyself,
Regard thy danger, and along with me !
   Val. I pray thee, Launce, an if thou seest
        my boy,
Bid him make haste and meet me at the North-
        gate.
   Pro. Go, sirrah, find him out. Come, Val-
        entine.
   Val. O my dear Silvia ! Hapless Valen-
        tine !   260
                        [*Exeunt Val. and Pro.*
   Launce. I am but a fool, look you ; and
yet I have the wit to think my master is a kind
of a knave : but that's all one, if he be but one
knave. He lives not now that knows me to be
in love ; yet I am in love ; but a team of horse
shall not pluck that from me ; nor who 'tis I
love ; and yet 'tis a woman ; but what woman,
I will not tell myself ; and yet 'tis a milkmaid ;
yet 'tis not a maid, for she hath had gossips ;
yet 'tis a maid, for she is her master's maid,
and serves for wages. She hath more qualities
than a water-spaniel ; which is much in a bare
Christian. [*Pulling out a paper.*] Here is
the cate-log of her condition. ' Imprimis : She
can fetch and carry.' Why, a horse can do no
more : nay, a horse cannot fetch, but only
carry ; therefore is she better than a jade.
' Item : She can milk ; ' look you, a sweet virtue in a maid with clean hands.

                   Enter SPEED.

   Speed. How now, Signior Launce ! what
news with your mastership ?   280
   Launce. With my master's ship ? why, it
is at sea.
   Speed. Well, your old vice still ; mistake
the word. What news, then, in your paper ?
   Launce. The blackest news that ever thou
heardest.
   Speed. Why, man, how black ?
   Launce. Why, as black as ink.
   Speed. Let me read them.   290
   Launce. Fie on thee, jolt-head ! thou canst
not read.
   Speed. Thou liest ; I can.
   Launce. I will try thee. Tell me this : who
begot thee ?
   Speed. Marry, the son of my grandfather.
   Launce. O illiterate loiterer ! it was the son
of thy grandmother : this proves that thou
canst not read.

   Speed. Come, fool, come ; try me in thy
paper.   300
   Launce. There ; and St. Nicholas be thy
        speed !
   Speed. [*Reads*] ' Imprimis : She can milk.'
   Launce. Ay, that she can.
   Speed. ' Item : She brews good ale.'
   Launce. And thereof comes the proverb :
' Blessing of your heart, you brew good ale.'
   Speed. ' Item : She can sew.'
   Launce. That's as much as to say, Can she
so ?
   Speed. ' Item : She can knit.'   310
   Launce. What need a man care for a stock
with a wench, when she can knit him a stock ?
   Speed. ' Item : She can wash and scour.'
   Launce. A special virtue : for then she
need not be washed and scoured.
   Speed. ' Item : She can spin.'
   Launce. Then may I set the world on
wheels, when she can spin for her living.
   Speed. ' Item : She hath many nameless
virtues.'   320
   Launce. That's as much as to say, bastard
virtues ; that, indeed, know not their fathers
and therefore have no names.
   Speed. ' Here follow her vices.'
   Launce. Close at the heels of her virtues.
   Speed. ' Item : She is not to be kissed fast-
ing, in respect of her breath.'
   Launce. Well, that fault may be mended
with a breakfast. Read on.
   Speed. ' Item : She hath a sweet mouth.'
   Launce. That makes amends for her sour
breath.   331
   Speed. ' Item : She doth talk in her sleep.'
   Launce. It's no matter for that, so she
sleep not in her talk.
   Speed. ' Item : She is slow in words.'
   Launce. O villain, that set this down
among her vices ! To be slow in words is a
woman's only virtue : I pray thee, out with't,
and place it for her chief virtue.   340
   Speed. ' Item : She is proud.'
   Launce. Out with that too ; it was Eve's
legacy, and cannot be ta'en from her.
   Speed. ' Item : She hath no teeth.'
   Launce. I care not for that neither, because I love crusts.
   Speed. ' Item : She is curst.'
   Launce. Well, the best is, she hath no teeth
to bite.
   Speed. ' Item : She will often praise her
liquor.'   351
   Launce. If her liquor be good, she shall :
if she will not, I will ; for good things should
be praised.
   Speed. ' Item : She is too liberal.'
   Launce. Of her tongue she cannot, for
that's writ down she is slow of ; of her purse
she shall not, for that I'll keep shut : now, of
another thing she may, and that cannot I help.
Well, proceed.   360
   Speed. ' Item : She hath more hair than
wit, and more faults than hairs, and more
wealth than faults.'
   Launce. Stop there ; I'll have her : she was
mine, and not mine, twice or thrice in that last
article. Rehearse that once more.
   Speed. ' Item : She hath more hair than
wit,'—
   Launce. More hair than wit ? It may be ;

I'll prove it. The cover of the salt hides the salt, and therefore it is more than the salt; the hair that covers the wit is more than the wit, for the greater hides the less. What's next ?

Speed. 'And more faults than hairs,'—
Launce. That's monstrous : O, that that were out !
Speed. 'And more wealth than faults.'
Launce. Why, that word makes the faults gracious. Well, I'll have her ; and if it be a match, as nothing is impossible,—
Speed. What then ?   380
Launce. Why, then will I tell thee—that thy master stays for thee at the North-gate.
Speed. For me ?
Launce. For thee ! ay, who art thou ? he hath stayed for a better man than thee.
Speed. And must I go to him ?
Launce. Thou must run to him, for thou hast stayed so long that going will scarce serve the turn.
Speed. Why didst not tell me sooner ? pox of your love letters !   [*Exit.* 391
Launce. Now will he be swinged for reading my letter; an unmannerly slave, that will thrust himself into secrets ! I'll after, to rejoice in the boy's correction.   [*Exit.*

SCENE II. *The same. The* DUKE'S *palace.*

Enter DUKE *and* THURIO.

Duke. Sir Thurio, fear not but that she will love you,
Now Valentine is banish'd from her sight.
Thu. Since his exile she hath despised me most,
Forsworn my company and rail'd at me,
That I am desperate of obtaining her.
Duke. This weak impress of love is as a figure
Trenched in ice, which with an hour's heat
Dissolves to water and doth lose his form.
A little time will melt her frozen thoughts
And worthless Valentine shall be forgot.   10

Enter PROTEUS.

How now, Sir Proteus ! Is your countryman
According to our proclamation gone ?
Pro. Gone, my good lord.
Duke. My daughter takes his going grievously.
Pro. A little time, my lord, will kill that grief.
Duke. So I believe ; but Thurio thinks not so.
Proteus, the good conceit I hold of thee—
For thou hast shown some sign of good desert—
Makes me the better to confer with thee.
Pro. Longer than I prove loyal to your grace   20
Let me not live to look upon your grace.
Duke. Thou know'st how willingly I would effect
The match between Sir Thurio and my daughter.
Pro. I do, my lord.
Duke. And also, I think, thou art not ignorant
How she opposes her against my will.
Pro. She did, my lord, when Valentine was here.

Duke. Ay, and perversely she persevers so.
What might we do to make the girl forget
The love of Valentine and love Sir Thurio ? 30
Pro. The best way is to slander Valentine
With falsehood, cowardice and poor descent,
Three things that women highly hold in hate.
Duke. Ay, but she'll think that it is spoke in hate.
Pro. Ay, if his enemy deliver it :
Therefore it must with circumstance be spoken
By one whom she esteemeth as his friend.
Duke. Then you must undertake to slander him.
Pro. And that, my lord, I shall be loath to do :   40
'Tis an ill office for a gentleman,
Especially against his very friend.
Duke. Where your good word cannot advantage him,
Your slander never can endamage him ;
Therefore the office is indifferent,
Being entreated to it by your friend.
Pro. You have prevail'd, my lord ; if I can do it
By ought that I can speak in his dispraise,
She shall not long continue love to him.
But say this weed her love from Valentine,
It follows not that she will love Sir Thurio. 50
Thu. Therefore, as you unwind her love from him,
Lest it should ravel and be good to none,
You must provide to bottom it on me ;
Which must be done by praising me as much
As you in worth dispraise Sir Valentine.
Duke. And, Proteus, we dare trust you in this kind,
Because we know, on Valentine's report,
You are already Love's firm votary
And cannot soon revolt and change your mind.
Upon this warrant shall you have access 60
Where you with Silvia may confer at large ;
For she is lumpish, heavy, melancholy,
And, for your friend's sake, will be glad of you ;
Where you may temper her by your persuasion
To hate young Valentine and love my friend.
Pro. As much as I can do, I will effect :
But you, Sir Thurio, are not sharp enough ;
You must lay lime to tangle her desires
By wailful sonnets, whose composed rhymes
Should be full-fraught with serviceable vows.
Duke. Ay,   71
Much is the force of heaven-bred poesy.
Pro. Say that upon the altar of her beauty
You sacrifice your tears, your sighs, your heart :
Write till your ink be dry, and with your tears
Moist it again, and frame some feeling line
That may discover such integrity :
For Orpheus' lute was strung with poets' sinews,
Whose golden touch could soften steel and stones,
Make tigers tame and huge leviathans   80
Forsake unsounded deeps to dance on sands.
After your dire-lamenting elegies,
Visit by night your lady's chamber-window
With some sweet concert ; to their instruments
Tune a deploring dump : the night's dead silence
Will well become such sweet-complaining grievance.

This, or else nothing, will inherit her.
Duke. This discipline shows thou hast been
in love.
Thu. And thy advice this night I'll put in
practice.
Therefore, sweet Proteus, my direction-giver,
Let us into the city presently   91
To sort some gentlemen well skill'd in music.
I have a sonnet that will serve the turn
To give the onset to thy good advice.
Duke. About it, gentlemen!
Pro. We'll wait upon your grace till after
supper,
And afterward determine our proceedings.
Duke. Even now about it! I will pardon
you.   [*Exeunt.*

ACT IV.

SCENE I. *The frontiers of Mantua. A forest.*

Enter certain Outlaws.

First Out. Fellows, stand fast; I see a
passenger.
Sec. Out. If there be ten, shrink not, but
down with 'em.

Enter VALENTINE *and* SPEED.

Third Out. Stand, sir, and throw us that
you have about ye:
If not, we'll make you sit and rifle you.
Speed. Sir, we are undone; these are the
villains
That all the travellers do fear so much.
Val. My friends,—
First Out. That's not so, sir: we are your
enemies.
Sec. Out. Peace! we'll hear him.
Third Out. Ay, by my beard, will we, for
he's a proper man.   10
Val. Then know that I have little wealth to
lose:
A man I am cross'd with adversity;
My riches are these poor habiliments,
Of which if you should here disfurnish me,
You take the sum and substance that I have.
Sec. Out. Whither travel you?
Val. To Verona.
First Out. Whence came you?
Val. From Milan.
Third Out. Have you long sojourned
there?
Val. Some sixteen months, and longer
might have stay'd,
If crooked fortune had not thwarted me.
First Out. What, were you banish'd
thence?
Val. I was.
Sec. Out. For what offence?
Val. For that which now torments me to
rehearse:
I kill'd a man, whose death I much repent;
But yet I slew him manfully in fight,
Without false vantage or base treachery.
First Out. Why, ne'er repent it, if it were
done so.   30
But were you banish'd for so small a fault?
Val. I was, and held me glad of such a
doom.
Sec. Out. Have you the tongues?

Val. My youthful travel therein made me
happy,
Or else I often had been miserable.
Third Out. By the bare scalp of Robin
Hood's fat friar,
This fellow were a king for our wild faction!
First Out. We'll have him. Sirs, a word.
Speed. Master, be one of them; it's an hon-
orable kind of thievery.   40
Val. Peace, villain!
Sec. Out. Tell us this: have you any thing
to take to?
Val. Nothing but my fortune.
Third Out. Know, then, that some of us are
gentlemen,
Such as the fury of ungovern'd youth
Thrust from the company of awful men:
Myself was from Verona banished
For practising to steal away a lady,
An heir, and near allied unto the duke.
Sec. Out. And I from Mantua, for a gen-
tleman,   50
Who, in my mood, I stabb'd unto the heart.
First Out. And I for such like petty crimes
as these,
But to the purpose—for we cite our faults,
That they may hold excus'd our lawless lives;
And partly, seeing you are beautified
With goodly shape and by your own report
A linguist and a man of such perfection
As we do in our quality much want—
Sec. Out. Indeed, because you are a ban-
ish'd man,
Therefore, above the rest, we parley to you:
Are you content to be our general?   61
To make a virtue of necessity
And live, as we do, in this wilderness?
Third Out. What say'st thou? wilt thou be
of our consort?
Say ay, and be the captain of us all:
We'll do thee homage and be ruled by thee,
Love thee as our commander and our king.
First Out. But if thou scorn our courtesy,
thou diest.
Sec. Out. Thou shalt not live to brag what
we have offer'd.
Val. I take your offer and will live with
you,   70
Provided that you do no outrages
On silly women or poor passengers.
Third Out. No, we detest such vile base
practices.
Come, go with us, we'll bring thee to our
crews,
And show thee all the treasure we have got,
Which, with ourselves, all rest at thy dispose.
[*Exeunt.*

SCENE II. *Milan. Outside the* DUKE's *palace, under* SILVIA's *chamber.*

Enter PROTEUS.

Pro. Already have I been false to Valentine
And now I must be as unjust to Thurio.
Under the color of commending him,
I have access my own love to prefer:
But Silvia is too fair, too true, too holy,
To be corrupted with my worthless gifts.
When I protest true loyalty to her,
She twits me with my falsehood to my friend;
When to her beauty I commend my vows,
She bids me think how I have been forsworn
In breaking faith with Julia whom I loved: 11

And notwithstanding all her sudden quips,
The least whereof would quell a lover's hope,
Yet, spaniel-like, the more she spurns my love,
The more it grows and fawneth on her still.
But here comes Thurio : now must we to her window,
And give some evening music to her ear.

Enter Thurio *and* Musicians.

Thu. How now, Sir Proteus, are you crept before us ?
Pro. Ay, gentle Thurio : for you know that love
Will creep in service where it cannot go.   20
Thu. Ay, but I hope, sir, that you love not here.
Pro. Sir, but I do ; or else I would be hence.
Thu. Who ? Silvia ?
Pro.   Ay, Silvia ; for your sake.
Thu. I thank you for your own. Now, gentlemen,
Let's tune, and to it lustily awhile.

Enter, at a distance, Host, *and* Julia *in boy's clothes.*

Host. Now, my young guest, methinks you're allycholly : I pray you, why is it ?
Jul. Marry, mine host, because I cannot be merry.
Host. Come, we'll have you merry : I'll bring you where you shall hear music and see the gentleman that you asked for.
Jul. But shall I hear him speak ?
Host. Ay, that you shall.
Jul. That will be music.   [*Music plays.*
Host. Hark, hark !
Jul. Is he among these ?
Host. Ay : but, peace ! let's hear 'em.

SONG.

Who is Silvia ? what is she,
    That all our swains commend her ?   40
Holy, fair and wise is she ;
    The heaven such grace did lend her,
That she might admired be.

Is she kind as she is fair ?
    For beauty lives with kindness.
Love doth to her eyes repair,
    To help him of his blindness,
And, being help'd, inhabits there.

Then to Silvia let us sing,
    That Silvia is excelling ;   50
She excels each mortal thing
    Upon the dull earth dwelling :
To her let us garlands bring.

Host. How now ! are you sadder than you were before ? How do you, man ? the music likes you not.
Jul. You mistake ; the musician likes me not.
Host. Why, my pretty youth ?
Jul. He plays false, father.
Host. How ? out of tune on the strings ?
Jul. Not so ; but yet so false that he grieves my very heart-strings.   61
Host. You have a quick ear.
Jul. Ay, I would I were deaf ; it makes me have a slow heart.
Host. I perceive you delight not in music.
Jul. Not a whit, when it jars so.

Host. Hark, what fine change is in the music !
Jul. Ay, that change is the spite.   70
Host. You would have them always play but one thing ?
Jul. I would always have one play but one thing.
But, host, doth this Sir Proteus that we talk on
Often resort unto this gentlewoman ?
Host. I tell you what Launce, his man, told me : he loved her out of all nick.
Jul. Where is Launce ?
Host. Gone to seek his dog ; which to-morrow, by his master's command, he must carry for a present to his lady.   80
Jul. Peace ! stand aside : the company parts.
Pro. Sir Thurio, fear not you : I will so plead
That you shall say my cunning drift excels.
Thu. Where meet we ?
Pro.   At Saint Gregory's well.
Thu.   Farewell.
    [*Exeunt* Thu. *and* Musicians.

Enter Silvia *above.*

Pro. Madam, good even to your ladyship.
Sil. I thank you for your music, gentlemen.
Who is that that spake ?
Pro. One, lady, if you knew his pure heart's truth,
You would quickly learn to know him by his voice.
Sil. Sir Proteus, as I take it.   90
Pro. Sir Proteus, gentle lady, and your servant.
Sil. What's your will ?
Pro.   That I may compass yours.
Sil. You have your wish ; my will is even this :
That presently you hie you home to bed.
Thou subtle, perjured, false, disloyal man !
Think'st thou I am so shallow, so conceitless,
To be seduced by thy flattery,
That hast deceived so many with thy vows ?
Return, return, and make thy love amends.
For me, by this pale queen of night I swear,
I am so far from granting thy request   101
That I despise thee for thy wrongful suit,
And by and by intend to chide myself
Even for this time I spend in talking to thee.
Pro. I grant, sweet love, that I did love a lady ;
But she is dead.
Jul. [*Aside*] 'Twere false, if I should speak it ;
For I am sure she is not buried.
Sil. Say that she be ; yet Valentine thy friend
Survives ; to whom, thyself art witness,   110
I am betroth'd : and art thou not ashamed
To wrong him with thy importunacy ?
Pro. I likewise hear that Valentine is dead.
Sil. And so suppose am I ; for in his grave
Assure thyself my love is buried.
Pro. Sweet lady, let me rake it from the earth.
Sil. Go to thy lady's grave and call hers thence,
Or, at the least, in hers sepulchre thine.
Jul. [*Aside*] He heard not that.
Pro. Madam, if your heart be so obdurate,

Vouchsafe me yet your picture for my love,
The picture that is hanging in your chamber;
To that I'll speak, to that I'll sigh and weep:
For since the substance of your perfect self
Is else devoted, I am but a shadow;
And to your shadow will I make true love.
Jul. [*Aside*] If 'twere a substance, you
     would, sure, deceive it,
And make it but a shadow, as I am.
Sil. I am very loath to be your idol, sir;
But since your falsehood shall become you
     well   130
To worship shadows and adore false shapes,
Send to me in the morning and I'll send it:
And so, good rest.
Pro.   As wretches have o'ernight
That wait for execution in the morn.
          [*Exeunt Pro. and Sil. severally.*
Jul. Host, will you go?
Host. By my halidom, I was fast asleep.
Jul. Pray you, where lies Sir Proteus?
Host. Marry, at my house. Trust me, I
think 'tis almost day.
Jul. Not so; but it hath been the longest
     night   140
That e'er I watch'd and the most heaviest.
                                        [*Exeunt.*

SCENE III. *The same.*

Enter EGLAMOUR.

Egl. This is the hour that Madam Silvia
Entreated me to call and know her mind:
There's some great matter she'ld employ me in.
Madam, madam!

Enter SILVIA above.

Sil.   Who calls?
Egl. Your servant and your friend;
One that attends your ladyship's command.
Sil. Sir Eglamour, a thousand times good
     morrow.
Egl. As many, worthy lady, to yourself:
According to your ladyship's impose,
I am thus early come to know what service
It is your pleasure to command me in.   10
Sil. O Eglamour, thou art a gentleman—
Think not I flatter, for I swear I do not—
Valiant, wise, remorseful, well accomplish'd:
Thou art not ignorant what dear good will
I bear unto the banish'd Valentine,
Nor how my father would enforce me marry
Vain Thurio, whom my very soul abhors.
Thyself hast loved; and I have heard thee say
No grief did ever come so near thy heart
As when thy lady and thy true love died,   20
Upon whose grave thou vow'dst pure chastity.
Sir Eglamour, I would to Valentine,
To Mantua, where I hear he makes abode;
And, for the ways are dangerous to pass,
I do desire thy worthy company,
Upon whose faith and honor I repose.
Urge not my father's anger, Eglamour,
But think upon my grief, a lady's grief,
And on the justice of my flying hence,
To keep me from a most unholy match,   30
Which heaven and fortune still rewards with
     plagues.
I do desire thee, even from a heart
As full of sorrows as the sea of sands,
To bear me company and go with me:
If not, to hide what I have said to thee,
That I may venture to depart alone.

Egl. Madam, I pity much your grievances;
Which since I know they virtuously are placed,
I give consent to go along with you,
Recking as little what betideth me   40
As much I wish all good befortune you.
When will you go?
Sil.   This evening coming.
Egl. Where shall I meet you?
Sil.   At Friar Patrick's cell.
Where I intend holy confession.
Egl. I will not fail your ladyship. Good
morrow, gentle lady.
Sil. Good morrow, kind Sir Eglamour.
                         [*Exeunt severally.*

SCENE IV. *The same.*

Enter LAUNCE, with his Dog.

Launce. When a man's servant shall play
the cur with him, look you, it goes hard: one
that I brought up of a puppy; one that I saved
from drowning, when three or four of his blind
brothers and sisters went to it. I have taught
him, even as one would say precisely, 'thus I
would teach a dog.' I was sent to deliver him
as a present to Mistress Silvia from my master; and I came no sooner into the dining-
chamber but he steps me to her trencher and
steals her capon's leg: O, 'tis a foul thing when
a cur cannot keep himself in all companies!
I would have, as one should say, one that takes
upon him to be a dog indeed, to be, as it were,
a dog at all things. If I had not had more wit
than he, to take a fault upon me that he did, I
think verily he had been hanged for't; sure as
I live, he had suffered for't; you shall judge.
He thrusts me himself into the company of
three or four gentlemanlike dogs, under the
duke's table: he had not been there—bless the
mark!—a pissing while, but all the chamber
smelt him. 'Out with the dog!' says one:
'What cur is that?' says another: 'Whip him
out' says the third: 'Hang him up' says the
duke. I, having been acquainted with the smell
before, knew it was Crab, and goes me to the
fellow that whips the dogs: 'Friend,' quoth I,
'you mean to whip the dog?' 'Ay, marry, do
I,' quoth he. 'You do him the more wrong,'
quoth I; ''twas I did the thing you wot of.'
He makes me no more ado, but whips me out
of the chamber. How many masters would do
this for his servant? Nay, I'll be sworn, I have
sat in the stocks for puddings he hath stolen,
otherwise he had been executed; I have stood
on the pillory for geese he hath killed, otherwise he had suffered for't. Thou thinkest not of
this now. Nay, I remember the trick you served
me when I took my leave of Madam Silvia:
did not I bid thee still mark me and do as I
do? when didst thou see me heave up my leg
and make water against a gentlewoman's farthingale? didst thou ever see me do such a
trick?

Enter PROTEUS and JULIA.

Pro. Sebastian is thy name? I like thee
     well
And will employ thee in some service pres-
     ently.
Jul. In what you please: I'll do what I
     can.
Pro. I hope thou wilt. [*To Launce*] How
     now, you whoreson peasant!

Where have you been these two days loitering ?
Launce. Marry, sir, I carried Mistress Silvia the dog you bade me.   50
  Pro. And what says she to my little jewel ?
  Launce. Marry, she says your dog was a
cur, and tells you currish thanks is good
enough for such a present.
  Pro. But she received my dog ?
  Launce. No, indeed, did she not : here
have I brought him back again.
  Pro. What, didst thou offer her this from
me ?
  Launce. Ay, sir : the other squirrel was
stolen from me by the hangman boys in the
market-place : and then I offered her mine
own, who is a dog as big as ten of yours, and
therefore the gift the greater.
  Pro. Go get thee hence, and find my dog
again,
Or ne'er return again into my sight.
Away, I say ! stay'st thou to vex me here ?
                                  [*Exit Launce.*
A slave, that still an end turns me to shame !
Sebastian, I have entertained thee,
Partly that I have need of such a youth
That can with some discretion do my business,
For 'tis no trusting to yond foolish lout,   71
But chiefly for thy face and thy behavior,
Which, if my augury deceive me not,
Witness good bringing up, fortune and truth :
Therefore know thou, for this I entertain thee.
Go presently and take this ring with thee,
Deliver it to Madam Silvia :
She loved me well deliver'd it to me.
  Jul. It seems you loved not her, to leave
her token.
She is dead, belike ?
  Pro.   Not so ; I think she lives. 80
  Jul. Alas !
  Pro. Why dost thou cry ' alas ' ?
  Jul.   I cannot choose
But pity her.
  Pro.   Wherefore shouldst thou pity her ?
  Jul. Because methinks that she loved you
as well
As you do love your lady Silvia :
She dreams of him that has forgot her love ;
You dote on her that cares not for your love.
'Tis pity love should be so contrary ;
And thinking of it makes me cry ' alas ! '
  Pro. Well, give her that ring and there-
withal
This letter. That's her chamber. Tell my lady
I claim the promise for her heavenly picture.
Your message done, hie home unto my
chamber,
Where thou shalt find me, sad and solitary.
                                  [*Exit.*
  Jul. How many women would do such a
message ?
Alas, poor Proteus ! thou hast entertain'd
A fox to be the shepherd of thy lambs.
Alas, poor fool ! why do I pity him
That with his very heart despiseth me ?
Because he loves her, he despiseth me ;   100
Because I love him I must pity him.
This ring I gave him when he parted from me,
To bind him to remember my good will ;
And now am I, unhappy messenger,
To plead for that which I would not obtain,
To carry that which I would have refused,

To praise his faith which I would have dis-
praised.
I am my master's true-confirmed love ;
But cannot be true servant to my master,
Unless I prove false traitor to myself.   110
Yet will I woo for him, but yet so coldly
As, heaven it knows, I would not have him
speed.

          Enter SILVIA, *attended.*

Gentlewoman, good day ! I pray you, be my
mean
To bring me where to speak with Madam
Silvia.
  Sil. What would you with her, if that I be
she ?
  Jul. If you be she, I do entreat your pa-
tience
To hear me speak the message I am sent on.
  Sil. From whom ?
  Jul. From my master, Sir Proteus, madam.
  Sil. O, he sends you for a picture.   120
  Jul. Ay, madam.
  Sil. Ursula, bring my picture here.
Go give your master this : tell him from me,
One Julia, that his changing thoughts forget,
Would better fit his chamber than this shadow.
  Jul. Madam, please you peruse this
letter.—
Pardon me, madam ; I have unadvised
Deliver'd you a paper that I should not :
This is the letter to your ladyship.
  Sil. I pray thee, let me look on that again.
  Jul. It may not be ; good madam, pardon
me.
  Sil. There, hold !
I will not look upon your master's lines :
I know they are stuff'd with protestations
And full of new-found oaths ; which he will
break
As easily as I do tear his paper.
  Jul. Madam, he sends your ladyship this
ring.
  Sil. The more shame for him that he sends
it me ;
For I have heard him say a thousand times
His Julia gave it him at his departure.   140
Though his false finger have profaned the ring,
Mine shall not do his Julia so much wrong.
  Jul. She thanks you.
  Sil. What say'st thou ?
  Jul. I thank you, madam, that you tender
her.
Poor gentlewoman ! my master wrongs her
much.
  Sil. Dost thou know her ?
  Jul. Almost as well as I do know myself :
To think upon her woes I do protest
That I have wept a hundred several times. 150
  Sil. Belike she thinks that Proteus hath for-
sook her.
  Jul. I think she doth ; and that's her cause
of sorrow.
  Sil. Is she not passing fair ?
  Jul. She hath been fairer, madam, than
she is :
When she did think my master loved her well,
She, in my judgment, was as fair as you :
But since she did neglect her looking-glass
And threw her sun-expelling mask away,
The air hath starved the roses in her cheeks
And pinch'd the lily-tincture of her face, 160

That now she is become as black as I.
Sil. How tall was she?
Jul. About my stature; for at Pentecost,
When all our pageants of delight were play'd,
Our youth got me to play the woman's part,
And I was trimm'd in Madam Julia's gown,
Which served me as fit, by all men's judg-
ments,
As if the garment had been made for me:
Therefore I know she is about my height.
And at that time I made her weep agood,   170
For I did play a lamentable part:
Madam, 'twas Ariadne passioning
For Theseus' perjury and unjust flight;
Which I so lively acted with my tears
That my poor mistress, moved therewithal,
Wept bitterly; and would I might be dead
If I in thought felt not her very sorrow!
Sil. She is beholding to thee, gentle youth.
Alas, poor lady, desolate and left!
I weep myself to think upon thy words.   180
Here, youth, there is my purse; I give thee this
For thy sweet mistress' sake, because thou lov-
est her.
Farewell.   [*Exit Silvia, with attendants.*
Jul. And she shall thank you for't, if e'er
you know her.
A virtuous gentlewoman, mild and beautiful
I hope my master's suit will be but cold,
Since she respects my mistress' love so much.
Alas, how love can trifle with itself!
Here is her picture: let me see; I think,
If I had such a tire, this face of mine   190
Were full as lovely as is this of hers:
And yet the painter flatter'd her a little,
Unless I flatter with myself too much.
Her hair is auburn, mine is perfect yellow:
If that be all the difference in his love,
I'll get me such a color'd periwig.
Her eyes are grey as glass, and so are mine:
Ay, but her forehead's low, and mine's as
high.
What should it be that he respects in her
But I can make respective in myself,   200
If this fond Love were not a blinded god?
Come, shadow, come and take this shadow up,
For 'tis thy rival. O thou senseless form,
Thou shalt be worshipp'd, kiss'd, loved and
adored!
And, were there sense in his idolatry,
My substance should be statue in thy stead.
I'll use thee kindly for thy mistress' sake,
That used me so; or else, by Jove I vow,
I should have scratch'd out your unseeing eyes
To make my master out of love with thee!
[*Exit.*

ACT V.

SCENE I. *Milan. An abbey.*

Enter EGLAMOUR.

Egl. The sun begins to gild the western
sky;
And now it is about the very hour
That Silvia, at Friar Patrick's cell, should meet
me.
She will not fail, for lovers break not hours,
Unless it be to come before their time;
So much they spur their expedition.
See where she comes.

Enter SILVIA.

Lady, a happy evening!
Sil. Amen, amen! Go on, good Eglamour,
Out at the postern by the abbey-wall:
I fear I am attended by some spies.   10
Egl. Fear not: the forest is not three
leagues off;
If we recover that, we are sure enough.
[*Exeunt.*

SCENE II. *The same. The* DUKE's *palace.*

Enter THURIO, PROTEUS, *and* JULIA.

Thu. Sir Proteus, what says Silvia to my
suit?
Pro. O, sir, I find her milder than she was;
And yet she takes exceptions at your person.
Thu. What, that my leg is too long?
Pro. No; that it is too little.
Thu. I'll wear a boot, to make it somewhat
rounder.
Jul. [*Aside*] But love will not be spurr'd
to what it loathes.
Thu. What says she to my face?
Pro. She says it is a fair one.
Thu. Nay then, the wanton lies; my face
is black.   10
Pro. But pearls are fair; and the old say-
ing is,
Black men are pearls in beauteous ladies' eyes.
Jul. [*Aside*] 'Tis true; such pearls as put
out ladies' eyes;
For I had rather wink than look on them.
Thu. How likes she my discourse?
Pro. Ill, when you talk of war.
Thu. But well, when I discourse of love
and peace?
Jul. [*Aside*] But better, indeed, when you
hold your peace.
Thu. What says she to my valor?
Pro. O, sir, she makes no doubt of that. 20
Jul. [*Aside*] She needs not, when she
knows it cowardice.
Thu. What says she to my birth?
Pro. That you are well derived.
Jul. [*Aside*] True; from a gentleman to a
fool.
Thu. Considers she my possessions?
Pro. O, ay; and pities them.
Thu. Wherefore?
Jul. [*Aside*] That such an ass should owe
them.
Pro. That they are out by lease.
Jul. Here comes the duke.   30

Enter DUKE.

Duke. How now, Sir Proteus! how now,
Thurio!
Which of you saw Sir Eglamour of late?
Thu. Not I.
Pro.   Nor I.
Duke.   Saw you my daughter?
Pro.   Neither.
Duke. Why then,
She's fled unto that peasant Valentine;
And Eglamour is in her company.
'Tis true; for Friar Laurence met them both,
As he in penance wander'd through the forest;
Him he knew well, and guess'd that it was
she,
But, being mask'd, he was not sure of it;   40
Besides, she did intend confession

At Patrick's cell this even ; and there she was
    not ;
These likelihoods confirm her flight from
    hence.
Therefore, I pray you, stand not to discourse,
But mount you presently and meet with me
Upon the rising of the mountain-foot
That leads towards Mantua, whither they are
    fled :
Dispatch, sweet gentlemen, and follow me.
                          [Exit.
  Thu. Why, this it is to be a peevish girl,
That flies her fortune when it follows her. 50
I'll after, more to be revenged on Eglamour
Than for the love of reckless Silvia.   *[Exit.*
  Pro. And I will follow, more for Silvia's
    love
Than hate of Eglamour that goes with her.
                          [Exit.
  Jul. And I will follow, more to cross that
    love
Than hate for Silvia that is gone for love.
                          [Exit.

SCENE III. *The frontiers of Mantua.*
            The forest.

   Enter Outlaws *with* SILVIA.

  First Out. Come, come,
Be patient ; we must bring you to our captain.
  Sil. A thousand more mischances than this
    one
Have learn'd me how to brook this patiently.
  Sec. Out. Come, bring her away.
  First Out. Where is the gentleman that was
    with her ?
  Third Out. Being nimble-footed, he hath
    outrun us,
But Moyses and Valerius follow him.
Go thou with her to the west end of the wood ;
There is our captain : we'll follow him that's
    fled ;   10
The thicket is beset ; he cannot 'scape.
  First Out. Come, I must bring you to our
    captain's cave :
Fear not ; he bears an honorable mind,
And will not use a woman lawlessly.
  Sil. O Valentine, this I endure for thee !
                        [Exeunt.

SCENE IV. *Another part of the forest.*

      Enter VALENTINE.

  Val. How use doth breed a habit in a
    man !
This shadowy desert, unfrequented woods,
I better brook than flourishing peopled towns :
Here can I sit alone, unseen of any,
And to the nightingale's complaining notes
Tune my distresses and record my woes.
O thou that dost inhabit in my breast,
Leave not the mansion so long tenantless,
Lest, growing ruinous, the building fall
And leave no memory of what it was !   10
Repair me with thy presence, Silvia ;
Thou gentle nymph, cherish thy forlorn swain !
What halloing and what stir is this to-day ?
These are my mates, that make their wills their
    law,
Have some unhappy passenger in chase.
They love me well ; yet I have much to do
To keep them from uncivil outrages.
Withdraw thee, Valentine : who's this comes
    here ?

   Enter PROTEUS, SILVIA, *and* JULIA.

  Pro. Madam, this service I have done for
    you,
Though you respect not aught your servant
    doth,   20
To hazard life and rescue you from him
That would have forced your honor and your
    love ;
Vouchsafe me, for my meed, but one fair
    look ;
A smaller boon than this I cannot beg
And less than this, I am sure, you cannot give.
  Val. [*Aside*] How like a dream is this I
    see and hear !
Love, lend me patience to forbear awhile.
  Sil. O miserable, unhappy that I am !
  Pro. Unhappy were you, madam, ere I
    came ;
But by my coming I have made you happy. 30
  Sil. By thy approach thou makest me most
    unhappy.
  Jul. [*Aside*] And me, when he approacheth
    to your presence.
  Sil. Had I been seized by a hungry lion,
I would have been a breakfast to the beast,
Rather than have false Proteus rescue me.
O, Heaven be judge how I love Valentine,
Whose life's as tender to me as my soul !
And full as much, for more there cannot be,
I do detest false perjured Proteus.
Therefore be gone ; solicit me no more.   40
  Pro. What dangerous action, stood it next
    to death,
Would I not undergo for one calm look !
O, 'tis the curse in love, and still approved,
When women cannot love where they're be-
    loved !
  Sil. When Proteus cannot love where he's
    beloved.
Read over Julia's heart, thy first best love,
For whose dear sake thou didst then rend thy
    faith
Into a thousand oaths ; and all those oaths
Descended into perjury, to love me.
Thou hast no faith left now, unless thou'dst
    two ;   50
And that's far worse than none ; better have
    none
Than plural faith which is too much by one :
Thou counterfeit to thy true friend !
  Pro.   In love
Who respects friend ?
  Sil.   All men but Proteus.
  Pro. Nay, if the gentle spirit of moving
    words
Can no way change you to a milder form,
I'll woo you like a soldier, at arms' end,
And love you 'gainst the nature of love,—force
    ye.
  Sil. O heaven !
  Pro.   I'll force thee yield to my desire.
  Val. Ruffian, let go that rude uncivil touch,
Thou friend of an ill fashion !   60
  Pro.   Valentine !
  Val. Thou common friend, that's without
    faith or love,
For such is a friend now ; treacherous man !
Thou hast beguiled my hopes ; nought but
    mine eye
Could have persuaded me : now I dare not say

I have one friend alive ; thou wouldst disprove
me.
Who should be trusted, when one's own right
hand
Is perjured to the bosom ? Proteus,
I am sorry I must never trust thee more,
But count the world a stranger for thy sake.
The private wound is deepest : O time most
accurst,   71
'Mongst all foes that a friend should be the
worst !
Pro. My shame and guilt confounds me.
Forgive me, Valentine : if hearty sorrow
Be a sufficient ransom for offence,
I tender 't here ; I do as truly suffer
As e'er I did commit.
Val.   Then I am paid ;
And once again I do receive thee honest.
Who by repentance is not satisfied
Is nor of heaven nor earth, for these are
pleased.   80
By penitence the Eternal's wrath's appeased :
And, that my love may appear plain and free,
All that was mine in Silvia I give thee.
Jul. O me unhappy !   [*Swoons.*
Pro. Look to the boy.
Val. Why, boy ! why, wag ! how now !
what's the matter ? Look up ; speak.
Jul. O good sir, my master charged me to
deliver a ring to Madam Silvia, which, out of
my neglect, was never done.   90
Pro. Where is that ring, boy ?
Jul.   Here 'tis ; this is it.
Pro. How ! let me see :
Why, this is the ring I gave to Julia.
Jul. O, cry you mercy, sir, I have mis-
took :
This is the ring you sent to Silvia.
Pro. But how camest thou by this ring ?
At my depart
I gave this unto Julia.
Jul. And Julia herself did give it me ;
And Julia herself hath brought it hither.
Pro. How ! Julia !   100
Jul. Behold her that gave aim to all thy
oaths,
And entertain'd 'em deeply in her heart.
How oft hast thou with perjury cleft the root !
O Proteus, let this habit make thee blush !
Be thou ashamed that I have took upon me
Such an immodest raiment, if shame live
In a disguise of love :
It is the lesser blot, modesty finds,
Women to change their shapes than men their
minds.
Pro. Than men their minds ! 'tis true. O
heaven ! were man   110
But constant, he were perfect. That one error
Fills him with faults ; makes him run through
all the sins ;
Inconstancy falls off ere it begins.
What is in Silvia's face, but I may spy
More fresh in Julia's with a constant eye ?
Val. Come, come, a hand from either :
Let me be blest to make this happy close ;
'Twere pity two such friends should be long
foes.
Pro. Bear witness, Heaven, I have my wish
for ever.
Jul. And I mine.   120

Enter Outlaws, *with* DUKE *and* THURIO.

Outlaws. A prize, a prize, a prize !
Val. Forbear, forbear, I say ! it is my lord
the duke.
Your grace is welcome to a man disgraced,
Banished Valentine.
Duke.   Sir Valentine !
Thu. Yonder is Silvia ; and Silvia's mine.
Val. Thurio, give back, or else embrace
thy death ;
Come not within the measure of my wrath ;
Do not name Silvia thine ; if once again,
Verona shall not hold thee. Here she stands ;
Take but possession of her with a touch : 130
I dare thee but to breathe upon my love.
Thu. Sir Valentine, I care not for her, I ;
I hold him but a fool that will endanger
His body for a girl that loves him not :
I claim her not, and therefore she is thine.
Duke. The more degenerate and base art
thou,
To make such means for her as thou hast done
And leave her on such slight conditions.
Now, by the honor of my ancestry,
I do applaud thy spirit, Valentine,   140
And think thee worthy of an empress' love :
Know then, I here forget all former griefs,
Cancel all grudge, repeal thee home again,
Plead a new state in thy unrival'd merit,
To which I thus subscribe : Sir Valentine,
Thou art a gentleman and well derived ;
Take thou thy Silvia, for thou hast deserved
her.
Val. I thank your grace ; the gift hath
made me happy.
I now beseech you, for your daughter's sake,
To grant one boom that I shall ask of you. 150
Duke. I grant it, for thine own, whate'er it
be.
Val. These banish'd men that I have kept
withal
Are men endued with worthy qualities :
Forgive them what they have committed here
And let them be recall'd from their exile :
They are reformed, civil, full of good
And fit for great employment, worthy lord.
Duke. Thou hast prevail'd ; I pardon them
and thee :
Dispose of them as thou know'st their deserts.
Come, let us go : we will include all jars   160
With triumphs, mirth and rare solemnity.
Val. And, as we walk along, I dare be bold
With our discourse to make your grace to
smile.
What think you of this page, my lord ?
Duke. I think the boy hath grace in him ;
he blushes.
Val. I warrant you, my lord, more grace
than boy.
Duke. What mean you by that saying ?
Val. Please you, I'll tell you as we pass
along,
That you will wonder what hath fortuned.
Come, Proteus, 'tis your penance but to hear
The story of your loves discovered :   171
That done, our day of marriage shall be
yours ;
One feast, one house, one mutual happiness.
                                          [*Exeunt*

A
MIDSUMMER NIGHT'S DREAM.

(WRITTEN ABOUT 1593-94.)

INTRODUCTION.

A Midsummer Night's Dream is a strange and beautiful web, woven delicately by a youthful poet's fancy. What is perhaps most remarkable about the play is the harmonious blending in it of widely different elements. It is as if threads of silken splendor were run together in its texture with a yarn of hempen homespun, and both these with lines of dewy gossamer and filaments drawn from the moonbeams. In North's *Plutarch*, or in Chaucer's *Knight's Tale*, Shakespeare may have found the figures of Theseus and his Amazonian bride ; from Chaucer also (*Wife of Bath's Tale*), may have come the figure of the elf-queen (though not her name, Titania), and the story of Pyramus and Thisbe (see Chaucer's *Legend of Good Women*) ; this last, however, was perhaps taken from Golding's translation of Ovid's *Metamorphoses*. Oberon, the fairy-king, had recently appeared in Greene's play *The Scottish History of James IV.* ; Puck, under his name of Robin Goodfellow, was a roguish sprite, well known in English fairy-lore. Finally, in Montemayor's *Diana*, which Shakespeare had made acquaintance with before *The Two Gentlemen of Verona* was written, occur some incidents which may have suggested the magic effects of the flower-juice laid upon the sleeping lovers' lids. Taking a little from this quarter and a little from that, Shakespeare created out of such slight materials his marvellous Dream. The marriage of Duke Theseus and Hippolyta—who are classical in name only, being in reality romantic mediæval figures—surrounds the whole, as it were, with a magnificent frame. Theseus is Shakespeare's early ideal of a heroic warrior and man of action. His life is one of splendid achievement and of joy ; his love is a kind of happy victory, his marriage a triumph. From early morning, when his hounds—themselves heroic creatures—fill the valley with their " musical confusion," until midnight, when the Athenian clowns end their " very tragical mirth " with a Bergomask dance, Theseus displays his joyous energy and the graciousness of power. In contrast with him and his warrior bride, the figures of the young lovers look slight and graceful, and their love-perplexities and errors are seen to be among the minor and remediable afflictions of the world. The mirth of the lovers' part of *A Midsummer Night's Dream* turns chiefly upon the incidents, and therefore, as with the brothers Antipholus, in *The Comedy of Errors*, differences of character are not made prominent. Here, as in the *Errors*, there are entanglements and cross-purposes. The one play has been named ' the mistakes of a day," and the other " the mistakes of a night : " but the difference lies deeper than such names intimate ; for in the *Errors*, the confusion is external to the mind, here it is internal ; in the *Errors*, the feelings of the actors remain constant, but the persons toward whom they are directed take the place, unobserved, one of another ; here the persons remain constant, but their feelings of love, indifference, or dislike are at the mercy of mischief-making accident. As the two extremes of exquisite delicacy, of dainty elegance, and, on the other hand, of thick-witted grossness and clumsiness, stand the fairy tribe and the group of Athenian handicraftsmen. The world of the poet's dream includes the two—a Titania, and a Bottom the weaver—and can bring them into grotesque conjunction. No such fairy poetry existed anywhere in English literature before Shakespeare. The tiny elves, to whom a cowslip is tall, for whom the third part of a minute is an important division of time, have a miniature perfection which is charming. They delight in all beautiful and dainty things, and war with things that creep and things that fly, if they be uncomely ; their lives are gay with fine frolic and delicate revelry. Puck, the jester of Fairyland, stands apart from the rest, the recognizable " lob of spirits," a rough, " fawn-faced, shock-pated little fellow, a very Shetlander among the gossamer-winged, dainty-limbed shapes around him." It has been conjectured that *A Midsummer Night's Dream* was written to grace the wedding of some noble person—Southampton who was married in 1598, or Essex who was married in 1590 ; but these dates are, the one too late, the other too early. A passage (Act II., Sc. I., L. 88–118) in which Titania describes the recent ill seasons, wintry summers, flood and fog, would very aptly correspond with the disastrous years 1593 and 1594. Perhaps we may incline towards 1594 as the date of the play. It contains a large proportion of rhyming lines ; but the character of the play naturally calls for this. It has the gaiety, the fancifulness, and the want of either deep thought or passion which we might expect in an early drama. It was probably acted before Elizabeth. The praise of " single-blessedness " (Act I., Sc. I., L. 74–78) may have been designed to please the ears of the maiden queen; and Oberon's vision (Act II., Sc. I., L. 148–168) contains a splendid piece of poetical homage to her. The " fair vestal throned by the west " is certainly Elizabeth. Two quarto editions of the play, of which the second was probably pirated, were issued in the year 1600.

DRAMATIS PERSONÆ.

THESEUS, Duke of Athens.
EGEUS, father to Hermia.
LYSANDER, } in love with Hermia.
DEMETRIUS,
PHILOSTRATE, master of the revels to Theseus.
QUINCE, a carpenter.
SNUG, a joiner.
BOTTOM, a weaver.
FLUTE, a bellows-mender.
SNOUT, a tinker.
STARVELING, a tailor.

HIPPOLYTA, queen of the Amazons, betrothed to Theseus.

HERMIA, daughter to Egeus, in love with Lysander.
HELENA, in love with Demetrius.
OBERON, king of the fairies.
TITANIA, queen of the fairies.
PUCK, or Robin Goodfellow.
PEASEBLOSSOM,
COBWEB, } fairies.
MOTH,
MUSTARDSEED,

Other fairies attending their King and Queen. Attendants on Theseus and Hippolyta.

SCENE : *Athens, and a wood near it.*

ACT I.

SCENE I. *Athens. The palace of* THESEUS.

Enter THESEUS, HIPPOLYTA, PHILOSTRATE, *and* Attendants.

The. Now, fair Hippolyta, our nuptial hour
Draws on apace; four happy days bring in
Another moon : but, O, methinks, how slow
This old moon wanes ! she lingers my desires,
Like to a step-dame or a dowager
Long withering out a young man's revenue.
    Hip. Four days will quickly steep themselves in night;
Four nights will quickly dream away the time;
And then the moon, like to a silver bow   10
New-bent in heaven, shall behold the night
Of our solemnities.
    The.   Go, Philostrate,
Stir up the Athenian youth to merriments;
Awake the pert and nimble spirit of mirth;
Turn melancholy forth to funerals;
The pale companion is not for our pomp.
                    [*Exit Philostrate.*
Hippolyta, I woo'd thee with my sword,
And won thy love, doing thee injuries;
But I will wed thee in another key,
With pomp, with triumph and with revelling.

Enter EGEUS, HERMIA, LYSANDER, *and*
DEMETRIUS.

    Ege. Happy be Theseus, our renowned
        duke !   20
    The. Thanks, good Egeus : what's the news
        with thee ?
    Ege. Full of vexation come I, with complaint
Against my child, my daughter Hermia.
Stand forth, Demetrius. My noble lord,
This man hath my consent to marry her.
Stand forth, Lysander : and, my gracious duke,
This man hath bewitch'd the bosom of my child;

Thou, thou, Lysander, thou hast given her
        rhymes,
And interchanged love-tokens with my child :
Thou hast by moonlight at her window sung,
With feigning voice verses of feigning love, 31
And stolen the impression of her fantasy
With bracelets of thy hair, rings, gawds, conceits,
Knacks, trifles, nosegays, sweetmeats, messengers
Of strong prevailment in unharden'd youth :
With cunning hast thou filch'd my daughter's
        heart,
Turn'd her obedience, which is due to me,
To stubborn harshness : and, my gracious
        duke,
Be it so she will not here before your grace
Consent to marry with Demetrius,   40
I beg the ancient privilege of Athens,
As she is mine, I may dispose of her :
Which shall be either to this gentleman
Or to her death, according to our law
Immediately provided in that case.
    The. What say you, Hermia ? be advised,
        fair maid :
To you your father should be as a god;
One that composed your beauties, yea, and one
To whom you are but as a form in wax
By him imprinted and within his power   50
To leave the figure or disfigure it.
Demetrius is a worthy gentleman.
    Her. So is Lysander.
    The.   In himself he is;
But in this kind, wanting your father's voice,
The other must be held the worthier.
    Her. I would my father look'd but with my
        eyes.
    The. Rather your eyes must with his judgment look.
    Her. I do entreat your grace to pardon me.
I know not by what power I am made bold,
Nor how it may concern my modesty,   60
In such a presence here to plead my thoughts;
But I beseech your grace that I may know
The worst that may befall me in this case,

If I refuse to wed Demetrius.
The.   Either to die the death or to abjure
For ever the society of men.
Therefore, fair Hermia, question your desires ;
Know of your youth, examine well your blood,
Whether, if you yield not to your father's
    choice,
You can endure the livery of a nun,   70
For aye to be in shady cloister mew'd,
To live a barren sister all your life,
Chanting faint hymns to the cold fruitless
    moon.
Thrice-blessed they that master so their blood,
To undergo such maiden pilgrimage ;
But earthlier happy is the rose distill'd,
Than that which withering on the virgin thorn
Grows, lives and dies in single blessedness.
Her.   So will I grow, so live, so die, my
    lord,
Ere I will yield my virgin patent up   80
Unto his lordship, whose unwished yoke
My soul consents not to give sovereignty.
The.   Take time to pause ; and, by the next
    new moon—
The sealing-day betwixt my love and me,
For everlasting bond of fellowship—
Upon that day either prepare to die
For disobedience to your father's will,
Or else to wed Demetrius, as he would ;
Or on Diana's altar to protest
For aye austerity and single life.   90
Dem.   Relent, sweet Hermia : and, Lysan-
    der, yield
Thy crazed title to my certain right.
Lys.   You have her father's love, Deme-
    trius ;
Let me have Hermia's : do you marry him.
Ege.   Scornful Lysander ! true, he hath my
    love,
And what is mine my love shall render him.
And she is mine, and all my right of her
I do estate unto Demetrius.
Lys.   I am, my lord, as well derived as he,
As well possess'd ; my love is more than his ;
My fortunes every way as fairly rank'd,   101
If not with vantage, as Demetrius' ;
And, which is more than all these boasts can
    be,
I am beloved of beauteous Hermia :
Why should not I then prosecute my right ?
Demetrius, I'll avouch it to his head,
Made love to Nedar's daughter, Helena,
And won her soul ; and she, sweet lady, dotes,
Devoutly dotes, dotes in idolatry,
Upon this spotted and inconstant man.   110
The.   I must confess that I have heard so
    much,
And with Demetrius thought to have spoke
    thereof ;
But, being over-full of self-affairs,
My mind did lose it. But, Demetrius, come ;
And come, Egeus ; you shall go with me,
I have some private schooling for you both.
For you, fair Hermia, look you arm yourself
To fit your fancies to your father's will ;
Or else the law of Athens yields you up—   120
Which by no means we may extenuate—
To death, or to a vow of single life.
Come, my Hippolyta : what cheer, my love ?
Demetrius and Egeus, go along :
I must employ you in some business
Against our nuptial and confer with you
Of something nearly that concerns yourselves.

Ege.   With duty and desire we follow you.
    [Exeunt all but Lysander and Hermia.
Lys.   How now, my love ! why is your
    cheek so pale ?
How chance the roses there do fade so fast ?
Her.   Belike for want of rain, which I could
    well   130
Beteem them from the tempest of my eyes.
Lys.   Ay me ! for aught that I could ever
    read,
Could ever hear by tale or history,
The course of true love never did run smooth ;
But, either it was different in blood,—
Her.   O cross ! too high to be enthrall'd to
    low.
Lys.   Or else misgraffed in respect of
    years,—
Her.   O spite ! too old to be engaged to
    young.
Lys.   Or else it stood upon the choice of
    friends,—
Her.   O hell ! to choose love by another's
    eyes.   140
Lys.   Or, if there were a sympathy in
    choice,
War, death, or sickness did lay siege to it,
Making it momentary as a sound,
Swift as a shadow, short as any dream ;
Brief as the lightning in the collied night,
That, in a spleen, unfolds both heaven and
    earth,
And ere a man hath power to say ' Behold ! '
The jaws of darkness do devour it up :
So quick bright things come to confusion.
Her.   If then true lovers have been ever
    cross'd,   150
It stands as an edict in destiny :
Then let us teach our trial patience,
Because it is a customary cross,
As due to love as thoughts and dreams and
    sighs,
Wishes and tears, poor fancy's followers.
Lys.   A good persuasion : therefore, hear
    me, Hermia.
I have a widow aunt, a dowager
Of great revenue, and she hath no child—
From Athens is her house remote seven
    leagues ;
And she respects me as her only son.   160
There, gentle Hermia, may I marry thee ;
And to that place the sharp Athenian law
Cannot pursue us. If thou lovest me then,
Steal forth thy father's house to-morrow
    night ;
And in the wood, a league without the town,
Where I did meet thee once with Helena,
To do observance to a morn of May,
There will I stay for thee.
Her.   My good Lysander !
I swear to thee, by Cupid's strongest bow,
By his best arrow with the golden head,   170
By the simplicity of Venus' doves,
By that which knitteth souls and prospers
    loves,
And by that fire which burn'd the Carthage
    queen,
When the false Troyan under sail was seen,
By all the vows that ever men have broke,
In number more than ever women spoke,
In that same place thou hast appointed me,
To-morrow truly will I meet with thee.
Lys.   Keep promise, love. Look, here comes
    Helena.

Enter HELENA.

Her. God speed fair Helena! whither
    away ?   180
Hel. Call you me fair ? that fair again un-
    say.
Demetrius loves your fair : O happy fair !
Your eyes are lode-stars ; and your tongue's
    sweet air
More tuneable than lark to shepherd's ear,
When wheat is green, when hawthorn buds
    appear.
Sickness is catching : O, were favor so,
Yours would I catch, fair Hermia, ere I go ;
My ear should catch your voice, my eye your
    eye,
My tongue should catch your tongue's sweet
    melody.
Were the world mine, Demetrius being bated,
The rest I'd give to be to you translated.   191
O, teach me how you look, and with what art
You sway the motion of Demetrius' heart.
Her. I frown upon him, yet he loves me
    still.
Hel. O that your frowns would teach my
    smiles such skill !
Her. I give him curses, yet he gives me
    love.
Hel. O that my prayers could such affec-
    tion move !
Her. The more I hate, the more he follows
    me.
Hel. The more I love, the more he hateth
    me.
Her. His folly, Helena, is no fault of mine.
Hel. None, but your beauty : would that
    fault were mine !   201
Her. Take comfort : he no more shall see
    my face ;
Lysander and myself will fly this place.
Before the time I did Lysander see,
Seem'd Athens as a paradise to me :
O, then, what graces in my love do dwell,
That he hath turn'd a heaven unto a hell !
Lys. Helen, to you our minds we will un-
    fold :
To-morrow night, when Phœbe doth behold
Her silver visage in the watery glass,   210
Decking with liquid pearl the bladed grass,
A time that lovers' flights doth still conceal,
Through Athens' gates have we devised to
    steal.
Her. And in the wood, where often you
    and I
Upon faint primrose-beds were wont to lie,
Emptying our bosoms of their counsel sweet,
There my Lysander and myself shall meet ;
And thence from Athens turn away our eyes,
To seek new friends and stranger companies.
Farewell, sweet playfellow : pray thou for us ;
And good luck grant thee thy Demetrius ! 221
Keep word, Lysander : we must starve our
    sight
From lovers' food till morrow deep midnight.
Lys. I will, my Hermia.   [*Exit Herm.*
                   Helena, adieu :
As you on him, Demetrius dote on you !
                                    [*Exit.*
Hel. How happy some o'er other some can
    be !
Through Athens I am thought as fair as she.
But what of that ? Demetrius thinks not so ;
He will not know what all but he do know :

And as he errs, doting on Hermia's eyes,   230
So I, admiring of his qualities ;
Things base and vile, holding no quantity,
Love can transpose to form and dignity :
Love looks not with the eyes, but with the
    mind ;
And therefore is wing'd Cupid painted blind :
Nor hath Love's mind of any judgment taste ;
Wings and no eyes figure unheedy haste :
And therefore is Love said to be a child,
Because in choice he is so oft beguiled.
As waggish boys in game themselves forswear,
So the boy Love is perjured every where : 241
For ere Demetrius look'd on Hermia's eyne,
He hail'd down oaths that he was only mine ;
And when this hail some heat from Hermia
    felt,
So he dissolved, and showers of oaths did melt.
I will go tell him of fair Hermia's flight :
Then to the wood will he to-morrow night
Pursue her ; and for this intelligence
If I have thanks, it is a dear expense :
But herein mean I to enrich my pain,   250
To have his sight thither and back again.
                                    [*Exit.*

SCENE II. *Athens.* QUINCE'S *house.*

Enter QUINCE, SNUG, BOTTOM, FLUTE, SNOUT,
    and STARVELING.

Quin. Is all our company here ?
Bot. You were best to call them generally,
man by man, according to the scrip.
Quin. Here is the scroll of every man's
name, which is thought fit, through all Athens,
to play in our interlude before the duke and
the duchess, on his wedding-day at night.
Bot. First, good Peter Quince, say what
the play treats on, then read the names of the
actors, and so grow to a point.   10
Quin. Marry, our play is, The most lamentable comedy, and most cruel death of
Pyramus and Thisby.
Bot. A very good piece of work, I assure
you, and a merry. Now, good Peter Quince,
call forth your actors by the scroll. Masters,
spread yourselves.
Quin. Answer as I call you. Nick Bottom,
the weaver.   20
Bot. Ready. Name what part I am for,
and proceed.
Quin. You, Nick Bottom, are set down for
Pyramus.
Bot. What is Pyramus ? a lover, or a tyrant ?
Quin. A lover, that kills himself most gallant for love.
Bot. That will ask some tears in the true
performing of it : if I do it, let the audience
look to their eyes ; I will move storms, I will
condole in some measure. To the rest : yet
my chief humor is for a tyrant : I could play
Ercles rarely, or a part to tear a cat in, to
make all split.
              The raging rocks
              And shivering shocks
              Shall break the locks
                 Of prison gates ;
              And Phibbus' car
              Shall shine from far
              And make and mar
                 The foolish Fates.   40
This was lofty ! Now name the rest of the

players. This is Ercles' vein, a tyrant's vein ; a lover is more condoling.

Quin. Francis Flute, the bellows-mender.

Flu. Here, Peter Quince.

Quin. Flute, you must take Thisby on you.

Flu. What is Thisby ? a wandering knight ?

Quin. It is the lady that Pyramus must love.

Flu. Nay, faith, let me not play a woman ; I have a beard coming.   50

Quin. That's all one : you shall play it in a mask, and you may speak as small as you will.

Bot. An I may hide my face, let me play Thisby too, I'll speak in a monstrous little voice, ' Thisne, Thisne ; ' ' Ah, Pyramus, my lover dear ! thy Thisby dear, and lady dear ! '

Quin. No, no ; you must play Pyramus : and, Flute, you Thisby.

Bot. Well, proceed.

Quin. Robin Starveling, the tailor.   60

Star. Here, Peter Quince.

Quin. Robin Starveling, you must play Thisby's mother. Tom Snout, the tinker.

Snout. Here, Peter Quince.

Quin. You, Pyramus' father : myself, Thisby's father : Snug, the joiner ; you, the lion's part : and, I hope, here is a play fitted.

Snug. Have you the lion's part written ? pray you, if it be, give it me, for I am slow of study.

Quin. You may do it extempore, for it is nothing but roaring.   71

Bot. Let me play the lion too : I will roar, that I will do any man's heart good to hear me ; I will roar, that I will make the duke say ' Let him roar again, let him roar again.'

Quin. An you should do it too terribly, you would fright the duchess and the ladies, that they would shriek ; and that were enough to hang us all.

All. That would hang us, every mother's son.

Bot. I grant you, friends, if that you should fright the ladies out of their wits, they would have no more discretion but to hang us : but I will aggravate my voice so that I will roar you as gently as any sucking dove ; I will roar you an 'twere any nightingale.

Quin. You can play no part but Pyramus ; for Pyramus is a sweet-faced man ; a proper man, as one shall see in a summer's day ; a most lovely gentleman-like man : therefore you must needs play Pyramus.   91

Bot. Well, I will undertake it. What beard were I best to play it in ?

Quin. Why, what you will.

Bot. I will discharge it in either your straw-color beard, your orange-tawny beard, your purple-in-grain beard, or your French-crown-color beard, your perfect yellow.

Quin. Some of your French crowns have no hair at all, and then you will play bare-faced. But, masters, here are your parts : and I am to entreat you, request you and desire you, to con them by to-morrow night ; and meet me in the palace wood, a mile without the town, by moonlight ; there will we re-hearse, for if we meet in the day, we shall be dogged with company, and our devices known. In the meantime I will draw a bill of proper-

ties, such as our play wants. I pray you, fail me not.

Bot. We will meet ; and there we may re-hearse most obscenely and courageously. Take pains ; be perfect : adieu.

Quin. At the duke's oak we meet.

Bot. Enough ; hold or cut bow-strings.
     [*Exeunt.*

ACT II.

Scene I. *A wood near Athens.*

Enter, from opposite sides, a Fairy, *and* Puck.

Puck. How now, spirit ! whither wander
          you ?

Fai. Over hill, over dale,
          Thorough bush, thorough brier,
     Over park, over pale,
          Thorough flood, thorough fire,
     I do wander everywhere,
     Swifter than the moon's sphere ;
     And I serve the fairy queen,
     To dew her orbs upon the green.
     The cowslips tall her pensioners be :   10
     In their gold coats spots you see ;
     Those be rubies, fairy favors,
     In those freckles live their savors :
I must go seek some dewdrops here
And hang a pearl in every cowslip's ear.
Farewell, thou lob of spirits ; I'll be gone :
Our queen and all our elves come here anon.

Puck. The king doth keep his revels here
          to-night :
Take heed the queen come not within his
          sight ;
For Oberon is passing fell and wrath,   20
Because that she as her attendant hath
A lovely boy, stolen from an Indian king ;
She never had so sweet a changeling ;
And jealous Oberon would have the child
Knight of his train, to trace the forests wild ;
But she perforce withholds the loved boy,
Crowns him with flowers and makes him all
          her joy :
And now they never meet in grove or green,
By fountain clear, or spangled starlight sheen,
But they do square, that all their elves for
          fear   30
Creep into acorn-cups and hide them there.

Fai. Either I mistake your shape and
          making quite,
Or else you are that shrewd and knavish sprite
Call'd Robin Goodfellow : are not you he
That frights the maidens of the villagery ;
Skim milk, and sometimes labor in the quern
And bootless make the breathless housewife
          churn ;
And sometime make the drink to bear no
          barm ;
Mislead night-wanderers, laughing at their
          harm ?
Those that Hobgoblin call you and sweet
          Puck,
You do their work, and they shall have good
          luck :
Are not you he ?

Puck.   Thou speak'st aright ;
I am that merry wanderer of the night.
I jest to Oberon and make him smile
When I a fat and bean-fed horse beguile,
Neighing in likeness of a filly foal :

And sometime lurk I in a gossip's bowl,
In very likeness of a roasted crab,
And when she drinks, against her lips I bob
And on her wither'd dewlap pour the ale.   50
The wisest aunt, telling the saddest tale,
Sometime for three-foot stool mistasketh me;
Then slip I from her bum, down topples she,
And ' tailor ' cries, and falls into a cough;
And then the whole quire hold their hips and
    laugh,
And waxen in their mirth and neeze and
    swear
A merrier hour was never wasted there.
But, room, fairy! here comes Oberon.
    Fai.   And here my mistress. Would that
        he were gone!

Enter, from one side, OBERON, *with his train;
    from the other,* TITANIA, *with hers.*

    Obe.   Ill met by moonlight, proud Titania.
    Tita.   What, jealous Oberon! Fairies, skip
        hence :   61
I have forsworn his bed and company.
    Obe.   Tarry, rash wanton: am not I thy
        lord?
    Tita.   Then I must be thy lady : but I know
When thou hast stolen away from fairy land,
And in the shape of Corin sat all day,
Playing on pipes of corn and versing love
To amorous Phillida. Why art thou here,
Come from the farthest steppe of India?
But that, forsooth, the bouncing Amazon,   70
Your buskin'd mistress and your warrior love,
To Theseus must be wedded, and you come
To give their bed joy and prosperity.
    Obe.   How canst thou thus for shame,
        Titania,
Glance at my credit with Hippolyta,
Knowing I know thy love to Theseus?
Didst thou not lead him through the glimmer-
    ing night
From Perigenia, whom he ravished?
And make him with fair Ægle break his faith,
With Ariadne and Antiopa?   80
    Tita.   These are the forgeries of jealousy :
And never, since the middle summer's spring,
Met we on hill, in dale, forest or mead,
By paved fountain or by rushy brook,
Or in the beached margent of the sea,
To dance our ringlets to the whistling wind,
But with thy brawls thou hast disturb'd our
    sport.
Therefore the winds, piping to us in vain,
As in revenge, have suck'd up from the sea
Contagious fogs; which falling in the land 90
Have every pelting river made so proud
That they have overborne their continents :
The ox hath therefore stretch'd his yoke in
    vain,
The ploughman lost his sweat, and the green
    corn
Hath rotted ere his youth attain'd a beard;
The fold stands empty in the drowned field,
And crows are fatted with the murrion flock;
The nine men's morris is fill'd up with mud,
And the quaint mazes in the wanton green
For lack of tread are undistinguishable : 100
The human mortals want their winter here;
No night is now with hymn or carol blest :
Therefore the moon, the governess of floods,
Pale in her anger, washes all the air,
That rheumatic diseases do abound :
And thorough this distemperature we see

The seasons alter : hoary-headed frosts
Fall in the fresh lap of the crimson rose,
And on old Hiems' thin and icy crown   109
An odorous chaplet of sweet summer buds
Is, as in mockery, set : the spring, the
    summer,
The childing autumn, angry winter, change
Their wonted liveries, and the mazed world,
By their increase, now knows not which is
    which :
And this same progeny of evils comes
From our debate, from our dissension ;
We are their parents and original.
    Obe.   Do you amend it then ; it lies in
        you :
Why should Titania cross her Oberon?
I do but beg a little changeling boy,   120
To be my henchman.
    Tita.   Set your heart at rest :
The fairy land buys not the child of me.
His mother was a votaress of my order :
And, in the spiced Indian air, by night,
Full often hath she gossip'd by my side,
And sat with me on Neptune's yellow sands,
Marking the embarked traders on the flood,
When we have laugh'd to see the sails con-
    ceive
And grow big-bellied with the wanton wind ;
Which she, with pretty and with swimming
    gait   130
Following,—her womb then rich with my
    young squire,—
Would imitate, and sail upon the land,
To fetch me trifles, and return again,
As from a voyage, rich with merchandise.
But she, being mortal, of that boy did die ;
And for her sake do I rear up her boy,
And for her sake I will not part with him.
    Obe.   How long within this wood intend
        you stay?
    Tita.   Perchance till after Theseus' wed-
        ding-day.
If you will patiently dance in our round   140
And see our moonlight revels, go with us ;
If not, shun me, and I will spare your haunts.
    Obe.   Give me that boy, and I will go with
        thee.
    Tita.   Not for thy fairy kingdom. Fairies,
        away!
We shall chide downright, if I longer stay.
        [*Exit Titania with her train.*
    Obe.   Well, go thy way : thou shalt not
        from this grove
Till I torment thee for this injury.
My gentle Puck, come hither. Thou remem-
    berest
Since once I sat upon a promontory,   149
And heard a mermaid on a dolphin's back
Uttering such dulcet and harmonious breath
That the rude sea grew civil at her song
And certain stars shot madly from their
    spheres,
To hear the sea-maid's music.
    Puck.   I remember.
    Obe.   That very time I saw, but thou
        couldst not,
Flying between the cold moon and the earth,
Cupid all arm'd : a certain aim he took
At a fair vestal throned by the west,
And loosed his love-shaft smartly from his
    bow,
As it should pierce a hundred thousand
    hearts ;   160

But I might see young Cupid's fiery shaft
Quench'd in the chaste beams of the watery
    moon,
And the imperial votaress passed on,
In maiden meditation, fancy-free.
Yet mark'd I where the bolt of Cupid fell :
It fell upon a little western flower,
Before milk-white, now purple with love's
    wound,
And maidens call it love-in-idleness.
Fetch me that flower ; the herb I shew'd thee
    once :
The juice of it on sleeping eye-lids laid   170
Will make or man or woman madly dote
Upon the next live creature that it sees.
Fetch me this herb ; and be thou here again
Ere the leviathan can swim a league.
    Puck. I'll put a girdle round about the
    earth
In forty minutes.   [*Exit.*
    Obe.   Having once this juice,
I'll watch Titania when she is asleep,
And drop the liquor of it in her eyes.
The next thing then she waking looks upon,
Be it on lion, bear, or wolf, or bull,   180
On meddling monkey, or on busy ape,
She shall pursue it with the soul of love :
And ere I take this charm from off her sight,
As I can take it with another herb,
I'll make her render up her page to me.
But who comes here ? I am invisible ;
And I will overhear their conference.

Enter DEMETRIUS, HELENA, *following him.*

    Dem. I love thee not, therefore pursue me
    not.
Where is Lysander and fair Hermia ?
The one I'll slay, the other slayeth me.   190
Thou told'st me they were stolen unto this
    wood ;
And here am I, and wode within this wood,
Because I cannot meet my Hermia.
Hence, get thee gone, and follow me no more.
    Hel. You draw me, you hard-hearted
    adamant ;
But yet you draw not iron, for my heart
Is true as steel : leave you your power to
    draw,
And I shall have no power to follow you.
    Dem. Do I entice you ? do I speak you
    fair ?
Or, rather, do I not in plainest truth   200
Tell you, I do not, nor I cannot love you ?
    Hel. And even for that do I love you the
    more.
I am your spaniel ; and, Demetrius,
The more you beat me, I will fawn on you :
Use me but as your spaniel, spurn me, strike
    me,
Neglect me, lose me ; only give me leave,
Unworthy as I am, to follow you.
What worser place can I beg in your love,—
And yet a place of high respect with me,—
Than to be used as you use your dog ?   210
    Dem. Tempt not too much the hatred of
    my spirit;
For I am sick when I do look on thee.
    Hel. And I am sick when I look not on
    you.
    Dem. You do impeach your modesty too
    much,

To leave the city and commit yourself
Into the hands of one that loves you not ;
To trust the opportunity of night
And the ill counsel of a desert place
With the rich worth of your virginity.
    Hel. Your virtue is my privilege : for that
It is not night when I do see your face,   221
Therefore I think I am not in the night ;
Nor doth this wood lack worlds of company,
For you in my respect are all the world :
Then how can it be said I am alone,
When all the world is here to look on me ?
    Dem. I'll run from thee and hide me in
    the brakes,
And leave thee to the mercy of wild beasts.
    Hel. The wildest hath not such a heart as
    you.
Run when you will, the story shall be
    changed :   230
Apollo flies, and Daphne holds the chase ;
The dove pursues the griffin ; the mild hind
Makes speed to catch the tiger ; bootless
    speed,
When cowardice pursues and valor flies.
    Dem. I will not stay thy questions ; let me
    go :
Or, if thou follow me, do not believe
But I shall do thee mischief in the wood.
    Hel. Ay, in the temple, in the town, the
    field,
You do me mischief. Fie, Demetrius !
Your wrongs do set a scandal on my sex : 240
We cannot fight for love, as men may do ;
We should be woo'd and were not made to
    woo.   [*Exit Dem.*
I'll follow thee and make a heaven of hell,
To die upon the hand I love so well. [*Exit.*
    Obe. Fare thee well, nymph : ere he do
    leave this grove,
Thou shalt fly him and he shall seek thy love.

Re-enter PUCK.

Hast thou the flower there ? Welcome, wan-
    derer.
    Puck. Ay, there it is.
    Obe.   I pray thee, give it me.
I know a bank where the wild thyme blows,
Where oxlips and the nodding violet grows,
Quite over-canopied with luscious woodbine,
With sweet musk-roses and with eglantine :
There sleeps Titania sometime of the night,
Lull'd in these flowers with dances and de-
    light ;
And there the snake throws her enamell'd
    skin,
Weed wide enough to wrap a fairy in :
And with the juice of this I'll streak her eyes,
And make her full of hateful fantasies.
Take thou some of it, and seek through this
    grove :
A sweet Athenian lady is in love   260
With a disdainful youth : anoint his eyes ;
But do it when the next thing he espies
May be the lady : thou shalt know the man
By the Athenian garments he hath on.
Effect it with some care, that he may prove
More fond on her than she upon her love :
And look thou meet me ere the first cock
    crow.
    Puck. Fear not, my lord, your servant
        shall do so.   [*Exeunt.*

SCENE II. *Another part of the wood.*

Enter TITANIA, *with her train.*

Tita. Come, now a roundel and a fairy
    song;
Then, for the third part of a minute, hence;
Some to kill cankers in the musk-rose buds,
Some war with rere-mice for their leathern
    wings,
To make my small elves coats, and some keep
    back
The clamorous owl that nightly hoots and
    wonders
At our quaint spirits. Sing me now asleep;
Then to your offices and let me rest.

The Fairies sing.

You spotted snakes with double tongue,
    Thorny hedgehogs, be not seen;   10
Newts and blind-worms, do no wrong,
    Come not near our fairy queen.
Philomel, with melody
Sing in our sweet lullaby;
Lulla, lulla, lullaby, lulla, lulla, lullaby:
    Never harm,
    Nor spell nor charm,
    Come our lovely lady nigh;
So, good night, with lullaby.

Weaving spiders, come not here;   20
    Hence, you long-legg'd spinners, hence!
Beetles black, approach not near;
    Worm nor snail, do no offence.
Philomel, with melody, &c.

A Fairy. Hence, away! now all is well:
    One aloof stand sentinel.

        [*Exeunt Fairies. Titania sleeps.*

Enter OBERON, *and squeezes the flower on
    Titania's eyelids.*

Obe. What thou seest when thou dost wake,
    Do it for thy true-love take,
    Love and languish for his sake:
    Be it ounce, or cat, or bear,   30
    Pard, or boar with bristled hair,
    In thy eye that shall appear
    When thou wakest, it is thy dear:
Wake when some vile thing is near.
        [*Exit.*

Enter LYSANDER *and* HERMIA.

Lys. Fair love, you faint with wandering
    in the wood;
And to speak troth, I have forgot our way:
We'll rest us, Hermia, if you think it good,
And tarry for the comfort of the day.
Her. Be it so, Lysander: find you out a
    bed;
For I upon this bank will rest my head.   40
Lys. One turf shall serve as pillow for us
    both;
One heart, one bed, two bosoms and one
    troth.
Her. Nay, good Lysander; for my sake,
    my dear,
Lie further off yet, do not lie so near.
Lys. O, take the sense, sweet, of my inno-
    cence!
Love takes the meaning in love's conference.
I mean, that my heart unto yours is knit
So that but one heart we can make of it;
Two bosoms interchained with an oath;
So then two bosoms and a single troth.   50

Then by your side no bed-room me deny;
For lying so, Hermia, I do not lie.
Her. Lysander riddles very prettily:
Now much beshrew my manners and my
    pride,
If Hermia meant to say Lysander lied.
But, gentle friend, for love and courtesy
Lie further off; in human modesty,
Such separation as may well be said
Becomes a virtuous bachelor and a maid,
So far be distant; and, good night, sweet
    friend: 60
Thy love ne'er alter till thy sweet life end!
Lys. Amen, amen, to that fair prayer, say
    I;
And then end life when I end loyalty!
Here is my bed: sleep give thee all his rest!
Her. With half that wish the wisher's eyes
    be press'd!   [*They sleep.*

Enter PUCK.

Puck. Through the forest have I gone.
    But Athenian found I none,
    On whose eyes I might approve
    This flower's force in stirring love.
Night and silence.—Who is here?   70
    Weeds of Athens he doth wear:
    This is he, my master said,
    Despised the Athenian maid;
    And here the maiden, sleeping sound,
    On the dank and dirty ground.
    Pretty soul! she durst not lie
    Near this lack-love, this kill-courtesy.
    Churl, upon thy eyes I throw
    All the power this charm doth owe.
When thou wakest, let love forbid   80
    Sleep his seat on thy eyelid:
    So awake when I am gone;
For I must now to Oberon.   [*Exit.*

Enter DEMETRIUS *and* HELENA, *running.*

Hel. Stay, though thou kill me, sweet
    Demetrius.
Dem. I charge thee, hence, and do not
    haunt me thus.
Hel. O, wilt thou darkling leave me? do
    not so.
Dem. Stay, on thy peril: I alone will go.
        [*Exit.*
Hel. O, I am out of breath in this fond
    chase!
The more my prayer, the lesser is my grace.
Happy is Hermia, wheresoe'er she lies;   90
For she hath blessed and attractive eyes.
How came her eyes so bright? Not with salt
    tears:
If so, my eyes are oftener wash'd than hers.
No, no, I am as ugly as a bear;
For beasts that meet me run away for fear:
Therefore no marvel though Demetrius
Do, as a monster, fly my presence thus.
What wicked and dissembling glass of mine
Made me compare with Hermia's sphery
    eyne?   99
But who is here? Lysander! on the ground!
Dead? or asleep? I see no blood, no wound.
Lysander, if you live, good sir, awake.
Lys. [*Awaking*] And run through fire I will
    for thy sweet sake.
Transparent Helena! Nature shows art,
That through thy bosom makes me see thy
    heart.
Where is Demetrius? O, how fit a word

Is that vile name to perish on my sword!
Hel. Do not say so, Lysander; say not so
What though he love your Hermia? Lord,
    what though?   109
Yet Hermia still loves you: then be content.
Lys. Content with Hermia! No; I do re-
    pent
The tedious minutes I with her have spent.
Not Hermia but Helena I love:
Who will not change a raven for a dove?
The will of man is by his reason sway'd;
And reason says you are the worthier maid.
Things growing are not ripe until their season:
So I, being young, till now ripe not to rea-
    son;
And touching now the point of human skill,
Reason becomes the marshal to my will   120
And leads me to your eyes, where I o'erlook
Love's stories written in love's richest book.
Hel. Wherefore was I to this keen mock-
    ery born?
When at your hands did I deserve this scorn?
Is't not enough, is't not enough, young man,
That I did never, no, nor never can,
Deserve a sweet look from Demetrius' eye,
But you must flout my insufficiency?
Good troth, you do me wrong, good sooth,
    you do,
In such disdainful manner me to woo.   130
But fare you well: perforce I must confess
I thought you lord of more true gentleness.
O, that a lady, of one man refused,
Should of another therefore be abused! [*Exit.*
Lys. She sees not Hermia. Hermia, sleep
    thou there:
And never mayst thou come Lysander near!
For as a surfeit of the sweetest things
The deepest loathing to the stomach brings,
Or as the heresies that men do leave
Are hated most of those they did deceive, 140
So thou, my surfeit and my heresy,
Of all be hated, but the most of me!
And, all my powers, address your love and
    might
To honor Helen and to be her knight! [*Exit.*
Her. [*Awaking*] Help me, Lysander, help
    me! do thy best
To pluck this crawling serpent from my
    breast!
Ay me, for pity! what a dream was here!
Lysander, look how I do quake with fear:
Methought a serpent eat my heart away,
And you sat smiling at his cruel prey.   150
Lysander! what, removed? Lysander! lord!
What, out of hearing? gone? no sound, no
    word?
Alack, where are you? speak, an if you hear;
Speak, of all loves! I swoon almost with fear.
No? then I well perceive you all not nigh:
Either death or you I'll find immediately.
                                       [*Exit.*

ACT III.

Scene I. *The wood.* Titania *lying asleep.*

Enter Quince, Snug, Bottom, Flute,
    Snout, *and* Starveling.

Bot. Are we all met?
Quin. Pat, pat; and here's a marvellous
convenient place for our rehearsal. This green
plot shall be our stage, this hawthorn-brake

our tiring-house; and we will do it in action
as we will do it before the duke.
Bot. Peter Quince,—
Quin. What sayest thou, bully Bottom?
Bot. There are things in this comedy of
Pyramus and Thisby that will never please.
First, Pyramus must draw a sword to kill himself; which the ladies cannot abide. How
answer you that?
Snout. By'r lakin, a parlous fear.
Star. I believe we must leave the killing
out, when all is done.
Bot. Not a whit: I have a device to make
all well. Write me a prologue; and let the
prologue seem to say, we will do no harm with
our swords, and that Pyramus is not killed
indeed; and, for the more better assurance,
tell them that I, Pyramus, am not Pyramus,
but Bottom the weaver: this will put them out
of fear.
Quin. Well, we will have such a prologue;
and it shall be written in eight and six.
Bot. No, make it two more; let it be written in eight and eight.
Snout. Will not the ladies be afeard of
the lion?
Star. I fear it, I promise you.
Bot. Masters, you ought to consider with
yourselves: to bring in—God shield us!—a
lion among ladies, is a most dreadful thing;
for there is not a more fearful wild-fowl than
your lion living; and we ought to look to 't.
Snout. Therefore another prologue must
tell he is not a lion.
Bot. Nay, you must name his name, and
half his face must be seen through the lion's
neck: and he himself must speak through,
saying thus, or to the same defect,—'Ladies,'
—or 'Fair ladies,—I would wish you,'—or 'I
would request you,'—or 'I would entreat you,
—not to fear, not to tremble: my life for
yours. If you think I come hither as a lion, it
were pity of my life: no, I am no such thing;
I am a man as other men are;' and there indeed let him name his name, and tell them
plainly he is Snug the joiner.
Quin. Well, it shall be so. But there is two
hard things; that is, to bring the moonlight
into a chamber; for, you know, Pyramus and
Thisby meet by moonlight.   51
Snout. Doth the moon shine that night we
play our play?
Bot. A calendar, a calendar! look in the
almanac; find out moonshine, find out moonshine.
Quin. Yes, it doth shine that night.
Bot. Why, then may you leave a casement
of the great chamber window, where we play,
open, and the moon may shine in at the casement.
Quin. Ay; or else one must come in with
a bush of thorns and a lanthorn, and say he
comes to disfigure, or to present, the person
of Moonshine. Then, there is another thing:
we must have a wall in the great chamber;
for Pyramus and Thisby, says the story, did
talk through the chink of a wall.
Snout. You can never bring in a wall.
What say you, Bottom?
Bot. Some man or other must present
Wall: and let him have some plaster, or some
loam, or some rough-cast about him, to signify
wall; and let him hold his fingers thus, and

through that cranny shall Pyramus and Thisby whisper.

Quin. If that may be, then all is well. Come, sit down, every mother's son, and rehearse your parts. Pyramus, you begin : when you have spoken your speech, enter into that brake : and so every one according to his cue.

Enter PUCK *behind.*

Puck. What hempen home-spuns have we swaggering here,
So near the cradle of the fairy queen ?   80
What, a play toward ! I'll be an auditor ;
An actor too, perhaps, if I see cause.

Quin. Speak, Pyramus. Thisby, stand forth.

Bot. Thisby, the flowers of odious savors sweet,—

Quin. Odors, odors.

Bot. —— odors savors sweet :
So hath thy breath, my dearest Thisby dear.
But hark, a voice ! stay thou but here awhile,
And by and by I will to thee appear. [*Exit.*

Puck. A stranger Pyramus than e'er played here.   [*Exit.*

Flu. Must I speak now ?   91

Quin. Ay, marry, must you ; for you must understand he goes but to see a noise that he heard, and is to come again.

Flu. Most radiant Pyramus, most lily-white of hue,
Of color like the red rose on triumphant brier,
Most brisky juvenal and eke most lovely Jew,
As true as truest horse that yet would never tire,
I'll meet thee, Pyramus, at Ninny's tomb.

Quin. 'Ninus' tomb,' man : why, you must not speak that yet ; that you answer to Pyramus : you speak all your part at once, cues and all. Pyramus enter : your cue is past ; it is, 'never tire.'

Flu. O,—As true as truest horse, that yet would never tire.

Re-enter PUCK, *and* BOTTOM *with an ass's head.*

Bot. If I were fair, Thisby, I were only thine.

Quin. O monstrous ! O strange ! we are haunted. Pray, masters ! fly, masters ! Help ! [*Exeunt Quince, Snug, Flute, Snout, and Starveling.*

Puck. I'll follow you, I'll lead you about a round,
Through bog, through bush, through brake, through brier :   110
Sometime a horse I'll be, sometime a hound,
A hog, a headless bear, sometime a fire ;
And neigh, and bark, and grunt, and roar, and burn,
Like horse, hound, hog, bear, fire, at every turn.   [*Exit.*

Bot. Why do they run away ? this is a knavery of them to make me afeard.

Re-enter SNOUT.

Snout. O Bottom, thou art changed ! what do I see on thee ?

Bot. What do you see ? you see an ass-head of your own, do you ?   [*Exit Snout.*

Re-enter QUINCE.

Quin. Bless thee, Bottom ! bless thee ! thou art translated.   [*Exit.*

Bot. I see their knavery : this is to make an ass of me ; to fright me, if they could. But I will not stir from this place, do what they can : I will walk up and down here, and I will sing, that they shall hear I am not afraid.
[*Sings.*
The ousel cock so black of hue,
    With orange-tawny bill,
The throstle with his note so true,   130
    The wren with little quill,—

Tita. [*Awaking*] What angel wakes me from my flowery bed ?

Bot. [*Sings*]
The finch, the sparrow and the lark,
    The plain-song cuckoo gray,
Whose note full many a man doth mark,
    And dares not answer nay ;—
for, indeed, who would set his wit to so foolish a bird ? who would give a bird the lie, though he cry 'cuckoo' never so ?

Tita. I pray thee, gentle mortal, sing again :   141
Mine ear is much enamour'd of thy note ;
So is mine eye enthralled to thy shape ;
And thy fair virtue's force perforce doth move me
On the first view to say, to swear, I love thee.

Bot. Methinks, mistress, you should have little reason for that : and yet, to say the truth, reason and love keep little company together now-a-days ; the more the pity that some honest neighbors will not make them friends. Nay, I can gleek upon occasion.   150

Tita. Thou art as wise as thou art beautiful.

Bot. Not so, neither : but if I had wit enough to get out of this wood, I have enough to serve mine own turn.

Tita. Out of this wood do not desire to go :
Thou shalt remain here, whether thou wilt or no.
I am a spirit of no common rate ;
The summer still doth tend upon my state ;
And I do love thee : therefore, go with me ;
I'll give thee fairies to attend on thee,   160
And they shall fetch thee jewels from the deep,
And sing while thou on pressed flowers dost sleep ;
And I will purge thy mortal grossness so
That thou shalt like an airy spirit go.
Peaseblossom ! Cobweb ! Moth ! and Mustardseed !

Enter PEASEBLOSSOM, COBWEB, MOTH, *and* MUSTARDSEED.

Peas. Ready.
Cob.   And I.
Moth.   And I.
Mus.   And I.
All.   Where shall we go ?

Tita. Be kind and courteous to this gentleman ;
Hop in his walks and gambol in his eyes ;
Feed him with apricocks and dewberries,
With purple grapes, green figs, and mulberries ;   170
The honey-bags steal from the humble-bees,
And for night-tapers crop their waxen thighs
And light them at the fiery glow-worm's eyes,
To have my love to bed and to arise ;

And pluck the wings from painted butterflies
To fan the moonbeams from his sleeping eyes :
Nod to him, elves, and do him courtesies.
    Peas. Hail, mortal !
    Cob. Hail !
    Moth. Hail !   180
    Mus. Hail !
    Bot. I cry your worship's mercy, heartily :
I beseech your worship's name.
    Cob. Cobweb.
    Bot. I shall desire you of more acquaint-
ance, good Master Cobweb : if I cut my finger,
I shall make bold with you. Your name,
honest gentleman ?
    Peas. Peaseblossom.
    Bot. I pray you, commend me to Mistress
Squash, your mother, and to Master Peascod,
your father. Good Master Peaseblossom, I
shall desire you of more acquaintance too.
Your name, I beseech you, sir ?
    Mus. Mustardseed.
    Bot. Good Master Mustardseed, I know
your patience well : that same cowardly, giant-
like ox-beef hath devoured many a gentleman
of your house : I promise you your kindred
hath made my eyes water ere now. I desire
your more acquaintance, good Master Mustardseed.   201
    Tita. Come, wait upon him ; lead him to
    my bower.
The moon methinks looks with a watery
    eye ;
And when she weeps, weeps every little flower,
Lamenting some enforced chastity.
Tie up my love's tongue, bring him silently.
                                        [*Exeunt.*

SCENE II. *Another part of the wood.*

Enter OBERON.

    Obe. I wonder if Titania be awaked ;
Then, what it was that next came in her eye,
Which she must dote on in extremity.

Enter PUCK.

Here comes my messenger.
                        How now, mad spirit !
What night-rule now about this haunted
    grove ?
    Puck. My mistress with a monster is in
    love.
Near to her close and consecrated bower,
While she was in her dull and sleeping hour,
A crew of patches, rude mechanicals,
That work for bread upon Athenian stalls, 10
Were met together to rehearse a play
Intended for great Theseus' nuptial-day.
The shallowest thick-skin of that barren sort,
Who Pyramus presented, in their sport
Forsook his scene and enter'd in a brake
When I did him at this advantage take,
An ass's nole I fixed on his head :
Anon his Thisbe must be answered,
And forth my mimic comes. When they him
    spy,
As wild geese that the creeping fowler eye, 20
Or russet-pated choughs, many in sort,
Rising and cawing at the gun's report,
Sever themselves and madly sweep the sky,
So, at his sight, away his fellows fly ;
And, at our stamp, here o'er and o'er one
    falls ;
He murder cries and help from Athens calls.

Their sense thus weak, lost with their fears
    thus strong,
Made senseless things begin to do them wrong ;
For briers and thorns at their apparel snatch ;
Some sleeves, some hats, from yielders all
    things catch.   30
I led them on in this distracted fear,
And left sweet Pyramus translated there :
When in that moment, so it came to pass,
Titania waked and straightway loved an ass.
    Obe. This falls out better than I could de-
    vise.
But hast thou yet latch'd the Athenian's eyes
With the love-juice, as I did bid thee do ?
    Puck. I took him sleeping,—that is finish'd
    too,—
And the Athenian woman by his side :
That, when he waked, of force she must be
    eyed.   40

Enter HERMIA *and* DEMETRIUS.

    Obe. Stand close : this is the same Athe-
    nian.
    Puck. This is the woman, but not this the
    man.
    Dem. O, why rebuke you him that loves
    you so ?
Lay breath so bitter on your bitter foe.
    Her. Now I but chide ; but I should use
    thee worse,
For thou, I fear, hast given me cause to curse,
If thou hast slain Lysander in his sleep,
Being o'er shoes in blood, plunge in the deep,
And kill me too.
The sun was not so true unto the day   50
As he to me : would he have stolen away
From sleeping Hermia ? I'll believe as soon
This whole earth may be bored and that the
    moon
May through the centre creep and so displease
Her brother's noontide with the Antipodes.
It cannot be but thou hast murder'd him ;
So should a murderer look, so dead, so grim.
    Dem. So should the murder'd look, and so
    should I,
Pierced through the heart with your stern
    cruelty :   59
Yet you, the murderer, look as bright, as clear,
As yonder Venus in her glimmering sphere.
    Her. What's this to my Lysander ? where
    is he ?
Ah, good Demetrius, wilt thou give him me ?
    Dem. I had rather give his carcass to my
    hounds.
    Her. Out, dog ! out, cur ! thou drivest me
    past the bounds
Of maiden's patience. Hast thou slain him,
    then ?
Henceforth be never number'd among men !
O, once tell true, tell true, even for my sake !
Durst thou have look'd upon him being awake,
And hast thou kill'd him sleeping ? O brave
    touch !   70
Could not a worm, an adder, do so much ?
An adder did it ; for with doubler tongue
Than thine, thou serpent, never adder stung.
    Dem. You spend your passion on a mis-
    prised mood :
I am not guilty of Lysander's blood ;
Nor is he dead, for aught that I can tell.
    Her. I pray thee, tell me then that he is
    well.

Dem. An if I could, what should I get
therefore ?
Her. A privilege never to see me more.
And from thy hated presence part I so :   80
See me no more, whether he be dead or no.
                              [*Exit.*
Dem. There is no following her in this
fierce vein :
Here therefore for a while I will remain.
So sorrow's heaviness doth heavier grow
For debt that bankrupt sleep doth sorrow
owe :
Which now in some slight measure it will pay,
If for his tender here I make some stay.
                    [*Lies down and sleeps.*
Obe. What hast thou done ? thou hast mis-
taken quite
And laid the love-juice on some true-love's
sight :
Of thy misprision must perforce ensue   90
Some true love turn'd and not a false turn'd
true.
Puck. Then fate o'er-rules, that, one man
holding troth,
A million fail, confounding oath on oath.
Obe. About the wood go swifter than the
wind,
And Helena of Athens look thou find :
All fancy-sick she is and pale of cheer,
With sighs of love, that costs the fresh blood
dear :
By some illusion see thou bring her here :
I'll charm his eyes against she do appear.
Puck. I go, I go ; look how I go,   100
Swifter than arrow from the Tartar's bow.
                              [*Exit.*
Obe.   Flower of this purple dye,
        Hit with Cupid's archery,
        Sink in apple of his eye.
        When his love he doth espy,
        Let her shine as gloriously
        As the Venus of the sky.
        When thou wakest, if she be by,
        Beg of her for remedy.

Re-enter PUCK.

Puck.   Captain of our fairy band,   110
        Helena is here at hand ;
        And the youth, mistook by me,
        Pleading for a lover's fee.
        Shall we their fond pageant see ?
        Lord, what fools these mortals be !
Obe.   Stand aside : the noise they make
        Will cause Demetrius to awake.
Puck.   Then will two at once woo one ;
        That must needs be sport alone ;
        And those things do best please me
        That befal preposterously.   121

Enter LYSANDER *and* HELENA.

Lys. Why should you think that I should
woo in scorn ?
Scorn and derision never come in tears :
Look, when I vow, I weep ; and vows so born,
In their nativity all truth appears.
How can these things in me seem scorn to you,
Bearing the badge of faith, to prove them
true ?
Hel. You do advance your cunning more
and more.
When truth kills truth, O devilish-holy fray !
These vows are Hermia's : will you give her
o'er ?   130

Weigh oath with oath, and you will nothing
weigh :
Your vows to her and me, put in two scales,
Will even weigh, and both as light as tales.
Lys. I had no judgment when to her I
swore.
Hel. Nor none, in my mind, now you give
her o'er.
Lys. Demetrius loves her, and he loves not
you.
Dem. [*Awaking*] O Helen, goddess, nymph,
perfect, divine !
To what, my love, shall I compare thine eyne ?
Crystal is muddy. O, how ripe in show
Thy lips, those kissing cherries, tempting
grow !   140
That pure congealed white, high Taurus snow,
Fann'd with the eastern wind, turns to a crow
When thou hold'st up thy hand : O, let me
kiss
This princess of pure white, this seal of bliss !
Hel. O spite ! O hell ! I see you all are
bent
To set against me for your merriment :
If you were civil and knew courtesy,
You would not do me thus much injury.
Can you not hate me, as I know you do,
But you must join in souls to mock me too ?
If you were men, as men you are in show, 151
You would not use a gentle lady so ;
To vow, and swear, and superpraise my parts,
When I am sure you hate me with your hearts.
You both are rivals, and love Hermia ;
And now both rivals, to mock Helena :
A trim exploit, a manly enterprise,
To conjure tears up in a poor maid's eyes
With your derision ! none of noble sort
Would so offend a virgin, and extort   160
A poor soul's patience, all to make you sport.
Lys. You are unkind, Demetrius ; be not
so ;
For you love Hermia ; this you know I know :
And here, with all good will, with all my
heart,
In Hermia's love I yield you up my part ;
And yours of Helena to me bequeath,
Whom I do love and will do till my death.
Hel. Never did mockers waste more idle
breath.
Dem. Lysander, keep thy Hermia ; I will
none :
If e'er I loved her, all that love is gone.   170
My heart to her but as guest-wise sojourn'd,
And now to Helen is it home return'd,
There to remain.
Lys.   Helen, it is not so.
Dem. Disparage not the faith thou dost
not know,
Lest, to thy peril, thou aby it dear.
Look, where thy love comes ; yonder is thy
dear.

Re-enter HERMIA.

Her. Dark night, that from the eye his
function takes,
The ear more quick of apprehension makes ;
Wherein it doth impair the seeing sense,
It pays the hearing double recompense.   180
Thou art not by mine eye, Lysander, found ;
Mine ear, I thank it, brought me to thy sound
But why unkindly didst thou leave me so ?
Lys. Why should he stay, whom love doth
press to go ?

Her. What love could press Lysander from
  my side ?
Lys. Lysander's love, that would not let
  him bide,
Fair Helena, who more engilds the night
Than all you fiery oes and eyes of light.
Why seek'st thou me ? could not this make
  thee know,
The hate I bear thee made me leave thee so ?
Her. You speak not as you think : it can-
  not be.   191
Hel. Lo, she is one of this confederacy !
Now I perceive they have conjoin'd all three
To fashion this false sport, in spite of me.
Injurious Hermia ! most ungrateful maid !
Have you conspired, have you with these con-
  trived
To bait me with this foul derision ?
Is all the counsel that we two have shared,
The sisters' vows, the hours that we have spent,
When we have chid the hasty-footed time 200
For parting us,—O, is it all forgot ?
All school-days' friendship, childhood inno-
  cence ?
We, Hermia, like two artificial gods,
Have with our needles created both one flower,
Both on one sampler, sitting on one cushion,
Both warbling of one song, both in one key,
As if our hands, our sides, voices and minds,
Had been incorporate. So we grew together,
Like to a double cherry, seeming parted,
But yet an union in partition ;   210
Two lovely berries moulded on one stem ;
So, with two seeming bodies, but one heart ;
Two of the first, like coats in heraldry,
Due but to one and crowned with one crest.
And will you rent our ancient love asunder,
To join with men in scorning your poor
  friend ?
It is not friendly, 'tis not maidenly :
Our sex, as well as I, may chide you for it,
Though I alone do feel the injury.
Her. I am amazed at your passionate
  words.   220
I scorn you not : it seems that you scorn me.
Hel. Have you not set Lysander, as in
  scorn,
To follow me and praise my eyes and face ?
And made your other love, Demetrius,
Who even but now did spurn me with his foot,
To call me goddess, nymph, divine and rare,
Precious, celestial ? Wherefore speaks he this
To her he hates ? and wherefore doth Lysan-
  der
Deny your love, so rich within his soul,
And tender me, forsooth, affection,   230
But by your setting on, by your consent ?
What though I be not so in grace as you,
So hung upon with love, so fortunate,
But miserable most, to love unloved ?
This you should pity rather than despise.
Her. I understand not what you mean by
  this.
Hel. Ay, do, persever, counterfeit sad
  looks,
Make mouths upon me when I turn my back ;
Wink each at other ; hold the sweet jest up :
This sport, well carried, shall be chronicled.
If you have any pity, grace, or manners, 241
You would not make me such an argument.
But fare ye well : 'tis partly my own fault ;
Which death or absence soon shall remedy.
Lys. Stay, gentle Helena ; hear my excuse :

My love, my life, my soul, fair Helena !
Hel. O excellent !
Her.   Sweet, do not scorn her so.
Dem. If she cannot entreat, I can compel.
Lys. Thou canst compel no more than she
  entreat :
Thy threats have no more strength than her
  weak prayers.   250
Helen, I love thee ; by my life, I do :
I swear by that which I will lose for thee,
To prove him false that says I love thee not.
Dem. I say I love thee more than he can
  do.
Lys. If thou say so, withdraw, and prove
  it too.
Dem. Quick, come !
Her.   Lysander, whereto tends all this ?
Lys. Away, you Ethiope !
Dem.   No, no ; he'll . . .
Seem to break loose ; take on as you would
  follow,
But yet come not : you are a tame man, go !
Lys. Hang off, thou cat, thou burr ! vile
  thing, let loose,   260
Or I will shake thee from me like a serpent !
Her. Why are you grown so rude ? what
  change is this ?
Sweet love,—
Lys.   Thy love ! out, tawny Tartar, out !
Out, loathed medicine ! hated potion, hence !
Her. Do you not jest ?
Hel.   Yes, sooth ; and so do you.
Lys. Demetrius, I will keep my word with
  thee.
Dem. I would I had your bond, for I per-
  ceive
A weak bond holds you : I'll not trust your
  word.
Lys. What, should I hurt her, strike her,
  kill her dead ?
Although I hate her, I'll not harm her so. 270
Her. What, can you do me greater harm
  than hate ?
Hate me ! wherefore ? O me ! what news, my
  love !
Am not I Hermia ? are not you Lysander ?
I am as fair now as I was erewhile.
Since night you loved me ; yet since night you
  left me :
Why, then you left me—O, the gods forbid !—
In earnest, shall I say ?
Lys.   Ay, by my life ;
And never did desire to see thee more.
Therefore be out of hope, of question, of
  doubt ;
Be certain, nothing truer ; 'tis no jest   280
That I do hate thee and love Helena.
Her. O me ! you juggler ! you canker-
  blossom !
You thief of love ! what, have you come by
  night
And stolen my love's heart from him ?
Hel.   Fine, i'faith !
Have you no modesty, no maiden shame,
No touch of bashfulness ? What, will you
  tear
Impatient answers from my gentle tongue ?
Fie, fie ! you counterfeit, you puppet, you !
Her. Puppet ? why so ? ay, that way goes
  the game.
Now I perceive that she hath made compare
Between our statures ; she hath urged her
  height ;   291

And with her personage, her tall personage,
Her height, forsooth, she hath prevail'd with
    him.
And are you grown so high in his esteem;
Because I am so dwarfish and so low?
How low am I, thou painted maypole? speak;
How low am I? I am not yet so low
But that my nails can reach unto thine eyes.
  Hel. I pray you, though you mock me,
    gentlemen,
Let her not hurt me: I was never curst; 300
I have no gift at all in shrewishness;
I am a right maid for my cowardice:
Let her not strike me. You perhaps may think,
Because she is something lower than myself,
That I can match her.
  Her.   Lower! hark, again.
  Hel. Good Hermia, do not be so bitter
    with me.
I evermore did love you, Hermia,
Did ever keep your counsels, never wrong'd
    you;
Save that, in love unto Demetrius,
I told him of your stealth unto this wood. 310
He follow'd you; for love I follow'd him;
But he hath chid me hence and threaten'd me
To strike me, spurn me, nay, to kill me too:
And now, so you will let me quiet go,
To Athens will I bear my folly back
And follow you no further: let me go:
You see how simple and how fond I am.
  Her. Why, get you gone: who is't that
    hinders you?
  Hel. A foolish heart, that I leave here be-
    hind.
  Her. What, with Lysander?
  Hel.   With Demetrius. 320
  Lys. Be not afraid; she shall not harm
    thee, Helena.
  Dem. No, sir, she shall not, though you
    take her part.
  Hel. O, when she's angry, she is keen and
    shrewd!
She was a vixen when she went to school;
And though she be but little, she is fierce.
  Her. 'Little' again! nothing but 'low'
    and 'little'!
Why will you suffer her to flout me thus?
Let me come to her.
  Lys.   Get you gone, you dwarf;
You minimus, of hindering knot-grass made;
You bead, you acorn.
  Dem.   You are too officious 330
In her behalf that scorns your services.
Let her alone: speak not of Helena;
Take not her part; for, if thou dost intend
Never so little show of love to her,
Thou shalt aby it.
  Lys.   Now she holds me not;
Now follow, if thou darest, to try whose right,
Of thine or mine, is most in Helena.
  Dem. Follow! nay, I'll go with thee, cheek
    by jole.
           [*Exeunt Lysander and Demetrius.*
  Her. You, mistress, all this coil is 'long of
    you:
Nay, go not back.
  Hel.   I will not trust you, I, 340
Nor longer stay in your curst company.
Your hands than mine are quicker for a fray,
My legs are longer though, to run away. [*Exit.*
  Her. I am amazed, and know not what to
    say.   [*Exit.*

  Obe. This is thy negligence: still thou mis-
    takest,
Or else committ'st thy knaveries wilfully.
  Puck. Believe me, king of shadows, I mis-
    took.
Did not you tell me I should know the man
By the Athenian garment he had on?
And so far blameless proves my enterprise, 350
That I have 'nointed an Athenian's eyes;
And so far am I glad it so did sort
As this their jangling I esteem a sport.
  Obe. Thou see'st these lovers seek a place
    to fight:
Hie therefore, Robin, overcast the night;
The starry welkin cover thou anon
With drooping fog as black as Acheron,
And lead these testy rivals so astray
As one come not within another's way.
Like to Lysander sometime frame thy tongue,
Then stir Demetrius up with bitter wrong; 361
And sometime rail thou like Demetrius;
And from each other look thou lead them
    thus,
Till o'er their brows death-counterfeiting sleep
With leaden legs and batty wings doth creep:
Then crush this herb into Lysander's eye;
Whose liquor hath this virtuous property,
To take from thence all error with his might,
And make his eyeballs roll with wonted sight.
When they next wake, all this derision 370
Shall seem a dream and fruitless vision,
And back to Athens shall the lovers wend,
With league whose date till death shall never
    end.
Whiles I in this affair do thee employ,
I'll to my queen and beg her Indian boy;
And then I will her charmed eye release
From monster's view, and all things shall be
    peace.
  Puck. My fairy lord, this must be done
    with haste,
For night's swift dragons cut the clouds full
    fast,
And yonder shines Aurora's harbinger; 380
At whose approach, ghosts, wandering here
    and there,
Troop home to churchyards: damned spirits
    all,
That in crossways and floods have burial,
Already to their wormy beds are gone;
For fear lest day should look their shames
    upon,
They wilfully themselves exile from light
And must for aye consort with black-brow'd
    night.
  Obe. But we are spirits of another sort:
I with the morning's love have oft made sport,
And, like a forester, the groves may tread, 390
Even till the eastern gate, all fiery-red,
Opening on Neptune with fair blessed beams,
Turns into yellow gold his salt green streams.
But, notwithstanding, haste; make no delay:
We may effect this business yet ere day.
                        [*Exit.*
  Puck. Up and down, up and down,
    I will lead them up and down:
    I am fear'd in field and town:
    Goblin, lead them up and down.
Here comes one.   400

          Re-enter LYSANDER.

  Lys. Where art thou, proud Demetrius?
speak thou now.

Puck. Here, villain; drawn and ready.
Where art thou?
Lys. I will be with thee straight.
Puck.   Follow me, then,
To plainer ground.
[*Exit Lysander, as following the voice.*

Re-enter Demetrius.

Dem.   Lysander! speak again:
Thou runaway, thou coward, art thou fled?
Speak! In some bush? Where dost thou hide
thy head?
Puck. Thou coward, art thou bragging to
the stars,
Telling the bushes that thou look'st for wars,
And wilt not come? Come, recreant; come,
thou child;
I'll whip thee with a rod: he is defiled   410
That draws a sword on thee.
Dem.   Yea, art thou there?
Puck. Follow my voice: we'll try no man-
hood here.   [*Exeunt.*

Re-enter Lysander.

Lys. He goes before me and still dares me
on:
When I come where he calls, then he is gone.
The villain is much lighter-heel'd than I:
I follow'd fast, but faster he did fly;
That fallen am I in dark uneven way,
And here will rest me. [*Lies down.*] Come,
thou gentle day!
For if but once thou show me thy grey light,
I'll find Demetrius and revenge this spite.
[*Sleeps.*

Re-enter Puck *and* Demetrius.

Puck. Ho, ho, ho! Coward, why comest
thou not?   421
Dem. Abide me, if thou darest; for well I
wot
Thou runn'st before me, shifting every place,
And darest not stand, nor look me in the face.
Where art thou now?
Puck.   Come hither: I am here.
Dem. Nay, then, thou mock'st me. Thou
shalt buy this dear,
If ever I thy face by daylight see:
Now, go thy way. Faintness constraineth me
To measure out my length on this cold bed.
By day's approach look to be visited.
[*Lies down and sleeps.*

Re-enter Helena.

Hel. O weary night, O long and tedious
night,
Abate thy hours! Shine comforts from the
east,
That I may back to Athens by daylight,
From these that my poor company detest:
And sleep, that sometimes shuts up sorrow's
eye,
Steal me awhile from mine own company.
[*Lies down and sleeps.*
Puck. Yet but three? Come one more;
Two of both kinds make up four.
Here she comes, curst and sad:
Cupid is a knavish lad,   440
Thus to make poor females mad.

Re-enter Hermia.

Her. Never so weary, never so in woe,
Bedabbled with the dew and torn with
briers,

I can no further crawl, no further go;
My legs can keep no pace with my desires.
Here will I rest me till the break of day.
Heavens shield Lysander, if they mean a fray!
[*Lies down and sleeps.*
Puck.   On the ground
Sleep sound:
I'll apply   450
To your eye,
Gentle lover, remedy.
[*Squeezing the juice on Lysander's eyes.*
When thou wakest,
Thou takest
True delight
In the sight
Of thy former lady's eye:
And the country proverb known,
That every man should take his own,
In your waking shall be shown: 460
Jack shall have Jill;
Nought shall go ill;
The man shall have his mare again, and all
shall be well.   [*Exit.*

ACT IV.

Scene I. *The same.* Lysander, Demetrius,
Helena, *and* Hermia *lying asleep.*

Enter Titania *and* Bottom; Peaseblossom,
Cobweb, Moth, Mustardseed, *and other
Fairies attending;* Oberon *behind unseen.*

Tita. Come, sit thee down upon this
flowery bed,
While I thy amiable cheeks do coy,
And stick musk-roses in thy sleek smooth
head,
And kiss thy fair large ears, my gentle joy.
Bot. Where's Peaseblossom?
Peas. Ready.
Bot. Scratch my head Peaseblossom.
Where's Mounsieur Cobweb?
Cob. Ready.
Bot. Mounsieur Cobweb, good mounsieur,
get you your weapons in your hand, and kill
me a red-hipped humble-bee on the top of a
thistle; and, good mounsieur, bring me the
honey-bag. Do not fret yourself too much in
the action, mounsieur; and, good mounsieur,
have a care the honey-bag break not; I would
be loath to have you overflown with a honey-
bag, signior. Where's Mounsieur Mustardseed?
Mus. Ready.
Bot. Give me your neaf, Mounsieur Mustardseed. Pray you, leave your courtesy, good
mounsieur.
Mus. What's your will?
Bot. Nothing, good mounsieur, but to help
Cavalery Cobweb to scratch. I must to the
barber's, mounsieur; for methinks I am marvellous hairy about the face; and I am such
a tender ass, if my hair do but tickle me, I
must scratch.
Tita. What, wilt thou hear some music,
my sweet love?   30
Bot. I have a reasonable good ear in
music. Let's have the tongs and the bones.
Tita. Or say, sweet love, what thou desirest
to eat.
Bot. Truly, a peck of provender: I could
munch your good dry oats. Methinks I have

a great desire to a bottle of hay : good hay,
sweet hay, hath no fellow.

Tita. I have a venturous fairy that shall
seek   39
The squirrel's hoard, and fetch thee new nuts.

Bot. I had rather have a handful or two of
dried peas. But, I pray you, let none of your
people stir me : I have an exposition of sleep
come upon me.

Tita. Sleep thou, and I will wind thee in
my arms.
Fairies, begone, and be all ways away.
             [*Exeunt fairies.*
So doth the woodbine the sweet honeysuckle
Gently entwist ; the female ivy so
Enrings the barky fingers of the elm.
O, how I love thee ! how I dote on thee !   50
             [*They sleep.*

Enter PUCK.

Obe. [*Advancing*] Welcome, good Robin.
See'st thou this sweet sight ?
Her dotage now I do begin to pity :
For, meeting her of late behind the wood,
Seeking sweet favors from this hateful fool,
I did upbraid her and fall out with her ;
For she his hairy temples then had rounded
With a coronet of fresh and fragrant flowers ;
And that same dew, which sometime on the
buds
Was wont to swell like round and orient
pearls,
Stood now within the pretty flowerets' eyes   60
Like tears that did their own disgrace bewail.
When I had at my pleasure taunted her
And she in mild terms begg'd my patience,
I then did ask of her her changeling child ;
Which straight she gave me, and her fairy sent
To bear him to my bower in fairy land.
And now I have the boy, I will undo
This hateful imperfection of her eyes :
And, gentle Puck, take this transformed scalp
From off the head of this Athenian swain ;   70
That, he awaking when the other do,
May all to Athens back again repair
And think no more of this night's accidents
But as the fierce vexation of a dream.
But first I will release the fairy queen.
     Be as thou wast wont to be ;
     See as thou wast wont to see :
     Dian's bud o'er Cupid's flower
     Hath such force and blessed power.
Now, my Titania ; wake you, my sweet queen.

Tita. My Oberon ! what visions have I
seen !
Methought I was enamour'd of an ass.

Obe. There lies your love.

Tita.   How came these things to pass ?
O, how mine eyes do loathe his visage now !

Obe. Silence awhile. Robin, take off this
head.
Titania, music call ; and strike more dead
Than common sleep of all these five the sense.

Tita. Music, ho ! music, such as charmeth
sleep !   [*Music, still.*

Puck. Now, when thou wakest, with thine
own fool's eyes peep.

Obe. Sound, music ! Come, my queen, take
hands with me,   90
And rock the ground whereon these sleepers
be.
Now thou and I are new in amity,
And will to-morrow midnight solemnly

Dance in Duke Theseus' house triumphantly,
And bless it to all fair prosperity :
There shall the pairs of faithful lovers be
Wedded, with Theseus, all in jollity.

Puck. Fairy king, attend, and mark :
I do hear the morning lark.

Obe. Then, my queen, in silence sad,   100
Trip we after the night's shade :
We the globe can compass soon,
Swifter than the wandering moon.

Tita. Come, my lord, and in our flight
Tell me how it came this night
That I sleeping here was found
With these mortals on the ground.
             [*Exeunt.*
       [*Horns winded within.*

Enter THESEUS, HIPPOLYTA, EGEUS, *and train.*

The. Go, one of you, find out the forester ;
For now our observation is perform'd ;
And since we have the vaward of the day,   110
My love shall hear the music of my hounds.
Uncouple in the western valley ; let them go :
Dispatch, I say, and find the forester.
         [*Exit an Attendant.*
We will, fair queen, up to the mountain's top,
And mark the musical confusion
Of hounds and echo in conjunction.

Hip. I was with Hercules and Cadmus
once,
When in a wood of Crete they bay'd the bear
With hounds of Sparta : never did I hear   119
Such gallant chiding : for, besides the groves,
The skies, the fountains, every region near
Seem'd all one mutual cry : I never heard
So musical a discord, such sweet thunder.

The. My hounds are bred out of the Spar-
tan kind,
So flew'd, so sanded, and their heads are
hung
With ears that sweep away the morning dew ;
Crook-knee'd, and dew-lapp'd like Thessalian
bulls ;
Slow in pursuit, but match'd in mouth like
bells,   120
Each under each. A cry more tuneable
Was never holla'd to, nor cheer'd with horn,
In Crete, in Sparta, nor in Thessaly :
Judge when you hear. But, soft ! what nymphs
are these ?

Ege. My lord, this is my daughter here
asleep ;
And this, Lysander ; this Demetrius is ;
This Helena, old Nedar's Helena :
I wonder of their being here together.

The. No doubt they rose up early to ob-
serve
The rite of May, and, hearing our intent,   130
Came here in grace of our solemnity.
But speak, Egeus ; is not this the day
That Hermia should give answer of her
choice ?

Ege. It is, my lord.

The. Go, bid the huntsmen wake them
with their horns.
    [*Horns and shout within. Lys., Dem., Hel.,*
         and Her., wake and start up.
Good morrow, friends. Saint Valentine is
past :
Begin these wood-birds but to couple now ?

Lys. Pardon, my lord.

The.   I pray you all, stand up.
I know you two are rival enemies :

How comes this gentle concord in the world,
That hatred is so far from jealousy, 141
To sleep by hate, and fear no enmity ?
    Lys. My lord, I shall reply amazedly,
Half sleep, half waking : but as yet, I swear,
I cannot truly say how I came here ;
But, as I think,—for truly would I speak,
And now do I bethink me, so it is,—
I came with Hermia hither : our intent
Was to be gone from Athens, where we might,
Without the peril of the Athenian law. 150
    Ege. Enough, enough, my lord ; you have enough :
I beg the law, the law, upon his head.
They would have stolen away ; they would, Demetrius,
Thereby to have defeated you and me,
You of your wife and me of my consent,
Of my consent that she should be your wife.
    Dem. My lord, fair Helen told me of their stealth,
Of this their purpose hither to this wood ;
And I in fury hither follow'd them,
Fair Helena in fancy following me. 160
But, my good lord, I wot not by what power,—
But by some power it is,—my love to Hermia,
Melted as the snow, seems to me now
As the remembrance of an idle gaud
Which in my childhood I did dote upon ;
And all the faith, the virtue of my heart,
The object and the pleasure of mine eye,
Is only Helena. To her, my lord,
Was I betroth'd ere I saw Hermia :
But, like in sickness, did I loathe this food ; 170
But, as in health, come to my natural taste,
Now I do wish it, love it, long for it,
And will for evermore be true to it.
    The. Fair lovers, you are fortunately met :
Of this discourse we more will hear anon.
Egeus, I will overbear your will ;
For in the temple, by and by, with us
These couples shall eternally be knit :
And, for the morning now is something worn,
Our purposed hunting shall be set aside. 180
Away with us to Athens ; three and three,
We'll hold a feast in great solemnity.
Come, Hippolyta.
    [*Exeunt The., Hip., Ege., and train.*
    Dem. These things seem small and undistinguishable,
Like far-off mountains turned into clouds.
    Her. Methinks I see these things with parted eye,
When every thing seems double.
    Hel.   So methinks :
And I have found Demetrius like a jewel,
Mine own, and not mine own.
    Dem.   Are you sure
That we are awake ? It seems to me 190
That yet we sleep, we dream. Do not you think
The duke was here, and bid us follow him ?
    Her. Yea ; and my father.
    Hel.   And Hippolyta.
    Lys. And he did bid us follow to the temple.
    Dem. Why, then, we are awake : let's follow him ;
And by the way let us recount our dreams.
    [*Exeunt.*
    Bot. [*Awaking*] When my cue comes, call me, and I will answer : my next is, ' Most fair

Pyramus.' Heigh-ho ! Peter Quince ! Flute, the bellows-mender ! Snout, the tinker ! Starveling ! God's my life, stolen hence, and left me asleep ! I have had a most rare vision. I have had a dream, past the wit of man to say what dream it was : man is but an ass, if he go about to expound this dream. Methought I was—there is no man can tell what. Methought I was,—and methought I had,—but man is but a patched fool, if he will offer to say what methought I had. The eye of man hath not heard, the ear of man hath not seen, man's hand is not able to taste, his tongue to conceive, nor his heart to report, what my dream was. I will get Peter Quince to write a ballad of this dream : it shall be called Bottom's Dream, because it hath no bottom ; and I will sing it in the latter end of a play, before the duke : peradventure, to make it the more gracious, I shall sing it at her death.
    [*Exit.*

SCENE II. *Athens.* QUINCE'S *house.*

Enter QUINCE, FLUTE, SNOUT, *and* STARVELING.

    Quin. Have you sent to Bottom's house ? is he come home yet ?
    Star. He cannot be heard of. Out of doubt he is transported.
    Flu. If he come not, then the play is marred : it goes not forward, doth it ?
    Quin. It is not possible : you have not a man in all Athens able to discharge Pyramus but he.
    Flu. No, he hath simply the best wit of any handicraft man in Athens. 10
    Quin. Yea and the best person too ; and he is a very paramour for a sweet voice.
    Flu. You must say ' paragon : ' a paramour is, God bless us, a thing of naught.

Enter SNUG.

    Snug. Masters, the duke is coming from the temple, and there is two or three lords and ladies more married : if our sport had gone forward, we had all been made men.
    Flu. O sweet bully Bottom ! Thus hath he lost sixpence a day during his life ; he could not have 'scaped sixpence a day : an the duke had not given him sixpence a day for playing Pyramus, I'll be hanged ; he would have deserved it : sixpence a day in Pyramus, or nothing.

Enter BOTTOM.

    Bot. Where are these lads ? where are these hearts ?
    Quin. Bottom ! O most courageous day ! O most happy hour !
    Bot. Masters, I am to discourse wonders : but ask me not what ; for if I tell you, I am no true Athenian. I will tell you every thing, right as it fell out.
    Quin. Let us hear, sweet Bottom.
    Bot. Not a word of me. All that I will tell you is, that the duke hath dined. Get your apparel together, good strings to your beards, new ribbons to your pumps ; meet presently at the palace ; every man look o'er his part ; for the short and the long is, our play is preferred. In any case, let Thisby have clean linen ; and let not him that plays the lion pair his nails, for they shall hang out for the lion's

claws. And, most dear actors, eat no onions
nor garlic, for we are to utter sweet breath;
and I do not doubt but to hear them say, it is
a sweet comedy. No more words: away! go,
away!   [*Exeunt.*

ACT V.

SCENE I. *Athens. The palace of* THESEUS.

Enter THESEUS, HIPPOLYTA, PHILOSTRATE,
    Lords *and* Attendants.

Hip. 'Tis strange, my Theseus, that these
        lovers speak of.
The.   More strange than true: I never may
        believe
These antique fables, nor these fairy toys.
Lovers and madmen have such seething
        brains,
Such shaping fantasies, that apprehend
More than cool reason ever comprehends.
The lunatic, the lover and the poet
Are of imagination all compact:
One sees more devils than vast hell can hold,
That is, the madman: the lover, all as frantic,
Sees Helen's beauty in a brow of Egypt: 11
The poet's eye, in a fine frenzy rolling,
Doth glance from heaven to earth, from earth
        to heaven;
And as imagination bodies forth
The forms of things unknown, the poet's pen
Turns them to shapes and gives to airy nothing
A local habitation and a name.
Such tricks hath strong imagination,
That, if it would but apprehend some joy,
It comprehends some bringer of that joy;   20
Or in the night, imagining some fear,
How easy is a bush supposed a bear!
Hip.   But all the story of the night told
        over,
And all their minds transfigured so together,
More witnesseth than fancy's images
And grows to something of great constancy;
But, howsoever, strange and admirable.
The.   Here come the lovers, full of joy and
        mirth.

Enter LYSANDER, DEMETRIUS, HERMIA, *and*
    HELENA.

Joy, gentle friends! joy and fresh days of love
Accompany your hearts!
Lys.   More than to us 30
Wait in your royal walks, your board, your
        bed!
The.   Come now; what masques, what
        dances shall we have,
To wear away this long age of three hours
Between our after-supper and bed-time?
Where is our usual manager of mirth?
What revels are in hand? Is there no play,
To ease the anguish of a torturing hour?
Call Philostrate.
Phil.   Here, mighty Theseus.
The.   Say, what abridgement have you for
        this evening?
What masque? what music? How shall we
        beguile   40
The lazy time, if not with some delight?
Phil.   There is a brief how many sports are
        ripe:
Make choice of which your highness will see
first.   [*Giving a paper.*

The.   [*Reads*] 'The battle with the Cen-
        taurs, to be sung
By an Athenian eunuch to the harp.'
We'll none of that: that have I told my love,
In glory of my kinsman Hercules.
[*Reads*] 'The riot of the tipsy Bacchanals,
Tearing the Thracian singer in their rage.'
That is an old device; and it was play'd   50
When I from Thebes came last a conqueror.
[*Reads*] 'The thrice three Muses mourning for
        the death
Of Learning, late deceased in beggary.'
That is some satire, keen and critical,
Not sorting with a nuptial ceremony.
[*Reads*] 'A tedious brief scene of young Pyra-
        mus
And his love Thisbe; very tragical mirth.'
Merry and tragical! tedious and brief!
That is, hot ice and wondrous strange snow.
How shall we find the concord of this dis-
        cord?
Phil.   A play there is, my lord, some ten
        words long,   61
Which is as brief as I have known a play;
But by ten words, my lord, it is too long,
Which makes it tedious; for in all the play
There is not one word apt, one player fitted:
And tragical, my noble lord, it is;
For Pyramus therein doth kill himself.
Which, when I saw rehearsed, I must confess,
Made mine eyes water; but more merry tears
The passion of loud laughter never shed.   70
The.   What are they that do play it?
Phil.   Hard-handed men that work in
        Athens here,
Which never labor'd in their minds till now,
And now have toil'd their unbreathed memo-
        ries
With this same play, against your nuptial.
The.   And we will hear it.
Phil.   No, my noble lord;
It is not for you: I have heard it over,
And it is nothing, nothing in the world;
Unless you can find sport in their intents,
Extremely stretch'd and conn'd with cruel
        pain,   80
To do you service.
The.   I will hear that play;
For never anything can be amiss,
When simpleness and duty tender it.
Go, bring them in: and take your places,
        ladies.   [*Exit Philostrate.*
Hip.   I love not to see wretchedness o'er-
        charged
And duty in his service perishing.
The.   Why, gentle sweet, you shall see no
        such thing.
Hip.   He says they can do nothing in this
        kind.
The.   The kinder we, to give them thanks
        for nothing.   89
Our sport shall be to take what they mistake:
And what poor duty cannot do, noble respect
Takes it in might, not merit.
Where I have come, great clerks have pur-
        posed
To greet me with premeditated welcomes;
Where I have seen them shiver and look pale,
Make periods in the midst of sentences,
Throttle their practised accent in their fears
And in conclusion dumbly have broke off,
Not paying me a welcome. Trust me, sweet,
Out of this silence yet I pick'd a welcome;

And in the modesty of fearful duty 101
I read as much as from the rattling tongue
Of saucy and audacious eloquence.
Love, therefore, and tongue-tied simplicity
In least speak most, to my capacity.

Re-enter PHILOSTRATE.

Phil. So please your grace, the Prologue is
address'd.
The. Let him approach.
[*Flourish of trumpets.*

Enter QUINCE *for the* Prologue.

Pro. If we offend, it is with our good will.
That you should think, we come not to
offend,
But with good will. To show our simple skill,
That is the true beginning of our end. 111
Consider then we come but in despite.
We do not come as minding to content you,
Our true intent is. All for your delight
We are not here. That you should here re-
pent you,
The actors are at hand and by their show
You shall know all that you are like to know.
The. This fellow doth not stand upon
points.
Lys. He hath rid his prologue like a rough
colt; he knows not the stop. A good moral,
my lord: it is not enough to speak, but to
speak true.
Hip. Indeed he hath played on his pro-
logue like a child on a recorder; a sound, but
not in government.
The. His speech, was like a tangled chain;
nothing impaired, but all disordered. Who is
next?

Enter PYRAMUS *and* THISBE, WALL,
MOONSHINE, *and* LION.

Pro. Gentles, perchance you wonder at
this show;
But wonder on, till truth make all things
plain.
This man is Pyramus, if you would know ;130
This beauteous lady Thisby is certain.
This man, with lime and rough-cast, doth pre-
sent
Wall, that vile Wall which did these lovers
sunder;
And through Wall's chink, poor souls, they
are content
To whisper. At the which let no man won-
der.
This man, with lanthorn, dog, and bush of
thorn,
Presenteth Moonshine; for, if you will
know,
By moonshine did these lovers think no scorn
To meet at Ninus' tomb, there, there to
woo.
This grisly beast, which Lion hight by name,
The trusty Thisby, coming first by night, 141
Did scare away, or rather did affright;
And, as she fled, her mantle she did fall,
Which Lion vile with bloody mouth did
stain.
Anon comes Pyramus, sweet youth and tall,
And finds his trusty Thisby's mantle slain:
Whereat, with blade, with bloody blameful
blade,
He bravely broach'd his boiling bloody
breast;

And Thisby, tarrying in mulberry shade,
His dagger drew, and died. For all the rest,
Let Lion, Moonshine, Wall, and lovers twain
At large discourse, while here they do remain.
[*Exeunt Prologue, Thisbe, Lion, and
Moonshine.*

The. I wonder if the lion be to speak.
Dem. No wonder, my lord: one lion may,
when many asses do.
Wall. In this same interlude it doth befall
That I, one Snout by name, present a wall;
And such a wall, as I would have you think,
That had in it a crannied hole or chink,
Through which the lovers, Pyramus and
Thisby, 160
Did whisper often very secretly.
This loam, this rough-cast and this stone doth
show
That I am that same wall; the truth is so:
And this the cranny is, right and sinister,
Through which the fearful lovers are to whis-
per.
The. Would you desire lime and hair to
speak better?
Dem. It is the wittiest partition that ever I
heard discourse, my lord.

Enter PYRAMUS.

The. Pyramus draws near the wall: si-
lence!
Pyr. O grim-look'd night! O night with
hue so black! 171
O night, which ever art when day is not!
O night, O night! alack, alack, alack,
I fear my Thisby's promise is forgot!
And thou, O wall, O sweet, O lovely wall,
That stand'st between her father's ground
and mine!
Thou wall, O wall, O sweet and lovely wall,
Show me thy chink, to blink through with
mine eyne! [*Wall holds up his fingers.*
Thanks, courteous wall: Jove shield thee well
for this!
But what see I? No Thisby do I see. 180
O wicked wall, through whom I see no bliss!
Cursed be thy stones for thus deceiving me!
The. The wall, methinks, being sensible,
should curse again.
Pyr. No, in truth, sir, he should not. 'De-
ceiving me' is Thisby's cue: she is to enter
now, and I am to spy her through the wall.
You shall see, it will fall pat as I told you.
Yonder she comes.

Enter THISBE.

This. O wall, full often hast thou heard
my moans, 190
For parting my fair Pyramus and me!
My cherry lips have often kiss'd thy stones,
Thy stones with lime and hair knit up in
thee.
Pyr. I see a voice: now will I to the chink,
To spy an I can hear my Thisby's face.
Thisby!
This. My love thou art, my love I think.
Pyr. Think what thou wilt, I am thy lov-
er's grace;
And, like Limander, am I trusty still.
This. And I like Helen, till the Fates me
kill.
Pyr. Not Shafalus to Procrus was so true.
This. As Shafalus to Procrus, I to you.

Pyr. O, kiss me through the hole of this
vile wall !
This. I kiss the wall's hole, not your lips
at all.
Pyr. Wilt thou at Ninny's tomb meet me
straightway ?
This. 'Tide life, 'tide death, I come without
delay. [*Exeunt Pyramus and Thisbe.*
Wall. Thus have I, Wall, my part discharged so ;
And, being done, thus Wall away doth go.
[*Exit.*
The. Now is the mural down between the
two neighbors.   210
Dem. No remedy, my lord, when walls are
so wilful to hear without warning.
Hip. This is the silliest stuff that ever I
heard.
The. The best in this kind are but shadows ; and the worst are no worse, if imagination amend them.
Hip. It must be your imagination then, and
not theirs.
The. If we imagine no worse of them than
they of themselves, they may pass for excellent men. Here come two noble beasts in, a
man and a lion.

Enter LION and MOONSHINE.

Lion. You, ladies, you, whose gentle hearts
do fear
The smallest monstrous mouse that creeps
on floor,
May now perchance both quake and tremble
here,
When lion rough in wildest rage doth roar,
Then know that I, one Snug the joiner, am
A lion-fell, nor else no lion's dam ;
For, if I should as lion come in strife
Into this place, 'twere pity on my life.   230
The. A very gentle beast, and of a good
conscience.
Dem. The very best at a beast, my lord,
that e'er I saw.
Lys. This lion is a very fox for his valor.
The. True ; and a goose for his discretion.
Dem. Not so, my lord ; for his valor can-
not carry his discretion ; and the fox carries
the goose.
The. His discretion, I am sure, cannot carry
his valor ; for the goose carries not the fox.
It is well : leave it to his discretion, and let
us listen to the moon.
Moon. This lanthorn doth the horned moon
present ;—
Dem. He should have worn the horns on
his head.
The. He is no crescent, and his horns are
invisible within the circumference.
Moon. This lanthorn doth the horned
moon present ;
Myself the man i' the moon do seem to be.
The. This is the greatest error of all the
rest : the man should be put into the lanthorn.
How is it else the man i' the moon ?
Dem. He dares not come there for the
candle ; for, you see, it is already in snuff.
Hip. I am aweary of this moon : would he
would change !
The. It appears, by his small light of dis-
cretion, that he is in the wane ; but yet, in
courtesy, in all reason, we must stay the time.
Lys. Proceed, Moon.   260

Moon. All that I have to say, is, to tell you
that the lanthorn is the moon ; I, the man in
the moon ; this thorn-bush, my thorn-bush ;
and this dog, my dog.
Dem. Why, all these should be in the lanthorn ; for all these are in the moon. But,
silence ! here comes Thisbe.

Enter THISBE.

This. This is old Ninny's tomb. Where is
my love ?
Lion. [*Roaring*] Oh—— [*Thisbe runs off.*
Dem. Well roared, Lion.   270
The. Well run, Thisbe.
Hip. Well shone, Moon. Truly, the moon
shines with a good grace.
[*The Lion shakes Thisbe's mantle, and exit.*
The. Well moused, Lion.
Lys. And so the lion vanished.
Dem. And then came Pyramus.

Enter PYRAMUS.

Pyr. Sweet Moon, I thank thee for thy
sunny beams ;
I thank thee, Moon, for shining now so
bright ;
For, by thy gracious, golden, glittering gleams,
I trust to take of truest Thisby sight.   280
But stay, O spite !
But mark, poor knight,
What dreadful dole is here !
Eyes, do you see ?
How can it be ?
O dainty duck ! O dear !
Thy mantle good,
What, stain'd with blood !
Approach, ye Furies fell !
O Fates, come, come,   290
Cut thread and thrum ;
Quail, crush, conclude, and quell !
The. This passion, and the death of a dear
friend, would go near to make a man look
sad.
Hip. Beshrew my heart, but I pity the
man.
Pyr. O wherefore, Nature, didst thou lions
frame ?
Since lion vile hath here deflower'd my
dear :
Which is—no, no—which was the fairest dame
That lived, that loved, that liked, that look'd
with cheer.
Come, tears, confound ;   300
Out, sword, and wound
The pap of Pyramus ;
Ay, that left pap,
Where heart doth hop : [*Stabs himself.*
Thus die I, thus, thus, thus.
Now am I dead,
Now am I fled ;
My soul is in the sky :
Tongue, lose thy light ;
Moon, take thy flight : [*Exit Moonshine.*
Now die, die, die, die, die.   [*Dies.*
Dem. No die, but an ace, for him ; for he
is but one.
Lys. Less than an ace, man ; for he is
dead ; he is nothing.
The. With the help of a surgeon he might
yet recover, and prove an ass.
Hip. How chance Moonshine is gone be-
fore Thisbe comes back and finds her lover ?
The. She will find him by starlight. Here

she comes ; and her passion ends the play. 321

Re-enter THISBE.

Hip. Methinks she should not use a long one for such a Pyramus : I hope she will be brief.

Dem. A mote will turn the balance, which Pyramus, which Thisbe, is the better ; he for a man, God warrant us ; she for a woman, God bless us.

Lys. She hath spied him already with those sweet eyes.

Dem. And thus she means, videlicet :—330

This. Asleep, my love ?
      What, dead, my dove ?
   O Pyramus, arise !
   Speak, speak. Quite dumb ?
   Dead, dead ? A tomb
Must cover thy sweet eyes.
      These lily lips,
      This cherry nose,
   These yellow cowslip cheeks,
      Are gone, are gone :   340
Lovers, make moan :
His eyes were green as leeks.
      O Sisters Three,
      Come, come to me,
With hands as pale as milk ;
      Lay them in gore,
   Since you have shore
With shears his thread of silk.
      Tongue, not a word :
      Come, trusty sword ;   350
Come, blade, my breast imbrue :
                    [*Stabs herself.*
      And, farewell, friends ;
      Thus Thisby ends :
   Adieu, adieu, adieu.   [*Dies.*

The. Moonshine and Lion are left to bury the dead.

Dem. Ay, and Wall too.

Bot. [*Starting up*] No, I assure you ; the wall is down that parted their fathers. Will it please you to see the epilogue, or to hear a Bergomask dance between two of our company ?   361

The. No epilogue, I pray you ; for your play needs no excuse. Never excuse ; for when the players are all dead, there needs none to be blamed. Marry, if he that writ it had played Pyramus and hanged himself in Thisbe's garter, it would have been a fine tragedy : and so it is, truly ; and very notably discharged. But come, your Bergomask : let your epilogue alone.   [*A dance.*
The iron tongue of midnight hath told twelve :
Lovers, to bed ; 'tis almost fairy time. 371
I fear we shall out-sleep the coming morn
As much as we this night have overwatch'd.
This palpable-gross play hath well beguiled
The heavy gait of night. Sweet friends, to bed.
A fortnight hold we this solemnity,
In nightly revels and new jollity.   [*Exeunt.*

Enter PUCK.

Puck. Now the hungry lion roars,
   And the wolf behowls the moon ;
Whilst the heavy ploughman snores,   380
   All with weary task fordone.

Now the wasted brands do glow,
   Whilst the screech-owl, screeching loud,
Puts the wretch that lies in woe
   In remembrance of a shroud.
Now it is the time of night
   That the graves all gaping wide,
Every one lets forth his sprite,
   In the church-way paths to glide :
And we fairies, that do run   390
   By the triple Hecate's team,
From the presence of the sun,
   Following darkness like a dream,
Now are frolic : not a mouse
Shall disturb this hallow'd house :
I am sent with broom before,
To sweep the dust behind the door.

Enter OBERON *and* TITANIA *with their train.*

Obe. Through the house give glimmering light,
   By the dead and drowsy fire :
Every elf and fairy sprite   400
   Hop as light as bird from brier ;
And this ditty, after me,
Sing, and dance it trippingly.

Tita. First, rehearse your song by rote
   To each word a warbling note :
Hand in hand, with fairy grace,
Will we sing, and bless this place.
                    [*Song and dance.*

Obe. Now, until the break of day,
   Through this house each fairy stray.
To the best bride-bed will we,   410
   Which by us shall blessed be ;
And the issue there create
   Ever shall be fortunate.
So shall all the couples three
   Ever true in loving be ;
And the blots of Nature's hand
   Shall not in their issue stand ;
Never mole, hare lip, nor scar,
   Nor mark prodigious, such as are
Despised in nativity,   420
   Shall upon their children be.
With this field-dew consecrate,
   Every fairy take his gait ;
And each several chamber bless,
   Through this palace, with sweet peace ;
And the owner of it blest
   Ever shall in safety rest.
Trip away ; make no stay ;
Meet me all by break of day.
            [*Exeunt Oberon, Titania, and train.*

Puck. If we shadows have offended,   430
   Think but this, and all is mended,
That you have but slumber'd here
   While these visions did appear.
And this weak and idle theme,
   No more yielding but a dream,
Gentles, do not reprehend :
   If you pardon, we will mend :
And, as I am an honest Puck,
   If we have unearned luck
Now to 'scape the serpent's tongue, 440
   We will make amends ere long ;
Else the Puck a liar call ;
   So, good night unto you all.
Give me your hands, if we be friends,
And Robin shall restore amends. [*Exit.*

KING HENRY VI. PART II.

(WRITTEN ABOUT 1591–92.)

INTRODUCTION.

The second and third parts of *King Henry VI.* are recasts of two older plays—*The First Part of the Contention* (published 1594) and *The True Tragedie of Richard Duke of York, &c.* (published 1595). About 3,241 lines of these old plays re-appear either in the same or in an altered form in 2 and 3 *Henry VI.;* what remains (2,736 lines) being altogether new. No question in Shakespeare scholarship is more perplexing and difficult than that of the author-ship of these four connected historical dramas. Various theories have been propounded, but the two which have superseded all others are : (1) that of Mr. Richard Grant White, that Marlowe, Greene, and Shakespeare (and perhaps Peele) were the authors of the old plays, and Shake-speare alone the reviser ; (2) that of Miss Jane Lee, that Marlowe and Greene (and possibly Peele) were the authors of the old plays, and Shakespeare and Marlowe (working as col-laborateurs) the revisers. The latter is perhaps the most generally accepted theory. Marlowe's hand is certainly visible in both the old plays and in some of the passages which appear for the first time in *Henry VI.* (see, for a striking example, 2 *Henry VI.*, Act IV. Sc. I., L. 1–11). Shakespeare and the " Dead Shepherd" whom he alludes to in *As You Like It*, were then fellow-workers, and if rivals, their rivalry was noble. But in truth, at this time, Marlowe, by virtue of his prestige, and because he had found his proper genius while Shakespeare was still feeling after his true direction, would be the superior, and the degree of independence of spirit shown in Shakespeare's work, although he is under the influence of Marlowe, is inter-esting and remarkable. It is evident that already in variety of imagination and sound judg-ment Shakespeare surpasses his great contemporary. Miss Lee has made a detailed apportion-ment of the work among the several writers, but her table is too long to be reproduced here. She says : " *The Third Part of Henry VI.* underwent a much less thorough revision than the second. Out of 3,075 lines in Part II. there are 1,715 new lines, some 840 altered lines (many but very slightly altered), and some 520 old lines. In Part III., out of 2,902 lines, there are about 1,021 new lines, about 871 altered lines, and about 1,010 old lines. Hence it is that in Part III. there are fewer resemblances of thought and verbal expression to Shakespeare's un-doubted writings than in Part II." When the revision of the old plays was made cannot be said with certainty—perhaps a short time before Marlowe's death, in 1593, perhaps at a date previous to Greene's sneering allusion to Shakespeare in the *Groatsworth of Wit*, 1592.

DRAMATIS PERSONÆ.

KING HENRY the Sixth.
HUMPHREY, Duke of Gloucester, his uncle.
CARDINAL BEAUFORT, Bishop of Winchester, great-uncle to the King.
RICHARD PLANTAGENET, Duke of York.
EDWARD and RICHARD, his sons.
DUKE OF SOMERSET.
DUKE OF SUFFOLK.
DUKE OF BUCKINGHAM.
LORD CLIFFORD.
Young CLIFFORD, his son.
EARL OF SALISBURY.
EARL OF WARWICK.
LORD SCALES.
LORD SAY.
SIR HUMPHREY STAFFORD, and WILLIAM STAFFORD, his brother.
SIR JOHN STANLEY.
VAUX.
MATTHEW GOFFE.
A Sea-captain, Master, and Master's-Mate, and WALTER WHITMORE.
Two Gentlemen, prisoners with Suffolk.

JOHN HUME and JOHN SOUTHWELL, priests.
BOLINGBROKE, a conjurer.
THOMAS HORNER, an armorer. PETER, his man.
Clerk of Chatham. Mayor of Saint Alban's.
SIMPCOX, an impostor.
ALEXANDER IDEN, a Kentish gentleman.
JACK CADE, a rebel.
GEORGE BEVIS, JOHN HOLLAND, DICK the butcher, SMITH the weaver, MICHAEL, &c., followers of Cade.
Two Murderers.
MARGARET, Queen to King Henry.
ELEANOR, Duchess of Gloucester.
MARGARET JOURDAIN, a witch.
Wife to Simpcox.
Lords, Ladies, and Attendants, Petitioners, Aldermen, a Herald, a Beadle, Sheriff, and Officers, Citizens, 'Prentices, Falconers, Guards, Soldiers, Messengers, &c.

A Spirit.

SCENE : *England.*

ACT I.

Scene I. *London. The palace.*

Flourish of trumpets : then hautboys. Enter the King, Humphrey, Duke *of* Glouces-ter, Salisbury, Warwick, *and* Cardinal Beaufort, *on the one side ; the* Queen, Suffolk, York, Somerset, *and* Bucking-ham, *on the other.*

Suf. As by your high imperial majesty
I had in charge at my depart for France,
As procurator to your excellence,
To marry Princess Margaret for your grace,
So, in the famous ancient city, Tours,
In presence of the Kings of France and Sicil,
The Dukes of Orleans, Calaber, Bretagne and
     Alençon,
Seven earls, twelve barons and twenty reverend
     bishops,
I have perform'd my task and was espoused :
And humbly now upon my bended knee,   10
In sight of England and her lordly peers,
Deliver up my title in the queen
To your most gracious hands, that are the
     substance
Of that great shadow I did represent ;
The happiest gift that ever marquess gave,
The fairest queen that ever king received.
     King. Suffolk, arise. Welcome, Queen
     Margaret :
I can express no kinder sign of love
Than this kind kiss. O Lord, that lends me life,
Lend me a heart replete with thankfulness ! 20
For thou hast given me in this beauteous face
A world of earthly blessings to my soul,
If sympathy of love unite our thoughts.
     Queen. Great King of England and my
     gracious lord,
The mutual conference that my mind hath
     had,
By day, by night, waking and in my dreams,
In courtly company or at my beads,
With you, mine alder-liefest sovereign,
Makes me the bolder to salute my king
With ruder terms, such as my wit affords 30
And over-joy of heart doth minister.
     King. Her sight did ravish ; but her grace
     in speech,
Her words y-clad with wisdom's majesty,
Makes me from wondering fall to weeping
     joys ;
Such is the fulness of my heart's content.
Lords, with one cheerful voice welcome my
     love.
     All [*kneeling*]. Long live Queen Margaret,
     England's happiness !
     Queen. We thank you all.   [*Flourish.*
     Suf. My lord protector, so it please your
     grace,
Here are the articles of contracted peace 40
Between our sovereign and the French king
     Charles,
For eighteen months concluded by consent.
     Glou. [*Reads*] ' Imprimis, it is agreed be-tween the French king Charles, and William de la Pole, Marquess of Suffolk, ambassador for Henry King of England, that the said Henry shall espouse the Lady Margaret, daugh-ter unto Reignier King of Naples, Sicilia and Jerusalem, and crown her Queen of England ere the thirtieth of May next ensuing. Item,

that the duchy of Anjou and the county of Maine shall be released and delivered to the king her father'—   [*Lets the paper fall.*
     King. Uncle, how now !
     Glou.   Pardon me, gracious lord ;
Some sudden qualm hath struck me at the
     heart
And dimm'd mine eyes, that I can read no fur-ther.
     King. Uncle of Winchester, I pray, read
     on.
     Car. [*Reads*] ' Item, It is further agreed between them, that the duchies of Anjou and Maine shall be released and delivered over to the king her father, and she sent over of the King of England's own proper cost and charges, without having any dowry.'
     King. They please us well. Lord marquess,
     kneel down :
We here create thee the first duke of Suffolk,
And gird thee with the sword. Cousin of York,
We here discharge your grace from being
     regent
I' the parts of France, till term of eighteen
     months
Be full expired. Thanks, uncle Winchester,
Gloucester, York, Buckingham, Somerset,
Salisbury, and Warwick ;   70
We thank you all for this great favor done,
In entertainment to my princely queen.
Come, let us in, and with all speed provide
To see her coronation be perform'd.
     [*Exeunt King, Queen, and Suffolk.*
     Glou. Brave peers of England, pillars of
     the state,
To you Duke Humphrey must unload his
     grief,
Your grief, the common grief of all the land.
What ! did my brother Henry spend his youth,
His valor, coin and people, in the wars ?
Did he so often lodge in open field,   80
In winter's cold and summer's parching heat,
To conquer France, his true inheritance ?
And did my brother Bedford toil his wits,
To keep by policy what Henry got ?
Have you yourselves, Somerset, Buckingham,
Brave York, Salisbury, and victorious War-wick,
Received deep scars in France and Normandy ?
Or hath mine uncle Beaufort and myself,
With all the learned council of the realm,
Studied so long, sat in the council-house   90
Early and late, debating to and fro
How France and Frenchmen might be kept in
     awe,
And had his highness in his infancy
Crowned in Paris in despite of foes ?
And shall these labors and these honors die ?
Shall Henry's conquest, Bedford's vigilance,
Your deeds of war and all our counsel die ?
O peers of England, shameful is this league !
Fatal this marriage, cancelling your fame,
Blotting your names from books of memory,
Razing the characters of your renown,   101
Defacing monuments of conquer'd France,
Undoing all, as all had never been !
     Car. Nephew, what means this passionate
     discourse,
This peroration with such circumstance ?
For France, 'tis ours ; and we will keep it still.
     Glou. Ay, uncle, we will keep it, if we
     can ;
But now it is impossible we should :

Suffolk, the new-made duke that rules the
  roast,
Hath given the duchy of Anjou and Maine 110
Unto the poor King Reignier, whose large
  style
Agrees not with the leanness of his purse.
  Sal. Now, by the death of Him that died
  for all,
These counties were the keys of Normandy.
But wherefore weeps Warwick, my valiant
  son ?
  War. For grief that they are past re-
  covery :
For, were there hope to conquer them again,
My sword should shed hot blood, mine eyes
  no tears.
Anjou and Maine ! myself did win them both ;
Those provinces these arms of mine did con-
  quer :   120
And are the cities, that I got with wounds,
Delivered up again with peaceful words ?
Mort Dieu !
  York. For Suffolk's duke, may he be suf-
  focate,
That dims the honor of this warlike isle !
France should have torn and rent my very
  heart,
Before I would have yielded to this league.
I never read but England's kings have had
Large sums of gold and dowries with their
  wives :
And our King Henry gives away his own, 130
To match with her that brings no vantages.
  Glou. A proper jest, and never heard be-
  fore,
That Suffolk should demand a whole fifteenth
For costs and charges in transporting her !
She should have stayed in France and starved
  in France,
Before—
  Car. My Lord of Gloucester, now ye grow
  too hot :
It was the pleasure of my lord the king.
  Glou. My Lord of Winchester, I know
  your mind ;
'Tis not my speeches that you do mislike, 140
But 'tis my presence that doth trouble ye.
Rancor will out : proud prelate, in thy face
I see thy fury : if I longer stay,
We shall begin our ancient bickerings.
Lordings, farewell ; and say, when I am gone,
I prophesied France will be lost ere long. [*Exit.*
  Car. So, there goes our protector in a rage.
'Tis known to you he is mine enemy,
Nay, more, an enemy unto you all,
And no great friend, I fear me, to the king.150
Consider, lords, he is the next of blood,
And heir apparent to the English crown :
Had Henry got an empire by his marriage,
And all the wealthy kingdoms of the west,
There's reason he should be displeased at it.
Look to it, lords ! let not his smoothing words
Bewitch your hearts ; be wise and circumspect.
What though the common people favor him,
Calling him 'Humphrey, the good Duke of
  Gloucester,'
Clapping their hands, and crying with loud
  voice,   160
'Jesu maintain your royal excellence !'
With 'God preserve the good Duke Hum-
  phrey !'
I fear me, lords, for all this flattering gloss,
He will be found a dangerous protector.

  Buck. Why should he, then, protect our
  sovereign,
He being of age to govern of himself ?
Cousin of Somerset, join you with me,
And all together, with the Duke of Suffolk,
We'll quickly hoise Duke Humphrey from his
  seat.
  Car. This weighty business will not brook
  delay :   170
I'll to the Duke of Suffolk presently. [*Exit.*
  Som. Cousin of Buckingham, though
  Humphrey's pride
And greatness of his place be grief to us,
Yet let us watch the haughty cardinal :
His insolence is more intolerable
Than all the princes in the land beside :
If Gloucester be displaced, he'll be protector.
  Buck. Or thou or I, Somerset, will be pro-
  tector,
Despite Duke Humphrey or the cardinal.
          [*Exeunt Buckingham and Somerset.*
  Sal. Pride went before, ambition follows
  him.   180
While these do labor for their own preferment,
Behoves it us to labor for the realm.
I never saw but Humphrey Duke of Gloucester
Did bear him like a noble gentleman.
Oft have I seen the haughty cardinal,
More like a soldier than a man o' the church,
As stout and proud as he were lord of all,
Swear like a ruffian and demean himself
Unlike the ruler of a commonweal.
Warwick, my son, the comfort of my age, 190
Thy deeds, thy plainness and thy housekeep-
  ing,
Hath won the greatest favor of the commons,
Excepting none but good Duke Humphrey :
And, brother York, thy acts in Ireland,
In bringing them to civil discipline,
Thy late exploits done in the heart of France,
When thou wert regent for our sovereign,
Have made thee fear'd and honor'd of the
  people :
Join we together, for the public good,
In what we can, to bridle and suppress   200
The pride of Suffolk and the cardinal,
With Somerset's and Buckingham's ambition ;
And, as we may, cherish Duke Humphrey's
  deeds,
While they do tend the profit of the land.
  War. So God help Warwick, as he loves
  the land,
And common profit of his country !
  York. [*Aside*] And so says York, for he
  hath greatest cause.
  Sal. Then let's make haste away, and look
  unto the main.
  War. Unto the main ! O father, Maine is
  lost ;
That Maine which by main force Warwick did
  win,
And would have kept so long as breath did
  last !
Main chance, father, you meant ; but I meant
  Maine,
Which I will win from France, or else be slain.
          [*Exeunt Warwick and Salisbury.*
  York. Anjou and Maine are given to the
  French ;
Paris is lost ; the state of Normandy
Stands on a tickle point, now they are gone :
Suffolk concluded on the articles,
The peers agreed, and Henry was well pleased

To change two dukedoms for a duke's fair
　　daughter.　　　　　　　　　　　　219
I cannot blame them all : what is't to them ?
'Tis thine they give away, and not their own.
Pirates may make cheap pennyworths of their
　　pillage
And purchase friends and give to courtezans,
Still revelling like lords till all be gone ;
While as the silly owner of the goods
Weeps over them and wrings his hapless hands
And shakes his head and trembling stands
　　aloof,
While all is shared and all is borne away,
Ready to starve and dare not touch his own :
So York must sit and fret and bite his tongue,
While his own lands are bargain'd for and
　　sold.　　　　　　　　　　　　　　231
Methinks the realms of England, France and
　　Ireland
Bear that proportion to my flesh and blood
As did the fatal brand Althæa burn'd
Unto the prince's heart of Calydon.
Anjou and Maine both given unto the French !
Cold news for me, for I had hope of France,
Even as I have of fertile England's soil.
A day will come when York shall claim his
　　own ;
And therefore I will take the Nevils' parts 240
And make a show of love to proud Duke
　　Humphrey,
And, when I spy advantage, claim the crown,
For that's the golden mark I seek to hit :
Nor shall proud Lancaster usurp my right,
Nor hold the sceptre in his childish fist,
Nor wear the diadem upon his head,
Whose church-like humors fits not for a
　　crown.
Then, York, be still awhile, till time do serve :
Watch thou and wake when others be asleep,
To pry into the secrets of the state ;　　250
Till Henry, surfeiting in joys of love,
With his new bride and England's dear-bought
　　queen,
And Humphrey with the peers be fall'n at
　　jars :
Then will I raise aloft the milk-white rose,
With whose sweet smell the air shall be per-
　　fumed ;
And in my standard bear the arms of York
To grapple with the house of Lancaster ;
And, force perforce, I'll make him yield the
　　crown,
Whose bookish rule hath pull'd fair England
　　down.　　　　　　　　　　　　　*[Exit.*

SCENE II.　*The* DUKE OF GLOUCESTER'S
　　　　　　house.

Enter DUKE HUMPHREY *and his wife*
ELEANOR.

Duch.　Why droops my lord, like over-
　　ripen'd corn,
Hanging the head at Ceres' plenteous load ?
Why doth the great Duke Humphrey knit his
　　brows,
As frowning at the favors of the world ?
Why are thine eyes fixed to the sullen earth,
Gazing on that which seems to dim thy sight ?
What seest thou there ? King Henry's diadem,
Enchased with all the honors of the world ?
If so, gaze on, and grovel on thy face,
Until thy head be circled with the same.　10
Put forth thy hand, reach at the glorious gold.

What, is't too short ? I'll lengthen it with
　　mine ;
And, having both together heaved it up,
We'll both together lift our heads to heaven,
And never more abase our sight so low
As to vouchsafe one glance unto the ground.
　　Glou.　O Nell, sweet Nell, if thou dost love
　　thy lord,
Banish the canker of ambitious thoughts.
And may that thought, when I imagine ill
Against my king and nephew, virtuous Henry,
Be my last breathing in this mortal world !　21
My troublous dream this night doth make me
　　sad.
　　Duch.　What dream'd my lord ? tell me,
　　and I'll requite it
With sweet rehearsal of my morning's dream.
　　Glou.　Methought this staff, mine office-
　　badge in court,
Was broke in twain ; by whom I have forgot,
But, as I think, it was by the cardinal ;
And on the pieces of the broken wand
Were placed the heads of Edmund Duke of
　　Somerset,
And William de la Pole, first duke of Suffolk.
This was my dream : what it doth bode, God
　　knows.　　　　　　　　　　　　　31
　　Duch.　Tut, this was nothing but an argu-
　　ment
That he that breaks a stick of Gloucester's
　　grove
Shall lose his head for his presumption.
But list to me, my Humphrey, my sweet duke :
Methought I sat in seat of majesty
In the cathedral church of Westminster,
And in that chair where kings and queens are
　　crown'd ;
Where Henry and dame Margaret kneel'd to
　　me
And on my head did set the diadem.　　40
　　Glou.　Nay, Eleanor, then must I chide out-
　　right :
Presumptuous dame, ill-nurtured Eleanor,
Art thou not second woman in the realm,
And the protector's wife, beloved of him ?
Hast thou not worldly pleasure at command,
Above the reach or compass of thy thought ?
And wilt thou still be hammering treachery,
To tumble down thy husband and thyself
From top of honor to disgrace's feet ?
Away from me, and let me hear no more !　50
　　Duch.　What, what, my lord ! are you so
　　choleric
With Eleanor, for telling but her dream ?
Next time I'll keep my dreams unto myself,
And not be check'd.
　　Glou.　Nay, be not angry ; I am pleased
　　again.

Enter Messenger.

　　Mess.　My lord protector, 'tis his highness'
　　pleasure
You do prepare to ride unto Saint Alban's,
Where as the king and queen do mean to
　　hawk.
　　Glou.　I go. Come, Nell, thou wilt ride with
　　us ?
　　Duch.　Yes, my good lord, I'll follow pres-
　　ently.　　　　　　　　　　　　　　60
　　　　　　　　[Exeunt Gloucester and Messenger.
Follow I must ; I cannot go before,
While Gloucester bears this base and humble
　　mind.

Were I a man, a duke, and next of blood,
I would remove these tedious stumbling-blocks
And smooth my way upon their headless
      necks;
And, being a woman, I will not be slack
To play my part in Fortune's pageant.
Where are you there? Sir John! nay, fear not,
      man,
We are alone; here's none but thee and I.

Enter HUME.

Hume. Jesus preserve your royal majesty!
Duch. What say'st thou? majesty! I am
      but grace.   71
Hume. But, by the grace of God, and
      Hume's advice,
Your grace's title shall be multiplied.
Duch. What say'st thou, man? hast thou
      as yet conferr'd
With Margery Jourdain, the cunning witch,
With Roger Bolingbroke, the conjurer?
And will they undertake to do me good?
Hume. This they have promised, to show
      your highness
A spirit raised from depth of under-ground,
That shall make answer to such questions 80
As by your grace shall be propounded him.
Duch. It is enough; I'll think upon the
      questions:
When from St. Alban's we do make return,
We'll see these things effected to the full.
Here, Hume, take this reward; make merry,
      man,
With thy confederates in this weighty cause.
                                          [*Exit.*
Hume. Hume must make merry with the
      duchess' gold;
Marry, and shall. But, how now, Sir John
      Hume!
Seal up your lips, and give no words but
      mum:
The business asketh silent secrecy.
Dame Eleanor gives gold to bring the witch:
Gold cannot come amiss, were she a devil.
Yet have I gold flies from another coast;
I dare not say, from the rich cardinal
And from the great and new-made Duke of
      Suffolk,
Yet I do find it so; for, to be plain,
They, knowing Dame Eleanor's aspiring hu-
      mor,
Have hired me to undermine the duchess
And buz these conjurations in her brain.
They say 'A crafty knave does need no bro-
      ker;'   100
Yet am I Suffolk and the cardinal's broker.
Hume, if you take not heed, you shall go near
To call them both a pair of crafty knaves.
Well, so it stands; and thus, I fear, at last
Hume's knavery will be the duchess' wreck,
And her attainture will be Humphrey's fall:
Sort how it will, I shall have gold for all.
                                          [*Exit.*

SCENE III. *The palace.*

Enter three or four Petitioners, PETER, *the
      Armorer's man, being one.*

First Petit. My masters, let's stand close:
my lord protector will come this way by and
by, and then we may deliver our supplications
in the quill.
Sec. Petit. Marry, the Lord protect him, for
he's a good man! Jesu bless him!

Enter SUFFOLK *and* QUEEN.

Peter. Here a' comes, methinks, and the
queen with him. I'll be the first, sure.
Sec. Petit. Come back, fool; this is the
Duke of Suffolk, and not my lord protector.10
Suf. How now, fellow! would'st anything
with me?
First Petit. I pray, my lord, pardon me; I
took ye for my lord protector.
Queen. [*Reading*] 'To my Lord Protector!' Are your supplications to his lordship?
Let me see them: what is thine?
First Petit. Mine is, an't please your grace,
against John Goodman, my lord cardinal's
man, for keeping my house, and lands, and
wife and all, from me.   21
Suf. Thy wife, too! that's some wrong, in-
deed. What's yours? What's here! [*Reads*]
'Against the Duke of Suffolk, for enclosing the
commons of Melford.' How now, sir knave!
Sec. Petit. Alas, sir, I am but a poor petitioner of our whole township.
Peter. [*Giving his petition*] Against my
master, Thomas Horner, for saying that the
Duke of York was rightful heir to the crown.
Queen. What sayst thou? did the Duke of
York say he was rightful heir to the crown?
Peter. That my master was? no, forsooth:
my master said that he was, and that the king
was an usurper.
Suf. Who is there? [*Enter Servant.*] Take
this fellow in, and send for his master with a
pursuivant presently: we'll hear more of your
matter before the king.
                          [*Exit Servant with Peter.*
Queen. And as for you, that love to be
      protected   40
Under the wings of our protector's grace,
Begin your suits anew, and sue to him.
                          [*Tears the supplication.*
Away, base cullions! Suffolk, let them go.
All. Come, let's be gone.   [*Exeunt.*
Queen. My Lord of Suffolk, say, is this the
      guise,
Is this the fashion in the court of England?
Is this the government of Britain's isle,
And this the royalty of Albion's king?
What, shall King Henry be a pupil still
Under the surly Gloucester's governance?
Am I a queen in title and in style,
And must be made a subject to a duke?
I tell thee, Pole, when in the city Tours
Thou ran'st a tilt in honor of my love
And stolest away the ladies' hearts of France,
I thought King Henry had resembled thee
In courage, courtship and proportion:
But all his mind is bent to holiness,
To number Ave-Maries on his beads;
His champions are the prophets and apostles,
His weapons holy saws of sacred writ,   61
His study is his tilt-yard, and his loves
Are brazen images of canonized saints.
I would the college of the cardinals
Would choose him pope, and carry him to
      Rome,
And set the triple crown upon his head:
That were a state fit for his holiness.
Suf. Madam, be patient: as I was cause
Your highness came to England, so will I
In England work your grace's full content. 70
Queen. Beside the haughty protector, have
      we Beaufort,

The imperious churchman, Somerset, Buck-
ingham,
And grumbling York : and not the least of
these
But can do more in England than the king.
  Suf. And he of these that can do most of
all
Cannot do more in England than the Nevils :
Salisbury and Warwick are no simple peers.
  Queen. Not all these lords do vex me half
so much
As that proud dame, the lord protector's wife.
She sweeps it through the court with troops of
ladies,   80
More like an empress than Duke Humphrey's
wife :
Strangers in court do take her for the queen :
She bears a duke's revenues on her back,
And in her heart she scorns our poverty :
Shall I not live to be avenged on her ?
Contemptuous base-born callet as she is,
She vaunted 'mongst her minions t'other day,
The very train of her worst wearing gown
Was better worth than all my father's lands,
Till Suffolk gave two dukedoms for his
daughter.   90
  Suf. Madam, myself have limed a bush for
her,
And placed a quire of such enticing birds,
That she will light to listen to the lays,
And never mount to trouble you again.
So, let her rest : and, madam, list to me ;
For I am bold to counsel you in this.
Although we fancy not the cardinal,
Yet must we join with him and with the lords,
Till we have brought Duke Humphrey in dis-
grace.
As for the Duke of York, this late com-
plaint   100
Will make but little for his benefit.
So, one by one, we'll weed them all at last,
And you yourself shall steer the happy helm.

Sound a sennet. Enter the King, Duke Humphrey *of Gloucester,* Cardinal Beaufort,
Buckingham, York, Somerset, Salisbury,
Warwick, *and the* Duchess of Gloucester.

  King. For my part, noble lords, I care not
which ;
Or Somerset or York, all's one to me.
  York. If York have ill demean'd himself
in France,
Then let him be denay'd the regentship.
  Som. If Somerset be unworthy of the
place,
Let York be regent ; I will yield to him.
  War. Whether your grace be worthy, yea or
no,
Dispute not that : York is the worthier.   110
  Car. Ambitious Warwick, let thy betters
speak.
  War. The cardinal's not my better in the
field.
  Buck. All in this presence are thy betters,
Warwick.
  War. Warwick may live to be the best of
all.
  Sal. Peace, son ! and show some reason,
Buckingham,
Why Somerset should be preferred in this.
  Queen. Because the king, forsooth, will
have it so.

  Glou. Madam, the king is old enough him-
self
To give his censure : these are no women's
matters.   120
  Queen. If he be old enough, what needs
your grace
To be protector of his excellence ?
  Glou. Madam, I am protector of the
realm ;
And, at his pleasure, will resign my place.
  Suf. Resign it then and leave thine inso-
lence.
Since thou wert king—as who is king but
thou ?—
The commonwealth hath daily run to wreck ;
The Dauphin hath prevail'd beyond the seas ;
And all the peers and nobles of the realm
Have been as bondmen to thy sovereignty. 130
  Car. The commons hast thou rack'd ; the
clergy's bags
Are lank and lean with thy extortions.
  Som. Thy sumptuous buildings and thy
wife's attire
Have cost a mass of public treasury.
  Buck. Thy cruelty in execution
Upon offenders, hath exceeded law,
And left thee to the mercy of the law.
  Queen. Thy sale of offices and towns in
France,
If they were known, as the suspect is great,
Would make thee quickly hop without thy
head.   140
    [*Exit Gloucester. The Queen drops her
fan.*
Give me my fan : what, minion ! can ye not ?
    [*She gives the Duchess a box on the ear.*
I cry you mercy, madam ; was it you ?
  Duch. Was't I ! yea, I it was, proud
Frenchwoman :
Could I come near your beauty with my nails,
I'd set my ten commandments in your face.
  King. Sweet aunt, be quiet ; 'twas against
her will.
  Duch. Against her will ! good king, look to
't in time ;
She'll hamper thee, and dandle thee like a
baby :
Though in this place most master wear no
breeches,
She shall not strike Dame Eleanor unrevenged.
    [*Exit.*
  Buck. Lord cardinal, I will follow Eleanor,
And listen after Humphrey, how he proceeds:
She's tickled now ; her fume needs no spurs,
She'll gallop far enough to her destruction.
    [*Exit.*

Re-enter Gloucester.

  Glou. Now, lords, my choler being over-
blown
With walking once about the quadrangle,
I come to talk of commonwealth affairs.
As for your spiteful false objections,
Prove them, and I lie open to the law :
But God in mercy so deal with my soul, 160
As I in duty love my king and country !
But, to the matter that we have in hand :
I say, my sovereign, York is meetest man
To be your regent in the realm of France.
  Suf. Before we make election, give me
leave
To show some reason, of no little force,
That York is most unmeet of any man.

York. I'll tell thee, Suffolk, why I am un-
meet :
First, for I cannot flatter thee in pride ;
Next, if I be appointed for the place, 170
My Lord of Somerset will keep me here,
Without discharge, money, or furniture,
Till France be won into the Dauphin's hands :
Last time, I danced attendance on his will
Till Paris was besieged, famish'd, and lost.
War. That can I witness ; and a fouler fact
Did never traitor in the land commit.
Suf. Peace, headstrong Warwick !
War. Image of pride, why should I hold my
peace ?

Enter HORNER, *the Armorer, and his man*
PETER, *guarded.*

Suf. Because here is a man accused of
treason : 180
Pray God the Duke of York excuse himself !
York. Doth any one accuse York for a
traitor ?
King. What mean'st thou, Suffolk ; tell me,
what are these ?
Suf. Please it your majesty, this is the man
That doth accuse his master of high treason :
His words were these : that Richard, Duke of
York,
Was rightful heir unto the English crown
And that your majesty was a usurper.
King. Say, man, were these thy words ?
Hor. An't shall please your majesty, I
never said nor thought any such matter : God
is my witness, I am falsely accused by the
villain.
Pet. By these ten bones, my lords, he did
speak them to me in the garret one night, as
we were scouring my Lord of York's armor.
York. Base dunghill villain and mechanical,
I'll have thy head for this thy traitor's speech.
I do beseech your royal majesty,
Let him have all the rigor of the law. 199
Hor. Alas, my lord, hang me, if ever I
spake the words. My accuser is my 'prentice ;
and when I did correct him for his fault the
other day, he did vow upon his knees he
would be even with me : I have good witness
of this : therefore I beseech your majesty, do
not cast away an honest man for a villain's
accusation.
King. Uncle, what shall we say to this in
law ?
Glou. This doom, my lord, if I may judge :
Let Somerset be regent o'er the French,
Because in York this breeds suspicion : 210
And let these have a day appointed them
For single combat in convenient place,
For he hath witness of his servant's malice :
This is the law, and this Duke Humphrey's
doom.
Som. I humbly thank your royal majesty.
Hor. And I accept the combat willingly.
Pet. Alas, my lord, I cannot fight ; for
God's sake, pity my case. The spite of man
prevaileth against me. O Lord, have mercy
upon me ! I shall never be able to fight a blow.
O Lord, my heart ! 221
Glou. Sirrah, or you must fight, or else be
hang'd.
King. Away with them to prison ; and the
day of combat shall be the last of the next

month. Come, Somerset, we'll see thee sent
away. [*Flourish. Exeunt.*

SCENE IV. GLOUCESTER'S *garden.*

Enter MARGERY JOURDAIN, HUME, SOUTH-
WELL, *and* BOLINGBROKE.

Hume. Come, my masters ; the duchess, I
tell you, expects performance of your promises.
Boling. Master Hume, we are therefore
provided : will her ladyship behold and hear
our exorcisms ?
Hume. Ay, what else ? fear you not her
courage.
Boling. I have heard her reported to be a
woman of an invincible spirit : but it shall be
convenient, Master Hume, that you be by her
aloft, while we be busy below ; and so, I pray
you, go, in God's name, and leave us. [*Exit
Hume.*] Mother Jourdain, be you prostrate
and grovel on the earth ; John Southwell, read
you ; and let us to our work.

Enter DUCHESS *aloft,* HUME *following.*

Duch. Well said, my masters ; and wel-
come all. To this gear the sooner the better.
Boling. Patience, good lady ; wizards know
their times :
Deep night, dark night, the silent of the night,
The time of night when Troy was set on fire ;
The time when screech-owls cry and ban-dogs
howl,
And spirits walk and ghosts break up their
graves,
That time best fits the work we have in hand.
Madam, sit you and fear not : whom we raise,
We will make fast within a hallow'd verge.

[*Here they do the ceremonies belonging, and make the circle ; Bolingbroke or Southwell reads,* Conjuro
te, &c. *It thunders and lightens terribly ; then the Spirit riseth.*

Spir. Adsum.
M. Jourd. Asmath,
By the eternal God, whose name and power
Thou tremblest at, answer that I shall ask ;
For, till thou speak, thou shalt not pass from
hence. 30
Spir. Ask what thou wilt. That I had said
and done !
Boling. 'First of the king : what shall of
him become ?' [*Reading out of a paper.*
Spir. The duke yet lives that Henry shall
depose ;
But him outlive, and die a violent death.
[*As the Spirit speaks, Southwell
writes the answer.*
Boling. 'What fates await the Duke of
Suffolk ?'
Spir. By water shall he die, and take his
end.
Boling. 'What shall befall the Duke of
Somerset ?'
Spir. Let him shun castles ;
Safer shall he be upon the sandy plains
Than where castles mounted stand. 40
Have done, for more I hardly can endure.
Boling. Descend to darkness and the burn-
ing lake !
False fiend, avoid !
[*Thunder and lightning. Exit Spirit.*

Enter the Duke of York *and the* Duke of
Buckingham *with their* Guard *and break in.*

York. Lay hands upon these traitors and
their trash.
Beldam, I think we watch'd you at an inch.
What, madam, are you there ? the king and
commonweal
Are deeply indebted for this piece of pains :
My lord protector will, I doubt it not,
See you well guerdon'd for these good deserts.
Duch. Not half so bad as thine to Eng-
land's king,   50
Injurious duke, that threatest where's no cause.
Buck. True, madam, none at all : what call
you this ?
Away with them ! let them be clapp'd up close.
And kept asunder. You, madam, shall with us.
Stafford, take her to thee.
[Exeunt above Duchess and Hume, guarded.
We'll see your trinkets here all forthcoming.
All, away !
[Exeunt guard with Jourdain, Southwell, &c.
York. Lord Buckingham, methinks, you
watch'd her well :
A pretty plot, well chosen to build upon !
Now, pray, my lord, let's see the devil's writ.
What have we here ?   *[Reads.* 61
' The duke yet lives, that Henry shall depose ;
But him outlive, and die a violent death.'
Why, this is just
' Aio te, Æacida, Romanos vincere posse.'
Well, to the rest :
' Tell me what fate awaits the Duke of Suf-
folk ?
By water shall he die, and take his end.
What shall betide the Duke of Somerset ?
Let him shun castles ;   70
Safer shall he be upon the sandy plains
Than where castles mounted stand.'
Come, come, my lords ;
These oracles are hardly attain'd,
And hardly understood.
The king is now in progress towards Saint
Alban's,
With him the husband of this lovely lady :
Thither go these news, as fast as horse can
carry them :
A sorry breakfast for my lord protector.
Buck. Your grace shall give me leave, my
Lord of York,   80
To be the post, in hope of his reward.
York. At your pleasure, my good lord.
Who's within there, ho !

Enter a Servingman.

Invite my Lords of Salisbury and Warwick
To sup with me to-morrow night. Away !
[Exeunt.

ACT II.

Scene I. *Saint Alban's.*

Enter the King, Queen, Gloucester, Cardinal, *and* Suffolk, *with* Falconers *halloing.*

Queen. Believe me, lords, for flying at the
brook,
I saw not better sport these seven years' day :
Yet, by your leave, the wind was very high ;
And, ten to one, old Joan had not gone out.
King. But what a point, my lord, your fal-
con made,
And what a pitch she flew above the rest !
To see how God in all his creatures works !
Yea, man and birds are fain of climbing high.
Suf. No marvel, an it like your majesty,
My lord protector's hawks do tower so well ;10
They know their master loves to be aloft,
And bears his thoughts above his falcon's
pitch.
Glou. My lord, 'tis but a base ignoble mind
That mounts no higher than a bird can soar.
Car. I thought as much ; he would be
above the clouds.
Glou. Ay, my lord cardinal ? how think
you by that ?
Were it not good your grace could fly to
heaven ?
King. The treasury of everlasting joy.
Car. Thy heaven is on earth ; thine eyes
and thoughts
Beat on a crown, the treasure of thy heart ; 20
Pernicious protector, dangerous peer,
That smooth'st it so with king and common-
weal !
Glou. What, cardinal, is your priesthood
grown peremptory ?
Tantæne animis cœlestibus iræ ?
Churchmen so hot ? good uncle, hide such
malice ;
With such holiness can you do it ?
Suf. No malice, sir ; no more than well be-
comes
So good a quarrel and so bad a peer.
Glou. As who, my lord ?
Suf.   Why, as you, my lord,
An't like your lordly lord-protectorship.   30
Glou. Why, Suffolk, England knows thine
insolence.
Queen. And thy ambition, Gloucester.
King. I prithee, peace, good queen,
And whet not on these furious peers ;
For blessed are the peacemakers on earth.
Car. Let me be blessed for the peace I
make,
Against this proud protector, with my sword !
Glou. [*Aside to Car.*] Faith, holy uncle,
would 'twere come to that !
Car. [*Aside to Glou.*] Marry, when thou
darest.
Glou. [*Aside to Car.*] Make up no factious
numbers for the matter ;   40
In thine own person answer thy abuse.
Car. [*Aside to Glou.*] Ay, where thou dar-
est not peep : an if thou darest,
This evening, on the east side of the grove.
King. How now, my lords !
Car.   Believe me, cousin Gloucester,
Had not your man put up the fowl so sud-
denly,
We had had more sport. [*Aside to Glou.*]
Come with thy two-hand sword.
Glou. True, uncle.
Car. [*Aside to Glou.*] Are ye advised ? the
east side of the grove ?
Glou. [*Aside to Car.*] Cardinal, I am with
you.
King. Why, how now, uncle Gloucester !
Glou. Talking of hawking ; nothing else,
my lord.   50
[*Aside to Car.*] Now, by God's mother, priest,
I'll shave your crown for this,
Or all my fence shall fail.

Car. [*Aside to Glou.*] Medice, teipsum—
Protector, see to't well, protect yourself.
King. The winds grow high; so do your
    stomachs, lords.
How irksome is this music to my heart!
When such strings jar, what hope of har-
    mony?
I pray, my lords, let me compound this strife.

Enter a Townsman *of Saint Alban's, crying*
    'A miracle!'

Glou. What means this noise?
Fellow, what miracle dost thou proclaim? 60
Towns. A miracle! a miracle!
Suf. Come to the king and tell him what
    miracle.
Towns. Forsooth, a blind man at Saint Al-
    ban's shrine,
Within this half-hour, hath received his sight;
A man that ne'er saw in his life before.
King. Now, God be praised, that to believ-
    ing souls
Gives light in darkness, comfort in despair!

Enter the Mayor *of Saint Alban's and his
brethren, bearing* SIMPCOX, *between two in a
chair,* SIMPCOX's Wife *following.*

Car. Here comes the townsmen on proces-
    sion,
To present your highness with the man.
King. Great is his comfort in this earthly
    vale, 70
Although by his sight his sin be multiplied.
Glou. Stand by, my masters: bring him
    near the king;
His highness' pleasure is to talk with him.
King. Good fellow, tell us here the circum-
    stance,
That we for thee may glorify the Lord.
What, hast thou been long blind and now re-
    stored?
Simp. Born blind, an't please your grace.
Wife. Ay, indeed, was he.
Suf. What woman is this?
Wife. His wife, an't like your worship. 80
Glou. Hadst thou been his mother, thou
    couldst have better told.
King. Where wert thou born?
Simp. At Berwick in the north, an't like
    your grace.
King. Poor soul, God's goodness hath been
    great to thee:
Let never day nor night unhallow'd pass,
But still remember what the Lord hath done.
Queen. Tell me, good fellow, camest thou
    here by chance,
Or of devotion, to this holy shrine?
Simp. God knows, of pure devotion; being
    call'd
A hundred times and oftener, in my sleep, 90
By good Saint Alban; who said, 'Simpcox,
    come,
Come, offer at my shrine, and I will help thee.'
Wife. Most true, forsooth; and many time
    and oft
Myself have heard a voice to call him so.
Car. What, art thou lame?
Simp.   Ay, God Almighty help me!
Suf. How camest thou so?
Simp.   A fall off of a tree.
Wife. A plum-tree, master.

Glou. How long hast thou been blind?
Simp. O, born so, master.
Glou. What, and wouldst climb a tree?
Simp. But that in all my life, when I was
    a youth.
Wife. Too true; and bought his climbing
    very dear. 100
Glou. Mass, thou lovedst plums well, that
    wouldst venture so.
Simp. Alas, good master, my wife desired
    some damsons,
And made me climb, with danger of my life.
Glou. A subtle knave! but yet it shall not
    serve.
Let me see thine eyes: wink now: now open
    them:
In my opinion yet thou see'st not well.
Simp. Yes, master, clear as day, I thank
    God and Saint Alban.
Glou. Say'st thou me so? What color is
    this cloak of?
Simp. Red, master; red as blood. 110
Glou. Why, that's well said. What color
    is my gown of?
Simp. Black, forsooth: coal-black as jet.
King. Why, then, thou know'st what color
    jet is of?
Suf. And yet, I think, jet did he never see.
Glou. But cloaks and gowns, before this
    day, a many.
Wife. Never, before this day, in all his life.
Glou. Tell me, sirrah, what's my name?
Simp. Alas, master, I know not.
Glou. What's his name?
Simp. I know not. 120
Glou. Nor his?
Simp. No, indeed, master.
Glou. What's thine own name?
Simp. Saunder Simpcox, an if it please
    you, master.
Glou. Then, Saunder, sit there, the lyingest
knave in Christendom. If thou hadst been
born blind, thou mightest as well have known
all our names as thus to name the several
colors we do wear. Sight may distinguish of
colors, but suddenly to nominate them all, it
is impossible. My lords, Saint Alban here hath
done a miracle; and would ye not think his
cunning to be great, that could restore this
cripple to his legs again?
Simp. O master, that you could!
Glou. My masters of Saint Alban's, have
you not beadles in your town, and things
called whips?
May. Yes, my lord, if it please your grace.
Glou. Then send for one presently. 140
May. Sirrah, go fetch the beadle hither
straight.   [*Exit an Attendant.*
Glou. Now fetch me a stool hither by and
by. Now, sirrah, if you mean to save yourself
from whipping, leap me over this stool and
run away.
Simp. Alas, master, I am not able to stand
    alone:
You go about to torture me in vain.

Enter a Beadle *with whips.*

Glou. Well, sir, we must have you find
your legs. Sirrah beadle, whip him till he leap
over that same stool. 150
Bead. I will, my lord. Come on, sirrah;
off with your doublet quickly.

Simp. Alas, master, what shall I do ? I am not able to stand.

> [*After the Beadle hath hit him once, he leaps over the stool and runs away ; and they follow and cry, 'A miracle !'*

King. O God, seest Thou this, and bearest so long ?

Queen. It made me laugh to see the villain run.

Glou. Follow the knave ; and take this drab away.

Wife. Alas, sir, we did it for pure need.

Glou. Let them be whipped through every market-town, till they come to Berwick, from whence they came.   160

> [*Exeunt Wife, Beadle, Mayor, &c.*

Car. Duke Humphrey has done a miracle to-day.

Suf. True ; made the lame to leap and fly away.

Glou. But you have done more miracles than I ;
You made in a day, my lord, whole towns to fly.

Enter Buckingham.

King. What tidings with our cousin Buckingham ?

Buck. Such as my heart doth tremble to unfold.
A sort of naughty persons, lewdly bent,
Under the countenance and confederacy
Of Lady Eleanor, the protector's wife,
The ringleader and head of all this rout,   170
Have practised dangerously against your state,
Dealing with witches and with conjurers :
Whom we have apprehended in the fact ;
Raising up wicked spirits from under ground,
Demanding of King Henry's life and death,
And other of your highness' privy-council ;
As more at large your grace shall understand.

Car. [*Aside to Glou.*] And so, my lord pro-
tector, by this means
Your lady is forthcoming yet at London.
This news, I think, hath turn'd your weapon's
edge ;   180
'Tis like, my lord, you will not keep your hour.

Glou. Ambitious churchman, leave to af-
flict my heart :
Sorrow and grief have vanquish'd all my
powers ;
And, vanquish'd as I am, I yield to thee,
Or to the meanest groom.

King. O God, what mischiefs work the
wicked ones,
Heaping confusion on their own heads
thereby !

Queen. Gloucester, see here the tainture of
thy nest,
And look thyself be faultless, thou wert best.

Glou. Madam, for myself, to heaven I do
appeal,   190
How I have loved my king and commonweal :
And, for my wife, I know not how it stands ;
Sorry I am to hear what I have heard :
Noble she is, but if she have forgot
Honor and virtue and conversed with such
As, like to pitch, defile nobility,
banish her my bed and company
and give her as a prey to law and shame,
that hath dishonor'd Gloucester's honest
name.

King. Well, for this night we will repose us
here :   200
To-morrow toward London back again,
To look into this business thoroughly
And call these foul offenders to their answers
And poise the cause in justice' equal scales,
Whose beam stands sure, whose rightful cause
prevails.   [*Flourish. Exeunt.*

Scene II. *London. The* Duke of York's
garden.

Enter York, Salisbury, *and* Warwick.

York. Now, my good Lords of Salisbury
and Warwick,
Our simple supper ended, give me leave
In this close walk to satisfy myself,
In craving your opinion of my title,
Which is infallible, to England's crown.

Sal. My lord, I long to hear it at full.

War. Sweet York, begin : and if thy claim
be good,
The Nevils are thy subjects to command.

York. Then thus :
Edward the Third, my lords, had seven sons :
The first, Edward the Black Prince, Prince of
Wales ;   11
The second, William of Hatfield, and the third,
Lionel Duke of Clarence : next to whom
Was John of Gaunt, the Duke of Lancaster ;
The fifth was Edmund Langley, Duke of York ;
The sixth was Thomas of Woodstock, Duke of
Gloucester ;
William of Windsor was the seventh and last.
Edward the Black Prince died before his father
And left behind him Richard, his only son,
Who after Edward the Third's death reign'd
as king ;   20
Till Henry Bolingbroke, Duke of Lancaster,
The eldest son and heir of John of Gaunt,
Crown'd by the name of Henry the Fourth,
Seized on the realm, deposed the rightful king,
Sent his poor queen to France, from whence
she came,
And him to Pomfret ; where, as all you know,
Harmless Richard was murder'd traitorously.

War. Father, the duke hath told the truth :
Thus got the house of Lancaster the crown.

York. Which now they hold by force and
not by right ;   30
For Richard, the first son's heir, being dead,
The issue of the next son should have reign'd.

Sal. But William of Hatfield died without
an heir.

York. The third son, Duke of Clarence,
from whose line
I claim the crown, had issue, Philippe, a
daughter,
Who married Edmund Mortimer, Earl of
March :
Edmund had issue, Roger Earl of March ;
Roger had issue, Edmund, Anne and Eleanor.

Sal. This Edmund, in the reign of Boling-
broke,
As I have read, laid claim unto the crown ;   40
And, but for Owen Glendower, had been king,
Who kept him in captivity till he died.
But to the rest.

York.   His eldest sister, Anne,
My mother, being heir unto the crown,
Married Richard Earl of Cambridge ; who was
son
To Edmund Langley, Edward the Third's fifth
son.

By her I claim the kingdom : she was heir
To Roger Earl of March, who was the son
Of Edmund Mortimer, who married Philippe,
Sole daughter unto Lionel Duke of Clarence :
So, if the issue of the elder son   51
Succeed before the younger, I am king.
  War. What plain proceeding is more plain
    than this ?
Henry doth claim the crown from John of
    Gaunt,
The fourth son ; York claims it from the third.
Till Lionel's issue fails, his should not reign :
It fails not yet, but flourishes in thee
And in thy sons, fair slips of such a stock.
Then, father Salisbury, kneel we together ;
And in this private plot be we the first   60
That shall salute our rightful sovereign
With honor of his birthright to the crown.
  Both. Long live our sovereign Richard,
    England's king !
  York. We thank you, lords. But I am not
    your king
Till I be crown'd and that my sword be stain'd
With heart-blood of the house of Lancaster ;
And that's not suddenly to be perform'd,
But with advice and silent secrecy.
Do you as I do in these dangerous days :
Wink at the Duke of Suffolk's insolence,   70
At Beaufort's pride, at Somerset's ambition,
At Buckingham and all the crew of them,
Till they have snared the shepherd of the flock,
That virtuous prince, the good Duke Hum-
    phrey :
'Tis that they seek, and they in seeking that
Shall find their deaths, if York can prophesy.
  Sal. My lord, break we off ; we know your
    mind at full.
  War. My heart assures me that the Earl of
    Warwick
Shall one day make the Duke of York a king.
  York. And, Nevil, this I do assure myself :
Richard shall live to make the Earl of Warwick
The greatest man in England but the king.
                                    [*Exeunt.*

SCENE III. *A hall of justice.*

Sound trumpets. Enter the KING, *the* QUEEN,
GLOUCESTER, YORK, SUFFOLK, *and* SALIS-
BURY ; *the* DUCHESS OF GLOUCESTER, MAR-
GERY JOURDAIN, SOUTHWELL, HUME, *and*
BOLINGBROKE, *under guard.*

  King. Stand forth, Dame Eleanor Cobham,
    Gloucester's wife :
In sight of God and us, your guilt is great :
Receive the sentence of the law for sins
Such as by God's book are adjudged to death.
You four, from hence to prison back again ;
From thence unto the place of execution :
The witch in Smithfield shall be burn'd to
    ashes,
And you three shall be strangled on the gal-
    lows.
You, madam, for you are more nobly born,
Despoiled of your honor in your life,   10
Shall, after three days' open penance done,
Live in your country here in banishment,
With Sir John Stanley, in the Isle of Man.
  Duch. Welcome is banishment ; welcome
    were my death.
  Glou. Eleanor, the law, thou see'st, hath
    judged thee :

I cannot justify whom the law condemns.
          [*Exeunt Duchess and other prisoners,
                                    guarded.*
Mine eyes are full of tears, my heart of grief.
Ah, Humphrey, this dishonor in thine age
Will bring thy head with sorrow to the
    ground !
I beseech your majesty, give me leave to go ;
Sorrow would solace and mine age would ease.
  King. Stay, Humphrey Duke of Glouces-
    ter : ere thou go,
Give up thy staff : Henry will to himself
Protector be ; and God shall be my hope,
My stay, my guide and lantern to my feet :
And go in peace, Humphrey, no less beloved
Than when thou wert protector to thy king.
  Queen. I see no reason why a king of years
Should be to be protected like a child.   29
God and King Henry govern England's realm.
Give up your staff, sir, and the king his realm.
  Glou. My staff ? here, noble Henry, is my
    staff :
As willingly do I the same resign
As e'er thy father Henry made it mine ;
And even as willingly at thy feet I leave it
As others would ambitiously receive it.
Farewell, good king : when I am dead and
    gone,
May honorable peace attend thy throne !
                                    [*Exit.*
  Queen. Why, now is Henry king, and Mar-
    garet queen ;
And Humphrey Duke of Gloucester scarce
    himself,   40
That bears so shrewd a maim ; two pulls at
    once ;
His lady banish'd, and a limb lopp'd off.
This staff of honor raught, there let it stand
Where it best fits to be, in Henry's hand.
  Suf. Thus droops this lofty pine and hangs
    his sprays ;
Thus Eleanor's pride dies in her youngest days.
  York. Lords, let him go. Please it your
    majesty,
This is the day appointed for the combat ;
And ready are the appellant and defendant,
The armorer and his man, to enter the lists, 50
So please your highness to behold the fight.
  Queen. Ay, good my lord ; for purposely
    therefore
Left I the court, to see this quarrel tried.
  King. O God's name, see the lists and all
    things fit :
Here let them end it ; and God defend the
    right !
  York. I never saw a fellow worse bested,
Or more afraid to fight, than is the appellant,
The servant of this armorer, my lords.

Enter at one door, HORNER, *the Armorer, and
his* Neighbors, *drinking to him so much that
he is drunk ; and he enters with a drum before him and his staff with a sand-bag fas-
tened to it ; and at the other door* PETER, *his
man, with a drum and sand-bag, and 'Prentices drinking to him.*

  First Neigh. Here, neighbor Horner, I
drink to you in a cup of sack : and fear not,
neighbor, you shall do well enough.   61
  Sec. Neigh. And here, neighbor, here's a
cup of charneco.
  Third Neigh. And here's a pot of good

double beer, neighbor : drink, and fear not
your man.
    Hor. Let it come, i' faith, and I'll pledge
you all ; and a fig for Peter !
    First 'Pren. Here, Peter, I drink to thee :
and be not afraid.
    Sec. 'Pren. Be merry, Peter, and fear not
thy master : fight for credit of the 'prentices.
    Peter. I thank you all : drink, and pray
for me, I pray you ; for I think I have taken
my last draught in this world. Here, Robin, an
if I die, I give thee my apron : and, Will, thou
shalt have my hammer : and here, Tom, take
all the money that I have. O Lord bless me !
I pray God ! for I am never able to deal with
my master, he hath learnt so much fence already.
    Sal. Come, leave your drinking, and fall to
blows. Sirrah, what's thy name ?   81
    Peter. Peter, forsooth.
    Sal. Peter ! what more ?
    Peter. Thump.
    Sal. Thump ! then see thou thump thy
master well.
    Hor. Masters, I am come hither, as it
were, upon my man's instigation, to prove him
a knave and myself an honest man : and
touching the Duke of York, I will take my
death, I never meant him any ill, nor the king,
nor the queen : and therefore, Peter, have at
thee with a downright blow !
    York. Dispatch : this knave's tongue be-
gins to double.
Sound, trumpets, alarum to the combatants !
    [*Alarum. They fight, and Peter strikes
            him down.*
    Hor. Hold, Peter, hold ! I confess, I con-
fess treason.   [*Dies.*
    York. Take away his weapon. Fellow,
thank God, and the good wine in thy master's
way.   99
    Peter. O God, have I overcome mine en-
emy in this presence ? O Peter, thou hast pre-
vailed in right !
    King. Go, take hence that traitor from our
sight ;
For by his death we do perceive his guilt :
And God in justice hath revealed to us
The truth and innocence of this poor fellow,
Which he had thought to have murder'd
wrongfully.
Come, fellow, follow us for thy reward.
    [*Sound a flourish. Exeunt.*

SCENE IV. *A street.*

Enter GLOUCESTER *and his Servingmen, in
mourning cloaks.*

    Glou. Thus sometimes hath the brightest
day a cloud ;
And after summer evermore succeeds
Barren winter, with his wrathful nipping cold :
So cares and joys abound, as seasons fleet.
Sirs, what's o'clock ?
    Serv.   Ten, my lord.
    Glou. Ten is the hour that was appointed
me
To watch the coming of my punish'd duchess :
Uneath may she endure the flinty streets,
To tread them with her tender-feeling feet.
Sweet Nell, ill can thy noble mind abrook   10
The abject people gazing on thy face,
With envious looks, laughing at thy shame,
That erst did follow thy proud chariot-wheels
When thou didst ride in triumph through the
streets.
But, soft ! I think she comes ; and I'll prepare
My tear-stain'd eyes to see her miseries.

Enter the DUCHESS OF GLOUCESTER *in a white
sheet, and a taper burning in her hand ; with*
SIR JOHN STANLEY, *the* Sheriff, *and* Officers.

    Serv. So please your grace, we'll take her
from the sheriff.
    Glou. No, stir not, for your lives ; let her
pass by.
    Duch. Come you, my lord, to see my open
shame ?
Now thou dost penance too. Look how they
gaze !
See how the giddy multitude do point,   21
And nod their heads, and throw their eyes on
thee !
Ah, Gloucester, hide thee from their hateful
looks,
And, in thy closet pent up, rue my shame,
And ban thine enemies, both mine and thine !
    Glou. Be patient, gentle Nell ; forget this
grief.
    Duch. Ah, Gloucester, teach me to forget
myself !
For whilst I think I am thy married wife
And thou a prince, protector of this land,
Methinks I should not thus be led along,   30
Mail'd up in shame, with papers on my back,
And followed with a rabble that rejoice
To see my tears and hear my deep-fet groans.
The ruthless flint doth cut my tender feet,
And when I start, the envious people laugh
And bid me be advised how I tread.
Ah, Humphrey, can I bear this shameful
yoke ?
Trow'st thou that e'er I'll look upon the world,
Or count them happy that enjoy the sun ?
No ; dark shall be my light and night my day ;
To think upon my pomp shall be my hell.   41
Sometime I'll say, I am Duke Humphrey's
wife,
And he a prince and ruler of the land :
Yet so he ruled and such a prince he was
As he stood by whilst I, his forlorn duchess,
Was made a wonder and a pointing-stock
To every idle rascal follower.
But be thou mild and blush not at my shame,
Nor stir at nothing till the axe of death
Hang over thee, as, sure, it shortly will ;   50
For Suffolk, he that can do all in all
With her that hateth thee and hates us all,
And York and impious Beaufort, that false
priest,
Have all limed bushes to betray thy wings,
And, fly thou how thou canst, they'll tangle
thee :
But fear not thou, until thy foot be snared,
Nor never seek prevention of thy foes.
    Glou. Ah, Nell, forbear ! thou aimest all
awry ;
I must offend before I be attainted ;
And had I twenty times so many foes,   60
And each of them had twenty times their
power,
All these could not procure me any scathe,
So long as I am loyal, true and crimeless.
Wouldst have me rescue thee from this re-
proach ?
Why, yet thy scandal were not wiped away
But I in danger for the breach of law.

Thy greatest help is quiet, gentle Nell :
I pray thee, sort thy heart to patience ;
These few days' wonder will be quickly worn.

Enter a Herald.

Her. I summon your grace to his majesty's
    parliament,   70
Holden at Bury the first of this next month.
    Glou. And my consent ne'er ask'd herein
        before !
This is close dealing. Well, I will be there.
                            [*Exit Herald.*
My Nell, I take my leave : and, master sheriff,
Let not her penance exceed the king's com-
    mission.
    Sher. An't please your grace, here my com-
        mission stays,
And Sir John Stanley is appointed now
To take her with him to the Isle of Man.
    Glou. Must you, Sir John, protect my lady
        here ?
    Stan. So am I given in charge, may't please
        your grace.   80
    Glou. Entreat her not the worse in that I
        pray
You use her well : the world may laugh again ;
And I may live to do you kindness if
You do it her : and so, Sir John, farewell !
    Duch. What, gone, my lord, and bid me
        not farewell !
    Glou. Witness my tears, I cannot stay to
        speak.
            [*Exeunt Gloucester and Servingmen.*
    Duch. Art thou gone too ? all comfort go
        with thee !
For none abides with me : my joy is death ;
Death, at whose name I oft have been afear'd,
Because I wish'd this world's eternity.   90
Stanley, I prithee, go, and take me hence ;
I care not whither, for I beg no favor,
Only convey me where thou art commanded.
    Stan. Why, madam, that is to the Isle of
        Man ;
There to be used according to your state.
    Duch. That's bad enough, for I am but re-
        proach :
And shall I then be used reproachfully ?
    Stan. Like to a duchess, and Duke Hum-
        phrey's lady ;
According to that state you shall be used.
    Duch. Sheriff, farewell, and better than I
        fare,   100
Although thou hast been conduct of my shame.
    Sher. It is my office ; and, madam, pardon
        me.
    Duch. Ay, ay, farewell ; thy office is dis-
        charged.
Come, Stanley, shall we go ?
    Stan. Madam, your penance done, throw
        off this sheet,
And go we to attire you for our journey.
    Duch. My shame will not be shifted with
        my sheet :
No, it will hang upon my richest robes
And show itself, attire me how I can.
Go, lead the way ; I long to see my prison. 110
                            [*Exeunt.*

ACT III.

SCENE I. *The Abbey at Bury St. Edmund's.*

Sound a sennet. Enter the KING, *the* QUEEN,
CARDINAL BEAUFORT, SUFFOLK, YORK, BUCK-
INGHAM, SALISBURY *and* WARWICK *to the
Parliament.*

King. I muse my Lord of Gloucester is not
    come :
'Tis not his wont to be the hindmost man,
Whate'er occasion keeps him from us now.
    Queen. Can you not see ? or will ye not
        observe
The strangeness of his alter'd countenance ?
With what a majesty he bears himself,
How insolent of late he is become,
How proud, how peremptory, and unlike him-
    self ?
We know the time since he was mild and af-
    fable,
And if we did but glance a far-off look,   10
Immediately he was upon his knee,
That all the court admired him for submis-
    sion :
But meet him now, and, be it in the morn,
When every one will give the time of day,
He knits his brow and shows an angry eye,
And passeth by with stiff unbowed knee,
Disdaining duty that to us belongs.
Small curs are not regarded when they grin ;
But great men tremble when the lion roars ;
And Humphrey is no little man in England. 20
First note that he is near you in descent,
And should you fall, he as the next will mount.
Me seemeth then it is no policy,
Respecting what a rancorous mind he bears
And his advantage following your decease,
That he should come about your royal person
Or be admitted to your highness' council.
By flattery hath he won the commons' hearts,
And when he please to make commotion,
'Tis to be fear'd they all will follow him.   30
Now 'tis the spring, and weeds are shallow-
    rooted ;
Suffer them now, and they'll o'ergrow the
    garden
And choke the herbs for want of husbandry.
The reverent care I bear unto my lord
Made me collect these dangers in the duke.
If it be fond, call it a woman's fear ;
Which fear if better reasons can supplant,
I will subscribe and say I wrong'd the duke.
My Lord of Suffolk, Buckingham, and York,
Reprove my allegation, if you can ;   40
Or else conclude my words effectual.
    Suf. Well hath your highness seen into this
        duke ;
And, had I first been put to speak my mind,
I think I should have told your grace's tale.
The duchess, by his subornation,
Upon my life, began her devilish practices :
Or, if he were not privy to those faults,
Yet, by reputing of his high descent,
As next the king he was successive heir,
And such high vaunts of his nobility,   50
Did instigate the bedlam brain-sick duchess
By wicked means to frame our sovereign's fall.
Smooth runs the water where the brook is
    deep ;
And in his simple show he harbors treason.
The fox barks not when he would steal the
    lamb.
No, no, my sovereign ; Gloucester is a man
Unsounded yet and full of deep deceit.
    Car. Did he not, contrary to form of law,
Devise strange deaths for small offences done ?

York. And did he not, in his protector-
ship,   60
Levy great sums of money through the realm
For soldiers' pay in France, and never sent it ?
By means whereof the towns each day re-
volted.
Buck. Tut, these are petty faults to faults
unknown,
Which time will bring to light in smooth Duke
Humphrey.
King. My lords, at once : the care you have
of us,
To mow down thorns that would annoy our
foot,
Is worthy praise : but, shall I speak my con-
science,
Our kinsman Gloucester is as innocent
From meaning treason to our royal person 70
As is the sucking lamb or harmless dove :
The duke is virtuous, mild and too well given
To dream on evil or to work my downfall.
Queen. Ah, what's more dangerous than
this fond affiance !
Seems he a dove ? his feathers are but bor-
rowed,
For he's disposed as the hateful raven :
Is he a lamb ? his skin is surely lent him,
For he's inclined as is the ravenous wolf.
Who cannot steal a shape that means deceit ?
Take heed, my lord ; the welfare of us all 80
Hangs on the cutting short that fraudful man.

Enter SOMERSET.

Som. All health unto my gracious sover-
eign !
King. Welcome, Lord Somerset. What
news from France ?
Som. That all your interest in those terri-
tories
Is utterly bereft you ; all is lost.
King. Cold news, Lord Somerset : but
God's will be done !
York. [*Aside*] Cold news for me ; for I
had hope of France
As firmly as I hope for fertile England.
Thus are my blossoms blasted in the bud
And caterpillars eat my leaves away ;   90
But I will remedy this gear ere long,
Or sell my title for a glorious grave.

Enter GLOUCESTER.

Glou. All happiness unto my lord the king !
Pardon, my liege, that I have stay'd so long.
Suf. Nay, Gloucester, know that thou art
come too soon,
Unless thou wert more loyal than thou art :
I do arrest thee of high treason here.
Glou. Well, Suffolk, thou shalt not see me
blush
Nor change my countenance for this arrest : 100
A heart unspotted is not easily daunted.
The purest spring is not so free from mud
As I am clear from treason to my sovereign :
Who can accuse me ? wherein am I guilty ?
York. 'Tis thought, my lord, that you took
bribes of France,
And, being protector, stayed the soldiers' pay ;
By means whereof his highness hath lost
France.
Glou. Is it but thought so ? what are they
that think it ?
I never robb'd the soldiers of their pay,
Nor ever had one penny bribe from France.

So help me God, as I have watch'd the night,
Ay, night by night, in studying good for Eng-
land,   111
That doit that e'er I wrested from the king,
Or any groat I hoarded to my use,
Be brought against me at my trial-day !
No ; many a pound of mine own proper store,
Because I would not tax the needy commons,
Have I disbursed to the garrisons,
And never ask'd for restitution.
Car. It serves you well, my lord, to say so
much.
Glou. I say no more than truth, so help me
God !   120
York. In your protectorship you did devise
Strange tortures for offenders never heard of,
That England was defamed by tyranny.
Glou. Why, 'tis well known that, whiles I
was protector,
Pity was all the fault that was in me ;
For I should melt at an offender's tears,
And lowly words were ransom for their fault.
Unless it were a bloody murderer,
Or foul felonious thief that fleeced poor pas-
sengers,
I never gave them condign punishment : 130
Murder indeed, that bloody sin, I tortured
Above the felon or what trespass else.
Suf. My lord, these faults are easy, quickly
answered :
But mightier crimes are laid unto your charge,
Whereof you cannot easily purge yourself.
I do arrest you in his highness' name ;
And here commit you to my lord cardinal
To keep, until your further time of trial.
King. My lord of Gloucester, 'tis my spe-
cial hope
That you will clear yourself from all suspect :
My conscience tells me you are innocent. 141
Glou. Ah, gracious lord, these days are
dangerous :
Virtue is choked with foul ambition
And charity chased hence by rancor's hand ;
Foul subornation is predominant
And equity exiled your highness' land.
I know their complot is to have my life,
And if my death might make this island happy,
And prove the period of their tyranny,
I would expend it with all willingness : 150
But mine is made the prologue to their play ;
For thousands more, that yet suspect no peril,
Will not conclude their plotted tragedy.
Beaufort's red sparkling eyes blab his heart's
malice,
And Suffolk's cloudy brow his stormy hate ;
Sharp Buckingham unburthens with his tongue
The envious load that lies upon his heart ;
And dogged York, that reaches at the moon,
Whose overweening arm I have pluck'd back,
By false accuse doth level at my life : 160
And you, my sovereign lady, with the rest,
Causeless have laid disgraces on my head,
And with your best endeavor have stirr'd up
My liefest liege to be mine enemy :
Ay, all you have laid your heads together—
Myself had notice of your conventicles—
And all to make away my guiltless life.
I shall not want false witness to condemn me,
Nor store of treasons to augment my guilt ;
The ancient proverb will be well effected : 170
' A staff is quickly found to beat a dog.'
Car. My liege, his railing is intolerable :
If those that care to keep your royal person

From treason's secret knife and traitors' rage
Be thus upbraided, chid and rated at,
And the offender granted scope of speech,
'Twill make them cool in zeal unto your grace.
   Suf. Hath he not twit our sovereign lady here
With ignominious words, though clerkly couch'd,
As if she had suborned some to swear   180
False allegations to o'erthrow his state ?
   Queen. But I can give the loser leave to chide.
   Glou. Far truer spoke than meant : I lose, indeed ;
Beshrew the winners, for they play'd me false !
And well such losers may have leave to speak.
   Buck. He'll wrest the sense and hold us here all day ;
Lord cardinal, he is your prisoner.
   Car. Sirs, take away the duke, and guard him sure.
   Glou. Ah ! thus King Henry throws away his crutch
Before his legs be firm to bear his body.   190
Thus is the shepherd beaten from thy side,
And wolves are gnarling who shall gnaw thee first.
Ah, that my fear were false ! ah, that it were !
For, good King Henry, thy decay I fear.
                   [Exit, guarded.
   King. My lords, what to your wisdoms seemeth best,
Do or undo, as if ourself were here.
   Queen. What, will your highness leave the parliament ?
   King. Ay, Margaret ; my heart is drown'd with grief,
Whose flood begins to flow within mine eyes,   200
My body round engirt with misery,
For what's more miserable than discontent ?
Ah, uncle Humphrey ! in thy face I see
The map of honor, truth and loyalty :
And yet, good Humphrey, is the hour to come
That e'er I proved thee false or fear'd thy faith.
What louring star now envies thy estate,
That these great lords and Margaret our queen
Do seek subversion of thy harmless life ?
Thou never didst them wrong, nor no man wrong ;
And as the butcher takes away the calf   210
And binds the wretch, and beats it when it strays,
Bearing it to the bloody slaughter-house,
Even so remorseless have they borne him hence ;
And as the dam runs lowing up and down,
Looking the way her harmless young one went,
And can do nought but wail her darling's loss,
Even so myself bewails good Gloucester's case
With sad unhelpful tears, and with dimm'd eyes
Look after him and cannot do him good,
So mighty are his vowed enemies.   220
His fortunes I will weep ; and, 'twixt each groan
Say ' Who's a traitor ? Gloucester he is none.'
       [Exeunt all but Queen, Cardinal Beaufort, Suffolk, and York ; Somerset remains apart.
   Queen. Free lords, cold snow melts with the sun's hot beams.
Henry my lord is cold in great affairs,

Too full of foolish pity, and Gloucester's show
Beguiles him as the mournful crocodile
With sorrow snares relenting passengers,
Or as the snake roll'd in a flowering bank,
With shining checker'd slough, doth sting a child
That for the beauty thinks it excellent.   230
Believe me, lords, were none more wise than I—
And yet herein I judge mine own wit good—
This Gloucester should be quickly rid the world,
To rid us of the fear we have of him.
   Car. That he should die is worthy policy ;
But yet we want a color for his death :
'Tis meet he be condemn'd by course of law.
   Suf. But, in my mind, that were no policy :
The king will labor still to save his life,
The commons haply rise, to save his life ;   240
And yet we have but trivial argument,
More than mistrust, that shows him worthy death.
   York. So that, by this, you would not have him die.
   Suf. Ah, York, no man alive so fain as I !
   York. 'Tis York that hath more reason for his death.
But, my lord cardinal, and you, my Lord of Suffolk,
Say as you think, and speak it from your souls,
Were't not all one, an empty eagle were set
To guard the chicken from a hungry kite,
As place Duke Humphrey for the king's protector ?   250
   Queen. So the poor chicken should be sure of death.
   Suf. Madam, 'tis true ; and were't not madness, then,
To make the fox surveyor of the fold ?
Who being accused a crafty murderer,
His guilt should be but idly put over,
Because his purpose is not executed.
No ; let him die, in that he is a fox,
By nature proved an enemy to the flock,
Before his chaps be stain'd with crimson blood,
As Humphrey, proved by reasons, to my liege.
And do not stand on quillets how to slay him :
Be it by gins, by snares, by subtlety,
Sleeping or waking, 'tis no matter how,
So he be dead ; for that is good deceit
Which mates him first that first intends deceit.
   Queen. Thrice-noble Suffolk, 'tis resolutely spoke.
   Suf. Not resolute, except so much were done ;
For things are often spoke and seldom meant :
But that my heart accordeth with my tongue,
Seeing the deed is meritorious,   270
And to preserve my sovereign from his foe,
Say but the word, and I will be his priest.
   Car. But I would have him dead, my Lord of Suffolk,
Ere you can take due orders for a priest :
Say you consent and censure well the deed,
And I'll provide his executioner,
I tender so the safety of my liege.
   Suf. Here is my hand, the deed is worthy doing.
   Queen. And so say I.
   York. And I : and now we three have spoke it,   280
It skills not greatly who impugns our doom.

Enter a Post.

Post. Great lords, from Ireland am I come amain,
To signify that rebels there are up
And put the Englishmen unto the sword :
Send succors, lords, and stop the rage betime,
Before the wound do grow uncurable ;
For, being green, there is great hope of help.
   Car. A breach that craves a quick expedient stop !
What counsel give you in this weighty cause ?
   York. That Somerset be sent as regent thither ?   290
'Tis meet that lucky ruler be employ'd ;
Witness the fortune he hath had in France.
   Som. If York, with all his far-fet policy,
Had been the regent there instead of me,
He never would have stay'd in France so long.
   York. No, not to lose it all, as thou hast done :
I rather would have lost my life betimes
Than bring a burthen of dishonor home
By staying there so long till all were lost.
Show me one scar character'd on thy skin :300
Men's flesh preserved so whole do seldom win.
   Queen. Nay, then, this spark will prove a raging fire,
If wind and fuel be brought to feed it with :
No more, good York ; sweet Somerset, be still :
Thy fortune, York, hadst thou been regent there,
Might happily have proved far worse than his.
   York. What, worse than nought ? nay, then, a shame take all !
   Som. And, in the number, thee that wishest shame !
   Car. My Lord of York, try what your fortune is.
The uncivil kerns of Ireland are in arms   310
And temper clay with blood of Englishmen :
To Ireland will you lead a band of men,
Collected choicely, from each county some,
And try your hap against the Irishmen ?
   York. I will, my lord, so please his majesty.
   Suf. Why, our authority is his consent,
And what we do establish he confirms :
Then, noble York, take thou this task in hand.
   York. I am content : provide me soldiers, lords,
Whiles I take order for mine own affairs.   320
   Suf. A charge, Lord York, that I will see perform'd.
But now return we to the false Duke Humphrey.
   Car. No more of him ; for I will deal with him
That henceforth he shall trouble us no more.
And so break off ; the day is almost spent :
Lord Suffolk, you and I must talk of that event.
   York. My Lord of Suffolk, within fourteen days
At Bristol I expect my soldiers ;
For there I'll ship them all for Ireland.
   Suf. I'll see it truly done, my Lord of York.
                    [*Exeunt all but York.*
   York. Now, York, or never, steel thy fearful thoughts,   331
And change misdoubt to resolution :

Be that thou hopest to be, or what thou art
Resign to death ; it is not worth the enjoying :
Let pale-faced fear keep with the mean-born man,
And find no harbor in a royal heart.
Faster than spring-time showers comes thought on thought,
And not a thought but thinks on dignity.
My brain more busy than the laboring spider
Weaves tedious snares to trap mine enemies.
Well, nobles, well, 'tis politicly done,
To send me packing with an host of men :
I fear me you but warm the starved snake,
Who, cherish'd in your breasts, will sting your hearts.
'Twas men I lack'd and you will give them me :
I take it kindly ; and yet be well assured
You put sharp weapons in a madman's hands.
Whiles I in Ireland nourish a mighty band,
I will stir up in England some black storm
Shall blow ten thousand souls to heaven or hell ;
And this fell tempest shall not cease to rage
Until the golden circuit on my head,
Like to the glorious sun's transparent beams,
Do calm the fury of this mad-bred flaw.
And, for a minister of my intent,
I have seduced a headstrong Kentishman,
John Cade of Ashford,
To make commotion, as full well he can,
Under the title of John Mortimer.
In Ireland have I seen this stubborn Cade 360
Oppose himself against a troop of kerns,
And fought so long, till that his thighs with darts
Were almost like a sharp-quill'd porpentine ;
And, in the end being rescued, I have seen
Him caper upright like a wild Morisco,
Shaking the bloody darts as he his bells.
Full often, like a shag-hair'd crafty kern,
Hath he conversed with the enemy,
And undiscover'd come to me again
And given me notice of their villanies.   370
This devil here shall be my substitute ;
For that John Mortimer, which now is dead,
In face, in gait, in speech, he doth resemble :
By this I shall perceive the commons' mind,
How they affect the house and claim of York.
Say he be taken, rack'd and tortured,
I know no pain they can inflict upon him
Will make him say I moved him to those arms.
Say that he thrive, as 'tis great like he will,
Why, then from Ireland come I with my strength
And reap the harvest which that rascal sow'd ;
For Humphrey being dead, as he shall be,
And Henry put apart, the next for me. [*Exit.*

Scene II. *Bury St. Edmund's. A room of state.*

Enter certain Murderers, *hastily.*

   First Mur. Run to my Lord of Suffolk ; let him know
We have dispatch'd the duke, as he commanded.
   Sec. Mur. O that it were to do ! What have we done ?
Didst ever hear a man so penitent ?

Enter Suffolk.

   First Mur. Here comes my lord.

Suf. Now, sirs, have you dispatch'd this
　thing ?
First Mur. Ay, my good lord, he's dead.
Suf. Why, that's well said. Go, get you to
　my house ;
I will reward you for this venturous deed.
The king and all the peers are here at hand. 10
Have you laid fair the bed ? Is all things well,
According as I gave directions ?
First Mur. 'Tis, my good lord.
Suf. Away ! be gone. [*Exeunt Murderers.*

Sound trumpets. Enter the KING, *the* QUEEN,
CARDINAL BEAUFORT, SOMERSET, *with Attendants.*

King. Go, call our uncle to our presence
　straight ;
Say we intend to try his grace to-day,
If he be guilty, as 'tis published.
Suf. I'll call him presently, my noble lord.
　　　　　　　　　　　　　　　　[*Exit.*
King. Lords, take your places ; and, I pray
　you all,
Proceed no straiter 'gainst our uncle Glouces-
　ter　　　　　　　　　　　　　　　　20
Than from true evidence of good esteem
He be approved in practice culpable.
Queen. God forbid any malice should pre-
　vail,
That faultless may condemn a nobleman !
Pray God he may acquit him of suspicion !
King. I thank thee, Meg ; these words con-
　tent me much.

Re-enter SUFFOLK.

How now ! why look'st thou pale ? why trem-
　blest thou ?
Where is our uncle ? what's the matter, Suf-
　folk ?
Suf. Dead in his bed, my lord ; Gloucester
　is dead.
Queen. Marry, God forfend !　　　　　30
Car. God's secret judgment : I did dream
　to-night
The duke was dumb and could not speak a
　word.　　　　　　　　　[*The King swoons.*
Queen. How fares my lord ? Help, lords !
　the king is dead.
Som. Rear up his body ; wring him by the
　nose.
Queen. Run, go, help, help ! O Henry, ope
　thine eyes !
Suf. He doth revive again : madam, be pa-
　tient.
King. O heavenly God !
Queen.　　　　　How fares my gracious lord ?
Suf. Comfort, my sovereign ! gracious
　Henry, comfort !
King. What, doth my Lord of Suffolk com-
　fort me ?
Came he right now to sing a raven's note, 40
Whose dismal tune bereft my vital powers ;
And thinks he that the chirping of a wren,
By crying comfort from a hollow breast,
Can chase away the first-conceived sound ?
Hide not thy poison with such sugar'd words ;
Lay not thy hands on me ; forbear, I say ;
Their touch affrights me as a serpent's sting.
Thou baleful messenger, out of my sight !
Upon thy eye-balls murderous tryanny
Sits in grim majesty, to fright the world.　50
Look not upon me, for thine eyes are wound-
　ing :

Yet do not go away : come, basilisk,
And kill the innocent gazer with thy sight ;
For in the shade of death I shall find joy ;
In life but double death, now Gloucester's
　dead.
Queen. Why do you rate my Lord of Suf-
　folk thus ?
Although the duke was enemy to him,
Yet he most Christian-like laments his death :
And for myself, foe as he was to me,
Might liquid tears or heart-offending groans
Or blood-consuming sighs recall his life,　61
I would be blind with weeping, sick with
　groans,
Look pale as primrose with blood-drinking
　sighs,
And all to have the noble duke alive.
What know I how the world may deem of me ?
For it is known we were but hollow friends :
It may be judged I made the duke away ;
So shall my name with slander's tongue be
　wounded,
And princes' courts be fill'd with my reproach.
This get I by his death : ay me, unhappy !　70
To be a queen, and crown'd with infamy !
King. Ah, woe is me for Gloucester,
　wretched man !
Queen. Be woe for me, more wretched
　than he is.
What, dost thou turn away and hide thy face ?
I am no loathsome leper ; look on me.
What ! art thou, like the adder, waxen deaf ?
Be poisonous too and kill thy forlorn queen.
Is all thy comfort shut in Gloucester's tomb ?
Why, then, dame Margaret was ne'er thy joy.
Erect his statue and worship it,　　　　80
And make my image but an alehouse sign.
Was I for this nigh wreck'd upon the sea
And twice by awkward wind from England's
　bank
Drove back again unto my native clime ?
What boded this, but well forewarning wind
Did seem to say ' Seek not a scorpion's nest,
Nor set no footing on this unkind shore ' ?
What did I then, but cursed the gentle gusts
And he that loosed them forth their brazen
　caves :
And bid them blow towards England's blessed
　shore,　　　　　　　　　　　　　90
Or turn our stern upon a dreadful rock
Yet Æolus would not be a murderer,
But left that hateful office unto thee :
The pretty-vaulting sea refused to drown me,
Knowing that thou wouldst have me drown'd
　on shore,
With tears as salt as sea, through thy unkind-
　ness :
The splitting rocks cower'd in the sinking
　sands
And would not dash me with their ragged
　sides,
Because thy flinty heart, more hard than they,
Might in thy palace perish Margaret.　　100
As far as I could ken thy chalky cliffs,
When from thy shore the tempest beat us back,
I stood upon the hatches in the storm,
And when the dusky sky began to rob
My earnest-gaping sight of thy land's view,
I took a costly jewel from my neck,
A heart it was, bound in with diamonds,
And threw it towards thy land : the sea re-
　ceived it,
And so I wish'd thy body might my heart :

And even with this I lost fair England's view
And bid mine eyes be packing with my heart
And call'd them blind and dusky spectacles,
For losing ken of Albion's wished coast.
How often have I tempted Suffolk's tongue,
The agent of thy foul inconstancy,
To sit and witch me, as Ascanius did
When he to madding Dido would unfold
His father's acts commenced in burning Troy!
Am I not witch'd like her? or thou not false
like him?
Ay me, I can no more! die, Margaret!   120
For Henry weeps that thou dost live so long.

Noise within. Enter WARWICK, SALISBURY,
and many Commons.

War. It is reported, mighty sovereign,
That good Duke Humphrey traitorously is
murder'd
By Suffolk and the Cardinal Beaufort's means.
The commons, like an angry hive of bees
That want their leader, scatter up and down
And care not who they sting in his revenge.
Myself have calm'd their spleenful mutiny,
Until they hear the order of his death.
King. That he is dead, good Warwick, 'tis
too true;
But how he died God knows, not Henry:
Enter his chamber, view his breathless corpse,
And comment then upon his sudden death.
War. That shall I do, my liege. Stay,
Salisbury,
With the rude multitude till I return.   [*Exit.*
King. O Thou that judgest all things, stay
my thoughts,
My thoughts, that labor to persuade my soul
Some violent hands were laid on Humphrey's
life!
If my suspect be false, forgive me, God,
For judgment only doth belong to Thee. 140
Fain would I go to chafe his paly lips
With twenty thousand kisses, and to drain
Upon his face an ocean of salt tears,
To tell my love unto his dumb deaf trunk,
And with my fingers feel his hand unfeeling:
But all in vain are these mean obsequies;
And to survey his dead and earthly image,
What were it but to make my sorrow greater?

Re-enter WARWICK *and others, bearing*
GLOUCESTER'S *body on a bed.*

War. Come hither, gracious sovereign,
view this body.
King. That is to see how deep my grave is
made;   150
For with his soul fled all my worldly solace,
For seeing him I see my life in death.
War. As surely as my soul intends to live
With that dread King that took our state upon
him
To free us from his father's wrathful curse,
I do believe that violent hands were laid
Upon the life of this thrice-famed duke.
Suf. A dreadful oath, sworn with a solemn
tongue!
What instance gives Lord Warwick for his
vow?
War. See how the blood is settled in his
face.   160
Oft have I seen a timely-parted ghost,
Of ashy semblance, meagre, pale and blood-
less,
Being all descended to the laboring heart;

Who, in the conflict that it holds with death,
Attracts the same for aidance 'gainst the
enemy;
Which with the heart there cools and ne'er re-
turneth
To blush and beautify the cheek again.
But see, his face is black and full of blood,
His eye-balls further out than when he lived,
Staring full ghastly like a strangled man; 170
His hair uprear'd, his nostrils stretched with
struggling;
His hands abroad display'd, as one that
grasp'd
And tugg'd for life and was by strength sub-
dued:
Look, on the sheets his hair you see, is
sticking;
His well-proportion'd beard made rough and
rugged,
Like to the summer's corn by tempest lodged.
It cannot be but he was murder'd here;
The least of all these signs were probable.
Suf. Why, Warwick, who should do the
duke to death?
Myself and Beaufort had him in protection;
And we, I hope, sir, are no murderers.   181
War. But both of you were vow'd Duke
Humphrey's foes,
And you, forsooth, had the good duke to
keep:
'Tis like you would not feast him like a friend;
And 'tis well seen he found an enemy.
Queen. Then you, belike, suspect these no-
blemen
As guilty of Duke Humphrey's timeless death.
War. Who finds the heifer dead and bleed-
ing fresh
And sees fast by a butcher with an axe,
But will suspect 'twas he that made the slaugh-
ter?   190
Who finds the partridge in the puttock's nest,
But may imagine how the bird was dead,
Although the kite soar with unbloodied beak?
Even so suspicious is this tragedy.
Queen. Are you the butcher, Suffolk?
Where's your knife?
Is Beaufort term'd a kite? Where are his
talons?
Suf. I wear no knife to slaughter sleeping
men;
But here's a vengeful sword, rusted with ease,
That shall be scoured in his rancorous heart
That slanders me with murder's crimson
badge.
Say, if thou darest, proud Lord of Warwick-
shire,
That I am faulty in Duke Humphrey's death.
[*Exeunt Cardinal, Somerset, and others.*
War. What dares not Warwick, if false
Suffolk dare him?
Queen. He dares not calm his contumelious
spirit
Nor cease to be an arrogant controller,
Though Suffolk dare him twenty thousand
times.
War. Madam, be still; with reverence may
I say;
For every word you speak in his behalf
Is slander to your royal dignity.
Suf. Blunt-witted lord, ignoble in de-
meanor!   210
If ever lady wrong'd her lord so much,
Thy mother took into her blameful bed

Some stern untutor'd churl, and noble stock
Was graft with crab-tree slip ; whose fruit thou
art,
And never of the Nevils' noble race.
    War. But that the guilt of murder bucklers
        thee
And I should rob the deathsman of his fee,
Quitting thee thereby of ten thousand shames,
And that my sovereign's presence makes me
        mild,   219
I would, false murderous coward, on thy knee
Make thee beg pardon for thy passed speech,
And say it was thy mother that thou meant'st
That thou thyself was born in bastardy ;
And after all this fearful homage done,
Give thee thy hire and send thy soul to hell,
Pernicious blood-sucker of sleeping men !
    Suf. Thou shall be waking while I shed thy
        blood,
If from this presence thou darest go with me.
    War. Away even now, or I will drag thee
        hence :   229
Unworthy though thou art, I'll cope with thee
And do some service to Duke Humphrey's
        ghost.   [*Exeunt Suffolk and Warwick.*
    King. What stronger breastplate than a
        heart untainted !
Thrice is he armed that hath his quarrel just,
And he but naked, though lock'd up in steel
Whose conscience with injustice is corrupted.
                             [*A noise within.*
    Queen. What noise is this ?

*Re-enter SUFFOLK and WARWICK, with their
    weapons drawn.*

    King. Why, how now, lords ! your wrath-
        ful weapons drawn
Here in our presence ! dare you be so bold ?
Why, what tumultuous clamor have we here ?
    Suf. The traitorous Warwick with the men
        of Bury   240
Set all upon me, mighty sovereign.
    Sal. [*To the Commons, entering*] Sirs,
        stand apart ; the king shall know your
        mind.
Dread lord, the commons send you word by
        me,
Unless Lord Suffolk straight be done to death,
Or banished fair England's territories,
They will by violence tear him from your
        palace
And torture him with grievous lingering death.
They say, by him the good Duke Humphrey
        died ;
They say, in him they fear your highness'
        death ;
And mere instinct of love and loyalty,   250
Free from a stubborn opposite intent,
As being thought to contradict your liking,
Makes them thus forward in his banishment.
They say, in care of your most royal person,
That if your highness should intend to sleep
And charge that no man should disturb your
        rest
In pain of your dislike or pain of death,
Yet, notwithstanding such a strait edict,
Were there a serpent seen, with forked tongue,
That slily glided towards your majesty,   260
It were but necessary you were waked,
Lest, being suffer'd in that harmful slumber,
The mortal worm might make the sleep
        eternal ;
And therefore do they cry, though you forbid,

That they will guard you, whether you will or
        no,
From such fell serpents as false Suffolk is,
With whose envenomed and fatal sting,
Your loving uncle, twenty times his worth,
They say, is shamefully bereft of life.
    Commons. [*Within*] An answer from the
        king, my Lord of Salisbury !   270
    Suf. 'Tis like the commons, rude unpolish'd
        hinds,
Could send such message to their sovereign :
But you, my lord, were glad to be employ'd,
To show how quaint an orator you are :
But all the honor Salisbury hath won
Is, that he was the lord ambassador
Sent from a sort of tinkers to the king.
    Commons. [*Within*] An answer from the
        king, or we will all break in !
    King. Go, Salisbury, and tell them all from
        me,
I thank them for their tender loving care ; 280
And had I not been cited so by them,
Yet did I purpose as they do entreat ;
For, sure, my thoughts do hourly prophesy
Mischance unto my state by Suffolk's means :
And therefore, by His majesty I swear,
Whose far unworthy deputy I am,
He shall not breathe infection in this air
But three days longer, on the pain of death.
                              [*Exit Salisbury.*
    Queen. O Henry, let me plead for gentle
        Suffolk !
    King. Ungentle queen, to call him gentle
        Suffolk !   290
No more, I say : if thou dost plead for him,
Thou wilt but add increase unto my wrath.
Had I but said, I would have kept my word,
But when I swear, it is irrevocable.
If, after three days' space, thou here be'st
        found
On any ground that I am ruler of,
The world shall not be ransom for thy life.
Come, Warwick, come, good Warwick, go with
        me ;
I have great matters to impart to thee.
                [*Exeunt all but Queen and Suffolk.*
    Queen. Mischance and sorrow go along
        with you !   300
Heart's discontent and sour affliction
Be playfellows to keep you company !
There's two of you ; the devil make a third !
And threefold vengeance tend upon your
        steps !
    Suf. Cease, gentle queen, these execrations,
And let thy Suffolk take his heavy leave.
    Queen. Fie, coward woman and soft-
        hearted wretch !
Hast thou not spirit to curse thine enemy ?
    Suf. A plague upon them ! wherefore
        should I curse them ?
Would curses kill, as doth the mandrake's
        groan,   310
I would invent as bitter-searching terms,
As curst, as harsh and horrible to hear,
Deliver'd strongly through my fixed teeth,
With full as many signs of deadly hate,
As lean-faced Envy in her loathsome cave :
My tongue should stumble in mine earnest
        words ;
Mine eyes should sparkle like the beaten flint ;
Mine hair be fixed on end, as one distract ;
Ay, every joint should seem to curse and ban :

And even now my burthen'd heart would
  break,   320
Should I not curse them. Poison be their
  drink !
Gall, worse than gall, the daintiest that they
  taste !
Their sweetest shade a grove of cypress trees !
Their chiefest prospect murdering basilisks !
Their softest touch as smart as lizards' sting !
Their music frightful as the serpent's hiss,
And boding screech-owls make the concert
  full !
All the foul terrors in dark-seated hell—
  Queen. Enough, sweet Suffolk ; thou tor-
    ment'st thyself ;
And these dread curses, like the sun 'gainst
  glass,   330
Or like an overcharged gun, recoil,
And turn the force of them upon thyself.
  Suf. You bade me ban, and will you bid
    me leave ?
Now, by the ground that I am banish'd from,
Well could I curse away a winter's night,
Though standing naked on a mountain top,
Where biting cold would never let grass grow,
And think it but a minute spent in sport.
  Queen. O, let me entreat thee cease. Give
    me thy hand,
That I may dew it with my mournful tears ;
Nor let the rain of heaven wet this place,   341
To wash away my woful monuments.
O, could this kiss be printed in thy hand,
That thou mightst think upon these by the seal,
Through whom a thousand sighs are breathed
  for thee !
So, get thee gone, that I may know my grief ;
'Tis but surmised whiles thou art standing by,
As one that surfeits thinking on a want.
I will repeal thee, or, be well assured,
Adventure to be banished myself :   350
And banished I am, if but from thee.
Go ; speak not to me ; even now be gone.
O, go not yet ! Even thus two friends con-
  demn'd
Embrace and kiss and take ten thousand
  leaves,
Loather a hundred times to part than die.
Yet now farewell ; and farewell life with thee !
  Suf. Thus is poor Suffolk ten times
    banished ;
Once by the king, and three times thrice by
  thee.
'Tis not the land I care for, wert thou thence ;
A wilderness is populous enough,   360
So Suffolk had thy heavenly company :
For where thou art, there is the world itself,
With every several pleasure in the world,
And where thou art not, desolation.
I can no more : live thou to joy thy life ;
Myself no joy in nought but that thou livest.

Enter Vaux.

  Queen. Whither goes Vaux so fast ? what
    news, I prithee ?
  Vaux. To signify unto his majesty
That Cardinal Beaufort is at point of death ;
For suddenly a grievous sickness took him, 370
That makes him gasp and stare and catch the
  air,
Blaspheming God and cursing men on earth.
Sometimes he talks as if Duke Humphrey's
  ghost
Were by his side ; sometime he calls the king,

And whispers to his pillow, as to him,
The secrets of his overcharged soul ;
And I am sent to tell his majesty
That even now he cries aloud for him.
  Queen. Go tell this heavy message to the
    king.   [*Exit Vaux.*
Ay me ! what is this world ! what news are
  these !   380
But wherefore grieve I at an hour's poor loss,
Omitting Suffolk's exile, my soul's treasure ?
Why only, Suffolk, mourn I not for thee,
And with the southern clouds contend in tears,
Theirs for the earth's increase, mine for my
  sorrows ?
Now get thee hence : the king, thou know'st,
  is coming ;
If thou be found by me, thou art but dead.
  Suf. If I depart from thee, I cannot live ;
And in thy sight to die, what were it else
But like a pleasant slumber in thy lap ?   390
Here could I breathe my soul into the air,
As mild and gentle as the cradle-babe
Dying with mother's dug between its lips :
Where, from thy sight, I should be raging mad,
And cry out for thee to close up mine eyes,
To have thee with thy lips to stop my mouth ;
So shouldst thou either turn my flying soul,
Or I should breathe it so into thy body,
And then it lived in sweet Elysium.
To die by thee were but to die in jest ;   400
From thee to die were torture more than
  death :
O, let me stay, befall what may befall !
  Queen. Away ! though parting be a fretful
    corrosive,
It is applied to a deathful wound.
To France, sweet Suffolk : let me hear from
  thee ;
For wheresoe'er thou art in this world's globe,
I'll have an Iris that shall find thee out.
  Suf. I go.
  Queen. And take my heart with thee.
  Suf. A jewel, lock'd into the wofull'st cask
That ever did contain a thing of worth.   410
Even as a splitted bark, so sunder we :
This way fall I to death.
  Queen.   This way for me.
                          [*Exeunt severally.*

SCENE III. *A bedchamber.*

Enter the King, Salisbury, Warwick, *to the*
  Cardinal *in bed.*

  King. How fares my lord ? speak, Beau-
    fort, to thy sovereign ?
  Car. If thou be'st death, I'll give thee Eng-
    land's treasure,
Enough to purchase such another island,
So thou wilt let me live, and feel no pain.
  King. Ah, what a sign it is of evil life,
Where death's approach is seen so terrible !
  War. Beaufort, it is thy sovereign speaks
    to thee.
  Car. Bring me unto my trial when you will.
Died he not in his bed ? where should he die ?
Can I make men live, whether they will or no ?
O, torture me no more ! I will confess.
Alive again ? then show me where he is :
I'll give a thousand pound to look upon him.
He hath no eyes, the dust hath blinded them.
Comb down his hair ; look, look ! it stands up-
  right,
Like lime-twigs set to catch my winged soul.

Give me some drink; and bid the apothecary
Bring the strong poison that I bought of him.
  King. O thou eternal Mover of the heav-
      ens,
Look with a gentle eye upon this wretch! 20
O, beat away the busy meddling fiend
That lays strong siege unto this wretch's soul,
And from his bosom purge this black despair!
  War. See, how the pangs of death do make
      him grin!
  Sal. Disturb him not; let him pass peace-
      ably.
  King. Peace to his soul, if God's good
      pleasure be!
Lord cardinal, if thou think'st on heaven's
      bliss,
Hold up thy hand, make signal of thy hope.
He dies, and makes no sign. O God, forgive
      him!
  War. So bad a death argues a monstrous
      life.   30
  King. Forbear to judge, for we are sinners
      all.
Close up his eyes and draw the curtain close;
And let us all to meditation.   [*Exeunt.*

ACT IV.

SCENE I. *The coast of Kent.*

*Alarum. Fight at sea. Ordnance goes off.
  Enter a* Captain, *a* Master, *a* Master's-Mate,
  WALTER WHITMORE, *and others; with them*
  SUFFOLK, *and others, prisoners.*

  Cap. The gaudy, blabbing and remorseful
      day
Is crept into the bosom of the sea;
And now loud-howling wolves arouse the jades
That drag the tragic melancholy night;
Who, with their drowsy, slow and flagging
      wings,
Clip dead men's graves and from their misty
      jaws
Breathe foul contagious darkness in the air.
Therefore bring forth the soldiers of our
      prize;
For, whilst our pinnace anchors in the Downs,
Here shall they make their ransom on the
      sand,   10
Or with their blood stain this discolor'd shore.
Master, this prisoner freely give I thee;
And thou that art his mate, make boot of this;
The other, Walter Whitmore, is thy share.
  First Gent. What is my ransom, master?
      let me know.
  Mast. A thousand crowns, or else lay down
      your head.
  Mate. And so much shall you give, or off
      goes yours.
  Cap. What, think you much to pay two
      thousand crowns,
And bear the name and port of gentlemen?
Cut both the villains' throats; for die you
      shall: 20
The lives of those which we have lost in fight
Be counterpoised with such a petty sum!
  First Gent. I'll give it, sir; and therefore
      spare my life.
  Sec. Gent. And so will I and write home
      for it straight.
  Whit. I lost mine eye in laying the prize
      aboard,

And therefore to revenge it, shalt thou die;
                                    [*To Suf.*
And so should these, if I might have my will.
  Cap. Be not so rash; take ransom, let him
      live.
  Suf. Look on my George; I am a gentle-
      man:
Rate me at what thou wilt, thou shalt be
      paid.   30
  Whit. And so am I; my name is Walter
      Whitmore.
How now! why start'st thou? what, doth
      death affright?
  Suf. Thy name affrights me, in whose
      sound is death.
A cunning man did calculate my birth
And told me that by water I should die:
Yet let not this make thee be bloody-minded;
Thy name is Gaultier, being rightly sounded.
  Whit. Gaultier or Walter, which it is, I
      care not:
Never yet did base dishonor blur our name,
But with our sword we wiped away the blot;
Therefore, when merchant-like I sell revenge,
Broke be my sword, my arms torn and de-
      faced,
And I proclaim'd a coward through the
      world!
  Suf. Stay, Whitmore; for thy prisoner is
      a prince,
The Duke of Suffolk, William de la Pole.
  Whit. The Duke of Suffolk muffled up in
      rags!
  Suf. Ay, but these rags are no part of the
      duke:
Jove sometimes went disguised, and why not
      I?
  Cap. But Jove was never slain, as thou
      shalt be.
  Suf. Obscure and lowly swain, King
      Henry's blood,   50
The honorable blood of Lancaster,
Must not be shed by such a jaded groom.
Hast thou not kiss'd thy hand and held my
      stirrup?
Bare-headed plodded by my foot-cloth mule
And thought thee happy when I shook my
      head?
How often hast thou waited at my cup,
Fed from my trencher, kneel'd down at the
      board,
When I have feasted with Queen Margaret?
Remember it and let it make thee crest-fall'n,
Ay, and allay this thy abortive pride;   60
How in our voiding lobby hast thou stood
And duly waited for my coming forth?
This hand of mine hath writ in thy behalf,
And therefore shall it charm thy riotous
      tongue.
  Whit. Speak, captain, shall I stab the for-
      lorn swain?
  Cap. First let my words stab him, as he
      hath me.
  Suf. Base slave, thy words are blunt and
      so art thou.
  Cap. Convey him hence and on our long-
      boat's side
Strike off his head.
  Suf.   Thou darest not, for thy own.
  Cap. Yes, Pole.
  Suf.   Pole!
  Cap.   Pool! Sir Pool! lord! 70
Ay, kennel, puddle, sink; whose filth and dirt

Troubles the silver spring where England
    drinks.
Now will I dam up this thy yawning mouth
For swallowing the treasure of the realm :
Thy lips that kiss'd the queen shall sweep the
    ground ;
And thou that smiledst at good Duke Hum-
    phrey's death,
Against the senseless winds shalt grin in vain,
Who in contempt shall hiss at thee again :
And wedded be thou to the hags of hell,
For daring to affy a mighty lord   80
Unto the daughter of a worthless king,
Having neither subject, wealth, nor diadem.
By devilish policy art thou grown great,
And, like ambitious Sylla, overgorged
With gobbets of thy mother's bleeding heart.
By thee Anjou and Maine were sold to France,
The false revolting Normans thorough thee
Disdain to call us lord, and Picardy
Hath slain their governors, surprised our forts,
And sent the ragged soldiers wounded home.
The princely Warwick, and the Nevils all,   91
Whose dreadful swords were never drawn in
    vain,
As hating thee, are rising up in arms :
And now the house of York, thrust from the
    crown
By shameful murder of a guiltless king
And lofty proud encroaching tyranny,
Burns with revenging fire ; whose hopeful
    colors
Advance our half-faced sun, striving to shine,
Under the which is writ ' Invitis nubibus.'
The commons here in Kent are up in
    arms :   100
And, to conclude, reproach and beggary
Is crept into the palace of our king.
And all by thee. Away ! convey him hence.
Suf. O that I were a god, to shoot forth
    thunder
Upon these paltry, servile, abject drudges !
Small things make base men proud : this vil-
    lain here,
Being captain of a pinnace, threatens more
Than Bargulus the strong Illyrian pirate.
Drones suck not eagles' blood but rob bee-
    hives :
It is impossible that I should die   110
By such a lowly vassal as thyself.
Thy words move rage and not remorse in me :
I go of message from the queen to France ;
I charge thee waft me safely cross the
    Channel.
Cap. Walter,—
Whit. Come, Suffolk, I must waft thee to
    thy death.
Suf. Gelidus timor occupat artus it is thee
    I fear.
Whit. Thou shalt have cause to fear before
    I leave thee.
What, are ye daunted now ? now will ye
    stoop ?
First Gent. My gracious lord, entreat him,
    speak him fair.   120
Suf. Suffolk's imperial tongue is stern and
    rough,
Used to command, untaught to plead for
    favor.
Far be it we should honor such as these
With humble suit : no, rather let my head
Stoop to the block than these knees bow to any
Save to the God of heaven and to my king ;

And sooner dance upon a bloody pole
Than stand uncover'd to the vulgar groom.
True nobility is exempt from fear :
More can I bear than you dare execute.   130
    Cap. Hale him away, and let him talk no
    more.
    Suf. Come, soldiers, show what cruelty ye
    can,
That this my death may never be forgot !
Great men oft die by vile bezonians :
A Roman sworder and banditto slave
Murder'd sweet Tully ; Brutus' bastard hand
Stabb'd Julius Cæsar ; savage islanders
Pompey the Great ; and Suffolk dies by pirates.
    [*Exeunt Whitmore and others with Suffolk.*
    Cap. And as for these whose ransom we
    have set,
It is our pleasure one of them depart ;   140
Therefore come you with us and let him go.
    [*Exeunt all but the First Gentleman.*

Re-enter WHITMORE *with* SUFFOLK'S *body.*

    Whit. There let his head and lifeless body
    lie,
Until the queen his mistress bury it.   [*Exit.*
    First Gent. O barbarous and bloody spec-
    tacle !
His body will I bear unto the king :
If he revenge it not, yet will his friends ;
So will the queen, that living held him dear.
    [*Exit with the body.*

    Scene II. *Blackheath.*

    Enter GEORGE BEVIS *and* JOHN HOLLAND.

    Bevis. Come, and get thee a sword, though
made of a lath ; they have been up these two
days.
    Holl. They have the more need to sleep
now, then.
    Bevis. I tell thee, Jack Cade the clothier
means to dress the commonwealth, and turn
it, and set a new nap upon it.
    Holl. So he had need, for 'tis threadbare.
Well, I say it was never merry world in England since gentlemen came up.   10
    Bevis. O miserable age ! virtue is not re-
garded in handicrafts-men.
    Holl. The nobility think scorn to go in
leather aprons.
    Bevis. Nay, more, the king's council are no
good workmen.
    Holl. True ; and yet it is said, labor in thy
vocation ; which is as much to say as, let the
magistrates be laboring men ; and therefore
should we be magistrates.   20
    Bevis. Thou hast hit it ; for there's no bet-
ter sign of a brave mind than a hard hand.
    Holl. I see them ! I see them ! there's Best's
son, the tanner of Wingham,—
    Bevis. He shall have the skin of our ene-
mies, to make dog's-leather of.
    Holl. And Dick the Butcher,—
    Bevis. Then is sin struck down like an ox,
and iniquity's throat cut like a calf.
    Holl. And Smith the weaver,—   30
    Bevis. Argo, their thread of life is spun.
    Holl. Come, come, let's fall in with them.

Drum. Enter CADE, DICK *the Butcher*, SMITH
    *the Weaver, and a Sawyer, with infinite
    numbers.*

    Cade. We John Cade, so termed of our
supposed father,—

Dick. [*Aside*] Or rather, of stealing a cade of horrings.

Cade. For our enemies shall fall before us, inspired with the spirit of putting down kings and princes,—Command silence.

Dick. Silence!   40

Cade. My father was a Mortimer,—

Dick. [*Aside*] He was an honest man, and a good bricklayer.

Cade. My mother a Plantagenet,—

Dick. [*Aside*] I knew her well; she was a midwife.

Cade. My wife descended of the Lacies,—

Dick. [*Aside*] She was, indeed, a pedler's daughter, and sold many laces.   49

Smith. [*Aside*] But now of late, notable to travel with her furred pack, she washes bucks here at home.

Cade. Therefore am I of an honorable house.

Dick. [*Aside*] Ay, by my faith, the field is honorable; and there was he borne, under a hedge, for his father had never a house but the cage.

Cade. Valiant I am.

Smith. [*Aside*] A' must needs; for beggary is valiant.

Cade. I am able to endure much.   60

Dick. [*Aside*] No question of that; for I have seen him whipped three market-days together.

Cade. I fear neither sword nor fire.

Smith. [*Aside*] He need not fear the sword; for his coat is of proof.

Dick. [*Aside*] But methinks he should stand in fear of fire, being burnt i' the hand for stealing of sheep.

Cade. Be brave, then; for your captain is brave, and vows reformation. There shall be in England seven halfpenny loaves sold for a penny: the three-hooped pot shall have ten hoops; and I will make it felony to drink small beer: all the realm shall be in common; and in Cheapside shall my palfrey go to grass: and when I am king, as king I will be,—

All. God save your majesty!

Cade. I thank you, good people: there shall be no money; all shall eat and drink on my score; and I will apparel them all in one livery, that they may agree like brothers and worship me their lord.

Dick. The first thing we do, let's kill all the lawyers.

Cade. Nay, that I mean to do. Is not this a lamentable thing, that of the skin of an innocent lamb should be made parchment? that parchment, being scribbled o'er, should undo a man? Some say the bee stings: but I say, 'tis the bee's wax; for I did but seal once to a thing, and I was never mine own man since. How now! who's there?   91

Enter some, bringing forward the Clerk *of Chatham.*

Smith. The clerk of Chatham: he can write and read and cast accompt.

Cade. O monstrous!

Smith. We took him setting of boys' copies.

Cade. Here's a villain!

Smith. Has a book in his pocket with red letters in't.

Cade. Nay, then, he is a conjurer.   100

Dick. Nay, he can make obligations, and write court-hand.

Cade. I am sorry for't: the man is a proper man, of mine honor; unless I find him guilty, he shall not die. Come hither, sirrah, I must examine thee: what is thy name?

Clerk. Emmanuel.

Dick. They use to write it on the top of letters: 'twill go hard with you.

Cade. Let me alone. Dost thou use to write thy name? or hast thou a mark to thyself, like an honest plain-dealing man?   111

Clerk. Sir, I thank God, I have been so well brought up that I can write my name.

All. He hath confessed: away with him! he's a villain and a traitor.

Cade. Away with him, I say! hang him with his pen and ink-horn about his neck.

[*Exit one with the Clerk.*

Enter MICHAEL.

Mich. Where's our general?

Cade. Here I am, thou particular fellow.   119

Mich. Fly, fly, fly! Sir Humphrey Stafford and his brother are hard by, with the king's forces.

Cade. Stand, villain, stand, or I'll fell thee down. He shall be encountered with a man as good as himself: he is but a knight, is a'?

Mich. No.

Cade. To equal him, I will make myself a knight presently. [*Kneels*] Rise up Sir John Mortimer. [*Rises*] Now have at him!

Enter SIR HUMPHREY STAFFORD *and his* Brother, *with drum and soldiers.*

Staf. Rebellious hinds, the filth and scum of Kent,   130
Mark'd for the gallows, lay your weapons down;
Home to your cottages, forsake this groom:
The king is merciful, if you revolt.

Bro. But angry, wrathful, and inclined to blood,
If you go forward; therefore yield, or die.

Cade. As for these silken-coated slaves, I pass not:
It is to you, good people, that I speak,
Over whom, in time to come, I hope to reign;
For I am rightful heir unto the crown.   139

Staf. Villain, thy father was a plasterer;
And thou thyself a shearman, art thou not?

Cade. And Adam was a gardener.

Bro. And what of that?

Cade. Marry, this: Edmund Mortimer, Earl of March,
Married the Duke of Clarence' daughter, did he not?

Staf. Ay, sir.

Cade. By her he had two children at one birth.

Bro. That's false.

Cade. Ay, there's the question; but I say, 'tis true:
The elder of them, being put to nurse,   150
Was by a beggar-woman stolen away;
And, ignorant of his birth and parentage,
Became a bricklayer when he came to age:
His son am I; deny it, if you can.

Dick. Nay, 'tis too true; therefore he shall be king.

Smith. Sir, he made a chimney in my father's house, and the bricks are alive at this day to testify it; therefore deny it not.

Staf. And will you credit this base drudge's words,
That speaks he knows not what ? 160

All. Ay, marry, will we; therefore get ye gone.

Bro. Jack Cade, the Duke of York hath taught you this.

Cade. [*Aside*] He lies, for I invented it myself,
Go to, sirrah, tell the king from me, that, for his father's sake, Henry the Fifth, in whose time boys went to span-counter for French crowns, I am content he shall reign; but I'll be protector over him.

Dick. And furthermore, we'll have the Lord Say's head for selling the dukedom of Maine.

Cade. And good reason; for thereby is England mained, and fain to go with a staff, but that my puissance holds it up. Fellow kings, I tell you that that Lord Say hath gelded the commonwealth, and made it an eunuch: and more than that, he can speak French; and therefore he is a traitor.

Staf. O gross and miserable ignorance !

Cade. Nay, answer, if you can: the Frenchmen are our enemies; go to, then, I ask but this: can he that speaks with the tongue of an enemy be a good counsellor, or no ?

All. No, no; and therefore we'll have his head.

Bro. Well, seeing gentle words will not prevail,
Assail them with the army of the king.

Staf. Herald, away; and throughout every town
Proclaim them traitors that are up with Cade;
That those which fly before the battle ends
May, even in their wives' and children's sight,
Be hang'd up for example at their doors: 190
And you that be the king's friends, follow me.
[*Exeunt the two Staffords, and soldiers.*

Cade. And you that love the commons, follow me.
Now show yourselves men; 'tis for liberty.
We will not leave one lord, one gentleman:
Spare none but such as go in clouted shoon;
For they are thrifty honest men, and such
As would, but that they dare not, take our parts.

Dick. They are all in order and march toward us.

Cade. But then are we in order when we are most out of order. Come, march forward. [*Exeunt.* 200

SCENE III. *Another part of Blackheath.*

Alarums to the fight, wherein both the STAFFORDS *are slain. Enter* CADE *and the rest.*

Cade. Where's Dick, the butcher of Ashford ?

Dick. Here, sir.

Cade. They fell before thee like sheep and oxen, and thou behavedst thyself as if thou hadst been in thine own slaughter-house: therefore thus will I reward thee, the Lent shall be as long again as it is; and thou shalt have a license to kill for a hundred lacking one.

Dick. I desire no more. 10

Cade. And, to speak truth, thou deservest no less. This monument of the victory will I bear [*putting on Sir Humphrey's brigandine*]; and the bodies shall be dragged at my horse' heels till I do come to London, where we will have the mayor's sword borne before us.

Dick. If we mean to thrive and do good, break open the gaols and let out the prisoners.

Cade. Fear not that, I warrant thee. Come, let's march towards London. [*Exeunt.* 20

SCENE IV. *London. The palace.*

Enter the KING *with a supplication, and the* QUEEN *with* SUFFOLK'S *head, the* DUKE OF BUCKINGHAM *and the* LORD SAY.

Queen. Oft have I heard that grief softens the mind,
And makes it fearful and degenerate;
Think therefore on revenge and cease to weep.
But who can cease to weep and look on this ?
Here may his head lie on my throbbing breast:
But where's the body that I should embrace ?

Buck. What answer makes your grace to the rebels' supplication ?

King. I'll send some holy bishop to entreat;
For God forbid so many simple souls 10
Should perish by the sword ! And I myself,
Rather than bloody war shall cut them short,
Will parley with Jack Cade their general:
But stay, I'll read it over once again.

Queen. Ah, barbarous villains ! hath this lovely face
Ruled, like a wandering planet, over me,
And could it not enforce them to relent,
That were unworthy to behold the same ?

King. Lord Say, Jack Cade hath sworn to have thy head.

Say. Ay, but I hope your highness shall have his. 20

King. How now, madam !
Still lamenting and mourning for Suffolk's death ?
I fear me, love, if that I had been dead,
Thou wouldst not have mourn'd so much for me.

Queen. No, my love, I should not mourn, but die for thee.

Enter a Messenger.

King. How now ! what news ? why comest thou in such haste ?

Mess. The rebels are in Southwark; fly, my lord !
Jack Cade proclaims himself Lord Mortimer,
Descended from the Duke of Clarence' house,
And calls your grace usurper openly 30
And vows to crown himself in Westminster.
His army is a ragged multitude
Of hinds and peasants, rude and merciless:
Sir Humphrey Stafford and his brother's death
Hath given them heart and courage to proceed:
All scholars, lawyers, courtiers, gentlemen,
They call false caterpillars, and intend their death.

King. O graceless men ! they know not what they do.

Buck. My gracious lord, return to Killingworth,
Until a power be raised to put them down. 40

Queen. Ah, were the Duke of Suffolk now
alive,
These Kentish rebels would be soon appeased !
King. Lord Say, the traitors hate thee ;
Therefore away with us to Killingworth.
Say. So might your grace's person be in
danger.
The sight of me is odious in their eyes ;
And therefore in this city will I stay
And live alone as secret as I may.

Enter another Messenger.

Mess. Jack Cade hath gotten London
bridge :
The citizens fly and forsake their houses :   50
The rascal people, thirsting after prey,
Join with the traitor, and they jointly swear
To spoil the city and your royal court.
Buck. Then linger not, my lord ; away, take
horse.
King. Come, Margaret ; God, our hope,
will succor us.
Queen. My hope is gone, now Suffolk is
deceased.
King. Farewell, my lord : trust not the
Kentish rebels.
Buck. Trust nobody, for fear you be be-
tray'd.
Say. The trust I have is in mine innocence,
And therefore am I bold and resolute.   60
                                        [*Exeunt.*

SCENE V. *London. The Tower.*

Enter LORD SCALES *upon the Tower, walking.
Then enter two or three* Citizens *below.*

Scales. How now ! is Jack Cade slain ?
First Cit. No, my lord, nor likely to be
slain ; for they have won the bridge, killing all
those that withstand them : the lord mayor
craves aid of your honor from the Tower, to
defend the city from the rebels.
Scales. Such aid as I can spare you shall
command ;
But I am troubled here with them myself ;
The rebels have assay'd to win the Tower.
But get you to Smithfield, and gather head,   10
And thither I will send you Matthew Goffe ;
Fight for your king, your country and your
lives ;
And so, farewell, for I must hence again.
                                        [*Exeunt.*

SCENE VI. *London. Cannon Street.*

Enter JACK CADE *and the rest, and strikes his
staff on London-stone.*

Cade. Now is Mortimer lord of this city.
And here, sitting upon London-stone, I charge
and command that, of the city's cost, the
pissing-conduit run nothing but claret wine this
first year of our reign. And now henceforward
it shall be treason for any that calls me other
than Lord Mortimer.

Enter a Soldier, *running.*

Sold. Jack Cade ! Jack Cade !
Cade. Knock him down there.
                                [*They kill him.*
Smith. If this fellow be wise, he'll never
call ye Jack Cade more : I think he hath a
very fair warning.
Dick. My lord, there's an army gathered
together in Smithfield.
Cade. Come, then, let's go fight with them ;

but first, go and set London bridge on fire ;
and, if you can, burn down the Tower too.
Come, let's away.   [*Exeunt.*

SCENE VII. *London. Smithfield.*

Alarums. MATTHEW GOFFE *is slain, and all
the rest. Then enter* JACK CADE, *with his
company.*

Cade. So, sirs : now go some and pull
down the Savoy ; others to the inns of court ;
down with them all.
Dick. I have a suit unto your lordship.
Cade. Be it a lordship, thou shalt have it
for that word.
Dick. Only that the laws of England may
come out of your mouth.
Holl. [*Aside*] Mass, 'twill be sore law,
then ; for he was thrust in the mouth with a
spear, and 'tis not whole yet.   11
Smith. [*Aside*] Nay, John, it will be stinking law ; for his breath stinks with eating
toasted cheese.
Cade. I have thought upon it, it shall be so.
Away, burn all the records of the realm : my
mouth shall be the parliament of England.
Holl. [*Aside*] Then we are like to have
biting statutes, unless his teeth be pulled out.
Cade. And henceforward all things shall
be in common.   21

Enter a Messenger.

Mess. My lord, a prize, a prize ! here's the
Lord Say, which sold the towns in France ; he
that made us pay one and twenty fifteens, and
one shilling to the pound, the last subsidy.

Enter GEORGE BEVIS, *with the* LORD SAY.

Cade. Well, he shall be beheaded for it ten
times. Ah, thou say, thou serge, nay, thou
buckram lord ! now art thou within point-
blank of our jurisdiction regal. What canst
thou answer to my majesty for giving up of
Normandy unto Mounsieur Basimecu, the dauphin of France ? Be it known unto thee by
these presence, even the presence of Lord Mortimer, that I am the besom that must sweep
the court clean of such filth as thou art. Thou
hast most traitorously corrupted the youth of
the realm in erecting a grammar school ; and
whereas, before, our forefathers had no other
books but the score and the tally, thou hast
caused printing to be used, and, contrary to
the king, his crown and dignity, thou hast built
a paper-mill. It will be proved to thy face that
thou hast men about thee that usually talk of a
noun and a verb, and such abominable words
as no Christian ear can endure to hear. Thou
hast appointed justices of peace, to call poor
men before them about matters they were not
able to answer. Moreover, thou hast put them
in prison ; and because they could not read,
thou hast hanged them ; when, indeed, only for
that cause they have been most worthy to live.
Thou dost ride in a foot-cloth, dost thou not ?
Say. What of that ?
Cade. Marry, thou oughtest not to let thy
horse wear a cloak, when honester men than
thou go in their hose and doublets.
Dick. And work in their shirt too ; as myself, for example, that am a butcher.
Say. You men of Kent,—
Dick. What say you of Kent ?   60

Say. Nothing but this; 'tis 'bona terra, mala gens.'

Cade. Away with him, away with him! he speaks Latin.

Say. Hear me but speak, and bear me where you will.

Kent, in the Commentaries Cæsar writ,
Is term'd the civil'st place of all this isle :
Sweet is the country, because full of riches ;
The people liberal, valiant, active, wealthy ;
Which makes me hope you are not void of pity.
I sold not Maine, I lost not Normandy,   70
Yet, to recover them, would lose my life.
Justice with favor have I always done ;
Prayers and tears have moved me, gifts could never.
When have I aught exacted at your hands,
But to maintain the king, the realm and you ?
Large gifts have I bestow'd on learned clerks,
Because my book preferr'd me to the king,
And seeing ignorance is the curse of God,
Knowledge the wing wherewith we fly to heaven,
Unless you be possess'd with devilish spirits,
You cannot but forbear to murder me :   81
This tongue hath parley'd unto foreign kings
For your behoof,—

Cade. Tut, when struck'st thou one blow in the field ?

Say. Great men have reaching hands : oft have I struck
Those that I never saw and struck them dead.

Geo. O monstrous coward ! what, to come behind folks ?

Say. These cheeks are pale for watching for your good.   90

Cade. Give him a box o' the ear and that will make 'em red again.

Say. Long sitting to determine poor men's causes
Hath made me full of sickness and diseases.

Cade. Ye shall have a hempen caudle, then, and the help of hatchet.

Dick. Why dost thou quiver, man ?

Say. The palsy, and not fear, provokes me.

Cade. Nay, he nods at us, as who should say, I'll be even with you : I'll see if his head will stand steadier on a pole, or no. Take him away, and behead him.

Say. Tell me wherein have I offended most ?
Have I affected wealth or honor ? speak.
Are my chests fill'd up with extorted gold ?
Is my apparel sumptuous to behold ?
Whom have I injured, that ye seek my death ?
These hands are free from guiltless blood-shedding,
This breast from harboring foul deceitful thoughts.
O, let me live !   110

Cade. [*Aside*] I feel remorse in myself with his words ; but I'll bridle it : he shall die, an it be but for pleading so well for his life. Away with him ! he has a familiar under his tongue ; he speaks not o' God's name. Go, take him away, I say, and strike off his head presently ; and then break into his son-in-law's house, Sir James Cromer, and strike off his head, and bring them both upon two poles hither.

All. It shall be done.   120

Say. Ah, countrymen ! if when you make your prayers,
God should be so obdurate as yourselves,
How would it fare with your departed souls ?
And therefore yet relent, and save my life.

Cade. Away with him ! and do as I command ye.   [*Exeunt some with Lord Say.*
The proudest peer in the realm shall not wear a head on his shoulders, unless he pay me tribute ; there shall not a maid be married, but she shall pay to me her maidenhead ere they have it : men shall hold of me in capite ; and we charge and command that their wives be as free as heart can wish or tongue can tell.

Dick. My lord, when shall we go to Cheapside and take up commodities upon our bills ?

Cade. Marry, presently.

All. O, brave !

Re-enter one with the heads.

Cade. But is not this braver ? Let them kiss one another, for they loved well when they were alive. Now part them again, lest they consult about the giving up of some more towns in France. Soldiers, defer the spoil of the city until night : for with these borne before us, instead of maces, will we ride through the streets, and at every corner have them kiss. Away !   [*Exeunt.*

Scene VIII. *Southwark.*

Alarum and retreat. Enter Cade *and all his rabblement.*

Cade. Up Fish Street ! down Saint Magnus' Corner ! kill and knock down ! throw them into Thames ! [*Sound a parley.*] What noise is this I hear ? Dare any be so bold to sound retreat or parley, when I command them kill ?

Enter Buckingham *and old* Clifford, *attended.*

Buck. Ay, here they be that dare and will disturb thee :
Know, Cade, we come ambassadors from the king
Unto the commons whom thou hast misled ;
And here pronounce free pardon to them all
That will forsake thee and go home in peace.

Clif. What say ye, countrymen ? will ye relent,   11
And yield to mercy whilst 'tis offer'd you ;
Or let a rebel lead you to your deaths ?
Who loves the king and will embrace his pardon,
Fling up his cap, and say 'God save his majesty !'
Who hateth him and honors not his father,
Henry the Fifth, that made all France to quake,
Shake he his weapon at us and pass by.

All. God save the king ! God save the king !

Cade. What, Buckingham and Clifford, are ye so brave ? And you, base peasants, do ye believe him ? will you needs be hanged with your pardons about your necks ? Hath my sword therefore broke through London gates, that you should leave me at the White Hart in Southwark ? I thought ye would never have given out these arms till you had recovered your ancient freedom : but you are all recreants and dastards, and delight to live in slavery to the nobility. Let them break your backs with burthens, take your houses over your heads, ravish your wives and daughters before your faces : for me, I will make shift for one ; and so, God's curse light upon you all !

All. We'll follow Cade, we'll follow Cade !

Clif. Is Cade the son of Henry the Fifth, That thus you do exclaim you'll go with him ? Will he conduct you through the heart of France, And make the meanest of you earls and dukes ? Alas, he hath no home, no place to fly to ; 40 Nor knows he how to live but by the spoil, Unless by robbing of your friends and us. Were't not a shame, that whilst you live at jar, The fearful French, whom you late vanquished, Should make a start o'er seas and vanquish you ? Methinks already in this civil broil I see them lording it in London streets, Crying ' Villiago ! ' unto all they meet. Better ten thousand base-born Cades miscarry Than you should stoop unto a Frenchman's mercy. 50 To France, to France, and get what you have lost ; Spare England, for it is your native coast ; Henry hath money, you are strong and manly ; God on our side, doubt not of victory.

All. A Clifford ! a Clifford ! we'll follow the king and Clifford.

Cade. Was ever feather so lightly blown to and fro as this multitude ? The name of Henry the Fifth hales them to an hundred mischiefs, and makes them leave me desolate. I see them lay their heads together to surprise me. My sword make way for me, for here is no staying. In despite of the devils and hell, have through the very middest of you ? and heavens and honor be witness, that no want of resolution in me, but only my followers' base and ignominious treasons, makes me betake me to my heels. [*Exit.*

Buck. What, is he fled ? Go some, and follow him ; And he that brings his head unto the king Shall have a thousand crowns for his reward. [*Exeunt some of them.* Follow me, soldiers : we'll devise a mean 71 To reconcile you all unto the king. [*Exeunt.*

SCENE IX. *Kenilworth Castle.*

Sound Trumpets. Enter KING, QUEEN, *and* SOMERSET, *on the terrace.*

King. Was ever king that joy'd an earthly throne, And could command no more content than I ? No sooner was I crept out of my cradle But I was made a king, at nine months old. Was never subject long'd to be a king As I do long and wish to be a subject.

Enter BUCKINGHAM *and old* CLIFFORD.

Buck. Health and glad tidings to your majesty !

King. Why, Buckingham, is the traitor Cade surprised ? Or is he but retired to make him strong ?

Enter below, multitudes, with halters about their necks.

Clif. He is fled, my lord, and all his powers do yield ; 10 And humbly thus, with halters on their necks, Expect your highness' doom of life or death.

King. Then, heaven, set ope thy everlasting gates, To entertain my vows of thanks and praise ! Soldiers, this day have you redeemed your lives, And show'd how well you love your prince and country : Continue still in this so good a mind, And Henry, though he be infortunate, Assure yourselves, will never be unkind : And so, with thanks and pardon to you all, 20 I do dismiss you to your several countries.

All. God save the king ! God save the king !

Enter a MESSENGER.

Mess. Please it your grace to be advertised The Duke of York is newly come from Ireland, And with a puissant and a mighty power Of gallowglasses and stout kerns Is marching hitherward in proud array, And still proclaimeth, as he comes along, His arms are only to remove from thee The Duke of Somerset, whom he terms traitor. 30

King. Thus stands my state, 'twixt Cade and York distress'd. Like to a ship that, having 'scaped a tempest, Is straightway calm'd and boarded with a pirate : But now is Cade driven back, his men dispersed ; And now is York in arms to second him. I pray thee, Buckingham, go and meet him, And ask him what's the reason of these arms. Tell him I'll send Duke Edmund to the Tower ; And, Somerset, we'll commit thee thither, Until his army be dismiss'd from him. 40

Som. My lord, I'll yield myself to prison willingly, Or unto death, to do my country good.

King. In any case, be not too rough in terms ; For he is fierce and cannot brook hard language.

Buck. I will, my lord ; and doubt not so to deal As all things shall redound unto your good.

King. Come, wife, let's in, and learn to govern better ; For yet may England curse my wretched reign. [*Flourish. Exeunt.*

SCENE X. *Kent. Iden's garden.*

Enter CADE.

Cade. Fie on ambition ! fie on myself, that have a sword, and yet am ready to famish ! These five days have I hid me in these woods and durst not peep out, for all the country is laid for me ; but now am I so hungry that if I might have a lease of my life for a thousand years I could stay no longer. Wherefore, on

a brick wall have I climbed into this garden,
to see if I can eat grass, or pick a sallet another while, which is not amiss to cool a
man's stomach this hot weather. And I think
this word 'sallet' was born to do me good:
for many a time, but for a sallet, my brain-
pan had been cleft with a brown bill; and
many a time, when I have been dry and
bravely marching, it hath served me instead
of a quart pot to drink in; and now the word
'sallet' must serve me to feed on.

Enter IDEN.

Iden. Lord, who would live turmoiled in
     the court,
And may enjoy such quiet walks as these?
This small inheritance my father left me   20
Contenteth me, and worth a monarchy.
I seek not to wax great by others' waning,
Or gather wealth, I care not, with what envy:
Sufficeth that I have maintains my state
And sends the poor well pleased from my gate.
Cade. Here's the lord of the soil come to
seize me for a stray, for entering his fee-sim-
ple without leave. Ah, villain, thou wilt betray
me, and get a thousand crowns of the king by
carrying my head to him: but I'll make thee
eat iron like an ostrich, and swallow my sword
like a great pin, ere thou and I part.
Iden. Why, rude companion, whatsoe'er
     thou be,
I know thee not; why, then, should I betray
     thee?
Is't not enough to break into my garden,
And, like a thief, to come to rob my grounds,
Climbing my walls in spite of me the owner,
But thou wilt brave me with these saucy
     terms?
Cade. Brave thee! ay, by the best blood
that ever was broached, and beard thee too.
Look on me well: I have eat no meat these
five days; yet, come thou and thy five men,
and if I do not leave you all as dead as a door-
nail, I pray God I may never eat grass more.
Iden. Nay, it shall ne'er be said, while
     England stands,
That Alexander Iden, an esquire of Kent,
Took odds to combat a poor famish'd man.
Oppose thy steadfast-gazing eyes to mine,
See if thou canst outface me with thy looks:
Set limb to limb, and thou art far the
     lesser;   50
Thy hand is but a finger to my fist,
Thy leg a stick compared with this truncheon;
My foot shall fight with all the strength thou
     hast;
And if mine arm be heaved in the air,
Thy grave is digg'd already in the earth.
As for words, whose greatness answers words,
Let this my sword report what speech for-
     bears.
Cade. By my valor, the most complete
champion that ever I heard! Steel, if thou
turn the edge, or cut not out the burly-boned
clown in chines of beef ere thou sleep in thy
sheath, I beseech God on my knees thou
mayst be turned to hobnails.
     [*Here they fight. Cade falls.*
O, I am slain! famine and no other hath
slain me: let ten thousand devils come
against me, and give me but the ten meals I
have lost, and I'll defy them all. Wither, gar-

den; and be henceforth a burying-place to all
that do dwell in this house, because the un-
conquered soul of Cade is fled.   70
Iden. Is't Cade that I have slain, that mon-
     strous traitor?
Sword, I will hollow thee for this thy deed,
And hang thee o'er my tomb when I am
     dead:
Ne'er shall this blood be wiped from thy
     point;
But thou shalt wear it as a herald's coat,
To emblaze the honor that thy master got.
Cade. Iden, farewell, and be proud of thy
victory. Tell Kent from me, she hath lost her
best man, and exhort all the world to be cow-
ards; for I, that never feared any, am van-
quished by famine, not by valor. [*Dies.* 81
Iden. How much thou wrong'st me,
     heaven be my judge.
Die, damned wretch, the curse of her that
     bare thee;
And as I thrust thy body in with my sword,
So wish I, I might thrust thy soul to hell.
Hence will I drag thee headlong by the heels
Unto a dunghill which shall be thy grave,
And there cut off thy most ungracious head;
Which I will bear in triumph to the king,
Leaving thy trunk for crows to feed upon. 90
                                    [*Exit.*

ACT V.

SCENE I. *Fields between Dartford and Black-*
                        heath.

Enter YORK, *and his army of Irish, with drum*
                  and colors.

York. From Ireland thus comes York to
     claim his right,
And pluck the crown from feeble Henry's
     head:
Ring, bells, aloud; burn, bonfires, clear and
     bright,
To entertain great England's lawful king.
Ah! sancta majestas, who would not buy thee
     dear?
Let them obey that know not how to rule;
This hand was made to handle naught but
     gold.
I cannot give due action to my words,
Except a sword or sceptre balance it:
A sceptre shall it have, have I a soul,   10
On which I'll toss the flower-de-luce of France.

Enter BUCKINGHAM.

Whom have we here? Buckingham, to dis-
     turb me?
The king hath sent him, sure: I must dis-
     semble.
Buck. York, if thou meanest well, I greet
     thee well.
York. Humphrey of Buckingham, I accept
     thy greeting.
Art thou a messenger, or come of pleasure?
Buck. A messenger from Henry, our dread
     liege,
To know the reason of these arms in peace;
Or why thou, being a subject as I am,
Against thy oath and true allegiance sworn, 20
Should raise so great a power without his
     leave,

Or dare to bring thy force so near the court.
York. [*Aside*] Scarce can I speak, my
   choler is so great :
O, I could hew up rocks and fight with flint,
I am so angry at these abject terms ;
And now, like Ajax Telamonius,
On sheep or oxen could I spend my fury.
I am far better born than is the king,
More like a king, more kingly in my
   thoughts :
But I must make fair weather yet a while, 30
Till Henry be more weak and I more strong,—
Buckingham, I prithee, pardon me,
That I have given no answer all this while ;
My mind was troubled with deep melancholy.
The cause why I have brought this army
   hither
Is to remove proud Somerset from the king,
Seditious to his grace and to the state.
Buck. That is too much presumption on
   thy part :
But if thy arms be to no other end,
The king hath yielded unto thy demand : 40
The Duke of Somerset is in the Tower.
York. Upon thine honor, is he prisoner ?
Buck. Upon mine honor, he is prisoner.
York. Then, Buckingham, I do dismiss my
   powers.
Soldiers, I thank you all ; disperse yourselves ;
Meet me to-morrow in St. George's field,
You shall have pay and every thing you wish.
And let my sovereign, virtuous Henry,
Command my eldest son, nay, all my sons,
As pledges of my fealty and love ;   50
I'll send them all as willing as I live :
Lands, goods, horse, armor, any thing I have,
Is his to use, so Somerset may die.
Buck. York, I commend this kind submis-
   sion :
We twain will go into his highness' tent.

    Enter KING *and* Attendants.

King. Buckingham, doth York intend no
   harm to us,
That thus he marcheth with thee arm in arm ?
York. In all submission and humility
York doth present himself unto your highness.
King. Then what intends these forces thou
   dost bring ?   60
York. To heave the traitor Somerset from
   hence,
And fight against that monstrous rebel Cade,
Who since I heard to be discomfited.

    Enter IDEN, *with* CADE'S head.

Iden. If one so rude and of so mean condi-
   tion
May pass into the presence of a king,
Lo, I present your grace a traitor's head,
The head of Cade, whom I in combat slew.
King. The head of Cade ! Great God, how
   just art Thou !
O, let me view his visage, being dead,
That living wrought me such exceeding
   trouble.
Tell me, my friend, art thou the man that slew
   him ?   71
Iden. I was, an't like your majesty.
King. How art thou call'd ? and what is
   thy degree ?
Iden. Alexander Iden, that's my name ;

A poor esquire of Kent, that loves his king.
Buck. So please it you, my lord, 'twere
   not amiss
He were created knight for his good service.
King. Iden, kneel down. [*He kneels.*] Rise
   up a knight.
We give thee for reward a thousand marks,
And will that thou henceforth attend on us. 80
Iden. May Iden live to merit such a
   bounty,
And never live but true unto his liege ! [*Rises.*

    Enter QUEEN *and* SOMERSET.

King. See, Buckingham, Somerset comes
   with the queen :
Go, bid her hide him quickly from the duke.
Queen. For thousand Yorks he shall not
   hide his head,
But boldly stand and front him to his face.
York. How now ! is Somerset at liberty ?
Then, York, unloose thy long-imprison'd
   thoughts,
And let thy tongue be equal with thy heart.
Shall I endure the sight of Somerset ?   90
False king ! why hast thou broken faith with
   me,
Knowing how hardly I can brook abuse ?
King did I call thee ? no, thou art not king,
Not fit to govern and rule multitudes,
Which darest not, no, nor canst not rule a
   traitor.
That head of thine doth not become a crown ;
Thy hand is made to grasp a palmer's staff,
And not to grace an awful princely sceptre.
That gold must round engirt these brows of
   mine,
Whose smile and frown, like to Achilles'
   spear,
Is able with the change to kill and cure.   101
Here is a hand to hold a sceptre up
And with the same to act controlling laws.
Give place : by heaven, thou shalt rule no
   more
O'er him whom heaven created for thy ruler.
Som. O monstrous traitor ! I arrest thee,
   York,
Of capital treason 'gainst the king and crown ;
Obey, audacious traitor ; kneel for grace.
York. Wouldst have me kneel ? first let
   me ask of these,
If they can brook I bow a knee to man.   110
Sirrah, call in my sons to be my bail ;
               [*Exit Attendant.*
I know, ere they will have me go to ward,
They'll pawn their swords for my enfranchise-
   ment.
Queen. Call hither Clifford ! bid him come
   amain,
To say if that the bastard boys of York
Shall be the surety for their traitor father.
               [*Exit Buckingham.*
York. O blood-besotted Neapolitan,
Outcast of Naples, England's bloody scourge !
The sons of York, thy betters in their birth,
Shall be their father's bail ; and bane to those
That for my surety will refuse the boys !   121

    Enter EDWARD *and* RICHARD.

See where they come : I'll warrant they'll
   make it good.

Enter old Clifford *and his* Son.

Queen. And here comes Clifford to deny
  their bail.
Clif. Health and all happiness to my lord
  the king!   [*Kneels.*
York. I thank thee, Clifford : say, what
  news with thee ?
Nay, do not fright us with an angry look ;
We are thy sovereign, Clifford, kneel again ;
For thy mistaking so, we pardon thee.
Clif. This is my king, York, I do not mis-
  take ;
But thou mistakest me much to think I do :130
To Bedlam with him ! is the man grown mad ?
King. Ay, Clifford ; a bedlam and ambi-
  tious humor
Makes him oppose himself against his king.
Clif. He is a traitor ; let him to the Tower,
And chop away that factious pate of his.
Queen. He is arrested, but will not obey ;
His sons, he says, shall give their words for
  him.
York. Will you not, sons ?
Edw. Ay, noble father, if our words will
  serve.
Rich. And if words will not, then our
  weapons shall.   140
Clif. Why, what a brood of traitors have
  we here !
York. Look in a glass, and call thy image
  so :
I am thy king, and thou a false-heart traitor.
Call hither to the stake my two brave bears,
That with the very shaking of their chains
They may astonish these fell-lurking curs :
Bid Salisbury and Warwick come to me.

Enter the Earls of Warwick *and* Salisbury.

Clif. Are these thy bears ? we'll bait thy
  bears to death.
And manacle the bear-ward in their chains,
If thou darest bring them to the baiting place.
Rich. Oft have I seen a hot o'erweening
  cur   151
Run back and bite, because he was withheld ;
Who, being suffer'd his the bear's fell paw,
Hath clapp'd his tail between his legs and
  cried :
And such a piece of service will you do,
If you oppose yourselves to match Lord War-
  wick.
Clif. Hence, heap of wrath, foul indigested
  lump,
As crooked in thy manners as thy shape !
York. Nay, we shall heat you thoroughly
  anon.
Clif. Take heed, lest by your heat you burn
  yourselves.   160
King. Why, Warwick, hath thy knee for-
  got to bow ?
Old Salisbury, shame to thy silver hair,
Thou mad misleader of thy brain-sick son !
What, wilt thou on thy death-bed play the
  ruffian,
And seek for sorrow with thy spectacles ?
O, where is faith ? O, where is loyalty ?
If it be banish'd from the frosty head,
Where shall it find a harbor in the earth ?
Wilt thou go dig a grave to find out war,
And shame thine honorable age with blood ?
Why art thou old, and want'st experience ?171

Or wherefore dost abuse it, if thou hast it ?
For shame ! in duty bend thy knee to me
That bows unto the grave with mickle age.
Sal. My lord, I have consider'd with my-
  self
The title of this most renowned duke ;
And in my conscience do repute his grace
The rightful heir to England's royal seat.
King. Hast thou not sworn allegiance unto
  me ?
Sal. I have.   180
King. Canst thou dispense with heaven for
  such an oath ?
Sal. It is great sin to swear unto a sin,
But greater sin to keep a sinful oath.
Who can be bound by any solemn vow
To do a murderous deed, to rob a man,
To force a spotless virgin's chastity,
To reave the orphan of his patrimony,
To wring the widow from her custom'd right,
And have no other reason for this wrong
But that he was bound by a solemn oath ?
Queen. A subtle traitor needs no sophister.
King. Call Buckingham, and bid him arm
  himself.
York. Call Buckingham, and all the friends
  thou hast,
I am resolved for death or dignity.
Clif. The first I warrant thee, if dreams
  prove true.
War. You were best to go to bed and
  dream again,
To keep thee from the tempest of the field.
Clif. I am resolved to bear a greater storm
Than any thou canst conjure up to-day ;
And that I'll write upon thy burgonet,   200
Might I but know thee by thy household
  badge.
War. Now, by my father's badge, old
  Nevil's crest,
The rampant bear chain'd to the ragged staff,
This day I'll wear aloft my burgonet,
As on a mountain top the cedar shows
That keeps his leaves in spite of any storm,
Even to affright thee with the view thereof.
Clif. And from thy burgonet I'll rend thy
  bear
And tread it under foot with all contempt,
Despite the bear-ward that protects the bear.
Y. Clif. And so to arms, victorious father,
To quell the rebels and their complices.
Rich. Fie ! charity, for shame ! speak not
  in spite,
For you shall sup with Jesu Christ to-night.
Y. Clif. Foul stigmatic, that's more than
  thou canst tell.
Rich. If not in heaven, you'll surely sup in
  hell.   [*Exeunt severally.*

Scene II. *Saint Alban's.*

Alarums to the battle. Enter Warwick.

War. Clifford of Cumberland, 'tis War-
  wick calls :
And if thou dost not hide thee from the bear,
Now, when the angry trumpet sounds alarum
And dead men's cries do fill the empty air,
Clifford, I say, come forth and fight with me :
Proud northern lord, Clifford of Cumberland,
Warwick is hoarse with calling thee to arms.

Enter York.

How now, my noble lord ! what, all afoot ?

York. The deadly-handed Clifford slew my
  steed,
But match to match I have encounter'd him 9
And made a prey for carrion kites and crows
Even of the bonny beast he loved so well.

Enter old CLIFFORD.

War. Of one or both of us the time is
  come.
York. Hold, Warwick, seek thee out some
  other chase,
For I myself must hunt this deer to death.
War. Then, nobly, York; 'tis for a crown
  thou fight'st.
As I intend, Clifford, to thrive to-day,
It grieves my soul to leave thee unassail'd.
                            [*Exit.*
Clif. What seest thou in me, York? why
  dost thou pause?
York. With thy brave bearing should I be
  in love, 20
But that thou art so fast mine enemy.
Clif. Nor should thy prowess want praise
  and esteem,
But that 'tis shown ignobly and in treason.
York. So let it help me now against thy
  sword
As I in justice and true right express it.
Clif. My soul and body on the action both!
York. A dreadful lay! Address thee in-
  stantly. [*They fight, and Clifford falls.*
Clif. La fin couronne les œuvres. [*Dies.*
York. Thus war hath given thee peace, for
  thou art still.
Peace with his soul, heaven, if it be thy will!
                            [*Exit.*

Enter young CLIFFORD.

Y. Clif. Shame and confusion! all is on
  the rout;
Fear frames disorder, and disorder wounds
Where it should guard. O war, thou son of
  hell,
Whom angry heavens do make their minister
Throw in the frozen bosoms of our part
Hot coals of vengeance! Let no soldier fly.
He that is truly dedicate to war
Hath no self-love, nor he that loves himself
Hath not essentially but by circumstance
The name of valor. [*Seeing his dead father.*
O, let the vile world end, 40
And the premised flames of the last day
Knit earth and heaven together!
Now let the general trumpet blow his blast,
Particularities and petty sounds
To cease! Wast thou ordain'd, dear father,
To lose thy youth in peace, and to achieve
The silver livery of advised age,
And, in thy reverence and thy chair-days, thus
To die in ruffian battle? Even at this sight
My heart is turn'd to stone: and while 'tis
  mine, 50
It shall be stony. York not our old men spares;
No more will I their babes: tears virginal
Shall be to me even as the dew to fire,
And beauty that the tyrant oft reclaims
Shall to my flaming wrath be oil and flax.
Henceforth I will not have to do with pity:
Meet I an infant of the house of York,
Into as many gobbets will I cut it
As wild Medea young Absyrtus did:
In cruelty will I seek out my fame. 60

Come, thou new ruin of old Clifford's house:
As did Æneas old Anchises bear,
So bear I thee upon my manly shoulders;
But then Æneas bare a living load,
Nothing so heavy as these woes of mine.
         [*Exit, bearing off his father.*

Enter RICHARD *and* SOMERSET *to fight.*
SOMERSET *is killed.*

Rich. So, lie thou there;
For underneath an alehouse' paltry sign,
The Castle in Saint Alban's, Somerset
Hath made the wizard famous in his death.
Sword, hold thy temper; heart, be wrathful
  still: 70
Priests pray for enemies, but princes kill. [*Exit.*

Fight: excursions. Enter KING, QUEEN, *and
others.*

Queen. Away, my lord! you are slow; for
  shame, away!
King. Can we outrun the heavens? good
  Margaret, stay.
Queen. What are you made of? you'll nor
  fight nor fly:
Now is it manhood, wisdom and defence,
To give the enemy way, and to secure us
By what we can, which can no more but fly.
                    [*Alarum afar off.*
If you be ta'en, we then should see the bottom
Of all our fortunes: but if we haply scape, 79
As well we may, if not through your neglect,
We shall to London get, where you are loved
And where this breach now in our fortunes
  made
May readily be stopp'd.

Re-enter young CLIFFORD.

Y. Clif. But that my heart's on future mis-
  chief set,
I would speak blasphemy ere bid you fly:
But fly you must; uncurable discomfit
Reigns in the hearts of all our present parts.
Away, for your relief! and we will live
To see their day and them our fortune give:
Away, my lord, away! [*Exeunt.*

SCENE III. *Fields near St. Alban's.*

Alarum. Retreat. Enter YORK, RICHARD,
WARWICK, *and* Soldiers, *with drum and colors.*

York. Of Salisbury, who can report of
  him,
That winter lion, who in rage forgets
Aged contusions and all brush of time,
And, like a gallant in the brow of youth,
Repairs him with occasion? This happy day
Is not itself, nor have we won one foot,
If Salisbury be lost.
Rich.   My noble father,
Three times to-day I holp him to his horse,
Three times bestrid him; thrice I led him off,
Persuaded him from any further act: 10
But still, where danger was, still there I met
  him;
And like rich hangings in a homely house,
So was his will in his old feeble body.
But, noble as he is, look where he comes.

Enter SALISBURY.

Sal. Now, by my sword, well hast thou
  fought to-day;

By the mass, so did we all. I thank you, Rich-
　　　　ard :
God knows how long it is I have to live ;
And it hath pleased him that three times
　　　　to-day
You have defended me from imminent death.
Well, lords, we have not got that which we
　　　　have :   20
'Tis not enough our foes are this time fled,
Being opposites of such repairing nature.
　York. I know our safety is to follow
　　　　them ;
For, as I hear, the king is fled to London,

To call a present court of parliament.
Let us pursue him ere the writs go forth.
What says Lord Warwick ? shall we after
　　　　them ?
　War. After them ! nay, before them, if
　　　　we can.
Now, by my faith, lords, 'twas a glorious day :
Saint Alban's battle won by famous York   30
Shall be eternized in all age to come.
Sound drums and trumpets, and to London
　　　　all :
And more such days as these to us befall !
　　　　　　　　　　　　　　　　　　[*Exeunt.*

KING HENRY VI. PART III.

(WRITTEN ABOUT 1591–92.)

INTRODUCTION.

[See Introduction to Part II.]

DRAMATIS PERSONÆ.

KING HENRY the Sixth.
EDWARD, PRINCE OF WALES, his son.
LEWIS XI. KING OF FRANCE.
DUKE OF SOMERSET.
DUKE OF EXETER.
EARL OF OXFORD.
EARL OF NORTHUMBERLAND.
EARL OF WESTMORELAND.
LORD CLIFFORD.
RICHARD PLANTAGENET, Duke of York.

EDWARD, Earl of March, afterwards
King Edward IV.,
EDMUND, Earl of Rutland,
GEORGE, afterwards Duke of Clarence, } his sons.
RICHARD, afterwards Duke of Gloucester,

DUKE OF NORFOLK.
MARQUESS OF MONTAGUE.
EARL OF WARWICK.
EARL OF PEMBROKE.

LORD HASTINGS.
LORD STAFFORD.
SIR JOHN MORTIMER, } uncles to the Duke
SIR HUGH MORTIMER, } of York.
HENRY, Earl of Richmond, a youth.
LORD RIVERS, brother to Lady Grey.
SIR WILLIAM STANLEY.
SIR JOHN MONTGOMERY.
SIR JOHN SOMERVILLE.
Tutor to Rutland. Mayor of York.
Lieutenant of the Tower. A Nobleman.
Two Keepers. A Huntsman.
A Son that has killed his father.
A Father that has killed his son.

QUEEN MARGARET.
LADY GREY, afterwards Queen to Edward IV.
BONA, sister to the French Queen.

Soldiers, Attendants, Messengers, Watchmen,
&c.

SCENE : *England and France.*

ACT I.

SCENE I. *London. The Parliament-house.*

Alarum. Enter the DUKE OF YORK, EDWARD,
RICHARD, NORFOLK, MONTAGUE, WARWICK,
and Soldiers.

War. I wonder how the king escaped our
hands.
York. While we pursued the horsemen of
the north,
He slily stole away and left his men :
Whereat the great Lord of Northumberland,
Whose warlike ears could never brook retreat,
Cheer'd up the drooping army ; and himself,
Lord Clifford and Lord Stafford, all abreast,
Charged our main battle's front, and breaking
in
Were by the swords of common soldiers slain.
Edw. Lord Stafford's father, Duke of
Buckingham, 10
Is either slain or wounded dangerously ;
I cleft his beaver with a downright blow :
That this is true, father, behold his blood.

Mont. And, brother, here's the Earl of
Wiltshire's blood,
Whom I encounter'd as the battles join'd.
Rich. Speak thou for me and tell them
what I did.
[*Throwing down the Duke of Somerset's head.*
York. Richard hath best deserved of all
my sons.
But is your grace dead, my Lord of Somerset ?
Norf. Such hope have all the line of John
of Gaunt !
Rich. Thus do I hope to shake King
Henry's head. 20
War. And so do I. Victorious Prince of
York,
Before I see thee seated in that throne
Which now the house of Lancaster usurps,
I vow by heaven these eyes shall never close.
This is the palace of the fearful king,
And this the regal seat : possess it, York ;
For this is thine and not King Henry's heirs'.
York. Assist me, then, sweet Warwick,
and I will ;
For hither we have broken in by force.

Norf. We'll all assist you; he that flies
    shall die.   30
York. Thanks, gentle Norfolk : stay by
    me, my lords ;
And, soldiers, stay and lodge by me this night.
                                [They go up.
War. And when the king comes, offer him
    no violence,
Unless he seek to thrust you out perforce.
York. The queen this day here holds her
    parliament,
But little thinks we shall be of her council :
By words or blows here let us win our right.
Rich. Arm'd as we are, let's stay within
    this house.
War. The bloody parliament shall this be
    call'd,
Unless Plantagenet, Duke of York, be king,40
And bashful Henry deposed, whose cowardice
Hath made us by-words to our enemies.
York. Then leave me not, my lords ; be
    resolute ;
I mean to take possession of my right.
War. Neither the king, nor he that loves
    him best,
The proudest he that holds up Lancaster,
Dares stir a wing, if Warwick shake his bells.
I'll plant Plantagenet, root him up who dares :
Resolve thee, Richard ; claim the English
    crown.

Flourish. Enter King Henry, Clifford,
Northumberland, Westmoreland, Exeter, *and the rest.*

K. Hen. My lords, look where the sturdy
    rebel sits,   50
Even in the chair of state : belike he means,
Back'd by the power of Warwick, that false
    peer,
To aspire unto the crown and reign as king.
Earl of Northumberland, he slew thy father.
And thine, Lord Clifford ; and you both have
    vow'd revenge
On him, his sons, his favorites and his friends.
North. If I be not, heavens be revenged on
    me !
Clif. The hope thereof makes Clifford
    mourn in steel.
West. What, shall we suffer this ? let's
    pluck him down :
My heart for anger burns ; I cannot brook it.
K. Hen. Be patient, gentle Earl of West-
    moreland.   61
Clif. Patience is for poltroons, such as he :
He durst not sit there, had your father lived.
My gracious lord, here in the parliament
Let us assail the family of York.
North. Well hast thou spoken, cousin : be
    it so.
K. Hen. Ah, know you not the city favors
    them,
And they have troops of soldiers at their
    beck ?
Exe. But when the duke is slain, they'll
    quickly fly.
K. Hen. Far be the thought of this from
    Henry's heart,   70
To make a shambles of the parliament-house !
Cousin of Exeter, frowns, words and threats
Shall be the war that Henry means to use.
Thou factious Duke of York, descend my
    throne,

And kneel for grace and mercy at my feet ;
I am thy sovereign.
York.   I am thine.
Exe. For shame, come down : he made
    thee Duke of York.
York. 'Twas my inheritance, as the earl-
    dom was.
Exe. Thy father was a traitor to the crown.
War. Exeter, thou art a traitor to the
    crown
In following this usurping Henry.   81
Clif. Whom should he follow but his
    natural king ?
War. True, Clifford ; and that's Richard
    Duke of York.
K. Hen. And shall I stand, and thou sit in
    my throne ?
York. It must and shall be so : content
    thyself.
War. Be Duke of Lancaster ; let him be
    king.
West. He is both king and Duke of Lan-
    caster ;
And that the Lord of Westmoreland shall
    maintain.
War. And Warwick shall disprove it. You
    forget
That we are those which chased you from the
    field   90
And slew your fathers, and with colors spread
March'd through the city to the palace gates.
North. Yes, Warwick, I remember it to
    my grief ;
And, by his soul, thou and thy house shall rue
    it.
West. Plantagenet, of thee and these thy
    sons,
Thy kinsmen and thy friends, I'll have more
    lives
Than drops of blood were in my father's veins.
Clif. Urge it no more ; lest that, instead
    of words,
I send thee, Warwick, such a messenger
As shall revenge his death before I stir.   100
War. Poor Clifford ! how I scorn his
    worthless threats !
York. Will you we show our title to the
    crown ?
If not, our swords shall plead it in the field.
K. Hen. What title hast thou, traitor, to
    the crown ?
Thy father was, as thou art, Duke of York ;
Thy grandfather, Roger Mortimer, Earl of
    March :
I am the son of Henry the Fifth,
Who made the Dauphin and the French to
    stoop
And seized upon their towns and provinces.
War. Talk not of France, sith thou hast
    lost it all.   110
K. Hen. The lord protector lost it, and
    not I :
When I was crown'd I was but nine months
    old.
Rich. You are old enough now, and yet,
    methinks, you lose.
Father, tear the crown from the usurper's
    head.
Edw. Sweet father, do so ; set it on your
    head.
Mont. Good brother, as thou lovest and
    honorest arms,

Let's fight it out and not stand cavilling thus.
Rich. Sound drums and trumpets, and the
  king will fly.
York. Sons, peace!
K. Hen. Peace, thou! and give King Henry
  leave to speak.   120
War. Plantagenet shall speak first: hear
  him, lords;
And be you silent and attentive too,
For he that interrupts him shall not live.
K. Hen. Think'st thou that I will leave my
  kingly throne,
Wherein my grandsire and my father sat?
No: first shall war unpeople this my realm;
Ay, and their colors, often borne in France,
And now in England to our heart's great
  sorrow,
Shall be my winding-sheet. Why faint you,
  lords?
My title's good, and better far than his. 130
War. Prove it, Henry, and thou shalt be
  king.
K. Hen. Henry the Fourth by conquest
  got the crown.
York. 'Twas by rebellion against his king.
K. Hen. [*Aside*] I know not what to say;
  my title's weak.—
Tell me, may not a king adopt an heir?
York. What then?
K. Hen. An if he may, then am I lawful
  king;
For Richard, in the view of many lords,
Resign'd the crown to Henry the Fourth,
Whose heir my father was, and I am his. 140
York. He rose against him, being his sov-
  ereign,
And made him to resign his crown perforce.
War. Suppose, my lords, he did it uncon-
  strain'd,
Think you 'twere prejudicial to his crown?
Exe. No; for he could not so resign his
  crown
But that the next heir should succeed and
  reign.
K. Hen. Art thou against us, Duke of
  Exeter?
Exe. His is the right, and therefore pardon
  me.
York. Why whisper you, my lords, and an-
  swer not?
Exe. My conscience tells me he is lawful
  king.   150
K. Hen. [*Aside*] All will revolt from me,
  and turn to him.
North. Plantagenet, for all the claim thou
  lay'st,
Think not that Henry shall be so deposed.
War. Deposed he shall be, in despite of all.
North. Thou art deceived: 'tis not thy
  southern power,
Of Essex, Norfolk, Suffolk, nor of Kent,
Which makes thee thus presumptuous and
  proud,
Can set the duke up in despite of me.
Clif. King Henry, be thy title right or
  wrong,
Lord Clifford vows to fight in thy defence :160
May that ground gape and swallow me alive,
Where I shall kneel to him that slew my fa-
  ther!
K. Hen. O Clifford, how thy words revive
  my heart!

York. Henry of Lancaster, resign thy
  crown
What mutter you, or what conspire you, lords?
War. Do right unto this princely Duke of
  York,
Or I will fill the house with armed men,
And over the chair of state, where now he sits,
Write up his title with usurping blood.
  [*He stamps with his foot and the soldiers
                              show themselves.*
K. Hen. My Lord of Warwick, hear me
  but one word: 170
Let me for this my life-time reign as king.
York. Confirm the crown to me and to
  mine heirs,
And thou shalt reign in quiet while thou
  livest.
King. I am content: Richard Plantagenet,
Enjoy the kingdom after my decease.
Clif. What wrong is this unto the prince
  your son!
War. What good is this to England and
  himself!
West. Base, fearful and despairing Henry!
Clif. How hast thou injured both thyself
  and us!
West. I cannot stay to hear these articles.
North. Nor I.   181
Clif. Come, cousin, let us tell the queen
  these news.
West. Farewell, faint-hearted and degen-
  erate king,
In whose cold blood no spark of honor bides.
North. Be thou a prey unto the house of
  York,
And die in bands for this unmanly deed!
Clif. In dreadful war mayst thou be over-
  come,
Or live in peace abandon'd and despised!
        [*Exeunt North., Clif., and West.*
War. Turn this way, Henry, and regard
  them not.
Exe. They seek revenge and therefore will
  not yield.   190
K. Hen. Ah, Exeter!
War.   Why should you sigh, my lord?
K. Hen. Not for myself, Lord Warwick,
  but my son,
Whom I unnaturally shall disinherit.
But be it as it may: I here entail
The crown to thee and to thine heirs for ever;
Conditionally, that here thou take an oath
To cease this civil war, and, whilst I live,
To honor me as thy king and sovereign,
And neither by treason nor hostility   199
To seek to put me down and reign thyself.
York. This oath I willingly take and will
  perform.
War. Long live King Henry! Plantagenet
  embrace him.
K. Hen. And long live thou and these thy
  forward sons!
York. Now York and Lancaster are rec-
  onciled.
Exe. Accursed be he that seeks to make
  them foes! [*Sennet. Here they come
                                         down.*
York. Farewell, my gracious lord; I'll to
  my castle.
War. And I'll keep London with my
  soldiers.
Norf. And I to Norfolk with my followers

Mont. And I unto the sea from whence I
came.
[*Exeunt York, and his Sons, Warwick, Norfolk, Montague, their Soldiers, and Attendants.*
K. Hen. And I, with grief and sorrow,
to the court.   210

Enter QUEEN MARGARET *and the* PRINCE OF
WALES.

Exe. Here comes the queen, whose looks
bewray her anger :
I'll steal away.
K. Hen. Exeter, so will I.
Q. Mar. Nay, go not from me ; I will fol-
low thee.
K. Hen. Be patient, gentle queen, and I
will stay.
Q. Mar. Who can be patient in such ex-
tremes ?
Ah, wretched man ! would I had died a maid
And never seen thee, never borne thee son,
Seeing thou hast proved so unnatural a father
Hath he deserved to lose his birthright thus ?
Hadst thou but loved him half so well as I,
Or felt that pain which I did for him once,
Or nourish'd him as I did with my blood,
Thou wouldst have left thy dearest heart-blood
there,
Rather than have that savage duke thine heir
And disinherited thine only son.
Prince. Father, you cannot disinherit me :
If you be king, why should not I succeed ?
K. Hen. Pardon me, Margaret ; pardon
me, sweet son :
The Earl of Warwick and the duke enforced
me.
Q. Mar. Enforced thee ! art thou king, and
wilt be forced ?   230
I shame to hear thee speak. Ah, timorous
wretch !
Thou hast undone thyself, thy son and me ;
And given unto the house of York such head
As thou shalt reign but by their sufferance.
To entail him and his heirs unto the crown,
What is it, but to make thy sepulchre
And creep into it far before thy time ?
Warwick is chancellor and the lord of Calais ;
Stern Falconbridge commands the narrow
seas ;
The duke is made protector of the realm ;240
And yet shalt thou be safe ? such safety finds
The trembling lamb environed with wolves.
Had I been there, which am a silly woman,
The soldiers should have toss'd me on their
pikes
Before I would have granted to that act.
But thou preferr'st thy life before thine honor :
And seeing thou dost, I here divorce myself
Both from thy table, Henry, and thy bed,
Until that act of parliament be repeal'd
Whereby my son is disinherited.   250
The northern lords that have forsworn thy
colors
Will follow mine, if once they see them
spread ;
And spread they shall be, to thy foul dis-
grace
And utter ruin of the house of York.
Thus do I leave thee. Come, son, let's away ;
Our army is ready ; come, we'll after them.

K. Hen. Stay, gentle Margaret, and hear
me speak.
Q. Mar. Thou hast spoke too much al-
ready : get thee gone.
K. Hen. Gentle son Edward, thou wilt
stay with me ?
Q. Mar. Ay, to be murder'd by his ene-
mies.   260
Prince. When I return with victory from
the field
I'll see your grace : till then I'll follow her.
Q. Mar. Come, son, away ; we may not
linger thus.
[*Exeunt Queen Margaret and the Prince.*
K. Hen. Poor queen ! how love to me and
to her son
Hath made her break out into terms of rage !
Revenged may she be on that hateful duke,
Whose haughty spirit, winged with desire,
Will cost my crown, and like an empty eagle
Tire on the flesh of me and of my son !
The loss of those three lords torments my
heart :   270
I'll write unto them and entreat them fair.
Come, cousin, you shall be the messenger.
Exe. And I, I hope, shall reconcile them
all.   [*Exeunt.*

SCENE II. *Sandal Castle.*

Enter RICHARD, EDWARD, *and* MONTAGUE.

Rich. Brother, though I be youngest, give
me leave.
Edw. No, I can better play the orator.
Mont. But I have reasons strong and forcible.

Enter the DUKE OF YORK.

York. Why, how now, sons and brother !
at a strife?
What is your quarrel ? how began it first ?
Edw. No quarrel, but a slight contention.
York. About what ?
Rich. About that which concerns your
grace and us ;
The crown of England, father, which is yours.
York. Mine, boy ? not till King Henry be
dead.   10
Rich. Your right depends not on his life
or death.
Edw. Now you are heir, therefore enjoy it
now :
By giving the house of Lancaster leave to
breathe,
It will outrun you, father, in the end.
York. I took an oath that he should
quietly reign.
Edw. But for a kingdom any oath may be
broken :
I would break a thousand oaths to reign one
year.
Rich. No ; God forbid your grace should
be forsworn.
York. I shall be, if I claim by open war.
Rich. I'll prove the contrary, if you'll hear
me speak.   20
York. Thou canst not, son ; it is impos-
sible.
Rich. An oath is of no moment, being not
took
Before a true and lawful magistrate,
That hath authority over him that swears :
Henry had none, but did usurp the place ;

Then, seeing 'twas he that made you to de-
pose,
Your oath, my lord, is vain and frivolous.
Therefore, to arms! And, father, do but
think
How sweet a thing it is to wear a crown;
Within whose circuit is Elysium   30
And all that poets feign of bliss and joy.
Why do we linger thus? I cannot rest
Until the white rose that I wear be dyed
Even in the lukewarm blood of Henry's heart.
    York. Richard, enough; I will be king, or
        die.
Brother, thou shalt to London presently,
And whet on Warwick to this enterprise.
Thou, Richard, shalt to the Duke of Norfolk,
And tell him privily of our intent.
You, Edward, shall unto my Lord Cobham, 40
With whom the Kentishmen will willingly
        rise:
In them I trust; for they are soldiers,
Witty, courteous, liberal, full of spirit.
While you are thus employ'd, what resteth
        more,
But that I seek occasion how to rise,
And yet the king not privy to my drift,
Nor any of the house of Lancaster?

Enter a Messenger.

But, stay: what news? Why comest thou in
        such post?
    Gabr. The queen with all the northern earls
        and lords
Intend here to besiege you in your castle: 50
She is hard by with twenty thousand men;
And therefore fortify your hold, my lord.
    York. Ay, with my sword. What! think'st
        thou that we fear them?
Edward and Richard, you shall stay with me;
My brother Montague shall post to London:
Let noble Warwick, Cobham, and the rest,
Whom we have left protectors of the king,
With powerful policy strengthen themselves,
And trust not simple Henry nor his oaths.
    Mont. Brother, I go; I'll win them, fear it
        not: 60
And thus most humbly I do take my leave.
        [*Exit.*

Enter SIR JOHN MORTIMER *and* SIR HUGH
        MORTIMER.

    York. Sir John and Sir Hugh Mortimer,
        mine uncles,
You are come to Sandal in a happy hour;
The army of the queen mean to besiege us.
    Sir John. She shall not need; we'll meet
        her in the field.
    York. What, with five thousand men?
    Rich. Ay, with five hundred, father, for a
        need:
A woman's general; what should we fear?
        [*A march afar off.*
    Edw. I hear their drums: let's set our men
        in order,   70
And issue forth and bid them battle straight.
    York. Five men to twenty! though the
        odds be great,
I doubt not, uncle, of our victory.
Many a battle have I won in France,
When as the enemy hath been ten to one:
Why should I not now have the like success?
        [*Alarum. Exeunt.*

SCENE III.   *Field of battle betwixt Sandal
        Castle and Wakefield.*

Alarums. Enter RUTLAND *and his Tutor.*

    Rut. Ah, whither shall I fly to 'scape their
        hands?
Ah, tutor, look where bloody Clifford comes!

Enter CLIFFORD *and* Soldiers.

    Clif. Chaplain, away! thy priesthood saves
        thy life.
As for the brat of this accursed duke,
Whose father slew my father, he shall die.
    Tut. And I, my lord, will bear him com-
        pany.
    Clif. Soldiers, away with him!
    Tut. Ah, Clifford, murder not this innocent
        child,
Lest thou be hated both of God and man!
        [*Exit, dragged off by Soldiers.*
    Clif. How now! is he dead already? or is
        it fear   10
That makes him close his eyes? I'll open
        them.
    Rut. So looks the pent-up lion o'er the
        wretch
That trembles under his devouring paws;
And so he walks, insulting o'er his prey,
And so he comes, to rend his limbs asunder.
Ah, gentle Clifford, kill me with thy sword,
And not with such a cruel threatening look.
Sweet Clifford, hear me speak before I die.
I am too mean a subject for thy wrath:
Be thou revenged on men, and let me live. 20
    Clif. In vain thou speak'st, poor boy; my
        father's blood
Hath stopp'd the passage where thy words
        should enter.
    Rut. Then let my father's blood open it
        again;
He is a man, and, Clifford, cope with him.
    Clif. Had I thy brethren here, their lives
        and thine
Were not revenge sufficient for me;
No, if I digg'd up thy forefathers' graves
And hung their rotten coffins up in chains,
It could not slake mine ire, nor ease my heart.
The sight of any of the house of York 30
Is as a fury to torment my soul;
And till I root out their accursed line
And leave not one alive, I live in hell.
Therefore—   [*Lifting his hand.*
    Rut. O, let me pray before I take my
        death!
To thee I pray; sweet Clifford, pity me!
    Clif. Such pity as my rapier's point affords.
    Rut. I never did thee harm: why wilt thou
        slay me?
    Clif. Thy father hath.
    Rut.   But 'twas ere I was born.
Thou hast one son; for his sake pity me, 40
Lest in revenge thereof, sith God is just,
He be as miserably slain as I.
Ah, let me live in prison all my days;
And when I give occasion of offence,
Then let me die, for now thou hast no cause
    Clif. No cause!
Thy father slew my father; therefore, die.
        [*Stabs him*
    Rut. Di faciant laudis summa sit ista tuæ.
        [*Dies*
    Clif. Plantagenet! I come, Plantagenet!

And this thy son's blood cleaving to my blade
Shall rust upon my weapon, till thy blood,   51
Congeal'd with this, do make me wipe off
both.   [*Exit.*

SCENE IV. *Another part of the field.*

Alarum. *Enter* RICHARD, Duke of York.

York. The army of the queen hath got the
field :
My uncles both are slain in rescuing me ;
And all my followers to the eager foe
Turn back and fly, like ships before the wind
Or lambs pursued by hunger-starved wolves.
My sons, God knows what hath bechanced
them :
But this I know, they have demean'd them-
selves
Like men born to renown by life or death.
Three times did Richard make a lane to me,
And thrice cried ' Courage, father ! fight it
out ! '   10
And full as oft came Edward to my side,
With purple falchion, painted to the hilt
In blood of those that had encounter'd him :
And when the hardiest warriors did retire,
Richard cried ' Charge ! and give no foot of
ground ! '
And cried ' A crown, or else a glorious tomb !
A sceptre, or an earthly sepulchre ! '
With this, we charged again : but, out, alas !
We bodged again ; as I have seen a swan
With bootless labor swim against the tide 20
And spend her strength with over-matching
waves.   [*A short alarum within.*
Ah, hark ! the fatal followers do pursue ;
And I am faint and cannot fly their fury :
And were I strong, I would not shun their
fury :
The sands are number'd that make up my
life ;
Here must I stay, and here my life must end.

Enter QUEEN MARGARET, CLIFFORD, NORTH-
UMBERLAND, *the* young Prince, *and* Soldiers.

Come, bloody Clifford, rough Northumber-
land,
I dare your quenchless fury to more rage :
I am your butt, and I abide your shot.
North. Yield to our mercy, proud Plantag-
enet.   30
Clif. Ay, to such mercy as his ruthless arm,
With downright payment, show'd unto my
father.
Now Phaëthon hath tumbled from his car,
And made an evening at the noontide prick.
York. My ashes, as the phœnix, may bring
forth
A bird that will revenge upon you all :
And in that hope I throw mine eyes to heaven,
Scorning whate'er you can afflict me with.
Why come you not ? what ! multitudes, and
fear ?
Clif. So cowards fight when they can fly
no further ;   40
So doves do peck the falcon's piercing talons ;
So desperate thieves, all hopeless of their lives,
Breathe out invectives 'gainst the officers.
York. O Clifford, but bethink thee once
again,
And in thy thought o'er-run my former time ;
And, if though canst for blushing, view this
face,

And bite thy tongue, that slanders him with
cowardice
Whose frown hath made thee faint and fly
ere this !
Clif. I will not bandy with thee word for
word,
But buckle with thee blows, twice two for one.
Q. Mar. Hold, valiant Clifford ! for a thou-
sand causes   51
I would prolong awhile the traitor's life.
Wrath makes him deaf : speak thou, North-
umberland.
North. Hold, Clifford ! do not honor him
so much
To prick thy finger, though to wound his
heart :
What valor were it, when a cur doth grin,
For one to thrust his hand between his teeth,
When he might spurn him with his foot away ?
It is war's prize to take all vantages ;
And ten to one is no impeach of valor.   60
   [*They lay hands on* York, *who struggles.*
Clif. Ay, ay, so strives the woodcock with
the gin.
North. So doth the cony struggle in the
net.
York. So triumph thieves upon their con-
quer'd booty ;
So true men yield, with robbers so o'ermatch'd.
North. What would your grace have done
unto him now ?
Q. Mar. Brave warriors, Clifford and
Northumberland,
Come, make him stand upon this molehill
here,
That raught at mountains with outstretched
arms,
Yet parted but the shadow with his hand.
What ! was it you that would be England's
king ?   70
Was't you that revell'd in our parliament,
And made a preachment of your high de-
scent ?
Where are your mess of sons to back you
now ?
The wanton Edward, and the lusty George ?
And where's that valiant crook-back prodigy,
Dicky your boy, that with his grumbling voice
Was wont to cheer his dad in mutinies ?
Or, with the rest, where is your darling Rut-
land ?
Look, York : I stain'd this napkin with the
blood
That valiant Clifford, with his rapier's point,80
Made issue from the bosom of the boy ;
And if thine eyes can water for his death,
I give thee this to dry thy cheeks withal.
Alas, poor York ! but that I hate thee deadly,
I should lament thy miserable state.
I prithee, grieve, to make me merry, York.
What, hath thy fiery heart so parch'd thine
entrails
That not a tear can fall for Rutland's death ?
Why art thou patient, man ? thou shouldst be
mad ;
And I, to make thee mad, do mock thee thus.
Stamp, rave, and fret, that I may sing and
dance.   91
Thou wouldst be fee'd, I see, to make me
sport :
York cannot speak, unless he wear a crown.

A crown for York! and, lords, bow low to
   him :
Hold you his hands, whilst I do set it on.
          [*Putting a paper crown on his head.*
Ay, marry, sir, now looks he like a king!
Ay, this is he that took King Henry's chair,
And this is he was his adopted heir.
But how is it that great Plantagenet
Is crown'd so soon, and broke his solemn
   oath ?
As I bethink me, you should not be king 101
Till our King Henry had shook hands with
   death.
And will you pale your head in Henry's glory,
And rob his temples of the diadem,
Now in his life, against your holy oath ?
O, 'tis a fault too too unpardonable !
Off with the crown ; and, with the crown, his
   head ;
And, whilst we breathe, take time to do him
   dead.
   Clif. That is my office, for my father's
      sake.
   Q. Mar. Nay, stay ; lets hear the orisons
      he makes.   110
   York. She-wolf of France, but worse than
      wolves of France,
Whose tongue more poisons than the adder's
   tooth !
How ill-beseeming is it in thy sex
To triumph, like an Amazonian trull,
Upon their woes whom fortune captivates !
But that thy face is, vizard-like, unchanging,
Made impudent with use of evil deeds,
I would assay, proud queen, to make thee
   blush.
To tell thee whence thou camest, of whom
   derived,
Were shame enough to shame thee, wert thou
   not shameless.   120
Thy father bears the type of King of Naples,
Of both the Sicils and Jerusalem,
Yet not so wealthy as an English yeoman.
Hath that poor monarch taught thee to in-
   sult ?
It needs not, nor it boots thee not, proud
   queen,
Unless the adage must be verified,
That beggars mounted run their horse to death.
'Tis beauty that doth oft make women proud ;
But, God he knows, thy share thereof is
   small :
'Tis virtue that doth make them most ad-
   mired ;
The contrary doth make thee wonder'd at :
'Tis government that makes them seem divine :
The want thereof makes thee abominable :
Thou art as opposite to every good
As the Antipodes are unto us,
Or as the south to the septentrion.
O tiger's heart wrapt in a woman's hide !
How couldst thou drain the life-blood of the
   child,
To bid the father wipe his eyes withal,
And yet be seen to bear a woman's face ? 140
Women are soft, mild, pitiful and flexible ;
Thou stern, obdurate, flinty, rough, remorse-
   less.
Bids't thou me rage ? why, now thou hast
   thy wish :
Wouldst have me weep ? why, now thou hast
   thy will :
For raging wind blows up incessant showers,

And when the rage allays, the rain begins.
These tears are my sweet Rutland's obsequies :
And every drop cries vengeance for his death,
'Gainst thee, fell Clifford, and thee, false
   Frenchwoman.
   North. Beshrew me, but his passion moves
      me so   150
That hardly can I check my eyes from tears.
   York. That face of his the hungry canni-
      bals
Would not have touch'd, would not have
   stain'd with blood :
But you are more inhuman, more inexorable,
O, ten times more, than tigers of Hyrcania.
See, ruthless queen, a hapless father's tears :
This cloth thou dip'dst in blood of my sweet
   boy,
And I with tears do wash the blood away.
Keep thou the napkin, and go boast of this :
And if thou tell'st the heavy story right, 160
Upon my soul, the hearers will shed tears ;
Yea even my foes will shed fast-falling tears,
And say ' Alas, it was a piteous deed ! '
There, take the crown, and, with the crown,
   my curse ;
And in thy need such comfort come to thee
As now I reap at thy too cruel hand !
Hard-hearted Clifford, take me from the
   world :
My soul to heaven, my blood upon your
   heads !
   North. Had he been slaughter-man to all
      my kin,
I should not for my life but weep with him.
To see how inly sorrow gripes his soul. 171
   Q. Mar. What, weeping-ripe, my Lord
      Northumberland ?
Think but upon the wrong he did us all,
And that will quickly dry thy melting tears.
   Clif. Here's for my oath, here's for my
      father's death.   [*Stabbing him.*
   Q. Mar. And here's to right our gentle-
      hearted king.   [*Stabbing him.*
   York. Open Thy gate of mercy, gracious
      God !
My soul flies through these wounds to seek out
      Thee.   [*Dies.*
   Q. Mar. Off with his head, and set it on
      York gates ;
So York may overlook the town of York. 180
                       [*Flourish. Exeunt.*

ACT II.

SCENE I. *A plain near Mortimer's Cross in
               Herefordshire.*

A march. Enter EDWARD, RICHARD, *and their
                     power.*

   Edw. I wonder how our princely father
      'scaped,
Or whether he be 'scaped away or no
From Clifford's and Northumberland's pur-
   suit :
Had he been ta'en, we should have heard the
   news ;
Had he been slain, we should have heard the
   news ;
Or had he 'scaped, methinks we should have
   heard
The happy tidings of his good escape.
How fares my brother ? why is he so sad

Rich. I cannot joy, until I be resolved
Where our right valiant father is become. 10
I saw him in the battle range about;
And watch'd him how he singled Clifford
    forth.
Methought he bore him in the thickest troop
As doth a lion in a herd of neat;
Or as a bear, encompass'd round with dogs,
Who having pinch'd a few and made them
    cry,
The rest stand all aloof, and bark at him.
So fared our father with his enemies;
So fled his enemies my warlike father:
Methinks, 'tis prize enough to be his son. 20
See how the morning opes her golden gates,
And takes her farewell of the glorious sun!
How well resembles it the prime of youth,
Trimm'd like a younker prancing to his love!
    Edw. Dazzle mine eyes, or do I see three
        suns?
    Rich. Three glorious suns, each one a per-
        fect sun;
Not separated with the racking clouds,
But sever'd in a pale clear-shining sky.
See, see! they join, embrace, and seem to kiss,
As if they vow'd some league inviolable: 30
Now are they but one lamp, one light, one sun.
In this the heaven figures some event.
    Edw. 'Tis wondrous strange, the like yet
    never heard of.
I think it cites us, brother, to the field,
That we, the sons of brave Plantagenet,
Each one already blazing by our meeds,
Should notwithstanding join our lights to-
    gether
And over-shine the earth as this the world.
Whate'er it bodes, henceforward will I bear
Upon my target three fair-shining suns. 40
    Rich. Nay, bear three daughters: by your
        leave I speak it,
You love the breeder better than the male.

Enter a Messenger.

But what art thou, whose heavy looks foretell
Some dreadful story hanging on thy tongue?
    Mess. Ah, one that was a woful looker-on
When as the noble Duke of York was slain,
Your princely father and my loving lord!
    Edw. O, speak no more, for I have heard
        too much.
    Rich. Say how he died, for I will hear it all.
    Mess. Environed he was with many
        foes,   50
And stood against them, as the hope of Troy
Against the Greeks that would have enter'd
    Troy.
But Hercules himself must yield to odds;
And many strokes, though with a little axe,
Hew down and fell the hardest-timber'd oak.
By many hands your father was subdued;
But only slaughter'd by the ireful arm
Of unrelenting Clifford and the queen,
Who crown'd the gracious duke in high de-
    spite,
Laugh'd in his face; and when with grief he
    wept,   60
The ruthless queen gave him to dry his cheeks
A napkin steeped in the harmless blood
Of sweet young Rutland, by rough Clifford
    slain:
And after many scorns, many foul taunts,
They took his head, and on the gates of York
They set the same; and there it doth remain,

The saddest spectacle that e'er I view'd.
    Edw. Sweet Duke of York, our prop to
        lean upon,
Now thou art gone, we have no staff, no stay.
O Clifford, boisterous Clifford! thou hast slain
The flower of Europe for his chivalry;   71
And treacherously hast thou vanquish'd him,
For hand to hand he would have vanquish'd
    thee.
Now my soul's palace is become a prison:
Ah, would she break from hence, that this my
    body
Might in the ground be closed up in rest!
For never henceforth shall I joy again,
Never, O never, shall I see more joy!
    Rich. I cannot weep; for all my body's
        moisture
Scarce serves to quench my furnace-burning
        heart: 80
Nor can my tongue unload my heart's great
        burthen;
For selfsame wind that I should speak withal
Is kindling coals that fires all my breast,
And burns me up with flames that tears would
    quench.
To weep is to make less the depth of grief:
Tears then for babes; blows and revenge for
    me
Richard, I bear thy name; I'll venge thy
    death,
Or die renowned by attempting it.
    Edw. His name that valiant duke hath left
        with thee;
His dukedom and his chair with me is left.90
    Rich. Nay, if thou be that princely eagle's
        bird,
Show thy descent by gazing 'gainst the sun:
For chair and dukedom, throne and kingdom
    say;
Either that is thine, or else thou wert not his.

    March. *Enter* WARWICK, MARQUESS OF
        MONTAGUE, *and their army.*

    War. How now, fair lords! What fare?
        what news abroad?
    Rich. Great Lord of Warwick, if we should
        recount
Our baleful news, and at each word's deliver-
    ance
Stab poniards in our flesh till all were told,
The words would add more anguish than the
    wounds.
O valiant lord, the Duke of York is slain!100
    Edw. O Warwick, Warwick! that Plantag-
        enet,
Which held three dearly as his soul's redemp-
    tion,
Is by the stern Lord Clifford done to death.
    War. Ten days ago I drown'd these news
        in tears;
And now, to add more measure to your woes,
I come to tell you things sith then befall'n.
After the bloody fray at Wakefield fought,
Where your brave father breathed his latest
    gasp,
Tidings, as swiftly as the posts could run,
Were brought me of your loss and his depart.
I, then in London, keeper of the king,   111
Muster'd my soldiers, gather'd flocks of
    friends,
And very well appointed, as I thought,
March'd toward Saint Alban's to intercept
    the queen,

Bearing the king in my behalf along;
For by my scouts I was advertised
That she was coming with a full intent
To dash our late decree in parliament
Touching King Henry's oath and your succession.
Short tale to make, we at Saint Alban's met
Our battles join'd, and both sides fiercely
    fought :   121
But whether 'twas the coldness of the king,
Who look'd full gently on his warlike queen,
That robb'd my soldiers of their heated
    spleen ;
Or whether 'twas report of her success ;
Or more than common fear of Clifford's rigor,
Who thunders to his captives blood and death,
I cannot judge : but, to conclude with truth,
Their weapons like to lightning came and
    went ;
Our soldiers', like the night-owl's lazy flight,
Or like an idle thresher with a flail,   131
Fell gently down, as if they struck their
    friends.
I cheer'd them up with justice of our cause,
With promise of high pay and great rewards :
But all in vain ; they had no heart to fight,
And we in them no hope to win the day ;
So that we fled ; the king unto the queen ;
Lord George your brother, Norfolk and myself,
In haste, post-haste, are come to join with you :
For in the marches here we heard you were,
Making another head to fight again.   141
    Edw.   Where is the Duke of Norfolk, gentle
        Warwick ?
And when came George from Burgundy to
    England ?
    War.   Some six miles off the duke is with
        the soldiers ;
And for your brother, he was lately sent
From your kind aunt, Duchess of Burgundy,
With aid of soldiers to this needful war.
    Rich.   'Twas odds, belike, when valiant
        Warwick fled :
Oft have I heard his praises in pursuit,
But ne'er till now his scandal of retire.   150
    War.   Nor now my scandal, Richard, dost
        thou hear ;
For thou shalt know this strong right hand of
    mine
Can pluck the diadem from faint Henry's
    head,
And wring the awful sceptre from his fist,
Were he as famous and as bold in war
As he is famed for mildness, peace, and
    prayer.
    Rich.   I know it well, Lord Warwick ;
        blame me not :
'Tis love I bear thy glories makes me speak.
But in this troublous time what's to be done ?
Shall we go throw away our coats of steel,   160
And wrap our bodies in black mourning
    gowns,
Numbering our Ave-Maries with our beads ?
Or shall we on the helmets of our foes
Tell our devotion with revengeful arms ?
If for the last, say ay, and to it, lords.
    War.   Why, therefore Warwick came to
        seek you out ;
And therefore comes my brother Montague.
Attend me, lords. The proud insulting queen,
With Clifford and the haught Northumberland,   169

And of their feather many more proud birds,
Have wrought the easy-melting king like wax.
He swore consent to your succession,
His oath enrolled in the parliament ;
And now to London all the crew are gone,
To frustrate both his oath and what beside
May make against the house of Lancaster.
Their power, I think, is thirty thousand strong :
Now, if the help of Norfolk and myself,
With all the friends that thou, brave Earl of
    March,   179
Amongst the loving Welshmen canst procure,
Will but amount to five and twenty thousand,
Why, Via ! to London will we march amain,
And once again bestride our foaming steeds,
And once again cry ' Charge upon our foes ! '
But never once again turn back and fly.
    Rich.   Ay, now methinks I hear great War-
        wick speak :
Ne'er may he live to see a sunshine day,
That cries ' Retire,' if Warwick bid him stay.
    Edw.   Lord Warwick, on thy shoulder will
        I lean ;
And when thou fail'st—as God forbid the
    hour !—   190
Must Edward fall, which peril heaven forfend !
    War.   No longer Earl of March, but Duke
        of York :
The next degree is England's royal throne ;
For King of England shalt thou be proclaim'd
In every borough as we pass along ;
And he that throws not up his cap for joy
Shall for the fault make forfeit of his head.
King Edward, valiant Richard, Montague,
Stay we no longer, dreaming of renown,
But sound the trumpets, and about our task.
    Rich.   Then, Clifford, were thy heart as
        hard as steel,   201
As thou hast shown it flinty by thy deeds,
I come to pierce it, or to give thee mine.
    Edw.   Then strike up drums : God and
        Saint George for us !

                Enter a Messenger.

    War.   How now ! what news ?
    Mess.   The Duke of Norfolk sends you
        word by me,
The queen is coming with a puissant host ;
And craves your company for speedy counsel.
    War.   Why then it sorts, brave warriors,
        let's away.   [*Exeunt.*

            SCENE II. *Before York.*

Flourish. Enter KING HENRY, QUEEN MAR-
    GARET, *the* PRINCE OF WALES, CLIFFORD,
    and NORTHUMBERLAND, *with drum and*
    trumpets.

    Q. Mar.   Welcome, my lord, to this brave
        town of York.
Yonder's the head of that arch-enemy
That sought to be encompass'd with your
    crown :
Doth not the object cheer your heart, my
    lord ?
    K. Hen.   Ay, as the rocks cheer them that
        fear their wreck :
To see this sight, it irks my very soul.
Withhold revenge, dear God ! 'tis not my
    fault,
Nor wittingly have I infringed my vow.
    Clif.   My gracious liege, this too much
        lenity

And harmful pity must be laid aside.   10
To whom do lions cast their gentle looks ?
Not to the beast that would usurp their den.
Whose hand is that the forest bear doth lick ?
Not his that spoils her young before her face.
Who 'scapes the lurking serpent's mortal
    sting ?
Not he that sets his foot upon her back.
The smallest worm will turn being trodden on,
And doves will peck in safeguard of their
    brood.
Ambitious York doth level at thy crown,   19
Thou smiling while he knit his angry brows :
He, but a duke, would have his son a king,
And raise his issue, like a loving sire ;
Thou, being a king, blest with a goodly son,
Didst yield consent to disinherit him,
Which argued thee a most unloving father.
Unreasonable creatures feed their young ;
And though man's face be fearful to their
    eyes,
Yet, in protection of their tender ones,
Who hath not seen them, even with those
    wings
Which sometime they have used with fearful
    flight,   30
Make war with him that climb'd unto their
    nest,
Offering their own lives in their young's de-
    fence ?
For shame, my liege, make them your prece-
    dent !
Were it not pity that this goodly boy
Should lose his birthright by his father's fault,
And long hereafter say unto his child,
' What my great-grandfather and grandsire
    got
My careless father fondly gave away ' ?
Ah, what a shame were this ! Look on the
    boy ;
And let his manly face, which promiseth   40
Successful fortune, steel thy melting heart
To hold thine own and leave thine own with
    him.
    K. Hen. Full well hath Clifford play'd the
    orator,
Inferring arguments of mighty force.
But, Clifford, tell me, didst thou never hear
That things ill-got had ever bad success ?
And happy always was it for that son
Whose father for his hoarding went to hell ?
I'll leave my son my virtuous deeds behind ;
And would my father had left me no more ! 50
For all the rest is held at such a rate
As brings a thousand-fold more care to keep
Than in possession any jot of pleasure.
Ah, cousin York ! would thy best friends did
    know
How it doth grieve me that thy head is here !
    Q. Mar. My lord, cheer up your spirits :
    our foes are nigh,
And this soft courage makes your followers
    faint.
You promised knighthood to our forward
    son :
Unsheathe your sword, and dub him presently.
Edward, kneel down.   60
    K. Hen. Edward Plantagenet, arise a
    knight ;
And learn this lesson, draw thy sword in right.
    Prince. My gracious father, by your kingly
    leave,
I'll draw it as apparent to the crown,

And in that quarrel use it to the death.
    Clif. Why, that is spoken like a toward
    prince.

Enter a Messenger.

    Mess. Royal commanders, be in readi-
    ness :
For with a band of thirty thousand men
Comes Warwick, backing of the Duke of
    York ;
And in the towns, as they do march along,   70
Proclaims him king, and many fly to him :
Darraign your battle, for they are at hand.
    Clif. I would your highness would depart
    the field :
The queen hath best success when you are
    absent.
    Q. Mar. Ay, good my lord, and leave us to
    our fortune.
    K. Hen. Why, that's my fortune too ;
    therefore I'll stay.
    North. Be it with resolution then to fight.
    Prince. My royal father, cheer these noble
    lords
And hearten those that fight in your defence :
Unsheathe your sword, good father ; cry
    ' Saint George ! '   80

March. Enter EDWARD, GEORGE, RICHARD,
    WARWICK, NORFOLK, MONTAGUE, *and* Sol-
    diers.

    Edw. Now, perjured Henry ! wilt thou
    kneel for grace,
And set thy diadem upon my head ;
Or bide the mortal fortune of the field ?
    Q. Mar. Go, rate thy minions, proud in-
    sulting boy !
Becomes it thee to be thus bold in terms
Before thy sovereign and thy lawful king ?
    Edw. I am his king, and he should bow
    his knee ;
I was adopted heir by his consent :
Since when, his oath is broke ; for, as I hear,
You, that are king, though he do wear the
    crown,   90
Have caused him, by new act of parliament,
To blot out me, and put his own son in.
    Clif. And reason too :
Who should succeed the father but the son ?
    Rich. Are you there, butcher ? O, I can-
    not speak !
    Clif. Ay, crook-back, here I stand to an-
    swer thee,
Or any he the proudest of thy sort.
    Rich. 'Twas you that kill'd young Rut-
    land, was it not ?
    Clif. Ay, and old York, and yet not satis-
    fied.
    Rich. For God's sake, lords, give signal to
    the fight.   100
    War. What say'st thou, Henry, wilt thou
    yield the crown ?
    Q. Mar. Why, how now, long-tongued
    Warwick ! dare you speak ?
When you and I met at Saint Alban's last,
Your legs did better service than your hands.
    War. Then 'twas my turn to fly, and now
    'tis thine.
    Clif. You said so much before, and yet
    you fled.
    War. 'Twas not your valor, Clifford, drove
    me thence.

North. No, nor your manhood that durst
make you stay.
Rich. Northumberland, I hold thee rever-
ently.
Break off the parley; for scarce I can refrain
The execution of my big-swoln heart   111
Upon that Clifford, that cruel child-killer.
Clif. I slew thy father, call'st thou him a
child ?
Rich. Ay, like a dastard and a treacherous
coward,
As thou didst kill our tender brother Rutland ;
But ere sunset I'll make thee curse the deed.
K. Hen. Have done with words, my lords,
and hear me speak.
Q. Mar. Defy them then, or else hold
close thy lips.
K. Hen. I prithee, give no limits to my
tongue :
I am a king, and privileged to speak.   120
Clif. My liege, the wound that bred this
meeting here
Cannot be cured by words ; therefore be still.
Rich. Then, executioner, unsheathe thy
sword :
By him that made us all, I am resolved
That Clifford's manhood lies upon his tongue.
Edw. Say, Henry, shall I have my right,
or no ?
A thousand men have broke their fasts to-day,
That ne'er shall dine unless thou yield the
crown.
War. If thou deny, their blood upon thy
head ;
For York in justice puts his armor on.   130
Prince. If that be right which Warwick
says is right,
There is no wrong, but every thing is right.
Rich. Whoever got thee, there thy mother
stands ;
For, well I wot, thou hast thy mother's tongue.
Q. Mar. But thou art neither like thy sire
nor dam ;
But like a foul mis-shapen stigmatic,
Mark'd by the destinies to be avoided,
As venom toads, or lizards' dreadful stings.
Rich. Iron of Naples hid with English gilt,
Whose father bears the title of a king,—   140
As if a channel should be call'd the sea,—
Shamest thou not, knowing whence thou art
extraught,
To let thy tongue detect thy base-born heart ?
Edw. A wisp of straw were worth a thou-
sand crowns,
To make this shameless callet know herself.
Helen of Greece was fairer far than thou,
Although thy husband may be Menelaus ;
And ne'er was Agamemnon's brother wrong'd
By that false woman, as this king by thee.
His father revell'd in the heart of France,   150
And tamed the king, and made the dauphin
stoop ;
And had he match'd according to his state,
He might have kept that glory to this day ;
But when he took a beggar to his bed,
And graced thy poor sire with his bridal-day,
Even then that sunshine brew'd a shower for
him,
That wash'd his father's fortunes forth of
France,
And heap'd sedition on his crown at home.
For what hath broach'd this tumult but thy
pride ?

Hadst thou been meek, our title still had slept ;
And we, in pity of the gentle king,   161
Had slipp'd our claim until another age.
Geo. But when we saw our sunshine made
thy spring,
And that thy summer bred us no increase,
We set the axe to thy usurping root ;
And though the edge hath something hit our-
selves,
Yet, know thou, since we have begun to strike,
We'll never leave till we have hewn thee down,
Or bathed thy growing with our heated bloods.
Edw. And, in this resolution, I defy thee ;
Not willing any longer conference,   171
Since thou deniest the gentle king to speak.
Sound trumpets ! let our bloody colors wave !
And either victory, or else a grave.
Q. Mar. Stay, Edward.
Edw. No, wrangling woman, we'll no
longer stay :
These words will cost ten thousand lives this
day.   [*Exeunt.*

SCENE III. *A field of battle between Towton
and Saxton, in Yorkshire.*

Alarum. Excursions. Enter WARWICK.

War. Forspent with toil, as runners with
a race,
I lay me down a little while to breathe ;
For strokes received, and many blows repaid,
Have robb'd my strong-knit sinews of their
strength,
And spite of spite needs must I rest awhile.

Enter EDWARD, *running.*

Edw. Smile, gentle heaven ! or strike, ungentle death !
For this world frowns, and Edward's sun is
clouded.
War. How now, my lord ! what hap ?
what hope of good ?

Enter GEORGE.

Geo. Our hap is loss, our hope but sad de-
spair ;
Our ranks are broke, and ruin follows us :   10
What counsel give you ? whither shall we fly ?
Edw. Bootless is flight, they follow us with
wings ;
And weak we are and cannot shun pursuit.

Enter RICHARD.

Rich. Ah, Warwick, why hast thou with-
drawn thyself ?
Thy brother's blood the thirsty earth hath
drunk,
Broach'd with the steely point of Clifford's
lance ;
And in the very pangs of death he cried,
Like to a dismal clangor heard from far,
' Warwick, revenge ! brother, revenge my
death ! '
So, underneath the belly of their steeds,   20
That stain'd their fetlocks in his smoking
blood,
The noble gentleman gave up the ghost.
War. Then let the earth be drunken with
our blood :
I'll kill my horse, because I will not fly.
Why stand we like soft-hearted women here,
Wailing our losses, whiles the foe doth rage,
And look upon, as if the tragedy
Were play'd in jest by counterfeiting actors

Here on my knee I vow to God above,
I'll never pause again, never stand still,   30
Till either death hath closed these eyes of
    mine
Or fortune given me measure of revenge.
    Edw. O Warwick, I do bend my knee with
        thine ;
And in this vow do chain my soul to thine !
And, ere my knee rise from the earth's cold
        face,
I throw my hands, mine eyes, my heart to
        thee,
Thou setter up and plucker down of kings,
Beseeching thee, if with thy will it stands
That to my foes this body must be prey,
Yet that thy brazen gates of heaven may
        ope,   40
And give sweet passage to my sinful soul !
Now, lords, take leave until we meet again,
Where'er it be, in heaven or in earth.
    Rich. Brother, give me thy hand ; and,
        gentle Warwick,
Let me embrace thee in my weary arms :
I, that did never weep, now melt with woe
That winter should cut off our spring-time so.
    War. Away, away ! Once more, sweet
        lords, farewell.
    Geo. Yet let us all together to our troops,
And give them leave to fly that will not stay ;
And call them pillars that will stand to us ;
And, if we thrive, promise them such rewards
As victors wear at the Olympian games :
This may plant courage in their quailing
        breasts ;
For yet is hope of life and victory.
Forslow no longer, make we hence amain.
                                        [*Exeunt.*

    SCENE IV.   *Another part of the field.*

Excursions. Enter RICHARD *and* CLIFFORD.

    Rich. Now, Clifford, I have singled thee
        alone :
Suppose this arm is for the Duke of York,
And this for Rutland ; both bound to revenge,
Wert thou environ'd with a brazen wall.
    Clif. Now, Richard, I am with thee here
        alone :
This is the hand that stabb'd thy father York ;
And this the hand that slew thy brother Rut-
        land ;
And here's the heart that triumphs in their
        death
And cheers these hands that slew thy sire and
        brother
To execute the like upon thyself ;   10
And so, have at thee !
    [*They fight. Warwick comes ; Clifford flies.*
    Rich. Nay, Warwick, single out some other
        chase ;
For I myself will hunt this wolf to death.
                                        [*Exeunt.*

    SCENE V.   *Another part of the field.*
    Alarum.   Enter KING HENRY *alone.*

    King. This battle fares like to the morn-
        ing's war,
When dying clouds contend with growing
        light,
What time the shepherd, blowing of his nails,
Can neither call it perfect day nor night.
Now sways it this way, like a mighty sea
Forced by the tide to combat with the wind ;
Now sways it that way, like the selfsame sea

Forced to retire by fury of the wind :
Sometime the flood prevails, and then the
        wind ;
Now one the better, then another best ;   10
Both tugging to be victors, breast to breast,
Yet neither conqueror nor conquered :
So is the equal poise of this fell war.
Here on this molehill will I sit me down.
To whom God will, there be the victory !
For Margaret my queen, and Clifford too,
Have chid me from the battle ; swearing both
They prosper best of all when I am thence.
Would I were dead ! if God's good will were
        so ;
For what is in this world but grief and woe ?
O God ! methinks it were a happy life,   21
To be no better than a homely swain ;
To sit upon a hill, as I do now,
To carve out dials quaintly, point by point,
Thereby to see the minutes how they run,
How many make the hour full complete ;
How many hours bring about the day ;
How many days will finish up the year ;
How many years a mortal man may live.
When this is known, then to divide the
        times :   30
So many hours must I tend my flock ;
So many hours must I take my rest ;
So many hours must I contemplate ;
So many hours must I sport myself ;
So many days my ewes have been with young ;
So many weeks ere the poor fools will ean :
So many years ere I shall shear the fleece :
So minutes, hours, days, months, and years,
Pass'd over to the end they were created,
Would bring white hairs unto a quiet grave. 40
Ah, what a life were this ! how sweet ! how
        lovely !
Gives not the hawthorn-bush a sweeter shade
To shepherds looking on their silly sheep,
Than doth a rich embroider'd canopy
To kings that fear their subjects' treachery ?
O, yes, it doth ; a thousand-fold it doth.
And to conclude, the shepherd's homely curds,
His cold thin drink out of his leather bottle,
His wonted sleep under a fresh tree's shade,
All which secure and sweetly he enjoys,   50
Is far beyond a prince's delicates,
His viands sparkling in a golden cup,
His body couched in a curious bed,
When care, mistrust, and treason waits on
        him.

*Alarum.   Enter a Son that has killed his
    father, dragging in the dead body.*

    Son. Ill blows the wind that profits no-
        body.
This man, whom hand to hand I slew in fight,
May be possessed with some store of crowns ;
And I, that haply take them from him now,
May yet ere night yield both my life and them
To some man else, as this dead man doth
        me.   60
Who's this ? O God ! it is my father's face,
Whom in this conflict I unwares have kill'd.
O heavy times, begetting such events !
From London by the king was I press'd forth ;
My father, being the Earl of Warwick's man,
Came on the part of York, press'd by his mas-
        ter ;
And I, who at his hands received my life,
Have by my hands of life bereaved him.
Pardon me, God, I knew not what I did !

And pardon, father, for I knew not thee !   70
My tears shall wipe away these bloody marks ;
And no more words till they have flow'd their
     fill.
    K. Hen.   O piteous spectacle ! O bloody
     times !
Whiles lions war and battle for their dens,
Poor harmless lambs abide their enmity.
Weep, wretched man, I'll aid thee tear for
     tear ;
And let our hearts and eyes, like civil war,
Be blind with tears, and break o'ercharged
     with grief.

Enter a Father *that has killed his son, bringing
in the body.*

    Fath.   Thou that so stoutly hast resisted
     me,
Give me thy gold, if thou hast any gold :   80
For I have bought it with an hundred blows.
But let me see : is this our foeman's face ?
Ah, no, no, no, it is mine only son !
Ah, boy, if any life be left in thee,
Throw up thine eye ! see, see what showers
     arise,
Blown with the windy tempest of my heart,
Upon thy wounds, that kill mine eye and
     heart !
O, pity, God, this miserable age !
What stratagems, how fell, how butcherly,
Erroneous, mutinous and unnatural,   90
This deadly quarrel daily doth beget !
O boy, thy father gave thee life too soon,
And hath bereft thee of thy life too late !
    K. Hen.   Woe above woe ! grief more than
     common grief !
O that my death would stay these ruthful
     deeds !
O, pity, pity, gentle heaven, pity !
The red rose and the white are on his face,
The fatal colors of our striving houses :
The one his purple blood right well resembles ;
The other his pale cheeks, methinks, pre-
     senteth :   100
Wither one rose, and let the other flourish ;
If you contend, a thousand lives must wither.
    Son.   How will my mother for a father's
     death
Take on with me and ne'er be satisfied !
    Fath.   How will my wife for slaughter of
     my son
Shed seas of tears and ne'er be satisfied !
    K. Hen.   How will the country for these
     woful chances
Misthink the king and not be satisfied !
    Son.   Was ever son so rued a father's
     death ?
    Fath.   Was ever father so bemoan'd his
     son ?   110
    K. Hen.   Was ever king so grieved for sub-
     jects' woe ?
Much is your sorrow ; mine ten times so much.
    Son.   I'll bear thee hence, where I may
     weep my fill.   [*Exit with the body.*
    Fath.   These arms of mine shall be thy
     winding-sheet ;
My heart, sweet boy, shall be thy sepulchre,
For from my heart thine image ne'er shall go ;
My sighing breast shall be thy funeral bell ;
And so obsequious will thy father be,
Even for the loss of thee, having no more,
As Priam was for all his valiant sons.   120

I'll bear thee hence ; and let them fight that
     will,
For I have murdered where I should not kill.
         [*Exit with the body.*
    K. Hen.   Sad-hearted men, much overgone
     with care,
Here sits a king more woful than you are.

Alarums : excursions. Enter QUEEN MARGA-
RET, *the* PRINCE, *and* EXETER.

    Prince.   Fly, father, fly ! for all your friends
     are fled,
And Warwick rages like a chafed bull :
Away ! for death doth hold us in pursuit.
    Q. Mar.   Mount you, my lord ; towards
     Berwick post amain :
Edward and Richard, like a brace of grey-
     hounds
Having the fearful flying hare in sight,   130
With fiery eyes sparkling for very wrath,
And bloody steel grasp'd in their ireful hands,
Are at our backs ; and therefore hence amain.
    Exe.   Away ! for vengeance comes along
     with them :
Nay, stay not to expostulate, make speed ;
Or else come after : I'll away before.
    K. Hen.   Nay, take me with thee, good
     sweet Exeter :
Not that I fear to stay, but love to go
Whither the queen intends. Forward ; away !
         [*Exeunt.*

    SCENE VI.   *Another part of the field.*

A loud alarum. Enter CLIFFORD, *wounded.*

    Clif.   Here burns my candle out ; ay, here
     it dies,
Which, whiles it lasted, gave King Henry light.
O Lancaster, I fear thy overthrow
More than my body's parting with my soul !
My love and fear glued many friends to thee ;
And, now I fall, thy tough commixture melts.
Impairing Henry, strengthening misproud
     York,
The common people swarm like summer flies ;
And whither fly the gnats but to the sun ?
And who shines now but Henry's enemies ? 10
O Phœbus, hadst thou never given consent
That Phaëthon should check thy fiery steeds,
Thy burning car never had scorch'd the earth !
And, Henry, hadst thou sway'd as kings should
     do,
Or as thy father and his father did,
Giving no ground unto the house of York,
They never then had sprung like summer flies ;
I and ten thousand in this luckless realm
Had left no mourning widows for our death ;
And thou this day hadst kept thy chair in
     peace.   20
For what doth cherish weeds but gentle air ?
And what makes robbers bold but too much
     lenity ?
Bootless are plaints, and cureless are my
     wounds ;
No way to fly, nor strength to hold out flight :
The foe is merciless, and will not pity ;
For at their hands I have deserved no pity.
The air hath got into my deadly wounds,
And much effuse of blood doth make me faint.
Come, York and Richard, Warwick and the
     rest ;
I stabb'd your fathers' bosoms, split my breast
         [*He faints*

Alarum and retreat. Enter EDWARD, GEORGE, RICHARD, MONTAGUE, WARWICK, *and* Soldiers.

Edw. Now breathe we, lords : good fortune bids us pause, 31
And smooth the frowns of war with peaceful looks.
Some troops pursue the bloody-minded queen,
That led calm Henry, though he were a king,
As doth a sail, fill'd with a fretting gust,
Command an argosy to stem the waves.
But think you, lords, that Clifford fled with them ?
War. No, 'tis impossible he should escape,
For, though before his face I speak the words
Your brother Richard mark'd him for the grave : 40
And wheresoe'er he is, he's surely dead.
    [*Clifford groans, and dies.*
Edw. Whose soul is that which takes her heavy leave ?
Rich. A deadly groan, like life and death's departing.
Edw. See who it is : and, now the battle's ended,
If friend or foe, let him be gently used.
Rich. Revoke that doom of mercy, for 'tis Clifford ;
Who not contented that he lopp'd the branch
In hewing Rutland when his leaves put forth,
But set his murdering knife unto the root
From whence that tender spray did sweetly spring, 50
I mean our princely father, Duke of York.
War. From off the gates of York fetch down the head,
Your father's head, which Clifford placed there ;
Instead whereof let this supply the room :
Measure for measure must be answered.
Edw. Bring forth that fatal screech-owl to our house,
That nothing sung but death to us and ours :
Now death shall stop his dismal threatening sound,
And his ill-boding tongue no more shall speak.
War. I think his understanding is bereft.
Speak, Clifford, dost thou know who speaks to thee ? 61
Dark cloudy death o'ershades his beams of life,
And he nor sees nor hears us what we say.
Rich. O, would he did ! and so perhaps he doth :
'Tis but his policy to counterfeit,
Because he would avoid such bitter taunts
Which in the time of death he gave our father.
Geo. If so thou think'st, vex him with eager words.
Rich. Clifford, ask mercy and obtain no grace.
Edw. Clifford, repent in bootless penitence.
War. Clifford, devise excuses for thy faults.
Geo. While we devise fell tortures for thy faults.
Rich. Thou didst love York, and I am son to York.
Edw. Thou pitied'st Rutland ; I will pity thee.
Geo. Where's Captain Margaret, to fence you now ?

War. They mock thee, Clifford : swear as thou wast wont.
Rich. What, not an oath ? nay, then the world goes hard
When Clifford cannot spare his friends an oath.
I know by that he's dead ; and, by my soul,
If this right hand would buy two hour's life,
That I in all despite might rail at him, 81
This hand should chop it off, and with the issuing blood
Stifle the villain whose unstanched thirst
York and young Rutland could not satisfy.
War. Ay, but he's dead : off with the traitor's head,
And rear it in the place your father's stands.
And now to London with triumphant march,
There to be crowned England's royal king :
From whence shall Warwick cut the sea to France,
And ask the Lady Bona for thy queen : 90
So shalt thou sinew both these lands together ;
And, having France thy friend, thou shalt not dread
The scatter'd foe that hopes to rise again ;
For though they cannot greatly sting to hurt,
Yet look to have them buzz to offend thine ears.
First will I see the coronation ;
And then to Brittany I'll cross the sea,
To effect this marriage, so it please my lord.
Edw. Even as thou wilt, sweet Warwick, let it be ;
For in thy shoulder do I build my seat, 100
And never will I undertake the thing
Wherein thy counsel and consent is wanting.
Richard, I will create thee Duke of Gloucester,
And George, of Clarence : Warwick, as ourself,
Shall do and undo as him pleaseth best.
Rich. Let me be Duke of Clarence, George of Gloucester ;
For Gloucester's dukedom is too ominous.
War. Tut, that's a foolish observation :
Richard, be Duke of Gloucester. Now to London,
To see these honors in possession. 110
    [*Exeunt.*

ACT III.

SCENE I. *A forest in the north of England.*

Enter two Keepers, *with cross-bows in their hands.*

First Keep. Under this thick-grown brake we'll shroud ourselves ;
For through this laund anon the deer will come ;
And in this covert will we make our stand,
Culling the principal of all the deer.
Sec. Keep. I'll stay above the hill, so both may shoot.
First Keep. That cannot be ; the noise of thy cross-bow
Will scare the herd, and so my shoot is lost.
Here stand we both, and aim we at the best :
And, for the time shall not seem tedious,
I'll tell thee what befell me on a day 10
In this self-place where now we mean to stand.
Sec. Keep. Here comes a man ; let's stay till he be past.

Enter KING HENRY, *disguised, with a prayer-book.*

K. Hen. From Scotland am I stol'n, even
　　of pure love,
To greet mine own land with my wishful sight.
No, Harry, Harry, 'tis no land of thine;
Thy place is fill'd, thy sceptre wrung from
　　thee,
Thy balm wash'd off wherewith thou wast
　　anointed :
No bending knee will call thee Cæsar now,
No humble suitors press to speak for right,
No, not a man comes for redress of thee ; 20
For how can I help them, and not myself ?
　　First Keep. Ay, here's a deer whose skin's
　　a keeper's fee :
This is the quondam king ; let's seize upon
　　him.
　　K. Hen. Let me embrace thee, sour ad-
　　versity,
For wise men say it is the wisest course.
　　Sec. Keep. Why linger we ? let us lay
　　hands upon him.
　　First Keep. Forbear awhile ; we'll hear a
　　little more.
　　K. Hen. My queen and son are gone to
　　France for aid ;
And, as I hear, the great commanding War-
　　wick
Is thither gone, to crave the French king's
　　sister　　　　　　　　　　　　　　30
To wife for Edward : if this news be true,
Poor queen and son, your labor is but lost ;
For Warwick is a subtle orator,
And Lewis a prince soon won with moving
　　words.
By this account then Margaret may win him ;
For she's a woman to be pitied much :
Her sighs will make a battery in his breast ;
Her tears will pierce into a marble heart ;
The tiger will be mild whiles she doth mourn ;
And Nero will be tainted with remorse,　　40
To hear and see her plaints, her brinish tears.
Ay, but she's come to beg, Warwick, to give ;
She, on his left side, craving aid for Henry,
He, on his right, asking a wife for Edward.
She weeps, and says her Henry is deposed ;
He smiles, and says his Edward is install'd ;
That she, poor wretch, for grief can speak no
　　more ;
Whiles Warwick tells his title, smooths the
　　wrong,
Inferreth arguments of mighty strength,
And in conclusion wins the king from her, 50
With promise of his sister, and what else,
To strengthen and support King Edward's
　　place.
O Margaret, thus 'twill be ; and thou, poor
　　soul,
Art then forsaken, as thou went'st forlorn !
　　Sec. Keep. Say, what art thou that talk'st
　　of kings and queens ?
　　K. Hen. More than I seem, and less than
　　I was born to :
A man at least, for less I should not be ;
And men may talk of kings, and why not I ?
　　Sec. Keep. Ay, but thou talk'st as if thou
　　wert a king.
　　K. Hen. Why, so I am, in mind ; and that's
　　enough.　　　　　　　　　　　　　60
　　Sec. Keep. But, if thou be a king, where is
　　thy crown ?

　　K. Hen. My crown is in my heart, not on
　　my head ;
Not deck'd with diamonds and Indian stones,
Nor to be seen : my crown is called content :
A crown it is that seldom kings enjoy.
　　Sec. Keep. Well, if you be a king crown'd
　　with content,
Your crown content and you must be con-
　　tented
To go along with us ; for, as we think,
You are the king King Edward hath deposed ;
And we his subjects sworn in all allegiance 70
Will apprehend you as his enemy.
　　K. Hen. But did you never swear, and
　　break an oath ?
　　Sec. Keep. No, never such an oath ; nor
　　will not now.
　　K. Hen. Where did you dwell when I was
　　King of England ?
　　Sec. Keep. Here in this country, where we
　　now remain.
　　K. Hen. I was anointed king at nine
　　months old ;
My father and my grandfather were kings,
And you were sworn true subjects unto me :
And tell me, then, have you not broke your
　　oaths ?
　　First Keep. No ;　　　　　　　　80
For we were subjects but while you were king.
　　K. Hen. Why, am I dead ? do I not
　　breathe a man ?
Ah, simple men, you know not what you
　　swear!
Look, as I blow this feather from my face,
And as the air blows it to me again,
Obeying with my wind when I do blow,
And yielding to another when it blows,
Commanded always by the greater gust ;
Such is the lightness of you common men.
But do not break your oaths ; for of that sin 90
My mild entreaty shall not make you guilty.
Go where you will, the king shall be com-
　　manded ;
And be you kings, command, and I'll obey.
　　First Keep. We are true subjects to the
　　king, King Edward.
　　K. Hen. So would you be again to Henry,
If he were seated as King Edward is.
　　First Keep. We charge you, in God's
　　name, and the king's,
To go with us unto the officers.
　　K. Hen. In God's name, lead ; your king's
　　name be obey'd :
And what God will, that let your king per-
　　form ;
And what he will, I humbly yield unto.　101
　　　　　　　　　　　　　　　　　　[Exeunt.

SCENE II. *London. The palace.*

Enter KING EDWARD, GLOUCESTER, CLARENCE
and LADY GREY.

　　K. Edw. Brother of Gloucester, at Sain
　　Alban's field
This lady's husband, Sir Richard Grey, was
　　slain,
His lands then seized on by the conqueror
Her suit is now to repossess those lands ;
Which we in justice cannot well deny,
Because in quarrel of the house of York
The worthy gentleman did lose his life.
　　Glou. Your highness shall do well to gran
　　her suit ;
It were dishonor to deny it her.

K. Edw. It were no less ; but yet I'll make
   a pause.   10
Glou. [*Aside to Clar.*] Yea, is it so ?
I see the lady hath a thing to grant,
Before the king will grant her humble suit.
Clar. [*Aside to Glou.*] He knows the
   game : how true he keeps the wind !
Glou. [*Aside to Clar.*] Silence !
K. Edw. Widow, we will consider of your
   suit ;
And come some other time to know our mind.
L. Grey. Right gracious lord, I cannot
   brook delay :
May it please your highness to resolve me
   now ;
And what your pleasure is, shall satisfy me. 20
Glou. [*Aside to Clar.*] Ay, widow ? then I'll
   warrant you all your lands,
An if what pleases him shall pleasure you.
Fight closer, or, good faith, you'll catch a
   blow.
Clar. [*Aside to Glou.*] I fear her not, un-
   less she chance to fall.
Glou. [*Aside to Clar.*] God forbid that !
   for he'll take vantages.
K. Edw. How many children hast thou,
   widow ? tell me.
Clar. [*Aside to Glou.*] I think he means to
   beg a child of her.
Glou. [*Aside to Clar.*] Nay, whip me then :
   he'll rather give her two.
L. Grey. Three, my most gracious lord.
Glou. [*Aside to Clar.*] You shall have four,
   if you'll be ruled by him.   30
K. Edw. 'Twere pity they should lose their
   father's lands.
L. Grey. Be pitiful, dread lord, and grant
   it then.
K. Edw. Lords, give us leave : I'll try this
   widow's wit.
Glou. [*Aside to Clar.*] Ay, good leave have
   you ; for you will have leave,
Till youth take leave and leave you to the
   crutch.   [*Glou. and Clar. retire.*
K. Edw. Now tell me, madam, do you love
   your children ?
L. Grey. Ay, full as dearly as I love my-
   self.
K. Edw. And would you not do much to
   do them good ?
L. Grey. To do them good, I would sus-
   tain some harm.
K. Edw. Then get your husband's lands, to
   do them good.   40
L. Grey. Therefore I came unto your
   majesty.
K. Edw. I'll tell you how these lands are
   to be got.
L. Grey. So shall you bind me to your
   highness' service.
K. Edw. What service wilt thou do me, if
   I give them ?
L. Grey. What you command, that rests in
   me to do.
K. Edw. But you will take exceptions to
   my boon.
L. Grey. No, gracious lord, except I can-
   not do it.
K. Edw. Ay, but thou canst do what I
   mean to ask.
L. Grey. Why, then I will do what your
   grace commands.

Glou. [*Aside to Clar.*] He plies her hard ;
   and much rain wears the marble.   50
Clar. [*Aside to Glou.*] As red as fire ! nay,
   then her wax must melt.
L. Grey. Why stops my lord, shall I not
   hear my task ?
K. Edw. An easy task ; 'tis but to love a
   king.
L. Grey. That's soon perform'd, because
   I am a subject.
K. Edw. Why, then, thy husband's lands I
   freely give thee.
L. Grey. I take my leave with many thou-
   sand thanks.
Glou. [*Aside to Clar.*] The match is made ;
   she seals it with a curtsy.
K. Edw. But stay thee, 'tis the fruits of
   love I mean.
L. Grey. The fruits of love I mean, my
   loving liege.
K. Edw. Ay, but, I fear me, in another
   sense.   60
What love, think'st thou, I sue so much to
   get ?
L. Grey. My love till death, my humble
   thanks, my prayers ;
That love which virtue begs and virtue grants.
K. Edw. No, by my troth, I did not mean
   such love.
L. Grey. Why, then you mean not as I
   thought you did.
K. Edw. But now you partly may perceive
   my mind.
L. Grey. My mind will never grant what I
   perceive
Your highness aims at, if I aim aright.
K. Edw. To tell thee plain, I aim to lie
   with thee.
L. Grey. To tell you plain, I had rather lie
   in prison.   70
K. Edw. Why, then thou shalt not have thy
   husband's lands.
L. Grey. Why, then mine honesty shall be
   my dower ;
For by that loss I will not purchase them.
K. Edw. Therein thou wrong'st thy chil-
   dren mightily.
L. Grey. Herein your highness wrongs
   both them and me.
But, mighty lord, this merry inclination
Accords not with the sadness of my suit :
Please you dismiss me either with ' ay ' or
   ' no.'
K. Edw. Ay, if thou wilt say ' ay ' to my
   request ;
No, if thou dost say ' no ' to my demand.   80
L. Grey. Then, no, my lord. My suit is at
   an end.
Glou. [*Aside to Clar.*] The widow likes him
   not, she knits her brows.
Clar. [*Aside to Glou.*] He is the bluntest
   wooer in Christendom.
K. Edw. [*Aside*] Her looks do argue her
   replete with modesty ;
Her words do show her wit incomparable ;
All her perfections challenge sovereignty :
One way or other, she is for a king ;
And she shall be my love, or else my queen.—
Say that King Edward take thee for his
   queen ?
L. Grey. 'Tis better said than done, my
   gracious lord :   90

I am a subject fit to jest withal,
But far unfit to be a sovereign.
   K. Edw. Sweet widow, by my state I swear
     to thee
I speak no more than what my soul intends ;
And that is, to enjoy thee for my love.
   L. Grey. And that is more than I will yield
     unto :
I know I am too mean to be your queen,
And yet too good to be your concubine.
   K. Edw. You cavil, widow : I did mean,
     my queen.
   L. Grey. 'Twill grieve your grace my sons
     should call you father.   100
   K. Edw. No more than when my daughters
     call thee mother.
Thou art a widow, and thou hast some chil-
     dren ;
And, by God's mother, I, being but a bach-
     elor,
Have other some : why, 'tis a happy thing
To be the father unto many sons.
Answer no more, for thou shalt be my queen.
   Glou. [*Aside to Clar.*] The ghostly father
     now hath done his shrift.
   Clar. [*Aside to Glou.*] When he was made
     a shriver, 'twas for shift.
   K. Edw. Brothers, you muse what chat we
     two have had.
   Glou. The widow likes it not, for she looks
     very sad.   110
   K. Edw. You'll think it strange if I should
     marry her.
   Clar. To whom, my lord ?
   K. Edw.   Why, Clarence, to myself.
   Glou. That would be ten days' wonder at
     the least.
   Clar. That's a day longer than a wonder
     lasts.
   Glou. By so much is the wonder in ex-
     tremes.
   K. Edw. Well, jest on, brothers : I can tell
     you both
Her suit is granted for her husband's lands.

     Enter a Nobleman.

   Nob. My gracious lord, Henry your foe is
     taken,
And brought your prisoner to your palace gate.
   K. Edw. See that he be convey'd unto the
     Tower :   120
And go we, brothers, to the man that took
     him,
To question of his apprehension.
Widow, go you along. Lords, use her hon-
     orably.   [*Exeunt all but Gloucester.*
   Glou. Ay, Edward will use women honor-
     ably.
Would he were wasted, marrow, bones and all,
That from his loins no hopeful branch may
     spring,
To cross me from the golden time I look for !
And yet, between my soul's desire and me—
The lustful Edward's title buried—   129
Is Clarence, Henry, and his son young Ed-
     ward,
And all the unlook'd for issue of their bodies,
To take their rooms, ere I can place myself :
A cold premeditation for my purpose !
Why, then, I do but dream on sovereignty ;
Like one that stands upon a promontory,

And spies a far-off shore where he would
     tread,
Wishing his foot were equal with his eye,
And chides the sea that sunders him from
     thence,
Saying, he'll lade it dry to have his way :
So do I wish the crown, being so far off ; 140
And so I chide the means that keeps me from
     it ;
And so I say, I'll cut the causes off,
Flattering me with impossibilities.
My eye's too quick, my heart o'erweens too
     much,
Unless my hand and strength could equal
     them.
Well, say there is no kingdom then for Rich-
     ard ;
What other pleasure can the world afford ?
I'll make my heaven in a lady's lap,
And deck my body in gay ornaments,
And witch sweet ladies with my words and
     looks.   150
O miserable thought ! and more unlikely
Than to accomplish twenty golden crowns !
Why, love forswore me in my mother's womb :
And, for I should not deal in her soft laws,
She did corrupt frail nature with some bribe,
To shrink mine arm up like a wither'd shrub ;
To make an envious mountain on my back,
Where sits deformity to mock my body ;
To shape my legs of an unequal size ;
To disproportion me in every part,   160
Like to a chaos, or an unlick'd bear-whelp
That carries no impression like the dam.
And am I then a man to be beloved ?
O monstrous fault, to harbor such a thought !
Then, since this earth affords no joy to me,
But to command, to check, to o'erbear such
As are of better person than myself,
I'll make my heaven to dream upon the crown,
And, whiles I live, to account this world but
     hell,
Until my mis-shaped trunk that bears this head
Be round impaled with a glorious crown. 171
And yet I know not how to get the crown,
For many lives stand between me and home :
And I,—like one lost in a thorny wood,
That rends the thorns and is rent with the
     thorns,
Seeking a way and straying from the way ;
Not knowing how to find the open air,
But toiling desperately to find it out,—
Torment myself to catch the English crown :
And from that torment I will free myself, 180
Or hew my way out with a bloody axe.
Why, I can smile, and murder whiles I smile,
And cry 'Content' to that which grieves my
     heart,
And wet my cheeks with artificial tears,
And frame my face to all occasions.
I'll drown more sailors than the mermaid
     shall ;
I'll slay more gazers than the basilisk ;
I'll play the orator as well as Nestor,
Deceive more slily than Ulysses could,
And, like a Sinon, take another Troy.   190
I can add colors to the chameleon,
Change shapes with Proteus for advantages,
And set the murderous Machiavel to school.
Can I do this, and cannot get a crown ?
Tut, were it farther off, I'll pluck it down.
          [*Exit*

SCENE III. *France. The* KING's *palace.*

Flourish. Enter LEWIS *the French King, his sister* BONA, *his Admiral, called* BOURBON : PRINCE EDWARD, QUEEN MARGARET, *and the* EARL OF OXFORD. LEWIS *sits, and riseth up again.*

K. *Lew.* Fair Queen of England, worthy Margaret,
Sit down with us : it ill befits thy state
And birth, that thou shouldst stand while Lewis doth sit.
Q. *Mar.* No, mighty King of France : now Margaret
Must strike her sail and learn awhile to serve
Where kings command. I was, I must confess,
Great Albion's queen in former golden days :
But now mischance hath trod my title down,
And with dishonor laid me on the ground ;
Where I must take like seat unto my fortune,   10
And to my humble seat conform myself.
K. *Lew.* Why, say, fair queen, whence springs this deep despair ?
Q. *Mar.* From such a cause as fills mine eyes with tears
And stops my tongue, while heart is drown'd in cares.
K. *Lew.* Whate'er it be, be thou still like thyself,
And sit thee by our side : [*Seats her by him*]
        Yield not thy neck
To fortune's yoke, but let thy dauntless mind
Still ride in triumph over all mischance.
Be plain, Queen Margaret, and tell thy grief ;
It shall be eased, if France can yield relief. 20
Q. *Mar.* Those gracious words revive my drooping thoughts
And give my tongue-tied sorrows leave to speak.
Now, therefore, be it known to noble Lewis,
That Henry, sole possessor of my love,
Is of a king become a banish'd man,
And forced to live in Scotland a forlorn ;
While proud ambitious Edward Duke of York
Usurps the regal title and the seat
Of England's true-anointed lawful king.
This is the cause that I, poor Margaret,   30
With this my son, Prince Edward, Henry's heir,
Am come to crave thy just and lawful aid ;
And if thou fail us, all our hope is done :
Scotland hath will to help, but cannot help ;
Our people and our peers are both misled,
Our treasures seized, our soldiers put to flight,
And, as thou seest, ourselves in heavy plight.
K. *Lew.* Renowned queen, with patience calm the storm,
While we bethink a means to break it off.
Q. *Mar.* The more we stay, the stronger grows our foe.   40
K. *Lew.* The more I stay, the more I'll succor thee.
Q. *Mar.* O, but impatience waiteth on true sorrow.
And see where comes the breeder of my sorrow !

Enter WARWICK.

K. *Lew.* What's he approacheth boldly to our presence ?
Q. *Mar.* Our Earl of Warwick, Edward's greatest friend.

K. *Lew.* Welcome, brave Warwick ! What brings thee to France ?
            [*He descends. She ariseth.*
Q. *Mar.* Ay, now begins a second storm to rise ;
For this is he that moves both wind and tide.
War. From worthy Edward, King of Albion,
My lord and sovereign, and thy vowed friend,
I come, in kindness and unfeigned love,
First, to do greetings to thy royal person ;
And then to crave a league of amity ;
And lastly, to confirm that amity
With nuptial knot, if thou vouchsafe to grant
That virtuous Lady Bona, thy fair sister,
To England's king in lawful marriage.
Q. *Mar.* [*Aside*] If that go forward, Henry's hope is done.
War. [*To Bona*] And, gracious madam, in our king's behalf,   59
I am commanded, with your leave and favor,
Humbly to kiss your hand, and with my tongue
To tell the passion of my sovereign's heart ;
Where fame, late entering at his heedful ears,
Hath placed thy beauty's image and thy virtue.
Q. *Mar.* King Lewis and Lady Bona, hear me speak,
Before you answer Warwick. His demand
Springs not from Edward's well-meant honest love,
But from deceit bred by necessity ;
For how can tyrants safely govern home,
Unless abroad they purchase great alliance ?70
To prove him tyrant this reason may suffice,
That Henry liveth still ; but were he dead,
Yet here Prince Edward stands, King Henry's son.
Look, therefore, Lewis, that by this league and marriage
Thou draw not on thy danger and dishonor ;
For though usurpers sway the rule awhile,
Yet heavens are just, and time suppresseth wrongs.
War. Injurious Margaret !
Prince.   And why not queen ?
War. Because thy father Henry did usurp ;
And thou no more are prince than she is queen.
Oxf. Then Warwick disannuls great John of Gaunt,   81
Which did subdue the greatest part of Spain ;
And, after John of Gaunt, Henry the Fourth,
Whose wisdom was a mirror to the wisest ;
And, after that wise prince, Henry the Fifth,
Who by his prowess conquered all France :
From these our Henry lineally descends.
War. Oxford, how haps it, in this smooth discourse,
You told not how Henry the Sixth hath lost
All that which Henry the Fifth had gotten ? 90
Methinks these peers of France should smile at that.
But for the rest, you tell a pedigree
Of threescore and two years ; a silly time
To make prescription for a kingdom's worth.
Oxf. Why, Warwick, canst thou speak against thy liege,
Whom thou obeyed'st thirty and six years,
And not bewray thy treason with a blush ?
War. Can Oxford, that did ever fence the right,
Now buckler falsehood with a pedigree ?

For shame! leave Henry, and call Edward
king.   100
Oxf. Call him my king by whose injurious
doom
My elder brother, the Lord Aubrey Vere,
Was done to death? and more than so, my
father,
Even in the downfall of his mellow'd years,
When nature brought him to the door of
death?
No, Warwick, no; while life upholds this arm,
This arm upholds the house of Lancaster.
War. And I the house of York.
K. Lew. Queen Margaret, Prince Edward,
and Oxford,
Vouchsafe, at our request, to stand aside,   110
While I use further conference with Warwick.
                         [*They stand aloof.*
Q. Mar. Heavens grant that Warwick's
words bewitch him not!
K. Lew. Now Warwick, tell me, even upon
thy conscience,
Is Edward your true king? for I were loath
To link with him that were not lawful chosen.
War. Thereon I pawn my credit and mine
honor.
K. Lew. But is he gracious in the people's
eye?
War. The more that Henry was unfortu-
nate.
K. Lew. Then further, all dissembling set
aside,
Tell me for truth the measure of his love   120
Unto our sister Bona.
War.   Such it seems
As may beseem a monarch like himself.
Myself have often heard him say and swear
That this his love was an eternal plant,
Whereof the root was fix'd in virtue's ground,
The leaves and fruit maintain'd with beauty's
sun,
Exempt from envy, but not from disdain,
Unless the Lady Bona quit his pain.
K. Lew. Now, sister, let us hear your firm
resolve.
Bona. Your grant, or your denial, shall be
mine: 130
[*To War.*] Yet I confess that often ere this
day,
When I have heard your king's desert re-
counted,
Mine ear hath tempted judgment to desire.
K. Lew. Then, Warwick, thus: our sister
shall be Edward's;
And now forthwith shall articles be drawn
Touching the jointure that your king must
make,
Which with her dowry shall be counterpoised.
Draw near, Queen Margaret, and be a witness
That Bona shall be wife to the English king.
Prince. To Edward, but not to the English
king.   140
Q. Mar. Deceitful Warwick! it was thy
device
By this alliance to make void my suit:
Before thy coming Lewis was Henry's friend.
K. Lew. And still is friend to him and
Margaret:
But if your title to the crown be weak,
As may appear by Edward's good success,
Then 'tis but reason that I be released
From giving aid which late I promised.
Yet shall you have all kindness at my hand

That your estate requires and mine can yield.
War. Henry now lives in Scotland at his
ease,
Where having nothing, nothing can he lose.
And as for you yourself, our quondam queen,
You have a father able to maintain you;
And better 'twere you troubled him than
France.
Q. Mar. Peace, impudent and shameless
Warwick, peace,
Proud setter up and puller down of kings!
I will not hence, till, with my talk and tears,
Both full of truth, I make King Lewis behold
Thy sly conveyance and thy lord's false love;
For both of you are birds of selfsame feather.
              [*Post blows a horn within.*
K. Lew. Warwick, this is some post to us
or thee.

              Enter a Post.

Post. [*To War.*] My lord ambassador,
these letters are for you,
Sent from your brother, Marquess Montague:
[*To Lewis.*] These from our king unto your
majesty:
[*To Margaret.*] And, madam, these for you;
from whom I know not.
              [*They all read their letters.*
Oxf. I like it well that our fair queen and
mistress
Smiles at her news, while Warwick frowns at
his.
Prince. Nay, mark how Lewis stamps, as
he were nettled:
I hope all's for the best.   170
K. Lew. Warwick, what are thy news? and
yours, fair queen?
Q. Mar. Mine, such as fill my heart with
unhoped joys.
War. Mine, full of sorrow and heart's dis-
content.
K. Lew. What! has your king married the
Lady Grey!
And now, to soothe your forgery and his,
Sends me a paper to persuade me patience?
Is this the alliance that he seeks with France?
Dare he presume to scorn us in this manner?
Q. Mar. I told your majesty as much be-
fore:
This proveth Edward's love and Warwick's
honesty.   180
War. King Lewis, I here protest, in sight
of heaven,
And by the hope I have of heavenly bliss,
That I am clear from this misdeed of Ed-
ward's,
No more my king, for he dishonors me,
But most himself, if he could see his shame.
Did I forget that by the house of York
My father came untimely to his death?
Did I let pass the abuse done to my niece?
Did I impale him with the regal crown?
Did I put Henry from his native right?   190
And am I guerdon'd at the last with shame?
Shame on himself! for my desert is honor:
And to repair my honor lost for him,
I here renounce him and return to Henry.
My noble queen, let former grudges pass,
And henceforth I am thy true servitor:
I will revenge his wrong to Lady Bona,
And replant Henry in his former state.
Q. Mar. Warwick, these words have turn'd
my hate to love;

And I forgive and quite forget old faults,   200
And joy that thou becomest King Henry's
     friend.
  War. So much his friend, ay, his unfeigned
     friend,
That, if King Lewis vouchsafe to furnish us
With some few bands of chosen soldiers,
I'll undertake to land them on our coast
And force the tyrant from his seat by war.
'Tis not his new-made bride shall succor him :
And as for Clarence, as my letters tell me,
He's very likely now to fall from him,
For matching more for wanton lust than
     honor,   210
Or than for strength and safety of our country.
  Bona. Dear brother, how shall Bona be re-
     venged
But by thy help to this distressed queen ?
  Q. Mar. Renowned prince, how shall poor
     Henry live,
Unless thou rescue him from foul despair ?
  Bona. My quarrel and this English queen's
     are one.
  War. And mine, fair lady Bona, joins with
     yours.
  K. Lew. And mine with hers, and thine,
     and Margaret's.
Therefore at last I firmly am resolved
You shall have aid.   220
  Q. Mar. Let me give humble thanks for all
     at once.
  K. Lew. Then, England's messenger, return
     in post,
And tell false Edward, thy supposed king,
That Lewis of France is sending over masquers
To revel it with him and his new bride :
Thou seest what's past, go fear thy king withal.
  Bona. Tell him, in hope he'll prove a wid-
     ower shortly,
I'll wear the willow garland for his sake.
  Q. Mar. Tell him, my mourning weeds are
     laid aside,
And I am ready to put armor on.   230
  War. Tell him from me that he hath done
     me wrong,
And therefore I'll uncrown him ere't be long.
There's thy reward : be gone.   [*Exit Post.*
  K. Lew.   But, Warwick,
Thou and Oxford, with five thousand men,
Shall cross the seas, and bid false Edward
     battle ;
And, as occasion serves, this noble queen
And prince shall follow with a fresh supply.
Yet, ere thou go, but answer me one doubt,
What pledge have we of thy firm loyalty ?   239
  War. This shall assure my constant loy-
     alty,
That if our queen and this young prince agree,
I'll join mine eldest daughter and my joy
To him forthwith in holy wedlock bands.
  Q. Mar. Yes, I agree, and thank you for
     your motion.
Son Edward, she is fair and virtuous,
Therefore delay not, give thy hand to War-
     wick ;
And, with thy hand, thy faith irrevocable,
That only Warwick's daughter shall be thine.
  Prince. Yes, I accept her, for she well de-
     serves it ;
And here, to pledge my vow, I give my hand.
     [*He gives his hand to Warwick.*
  K. Lew. Why stay we now ? These soldiers
     shall be levied,

And thou, Lord Bourbon, our high admiral,
Shalt waft them over with our royal fleet.
I long till Edward fall by war's mischance,
For mocking marriage with a dame of France.
                   [*Exeunt all but Warwick.*
  War. I came from Edward as ambassador,
But I return his sworn and mortal foe :
Matter of marriage was the charge he gave me,
But dreadful war shall answer his demand.
Had he none else to make a stale but me ?   260
Then none but I shall turn his jest to sorrow.
I was the chief that raised him to the crown,
And I'll be chief to bring him down again :
Not that I pity Henry's misery,
But seek revenge on Edward's mockery. [*Exit.*

ACT IV.

Scene I. London. The palace.

Enter Gloucester, Clarence, Somerset, *and*
                Montague.

  Glou. Now tell me, brother Clarence, what
     think you
Of this new marriage with the Lady Grey ?
Hath not our brother made a worthy choice ?
  Clar. Alas, you know, 'tis far from hence
     to France ;
How could he stay till Warwick made return ?
  Som. My lords, forbear this talk ; here
     comes the king.
  Glou. And his well-chosen bride.
  Clar. I mind to tell him plainly what I
     think.

Flourish. Enter King Edward, *attended ;*
  Lady Grey, *as Queen ;* Pembroke, Stafford, Hastings, *and others.*

  K. Edw. Now, brother of Clarence, how
     like you our choice,
That you stand pensive, as half malcontent ?
  Clar. As well as Lewis of France, or the
     Earl of Warwick,   11
Which are so weak of courage and in judg-
     ment
That they'll take no offence at our abuse.
  K. Edw. Suppose they take offence without
     a cause,
They are but Lewis and Warwick : I am Ed-
     ward,
Your king and Warwick's, and must have my
     will.
  Glou. And shall have your will, because
     our king :
Yet hasty marriage seldom proveth well.
  K. Edw. Yea, brother Richard, are you of-
     fended too ?
  Glou. Not I :   20
No, God forbid that I should wish them
     sever'd
Whom God hath join'd together ; ay, and
     'twere pity
To sunder them that yoke so well together.
  K. Edw. Setting your scorns and your mis-
     like aside,
Tell me some reason why the Lady Grey
Should not become my wife and England's
     queen.
And you too, Somerset and Montague,
Speak freely what you think.
  Clar. Then this is mine opinion : that
     King Lewis

Becomes your enemy, for mocking him   30
About the marriage of the Lady Bona.
Glou.   And Warwick, doing what you gave
    in charge,
Is now dishonored by this new marriage.
K. Edw.   What if both Lewis and Warwick
    be appeased
By such invention as I can devise ?
Mont.   Yet, to have join'd with France in
    such alliance
Would more have strengthen'd this our com-
    monwealth
'Gainst foreign storms than any home-bred
    marriage.
Hast.   Why, knows not Montague that of
    itself
England is safe, if true within itself ?   40
Mont.   But the safer when 'tis back'd with
    France.
Hast.   'Tis better using France than trusting
    France :
Let us be back'd with God and with the seas
Which He hath given for fence impregnable,
And with their helps only defend ourselves ;
In them and in ourselves our safety lies.
Clar.   For this one speech Lord Hastings
    well deserves
To have the heir of the Lord Hungerford.
K. Edw.   Ay, what of that ? it was my will
    and grant ;
And for this once my will shall stand for law.
Glou.   And yet methinks your grace hath
    not done well,   51
To give the heir and daughter of Lord Scales
Unto the brother of your loving bride :
She better would have fitted me or Clarence :
But in your bride you bury brotherhood.
Clar.   Or else you would not have bestow'd
    the heir
Of the Lord Bonville on your new wife's son,
And leave your brothers to go speed elsewhere.
K. Edw.   Alas, poor Clarence ! is it for a
    wife
That thou art malcontent ? I will provide thee.
Clar.   In choosing for yourself, you show'd
    your judgment,   61
Which being shallow, you shall give me leave
To play the broker in mine own behalf ;
And to that end I shortly mind to leave you.
K. Edw.   Leave me, or tarry, Edward will
    be king,
And not be tied unto his brother's will.
Q. Eliz.   My lords, before it pleased his
    majesty
To raise my state to title of a queen,
Do me but right, and you must all confess
That I was not ignoble of descent ;   70
And meaner than myself have had like fortune.
But as this title honors me and mine,
So your dislike, to whom I would be pleasing,
Doth cloud my joys with danger and with
    sorrow.
K. Edw.   My love, forbear to fawn upon
    their frowns :
What danger or what sorrow can befall thee,
So long as Edward is thy constant friend,
And their true sovereign, whom they must
    obey ?
Nay, whom they shall obey, and love thee too,
Unless they seek for hatred at my hands ;   80
Which if they do, yet will I keep thee safe,
And they shall feel the vengeance of my wrath.

Glou.   I hear, yet say not much, but think
    the more.   [*Aside.*

Enter a Post.

K. Edw.   Now, messenger, what letters or
    what news
From France ?
Post.   My sovereign liege, no letters ; and
    few words,
But such as I, without your special pardon,
Dare not relate.
K. Edw.   Go to, we pardon thee : therefore,
    in brief,
Tell me their words as near as thou canst guess
    them.   90
What answer makes King Lewis unto our let-
    ters ?
Post.   At my depart, these were his very
    words :
' Go tell false Edward, thy supposed king,
That Lewis of France is sending over masquers   100
To revel it with him and his new bride.'
K. Edw.   Is Lewis so brave ? belike he
    thinks me Henry.
But what said Lady Bona to my marriage ?
Post.   These were her words, utter'd with
    mild disdain :
Tell him, in hope he'll prove a widower shortly,
I'll wear the willow garland for his sake.'   100
K. Edw.   I blame not her, she could say lit-
    tle less ;
She had the wrong. But what said Henry's
    queen ?
For I have heard that she was there in place.
Post.   ' Tell him,' quoth she, ' my mourning
    weeds are done,
And I am ready to put armor on.'
K. Edw.   Belike she minds to play the Am-
    azon.
But what said Warwick to these injuries ?
Post.   He, more incensed against your maj-
    esty
Than all the rest, discharged me with these
    words :
' Tell him from me that he hath done me
    wrong,
And therefore I'll uncrown him ere't be long.'
K. Edw.   Ha ! durst the traitor breathe out
    so proud words ?
Well I will arm me, being thus forewarn'd :
They shall have wars and pay for their pre-
    sumption.
But say, is Warwick friends with Margaret ?
Post.   Ay, gracious sovereign ; they are so
    link'd in friendship,
That young Prince Edward marries Warwick's
    daughter.
Clar.   Belike the elder ; Clarence will have
    the younger.
Now, brother king, farewell, and sit you fast,
For I will hence to Warwick's other daughter ;
That, though I want a kingdom, yet in mar-
    riage
I may not prove inferior to yourself.
You that love me and Warwick, follow me.
    [*Exit Clarence, and Somerset follows.*
Glou.   [*Aside.*] Not I :
My thoughts aim at a further matter ; I
Stay not for the love of Edward, but the
    crown.
K. Edw.   Clarence and Somerset both gone
    to Warwick !

Yet am I arm'd against the worst can happen;
And haste is needful in this desperate case.
Pembroke and Stafford, you in our behalf 130
Go levy men, and make prepare for war;
They are already, or quickly will be landed:
Myself in person will straight follow you.
    [Exeunt Pembroke and Stafford.
But, ere I go, Hastings and Montague,
Resolve my doubt. You twain, of all the rest,
Are near to Warwick by blood and by al-
    liance:
Tell me if you love Warwick more than me?
If it be so, then both depart to him;
I rather wish you foes than hollow friends:
But if you mind to hold your true obedience,
Give me assurance with some friendly vow,
That I may never have you in suspect.
    Mont. So God help Montague as he proves
    true!
    Hast. And Hastings as he favors Edward's
    cause!
    K. Edw. Now, brother Richard, will you
    stand by us?
    Glou. Ay, in despite of all that shall with-
    stand you.
    K. Edw. Why, so! then am I sure of vic-
    tory.
Now therefore let us hence; and lose no hour,
Till we meet Warwick with his foreign power.
    [Exeunt.

    SCENE II. *A plain in Warwickshire.*

Enter WARWICK *and* OXFORD, *with French*
    soldiers.

    War. Trust me, my lord, all hitherto goes
    well;
The common people by numbers swarm to us.

    Enter CLARENCE *and* SOMERSET.

But see where Somerset and Clarence come!
Speak suddenly, my lords, are we all friends?
    Clar. Fear not that, my lord.
    War. Then, gentle Clarence, welcome unto
    Warwick;
And welcome, Somerset: I hold it cowardice
To rest mistrustful where a noble heart
Hath pawn'd an open hand in sign of love;
Else might I think that Clarence, Edward's
    brother, 10
Were but a feigned friend to our proceedings:
But welcome, sweet Clarence; my daughter
    shall be thine.
And now what rests but, in night's coverture,
Thy brother being carelessly encamp'd,
His soldiers lurking in the towns about,
And but attended by a simple guard,
We may surprise and take him at our pleas-
    ure?
Our scouts have found the adventure very
    easy:
That as Ulysses and stout Diomede
With sleight and manhood stole to Rhesus'
    tents, 20
And brought from thence the Thracian fatal
    steeds,
So we, well cover'd with the night's black
    mantle,
At unawares may beat down Edward's guard
And seize himself; I say not, slaughter him,
For I intend but only to surprise him.
You that will follow me to this attempt,
Applaud the name of Henry with your leader.
    [They all cry, 'Henry!'

Why, then, let's on our way in silent sort:
For Warwick and his friends, God and Saint
    George!   *[Exeunt.*

    SCENE III. *Edward's camp, near Warwick.*

Enter three Watchmen, *to guard the* KING'S
    tent.

    First Watch. Come on, my masters, each
    man take his stand:
The king by this is set him down to sleep.
    Second Watch. What, will he not to bed?
    First Watch. Why, no; for he hath made a
    solemn vow
Never to lie and take his natural rest
Till Warwick or himself be quite suppress'd.
    Second Watch. To-morrow then belike
    shall be the day,
If Warwick be so near as men report.
    Third Watch. But say, I pray, what noble-
    man is that
That with the king here resteth in his tent? 10
    First Watch. 'Tis the Lord Hastings, the
    king's chiefest friend.
    Third Watch. O, is it so? But why com-
    mands the king
That his chief followers lodge in towns about
    him,
While he himself keeps in the cold field?
    Second Watch. 'Tis the more honor, be-
    cause more dangerous.
    Third Watch. Ay, but give me worship and
    quietness;
I like it better than a dangerous honor.
If Warwick knew in what estate he stands,
'Tis to be doubted he would waken him.
    First Watch. Unless our halberds did shut
    up his passage. 20
    Second Watch. Ay, wherefore else guard
    we his royal tent,
But to defend his person from night-foes?

Enter WARWICK, CLARENCE, OXFORD, SOMER-
    SET, *and French soldiers, silent all.*

    War. This is his tent; and see where stand
    his guard.
Courage, my masters! honor now or never!
But follow me, and Edward shall be ours.
    First Watch. Who goes there?
    Second Watch. Stay, or thou diest!
    [Warwick and the rest cry all, 'War-
    wick! Warwick!' and set upon the
    Guard, who fly, crying, 'Arm!
    arm!' Warwick and the rest follow-
    ing them.

The drum playing and trumpet sounding, re-
    enter WARWICK, SOMERSET, *and the rest,*
    bringing the KING *out in his gown, sitting in*
    a chair. RICHARD *and* HASTINGS *fly over*
    the stage.
    Som. What are they that fly there?
    War. Richard and Hastings: let them go;
    here is
The duke.
    K. Edw. The duke! Why, Warwick, when
    we parted, 30
Thou call'dst me king.
    War.   Ay, but the case is alter'd:
When you disgraced me in my embassade,
Then I degraded you from being king,
And come now to create you Duke of York.
Alas! how should you govern any kingdom,

That know not how to use ambassadors,
Nor how to be contented with one wife,
Nor how to use your brothers brotherly,
Nor how to study for the people's welfare,
Nor how to shroud yourself from enemies ? 40
  K. Edw. Yea, brother of Clarence, are
    thou here too ?
Nay, then I see that Edward needs must down.
Yet, Warwick, in despite of all mischance,
Of thee thyself and all thy complices,
Edward will always bear himself as king :
Though fortune's malice overthrow my state,
My mind exceeds the compass of her wheel.
  War. Then, for his mind, be Edward Eng-
    land's king :   [*Takes off his crown.*
But Henry now shall wear the English crown,
And be true king indeed, thou but the shadow.
My Lord of Somerset, at my request,   51
See that forthwith Duke Edward be convey'd
Unto my brother, Archbishop of York.
When I have fought with Pembroke and his
    fellows,
I'll follow you, and tell what answer
Lewis and the Lady Bona send to him.
Now, for a while farewell, good Duke of York.
        [*They lead him out forcibly.*
  K. Edw. What fates impose, that men must
    needs abide ;
It boots not to resist both wind and tide.
        [*Exit, guarded.*
  Oxf. What now remains, my lords, for us
    to do   60
But march to London with our soldiers ?
  War. Ay, that's the first thing that we have
    to do ;
To free King Henry from imprisonment
And see him seated in the regal throne.
        [*Exeunt.*

SCENE IV. *London. The palace.*

Enter QUEEN ELIZABETH *and* RIVERS.

  Riv. Madam, what makes you in this sud-
    den change ?
  Q. Eliz. Why, brother Rivers, are you yet
    to learn
What late misfortune is befall'n King Edward ?
  Riv. What ! loss of some pitch'd battle
    against Warwick ?
  Q. Eliz. No, but the loss of his own royal
    person.
  Riv. Then is my sovereign slain ?
  Q. Eliz. Ay, almost slain, for he is taken
    prisoner,
Either betray'd by falsehood of his guard
Or by his foe surprised at unawares :
And, as I further have to understand,   10
Is new committed to the Bishop of York,
Fell Warwick's brother and by that our foe.
  Riv. These news I must confess are full of
    grief ;
Yet, gracious madam, bear it as you may :
Warwick may lose, that now hath won the day.
  Q. Eliz. Till then fair hope must hinder
    life's decay.
And I the rather wean me from despair
For love of Edward's offspring in my womb :
This is it that makes me bridle passion
And bear with mildness my misfortune's
    cross ;   20
Ay, ay, for this I draw in many a tear
And stop the rising of blood-sucking sighs,
Lest with my sighs or tears I blast or drown

King Edward's fruit, true heir to the English
    crown.
  Riv. But, madam, where is Warwick then
    become ?
  Q. Eliz. I am inform'd that he comes to-
    wards London,
To set the crown once more on Henry's head :
Guess thou the rest ; King Edward's friends
    must down,
But, to prevent the tyrant's violence,—
For trust not him that hath once broken
    faith,—   30
I'll hence forthwith unto the sanctuary,
To save at least the heir of Edward's right :
There shall I rest secure from force and fraud.
Come, therefore, let us fly while we may fly :
If Warwick take us we are sure to die.
        [*Exeunt.*

SCENE V. *A park near Middleham Castle in
    Yorkshire.*

Enter GLOUCESTER, LORD HASTINGS, *and* SIR
    WILLIAM STANLEY.

  Glou. Now, my Lord Hastings and Sir Wil-
    liam Stanley,
Leave off to wonder why I drew you hither,
Into this chiefest thicket of the park.
Thus stands the case : you know our king, my
    brother,
Is prisoner to the bishop here, at whose hands
He hath good usage and great liberty,
And, often but attended with weak guard,
Comes hunting this way to disport himself.
I have advertised him by secret means
That if about this hour he make this way   10
Under the color of his usual game,
He shall here find his friends with horse and
    men
To set him free from his captivity.

Enter KING EDWARD *and a* Huntsman *with
    him.*

  Hunt. This way, my lord ; for this way lies
    the game.
  K. Edw. Nay, this way, man : see where
    the huntsmen stand.
Now, brother of Gloucester, Lord Hastings,
    and the rest,
Stand you thus close, to steal the bishop's
    deer ?
  Glou. Brother, the time and case requireth
    haste :
Your horse stands ready at the park-corner.
  K. Edw. But whither shall we then ?
  Hast.   To Lynn, my lord, 20
And ship from thence to Flanders.
  Glou. Well guess'd, believe me ; for that
    was my meaning.
  K. Edw. Stanley, I will requite thy for-
    wardness.
  Glou. But wherefore stay we ? 'tis no time
    to talk.
  K. Edw. Huntsman, what say'st thou ? wilt
    thou go along ?
  Hunt. Better do so than tarry and be
    hang'd.
  Glou. Come then, away ; let's ha' no more
    ado.
  K. Edw. Bishop, farewell : shield thee from
    Warwick's frown.
And pray that I may repossess the crown.
        [*Exeunt.*

SCENE VI. *London. The Tower.*

Flourish. Enter KING HENRY, CLARENCE,
WARWICK, SOMERSET, *young* RICHMOND, OX-
FORD, MONTAGUE, *and* Lieutenant of the
Tower.

K. Hen. Master lieutenant, now that God
  and friends
Have shaken Edward from the regal seat,
And turn'd my captive state to liberty,
My fear to hope, my sorrows unto joys,
At our enlargement what are thy due fees ?
  Lieu. Subjects may challenge nothing of
    their sovereigns ;
But if an humble prayer may prevail,
I then crave pardon of your majesty.
  K. Hen. For what, lieutenant ? for well
    using me ?
Nay, be thou sure I'll well requite thy kind-
    ness,   10
For that it made my imprisonment a pleasure ;
Ay, such a pleasure as incaged birds
Conceive when after many moody thoughts
At last by notes of household harmony
They quite forget their loss of liberty.
But, Warwick, after God, thou set'st me free,
And chiefly therefore I thank God and thee ;
He was the author, thou the instrument.
Therefore, that I may conquer fortune's spite
By living low, where fortune cannot hurt me,
And that the people of this blessed land   21
May not be punish'd with my thwarting stars,
Warwick, although my head still wear the
    crown,
I here resign my government to thee,
For thou art fortunate in all thy deeds.
  War. Your grace hath still been famed for
    virtuous ;
And now may seem as wise as virtuous,
By spying and avoiding fortune's malice,
For few men rightly temper with the stars :
Yet in this one thing let me blame your grace,
For choosing me when Clarence is in place.   31
  Clar. No, Warwick, thou art worthy of the
    sway,
To whom the heavens in thy nativity
Adjudged an olive branch and laurel crown,
As likely to be blest in peace and war ;
And therefore I yield thee my free consent.
  War. And I choose Clarence only for pro-
    tector.
  K. Hen. Warwick and Clarence give me
    both your hands :
Now join your hands, and with your hands
    your hearts,
That no dissension hinder government :   40
I make you both protectors of this land,
While I myself will lead a private life
And in devotion spend my latter days,
To sin's rebuke and my Creator's praise.
  War. What answers Clarence to his sover-
    eign's will ?
  Clar. That he consents, if Warwick yield
    consent ;
For on thy fortune I repose myself.
  War. Why, then, though loath, yet must I
    be content :
We'll yoke together, like a double shadow
To Henry's body, and supply his place ;   50
I mean, in bearing weight of government,
While he enjoys the honor and his ease.
And, Clarence, now then it is more than need-
    ful

Forthwith that Edward be pronounced a trai-
    tor,
And all his lands and goods be confiscate.
  Clar. What else ? and that succession be
    determined.
  War. Ay, therein Clarence shall not want
    his part.
  K. Hen. But, with the first of all your chief
    affairs,
Let me entreat, for I command no more,
That Margaret your queen and my son Ed-
    ward   60
Be sent for, to return from France with speed ;
For, till I see them here, by doubtful fear
My joy of liberty is half eclipsed.
  Clar. It shall be done, my sovereign, with
    all speed.
  K. Hen. My Lord of Somerset, what youth
    is that,
Of whom you seem to have so tender care ?
  Som. My liege, it is young Henry, earl of
    Richmond.
  K. Hen. Come hither, England's hope.
[*Lays his hand on his head*]   If secret powers
Suggest but truth to my divining thoughts,
This pretty lad will prove our country's bliss.
His looks are full of peaceful majesty,   71
His head by nature framed to wear a crown,
His hand to wield a sceptre, and himself
Likely in time to bless a regal throne.
Make much of him, my lords, for this is he
Must help you more than you are hurt by me.

Enter a POST.

  War. What news, my friend ?
  Post. That Edward is escaped from your
    brother,
And fled, as he hears since, to Burgundy.
  War. Unsavory news ! but how made he
    escape ?   80
  Post. He was convey'd by Richard Duke of
    Gloucester
And the Lord Hastings, who attended him
In secret ambush on the forest side
And from the bishop's huntsmen rescued him ;
For hunting was his daily exercise.
  War. My brother was too careless of his
    charge.
But let us hence, my sovereign, to provide
A salve for any sore that may betide.
    [*Exeunt all but Somerset, Richmond, and
                                    Oxford.*
  Som. My lord, I like not of this flight of
    Edward's ;   89
For doubtless Burgundy will yield him help,
And we shall have more wars before 't be long.
As Henry's late presaging prophecy
Did glad my heart with hope of this young
    Richmond,
So doth my heart misgive me, in these con-
    flicts
What may befall him, to his harm and ours :
Therefore, Lord Oxford, to prevent the worst,
Forthwith we'll send him hence to Brittany,
Till storms be past of civil enmity.
  Oxf. Ay, for if Edward repossess the
    crown,
'Tis like that Richmond with the rest shall
    down.   100
  Som. It shall be so ; he shall to Brittany.
Come, therefore, let's about it speedily.
    [*Exeunt.*

SCENE VII. *Before York.*

Flourish.   Enter KING EDWARD, GLOUCESTER,
HASTINGS, *and* Soldiers.

K. *Edw.* Now, brother Richard, Lord Has-
tings, and the rest,
Yet thus far fortune maketh us amends,
And says that once more I shall interchange
My waned state for Henry's regal crown.
Well have we pass'd and now repass'd the seas
And brought desired help from Burgundy :
What then remains, we being thus arrived
From Ravenspurgh haven before the gates of
York,
But that we enter, as into our dukedom ?
Glou. The gates made fast ! Brother, I like
not this ;   10
For many men that stumble at the threshold
Are well foretold that danger lurks within.
K. *Edw.* Tush, man, abodements must not
now affright us :
By fair or foul means we must enter in,
For hither will our friends repair to us.
Hast. My liege, I'll knock once more to
summon them.

Enter, on the walls, the Mayor of York, *and
his Brethren.*

May. My lords, we were forewarned of
your coming,
And shut the gates for safety of ourselves ;
For now we owe allegiance unto Henry.
K. *Edw.* But, master mayor, if Henry be
your king,   20
Yet Edward at the least is Duke of York.
May. True, my good lord ; I know you for
no less.
K. *Edw.* Why, and I challenge nothing but
my dukedom,
As being well content with that alone.
Glou. [*Aside*] But when the fox hath once
got in his nose,
He'll soon find means to make the body follow.
Hast. Why, master mayor, why stand you
in a doubt ?
Open the gates ; we are King Henry's friends.
May. Ay, say you so ? the gates shall then
be open'd.   [*They descend.*
Glou. A wise stout captain, and soon per-
suaded !   30
Hast. The good old man would fain that all
were well,
So 'twere not 'long of him ; but being enter'd,
I doubt not, I, but we shall soon persuade
Both him and all his brothers unto reason.

Enter the Mayor *and two* Aldermen, *below.*

K. *Edw.* So, master mayor : these gates
must not be shut
But in the night or in the time of war.
What ! fear not, man, but yield me up the
keys ;   [*Takes his keys.*
For Edward will defend the town and thee,
And all those friends that deign to follow me.

March.   Enter MONTGOMERY, *with drum and
soldiers.*

Glou. Brother, this is Sir John Montgomery,
Our trusty friend, unless I be deceived.   41
K. *Edw.* Welcome, Sir John ! But why
come you in arms ?

Mont. To help King Edward in his time of
storm,
As every loyal subject ought to do.
K. *Edw.* Thanks, good Montgomery ; but
we now forget
Our title to the crown and only claim
Our dukedom till God please to send the rest.
Mont. Then fare you well, for I will hence
again :
I came to serve a king and not a duke.
Drummer, strike up, and let us march away.50
                        [*The drum begins to march.*
K. *Edw.* Nay, stay, Sir John, awhile, and
we'll debate
By what safe means the crown may be re-
cover'd.
Mont. What talk you of debating ? in few
words,
If you'll not here proclaim yourself our king,
I'll leave you to your fortune and be gone
To keep them back that come to succor you :
Why shall we fight, if you pretend no title ?
Glou. Why, brother, wherefore stand you
on nice points ?
K. *Edw.* When we grow stronger, then
we'll make our claim :
Till then, 'tis wisdom to conceal our meaning.
Hast. Away with scrupulous wit ! now arms
must rule.   61
Glou. And fearless minds climb soonest
unto crowns.
Brother, we will proclaim you out of hand :
The bruit thereof will bring you many friends.
K. *Edw.* Then be it as you will ; for 'tis my
right,
And Henry but usurps the diadem.
Mont. Ay, now my sovereign speaketh like
himself ;
And now will I be Edward's champion.
Hast. Sound trumpet ; Edward shall be
here proclaim'd :   69
Come, fellow-soldier, make thou proclamation.
                                                   [*Flourish.*
Sold. Edward the Fourth, by the grace of
God, king of England and France, and lord of
Ireland, &c.
Mont. And whosoe'er gainsays King Ed-
ward's right,
By this I challenge him to single fight.
                        [*Throws down his gauntlet.*
All. Long live Edward the Fourth !
K. *Edw.* Thanks, brave Montgomery ; and
thanks unto you all :
If fortune serve me, I'll requite this kindness.
Now, for this night, let's harbor here in
York ;
And when the morning sun shall raise his car
Above the border of this horizon,
We'll forward towards Warwick and his mates ;
For well I wot that Henry is no soldier.
Ah, froward Clarence ! how evil it beseems
thee,
To flatter Henry and forsake thy brother !
Yet, as we may, we'll meet both thee and War-
wick.
Come on, brave soldiers : doubt not of the day,
And, that once gotten, doubt not of large pay.
                                                   [*Exeunt.*

SCENE VIII. *London. The palace.*

Flourish.   Enter KING HENRY, WARWICK,
MONTAGUE, CLARENCE, EXETER, *and* OX-
FORD.

War. What counsel, lords ? Edward from
  Belgia,
With hasty Germans and blunt Hollanders,
Hath pass'd in safety through the narrow seas,
And with his troops doth march amain to Lon-
  don ;
And many giddy people flock to him.
  K. Hen. Let's levy men, and beat him back
  again.
  Clar. A little fire is quickly trodden out ;
Which, being suffer'd, rivers cannot quench.
  War. In Warwickshire I have true-hearted
  friends,
Not mutinous in peace, yet bold in war ;   10
Those will I muster up : and thou, son Clar-
  ence,
Shalt stir up in Suffolk, Norfolk and in Kent,
The knights and gentlemen to come with thee :
Thou, brother Montague, in Buckingham,
Northampton and in Leicestershire, shalt find
Men well inclined to hear what thou com-
  mand'st :
And thou, brave Oxford, wondrous well be-
  loved,
In Oxfordshire shalt muster up thy friends.
My sovereign, with the loving citizens,
Like to his island girt in with the ocean,
Or modest Dian circled with her nymphs,
Shall rest in London till we come to him.
Fair lords, take leave and stand not to reply.
Farewell, my sovereign.
  K. Hen. Farewell, my Hector, and my
  Troy's true hope.
  Clar. In sign of truth, I kiss your highness'
  hand.
  K. Hen. Well-minded Clarence, be thou
  fortunate !
  Mont. Comfort, my lord ; and so I take my
  leave.
  Oxf. And thus I seal my truth, and bid
  adieu.
  K. Hen. Sweet Oxford, and my loving
  Montague,   30
And all at once, once more a happy farewell.
  War. Farewell, sweet lords : let's meet at
  Coventry.
  [*Exeunt all but King Henry and Exeter.*
  K. Hen. Here at the palace will I rest
  awhile.
Cousin of Exeter, what thinks your lordship ?
Methinks the power that Edward hath in field
Should not be able to encounter mine.
  Exe. The doubt is that he will seduce the
  rest.
  K. Hen. That's not my fear ; my meed hath
  got me fame :
I have not stopp'd mine ears to their demands,
Nor posted off their suits with slow delays ;   40
My pity hath been balm to heal their wounds,
My mildness hath allay'd their swelling griefs,
My mercy dried their water-flowing tears ;
I have not been desirous of their wealth,
Nor much oppress'd them with great subsidies.
Nor forward of revenge, though they much
  err'd :
Then why should they love Edward more than
  me ?
No, Exeter, these graces challenge grace :
And when the lion fawns upon the lamb,
The lamb will never cease to follow him.   50
  [*Shout within.* 'A Lancaster ! A Lancaster !'
  Exe. Hark, hark, my lord ! what shouts are
  these ?

Enter King Edward, Gloucester, *and
  soldiers.*

  K. Edw. Seize on the shame-faced Henry,
  bear him hence ;
And once again proclaim us King of England.
You are the fount that makes small brooks to
  flow :
Now stops thy spring ; my sea shall suck them
  dry,
And swell so much the higher by their ebb.
Hence with him to the Tower ; let him not
  speak. [*Exeunt some with King Henry.*
And, lords, towards Coventry bend we our
  course,
Where peremptory Warwick now remains :   60
The sun shines hot ; and, if we use delay,
Cold biting winter mars our hoped-for hay.
  Glou. Away betimes, before his forces join,
And take the great-grown traitor unawares :
Brave warriors, march amain towards Coven-
  try.   [*Exeunt.*

ACT V.

Scene I. *Coventry.*

Enter Warwick, *the* Mayor of Coventry, *two*
  Messengers, *and others upon the walls.*

  War. Where is the post that came from
  valiant Oxford ?
How far hence is thy lord, mine honest fellow ?
  First Mess. By this at Dunsmore, march-
  ing hitherward.
  War. How far off is our brother Mon-
  tague ?
Where is the post that came from Montague ?
  Second Mess. By this at Daintry, with a
  puissant troop.

Enter Sir John Somerville.

  War. Say, Somerville, what says my loving
  son ?
And, by thy guess, how nigh is Clarence now ?
  Som. At Southam I did leave him with his
  forces,
And do expect him here some two hours
  hence.
                                   [*Drum heard.*
  War. Then Clarence is at hand, I hear his
  drum.   11
  Som. It is not his, my lord ; here Southam
  lies :
The drum your honor hears marcheth from
  Warwick.
  War. Who should that be ? belike, un-
  look'd-for friends.
  Som. They are at hand, and you shall
  quickly know.

March : flourish. Enter King Edward,
  Gloucester, *and soldiers.*

  K. Edw. Go, trumpet, to the walls, and
  sound a parle.
  Glou. See how the surly Warwick mans the
  wall !
  War. O unbid spite ! is sportful Edward
  come ?
Where slept our scouts, or how are they seduced,
That we could hear no news of his repair ?   20

K. Edw. Now, Warwick, wilt thou ope the
city gates,
Speak gentle words and humbly bend thy
knee,
Call Edward king and at his hands beg
mercy ?
And he shall pardon thee these outrages.
War. Nay, rather, wilt thou draw thy forces
hence,
Confess who set thee up and pluck'd thee
down,
Call Warwick patron and be penitent ?
And thou shalt still remain the Duke of York.
Glou. I thought, at least, he would have
said the king ;
Or did he make the jest against his will ?   30
War. Is not a dukedom, sir, a goodly gift ?
Glou. Ay, by my faith, for a poor earl to
give :
I'll do thee service for so good a gift.
War. 'Twas I that gave the kingdom to thy
brother.
K. Edw. Why then 'tis mine, if but by War-
wick's gift.
War. Thou art no Atlas for so great a
weight :
And, weakling, Warwick takes his gift again ;
And Henry is my king, Warwick his subject.
K. Edw. But Warwick's king is Edward's
prisoner :
And, gallant Warwick, do but answer this : 40
What is the body when the head is off ?
Glou. Alas, that Warwick had no more
forecast,
But, whiles he thought to steal the single ten,
The king was slily finger'd from the deck !
You left poor Henry at the Bishop's palace,
And, ten to one, you'll meet him in the Tower.
K. Edw. 'Tis even so ; yet you are Warwick
still.
Glou. Come, Warwick, take the time ;
kneel down, kneel down :
Nay, when ? strike now, or else the iron cools.
War. I had rather chop this hand off at a
blow,   50
And with the other fling it at thy face,
Than bear so low a sail, to strike to thee.
K. Edw. Sail how thou canst, have wind
and tide thy friend,
This hand, fast wound about thy coal-black
hair,
Shall, whiles thy head is warm and new cut
off,
Write in the dust this sentence with thy blood,
' Wind-changing Warwick now can change no
more.'

Enter OXFORD, *with drum and colors.*

War. O cheerful colors ! see where Oxford
comes !
Oxf. Oxford, Oxford, for Lancaster !
          [*He and his forces enter the city.*
Glou. The gates are open, let us enter too.
K. Edw. So other foes may set upon our
backs.   61
Stand we in good array ; for they no doubt
Will issue out again and bid us battle :
If not, the city being but of small defence,
We'll quickly rouse the traitors in the same.
War. O, welcome, Oxford ! for we want
thy help.

Enter MONTAGUE *with drum and colors.*

Mont. Montague, Montague, for Lancas-
ter !
          [*He and his forces enter the city.*
Glou. Thou and thy brother both shall buy
this treason
Even with the dearest blood your bodies bear.
K. Edw. The harder match'd, the greater
victory :   70
My mind presageth happy gain and conquest.

Enter SOMERSET, *with drum and colors.*

Som. Somerset, Somerset, for Lancaster !
          [*He and his forces enter the city.*
Glou. Two of thy name, both Dukes of
Somerset,
Have sold their lives unto the house of York ;
And thou shalt be the third if this sword hold.

Enter CLARENCE, *with drum and colors.*

War. And lo, where George of Clarence
sweeps along,
Of force enough to bid his brother battle ;
With whom an upright zeal to right prevails
More than the nature of a brother's love :
Come, Clarence, come ; thou wilt, if Warwick
call.   80
Clar. Father of Warwick, know you what
this means ?
          [*Taking his red rose out of his hat.*
Look here, I throw my infamy at thee :
I will not ruinate my father's house,
Who gave his blood to lime the stones together,
And set up Lancaster. Why, trow'st thou,
Warwick,
That Clarence is so harsh, so blunt, unnatural,
To bend the fatal instruments of war
Against his brother and his lawful king ?
Perhaps thou wilt object my holy oath :
To keep that oath were more impiety   90
Than Jephthah's, when he sacrificed his daugh-
ter.
I am so sorry for my trespass made
That, to deserve well at my brother's hands,
I here proclaim myself thy mortal foe,
With resolution, wheresoe'er I meet thee—
As I will meet thee, if thou stir abroad—
To plague thee for thy foul misleading me.
And so, proud-hearted Warwick, I defy thee,
And to my brother turn my blushing cheeks.
Pardon me, Edward, I will make amends : 100
And, Richard, do not frown upon my faults,
For I will henceforth be no more unconstant.
K. Edw. Now welcome more, and ten
times more beloved,
Than if thou never hadst deserved our hate.
Glou. Welcome, good Clarence ; this is
brotherlike.
War. O passing traitor, perjured and un-
just !
K. Edw. What, Warwick, wilt thou leave
the town and fight ?
Or shall we beat the stones about thine ears ?
War. Alas, I am not coop'd here for de-
fence !
I will away towards Barnet presently,   110
And bid thee battle, Edward, if thou darest.
K. Edw. Yes, Warwick, Edward dares, and
leads the way.
Lords, to the field ; Saint George and victory !
          [*Exeunt King Edward and his company.
          March. Warwick and his com-
          pany follow.*

SCENE II.   *A field of battle near Barnet.*

Alarum and excursions. Enter KING EDWARD, *bringing forth* WARWICK *wounded.*

K. Edw. So, lie thou there : die thou, and
    die our fear ;
For Warwick was a bug that fear'd us all.
Now, Montague, sit fast ; I seek for thee,
That Warwick's bones may keep thine com-
    pany.   [*Exit.*
  War. Ah, who is nigh ? come to me, friend
    or foe,
And tell me who is victor, York or Warwick ?
Why ask I that ? my mangled body shows,
My blood, my want of strength, my sick heart
    shows,
That I must yield my body to the earth
And, by my fall, the conquest to my foe.   10
Thus yields the cedar to the axe's edge,
Whose arms gave shelter to the princely eagle,
Under whose shade the ramping lion slept,
Whose top-branch overpeer'd Jove's spreading
    tree
And kept low shrubs from winter's powerful
    wind.
These eyes, that now are dimm'd with death's
    black veil,
Have been as piercing as the mid-day sun,
To search the secret treasons of the world :
The wrinkles in my brows, now filled with
    blood,
Were liken'd oft to kingly sepulchres ;   20
For who lived king, but I could dig his grave ?
And who durst smile when Warwick bent his
    brow ?
Lo, now my glory smear'd in dust and blood !
My parks, my walks, my manors that I had,
Even now forsake me, and of all my lands
Is nothing left me but my body's length.
Why, what is pomp, rule, reign, but earth and
    dust ?
And, live we how we can, yet die we must.

Enter OXFORD *and* SOMERSET.

  Som. Ah, Warwick, Warwick ! wert thou
    as we are,
We might recover all our loss again :   30
The queen from France hath brought a puis-
    sant power :
Even now we heard the news : ah, could'st
    thou fly !
  War. Why, then I would not fly.
    Ah, Montague,
If thou be there, sweet brother, take my hand,
And with thy lips keep in my soul awhile !
Thou lovest me not ; for, brother, if thou didst,
Thy tears would wash this cold congealed
    blood
That glues my lips and will not let me speak.
Come quickly, Montague, or I am dead.
  Som. Ah, Warwick ! Montague hath
    breathed his last ;   40
And to the latest gasp cried out for Warwick,
And said ' Commend me to my valiant
    brother.'
And more he would have said, and more he
    spoke,
Which sounded like a clamor in a vault,
That mought not be distinguished ; but at last
I well might hear, delivered with a groan,
' O, farewell, Warwick ! '
  War. Sweet rest his soul ! Fly, lords, and
    save yourselves ;

For Warwick bids you all farewell to meet in
    heaven.   [*Dies.*
  Oxf. Away, away, to meet the queen's
    great power ! [*Here they bear away his
    body.*   *Exeunt.*

SCENE III.   *Another part of the field.*

Flourish. Enter KING EDWARD *in triumph ;
with* GLOUCESTER, CLARENCE, *and the rest.*

  K. Edw. Thus far our fortune keeps an up-
    ward course,
And we are graced with wreaths of victory.
But, in the midst of this bright-shining day,
I spy a black, suspicious, threatening cloud,
That will encounter with our glorious sun,
Ere he attain his easeful western bed :
I mean, my lords, those powers that the queen
Hath raised in Gallia have arrived our coast
And, as we hear, march on to fight with us.
  Clar. A little gale will soon disperse that
    cloud   10
And blow it to the source from whence it
    came :
The very beams will dry those vapors up,
For every cloud engenders not a storm.
  Glou. The queen is valued thirty thousand
    strong,
And Somerset, with Oxford, fled to her :
If she have time to breathe be well assured
Her faction will be full as strong as ours.
  K. Edw. We are advertised by our loving
    friends
That they do hold their course toward Tewks-
    bury :
We, having now the best at Barnet field,   20
Will thither straight, for willingness rids way ;
And, as we march, our strength will be aug-
    mented
In every county as we go along.
Strike up the drum ; cry ' Courage ! ' and
    away.   [*Exeunt.*

SCENE IV.   *Plains near Tewksbury.*

March. Enter QUEEN MARGARET, PRINCE
EDWARD, SOMERSET, OXFORD, *and soldiers.*

  Q. Mar. Great lords, wise men ne'er sit and
    wail their loss,
But cheerly seek how to redress their harms.
What though the mast be now blown over-
    board,
The cable broke, the holding-anchor lost,
And half our sailors swallow'd in the flood ?
Yet lives our pilot still. Is't meet that he
Should leave the helm and like a fearful lad
With tearful eyes add water to the sea
And give more strength to that which hath too
    much,
Whiles, in his moan, the ship splits on the
    rock,
Which industry and courage might have
    saved ?
Ah, what a shame ! ah, what a fault were this !
Say Warwick was our anchor ; what of that ?
And Montague our topmast ; what of him ?
Our slaughter'd friends the tackles ; what of
    these ?
Why, is not Oxford here another anchor ?
And Somerset another goodly mast ?
The friends of France our shrouds and tack-
    lings ?
And, though unskilful, why not Ned and I
For once allow'd the skilful pilot's charge ?   20

We will not from the helm to sit and weep,
But keep our course, though the rough wind
        say no,
From shelves and rocks that threaten us with
        wreck.
As good to chide the waves as speak them fair.
And what is Edward but a ruthless sea ?
What Clarence but a quicksand of deceit ?
And Richard but a ragged fatal rock ?
All these the enemies to our poor bark.
Say you can swim ; alas, 'tis but a while !
Tread on the sand ; why, there you quickly
        sink :   30
Bestride the rock ; the tide will wash you off,
Or else you famish ; that's a threefold death.
This speak I, lords, to let you understand,
If case some one of you would fly from us,
That there's no hoped-for mercy with the
        brothers
More than with ruthless waves, with sands and
        rocks.
Why, courage then ! what cannot be avoided
'Twere childish weakness to lament or fear.
    Prince. Methinks a woman of this valiant
        spirit
Should, if a coward heard her speak these
        words,   40
Infuse his breast with magnanimity
And make him, naked, foil a man at arms.
I speak not this as doubting any here ;
For did I but suspect a fearful man
He should have leave to go away betimes,
Lest in our need he might infect another
And make him of like spirit to himself.
If any such be here—as God forbid !—
Let him depart before we need his help.
    Oxf. Women and children of so high a
        courage,   50
And warriors faint ! why, 'twere perpetual
        shame.
O brave young prince ! thy famous grand-
        father
Doth live again in thee : long mayst thou live
To bear his image and renew his glories !
    Som. And he that will not fight for such a
        hope,
Go home to bed, and like the owl by day,
If he arise, be mock'd and wonder'd at.
    Q. Mar. Thanks, gentle Somerset ; sweet
        Oxford, thanks.
    Prince. And take his thanks that yet hath
        nothing else.

            Enter a Messenger.

    Mess. Prepare you, lords, for Edward is at
        hand,   60
Ready to fight ; therefore be resolute.
    Oxf. I thought no less : it is his policy
To haste thus fast, to find us unprovided.
    Som. But he's deceived ; we are in readi-
        ness.
    Q. Mar. This cheers my heart, to see your
        forwardness.
    Oxf. Here pitch our battle ; hence we will
        not budge.

Flourish and march. Enter KING EDWARD,
    GLOUCESTER, CLARENCE, *and soldiers.*

    K. Edw. Brave followers, yonder stands the
        thorny wood,
Which, by the heavens' assistance and your
        strength,
Must by the roots be hewn up yet ere night.

I need not add more fuel to your fire,   70
For well I wot ye blaze to burn them out
Give signal to the fight, and to it, lords !
    Q. Mar. Lords, knights, and gentlemen,
        what I should say
My tears gainsay ; for every word I speak,
Ye see, I drink the water of mine eyes.
Therefore, no more but this : Henry, your
        sovereign,
Is prisoner to the foe ; his state usurp'd,
His realm a slaughter-house, his subjects slain,
His statutes cancell'd and his treasure spent ;
And yonder is the wolf that makes this spoil.
You fight in justice : then, in God's name,
        lords,   81
Be valiant and give signal to the fight.
    [*Alarum : Retreat : Excursions. Exeunt.*

    SCENE V.   *Another part of the field.*

Flourish. Enter KING EDWARD, GLOUCESTER,
    CLARENCE, *and soldiers ; with* QUEEN MAR-
    GARET, OXFORD, *and* SOMERSET, *prisoners.*

    K. Edw. Now here a period of tumultuous
        broils.
Away with Oxford to Hames Castle straight :
For Somerset, off with his guilty head.
Go, bear them hence ; I will not hear them
        speak.
    Oxf. For my part, I'll not trouble thee with
        words.
    Som. Nor I, but stoop with patience to my
        fortune.
    [*Exeunt Oxford and Somerset, guarded.*
    Q. Mar. So part we sadly in this troublous
        world,
To meet with joy in sweet Jerusalem.
    K. Edw. Is proclamation made, that who
        finds Edward
Shall have a high reward, and he his life ?   10
    Glou. It is : and lo, where youthful Ed-
        ward comes !

    Enter soldiers, with PRINCE EDWARD.

    K. Edw. Bring forth the gallant, let us
        hear him speak.
What ! can so young a thorn begin to prick ?
Edward, what satisfaction canst thou make
For bearing arms, for stirring up my subjects,
And all the trouble thou hast turn'd me to ?
    Prince. Speak like a subject, proud am-
        bitious York !
Suppose that I am now my father's mouth ;
Resign thy chair, and where I stand kneel thou,
Whilst I propose the selfsame words to thee,
Which, traitor, thou wouldst have me answer
        to.   21
    Q. Mar. Ah, that thy father had been so
        resolved !
    Glou. That you might still have worn the
        petticoat,
And ne'er have stol'n the breech from Lan-
        caster.
    Prince. Let Æsop fable in a winter's night ;
His currish riddles sort not with this place.
    Glou. By heaven, brat, I'll plague ye for
        that word.
    Q. Mar. Ay, thou wast born to be a plague
        to men.
    Glou. For God's sake, take away this cap-
        tive scold.
    Prince. Nay, take away this scolding crook-
        back rather.   30

K. Edw. Peace, wilful boy, or I will charm your tongue.
Clar. Untutor'd lad, thou art too malapert.
Prince. I know my duty; you are all un-dutiful :
Lascivious Edward, and thou perjured George,
And thou mis-shapen Dick, I tell ye all
I am your better, traitors as ye are :
And thou usurp'st my father's right and mine.
K. Edw. Take that, thou likeness of this railer here.   [*Stabs him.*
Glou. Sprawl'st thou ? take that, to end thy agony.   [*Stabs him.*
Clar. And there's for twitting me with per-jury.   [*Stabs him.* 40
Q. Mar. O, kill me too !
Glou. Marry, and shall. [*Offers to kill her.*
K. Edw. Hold, Richard, hold ; for we have done too much.
Glou. Why should she live, to fill the world with words ?
K. Edw. What, doth she swoon ? use means for her recovery.
Glou. Clarence, excuse me to the king my brother ;
I'll hence to London on a serious matter :
Ere ye come there, be sure to hear some news.
Clar. What ? what ?
Glou. The Tower, the Tower.   [*Exit.* 50
Q. Mar. O Ned, sweet Ned ! speak to thy mother, boy !
Canst thou not speak ? O traitors ! murder-ers !
They that stabb'd Cæsar shed no blood at all,
Did not offend, nor were not worthy blame,
If this foul deed were by to equal it :
He was a man ; this, in respect, a child :
And men ne'er spend their fury on a child.
What's worse than murderer, that I may name it ?
No, no, my heart will burst, an if I speak :
And I will speak, that so my heart may burst.
Butchers and villains ! bloody cannibals ! 61
How sweet a plant have you untimely cropp'd !
You have no children, butchers ! if you had,
The thought of them would have stirr'd up re-morse :
But if you ever chance to have a child,
Look in his youth to have him so cut off
As, deathsmen, you have rid this sweet young prince !
K. Edw. Away with her ; go, bear her hence perforce.
Q. Mar. Nay, never bear me hence, dis-patch me here,
Here sheathe thy sword, I'll pardon thee my death :   70
What, wilt thou not ? then, Clarence, do it thou.
Clar. By heaven, I will not do thee so much ease.
Q. Mar. Good Clarence, do ; sweet Clar-ence, do thou do it.
Clar. Didst thou not hear me swear I would not do it ?
Q. Mar. Ay, but thou usest to forswear thyself :
'Twas sin before, but now 'tis charity.
What, wilt thou not ? Where is that devil's butcher,
Hard-favor'd Richard ? Richard, where art thou ?
Thou art not here : murder is thy alms-deed ;

Petitioners for blood thou ne'er put'st back. 80
K. Edw. Away, I say ; I charge ye, bear her hence.
Q. Mar. So come to you and yours, as to this prince !   [*Exit, led out forcibly.*
K. Edw. Where's Richard gone ?
Clar. To London, all in post ; and, as I guess,
To make a bloody supper in the Tower.
K. Edw. He's sudden, if a thing comes in his head.
Now march we hence : discharge the common sort
With pay and thanks, and let's away to Lon-don
And see our gentle queen how well she fares :
By this, I hope, she hath a son for me.   90
[*Exeunt.*

SCENE VI. *London. The Tower.*

Enter KING HENRY *and* GLOUCESTER, *with the* Lieutenant, *on the walls.*

Glou. Good day, my lord. What, at your book so hard ?
K. Hen. Ay, my good lord :—my lord, I should say rather ;
'Tis sin to flatter ; ' good ' was little better :
' Good Gloucester ' and ' good devil ' were alike,
And both preposterous ; therefore, not ' good lord.'
Glou. Sirrah, leave us to ourselves : we must confer.   [*Exit Lieutenant.*
K. Hen. So flies the reckless shepherd from the wolf ;
So first the harmless sheep doth yield his fleece
And next his throat unto the butcher's knife.
What scene of death hath Roscius now to act ?
Glou. Suspicion always haunts the guilty mind ;   11
The thief doth fear each bush an officer.
K. Hen. The bird that hath been limed in a bush,
With trembling wings misdoubteth every bush ;
And I, the hapless male to one sweet bird,
Have now the fatal object in my eye
Where my poor young was limed, was caught and kill'd.
Glou. Why, what a peevish fool was that of Crete,
That taught his son the office of a fowl ! 19
And yet, for all his wings, the fool was drown'd.
K. Hen. I, Dædalus ; my poor boy, Icarus ;
Thy father, Minos, that denied our course ;
The sun that sear'd the wings of my sweet boy
Thy brother Edward, and thyself the sea
Whose envious gulf did swallow up his life.
Ah, kill me with thy weapon, not with words !
My breast can better brook thy dagger's point
Than can my ears that tragic history.
But wherefore dost thou come ? is't for my life ?   29
Glou. Think'st thou I am an executioner ?
K. Hen. A persecutor, I am sure, thou art :
If murdering innocents be executing,
Why, then thou art an executioner.
Glou. Thy son I kill'd for his presumption.
K. Hen. Hadst thou been kill'd when first thou didst presume,
Thou hadst not lived to kill a son of mine.

And thus I prophesy, that many a thousand,
Which now mistrust no parcel of my fear,
And many an old man's sigh and many a
　　widow's,　　　　　　　　　　　　　39
And many an orphan's water-standing eye—
Men for their sons, wives for their husbands,
And orphans for their parents timeless death—
Shall rue the hour that ever thou wast born.
The owl shriek'd at thy birth,—an evil sign ;
The night-crow cried, aboding luckless time ;
Dogs howl'd, and hideous tempest shook down
　　trees ;
The raven rook'd her on the chimney's top,
And chattering pies in dismal discords sung.
Thy mother felt more than a mother's pain,
And yet brought forth less than a mother's
　　hope,　　　　　　　　　　　　　　50
To wit, an indigested and deformed lump,
Not like the fruit of such a goodly tree.
Teeth hadst thou in thy head when thou wast
　　born,
To signify thou camest to bite the world :
And, if the rest be true which I have heard,
Thou camest—
　　Glou.　I'll hear no more : die, prophet, in
　　　thy speech :　　　　　　　　[*Stabs him.*
For this amongst the rest, was I ordain'd.
　　K. Hen.　Ay, and for much more slaughter
　　　after this.
O, God forgive my sins, and pardon thee !
　　　　　　　　　　　　　　　　[*Dies.* 60
　　Glou.　What, will the aspiring blood of
　　　Lancaster
Sink in the ground ? I thought it would have
　　mounted.
See how my sword weeps for the poor king's
　　death !
O, may such purple tears be alway shed
From those that wish the downfall of our
　　house !
If any spark of life be yet remaining,
Down, down to hell ; and say I sent thee
　　thither :　　　　　　[*Stabs him again.*
I, that have neither pity, love, nor fear.
Indeed, 'tis true that Henry told me of ;
For I have often heard my mother say　　70
I came into the world with my legs forward :
Had I not reason, think ye, to make haste,
And seek their ruin that usurp'd our right ?
The midwife wonder'd and the women cried
' O, Jesus bless us, he is born with teeth ! '
And so I was ; which plainly signified
That I should snarl and bite and play the dog.
Then, since the heavens have shaped my body
　　so,
Let hell make crook'd my mind to answer it.
I have no brother, I am like no brother ;　80
And this word ' love,' which greybeards call
　　divine,
Be resident in men like one another
And not in me : I am myself alone.
Clarence, beware ; thou keep'st me from the
　　light :
But I will sort a pitchy day for thee ;
For I will buz abroad such prophecies
That Edward shall be fearful of his life,
And then, to purge his fear, I'll be thy death.
King Henry and the prince his son are gone :
Clarence, thy turn is next, and then the rest,
Counting myself but bad till I be best.　　91
I'll throw thy body in another room

And triumph, Henry, in thy day of doom.
　　　　　　　　　　[*Exit, with the body.*

SCENE VII.　*London.　The palace.*

Flourish.　Enter KING EDWARD, QUEEN ELIZ-
ABETH, CLARENCE, GLOUCESTER, HASTINGS, *a*
Nurse *with the young Prince, and* Attend-
ants.

　　K. Edw.　Once more we sit in England's
　　　royal throne,
Re-purchased with the blood of enemies.
What valiant foemen, like to autumn's corn,
Have we mow'd down in tops of all their pride !
Three Dukes of Somerset, threefold renown'd
For hardy and undoubted champions,
Two Cliffords, as the father and the son,
And two Northumberlands ; two braver men
Ne'er spurr'd their coursers at the trumpet's
　　sound ;
With them, the two brave bears, Warwick and
　　Montague,
That in their chains fetter'd the kingly lion
And made the forest tremble when they roar'd.
Thus have we swept suspicion from our seat
And made our footstool of security.
Come hither, Bess, and let me kiss my boy.
Young Ned, for thee, thine uncles and myself
Have in our armors watch'd the winter's night,
Went all afoot in summer's scalding heat,
That thou mightst repossess the crown in
　　peace ;
And of our labors thou shalt reap the gain.20
　　Glou.　[*Aside*] I'll blast his harvest, if your
　　　head were laid ;
For yet I am not look'd on in the world.
This shoulder was ordain'd so thick to heave ;
And heave it shall some weight, or break my
　　back :
Work thou the way,—and thou shalt execute.
　　K. Edw.　Clarence and Gloucester, love my
　　　lovely queen ;
And kiss your princely nephew, brothers both.
　　Clar.　The duty that I owe unto your maj-
　　　esty
I seal upon the lips of this sweet babe.
　　Q. Eliz.　Thanks, noble Clarence ; worthy
　　　brother, thanks.
　　Glou.　And, that I love the tree from
　　　whence thou sprang'st,
Witness the loving kiss I give the fruit.
[*Aside*] To say the truth, so Judas kiss'd his
　　master,
And cried 'all hail ! ' when as he meant all
　　harm.
　　K. Edw.　Now am I seated as my soul de-
　　　lights,
Having my country's peace and brothers' loves.
　　Clar.　What will your grace have done
　　　with Margaret ?
Reignier, her father, to the king of France
Hath pawn'd the Sicils and Jerusalem,
And hither have they sent it for her ransom.
　　K. Edw.　Away with her, and waft her
　　　hence to France.
And now what rests but that we spend the time
With stately triumphs, mirthful comic shows,
Such as befits the pleasure of the court ?
Sound drums and trumpets ! farewell sour an-
　　noy !
For here, I hope, begins our lasting joy.
　　　　　　　　　　　　　　　　[*Exeunt.*

KING RICHARD III.

(WRITTEN IN 1593.)

INTRODUCTION.

This play, because among other alleged reasons it exhibits so much smaller a proportion of rhyme than *Richard II.*, is held by some critics to be the later of the two in chronological order; but here Shakespeare was working, though not in the presence, yet under the influence and in the manner of the great master of dramatic blank verse, Marlowe. *Richard III.* carries on with the highest energy, and we may suppose, after brief delay on Shakespeare's part, the subject of the fortunes of the house of York from the point when it was dropped in 3 *Henry VI.* It would hardly be possible that Shakespeare should subsequently continue to write in a manner so Marlowesque as that of *Richard III.;* he was not yet in comedy or tragedy delivered from rhyme. What more natural than that he should pass in *Richard II.* to a manner perhaps inferior but more his own, more varied, more subtle, and marked by finer if less forcible characterization? *Richard III.* can hardly be later in date than 1593. Shakespeare was indebted little, if at all, to the old play *The True Tragedie of Richard III.*, and certainly not at all to Dr. Legge's Latin play upon the same subject. A highly popular subject with Elizabethan audiences this was—the fall of the Yorkist usurper, and the accession of the first Tudor king as champion of justice. Shakespeare's play was printed in quarto in seven editions between 1597 and 1630. His materials the dramatist found in the chronicles of Holinshed and Hall. The entire play may be said to be the exhibition of the one central character of Richard; all subordinate persons are created that he may wreak his will upon them. This is quite in the manner of Marlowe. Like Marlowe also is the fierce energy of the central character, untempered by moral restraints, the heaping up of violent deeds, the absence of all reserve or mystery in the characterization, the broad and bold touches, the demoniac force and intensity of the whole. There is something sublime and terrible in so great and fierce a human energy as that of Richard, concentrated within one withered and distorted body. This is the evil offspring and flower of the long and cruel civil wars—this distorted creature, a hater and scorner of man, an absolute cynic, loveless and alone, disregarding all human bonds and human affections, yet full of intellect, of fire, of power. The accumulated crimes of civil war are at last atoned for, and the evil which culminates in Richard falls with Richard from its bad eminence.

DRAMATIS PERSONÆ.

KING EDWARD the Fourth.
EDWARD, Prince of Wales, afterwards King Edward V., RICHARD, Duke of York, } sons to the King.
GEORGE, Duke of Clarence, RICHARD, Duke of Gloucester, afterwards King Richard III., } brothers to the King.
A young son of Clarence.
HENRY, Earl of Richmond, afterwards King Henry VII.
CARDINAL BOURCHIER, Archbishop of Canterbury.
THOMAS ROTHERHAM, Archbishop of York.
JOHN MORTON, Bishop of Ely.
DUKE OF BUCKINGHAM.
DUKE OF NORFOLK.
EARL OF SURREY, his son.
EARL RIVERS, brother to Elizabeth.
MARQUIS OF DORSET and LORD GREY, sons to Elizabeth.
EARL OF OXFORD.
LORD HASTINGS.
LORD STANLEY, called also EARL OF DERBY.
LORD LOVEL.
SIR THOMAS VAUGHAN.

SIR RICHARD RATCLIFF.
SIR WILLIAM CATESBY.
SIR JAMES TYRREL.
SIR JAMES BLOUNT.
SIR WALTER HERBERT.
SIR ROBERT BRAKENBURY, Lieutenant of the Tower.
CHRISTOPHER URSWICK, a priest. Another Priest.
TRESSEL and BERKELEY, gentlemen attending on the Lady Anne.
Lord Mayor of London. Sheriff of Wiltshire.
ELIZABETH, queen to King Edward IV.
MARGARET, widow of King Henry VI.
DUCHESS OF YORK, mother to King Edward IV.
LADY ANNE, widow of Edward Prince of Wales, son to King Henry VI.; afterwards married to Richard.
A young Daughter of Clarence (MARGARET PLANTAGENET).

Ghosts of those murdered by Richard III., Lords and other Attendants; a Pursuivant, Scrivener, Citizens, Murderers, Messengers, Soldiers, &c.

SCENE : *England.*

ACT I.

SCENE I. *London. A street.*

Enter RICHARD, DUKE OF GLOUCESTER, *solus.*

Glou. Now is the winter of our discontent
Made glorious summer by this sun of York;
And all the clouds that lour'd upon our house
In the deep bosom of the ocean buried.
Now are our brows bound with victorious
    wreaths;
Our bruised arms hung up for monuments;
Our stern alarums changed to merry meetings,
Our dreadful marches to delightful measures.
Grim-visaged war hath smooth'd his wrinkled
    front;
And now, instead of mounting barded steeds
To fright the souls of fearful adversaries,   11
He capers nimbly in a lady's chamber
To the lascivious pleasing of a lute.
But I, that am not shaped for sportive tricks,
Nor made to court an amorous looking-glass;
I, that am rudely stamp'd, and want love's
    majesty
To strut before a wanton ambling nymph;
I, that am curtail'd of this fair proportion,
Cheated of feature by dissembling nature,
Deformed, unfinish'd, sent before my time   20
Into this breathing world, scarce half made
    up,
And that so lamely and unfashionable
That dogs bark at me as I halt by them;
Why, I, in this weak piping time of peace,
Have no delight to pass away the time,
Unless to spy my shadow in the sun
And descant on mine own deformity:
And therefore, since I cannot prove a lover,
To entertain these fair well-spoken days,
I am determined to prove a villain   30
And hate the idle pleasures of these days.
Plots have I laid, inductions dangerous,
By drunken prophecies, libels and dreams,
To set my brother Clarence and the king
In deadly hate the one against the other:
And if King Edward be as true and just
As I am subtle, false and treacherous,
This day should Clarence closely be mew'd up,
About a prophecy, which says that G
Of Edward's heirs the murderer shall be.   40
Dive, thoughts, down to my soul: here Clarence comes.

Enter CLARENCE, *guarded, and* BRAKENBURY.

Brother, good day; what means this armed
    guard
That waits upon your grace?
    Clar.   His majesty,
Tendering my person's safety, hath appointed
This conduct to convey me to the Tower.
    Glou. Upon what cause?
    Clar.   Because my name is George.
    Glou. Alack, my lord, that fault is none of
    yours;
He should, for that, commit your godfathers:
O, belike his majesty hath some intent
That you shall be new-christen'd in the Tower.
But what's the matter, Clarence? may I
    know?
    Clar. Yea, Richard, when I know; for I
    protest
As yet I do not: but, as I can learn,
He hearkens after prophecies and dreams;

And from the cross-row plucks the letter G,
And says a wizard told him that by G
His issue disinherited should be;
And, for my name of George begins with G,
It follows in his thought that I am he.   59
These, as I learn, and such like toys as these
Have moved his highness to commit me now.
    Glou. Why, this it is, when men are ruled
    by women:
'Tis not the king that sends you to the Tower:
My Lady Grey his wife, Clarence, 'tis she
That tempers him to this extremity.
Was it not she and that good man of worship,
Anthony Woodville, her brother there,
That made him send Lord Hastings to the
    Tower,
From whence this present day he is deliver'd?
We are not safe, Clarence; we are not safe.   70
    Clar. By heaven, I think there's no man is
    secure
But the queen's kindred and night-walking
    heralds
That trudge betwixt the king and Mistress
    Shore.
Heard ye not what an humble suppliant
Lord Hastings was to her for his delivery?
    Glou. Humbly complaining to her deity
Got my lord chamberlain his liberty.
I'll tell you what; I think it is our way,
If we will keep in favor with the king,
To be her men and wear her livery: 80
The jealous o'erworn widow and herself,
Since that our brother dubb'd them gentle-
    women,
Are mighty gossips in this monarchy.
    Brak. I beseech your graces both to pardon
    me;
His majesty hath straitly given in charge
That no man shall have private conference,
Of what degree soever, with his brother.
    Glou. Even so; an't please your worship,
    Brakenbury,
You may partake of any thing we say: 89
We speak no treason, man: we say the king
Is wise and virtuous, and his noble queen
Well struck in years, fair, and not jealous;
We say that Shore's wife hath a pretty foot,
A cherry lip, a bonny eye, a passing pleasing
    tongue;
And that the queen's kindred are made gentle-
    folks:
How say you, sir? can you deny all this?
    Brak. With this, my lord, myself have
    nought to do.
    Glou. Naught to do with Mistress Shore! I
    tell thee, fellow,
He that doth naught with her, excepting one,
Were best he do it secretly, alone.   100
    Brak. What one, my lord?
    Glou. Her husband, knave: wouldst thou
    betray me?
    Brak. I beseech your grace to pardon me,
    and withal
Forbear your conference with the noble duke.
    Clar. We know thy charge, Brakenbury,
    and will obey.
    Glou. We are the queen's abjects, and must
    obey.
Brother, farewell: I will unto the king;
And whatsoever you will employ me in,
Were it to call King Edward's widow sister,
I will perform it to enfranchise you.   110

Meantime, this deep disgrace in brotherhood
Touches me deeper than you can imagine.
  Clar. I know it pleaseth neither of us well.
  Glou. Well, your imprisonment shall not be
    long;
I will deliver you, or else lie for you :
Meantime, have patience.
  Clar.   I must perforce. Farewell.
  [Exeunt Clarence, Brakenbury, and Guard.
  Glou. Go, tread the path that thou shalt
    ne'er return,
Simple, plain Clarence ! I do love thee so,
That I will shortly send thy soul to heaven,
If heaven will take the present at our hands.
But who comes here ? the new-deliver'd Has-
    tings ?

      Enter LORD HASTINGS.

  Hast. Good time of day unto my gracious
    lord !
  Glou. As much unto my good lord cham-
    berlain !
Well are you welcome to the open air.
How hath your lordship brook'd imprison-
    ment ?
  Hast. With patience, noble lord, as prison-
    ers must :
But I shall live, my lord, to give them thanks
That were the cause of my imprisonment.
  Glou. No doubt, no doubt ; and so shall
    Clarence too ;
For they that were your enemies are his,   130
And have prevail'd as much on him as you.
  Hast. More pity that the eagle should be
    mew'd,
While kites and buzzards prey at liberty.
  Glou. What news abroad ?
  Hast. No news so bad abroad as this at
    home ;
The king is sickly, weak and melancholy,
And his physicians fear him mightily.
  Glou. Now, by Saint Paul, this news is bad
    indeed.
O, he hath kept an evil diet long,   139
And overmuch consumed his royal person :
'Tis very grievous to be thought upon.
What, is he in his bed ?
  Hast. He is.
  Glou. Go you before, and I will follow
    you.   *[Exit Hastings.*
He cannot live, I hope ; and must not die
Till George be pack'd with post-horse up to
    heaven.
I'll in, to urge his hatred more to Clarence,
With lies well steel'd with weighty arguments ;
And, if I fail not in my deep intent,
Clarence hath not another day to live :   150
Which done, God take King Edward to his
    mercy,
And leave the world for me to bustle in !
For then I'll marry Warwick's youngest
    daughter.
What though I kill'd her husband and her
    father ?
The readiest way to make the wench amends
Is to become her husband and her father :
The which will I ; not all so much for love
As for another secret close intent,
By marrying her which I must reach unto.
But yet I run before my horse to market :   160
Clarence still breathes ; Edward still lives and
    reigns :

When they are gone, then must I count my
    gains.   *[Exit.*

SCENE II. *The same. Another street.*

Enter the corpse of KING HENRY *the Sixth,*
  Gentlemen *with halberds to guard it ;* LADY
  ANNE *being the mourner.*

  Anne. Set down, set down your honorable
    load,
If honor may be shrouded in a hearse,
Whilst I awhile obsequiously lament
The untimely fall of virtuous Lancaster.
Poor key-cold figure of a holy king !
Pale ashes of the house of Lancaster !
Thou bloodless remnant of that royal blood !
Be it lawful that I invocate thy ghost,
To hear the lamentations of Poor Anne,
Wife to thy Edward, to thy slaughter'd son, 10
Stabb'd by the selfsame hand that made these
    wounds !
Lo, in these windows that let forth thy life,
I pour the helpless balm of my poor eyes.
Cursed be the hand that made these fatal
    holes !
Cursed be the heart that had the heart to do
    it !
Cursed be the blood that let this blood from
    hence !
More direful hap betide that hated wretch,
That makes us wretched by the death of thee,
Than I can wish to adders, spiders, toads,
Or any creeping venom'd thing that lives ! 20
If ever he have child, abortive be it,
Prodigious, and untimely brought to light,
Whose ugly and unnatural aspect
May fright the hopeful mother at the view ;
And that be heir to his unhappiness !
If ever he have wife, let her be made
As miserable by the death of him
As I am made by my poor lord and thee !
Come, now towards Chertsey with your holy
    load,
Taken from Paul's to be interred there ; 30
And still, as you are weary of the weight,
Rest you, whiles I lament King Henry's corse.

      Enter GLOUCESTER.

  Glou. Stay, you that bear the corse, and
    set it down.
  Anne. What black magician conjures up
    this fiend,
To stop devoted charitable deeds ?
  Glou. Villains, set down the corse ; or, by
    Saint Paul,
I'll make a corse of him that disobeys.
  Gent. My lord, stand back, and let the
    coffin pass.
  Glou. Unmanner'd dog ! stand thou, when
    I command :   39
Advance thy halbert higher than my breast,
Or, by Saint Paul, I'll strike thee to my foot,
And spurn upon thee, beggar, for thy boldness.
  Anne. What, do you tremble ? are you all
    afraid ?
Alas, I blame you not ; for you are mortal,
And mortal eyes cannot endure the devil.
Avaunt, thou dreadful minister of hell !
Thou hadst but power over his mortal body,
His soul thou canst not have ; therefore be
    gone.
  Glou. Sweet saint, for charity, be not so
    curst.

Anne. Foul devil, for God's sake, hence,
    and trouble us not ;   50
For thou hast made the happy earth thy hell,
Fill'd it with cursing cries and deep exclaims.
If thou delight to view thy heinous deeds,
Behold this pattern of thy butcheries.
O, gentlemen, see, see ! dead Henry's wounds
Open their congeal'd mouths and bleed afresh !
Blush, blush, thou lump of foul deformity ;
For 'tis thy presence that exhales this blood
From cold and empty veins, where no blood
    dwells ;
Thy deed, inhuman and unnatural,   60
Provokes this deluge most unnatural.
O God, which this blood madest, revenge his
    death !
O earth, which this blood drink'st revenge his
    death !
Either heaven with lightning strike the mur-
    derer dead,
Or earth, gape open wide and eat him quick,
As thou dost swallow up this good king's
    blood,
Which his hell-govern'd arm hath butchered !
Glou. Lady, you know no rules of charity,
Which renders good for bad, blessings for
    curses.
Anne. Villain, thou know'st no law of God
    nor man :   70
No beast so fierce but knows some touch of
    pity.
Glou. But I know none, and therefore am
    no beast.
Anne. O wonderful, when devils tell the
    truth !
Glou. More wonderful, when angels are so
    angry.
Vouchsafe, divine perfection of a woman,
Of these supposed evils, to give me leave,
By circumstance, but to acquit myself.
Anne. Vouchsafe, defused infection of a
    man,
For these known evils, but to give me leave,
By circumstance, to curse thy cursed self. 80
Glou. Fairer than tongue can name thee,
    let me have
Some patient leisure to excuse myself.
Anne. Fouler than heart can think thee,
    thou canst make
No excuse current, but to hang thyself.
Glou. By such despair, I should accuse
    myself.
Anne. And, by despairing, shouldst thou
    stand excused ;
For doing worthy vengeance on thyself,
Which didst unworthy slaughter upon others.
Glou. Say that I slew them not ?
Anne. Why, then they are not dead :
But dead they are, and, devilish slave, by thee.
Glou. I did not kill your husband.   91
Anne. Why, then he is alive.
Glou. Nay, he is dead ; and slain by Ed-
    ward's hand.
Anne. In thy foul throat thou liest : Queen
    Margaret saw
Thy murderous falchion smoking in his blood ;
The which thou once didst bend against her
    breast,
But that thy brothers beat aside the point.
Glou. I was provoked by her slanderous
    tongue,
Which laid their guilt upon my guiltless
    shoulders.

Anne. Thou wast provoked by thy bloody
    mind.
Which never dreamt on aught but butcheries :
Didst thou not kill this king ?   101
Glou. .   I grant ye.
Anne. Dost grant me, hedgehog ? then,
    God grant me too
Thou mayst be damned for that wicked deed !
O, he was gentle, mild, and virtuous !
Glou. The fitter for the King of heaven,
    that hath him.
Anne. He is in heaven, where thou shalt
    never come.
Glou. Let him thank me, that holp to send
    him thither ;
For he was fitter for that place than earth.
Anne. And thou unfit for any place but
    hell.
Glou. Yes, one place else, if you will hear
    me name it.   110
Anne. Some dungeon.
Glou.   Your bed-chamber.
Anne. I'll rest betide the chamber where
    thou liest !
Glou. So will it, madam, till I lie with you.
Anne. I hope so.
Glou. I know so. But, gentle Lady Anne,
To leave this keen encounter of our wits,
And fall somewhat into a slower method,
Is not the causer of the timeless deaths
Of these Plantagenets, Henry and Edward,
As blameful as the executioner ?
Anne. Thou art the cause, and most ac-
    cursed effect.   120
Glou. Your beauty was the cause of that
    effect ;
Your beauty, which did haunt me in my sleep
To undertake the death of all the world,
So I might live one hour in your sweet bosom.
Anne. If I thought that, I tell thee, homi-
    cide,
These nails should rend that beauty from my
    cheeks.
Glou. These eyes could never endure sweet
    beauty's wreck ;
You should not blemish it, if I stood by :
As all the world is cheered by the sun,
So I by that ; it is my day, my life.   130
Anne. Black night o'ershade thy day, and
    death thy life !
Glou. Curse not thyself, fair creature ;
    thou art both.
Anne. I would I were, to be revenged on
    thee.
Glou. It is a quarrel most unnatural,
To be revenged on him that loveth you.
Anne. It is a quarrel just and reasonable,
To be revenged on him that slew my husband.
Glou. He that bereft thee, lady, of thy hus-
    band,
Did it to help thee to a better husband.
Anne. His better doth not breathe upon
    the earth.   140
Glou. He lives that loves thee better than
    he could.
Anne. Name him.
Glou.   Plantagenet.
Anne.   Why, that was he
Glou. The selfsame name, but one of better
    nature.
Anne. Where is he ?
Glou.   Here. [*She spitteth at him.*]
    Why dost thou spit at me ?

Anne. Would it were mortal poison, for
  thy sake !
Glou. Never came poison from so sweet a
  place.
Anne. Never hung poison on a fouler toad.
Out of my sight ! thou dost infect my eyes.
Glou. Thine eyes, sweet lady, have in-
  fected mine.   150
Anne. Would they were basilisks, to strike
  thee dead !
Glou. I would they were, that I might die
  at once !
For now they kill me with a living death.
Those eyes of thine from mine have drawn salt
  tears,
Shamed their aspect with store of childish
  drops :
These eyes, which never shed remorseful tear,
No, when my father York and Edward wept,
To hear the piteous moan that Rutland made
When black-faced Clifford shook his sword at
  him ;
Nor when thy warlike father, like a child, 160
Told the sad story of my father's death,
And twenty times made pause to sob and
  weep,
That all the standers-by had wet their cheeks,
Like trees bedash'd with rain : in that sad
  time
My manly eyes did scorn an humble tear ;
And what these sorrows could not thence ex-
  hale,
Thy beauty hath, and made them blind with
  weeping.
I never sued to friend nor enemy ;
My tongue could never learn sweet smoothing
  words ;
But, now thy beauty is proposed my fee, 170
My proud heart sues and prompts my tongue
  to speak. [*She looks scornfully at him.*
Teach not thy lips such scorn, for they were
  made
For kissing, lady, not for such contempt.
If thy revengeful heart cannot forgive,
Lo, here I lend thee this sharp-pointed sword ;
Which if thou please to hide in this true
  bosom,
And let the soul forth that adoreth thee,
I lay it naked to the deadly stroke,
And humbly beg the death upon my knee.
  [*He lays his breast open : she offers at
           it with his sword.*
Nay, do not pause ; for I did kill King Henry,
But 'twas thy beauty that provoked me. 181
Nay, now dispatch ; 'twas I that stabb'd young
  Edward,
But 'twas thy heavenly face that set me on.
        [*Here she lets fall the sword.*
Take up the sword again, or take up me.
Anne. Arise, dissembler : though I wish
  thy death,
I will not be the executioner.
Glou. Then bid me kill myself, and I will
  do it.
Anne. I have already.
Glou.   Tush, that was in thy rage :
Speak it again, and, even with the word,
That hand, which, for thy love, did kill thy
  love,   190
Shall, for thy love, kill a far truer love ;
To both their deaths thou shalt be accessary.
Anne. I would I knew thy heart.
Glou. 'Tis figured in my tongue.

Anne. I fear me both are false.
Glou. Then never man was true.
Anne. Well, well, put up your sword.
Glou. Say, then, my peace is made.
Anne. That shall you know hereafter.
Glou. But shall I live in hope ?   200
Anne. All men, I hope, live so.
Glou. Vouchsafe to wear this ring.
Anne. To take is not to give.
Glou. Look, how this ring encompasseth
  thy finger.
Even so thy breast encloseth my poor heart ;
Wear both of them, for both of them are
  thine.
And if thy poor devoted suppliant may
But beg one favor at thy gracious hand,
Thou dost confirm his happiness for ever.
Anne. What is it ?   210
Glou. That it would please thee leave these
  sad designs
To him that hath more cause to be a mourner,
And presently repair to Crosby Place ;
Where, after I have solemnly interr'd
At Chertsey monastery this noble king,
And wet his grave with my repentant tears,
I will with all expedient duty see you :
For divers unknown reasons, I beseech you,
Grant me this boon.
Anne.   With all my heart ; and much it
  joys me too,   220
To see you are become so penitent.
Tressel and Berkeley, go along with me.
Glou. Bid me farewell.
Anne.   'Tis more than you deserve ;
But since you teach me how to flatter you,
Imagine I have said farewell already.
  [*Exeunt Lady Anne, Tressel, and Berkeley.*
Glou. Sirs, take up the corse.
Gent.   Towards Chertsey, noble lord ?
Glou. No, to White-Friars ; there attend
  my coming. [*Exeunt all but Gloucester.*
Was ever woman in this humor woo'd ?
Was ever woman in this humor won ?
I'll have her ; but I will not keep her long. 230
What ! I, that kill'd her husband and his
  father,
To take her in her heart's extremest hate,
With curses in her mouth, tears in her eyes,
The bleeding witness of her hatred by ;
Having God, her conscience, and these bars
  against me,
And I nothing to back my suit at all,
But the plain devil and dissembling looks,
And yet to win her, all the world to nothing !
Ha !
Hath she forgot already that brave prince, 240
Edward, her lord, whom I, some three months
  since,
Stabb'd in my angry mood at Tewksbury ?
A sweeter and a lovelier gentleman,
Framed in the prodigality of nature,
Young, valiant, wise, and, no doubt, right
  royal,
The spacious world cannot again afford :
And will she yet debase her eyes on me,
That cropp'd the golden prime of this sweet
  prince,
And made her widow to a woful bed ?
On me, whose all not equals Edward's
  moiety ?
On me, that halt and am unshapen thus ? 251
My dukedom to a beggarly denier,
I do mistake my person all this while :

Upon my life, she finds, although I cannot,
Myself to be a marvellous proper man.
I'll be at charges for a looking-glass,
And entertain some score or two of tailors,
To study fashions to adorn my body:
Since I am crept in favor with myself,
I will maintain it with some little cost.   260
But first I'll turn yon fellow in his grave;
And then return lamenting to my love.
Shine out, fair sun, till I have bought a glass,
That I may see my shadow as I pass.   [*Exit.*

SCENE III. *The palace.*

Enter QUEEN ELIZABETH, LORD RIVERS, *and*
LORD GREY.

Riv. Have patience, madam: there's no
  doubt his majesty
Will soon recover his accustom'd health.
  Grey. In that you brook it ill, it makes
  him worse:
Therefore, for God's sake, entertain good com-
  fort,
And cheer his grace with quick and merry
  words.
  Q. Eliz. If he were dead, what would be-
  tide of me?
  Riv. No other harm but loss of such a lord.
  Q. Eliz. The loss of such a lord includes
  all harm.
  Grey. The heavens have bless'd you with a
  goodly son,
To be your comforter when he is gone.   10
  Q. Eliz. Oh, he is young, and his minority
Is put unto the trust of Richard Gloucester,
A man that loves not me, nor none of you.
  Riv. Is it concluded he shall be protector?
  Q. Eliz. It is determined, not concluded
  yet:
But so it must be, if the king miscarry.

Enter BUCKINGHAM *and* DERBY.

Grey. Here come the lords of Buckingham
  and Derby.
  Buck. Good time of day unto your royal
  grace!
  Der. God make your majesty joyful as
  you have been!
  Q. Eliz. The Countess Richmond, good my
  Lord of Derby,   20
To your good prayers will scarcely say amen.
Yet, Derby, notwithstanding she's your wife,
And loves not me, be you, good lord, assured
I hate not you for her proud arrogance.
  Der. I do beseech you, either not believe
The envious slanders of her false accusers;
Or, if she be accused in true report,
Bear with her weakness, which, I think, pro-
  ceeds
From wayward sickness, and no grounded
  malice.
  Riv. Saw you the king to-day, my Lord of
  Derby?   30
  Der. But now the Duke of Buckingham
  and I
Are come from visiting his majesty.
  Q. Eliz. What likelihood of his amend-
  ment, lords?
  Buck. Madam, good hope; his grace
  speaks cheerfully.
  Q. Eliz. God grant him health! Did you
  confer with him?
  Buck. Madam, we did: he desires to make
  atonement

Betwixt the Duke of Gloucester and your
  brothers,
And betwixt them and my lord chamberlain;
And sent to warn them to his royal presence.
  Q. Eliz. Would all were well! but that
  will never be   40
I fear our happiness is at the highest.

Enter GLOUCESTER, HASTINGS, *and* DORSET.

  Glou. They do me wrong, and I will not
  endure it:
Who are they that complain unto the king,
That I, forsooth, am stern, and love them not?
By holy Paul, they love his grace but lightly
That fill his ears with such dissentious ru-
  mors.
Because I cannot flatter and speak fair,
Smile in men's faces, smooth, deceive and cog,
Duck with French nods and apish courtesy,
I must be held a rancorous enemy.   50
Cannot a plain man live and think no harm,
But thus his simple truth must be abused
By silken, sly, insinuating Jacks?
  Riv. To whom in all this presence speaks
  your grace?
  Glou. To thee, that hast nor honesty nor
  grace.
When have I injured thee? when done thee
  wrong?
Or thee? or thee? or any of your faction?
A plague upon you all! His royal person,—
Whom God preserve better than you would
  wish!—
Cannot be quiet scarce a breathing-while,   60
But you must trouble him with lewd com-
  plaints.
  Q. Eliz. Brother of Gloucester, you mis-
  take the matter.
The king, of his own royal disposition,
And not provoked by any suitor else;
Aiming, belike, at your interior hatred,
Which in your outward actions shows itself
Against my kindred, brothers, and myself,
Makes him to send; that thereby he may
  gather
The ground of your ill-will, and so remove it.
  Glou. I cannot tell: the world is grown
  so bad,   70
That wrens make prey where eagles dare not
  perch:
Since every Jack became a gentleman,
There's many a gentle person made a Jack.
  Q. Eliz. Come, come, we know your mean-
  ing, brother Gloucester;
You envy my advancement and my friends':
God grant we never may have need of you!
  Glou. Meantime, God grants that we have
  need of you:
Our brother is imprison'd by your means,
Myself disgraced, and the nobility
Held in contempt; whilst many fair promo-
  tions   80
Are daily given to ennoble those
That scarce, some two days since, were worth
  a noble.
  Q. Eliz. By Him that raised me to this
  careful height
From that contented hap which I enjoy'd,
I never did incense his majesty
Against the Duke of Clarence, but have been
An earnest advocate to plead for him.
My lord, you do me shameful injury,
Falsely to draw me in these vile suspects.

Glou. You may deny that you were not the
cause 90
Of my Lord Hastings' late imprisonment.
Riv. She may, my lord, for—
Glou. She may, Lord Rivers! why, who
knows not so?
She may do more, sir, than denying that:
She may help you to many fair preferments,
And then deny her aiding hand therein,
And lay those honors on your high deserts.
What may she not? She may, yea, marry,
may she,—
Riv. What, marry, may she?
Glou. What, marry, may she! marry with
a king, 100
A bachelor, a handsome stripling too:
I wis your grandam had a worser match.
Q. Eliz. My Lord of Gloucester, I have too
long borne
Your blunt upbraidings and your bitter
scoffs:
By heaven, I will acquaint his majesty
With those gross taunts I often have endured.
I had rather be a country servant-maid
Than a great queen, with this condition,
To be thus taunted, scorn'd, and baited at:

Enter QUEEN MARGARET, *behind.*

Small joy have I in being England's queen. 110
Q. Mar. And lessen'd be that small, God,
I beseech thee!
Thy honor, state and seat is due to me.
Glou. What! threat you me with telling of
the king?
Tell him, and spare not: look, what I have
said
I will avouch in presence of the king:
I dare adventure to be sent to the Tower.
'Tis time to speak; my pains are quite forgot.
Q. Mar. Out, devil! I remember them too
well:
Thou slewest my husband Henry in the
Tower,
And Edward, my poor son, at Tewksbury. 120
Glou. Ere you were queen, yea, or your
husband king,
I was a pack-horse in his great affairs;
A weeder-out of his proud adversaries,
A liberal rewarder of his friends:
To royalize his blood I spilt mine own.
Q. Mar. Yea, and much better blood than
his or thine.
Glou. In all which time you and your hus-
band Grey
Were factious for the house of Lancaster;
And, Rivers, so were you. Was not your hus-
band
In Margaret's battle at Saint Alban's slain?
Let me put in your minds, if you forget, 131
What you have been ere now, and what you
are;
Withal, what I have been, and what I am.
Q. Mar. A murderous villain, and so still
thou art.
Glou. Poor Clarence did forsake his
father, Warwick;
Yea, and forswore himself,—which Jesu par-
don!—
Q. Mar. Which God revenge!
Glou. To fight on Edward's party for the
crown;
And for his meed, poor lord, he is mew'd up.

I would to God my heart were flint, like Ed-
ward's; 140
Or Edward's soft and pitiful, like mine:
I am too childish-foolish for this world.
Q. Mar. Hie thee to hell for shame, and
leave the world,
Thou cacodemon! there thy kingdom is.
Riv. My Lord of Gloucester, in those busy
days
Which here you urge to prove us enemies,
We follow'd then our lord, our lawful king:
So should we you, if you should be our king.
Glou. If I should be! I had rather be a
pedlar:
Far be it from my heart, the thought of it!
Q. Eliz. As little joy, my lord, as you sup-
pose 151
You should enjoy, were you this country's
king,
As little joy may you suppose in me,
That I enjoy, being the queen thereof.
Q. Mar. A little joy enjoys the queen
thereof;
For I am she, and altogether joyless.
I can no longer hold me patient. [*Advancing.*
Hear me, you wrangling pirates, that fall out
In sharing that which you have pill'd from
me!
Which of you trembles not that looks on me?
If not, that, I being queen, you bow like sub-
jects, 161
Yet that, by you deposed, you quake like
rebels?
O gentle villain, do not turn away!
Glou. Foul wrinkled witch, what makest
thou in my sight?
Q. Mar. But repetition of what thou hast
marr'd;
That will I make before I let thee go.
Glou. Wert thou not banished on pain of
death?
Q. Mar. I was; but I do find more pain in
banishment
Than death can yield me here by my abode.
A husband and a son thou owest to me; 170
And thou a kingdom; all of you allegiance:
The sorrow that I have, by right is yours,
And all the pleasures you usurp are mine.
Glou. The curse my noble father laid on
thee,
When thou didst crown his warlike brows with
paper
And with thy scorns drew'st rivers from his
eyes,
And then, to dry them, gavest the duke a
clout
Steep'd in the faultless blood of pretty Rut-
land,—
His curses, then from bitterness of soul
Denounced against thee, are all fall'n upon
thee; 180
And God, not we, hath plagued thy bloody
deed.
Q. Eliz. So just is God, to right the inno-
cent.
Hast. O, 'twas the foulest deed to slay that
babe,
And the most merciless that e'er was heard
of!
Riv. Tyrants themselves wept when it was
reported.
Dor. No man but prophesied revenge for it.

Buck. Northumberland, then present, wept
    to see it.
Q. Mar. What were you snarling all be-
    fore I came,
Ready to catch each other by the throat, 189
And turn you all your hatred now on me ?
Did York's dread curse prevail so much with
    heaven
That Henry's death, my lovely Edward's
    death,
Their kingdom's loss, my woful banishment,
Could all but answer for that peevish brat ?
Can curses pierce the clouds and enter
    heaven ?
Why, then, give way, dull clouds, to my quick
    curses !
If not by war, by surfeit die your king,
As ours by murder, to make him a king !
Edward thy son, which now is Prince of
    Wales,
For Edward my son, which was Prince of
    Wales, 200
Die in his youth by like untimely violence !
Thyself a queen, for me that was a queen,
Outlive thy glory, like my wretched self !
Long mayst thou live to wail thy children's
    loss ;
And see another, as I see thee now,
Deck'd in thy rights, as thou art stall'd in
    mine !
Long die thy happy days before thy death ;
And, after many lengthen'd hours of grief,
Die neither mother, wife, nor England's
    queen !
Rivers and Dorset, you were standers by, 210
And so wast thou, Lord Hastings, when my
    son
Was stabb'd with bloody daggers : God, I
    pray him,
That none of you may live your natural age,
But by some unlook'd accident cut off !
    Glou. Have done thy charm, thou hateful
    wither'd hag !
    Q. Mar. And leave out thee ? stay, dog, for
    thou shalt hear me.
If heaven have any grievous plague in store
Exceeding those that I can wish upon thee,
O, let them keep it till thy sins be ripe,
And then hurl down their indignation   220
On thee, the troubler of the poor world's
    peace !
The worm of conscience still begnaw thy soul !
Thy friends suspect for traitors while thou
    livest,
And take deep traitors for thy dearest friends !
No sleep close up that deadly eye of thine,
Unless it be whilst some tormenting dream
Affrights thee with a hell of ugly devils !
Thou elvish-mark'd, abortive, rooting hog !
Thou that wast seal'd in thy nativity
The slave of nature and the son of hell ! 230
Thou slander of thy mother's heavy womb !
Thou loathed issue of thy father's loins !
Thou rag of honor ! thou detested—
    Glou. Margaret.
    Q. Mar.   Richard !
    Glou.   Ha !
    Q. Mar.   I call thee not.
    Glou. I cry thee mercy then, for I had
    thought
That thou hadst call'd me all these bitter
    names.

    Q. Mar. Why, so I did ; but look'd for no
    reply.
O, let me make the period to my curse !
    Glou. 'Tis done by me, and ends in ' Mar-
    garet.'
    Q. Eliz. Thus have you breathed your curse
    against yourself.   240
    Q. Mar. Poor painted queen, vain flourish
    of my fortune !
Why strew'st thou sugar on that bottled spider,
Whose deadly web ensnareth thee about ?
Fool, fool ! thou whet'st a knife to kill thyself.
The time will come when thou shalt wish for
    me
To help thee curse that poisonous bunch-
    back'd toad.
    Hast. False-boding woman, end thy frantic
    curse,
Lest to thy harm thou move our patience.
    Q. Mar. Foul shame upon you ! you have
    all moved mine.
    Riv. Were you well served, you would be
    taught your duty.   250
    Q. Mar. To serve me well, you all should
    do me duty,
Teach me to be your queen, and you my sub-
    jects :
O, serve me well, and teach yourselves that
    duty !
    Dor. Dispute not with her ; she is lunatic.
    Q. Mar. Peace, master marquess, you are
    malapert :
Your fire-new stamp of honor is scarce cur-
    rent.
O, that your young nobility could judge
What 'twere to lose it, and be miserable !
They that stand high have many blasts to
    shake them ;
And if they fall, they dash themselves to
    pieces.   260
    Glou. Good counsel, marry : learn it, learn
    it, marquess.
    Dor. It toucheth you, my lord, as much as
    me.
    Glou. Yea, and much more : but I was
    born so high,
Our aery buildeth in the cedar's top,
And dallies with the wind and scorns the sun.
    Q. Mar. And turns the sun to shade ; alas !
    alas !
Witness my son, now in the shade of death ;
Whose bright out-shining beams thy cloudy
    wrath
Hath in eternal darkness folded up.
Your aery buildeth in our aery's nest.   270
O God, that seest it, do not suffer it !
As it was won with blood, lost be it so !
    Buck. Have done ! for shame, if not for
    charity.
    Q. Mar. Urge neither charity nor shame to
    me :
Uncharitably with me have you dealt,
And shamefully by you my hopes are butch-
    er'd.
My charity is outrage, life my shame ;
And in that shame still live my sorrow's rage !
    Buck. Have done, have done.
    Q. Mar. O princely Buckingham, I'll kiss
    thy hand,   280
In sign of league and amity with thee :
Now fair befal thee and thy noble house !
Thy garments are not spotted with our blood,
Nor thou within the compass of my curse.

Buck. Nor no one here ; for curses never
    pass
The lips of those that breathe them in the air.
Q. Mar. I'll not believe but they ascend the
    sky,
And there awake God's gentle-sleeping peace.
O Buckingham, take heed of yonder dog !
Look, when he fawns, he bites ; and when he
    bites,   290
His venom tooth will rankle to the death :
Have not to do with him, beware of him ;
Sin, death, and hell have set their marks on
    him,
And all their ministers attend on him.
    Glou. What doth she say, my Lord of
    Buckingham ?
    Buck. Nothing that I respect, my gracious
    lord.
    Q. Mar. What, dost thou scorn me for my
    gentle counsel ?
And soothe the devil that I warn thee from ?
O, but remember this another day,
When he shall split thy very heart with sor-
    row,   300
And say poor Margaret was a prophetess !
Live each of you the subjects to his hate,
And he to yours, and all of you to God's !
                   [Exit.
    Hast. My hair doth stand on end to hear
    her curses.
    Riv. And so doth mine : I muse why she's
    at liberty.
    Glou. I cannot blame her : by God's holy
    mother,
She hath had too much wrong ; and I repent
My part thereof that I have done to her.
    Q. Eliz. I never did her any, to my knowl-
    edge.
    Glou. But you have all the vantage of her
    wrong.   310
I was too hot to do somebody good,
That is too cold in thinking of it now.
Marry, as for Clarence, he is well repaid,
He is frank'd up to fatting for his pains :
God pardon them that are the cause of it !
    Riv. A virtuous and a Christian-like con-
    clusion,
To pray for them that have done scathe to us.
    Glou. So do I ever : *[Aside]* being well-
    advised.
For had I cursed now, I had cursed myself.

            Enter Catesby.

    Cates. Madam, his majesty doth call for
    you ;   320
And for your grace ; and you, my noble lords.
    Q. Eliz. Catesby, we come. Lords, will you
    go with us ?
    Riv. Madam, we will attend your grace.
          [Exeunt all but Gloucester.
    Glou. I do the wrong, and first begin to
    brawl.
The secret mischiefs that I set abroach
I lay unto the grievous charge of others.
Clarence, whom I, indeed, have laid in dark-
    ness,
I do beweep to many simple gulls ;
Namely, to Hastings, Derby, Buckingham ;
And say it is the queen and her allies   330
That stir the king against the duke my brother.
Now, they believe it ; and withal whet me
To be revenged on Rivers, Vaughan, Grey :
But then I sigh ; and, with a piece of scripture,

Tell them that God bids us do good for evil :
And thus I clothe my naked villany
With old odd ends stolen out of holy writ ;
And seem a saint, when most I play the devil.

         Enter two Murderers.

But, soft ! here come my executioners.
How now, my hardy, stout resolved mates !
Are you now going to dispatch this deed ? 341
    First Murd. We are, my lord ; and come
    to have the warrant,
That we may be admitted where he is.
    Glou. Well thought upon ; I have it here
    about me.   *[Gives the warrant.*
When you have done, repair to Crosby Place.
But, sirs, be sudden in the execution,
Withal obdurate, do not hear him plead ;
For Clarence is well-spoken, and perhaps
May move your hearts to pity if you mark
    him.
    First Murd. Tush !   350
Fear not, my lord, we will not stand to prate ;
Talkers are no good doers : be assured
We come to use our hands and not our
    tongues.
    Glou. Your eyes drop millstones, when
    fools' eyes drop tears :
I like you, lads ; about your business straight ;
Go, go, dispatch.
    First Murd. We will, my noble lord.
                   [Exeunt.

    Scene IV. *London. The Tower.*

    Enter Clarence *and* Brakenbury.

    Brak. Why looks your grace so heavily to-
    day ?
    Clar. O, I have pass'd a miserable night,
So full of ugly sights, of ghastly dreams,
That, as I am a Christian faithful man,
I would not spend another such a night,
Though 'twere to buy a world of happy days,
So full of dismal terror was the time !
    Brak. What was your dream ? I long to
    hear you tell it.
    Clar. Methoughts that I had broken from
    the Tower,
And was embark'd to cross to Burgundy ; 10
And, in my company, my brother Gloucester ;
Who from my cabin tempted me to walk
Upon the hatches : thence we looked toward
    England,
And cited up a thousand fearful times,
During the wars of York and Lancaster
That had befall'n us. As we paced along
Upon the giddy footing of the hatches,
Methought that Gloucester stumbled ; and, in
    falling,
Struck me, that thought to stay him, over-
    board,
Into the tumbling billows of the main.   20
Lord, Lord ! methought, what pain it was to
    drown !
What dreadful noise of waters in mine ears !
What ugly sights of death within mine eyes !
Methought I saw a thousand fearful wrecks ;
Ten thousand men that fishes gnaw'd upon ;
Wedges of gold, great anchors, heaps of pearl,
Inestimable stones, unvalued jewels,
All scatter'd in the bottom of the sea :
Some lay in dead men's skulls ; and, in those
    holes   29
Where eyes did once inhabit, there were crept,
As 'twere in scorn of eyes, reflecting gems,

Which woo'd the slimy bottom of the deep,
And mock'd the dead bones that lay scatter'd
    by.
  Brak. Had you such leisure in the time of
    death
To gaze upon the secrets of the deep ?
  Clar. Methought I had ; and often did I
    strive
To yield the ghost : but still the envious flood
Kept in my soul, and would not let it forth
To seek the empty, vast and wandering air ;
But smother'd it within my panting bulk,   40
Which almost burst to belch it in the sea.
  Brak. Awaked you not with this sore
    agony ?
  Clar. O, no, my dream was lengthen'd
    after life ;
O, then began the tempest to my soul,
Who pass'd, methought, the melancholy flood,
With that grim ferryman which poets write of,
Unto the kingdom of perpetual night.
The first that there did greet my stranger soul,
Was my great father-in-law, renowned War-
    wick ;   49
Who cried aloud, ' What scourge for perjury
Can this dark monarchy afford false Clar-
    ence ? '
And so he vanish'd : then came wandering by
A shadow like an angel, with bright hair
Dabbled in blood ; and he squeak'd out aloud,
' Clarence is come ; false, fleeting, perjured
    Clarence,
That stabb'd me in the field by Tewksbury ;
Seize on him, Furies, take him to your tor-
    ments ! '
With that, methoughts, a legion of foul fiends
Environ'd me about, and howled in mine ears
Such hideous cries, that with the very noise
I trembling waked, and for a season after   61
Could not believe but that I was in hell,
Such terrible impression made the dream.
  Brak. No marvel, my lord, though it af-
    frighted you ;
I promise you, I am afraid to hear you tell it.
  Clar. O Brakenbury, I have done those
    things,
Which now bear evidence against my soul,
For Edward's sake ; and see how he requites
    me !
O God ! if my deep prayers cannot appease
    thee,
But thou wilt be avenged on my misdeeds,   70
Yet execute thy wrath in me alone,
O, spare my guiltless wife and my poor chil-
    dren !
I pray thee, gentle keeper, stay by me ;
My soul is heavy, and I fain would sleep.
  Brak. I will, my lord : God give your grace
    good rest !   [*Clarence sleeps.*
Sorrow breaks seasons and reposing hours,
Makes the night morning, and the noon-tide
    night.
Princes have but their titles for their glories,
An outward honor for an inward toil ;
And, for unfelt imagination,   80
They often feel a world of restless cares :
So that, betwixt their titles and low names,
There's nothing differs but the outward fame.

Enter the two Murderers.

  First Murd. Ho ! who's here ?
  Brak. In God's name what are you, and
    how came you hither ?

First Murd. I would speak with Clarence,
    and I came hither on my legs.
  Brak. Yea, are you so brief ?
  Sec. Murd. O sir, it is better to be brief
    than tedious. Show him our commission ; talk
    no more.   [*Brakenbury reads it.*
  Brak. I am, in this, commanded to deliver
The noble Duke of Clarence to your hands :
I will not reason what is meant hereby,
Because I will be guiltless of the meaning.
Here are the keys, there sits the duke asleep :
I'll to the king ; and signify to him
That thus I have resign'd my charge to you.
  First Murd. Do so, it is a point of wis-
    dom : fare you well. [*Exit Brakenbury.* 100
  Sec. Murd. What, shall we stab him as he
    sleeps ?
  First Murd. No ; then he will say 'twas
    done cowardly, when he wakes.
  Sec. Murd. When he wakes ! why, fool, he
    shall never wake till the judgment-day.
  First Murd. Why, then he will say we
    stabbed him sleeping.
  Sec. Murd. The urging of that word ' judg-
    ment ' hath bred a kind of remorse in me. 110
  First Murd. What, art thou afraid ?
  Sec. Murd. Not to kill him, having a war-
    rant for it ; but to be damned for killing him,
    from which no warrant can defend us.
  First Murd. I thought thou hadst been res-
    olute.
  Sec. Murd. So I am, to let him live.
  First Murd. Back to the Duke of Glouces-
    ter, tell him so.
  Sec. Murd. I pray thee, stay a while : I
    hope my holy humor will change ; 'twas wont
    to hold me but while one would tell twenty.
  First Murd. How dost thou feel thyself
    now ?
  Sec. Murd. 'Faith, some certain dregs of
    conscience are yet within me.
  First Murd. Remember our reward, when
    the deed is done.
  Sec. Murd. 'Zounds, he dies : I had forgot
    the reward.   129
  First Murd. Where is thy conscience now ?
  Sec. Murd. In the Duke of Gloucester's
    purse.
  First Murd. So when he opens his purse to
    give us our reward, thy conscience flies out.
  Sec. Murd. Let it go ; there's few or none
    will entertain it.
  First Murd. How if it come to thee again ?
  Sec. Murd. I'll not meddle with it : it is a
    dangerous thing : it makes a man a coward :
    a man cannot steal, but it accuseth him ; he
    cannot swear, but it checks him ; he cannot
    lie with his neighbor's wife, but it detects
    him : 'tis a blushing shamefast spirit that
    mutinies in a man's bosom : it fills one full of
    obstacles : it made me once restore a purse of
    gold that I found ; it beggars any man that
    keeps it : it is turned out of all towns and
    cities for a dangerous thing ; and every man
    that means to live well endeavors to trust to
    himself and to live without it.
  First Murd. 'Zounds, it is even now at my
    elbow, persuading me not to kill the duke. 150
  Sec. Murd. Take the devil in thy mind
    and believe him not : he would insinuate with
    thee but to make thee sigh.
  First Murd. Tut, I am strong-framed, he
    cannot prevail with me, I warrant thee.

Sec. Murd. Spoke like a tall fellow that respects his reputation. Come, shall we to this gear ?

First Murd. Take him over the costard with the hilts of thy sword, and then we will chop him in the malmsey-butt in the next room.   161

Sec. Murd. O excellent devise ! make a sop of him.

First Murd. Hark ! he stirs : shall I strike ?

Sec. Murd. No, first let's reason with him.

Clar. Where art thou, keeper ? give me a cup of wine.

Sec. Murd. You shall have wine enough, my lord, anon.

Clar. In God's name, what art thou ?

Sec. Murd. A man, as you are.   170

Clar. But not, as I am, royal.

Sec. Murd. Nor you, as we are, loyal.

Clar. Thy voice is thunder, but thy looks are humble.

Sec. Murd. My voice is now the king's, my looks mine own.

Clar. How darkly and how deadly dost thou speak !
Your eyes do menace me : why look you pale ?
Who sent you hither ? Wherefore do you come ?

Both. To, to, to—

Clar. To murder me ?

Both. Ay, ay.

Clar. You scarcely have the hearts to tell me so,   180
And therefore cannot have the hearts to do it.
Wherein, my friends, have I offended you ?

First Murd. Offended us you have not, but the king.

Clar. I shall be reconciled to him again.

Sec. Murd. Never, my lord ; therefore prepare to die.

Clar. Are you call'd forth from out a world of men
To slay the innocent ? What is my offence ?
Where are the evidence that do accuse me ?
What lawful quest have given their verdict up
Unto the frowning judge ? or who pronounced
The bitter sentence of poor Clarence' death ?
Before I be convict by course of law,
To threaten me with death is most unlawful.
I charge you, as you hope to have redemption
By Christ's dear blood shed for our grievous sins,
That you depart and lay no hands on me :
The deed you undertake is damnable.

First Murd. What we will do, we do upon command.

Sec. Murd. And he that hath commanded is the king.

Clar. Erroneous vassal ! the great King of kings   200
Hath in the tables of his law commanded
That thou shalt do no murder : and wilt thou, then,
Spurn at his edict and fulfil a man's ?
Take heed ; for he holds vengeance in his hands,
To hurl upon their heads that break his law.

Sec. Murd. And that same vengeance doth he hurl on thee,
For false forswearing and for murder too :
Thou didst receive the holy sacrament,

To fight in quarrel of the house of Lancaster.

First Murd. And, like a traitor to the name of God,   210
Didst break that vow ; and with thy treacherous blade
Unrip'dst the bowels of thy sovereign's son.

Sec. Murd. Whom thou wert sworn to cherish and defend.

First Murd. How canst thou urge God's dreadful law to us,
When thou hast broke it in so dear degree ?

Clar. Alas ! for whose sake did I that ill deed ?
For Edward, for my brother, for his sake :
Why, sirs,
He sends ye not to murder me for this ;
For in this sin he is as deep as I.   220
If God will be revenged for this deed,
O, know you yet, he doth it publicly :
Take not the quarrel from his powerful arm ;
He needs no indirect nor lawless course
To cut off those that have offended him.

First Murd. Who made thee, then, a bloody minister,
When gallant-springing brave Plantagenet,
That princely novice, was struck dead by thee ?

Clar. My brother's love, the devil, and my rage.

First Murd. Thy brother's love, our duty, and thy fault,   230
Provoke us hither now to slaughter thee.

Clar. Oh, if you love my brother, hate not me ;
I am his brother, and I love him well.
If you be hired for meed, go back again,
And I will send you to my brother Gloucester,
Who shall reward you better for my life
Than Edward will for tidings of my death.

Sec. Murd. You are deceived, your brother Gloucester hates you.

Clar. O, no, he loves me, and he holds me dear :
Go you to him from me.

Both.   Ay, so we will.   240

Clar. Tell him, when that our princely father York
Bless'd his three sons with his victorious arm,
And charged us from his soul to love each other,
He little thought of this divided friendship :
Bid Gloucester think of this, and he will weep.

First Murd. Ay, millstones ; as he lesson'd us to weep.

Clar. O, do not slander him, for he is kind.

First Murd. Right,
As snow in harvest. Thou deceivest thyself :
'Tis he that sent us hither now to slaughter thee.

Clar. It cannot be ; for when I parted with him,
He hugg'd me in his arms, and swore, with sobs,
That he would labor my delivery.

Sec. Murd. Why, so he doth, now he delivers thee
From this world's thraldom to the joys of heaven.

First Murd. Make peace with God, for you must die, my lord.

Clar. Hast thou that holy feeling in thy soul,

To counsel me to make my peace with God,
And art thou yet to thy own soul so blind,
That thou wilt war with God by murdering
   me?   260
Ah, sirs, consider, he that set you on
To do this deed will hate you for the deed.
  Sec. Murd. What shall we do?
  Clar.   Relent, and save your souls.
  First Murd. Relent! 'tis cowardly and
   womanish.
  Clar. Not to relent is beastly, savage,
   devilish.
Which of you, if you were a prince's son,
Being pent from liberty, as I am now,
If two such murderers as yourselves came to
   you,
Would not entreat for life?
My friend, I spy some pity in thy looks: 270
O, if thine eye be not a flatterer,
Come thou on my side, and entreat for me,
As you would beg, were you in my distress:
A begging prince what beggar pities not?
  Sec. Murd. Look behind you, my lord.
  First Murd. Take that, and that: if all this
   will not do,   [*Stabs him.*
I'll drown you in the malmsey-butt within.
                [*Exit, with the body.*
  Sec. Murd. A bloody deed, and desperately
   dispatch'd!
How fain, like Pilate, would I wash my hands
Of this most grievous guilty murder done!

        Re-enter First Murderer.

  First Murd. How now! what mean'st
   thou, that thou help'st me not?   281
By heavens, the duke shall know how slack
   thou art!
  Sec. Murd. I would he knew that I had
   saved his brother!
Take thou the fee, and tell him what I say;
For I repent me that the duke is slain.   [*Exit.*
  First Murd. So do not I: go, coward as
   thou art.
Now must I hide his body in some hole,
Until the duke take order for his burial:
And when I have my meed, I must away;   289
For this will out, and here I must not stay.

ACT II.

SCENE I. *London. The palace.*

Flourish. Enter KING EDWARD *sick,* QUEEN
ELIZABETH, DORSET, RIVERS, HASTINGS,
BUCKINGHAM, GREY, *and others.*

  K. Edw. Why, so: now have I done a
   good day's work:
You peers, continue this united league:
I every day expect an embassage
From my Redeemer to redeem me hence;
And now in peace my soul shall part to
   heaven,
Since I have set my friends at peace on earth.
Rivers and Hastings, take each other's hand;
Dissemble not your hatred, swear your love.
  Riv. By heaven, my heart is purged from
   grudging hate: 9
And with my hand I seal my true heart's love.
  Hast. So thrive I, as I truly swear the like!
  K. Edw. Take heed you dally not before
   your king;
Lest he that is the supreme King of kings

Confound your hidden falsehood, and award
Either of you to be the other's end.
  Hast. So prosper I, as I swear perfect
   love!
  Riv. And I, as I love Hastings with my
   heart!
  K. Edw. Madam, yourself are not exempt
   in this,
Nor your son Dorset, Buckingham, nor you;
You have been factious one against the other,
Wife, love Lord Hastings, let him kiss your
   hand;   21
And what you do, do it unfeignedly.
  Q. Eliz. Here, Hastings; I will never more
   remember
Our former hatred, so thrive I and mine!
  K. Edw. Dorset, embrace him; Hastings,
   love lord marquess.
  Dor. This interchange of love, I here pro-
   test,
Upon my part shall be unviolable.
  Hast. And so swear I, my lord
                   [*They embrace.*
  K. Edw. Now, princely Buckingham, seal
   thou this league
With thy embracements to my wife's allies,
And make me happy in your unity.   31
  Buck. Whenever Buckingham doth turn
   his hate
On you or yours [*to the Queen*], but with all
   duteous love
Doth cherish you and yours, God punish me
With hate in those where I expect most love!
When I have most need to employ a friend,
And most assured that he is a friend,
Deep, hollow, treacherous, and full of guile,
Be he unto me! this do I beg of God,
When I am cold in zeal to you or yours.   40
                   [*They embrace.*
  K. Edw. A pleasing cordial, princely Buck-
   ingham,
Is this thy vow unto my sickly heart.
There wanteth now our brother Gloucester
   here,
To make the perfect period of this peace.
  Buck. And, in good time, here comes the
   noble duke.

        Enter GLOUCESTER.

  Glou. Good morrow to my sovereign king
   and queen:
And, princely peers, a happy time of day!
  K. Edw. Happy, indeed, as we have spent
   the day.
Brother, we have done deeds of charity;
Made peace of enmity, fair love of hate,   50
Between these swelling wrong-incensed peers.
  Glou. A blessed labor, my most sovereign
   liege:
Amongst this princely heap, if any here,
By false intelligence, or wrong surmise,
Hold me a foe;
If I unwittingly, or in my rage,
Have aught committed that is hardly borne
By any in this presence, I desire
To reconcile me to his friendly peace:
'Tis death to me to be at enmity;   60
I hate it, and desire all good men's love.
First, madam, I entreat true peace of you,
Which I will purchase with my duteous serv-
   ice;
Of you, my noble cousin Buckingham,
If ever any grudge were lodged between us;

Of you, Lord Rivers, and, Lord Grey, of you ;
That all without desert have frown'd on me ;
Dukes, earls, lords, gentlemen ; indeed, of all.
I do not know that Englishman alive
With whom my soul is any jot at odds   70
More than the infant that is born to-night :
I thank my God for my humility.
  Q. Eliz. A holy day shall this be kept here-
    after :
I would to God all strifes were well com-
    pounded.
My sovereign liege, I do beseech your majesty
To take our brother Clarence to your grace.
  Glou. Why, madam, have I offer'd love for
    this,
To be so flouted in this royal presence ?
Who knows not that the noble duke is dead ?
                   [They all start.
You do him injury to scorn his corse.   80
  Riv. Who knows not he is dead ! who
    knows he is ?
  Q. Eliz. All-seeing heaven, what a world
    is this !
  Buck. Look I so pale, Lord Dorset, as the
    rest ?
  Dor. Ay, my good lord ; and no one in
    this presence
But his red color hath forsook his cheeks.
  K. Edw. Is Clarence dead ? the order was
    reversed.
  Glou. But he, poor soul, by your first or-
    der died,
And that a winged Mercury did bear ;
Some tardy cripple bore the countermand,
That came too lag to see him buried.   90
God grant that some, less noble and less loyal,
Nearer in bloody thoughts, but not in blood,
Deserve not worse than wretched Clarence did,
And yet go current from suspicion !

           Enter DERBY.

  Der. A boon, my sovereign, for my service
    done !
  K. Edw. I pray thee, peace : my soul is
    full of sorrow.
  Der. I will not rise, unless your highness
    grant.
  K. Edw. Then speak at once what is it
    thou demand'st.
  Der. The forfeit, sovereign, of my servant's
    life ;
Who slew to-day a righteous gentleman   100
Lately attendant on the Duke of Norfolk.
  K. Edw. Have I a tongue to doom my
    brother's death,
And shall the same give pardon to a slave ?
My brother slew no man ; his fault was
    thought,
And yet his punishment was cruel death.
Who sued to me for him ? who, in my rage,
Kneel'd at my feet, and bade me be advised ?
Who spake of brotherhood ? who spake of
    love ?
Who told me how the poor soul did forsake
The mighty Warwick, and did fight for me ?
Who told me, in the field by Tewksbury,   111
When Oxford had me down, he rescued me,
And said, ' Dear brother, live, and be a king ' ?
Who told me, when we both lay in the field
Frozen almost to death, how he did lap me
Even in his own garments, and gave himself,
All thin and naked, to the numb cold night ?
All this from my remembrance brutish wrath

Sinfully pluck'd, and not a man of you
Had so much grace to put it in my mind.   120
But when your carters or your waiting-vassals
Have done a drunken slaughter, and defaced
The precious image of our dear Redeemer,
You straight are on your knees for pardon,
    pardon ;
And I unjustly too, must grant it you :
But for my brother not a man would speak,
Nor I, ungracious, speak unto myself
For him, poor soul. The proudest of you all
Have been beholding to him in his life ;
Yet none of you would once plead for his life.
O God, I fear thy justice will take hold   131
On me, and you, and mine, and yours for this !
Come, Hastings, help me to my closet. Oh,
    poor Clarence !
     [Exeunt some with King and Queen.
  Glou. This is the fruit of rashness ! Mark'd
    you not
How that the guilty kindred of the queen
Look'd pale when they did hear of Clarence'
    death ?
O, they did urge it still unto the king !
God will revenge it. But come, let us in,
To comfort Edward with our company.
  Buck. We wait upon your grace. [*Exeunt.*

       SCENE II. *The palace.*

Enter the DUCHESS OF YORK, *with the two
    children of* CLARENCE.

  Boy. Tell me, good grandam, is our father
    dead ?
  Duch. No, boy.
  Boy. Why do you wring your hands, and
    beat your breast,
And cry ' O Clarence, my unhappy son ! '
  Girl. Why do you look on us, and shake
    your head,
And call us wretches, orphans, castaways,
If that our noble father be alive ?
  Duch. My pretty cousins, you mistake me
    much ;
I do lament the sickness of the king,
As loath to lose him, not your father's death ;
It were lost sorrow to wail one that's lost.   11
  Boy. Then, grandam, you conclude that he
    is dead.
The king my uncle is to blame for this :
God will revenge it ; whom I will importune
With daily prayers all to that effect.
  Girl. And so will I.
  Duch. Peace, children, peace ! the king
    doth love you well :
Incapable and shallow innocents,
You cannot guess who caused your father's
    death.
  Boy. Grandam, we can ; for my good un-
    cle Gloucester   20
Told me, the king, provoked by the queen,
Devised impeachments to imprison him :
And when my uncle told me so, he wept,
And hugg'd me in his arm, and kindly kiss'd
    my cheek ;
Bade me rely on him as on my father,
And he would love me dearly as his child.
  Duch. Oh, that deceit should steal such
    gentle shapes,
And with a virtuous vizard hide foul guile !
He is my son ; yea, and therein my shame ;
Yet from my dugs he drew not this deceit.   30
  Son. Think you my uncle did dissemble,
    grandam ?

Duch. Ay, boy.

Son. I cannot think it. Hark! what noise
is this?

Enter QUEEN ELIZABETH, *with her hair about
her ears;* RIVERS, *and* DORSET *after her.*

Q. Eliz. Oh, who shall hinder me to wail
and weep,
To chide my fortune, and torment myself?
I'll join with black despair against my soul,
And to myself become an enemy.

Duch. What means this scene of rude impatience?

Q. Eliz. To make an act of tragic violence:
Edward, my lord, your son, our king, is dead.
Why grow the branches now the root is
wither'd? 41
Why wither not the leaves the sap being
gone?
If you will live, lament; if die, be brief,
That our swift-winged souls may catch the
king's;
Or, like obedient subjects, follow him
To his new kingdom of perpetual rest.

Duch. Ah, so much interest have I in thy
sorrow
As I had title in thy noble husband!
I have bewept a worthy husband's death,
And lived by looking on his images: 50
But now two mirrors of his princely semblance
Are crack'd in pieces by malignant death,
And I for comfort have but one false glass,
Which grieves me when I see my shame in
him.
Thou art a widow; yet thou art a mother,
And hast the comfort of thy children left
thee:
But death hath snatch'd my husband from
mine arms,
And pluck'd two crutches from my feeble
limbs,
Edward and Clarence. O, what cause have I,
Thine being but a moiety of my grief, 60
To overgo thy plaints and drown thy cries!

Boy. Good aunt, you wept not for our
father's death;
How can we aid you with our kindred tears?

Girl. Our fatherless distress was left un-
moan'd;
Your widow-dolor likewise be unwept!

Q. Eliz. Give me no help in lamentation;
I am not barren to bring forth complaints:
All springs reduce their currents to mine eyes,
That I, being govern'd by the watery moon,
May send forth plenteous tears to drown the
world! 70
Oh for my husband, for my dear lord Ed-
ward!

Chil. Oh for our father, for our dear lord
Clarence!

Duch. Alas for both, both mine, Edward
and Clarence!

Q. Eliz. What stay had I but Edward? and
he's gone.

Chil. What stay had we but Clarence? and
he's gone.

Duch. What stays had I but they? and
they are gone.

Q. Eliz. Was never widow had so dear a
loss!

Chil. Were never orphans had so dear a
loss!

Duch. Was never mother had so dear a
loss! 80
Alas, I am the mother of these moans!
Their woes are parcell'd, mine are general.
She for an Edward weeps, and so do I;
I for a Clarence weep, so doth not she:
These babes for Clarence weep and so do I;
I for an Edward weep, so do not they:
Alas, you three, on me, threefold distress'd,
Pour all your tears! I am your sorrow's nurse,
And I will pamper it with lamentations.

Dor. Comfort, dear mother: God is much
displeased
That you take with unthankfulness his doing:
In common worldly things, 'tis call'd ungrate-
ful,
With dull unwillingness to repay a debt
Which with a bounteous hand was kindly
lent;
Much more to be thus opposite with heaven,
For it requires the royal debt it lent you.

Riv. Madam, bethink you, like a careful
mother,
Of the young prince your son: send straight
for him;
Let him be crown'd; in him your comfort
lives:
Drown desperate sorrow in dead Edward's
grave,
And plant your joys in living Edward's throne.

Enter GLOUCESTER, BUCKINGHAM, DERBY,
HASTINGS, *and* RATCLIFF.

Glou. Madam, have comfort: all of us
have cause 101
To wail the dimming of our shining star;
But none can cure their harms by wailing
them.
Madam, my mother, I do cry you mercy;
I did not see your grace: humbly on my knee
I crave your blessing.

Duch. God bless thee; and put meekness
in thy mind,
Love, charity, obedience, and true duty!

Glou. [*Aside*] Amen; and make me die
a good old man!
That is the butt-end of a mother's blessing:
I marvel why her grace did leave it out. 111

Buck. You cloudy princes and heart-sor-
rowing peers,
That bear this mutual heavy load of moan,
Now cheer each other in each other's love:
Though we have spent our harvest of this
king,
We are to reap the harvest of his son.
The broken rancor of your high-swoln hearts,
But lately splinter'd, knit, and join'd together,
Must gently be preserved, cherish'd, and
kept:
Me seemeth good, that, with some little train,
Forthwith from Ludlow the young prince be
fetch'd
Hither to London, to be crown'd our king.

Riv. Why with some little train, my Lord
of Buckingham?

Buck. Marry, my lord, lest, by a multitude,
The new-heal'd wound of malice should break
out;
Which would be so much the more dangerous,
By how much the estate is green and yet ungovern'd:

Where every horse bears his commanding
  rein,
And may direct his course as please himself,
As well the fear of harm, as harm apparent,
In my opinion, ought to be prevented.   131
  Glou. I hope the king made peace with all
    of us ;
And the compact is firm and true in me.
  Riv. And so in me ; and so, I think, in all :
Yet, since it is but green, it should be put
To no apparent likelihood of breach,
Which haply by much company might be
  urged :
Therefore I say with noble Buckingham,
That it is meet so few should fetch the prince.
  Hast. And so say I.   140
  Glou. Then be it so ; and go we to de-
termine
Who they shall be that straight shall post to
  Ludlow.
Madam, and you, my mother, will you go
To give your censures in this weighty busi-
  ness ?
  Q. Eliz. }
  Duch. } With all our hearts.
  [*Exeunt all but Buckingham and Gloucester.*
  Buck. My lord, whoever journeys to the
    prince,
For God's sake, let not us two be behind ;
For, by the way, I'll sort occasion,
As index to the story we late talk'd of,
To part the queen's proud kindred from the
  king.   150
  Glou. My other self, my counsel's consis-
tory,
My oracle, my prophet ! My dear cousin,
I, like a child, will go by thy direction.
Towards Ludlow then, for we'll not stay be-
  hind.   [*Exeunt.*

Scene III. *London. A street.*

Enter two Citizens *meeting.*

  First Cit. Neighbor, well met : whither
    away so fast ?
  Sec. Cit. I promise you, I scarcely know
    myself :
Hear you the news abroad ?
  First Cit.   Ay, that the king is dead.
  Sec. Cit. Bad news, by'r lady ; seldom
    comes the better :
I fear, I fear 'twill prove a troublous world.

Enter another Citizen.

  Third Cit. Neighbors, God speed !
  First Cit.   Give you good morrow, sir.
  Third Cit. Doth this news hold of good
    King Edward's death ?
  Sec. Cit. Ay, sir, it is too true ; God help
    the while !
  Third Cit. Then, masters, look to see a
    troublous world.
  First Cit. No, no ; by God's good grace
    his son shall reign.   10
  Third Cit. Woe to the land that's govern'd
    by a child !
  Sec. Cit. In him there is a hope of govern-
    ment,
That in his nonage council under him,
And in his full and ripen'd years himself,
No doubt, shall then and till then govern well.
  First Cit. So stood the state when Henry
    the Sixth
Was crown'd in Paris but at nine months old.

  Third Cit. Stood the state so ? No, no,
    good friends, God wot ;
For then this land was famously enrich'd
With politic grave counsel ; then the king   20
Had virtuous uncles to protect his grace.
  First Cit. Why, so hath this, both by the
    father and mother.
  Third Cit. Better it were they all came by
    the father,
Or by the father there were none at all ;
For emulation now, who shall be nearest,
Will touch us all too near, if God prevent
  not.
O, full of danger is the Duke of Gloucester !
And the queen's sons and brothers haught and
  proud :
And were they to be ruled, and not to rule,
This sickly land might solace as before.   30
  First Cit. Come, come, we fear the worst ;
    all shall be well.
  Third Cit. When clouds appear, wise men
    put on their cloaks ;
When great leaves fall, the winter is at hand ;
When the sun sets, who doth not look for
  night ?
Untimely storms make men expect a dearth.
All may be well ; but, if God sort it so,
'Tis more than we deserve, or I expect.
  Sec. Cit. Truly, the souls of men are full
    of dread :
Ye cannot reason almost with a man
That looks not heavily and full of fear.   40
  Third Cit. Before the times of change, still
    is it so :
By a divine instinct men's minds mistrust
Ensuing dangers ; as, by proof, we see
The waters swell before a boisterous storm.
But leave it all to God. Whither away ?
  Sec. Cit. Marry, we were sent for to the
    justices.
  Third Cit. And so was I : I'll bear you
    company.   [*Exeunt.*

Scene IV. *London. The palace.*

Enter the Archbishop of York, *the young*
  Duke of York, Queen Elizabeth, *and*
  the Duchess of York.

  Arch. Last night, I hear, they lay at North-
    ampton ;
At Stony-Stratford will they be to-night :
To-morrow, or next day, they will be here.
  Duch. I long with all my heart to see the
    prince :
I hope he is much grown since last I saw him.
  Q. Eliz. But I hear, no ; they say my son
    of York
Hath almost overta'en him in his growth.
  York. Ay, mother ; but I would not have
    it so.
  Duch. Why, my young cousin, it is good
    to grow.
  York. Grandam, one night, as we did sit
    at supper,   10
My uncle Rivers talk'd how I did grow
More than my brother : ' Ay,' quoth my uncle
  Gloucester,
' Small herbs have grace, great weeds do grow
  apace : '
And since, methinks, I would not grow so
  fast,
Because sweet flowers are slow and weeds
  make haste.

Duch. Good faith, good faith, the saying did not hold
In him that did object the same to thee;
He was the wretched'st thing when he was young,
So long a-growing and so leisurely,
That, if this rule were true, he should be gracious. 20
Arch. Why, madam, so, no doubt, he is.
Duch. I hope he is; but yet let mothers doubt.
York. Now, by my troth, if I had been remember'd,
I could have given my uncle's grace a flout,
To touch his growth nearer than he touch'd mine.
Duch. How, my pretty York? I pray thee, let me hear it.
York. Marry, they say my uncle grew so fast
That he could gnaw a crust at two hours old:
'Twas full two years ere I could get a tooth.
Grandam, this would have been a biting jest.
Duch. I pray thee, pretty York, who told thee this? 31
York. Grandam, his nurse.
Duch. His nurse! why, she was dead ere thou wert born.
York. If 'twere not she, I cannot tell who told me.
Q. Eliz. A parlous boy: go to, you are too shrewd.
Arch. Good madam, be not angry with the child.
Q. Eliz. Pitchers have ears.

Enter a Messenger.

Arch. Here comes a messenger. What news?
Mess. Such news, my lord, as grieves me to unfold.
Q. Eliz. How fares the prince?
Mess. Well, madam, and in health. 40
Duch. What is thy news then?
Mess. Lord Rivers and Lord Grey are sent to Pomfret,
With them Sir Thomas Vaughan, prisoners.
Duch. Who hath committed them?
Mess. The mighty dukes
Gloucester and Buckingham.
Q. Eliz. For what offence?
Mess. The sum of all I can, I have disclosed;
Why or for what these nobles were committed
Is all unknown to me, my gracious lady.
Q. Eliz. Ay me, I see the downfall of our house!
The tiger now hath seized the gentle hind; 50
Insulting tyranny begins to jet
Upon the innocent and aweless throne:
Welcome, destruction, death, and massacre!
I see, as in a map, the end of all.
Duch. Accursed and unquiet wrangling days,
How many of you have mine eyes beheld!
My husband lost his life to get the crown;
And often up and down my sons were toss'd,
For me to joy and weep their gain and loss:
And being seated, and domestic broils 60
Clean over-blown, themselves, the conquerors,
Make war upon themselves; blood against blood,
Self against self: O, preposterous

And frantic outrage, end thy damned spleen;
Or let me die, to look on death no more!
Q. Eliz. Come, come, my boy; we will to sanctuary.
Madam, farewell.
Duch. I'll go along with you.
Q. Eliz. You have no cause.
Arch. My gracious lady, go;
And thither bear your treasure and your goods.
For my part, I'll resign unto your grace 70
The seal I keep: and so betide to me
As well I tender you and all of yours!
Come, I'll conduct you to the sanctuary.
[*Exeunt.*

ACT III.

SCENE I. *London. A street.*

The trumpets sound. Enter the young PRINCE, *the Dukes of* GLOUCESTER *and* BUCKINGHAM, CARDINAL BOURCHIER, CATESBY, *and others.*

Buck. Welcome, sweet prince, to London, to your chamber.
Glou. Welcome, dear cousin, my thoughts' sovereign:
The weary way hath made you melancholy.
Prince. No, uncle; but our crosses on the way
Have made it tedious, wearisome, and heavy:
I want more uncles here to welcome me.
Glou. Sweet prince, the untainted virtue of your years
Hath not yet dived into the world's deceit
Nor more can you distinguish of a man
Than of his outward show; which, God he knows, 10
Seldom or never jumpeth with the heart.
Those uncles which you want were dangerous;
Your grace attended to their sugar'd words,
But look'd not on the poison of their hearts:
God keep you from them, and from such false friends!
Prince. God keep me from false friends! but they were none.
Glou. My lord, the mayor of London comes to greet you.

Enter the LORD MAYOR *and his train.*

May. God bless your grace with health and happy days!
Prince. I thank you, good my lord; and thank you all.
I thought my mother, and my brother York,
Would long ere this have met us on the way:
Fie, what a slug is Hastings, that he comes not
To tell us whether they will come or no!

Enter LORD HASTINGS.

Buck. And, in good time, here comes the sweating lord.
Prince. Welcome, my lord: what, will our mother come?
Hast. On what occasion, God he knows, not I,
The queen your mother, and your brother York,
Have taken sanctuary: the tender prince

Would fain have come with me to meet your
  grace,
But by his mother was perforce withheld. 30
  Buck. Fie, what an indirect and peevish
  course
Is this of hers! Lord cardinal, will your grace
Persuade the queen to send the Duke of York
Unto his princely brother presently?
If she deny, Lord Hastings, go with him,
And from her jealous arms pluck him perforce.
  Card. My Lord of Buckingham, if my weak
  oratory
Can from his mother win the Duke of York,
Anon expect him here; but if she be obdurate
To mild entreaties, God in heaven forbid 40
We should infringe the holy privilege
Of blessed sanctuary! not for all this land
Would I be guilty of so deep a sin.
  Buck. You are too senseless-obstinate, my
  lord,
Too ceremonious and traditional:
Weigh it but with the grossness of this age,
You break not sanctuary in seizing him.
The benefit thereof is always granted
To those whose dealings have deserved the
  place,   50
And those who have the wit to claim the
  place:
This prince hath neither claim'd it nor deserved
  it;
And therefore, in mine opinion, cannot have
  it:
Then, taking him from thence that is not there,
You break no privilege nor charter there.
Oft have I heard of sanctuary men;
But sanctuary children ne'er till now.
  Card. My lord, you shall o'er-rule my
  mind for once.
Come on, Lord Hastings, will you go with me?
  Hast. I go, my lord.
  Prince. Good lords, make all the speedy
  haste you may.   60
                [Exeunt Cardinal and Hastings.
Say, uncle Gloucester, if our brother come,
Where shall we sojourn till our coronation?
  Glou. Where it seems best unto your royal
  self.
If I may counsel you, some day or two
Your highness shall repose you at the Tower:
Then where you please, and shall be thought
  most fit
For your best health and recreation.
  Prince. I do not like the Tower, of any
  place.
Did Julius Cæsar build that place, my lord?
  Buck. He did, my gracious lord, begin
  that place;   70
Which, since, succeeding ages have re-edified.
  Prince. Is it upon record, or else reported
Successively from age to age, he built it?
  Buck. Upon record, my gracious lord.
  Prince. But say, my lord, it were not reg-
  ister'd,
Methinks the truth should live from age to
  age,
As 'twere retail'd to all posterity,
Even to the general all-ending day.
  Glou. [*Aside*] So wise so young, they say,
  do never live long.
  Prince. What say you, uncle?   80
  Glou. I say, without characters, fame lives
  long.
[*Aside*] Thus, like the formal vice, Iniquity,

I moralize two meanings in one word.
  Prince. That Julius Cæsar was a famous
  man;
With what his valor did enrich his wit,
His wit set down to make his valor live:
Death makes no conquest of this conqueror;
For now he lives in fame, though not in life.
I'll tell you what, my cousin Buckingham,—
  Buck. What, my gracious lord?   90
  Prince. An if I live until I be a man,
I'll win our ancient right in France again,
Or die a soldier, as I lived a king.
  Glou. [*Aside*] Short summers lightly have a
  forward spring.

          Enter young York, Hastings, *and the*
                          Cardinal.

  Buck. Now, in good time, here comes the
  Duke of York.
  Prince. Richard of York! how fares our
  loving brother?
  York. Well, my dread lord; so must I call
  you now.
  Prince. Ay, brother, to our grief, as it is
  yours:
Too late he died that might have kept that
  title,
Which by his death hath lost much majesty.
  Glou. How fares our cousin, noble Lord of
  York?   101
  York. I thank you, gentle uncle. O, my
  lord,
You said that idle weeds are fast in growth:
The prince my brother hath outgrown me far.
  Glou. He hath, my lord.
  York.   And therefore is he idle?
  Glou. O, my fair cousin, I must not say so.
  York. Then is he more beholding to you
  than I.
  Glou. He may command me as my sover-
  eign;
But you have power in me as in a kinsman.
  York. I pray you, uncle, give me this dag-
  ger.   110
  Glou. My dagger, little cousin? with all
  my heart.
  Prince. A beggar, brother?
  York. Of my kind uncle, that I know will
  give;
And being but a toy, which is no grief to
  give.
  Glou. A greater gift than that I'll give my
  cousin.
  York. A greater gift! O, that's the sword
  to it.
  Glou. Ay, gentle cousin, were it light
  enough.
  York. O, then, I see, you will part but
  with light gifts;
In weightier things you'll say a beggar nay.
  Glou. It is too heavy for your grace to
  wear.   120
  York. I weigh it lightly, were it heavier.
  Glou. What, would you have my weapon,
  little lord?
  York. I would, that I might thank you as
  you call me.
  Glou. How?
  York. Little.
  Prince. My Lord of York will still be cross
  in talk:
Uncle, your grace knows how to bear with
  him.

York. You mean, to bear me, not to bear
with me :
Uncle, my brother mocks both you and me ;
Because that I am little, like an ape,   130
He thinks that you should bear me on your
shoulders.
Buck. With what a sharp-provided wit he
reasons !
To mitigate the scorn he gives his uncle,
He prettily and aptly taunts himself :
So cunning and so young is wonderful.
Glou. My lord, will't please you pass
along ?
Myself and my good cousin Buckingham
Will to your mother, to entreat of her
To meet you at the Tower and welcome you.
York. What, will you go unto the Tower,
my lord ?   140
Prince. My lord protector needs will have
it so.
York. I shall not sleep in quiet at the
Tower.
Glou. Why, what should you fear ?
York. Marry, my uncle Clarence' angry
ghost :
My grandam told me he was murder'd there.
Prince. I fear no uncles dead.
Glou. Nor none that live, I hope.
Prince. An if they live, I hope I need not
fear.
But come, my lord ; and with a heavy heart,
Thinking on them, go I unto the Tower.   150
    [*A Sennet. Exeunt all but Gloucester,
        Buckingham and Catesby.*
Buck. Think you, my lord, this little prat-
ing York
Was not incensed by his subtle mother
To taunt and scorn you thus opprobriously ?
Glou. No doubt, no doubt ; O, 'tis a par-
lous boy ;
Bold, quick, ingenious, forward, capable :
He is all the mother's, from the top to toe.
Buck. Well, let them rest. Come hither,
Catesby.
Thou art sworn as deeply to effect what we
intend
As closely to conceal what we impart :
Thou know'st our reasons urged upon the
way ;   160
What think'st thou ? is it not an easy matter
To make William Lord Hastings of our mind,
For the instalment of this noble duke
In the seat royal of this famous isle ?
Cate. He for his father's sake so loves the
prince,
That he will not be won to aught against him.
Buck. What think'st thou, then, of Stan-
ley ? what will he ?
Cate. He will do all in all as Hastings
doth.
Buck. Well, then, no more but this : go,
gentle Catesby,
And, as it were far off, sound thou Lord Has-
tings,   170
How doth he stand affected to our purpose ;
And summon him to-morrow to the Tower,
To sit about the coronation.
If thou dost find him tractable to us,
Encourage him, and show him all our rea-
sons :
If he be leaden, icy-cold, unwilling,
Be thou so too ; and so break off your talk,
And give us notice of his inclination :

For we to-morrow hold divided councils,
Wherein thyself shalt highly be employ'd. 180
Glou. Commend me to Lord William ;
tell him, Catesby,
His ancient knot of dangerous adversaries
To-morrow are let blood at Pomfret-castle ;
And bid my friend, for joy of this good news,
Give mistress Shore one gentle kiss the more.
Buck. Good Catesby, go, effect this busi-
ness soundly.
Cate. My good lords both, with all the heed
I may.
Glou. Shall we hear from you, Catesby,
ere we sleep ?
Cate. You shall, my lord.
Glou. At Crosby Place, there shall you
find us both.   [*Exit Catesby.* 190
Buck. Now, my lord, what shall we do, if
we perceive
Lord Hastings will not yield to our complots ?
Glou. Chop off his head, man ; somewhat
we will do :
And, look, when I am king, claim thou of me
The earldom of Hereford, and the moveables
Whereof the king my brother stood possess'd.
Buck. I'll claim that promise at your
grace's hands.
Glou. And look to have it yielded with all
willingness.
Come, let us sup betimes, that afterwards 199
We may digest our complots in some form.
    [*Exeunt.*

SCENE II. *Before Lord Hastings' house.*

Enter a Messenger.

Mess. What, ho ! my lord !
Hast. [*Within*] Who knocks at the door ?
Mess. A messenger from the Lord Stanley.

Enter LORD HASTINGS.

Hast. What is't o'clock ?
Mess. Upon the stroke of four.
Hast. Cannot thy master sleep these tedi-
ous nights ?
Mess. So it should seem by that I have to
say.
First, he commends him to your noble lord-
ship.
Hast. And then ?
Mess. And then he sends you word   10
He dreamt to-night the boar had razed his
helm :
Besides, he says there are two councils held ;
And that may be determined at the one
Which may make you and him to rue at the
other.
Therefore he sends to know your lordship's
pleasure,
If presently you will take horse with him,
And with all speed post with him toward the
north,
To shun the danger that his soul divines.
Hast. Go, fellow, go, return unto thy lord ;
Bid him not fear the separated councils : 20
His honor and myself are at the one,
And at the other is my servant Catesby ;
Where nothing can proceed that toucheth us
Whereof I shall not have intelligence.
Tell him his fears are shallow, wanting in-
stance :
And for his dreams, I wonder he is so fond
To trust the mockery of unquiet slumbers :
To fly the boar before the boar pursues,

Were to incense the boar to follow us
And make pursuit where he did mean no
   chase.   30
Go, bid thy master rise and come to me;
And we will both together to the Tower,
Where, he shall see, the boar will use us
   kindly.
  Mess. My gracious lord, I'll tell him what
   you say.   [*Exit.*

        Enter CATESBY.

  Cate. Many good morrows to my noble
   lord!
  Hast. Good morrow, Catesby; you are
   early stirring:
What news, what news, in this our tottering
   state?
  Cate. It is a reeling world, indeed, my
   lord;
And I believe 'twill never stand upright   39
Till Richard wear the garland of the realm.
  Hast. How! wear the garland! dost thou
   mean the crown?
  Cate. Ay, my good lord.
  Hast. I'll have this crown of mine cut from
   my shoulders
Ere I will see the crown so foul misplaced.
But canst thou guess that he doth aim at it?
  Cate. Ay, on my life; and hopes to find
   you forward
Upon his party for the gain thereof:
And thereupon he sends you this good news,
That this same very day your enemies,
The kindred of the queen, must die at Pom-
   fret.   50
  Hast. Indeed, I am no mourner for that
   news,
Because they have been still mine enemies:
But, that I'll give my voice on Richard's side,
To bar my master's heirs in true descent,
God knows I will not do it, to the death.
  Cate. God keep your lordship in that gra-
   cious mind!
  Hast. But I shall laugh at this a twelve-
   month hence,
That they who brought me in my master's
   hate,
I live to look upon their tragedy.
I tell thee, Catesby,—   60
  Cate. What, my lord?
  Hast. Ere a fortnight make me elder,
I'll send some packing that yet think not on it.
  Cate. 'Tis a vile thing to die, my gracious
   lord,
When men are unprepared and look not for it.
  Hast. O monstrous, monstrous! and so
   falls it out
With Rivers, Vaughan, Grey: and so 'twill do
With some men else, who think themselves as
   safe
As thou and I; who, as thou know'st, are dear
To princely Richard and to Buckingham. 70
  Cate. The princes both make high account
   of you;
[*Aside*] For they account his head upon the
   bridge.
  Hast. I know they do; and I have well de-
   served it.

      Enter LORD STANLEY.

Come on, come on; where is your boar-spear,
   man?
Fear you the boar, and go so unprovided?

  Stan. My lord, good morrow; good mor-
   row, Catesby:
You may jest on, but, by the holy rood,
I do not like these several councils, I.
  Hast. My lord,
I hold my life as dear as you do yours;   80
And never in my life, I do protest,
Was it more precious to me than 'tis now:
Think you, but that I know our state secure,
I would be so triumphant as I am?
  Stan. The lords at Pomfret, when they rode
   from London,
Were jocund, and supposed their state was
   sure,
And they indeed had no cause to mistrust;
But yet, you see, how soon the day o'ercast.
This sudden stab of rancor I misdoubt:
Pray God, I say, I prove a needless coward!
What, shall we toward the Tower? the day is
   spent.   91
  Hast. Come, come, have with you. Wot
   you what, my lord?
To-day the lords you talk of are beheaded.
  Stan. They, for their truth, might better
   wear their heads
Than some that have accused them wear their
   hats.
But come, my lord, let us away.

      Enter a Pursuivant.

  Hast. Go on before; I'll talk with this
   good fellow.
        [*Exeunt Stanley and Catesby.*
How now, sirrah! how goes the world with
   thee?
  Purs. The better that your lordship please
   to ask.
  Hast. I tell thee, man, 'tis better with me
   now   100
Than when I met thee last where now we
   meet:
Then was I going prisoner to the Tower,
By the suggestion of the queen's allies;
But now, I tell thee—keep it to thyself—
This day those enemies are put to death,
And I in better state than e'er I was.
  Purs. God hold it, to your honor's good
   content!
  Hast. Gramercy, fellow: there, drink that
   for me.   [*Throws him his purse.*
  Purs. God save your lordship!   [*Exit.*

       Enter a Priest.

  Priest. Well met, my lord; I am glad to
   see your honor.   110
  Hast. I thank thee, good Sir John, with all
   my heart.
I am in your debt for your last exercise;
Come the next Sabbath, and I will content
   you.   [*He whispers in his ear.*

      Enter BUCKINGHAM.

  Buck. What, talking with a priest, lord
   chamberlain?
Your friends at Pomfret, they do need the
   priest;
Your honor hath no shriving work in hand.
  Hast. Good faith, and when I met this holy
   man,
Those men you talk of came into my mind.
What, go you toward the Tower?
  Buck. I do, my lord; but long I shall not
   stay: 120

I shall return before your lordship thence.
Hast. 'Tis like enough, for I stay dinner
    there.
Buck. [Aside] And supper too, although
    thou know'st it not.
Come, will you go?
Hast. I'll wait upon your lordship.
                                    [Exeunt.

SCENE III. *Pomfret Castle.*

Enter SIR RICHARD RATCLIFF, *with halberds,*
    carrying RIVERS, GREY, *and* VAUGHAN *to*
    death.

Rat. Come, bring forth the prisoners.
Riv. Sir Richard Ratcliff, let me tell thee
    this:
To-day shalt thou behold a subject die
For truth, for duty, and for loyalty.
Grey. God keep the prince from all the
    pack of you!
A knot you are of damned blood-suckers.
Vaug. You live that shall cry woe for this
    hereafter.
Rat. Dispatch; the limit of your lives is
    out.
Riv. O Pomfret, Pomfret! O thou bloody
    prison,
Fatal and ominous to noble peers!   10
Within the guilty closure of thy walls
Richard the second here was hack'd to death;
And, for more slander to thy dismal seat,
We give thee up our guiltless blood to drink.
Grey. Now Margaret's curse is fall'n upon
    our heads,
For standing by when Richard stabb'd her son.
Riv. Then cursed she Hastings, then cursed
    she Buckingham,
Then cursed she Richard. O, remember, God,
To hear her prayers for them, as now for us!
And for my sister and her princely sons, 20
Be satisfied, dear God, with our true blood,
Which, as thou know'st, unjustly must be
    spilt.
Rat. Make haste; the hour of death is ex-
    piate.
Riv. Come, Grey, come, Vaughan, let us
    all embrace:
And take our leave, until we meet in heaven.
                                    [Exeunt.

SCENE IV. *The Tower of London.*

Enter BUCKINGHAM, DERBY, HASTINGS, *the*
    BISHOP OF ELY, RATCLIFF, LOVEL, *with*
    others, and take their seats at a table.

Hast. My lords, at once: the cause why we
    are met
Is, to determine of the coronation.
In God's name, speak: when is the royal day?
Buck. Are all things fitting for that royal
    time?
Der. It is, and wants but nomination.
Ely. To-morrow, then, I judge a happy
    day.
Buck. Who knows the lord protector's
    mind herein?
Who is most inward with the royal duke?
Ely. Your grace, we think, should soonest
    know his mind.
Buck. Who, I, my lord! we know each
    other's faces,   10
But for our hearts, he knows no more of
    mine,
Than I of yours;

Nor I no more of his, than you of mine.
Lord Hastings, you and he are near in love.
Hast. I thank his grace, I know he loves
    me well;
But, for his purpose in the coronation,
I have not sounded him, nor he deliver'd
His gracious pleasure any way therein:
But you, my noble lords, may name the time;
And in the duke's behalf I'll give my voice,
Which, I presume, he'll take in gentle part. 21

Enter GLOUCESTER.

Ely. Now in good time, here comes the
    duke himself.
Glou. My noble lords and cousins all,
    good morrow.
I have been long a sleeper; but, I hope,
My absence doth neglect no great designs,
Which by my presence might have been con-
    cluded.
Buck. Had not you come upon your cue,
    my lord,
William Lord Hastings had pronounced your
    part,—
I mean, your voice,—for crowning of the king.
Glou. Than my Lord Hastings no man
    might be bolder;   30
His lordship knows me well, and loves me
    well.
Hast. I thank your grace.
Glou.   My lord of Ely!
Ely.   My lord?
Glou. When I was last in Holborn,
I saw good strawberries in your garden there:
I do beseech you send for some of them.
Ely. Marry, and will, my lord, with all my
    heart.   [Exit.
Glou. Cousin of Buckingham, a word with
    you.   [Drawing him aside.
Catesby hath sounded Hastings in our busi-
    ness,
And finds the testy gentleman so hot,
As he will lose his head ere give consent 40
His master's son, as worshipful he terms it,
Shall lose the royalty of England's throne.
Buck. Withdraw you hence, my lord, I'll
    follow you.
    [Exit Gloucester, Buckingham following.
Der. We have not yet set down this day of
    triumph.
To-morrow, in mine opinion, is too sudden;
For I myself am not so well provided
As else I would be, were the day prolong'd.

Re-enter BISHOP OF ELY.

Ely. Where is my lord protector? I have
sent for these strawberries.
Hast. His grace looks cheerfully and
    smooth to-day;   50
There's some conceit or other likes him well,
When he doth bid good morrow with such a
    spirit.
I think there's never a man in Christendom
That can less hide his love or hate than he;
For by his face straight shall you know his
    heart.
Der. What of his heart perceive you in
    his face
By any likelihood he show'd to-day?
Hast. Marry, that with no man here he is
    offended;
For, were he, he had shown it in his looks.
Der. I pray God he be not, I say.   60

Re-enter GLOUCESTER *and* BUCKINGHAM.

Glou. I pray you all, tell me what they
    deserve
That do conspire my death with devilish plots
Of damned witchcraft, and that have prevail'd
Upon my body with their hellish charms ?
Hast. The tender love I bear your grace,
    my lord,
Makes me most forward in this noble presence
To doom the offenders, whatsoever they be :
I say, my lord, they have deserved death.
Glou. Then be your eyes the witness of
    this ill :
See how I am bewitch'd ; behold mine arm 70
Is, like a blasted sapling, wither'd up :
And this is Edward's wife, that monstrous
    witch,
Consorted with that harlot strumpet Shore,
That by their witchcraft thus have marked me.
Hast. If they have done this thing, my
    gracious lord,—
Glou. If ! thou protector of this damned
    strumpet,
Tellest thou me of ' ifs ' ? Thou art a traitor :
Off with his head ! Now, by Saint Paul I
    swear,
I will not dine until I see the same.
Lovel and Ratcliff, look that it be done :   80
The rest, that love me, rise and follow me.
[*Exeunt all but Hastings, Ratcliff, and Lovel.*
Hast. Woe, woe for England ! not a whit
    for me ;
For I, too fond, might have prevented this.
Stanley did dream the boar did raze his helm ;
But I disdain'd it, and did scorn to fly :
Three times to-day my foot-cloth horse did
    stumble,
And startled, when he look'd upon the Tower,
As loath to bear me to the slaughter-house.
O, now I want the priest that spake to me :
I now repent I told the pursuivant,   90
As 'twere triumphing at mine enemies,
How they at Pomfret bloodily were butcher'd,
And I myself secure in grace and favor.
O Margaret, Margaret, now thy heavy curse
Is lighted on poor Hastings' wretched head !
Rat. Dispatch, my lord ; the duke would
    be at dinner :
Make a short shrift ; he longs to see your head.
Hast. O momentary grace of mortal men,
Which we more hunt for than the grace of
    God !
Who builds his hopes in air of your good
    looks,   100
Lives like a drunken sailor on a mast,
Ready, with every nod, to tumble down
Into the fatal bowels of the deep.
Lov. Come, come, dispatch ; 'tis bootless
    to exclaim.
Hast. O bloody Richard ! miserable Eng-
    land !
I prophesy the fearfull'st time to thee
That ever wretched age hath look'd upon.
Come, lead me to the block ; bear him my
    head.
They smile at me that shortly shall be dead.
                         [*Exeunt.*

SCENE V. *The Tower-walls.*

Enter GLOUCESTER *and* BUCKINGHAM, *in rotten armor, marvellous ill-favored.*

Glou. Come, cousin, canst thou quake, and
    change thy color,
Murder thy breath in the middle of a word,
And then begin again, and stop again,
As if thou wert distraught and mad with ter-
    ror ?
Buck. Tut, I can counterfeit the deep tra-
    gedian ;
Speak and look back, and pry on every side,
Tremble and start at wagging of a straw,
Intending deep suspicion : ghastly looks
Are at my service, like enforced smiles ;
And both are ready in their offices,   10
At any time, to grace my stratagems.
But what, is Catesby gone ?
Glou. He is ; and, see, he brings the mayor
    along.

Enter the Mayor *and* CATESBY.

Buck. Lord mayor,—
Glou. Look to the drawbridge there !
Buck. Hark ! a drum.
Glou. Catesby, o'erlook the walls.
Buck. Lord mayor, the reason we have
    sent—
Glou. Look back, defend thee, here are
    enemies.
Buck. God and our innocency defend and
    guard us !   20
Glou. Be patient, they are friends, Ratcliff
    and Lovel.

Enter LOVEL *and* RATCLIFF, *with* HASTINGS'
    head.

Lov. Here is the head of that ignoble
    traitor,
The dangerous and unsuspected Hastings.
Glou. So dear I loved the man, that I must
    weep.
I took him for the plainest harmless creature
That breathed upon this earth a Christian ;
Made him my book, wherein my soul recorded
The history of all her secret thoughts :
So smooth he daub'd his vice with show of
    virtue,
That, his apparent open guilt omitted,   30
I mean, his conversation with Shore's wife,
He lived from all attainder of suspect.
Buck. Well, well, he was the covert'st
    shelter'd traitor
That ever lived.
Would you imagine, or almost believe,
Were't not that, by great preservation,
We live to tell it you, the subtle traitor
This day had plotted, in the council-house
To murder me and my good Lord of Glouces-
    ter ?
May. What, had he so ?   40
Glou. What, think you we are Turks or
    infidels ?
Or that we would, against the form of law,
Proceed thus rashly to the villain's death,
But that the extreme peril of the case,
The peace of England and our persons' safety,
Enforced us to this execution ?
May. Now, fair befall you ! he deserved
    his death ;
And you my good lords, both have well pro-
    ceeded,
To warn false traitors from the like attempts.
I never look'd for better at his hands,   50
After he once fell in with Mistress Shore.

Glou. Yet had not we determined he
    should die,
Until your lordship came to see his death ;
Which now the loving haste of these our
    friends,
Somewhat against our meaning, have pre-
    vented :
Because, my lord, we would have had you
    heard
The traitor speak, and timorously confess
The manner and the purpose of his treason ;
That you might well have signified the same
Unto the citizens, who haply may   60
Misconstrue us in him and wail his death.
    May. But, my good lord, your grace's word
        shall serve,
As well as I had seen and heard him speak :
And doubt you not, right noble princes both,
But I'll acquaint our duteous citizens
With all your just proceedings in this cause.
    Glou. And to that end we wish'd your lord-
        ship here,
To avoid the carping censures of the world.
    Buck. But since you come too late of our
        intents,
Yet witness what you hear we did intend : 70
And so, my good lord mayor, we bid farewell.
                            [*Exit Mayor.*
    Glou. Go, after, after, cousin Buckingham.
The mayor towards Guildhall hies him in all
    post :
There, at your meet'st advantage of the time,
Infer the bastardy of Edward's children :
Tell them how Edward put to death a citizen,
Only for saying he would make his son
Heir to the crown ; meaning indeed his house,
Which, by the sign thereof, was termed so.
Moreover, urge his hateful luxury,   80
And bestial appetite in change of lust ;
Which stretched to their servants, daughters,
    wives,
Even where his lustful eye or savage heart,
Without control, listed to make his prey.
Nay, for a need, thus far come near my per-
    son :
Tell them, when that my mother went with
    child
Of that unsatiate Edward, noble York
My princely father then had wars in France ;
And, by just computation of the time,
Found that the issue was not his begot ; 90
Which well appeared in his lineaments,
Being nothing like the noble duke my father :
But touch this sparingly, as 'twere far off ;
Because you know, my lord, my mother lives.
    Buck. Fear not, my lord, I'll play the
        orator
As if the golden fee for which I plead
Were for myself : and so, my lord, adieu.
    Glou. If you thrive well, bring them to
        Baynard's Castle ;
Where you shall find me well accompanied
With reverend fathers and well-learned
    bishops.
    Buck. I go : and towards three or four
        o'clock
Look for the news that the Guildhall affords.
                            [*Exit.*
    Glou. Go, Lovel, with all speed to Doctor
        Shaw ;
[*To Cate.*] Go thou to Friar Penker ; bid them
    both

Meet me within this hour at Baynard's Castle.
            [*Exeunt all but Gloucester.*
Now will I in, to take some privy order,
To draw the brats of Clarence out of sight ;
And to give notice, that no manner of person
At any time have recourse unto the princes.
                            [*Exit.*

SCENE VI. *The same. A street.*

Enter a Scrivener, *with a paper in his hand.*

    Scriv. This is the indictment of the good
        Lord Hastings ;
Which in a set hand fairly is engross'd,
That it may be this day read over in Paul's.
And mark how well the sequel hangs to-
    gether :
Eleven hours I spent to write it over,
For yesternight by Catesby was it brought me ;
The precedent was full as long a-doing :
And yet within these five hours lived Lord
    Hastings,
Untainted, unexamined, free, at liberty.
Here's a good world the while ! Why who's
    so gross,   10
That seeth not this palpable device ?
Yet who's so blind, but says he sees it not ?
Bad is the world ; and all will come to nought,
When such bad dealings must be seen in
    thought.   [*Exit.*

SCENE VII. *Baynard's Castle.*

Enter GLOUCESTER *and* BUCKINGHAM, *at
        several doors.*

    Glou. How now, my lord, what say the
        citizens ?
    Buck. Now, by the holy mother of our
        Lord,
The citizens are mum and speak not a word.
    Glou. Touch'd you the bastardy of Ed-
        ward's children ?
    Buck. I did ; with his contract with Lady
        Lucy,
And his contract by deputy in France ;
The insatiate greediness of his desires,
And his enforcement of the city wives ;
His tyranny for trifles ; his own bastardy,
As being got, your father then in France, 10
And his resemblance, being not like the duke :
Withal I did infer your lineaments,
Being the right idea of your father,
Both in your form and nobleness of mind ;
Laid open all your victories in Scotland,
Your discipline in war, wisdom in peace,
Your bounty, virtue, fair humility ;
Indeed, left nothing fitting for the purpose
Untouch'd, or slightly handled, in discourse :
And when mine oratory grew to an end,   20
I bid them that did love their country's good
Cry 'God save Richard, England's royal
    king ! '
    Glou. Ah ! and did they so ?
    Buck. No, so God help me, they spake not
        a word ;
But, like dumb statuas or breathing stones,
Gazed each on other, and look'd deadly pale.
Which when I saw, I reprehended them ;
And ask'd the mayor what meant this wilful
    silence :
His answer was, the people were not wont
To be spoke to but by the recorder.   30
Then he was urged to tell my tale again,
' Thus saith the duke, thus hath the duke in-
    ferr'd ; '

But nothing spake in warrant from himself.
When he had done, some followers of mine
    own,
At the lower end of the hall, hurl'd up their
    caps,
And some ten voices cried ' God save King
    Richard ! '
And thus I took the vantage of those few,
' Thanks, gentle citizens and friends,' quoth I ;
' This general applause and loving shout
Argues your wisdoms and your love to
    Richard : '   40
And even here brake off, and came away.
    Glou. What tongueless blocks were they !
        would not they speak ?
    Buck. No, by my troth, my lord.
    Glou. Will not the mayor then and his
        brethren come ?
    Buck. The mayor is here at hand : intend
        some fear ;
Be not you spoke with, but by mighty suit :
And look you get a prayer-book in your hand,
And stand betwixt two churchmen, good my
    lord ;
For on that ground I'll build a holy descant :
And be not easily won to our request :   50
Play the maid's part, still answer nay, and take
    it.
    Glou. I go ; and if you plead as well for
        them
As I can say nay to thee for myself,
No doubt we'll bring it to a happy issue.
    Buck. Go, go, up to the leads ; the lord
mayor knocks.   *[Exit Gloucester.*

        Enter the Mayor *and* Citizens.

Welcome, my lord ; I dance attendance here ;
I think the duke will not be spoke withal.

            Enter Catesby.

Here comes his servant : how now, Catesby,
What says he ?
    Cate. My lord : he doth entreat your
        grace ;
To visit him to-morrow or next day :   60
He is within, with two right reverend fathers,
Divinely bent to meditation ;
And in no worldly suit would he be moved,
To draw him from his holy exercise.
    Buck. Return, good Catesby, to thy lord
        again ;
Tell him, myself, the mayor and citizens,
In deep designs and matters of great moment,
No less importing than our general good,
Are come to have some conference with his
    grace.
    Cate. I'll tell him what you say, my lord.
                                        [Exit.
    Buck. Ah, ha, my lord, this prince is not
        an Edward !   71
He is not lolling on a lewd day-bed,
But on his knees at meditation ;
Not dallying with a brace of courtezans,
But meditating with two deep divines ;
Not sleeping, to engross his idle body,
But praying, to enrich his watchful soul :
Happy were England, would this gracious
    prince
Take on himself the sovereignty thereof :
But, sure, I fear, we shall ne'er win him to it.
    May. Marry, God forbid his grace should
        say us nay !   81
    Buck. I fear he will.

            Re-enter Catesby.

How now, Catesby, what says your lord ?
    Cate.   My lord,
He wonders to what end you have assembled
Such troops of citizens to speak with him,
His grace not being warn'd thereof before :
My lord, he fears you mean no good to him.
    Buck. Sorry I am my noble cousin should
Suspect me, that I mean no good to him :
By heaven, I come in perfect love to him ;   90
And so once more return and tell his grace.
                                    [Exit Catesby.
When holy and devout religious men
Are at their beads, 'tis hard to draw them
    thence,
So sweet is zealous contemplation.

Enter Gloucester *aloft, between two* Bishops.
            Catesby *returns.*

    May. See, where he stands between two
        clergymen !
    Buck. Two props of virtue for a Christian
        prince,
To stay him from the fall of vanity :
And, see, a book of prayer in his hand,
True ornaments to know a holy man.
Famous Plantagenet, most gracious prince,
Lend favorable ears to our request ;   101
And pardon us the interruption
Of thy devotion and right Christian zeal.
    Glou. My lord, there needs no such
        apology :
I rather do beseech you pardon me,
Who, earnest in the service of my God,
Neglect the visitation of my friends.
But, leaving this, what is your grace's pleas-
    ure ?
    Buck. Even that, I hope, which pleaseth
        God above,
And good men of this ungovern'd isle.   110
    Glou. I do suspect I have done some
        offence
That seems disgracious in the city's eyes,
And that you come to reprehend my igno-
    rance.
    Buck. You have, my lord : would it might
        please your grace,
At our entreaties, to amend that fault !
    Glou. Else wherefore breathe I in a Chris-
        tian land ?
    Buck. Then know, it is your fault that you
        resign
The supreme seat, the throne majestical,
The scepter'd office of your ancestors,
Your state of fortune and your due of birth,
The lineal glory of your royal house,   120
To the corruption of a blemish'd stock :
Whilst, in the mildness of your sleepy
    thoughts,
Which here we waken to our country's good,
This noble isle doth want her proper limbs ;
Her face defaced with scars of infamy,
Her royal stock graft with ignoble plants,
And almost shoulder'd in the swallowing gulf
Of blind forgetfulness and dark oblivion.
Which to recure, we heartily solicit   130
Your gracious self to take on you the charge
And kingly government of this your land,
Not as protector, steward, substitute,
Or lowly factor for another's gain ;
But as successively from blood to blood,
Your right of birth, your empery, your own.

For this, consorted with the citizens,
Your very worshipful and loving friends,
And by their vehement instigation,   139
In this just suit come I to move your grace.
   Glou. I know not whether to depart in
     silence,
Or bitterly to speak in your reproof,
Best fitteth my degree or your condition :
If not to answer, you might haply think
Tongue-tied ambition, not replying, yielded
To bear the golden yoke of sovereignty,
Which fondly you would here impose on me ;
If to reprove you for this suit of yours,
So season'd with your faithful love to me,
Then, on the other side, I check'd my friends.
Therefore, to speak, and to avoid the first, 151
And then, in speaking, not to incur the last,
Definitively thus I answer you.
Your love deserves my thanks ; but my desert
Unmeritable shuns your high request.
First, if all obstacles were cut away,
And that my path were even to the crown,
As my ripe revenue and due by birth ;
Yet so much is my poverty of spirit,
So mighty and so many my defects,   160
As I had rather hide me from my greatness,
Being a bark to brook no mighty sea,
Than in my greatness covet to be hid,
And in the vapor of my glory smother'd.
But, God be thank'd, there's no need of me,
And much I need to help you, if need were ;
The royal tree hath left us royal fruit,
Which, mellow'd by the stealing hours of time,
Will well become the seat of majesty,
And make, no doubt, us happy by his reign.
On him I lay what you would lay on me,   171
The right and fortune of his happy stars ;
Which God defend that I should wring from
     him !
   Buck. My lord, this argues conscience in
     your grace ;
But the respects thereof are nice and trivial,
All circumstances well considered.
You say that Edward is your brother's son :
So say we too, but not by Edward's wife ;
For first he was contract to Lady Lucy—
Your mother lives a witness to that vow— 180
And afterward by substitute betroth'd
To Bona, sister to the King of France.
These both put by, a poor petitioner,
A care-crazed mother of a many children,
A beauty-waning and distressed widow,
Even in the afternoon of her best days,
Made prize and purchase of his lustful eye,
Seduced the pitch and height of all his
     thoughts
To base declension and loathed bigamy :
By her, in his unlawful bed, he got   190
This Edward, whom our manners term the
     prince.
More bitterly could I expostulate,
Save that, for reverence to some alive,
I give a sparing limit to my tongue.
Then, good my lord, take to your royal self
This proffer'd benefit of dignity ;
If not to bless us and the land withal,
Yet to draw forth your noble ancestry
From the corruption of abusing times,
Unto a lineal true-derived course.   200
   May. Do, good my lord, your citizens en-
     treat you.
   Buck. Refuse not, mighty lord, this prof-
     fer'd love.

   Cate. O, make them joyful, grant their
     lawful suit !
   Glou. Alas, why would you heap these
     cares on me ?
I am unfit for state and majesty :
I do beseech you, take it not amiss ;
I cannot nor I will not yield to you.
   Buck. If you refuse it,—as, in love and
     zeal,
Loath to depose the child, your brother's son ;
As well we know your tenderness of heart 210
And gentle, kind, effeminate remorse,
Which we have noted in you to your kin,
And egally indeed to all estates,—
Yet whether you accept our suit or no,
Your brother's son shall never reign our king ;
But we will plant some other in the throne,
To the disgrace and downfall of your house :
And in this resolution here we leave you.—
Come, citizens : 'zounds ! I'll entreat no more.
   Glou. O, do not swear, my lord of Buck-
     ingham.   220
          [*Exit Buckingham with the Citizens.*
   Cate. Call them again, my lord, and accept
     their suit.
   Another. Do, good my lord, lest all the
     land do rue it.
   Glou. Would you enforce me to a world of
     care ?
Well, call them again. I am not made of stone,
But penetrable to your kind entreats,
Albeit against my conscience and my soul.

     Re-enter BUCKINGHAM *and the rest.*

Cousin of Buckingham, and you sage, grave
     men,
Since you will buckle fortune on my back,
To bear her burthen, whether I will or no,
I must have patience to endure the load :   230
But if black scandal or foul-faced reproach
Attend the sequel of your imposition,
Your mere enforcement shall acquittance me
From all the impure blots and stains thereof ;
For God he knows, and you may partly see,
How far I am from the desire thereof.
   May. God bless your grace ! we see it, and
     will say it.
   Glou. In saying so, you shall but say the
     truth.
   Buck. Then I salute you with this kingly
     title :
Long live Richard, England's royal king ! 240
   May and Cit. Amen.
   Buck. To-morrow will it please you to be
     crown'd ?
   Glou. Even when you please, since you will
     have it so.
   Buck. To-morrow, then, we will attend
     your grace :
And so most joyfully we take our leave.
   Glou. Come, let us to our holy task again.
Farewell, good cousin ; farewell, gentle friends.
                      [*Exeunt.*

ACT IV.

SCENE I. *Before the Tower.*

Enter, on one side, QUEEN ELIZABETH, DUCH-
ESS OF YORK, *and* MARQUESS OF DORSET ;
on the other, ANNE, DUCHESS OF GLOUCES-
TER, *leading* LADY MARGARET PLANTAGENET,
CLARENCE'S *young Daughter.*

Duch.   Who meets us here ? my niece Plan-
tagenet
Led in the hand of her kind aunt of Glouces-
ter ?
Now, for my life, she's wandering to the
Tower,
On pure heart's love to greet the tender
princes.
Daughter, well met.
Anne.   God give your graces both
A happy and a joyful time of day !
Q. Eliz.   As much to you, good sister !
Whither away ?
Anne.   No farther than the Tower ; and, as
I guess,
Upon the like devotion as yourselves,
To gratulate the gentle princes there.   10
Q. Eliz.   Kind sister, thanks : we'll enter all
together.

Enter BRAKENBURY.

And, in good time, here the lieutenant comes.
Master lieutenant, pray you, by your leave,
How doth the prince, and my young son of
York ?
Brak.   Right well, dear madam. By your
patience,
I may not suffer you to visit them ;
The king hath straitly charged the contrary.
Q. Eliz.   The king ! why, who's that ?
Brak.   I cry you mercy : I mean the lord
protector.
Q. Eliz.   The Lord protect him from that
kingly title !   20
Hath he set bounds betwixt their love and me ?
I am their mother ; who should keep me from
them ?
Duch.   I am their father's mother ; I will
see them.
Anne.   Their aunt I am in law, in love their
mother :
Then bring me to their sights ; I'll bear thy
blame
And take thy office from thee, on my peril.
Brak.   No, madam, no ; I may not leave it
so :
I am bound by oath, and therefore pardon me.
                                               [*Exit.*

Enter LORD STANLEY.

Stan.   Let me but meet you, ladies, one
hour hence,   29
And I'll salute your grace of York as mother,
And reverend looker on, of two fair queens.
[*To Anne*] Come, madam, you must straight
to Westminster,
There to be crowned Richard's royal queen.
Q. Eliz.   O, cut my lace in sunder, that my
pent heart
May have some scope to beat, or else I swoon
With this dead-killing news !
Anne.   Despiteful tidings ! O unpleasing
news !
Dor.   Be of good cheer : mother, how fares
your grace ?
Q. Eliz.   O Dorset, speak not to me, get
thee hence !
Death and destruction dog thee at the heels ;
Thy mother's name is ominous to children.   41
If thou wilt outstrip death, go cross the seas,
And live with Richmond, from the reach of
hell :

Go, hie thee, hie thee from this slaughter-
house,
Lest thou increase the number of the dead ;
And make me die the thrall of Margaret's
curse,
Nor mother, wife, nor England's counted
queen.
Stan.   Full of wise care is this your coun-
sel, madam.
Take all the swift advantage of the hours ;
You shall have letters from me to my son   50
To meet you on the way, and welcome you.
Be not ta'en tardy by unwise delay.
Duch.   O ill-dispersing wind of misery !
O my accursed womb, the bed of death !
A cockatrice hast thou hatch'd to the world,
Whose unavoided eye is murderous.
Stan.   Come, madam, come ; I in all haste
was sent.
Anne.   And I in all unwillingness will go.
I would to God that the inclusive verge
Of golden metal that must round my brow   60
Were red-hot steel, to sear me to the brain !
Anointed let me be with deadly venom,
And die, ere men can say, God save the
queen !
Q. Eliz.   Go, go, poor soul, I envy not thy
glory ;
To feed my humor, wish thyself no harm.
Anne.   No ! why ? When he that is my hus-
band now
Came to me, as I follow'd Henry's corse,
When scarce the blood was well wash'd from
his hands
Which issued from my other angel husband
And that dead saint which then I weeping fol-
low'd ;   70
O, when, I say, I look'd on Richard's face,
This was my wish : ' Be thou,' quoth I, ' ac-
cursed,
For making me, so young, so old a widow !
And, when thou wed'st, let sorrow haunt thy
bed ;
And be thy wife—if any be so mad—
As miserable by the life of thee
As thou hast made me by my dear lord's
death ! '
Lo, ere I can repeat this curse again,
Even in so short a space, my woman's heart
Grossly grew captive to his honey words   80
And proved the subject of my own soul's
curse,
Which ever since hath kept my eyes from rest ;
For never yet one hour in his bed
Have I enjoy'd the golden dew of sleep,
But have been waked by his timorous dreams.
Besides, he hates me for my father Warwick ;
And will, no doubt, shortly be rid of me.
Q. Eliz.   Poor heart, adieu ! I pity thy com-
plaining.
Anne.   No more than from my soul I
mourn for yours.
Q. Eliz.   Farewell, thou woful welcomer of
glory !   90
Anne.   Adieu, poor soul, that takest thy
leave of it !
Duch.   [*To Dorset*] Go thou to Richmond,
and good fortune guide thee !
[*To Anne*] Go thou to Richard, and good an-
gels guard thee !
[*To Queen Eliz.*] Go thou to sanctuary, and
good thoughts possess thee !

I to my grave, where peace and rest lie with
   me!
Eighty odd years of sorrow have I seen,
And each hour's joy wrecked with a week of
   teen.
Q. Eliz. Stay, yet look back with me unto
   the Tower.
Pity, you ancient stones, those tender babes
Whom envy hath immured within your walls!
Rough cradle for such little pretty ones!   101
Rude ragged nurse, old sullen playfellow
For tender princes, use my babies well!
So foolish sorrow bids your stones farewell.
                                    [*Exeunt.*

SCENE II. *London. The palace.*

Sennet. Enter RICHARD, *in pomp, crowned;*
   BUCKINGHAM, CATESBY, *a page, and others.*

K. Rich. Stand all apart. Cousin of Buck-
   ingham!
Buck. My gracious sovereign?
K. Rich. Give me thy hand. [*Here he as-
cendeth his throne.*] Thus high, by thy advice
And thy assistance, is King Richard seated;
But shall we wear these honors for a day?
Or shall they last, and we rejoice in them?
Buck. Still live they and for ever may they
   last!
K. Rich. O Buckingham, now do I play
   the touch,
To try if thou be current gold indeed:
Young Edward lives: think now what I would
   say.   10
Buck. Say on, my loving lord.
K. Rich. Why, Buckingham, I say, I would
   be king,
Buck. Why, so you are, my thrice re-
   nowned liege.
K. Rich. Ha! am I king? 'tis so: but Ed-
   ward lives.
Buck. True, noble prince.
K. Rich.   O bitter consequence,
That Edward still should live! 'True, noble
   prince!'
Cousin, thou wert not wont to be so dull:
Shall I be plain? I wish the bastards dead;
And I would have it suddenly perform'd.
What sayest thou? speak suddenly; be brief.
Buck. Your grace may do your pleasure.
K. Rich. Tut, tut, thou art all ice, thy kind-
   ness freezeth!
Say, have I thy consent that they shall die?
Buck. Give me some breath, some little
   pause, my lord,
Before I positively speak herein:
I will resolve your grace immediately. [*Exit.*
Cate. [*Aside to a stander by*] The king is
   angry: see, he bites the lip.
K. Rich. I will converse with iron-witted
   fools
And unrespective boys: none are for me
That look into me with considerate eyes: 30
High-reaching Buckingham grows circumspect.
Boy!
Page. My lord?
K. Rich. Know'st thou not any whom cor-
   rupting gold
Would tempt unto a close exploit of death?
Page. My lord, I know a discontented gen-
   tleman,
Whose humble means match not his haughty
   mind:
Gold were as good as twenty orators,

And will, no doubt, tempt him to any thing.
K. Rich. What is his name?   40
Page.   His name, my lord, is Tyrrel.
K. Rich. I partly know the man: go, call
   him hither.   [*Exit Page.*
The deep-revolving witty Buckingham
No more shall be the neighbor to my counsel:
Hath he so long held out with me untired,
And stops he now for breath?

Enter STANLEY.

              How now! what news with you?
Stan. My lord, I hear the Marquis Dorset's
   fled
To Richmond, in those parts beyond the sea
Where he abides.   [*Stands apart.*
K. Rich. Catesby!
Cate. My lord?   50
K. Rich. Rumor it abroad
That Anne, my wife, is sick and like to die:
I will take order for her keeping close.
Inquire me out some mean-born gentleman,
Whom I will marry straight to Clarence'
   daughter:
The boy is foolish, and I fear not him.
Look, how thou dream'st! I say again, give
   out
That Anne my wife is sick and like to die:
About it; for it stands me much upon,
To stop all hopes whose growth may damage
   me.   [*Exit Catesby.* 60
I must be married to my brother's daughter,
Or else my kingdom stands on brittle glass.
Murder her brothers, and then marry her!
Uncertain way of gain! But I am in
So far in blood that sin will pluck on sin:
Tear-falling pity dwells not in this eye.

Re-enter PAGE, *with* TYRREL.

Is thy name Tyrrel?
Tyr. James Tyrrel, and your most obedient
   subject.
K. Rich. Art thou, indeed?
Tyr.   Prove me, my gracious sovereign.
K. Rich. Darest thou resolve to kill a
   friend of mine?   70
Tyr. Ay, my lord;
But I had rather kill two enemies.
K. Rich. Why, there thou hast it: two
   deep enemies,
Foes to my rest and my sweet sleep's dis-
   turbers
Are they that I would have thee deal upon:
Tyrrel, I mean those bastards in the Tower.
Tyr. Let me have open means to come to
   them,
And soon I'll rid you from the fear of them.
K. Rich. Thou sing'st sweet music. Hark,
   come hither, Tyrrel.
Go, by this token: rise, and lend thine ear: 80
                                  [*Whispers.*
There is no more but so: say it is done,
And I will love thee, and prefer thee too.
Tyr. 'Tis done, my gracious lord.
K. Rich. Shall we hear from thee, Tyrrel,
   ere we sleep?
Tyr. Ye shall, my Lord.   [*Exit.*

Re-enter BUCKINGHAM.

Buck. My Lord, I have consider'd in my
   mind
The late demand that you did sound me in.

K. Rich. Well, let that pass. Dorset is fled
to Richmond.
Buck. I hear that news, my lord.
K. Rich. Stanley, he is your wife's son :
well, look to it.   90
Buck. My lord, I claim your gift, my due
by promise,
For which your honor and your faith is
pawn'd ;
The earldom of Hereford and the moveables
The which you promised I should possess.
K. Rich. Stanley, look to your wife ; if she
convey
Letters to Richmond, you shall answer it.
Buck. What says your highness to my just
demand ?
K. Rich. As I remember, Henry the Sixth
Did prophesy that Richmond should be king,
When Richmond was a little peevish boy. 100
A king, perhaps, perhaps,—
Buck. My lord !
K. Rich. How chance the prophet could
not at that time
Have told me, I being by, that I should kill
him ?
Buck. My lord, your promise for the earl-
dom,—
K. Rich. Richmond ! When last I was at
Exeter,
The mayor in courtesy show'd me the castle,
And call'd it Rougemont : at which name I
started,
Because a bard of Ireland told me once,
I should not live long after I saw Richmond.
Buck. My Lord !   111
K. Rich. Ay, what's o'clock ?
Buck. I am thus bold to put your grace in
mind
Of what you promised me.
K. Rich.   Well, but what's o'clock ?
Buck. Upon the stroke of ten.
K. Rich.   Well, let it strike.
Buck. Why let it strike ?
K. Rich. Because that, like a Jack, thou
keep'st the stroke
Betwixt thy begging and my meditation.
I am not in the giving vein to-day.
Buck. Why, then resolve me whether you
will or no.   120
K. Rich. Tut, tut,
Thou troublest me ; I am not in the vein.
                                  [*Exeunt all but Buckingham.*
Buck. Is it even so ? rewards he my true
service
With such deep contempt ? made I him king
for this ?
O, let me think on Hastings, and be gone
To Brecknock, while my fearful head is on !
                                                                       [*Exit.*

SCENE III. *The same.*
Enter TYRREL.

Tyr. The tyrannous and bloody deed is
done,
The most arch act of piteous massacre
That ever yet this land was guilty of.
Dighton and Forrest, whom I did suborn
To do this ruthless piece of butchery,
Although they were flesh'd villains, bloody
dogs,
Melting with tenderness and kind compassion
Wept like two children in their deaths' sad
stories.

' Lo, thus ' quoth Dighton, ' lay those tender
babes : '
' Thus, thus,' quoth Forrest, ' girdling one an-
other   10
Within their innocent alabaster arms :
Their lips were four red roses on a stalk,
Which in their summer beauty kiss'd each
other.
A book of prayers on their pillow lay ;
Which once,' quoth Forrest, ' almost changed
my mind ;
But O ! the devil '—there the villain stopp'd :
Whilst Dighton thus told on : ' We smothered
The most replenished sweet work of nature,
That from the prime creation e'er she framed.'
Thus both are gone with conscience and re-
morse ;   20
They could not speak ; and so I left them both,
To bring this tidings to the bloody king.
And here he comes.

Enter KING RICHARD.

                        All hail, my sovereign liege !
K. Rich. Kind Tyrrel, am I happy in thy
news ?
Tyr. If to have done the thing you gave in
charge
Beget your happiness, be happy then,
For it is done, my lord.
K. Rich.   But didst thou see them dead ?
Tyr. I did, my lord.
K. Rich.   And buried, gentle Tyrrel ?
Tyr. The chaplain of the Tower hath bur-
ied them ;
But how or in what place I do not know.   30
K. Rich. Come to me, Tyrrel, soon at after
supper,
And thou shalt tell the process of their death.
Meantime, but think how I may do thee good,
And be inheritor of thy desire.
Farewell till soon.   [*Exit Tyrrel.*
The son of Clarence have I pent up close ;
His daughter meanly have I match'd in mar-
riage ;
The sons of Edward sleep in Abraham's
bosom,
And Anne my wife hath bid the world good
night.   39
Now, for I know the Breton Richmond aims
At young Elizabeth, my brother's daughter,
And, by that knot, looks proudly o'er the
crown,
To her I go, a jolly thriving wooer.

Enter CATESBY.

Cate. My lord !
K. Rich. Good news or bad, that thou
comest in so bluntly ?
Cate. Bad news, my lord : Ely is fled to
Richmond ;
And Buckingham, back'd with the hardy
Welshmen,
Is in the field, and still his power increaseth.
K. Rich. Ely with Richmond troubles me
more near   49
Than Buckingham and his rash-levied army.
Come, I have heard that fearful commenting
Is leaden servitor to dull delay ;
Delay leads impotent and snail-paced beggary :
Then fiery expedition be my wing,
Jove's Mercury, and herald for a king !
Come, muster men : my counsel is my shield ;

We must be brief when traitors brave the field. [*Exeunt.*

SCENE IV. *Before the palace.*

Enter QUEEN MARGARET.

Q. Mar. So, now prosperity begins to mellow
And drop into the rotten mouth of death.
Here in these confines slily have I lurk'd,
To watch the waning of mine adversaries.
A dire induction am I witness to,
And will to France, hoping the consequence
Will prove as bitter, black, and tragical.
Withdraw thee, wretched Margaret : who comes here ?

Enter QUEEN ELIZABETH *and the* DUCHESS OF YORK.

Q. Eliz. Ah, my young princes ! ah, my tender babes !
My unblown flowers, new-appearing sweets !
If yet your gentle souls fly in the air   11
And be not fix'd in doom perpetual,
Hover about me with your airy wings
And hear your mother's lamentation !
Q. Mar. Hover about her ; say, that right for right
Hath dimm'd your infant morn to aged night.
Duch. So many miseries have crazed my voice,
That my woe-wearied tongue is mute and dumb,
Edward Plantagenet, why art thou dead ?
Q. Mar. Plantagenet doth quit Plantagenet.
Edward for Edward pays a dying debt.   21
Q. Eliz. Wilt thou, O God, fly from such gentle lambs,
And throw them in the entrails of the wolf ?
When didst thou sleep when such a deed was done ?
Q. Mar. When holy Harry died, and my sweet son.
Duch. Blind sight, dead life, poor mortal living ghost,
Woe's scene, world's shame, grave's due by life usurp'd,
Brief abstract and record of tedious days,
Rest thy unrest on England's lawful earth,
[*Sitting down.*
Unlawfully made drunk with innocents' blood !
Q. Eliz. O, that thou wouldst as well afford a grave   31
As thou canst yield a melancholy seat !
Then would I hide my bones, not rest them here.
O, who hath any cause to mourn but I ?
[*Sitting down by her.*
Q. Mar. If ancient sorrow be most reverend,
Give mine the benefit of seniory,
And let my woes frown on the upper hand.
If sorrow can admit society,
[*Sitting down with them.*
Tell o'er your woes again by viewing mine :
I had an Edward, till a Richard kill'd him ;   40
I had a Harry, till a Richard kill'd him :
Thou hadst an Edward, till a Richard kill'd him ;
Thou hadst a Richard, till a Richard killed him ;
Duch. I had a Richard too, and thou didst kill him ;
I had a Rutland too, thou holp'st to kill him.

Q. Mar. Thou hadst a Clarence too, and Richard kill'd him.
From forth the kennel of thy womb hath crept
A hell-hound that doth hunt us all to death :
That dog, that had his teeth before his eyes,
To worry lambs and lap their gentle blood,   50
That foul defacer of God's handiwork,
That excellent grand tyrant of the earth,
That reigns in galled eyes of weeping souls,
Thy womb let loose, to chase us to our graves.
O upright, just, and true-disposing God,
How do I thank thee, that this carnal cur
Preys on the issue of his mother's body,
And makes her pew-fellow with others' moan !
Duch. O Harry's wife, triumph not in my woes !
God witness with me, I have wept for thine.
Q. Mar. Bear with me ; I am hungry for revenge,   61
And now I cloy me with beholding it.
Thy Edward he is dead, that stabb'd my Edward ;
Thy other Edward dead, to quit my Edward ;
Young York he is but boot, because both they
Match not the high perfection of my loss :
Thy Clarence he is dead that kill'd my Edward ;
And the beholders of this tragic play,
The adulterate Hastings, Rivers, Vaughan, Grey,
Untimely smother'd in their dusky graves.   70
Richard yet lives, hell's black intelligencer,
Only reserved their factor, to buy souls
And send them thither : but at hand, at hand,
Ensues his piteous and unpitied end :
Earth gapes, hell burns, fiends roar, saints pray,
To have him suddenly convey'd away.
Cancel his bond of life, dear God, I pray,
That I may live to say, The dog is dead !
Q. Eliz. O, thou didst prophesy the time would come   80
That I should wish for thee to help me curse
That bottled spider, that foul bunch-back'd toad !
Q. Mar. I call'd thee then vain flourish of my fortune ;
I call'd thee then poor shadow, painted queen ;
The presentation of but what I was ;
The flattering index of a direful pageant ;
One heaved a-high, to be hurl'd down below ;
A mother only mock'd with two sweet babes ;
A dream of what thou wert, a breath, a bubble,
A sign of dignity, a garish flag,
To be the aim of every dangerous shot,   90
A queen in jest, only to fill the scene.
Where is thy husband now ? where be thy brothers ?
Where are thy children ? wherein dost thou joy ?
Who sues to thee and cries ' God save the queen ' ?
Where be the bending peers that flatter'd thee ?
Where be the thronging troops that follow'd thee ?
Decline all this, and see what now thou art :
For happy wife, a most distressed widow ;
For joyful mother, one that wails the name ;
For queen, a very caitiff crown'd with care ;
For one being sued to, one that humbly sues ;
For one that scorn'd at me, now scorn'd of me ;
For one being fear'd of all, now fearing one ;

For one commanding all, obey'd of none.
Thus hath the course of justice wheel'd about,
And left thee but a very prey to time ;
Having no more but thought of what thou wert,
To torture thee the more, being what thou art.
Thou didst usurp my place, and dost thou not
Usurp the just proportion of my sorrow ? 110
Now thy proud neck bears half my burthen'd
        yoke ;
From which even here I slip my weary neck,
And leave the burthen of it all on thee.
Farewell, York's wife, and queen of sad mis-
        chance :
These English woes will make me smile in
        France.
Q. Eliz. O thou well skill'd in curses, stay
        awhile,
And teach me how to curse mine enemies !
Q. Mar. Forbear to sleep the nights, and
        fast the days ;
Compare dead happiness with living woe ;
Think that thy babes were fairer than they
        were,   120
And he that slew them fouler than he is :
Bettering thy loss makes the bad causer
        worse :
Revolving this will teach thee how to curse.
Q. Eliz. My words are dull ; O, quicken
        them with thine !
Q. Mar. Thy woes will make them sharp,
        and pierce like mine.   [*Exit.*
Duch. Why should calamity be full of
        words ?
Q. Eliz. Windy attorneys to their client
        woes,
Airy succeeders of intestate joys,
Poor breathing orators of miseries !
Let them have scope : though what they do
        impart   130
Help not at all, yet do they ease the heart.
Duch. If so, then be not tongue-tied : go
        with me,
And in the breath of bitter words let's smother
My damned son, which thy two sweet sons
        smother'd.
I hear his drum : be copious in exclaims.

Enter King Richard, *marching, with drums
        and trumpets.*

K. Rich. Who intercepts my expedition ?
Duch. O, she that might have intercepted
        thee,
By strangling thee in her accursed womb,
From all the slaughters, wretch, that thou hast
        done !
Q. Eliz. Hidest thou that forehead with a
        golden crown,   140
Where should be graven, if that right were
        right,
The slaughter of the prince that owed that
        crown,
And the dire death of my two sons and
        brothers ?
Tell me, thou villain slave, where are my chil-
        dren ?
Duch. Thou toad, thou toad, where is thy
        brother Clarence ?
And little Ned Plantagenet, his son ?
Q. Eliz. Where is kind Hastings, Rivers,
        Vaughan, Grey ?
K. Rich. A flourish, trumpets ! strike
        alarum, drums !
Let not the heavens hear these tell-tale women

Rail on the Lord's anointed : strike, I say !
        [*Flourish. Alarums.*
Either be patient, and entreat me fair,   151
Or with the clamorous report of war
Thus will I drown your exclamations.
Duch. Art thou my son ?
K. Rich. Ay, I thank God, my father, and
        yourself.
Duch. Then patiently hear my impatience.
K. Rich. Madam, I have a touch of your
        condition,
Which cannot brook the accent of reproof.
Duch. O, let me speak !
K. Rich. Do then ; but I'll not hear.
Duch. I will be mild and gentle in my
        speech.   160
K. Rich. And brief, good mother ; for I am
        in haste.
Duch. Art thou so hasty ? I have stay'd for
        thee,
God knows, in anguish, pain and agony.
K. Rich. And came I not at last to comfort
        you ?
Duch. No, by the holy rood, thou know'st
        it well,
Thou camest on earth to make the earth my
        hell.
A grievous burthen was thy birth to me ;
Tetchy and wayward was thy infancy ;
Thy school-days frightful, desperate, wild, and
        furious,
Thy prime of manhood daring, bold, and ven-
        turous,   170
Thy age confirm'd, proud, subtle, bloody,
        treacherous,
More mild, but yet more harmful, kind in
        hatred :
What comfortable hour canst thou name,
That ever graced me in thy company ?
K. Rich. Faith, none, but Humphrey Hour,
        that call'd your grace
To breakfast once forth of my company.
If I be so disgracious in your sight,
Let me march on, and not offend your grace.
Strike up the drum.
Duch.   I prithee, hear me speak.
K. Rich. You speak too bitterly.
Duch.   Hear me a word ;   180
For I shall never speak to thee again.
K. Rich. So.
Duch. Either thou wilt die, by God's just
        ordinance,
Ere from this war thou turn a conqueror,
Or I with grief and extreme age shall perish
And never look upon thy face again.
Therefore take with thee my most heavy curse ;
Which, in the day of battle, tire thee more
Than all the complete armor that thou
        wear'st !
My prayers on the adverse party fight ;   190
And there the little souls of Edward's children
Whisper the spirits of thine enemies
And promise them success and victory.
Bloody thou art, bloody will be thy end ;
Shame serves thy life and doth thy death at-
        tend.   [*Exit.*
Q. Eliz. Though far more cause, yet much
        less spirit to curse
Abides in me ; I say amen to all.
K. Rich. Stay, madam ; I must speak a
        word with you.
Q. Eliz. I have no more sons of the royal
        blood

For thee to murder : for my daughters, Rich-
   ard,   200
They shall be praying nuns, not weeping
   queens ;
And therefore level not to hit their lives.
   K. Rich. You have a daughter call'd Eliza-
     beth,
Virtuous and fair, royal and gracious.
   Q. Eliz. And must she die for this ? O, let
     her live,
And I'll corrupt her manners, stain her beauty ;
Slander myself as false to Edward's bed ;
Throw over her the veil of infamy :
So she may live unscarr'd of bleeding slaugh-
   ter,
I will confess she was not Edward's daughter.
   K. Rich. Wrong not her birth, she is of
     royal blood.   211
   Q. Eliz. To save her life, I'll say she is not
     so.
   K. Rich. Her life is only safest in her birth.
   Q. Eliz. And only in that safety died her
     brothers.
   K. Rich. Lo, at their births good stars were
     opposite.
   Q. Eliz. No, to their lives bad friends were
     contrary.
   K. Rich. All unavoided is the doom of
     destiny.
   Q. Eliz. True, when avoided grace makes
     destiny :
My babes were destined to a fairer death,
If grace had bless'd thee with a fairer life. 220
   K. Rich. You speak as if that I had slain
     my cousins.
   Q. Eliz. Cousins, indeed ; and by their
     uncle cozen'd
Of comfort, kingdom, kindred, freedom, life.
Whose hand soever lanced their tender hearts,
Thy head, all indirectly, gave direction :
No doubt the murderous knife was dull and
   blunt
Till it was whetted on thy stone-hard heart,
To revel in the entrails of my lambs.
But that still use of grief makes wild grief
   tame,
My tongue should to thy ears not name my
   boys   230
Till that my nails were anchor'd in thine eyes ;
And I, in such a desperate bay of death,
Like a poor bark, of sails and tackling reft,
Rush all to pieces on thy rocky bosom.
   K. Rich. Madam, so thrive I in my enter-
     prise
And dangerous success of bloody wars,
As I intend more good to you and yours
Than ever you or yours were by me wrong'd !
   Q. Eliz. What good is cover'd with the face
     of heaven,
To be discover'd, that can do me good ?   240
   K. Rich. The advancement of your chil-
     dren, gentle lady.
   Q. Eliz. Up to some scaffold, there to lose
     their heads ?
   K. Rich. No, to the dignity and height of
     honor,
The high imperial type of this earth's glory.
   Q. Eliz. Flatter my sorrows with report of
     it ;
Tell me what state, what dignity, what honor,
Canst thou demise to any child of mine ?
   K. Rich. Even all I have ; yea, and myself
     and all,

Will I withal endow a child of thine ;
So in the Lethe of thy angry soul   250
Thou drown the sad remembrance of those
   wrongs
Which thou supposest I have done to thee.
   Q. Eliz. Be brief, lest that be process of
     thy kindness
Last longer telling than thy kindness' date.
   K. Rich. Then know, that from my soul I
     love thy daughter.
   Q. Eliz. My daughter's mother thinks it
     with her soul.
   K. Rich. What do you think ?
   Q. Eliz. That thou dost love my daughter
     from thy soul :
So from thy soul's love didst thou love her
   brothers ;
And from my heart's love I do thank thee for
   it.   260
   K. Rich. Be not so hasty to confound my
     meaning :
I mean, that with my soul I love thy daughter,
And mean to make her queen of England.
   Q. Eliz. Say then, who dost thou mean
     shall be her king ?
   K. Rich. Even he that makes her queen :
     who should be else ?
   Q. Eliz. What, thou ?
   K. Rich. I, even I : what think you of it,
     madam ?
   Q. Eliz. How canst thou woo her ?
   K. Rich.   That would I learn of you,
As one that are best acquainted with her hu-
   mor.
   Q. Eliz. And wilt thou learn of me ?
   K. Rich.   Madam, with all my heart. 270
   Q. Eliz. Send to her, by the man that slew
     her brothers,
A pair of bleeding hearts ; thereon engrave
Edward and York ; then haply she will weep :
Therefore present to her,—as sometime Mar-
   garet
Did to thy father, steep'd in Rutland's blood,—
A handkerchief ; which, say to her, did drain
The purple sap from her sweet brother's body,
And bid her dry her weeping eyes therewith.
If this inducement force her not to love,
Send her a story of thy noble acts ;   280
Tell her thou madest away her uncle Clarence,
Her uncle Rivers ; yea, and, for her sake,
Madest quick conveyance with her good aunt
   Anne.
   K. Rich. Come, come, you mock me ; this
     is not the way
To win your daughter.
   Q. Eliz.   There is no other way ;
Unless thou couldst put on some other shape,
And not be Richard that hath done all this.
   K. Rich. Say that I did all this for love of
     her.
   Q. Eliz. Nay, then indeed she cannot
     choose but hate thee,
Having bought love with such a bloody spoil.
   K. Rich. Look, what is done cannot be now
     amended :   291
Men shall deal unadvisedly sometimes,
Which after hours give leisure to repent.
If I did take the kingdom from your sons,
To make amends, I'll give it to your daughter.
If I have kill'd the issue of your womb,
To quicken your increase, I will beget
Mine issue of your blood upon your daughter :
A grandam's name is little less in love

Than is the doting title of a mother; 300
They are as children but one step below,
Even of your mettle, of your very blood;
Of all one pain, save for a night of groans
Endured of her, for whom you bid like sorrow.
Your children were vexation to your youth,
But mine shall be a comfort to your age.
The loss you have is but a son being king,
And by that loss your daughter is made queen.
I cannot make you what amends I would,
Therefore accept such kindness as I can. 310
Dorset your son, that with a fearful soul
Leads discontented steps in foreign soil,
This fair alliance quickly shall call home
To high promotions and great dignity:
The king, that calls your beauteous daughter wife,
Familiarly shall call thy Dorset brother;
Again shall you be mother to a king,
And all the ruins of distressful times
Repair'd with double riches of content.
What! we have many goodly days to see: 320
The liquid drops of tears that you have shed
Shall come again, transform'd to orient pearl,
Advantaging their loan with interest
Of ten times double gain of happiness.
Go, then, my mother, to thy daughter go;
Make bold her bashful years with your experience;
Prepare her ears to hear a wooer's tale;
Put in her tender heart the aspiring flame
Of golden sovereignty; acquaint the princess
With the sweet silent hours of marriage joys:
And when this arm of mine hath chastised 331
The petty rebel, dull-brain'd Buckingham,
Bound with triumphant garlands will I come
And lead thy daughter to a conqueror's bed;
To whom I will retail my conquest won,
And she shall be sole victress, Cæsar's Cæsar.
Q. Eliz.	What were I best to say? her father's brother
Would be her lord? or shall I say, her uncle?
Or, he that slew her brothers and her uncles?
Under what title shall I woo for thee, 340
That God, the law, my honor and her love,
Can make seem pleasing to her tender years?
K. Rich.	Infer fair England's peace by this alliance.
Q. Eliz.	Which she shall purchase with still lasting war.
K. Rich.	Say that the king, which may command, entreats.
Q. Eliz.	That at her hands which the king's King forbids.
K. Rich.	Say, she shall be a high and mighty queen.
Q. Eliz.	To wail the title, as her mother doth.
K. Rich.	Say, I will love her everlastingly.
Q. Eliz.	But how long shall that title 'ever' last? 350
K. Rich.	Sweetly in force unto her fair life's end.
Q. Eliz.	But how long fairly shall her sweet life last?
K. Rich.	So long as heaven and nature lengthens it.
Q. Eliz.	So long as hell and Richard likes of it.
K. Rich.	Say, I, her sovereign, am her subject love.
Q. Eliz.	But she, your subject, loathes such sovereignty.

K. Rich.	Be eloquent in my behalf to her.
Q. Eliz.	An honest tale speeds best being plainly told.
K. Rich.	Then in plain terms tell her my loving tale.
Q. Eliz.	Plain and not honest is too harsh a style. 360
K. Rich.	Your reasons are too shallow and too quick.
Q. Eliz.	O no, my reasons are too deep and dead;
Too deep and dead, poor infants, in their grave.
K. Rich.	Harp not on that string, madam; that is past.
Q. Eliz.	Harp on it still shall I till heart-strings break.
K. Rich.	Now, by my George, my garter, and my crown,—
Q. Eliz.	Profaned, dishonor'd, and the third usurp'd.
K. Rich.	I swear—
Q. Eliz.	By nothing; for this is no oath:
The George, profaned, hath lost his holy honor;
The garter, blemish'd, pawn'd his knightly virtue;
The crown, usurp'd, disgraced his kingly glory.
If something thou wilt swear to be believed,
Swear then by something that thou hast not wrong'd.
K. Rich.	Now, by the world—
Q. Eliz.	'Tis full of thy foul wrongs.
K. Rich.	My father's death—
Q. Eliz.	Thy life hath that dishonor'd.
K. Rich.	Then, by myself—
Q. Eliz.	Thyself thyself misusest.
K. Rich.	Why then, by God—
Q. Eliz.	God's wrong is most of all.
If thou hadst fear'd to break an oath by Him,
The unity the king thy brother made 379
Had not been broken, nor my brother slain:
If thou hadst fear'd to break an oath by Him,
The imperial metal, circling now thy brow,
Had graced the tender temples of my child,
And both the princes had been breathing here,
Which now, two tender playfellows for dust,
Thy broken faith hath made a prey for worms.
What canst thou swear by now?
K. Rich.	The time to come.
Q. Eliz.	That thou hast wronged in the time o'erpast;
For I myself have many tears to wash
Hereafter time, for time past wrong'd by thee.
The children live, whose parents thou hast slaughter'd, 391
Ungovern'd youth, to wail it in their age;
The parents live, whose children thou hast butcher'd,
Old wither'd plants, to wail it with their age.
Swear not by time to come; for that thou hast
Misused ere used, by time misused o'erpast.
K. Rich.	As I intend to prosper and repent,
So thrive I in my dangerous attempt
Of hostile arms! myself myself confound!
Heaven and fortune bar me happy hours! 400
Day, yield me not thy light; nor, night, thy rest!
Be opposite all planets of good luck
To my proceedings, if, with pure heart's love,
Immaculate devotion, holy thoughts,
I tender not thy beauteous princely daughter!
In her consists my happiness and thine;

Without her, follows to this land and me,
To thee, herself, and many a Christian soul,
Death, desolation, ruin and decay:
It cannot be avoided but by this;				410
It will not be avoided but by this.
Therefore, good mother,—I must call you so—
Be the attorney of my love to her:
Plead what I will be, not what I have been;
Not my deserts, but what I will deserve:
Urge the necessity and state of times,
And be not peevish-fond in great designs.
Q. Eliz. Shall I be tempted of the devil
thus?
K. Rich. Ay, if the devil tempt thee to do
good.
Q. Eliz. Shall I forget myself to be myself?
K. Rich. Ay, if yourself's remembrance
wrong yourself.				421
Q. Eliz. But thou didst kill my children.
K. Rich. But in your daughter's womb I
bury them:
Where in that nest of spicery they shall breed
Selves of themselves, to your recomforture.
Q. Eliz. Shall I go win my daughter to thy
will?
K. Rich. And be a happy mother by the
deed.
Q. Eliz. I go. Write to me very shortly,
And you shall understand from me her mind.
K. Rich. Bear her my true love's kiss; and
so, farewell. [*Exit Queen Elizabeth.* 430
Relenting fool, and shallow, changing woman!

Enter RATCLIFF; CATESBY *following.*

How now! what news?
Rat. My gracious sovereign, on the western
coast
Rideth a puissant navy; to the shore
Throng many doubtful hollow-hearted friends,
Unarm'd, and unresolved to beat them back:
'Tis thought that Richmond is their admiral;
And there they hull, expecting but the aid
Of Buckingham to welcome them ashore.
K. Rich. Some light-foot friend post to the
Duke of Norfolk:				440
Ratcliff, thyself, or Catesby; where is he?
Cate. Here, my lord.
K. Rich. Fly to the duke: [*To Ratcliff*]
Post thou to Salisbury:
When thou comest thither,—[*To Catesby*]
Dull, unmindful villain,
Why stand'st thou still, and go'st not to the
duke?
Cate. First, mighty sovereign, let me know
your mind,
What from your grace I shall deliver to him.
K. Rich. O, true, good Catesby: bid him
levy straight
The greatest strength and power he can make,
And meet me presently at Salisbury.				450
Cate. I go. [*Exit.*
Rat. What is't your highness' pleasure I
shall do at Salisbury?
K. Rich. Why, what wouldst thou do there
before I go?
Rat. Your highness told me I should post
before.
K. Rich. My mind is changed, sir, my mind
is changed.

Enter LORD STANLEY.

How now, what news with you?

Stan. None good, my lord, to please you
with the hearing;
Nor none so bad, but it may well be told.
K. Rich. Hoyday, a riddle! neither good
nor bad!				460
Why dost thou run so many mile about,
When thou mayst tell thy tale a nearer way?
Once more, what news?
Stan.				Richmond is on the seas.
K. Rich. There let him sink, and be the
seas on him!
White-liver'd runagate, what doth he there?
Stan. I know not, mighty sovereign, but by
guess.
K. Rich. Well, sir, as you guess, as you
guess?
Stan. Stirr'd up by Dorset, Buckingham,
and Ely,
He makes for England, there to claim the
crown.
K. Rich. Is the chair empty? is the sword
unsway'd?				470
Is the king dead? the empire unpossess'd?
What heir of York is there alive but we?
And who is England's king but great York's
heir?
Then, tell me, what doth he upon the sea?
Stan. Unless for that, my liege, I cannot
guess.
K. Rich. Unless for that he comes to be
your liege,
You cannot guess wherefore the Welshman
comes.
Thou wilt revolt, and fly to him, I fear.
Stan. No, mighty liege; therefore mistrust
me not.
K. Rich. Where is thy power, then, to beat
him back?				480
Where are thy tenants and thy followers?
Are they not now upon the western shore,
Safe-conducting the rebels from their ships?
Stan. No, my good lord, my friends are in
the north.
K. Rich. Cold friends to Richard: what do
they in the north,
When they should serve their sovereign in the
west?
Stan. They have not been commanded,
mighty sovereign:
Please it your majesty to give me leave,
I'll muster up my friends, and meet your grace
Where and what time your majesty shall
please.
K. Rich. Ay, ay, thou wouldst be gone to
join with Richmond:
I will not trust you, sir.
Stan.				Most mighty sovereign,
You have no cause to hold my friendship
doubtful:
I never was nor never will be false.
K. Rich. Well,
Go muster men; but, hear you, leave behind
Your son, George Stanley: look your faith be
firm,
Or else his head's assurance is but frail.
Stan. So deal with him as I prove true to
you. [*Exit.*

Enter a Messenger.

Mess. My gracious sovereign, now in Dev-
onshire,				500
As I by friends am well advertised,
Sir Edward Courtney, and the haughty prelate

Bishop of Exeter, his brother there,
With many more confederates, are in arms.

Enter another Messenger.

Sec. Mess.　My liege, in Kent the Guildfords
　are in arms;
And every hour more competitors
Flock to their aid, and still their power in-
　creaseth.

Enter another Messenger.

Third Mess.　My lord, the army of the
　Duke of Buckingham—
K. Rich.　Out on you, owls! nothing but
　songs of death?　　[*He striketh him.*
Take that, until thou bring me better news. 510
Third Mess.　The news I have to tell your
　majesty
Is, that by sudden floods and fall of waters,
Buckingham's army is dispersed and scatter'd;
And he himself wander'd away alone,
No man knows whither.
K. Rich.　　　　　　I cry thee mercy:
There is my purse to cure that blow of thine.
Hath any well-advised friend proclaim'd
Reward to him that brings the traitor in?
Third Mess.　Such proclamation hath been
　made, my liege.

Enter another Messenger.

Fourth Mess.　Sir Thomas Lovel and Lord
　Marquis Dorset,　　　　　　　520
'Tis said, my liege, in Yorkshire are in arms.
Yet this good comfort bring I to your grace,
The Breton navy is dispersed by tempest:
Richmond, in Dorsetshire, sent out a boat
Unto the shore, to ask those on the banks
If they were his assistants, yea or no;
Who answer'd him, they came from Bucking-
　ham
Upon his party: he, mistrusting them,
Hoisted sail and made away for Brittany.
K. Rich.　March on, march on, since we are
　up in arms;　　　　　　　　530
If not to fight with foreign enemies,
Yet to beat down these rebels here at home.

Re-enter CATESBY.

Cate.　My liege, the Duke of Buckingham
　is taken;
That is the best news: that the Earl of Rich-
　mond
Is with a mighty power landed at Milford,
Is colder tidings, yet they must be told.
K. Rich.　Away towards Salisbury! while
　we reason here,
A royal battle might be won and lost:
Some one take order Buckingham be brought
To Salisbury; the rest march on with me. 540
　　　　　　　　　　[*Flourish. Exeunt.*

SCENE V.　*Lord Derby's house.*

Enter DERBY *and* SIR CHRISTOPHER URSWICK.

Der.　Sir Christopher, tell Richmond this
　from me:
That in the sty of this most bloody boar
My son George Stanley is frank'd up in hold:
If I revolt, off goes young George's head;
The fear of that withholds my present aid.
But, tell me, where is princely Richmond now?
Chris.　At Pembroke, or at Ha'rford-west,
　in Wales.
Der.　What men of name resort to him?

Chris.　Sir Walter Herbert, a renowned sol-
　dier;
Sir Gilbert Talbot, Sir William Stanley;　10
Oxford, redoubted Pembroke, Sir James Blunt,
And Rice ap Thomas with a valiant crew;
And many more of noble fame and worth:
And towards London they do bend their
　course,
If by the way they be not fought withal.
Der.　Return unto thy lord; commend me
　to him:
Tell him the queen hath heartily consented
He shall espouse Elizabeth her daughter.
These letters will resolve him of my mind.
Farewell.　　　　　　　　　　[*Exeunt.*

ACT V.

SCENE I.　*Salisbury. An open place.*

Enter the Sheriff, *and* BUCKINGHAM, *with hal-
　berds, led to execution.*

Buck.　Will not King Richard let me speak
　with him?
Sher.　No, my good lord; therefore be pa-
　tient.
Buck.　Hastings, and Edward's children,
　Rivers, Grey,
Holy King Henry, and thy fair son Edward,
Vaughan, and all that have miscarried
By underhand corrupted foul injustice,
If that your moody discontented souls
Do through the clouds behold this present
　hour,
Even for revenge mock my destruction!
This is All-Souls' day, fellows, is it not?　10
Sher.　It is, my lord.
Buck.　Why, then All-Souls' day is my
　body's doomsday.
This is the day that, in King Edward's time,
I wish't might fall on me, when I was found
False to his children or his wife's allies;
This is the day wherein I wish'd to fall
By the false faith of him I trusted most;
This, this All-Souls' day to my fearful soul
Is the determined respite of my wrongs:
That high All-Seer that I dallied with　20
Hath turn'd my feigned prayer on my head
And given in earnest what I begg'd in jest.
Thus doth he force the swords of wicked men
To turn their own points on their masters'
　bosoms:
Now Margaret's curse is fallen upon my head;
'When he,' quoth she, 'shall split thy heart
　with sorrow,
Remember Margaret was a prophetess.'
Come, sirs, convey me to the block of shame;
Wrong hath but wrong, and blame the due of
　blame.　　　　　　　　　　[*Exeunt.*

SCENE II.　*The camp near Tamworth.*

Enter RICHMOND, OXFORD, BLUNT, HERBERT,
　and others, with drum and colors.

Richm.　Fellows in arms, and my most lov-
　ing friends,
Bruised underneath the yoke of tyranny,
Thus far into the bowels of the land
Have we march'd on without impediment;
And here receive we from our father Stanley
Lines of fair comfort and encouragement.
The wretched, bloody, and usurping boar,

That spoil'd your summer fields and fruitful vines,
Swills your warm blood like wash, and makes his trough
In your embowell'd bosoms, this foul swine 10
Lies now even in the centre of this isle,
Near to the town of Leicester, as we learn :
From Tamworth thither is but one day's march.
In God's name, cheerly on, courageous friends,
To reap the harvest of perpetual peace
By this one bloody trial of sharp war.
Oxf.	Every man's conscience is a thousand swords,
To fight against that bloody homicide.
Herb.	I doubt not but his friends will fly to us.
Blunt.	He hath no friends but who are friends for fear, 20
Which in his greatest need will shrink from him.
Richm.	All for our vantage. Then, in God's name, march :
True hope is swift, and flies with swallow's wings :
Kings it makes gods, and meaner creatures kings.	[*Exeunt.*

SCENE III.	*Bosworth Field.*

Enter KING RICHARD *in arms, with* NORFOLK, *the* EARL *of* SURREY, *and others.*

K. Rich.	Here pitch our tents, even here in Bosworth field.
My Lord of Surrey, why look you so sad ?
Sur.	My heart is ten times lighter than my looks.
K. Rich.	My Lord of Norfolk,—
Nor.	Here, most gracious liege.
K. Rich.	Norfolk, we must have knocks ; ha ! must we not ?
Nor.	We must both give and take, my gracious lord.
K. Rich.	Up with my tent there ! here will I lie to-night ;
But where to-morrow ? Well, all's one for that.
Who hath descried the number of the foe ?
Nor.	Six or seven thousand is their utmost power. 10
K. Rich.	Why, our battalion trebles that account :
Besides, the king's name is a tower of strength,
Which they upon the adverse party want.
Up with my tent there ! Valiant gentlemen,
Let us survey the vantage of the field ;
Call for some men of sound direction :
Let's want no discipline, make no delay,
For, lords, to-morrow is a busy day. [*Exeunt.*

Enter, on the other side of the field, RICH-MOND, SIR WILLIAM BRANDON, OXFORD, *and others. Some of the* Soldiers *pitch Richmond's tent.*

Richm.	The weary sun hath made a golden set,
And, by the bright track of his fiery car, 20
Gives signal of a goodly day to-morrow.
Sir William Brandon, you shall bear my standard.
Give me some ink and paper in my tent :
I'll draw the form and model of our battle,
Limit each leader to his several charge,
And part in just proportion our small strength,

My Lord of Oxford, you, Sir William Brandon,
And you, Sir Walter Herbert, stay with me.
The Earl of Pembroke keeps his regiment :
Good Captain Blunt, bear my good night to him, 30
And by the second hour in the morning
Desire the earl to see me in my tent :
Yet one thing more, good Blunt, before thou go'st,
Where is Lord Stanley quarter'd, dost thou know ?
Blunt.	Unless I have mista'en his colors much,
Which well I am assured I have not done,
His regiment lies half a mile at least
South from the mighty power of the king.
Richm.	If without peril it be possible,
Good Captain Blunt, bear my good-night to him, 40
And give him from me this most needful scroll.
Blunt.	Upon my life, my lord, I'll undertake it ;
And so, God give you quiet rest to-night !
Richm.	Good night, good Captain Blunt.
Come, gentlemen,
Let us consult upon to-morrow's business :
In to our tent ; the air is raw and cold.
[*They withdraw into the tent.*

Enter, to his tent, KING RICHARD, NORFOLK, RATCLIFF, CATESBY, *and others.*

K. Rich.	What is't o'clock ?
Cate.	It's supper-time, my lord ;
It's nine o'clock.
K. Rich.	I will not sup to-night.
Give me some ink and paper.
What, is my beaver easier than it was ? 50
And all my armor laid into my tent ?
Cate.	It is, my liege ; and all things are in readiness.
K. Rich.	Good Norfolk, hie thee to thy charge ;
Use careful watch, choose trusty sentinels.
Nor.	I go, my lord.
K. Rich.	Stir with the lark to-morrow, gentle Norfolk.
Nor.	I warrant you, my lord.	[*Exit.*
K. Rich.	Catesby !
Cate.	My lord ?
K. Rich.	Send out a pursuivant at arms
To Stanley's regiment ; bid him bring his power 60
Before sunrising, lest his son George fall
Into the blind cave of eternal night.
[*Exit Catesby.*
Fill me a bowl of wine. Give me a watch.
Saddle white Surrey for the field to-morrow.
Look that my staves be sound, and not too heavy.
Ratcliff !
Rat.	My lord ?
K. Rich.	Saw'st thou the melancholy Lord Northumberland ?
Rat.	Thomas the Earl of Surrey, and himself,
Much about cock-shut time, from troop to troop 70
Went through the army, cheering up the soldiers.
K. Rich.	So, I am satisfied. Give me a bowl of wine :
I have not that alacrity of spirit,

Nor cheer of mind, that I was wont to have.
Set it down. Is ink and paper ready ?
 Rat. It is, my lord.
 K. Rich. Bid my guard watch ; leave me.
Ratcliff, about the mid of night come to my
    tent
And help to arm me. Leave me, I say.
   [*Exeunt Ratcliff and the other Attendants.*

Enter Derby *to* Richmond *in his tent, Lords
    and others attending.*

 Der. Fortune and victory sit on thy helm !
 Richm. All comfort that the dark night can
    afford   80
Be to thy person, noble father-in-law !
Tell me, how fares our loving mother ?
 Der. I, by attorney, bless thee from thy
    mother,
Who prays continually for Richmond's good :
So much for that. The silent hours steal on,
And flaky darkness breaks within the east.
In brief,—for so the season bids us be,—
Prepare thy battle early in the morning,
And put thy fortune to the arbitrement
Of bloody strokes and mortal-staring war.   90
I, as I may—that which I would I cannot,—
With best advantage will deceive the time,
And aid thee in this doubtful shock of arms :
But on thy side I may not be too forward
Lest, being seen, thy brother, tender George,
Be executed in his father's sight.
Farewell : the leisure and the fearful time
Cuts off the ceremonious vows of love
And ample interchange of sweet discourse,
Which so long sunder'd friends should dwell
    upon :   100
God give us leisure for these rites of love !
Once more, adieu : be valiant, and speed
    well !
 Richm. Good lords, conduct him to his
    regiment :
I'll strive, with troubled thoughts, to take a
    nap,
Lest leaden slumber peise me down to-morrow,
When I should mount with wings of victory :
Once more, good night, kind lords and gentle-
    men.   [*Exeunt all but Richmond.*
O Thou, whose captain I account myself,
Look on my forces with a gracious eye ;   109
Put in their hands thy bruising irons of wrath,
That they may crush down with a heavy fall
The usurping helmets of our adversaries !
Make us thy ministers of chastisement,
That we may praise thee in the victory !
To thee I do commend my watchful soul,
Ere I let fall the windows of mine eyes :
Sleeping and waking, O, defend me still !
                                      [*Sleeps.*

Enter the Ghost of Prince Edward, *son to*
    Henry *the Sixth.*

 Ghost. [*To Richard*] Let me sit heavy on
    thy soul to-morrow !
Think, how thou stab'dst me in my prime of
    youth
At Tewksbury : despair, therefore, and die !
 [*To Richmond*] Be cheerful, Richmond ; for
    the wronged souls
Of butcher'd princes fight in thy behalf :
King Henry's issue, Richmond, comforts thee.

Enter the Ghost of Henry *the Sixth.*

 Ghost. [*To Richard*] When I was mortal,
    my anointed body
By thee was punched full of deadly holes :
Think on the Tower and me : despair, and
    die !
Harry the Sixth bids thee despair, and die !
 [*To Richmond*] Virtuous and holy, be thou
    conqueror !
Harry, that prophesied thou shouldst be king,
Doth comfort thee in thy sleep : live, and
    flourish !   130

Enter the Ghost of Clarence.

 Ghost. [*To Richard*] Let me sit heavy on
    thy soul to-morrow !
I, that was wash'd to death with fulsome wine,
Poor Clarence, by thy guile betrayed to death !
To-morrow in the battle think on me,
And fall thy edgeless sword : despair, and
    die !—
 [*To Richmond*] Thou offspring of the house
    of Lancaster,
The wronged heirs of York do pray for thee :
Good angels guard thy battle ! live, and flour-
    ish !

Enter the Ghosts of Rivers, Grey, *and*
    Vaughan.

 Ghost of R. [*To Richard*] Let me sit
    heavy on thy soul to-morrow,
Rivers, that died at Pomfret ! despair, and die !
 Ghost of G. [*To Richard*] Think upon
    Grey, and let thy soul despair !   141
 Ghost of V. [*To Richard*] Think upon
    Vaughan, and, with guilty fear,
Let fall thy lance : despair, and die !
 All. [*To Richmond*] Awake, and think our
    wrongs in Richard's bosom
Will conquer him ! awake, and win the day !

Enter the Ghost of Hastings.

 Ghost. [*To Richard*] Bloody and guilty,
    guiltily awake,
And in a bloody battle end thy days !
Think on Lord Hastings : despair, and die !
 [*To Richmond*] Quiet untroubled soul, awake,
    awake !
Arm, fight, and conquer, for fair England's
    sake !   150

Enter the Ghosts of the two young Princes.

 Ghosts. [*To Richard*] Dream on thy cous-
    ins smother'd in the Tower :
Let us be led within thy bosom, Richard,
And weigh thee down to ruin, shame, and
    death !
Thy nephews' souls bid thee despair and die !
 [*To Richmond*] Sleep, Richmond, sleep in
    peace, and wake in joy ;
Good angels guard thee from the boar's an-
    noy !
Live, and beget a happy race of kings !
Edward's unhappy sons do bid thee flourish.

Enter the Ghost of Lady Anne.

 Ghost. [*To Richard*] Richard, thy wife,
    that wretched Anne thy wife,
That never slept a quiet hour with thee,   160
Now fills thy sleep with perturbations :
To-morrow in the battle think on me,
And fall thy edgeless sword : despair, and die !
 [*To Richmond*] Thou quiet soul, sleep thou a
    quiet sleep ;

Dream of success and happy victory!
Thy adversary's wife doth pray for thee.

Enter the Ghost of BUCKINGHAM.

Ghost. [*To Richard*] The first was I that
helped thee to the crown;
The last was I that felt thy tyranny:
O, in the battle think on Buckingham,
And die in terror of thy guiltiness!　　170
Dream on, dream on, of bloody deeds and
death:
Fainting, despair; despairing, yield thy breath!
[*To Richmond*] I died for hope ere I could
lend thee aid:
But cheer thy heart, and be thou not dis-
may'd:
God and good angels fight on Richmond's
side;
And Richard falls in height of all his pride.
　　[*The Ghosts vanish. King Richard starts
　　　　　out of his dream.*
　K. Rich. Give me another horse: bind up
my wounds.
Have mercy, Jesu!—Soft! I did but dream.
O coward conscience, how dost thou afflict
me!
The lights burn blue. It is now dead midnight.
Cold fearful drops stand on my trembling
flesh.
What do I fear? myself? there's none else by:
Richard loves Richard; that is, I am I.
Is there a murderer here? No. Yes, I am:
Then fly. What, from myself? Great reason
why:
Lest I revenge. What, myself upon myself?
Alack, I love myself. Wherefore? for any good
That I myself have done unto myself?
O, no! alas, I rather hate myself
For hateful deeds committed by myself!　190
I am a villain: yet I lie, I am not.
Fool, of thyself speak well: fool, do not
flatter.
My conscience hath a thousand several
tongues,
And every tongue brings in a several tale,
And every tale condemns me for a villain.
Perjury, perjury, in the high'st degree;
Murder, stern murder, in the direst degree;
All several sins, all used in each degree,
Throng to the bar, crying all, Guilty! guilty!
I shall despair. There is no creature loves me;
And if I die, no soul shall pity me:　　201
Nay, wherefore should they, since that I myself
Find in myself no pity to myself?
Methought the souls of all that I had murder'd
Came to my tent; and every one did threat
To-morrow's vengeance on the head of Rich-
ard.

Enter RATCLIFF.

Rat. My lord!
K. Rich. 'Zounds! who is there?
Rat. Ratcliff, my lord; 'tis I. The early
village-cock
Hath twice done salutation to the morn;　210
Your friends are up, and buckle on their
armor.
K. Rich. O Ratcliff, I have dream'd a fear-
ful dream!
What thinkest thou, will our friends prove all
true?
Rat. No doubt, my lord.
K. Rich.　　　　　O Ratcliff, I fear, I fear,—

Rat. Nay, good my lord, be not afraid of
shadows.
K. Rich. By the apostle Paul, shadows to-
night
Have struck more terror to the soul of Richard
Than can the substance of ten thousand sol-
diers
Armed in proof, and led by shallow Richmond.
It is not yet near day. Come, go with me;　220
Under our tents I'll play the eaves-dropper,
To see if any mean to shrink from me.
　　　　　　　　　　　　　　　[*Exeunt.*

Enter the Lords *to* RICHMOND, *sitting in his
tent.*

Lords. Good morrow, Richmond!
Richm. Cry mercy, lords and watchful
gentlemen,
That you have ta'en a tardy sluggard here.
Lords. How have you slept, my lord?
Richm. The sweetest sleep, and fairest-bod-
ing dreams
That ever enter'd in a drowsy head,
Have I since your departure had, my lords.
Methought their souls, whose bodies Richard
murder'd,　　　　　　　　　　　　　230
Came to my tent, and cried on victory:
I promise you, my soul is very jocund
In the remembrance of so fair a dream.
How far into the morning is it, lords?
Lords. Upon the stroke of four.
Richm. Why, then 'tis time to arm and give
direction.

His oration to his soldiers.

More than I have said, loving countrymen,
The leisure and enforcement of the time
Forbids to dwell upon: yet remember this,
God and our good cause fight upon our side;
The prayers of holy saints and wronged souls,
Like high-rear'd bulwarks, stand before our
faces;
Richard except, those whom we fight against
Had rather have us win than him they follow:
For what is he they follow? truly, gentlemen,
A bloody tyrant and a homicide;
One raised in blood, and one in blood estab-
lish'd;
One that made means to come by what he
hath,
And slaughter'd those that were the means to
help him;　　　　　　　　　　　　249
A base foul stone, made precious by the foil
Of England's chair, where he is falsely set;
One that hath ever been God's enemy:
Then, if you fight against God's enemy,
God will in justice ward you as his soldiers;
If you do sweat to put a tyrant down,
You sleep in peace, the tyrant being slain;
If you do fight against your country's foes,
Your country's fat shall pay your pains the
hire;
If you do fight in safeguard of your wives,
Your wives shall welcome home the conquer
ors;　　　　　　　　　　　　　　260
If you do free your children from the sword,
Your children's children quit it in your age
Then, in the name of God and all these rights
Advance your standards, draw your willing
swords.
For me, the ransom of my bold attempt
Shall be this cold corpse on the earth's cold
face;

But if I thrive, the gain of my attempt
The least of you shall share his part thereof.
Sound drums and trumpets boldly and cheer-
  fully;
God and Saint George! Richmond and vic-
  tory!   [*Exeunt.* 270

Re-enter KING RICHARD, RATCLIFF, *Attendants and Forces.*

K. Rich. What said Northumberland as
  touching Richmond?
Rat. That he was never trained up in arms.
K. Rich. He said the truth : and what said
  Surrey then?
Rat. He smiled and said ' The better for our
  purpose.'
K. Rich. He was in the right; and so in-
  deed it is.   [*Clock striketh.*
Tell the clock there. Give me a calendar.
Who saw the sun to-day?
  Rat.   Not I, my lord.
K. Rich. Then he disdains to shine; for by
  the book
He should have braved the east an hour ago :
A black day will it be to somebody.   280
Ratcliff!
  Rat. My lord?
  K. Rich. The sun will not be seen to-day;
The sky doth frown and lour upon our army.
I would these dewy tears were from the
  ground.
Not shine to-day! Why, what is that to me
More than to Richmond? for the selfsame
  heaven
That frowns on me looks sadly upon him.

Enter NORFOLK.

Nor. Arm, arm, my lord; the foe vaunts in
  the field.
K. Rich. Come, bustle, bustle; caparison
  my horse.
Call up Lord Stanley, bid him bring his power :
I will lead forth my soldiers to the plain, 291
And thus my battle shall be ordered :
My foreward shall be drawn out all in length,
Consisting equally of horse and foot;
Our archers shall be placed in the midst :
John Duke of Norfolk, Thomas Earl of Sur-
  rey,
Shall have the leading of this foot and horse.
They thus directed, we will follow
In the main battle, whose puissance on either
  side
Shall be well winged with our chiefest horse.
This, and Saint George to boot! What think'st
  thou, Norfolk?   301
Nor. A good direction, warlike sovereign.
This found I on my tent this morning.
                     [*He sheweth him a paper.*
K. Rich. [*Reads*] ' Jockey of Norfolk, be
  not too bold,
For Dickon thy master is bought and sold.'
A thing devised by the enemy.
Go, gentleman, every man unto his charge :
Let not our babbling dreams affright our
  souls :
Conscience is but a word that cowards use,
Devised at first to keep the strong in awe : 310
Our strong arms be our conscience, swords
  our law.
March on, join bravely, let us to't pell-mell;
If not to heaven, then hand in hand to hell.

His oration to his Army.

What shall I say more than I have inferr'd?
Remember whom you are to cope withal;
A sort of vagabonds, rascals, and runaways,
A scum of Bretons, and base lackey peasants,
Whom their o'er-cloyed country vomits forth
To desperate ventures and assured destruction.
You sleeping safe, they bring to you unrest;
You having lands, and blest with beauteous
  wives,   321
They would restrain the one, distain the other.
And who doth lead them but a paltry fellow,
Long kept in Bretagne at our mother's cost?
A milk-sop, one that never in his life
Felt so much cold as over shoes in snow?
Let's whip these stragglers o'er the seas again;
Lash hence these overweening rags of France,
These famish'd beggars, weary of their lives;
Who, but for dreaming on this fond exploit,
For want of means, poor rats, had hang'd
  themselves :   331
If we be conquer'd, let men conquer us,
And not these bastard Bretons; whom our
  fathers
Have in their own land beaten, bobb'd, and
  thump'd,
And in record, left them the heirs of shame.
Shall these enjoy our lands? lie with our
  wives?
Ravish our daughters?   [*Drum afar off.*]
  Hark! I hear their drum.
Fight, gentlemen of England! fight, bold yoe-
  men!
Draw, archers, draw your arrows to the head!
Spur your proud horses hard, and ride in
  blood;   340
Amaze the welkin with your broken staves!

Enter a Messenger.

What says Lord Stanley? will he bring his
  power?
Mess. My lord, he doth deny to come.
K. Rich. Off with his son George's head!
Nor. My lord, the enemy is past the marsh :
After the battle let George Stanley die.
K. Rich. A thousand hearts are great within
  my bosom :
Advance our standards, set upon our foes;
Our ancient word of courage, fair
  Saint George,
Inspire us with the spleen of fiery dragons!
Upon them! victory sits on our helms.   351
                                [*Exeunt.*

SCENE IV. *Another part of the field.*

Alarum : excursions. Enter NORFOLK *and
  forces fighting; to him* CATESBY.

Cate. Rescue, my Lord of Norfolk, rescue,
  rescue!
The king enacts more wonders than a man,
Daring an opposite to every danger :
His horse is slain, and all on foot he fights,
Seeking for Richmond in the throat of death.
Rescue, fair lord, or else the day is lost!

Alarums. Enter KING RICHARD.

K. Rich. A horse! a horse! my kingdom
  for a horse!
Cate. Withdraw, my lord; I'll help you to
  a horse.
K. Rich. Slave, I have set my life upon a
  cast,

And I will stand the hazard of the die : 10
I think there be six Richmonds in the field ;
Five have I slain to-day instead of him.
A horse ! a horse ! my kingdom for a horse !
                                              [*Exeunt.*

SCENE V. *Another part of the field.*

Alarum. Enter RICHARD *and* RICHMOND ; *they
fight.* RICHARD *is slain. Retreat and flourish. Re-enter* RICHMOND, DERBY *bearing the
crown, with divers other Lords.*

Richm. God and your arms be praised,
      victorious friends,
The day is ours, the bloody dog is dead.

Der. Courageous Richmond, well hast thou
      acquit thee.
Lo, here, this long-usurped royalty
From the dead temples of this bloody wretch
Have I pluck'd off, to grace thy brows withal :
Wear it, enjoy it, and make much of it.

Richm. Great God of heaven, say Amen to
      all !
But, tell me, is young George Stanley living ?

Der. He is, my lord, and safe in Leicester
      town ;
Whither, if it please you, we may now with-
      draw us.

Richm. What men of name are slain on
      either side ?

Der. John Duke of Norfolk, Walter Lord
      Ferrers,
Sir Robert Brackenbury, and Sir William
      Brandon.

Richm. Inter their bodies as becomes their
      births :
Proclaim a pardon to the soldiers fled
That in submission will return to us ;
And then, as we have ta'en the sacrament,
We will unite the white rose and the red :
Smile heaven upon this fair conjunction,   20
That long have frown'd upon their enmity !
What traitor hears me, and says not amen ?
England hath long been mad, and scarr'd her-
      self ;
The brother blindly shed the brother's blood,
The father rashly slaughter'd his own son,
The son, compell'd, been butcher to the sire :
All this divided York and Lancaster,
Divided in their dire division,
O, now, let Richmond and Elizabeth,
The true succeeders of each royal house,   30
By God's fair ordinance conjoin together !
And let their heirs, God, if thy will be so,
Enrich the time to come with smooth-faced
      peace,
With smiling plenty and fair prosperous days !
Abate the edge of traitors, gracious Lord,
That would reduce these bloody days again,
And make poor England weep in streams of
      blood !
Let them not live to taste this land's increase
That would with treason wound this fair land's
      peace !
Now civil wounds are stopp'd, peace lives
      again :
That she may long live here, God say amen !
                                              [*Exeunt.*

ROMEO AND JULIET.

(TWO DATES ARE ASSIGNED TO IT, 1591 AND 1596–97.)

INTRODUCTION.

The story of the unhappy lovers of Verona, as a supposed historical occurrence, is referred to the year 1303 ; but no account of it exists of an earlier date than that of Luigi da Porto, about 1530. The story quickly acquired a European celebrity. Published by Bandello in his collection of Italian novels in 1554, it was translated into French in 1559 by Pierre Boisteau, and in three years more touched English soil. Arthur Brooke in 1562 produced his long metrical version, founded upon Boisteau's novel, and a pure translation of Boisteau's work appeared in Paynter's *Palace of Pleasure* in 1567. We have here reached Shakespeare's sources : Paynter he probably consulted ; in nearly all essentials he follows the *Romeus and Juliet* of Brooke. The precise date of Shakespeare's play is uncertain. In 1597 it was published in quarto, " as it hath been often (with great applause) plaid publiquely by the right Honorable the Lord of Hunsdon his servants." Now the Lord Chamberlain, Henry Lord Hunsdon, died July 22, 1596 ; his son, George Lord Hunsdon, was appointed Chamberlain in April, 1597. Before July, 1596, or after April, 1597, the theatrical company would have been styled by the more honorable designation, " the Lord Chamberlain's servants ; " but during the interval they would have been described as on the title-page of the quarto. The Nurse's mention of the earthquake (Act I., Sc. III., L. 23), " 'Tis since the earthquake now eleven years," has been referred to as giving the date 1591, a memorable earthquake, felt in London, having occurred in 1580 ; but, while professing an infallibly accurate recollection, the old woman blunders sadly about her dates, so that even if an actual English earthquake were alluded to, the point of the jest may have been in the inaccuracy of the reference. The internal evidence favors the opinion that this tragedy was an early work of the poet, and that it was subsequently revised and enlarged. There is much rhyme, and much of this is in the form of alternate rhyme ; the forced playing upon words, and the overstrained conceits point to an early date. We may perhaps accept the opinion that the play was begun, and in part written, as early as 1591, and that it assumed its final form about 1597. Apart from its intrinsic beauty, *Romeo and Juliet* is of deep interest when viewed as Shakespeare's first tragedy, and as a work which probably occupied his thoughts, from time to time, during a series of years. It is a young man's tragedy, in which Youth and Love are brought face to face with Hatred and Death. The scene is essentially Italian : the burning noons of July in the Italian city inflame the blood of the street quarrelers ; the voluptuous moonlit nights are only like a softer day. And the characters are Italian, with their lyrical ardor, their southern impetuosity of passion, and the southern forms and color of their speech. Romeo's nature is prone to enthusiastic feeling, and, as it were, vaguely trembling in the direction of love before he sees Juliet ; to meet her gives form and fixity to his vague emotion. To Juliet—a girl of fourteen—love comes as a thing previously unknown ; it is at once terrible and blissful ; she rises, through love, and sorrow, and trial, from a child into a heroic woman. After Shakespeare has exalted their enthusiastic joy and rapture to the highest point, he suddenly casts it down. Romeo is at first completely unmanned ; but Juliet exhibits a noble fortitude and self-command. Mercutio and the Nurse are almost creations of Shakespeare. Brooke had described Mercutio as " a lion among maidens," and speaks of his " ice-cold hand ; " but it was the dramatist who drew at full length the figure of this brilliant being, who though with wit running beyond what is becoming, and effervescent animal spirits, yet acts as a guardian of Romeo, and is always a gallant gentleman. He dies forcing a jest through his bodily anguish, but he dies on Romeo's behalf : the scene darkens as his figure disappears. The action is accelerated by Shakespeare to the utmost, the four or five months of Brooke's poem being reduced to as many days. On Sunday the lovers meet, next day they are made one in marriage, on Tuesday morning at dawn they part, and they are finally re-united in the tomb on the night of Thursday. Shakespeare does not close the tragedy with Juliet's death : as he has shown in the first scene the hatred of the houses through the comic quarrel of the servants, thereby introducing the causes which produce the tragic issue, so in the last scene he shows us the houses sorrowfully reconciled over the dead bodies of a son and daughter.

DRAMATIS PERSONÆ.

ESCALUS, prince of Verona.
PARIS, a young nobleman, kinsman to the prince.

MONTAGUE, } heads of two houses at vari-
CAPULET, } ance with each other.
An old man, cousin to Capulet.

ROMEO, son to Montague.
MERCUTIO, kinsman to the prince, and friend
    to Romeo.
BENVOLIO, nephew to Montague, and friend to
    Romeo.
TYBALT, nephew to Lady Capulet.
FRIAR LAURENCE, } Franciscans.
FRIAR JOHN,   }
BALTHASAR, servant to Romeo.
SAMPSON, } servants to Capulet.
GREGORY, }
PETER, servant to Juliet's nurse.
ABRAHAM, servant to Montague.

An Apothecary.
Three Musicians.
Page to Paris ; another Page ; an officer.
LADY MONTAGUE, wife to Montague.
LADY CAPULET, wife to Capulet.
JULIET, daughter to Capulet.
Nurse to Juliet.
Citizens of Verona ; several Men and Women,
    relations to both houses ; Maskers,
    Guards, Watchmen, and Attendants.

Chorus.

SCENE : *Verona : Mantua.*

PROLOGUE.

Two households, both alike in dignity,
    In fair Verona, where we lay our scene,
From ancient grudge break to new mutiny,
    Where civil blood makes civil hands un-
    clean.
From forth the fatal loins of these two foes
    A pair of star-cross'd lovers take their life ;
Whose misadventured piteous overthrows
Do with their death bury their parents' strife.
The fearful passage of their death-mark'd love,
    And the continuance of their parents' rage,
Which, but their children's end, nought could
    remove,   11
Is now the two hours' traffic of our stage ;
The which if you with patient ears attend,
    What here shall miss, our toil shall strive to
    mend.

ACT I.

SCENE I. *Verona. A public place.*

Enter SAMPSON *and* GREGORY, *of the house of
    Capulet, armed with swords and bucklers.*

Sam. Gregory, o' my word, we'll not carry
coals.
Gre. No, for then we should be colliers.
Sam. I mean, an we be in choler, we'll
draw.
Gre. Ay, while you live, draw your neck
out o' the collar.
Sam. I strike quickly, being moved.
Gre. But thou art not quickly moved to
strike.
Sam. A dog of the house of Montague
moves me.   10
Gre. To move is to stir ; and to be valiant
is to stand : therefore, if thou art moved, thou
runn'st away.
Sam. A dog of that house shall move me
to stand : I will take the wall of any man or
maid of Montague's.
Gre. That shows thee a weak slave ; for the
weakest goes to the wall.
Sam. True ; and therefore women, being
the weaker vessels, are ever thrust to the wall :
therefore I will push Montague's men from
the wall, and thrust his maids to the wall.
Gre. The quarrel is between our masters
and us their men.
Sam. 'Tis all one, I will show myself a
tyrant : when I have fought with the men, I

will be cruel with the maids, and cut off their
heads.
Gre. The heads of the maids ?   29
Sam. Ay, the heads of the maids, or their
maidenheads ; take it in what sense thou wilt.
Gre. They must take it in sense that feel it.
Sam. Me they shall feel while I am able to
stand : and 'tis known I am a pretty piece of
flesh.
Gre. 'Tis well thou art not fish ; if thou
hadst, thou hadst been poor John. Draw thy
tool ; here comes two of the house of the
Montagues.
Sam. My naked weapon is out : quarrel, I
will back thee.   40
Gre. How ! turn thy back and run ?
Sam. Fear me not.
Gre. No, marry ; I fear thee !
Sam. Let us take the law of our sides ; let
them begin.
Gre. I will frown as I pass by, and let them
take it as they list.
Sam. Nay, as they dare. I will bite my
thumb at them ; which is a disgrace to them,
if they bear it.   50

Enter ABRAHAM *and* BALTHASAR.

Abr. Do you bite your thumb at us, sir ?
Sam. I do bite my thumb, sir.
Abr. Do you bite your thumb at us, sir ?
Sam. [*Aside to Gre.*] Is the law of our
side, if I say ay ?
Gre. No.
Sam. No, sir, I do not bite my thumb at
you, sir, but I bite my thumb, sir.
Gre. Do you quarrel, sir ?
Abr. Quarrel, sir ! no, sir.   60
Sam. If you do, sir, I am for you : I serve
as good a man as you.
Abr. No better.
Sam. Well, sir.
Gre. Say ' better : ' here comes one of my
master's kinsmen.
Sam. Yes, better, sir.
Abr. You lie.
Sam. Draw, if you be men. Gregory, re-
member thy swashing blow. [*They fight.*   70

Enter BENVOLIO.

Ben. Part, fools !
Put up your swords ; you know not what you
    do.   [*Beats down their sword.*

Enter TYBALT.

Tyb. What, art thou drawn among these
    heartless hinds ?

Turn thee, Benvolio, look upon thy death.
  Ben. I do but keep the peace : put up thy
    sword,
Or manage it to part these men with me.
  Tyb. What, drawn, and talk of peace! I
    hate the word,
As I hate hell, all Montagues, and thee :
Have at thee, coward!   [*They fight.*

*Enter several of both houses, who join the
  fray ; then enter* Citizens, *with clubs.*

  First Cit. Clubs, bills, and partisans!
    strike! beat them down!   80
Down with the Capulets! down with the
  Montagues!

Enter Capulet *in his gown, and* Lady
    Capulet.

  Cap. What noise is this? Give me my long
    sword, ho!
  La. Cap. A crutch, a crutch! why call you
    for a sword?
  Cap. My sword, I say! Old Montague is
    come,
And flourishes his blade in spite of me.

Enter Montague *and* Lady Montague.

  Mon. Thou villain Capulet,—Hold me not,
    let me go.
  La. Mon. Thou shalt not stir a foot to seek
    a foe.

Enter Prince, *with* Attendants.

  Prin. Rebellious subjects, enemies to peace,
Profaners of this neighbor-stained steel,—
Will they not hear? What, ho! you men, you
  beasts,   90
That quench the fire of your pernicious rage
With purple fountains issuing from your veins,
On pain of torture, from those bloody hands
Throw your mistemper'd weapons to the
  ground,
And hear the sentence of your moved prince.
Three civil brawls, bred of an airy word,
By thee, old Capulet, and Montague,
Have thrice disturb'd the quiet of our streets,
And made Verona's ancient citizens
Cast by their grave beseeming ornaments, 100
To wield old partisans, in hands as old,
Canker'd with peace, to part your canker'd
  hate :
If ever you disturb our streets again,
Your lives shall pay the forfeit of the peace.
For this time, all the rest depart away :
You, Capulet, shall go along with me :
And, Montague, come you this afternoon,
To know our further pleasure in this case,
To old Free-town, our common judgment-
  place.   109
Once more, on pain of death, all men depart.
    [*Exeunt all but Montague, Lady Mon-
        tague, and Benvolio.*
  Mon. Who set this ancient quarrel new
    abroach?
Speak, nephew, were you by when it began?
  Ben. Here were the servants of your ad-
    versary,
And yours, close fighting ere I did approach :
I drew to part them : in the instant came
The fiery Tybalt, with his sword prepared,
Which, as he breathed defiance to my ears,
He swung about his head and cut the winds,
Who nothing hurt withal hiss'd him in scorn :

While we were interchanging thrusts and
  blows,   120
Came more and more and fought on part and
  part,
Till the prince came, who parted either part.
  La. Mon. O, where is Romeo? saw you
    him to-day?
Right glad I am he was not at this fray.
  Ben. Madam, an hour before the wor-
    shipp'd sun
Peer'd forth the golden window of the east,
A troubled mind drave me to walk abroad ;
Where, underneath the grove of sycamore
That westward rooteth from the city's side,
So early walking did I see your son :   130
Towards him I made, but he was ware of me
And stole into the covert of the wood :
I, measuring his affections by my own,
That most are busied when they're most alone,
Pursued my humor not pursuing his,
And gladly shunn'd who gladly fled from me.
  Mon. Many a morning hath he there been
    seen,
With tears augmenting the fresh morning's
  dew,
Adding to clouds more clouds with his deep
  sighs ;
But all so soon as the all-cheering sun   140
Should in the furthest east begin to draw
The shady curtains from Aurora's bed,
Away from light steals home my heavy son,
And private in his chamber pens himself,
Shuts up his windows, locks fair daylight out
And makes himself an artificial night :
Black and portentous must this humor prove,
Unless good counsel may the cause remove.
  Ben. My noble uncle, do you know the
    cause?
  Mon. I neither know it nor can learn of
    him.   150
  Ben. Have you importuned him by any
    means?
  Mon. Both by myself and many other
    friends :
But he, his own affections' counsellor,
Is to himself—I will not say how true—
But to himself so secret and so close,
So far from sounding and discovery,
As is the bud bit with an envious worm,
Ere he can spread his sweet leaves to the air,
Or dedicate his beauty to the sun.
Could we but learn from whence his sorrows
  grow.   160
We would as willingly give cure as know.

Enter Romeo.

  Ben. See, where he comes : so please you,
    step aside ;
I'll know his grievance, or be much denied.
  Mon. I would thou wert so happy by thy
    stay,
To hear true shrift. Come, madam, let's away.
    [*Exeunt Montague and Lady.*
  Ben. Good-morrow, cousin.
  Rom.   Is the day so young?
  Ben. But new struck nine.
  Rom.   Ay me! sad hours seem long.
Was that my father that went hence so fast?
  Ben. It was. What sadness lengthens Ro-
    meo's hours?
  Rom. Not having that, which, having,
    makes them short.   170
  Ben. In love?

Rom. Out—
Ben. Of love?
Rom. Out of her favor, where I am in love.
Ben. Alas, that love, so gentle in his view,
Should be so tyrannous and rough in proof!
Rom. Alas, that love, whose view is muf-
fled still,
Should, without eyes, see pathways to his will!
Where shall we dine? O me! What fray was
here?
Yet tell me not, for I have heard it all.   180
Here's much to do with hate, but more with
love.
Why, then, O brawling love! O loving hate!
O any thing, of nothing first create!
O heavy lightness! serious vanity!
Mis-shapen chaos of well-seeming forms!
Feather of lead, bright smoke, cold fire, sick
health!
Still-waking sleep, that is not what it is!
This love feel I, that feel no love in this.
Dost thou not laugh?
Ben.   No, coz, I rather weep.
Rom. Good heart, at what?   190
Ben.   At thy good heart's oppression.
Rom. Why, such is love's transgression.
Griefs of mine own lie heavy in my breast,
Which thou wilt propagate, to have it prest
With more of thine: this love that thou hast
shown
Doth add more grief to too much of mine own.
Love is a smoke raised with the fume of sighs;
Being purged, a fire sparkling in lovers' eyes;
Being vex'd, a sea nourish'd with lovers' tears:
What is it else? a madness most discreet,
A choking gall and a preserving sweet.   200
Farewell, my coz.
Ben.   Soft! I will go along;
An if you leave me so, you do me wrong.
Rom. Tut, I have lost myself; I am not
here;
This is not Romeo, he's some other where.
Ben. Tell me in sadness, who is that you
love.
Rom. What, shall I groan and tell thee?
Ben.   Groan! why, no.
But sadly tell me who.
Rom. Bid a sick man in sadness make his
will:
Ah, word ill urged to one that is so ill!
In sadness, cousin, I do love a woman.   210
Ben. I aim'd so near, when I supposed you
loved.
Rom. A right good mark-man! And she's
fair I love.
Ben. A right fair mark, fair coz, is soonest
hit.
Rom. Well, in that hit you miss: she'll not
be hit
With Cupid's arrow; she hath Dian's wit;
And, in strong proof of chastity well arm'd,
From love's weak childish bow she lives un-
harm'd.
She will not stay the siege of loving terms,
Nor bide the encounter of assailing eyes,
Nor ope her lap to saint-seducing gold: 220
O, she is rich in beauty, only poor,
That when she dies with beauty dies her store.
Ben. Then she hath sworn that she will still
live chaste?
Rom. She hath, and in that sparing makes
huge waste,
For beauty starved with her severity

Cuts beauty off from all posterity.
She is too fair, too wise, wisely too fair,
To merit bliss by making me despair:
She hath forsworn to love, and in that vow
Do I live dead that live to tell it now.   230
Ben. Be ruled by me, forget to think of her.
Rom. O, teach me how I should forget to
think.
Ben. By giving liberty unto thine eyes;
Examine other beauties.
Rom.   'Tis the way
To call hers exquisite, in question more:
These happy masks that kiss fair ladies' brows
Being black put us in mind they hide the fair;
He that is strucken blind cannot forget
The precious treasure of his eyesight lost:
Show me a mistress that is passing fair,   240
What doth her beauty serve, but as a note
Where I may read who pass'd that passing
fair?
Farewell: thou canst not teach me to forget.
Ben. I'll pay that doctrine, or else die in
debt.   [*Exeunt.*

SCENE II. *A street.*

Enter CAPULET, PARIS, *and* Servant.

Cap. But Montague is bound as well as I,
In penalty alike; and 'tis not hard, I think,
For men so old as we to keep the peace.
Par. Of honorable reckoning are you
both;
And pity 'tis you lived at odds so long.
But now, my lord, what say you to my suit?
Cap. But saying o'er what I have said be-
fore:
My child is yet a stranger in the world;
She hath not seen the change of fourteen
years;
Let two more summers wither in their pride,
Ere we may think her ripe to be a bride.   11
Par. Younger than she are happy mothers
made.
Cap. And too soon marr'd are those so
early made.
The earth hath swallow'd all my hopes but she,
She is the hopeful lady of my earth:
But woo her, gentle Paris, get her heart,
My will to her consent is but a part;
An she agree, within her scope of choice
Lies my consent and fair according voice.
This night I hold an old accustom'd feast,   20
Whereto I have invited many a guest,
Such as I love; and you, among the store,
One more, most welcome, makes my number
more.
At my poor house look to behold this night
Earth-treading stars that make dark heaven
light:
Such comfort as do lusty young men feel
When well-apparell'd April on the heel
Of limping winter treads, even such delight
Among fresh female buds shall you this night
Inherit at my house; hear all, all see,   30
And like her most whose merit most shall be:
Which on more view, of many mine being
one
May stand in number, though in reckoning
none,
Come, go with me. [*To Serv., giving a paper.*
Go, sirrah, trudge about
Through fair Verona; find those persons out
Whose names are written there, and to them
say,

My house and welcome on their pleasure stay.
[*Exeunt Capulet and Paris.*
  Serv. Find them out whose names are written here! It is written, that the shoemaker
should meddle with his yard, and the tailor
with his last, the fisher with his pencil, and the
painter with his nets; but I am sent to find
those persons whose names are here writ, and
can never find what names the writing person
hath here writ. I must to the learned.—In good
time.

Enter Benvolio and Romeo.

  Ben. Tut, man, one fire burns out another's
    burning,
One pain is lessen'd by another's anguish;
Turn giddy, and be holp by backward turning;
  One desperate grief cures with another's
    languish:
Take thou some new infection to thy eye,   50
And the rank poison of the old will die.
  Rom. Your plaintain-leaf is excellent for
    that.
  Ben. For what, I pray thee?
  Rom.   For your broken shin.
  Ben. Why, Romeo, art thou mad?
  Rom. Not mad, but bound more than a
    mad-man is;
Shut up in prison, kept without my food,
Whipp'd and tormented and—God-den, good
    fellow.
  Serv. God gi' god-den. I pray, sir, can you
read?   59
  Rom. Ay, mine own fortune in my misery.
  Serv. Perhaps you have learned it without
book: but, I pray, can you read any thing you
see?
  Rom. Ay, if I know the letters and the lan-
guage.
  Serv. Ye say honestly: rest you merry!
  Rom. Stay, fellow; I can read. [*Reads.*
' Signior Martino and his wife and daugh-
ters; County Anselme and his beauteous sis-
ters; the lady widow of Vitravio; Signior
Placentio and his lovely nieces; Mercutio and
his brother Valentine; mine uncle Capulet, his
wife, and daughters; my fair niece Rosaline;
Livia; Signior Valentio and his cousin Tybalt,
Lucio and the lively Helena.'
A fair assembly: whither should they come?
  Serv. Up.
  Rom. Whither?
  Serv. To supper; to our house.
  Rom. Whose house?
  Serv. My master's.   80
  Rom. Indeed, I should have ask'd you that
before.
  Serv. Now I'll tell you without asking: my
master is the great rich Capulet; and if you be
not of the house of Montagues, I pray, come
and crush a cup of wine. Rest you merry!
[*Exit.*
  Ben. At this same ancient feast of Capu-
let's
Sups the fair Rosaline whom thou so lovest,
With all the admired beauties of Verona:
Go thither; and, with unattainted eye,   90
Compare her face with some that I shall show,
And I will make thee think thy swan a crow.
  Rom. When the devout religion of mine eye
Maintains such falsehood, then turn tears to
    fires;
And these, who often drown'd could never die,

Transparent heretics, be burnt for liars!
One fairer than my love! the all-seeing sun
Ne'er saw her match since first the world be-
    gun.
  Ben. Tut, you saw her fair, none else being
    by,
Herself poised with herself in either eye: 100
But in that crystal scales let there be weigh'd
Your lady's love against some other maid
That I will show you shining at this feast,
And she shall scant show well that now shows
    best.
  Rom. I'll go along, no such sight to be
    shown,
But to rejoice in splendor of mine own.
[*Exeunt.*

Scene III. *A room in Capulet's house.*
Enter Lady Capulet and Nurse.

  La. Cap. Nurse, where's my daughter? call
    her forth to me.
  Nurse. Now, by my maidenhead, at twelve
    year old,
I bade her come. What, lamb! what, lady-
    bird!
God forbid! Where's this girl? What, Juliet!

Enter Juliet.

  Jul. How now! who calls?
  Nurse.   Your mother.
  Jul.   Madam, I am here.
What is your will?
  La. Cap. This is the matter:—Nurse, give
    leave awhile,
We must talk in secret:—nurse, come back
    again;
I have remember'd me, thou's hear our coun-
    sel.
Thou know'st my daughter's of a pretty age.
  Nurse. Faith, I can tell her age unto an
    hour.   11
  La. Cap. She's not fourteen.
  Nurse.   I'll lay fourteen of my teeth,—
And yet, to my teen be it spoken, I have but
    four,—
She is not fourteen. How long is it now
To Lammas-tide?
  La. Cap.   A fortnight and odd days.
  Nurse. Even or odd, of all days in the year,
Come Lammas-eve at night shall she be four-
    teen.
Susan and she—God rest all Christian souls!—
Were of an age: well, Susan is with God;
She was too good for me: but, as I said,   20
On Lammas-eve at night shall she be fourteen;
That shall she, marry; I remember it well.
'Tis since the earthquake now eleven years;
And she was wean'd,—I never shall forget it,—
Of all the days of the year, upon that day:
For I had then laid wormwood to my dug,
Sitting in the sun under the dove-house wall;
My lord and you were then at Mantua:—
Nay, I do bear a brain:—but, as I said,
When it did taste the wormwood on the nipple
Of my dug and felt it bitter, pretty fool,   31
To see it tetchy and fall out with the dug!
Shake quoth the dove-house: 'twas no need,
    I trow,
To bid me trudge:
And since that time it is eleven years;
For then she could stand alone; nay, by the
    rood,
She could have run and waddled all about;

For even the day before, she broke her brow :
And then my husband—God be with his soul !
A' was a merry man—took up the child :   40
' Yea,' quoth he, ' dost thou fall upon thy
        face ?
Thou wilt fall backward when thou hast more
        wit ;
Wilt thou not, Jule ?' and, by my holidame,
The pretty wretch left crying and said ' Ay.'
To see, now, how a jest shall come about !
I warrant, an I should live a thousand years,
I never should forget it : ' Wilt thou not,
        Jule ?' quoth he ;
And, pretty fool, it stinted and said ' Ay.'
    La. Cap. Enough of this ; I pray thee, hold
        thy peace.
    Nurse. Yes, madam : yet I cannot choose
        but laugh,   50
To think it should leave crying and say ' Ay.'
And yet, I warrant, it had upon its brow
A bump as big as a young cockerel's stone ;
A parlous knock ; and it cried bitterly :
' Yea,' quoth my husband, ' fall'st upon thy
        face ?
Thou wilt fall backward when thou comest to
        age ;
Wilt thou not, Jule ?' it stinted and said ' Ay.'
    Jul. And stint thou too, I pray thee, nurse,
        say I.
    Nurse. Peace, I have done. God mark thee
        to his grace !
Thou wast the prettiest babe that e'er I
        nursed :   60
An I might live to see thee married once,
I have my wish.
    La. Cap. Marry, that ' marry ' is the very
        theme
I came to talk of. Tell me, daughter Juliet,
How stands your disposition to be married ?
    Jul. It is an honor that I dream not of.
    Nurse. An honor ! were not I thine only
        nurse,
I would say thou hadst suck'd wisdom from
        thy teat.
    La. Cap. Well, think of marriage now ;
        younger than you,
Here in Verona, ladies of esteem,   70
Are made already mothers : by my count,
I was your mother much upon these years
That you are now a maid. Thus then in brief :
The valiant Paris seeks you for his love.
    Nurse. A man, young lady ! lady, such a
        man
As all the world—why, he's a man of wax.
    La. Cap. Verona's summer hath not such
        a flower.
    Nurse. Nay, he's a flower ; in faith, a very
        flower.
    La. Cap. What say you ? can you love the
        gentleman ?
This night you shall behold him at our feast ;
Read o'er the volume of young Paris' face,   81
And find delight writ there with beauty's pen ;
Examine every married lineament,
And see how one another lends content ;
And what obscured in this fair volume lies
Find written in the margent of his eyes.
This precious book of love, this unbound lover,
To beautify him, only lacks a cover :
The fish lives in the sea, and 'tis much pride
For fair without the fair within to hide :   90
That book in many's eyes doth share the glory,
That in gold clasps locks in the golden story ;

So shall you share all that he doth possess,
By having him, making yourself no less.
    Nurse. No less ! nay, bigger ; women grow
        by men.
    La. Cap. Speak briefly, can you like of
        Paris' love ?
    Jul. I'll look to like, if looking liking
        move :
But no more deep will I endart mine eye
Than your consent gives strength to make it fly.

Enter a Servant.

    Serv. Madam, the guests are come, supper
served up, you called, my young lady asked for,
the nurse cursed in the pantry, and every thing
in extremity. I must hence to wait ; I beseech
you, follow straight.
    La. Cap. We follow thee. [*Exit Servant.*]
        Juliet, the county stays.
    Nurse. Go, girl, seek happy nights to happy
        days.   [*Exeunt.*

SCENE IV. *A street.*

Enter ROMEO, MERCUTIO, BENVOLIO, *with five
    or six* Maskers, Torch-bearers, *and others.*

    Rom. What, shall this speech be spoke for
        our excuse ?
Or shall we on without apology ?
    Ben. The date is out of such prolixity :
We'll have no Cupid hoodwink'd with a scarf,
Bearing a Tartar's painted bow of lath,
Scaring the ladies like a crow-keeper ;
Nor no without-book prologue, faintly spoke
After the prompter, for our entrance :
But let them measure us by what they will ;
We'll measure them a measure, and be gone.
    Rom. Give me a torch : I am not for this
        ambling ;   11
Being but heavy, I will bear the light.
    Mer. Nay, gentle Romeo, we must have
        you dance.
    Rom. Not I, believe me : you have dancing
        shoes
With nimble soles : I have a soul of lead
So stakes me to the ground I cannot move.
    Mer. You are a lover ; borrow Cupid's
        wings,
And soar with them above a common bound.
    Rom. I am too sore enpierced with his
        shaft
To soar with his light feathers, and so bound,
I cannot bound a pitch above dull woe :   21
Under love's heavy burden do I sink.
    Mer. And, to sink in it, should you burden
        love ;
Too great oppression for a tender thing.
    Rom. Is love a tender thing ? it is too
        rough,
Too rude, too boisterous, and it pricks like
        thorn.
    Mer. If love be rough with you, be rough
        with love ;
Prick love for pricking, and you beat love
        down.
Give me a case to put my visage in :
A visor for a visor ! what care I   30
What curious eye doth quote deformities ?
Here are the beetle brows shall blush for me.
    Ben. Come, knock and enter ; and no
        sooner in,
But every man betake him to his legs.
    Rom. A torch for me : let wantons light o
        heart

Tickle the senseless rushes with their heels,
For I am proverb'd with a grandsire phrase ;
I'll be a candle-holder, and look on.
The game was ne'er so fair, and I am done.
  Mer. Tut, dun's the mouse, the constable's
    own word :   40
If thou art dun, we'll draw thee from the mire
Of this sir-reverence love, wherein thou stick'st
Up to the ears. Come, we burn daylight, ho !
  Rom. Nay, that's not so.
  Mer.   I mean, sir, in delay
We waste our lights in vain, like lamps by day.
Take our good meaning, for our judgment sits
Five times in that ere once in our five wits.
  Rom. And we mean well in going to this
    mask ;
But 'tis no wit to go.
  Mer.   Why, may one ask ?
  Rom. I dream'd a dream to-night.
  Mer.   And so did I. 50
  Rom. Well, what was yours ?
  Mer.   That dreamers often lie.
  Rom. In bed asleep, while they do dream
    things true.
  Mer. O, then, I see Queen Mab hath been
    with you.
She is the fairies' midwife, and she comes
In shape no bigger than an agate-stone
On the fore-finger of an alderman,
Drawn with a team of little atomies
Athwart men's noses as they lie asleep ;
Her wagon-spokes made of long spiders' legs,
The cover of the wings of grasshoppers, 60
The traces of the smallest spider's web,
The collars of the moonshine's watery beams,
Her whip of cricket's bone, the lash of film,
Her wagoner a small grey-coated gnat,
Not half so big as a round little worm
Prick'd from the lazy finger of a maid ;
Her chariot is an empty hazel-nut
Made by the joiner squirrel or old grub,
Time out o' mind the fairies' coachmakers.
And in this state she gallops night by night 70
Through lovers' brains, and then they dream
    of love ;
O'er courtiers' knees, that dream on court'sies
    straight,
O'er lawyers' fingers, who straight dream on
    fees,
O'er ladies' lips, who straight on kisses dream,
Which oft the angry Mab with blisters plagues,
Because their breaths with sweetmeats tainted
    are :
Sometime she gallops o'er a courtier's nose,
And then dreams he of smelling out a suit ;
And sometime comes she with a tithe-pig's tail
Tickling a parson's nose as a' lies asleep, 80
Then dreams he of another benefice :
Sometime she driveth o'er a soldier's neck,
And then dreams he of cutting foreign throats,
Of breaches, ambuscadoes, Spanish blades,
Of healths five-fathom deep ; and then anon
Drums in his ear, at which he starts and wakes,
And being thus frighted swears a prayer or two
And sleeps again. This is that very Mab
That plats the manes of horses in the night,
And bakes the elf-locks in foul sluttish hairs,
Which once untangled, much misfortune
    bodes :   91
This is the hag, when maids lie on their backs,
That presses them and learns them first to bear,
Making them women of good carriage :
This is she—

  Rom.   Peace, peace, Mercutio, peace !
Thou talk'st of nothing.
  Mer.   True, I talk of dreams,
Which are the children of an idle brain,
Begot of nothing but vain fantasy,
Which is as thin of substance as the air
And more inconstant than the wind, who
    wooes
Even now the frozen bosom of the north, 101
And, being anger'd, puffs away from thence,
Turning his face to the dew-dropping south.
  Ben. This wind, you talk of, blows us from
    ourselves ;
Supper is done, and we shall come too late.
  Rom. I fear, too early : for my mind mis-
    gives
Some consequence yet hanging in the stars
Shall bitterly begin his fearful date
With this night's revels and expire the term
Of a despised life closed in my breast 110
By some vile forfeit of untimely death.
But He, that hath the steerage of my course,
Direct my sail ! On, lusty gentlemen.
  Ben. Strike, drum.   [*Exeunt.*

    Scene V. *A hall in Capulet's house.*

Musicians *waiting. Enter* Servingmen *with
    napkins.*

  First Serv. Where's Potpan, that he helps
not to take away ? He shift a trencher ? he
scrape a trencher !
  Sec. Serv. When good manners shall lie all
in one or two men's hands and they unwashed
too, 'tis a foul thing.
  First Serv. Away with the joint-stools, remove the court-cupboard, look to the plate.
Good thou, save me a piece of marchpane ;
and, as thou lovest me, let the porter let in
Susan Grindstone and Nell. Antony, and Potpan !   11
  Sec. Serv. Ay, boy, ready.
  First Serv. You are looked for and called
for, asked for and sought for, in the great
chamber.
  Sec. Serv. We cannot be here and there
too. Cheerly, boys ; be brisk awhile, and the
longer liver take all.

Enter Capulet, *with* Juliet *and others of his
  house, meeting the* Guests *and* Maskers.

  Cap. Welcome, gentlemen! ladies that have
    their toes
Unplagued with corns will have a bout with
    you.
Ah ha, my mistresses ! which of you all 20
Will now deny to dance ? she that makes
    dainty,
She, I'll swear, hath corns ; am I come near ye
    now ?
Welcome, gentlemen ! I have seen the day
That I have worn a visor and could tell
A whispering tale in a fair lady's ear,
Such as would please : 'tis gone, 'tis gone, 'tis
    gone :
You are welcome, gentlemen ! come, musi-
    cians, play.
A hall, a hall ! give room ! and foot it, girls.
        [*Music plays, and they dance.*
More light, you knaves ; and turn the tables
    up,
And quench the fire, the room is grown too
    hot.   30
Ah, sirrah, this unlook'd-for sport comes well.

Nay, sit, nay, sit, good cousin Capulet;
For you and I are past our dancing days :
How long is't now since last yourself and I
Were in a mask ?
　　Sec. Cap.　By'r lady, thirty years.
　　Cap.　What, man ! 'tis not so much, 'tis not
　　　so much :
'Tis since the nuptials of Lucentio,
Come pentecost as quickly as it will,
Some five and twenty years ; and then we
　　mask'd.
　　Sec. Cap.　'Tis more, 'tis more, his son is
　　　elder, sir ;　　　　　　　　　　40
His son is thirty.
　　Cap.　　　　　Will you tell me that ?
His son was but a ward two years ago.
　　Rom.　[*To a Servingman*] What lady is
　　　that, which doth enrich the hand
Of yonder knight ?
　　Serv.　I know not, sir.
　　Rom.　O, she doth teach the torches to burn
　　　bright !
It seems she hangs upon the cheek of night
Like a rich jewel in an Ethiope's ear ;
Beauty too rich for use, for earth too dear !
So shows a snowy dove trooping with crows,
As yonder lady o'er her fellows shows.　　51
The measure done, I'll watch her place of
　　stand,
And, touching hers, make blessed my rude
　　hand.
Did my heart love till now ? forswear it, sight !
For I ne'er saw true beauty till this night.
　　Tyb.　This, by his voice, should be a Mon-
　　　tague.
Fetch me my rapier, boy. What dares the
　　slave
Come hither, cover'd with an antic face,
To fleer and scorn at our solemnity ?
Now, by the stock and honor of my kin,　　60
To strike him dead, I hold it not a sin.
　　Cap.　Why, how now, kinsman ! wherefore
　　　storm you so ?
　　Tyb.　Uncle, this is a Montague, our foe,
A villain that is hither come in spite,
To scorn at our solemnity this night.
　　Cap.　Young Romeo is it ?
　　Tyb.　　　　　'Tis he, that villain Romeo.
　　Cap.　Content thee, gentle coz, let him
　　　alone ;
He bears him like a portly gentleman ;
And, to say truth, Verona brags of him
To be a virtuous and well-govern'd youth :　70
I would not for the wealth of all the town
Here in my house do him disparagement :
Therefore be patient, take no note of him :
It is my will, the which if thou respect,
Show a fair presence and put off these frowns,
And ill-beseeming semblance for a feast.
　　Tyb.　It fits, when such a villain is a guest :
I'll not endure him.
　　Cap.　　　　　He shall be endured :
What, goodman boy ! I say, he shall : go to ;
Am I the master here, or you ? go to.　　80
You'll not endure him ! God shall mend my
　　soul !
You'll make a mutiny among my guests !
You will set cock-a-hoop ! you'll be the man !
　　Tyb.　Why, uncle, 'tis a shame.
　　Cap.　　　　　　　　Go to, go to ;
You are a saucy boy : is't so, indeed ?
This trick may chance to scathe you, I know
　　what :

You must contrary me ! marry, 'tis time.
Well said, my hearts ! You are a princox ; go :
Be quiet, or—More light, more light ! For
　　shame !
I'll make you quiet. What, cheerly, my
　　hearts !　　　　　　　　　　90
　　Tyb.　Patience perforce with wilful choler
　　　meeting
Makes my flesh tremble in their different
　　greeting.
I will withdraw : but this intrusion shall
Now seeming sweet convert to bitter gall.
　　　　　　　　　　　　　　[*Exit.*
　　Rom.　[*To Juliet*] If I profane with my un-
　　　worthiest hand
This holy shrine, the gentle fine is this :
My lips, two blushing pilgrims, ready stand
To smooth that rough touch with a tender
　　kiss.
　　Jul.　Good pilgrim, you do wrong your hand
　　　too much,　　　　　　　　　　99
Which mannerly devotion shows in this ;
For saints have hands that pilgrims' hands do
　　touch,
And palm to palm is holy palmers' kiss.
　　Rom.　Have not saints lips, and holy palm-
　　　ers too ?
　　Jul.　Ay, pilgrim, lips that they must use in
　　　prayer.
　　Rom.　O, then, dear saint, let lips do what
　　　hands do ;
They pray, grant thou, lest faith turn to de-
　　spair.
　　Jul.　Saints do not move, though grant for
　　　prayers' sake.
　　Rom.　Then move not, while my prayer's
　　　effect I take.
Thus from my lips, by yours, my sin is purged.
　　Jul.　Then have my lips the sin that they
　　　have took.　　　　　　　　　　110
　　Rom.　Sin from thy lips ? O trespass sweetly
　　　urged !
Give me my sin again.
　　Jul.　　　　　　You kiss by the book.
　　Nurse.　Madam, your mother craves a word
　　　with you.
　　Rom.　What is her mother ?
　　Nurse.　　　　　Marry, bachelor,
Her mother is the lady of the house,
And a good lady, and a wise and virtuous :
I nursed her daughter, that you talk'd withal ;
I tell you, he that can lay hold of her
Shall have the chinks.
　　Rom.　　　　　Is she a Capulet ?
O dear account ! my life is my foe's debt.　120
　　Ben.　Away, begone ; the sport is at the
　　　best.
　　Rom.　Ay, so I fear ; the more is my unrest.
　　Cap.　Nay, gentlemen, prepare not to be
　　　gone ;
We have a trifling foolish banquet towards.
Is it e'en so ? why, then, I thank you all ;
I thank you, honest gentlemen ; good night.
More torches here ! Come on then, let's to bed.
Ah, sirrah, by my fay, it waxes late :
I'll to my rest.
　　　　　[*Exeunt all but Juliet and Nurse.*
　　Jul.　Come hither, nurse. What is yond gen-
　　　tleman ?　　　　　　　　　　130
　　Nurse.　The son and heir of old Tiberio.
　　Jul.　What's he that now is going out of
　　　door ?

Nurse. Marry, that, I think, be young
  Petrucio.
Jul. What's he that follows there, that
  would not dance ?
Nurse. I know not.
Jul. Go, ask his name : if he be married,
My grave is like to be my wedding bed.
Nurse. His name is Romeo, and a Monta-
  gue ;
The only son of your great enemy.
Jul. My only love sprung from my only
  hate !   140
Too early seen unknown, and known too late !
Prodigious birth of love it is to me,
That I must love a loathed enemy.
Nurse. What's this ? what's this ?
Jul.   A rhyme I learn'd even now
Of one I danced withal. [*One calls within*
  ' Juliet.'
Nurse.   Anon, anon !
Come, let's away ; the strangers all are gone.
                    [*Exeunt.*

ACT II.

PROLOGUE.

Enter Chorus.

Chor. Now old desire doth in his death-bed
  lie,
  And young affection gapes to be his heir ;
That fair for which love groan'd for and would
  die,
  With tender Juliet match'd, is now not fair.
Now Romeo is beloved and loves again,
  Alike betwitched by the charm of looks,
But to his foe supposed he must complain,
  And she steal love's sweet bait from fearful
    hooks :
Being held a foe, he may not have access 9
  To breathe such vows as lovers use to
    swear ;
And she as much in love, her means much less
  To meet her new-beloved any where :
But passion lends them power, time means, to
  meet,
Tempering extremities with extreme sweet.
                      [*Exit.*

SCENE I. *A lane by the wall of Capulet's
    orchard.*

Enter ROMEO.

Rom. Can I go forward when my heart is
  here ?
Turn back, dull earth, and find thy centre out.
  [*He climbs the wall, and leaps down
                    within it.*

Enter BENVOLIO *and* MERCUTIO.

Ben. Romeo ! my cousin Romeo !
Mer.   He is wise ;
And, on my life, hath stol'n him home to bed.
Ben. He ran this way, and leap'd this
  orchard wall :
Call, good Mercutio.
Mer.   Nay, I'll conjure too.
Romeo ! humors ! madman ! passion ! lover !
Appear thou in the likeness of a sigh :
Speak but one rhyme, and I am satisfied ;
Cry but ' Ay me ! ' pronounce but ' love ' and
  ' dove ; '   10
Speak to my gossip Venus one fair word,

One nick-name for her purblind son and heir,
Young Adam Cupid, he that shot so trim,
When King Cophetua loved the beggar-maid !
He heareth not, he stirreth not, he moveth not ;
The ape is dead, and I must conjure him.
I conjure thee by Rosaline's bright eyes,
By her high forehead and her scarlet lip,
By her fine foot, straight leg and quivering
  thigh
And the demesnes that there adjacent lie, 20
That in thy likeness thou appear to us !
Ben. And if he hear thee, thou wilt anger
  him.
Mer. This cannot anger him : 'twould an-
  ger him
To raise a spirit in his mistress' circle
Of some strange nature, letting it there stand
Till she had laid it and conjured it down ;
That were some spite : my invocation
Is fair and honest, and in his mistress' name
I conjure only but to raise up him.
Ben. Come, he hath hid himself among
  these trees,   30
To be consorted with the humorous night :
Blind is his love and best befits the dark.
Mer. If love be blind, love cannot hit the
  mark.
Now will he sit under a medlar tree,
And wish his mistress were that kind of fruit
As maids call medlars, when they laugh alone.
O, Romeo, that she were, O, that she were
An open et cætera, thou a poperin pear !
Romeo, good night : I'll to my truckle-bed.
This field-bed is too cold for me to sleep : 40
Come, shall we go ?
Ben.   Go, then ; for 'tis in vain
To seek him here that means not to be found.
                    [*Exeunt.*

SCENE II. *Capulet's orchard.*

Enter ROMEO.

Rom. He jests at scars that never felt a
  wound.
  [*Juliet appears above at a window.*
But, soft ! what light through yonder window
  breaks ?
It is the east, and Juliet is the sun.
Arise, fair sun, and kill the envious moon,
Who is already sick and pale with grief,
That thou her maid art far more fair than
  she :
Be not her maid, since she is envious ;
Her vestal livery is but sick and green
And none but fools do wear it ; cast it off.
It is my lady, O, it is my love !   10
O, that she knew she were !
She speaks, yet she says nothing : what of
  that ?
Her eye discourses ; I will answer it.
I am too bold, 'tis not to me she speaks :
Two of the fairest stars in all the heaven,
Having some business, do entreat her eyes
To twinkle in their spheres till they return.
What if her eyes were there, they in her head ?
The brightness of her cheek would shame those
  stars,   19
As daylight doth a lamp ; her eyes in heaven
Would through the airy region stream so
  bright
That birds would sing and think it were not
  night.
See, how she leans her cheek upon her hand !
O, that I were a glove upon that hand,

That I might touch that cheek !
Jul.   Ay me !
Rom.   She speaks :
O, speak again, bright angel ! for thou art
As glorious to this night, being o'er my head
As is a winged messenger of heaven
Unto the white-upturned wondering eyes
Of mortals that fall back to gaze on him
When he bestrides the lazy-pacing clouds
And sails upon the bosom of the air.
Jul. O Romeo, Romeo ! wherefore art thou
      Romeo ?
Deny thy father and refuse thy name ;
Or, if thou wilt not, be but sworn my love,
And I'll no longer be a Capulet.
Rom. [*Aside*] Shall I hear more, or shall I
      speak at this ?
Jul. 'Tis but thy name that is my enemy ;
Thou art thyself, though not a Montague.
What's Montague ? it is nor hand, nor foot, 40
Nor arm, nor face, nor any other part
Belonging to a man. O, be some other name !
What's in a name ? that which we call a rose
By any other name would smell as sweet ;
So Romeo would, were he not Romeo call'd,
Retain that dear perfection which he owes
Without that title. Romeo, doff thy name,
And for that name which is no part of thee
Take all myself.
Rom.   I take thee at thy word :
Call me but love, and I'll be new baptized ;   50
Henceforth I never will be Romeo.
Jul. What man art thou that thus be-
      screen'd in night
So stumblest on my counsel ?
Rom.   By a name
I know not how to tell thee who I am :
My name, dear saint, is hateful to myself,
Because it is an enemy to thee ;
Had I it written, I would tear the word.
Jul. My ears have not yet drunk a hundred
      words
Of that tongue's utterance, yet I know the
      sound :
Art thou not Romeo and a Montague ?   60
Rom. Neither, fair saint, if either thee dis-
      like.
Jul. How camest thou hither, tell me, and
      wherefore ?
The orchard walls are high and hard to climb,
And the place death, considering who thou art,
If any of my kinsmen find thee here.
Rom. With love's light wings did I o'er-
      perch these walls ;
For stony limits cannot hold love out,
And what love can do that dares love attempt ;
Therefore thy kinsmen are no let to me.
Jul. If they do see thee, they will murder
      thee.   70
Rom. Alack, there lies more peril in thine
      eye
Than twenty of their swords : look thou but
      sweet,
And I am proof against their enmity.
Jul. I would not for the world they saw
      thee here.
Rom. I have night's cloak to hide me from
      their sight ;
And but thou love me, let them find me here :
My life were better ended by their hate,
Than death prorogued, wanting of thy love.
Jul. By whose direction found'st thou out
      this place ?

Rom. By love, who first did prompt me to
      inquire ;   80
He lent me counsel and I lent him eyes.
I am no pilot ; yet, wert thou as far
As that vast shore wash'd with the farthest sea,
I would adventure for such merchandise.
Jul. Thou know'st the mask of night is on
      my face,
Else would a maiden blush bepaint my cheek
For that which thou hast heard me speak to-
      night.
Fain would I dwell on form, fain, fain deny
What I have spoke : but farewell compliment !
Dost thou love me ? I know thou wilt say ' Ay,'
And I will take thy word : yet, if thou swear'st,
Thou mayst prove false ; at lovers' perjuries,
Then say, Jove laughs. O gentle Romeo,
If thou dost love, pronounce it faithfully :
Or if thou think'st I am too quickly won,
I'll frown and be perverse and say thee nay,
So thou wilt woo ; but else, not for the world.
In truth, fair Montague, I am too fond,
And therefore thou mayst think my 'havior
      light :
But trust me, gentleman, I'll prove more true
Than those that have more cunning to be
      strange.   101
I should have been more strange, I must con-
      fess,
But that thou overheard'st, ere I was ware,
My true love's passion : therefore pardon me,
And not impute this yielding to light love,
Which the dark night hath so discovered.
Rom. Lady, by yonder blessed moon I
      swear
That tips with silver all these fruit-tree tops—
Jul. O, swear not by the moon, the incon-
      stant moon,
That monthly changes in her circled orb,   110
Lest that thy love prove likewise variable.
Rom. What shall I swear by ?
Jul.   Do not swear at all ;
Or, if thou wilt, swear by thy gracious self,
Which is the god of my idolatry,
And I'll believe thee.
Rom.   If my heart's dear love—
Jul. Well, do not swear : although I joy in
      thee,
I have no joy of this contract to-night :
It is too rash, too unadvised, too sudden ;
Too like the lightning, which doth cease to be
Ere one can say ' It lightens.' Sweet, good
      night !   120
This bud of love, by summer's ripening breath,
May prove a beauteous flower when next we
      meet.
Good night, good night ! as sweet repose and
      rest
Come to thy heart as that within my breast !
Rom. O, wilt thou leave me so unsatisfied ?
Jul. What satisfaction canst thou have to-
      night ?
Rom. The exchange of thy love's faithful
      vow for mine.
Jul. I gave thee mine before thou didst re-
      quest it :
And yet I would it were to give again.
Rom. Wouldst thou withdraw it ? for what
      purpose, love ?   130
Jul. But to be frank, and give it thee again
And yet I wish but for the thing I have :
My bounty is as boundless as the sea,
My love as deep ; the more I give to thee,

The more I have, for both are infinite.
                              [*Nurse calls within.*
I hear some noise within ; dear love, adieu !
Anon, good nurse ! Sweet Montague, be true.
Stay but a little, I will come again.
                              [*Exit, above.*
Rom. O blessed, blessed night ! I am
    afeard,
Being in night, all this is but a dream,   140
Too flattering-sweet to be substantial.

Re-enter JULIET, *above.*

Jul. Three words, dear Romeo, and good
    night indeed.
If that thy bent of love be honorable,
Thy purpose marriage, send me word to-mor-
    row,
By one that I'll procure to come to thee,
Where and what time thou wilt perform the
    rite ;
And all my fortunes at thy foot I'll lay
And follow thee my lord throughout the
    world.
Nurse. [*Within*] Madam !
Jul. I come, anon.—But if thou mean'st
    not well,   150
I do beseech thee—
Nurse. [*Within*] Madam!
Jul.   By and by, I come :—
To cease thy suit, and leave me to my grief :
To-morrow will I send.
Rom.   So thrive my soul—
Jul. A thousand times good night !
                              [*Exit, above.*
Rom. A thousand times the worse, to want
    thy light.
Love goes toward love, as schoolboys from
    their books,
But love from love, toward school with heavy
    looks.   [*Retiring.*

Re-enter JULIET, *above.*

Jul. Hist ! Romeo, hist ! O, for a falconer's
    voice,
To lure this tassel-gentle back again !   160
Bondage is hoarse, and may not speak aloud ;
Else would I tear the cave where Echo lies,
And make her airy tongue more hoarse than
    mine,
With repetition of my Romeo's name.
Rom. It is my soul that calls upon my
    name :
How silver-sweet sound lovers' tongues by
    night,
Like softest music to attending ears !
Jul. Romeo !
Rom.   My dear ?
Jul.   At what o'clock to-morrow
Shall I send to thee ?
Rom.   At the hour of nine.
Jul. I will not fail : 'tis twenty years till
    then.   170
I have forgot why I did call thee back.
Rom. Let me stand here till thou remem-
    ber it.
Jul. I shall forget, to have thee still stand
    there,
Remembering how I love thy company.
Rom. And I'll still stay, to have thee still
    forget,
Forgetting any other home but this.
Jul. 'Tis almost morning ; I would have
    thee gone :

And yet no further than a wanton's bird ;
Who lets it hop a little from her hand,
Like a poor prisoner in his twisted gyves, 180
And with a silk thread plucks it back again,
So loving-jealous of his liberty.
Rom. I would I were thy bird.
Jul.   Sweet, so would I :
Yet I should kill thee with much cherishing.
Good night, good night ! parting is such sweet
    sorrow,
That I shall say good night till it be morrow.
                              [*Exit above.*
Rom. Sleep dwell upon thine eyes, peace
    in thy breast !
Would I were sleep and peace, so sweet to
    rest !
Hence will I to my ghostly father's cell,   189
His help to crave, and my dear hap to tell.
                              [*Exit.*

SCENE III. *Friar Laurence's cell.*

Enter FRIAR LAURENCE, *with a basket.*

Fri. L. The grey-eyed morn smiles on the
    frowning night,
Chequering the eastern clouds with streaks of
    light,
And flecked darkness like a drunkard reels
From forth day's path and Titan's fiery
    wheels :
Now, ere the sun advance his burning eye,
The day to cheer and night's dank dew to dry,
I must up-fill this osier cage of ours
With baleful weeds and precious-juiced
    flowers.
The earth that's nature's mother is her tomb ;
What is her burying grave that is her womb,
And from her womb children of divers kind 11
We sucking on her natural bosom find,
Many for many virtues excellent,
None but for some and yet all different.
O, mickle is the powerful grace that lies
In herbs, plants, stones, and their true qual-
    ities :
For nought so vile that on the earth doth live
But to the earth some special good doth give,
Nor aught so good but strain'd from that fair
    use
Revolts from true birth, stumbling on abuse :
Virtue itself turns vice, being misapplied ; 21
And vice sometimes by action dignified.
Within the infant rind of this small flower
Poison hath residence and medicine power :
For this, being smelt, with that part cheers
    each part ;
Being tasted, slays all senses with the heart.
Two such opposed kings encamp them still
In man as well as herbs, grace and rude will ;
And where the worser is predominant,
Full soon the canker death eats up that plant.

Enter ROMEO.

Rom. Good morrow, father.   31
Fri. L.   Benedicite !
What early tongue so sweet saluteth me ?
Young son, it argues a distemper'd head
So soon to bid good morrow to thy bed :
Care keeps his watch in every old man's eye,
And where care lodges, sleep will never lie ;
But where unbruised youth with unstuff'd
    brain
Doth couch his limbs, there golden sleep doth
    reign :
Therefore thy earliness doth me assure

Thou art up-roused by some distemperature ;
Or if not so, then here I hit it right,   41
Our Romeo hath not been in bed to-night.
  Rom. That last is true ; the sweeter rest
    was mine.
  Fri. L. God pardon sin ! wast thou with
    Rosaline ?
  Rom. With Rosaline, my ghostly father ?
    no ;
I have forgot that name, and that name's woe.
  Fri. L. That's my good son : but where
    hast thou been, then ?
  Rom. I'll tell thee, ere thou ask it me
    again.
I have been feasting with mine enemy,
Where on a sudden one hath wounded me, 50
That's by me wounded : both our remedies
Within thy help and holy physic lies :
I bear no hatred, blessed man, for, lo,
My intercession likewise steads my foe.
  Fri. L. Be plain, good son, and homely in
    thy drift ;
Riddling confession finds but riddling shrift.
  Rom. Then plainly know my heart's dear
    love is set
On the fair daughter of rich Capulet :
As mine on hers, so hers is set on mine ;
And all combined, save what thou must com-
    bine   60
By holy marriage : when and where and how
We met, we woo'd and made exchange of vow,
I'll tell thee as we pass ; but this I pray,
That thou consent to marry us to-day.
  Fri. L. Holy Saint Francis, what a change
    is here !
Is Rosaline, whom thou didst love so dear,
So soon forsaken ? young men's love then lies
Not truly in their hearts, but in their eyes.
Jesu Maria, what a deal of brine   69
Hath wash'd thy sallow cheeks for Rosaline !
How much salt water thrown away in waste,
To season love, that of it doth not taste !
The sun not yet thy sighs from heaven clears,
Thy old groans ring yet in my ancient ears ;
Lo, here upon thy cheek the stain doth sit
Of an old tear that is not wash'd off yet :
If e'er thou wast thyself and these woes thine,
Thou and these woes were all for Rosaline :
And art thou changed ? pronounce this sen-
    tence then,
Women may fall, when there's no strength in
    men.   80
  Rom. Thou chid'st me oft for loving Ro-
    saline.
  Fri. L. For doting, not for loving, pupil
    mine.
  Rom. And bad'st me bury love.
  Fri. L.   Not in a grave,
To lay one in, another out to have.
  Rom. I pray thee, chide not ; she whom I
    love now
Doth grace for grace and love for love allow ;
The other did not so.
  Fri. L.   O, she knew well
Thy love did read by rote and could not spell.
But come, young waverer, come, go with me,
In one respect I'll thy assistant be ;   90
For this alliance may so happy prove,
To turn your households' rancor to pure love.
  Rom. O, let us hence ; I stand on sudden
    haste.
  Fri. L. Wisely and slow ; they stumble that
    run fast.   *[Exeunt.*

SCENE IV. *A street.*

Enter BENVOLIO *and* MERCUTIO.

  Mer. Where the devil should this Romeo
    be ?
Came he not home to-night ?
  Ben. Not to his father's ; I spoke with his
    man.
  Mer. Ah, that same pale hard-hearted
    wench, that Rosaline,
Torments him so, that he will sure run mad.
  Ben. Tybalt, the kinsman of old Capulet,
Hath sent a letter to his father's house.
  Mer. A challenge, on my life.
  Ben. Romeo will answer it.
  Mer. Any man that can write may answer
    a letter.   10
  Ben. Nay, he will answer the letter's mas-
ter, how he dares, being dared.
  Mer. Alas, poor Romeo ! he is already
dead ; stabbed with a white wench's black eye ;
shot through the ear with a love-song ; the very
pin of his heart cleft with the blind bow-boy's
butt-shaft : and is he a man to encounter
Tybalt ?
  Ben. Why, what is Tybalt ?
  Mer. More than prince of cats, I can tell
you. O, he is the courageous captain of compliments. He fights as you sing prick-song,
keeps time, distance, and proportion ; rests his
his minim rest, one, two, and the third in your
bosom : the very butcher of a silk button, a
duellist, a duellist ; a gentleman of the very
first house, of the first and second cause : ah,
the immortal passado ! the punto reverso ! the
hai !
  Ben. The what ?
  Mer. The pox of such antic, lisping, affecting fantasticoes ; these new tuners of accents !
' By Jesu, a very good blade ! a very tall man !
a very good whore ! ' Why, is not this a lamentable thing, grandsire, that we should be thus
afflicted with these strange flies, these fashion-
mongers, these perdona-mi's, who stand so
much on the new form, that they cannot sit at
ease on the old bench ? O, their bones, their
bones !

Enter ROMEO.

  Ben. Here comes Romeo, here comes
    Romeo.
  Mer. Without his roe, like a dried herring :
O flesh, flesh, how art thou fishified ! Now is
he for the numbers that Petrarch flowed in :
Laura to his lady was but a kitchen-wench ;
marry, she had a better love to be-rhyme her ;
Dido a dowdy ; Cleopatra a gipsy ; Helen
and Hero hildings and harlots ; Thisbe a grey
eye or so, but not to the purpose. Signior
Romeo, bon jour ! there's a French salutation
to your French slop. You gave us the counterfeit fairly last night.
  Rom. Good morrow to you both. What
counterfeit did I give you ?   50
  Mer. The slip, sir, the slip ; can you not
conceive ?
  Rom. Pardon, good Mercutio, my business
was great ; and in such a case as mine a man
may strain courtesy.
  Mer. That's as much as to say, such a case
as yours constrains a man to bow in the hams
  Rom. Meaning, to court'sy.
  Mer. Thou hast most kindly hit it.

Rom. A most courteous exposition. 60
Mer. Nay, I am the very pink of courtesy.
Rom. Pink for flower.
Mer. Right.
Rom. Why, then is my pump well flowered.
Mer. Well said : follow me this jest now
till thou hast worn out thy pump, that when
the single sole of it is worn, the jest may re-
main after the wearing sole singular.
Rom. O single-soled jest, solely singular
for the singleness ! 70
Mer. Come between us, good Benvolio ;
my wits faint.
Rom. Switch and spurs, switch and spurs ;
or I'll cry a match.
Mer. Nay, if thy wits run the wild-goose
chase, I have done, for thou hast more of the
wild-goose in one of thy wits than, I am sure,
I have in my whole five : was I with you there
for the goose ? 79
Rom. Thou wast never with me for any
thing when thou wast not there for the goose.
Mer. I will bite thee by the ear for that
jest.
Rom. Nay, good goose, bite not.
Mer. Thy wit is a very bitter sweeting ; it
is a most sharp sauce.
Rom. And is it not well served in to a
sweet goose ?
Mer. O, here's a wit of cheveril, that
stretches from an inch narrow to an ell broad !
Rom. I stretch it out for that word
' broad ; ' which added to the goose, proves
thee far and wide a broad goose. 91
Mer. Why, is not this better now than
groaning for love ? now art thou sociable, now
art thou Romeo ; now art thou what thou art,
by art as well as by nature : for this drivelling
love is like a great natural, that runs lolling
up and down to hide his bauble in a hole.
Ben. Stop there, stop there.
Mer. Thou desirest me to stop in my tale
against the hair. 100
Ben. Thou wouldst else have made thy tale
large.
Mer. O, thou art deceived ; I would have
made it short : for I was come to the whole
depth of my tale ; and meant, indeed, to oc-
cupy the argument no longer.
Rom. Here's goodly gear !

Enter Nurse *and* Peter.

Mer. A sail, a sail !
Ben. Two, two ; a shirt and a smock.
Nurse. Peter ! 110
Peter. Anon !
Nurse. My fan, Peter.
Mer. Good Peter, to hide her face ; for her
fan's the fairer face.
Nurse. God ye good morrow, gentlemen.
Mer. God ye good den, fair gentlewoman.
Nurse. Is it good den ?
Mer. 'Tis no less, I tell you, for the bawdy
hand of the dial is now upon the prick of
noon.
Nurse. Out upon you ! what a man are
you ! 120
Rom. One, gentlewoman, that God hath
made for himself to mar.
Nurse. By my troth, it is well said ; ' for
himself to mar,' quoth a' ? Gentlemen, can
any of you tell me where I may find the young
Romeo ?

Rom. I can tell you ; but young Romeo
will be older when you have found him than
he was when you sought him : I am the youngest of that name, for fault of a worse.
Nurse. You say well. 130
Mer. Yea, is the worst well ? very well
took, i' faith ; wisely, wisely.
Nurse. If you be he, sir, I desire some confidence with you.
Ben. She will indite him to some supper.
Mer. A bawd, a bawd, a bawd ! so ho !
Rom. What hast thou found ?
Mer. No hare, sir ; unless a hare, sir, in a
lenten pie, that is something stale and hoar
ere it be spent. [*Sings.* 140
        An old hare hoar,
        And an old hare hoar,
    Is very good meat in lent :
        But a hare that is hoar
        Is too much for a score,
    When it hoars ere it be spent.
Romeo, will you come to your father's ? we'll
to dinner, thither.
Rom. I will follow you.
Mer. Farewell, ancient lady ; farewell,
[*singing*] ' lady, lady, lady.' 151
        [*Exeunt Mercutio and Benvolio.*
Nurse. Marry, farewell ! I pray you, sir,
what saucy merchant was this, that was so full
of his ropery ?
Rom. A gentleman, nurse, that loves to
hear himself talk, and will speak more in a
minute than he will stand to in a month.
Nurse. An a' speak any thing against me,
I'll take him down, an a' were lustier than he
is, and twenty such Jacks ; and if I cannot, I'll
find those that shall. Scurvy knave ! I am none
of his flirt-gills ; I am none of his skains-
mates. And thou must stand by too, and suffer every knave to use me at his pleasure ?
Peter. I saw no man use you at his pleasure ; if I had, my weapon should quickly have
been out, I warrant you : I dare draw as soon
as another man, if I see occasion in a good
quarrel, and the law on my side. 169
Nurse. Now, afore God, I am so vexed,
that every part about me quivers. Scurvy
knave ! Pray you, sir, a word : and as I told
you, my young lady bade me inquire you out ;
what she bade me say, I will keep to myself :
but first let me tell ye, if ye should lead her
into a fool's paradise, as they say, it were a
very gross kind of behavior, as they say : for
the gentlewoman is young ; and, therefore, if
you should deal double with her, truly it were
an ill thing to be offered to any gentlewoman,
and very weak dealing. 181
Rom. Nurse, commend me to thy lady and
mistress. I protest unto thee—
Nurse. Good heart, and, i' faith, I will tell
her as much : Lord, Lord, she will be a joyful
woman.
Rom. What wilt thou tell her, nurse ? thou
dost not mark me.
Nurse. I will tell her, sir, that you do protest ; which, as I take it, is a gentlemanlike
offer. 190
Rom. Bid her devise
Some means to come to shrift this afternoon ;
And there she shall at Friar Laurence' cell
Be shrived and married. Here is for thy pains.
Nurse. No, truly, sir ; not a penny.
Rom. Go to ; I say you shall.

Nurse. This afternoon, sir? well, she shall
be there.

Rom. And stay, good nurse, behind the
abbey wall:
Within this hour my man shall be with thee,
And bring thee cords made like a tackled
stair; 201
Which to the high top-gallant of my joy
Must be my convoy in the secret night.
Farewell; be trusty, and I'll quit thy pains:
Farewell; commend me to thy mistress.

Nurse. Now God in heaven bless thee!
Hark you, sir.

Rom. What say'st thou, my dear nurse?

Nurse. Is your man secret? Did you ne'er
hear say,
Two may keep counsel, putting one away?

Rom. I warrant thee, my man's as true as
steel. 210

Nurse. Well, sir; my mistress is the sweetest lady—Lord, Lord! when 'twas a little
prating thing:—O, there is a nobleman in
town, one Paris, that would fain lay knife
aboard; but she, good soul, had as lief see a
toad, a very toad, as see him. I anger her
sometimes and tell her that Paris is the properer man; but, I'll warrant you, when I say
so, she looks as pale as any clout in the versal
world. Doth not rosemary and Romeo begin
both with a letter? 220

Rom. Ay, nurse; what of that? both with
an R.

Nurse. Ah, mocker! that's the dog's
name; R is for the— No; I know it begins
with some other letter:—and she hath the
prettiest sententious of it, of you and rosemary,
that it would do you good to hear it.

Rom. Commend me to thy lady.

Nurse. Ay, a thousand times.
[*Exit Romeo.*

Peter! 230

Pet. Anon!

Nurse. Peter, take my fan, and go before,
and apace. [*Exeunt.*

SCENE V. *Capulet's orchard.*

Enter JULIET.

Jul. The clock struck nine when I did send
the nurse;
In half an hour she promised to return.
Perchance she cannot meet him: that's not
so.
O, she is lame! love's heralds should be
thoughts,
Which ten times faster glide than the sun's
beams,
Driving back shadows over louring hills:
Therefore do nimble-pinion'd doves draw love,
And therefore hath the wind-swift Cupid
wings.
Now is the sun upon the highmost hill
Of this day's journey, and from nine till twelve
Is three long hours, yet she is not come. 11
Had she affections and warm youthful blood,
She would be as swift in motion as a ball;
My words would bandy her to my sweet love,
And his to me:
But old folks, many feign as they were dead;
Unwieldy, slow, heavy and pale as lead.
O God, she comes!

Enter Nurse *and* PETER.

O honey nurse, what news?

Hast thou met with him? Send thy man away.

Nurse. Peter, stay at the gate. [*Exit Peter.*

Jul. Now, good sweet nurse, O Lord, why
look'st thou sad?
Though news be sad, yet tell them merrily;
If good, thou shamest the music of sweet news
By playing it to me with so sour a face.

Nurse. I am a-weary, give me leave
awhile:
Fie, how my bones ache! what a jaunt have
I had!

Jul. I would thou hadst my bones, and I
thy news:
Nay, come, I pray thee, speak; good, good
nurse, speak.

Nurse. Jesu, what haste? can you not stay
awhile?
Do you not see that I am out of breath? 30

Jul. How art thou out of breath, when
thou hast breath
To say to me that thou art out of breath?
The excuse that thou dost make in this delay
Is longer than the tale thou dost excuse.
Is thy news good, or bad? answer to that;
Say either, and I'll stay the circumstance:
Let me be satisfied, is't good or bad?

Nurse. Well, you have made a simple
choice; you know not how to choose a man:
Romeo! no, not he; though his face be better
than any man's, yet his leg excels all men's;
and for a hand, and a foot, and a body,
though they be not to be talked on, yet they
are past compare: he is not the flower of
courtesy, but, I'll warrant him, as gentle as a
lamb. Go thy ways, wench; serve God. What,
have you dined at home?

Jul. No, no: but all this did I know before. What says he of our marriage? what of
that?

Nurse. Lord, how my head aches! what a
head have I!
It beats as it would fall in twenty pieces. 50
My back o' t' other side,—O, my back, my
back!
Beshrew your heart for sending me about,
To catch my death with jaunting up and
down!

Jul. I' faith, I am sorry that thou art not
well.
Sweet, sweet, sweet nurse, tell me, what says
my love?

Nurse. Your love says, like an honest gentleman, and a courteous, and a kind, and a
handsome, and, I warrant, a virtuous,—Where
is your mother?

Jul. Where is my mother! why, she is
within; 60
Where should she be? How oddly thou re-
pliest!
'Your love says, like an honest gentleman,
Where is your mother?'

Nurse. O God's lady dear!
Are you so hot? marry, come up, I trow;
Is this the poultice for my aching bones?
Henceforward do your messages yourself.

Jul. Here's such a coil! come, what says
Romeo?

Nurse. Have you got leave to go to shrift
to-day?

Jul. I have.

Nurse. Then hie you hence to Friar Laurence' cell; 70
There stays a husband to make you a wife:

Now comes the wanton blood up in your
    cheeks,
They'll be in scarlet straight at any news.
Hie you to church; I must another way,
To fetch a ladder, by the which your love
Must climb a bird's nest soon when it is dark:
I am the drudge and toil in your delight,
But you shall bear the burden soon at night.
Go; I'll to dinner: hie you to the cell.

Jul. Hie to high fortune! Honest nurse,
    farewell.   [*Exeunt.* 80

SCENE VI. *Friar Laurence's cell.*

Enter FRIAR LAURENCE *and* ROMEO.

Fri. L. So smile the heavens upon this holy
    act,
That after hours with sorrow chide us not!

Rom. Amen, amen! but come what sor-
    row can,
It cannot countervail the exchange of joy
That one short minute gives me in her sight:
Do thou but close our hands with holy words,
Then love-devouring death do what he dare;
It is enough I may but call her mine.

Fri. L. These violent delights have violent
    ends
And in their triumph die, like fire and pow-
    der,   10
Which as they kiss consume: the sweetest
    honey
Is loathsome in his own deliciousness
And in the taste confounds the appetite:
Therefore love moderately; long love doth so;
Too swift arrives as tardy as too slow.

Enter JULIET.

Here comes the lady: O, so light a foot
Will ne'er wear out the everlasting flint:
A lover may bestride the gossamer
That idles in the wanton summer air,
And yet not fall; so light is vanity.   20

Jul. Good even to my ghostly confessor.

Fri. L. Romeo shall thank thee, daughter,
    for us both.

Jul. As much to him, else is his thanks too
    much.

Rom. Ah, Juliet, if the measure of thy joy
Be heap'd like mine and that thy skill be more
To blazon it, then sweeten with thy breath
This neighbor air, and let rich music's tongue
Unfold the imagined happiness that both
Receive in either by this dear encounter.

Jul. Conceit, more rich in matter than in
    words,   30
Brags of his substance, not of ornament:
They are but beggars that can count their
    worth;
But my true love is grown to such excess
I cannot sum up sum of half my wealth.

Fri. L. Come, come with me, and we will
    make short work;
For, by your leaves, you shall not stay alone
Till holy church incorporate two in one.
          [*Exeunt.*

ACT III.

SCENE I. *A public place.*

Enter MERCUTIO, BENVOLIO, Page, *and*
Servants.

Ben. I pray thee, good Mercutio, let's re-
    tire:
The day is hot, the Capulets abroad,
And, if we meet, we shall not scape a brawl;
For now, these hot days, is the mad blood
    stirring.

Mer. Thou art like one of those fellows
that when he enters the confines of a tavern
claps me his sword upon the table and says
'God send me no need of thee!' and by the
operation of the second cup draws it on the
drawer, when indeed there is no need.   10

Ben. Am I like such a fellow?

Mer. Come, come, thou art as hot a Jack
in thy mood as any in Italy, and as soon
moved to be moody, and as soon moody to
be moved.

Ben. And what to?

Mer. Nay, an there were two such, we
should have none shortly, for one would kill
the other. Thou! why, thou wilt quarrel with
a man that hath a hair more, or a hair less, in
his beard, than thou hast: thou wilt quarrel
with a man for cracking nuts, having no other
reason but because thou hast hazel eyes: what
eye but such an eye would spy out such a
quarrel? Thy head is as full of quarrels as an
egg is full of meat, and yet thy head hath been
beaten as addle as an egg for quarrelling:
thou hast quarrelled with a man for coughing
in the street, because he hath wakened thy dog
that hath lain asleep in the sun: didst thou
not fall out with a tailor for wearing his new
doublet before Easter? with another, for tying
his new shoes with old riband? and yet thou
wilt tutor me from quarrelling!

Ben. An I were so apt to quarrel as thou
art, any man should buy the fee-simple of my
life for an hour and a quarter.

Mer. The fee-simple! O simple!

Ben. By my head, here come the Capulets.

Mer. By my heel, I care not.

Enter TYBALT *and others.*

Tyb. Follow me close, for I will speak to
    them.   40
Gentlemen, good den: a word with one of
    you.

Mer. And but one word with one of us?
couple it with something; make it a word
and a blow.

Tyb. You shall find me apt enough to that,
sir, an you will give me occasion.

Mer. Could you not take some occasion
without giving?

Tyb. Mercutio, thou consort'st with Romeo,—

Mer. Consort! what, dost thou make us
minstrels? an thou make minstrels of us, look
to hear nothing but discords: here's my fiddlestick; here's that shall make you dance.
'Zounds, consort!

Ben. We talk here in the public haunt of
    men:
Either withdraw unto some private place,
And reason coldly of your grievances,
Or else depart; here all eyes gaze on us.

Mer. Men's eyes were made to look, and
    let them gaze;
I will not budge for no man's pleasure, I.

Enter ROMEO.

Tyb. Well, peace be with you, sir : here
comes my man.

Mer. But I'll be hang'd, sir, if he wear
your livery : 60
Marry, go before to field, he'll be your follower ;
Your worship in that sense may call him
'man.'

Tyb. Romeo, the hate I bear thee can afford
No better term than this,—thou art a villain.

Rom. Tybalt, the reason that I have to love
thee
Doth much excuse the appertaining rage
To such a greeting : villain am I none ;
Therefore farewell ; I see thou know'st me not.

Tyb. Boy, this shall not excuse the injuries
That thou hast done me ; therefore turn and
draw. 70

Rom. I do protest, I never injured thee,
But love thee better than thou canst devise,
Till thou shalt know the reason of my love :
And so, good Capulet,—which name I tender
As dearly as my own,—be satisfied.

Mer. O calm, dishonorable, vile submis-
sion !
Alla stoccata carries it away. [*Draws.*
Tybalt, you rat-catcher, will you walk ?

Tyb. What wouldst thou have with me ? 79

Mer. Good king of cats, nothing but one
of your nine lives ; that I mean to make bold
withal, and as you shall use me hereafter, dry-
beat the rest of the eight. Will you pluck your
sword out of his pilcher by the ears ? make
haste, lest mine be about your ears ere it be
out.

Tyb. I am for you. [*Drawing.*

Rom. Gentle Mercutio, put thy rapier up.

Mer. Come, sir, your passado. [*They fight.*

Rom. Draw, Benvolio ; beat down their
weapons. 89
Gentlemen, for shame, forbear this outrage !
Tybalt, Mercutio, the prince expressly hath
Forbidden bandying in Verona streets :
Hold, Tybalt ! good Mercutio !
[*Tybalt under Romeo's arm stabs Mercutio,
and flies with his followers.*

Mer. I am hurt.
A plague o' both your houses ! I am sped.
Is he gone, and hath nothing ?

Ben. What, art thou hurt ?

Mer. Ay, ay, a scratch, a scratch ; marry,
'tis enough.
Where is my page ? Go, villain, fetch a surgeon. [*Exit Page.*

Rom. Courage, man ; the hurt cannot be
much.

Mer. No, 'tis not so deep as a well, nor so
wide as a church-door ; but 'tis enough, 'twill
serve : ask for me to-morrow, and you shall
find me a grave man. I am peppered, I warrant, for this world. A plague o' both your
houses ! 'Zounds, a dog, a rat, a mouse, a cat,
to scratch a man to death ! a braggart, a
rogue, a villain, that fights by the book of
arithmetic ! Why the devil came you between
us ? I was hurt under your arm.

Rom. I thought all for the best.

Mer. Help me into some house, Benvolio,
Or I shall faint. A plague o' both your
houses ! 111
They have made worms' meat of me : I have
it,
And soundly too : your houses !
[*Exeunt Mercutio and Benvolio.*

Rom. This gentleman, the prince's near
ally,
My very friend, hath got his mortal hurt
In my behalf ; my reputation stain'd
With Tybalt's slander,—Tybalt, that an hour
Hath been my kinsman ! O sweet Juliet,
Thy beauty hath made me effeminate
And in my temper soften'd valor's steel ! 120

Re-enter BENVOLIO.

Ben. O Romeo, Romeo, brave Mercutio's
dead !
That gallant spirit hath aspired the clouds,
Which too untimely here did scorn the earth.

Rom. This day's black fate on more days
doth depend ;
This but begins the woe, others must end.

Ben. Here comes the furious Tybalt back
again.

Rom. Alive, in triumph ! and Mercutio
slain !
Away to heaven, respective lenity,
And fire-eyed fury be my conduct now !

Re-enter TYBALT.

Now, Tybalt, take the villain back again, 130
That late thou gavest me ; for Mercutio's soul
Is but a little way above our heads,
Staying for thine to keep him company :
Either thou, or I, or both, must go with him.

Tyb. Thou, wretched boy, that didst consort him here,
Shalt with him hence.

Rom. This shall determine that.
[*They fight ; Tybalt falls.*

Ben. Romeo, away, be gone !
The citizens are up, and Tybalt slain.
Stand not amazed : the prince will doom thee
death,
If thou art taken : hence, be gone, away ! 140

Rom. O, I am fortune's fool !

Ben. Why dost thou stay ?
[*Exit Romeo.*

Enter Citizens, &c.

First Cit. Which way ran he that kill'd
Mercutio ?
Tybalt, that murderer, which way ran he ?

Ben. There lies that Tybalt.

First Cit. Up, sir, go with me ;
I charge thee in the prince's name, obey.

Enter Prince, *attended ;* MONTAGUE, CAP-
ULET, *their* Wives, *and others.*

Prin. Where are the vile beginners of this
fray ?

Ben. O noble prince, I can discover all
The unlucky manage of this fatal brawl :
There lies the man, slain by young Romeo,
That slew thy kinsman, brave Mercutio. 150

La. Cap. Tybalt, my cousin ! O my broth-
er's child !
O prince ! O cousin ! husband ! O, the blood
is spilt
O my dear kinsman ! Prince, as thou art true,
For blood of ours, shed blood of Montague.
O cousin, cousin !

Prin. Benvolio, who began this bloody
fray ?

Ben. Tybalt, here slain, whom Romeo's
hand did slay ;
Romeo that spoke him fair, bade him bethink

How nice the quarrel was, and urged withal
Your high displeasure : all this uttered 160
With gentle breath, calm look, knees humbly
    bow'd,
Could not take truce with the unruly spleen
Of Tybalt deaf to peace, but that he tilts
With piercing steel at bold Mercutio's breast,
Who, all as hot, turns deadly point to point,
And, with a martial scorn, with one hand
    beats
Cold death aside, and with the other sends
It back to Tybalt, whose dexterity
Retorts it : Romeo he cries aloud,
'Hold, friends! friends, part!' and, swifter
    than his tongue, 170
His agile arm beats down their fatal points,
And 'twixt them rushes ; underneath whose
    arm
An envious thrust from Tybalt hit the life
Of stout Mercutio, and then Tybalt fled ;
But by and by comes back to Romeo,
Who had but newly entertain'd revenge,
And to 't they go like lightning, for, ere I
Could draw to part them, was stout Tybalt
    slain,
And, as he fell, did Romeo turn and fly.
This is the truth, or let Benvolio die. 180
    La. Cap. He is a kinsman to the Monta-
    gue ;
Affection makes him false ; he speaks not
    true :
Some twenty of them fought in this black
    strife,
And all those twenty could but kill one life.
I beg for justice, which thou, prince, must
    give ;
Romeo slew Tybalt, Romeo must not live.
    Prin. Romeo slew him, he slew Mercutio ;
Who now the price of his dear blood doth
    owe?
    Mon. Not Romeo, prince, he was Mercu-
    tio's friend ;
His fault concludes but what the law should
    end, 190
The life of Tybalt.
    Prin. And for that offence
Immediately we do exile him hence :
I have an interest in your hate's proceeding,
My blood for your rude brawls doth lie
    a-bleeding ;
But I'll amerce you with so strong a fine
That you shall all repent the loss of mine :
I will be deaf to pleading and excuses ;
Nor tears nor prayers shall purchase out
    abuses :
Therefore use none : let Romeo hence in haste,
Else, when he's found, that hour is his last.
Bear hence this body and attend our will : 201
Mercy but murders, pardoning those that kill.
        [*Exeunt.*

Scene II. *Capulet's orchard.*
        Enter JULIET.

    Jul. Gallop apace, you fiery-footed steeds,
Towards Phœbus' lodging : such a wagoner
As Phaethon would whip you to the west,
And bring in cloudy night immediately.
Spread thy close curtain, love-performing
    night,
That runaway's eyes may wink, and Romeo
Leap to these arms, untalk'd of and unseen.
Lovers can see to do their amorous rites
By their own beauties ; or, if love be blind,

It best agrees with night. Come, civil night,
Thou sober-suited matron, all in black, 11
And learn me how to lose a winning match,
Play'd for a pair of stainless maidenhoods :
Hood my unmann'd blood, bating in my
    cheeks,
With thy black mantle ; till strange love,
    grown bold,
Think true love acted simple modesty.
Come, night ; come, Romeo ; come, thou day
    in night ;
For thou wilt lie upon the wings of night
Whiter than new snow on a raven's back.
Come, gentle night, come, loving, black-brow'd
    night, 20
Give me my Romeo ; and, when he shall die,
Take him and cut him out in little stars,
And he will make the face of heaven so fine
That all the world will be in love with night
And pay no worship to the garish sun.
O, I have bought the mansion of a love,
But not possess'd it, and, though I am sold,
Not yet enjoy'd : so tedious is this day
As is the night before some festival
To an impatient child that hath new robes 30
And may not wear them. O, here comes my
    nurse,
And she brings news ; and every tongue that
    speaks
But Romeo's name speaks heavenly eloquence.

        Enter Nurse, *with cords.*

Now, nurse, what news ? What hast thou
    there ? the cords
That Romeo bid thee fetch ?
    Nurse. Ay, ay, the cords.
            [*Throws them down.*
    Jul. Ay me! what news ? why dost thou
        wring thy hands ?
    Nurse. Ah, well-a-day! he's dead, he's
        dead, he's dead!
We are undone, lady, we are undone!
Alack the day! he's gone, he's kill'd, he's
    dead!
    Jul. Can heaven be so envious ?
    Nurse. Romeo can, 40
Though heaven cannot : O Romeo, Romeo!
Who ever would have thought it ? Romeo!
    Jul. What devil art thou, that dost torment
        me thus ?
This torture should be roar'd in dismal hell.
Hath Romeo slain himself? say thou but 'I,'
And that bare vowel 'I' shall poison more
Than the death-darting eye of cockatrice :
I am not I, if there be such an I ;
Or those eyes shut, that make thee answer 'I.'
If he be slain, say 'I'; or if not, no : 50
Brief sounds determine of my weal or woe.
    Nurse. I saw the wound, I saw it with
        mine eyes,—
God save the mark!—here on his manly
    breast :
A piteous corse, a bloody piteous corse ;
Pale, pale as ashes, all bedaub'd in blood,
All in gore-blood ; I swounded at the sight.
    Jul. O, break, my heart! poor bankrupt,
        break at once!
To prison, eyes, ne'er look on liberty!
Vile earth, to earth resign ; end motion here ;
And thou and Romeo press one heavy bier!
    Nurse. O Tybalt, Tybalt, the best friend I
        had! 61
O courteous Tybalt! honest gentleman!

That ever I should live to see thee dead!
 Jul. What storm is this that blows so con-
  trary?
Is Romeo slaughter'd, and is Tybalt dead?
My dear-loved cousin, and my dearer lord?
Then, dreadful trumpet, sound the general
  doom!
For who is living, if those two are gone?
 Nurse. Tybalt is gone, and Romeo ban-
  ished;
Romeo that kill'd him, he is banished. 70
 Jul. O God! did Romeo's hand shed Ty-
  balt's blood?
 Nurse. It did, it did; alas the day, it did!
 Jul. O serpent heart, hid with a flowering
  face!
Did ever dragon keep so fair a cave?
Beautiful tyrant! fiend angelical!
Dove-feather'd raven! wolvish-ravening lamb!
Despised substance of divinest show!
Just opposite to what thou justly seem'st,
A damned saint, an honorable villain!
O nature, what hadst thou to do in hell, 80
When thou didst bower the spirit of a fiend
In moral paradise of such sweet flesh?
Was ever book containing such vile matter
So fairly bound? O, that deceit should dwell
In such a gorgeous palace!
 Nurse.   There's no trust,
No faith, no honesty in men; all perjured,
All forsworn, all naught, all dissemblers.
Ah, where's my man? give me some aqua
  vitæ:
These griefs, these woes, these sorrows make
  me old.
Shame come to Romeo!
 Jul.   Blister'd be thy tongue 90
For such a wish! he was not born to shame:
Upon his brow shame is ashamed to sit;
For 'tis a throne where honor may be crown'd
Sole monarch of the universal earth.
O, what a beast was I to chide at him!
 Nurse. Will you speak well of him that
  kill'd your cousin?
 Jul. Shall I speak ill of him that is my hus-
  band?
Ah, poor my lord, what tongue shall smooth
  thy name,
When I, thy three-hours wife, have mangled
  it?
But, wherefore, villain, didst thou kill my
  cousin? 100
That villain cousin would have kill'd my hus-
  band:
Back, foolish tears, back to your native
  spring;
Your tributary drops belong to woe,
Which you, mistaking, offer up to joy.
My husband lives, that Tybalt would have
  slain;
And Tybalt's dead, that would have slain my
  husband:
All this is comfort; wherefore weep I then?
Some word there was, worser than Tybalt's
  death,
That murder'd me: I would forget it fain;
But, O, it presses to my memory, 110
Like damned guilty deeds to sinners' minds:
'Tybalt is dead, and Romeo—banished;'
That 'banished,' that one word 'banished,'
Hath slain ten thousand Tybalts. Tybalt's
  death
Was woe enough, if it had ended there:

Or, if sour woe delights in fellowship
And needly will be rank'd with other griefs,
Why follow'd not, when she said 'Tybalt's
  dead,'
Thy father, or thy mother, nay, or both,
Which modern lamentations might have
  moved? 120
But with a rear-ward following Tybalt's death,
'Romeo is banished,' to speak that word,
Is father, mother, Tybalt, Romeo, Juliet,
All slain, all dead. 'Romeo is banished!'
There is no end, no limit, measure, bound,
In that word's death; no words can that woe
  sound.
Where is my father, and my mother, nurse?
 Nurse. Weeping and wailing over Tybalt's
  corse:
Will you go to them? I will bring you thither.
 Jul. Wash they his wounds with tears:
  mine shall be spent, 130
When theirs are dry, for Romeo's banishment.
Take up those cords: poor ropes, you are be-
  guiled,
Both you and I; for Romeo is exiled:
He made you for a highway to my bed;
But I, a maid, die maiden-widowed.
Come, cords, come, nurse; I'll to my wedding-
  bed;
And death, not Romeo, take my maidenhead!
 Nurse. Hie to your chamber: I'll find
  Romeo
To comfort you: I wot well where he is.
Hark ye, your Romeo will be here at night:
I'll to him; he is hid at Laurence' cell.
 Jul. O, find him! give this ring to my true
  knight,
And bid him come to take his last farewell.
            [*Exeunt.*

SCENE III. *Friar Laurence's cell.*

Enter FRIAR LAURENCE.

 Fri. L. Romeo, come forth; come forth,
  thou fearful man:
Affliction is enamor'd of thy parts,
And thou art wedded to calamity.

Enter ROMEO.

 Rom. Father, what news? what is the
  prince's doom?
What sorrow craves acquaintance at my hand,
That I yet know not?
 Fri. L.   Too familiar
Is my dear son with such sour company:
I bring thee tidings of the prince's doom.
 Rom. What less than dooms-day is the
  prince's doom?
 Fri. L. A gentler judgment vanish'd from
  his lips, 10
Not body's death, but body's banishment.
 Rom. Ha, banishment! be merciful, say
  'death;'
For exile hath more terror in his look,
Much more than death: do not say 'banish-
  ment.'
 Fri. L. Hence from Verona art thou ban-
  ished:
Be patient, for the world is broad and wide.
 Rom. There is no world without Verona
  walls,
But purgatory, torture, hell itself.
Hence-banished is banish'd from the world,
And world's exile is death: then banished, 20
Is death mis-term'd: calling death banishment,

Thou cutt'st my head off with a golden axe,
And smilest upon the stroke that murders me.
  Fri. L. O deadly sin! O rude unthankful-
      ness!
Thy fault our law calls death; but the kind
      prince,
Taking thy part, hath rush'd aside the law,
And turn'd that black word death to banish-
      ment:
This is dear mercy, and thou seest it not.
  Rom. 'Tis torture, and not mercy: heaven
      is here,
Where Juliet lives; and every cat and dog 30
And little mouse, every unworthy thing,
Live here in heaven and may look on her;
But Romeo may not: more validity,
More honorable state, more courtship lives
In carrion-flies than Romeo: they may seize
On the white wonder of dear Juliet's hand
And steal immortal blessing from her lips,
Who, even in pure and vestal modesty,
Still blush, as thinking their own kisses sin;
But Romeo may not; he is banished: 40
Flies may do this, but I from this must fly:
They are free men, but I am banished.
And say'st thou yet that exile is not death?
Hadst thou no poison mix'd, no sharp-ground
      knife,
No sudden mean of death, though ne'er so
      mean,
But 'banished' to kill me?—'banished'?
O friar, the damned use that word in hell;
Howlings attend it: how hast thou the heart,
Being a divine, a ghostly confessor,
A sin-absolver, and my friend profess'd, 50
To mangle me with that word 'banished'?
  Fri. L. Thou fond mad man, hear me
      but speak a word.
  Rom. O, thou wilt speak again of banish-
      ment.
  Fri. L. I'll give thee armor to keep off that
      word:
Adversity's sweet milk, philosophy,
To comfort thee, though thou art banished.
  Rom. Yet 'banished'? Hang up philos-
      ophy!
Unless philosophy can make a Juliet,
Displant a town, reverse a prince's doom,
It helps not, it prevails not: talk no more. 60
  Fri. L. O, then I see that madmen have
      no ears.
  Rom. How should they, when that wise
      men have no eyes?
  Fri. L. Let me dispute with thee of thy
      estate.
  Rom. Thou canst not speak of that thou
      dost not feel:
Wert thou as young as I, Juliet thy love,
An hour but married, Tybalt murdered,
Doting like me and like me banished,
Then mightst thou speak, then mightst thou
      tear thy hair,
And fall upon the ground, as I do now,
Taking the measure of an unmade grave. 70
                    [*Knocking within.*
  Fri. L. Arise; one knocks; good Romeo,
      hide thyself.
  Rom. Not I; unless the breath of heart-
      sick groans,
Mist-like, infold me from the search of eyes.
                              [*Knocking.*
  Fri. L. Hark, how they knock! Who's
      there? Romeo, arise;

Thou wilt be taken. Stay awhile! Stand up;
                              [*Knocking.*
Run to my study. By and by! God's will,
What simpleness is this! I come, I come!
                              [*Knocking.*
Who knocks so hard? whence come you?
      what's your will?
  Nurse. [*Within*] Let me come in, and you
      shall know my errand;
I come from Lady Juliet.
  Fri. L.   Welcome, then. 80

              Enter Nurse.

  Nurse. O holy friar, O, tell me, holy friar,
Where is my lady's lord, where's Romeo?
  Fri. L. There on the ground, with his own
      tears made drunk.
  Nurse. O, he is even in my mistress' case,
Just in her case! O woful sympathy!
Piteous predicament! Even so lies she,
Blubbering and weeping, weeping and blubber-
      ing.
Stand up, stand up; stand, and you be a
      man:
For Juliet's sake, for her sake, rise and stand;
Why should you fall into so deep an O? 90
  Rom. Nurse!
  Nurse. Ah sir! ah sir! Well, death's the
      end of all.
  Rom. Spakest thou of Juliet? how is it
      with her?
Doth she not think me an old murderer,
Now I have stain'd the childhood of our joy
With blood removed but little from her own?
Where is she? and how doth she? and what
      says
My conceal'd lady to our cancell'd love?
  Nurse. O, she says nothing, sir, but weeps
      and weeps;   99
And now falls on her bed; and then starts up,
And Tybalt calls; and then on Romeo cries,
And then down falls again.
  Rom.   As if that name,
Shot from the deadly level of a gun,
Did murder her; as that name's cursed hand
Murder'd her kinsman. O, tell me, friar, tell
      me,
In what vile part of this anatomy
Doth my name lodge? tell me, that I may
      sack
The hateful mansion. [*Drawing his sword.*
  Fri. L.   Hold thy desperate hand!
Art thou a man? thy form cries out thou art:
Thy tears are womanish; thy wild acts denote
The unreasonable fury of a beast: 111
Unseemly woman in a seeming man!
Or ill-beseeming beast in seeming both!
Thou hast amazed me: by my holy order,
I thought thy disposition better temper'd.
Hast thou slain Tybalt? wilt thou slay thy-
      self?
And slay thy lady too that lives in thee,
By doing damned hate upon thyself?
Why rail'st thou on thy birth, the heaven, and
      earth?
Since birth, and heaven, and earth, all three
      do meet   120
In thee at once; which thou at once wouldst
      lose.
Fie, fie, thou shamest thy shape, thy love, thy
      wit;
Which, like a usurer, abound'st in all,
And usest none in that true use indeed

Which should bedeck thy shape, thy love,
  thy wit :
Thy noble shape is but a form of wax,
Digressing from the valor of a man ;
Thy dear love sworn but hollow perjury,
Killing that love which thou hast vow'd to
  cherish ;
Thy wit, that ornament to shape and love, 130
Mis-shapen in the conduct of them both,
Like powder in a skilless soldier's flask,
Is set a-fire by thine own ignorance,
And thou dismember'd with thine own de-
  fence.
What, rouse thee, man ! thy Juliet is alive,
For whose dear sake thou wast but lately
  dead ;
There art thou happy : Tybalt would kill thee,
But thou slew'st Tybalt ; there are thou happy
  too :
The law that threaten'd death becomes thy
  friend
And turns it to exile ; there art thou happy :
A pack of blessings lights upon thy back ; 141
Happiness courts thee in her best array ;
But, like a misbehaved and sullen wench,
Thou pout'st upon thy fortune and thy love :
Take heed, take heed, for such die miserable.
Go, get thee to thy love, as was decreed,
Ascend her chamber, hence and comfort her :
But look thou stay not till the watch be set,
For then thou canst not pass to Mantua ; 149
Where thou shalt live, till we can find a time
To blaze your marriage, reconcile your
  friends,
Beg pardon of the prince, and call thee back
With twenty hundred thousand times more joy
Than thou went'st forth in lamentation.
Go before, nurse : commend me to thy lady ;
And bid her hasten all the house to bed,
Which heavy sorrow makes them apt unto :
Romeo is coming.
  Nurse. O Lord, I could have stay'd here
  all the night
To hear good counsel : O, what learning is !
My lord, I'll tell my lady you will come. 161
  Rom. Do so, and bid my sweet prepare to
  chide.
  Nurse. Here, sir, a ring she bid me give
  you, sir :
Hie you, make haste, for it grows very late.
                                        [*Exit.*
  Rom. How well my comfort is revived by
  this !
  Fri. L. Go hence ; good night ; and here
  stands all your state :
Either be gone before the watch be set,
Or by the break of day disguised from hence :
Sojourn in Mantua ; I'll find out your man,
And he shall signify from time to time   170
Every good hap to you that chances here :
Give me thy hand ; 'tis late : farewell ; good
  night.
  Rom. But that a joy past joy calls out on
  me,
It were a grief, so brief to part with thee :
Farewell.   [*Exeunt.*

SCENE IV. *A room in Capulet's house.*

Enter CAPULET, LADY CAPULET, *and* PARIS.
  Cap. Things have fall'n out, sir, so unluckily,
That we have had no time to move our daughter :

Look you, she loved her kinsman Tybalt
  dearly,
And so did I :—Well, we were born to die.
'Tis very late, she'll not come down to-night :
I promise you, but for your company,
I would have been a-bed an hour ago.
  Par. These times of woe afford no time to
  woo.
Madam, good night : commend me to your
  daughter.
  La. Cap. I will, and know her mind early
  to-morrow ;   10
To-night she is mew'd up to her heaviness.
  Cap. Sir Paris, I will make a desperate
  tender
Of my child's love : I think she will be ruled
In all respects by me ; nay, more, I doubt it
  not.
Wife, go you to her ere you go to bed,
Acquaint her here of my son Paris' love ;
And bid her, mark you me, on Wednesday
  next—
But, soft ! what day is this ?
  Par.   Monday, my lord.
  Cap. Monday ! ha, ha ! Well, Wednesday
  is too soon,
O' Thursday let it be : o' Thursday, tell her,
She shall be married to this noble earl.   21
Will you be ready ? do you like this haste ?
We'll keep no great ado,—a friend or two ;
For, hark you, Tybalt being slain so late,
It may be thought we held him carelessly,
Being our kinsman, if we revel much :
Therefore we'll have some half a dozen
  friends,
And there an end. But what say you to Thurs-
  day ?
  Par. My lord, I would that Thursday were
  to-morrow.
  Cap. Well, get you gone : o' Thursday be
  it, then.   30
Go you to Juliet ere you go to bed,
Prepare her, wife, against this wedding-day.
Farewell, my lord. Light to my chamber, ho !
Afore me ! it is so very very late,
That we may call it early by and by.
Good night.   [*Exeunt.*

SCENE V. *Capulet's orchard.*

Enter ROMEO *and* JULIET *above, at the window.*
  Jul. Wilt thou be gone ? it is not yet near
  day :
It was the nightingale, and not the lark,
That pierced the fearful hollow of thine ear ;
Nightly she sings on yon pomegranate-tree :
Believe me, love, it was the nightingale.
  Rom. It was the lark, the herald of the
  morn,
No nightingale : look, love, what envious
  streaks
Do lace the severing clouds in yonder east :
Night's candles are burnt out, and jocund day
Stands tiptoe on the misty mountain tops. 10
I must be gone and live, or stay and die.
  Jul. Yon light is not day-light, I know it, I :
It is some meteor that the sun exhales,
To be this night a torch-bearer,
And light thee on thy way to Mantua :
Therefore stay yet ; thou need'st not to be
  gone.
  Rom. Let me be ta'en, let me be put to
  death ;
I am content, so thou wilt have it so.

I'll say yon grey is not the morning's eye,
'Tis but the pale reflex of Cynthia's brow ; 20
Nor that is not the lark, whose notes do beat
The vaulty heaven so high above our heads :
I have more care to stay than will to go :
Come, death, and welcome ! Juliet wills it so.
How is't, my soul ? let's talk ; it is not day.

Jul. It is, it is : hie hence, be gone, away !
It is the lark that sings so out of tune,
Straining harsh discords and unpleasing sharps.
Some say the lark makes sweet division ;
This doth not so, for she divideth us :   30
Some say the lark and loathed toad change
    eyes ;
O, now I would they had changed voices too !
Since arm from arm that voice doth us affray,
Hunting thee hence with hunt's-up to the day,
O, now be gone ; more light and light it grows.

Rom. More light and light ; more dark and
    dark our woes !

Enter Nurse, *to the chamber.*

Nurse. Madam !

Jul. Nurse ?

Nurse. Your lady mother is coming to
    your chamber :
The day is broke ; be wary, look about. [*Exit.*

Jul. Then, window, let day in, and let life
    out.   41

Rom. Farewell, farewell ! one kiss, and I'll
    descend.   [*He goeth down.*

Jul. Art thou gone so ? love, lord, ay, hus-
    band, friend !
I must hear from thee every day in the hour,
For in a minute there are many days :
O, by this count I shall be much in years
Ere I again behold my Romeo !

Rom. Farewell !
I will omit no opportunity
That may convey my greetings, love, to thee.

Jul. O think'st thou we shall ever meet
    again ?   51

Rom. I doubt it not ; and all these woes
    shall serve
For sweet discourses in our time to come.

Jul. O God, I have an ill-divining soul !
Methinks I see thee, now thou art below,
As one dead in the bottom of a tomb :
Either my eyesight fails, or thou look'st pale.

Rom. And trust me, love, in my eye so do
    you :
Dry sorrow drinks our blood. Adieu, adieu !
                         [*Exit.*

Jul. O fortune, fortune ! all men call thee
    fickle :   60
If thou art fickle, what dost thou with him.
That is renown'd for faith ? Be fickle, fortune ;
For then, I hope, thou wilt not keep him long,
But send him back.

La. Cap. [*Within*] Ho, daughter ! are you
    up ?

Jul. Who is't that calls ? is it my lady
    mother ?
Is she not down so late, or up so early ?
What unaccustom'd cause procures her
    hither ?

Enter LADY CAPULET.

La. Cap. Why, how now, Juliet !

Jul.   Madam, I am not well.

La. Cap. Evermore weeping for your cous-
    in's death ?   70

What, wilt thou wash him from his grave with
    tears ?
An if thou couldst, thou couldst not make him
    live ;
Therefore, have done : some grief shows much
    of love ;
But much of grief shows still some want of
    wit.

Jul. Yet let me weep for such a feeling loss.

La. Cap. So shall you feel the loss, but not
    the friend
Which you weep for.

Jul.   Feeling so the loss,
I cannot choose but ever weep the friend.

La. Cap. Well, girl, thou weep'st not so
    much for his death,
As that the villain lives which slaughter'd him.

Jul. What villain, madam ?   81

La. Cap.   That same villain, Romeo.

Jul. [*Aside*] Villain and he be many miles
    asunder.—
God pardon him ! I do, with all my heart ;
And yet no man like he doth grieve my heart.

La. Cap. That is, because the traitor mur-
    derer lives.

Jul. Ay, madam, from the reach of these
    my hands :
Would none but I might venge my cousin's
    death !

La. Cap. We will have vengeance for it,
    fear thou not :
Then weep no more. I'll send to one in Man-
    tua,   89
Where that same banish'd runagate doth
    live,
Shall give him such an unaccustom'd dram,
That he shall soon keep Tybalt company :
And then, I hope, thou wilt be satisfied.

Jul. Indeed, I never shall be satisfied
With Romeo, till I behold him—dead—
Is my poor heart so for a kinsman vex'd.
Madam, if you could find out but a man
To bear a poison, I would temper it ;
That Romeo should, upon receipt thereof, 99
Soon sleep in quiet. O, how my heart abhors
To hear him named, and cannot come to him,
To wreak the love I bore my cousin
Upon his body that hath slaughter'd him !

La. Cap. Find thou the means, and I'll
    find such a man.
But now I'll tell thee joyful tidings, girl.

Jul. And joy comes well in such a needy
    time :
What are they, I beseech your ladyship ?

La. Cap. Well, well, thou hast a careful
    father, child ;
One who, to put thee from thy heaviness,
Hath sorted out a sudden day of joy,   110
That thou expect'st not nor I look'd not for.

Jul. Madam, in happy time, what day is
    that ?

La. Cap. Marry, my child, early next
    Thursday morn,
The gallant, young and noble gentleman,
The County Paris, at Saint Peter's Church,
Shall happily make thee there a joyful bride.

Jul. Now, by Saint Peter's Church and
    Peter too,
He shall not make me there a joyful bride.
I wonder at this haste ; that I must wed
Ere he, that should be husband, comes to
    woo.
I pray you, tell my lord and father, madam,

I will not marry yet; and, when I do, I swear,
It shall be Romeo, whom you know I hate,
Rather than Paris. These are news indeed!
La. Cap. Here comes your father; tell
him so yourself,
And see how he will take it at your hands.

Enter CAPULET *and* Nurse.

Cap. When the sun sets, the air doth driz-
zle dew;
But for the sunset of my brother's son
It rains downright.
How now! a conduit, girl? what, still in
tears?
Evermore showering? In one little body 131
Thou counterfeit'st a bark, a sea, a wind;
For still thy eyes, which I may call the sea,
Do ebb and flow with tears; the bark thy
body is,
Sailing in this salt flood; the winds, thy sighs;
Who, raging with thy tears, and they with
them,
Without a sudden calm, will overset
Thy tempest-tossed body. How now, wife!
Have you deliver'd to her our decree?
La. Cap. Ay, sir; but she will none, she
gives you thanks.   140
I would the fool were married to her grave!
Cap. Soft! take me with you, take me
with you, wife.
How! will she none? doth she not give us
thanks?
Is she not proud? doth she not count her
blest,
Unworthy as she is, that we have wrought
So worthy a gentleman to be her bride-
groom?
Jul. Not proud, you have; but thankful,
that you have:
Proud can I never be of what I hate;
But thankful even for hate, that is meant love.
Cap. How now, how now, chop-logic!
What is this?   150
'Proud,' and 'I thank you,' and 'I thank you
not;'
And yet 'not proud,' mistress minion, you,
Thank me no thankings, nor, proud me no
prouds,
But fettle your fine joints 'gainst Thursday
next,
To go with Paris to Saint Peter's Church,
Or I will drag thee on a hurdle thither.
Out, you green-sickness carrion! out, you bag-
gage!
You tallow-face!
La. Cap. Fie, fie! what, are you mad?
Jul. Good father, I beseech you on my
knees,
Hear me with patience but to speak a word.
Cap. Hang thee, young baggage! disobe-
dient wretch!   161
I tell thee what: get thee to church o' Thurs-
day,
Or never after look me in the face:
Speak not, reply not, do not answer me;
My fingers itch. Wife, we scarce thought us
blest
That God had lent us but this only child;
But now I see this one is one too much,
And that we have a curse in having her:
Out on her, hilding!
Nurse.   God in heaven bless her!
You are to blame, my lord, to rate her so. 170

Cap. And why, my lady wisdom? hold your
tongue,
Good prudence; smatter with your gossips, go.
Nurse. I speak no treason.
Cap.   O, God ye god-den.
Nurse. May not one speak?
Cap.   Peace, you mumbling fool!
Utter your gravity o'er a gossip's bowl;
For here we need it not.
La. Cap.   You are too hot.
Cap. God's bread! it makes me mad:
Day, night, hour, tide, time, work, play,
Alone, in company, still my care hath been
To have her match'd: and having now pro-
vided   180
A gentleman of noble parentage,
Of fair demesnes, youthful, and nobly train'd,
Stuff'd, as they say, with honorable parts,
Proportion'd as one's thought would wish a
man;
And then to have a wretched puling fool,
A whining mammet, in her fortune's tender,
To answer 'I'll not wed; I cannot love,
I am too young; I pray you, pardon me.'
But, as you will not wed, I'll pardon you:
Graze where you will, you shall not house with
me: 190
Look to't, think on't, I do not use to jest.
Thursday is near; lay hand on heart, advise:
An you be mine, I'll give you to my friend;
And you be not, hang, beg, starve, die in the
streets,
For, by my soul, I'll ne'er acknowledge thee,
Nor what is mine shall never do thee good:
Trust to't, bethink you; I'll not be forsworn.
          [Exit.
Jul. Is there no pity sitting in the clouds,
That sees into the bottom of my grief?
O, sweet my mother, cast me not away! 200
Delay this marriage for a month, a week;
Or, if you do not, make the bridal bed
In that dim monument where Tybalt lies.
La. Cap. Talk not to me, for I'll not
speak a word:
Do as thou wilt, for I have done with thee.
          [Exit.
Jul. O God!—O nurse, how shall this be
prevented?
My husband is on earth, my faith in heaven;
How shall that faith return again to earth,
Unless that husband send it me from heaven
By leaving earth? comfort me, counsel me.
Alack, alack, that heaven should practise
stratagems   211
Upon so soft a subject as myself!
What say'st thou? hast thou not a word of
joy?
Some comfort, nurse.
Nurse.   Faith, here it is.
Romeo is banish'd; and all the world to noth-
ing,
That he dares ne'er come back to challenge
you;
Or, if he do, it needs must be by stealth.
Then, since the case so stands as now it doth,
I think it best you married with the county.
O, he's a lovely gentleman!   220
Romeo's a dishclout to him: an eagle, madam,
Hath not so green, so quick, so fair an eye
As Paris hath. Beshrew my very heart,
I think you are happy in this second match,
For it excels your first: or if it did not,
Your first is dead; or 'twere as good he were,

As living here and you no use of him.
 Jul. Speakest thou from thy heart ?
 Nurse.   And from my soul too ;
Or else beshrew them both.
 Jul.   Amen !
 Nurse.   What ?
 Jul. Well, thou hast comforted me marvel-
  lous much.   230
Go in ; and tell my lady, I am gone,
Having displeased my father, to Laurence'
  cell,
To make confession and to be absolved.
 Nurse. Marry, I will ; and this is wisely
  done.   [*Exit.*
 Jul. Ancient damnation ! O most wicked
  fiend !
Is it more sin to wish me thus forsworn,
Or to dispraise my lord with that same tongue
Which she hath praised him with above com-
  pare
So many thousand times ? Go, counsellor ;
Thou and my bosom henceforth shall be twain.
I'll to the friar, to know his remedy :   241
If all else fail, myself have power to die.
                    [*Exit.*

ACT IV.

Scene I. *Friar Laurence's cell.*

Enter Friar Laurence *and* Paris.

 Fri. L. On Thursday, sir ? the time is very
  short.
 Par. My father Capulet will have it so ;
And I am nothing slow to slack his haste.
 Fri. L. You say you do not know the lady's
  mind :
Uneven is the course, I like it not.
 Par. Immoderately she weeps for Tybalt's
  death,
And therefore have I little talk'd of love ;
For Venus smiles not in a house of tears.
Now, sir, her father counts it dangerous
That she doth give her sorrow so much sway,
And in his wisdom hastes our marriage,   11
To stop the inundation of her tears ;
Which, too much minded by herself alone,
May be put from her by society :
Now do you know the reason of this haste.
 Fri. L. [*Aside*] I would I knew not why it
  should be slow'd.
Look, sir, here comes the lady towards my
  cell.

Enter Juliet.

 Par. Happily met, my lady and my wife !
 Jul. That may be, sir, when I may be a
  wife.
 Par. That may be must be, love, on Thurs-
  day next.   20
 Jul. What must be shall be.
 Fri. L.   That's a certain text.
 Par. Come you to make confession to this
  father ?
 Jul. To answer that, I should confess to
  you.
 Par. Do not deny to him that you love me.
 Jul. I will confess to you that I love him.
 Par. So will ye, I am sure, that you love
  me.
 Jul. If I do so, it will be of more price,

Being spoke behind your back, than to your
  face.
 Par. Poor soul, thy face is much abused
  with tears.
 Jul. The tears have got small victory by
  that ;   30
For it was bad enough before their spite.
 Par. Thou wrong'st it, more than tears,
  with that report.
 Jul. That is no slander, sir, which is a
  truth ;
And what I spake, I spake it to my face.
 Par. Thy face is mine, and thou hast
  slander'd it.
 Jul. It may be so, for it is not mine own.
Are you at leisure, holy father, now ;
Or shall I come to you at evening mass ?
 Fri. L. My leisure serves me, pensive
  daughter, now.
My lord, we must entreat the time alone.   40
 Par. God shield I should disturb devo-
  tion !
Juliet, on Thursday early will I rouse ye :
Till then, adieu ; and keep this holy kiss.
                    [*Exit.*
 Jul. O, shut the door ! and when thou hast
  done so,
Come weep with me ; past hope, past cure,
  past help !
 Fri. L. Ah, Juliet, I already know thy
  grief ;
It strains me past the compass of my wits :
I hear thou must, and nothing may prorogue
  it,
On Thursday next be married to this county.
 Jul. Tell me not, friar, that thou hear'st of
  this,   50
Unless thou tell me how I may prevent it :
If, in thy wisdom, thou canst give no help,
Do thou but call my resolution wise,
And with this knife I'll help it presently.
God join'd my heart and Romeo's, thou our
  hands ;
And ere this hand, by thee to Romeo seal'd,
Shall be the label to another deed,
Or my true heart with treacherous revolt
Turn to another, this shall slay them both :
Therefore, out of thy long-experienced time,
Give me some present counsel, or, behold, 61
'Twixt my extremes and me this bloody knife
Shall play the umpire, arbitrating that
Which the commission of thy years and art
Could to no issue of true honor bring.
Be not so long to speak ; I long to die,
If what thou speak'st speak not of remedy.
 Fri. L. Hold, daughter : I do spy a kind
  of hope,
Which craves as desperate an execution.
As that is desperate which we would prevent.
If, rather than to marry County Paris,   71
Thou hast the strength of will to slay thyself,
Then is it likely thou wilt undertake
A thing like death to chide away this shame,
That copest with death himself to scape from
  it :
And, if thou darest, I'll give thee remedy.
 Jul. O, bid me leap, rather than marry
  Paris,
From off the battlements of yonder tower ;
Or walk in thievish ways ; or bid me lurk
Where serpents are ; chain me with roaring
  bears ;   80
Or shut me nightly in a charnel-house,

O'er-cover'd quite with dead men's rattling bones,
With reeky shanks and yellow chapless skulls ;
Or bid me go into a new-made grave
And hide me with a dead man in his shroud ;
Things that, to hear them told, have made me tremble ;
And I will do it without fear or doubt,
To live an unstain'd wife to my sweet love.
Fri. L. Hold, then ; go home, be merry, give consent
To marry Paris : Wednesday is to-morrow :
To-morrow night look that thou lie alone ; 91
Let not thy nurse lie with thee in thy chamber :
Take thou this vial, being then in bed,
And this distilled liquor drink thou off ;
When presently through all thy veins shall run
A cold and drowsy humor, for no pulse
Shall keep his native progress, but surcease :
No warmth, no breath, shall testify thou livest ;
The roses in thy lips and cheeks shall fade
To paly ashes, thy eyes' windows fall, 100
Like death, when he shuts up the day of life ;
Each part, deprived of supple government,
Shall, stiff and stark and cold, appear like death :
And in this borrow'd likeness of shrunk death
Thou shalt continue two and forty hours,
And then awake as from a pleasant sleep.
Now, when the bridegroom in the morning comes
To rouse thee from thy bed, there art thou dead :
Then, as the manner of our country is,
In thy best robes uncover'd on the bier 110
Thou shalt be borne to that same ancient vault
Where all the kindred of the Capulets lie.
In the mean time, against thou shalt awake,
Shall Romeo by my letters know our drift,
And hither shall he come : and he and I
Will watch thy waking, and that very night
Shall Romeo bear thee hence to Mantua.
And this shall free thee from this present shame ;
If no inconstant toy, nor womanish fear,
Abate thy valor in the acting it. 120
Jul. Give me, give me ! O, tell not me of fear !
Fri. L. Hold ; get you gone, be strong and prosperous
In this resolve : I'll send a friar with speed
To Mantua, with my letters to thy lord.
Jul. Love give me strength ! and strength shall help afford.
Farewell, dear father ! [*Exeunt.*

SCENE II. *Hall in Capulet's house.*

Enter CAPULET, LADY CAPULET, Nurse, *and two* Servingmen.

Cap. So many guests invite as here are writ. [*Exit First Servant.*
Sirrah, go hire me twenty cunning cooks.
Sec. Serv. You shall have none ill, sir ; for I'll try if they can lick their fingers.
Cap. How canst thou try them so ?
Sec. Serv. Marry, sir, 'tis an ill cook that cannot lick his own fingers : therefore he that cannot lick his fingers goes not with me.
Cap. Go, be gone. [*Exit Sec. Servant.*
We shall be much unfurnished for this time.

What, is my daughter gone to Friar Laurence ? 11
Nurse. Ay, forsooth.
Cap. Well, he may chance to do some good on her :
A peevish self-will'd harlotry it is.
Nurse. See where she comes from shrift with merry look.

Enter JULIET.

Cap. How now, my headstrong ! where have you been gadding ?
Jul. Where I have learn'd me to repent the sin
Of disobedient opposition
To you and your behests, and am enjoin'd
By holy Laurence to fall prostrate here, 20
And beg your pardon : pardon, I beseech you !
Henceforward I am ever ruled by you.
Cap. Send for the county ; go tell him of this :
I'll have this knot knit up to-morrow morning.
Jul. I met the youthful lord at Laurence' cell ;
And gave him what becomed love I might,
Not stepping o'er the bounds of modesty.
Cap. Why, I am glad on't ; this is well : stand up :
This is as't should be. Let me see the county ;
Ay, marry, go, I say, and fetch him hither. 30
Now, afore God ! this reverend holy friar,
Our whole city is much bound to him.
Jul. Nurse, will you go with me into my closet,
To help me sort such needful ornaments
As you think fit to furnish me to-morrow ?
La. Cap. No, not till Thursday ; there is time enough.
Cap. Go, nurse, go with her : we'll to church to-morrow.
 [*Exeunt Juliet and Nurse.*
La. Cap. We shall be short in our provision :
'Tis now near night.
Cap.   Tush, I will stir about,
And all things shall be well, I warrant thee, wife : 40
Go thou to Juliet, help to deck up her ;
I'll not to bed to-night ; let me alone ;
I'll play the housewife for this once. What, ho !
They are all forth. Well, I will walk myself
To County Paris, to prepare him up
Against to-morrow : my heart is wondrous light,
Since this same wayward girl is so reclaim'd.
 [*Exeunt.*

SCENE III. *Juliet's chamber.*

Enter JULIET *and* Nurse.

Jul. Ay, those attires are best : but, gentle nurse,
I pray thee, leave me to myself to-night,
For I have need of many orisons
To move the heavens to smile upon my state,
Which, well thou know'st, is cross, and full of sin.

Enter LADY CAPULET.

La. Cap. What, are you busy, ho ? need you my help ?

Jul. No, madam; we have cull'd such nec-
    essaries
As are behoveful for our state to-morrow :
So please you, let me now be left alone,   9
And let the nurse this night sit up with you ;
For, I am sure, you have your hands full all,
In this so sudden business.
    La. Cap.   Good night :
Get thee to bed, and rest ; for thou hast need.
         [*Exeunt Lady Capulet and Nurse.*
Jul. Farewell ! God knows when we shall
    meet again.
I have a faint cold fear thrills through my
    veins,
That almost freezes up the heat of life :
I'll call them back again to comfort me :
Nurse ! What should she do here ?
My dismal scene I needs must act alone.
Come, vial.   20
What if this mixture do not work at all ?
Shall I be married then to-morrow morning ?
No, no : this shall forbid it : lie thou there.
         [*Laying down her dagger.*
What if it be a poison, which the friar
Subtly hath minister'd to have me dead,
Lest in this marriage he should be dishonor'd,
Because he married me before to Romeo ?
I fear it is : and yet, methinks, it should not,
For he hath still been tried a holy man.
How if, when I am laid into the tomb,   30
I wake before the time that Romeo
Come to redeem me ? there's a fearful point !
Shall I not, then, be stifled in the vault,
To whose foul mouth no healthsome air
    breathes in,
And there die strangled ere my Romeo comes ?
Or, if I live, is it not very like,
The horrible conceit of death and night,
Together with the terror of the place,—
As in a vault, an ancient receptacle,
Where, for these many hundred years, the
    bones   40
Of all my buried ancestors are packed :
Where bloody Tybalt, yet but green in earth,
Lies festering in his shroud ; where, as they
    say,
At some hours in the night spirits resort ;—
Alack, alack, is it not like that I,
So early waking, what with loathsome smells,
And shrieks like mandrakes' torn out of the
    earth,
That living mortals, hearing them, run mad :—
O, if I wake, shall I not be distraught,   50
Environed with all these hideous fears ?
And madly play with my forefather's joints ?
And pluck the mangled Tybalt from his
    shroud ?
And, in this rage, with some great kinsman's
    bone,
As with a club, dash out my desperate brains ?
O, look ! methinks I see my cousin's ghost
Seeking out Romeo, that did spit his body
Upon a rapier's point : stay, Tybalt, stay !
Romeo, I come ! this do I drink to thee.
    [*She falls upon her bed, within the curtains.*

    Scene IV. *Hall in Capulet's house.*
    Enter Lady Capulet *and* Nurse.

La. Cap. Hold, take these keys, and fetch
    more spices, nurse.
Nurse. They call for dates and quinces in
    the pastry.

    Enter Capulet.

Cap. Come, stir, stir, stir ! the second
    cock hath crow'd,
The curfew-bell hath rung, 'tis three o'clock :
Look to the baked meats, good Angelica :
Spare not for cost.
    Nurse.   Go, you cot-quean, go,
Get you to bed ; faith, you'll be sick to-mor-
    row
For this night's watching.
    Cap. No, not a whit : what ! I have
    watch'd ere now
All night for lesser cause, and ne'er been sick.
    La. Cap. Ay, you have been a mouse-hunt
    in your time ;   11
But I will watch you from such watching now.
        [*Exeunt Lady Capulet and Nurse.*
Cap. A jealous hood, a jealous hood !

Enter three or four Servingmen, *with spits,
    logs, and baskets.*

                           Now, fellow,
What's there ?
    First Serv. Things for the cook, sir ; but I
    know not what.
    Cap. Make haste, make haste.
                        [*Exit First Serv.*
Sirrah, fetch drier logs :
Call Peter, he will show thee where they are.
    Sec. Serv. I have a head, sir, that will
    find out logs,
And never trouble Peter for the matter. [*Exit.*
    Cap. Mass, and well said ; a merry whore-
    son, ha !
Thou shalt be logger-head. Good faith, 'tis
    day :   20
The county will be here with music straight,
For so he said he would : I hear him near.
                        [*Music within.*
Nurse ! Wife ! What, ho ! What, nurse, I say !

    Re-enter Nurse.

Go waken Juliet, go and trim her up ;
I'll go and chat with Paris : hie, make haste,
Make haste ; the bridegroom he is come al-
    ready :
Make haste, I say.   [*Exeunt.*

    Scene V. *Juliet's chamber.*
    Enter Nurse.

Nurse. Mistress ! what, mistress ! Juliet !
    fast, I warrant her, she :
Why, lamb ! why, lady ! fie, you slug-a-bed !
Why, love, I say ! madam ! sweet-heart ! why,
    bride !
What, not a word ? you take your penny-
    worths now ;
Sleep for a week ; for the next night, I war-
    rant,
The County Paris hath set up his rest,
That you shall rest but little. God forgive me,
Marry, and amen, how sound is she asleep !
I must needs wake her. Madam, madam,
    madam !
Ay, let the county take you in your bed ;   10
He'll fright you up, i' faith. Will it not be ?
                [*Undraws the curtains.*
What, dress'd ! and in your clothes ! and
    down again !
I must needs wake you ; Lady ! lady ! lady !
Alas, alas ! Help, help ! my lady's dead !
O, well-a-day, that ever I was born !

Some aqua vitæ, ho! My lord! my lady!

Enter LADY CAPULET.

La. Cap. What noise is here?
Nurse.   O lamentable day!
La. Cap. What is the matter?
Nurse.   Look, look! O heavy day!
La. Cap. O me, O me! My child, my
    only life,
Revive, look up, or I will die with thee!   20
Help, help! Call help.

Enter CAPULET.

Cap. For shame, bring Juliet forth; her
    lord is come.
Nurse. She's dead, deceased, she's dead;
    alack the day!
La. Cap. Alack the day, she's dead, she's
    dead, she's dead!
Cap. Ha! let me see her: out, alas! she's
    cold;
Her blood is settled, and her joints are stiff;
Life and these lips have long been separated:
Death lies on her like an untimely frost
Upon the sweetest flower of all the field.
Nurse. O lamentable day!
La. Cap.   O woful time! 30
Cap. Death, that hath ta'en her hence to
    make me wail,
Ties up my tongue, and will not let me speak.

Enter FRIAR LAURENCE *and* PARIS, *with*
    Musicians.

Fri. L. Come, is the bride ready to go to
    church?
Cap. Ready to go, but never to return.
O son! the night before thy wedding-day
Hath Death lain with thy wife. There she lies,
Flower as she was, deflowered by him.
Death is my son-in-law, Death is my heir;
My daughter he hath wedded: I will die,
And leave him all; life, living, all is Death's.
Par. Have I thought long to see this morn-
    ing's face,   41
And doth it give me such a sight as this?
La. Cap. Accursed, unhappy, wretched,
    hateful day!
Most miserable hour that e'er time saw
In lasting labor of his pilgrimage!
But one, poor one, one poor and loving child,
But one thing to rejoice and solace in,
And cruel death hath catch'd it from my
    sight!
Nurse. O woe! O woful, woful, woful
    day!
Most lamentable day, most woful day,   50
That ever, ever, I did yet behold!
O day! O day! O day! O hateful day!
Never was seen so black a day as this:
O woful day, O woful day!
Par. Beguiled, divorced, wronged, spited,
    slain!
Most detestable death, by thee beguil'd,
By cruel cruel thee quite overthrown!
O love! O life! not life, but love in death!
Cap. Despised, distressed, hated, martyr'd,
    kill'd!
Uncomfortable time, why camest thou now 60
To murder, murder our solemnity?
O child! O child! my soul, and not my child!
Dead art thou! Alack! my child is dead;
And with my child my joys are buried.

Fri. L. Peace, ho, for shame! confusion's
    cure lives not
In these confusions. Heaven and yourself
Had part in this fair maid; now heaven hath
    all,
And all the better is it for the maid:
Your part in her you could not keep from
    death,
But heaven keeps his part in eternal life.   70
The most you sought was her promotion;
For 'twas your heaven she should be ad-
    vanced:
And weep ye now, seeing she is advanced
Above the clouds, as high as heaven itself?
O, in this love, you love your child so ill,
That you run mad, seeing that she is well:
She's not well married that lives married
    long;
But she's best married that dies married
    young.
Dry up your tears, and stick your rosemary
On this fair corse; and, as the custom is,   80
In all her best array bear her to church:
For though fond nature bids us all lament,
Yet nature's tears are reason's merriment.
Cap. All things that we ordained festival,
Turn from their office to black funeral;
Our instruments to melancholy bells,
Our wedding cheer to a sad burial feast,
Our solemn hymns to sullen dirges change,
Our bridal flowers serve for a buried corse,
And all things change them to the contrary.
Fri. L. Sir, go you in; and, madam, go
    with him;
And go, Sir Paris; every one prepare
To follow this fair corse unto her grave:
The heavens do lour upon you for some ill;
Move them no more by crossing their high
    will.
    [*Exeunt Capulet, Lady Capulet,
        Paris, and Friar.*
First Mus. Faith, we may put up our
    pipes, and be gone.
Nurse. Honest goodfellows, ah, put up, put
    up;
For, well you know, this is a pitiful case. 100
    [*Exit.*
First Mus. Ay, by my troth, the case
    may be amended.

Enter PETER.

Pet. Musicians, O, musicians, 'Heart's
ease, Heart's ease:' O, an you will have me
live, play 'Heart's ease.'
First Mus. Why 'Heart's ease?'
Pet. O, musicians, because my heart itself
plays 'My heart is full of woe:' O, play me
some merry dump, to comfort me.
First Mus. Not a dump we; 'tis no time to
play now.   110
Pet. You will not, then?
First Mus. No.
Pet. I will then give it you soundly.
First Mus. What will you give us?
Pet. No money, on my faith, but the gleek;
I will give you the minstrel.
First Mus. Then will I give you the serv-
ing-creature.
Pet. Then will I lay the serving-creature's
dagger on your pate. I will carry no crotch-
ets: I'll re you, I'll fa you; do you note me?
First Mus. An you re us and fa us, you
note us.

Sec. Mus. Pray you, put up your dagger,
and put out your wit.

Pet. Then have at you with my wit! I will
dry-beat you with an iron wit, and put up my
iron dagger. Answer me like men :

  ' When griping grief the heart doth wound,
    And doleful dumps the mind oppress,
  Then music with her silver sound '—   130
why ' silver sound ' ? why ' music with her
silver sound ' ? What say you, Simon Cat-
ling ?

First Mus. Marry, sir, because silver hath
a sweet sound.

Pet. Pretty ! What say you, Hugh Re-
beck ?

Sec. Mus. I say ' silver sound,' because
musicians sound for silver.

Pet. Pretty too ! What say you, James
Soundpost ?   139

Third Mus. Faith, I know not what to say.

Pet. O, I cry you mercy ; you are the
singer : I will say for you. It is ' music with
her silver sound,' because musicians have no
gold for sounding :

  ' Then music with her silver sound
  With speedy help doth lend redress.'
                     [Exit.

First Mus. What a pestilent knave is this
same !

Sec. Mus. Hang him, Jack ! Come, we'll in
here ; tarry for the mourners, and stay dinner.   *[Exeunt.*

ACT V.

Scene I. *Mantua. A street.*

Enter Romeo.

Rom. If I may trust the flattering truth of
  sleep,
My dreams presage some joyful news at
  hand :
My bosom's lord sits lightly in his throne ;
And all this day an unaccustom'd spirit
Lifts me above the ground with cheerful
  thoughts.
I dreamt my lady came and found me dead—
Strange dream, that gives a dead man leave to
  think !—
And breathed such life with kisses in my lips,
That I revived, and was an emperor.
Ah me! how sweet is love itself possess'd, 10
When but love's shadows are so rich in joy !

Enter Balthasar, *booted.*

News from Verona !—How now, Balthasar !
Dost thou not bring me letters from the friar ?
How doth my lady ? Is my father well ?
How fares my Juliet ? that I ask again ;
For nothing can be ill, if she be well.

Bal. Then she is well, and nothing can be
  ill :
Her body sleeps in Capel's monument,
And her immortal part with angels lives.
I saw her laid low in her kindred's vault, 20
And presently took post to tell it you :
O, pardon me for bringing these ill news,
Since you did leave it for my office, sir.

Rom. Is it even so ? then I defy you, stars !
Thou know'st my lodging : get me ink and
  paper,
And hire post-horses ; I will hence to-night.

Bal. I do beseech you, sir, have patience :
Your looks are pale and wild, and do im-
  port
Some misadventure.

Rom.   Tush, thou art deceived :
Leave me, and do the thing I bid thee do. 30
Hast thou no letters to me from the friar ?

Bal. No, my good lord.

Rom.   No matter : get thee gone,
And hire those horses ; I'll be with thee
  straight.   *[Exit Balthasar.*
Well, Juliet, I will lie with thee to-night.
Let's see for means : O mischief, thou art
  swift
To enter in the thoughts of desperate men !
I do remember an apothecary,—
And hereabouts he dwells,—which late I
  noted
In tatter'd weeds, with overwhelming brows,
Culling of simples ; meagre were his looks, 40
Sharp misery had worn him to the bones :
And in his needy shop a tortoise hung,
An alligator stuff'd, and other skins
Of ill-shaped fishes ; and about his shelves
A beggarly account of empty boxes,
Green earthen pots, bladders and musty
  seeds,
Remnants of packthread and old cakes of
  roses,
Were thinly scatter'd, to make up a show.
Noting this penury, to myself I said
' An if a man did need a poison now, 50
Whose sale is present death in Mantua,
Here lives a caitiff wretch would sell it him.'
O, this same thought did but forerun my
  need ;
And this same needy man must sell it me.
As I remember, this should be the house.
Being holiday, the beggar's shop is shut.
What, ho ! apothecary !

Enter Apothecary.

Ap.   Who calls so loud ?

Rom. Come hither, man. I see that thou
  art poor :
Hold, there is forty ducats : let me have
A dram of poison, such soon-speeding gear 60
As will disperse itself through all the veins
That the life-weary taker may fall dead
And that the trunk may be discharged of
  breath
As violently as hasty powder fired
Doth hurry from the fatal cannon's womb.

Ap. Such mortal drugs I have ; but Mantua's law
Is death to any he that utters them.

Rom. Art thou so bare and full of
  wretchedness,
And fear'st to die ? famine is in thy cheeks,
Need and oppression starveth in thine eyes, 70
Contempt and beggary hangs upon thy back ;
The world is not thy friend nor the world's
  law ;
The world affords no law to make thee rich ;
Then be not poor, but break it, and take this.

Ap. My poverty, but not my will, consents.

Rom. I pay thy poverty, and not thy will.

Ap. Put this in any liquid thing you will,
And drink it off ; and, if you had the strength
Of twenty men, it would dispatch you straight.

Rom. There is thy gold, worse poison to
  men's souls, 80
Doing more murders in this loathsome world,

Than these poor compounds that thou mayst
not sell.
I sell thee poison ; thou hast sold me none.
Farewell : buy food, and get thyself in flesh.
Come, cordial and not poison, go with me
To Juliet's grave ; for there must I use thee.
[*Exeunt.*

SCENE II. *Friar Laurence's cell.*

Enter FRIAR JOHN.

Friar J. Holy Franciscan friar ! brother,
ho !

Enter FRIAR LAURENCE.

Fri. L. This same should be the voice of
Friar John.
Welcome from Mantua : what says Romeo ?
Or, if his mind be writ, give me his letter.
Fri. J. Going to find a bare-foot brother
out,
One of our order, to associate me,
Here in this city visiting the sick,
And finding him, the searchers of the town,
Suspecting that we both were in a house
Where the infectious pestilence did reign,   10
Seal'd up the doors, and would not let us
forth ;
So that my speed to Mantua there was stay'd.
Fri. L. Who bare my letter, then, to
Romeo ?
Fri. J. I could not send it,—here it is
again,—
Nor get a messenger to bring it thee,
So fearful were they of infection.
Fri. L. Unhappy fortune ! by my brother-
hood,
The letter was not nice but full of charge
Of dear import, and the neglecting it
May do much danger. Friar John, go hence ;
Get me an iron crow, and bring it straight 21
Unto my cell.
Fri. J. Brother, I'll go and bring it thee.
[*Exit.*
Fri. L. Now must I to the monument
alone ;
Within this three hours will fair Juliet wake :
She will beshrew me much that Romeo
Hath had no notice of these accidents ;
But I will write again to Mantua,
And keep her at my cell till Romeo come ;
Poor living corse, closed in a dead man's
tomb !   [*Exit.*

SCENE III. *A churchyard ; in it a tomb
belonging to the Capulets.*

Enter PARIS, *and his* Page *bearing flowers
and a torch.*

Par. Give me thy torch, boy : hence, and
stand aloof :
Yet put it out, for I would not be seen.
Under yond yew-trees lay thee all along,
Holding thine ear close to the hollow ground ;
So shall no foot upon the churchyard tread,
Being loose, unfirm, with digging up of graves,
But thou shalt hear it : whistle then to me,
As signal that thou hear'st something approach.
Give me those flowers. Do as I bid thee, go.
Page. [*Aside*] I am almost afraid to stand
alone   10
Here in the churchyard ; yet I will adventure.
[*Retires.*

Par. Sweet flower, with flowers thy bridal
bed I strew,—
O woe ! thy canopy is dust and stones ;—
Which with sweet water nightly I will dew,
Or, wanting that, with tears distill'd by
moans :
The obsequies that I for thee will keep
Nightly shall be to strew thy grave and weep.
[*The Page whistles.*
The boy gives warning something doth ap-
proach.
What cursed foot wanders this way to-night,
To cross my obsequies and true love's rite ? 20
What with a torch ! muffle me, night, awhile.
[*Retires.*

Enter ROMEO *and* BALTHASAR, *with a torch,
mattock, &c.*

Rom. Give me that mattock and the
wrenching iron.
Hold, take this letter ; early in the morning
See thou deliver it to my lord and father.
Give me the light : upon thy life, I charge
thee,
Whate'er thou hear'st or seest, stand all aloof,
And do not interrupt me in my course.
Why I descend into this bed of death,
Is partly to behold my lady's face ;
But chiefly to take thence from her dead
finger
A precious ring, a ring that I must use   31
In dear employment : therefore hence, be
gone :
But if thou, jealous, dost return to pry
In what I further shall intend to do,
By heaven, I will tear thee joint by joint
And strew this hungry churchyard with thy
limbs :
The time and my intents are savage-wild,
More fierce and more inexorable far
Than empty tigers or the roaring sea.
Bal. I will be gone, sir, and not trouble
you.
Rom. So shalt thou show me friendship.
Take thou that :   41
Live, and be prosperous : and farewell, good
fellow.
Bal. [*Aside*] For all this same, I'll hide
me hereabout :
His looks I fear, and his intents I doubt.
[*Retires.*
Rom. Thou detestable maw, thou womb
of death,
Gorged with the dearest morsel of the earth,
Thus I enforce thy rotten jaws to open,
And, in despite, I'll cram thee with more
food !   [*Opens the tomb.*
Par. This is that banish'd haughty Mon-
tague,
That murder'd my love's cousin, with which
grief,   50
It is supposed, the fair creature died ;
And here is come to do some villanous shame
To the dead bodies : I will apprehend him.
[*Comes forward.*
Stop thy unhallow'd toil, vile Montague !
Can vengeance be pursued further than
death ?
Condemned villain, I do apprehend thee :
Obey, and go with me ; for thou must die.
Rom. I must indeed ; and therefore came
I hither.

Good gentle youth, tempt not a desperate
    man ;
Fly hence, and leave me : think upon these
    gone ;   60
Let them affright thee. I beseech thee, youth,
Put not another sin upon my head,
By urging me to fury : O, be gone !
By heaven, I love thee better than myself ;
For I come hither arm'd against myself :
Stay not, be gone ; live, and hereafter say,
A madman's mercy bade thee run away.
  Par.   I do defy thy conjurations,
And apprehend thee for a felon here.
  Rom.   Wilt thou provoke me ? then have at
    thee, boy !   [*They fight.* 70
  Page.   O Lord, they fight ! I will go call
    the watch.   [*Exit.*
  Par.   O, I am slain ! [*Falls.*] If thou be
    merciful,
Open the tomb, lay me with Juliet.   [*Dies.*
  Rom.   In faith, I will. Let me peruse this
    face.
Mercutio's kinsman, noble County Paris !
What said my man, when my betossed soul
Did not attend him as we rode ? I think
He told me Paris should have married Juliet :
Said he not so ? or did I dream it so ?
Or am I mad, hearing him talk of Juliet,   80
To think it was so ? O, give me thy hand,
One writ with me in sour misfortune's book !
I'll bury thee in a triumphant grave ;
A grave ? O, no ! a lantern, slaughter'd youth,
For here lies Juliet, and her beauty makes
This vault a feasting presence full of light.
Death, lie thou there, by a dead man interr'd.
    [*Laying Paris in the tomb.*
How oft when men are at the point of death
Have they been merry ! which their keepers
    call
A lightning before death : O, how may I   90
Call this a lightning ? O my love ! my wife !
Death, that hath suck'd the honey of thy
    breath,
Hath had no power yet upon thy beauty :
Thou art not conquer'd ; beauty's ensign yet
Is crimson in thy lips and in thy cheeks,
And death's pale flag is not advanced there.
Tybalt, liest thou there in thy bloody sheet ?
O, what more favor can I do to thee,
Than with that hand that cut thy youth in
    twain
To sunder his that was thine enemy ?   100
Forgive me, cousin ! Ah, dear Juliet,
Why art thou yet so fair ? shall I believe
That unsubstantial death is amorous,
And that the lean abhorred monster keeps
Thee here in dark to be his paramour ?
For fear of that, I still will stay with thee ;
And never from this palace of dim night
Depart again : here, here will I remain
With worms that are thy chamber-maids ; O,
    here
Will I set up my everlasting rest,   110
And shake the yoke of inauspicious stars
From this world-wearied flesh. Eyes, look
    your last !
Arms, take your last embrace ! and, lips, O
    you
The doors of breath, seal with a righteous kiss
A dateless bargain to engrossing death !
Come, bitter conduct, come, unsavory guide !
Thou desperate pilot, now at once run on
The dashing rocks thy sea-sick weary bark !

Here's to my love ! [*Drinks.*] O true apothe-
    cary !   119
Thy drugs are quick. Thus with a kiss I die.
    [*Dies.*

Enter, at the other end of the churchyard,
FRIAR LAURENCE, *with a lantern, crow, and
spade.*
  Fri. L.   Saint Francis be my speed ! how
    oft to-night
Have my old feet stumbled at graves ! Who's
    there ?
  Bal.   Here's one, a friend, and one that
    knows you well.
  Fri. L.   Bliss be upon you ! Tell me, good
    my friend,
What torch is yond, that vainly lends his light
To grubs and eyeless skulls ? as I discern,
It burneth in the Capel's monument.
  Bal.   It doth so, holy sir ; and there's my
    master,
One that you love.
  Fri. L.   Who is it ?
  Bal.   Romeo.
  Fri. L.   How long hath he been there ?
  Bal.   Full half an hour. 130
  Fri. L.   Go with me to the vault.
  Bal.   I dare not, sir :
My master knows not but I am gone hence ;
And fearfully did menace me with death,
If I did stay to look on his intents.
  Fri. L.   Stay, then ; I'll go alone. Fear
    comes upon me :
O, much I fear some ill unlucky thing.
  Bal.   As I did sleep under this yew-tree
    here,
I dreamt my master and another fought,
And that my master slew him.
  Fri. L.   Romeo !
    [*Advances.*
Alack, alack, what blood is this, which stains
The stony entrance of this sepulchre ?
What mean these masterless and gory swords
To lie discolor'd by this place of peace ?
    [*Enters the tomb.*
Romeo ! O, pale ! Who else ? what, Paris too ?
And steep'd in blood ? Ah, what an unkind
    hour
Is guilty of this lamentable chance !
The lady stirs.   [*Juliet wakes.*
  Jul.   O comfortable friar ! where is my
    lord ?
I do remember well where I should be,
And there I am. Where is my Romeo ?   150
    [*Noise within.*
  Fri. L.   I hear some noise. Lady, come
    from that nest
Of death, contagion, and unnatural sleep :
A greater power than we can contradict
Hath thwarted our intents. Come, come away.
Thy husband in thy bosom there lies dead ;
And Paris too. Come, I'll dispose of thee
Among a sisterhood of holy nuns :
Stay not to question, for the watch is coming ;
Come, go, good Juliet [*Noise again*], I dare
    no longer stay.
  Jul.   Go, get thee hence, for I will not
    away.   [*Exit Fri. L.* 160
What's here ? a cup, closed in my true love's
    hand ?
Poison, I see, hath been his timeless end :
O churl ! drunk all, and left no friendly drop
To help me after ? I will kiss thy lips ;

Haply some poison yet doth hang on them,
To make me die with a restorative.
                              [*Kisses him.*
Thy lips are warm.
  First Watch. [*Within*] Lead, boy : which
      way ?
  Jul. Yea, noise ? then I'll be brief. O
      happy dagger !
                [*Snatching Romeo's dagger.*
This is thy sheath [*Stabs herself*] ; there rust,
      and let me die.   170
      [*Falls on Romeo's body, and dies.*

  Enter Watch, *with the* Page *of* PARIS.

  Page. This is the place ; there, where the
      torch doth burn.
  First Watch. The ground is bloody ; search
      about the churchyard :
Go, some of you, whoe'er you find attach.
Pitiful sight ! here lies the county slain ;
And Juliet bleeding, warm, and newly dead,
Who here hath lain these two days buried.
Go, tell the prince : run to the Capulets :
Raise up the Montagues : some others search :
We see the ground whereon these woes do lie ;
But the true ground of all these piteous woes
We cannot without circumstance descry.   181

  Re-enter some of the Watch, *with* BALTHASAR.

  Sec. Watch. Here's Romeo's man ; we
      found him in the churchyard.
  First Watch. Hold him in safety, till the
      prince come hither.

  Re-enter others of the Watch, *with* FRIAR
      LAURENCE.

  Third Watch. Here is a friar, that trem-
      bles, sighs and weeps :
We took this mattock and this spade from
      him,
As he was coming from this churchyard side.
  First Watch. A great suspicion : stay the
      friar too.

  Enter the PRINCE *and* Attendants.

  Prince. What misadventure is so early up,
That calls our person from our morning's
      rest ?

  Enter CAPULET, LADY CAPULET, *and others.*

  Cap. What should it be, that they so
      shriek abroad ?   190
  La. Cap. The people in the street cry
      Romeo,
Some Juliet, and some Paris ; and all run,
With open outcry toward our monument.
  Prince. What fear is this which startles in
      our ears ?
  First Watch. Sovereign, here lies the
      County Paris slain ;
And Romeo dead ; and Juliet, dead before,
Warm and new kill'd.
  Prince. Search, seek, and know how this
      foul murder comes.
  First Watch. Here is a friar, and slaugh-
      ter'd Romeo's man ;
With instruments upon them, fit to open   200
These dead men's tombs.
  Cap. O heavens ! O wife, look how our
      daughter bleeds !
This dagger hath mista'en—for, lo, his house
Is empty on the back of Montague,—
And it mis-sheathed in my daughter's bosom !

  La. Cap. O me ! this sight of death is as a
      bell,
That warns my old age to a sepulchre.

  Enter MONTAGUE *and others.*

  Prince. Come, Montague ; for thou art
      early up,
To see thy son and heir more early down.
  Mon. Alas, my liege, my wife is dead to-
      night ;   210
Grief of my son's exile hath stopp'd her
      breath :
What further woe conspires against mine age ?
  Prince. Look, and thou shalt see.
  Mon. O thou untaught ! what manners is
      in this ?
To press before thy father to a grave ?
  Prince. Seal up the mouth of outrage for
      a while,
Till we can clear these ambiguities,
And know their spring, their head, their true
      descent ;
And then will I be general of your woes,
And lead you even to death : meantime for-
      bear,   220
And let mischance be slave to patience.
Bring forth the parties of suspicion.
  Fri. L. I am the greatest, able to do least,
Yet most suspected, as the time and place
Doth make against me of this direful murder ;
And here I stand, both to impeach and purge
Myself condemned and myself excused.
  Prince. Then say at once what thou dost
      know in this.
  Fr. L. I will be brief, for my short date
      of breath
Is not so long as is a tedious tale.   230
Romeo, there dead, was husband to that
      Juliet ;
And she, there dead, that Romeo's faithful
      wife :
I married them ; and their stol'n marriage-day
Was Tybalt's dooms-day, whose untimely
      death
Banish'd the new-made bridegroom from the
      city,
For whom, and not for Tybalt, Juliet pined.
You, to remove that siege of grief from her,
Betroth'd and would have married her per-
      force
To County Paris : then comes she to me,
And, with wild looks, bid me devise some
      mean
To rid her from this second marriage,   241
Or in my cell there would she kill herself.
Then gave I her, so tutor'd by my art,
A sleeping potion ; which so took effect
As I intended, for it wrought on her
The form of death : meantime I writ to
      Romeo,
That he should hither come as this dire night,
To help to take her from her borrow'd grave,
Being the time the potion's force should cease.
But he which bore my letter, Friar John, 250
Was stay'd by accident, and yesternight
Return'd my letter back. Then all alone
At the prefixed hour of her waking,
Came I to take her from her kindred's vault ;
Meaning to keep her closely at my cell,
Till I conveniently could send to Romeo :
But when I came, some minute ere the time
Of her awaking, here untimely lay
The noble Paris and true Romeo dead.

She wakes ; and I entreated her come forth,
And bear this work of heaven with patience :
But then a noise did scare me from the tomb ;
And she, too desperate, would not go with me,
But, as it seems, did violence on herself.
All this I know ; and to the marriage
Her nurse is privy : and, if aught in this
Miscarried by my fault, let my old life
Be sacrificed, some hour before his time,
Unto the rigor of severest law.

   Prince. We still have known thee for a
      holy man.   270
Where's Romeo's man ? what can he say in
      this ?

   Bal. I brought my master news of Juliet's
      death ;
And then in post he came from Mantua
To this same place, to this same monument.
This letter he early bid me give his father,
And threatened me with death, going in the
      vault,
If I departed not and left him there.

   Prince. Give me the letter ; I will look on
      it.
Where is the county's page, that raised the
      watch ?
Sirrah, what made your master in this place ?

   Page. He came with flowers to strew his
      lady's grave ;   281
And bid me stand aloof, and so I did :
Anon comes one with light to ope the tomb ;
And by and by my master drew on him ;
And then I ran away to call the watch.

   Prince. This letter doth make good the
      friar's words,

Their course of love, the tidings of her death :
And here he writes that he did buy a poison
Of a poor 'pothecary, and therewithal
Came to this vault to die, and lie wth Juliet.
Where be these enemies ? Capulet ! Monta-
      gue !   291
See, what a scourge is laid upon your hate,
That heaven finds means to kill your joys with
      love.
And I for winking at your discords too
Have lost a brace of kinsmen : all are pun-
      ish'd.

   Cap. O brother Montague, give me thy
      hand :
This is my daughter's jointure, for no more
Can I demand.

   Mon.   But I can give thee more :
For I will raise her statue in pure gold ;
That while Verona by that name is known,
There shall no figure at such rate be set
As that of true and faithful Juliet.

   Cap. As rich shall Romeo's by his lady's
      lie ;
Poor sacrifices of our enmity !

   Prince. A glooming peace this morning
      with it brings ;
The sun, for sorrow, will not show his
      head :
Go hence, to have more talk of these sad
      things ;
Some shall be pardon'd, and some pun-
      ished :
For never was a story of more woe   309
Than this of Juliet and her Romeo. [*Exeunt.*

KING RICHARD II.

(WRITTEN ABOUT 1594.)

INTRODUCTION.

King Richard II. appeared in quarto in 1597. In 1608 a third edition was published "with new additions of the Parliament Scene and the deposing of King Richard," that is to say, with the added lines 154–318 in Act IV., Sc. I. It is probable that these lines were written as part of the original play, but relating as they did to the deposition of a king, had been omitted for fear of giving offence at a time when the Pope and Catholic princes were exhorting her subjects to dethrone Elizabeth. The date of the play is not ascertained, but it has been assigned, with an appearance of probability, to the year 1593 or 1594. Whether it preceded or followed *Richard III.* is a question in dispute. It is the inferior scenes which contain most rhymed verse ; the dramatist exhibits, as in *Romeo and Juliet,* mastery over blank verse, but is not yet free from the tendency to fall back into rhyme. Upon the whole *Richard II.* bears closer affinity to *King John* than to any other of Shakespeare's plays. Marlowe's genius, however, still exercises an influence over Shakespeare's imagination while he was fashioning his *Richard II.* Having in *Richard III.* (if it preceded the present play) brought the civil wars of England to an issue and an end, Shakespeare turned back to the reign of the earlier Richard, whose deposition led the way to the disputed succession and the conflicts of half a century later. The interest of the play centres in two connected things—the personal contrast between the falling and the rising kings, and the political action of each ; the misgovernment of the one inviting and almost justifying the usurpation of the other. Richard, though possessed of a certain regal charm and power of attaching tender natures to himself, is deficient in all that is sterling and real in manhood. He is self-indulgent, has much superficial sensitiveness, loves to contemplate in a romantic way whatever is pathetic or passionate in life, possesses a kind of rhetorical imagination, and has abundant command of delicate and gleaming words. His will is nerveless, he is incapable of consistency of feeling, incapable of strenuous action. Bolingbroke, on the other hand, who pushes Richard from his throne, is a man framed for such material success as waits on personal ambition. His is a resolute gaze which sees his object far off, and he has persistency and energy of will to carry him forward without faltering. His faculties are strong and well-knit ; he is not cruel, but shrinks from no deed that is needful to his purpose because the deed is cruel. There is no finer contrast in Shakespeare's historical plays than that between the figures of the formidable king of deeds and the romantic king of hectic feelings and brilliant words.

DRAMATIS PERSONÆ.

KING RICHARD the Second.
JOHN OF GAUNT, Duke of Lancaster,
EDMUND OF LANGLEY, Duke of York,
} uncles to the King.

HENRY, surnamed BOLINGBROKE, Duke of Hereford, son to John of Gaunt ; afterwards KING HENRY IV.
DUKE OF AUMERLE, son to the Duke of York.
THOMAS MOWBRAY, Duke of Norfolk.
DUKE OF SURREY.
EARL OF SALISBURY.
LORD BERKELEY.
BUSHY,
BAGOT,
GREEN,
} servants to King Richard.
EARL OF NORTHUMBERLAND.
HENRY PERCY, surnamed Hotspur, his son.

LORD ROSS.
LORD WILLOUGHBY.
LORD FITZWATER.
Bishop of Carlisle.
Abbot of Westminster.
Lord Marshal.
SIR STEPHEN SCROOP.
SIR PIERCE of Exton.
Captain of a band of Welshmen.

QUEEN to King Richard.
DUCHESS OF YORK.
DUCHESS OF GLOUCESTER.
Lady attending on the Queen.

Lords, Heralds, Officers, Soldiers, two Gardeners, Keeper, Messenger, Groom, and other Attendants.

SCENE : *England and Wales.*

ACT I.

Scene I. *London.* King Richard's *palace.*

Enter King Richard, John of Gaunt, *with other* Nobles *and* Attendants

K. Rich. Old John of Gaunt, time-honor'd
        Lancaster,
Hast thou, according to thy oath and band,
Brought hither Henry Hereford thy bold son,
Here to make good the boisterous late appeal,
Which then our leisure would not let us hear,
Against the Duke of Norfolk, Thomas Mow-
        bray?
    Gaunt. I have, my liege.
    K. Rich. Tell me, moreover, hast thou
        sounded him,
If he appeal the duke on ancient malice;
Or worthily, as a good subject should,   10
On some known ground of treachery in him?
    Gaunt. As near as I could sift him on that
        argument,
On some apparent danger seen in him
Aim'd at your highness, no inveterate malice.
    K. Rich. Then call them to our presence;
        face to face,
And frowning brow to brow, ourselves will
        hear
The accuser and the accused freely speak:
High-stomach'd are they both, and full of ire,
In rage deaf as the sea, hasty as fire.

Enter Bolingbroke *and* Mowbray.

    Boling. Many years of happy days befal 20
My gracious sovereign, my most loving liege!
    Mow. Each day still better other's happi-
        ness;
Until the heavens, envying earth's good hap,
Add an immortal title to your crown!
    K. Rich. We thank you both: yet one but
        flatters us,
As well appeareth by the cause you come;
Namely, to appeal each other of high treason.
Cousin of Hereford, what dost thou object
Against the Duke of Norfolk, Thomas Mow-
        bray?
    Boling. First, heaven be the record to my
        speech!   30
In the devotion of a subject's love,
Tendering the precious safety of my prince,
And free from other misbegotten hate,
Come I appellant to this princely presence.
Now, Thomas Mowbray, do I turn to thee,
And mark my greeting well; for what I speak
My body shall make good upon this earth,
Or my divine soul answer it in heaven.
Thou art a traitor and a miscreant,
Too good to be so and too bad to live,   40
Since the more fair and crystal is the sky,
The uglier seem the clouds that in it fly.
Once more, the more to aggravate the note,
With a foul traitor's name stuff I thy throat;
And wish, so please my sovereign, ere I move,
What my tongue speaks my right drawn sword
        may prove.
    Mow. Let not my cold words here accuse
        my zeal:
'Tis not the trial of a woman's war,
The bitter clamor of two eager tongues,
Can arbitrate this cause betwixt us twain; 50
The blood is hot that must be cool'd for this:
Yet can I not of such tame patience boast

As to be hush'd and nought at all to say:
First, the fair reverence of your highness curbs
        me
From giving reins and spurs to my free
        speech;
Which else would post until it had return'd
These terms of treason doubled down his
        throat.
Setting aside his high blood's royalty,
And let him be no kinsman to my liege,
I do defy him, and I spit at him;   60
Call him a slanderous coward and a villain:
Which to maintain I would allow him odds,
And meet him, were I tied to run afoot
Even to the frozen ridges of the Alps,
Or any other ground inhabitable,
Where ever Englishman durst set his foot.
Mean time let this defend my loyalty,
By all my hopes, most falsely doth he lie.
    Boling. Pale trembling coward, there I
        throw my gage,
Disclaiming here the kindred of the king, 70
And lay aside my high blood's royalty,
Which fear, not reverence, makes thee to ex-
        cept.
If guilty dread have left thee so much strength
As to take up mine honor's pawn, then stoop:
By that and all the rites of knighthood else,
Will I make good against thee, arm to arm,
What I have spoke, or thou canst worse devise.
    Mow. I take it up; and by that sword I
        swear
Which gently laid my knighthood on my
        shoulder,
I'll answer thee in any fair degree,   80
Or chivalrous design of knightly trial:
And when I mount, alive may I not light,
If I be traitor or unjustly fight!
    K. Rich. What doth our cousin lay to
        Mowbray's charge?
It must be great that can inherit us
So much as of a thought of ill in him.
    Boling. Look, what I speak, my life shall
        prove it true;
That Mowbray hath received eight thousand
        nobles
In name of lendings for your highness' sol-
        diers,
The which he hath detain'd for lewd employ-
        ments,
Like a false traitor and injurious villain. 91
Besides I say and will in battle prove,
Or here or elsewhere to the furthest verge
That ever was survey'd by English eye,
That all the treasons for these eighteen years
Complotted and contrived in this land
Fetch from false Mowbray their first head and
        spring.
Further I say and further will maintain
Upon his bad life to make all this good,
That he did plot the Duke of Gloucester's
        death,   100
Suggest his soon-believing adversaries,
And consequently, like a traitor coward,
Sluiced out his innocent soul through streams
        of blood:
Which blood, like sacrificing Abel's, cries,
Even from the tongueless caverns of the earth,
To me for justice and rough chastisement;
And, by the glorious worth of my descent,
This arm shall do it, or this life be spent.
    K. Rich. How high a pitch his resolution
        soars!

Thomas of Norfolk, what say'st thou to this?

Mow. O, let my sovereign turn away his
 face   110
And bid his ears a little while be deaf,
Till I have told this slander of his blood,
How God and good men hate so foul a liar.

K. Rich. Mowbray, impartial are our eyes
 and ears:
Were he my brother, nay, my kingdom's heir,
As he is but my father's brother's son,
Now, by my sceptre's awe, I make a vow,
Such neighbor nearness to our sacred blood
Should nothing privilege him, nor partialize
The unstooping firmness of my upright soul:
He is our subject, Mowbray; so art thou:
Free speech and fearless I to thee allow.

Mow. Then, Bolingbroke, as low as to thy
 heart,
Through the false passage of thy throat, thou
 liest.
Three parts of that receipt I had for Calais
Disbursed I duly to his highness' soldiers;
The other part reserved I by consent,
For that my sovereign liege was in my debt
Upon remainder of a dear account, 130
Since last I went to France to fetch his queen:
Now swallow down that lie. For Gloucester's
 death,
I slew him not; but to my own disgrace
Neglected my sworn duty in that case.
For you, my noble Lord of Lancaster,
The honorable father to my foe
Once did I lay an ambush for your life,
A trespass that doth vex my grieved soul
But ere I last received the sacrament
I did confess it, and exactly begg'd 140
Your grace's pardon, and I hope I had it.
This is my fault: as for the rest appeal'd,
It issues from the rancor of a villain,
A recreant and most degenerate traitor:
Which in myself I boldly will defend;
And interchangeably hurl down my gage
Upon this overweening traitor's foot,
To prove myself a loyal gentleman
Even in the best blood chamber'd in his
 bosom.
In haste whereof, most heartily I pray 150
Your highness to assign our trial day.

K. Rich. Wrath-kindled gentlemen, be
 ruled by me:
Let's purge this choler without letting blood:
This we prescribe, though no physician;
Deep malice makes too deep incision;
Forget, forgive; conclude and be agreed;
Our doctors say this is no month to bleed:
Good uncle, let this end where it begun;
We'll calm the Duke of Norfolk, you your
 son.

Gaunt. To be a make-peace shall become
 my age: 160
Throw down, my son, the Duke of Norfolk's
 gage.

K. Rich. And, Norfolk, throw down his.

Gaunt.   When, Harry, when?
Obedience bids I should not bid again.

K. Rich. Norfolk, throw down, we bid;
 there is no boot.

Mow. Myself I throw, dread sovereign, at
 thy foot.
My life thou shalt command, but not my
 shame:
The one my duty owes; but my fair name,
Despite of death that lives upon my grave,

To dark dishonor's use thou shalt not have.
I am disgraced, impeach'd and baffled here,
Pierced to the soul with slander's venom'd
 spear,   171
The which no balm can cure but his heart-
 blood
Which breathed this poison.

K. Rich.   Rage must be withstood:
Give me his gage: lions make leopards tame.

Mow. Yea, but not change his spots: take
 but my shame,
And I resign my gage. My dear dear lord,
The purest treasure mortal times afford
Is spotless reputation: that away,
Men are but gilded loam or painted clay.
A jewel in a ten-times-barr'd-up chest 180
Is a bold spirit in a loyal breast.
Mine honor is my life; both grow in one;
Take honor from me, and my life is done:
Then, dear my liege, mine honor let me try;
In that I live and for that will I die.

K. Rich. Cousin, throw up your gage; do
 you begin.

Boling. O, God defend my soul from such
 deep sin!
Shall I seem crest-fall'n in my father's sight?
Or with pale beggar-fear impeach my height
Before this out-dared dastard? Ere my tongue
Shall wound my honor with such feeble wrong,
Or sound so base a parle, my teeth shall tear
The slavish motive of recanting fear, 193
And spit it bleeding in his high disgrace,
Where shame doth harbor, even in Mowbray's
 face.   [*Exit Gaunt.*

K. Rich. We were not born to sue, but to
 command;
Which since we cannot do to make you
 friends,
Be ready, as your lives shall answer it,
At Coventry, upon Saint Lambert's day: 199
There shall your swords and lances arbitrate
The swelling difference of your settled hate:
Since we can not atone you, we shall see
Justice design the victor's chivalry.
Lord marshal, command our officers at arms
Be ready to direct these home alarms.
          [*Exeunt.*

SCENE II. *The* DUKE OF LANCASTER'S *palace.*

Enter JOHN OF GAUNT *with the* DUCHESS
OF GLOUCESTER.

Gaunt. Alas, the part I had in Wood-
 stock's blood
Doth more solicit me than your exclaims,
To stir against the butchers of his life!
But since correction lieth in those hands
Which made the fault that we cannot correct,
Put we our quarrel to the will of heaven;
Who, when they see the hours ripe on earth,
Will rain hot vengeance on offenders' heads.

Duch. Finds brotherhood in thee no
 sharper spur?
Hath love in thy old blood no living fire? 10
Edward's seven sons, whereof thyself art one,
Were as seven vials of his sacred blood,
Or seven fair branches springing from one
 root:
Some of those seven are dried by nature's
 course,
Some of those branches by the Destinies cut;
But Thomas, my dear lord, my life, my Glou-
 cester,
One vial full of Edward's sacred blood,

One flourishing branch of his most royal root,
Is crack'd, and all the precious liquor spilt,
Is hack'd down, and his summer leaves all
    faded,
By envy's hand and murder's bloody axe. 21
Ah, Gaunt, his blood was thine! that bed, that
    womb,
That metal, that self-mould, that fashion'd thee
Made him a man; and though thou livest and
    breathest,
Yet art thou slain in him : thou dost consent
In some large measure to thy father's death,
In that thou seest thy wretched brother die,
Who was the model of thy father's life.
Call it not patience, Gaunt ; it is despair : 29
In suffering thus thy brother to be slaughter'd,
Thou showest the naked pathway to thy life,
Teaching stern murder how to butcher thee :
That which in mean men we intitle patience
Is pale cold cowardice in noble breasts.
What shall I say? to safeguard thine own life,
The best way is to venge my Gloucester's
    death.
   Gaunt. God's is the quarrel ; for God's
    substitute,
His deputy anointed in His sight,
Hath caused his death : the which if wrong-
    fully,
Let heaven revenge ; for I may never lift 40
An angry arm against His minister.
   Duch. Where then, alas, may I complain
    myself?
   Gaunt. To God, the widow's champion and
    defence.
   Duch. Why, then, I will. Farewell, old
    Gaunt.
Thou goest to Coventry, there to behold
Our cousin Hereford and fell Mowbray fight :
O, sit my husband's wrongs on Hereford's
    spear,
That it may enter butcher Mowbray's breast!
Or, if misfortune miss the first career,
Be Mowbray's sins so heavy in his bosom, 50
That they may break his foaming courser's
    back,
And throw the rider headlong in the lists,
A caitiff recreant to my cousin Hereford!
Farewell, old Gaunt : thy sometimes brother's
    wife
With her companion grief must end her life.
   Gaunt. Sister, farewell ; I must to Cov-
    entry :
As much good stay with thee as go with me!
   Duch. Yet one word more : grief boundeth
    where it falls,
Not with the empty hollowness, but weight :
I take my leave before I have begun, 60
For sorrow ends not when it seemeth done.
Commend me to thy brother, Edmund York.
Lo, this is all :—nay, yet depart not so ;
Though this be all, do not so quickly go ;
I shall remember more. Bid him—ah, what?—
With all good speed at Plashy visit me.
Alack, and what shall good old York there see
But empty lodgings and unfurnish'd walls,
Unpeopled offices, untrodden stones?
And what hear there for welcome but my
    groans? 70
Therefore commend me ; let him not come
    there,
To seek out sorrow that dwells every where.
Desolate, desolate, will I hence and die :

The last leave of thee takes my weeping eye.
                       [Exeunt.

SCENE III. *The lists at Coventry.*

Enter the Lord Marshal *and the* DUKE OF
AUMERLE.

   Mar. My Lord Aumerle, is Harry Hereford
    arm'd?
   Aum. Yea, at all points ; and longs to en-
    ter in.
   Mar. The Duke of Norfolk, sprightfully
    and bold,
Stays but the summons of the appellant's
    trumpet.
   Aum. Why, then, the champions are pre-
    pared, and stay
For nothing but his majesty's approach.

The trumpets sound, and the KING *enters with
his nobles,* GAUNT, BUSHY, BAGOT, GREEN,
and others. When they are set, enter MOW-
BRAY *in arms, defendant, with a Herald.*

   K. Rich. Marshal, demand of yonder
    champion
The cause of his arrival here in arms :
Ask him his name and orderly proceed
To swear him in the justice of his cause. 10
   Mar. In God's name and the king's, say
    who thou art
And why thou comest thus knightly clad in
    arms,
Against what man thou comest, and what thy
    quarrel :
Speak truly, on thy knighthood and thy oath ;
As so defend thee heaven and thy valor!
   Mow. My name is Thomas Mowbray, Duke
    of Norfolk ;
Who hither come engaged by my oath—
Which God defend a knight should violate!—
Both to defend my loyalty and truth
To God, my king and my succeeding issue, 20
Against the Duke of Hereford that appeals
    me ;
And, by the grace of God and this mine arm,
To prove him, in defending of myself,
A traitor to my God, my king, and me :
And as I truly fight, defend me heaven!

The trumpets sound. Enter BOLINGBROKE, *appellant, in armor, with a Herald.*

   K. Rich. Marshal, ask yonder knight in
    arms,
Both who he is and why he cometh hither
Thus plated in habiliments of war,
And formally, according to our law,
Depose him in the justice of his cause. 30
   Mar. What is thy name? and wherefore
    comest thou hither,
Before King Richard in his royal lists?
Against whom comest thou? and what's thy
    quarrel?
Speak like a true knight, so defend thee
    heaven!
   Boling. Harry of Hereford, Lancaster and
    Derby
Am I ; who ready here do stand in arms,
To prove, by God's grace and my body's valor,
In lists, on Thomas Mowbray, Duke of Nor-
    folk,
That he is a traitor, foul and dangerous,
To God of heaven, King Richard and to me ;
And as I truly fight, defend me heaven! 41

Mar. On pain of death, no person be so
  bold
Or daring-hardy as to touch the lists,
Except the marshal and such officers
Appointed to direct these fair designs.
  Boling. Lord marshal, let me kiss my sov-
    ereign's hand,
And bow my knee before his majesty :
For Mowbray and myself are like two men
That vow a long and weary pilgrimage ;
Then let us take a ceremonious leave   50
And loving farewell of our several friends.
  Mar. The appellant in all duty greets your
    highness,
And craves to kiss your hand and take his
    leave.
  K. Rich. We will descend and fold him in
    our arms.
Cousin of Hereford, as thy cause is right,
So be thy fortune in this royal fight !
Farewell, my blood ; which if to-day thou shed,
Lament we may, but not revenge thee dead.
  Boling. O, let no noble eye profane a tear
For me, if I be gored with Mowbray's spear :
As confident as is the falcon's flight   61
Against a bird, do I with Mowbray fight.
My loving lord, I take my leave of you ;
Of you, my noble cousin, Lord Aumerle ;
Not sick, although I have to do with death,
But lusty, young, and cheerly drawing breath.
Lo, as at English feasts, so I regreet
The daintiest last, to make the end most
    sweet :
O thou, the earthly author of my blood,
Whose youthful spirit, in me regenerate,   70
Doth with a twofold vigor lift me up
To reach at victory above my head,
Add proof unto mine armor with thy prayers ;
And with thy blessings steel my lance's point,
That it may enter Mowbray's waxen coat,
And furbish new the name of John a Gaunt,
Even in the lusty havior of his son.
  Gaunt. God in thy good cause make thee
    prosperous !
Be swift like lightning in the execution ;
And let thy blows, doubly redoubled,   80
Fall like amazing thunder on the casque
Of thy adverse pernicious enemy :
Rouse up thy youthful blood, be valiant and
    live.
  Boling. Mine innocency and Saint George
    to thrive !
  Mow. However God or fortune cast my
    lot,
There lives or dies, true to King Richard's
    throne,
A loyal, just and upright gentleman :
Never did captive with a freer heart
Cast off his chains of bondage and embrace
His golden uncontroll'd enfranchisement,   90
More than my dancing soul doth celebrate
This feast of battle with mine adversary.
Most mighty liege, and my companion peers,
Take from my mouth the wish of happy years :
As gentle and as jocund as to jest
Go I to fight : truth hath a quiet breast.
  K. Rich. Farewell, my lord : securely I
    espy
Virtue with valor couched in thine eye.
Order the trial, marshal, and begin.
  Mar. Harry of Hereford, Lancaster and
    Derby,   100
Receive thy lance ; and God defend the right !

  Boling. Strong as a tower in hope, I cry
    amen.
  Mar. Go bear this lance to Thomas, Duke
    of Norfolk.
  First Her. Harry of Hereford, Lancaster
    and Derby,
Stands here for God, his sovereign and him-
    self,
On pain to be found false and recreant,
To prove the Duke of Norfolk, Thomas Mow-
    bray,
A traitor to his God, his king and him ;
And dares him to set forward to the fight.
  Sec. Her. Here standeth Thomas Mow-
    bray, Duke of Norfolk,   110
On pain to be found false and recreant,
Both to defend himself and to approve
Henry of Hereford, Lancaster, and Derby,
To God, his sovereign and to him disloyal ;
Courageously and with a free desire
Attending but the signal to begin.
  Mar. Sound, trumpets ; and set forward,
    combatants.   [*A charge sounded.*
Stay, the king hath thrown his warder down.
  K. Rich. Let them lay by their helmets and
    their spears,
And both return back to their chairs again :
Withdraw with us : and let the trumpets
    sound   121
While we return these dukes what we decree.
                            [*A long flourish.*
Draw near,
And list what with our council we have done.
For that our kingdom's earth should not be
    soil'd
With that dear blood which it hath fostered ;
And for our eyes do hate the dire aspect
Of civil wounds plough'd up with neighbors'
    sword ;
And for we think the eagle-winged pride
Of sky-aspiring and ambitious thoughts,   130
With rival-hating envy, set on you
To wake our peace, which in our country's
    cradle
Draws the sweet infant breath of gentle sleep ;
Which so roused up with boisterous untuned
    drums,
With harsh resounding trumpets' dreadful
    bray,
And grating shock of wrathful iron arms,
Might from our quiet confines fright fair peace
And make us wade even in our kindred's
    blood :
Therefore, we banish you our territories :
You, cousin Hereford, upon pain of life,   140
Till twice five summers have enrich'd our fields
Shall not regreet our fair dominions,
But tread the stranger paths of banishment.
  Boling. Your will be done : this must my
    comfort be,
That sun that warms you here shall shine on
    me ;
And those his golden beams to you here lent
Shall point on me and gild my banishment.
  K. Rich. Norfolk, for thee remains a heav-
    ier doom,
Which I with some unwillingness pronounce :
The sly slow hours shall not determinate   150
The dateless limit of thy dear exile ;
The hopeless word of ' never to return '
Breathe I against thee, upon pain of life.
  Mow. A heavy sentence, my most sover-
    eign liege,

And all unlook'd for from your highness'
    mouth :
A dearer merit, not so deep a maim
As to be cast forth in the common air,
Have I deserved at your highness' hands.
The language I have learn'd these forty years,
My native English, now I must forego :   160
And now my tongue's use is to me no more
Than an unstringed viol or a harp,
Or like a cunning instrument cased up,
Or, being open, put into his hands
That knows no touch to tune the harmony :
Within my mouth you have engaol'd my
    tongue,
Doubly portcullis'd with my teeth and lips ;
And dull unfeeling barren ignorance
Is made my gaoler to attend on me.
I am too old to fawn upon a nurse,   170
Too far in years to be a pupil now :
What is thy sentence then but speechless
    death,
Which robs my tongue from breathing native
    breath ?
    K. Rich. It boots thee not to be compas-
    sionate :
After our sentence plaining comes too late.
    Mow. Then thus I turn me from my coun-
    try's light,
To dwell in solemn shades of endless night.
    K. Rich. Return again, and take an oath
    with thee.
Lay on our royal sword your banish'd hands ;
Swear by the duty that you owe to God— 180
Our part therein we banish with yourselves—
To keep the oath that we administer :
You never shall, so help you truth and God !
Embrace each other's love in banishment ;
Nor never look upon each other's face ;
Nor never write, regreet, nor reconcile
This louring tempest of your home-bred hate ;
Nor never by advised purpose meet
To plot, contrive, or complot any ill
'Gainst us, our state, our subjects, or our land.
    Boling. I swear.   191
    Mow. And I, to keep all this.
    Boling. Norfolk, so far as to mine en-
    emy :—
By this time, had the king permitted us,
One of our souls had wander'd in the air,
Banish'd this frail sepulchre of our flesh,
As now our flesh is banish'd from this land :
Confess thy treasons ere thou fly the realm ;
Since thou hast far to go, bear not along
The clogging burthen of a guilty soul.   200
    Mow. No, Bolingbroke : if ever I were
    traitor,
My name be blotted from the book of life,
And I from heaven banish'd as from hence !
But what thou art, God, thou, and I do know ;
And all too soon, I fear, the king shall rue.
Farewell, my liege. Now no way can I stray ;
Save back to England, all the world's my way.
    [*Exit.*
    K. Rich. Uncle, even in the glasses of thine
    eyes
I see thy grieved heart : thy sad aspect
Hath from the number of his banish'd years
Pluck'd four away. [*To Boling.*] Six frozen
    winters spent,   211
Return with welcome home from banishment.
    Boling. How long a time lies in one little
    word !
Four lagging winters and four wanton springs

End in a word : such is the breath of kings.
    Gaunt. I thank my liege, that in regard of
    me
He shortens four years of my son's exile :
But little vantage shall I reap thereby ;
For, ere the six years that he hath to spend
Can change their moons and bring their times
    about,   220
My oil-dried lamp and time-bewasted light
Shall be extinct with age and endless night ;
My inch of taper will be burnt and done,
And blindfold death not let me see my son.
    K. Rich. Why, uncle, thou hast many years
    to live.
    Gaunt. But not a minute, king, that thou
    canst give :
Shorten my days thou canst with sullen sor-
    row,
And pluck nights from me, but not lend a
    morrow ;
Thou canst help time to furrow me with age,
But stop no wrinkle in his pilgrimage ;   230
Thy word is current with him for my death,
But dead, thy kingdom cannot buy my breath.
    K. Rich. Thy son is banish'd upon good
    advice,
Whereto thy tongue a party-verdict gave :
Why at our justice seem'st thou then to lour ?
    Gaunt. Things sweet to taste prove in di-
    gestion sour.
You urged me as a judge ; but I had rather
You would have bid me argue like a father.
O, had it been a stranger, not my child,
To smooth his fault I should have been more
    mild :   240
A partial slander sought I to avoid,
And in the sentence my own life destroy'd.
Alas, I look'd when some of you should say,
I was too strict to make mine own away ;
But you gave leave to my unwilling tongue
Against my will to do myself this wrong.
    K. Rich. Cousin, farewell ; and, uncle, bid
    him so :
Six years we banish him, and he shall go.
    [*Flourish. Exeunt King Richard and train.*
    Aum. Cousin, farewell : what presence
    must not know,
From where you do remain let paper show.
    Mar. My lord, no leave take I ; for I will
    ride,   251
As far as land will let me, by your side.
    Gaunt. O, to what purpose dost thou hoard
    thy words,
That thou return'st no greeting to thy friends ?
    Boling. I have too few to take my leave of
    you,
When the tongue's office should be prodigal
To breathe the abundant dolor of the heart.
    Gaunt. Thy grief is but thy absence for a
    time.
    Boling. Joy absent, grief is present for that
    time.
    Gaunt. What is six winters ? they are
    quickly gone.   260
    Boling. To men in joy ; but grief makes
    one hour ten.
    Gaunt. Call it a travel that thou takest for
    pleasure.
    Boling. My heart will sigh when I miscall
    it so,
Which finds it an inforced pilgrimage.
    Gaunt. The sullen passage of thy weary
    steps

Esteem as foil wherein thou art to set
The precious jewel of thy home return.
  Boling. Nay, rather, every tedious stride I
    make
Will but remember me what a deal of world
I wander from the jewels that I love.   270
Must I not serve a long apprenticehood
To foreign passages, and in the end,
Having my freedom, boast of nothing else
But that I was a journeyman to grief ?
  Gaunt. All places that the eye of heaven
    visits
Are to a wise man ports and happy havens.
Teach thy necessity to reason thus ;
There is no virtue like necessity.
Think not the king did banish thee,
But thou the king. Woe doth the heavier sit,
Where it perceives it is but faintly borne. 281
Go, say I sent thee forth to purchase honor
And not the king exiled thee ; or suppose
Devouring pestilence hangs in our air
And thou art flying to a fresher clime :
Look, what thy soul holds dear, imagine it
To lie that way thou go'st, not whence thou
    comest :
Suppose the singing birds musicians,
The grass whereon thou tread'st the presence
    strew'd,
The flowers fair ladies, and thy steps no more
Than a delightful measure or a dance ;
For gnarling sorrow hath less power to bite
The man that mocks at it and sets it light.
  Boling. O, who can hold a fire in his hand
By thinking on the frosty Caucasus ?
Or cloy the hungry edge of appetite
By bare imagination of a feast ?
Or wallow naked in December snow
By thinking on fantastic summer's heat ?
O, no ! the apprehension of the good   300
Gives but the greater feeling to the worse :
Fell sorrow's tooth doth never rankle more
Than when he bites, but lanceth not the sore.
  Gaunt. Come, come, my son, I'll bring thee
    on thy way :
Had I thy youth and cause, I would not stay.
  Boling. Then, England's ground, farewell ;
    sweet soil, adieu ;
My mother, and my nurse, that bears me yet !
Where'er I wander, boast of this I can,
Though banish'd, yet a trueborn Englishman.
                                    [*Exeunt.*

SCENE IV. *The court.*

Enter the KING, *with* BAGOT *and* GREEN *at one
door ; and the* DUKE OF AUMERLE *at another.*

  K. Rich. We did observe. Cousin Aumerle,
How far brought you high Hereford on his
    way ?
  Aum. I brought high Hereford, if you call
    him so,
But to the next highway, and there I left him.
  K. Rich. And say, what store of parting
    tears were shed ?
  Aum. Faith, none for me ; except the north-
    east wind,
Which then blew bitterly against our faces,
Awaked the sleeping rheum, and so by chance
Did grace our hollow parting with a tear.
  K. Rich. What said our cousin when you
    parted with him ?   10
  Aum. ' Farewell : '
And, for my heart disdained that my tongue

Should so profane the word, that taught me
    craft
To counterfeit oppression of such grief
That words seem'd buried in my sorrow's
    grave.
Marry, would the word ' farewell ' have
    lengthen'd hours
And added years to his short banishment,
He should have had a volume of farewells ;
But since it would not, he had none of me.
  K. Rich. He is our cousin, cousin ; but 'tis
    doubt,   20
When time shall call him home from banish-
    ment,
Whether our kinsman come to see his friends.
Ourself and Bushy, Bagot here and Green
Observed his courtship to the common peo-
    ple ;
How he did seem to dive into their hearts
With humble and familiar courtesy,
What reverence he did throw away on slaves,
Wooing poor craftsmen with the craft of
    smiles
And patient underbearing of his fortune,
As 'twere to banish their affects with him. 30
Off goes his bonnet to an oyster-wench ;
A brace of draymen bid God speed him well
And had the tribute of his supple knee,
With ' Thanks, my countrymen, my loving
    friends ; '
As were our England in reversion his,
And he our subjects' next degree in hope.
  Green. Well, he is gone ; and with him go
    these thoughts.
Now for the rebels which stand out in Ire-
    land,
Expedient manage must be made, my liege,
Ere further leisure yield them further means
For their advantage and your highness' loss.
  K. Rich. We will ourself in person to this
    war :
And, for our coffers, with too great a court
And liberal largess, are grown somewhat light,
We are inforced to farm our royal realm ;
The revenue whereof shall furnish us
For our affairs in hand : if that come short,
Our substitutes at home shall have blank
    charters ;
Whereto, when they shall know what men are
    rich,
They shall subscribe them for large sums of
    gold
And send them after to supply our wants ; 51
For we will make for Ireland presently.

Enter BUSHY.

Bushy, what news ?
  Bushy. Old John of Gaunt is grievous sick,
    my lord,
Suddenly taken ; and hath sent post haste
To entreat your majesty to visit him.
  K. Rich. Where lies he ?
  Bushy. At Ely House.
  K. Rich. Now put it, God, in the physi-
    cian's mind
To help him to his grave immediately !   60
The lining of his coffers shall make coats
To deck our soldiers for these Irish wars.
Come, gentlemen, let's all go visit him :
Pray God we may make haste, and come too
    late !
  All. Amen.   [*Exeunt.*

ACT II.

SCENE I. *Ely House.*

Enter JOHN OF GAUNT *sick, with the* DUKE
OF YORK, *&c.*

Gaunt. Will the king come, that I may
  breathe my last
In wholesome counsel to his unstaid youth ?
York. Vex not yourself, nor strive not with
  your breath ;
For all in vain comes counsel to his ear.
Gaunt. O, but they say the tongues of dy-
  ing men
Enforce attention like deep harmony :
Where words are scarce, they are seldom
  spent in vain,
For they breathe truth that breathe their words
  in pain.
He that no more must say is listen'd more
Than they whom youth and ease have taught
  to glose ;   10
More are men's ends mark'd than their lives
  before :
The setting sun, and music at the close,
As the last taste of sweets, is sweetest last,
Writ in remembrance more than things long
  past :
Though Richard my life's counsel would not
  hear,
My death's sad tale may yet undeaf his ear.
York. No ; it is stopp'd with other flatter-
  ing sounds,
As praises, of whose taste the wise are fond,
Lascivious metres, to whose venom sound
The open ear of youth doth always listen ;   20
Report of fashions in proud Italy,
Whose manners still our tardy apish nation
Limps after in base imitation.
Where doth the world thrust forth a vanity—
So it be new, there's no respect how vile—
That is not quickly buzz'd into his ears ?
Then all too late comes counsel to be heard,
Where will doth mutiny with wit's regard.
Direct not him whose way himself will
  choose :
'Tis breath thou lack'st, and that breath wilt
  thou lose.   30
Gaunt. Methinks I am a prophet new in-
  spired
And thus expiring do foretell of him :
His rash fierce blaze of riot cannot last,
For violent fires soon burn out themselves ;
Small showers last long, but sudden storms are
  short ;
He tires betimes that spurs too fast betimes ;
With eager feeding food doth choke the
  feeder :
Light vanity, insatiate cormorant,
Consuming means, soon preys upon itself.
This royal throne of kings, this scepter'd isle,
This earth of majesty, this seat of Mars,   41
This other Eden, demi-paradise,
This fortress built by Nature for herself
Against infection and the hand of war,
This happy breed of men, this little world,
This precious stone set in the silver sea,
Which serves it in the office of a wall,
Or as a moat defensive to a house,
Against the envy of less happier lands,

This blessed plot, this earth, this realm, this
  England,   50
This nurse, this teeming womb of royal kings,
Fear'd by their breed and famous by their
  birth,
Renowned for their deeds as far from home,
For Christian service and true chivalry,
As is the sepulchre in stubborn Jewry,
Of the world's ransom, blessed Mary's Son,
This land of such dear souls, this dear dear
  land,
Dear for her reputation through the world,
Is now leased out, I die pronouncing it,
Like to a tenement or pelting farm :   60
England, bound in with the triumphant sea,
Whose rocky shore beats back the envious
  siege
Of watery Neptune, is now bound in with
  shame,
With inky blots and rotten parchment bonds :
That England, that was wont to conquer
  others,
Hath made a shameful conquest of itself.
Ah, would the scandal vanish with my life,
How happy then were my ensuing death !

Enter KING RICHARD *and* QUEEN, AUMERLE,
BUSHY, GREEN, BAGOT, ROSS, *and* WIL-
LOUGHBY.

York. The king is come : deal mildly with
  his youth ;
For young hot colts being raged do rage the
  more.   70
Queen. How fares our noble uncle, Lan-
  caster ?
K. Rich. What comfort, man ? how is't
with aged Gaunt ?
Gaunt. O, how that name befits my com-
  position !
Old Gaunt indeed, and gaunt in being old :
Within me grief hath kept a tedious fast ;
And who abstains from meat that is not
  gaunt ?
For sleeping England long time have I
  watch'd;
Watching breeds leanness, leanness is all
  gaunt :
The pleasure that some fathers feed upon,   79
Is my strict fast ; I mean, my children's looks ;
And therein fasting, hast thou made me gaunt :
Gaunt am I for the grave, gaunt as a grave,
Whose hollow womb inherits nought but
  bones.
K. Rich. Can sick men play so nicely with
  their names ?
Gaunt. No, misery makes sport to mock
  itself :
Since thou dost seek to kill my name in me,
I mock my name, great king, to flatter thee.
K. Rich. Should dying men flatter with
  those that live ?
Gaunt. No, no, men living flatter those that
  die.
K. Rich. Thou, now a-dying, say'st thou
  flatterest me.   90
Gaunt. O, no ! thou diest, though I the
  sicker be.
K. Rich. I am in health, I breathe, and see
  thee ill.
Gaunt. Now He that made me knows I see
  thee ill ;
Ill in myself to see, and in thee seeing ill.
Thy death-bed is no lesser than thy land

Wherein thou liest in reputation sick ;
And thou, too careless patient as thou art,
Commit'st thy anointed body to the cure
Of those physicians that first wounded thee :
A thousand flatterers sit within thy crown, 100
Whose compass is no bigger than thy head ;
And yet, incaged in so small a verge,
The waste is no whit lesser than thy land.
O, had thy grandsire with a prophet's eye
Seen how his son's son should destroy his sons,
From forth thy reach he would have laid thy
          shame,
Deposing thee before thou wert possess'd,
Which art possess'd now to depose thyself.
Why, cousin, wert thou regent of the world,
It were a shame to let this land by lease ; 110
But for thy world enjoying but this land,
Is it not more than shame to shame it so ?
Landlord of England art thou now, not king :
Thy state of law is bondslave to the law ;
And thou—
    K. Rich.   A lunatic lean-witted fool,
Presuming on an ague's privilege,
Darest with thy frozen admonition
Make pale our cheek, chasing the royal blood
With fury from his native residence.
Now, by my seat's right royal majesty, 120
Wert thou not brother to great Edward's son,
This tongue that runs so roundly in thy head
Should run thy head from thy unreverent
          shoulders.
    Gaunt.   O, spare me not, my brother Ed-
          ward's son,
For that I was his father Edward's son ;
That blood already, like the pelican,
Hast thou tapp'd out and drunkenly caroused :
My brother Gloucester, plain well-meaning
          soul,
Whom fair befal in heaven 'mongst happy
          souls !
May be a precedent and witness good 130
That thou respect'st not spilling Edward's
          blood :
Join with the present sickness that I have ;
And thy unkindness be like crooked age,
To crop at once a too long wither'd flower.
Live in thy shame, but die not shame with
          thee !
These words hereafter thy tormentors be !
Convey me to my bed, then to my grave :
Love they to live that love and honor have.
          [*Exit, borne off by his Attendants.*
    K. Rich.   And let them die that age and sul-
          lens have ;
For both hast thou, and both become the
          grave.
    York.   I do beseech your majesty, impute
          his words   141
To wayward sickliness and age in him :
He loves you, on my life, and holds you dear
As Harry Duke of Hereford, were he here.
    K. Rich.   Right, you say true : as Here-
          ford's love, so his ;
As theirs, so mine ; and all be as it is.

Enter NORTHUMBERLAND.

    North.   My liege, old Gaunt commends him
          to your majesty.
    K. Rich.   What says he ?
    North.   Nay, nothing ; all is said :
His tongue is now a stringless instrument ;
Words, life and all, old Lancaster hath spent.

    York.   Be York the next that must be bank-
          rupt so !   151
Though death be poor, it ends a mortal woe.
    K. Rich.   The ripest fruit first falls, and so
          doth he ;
His time is spent, our pilgrimage must be.
So much for that. Now for our Irish wars :
We must supplant those rough rug-headed
          kerns,
Which live like venom where no venom else
But only they have privilege to live.
And for these great affairs do ask some charge,
Towards our assistance we do seize to us 160
The plate, coin, revenues and moveables,
Whereof our uncle Gaunt did stand possess'd.
    York.   How long shall I be patient ? ah,
          how long
Shall tender duty make me suffer wrong ?
Not Gloucester's death, nor Hereford's banish-
          ment,
Not Gaunt's rebukes, nor England's private
          wrongs,
Nor the prevention of poor Bolingbroke
About his marriage, nor my own disgrace,
Have ever made me sour my patient cheek,
Or bend one wrinkle on my sovereign's face.
I am the last of noble Edward's sons,   171
Of whom thy father, Prince of Wales, was
          first :
In war was never lion raged more fierce,
In peace was never gentle lamb more mild,
Than was that young and princely gentleman.
His face thou hast, for even so look'd he,
Accomplish'd with the number of thy hours ;
But when he frown'd, it was against the French
And not against his friends ; his noble hand
Did win what he did spend and spent not that
Which his triumphant father's hand had won ;
His hands were guilty of no kindred blood,
But bloody with the enemies of his kin.
O Richard ! York is too far gone with grief,
Or else he never would compare between.
    K. Rich.   Why, uncle, what's the matter ?
    York.   O my liege,
Pardon me, if you please ; if not, I, pleased
Not to be pardon'd, am content withal.
Seek you to seize and gripe into your hands
The royalties and rights of banish'd Hereford ?
Is not Gaunt dead, and doth not Hereford
          live ?
Was not Gaunt just, and is not Harry true ?
Did not the one deserve to have an heir ?
Is not his heir a well-deserving son ?
Take Hereford's rights away, and take from
          Time
His charters and his customary rights ;
Let not to-morrow then ensue to-day ;
Be not thyself ; for how art thou a king
But by fair sequence and succession ?
Now, afore God—God forbid I say true !—200
If you do wrongfully seize Hereford's rights,
Call in the letters patent that he hath
By his attorneys-general to sue
His livery, and deny his offer'd homage,
You pluck a thousand dangers on your head,
You lose a thousand well-disposed hearts
And prick my tender patience to those
          thoughts
Which honor and allegiance cannot think.
    K. Rich.   Think what you will, we seize
          into our hands
His plate, his goods, his money and his lands

York. I'll not be by the while : my liege,
　　farewell :　　　　　　　　　　　　211
What will ensue hereof, there's none can tell ;
But by bad courses may be understood
That their events can never fall out good.
　　　　　　　　　　　　　　　　[*Exit.*
K. Rich. Go, Bushy, to the Earl of Wilt-
　　shire straight :
Bid him repair to us to Ely House
To see this business. To-morrow next
We will for Ireland ; and 'tis time, I trow :
And we create, in absence of ourself,　　219
Our uncle York lord governor of England ;
For he is just and always loved us well.
Come on, our queen : to-morrow must we
　　part ;
Be merry, for our time of stay is short.
　　[*Flourish. Exeunt King, Queen, Aumerle,
　　　　　Bushy, Green, and Bagot.*
North. Well, lords, the Duke of Lancaster
　　is dead.
Ross. And living too ; for now his son is
　　duke.
Willo. Barely in title, not in revenue.
North. Richly in both, if justice had her
　　right.
Ross. My heart is great ; but it must break
　　with silence,
Ere't be disburden'd with a liberal tongue.
North. Nay, speak thy mind ; and let him
　　ne'er speak more　　　　　　　　230
That speaks thy words again to do thee harm !
Willo. Tends that thou wouldst speak to
　　the Duke of Hereford ?
If it be so, out with it boldly, man ;
Quick is mine ear to hear of good towards him.
Ross. No good at all that I can do for
　　him ;
Unless you call it good to pity him,
Bereft and gelded of his patrimony.
North. Now, afore God, 'tis shame such
　　wrongs are borne
In him, a royal prince, and many moe
Of noble blood in this declining land.　　240
The king is not himself, but basely led
By flatterers ; and what they will inform,
Merely in hate, 'gainst any of us all,
That will the king severely prosecute
'Gainst us, our lives, our children, and our
　　heirs.
Ross. The commons hath he pill'd with
　　grievous taxes,
And quite lost their hearts : the nobles hath
　　he fined
For ancient quarrels, and quite lost their
　　hearts,
Willo. And daily new exactions are de-
　　vised,
As blanks, benevolences, and I wot not what :
But what, o' God's name, doth become of
　　this ?　　　　　　　　　　　　　251
North. Wars have not wasted it, for warr'd
　　he hath not,
But basely yielded upon compromise
That which his noble ancestors achieved with
　　blows :
More hath he spent in peace than they in wars.
Ross. The Earl of Wiltshire hath the realm
　　in farm.
Willo. The king's grown bankrupt, like a
　　broken man.
North. Reproach and dissolution hangeth
　　over him.

Ross. He hath not money for these Irish
　　wars,
His burthenous taxations notwithstanding,　260
But by the robbing of the banish'd duke.
North. His noble kinsman : most degener-
　　ate king !
But, lords, we hear this fearful tempest sing,
Yet see no shelter to avoid the storm ;
We see the wind sit sore upon our sails,
And yet we strike not, but securely perish.
Ross. We see the very wreck that we must
　　suffer ;
And unavoided is the danger now,
For suffering so the causes of our wreck.
North. Not so ; even through the hollow
　　eyes of death　　　　　　　　270
I spy life peering ; but I dare not say
How near the tidings of our comfort is.
Willo. Nay, let us share thy thoughts, as
　　thou dost ours.
Ross. Be confident to speak, Northumber-
　　land :
We three are but thyself ; and, speaking so,
Thy words are but as thoughts ; therefore, be
　　bold.
North. Then thus : I have from Port le
　　Blanc, a bay
In Brittany, received intelligence
That Harry Duke of Hereford, Rainold Lord
　　Cobham,
. . . . 280
That late broke from the Duke of Exeter,
His brother, Archbishop late of Canterbury,
Sir Thomas Erpingham, Sir John Ramston,
Sir John Norbery, Sir Robert Waterton and
　　Francis Quoint,
All these well furnish'd by the Duke of Bre-
　　tagne
With eight tall ships, three thousand men of
　　war,
Are making hither with all due expedience
And shortly mean to touch our northern
　　shore :
Perhaps they had ere this, but that they stay
The first departing of the king for Ireland.
If then we shall shake off our slavish yoke,
Imp out our drooping country's broken wing,
Redeem from broking pawn the blemish'd
　　crown,
Wipe off the dust that hides our sceptre's gilt
And make high majesty look like itself,　　295
Away with me in post to Ravenspurgh ;
But if you faint, as fearing to do so,
Stay and be secret, and myself will go.
Ross. To horse, to horse ! urge doubts to
　　them that fear.
Willo. Hold out my horse, and I will first
　　be there.　　　　　　　　[*Exeunt* 300

Scene II. *The palace.*

Enter Queen, Bushy, *and* Bagot.

Bushy. Madam, your majesty is too much
　　sad :
You promised, when you parted with the king,
To lay aside life-harming heaviness
And entertain a cheerful disposition.
Queen. To please the king I did ; to please
　　myself
I cannot do it ; yet I know no cause
Why I should welcome such a guest as grief,
Save bidding farewell to so sweet a guest
As my sweet Richard : yet again, methinks,
Some unborn sorrow, ripe in fortune's womb,

Is coming towards me, and my inward soul 11
With nothing trembles : at some thing it
grieves,
More than with parting from my lord the king.
Bushy. Each substance of a grief hath
twenty shadows,
Which shows like grief itself, but is not so ;
For sorrow's eye, glazed with blinding tears,
Divides one thing entire to many objects ;
Like perspectives, which rightly gazed upon
Show nothing but confusion, eyed awry
Distinguish form : so your sweet majesty, 20
Looking awry upon your lord's departure,
Find shapes of grief, more than himself, to
wail ;
Which, look'd on as it is, is nought but
shadows
Of what it is not. Then, thrice-gracious queen,
More than your lord's departure weep not :
more's not seen ;
Or if it be, 'tis with false sorrow's eye,
Which for things true weeps things imaginary.
Queen. It may be so ; but yet my inward
soul
Persuades me it is otherwise : howe'er it be,
I cannot but be sad ; so heavy sad 30
As, though on thinking on no thought I think,
Makes me with heavy nothing faint and shrink.
Bushy. 'Tis nothing but conceit, my gra-
cious lady.
Queen. 'Tis nothing less : conceit is still
derived
From some forefather grief ; mine is not so,
For nothing had begot my something grief ;
Or something hath the nothing that I grieve :
'Tis in reversion that I do possess ;
But what it is, that is not yet known ; what
I cannot name ; 'tis nameless woe, I wot. 40

Enter GREEN.

Green. God save your majesty ! and well
met, gentlemen :
I hope the king is not yet shipp'd for Ireland.
Queen. Why hopest thou so ? 'tis better
hope he is ;
For his designs crave haste, his haste good
hope :
Then wherefore dost thou hope he is not
shipp'd ?
Green. That he, our hope, might have re-
tired his power,
And driven into despair an enemy's hope,
Who strongly hath set footing in this land :
The banish'd Bolingbroke repeals himself,
And with uplifted arms is safe arrived 50
At Ravenspurgh.
Queen. Now God in heaven forbid !
Green. Ah, madam, 'tis too true : and that
is worse,
The Lord Northumberland, his son young
Henry Percy,
The Lords of Ross, Beaumond, and Wil-
loughby,
With all their powerful friends, are fled to him.
Bushy. Why have you not proclaim'd
Northumberland
And all the rest revolted faction traitors ?
Green. We have : whereupon the Earl of
Worcester
Hath broke his staff, resign'd his stewardship,
And all the household servants fled with him
To Bolingbroke. 61

Queen. So, Green, thou art the midwife to
my woe,
And Bolingbroke my sorrow's dismal heir :
Now hath my soul brought forth her prodigy,
And I, a gasping new-deliver'd mother,
Have woe to woe, sorrow to sorrow join'd.
Bushy. Despair not, madam.
Queen. Who shall hinder me ?
I will despair, and be at enmity
With cozening hope : he is a flatterer,
A parasite, a keeper back of death, 70
Who gently would dissolve the bands of life,
Which false hope lingers in extremity.

Enter YORK.

Green. Here comes the Duke of York.
Queen. With signs of war about his aged
neck :
O, full of careful business are his looks !
Uncle, for God's sake, speak comfortable
words.
York. Should I do so, I should belie my
thoughts :
Comfort's in heaven ; and we are on the earth,
Where nothing lives but crosses, cares and
grief.
Your husband, he is gone to save far off, 80
Whilst others come to make him lose at
home :
Here am I left to underprop his land,
Who, weak with age, cannot support myself :
Now comes the sick hour that his surfeit
made ;
Now shall he try his friends that flatter'd him.

Enter a Servant.

Serv. My lord, your son was gone before I
came.
York. He was ? Why, so ! go all which way
it will !
The nobles they are fled, the commons they are
cold,
And will, I fear, revolt on Hereford's side.
Sirrah, get thee to Plashy, to my sister
Gloucester ; 90
Bid her send me presently a thousand pound :
Hold, take my ring.
Serv. My lord, I had forgot to tell your
lordship,
To-day, as I came by, I called there ;
But I shall grieve you to report the rest.
York. What is't, knave ?
Serv. An hour before I came, the duchess
died.
York. God for his mercy ! what a tide of
woes
Comes rushing on this woeful land at once !
I know not what to do : I would to God, 100
So my untruth had not provoked him to it,
The king had cut off my head with my
brother's.
What, are there no posts dispatch'd for Ire-
land ?
How shall we do for money for these wars ?
Come, sister,—cousin, I would say,—pray
pardon me.
Go, fellow, get thee home, provide some cart
And bring away the armor that is there.
[*Exit Servant*
Gentlemen, will you go muster men ?
If I know how or which way to order these
affairs
Thus thrust disorderly into my hands, 110

Never believe me. Both are my kinsmen :
The one is my sovereign, whom both my oath
And duty bids defend ; the other again
Is my kinsman, whom the king hath wrong'd,
Whom conscience and my kindred bids to
    right.
Well, somewhat we must do. Come, cousin, I'll
Dispose of you.
Gentlemen, go, muster up your men,
And meet me presently at Berkeley.
I should to Plashy too ;   120
But time will not permit : all is uneven,
And every thing is left at six and seven.
               [*Exeunt York and Queen.*
  Bushy. The wind sits fair for news to go to
    Ireland,
But none returns. For us to levy power
Proportionable to the enemy
Is all unpossible.
  Green. Besides, our nearness to the king in
    love
Is near the hate of those love not the king.
  Bagot. And that's the wavering commons :
    for their love   129
Lies in their purses, and whoso empties them
By so much fills their hearts with deadly hate.
  Bushy. Wherein the king stands generally
    condemn'd.
  Bagot. If judgement lie in them, then so do
    we,
Because we ever have been near the king.
  Green. Well, I will for refuge straight to
    Bristol castle :
The Earl of Wiltshire is already there.
  Bushy. Thither will I with you ; for little
    office
The hateful commons will perform for us,
Except like curs to tear us all to pieces.
Will you go along with us ?   140
  Bagot. No ; I will to Ireland to his majesty.
Farewell : if heart's presages be not vain,
We three here part that ne'er shall meet again.
  Bushy. That's as York thrives to beat back
    Bolingbroke.
  Green. Alas, poor duke ! the task he under-
    takes
Is numbering sands and drinking oceans dry :
Where one on his side fights, thousands will
    fly.
Farewell at once, for once, for all, and ever.
  Bushy. Well, we may meet again.
  Bagot.   I fear me, never. 150
                     [*Exeunt.*

    Scene III. *Wilds in Gloucestershire.*

Enter Bolingbroke *and* Northumberland,
    with Forces.

  Boling. How far is it, my lord, to Berkeley
    now ?
  North. Believe me, noble lord,
I am a stranger here in Gloucestershire.
These high wild hills and rough uneven ways
Draws out our miles, and makes them weari-
    some ;
And yet your fair discourse hath been as sugar,
Making the hard way sweet and delectable.
But I bethink me what a weary way
From Ravenspurgh to Cotswold will be found
In Ross and Willoughby, wanting your com-
    pany,   10
Which, I protest, hath very much beguiled
The tediousness and process of my travel :
But theirs is sweetened with the hope to have

The present benefit which I possess ;
And hope to joy is little less in joy
Than hope enjoy'd : by this the weary lords
Shall make their way seem short, as mine hath
    done
By sight of what I have, your noble company.
  Boling. Of much less value is my company
Than your good words. But who comes here ?

     Enter Henry Percy.

  North. It is my son, young Harry Percy, 21
Sent from my brother Worcester, whenceso-
    ever.
Harry, how fares your uncle ?
  Percy. I had thought, my lord, to have
    learn'd his health of you.
  North. Why, is he not with the queen ?
  Percy. No, my good Lord ; he hath for-
    sook the court,
Broken his staff of office and dispersed
The household of the king.
  North.   What was his reason ?
He was not so resolved when last we spake to-
    gether.
  Percy. Because your lordship was pro-
    claimed traitor.   30
But he, my lord, is gone to Ravenspurgh,
To offer service to the Duke of Hereford,
And sent me over by Berkeley, to discover
What power the Duke of York had levied
    there ;
Then with directions to repair to Ravenspurgh.
  North. Have you forgot the Duke of Here-
    ford, boy ?
  Percy. No, my good lord, for that is not
    forgot
Which ne'er I did remember : to my knowl-
    edge,
I never in my life did look on him.
  North. Then learn to know him now ; this
    is the duke.   40
  Percy. My gracious lord, I tender you my
    service,
Such as it is, being tender, raw and young :
Which elder days shall ripen and confirm
To more approved service and desert.
  Boling. I thank thee, gentle Percy ; and be
    sure
I count myself in nothing else so happy
As in a soul remembering my good friends ;
And, as my fortune ripens with thy love,
It shall be still thy true love's recompense :
My heart this covenant makes, my hand thus
    seals it.   50
  North. How far is it to Berkeley ? and
    what stir
Keeps good old York there with his men of
    war ?
  Percy. There stands the castle, by yon tuft
    of trees,
Mann'd with three hundred men, as I have
    heard ;
And in it are the Lords of York, Berkeley, and
    Seymour ;
None else of name and noble estimate.

    Enter Ross *and* Willoughby.

  North. Here come the Lords of Ross and
    Willoughby,
Bloody with spurring, fiery-red with haste.
  Boling. Welcome, my lords. I wot your
    love pursues
A banish'd traitor : all my treasury   60

Is yet but unfelt thanks, which more enrich'd
Shall be your love and labor's recompense.
  Ross. Your presence makes us rich, most
    noble lord.
  Willo. And far surmounts our labor to at-
    tain it.
  Boling. Evermore thanks, the exchequer of
    the poor;
Which, till my infant fortune comes to years,
Stands for my bounty. But who comes here?

       Enter BERKELEY.

  North. It is my Lord of Berkeley, as I
    guess.
  Berk. My Lord of Hereford, my message is
    to you.
  Boling. My lord, my answer is—to Lancas-
    ter;   70
And I am come to seek that name in England;
And I must find that title in your tongue,
Before I make reply to aught you say.
  Berk. Mistake me not, my lord; 'tis not
    my meaning
To raze one title of your honor out:
To you, my lord, I come, what lord you will,
From the most gracious regent of this land,
The Duke of York, to know what pricks you
    on
To take advantage of the absent time
And fright our native peace with self-born
    arms.   80

    Enter YORK *attended.*

  Boling. I shall not need transport my
    words by you;
Here comes his grace in person.
           My noble uncle! [*Kneels.*
  York. Show me thy humble heart, and not
    thy knee,
Whose duty is deceiveable and false.
  Boling. My gracious uncle—
  York. Tut, tut!
Grace me no grace, nor uncle me no uncle:
I am no traitor's uncle; and that word 'grace'
In an ungracious mouth is but profane. 89
Why have those banish'd and forbidden legs
Dared once to touch a dust of England's
    ground?
But then more 'why?' why have they dared
    to march
So many miles upon her peaceful bosom,
Frighting her pale-faced villages with war
And ostentation of despised arms?
Comest thou because the anointed king is
    hence?
Why, foolish boy, the king is left behind,
And in my loyal bosom lies his power.
Were I but now the lord of such youth
As when brave Gaunt, thy father, and myself
Rescued the Black Prince, that young Mars of
    men,   101
From forth the ranks of many thousand
    French,
O, then how quickly should this arm of mine,
Now prisoner to the palsy, chastise thee
And minister correction to thy fault!
  Boling. My gracious uncle, let me know
    my fault:
On what condition stands it and wherein?
  York. Even in condition of the worst de-
    gree,
In gross rebellion and detested treason:
Thou art a banish'd man, and here art come

Before the expiration of thy time,   111
In braving arms against thy sovereign.
  Boling. As I was banish'd, I was banish'd
    Hereford;
But as I come, I come for Lancaster.
And, noble uncle, I beseech your grace
Look on my wrongs with an indifferent eye:
You are my father, for methinks in you
I see old Gaunt alive; O, then, my father,
Will you permit that I shall stand condemn'd
A wandering vagabond; my rights and royal-
    ties   120
Pluck'd from my arms perforce and given
    away
To upstart unthrifts? Wherefore was I born?
If that my cousin king be King of England,
It must be granted I am Duke of Lancaster.
You have a son, Aumerle, my noble cousin;
Had you first died, and he been thus trod
    down,
He should have found his uncle Gaunt a fa-
    ther,
To rouse his wrongs and chase them to the
    bay.
I am denied to sue my livery here,
And yet my letters-patents give me leave: 130
My father's goods are all distrain'd and sold,
And these and all are all amiss employ'd.
What would you have me do? I am a subject,
And I challenge law: attorneys are denied
    me;
And therefore personally I lay my claim
To my inheritance of free descent.
  North. The noble duke hath been too
    much abused.
  Ross. It stands your grace upon to do him
    right.
  Willo. Base men by his endowments are
    made great.
  York. My lords of England, let me tell you
    this: 140
I have had feeling of my cousin's wrongs
And labored all I could to do him right;
But in this kind to come, in braving arms,
Be his own carver and cut out his way,
To find out right with wrong, it may not be;
And you that do abet him in this kind
Cherish rebellion and are rebels all.
  North. The noble duke hath sworn his
    coming is
But for his own; and for the right of that
We all have strongly sworn to give him aid;
And let him ne'er see joy that breaks that
    oath!   151
  York. Well, well, I see the issue of these
    arms:
I cannot mend it, I must needs confess,
Because my power is weak and all ill left:
But if I could, by Him that gave me life,
I would attach you all and make you stoop
Unto the sovereign mercy of the king;
But since I cannot, be it known to you
I do remain as neuter. So, fare you well;
Unless you please to enter in the castle 160
And there repose you for this night.
  Boling. An offer, uncle, that we will ac-
    cept:
But we must win your grace to go with us
To Bristol castle, which they say is held
By Bushy, Bagot and their complices,
The caterpillars of the commonwealth,
Which I have sworn to weed and pluck away

York. It may be I will go with you : but
    yet I'll pause ;
For I am loath to break our country's laws.
Nor friends nor foes, to me welcome you are :
Things past redress are now with me past
    care.   *[Exeunt.* 171

    SCENE IV. *A camp in Wales.*

    Enter SALISBURY *and a* Welsh Captain.

  Cap. My lord of Salisbury, we have stay'd
    ten days,
And hardly kept our countrymen together,
And yet we hear no tidings from the king ;
Therefore we will disperse ourselves : farewell.
  Sal. Stay yet another day, thou trusty
    Welshman :
The king reposeth all his confidence in thee.
  Cap. 'Tis thought the king is dead ; we will
    not stay.
The bay-trees in our country are all wither'd
And meteors fright the fixed stars of heaven ;
The pale-faced moon looks bloody on the
    earth   10
And lean-look'd prophets whisper fearful
    change ;
Rich men look sad and ruffians dance and
    leap,
The one in fear to lose what they enjoy,
The other to enjoy by rage and war :
These signs forerun the death or fall of kings.
Farewell : our countrymen are gone and fled,
As well assured Richard their king is dead.
                                    [Exit.
  Sal. Ah, Richard, with the eyes of heavy
    mind
I see thy glory like a shooting star
Fall to the base earth from the firmament. 20
Thy sun sets weeping in the lowly west,
Witnessing storms to come, woe and unrest :
Thy friends are fled to wait upon thy foes,
And crossly to thy good all fortune goes.
                                    [Exit.

          ACT III.

  SCENE I. *Bristol. Before the castle.*

Enter BOLINGBROKE, YORK, NORTHUMBER-
    LAND, ROSS, PERCY, WILLOUGHBY, *with*
    BUSHY *and* GREEN, *prisoners.*

  Boling. Bring forth these men.
Bushy and Green, I will not vex your souls—
Since presently your souls must part your
    bodies—
With too much urging your pernicious lives,
For 'twere no charity ; yet, to wash your
    blood
From off my hands, here in the view of men
I will unfold some causes of your deaths.
You have misled a prince, a royal king,
A happy gentleman in blood and lineaments,
By you unhappied and disfigured clean : 10
You have in manner with your sinful hours
Made a divorce betwixt his queen and him,
Broke the possession of a royal bed
And stain'd the beauty of a fair queen's
    cheeks
With tears drawn from her eyes by your foul
    wrongs.
Myself, a prince by fortune of my birth,
Near to the king in blood, and near in love
Till you did make him misinterpret me,

Have stoop'd my neck under your injuries,
And sigh'd my English breath in foreign
    clouds,   20
Eating the bitter bread of banishment ;
Whilst you have fed upon my signories,
Dispark'd my parks and fell'd my forest
    woods,
From my own windows torn my household
    coat,
Razed out my imprese, leaving me no sign,
Save men's opinions and my living blood,
To show the world I am a gentleman.
This and much more, much more than twice
    all this,
Condemns you to the death. See them deliv-
    er'd over
To execution and the hand of death.   30
  Bushy. More welcome is the stroke of
    death to me
Than Bolingbroke to England. Lords, fare-
    well.
  Green. My comfort is that heaven will
    take our souls
And plague injustice with the pains of hell.
  Boling. My Lord Northumberland, see
    them dispatch'd.
      [Exeunt Northumberland and others,
                         with the prisoners.
Uncle, you say the queen is at your house ;
For God's sake, fairly let her be entreated :
Tell her I send to her my kind commends ;
Take special care my greetings be deliver'd.
  York. A gentleman of mine I have dis-
    patch'd   40
With letters of your love to her at large.
  Boling. Thanks, gentle uncle. Come, lords,
    away,
To fight with Glendower and his complices :
Awhile to work, and after holiday.   *[Exeunt.*

  SCENE II. *The coast of Wales. A castle in*
                view.

Drums ; flourish and colors. Enter KING
    RICHARD, *the* BISHOP OF CARLISLE, AU-
    MERLE, *and Soldiers.*

  K. Rich. Barkloughly castle call they this
    at hand ?
  Aum. Yea, my lord. How brooks your
    grace the air,
After your late tossing on the breaking seas ?
  K. Rich. Needs must I like it well : I weep
    for joy
To stand upon my kingdom once again.
Dear earth, I do salute thee with my hand,
Though rebels wound thee with their horses'
    hoofs :
As a long-parted mother with her child
Plays fondly with her tears and smiles in
    meeting,
So, weeping, smiling, greet I thee, my earth,
And do thee favors with my royal hands. 11
Feed not thy sovereign's foe, my gentle earth,
Nor with thy sweets comfort his ravenous
    sense ;
But let thy spiders, that suck up thy venom,
And heavy-gaited toads lie in their way,
Doing annoyance to the treacherous feet
Which with usurping steps do trample thee :
Yield stinging nettles to mine enemies ;
And when they from thy bosom pluck a
    flower,
Guard it, I pray thee, with a lurking adder 20

Whose double tongue may with a mortal
    touch
Throw death upon thy sovereign's enemies.
Mock not my senseless conjuration, lords :
This earth shall have a feeling and these
    stones
Prove armed soldiers, ere her native king
Shall falter under foul rebellion's arms.
    Car. Fear not, my lord : that Power that
    made you king
Hath power to keep you king in spite of all.
The means that heaven yields must be em-
    braced,
And not neglected ; else, if heaven would, 30
And we will not, heaven's offer we refuse,
The proffer'd means of succor and redress.
    Aum. He means, my lord, that we are too
    remiss ;
Whilst Bolingbroke, through our security,
Grows strong and great in substance and in
    power.
    K. Rich. Discomfortable cousin ! know'st
    thou not
That when the searching eye of heaven is hid,
Behind the globe, that lights the lower world,
Then thieves and robbers range abroad unseen
In murders and in outrage, boldly here ; 40
But when from under this terrestrial ball
He fires the proud tops of the eastern pines
And darts his light through every guilty hole,
Then murders, treasons, and detested sins,
The cloak of night being pluck'd from off
    their backs,
Stand bare and naked, trembling at them-
    selves ?
So when this thief, this traitor, Bolingbroke,
Who all this while did revell'd in the night
Whilst we were wandering with the antipodes,
Shall see us rising in our throne, the east, 50
His treasons will sit blushing in his face,
Not able to endure the sight of day,
But self-affrighted tremble at his sin.
Not all the water in the rough rude sea
Can wash the balm off from an anointed
    king ;
The breath of worldly men cannot depose
The deputy elected by the Lord :
For every man that Bolingbroke hath press'd
To lift shrewd steel against our golden crown,
God for his Richard hath in heavenly pay
A glorious angel : then, if angels fight, 61
Weak men must fall, for heaven still guards
    the right.

        Enter SALISBURY.

Welcome, my lord : how far off lies your
    power ?
    Sal. Nor near nor farther off, my gracious
    lord,
Than this weak arm : discomfort guides my
    tongue
And bids me speak of nothing but despair.
One day too late, I fear me, noble lord,
Hath clouded all thy happy days on earth :
O, call back yesterday, bid time return,
And thou shalt have twelve thousand fighting
    men ! 70
To-day, to-day, unhappy day, too late,
O'erthrows thy joys, friends, fortune and thy
    state :
For all the Welshmen, hearing thou wert
    dead,
Are gone to Bolingbroke, dispersed and fled.

    Aum. Comfort, my liege ; why looks your
    grace so pale ?
    K. Rich. But now the blood of twenty
    thousand men
Did triumph in my face, and they are fled ;
And, till so much blood thither come again,
Have I not reason to look pale and dead ? 80
All souls that will be safe fly from my side,
For time hath set a blot upon my pride.
    Aum. Comfort, my liege ; remember who
    you are.
    K. Rich. I had forgot myself ; am I not
    king ?
Awake, thou coward majesty ! thou sleepest.
Is not the king's name twenty thousand
    names ?
Arm, arm, my name ! a puny subject strikes
At thy great glory. Look not to the ground,
Ye favorites of a king : are we not high ?
High be our thoughts : I know my uncle York
Hath power enough to serve our turn. But
    who comes here ? 90

        Enter SCROOP.

    Scroop. More health and happiness betide
    my liege
Than can my care-tuned tongue deliver him !
    K. Rich. Mine ear is open and my heart
    prepared ;
The worst is worldly loss thou canst unfold.
Say, is my kingdom lost ? why, 'twas my care
And what loss is it to be rid of care ?
Strives Bolingbroke to be as great as we ?
Greater he shall not be ; if he serve God,
We'll serve Him too and be his fellow so : 99
Revolt our subjects ? that we cannot mend ;
They break their faith to God as well as us :
Cry woe, destruction, ruin and decay :
The worst is death, and death will have his
    day.
    Scroop. Glad am I that your highness is so
    arm'd
To bear the tidings of calamity.
Like an unseasonable stormy day,
Which makes the silver rivers drown their
    shores,
As if the world were all dissolved to tears,
So high above his limits swells the rage
Of Bolingbroke, covering your fearful land
With hard bright steel and hearts harder than
    steel. 111
White-beards have arm'd their thin and hair-
    less scalps
Against thy majesty ; boys, with women's
    voices,
Strive to speak big and clap their female joints
In stiff unwieldy arms against thy crown :
The very beadsmen learn to bend their bows
Of double-fatal yew against thy state ;
Yea, distaff-women manage rusty bills
Against thy seat : both young and old rebel,
And all goes worse than I have power to tell.
    K. Rich. Too well, too well thou tell'st a
    tale so ill. 121
Where is the Earl of Wiltshire ? where is
    Bagot ?
What is become of Bushy ? where is Green ?
That they have let the dangerous enemy
Measure our confines with such peaceful steps?
If we prevail, their heads shall pay for it :
I warrant they have made peace with Boling-
    broke.

Scroop. Peace have they made with him in-
deed, my lord.
K. Rich. O villains, vipers, damn'd without
redemption !
Dogs, easily won to fawn on any man ! 130
Snakes, in my heart-blood warm'd, that sting
my heart !
Three Judases, each one thrice worse than
Judas !
Would they make peace ? terrible hell make
war
Upon their spotted souls for this offence !
Scroop. Sweet love, I see, changing his
property,
Turns to the sourest and most deadly hate :
Again uncurse their souls ; their peace is made
With heads, and not with hands ; those whom
you curse
Have felt the worst of death's destroying
wound
And lie full low, graved in the hollow ground.
Aum. Is Bushy, Green, and the Earl of
Wiltshire dead ? 141
Scroop. Ay, all of them at Bristol lost their
heads.
Aum. Where is the duke my father with
his power ?
K. Rich. No matter where ; of comfort no
man speak :
Let's talk of graves, of worms, and epitaphs ;
Make dust our paper and with rainy eyes
Write sorrow on the bosom of the earth,
Let's choose executors and talk of wills :
And yet not so, for what can we bequeath
Save our deposed bodies to the ground ? 150
Our lands, our lives and all are Bolingbroke's,
And nothing can we call our own but death
And that small model of the barren earth
Which serves as paste and cover to our bones.
For God's sake, let us sit upon the ground
And tell sad stories of the death of kings :
How some have been deposed ; some slain in
war ;
Some haunted by the ghosts they have de-
posed ;
Some poison'd by their wives : some sleeping
kill'd ;
All murder'd : for within the hollow crown
That rounds the mortal temples of a king 161
Keeps Death his court and there the antic sits,
Scoffing his state and grinning at his pomp,
Allowing him a breath, a little scene,
To monarchize, be fear'd and kill with looks,
Infusing him with self and vain conceit,
As if this flesh which walls about our life,
Were brass impregnable, and humor'd thus
Comes at the last and with a little pin
Bores through his castle wall, and farewell
king ! 170
Cover your heads and mock not flesh and
blood
With solemn reverence : throw away respect,
Tradition, form and ceremonious duty,
For you have but mistook me all this while :
I live with bread like you, feel want,
Taste grief, need friends : subjected thus,
How can you say to me, I am a king ?
Car. My lord, wise men ne'er sit and wail
their woes,
But presently prevent the ways to wail. 179
To fear the foe, since fear oppresseth strength,
Gives in your weakness strength unto your foe,
And so your follies fight against yourself.

Fear and be slain ; no worse can come to
fight :
And fight and die is death destroying death ;
Where fearing dying pays death servile breath.
Aum. My father hath a power ; inquire of
him,
And learn to make a body of a limb.
K. Rich. Thou chidest me well : proud
Bolingbroke, I come
To change blows with thee for our day of
doom.
This ague fit of fear is over-blown; 190
An easy task it is to win our own.
Say, Scroop, where lies our uncle with his
power ?
Speak sweetly, man, although thy looks be
sour.
Scroop. Men judge by the complexion of
the sky
The state and inclination of the day :
So may you by my dull and heavy eye,
My tongue hath but a heavier tale to say.
I play the torturer, by small and small
To lengthen out the worst that must be
spoken :
Your uncle York is join'd with Bolingbroke,
And all your northern castles yielded up, 201
And all your southern gentlemen in arms
Upon his party.
K. Rich.   Thou hast said enough.
Beshrew thee, cousin, which didst lead me
forth   [*To Aumerle.*
Of that sweet way I was in to despair !
What say you now ? what comfort have we
now ?
By heaven, I'll hate him everlastingly
That bids me be of comfort any more.
Go to Flint castle : there I'll pine away ;
A king, woe's slave, shall kingly woe obey. 210
That power I have, discharge ; and let them
go
To ear the land that hath some hope to grow,
For I have none : let no man speak again
To alter this, for counsel is but vain.
Aum. My liege, one word.
K. Rich.   He does me double wrong
That wounds me with the flatteries of his
tongue.
Discharge my followers : let them hence away,
From Richard's night to Bolingbroke's fair
day.   [*Exeunt.*

SCENE III. *Wales. Before Flint castle.*

Enter, with drum and colors, BOLINGBROKE,
YORK, NORTHUMBERLAND, Attendants, *and
forces.*

Boling. So that by this intelligence we
learn
The Welshmen are dispersed, and Salisbury
Is gone to meet the king, who lately landed
With some few private friends upon this coast.
North. The news is very fair and good, my
lord :
Richard not far from hence hath hid his head.
York. It would beseem the Lord Northum-
berland
To say 'King Richard :' alack the heavy day
When such a sacred king should hide his head.
North. Your grace mistakes ; only to be
brief,
Left I his title out.
York.   The time hath been, 10

Would you have been so brief with him, he
    would
Have been so brief with you, to shorten you,
For taking so the head, your whole head's
    length.
  Boling. Mistake not, uncle, further than
    you should.
  York. Take not, good cousin, further than
    you should.
Lest you mistake the heavens are o'er our
    heads.
  Boling. I know it, uncle, and oppose not
    myself
Against their will. But who comes here ?   19

         Enter PERCY.

Welcome, Harry : what, will not this castle
    yield ?
  Percy. The castle royally is mann'd, my
    lord,
Against thy entrance.
  Boling. Royally !
Why, it contains no king ?
  Percy.   Yes, my good lord,
It doth contain a king ; King Richard lies
Within the limits of yon lime and stone :
And with him are the Lord Aumerle, Lord
    Salisbury,
Sir Stephen Scroop, besides a clergyman
Of holy reverence ; who, I cannot learn.
  North. O, belike it is the Bishop of Car-
    lisle.
  Boling. Noble lords,   31
Go to the rude ribs of that ancient castle ;
Through brazen trumpet send the breath of
    parley
Into his ruin'd ears, and thus deliver :
Henry Bolingbroke
On both his knees doth kiss King Richard's
    hand
And sends allegiance and true faith of heart
To his most royal person, hither come
Even at his feet to lay my arms and power,
Provided that my banishment repeal'd   40
And lands restored again be freely granted :
If not, I'll use the advantage of my power
And lay the summer's dust with showers of
    blood
Rain'd from the wounds of slaughter'd English-
    men :
The which, how far off from the mind of Bol-
    ingbroke
It is, such crimson tempest should bedrench
The fresh green lap of fair King Richard's
    land,
My stooping duty tenderly shall show.
Go, signify as much, while here we march
Upon the grassy carpet of this plain.   50
Let's march without the noise of threatening
    drum,
That from this castle's tatter'd battlements
Our fair appointments may be well perused.
Methinks King Richard and myself should
    meet
With no less terror than the elements
Of fire and water, when their thundering shock
At meeting tears the cloudy cheeks of heaven.
Be he the fire, I'll be the yielding water :
The rage be his, whilst on the earth I rain
My waters ; on the earth, and not on him. 60
March on, and mark King Richard how he
    looks.

*Parle without, and answer within. Then a
flourish. Enter on the walls,* KING RICHARD,
the BISHOP OF CARLISLE, AUMERLE, SCROOP,
and SALISBURY.

See, see, King Richard doth himself appear,
As doth the blushing discontented sun
From out the fiery portal of the east,
When he perceives the envious clouds are bent
To dim his glory and to stain the track
Of his bright passage to the occident.
  York. Yet looks he like a king : behold, his
    eye,
As bright as is the eagle's, lightens forth
Controlling majesty : alack, alack, for woe, 70
That any harm should stain so fair a show !
  K. Rich. We are amazed ; and thus long
    have we stood
To watch the fearful bending of thy knee,
                       [*To* North.
Because we thought ourself thy lawful king :
And if we be, how dare thy joints forget
To pay their awful duty to our presence ?
If we be not, show us the hand of God
That hath dismiss'd us from our stewardship ;
For well we know, no hand of blood and bone
Can gripe the sacred handle of our sceptre, 80
Unless he do profane, steal, or usurp.
And though you think that all, as you have
    done,
Have torn their souls by turning them from us,
And we are barren and bereft of friends ;
Yet know, my master, God omnipotent,
Is mustering in his clouds on our behalf
Armies of pestilence ; and they shall strike
Your children yet unborn and unbegot,
That lift your vassal hands against my head
And threat the glory of my precious crown. 90
Tell Bolingbroke—for yond methinks he
    stands—
That every stride he makes upon my land
Is dangerous treason : he is come to open
The purple testament of bleeding war ;
But ere the crown he looks for live in peace,
Ten thousand bloody crowns of mothers' sons
Shall ill become the flower of England's face,
Change the complexion of her maid-pale peace
To scarlet indignation and bedew
Her pastures' grass with faithful English blood.
  North. The king of heaven forbid our lord
    the king   101
Should so with civil and uncivil arms
Be rush'd upon ! Thy thrice noble cousin
Harry Bolingbroke doth humbly kiss thy
    hand ;
And by the honorable tomb he swears,
That stands upon your royal grandsire's bones,
And by the royalties of both your bloods,
Currents that spring from one most gracious
    head,
And by the buried hand of warlike Gaunt,
And by the worth and honor of himself, 110
Comprising all that may be sworn or said,
His coming hither hath no further scope
Than for his lineal royalties and to beg
Enfranchisement immediate on his knees :
Which on thy royal party granted once,
His glittering arms he will commend to rust,
His barbed steeds to stables, and his heart
To faithful service of your majesty.
This swears he, as he is a prince, is just ;
And, as I am a gentleman, I credit him. 120

K. Rich. Northumberland, say thus the
　　king returns :
His noble cousin is right welcome hither ;
And all the number of his fair demands
Shall be accomplish'd without contradiction :
With all the gracious utterance thou hast
Speak to his gentle hearing kind commends.
We do debase ourselves, cousin, do we not,
　　　　　　　　　　　　　　[To Aumerle.
To look so poorly and to speak so fair ?
Shall we call back Northumberland, and send
Defiance to the traitor, and so die ?　　　130
　Aum. No, good my lord ; let's fight with
　　gentle words
Till time lend friends and friends their helpful
　　swords.
　K. Rich. O God, O God ! that e'er this
　　tongue of mine,
That laid the sentence of dread banishment
On yon proud man, should take it off again
With words of sooth ! O that I were as great
As is my grief, or lesser than my name !
Or that I could forget what I have been,
Or not remember what I must be now !
Swell'st thou, proud heart ? I'll give thee scope
　　to beat,　　　　　　　　　　　　　140
Since foes have scope to beat both thee and
　　me.
　Aum. Northumberland comes back from
　　Bolingbroke.
　K. Rich. What must the king do now ?
　　must he submit ?
The king shall do it : must he be deposed ?
The king shall be contented : must he lose
The name of king ? o' God's name, let it go :
I'll give my jewels for a set of beads,
My gorgeous palace for a hermitage,
My gay apparel for an almsman's gown,
My figured goblets for a dish of wood,　　150
My sceptre for a palmer's walking staff,
My subjects for a pair of carved saints
And my large kingdom for a little grave,
A little little grave, an obscure grave ;
Or I'll be buried in the king's highway,
Some way of common trade, where subjects'
　　feet
May hourly trample on their sovereign's head ;
For on my heart they tread now whilst I live ;
And buried once, why not upon my head ?
Aumerle, thou weep'st, my tender-hearted
　　cousin !　　　　　　　　　　　　　160
We'll make foul weather with despised tears ;
Our sighs and they shall lodge the summer
　　corn,
And make a dearth in this revolting land.
Or shall we play the wantons with our woes,
And make some pretty match with shedding
　　tears ?
As thus, to drop them still upon one place,
Till they have fretted us a pair of graves
Within the earth ; and, therein laid,—there lies
Two kinsmen digg'd their graves with weep-
　　ing eyes.
Would not this ill do well ? Well, well, I see
I talk but idly, and you laugh at me.　　171
Most mighty prince, my Lord Northumber-
　　land,
What says King Bolingbroke ? will his majesty
Give Richard leave to live till Richard die ?
You make a leg, and Bolingbroke says ay.
　North. My lord, in the base court he doth
　　attend

To speak with you ; may it please you to come
　　down.
　K. Rich. Down, down I come ; like glis-
　　tering Phaethon,
Wanting the manage of unruly jades.
In the base court ? Base court, where kings
　　grow base,　　　　　　　　　　　　180
To come at traitors' calls and do them grace.
In the base court ? Come down ? Down,
　　court ! down, king !
For night-owls shriek where mounting larks
　　should sing.　　　　　*[Exeunt from above
　Boling. What says his majesty ?
　North.　　　　　Sorrow and grief of heart
Makes him speak fondly, like a frantic man :
Yet he is come.

Enter King Richard *and his attendants below.*

　Boling. Stand all apart,
And show fair duty to his majesty.
　　　　　　　　　　　　　[He kneels down.
My gracious lord,—
　K. Rich. Fair cousin, you debase your
　　princely knee　　　　　　　　　　190
To make the base earth proud with kissing it :
Me rather had my heart might feel your love
Than my unpleased eye see your courtesy.
Up, cousin, up ; your heart is up, I know,
Thus high at least, although your knee be low.
　Boling. My gracious lord, I come but for
　　mine own.
　K. Rich. Your own is yours, and I am
　　yours, and all.
　Boling. So far be mine, my most redoubted
　　lord,
As my true service shall deserve your love.
　K. Rich. Well you deserve : they well de-
　　serve to have,　　　　　　　　　　200
That know the strong'st and surest way to get.
Uncle, give me your hands : nay, dry your
　　eyes ;
Tears show their love, but want their remedies.
Cousin, I am too young to be your father,
Though you are old enough to be my heir.
What you will have, I'll give, and willing too ;
For do we must what force will have us do.
Set on towards London, cousin, is it so ?
　Boling. Yea, my good lord.
　K. Rich.　　　Then I must not say no.　210
　　　　　　　　　　　　　[Flourish. Exeunt.

Scene IV. *Langley. The* Duke of York's
　　　　　　　garden.

Enter the Queen *and two* Ladies.

　Queen. What sport shall we devise here in
　　this garden,
To drive away the heavy thought of care ?
　Lady. Madam, we'll play at bowls.
　Queen. 'Twill make me think the world is
　　full of rubs,
And that my fortune rubs against the bias.
　Lady. Madam, we'll dance.
　Queen.　　　My legs can keep no measure in
　　delight,
When my poor heart no measure keeps in
　　grief :
Therefore, no dancing, girl ; some other sport.
　Lady. Madam, we'll tell tales.　　　　10
　Queen. Of sorrow or of joy ?
　Lady.　　　　　Of either, madam.
　Queen. Of neither, girl :
For if of joy, being altogether wanting,
It doth remember me the more of sorrow ;

Or if of grief, being altogether had,
It adds more sorrow to my want of joy:
For what I have I need not to repeat;
And what I want it boots not to complain.
	Lady. Madam, I'll sing.
	Queen.		'Tis well that thou hast cause
But thou shouldst please me better, wouldst
		thou weep.			20
	Lady. I could weep, madam, would it do
		you good.
	Queen. And I could sing, would weeping
		do me good,
And never borrow any tear of thee.

		Enter a Gardener, *and two* Servants.

But stay, here come the gardeners:
Let's step into the shadow of these trees.
My wretchedness unto a row of pins,
They'll talk of state; for every one doth so
Against a change; woe is forerun with woe.
			[*Queen and Ladies retire.*
	Gard. Go, bind thou up yon dangling apri-
		cocks,
Which, like unruly children, make their sire 30
Stoop with oppression of their prodigal
		weight:
Give some supportance to the bending twigs.
Go thou, and like an executioner,
Cut off the heads of too fast growing sprays,
That look too lofty in our commonwealth:
All must be even in our government.
You thus employ'd, I will go root away
The noisome weeds, which without profit suck
The soil's fertility from wholesome flowers.
	Serv. Why should we in the compass of a
		pale			40
Keep law and form and due proportion,
Showing, as in a model, our firm estate,
When our sea-walled garden, the whole land,
Is full of weeds, her fairest flowers choked up,
Her fruit-trees all upturned, her hedges ruin'd,
Her knots disorder'd and her wholesome herbs
Swarming with caterpillars?
	Gard.			Hold thy peace:
He that hath suffer'd this disorder'd spring
Hath now himself met with the fall of leaf:
The weeds which his broad-spreading leaves
		did shelter,			50
That seem'd in eating him to hold him up,
Are pluck'd up root and all by Bolingbroke,
I mean the Earl of Wiltshire, Bushy, Green.
	Serv. What, are they dead?
	Gard.		They are; and Bolingbroke
Hath seized the wasteful king. O, what pity
		is it
That he had not so trimm'd and dress'd his
		land
As we this garden! We at time of year
Do wound the bark, the skin of our fruit-trees,
Lest, being over-proud in sap and blood,
With too much riches it confound itself:	60
Had he done so to great and growing men,
They might have lived to bear and he to taste
Their fruits of duty: superfluous branches
We lop away, that bearing boughs may live:
Had he done so, himself had borne the crown,
Which waste of idle hours hath quite thrown
		down.
	Serv. What, think you then the king shall
		be deposed?
	Gard. Depress'd he is already, and deposed
'Tis doubt he will be: letters came last night

To a dear friend of the good Duke of York's,
That tell black tidings.			71
	Queen. O, I am press'd to death through
		want of speaking!	[*Coming forward.*
Thou, old Adam's likeness, set to dress this
		garden,
How dares thy harsh rude tongue sound this
		unpleasing news?
What Eve, what serpent, hath suggested thee
To make a second fall of cursed man?
Why dost thou say King Richard is deposed?
Darest thou, thou little better thing than earth,
Divine his downfall? Say, where, when, and
		how,
Camest thou by this ill tidings? speak, thou
		wretch.			80
	Gard. Pardon me, madam: little joy have I
To breathe this news; yet what I say is true.
King Richard, he is in the mighty hold
Of Bolingbroke: their fortunes both are
		weigh'd:
In your lord's scale is nothing but himself,
And some few vanities that make him light;
But in the balance of great Bolingbroke,
Besides himself, are all the English peers,
And with that odds he weighs King Richard
		down.
Post you to London, and you will find it so;
I speak no more than every one doth know. 91
	Queen. Nimble mischance, that art so light
		of foot,
Doth not thy embassage belong to me,
And am I last that knows it? O, thou think'st
To serve me last, that I may longest keep
Thy sorrow in my breast. Come, ladies, go,
To meet at London London's king in woe.
What, was I born to this, that my sad look
Should grace the triumph of great Boling-
		broke?			99
Gardener, for telling me these news of woe,
Pray God the plants thou graft'st may never
		grow.		[*Exeunt Queen and Ladies.*
	Gard. Poor queen! so that thy state might
		be no worse,
I would my skill were subject to thy curse.
Here did she fall a tear; here in this place
I'll set a bank of rue, sour herb of grace:
Rue, even for ruth, here shortly shall be seen,
In the remembrance of a weeping queen.
			[*Exeunt.*

ACT IV.

SCENE I. *Westminster Hall.*

Enter, as to the Parliament, BOLINGBROKE,
AUMERLE, NORTHUMBERLAND, PERCY, FITZ-
WATER, SURREY, *the* BISHOP OF CARLISLE,
the ABBOT OF WESTMINSTER, *and another*
Lord, Herald, Officers, *and* BAGOT.

	Boling. Call forth Bagot.
Now, Bagot, freely speak thy mind;
What thou dost know of noble Gloucester's
		death,
Who wrought it with the king, and who per-
		form'd
The bloody office of his timeless end.
	Bagot. Then set before my face the Lord
		Aumerle.
	Boling. Cousin, stand forth, and look upon
		that man.

Bagot. My Lord Aumerle, I know your
daring tongue
Scorns to unsay what once it hath deliver'd.
In that dead time when Gloucester's death was
plotted,   10
I heard you say, ' Is not my arm of length,
That reacheth from the restful English court
As far as Calais, to mine uncle's head ? '
Amongst much other talk, that very time,
I heard you say that you had rather refuse
The offer of an hundred thousand crowns
Than Bolingbroke's return to England ;
Adding withal, how blest this land would be
In this your cousin's death.
  Aum.   Princes and noble lords,
What answer shall I make to this base man ?   21
Shall I so much dishonor my fair stars,
On equal terms to give him chastisement ?
Either I must, or have mine honor soil'd
With the attainder of his slanderous lips.
There is my gage, the manual seal of death,
That marks thee out for hell : I say, thou liest,
And will maintain what thou hast said is false
In thy heart-blood, though being all too base
To stain the temper of my knightly sword.
  Boling. Bagot, forbear ; thou shalt not take
it up.   30
  Aum. Excepting one, I would he were the
best
In all this presence that hath moved me so.
  Fitz. If that thy valor stand on sympathy,
There is my gage, Aumerle, in gage to thine :
By that fair sun which shows me where thou
stand'st,
I heard thee say, and vauntingly thou spakest
it,
That thou wert cause of noble Gloucester's
death.
If thou deny'st it twenty times, thou liest ;
And I will turn thy falsehood to thy heart,
Where it was forged, with my rapier's point.
  Aum. Thou darest not, coward, live to see
that day.   41
  Fitz. Now, by my soul, I would it were this
hour.
  Aum. Fitzwater, thou art damn'd to hell
for this.
  Percy. Aumerle, thou liest ; his honor is as
true
In this appeal as thou art all unjust ;
And that thou art so, there I throw my gage,
To prove it on thee to the extremest point
Of mortal breathing : seize it, if thou darest.
  Aum. An if I do not, may my hands rot off
And never brandish more revengeful steel   50
Over the glittering helmet of my foe !
  Another Lord. I task the earth to the like,
forsworn Aumerle ;
And spur thee on with full as many lies
As may be holloa'd in thy treacherous ear
From sun to sun : there is my honor's pawn ;
Engage it to the trial, if thou darest.
  Aum. Who sets me else ? by heaven, I'll
throw at all :
I have a thousand spirits in one breast,
To answer twenty thousand such as you.
  Surrey. My Lord Fitzwater, I do remem-
ber well   60
The very time Aumerle and you did talk.
  Fitz. 'Tis very true : you were in presence
then ;
And you can witness with me this is true.

  Surrey. As false, by heaven, as heaven it-
self is true.
  Fitz. Surrey, thou liest.
  Surrey.   Dishonorable boy !
That lie shall lie so heavy on my sword,
That it shall render vengeance and revenge
Till thou the lie-giver and that lie do lie
In earth as quiet as thy father's skull :
In proof whereof, there is my honor's pawn ;
Engage it to the trial, if thou darest.   71
  Fitz. How fondly dost thou spur a forward
horse !
If I dare eat, or drink, or breathe, or live,
I dare meet Surrey in a wilderness,
And spit upon him, whilst I say he lies,
And lies, and lies : there is my bond of faith,
To tie thee to my strong correction.
As I intend to thrive in this new world,
Aumerle is guilty of my true appeal :
Besides, I heard the banish'd Norfolk say   80
That thou, Aumerle, didst send two of thy
men
To execute the noble duke at Calais.
  Aum. Some honest Christian trust me with
a gage,
That Norfolk lies : here do I throw down this,
If he may be repeal'd, to try his honor.
  Boling. These differences shall all rest
under gage
Till Norfolk be repeal'd : repeal'd he shall be,
And, though mine enemy, restored again
To all his lands and signories : when he's
return'd,
Against Aumerle we will enforce his trial.   90
  Car. That honorable day shall ne'er be
seen.
Many a time hath banish'd Norfolk fought
For Jesu Christ in glorious Christian field,
Streaming the ensign of the Christian cross
Against black pagans, Turks, and Saracens :
And toil'd with works of war, retired himself
To Italy ; and there at Venice gave
His body to that pleasant country's earth,
And his pure soul unto his captain Christ,
Under whose colors he had fought so long.   100
  Boling. Why, bishop, is Norfolk dead ?
  Car. As surely as I live, my lord.
  Boling. Sweet peace conduct his sweet soul
to the bosom
Of good old Abraham ! Lords appellants,
Your differences shall all rest under gage
Till we assign you to your days of trial.

  Enter YORK, *attended.*

  York. Great Duke of Lancaster, I come to
thee
From plume-pluck'd Richard ; who with will-
ing soul
Adopts thee heir, and his high sceptre yields
To the possession of thy royal hand :   110
Ascend his throne, descending now from him ;
And long live Henry, fourth of that name !
  Boling. In God's name, I'll ascend the
regal throne.
  Car. Marry. God forbid !
Worst in this royal presence may I speak,
Yet best beseeming me to speak the truth.
Would God that any in this noble presence
Were enough noble to be upright judge
Of noble Richard ! then true noblesse would
Learn him forbearance from so foul a wrong.
What subject can give sentence on his king ?

And who sits here that is not Richard's sub-
    ject ?
Thieves are not judged but they are by to hear,
Although apparent guilt be seen in them ;
And shall the figure of God's majesty,
His captain, steward, deputy-elect,
Anointed, crowned, planted many years,
Be judged by subject and inferior breath,
And he himself not present ? O, forfend it,
    God,
That in a Christian climate souls refined   130
Should show so heinous, black, obscene a
    deed !
I speak to subjects, and a subject speaks,
Stirr'd up by God, thus boldly for his king.
My Lord of Hereford here, whom you call
    king,
Is a foul traitor to proud Hereford's king :
And if you crown him, let me prophesy :
The blood of English shall manure the ground,
And future ages groan for this foul act ;
Peace shall go sleep with Turks and infidels,
And in this seat of peace tumultuous wars 140
Shall kin with kin and kind with kind con-
    found ;
Disorder, horror, fear and mutiny
Shall here inhabit, and this land be call'd
The field of Golgotha and dead men's skulls.
O, if you raise this house against this house,
It will the woefullest division prove
That ever fell upon this cursed earth.
Prevent it, resist it, let it not be so,
Lest child, child's children, cry against you
    ' woe ! '
   North.   Well have you argued, sir ; and, for
    your pains,   150
Of capital treason we arrest you here.
My Lord of Westminster, be it your charge
To keep him safely till his day of trial.
May it please you, lords, to grant the com-
    mons' suit.
   Boling. Fetch hither Richard, that in com-
    mon view
He may surrender ; so we shall proceed
Without suspicion.
   York.   I will be his conduct. [*Exit.*
   Boling. Lords, you that here are under our
    arrest,
Procure your sureties for your days of answer.
Little are we beholding to your love,   160
And little look'd for at your helping hands.

Re-enter YORK, *with* RICHARD, *and* Officers
    bearing the regalia.

   K. Rich. Alack, why am I sent for to a
    king,
Before I have shook off the regal thoughts
Wherewith I reign'd ? I hardly yet have learn'd
To insinuate, flatter, bow, and bend my limbs :
Give sorrow leave awhile to tutor me
To this submission. Yet I well remember
The favors of these men : were they not mine ?
Did they not sometime cry, ' all hail ! ' to me ?
So Judas did to Christ : but he, in twelve, 170
Found truth in all but one : I, in twelve thou-
    sand, none.
God save the king ! Will no man say amen ?
Am I both priest and clerk ? well then, amen.
God save the king ! although I be not he ;
And yet, amen, if heaven do think him me.
To do what service am I sent for hither ?
   York. To do that office of thine own good
    will

Which tired majesty did make thee offer,
The resignation of thy state and crown
To Henry Bolingbroke   180
   K. Rich. Give me the crown. Here, cousin,
    seize the crown ;
Here cousin :
On this side my hand, and on that side yours.
Now is this golden crown like a deep well
That owes two buckets, filling one another,
The emptier ever dancing in the air,
The other down, unseen and full of water :
That bucket down and full of tears am I,
Drinking my griefs, whilst you mount up on
    high.
   Boling. I thought you had been willing to
    resign.   190
   K. Rich. My crown I am ; but still my
    griefs are mine :
You may my glories and my state depose,
But not my griefs ; still am I king of those.
   Boling. Part of your cares you give me
    with your crown.
   K. Rich. Your cares set up do not pluck
    my cares down.
My care is loss of care, by old care done ;
Your care is gain of care, by new care won :
The cares I give I have, though given away ;
They tend the crown, yet still with me they
    stay.
   Boling. Are you contented to resign the
    crown ?   200
   K. Rich. Ay, no ; no, ay ; for I must noth-
    ing be ;
Therefore no no, for I resign to thee.
Now mark me, how I will undo myself ;
I give this heavy weight from off my head
And this unwieldy sceptre from my hand,
The pride of kingly sway from out my heart ;
With mine own tears I wash away my balm,
With mine own hands I give away my crown,
With mine own tongue deny my sacred state,
With mine own breath release all duty's rites :
All pomp and majesty I do forswear ;   211
My manors, rents, revenues I forego ;
My acts, decrees, and statutes I deny :
God pardon all oaths that are broke to me !
God keep all vows unbroke that swear to thee !
Make me, that nothing have, with nothing
    grieved,
And thou with all pleased, that hast all
    achieved !
Long mayst thou live in Richard's seat to sit,
And soon lie Richard in an earthly pit !   219
God save King Harry, unking'd Richard says,
And send him many years of sunshine days !
What more remains ?
   North.   No more, but that you read
These accusations and these grievous crimes
Committed by your person and your followers
Against the state and profit of this land ;
That, by confessing them, the souls of men
May deem that you are worthily deposed.
   K. Rich. Must I do so ? and must I ravel
    out
My weaved-up folly ? Gentle Northumberland,
If thy offences were upon record,   230
Would it not shame thee in so fair a troop
To read a lecture of them ? If thou wouldst,
There shouldst thou find one heinous article,
Containing the deposing of a king
And cracking the strong warrant of an oath,
Mark'd with a blot, damn'd in the book of
    heaven :

Nay, all of you that stand and look upon,
Whilst that my wretchedness doth bait myself,
Though some of you with Pilate wash your
    hands
Showing an outward pity ; yet you Pilates 240
Have here deliver'd me to my sour cross,
And water cannot wash away your sin.
   North. My lord, dispatch ; read o'er these
    articles.
   K. Rich. Mine eyes are full of tears, I can-
    not see :
And yet salt water blinds them not so much
But they can see a sort of traitors here.
Nay, if I turn mine eyes upon myself,
I find myself a traitor with the rest ;
For I have given here my soul's consent
To undeck the pompous body of a king ; 250
Made glory base and sovereignty a slave,
Proud majesty a subject, state a peasant.
   North. My lord,—
   K. Rich. No lord of thine, thou haught in-
    sulting man,
Nor no man's lord ; I have no name, no title,
No, not that name was given me at the font,
But 'tis usurp'd : alack the heavy day,
That I have worn so many winters out,
And know not now what name to call myself !
O that I were a mockery king of snow, 260
Standing before the sun of Bolingbroke,
To melt myself away in water-drops !
Good king, great king, and yet not greatly
    good,
An if my word be sterling yet in England,
Let it command a mirror hither straight,
That it may show me what a face I have,
Since it is bankrupt of his majesty.
   Boling. Go some of you and fetch a look-
    ing-glass.   [*Exit an attendant.*
   North. Read o'er this paper while the glass
    doth come.
   K. Rich. Fiend, thou torment'st me ere I
    come to hell !   270
   Boling. Urge it no more, my Lord North-
    umberland.
   North. The commons will not then be sat-
    isfied.
   K. Rich. They shall be satisfied : I'll read
    enough,
When I do see the very book indeed
Where all my sins are writ, and that's myself.

    Re-enter Attendant, *with a glass.*

Give me the glass, and therein will I read.
No deeper wrinkles yet ? hath sorrow struck
So many blows upon this face of mine,
And made no deeper wounds ? O flattering
    glass,
Like to my followers in prosperity, 280
Thou dost beguile me ! Was this face the face
That every day under his household roof
Did keep ten thousand men ? was this the face
That, like the sun, did make beholders wink ?
Was this the face that faced so many follies,
And was at last out-faced by Bolingbroke ?
A brittle glory shineth in this face :
As brittle as the glory is the face ;
    [*Dashes the glass against the ground.*
For there it is, crack'd in a hundred shivers.
Mark, silent king, the moral of this sport, 290
How soon my sorrow hath destroy'd my face.
   Boling. The shadow of your sorrow hath
    destroy'd
The shadow of your face.

   K. Rich.   Say that again.
The shadow of my sorrow ! ha ! let's see :
'Tis very true, my grief lies all within ;
And these external manners of laments
Are merely shadows to the unseen grief
That swells with silence in the tortured soul ;
There lies the substance : and I thank thee,
    king,
For thy great bounty, that not only givest 300
Me cause to wail but teachest me the way
How to lament the cause. I'll beg one boon,
And then be gone and trouble you no more.
Shall I obtain it ?
   Boling.   Name it, fair cousin.
   K. Rich. 'Fair cousin' ? I am greater than
    a king :
For when I was a king, my flatterers
Were then but subjects ; being now a subject,
I have a king here to my flatterer.
Being so great, I have no need to beg.
   Boling. Yet ask.
   K. Rich. And shall I have ?
   Boling. You shall.   310
   K. Rich. Then give me leave to go.
   Boling. Whither ?
   K. Rich. Whither you will, so I were from
    your sights.
   Boling. Go, some of you convey him to the
    Tower.
   K. Rich. O, good ! convey ? conveyers are
    you all,
That rise thus nimbly by a true king's fall.
    [*Exeunt King Richard, some Lords,*
               and a Guard.
   Boling. On Wednesday next we solemnly
    set down
Our coronation : lords, prepare yourselves.
    [*Exeunt all except the Bishop of Carlisle, the*
       Abbot of Westminster, and Aumerle.
   Abbot. A woeful pageant have we here be-
    held.   321
   Car. The woe's to come ; the children yet
    unborn.
Shall feel this day as sharp to them as thorn.
   Aum. You holy clergymen, is there no plot
To rid the realm of this pernicious blot ?
   Abbot. My lord,
Before I freely speak my mind herein,
You shall not only take the sacrament
To bury mine intents, but also to effect
Whatever I shall happen to devise. 330
I see your brows are full of discontent,
Your hearts of sorrow and your eyes of tears :
Come home with me to supper ; and I'll lay
A plot shall show us all a merry day. [*Exeunt.*

            ———

ACT V.

SCENE I. *London. A street leading to the*
             Tower.

     Enter QUEEN *and* Ladies.

   Queen. This way the king will come ; this
    is the way
To Julius Cæsar's ill-erected tower,
To whose flint bosom my condemned lord
Is doom'd a prisoner by proud Bolingbroke :
Here let us rest, if this rebellious earth
Have any resting for her true king's queen.

     Enter RICHARD *and* Guard.

But soft, but see, or rather do not see,

My fair rose wither : yet look up, behold,
That you in pity may dissolve to dew, 9
And wash him fresh again with true-love tears.
Ah, thou, the model where old Troy did stand,
Thou map of honor, thou King Richard's
tomb,
And not King Richard ; thou most beauteous
inn,
Why should hard-favor'd grief be lodged in
thee,
When triumph is become an alehouse guest ?
    K. Rich. Join not with grief, fair woman,
do not so,
To make my end too sudden : learn, good soul,
To think our former state a happy dream ;
From which awaked, the truth of what we are
Shows us but this : I am sworn brother, sweet,
To grim Necessity, and he and I 21
Will keep a league till death. Hie thee to
France
And cloister thee in some religious house :
Our holy lives must win a new world's crown,
Which our profane hours here have stricken
down.
    Queen. What, is my Richard both in shape
and mind
Transform'd and weaken'd ? hath Bolingbroke
deposed
Thine intellect ? hath he been in thy heart ?
The lion dying thrusteth forth his paw,
And wounds the earth, if nothing else, with
rage 30
To be o'erpower'd ; and wilt thou, pupil-like,
Take thy correction mildly, kiss the rod,
And fawn on rage with base humility,
Which art a lion and a king of beasts ?
    K. Rich. A king of beasts, indeed ; if
aught but beasts,
I had been still a happy king of men.
Good sometime queen, prepare thee hence for
France :
Think I am dead and that even here thou
takest,
As from my death-bed, thy last living leave.
In winter's tedious nights sit by the fire 40
With good old folks and let them tell thee
tales
Of woeful ages long ago betid ;
And ere thou bid good night, to quit their
griefs,
Tell thou the lamentable tale of me
And send the hearers weeping to their beds :
For why, the senseless brands will sympathize
The heavy accent of thy moving tongue
And in compassion weep the fire out ;
And some will mourn in ashes, some coal-
black,
For the deposing of a rightful king. 50

    Enter NORTHUMBERLAND *and others.*

    North. My lord, the mind of Bolingbroke
is changed :
You must to Pomfret, not unto the Tower.
And, madam, there is order ta'en for you ;
With all swift speed you must away to
France.
    K. Rich. Northumberland, thou ladder
wherewithal
The mounting Bolingbroke ascends my throne,
The time shall not be many hours of age
More than it is ere foul sin gathering head
Shalt break into corruption : thou shalt think,

Though he divide the realm and give thee
half, 60
It is too little, helping him to all ;
And he shall think that thou, which know'st
the way
To plant unrightful kings, wilt know again,
Being ne'er so little urged, another way
To pluck him headlong from the usurped
throne.
The love of wicked men converts to fear ;
That fear to hate, and hate turns one or both
To worthy danger and deserved death.
    North. My guilt be on my head, and there
an end.
Take leave and part ; for you must part forth-
with. 70
    K. Rich. Doubly divorced ! Bad men, you
violate
A twofold marriage, 'twixt my crown and me,
And then betwixt me and my married wife.
Let me unkiss the oath 'twixt thee and me ;
And yet not so, for with a kiss 'twas made.
Part us, Northumberland ; I towards the
north,
Where shivering cold and sickness pines the
clime ;
My wife to France : from whence, set forth in
pomp,
She came adorned hither like sweet May,
Sent back like Hallowmas or short'st of day.
    Queen. And must we be divided ? must we
part ? 81
    K. Rich. Ay, hand from hand, my love,
and heart from heart.
    Queen. Banish us both and send the king
with me.
    North. That were some love but little
policy.
    Queen. Then whither he goes, thither let
me go.
    K. Rich. So two, together weeping, make
one woe.
Weep thou for me in France, I for thee here ;
Better far off than near, be ne'er the near.
Go, count thy way with sighs ; I mine with
groans.
    Queen. So longest way shall have the long-
est moans. 90
    K. Rich. Twice for one step I'll groan, the
way being short,
And piece the way out with a heavy heart.
Come, come, in wooing sorrow let's be brief,
Since, wedding it, there is such length in
grief ;
One kiss shall stop our mouths, and dumbly
part ;
Thus give I mine, and thus take I thy heart.
    Queen. Give me mine own again ; 'twere
no good part
To take on me to keep and kill thy heart.
So, now I have mine own again, be gone,
That I might strive to kill it with a groan. 100
    K. Rich. We make woe wanton with this
fond delay :
Once more, adieu ; the rest let sorrow say.
                                    [*Exeunt.*

    SCENE II. *The* DUKE OF YORK'S *palace.*
        Enter YORK *and his* DUCHESS.

    Duch. My lord, you told me you would tell
the rest,
When weeping made you break the story off,
Of our two cousins coming into London.

York. Where did I leave?
Duch.   At that sad stop, my lord,
Where rude misgovern'd hands from windows' tops
Threw dust and rubbish on King Richard's head.
York. Then, as I said, the duke, great Bolingbroke,
Mounted upon a hot and fiery steed
Which his aspiring rider seem'd to know,
With slow but stately pace kept on his course,
Whilst all tongues cried 'God save thee, Bolingbroke!'   11
You would have thought the very windows spake,
So many greedy looks of young and old
Through casements darted their desiring eyes
Upon his visage, and that all the walls
With painted imagery had said at once
'Jesu preserve thee! welcome, Bolingbroke!'
Whilst he, from the one side to the other turning,
Bareheaded, lower than his proud steed's neck,
Bespake them thus: 'I thank you, countrymen:'   20
And thus still doing, thus he pass'd along.
Duch. Alack, poor Richard! where rode he the whilst?
York. As in a theatre, the eyes of men,
After a well-graced actor leaves the stage,
Are idly bent on him that enters next,
Thinking his prattle to be tedious;
Even so, or with much more contempt, men's eyes
Did scowl on gentle Richard; no man cried 'God save him!'
No joyful tongue gave him his welcome home:
But dust was thrown upon his sacred head:
Which with such gentle sorrow he shook off,
His face still combating with tears and smiles,
The badges of his grief and patience,
That had not God, for some strong purpose, steel'd
The hearts of men, they must perforce have melted
And barbarism itself have pitied him.
But heaven hath a hand in these events,
To whose high will we bound our calm contents.
To Bolingbroke are we sworn subjects now,
Whose state and honor I for aye allow.   40
Duch. Here comes my son Aumerle.
York.   Aumerle that was;
But that is lost for being Richard's friend,
And, madam, you must call him Rutland now:
I am in parliament pledge for his truth
And lasting fealty to the new-made king.

Enter AUMERLE.

Duch. Welcome, my son: who are the violets now
That strew the green lap of the new come spring?
Aum. Madam, I know not, nor I greatly care not:
God knows I had as lief be none as one.
York. Well, bear you well in this new spring of time,   50
Lest you be cropp'd before you come to prime.

What news from Oxford? hold those justs and triumphs?
Aum. For aught I know, my lord, they do.
York. You will be there, I know.
Aum. If God prevent not, I purpose so.
York. What seal is that, that hangs without thy bosom?
Yea, look'st thou pale? let me see the writing.
Aum. My lord, 'tis nothing.
York.   No matter, then, who see it;
I will be satisfied; let me see the writing.
Aum. I do beseech your grace to pardon me: 60
It is a matter of small consequence,
Which for some reasons I would not have seen.
York. Which for some reasons, sir, I mean to see.
I fear, I fear,—
Duch.   What should you fear?
'Tis nothing but some bond, that he is enter'd into
For gay apparel 'gainst the triumph day.
York. Bound to himself! what doth he with a bond
That he is bound to? Wife, thou art a fool.
Boy, let me see the writing.
Aum. I do beseech you, pardon me; I may not show it.   70
York. I will be satisfied; let me see it, I say.
[He plucks it out of his bosom and reads it.
Treason! foul treason! Villain! traitor! slave!
Duch. What is the matter, my lord?
York. Ho! who is within there?

Enter a Servant.

                                Saddle my horse.
God for his mercy, what treachery is here!
Duch. Why, what is it, my lord?
York. Give me my boots, I say; saddle my horse.   [*Exit Servant.*
Now, by mine honor, by my life, by my troth,
I will appeach the villain.
Duch.   What is the matter?
York. Peace, foolish woman.   80
Duch. I will not peace. What is the matter, Aumerle?
Aum. Good mother, be content; it is no more
Than my poor life must answer.
Duch.   Thy life answer!
York. Bring me my boots: I will unto the king.

Re-enter Servant with boots.

Duch. Strike him, Aumerle. Poor boy, thou art amazed.
Hence, villain! never more come in my sight.
York. Give me my boots, I say.
Duch. Why, York, what wilt thou do?
Wilt thou not hide the trespass of thine own?
Have we more sons? or are we like to have?
Is not my teeming date drunk up with time?
And wilt thou pluck my fair son from mine age,
And rob me of a happy mother's name?
Is he not like thee? is he not thine own?
York. Thou fond mad woman,
Wilt thou conceal this dark conspiracy?

A dozen of them here have ta'en the sacra-
ment,
And interchangeably set down their hands,
To kill the king at Oxford.
   Duch.   .   He shall be none;
We'll keep him here : then what is that to
   him ?   100
   York. Away, fond woman! were he
   twenty times my son,
I would appeach him.
   Duch.   Hadst thou groan'd for him
As I have done, thou wouldst be more pitiful.
But now I know thy mind ; thou dost suspect
That I have been disloyal to thy bed,
And that he is a bastard, not thy son :
Sweet York, sweet husband, be not of that
   mind :
He is as like thee as a man may be,
Not like to me, or any of my kin,
And yet I love him.
   York.   Make way, unruly woman! 110
                          [*Exit.*
   Duch. After, Aumerle! mount thee upon
   his horse ;
Spur post, and get before him to the king,
And beg thy pardon ere he do accuse thee.
I'll not be long behind ; though I be old,
I doubt not but to ride as fast as York :
And never will I rise up from the ground
Till Bolingbroke have pardon'd thee. Away,
   be gone !   [*Exeunt.*

      SCENE III. *A royal palace.*

Enter BOLINGBROKE, PERCY, *and other* Lords.
   Boling. Can no man tell me of my un-
   thrifty son ?
'Tis full three months since I did see him last ;
If any plague hang over us, 'tis he.
I would to God, my lords, he might be found :
Inquire at London, 'mongst the taverns there,
For there, they say, he daily doth frequent,
With unrestrained loose companions,
Even such, they say, as stand in narrow lanes,
And beat our watch, and rob our passengers ;
Which he, young wanton and effeminate boy,
Takes on the point of honor to support   11
So dissolute a crew.
   Percy. My lord, some two days since I saw
   the prince,
And told him of those triumphs held at Ox-
   ford.
   Boling. And what said the gallant ?
   Percy. His answer was, he would unto the
   stews,
And from the common'st creature pluck a
   glove,
And wear it as a favor ; and with that
He would unhorse the lustiest challenger.
   Boling. As dissolute as desperate ; yet
   through both   20
I see some sparks of better hope, which elder
   years
May happily bring forth. But who comes
   here ?

        Enter AUMERLE.
   Aum. Where is the king ?
   Boling. What means our cousin, that he
   stares and looks
So wildly ?
   Aum. God save your grace ! I do beseech
   your majesty,

To have some conference with your grace
   alone.
   Boling. Withdraw yourselves, and leave
   us here alone. [*Exeunt Percy and Lords.*
What is the matter with our cousin now ?
   Aum. For ever may my knees grow to the
   earth,   30
My tongue cleave to my roof within my
   mouth,
Unless a pardon ere I rise or speak.
   Boling. Intended or committed was this
   fault ?
If on the first, how heinous e'er it be,
To win thy after-love I pardon thee.
   Aum. Then give me leave that I may turn
   the key,
That no man enter till my tale be done.
   Boling. Have thy desire.
   York. [*Within*] My liege, beware ; look to
   thyself ;
Thou hast a traitor in thy presence there.   40
   Boling. Villain, I'll make thee safe.
                        [*Drawing.*
   Aum. Stay thy revengeful hand ; thou hast
   no cause to fear.
   York. [*Within*] Open the door, secure, fool-
   hardy king :
Shall I for love speak treason to thy face ?
Open the door, or I will break it open.

          Enter YORK.

   Boling. What is the matter, uncle ? speak ;
Recover breath ; tell us how near is danger,
That we may arm us to encounter it.
   York. Peruse this writing here, and thou
   shalt know   49
The treason that my haste forbids me show.
   Aum. Remember, as thou read'st, thy
   promise pass'd :
I do repent me ; read not my name there ;
My heart is not confederate with my hand.
   York. It was, villain, ere thy hand did
   set it down.
I tore it from the traitor's bosom, king ;
Fear, and not love, begets his penitence :
Forget to pity him, lest thy pity prove
A serpent that will sting thee to the heart.
   Boling. O heinous, strong and bold con-
   spiracy !
O loyal father of a treacherous son !   60
Thou sheer, immaculate and silver fountain,
From whence this stream through muddy pas-
   sages
Hath held his current and defiled himself !
Thy overflow of good converts to bad,
And thy abundant goodness shall excuse
This deadly blot in thy digressing son.
   York. So shall my virtue be his vice's
   bawd ;
And he shall spend mine honor with his
   shame,
As thriftless sons their scraping fathers' gold.
Mine honor lives when his dishonor dies,   70
Or my shamed life in his dishonor lies :
Thou kill'st me in his life ; giving him breath,
The traitor lives, the true man's put to
   death.
   Duch. [*Within*] What ho, my liege ! for
   God's sake, let me in.
   Boling. What shrill-voiced suppliant makes
   this eager cry ?
   Duch. A woman, and thy aunt, great king ;
   'tis I.

Speak with me, pity me, open the door :
A beggar begs that never begg'd before.
  Boling. Our scene is alter'd from a serious
     thing,
And now changed to 'The Beggar and the
     King.'   80
My dangerous cousin, let your mother in :
I know she is come to pray for your foul sin.
  York. If thou do pardon, whosoever pray,
More sins for this forgiveness prosper may.
This fester'd joint cut off, the rest rest sound ;
This let alone will all the rest confound.

Enter Duchess.

  Duch. O king, believe not this hard-hearted
     man !
Love loving not itself none other can.
  York. Thou frantic woman, what dost thou
     make here ?
Shall thy old dugs once more a traitor rear ?
  Duch. Sweet York, be patient. Hear me,
     gentle liege.   [*Kneels.* 91
  Boling. Rise up, good aunt.
  Duch.   Not yet, I thee beseech :
For ever will I walk upon my knees,
And never see day that the happy sees,
Till thou give joy ; until thou bid me joy,
By pardoning Rutland, my transgressing boy.
  Aum. Unto my mother's prayers I bend
     my knee.
  York. Against them both my true joints
     bended be.
Ill mayst thou thrive, if thou grant any grace !
  Duch. Pleads he in earnest ? look upon his
     face ;   100
His eyes do drop no tears, his prayers are in
     jest ;
His words come from his mouth, ours from
     our breast :
He prays but faintly and would be denied ;
We pray with heart and soul and all beside :
His weary joints would gladly rise, I know ;
Our knees shall kneel till to the ground they
     grow :
His prayers are full of false hypocrisy ;
Ours of true zeal and deep integrity.
Our prayers do out-pray his ; then let them
     have
That mercy which true prayer ought to have.
  Boling. Good aunt, stand up.   111
  Duch.   Nay, do not say, 'stand up ;'
Say, 'pardon' first, and afterwards 'stand up.'
And if I were thy nurse, thy tongue to teach,
'Pardon' should be the first word of thy
     speech,
I never long'd to hear a word till now ;
Say 'pardon,' king ; let pity teach thee how :
The word is short, but not so short as sweet ;
No word like 'pardon' for kings' mouths so
     meet.
  York. Speak it in French, king ; say, 'par-
     donne moi.'
  Duch. Dost thou teach pardon pardon to
     destroy ?   120
Ah, my sour husband, my hard-hearted lord,
That set'st the word itself against the word !
Speak 'pardon' as 'tis current in our land ;
The chopping French we do not understand.
Thine eye begins to speak ; set thy tongue
     there ;
Or in thy piteous heart plant thou thine ear ;
That hearing how our plaints and prayers do
     pierce,

Pity may move thee 'pardon' to rehearse.
  Boling. Good aunt, stand up.
  Duch.   I do not sue to stand ;
Pardon is all the suit I have in hand.   130
  Boling. I pardon him, as God shall pardon
     me.
  Duch. O happy vantage of a kneeling
     knee !
Yet am I sick for fear : speak it again ;
Twice saying 'pardon' doth not pardon twain,
But makes one pardon strong.
  Boling.   With all my heart
I pardon him.
  Duch.   A god on earth thou art.
  Boling. But for our trusty brother-in-law
     and the abbot,
With all the rest of that consorted crew,
Destruction straight shall dog them at the
     heels.
Good uncle, help to order several powers 140
To Oxford, or where'er these traitors are :
They shall not live within this world, I swear,
But I will have them, if I once know where.
Uncle, farewell : and, cousin too, adieu :
Your mother well hath pray'd, and prove you
     true.
  Duch. Come, my old son : I pray God
     make thee new.   [*Exeunt.*

SCENE IV. *The same.*

Enter Exton *and* Servant.

  Exton. Didst thou not mark the king,
     what words he spake,
'Have I no friend will rid me of this living
     fear ?'
Was it not so ?
  Serv.   These were his very words.
  Exton. 'Have I no friend ?' quoth he : he
     spake it twice,
And urged it twice together, did he not ?
  Serv. He did.
  Exton. And speaking it, he wistly look'd
     on me ;
And who should say, 'I would thou wert the
     man
That would divorce this terror from my
     heart ;'
Meaning the king at Pomfret. Come, let's go :
I am the king's friend, and will rid his foe. 11
                         [*Exeunt.*

SCENE V. *Pomfret castle.*

Enter King Richard.

  K. Rich. I have been studying how I may
     compare
This prison where I live unto the world :
And for because the world is populous
And here is not a creature but myself,
I cannot do it ; yet I'll hammer it out.
My brain I'll prove the female to my soul,
My soul the father ; and these two beget
A generation of still-breeding thoughts,
And these same thoughts people this little
     world,
In humors like the people of this world,   10
For no thought is contented. The better sort,
As thoughts of things divine, are intermix'd
With scruples and do set the word itself
Against the word :
As thus, 'Come, little ones,' and then again,
'It is as hard to come as for a camel
To thread the postern of a small needle's eye.'
Thoughts tending to ambition, they do plot

Unlikely wonders; how these vain weak nails
May tear a passage through the flinty ribs 20
Of this hard world, my ragged prison walls,
And, for they cannot, die in their own pride.
Thoughts tending to content flatter themselves
That they are not the first of fortune's slaves,
Nor shall not be the last; like silly beggars
Who sitting in the stocks refuge their shame,
That many have and others must sit there;
And in this thought they find a kind of ease,
Bearing their own misfortunes on the back
Of such as have before endured the like. 30
Thus play I in one person many people,
And none contented: sometimes am I king;
Then treasons make me wish myself a beggar,
And so I am: then crushing penury
Persuades me I was better when a king;
Then am I king'd again: and by and by
Think that I am unking'd by Bolingbroke,
And straight am nothing: but whate'er I be,
Nor I nor any man that but man is
With nothing shall be pleased, till he be eased
With being nothing. Music do I hear? 41
[*Music.*
Ha, ha! keep time: how sour sweet music is,
When time is broke and no proportion kept!
So is it in the music of men's lives.
And here have I the daintiness of ear
To check time broke in a disorder'd string;
But for the concord of my state and time
Had not an ear to hear my true time broke.
I wasted time, and now doth time waste me;
For now hath time made me his numbering
clock: 50
My thoughts are minutes; and with sighs they
jar
Their watches on unto mine eyes, the outward
watch,
Whereto my finger, like a dial's point,
Is pointing still, in cleansing them from tears.
Now sir, the sound that tells what hour it is
Are clamorous groans, which strike upon my
heart,
Which is the bell: so sighs and tears and
groans
Show minutes, times, and hours: but my time
Runs posting on in Bolingbroke's proud joy,
While I stand fooling here, his Jack o' the
clock. 60
This music mads me; let it sound no more;
For though it have holp madmen to their wits,
In me it seems it will make wise men mad.
Yet blessing on his heart that gives it me!
For 'tis a sign of love; and love to Richard
Is a strange brooch in this all-hating world.

Enter a Groom *of the Stable.*

Groom. Hail, royal prince!
K. Rich.   Thanks, noble peer;
The cheapest of us is ten groats too dear.
What art thou? and how comest thou hither,
Where no man never comes but that sad dog
That brings me food to make misfortune live?
Groom. I was a poor groom of thy stable,
king,
When thou wert king; who, travelling towards
York,
With much ado at length have gotten leave
To look upon my sometimes royal master's
face.
O, how it yearn'd my heart when I beheld
In London streets, that coronation-day,

When Bolingbroke rode on roan Barbary,
That horse that thou so often hast bestrid, 79
That horse that I so carefully have dress'd!
K. Rich. Rode he on Barbary? Tell me,
gentle friend,
How went he under him?
Groom. So proudly as if he disdain'd the
ground.
K. Rich. So proud that Bolingbroke was
on his back!
That jade hath eat bread from my royal hand;
This hand hath made him proud with clap-
ping him.
Would he not stumble? would he not fall
down,
Since pride must have a fall, and break the
neck
Of that proud man that did usurp his back?
Forgiveness, horse! why do I rail on thee, 90
Since thou, created to be awed by man,
Wast born to bear? I was not made a horse;
And yet I bear a burthen like an ass,
Spurr'd, gall'd and tired by jauncing Boling-
broke.

Enter Keeper, *with a dish.*

Keep. Fellow, give place; here is no longer
stay.
K. Rich. If thou love me, 'tis time thou
wert away.
Groom. What my tongue dares not, that
my heart shall say. [*Exit.*
Keep. My lord, will't please you to fall to?
K. Rich. Taste of it first, as thou art wont
to do. 99
Keep. My lord, I dare not: Sir Pierce of
Exton, who lately came from the king,
commands the contrary.
K. Rich. The devil take Henry of Lancas-
ter and thee!
Patience is stale, and I am weary of it.
[*Beats the keeper.*
Keep. Help, help, help!

Enter EXTON *and* Servants, *armed.*

K. Rich. How now! what means death in
this rude assault?
Villain, thy own hand yields thy death's instru-
ment.
[*Snatching an axe from a* Servant *and kill-
ing him.*
Go thou, and fill another room in hell.
[*He kills another. Then* Exton *strikes him
down.*
That hand shall burn in never-quenching fire
That staggers thus my person. Exton, thy
fierce hand 110
Hath with the king's blood stain'd the king's
own land.
Mount, mount, my soul! thy seat is up on
high;
Whilst my gross flesh sinks downward, here
to die. [*Dies.*
Exton. As full of valor as of royal blood:
Both have I spill'd; O would the deed were
good!
For now the devil, that told me I did well,
Says that this deed is chronicled in hell.
This dead king to the living king I'll bear:
Take hence the rest, and give them burial
here. [*Exeunt.*

Scene VI. *Windsor castle.*

Flourish. Enter Bolingbroke, York, *with other* Lords, *and* Attendants.

Boling. Kind uncle York, the latest news we hear
Is that the rebels have consumed with fire
Our town of Cicester in Gloucestershire ;
But whether they be ta'en or slain we hear not.

Enter Northumberland.

Welcome, my lord : what is the news ?
  North. First, to thy sacred state wish I all happiness.
The next news is, I have to London sent
The heads of Oxford, Salisbury, Blunt, and Kent :
The manner of their taking may appear
At large discoursed in this paper here.   10
  Boling. We thank thee, gentle Percy, for thy pains ;
And to thy worth will add right worthy gains.

Enter Fitzwater.

Fitz. My lord, I have from Oxford sent to London
The heads of Brocas and Sir Bennet Seely,
Two of the dangerous consorted traitors
That sought at Oxford thy dire overthrow.
  Boling. Thy pains, Fitzwater, shall not be forgot ;
Right noble is thy merit, well I wot.

Enter Percy, *and the* Bishop of Carlisle.

Percy. The grand conspirator, Abbot of Westminster,
With clog of conscience and sour melancholy
Hath yielded up his body to the grave ;   21
But here is Carlisle living, to abide

Thy kingly doom and sentence of his pride.
  Boling. Carlisle, this is your doom :
Choose out some secret place, some reverend room,
More than thou hast, and with it joy thy life ;
So as thou livest in peace, die free from strife :
For though mine enemy thou hast ever been,
High sparks of honor in thee have I seen.

Enter Exton, *with persons bearing a coffin.*

  Exton. Great king, within this coffin I present   30
Thy buried fear : herein all breathless lies
The mightiest of thy greatest enemies,
Richard of Bordeaux, by me hither brought.
  Boling. Exton, I thank thee not ; for thou hast wrought
A deed of slander with thy fatal hand
Upon my head and all this famous land.
  Exton. From your own mouth, my lord, did I this deed.
  Boling. They love not poison that do poison need,
Nor do I thee : though I did wish him dead,
I hate the murderer, love him murdered.   40
The guilt of conscience take thou for thy labor,
But neither my good word nor princely favor :
With Cain go wander through shades of night,
And never show thy head by day nor light.
Lords, I protest, my soul is full of woe,
That blood should sprinkle me to make me grow :
Come, mourn with me for that I do lament,
And put on sullen black incontinent :
I'll make a voyage to the Holy Land,   49
To wash this blood off from my guilty hand :
March sadly after ; grace my mournings here ;
In weeping after this untimely bier. [*Exeunt.*

KING JOHN.

(WRITTEN ABOUT 1595.)

INTRODUCTION.

King John departs farther from the facts of history than any other of Shakespeare's historical plays. He here follows for the most part not Holinshed, but an old play which appeared in 1591 entitled *The Troublesome Raigne of King John of England*. He follows it, however, not in the close way in which he had previously worked when writing 2 and 3 *Henry VI.*; the main incidents are the same, but Shakespeare elevates and almost re-creates the characters; for the most eloquent and poetical passages no original is to be found in the old play. The character of the king grows more darkly treacherous in Shakespeare's: barely a hint of the earlier author suggested the scene, so powerful and so subtle, in which John insinuates to Hubert his murderous desires; the boyish innocence of Arthur and the pathos of his life become real and living as they are dealt with by the imagination of Shakespeare; Constance is no longer a fierce and ambitious virago, but a passionate, sorrowing mother; Faulconbridge is ennobled by a manly tenderness and a purer patriotism. Shakespeare depicts, with true English spirit, the faithlessness, the ambition, the political greed, and the sophistry of the court of Rome; but he wholly omits a ribald scene of the old play, in which the licentiousness of monasteries is exposed to ridicule. As to the date of *King John* all that can be asserted with confidence is that it lies somewhere between the early histories (*Henry VI.* with *Richard III.*) and the group of later histories, the trilogy consisting of 1 and 2 *Henry IV.* and *Henry V.* Thus in the historical series it is brought close to *Richard II.* Neither play contains prose, but the treatment of Faulconbridge's part shows more approach to the alliance of a humorous or comic element with history (which becomes complete in *Henry IV.*) than does anything in the play of *Richard II.* *King John* and *Richard II.* have the common characteristic of containing very inferior dramatic work side by side with work of a high and difficult kind. The chief point of difference with respect to form is that *Richard II.* contains a much larger proportion of rhymed verse, and on the whole we shall perhaps not err in regarding *Richard II.* as the earlier of the two.

DRAMATIS PERSONÆ.

KING JOHN.
PRINCE HENRY, son to the king.
ARTHUR, Duke of Bretagne, nephew to the king.
The Earl of PEMBROKE.
The Earl of ESSEX.
The Earl of SALISBURY.
The Lord BIGOT.
HUBERT DE BURGH.
ROBERT FAULCONBRIDGE, son to Sir Robert Faulconbridge.
PHILIP the BASTARD, his half-brother.
JAMES GURNEY, servant to Lady Faulconbridge.
PETER of Pomfret, a prophet.
PHILIP, King of France.

LEWIS, the Dauphin.
LYMOGES, Duke of AUSTRIA.
CARDINAL PANDULPH, the Pope's legate.
MELUN, a French Lord.
CHATILLON, ambassador from France to King John.

QUEEN ELINOR, mother to King John.
CONSTANCE, mother to Arthur.
BLANCH of Spain, niece to King John.
LADY FAULCONBRIDGE.

Lords, Citizens of Angiers, Sheriff, Heralds, Officers, Soldiers, Messengers, and other Attendants.

SCENE: *Partly in England, and partly in France.*

ACT I.

SCENE I. KING JOHN'S *palace.*

Enter KING JOHN, QUEEN ELINOR, PEMBROKE, ESSEX, SALISBURY, *and others, with* CHATILLON.

K. John. Now, say, Chatillon, what would France with us?
Chat. Thus, after greeting, speaks the King of France
In my behavior to the majesty,
The borrow'd majesty, of England here.
Eli. A strange beginning: 'borrow'd majesty!'
K. John. Silence, good mother; hear the embassy.
Chat. Philip of France, in right and true behalf
Of thy deceased brother Geffrey's son,
Arthur Plantagenet, lays most lawful claim
To this fair island and the territories,   10
To Ireland, Poictiers, Anjou, Touraine, Maine,
Desiring thee to lay aside the sword
Which sways usurpingly these several titles,

And put the same into young Arthur's hand,
Thy nephew and right royal sovereign.
K. John. What follows if we disallow of
this ?
Chat. The proud control of fierce and
bloody war,
To enforce these rights so forcibly withheld.
K. John. Here have we war for war and
blood for blood,
Controlment for controlment : so answer
France. 20
Chat. Then take my king's defiance from
my mouth,
The farthest limit of my embassy.
K. John. Bear mine to him, and so depart
in peace :
Be thou as lightning in the eyes of France ;
For ere thou canst report I will be there,
The thunder of my cannon shall be heard :
So hence ! Be thou the trumpet of our wrath
And sullen presage of your own decay.
An honorable conduct let him have :
Pembroke, look to 't. Farewell, Chatillon. 30
  [*Exeunt Chatillon and Pembroke.*
Eli. What now, my son ! have I not ever
said
How that ambitious Constance would not
cease
Till she had kindled France and all the world,
Upon the right and party of her son ?
This might have been prevented and made
whole
With very easy arguments of love,
Which now the manage of two kingdoms
must
With fearful bloody issue arbitrate.
K. John. Our strong possession and our
right for us.
Eli. Your strong possession much more
than your right, 40
Or else it must go wrong with you and me :
So much my conscience whispers in your ear,
Which none but heaven and you and I shall
hear.

Enter a Sheriff.

Essex. My liege, here is the strangest con-
troversy
Come from the country to be judged by you,
That e'er I heard : shall I produce the men ?
K. John. Let them approach.
Our abbeys and our priories shall pay
This expedition's charge.

Enter ROBERT FAULCONBRIDGE *and* PHILIP
his bastard brother.

                  What men are you ?
Bast. Your faithful subject I, a gentleman
Born in Northamptonshire and eldest son, 51
As I suppose, to Robert Faulconbridge,
A soldier, by the honor-giving hand
Of Cœur-de-lion knighted in the field.
K. John. What art thou ?
Rob. The son and heir to that same Faul-
conbridge.
K. John. Is that the elder, and art thou the
heir ?
You came not of one mother then, it seems.
Bast. Most certain of one mother, mighty
king ;
That is well known ; and, as I think, one
father : 60
But for the certain knowledge of that truth

I put you o'er to heaven and to my mother :
Of that I doubt, as all men's children may.
Eli. Out on thee, rude man ! thou dost
shame thy mother
And wound her honor with this diffidence.
Bast. I, madam ? no, I have no reason for
it ;
That is my brother's plea and none of mine ;
The which if he can prove, a' pops me out
At least from fair five hundred pound a year :
Heaven guard my mother's honor and my
land ! 70
K. John. A good blunt fellow. Why, being
younger born,
Doth he lay claim to thine inheritance ?
Bast. I know not why, except to get the
land.
But once he slander'd me with bastardy :
But whether I be as true begot or no,
That still I lay upon my mother's head,
But that I am as well begot, my liege,—
Fair fall the bones that took the pains for
me !—
Compare our faces and be judge yourself.
If old sir Robert did beget us both 80
And were our father and this son like him,
O old sir Robert, father, on my knee
I give heaven thanks I was not like to thee !
K. John. Why, what a madcap hath
heaven lent us here !
Eli. He hath a trick of Cœur-de-lion's
face ;
The accent of his tongue affecteth him.
Do you not read some tokens of my son
In the large composition of this man ?
K. John. Mine eye hath well examined his
parts
And finds them perfect Richard. Sirrah,
speak, 90
What doth move you to claim your brother's
land ?
Bast. Because he hath a half-face, like my
father.
With half that face would he have all my
land :
A half-faced groat five hundred pound a
year !
Rob. My gracious liege, when that my
father lived,
Your brother did employ my father much,—
Bast. Well, sir, by this you cannot get my
land :
Your tale must be how he employ'd my
mother.
Rob. And once dispatch'd him in an em-
bassy
To Germany, there with the emperor 100
To treat of high affairs touching that time.
The advantage of his absence took the king
And in the mean time sojourn'd at my
father's ;
Where how he did prevail I shame to speak,
But truth is truth : large lengths of seas and
shores
Between my father and my mother lay,
As I have heard my father speak himself,
When this same lusty gentleman was got.
Upon his death-bed he by will bequeath'd
His lands to me, and took it on his death 110
That this my mother's son was none of his ;
And if he were, he came into the world
Full fourteen weeks before the course of time.
Then, good my liege, let me have what is mine,

My father's land, as was my father's will.

K. John. Sirrah, your brother is legitimate;
Your father's wife did after wedlock bear him,
And if she did play false, the fault was hers;
Which fault lies on the hazards of all husbands 119
That marry wives. Tell me, how if my brother,
Who, as you say, took pains to get this son,
Had of your father claim'd this son for his?
In sooth, good friend, your father might have kept
This calf bred from his cow from all the world;
In sooth he might; then, if he were my brother's,
My brother might not claim him; nor your father,
Being none of his, refuse him: this concludes;
My mother's son did get your father's heir;
Your father's heir must have your father's land.

Rob. Shall then my father's will be of no force 130
To dispossess that child which is not his?

Bast. Of no more force to dispossess me, sir,
Than was his will to get me, as I think.

Eli. Whether hadst thou rather be a Faulconbridge
And like thy brother, to enjoy thy land,
Or the reputed son of Cœur-de-lion,
Lord of thy presence and no land beside?

Bast. Madam, an if my brother had my shape,
And I had his, sir Robert's his, like him;
And if my legs were two such riding-rods, 140
My arms such eel-skins stuff'd, my face so thin
That in mine ear I durst not stick a rose
Lest men should say 'Look, where three-farthings goes!'
And, to his shape, were heir to all this land,
Would I might never stir from off this place,
I would give it every foot to have this face;
I would not be sir Nob in any case.

Eli. I like thee well: wilt thou forsake thy fortune,
Bequeath thy land to him and follow me?
I am a soldier and now bound to France. 150

Bast. Brother, take you my land, I'll take my chance.
Your face hath got five hundred pound a year,
Yet sell your face for five pence and 'tis dear.
Madam, I'll follow you unto the death.

Eli. Nay, I would have you go before me thither.

Bast. Our country manners give our betters way.

K. John. What is thy name?

Bast. Philip, my liege, so is my name begun;
Philip, good old sir Robert's wife's eldest son.

K. John. From henceforth bear his name whose form thou bear'st: 160
Kneel thou down Philip, but rise more great,
Arise sir Richard and Plantagenet.

Bast. Brother by the mother's side, give me your hand:
My father gave me honor, yours gave land.
Now blessed by the hour, by night or day,
When I was got, sir Robert was away!

Eli. The very spirit of Plantagenet!
I am thy grandam, Richard; call me so.

Bast. Madam, by chance but not by truth; what though? 170
Something about, a little from the right,
In at the window, or else o'er the hatch:
Who dares not stir by day must walk by night,
And have is have, however men do catch:
Near or far off, well won is still well shot,
And I am I, howe'er I was begot.

K. John. Go, Faulconbridge: now hast thou thy desire;
A landless knight makes thee a landed squire.
Come, madam, and come, Richard, we must speed
For France, for France, for it is more than need.

Bast. Brother, adieu: good fortune come to thee! 180
For thou wast got i' the way of honesty.
[*Exeunt all but Bastard.*
A foot of honor better than I was;
But many a many foot of land the worse.
Well, now can I make any Joan a lady.
'Good den, sir Richard!'—'God-a-mercy, fellow!'—
And if his name be George, I'll call him Peter;
For new-made honor doth forget men's names;
'Tis too respective and too sociable
For your conversion. Now your traveller, 189
He and his toothpick at my worship's mess,
And when my knightly stomach is sufficed,
Why then I suck my teeth and catechize
My picked man of countries: 'My dear sir,'
Thus, leaning on mine elbow, I begin,
'I shall beseech you'—that is question now;
And then comes answer like an Absey book:
'O sir,' says answer, 'at your best command;
At your employment; at your service, sir;'
'No, sir,' says question, 'I, sweet sir, at yours:'
And so, ere answer knows what question would, 200
Saving in dialogue of compliment,
And talking of the Alps and Apennines,
The Pyrenean and the river Po,
It draws toward supper in conclusion so.
But this is worshipful society
And fits the mounting spirit like myself,
For he is but a bastard to the time
That doth not smack of observation;
And so am I, whether I smack or no;
And not alone in habit and device, 210
Exterior form, outward accoutrement,
But from the inward motion to deliver
Sweet, sweet, sweet poison for the age's tooth:
Which, though I will not practise to deceive,
Yet, to avoid deceit, I mean to learn;
For it shall strew the footsteps of my rising.
But who comes in such haste in riding-robes?
What woman-post is this? hath she no husband
That will take pains to blow a horn before her?

Enter LADY FAULCONBRIDGE *and* JAMES GURNEY.

O me! it is my mother. How now, good lady!
What brings you here to court so hastily? 221

Lady F. Where is that slave, thy brother? where is he,
That holds in chase mine honor up and down?

Bast. My brother Robert? old sir Robert's son?

Colbrand the giant, that same mighty man ?
Is it sir Robert's son that you seek so ?
    Lady F. Sir Robert's son ! Ay, thou un-
        reverend boy,
Sir Robert's son : why scorn'st thou at sir
        Robert ?
He is sir Robert's son, and so art thou.
    Bast. James Gurney, wilt thou give us
        leave awhile ?   230
    Gur. Good leave, good Philip.
    Bast.   Philip ! sparrow : James,
There's toys abroad : anon I'll tell thee more.
                                    [*Exit Gurney.*
Madam, I was not old sir Robert's son :
Sir Robert might have eat his part in me
Upon Good-Friday and ne'er broke his fast :
Sir Robert could do well : marry, to confess,
Could he get me ? Sir Robert could not do it :
We know his handiwork : therefore, good
        mother,
To whom am I beholding for these limbs ?
Sir Robert never holp to make this leg.   240
    Lady F. Hast thou conspired with thy
        brother too,
That for thine own gain shouldst defend mine
        honor ?
What means this scorn, thou most untoward
        knave ?
    Bast. Knight, knight, good mother, Basil-
        isco-like.
What ! I am dubb'd ! I have it on my shoulder.
But, mother, I am not sir Robert's son ;
I have disclaim'd sir Robert and my land ;
Legitimation, name and all is gone :
Then, good my mother, let me know my fa-
        ther ;
Some proper man, I hope : who was it,
        mother ?   250
    Lady F. Hast thou denied thyself a Faul-
        conbridge ?
    Bast. As faithfully as I deny the devil.
    Lady F. King Richard Cœur-de-lion was
        thy father :
By long and vehement suit I was seduced
To make room for him in my husband's bed :
Heaven lay not my transgression to my
        charge !
Thou art the issue of my dear offence,
Which was so strongly urged past my defence.
    Bast. Now, by this light, were I to get
        again,
Madam, I would not wish a better father.   260
Some sins do bear their privilege on earth,
And so doth yours ; your fault was not your
        folly :
Needs must you lay your heart at his dispose,
Subjected tribute to commanding love,
Against whose fury and unmatched force
The aweless lion could not wage the fight,
Nor keep his princely heart from Richard's
        hand.
He that perforce robs lions of their hearts
May easily win a woman's. Ay, my mother,
With all my heart I thank thee for my father !
Who lives and dares but say thou didst not
        well   271
When I was got, I'll send his soul to hell.
Come, lady, I will show thee to my kin ;
    And they shall say, when Richard me begot,
If thou hadst said him nay, it had been sin :
Who says it was, he lies ; I say 'twas not.
                                    [*Exeunt.*

ACT II.

SCENE I. *France. Before Angiers.*

Enter AUSTRIA *and forces, drums, etc. on one
    side : on the other* KING PHILIP *of France
    and his power ;* LEWIS, ARTHUR, CON-
    STANCE *and attendants.*

    Lew. Before Angiers well met, brave
        Austria.
Arthur, that great forerunner of thy blood,
Richard, that robb'd the lion of his heart
And fought the holy wars in Palestine,
By this brave duke came early to his grave :
And for amends to his posterity,
At our importance hither is he come,
To spread his colors, boy, in thy behalf,
And to rebuke the usurpation
Of thy unnatural uncle, English John :   10
Embrace him, love him, give him welcome
        hither.
    Arth. God shall forgive you Cœur-de-
        lion's death
The rather that you give his offspring life,
Shadowing their right under your wings of
        war :
I give you welcome with a powerless hand,
But with a heart full of unstained love :
Welcome before the gates of Angiers, duke.
    Lew. A noble boy ! Who would not do
        thee right ?
    Aust. Upon thy cheek lay I this zealous
        kiss,
As seal to this indenture of my love,   20
That to my home I will no more return,
Till Angiers and the right thou hast in France,
Together with that pale, that white-faced
        shore,
Whose foot spurns back the ocean's roaring
        tides
And coops from other lands her islanders,
Even till that England, hedged in with the
        main,
That water-walled bulwark, still secure
And confident from foreign purposes,
Even till that utmost corner of the west
Salute thee for her king : till then, fair boy, 30
Will I not think of home, but follow arms.
    Const. O, take his mother's thanks, a wid-
        ow's thanks,
Till your strong hand shall help to give him
        strength
To make a more requital to your love !
    Aust. The peace of heaven is theirs that
        lift their swords
In such a just and charitable war.
    K. Phi. Well then, to work : our cannon
        shall be bent
Against the brows of this resisting town.
Call for our chiefest men of discipline,
To cull the plots of best advantages :   40
We'll lay before this town our royal bones,
Wade to the market-place in Frenchmen's
        blood,
But we will make it subject to this boy.
    Const. Stay for an answer to your embassy,
Lest unadvised you stain your swords with
        blood :
My Lord Chatillon may from England bring,
That right in peace which here we urge in
        war,

And then we shall repent each drop of blood
That hot rash haste so indirectly shed.

Enter CHATILLON.

K. Phi. A wonder, lady! lo, upon thy
        wish,   50
Our messenger Chatillon is arrived!
What England says, say briefly, gentle lord;
We coldly pause for thee; Chatillon, speak.
    Chat. Then turn your forces from this
        paltry siege
And stir them up against a mightier task.
England, impatient of your just demands,
Hath put himself in arms: the adverse winds,
Whose leisure I have stay'd, have given him
        time
To land his legions all as soon as I;
His marches are expedient to this town,   60
His forces strong, his soldiers confident.
With him along is come the mother-queen,
An Ate, stirring him to blood and strife;
With her her niece, the Lady Blanch of Spain;
With them a bastard of the king's deceased;
And all the unsettled humors of the land,
Rash, inconsiderate, fiery voluntaries,
With ladies' faces and fierce dragons' spleens,
Have sold their fortunes at their native homes,
Bearing their birthrights proudly on their
        backs,   70
To make a hazard of new fortunes here:
In brief, a braver choice of dauntless spirits
Than now the English bottoms have waft o'er
Did nearer float upon the swelling tide,
To do offence and scath in Christendom.
                        [*Drum beats.*
The interruption of their churlish drums
Cuts off more circumstance: they are at hand,
To parley or to fight; therefore prepare.
    K. Phi. How much unlook'd for is this
        expedition!
    Aust. By how much unexpected, by so
        much   80
We must awake endeavor for defence;
For courage mounteth with occasion:
Let them be welcome then: we are prepared.

Enter KING JOHN, ELINOR, BLANCH, *the Bas-
        tard, Lords, and forces.*

    K. John. Peace be to France, if France in
        peace permit
Our just and lineal entrance to our own;
If not, bleed France, and peace ascend to
        heaven,
Whiles we, God's wrathful agent, do correct
Their proud contempt that beats His peace to
        heaven.
    K. Phi. Peace be to England, if that war
        return   89
From France to England, there to live in
        peace.
England we love; and for that England's sake
With burden of our armor here we sweat.
This toil of ours should be a work of thine;
But thou from loving England art so far,
That thou hast under-wrought his lawful king
Cut off the sequence of posterity,
Out-faced infant state and done a rape
Upon the maiden virtue of the crown.
Look here upon thy brother Geffrey's face;
These eyes, these brows, were moulded out of
        his: 100
This little abstract doth contain that large
Which died in Geffrey, and the hand of time

Shall draw this brief into as huge a volume.
That Geffrey was thy elder brother born,
And this his son; England was Geffrey's right
And this is Geffrey's: in the name of God
How comes it then that thou art call'd a king,
When living blood doth in these temples beat,
Which owe the crown that thou o'ermasterest?
    K. John. From whom hast thou this great
        commission, France,   110
To draw my answer from thy articles?
    K. Phi. From that supernal judge, that
        stirs good thoughts
In any breast of strong authority,
To look into the blots and stains of right:
That judge hath made me guardian to this
        boy:
Under whose warrant I impeach thy wrong
And by whose help I mean to chastise it.
    K. John. Alack, thou dost usurp authority.
    K. Phi. Excuse; it is to beat usurping
        down.
    Eli. Who is it thou dost call usurper,
        France?
    Const. Let me make answer; thy usurping
        son.
    Eli. Out, insolent! thy bastard shall be
        king,
That thou mayst be a queen, and check the
        world!
    Const. My bed was ever to thy son as true
As thine was to thy husband; and this boy
Liker in feature to his father Geffrey
Than thou and John in manners; being as like
As rain to water, or devil to his dam.
My boy a bastard! By my soul, I think
His father never was so true begot: 130
It cannot be, an if thou wert his mother.
    Eli. There's a good mother, boy, that blots
        thy father.
    Const. There's a good grandam, boy, that
        would blot thee.
    Aust. Peace!
    Bast.   Hear the crier.
    Aust.   What the devil art thou?
    Bast. One that will play the devil, sir, with
        you,
An a' may catch your hide and you alone:
You are the hare of whom the proverb goes,
Whose valor plucks dead lions by the beard;
I'll smoke your skin-coat, an I catch you
        right;
Sirrah, look to't; i' faith, I will, i' faith.   140
    Blanch. O, well did he become that lion's
        robe
That did disrobe the lion of that robe!
    Bast. It lies as sightly on the back of him
As great Alcides' shows upon an ass:
But, ass, I'll take that burthen from your back,
Or lay on that shall make your shoulders
        crack.
    Aust. What craker is this same that deafs
        our ears
With this abundance of superfluous breath?
    K. Phi. Lewis, determine what we shall do
        straight.
    Lew. Women and fools, break off your
        conference.   150
King John, this is the very sum of all;
England and Ireland, Anjou, Touraine, Maine,
In right of Arthur do I claim of thee:
Wilt thou resign them and lay down thy arms?
    K. John. My life as soon: I do defy thee,
        France.

Arthur of Bretagne, yield thee to my hand ;
And out of my dear love I'll give thee more
Than e'er the coward hand of France can win :
Submit thee, boy.

Eli.   Come to thy grandam, child.

Const. Do, child, go to it grandam, child :
Give grandam kingdom, and it grandam will
Give it a plum, a cherry, and a fig :
There's a good grandam.

Arth.   Good my mother, peace !
I would that I were low laid in my grave :
I am not worth this coil that's made for me.

Eli.   His mother shames him so, poor boy,
  he weeps.

Const.   Now shame upon you, whether she
  does or no !
His grandam's wrongs, and not his mother's
  shames,
Draws those heaven-moving pearls from his
  poor eyes,
Which heaven shall take in nature of a fee ;
Ay, with these crystal beads heaven shall be
  bribed   171
To do him justice and revenge on you.

Eli.   Thou monstrous slanderer of heaven
  and earth !

Const.   Thou monstrous injurer of heaven
  and earth !
Call not me slanderer ; thou and thine usurp
The dominations, royalties and rights
Of this oppressed boy : this is thy eld'st son's
  son,
Infortunate in nothing but in thee :
Thy sins are visited in this poor child ;
The canon of the law is laid on him,   180
Being the second generation
Removed from thy sin-conceiving womb.

K. John.   Bedlam, have done.

Const.   I have but this to say,
That he is not only plagued for her sin,
But God hath made her sin and her the plague
On this removed issue, plague for her
And with her plague ; her sin his injury,
Her injury the beadle to her sin,
All punish'd in the person of this child,
And all for her ; a plague upon her !   190

Eli.   Thou unadvised scold, I can produce
A will that bars the title of thy son.

Const.   Ay, who doubts that ? a will ! a
  wicked will ;
A woman's will ; a canker'd grandam's will !

K. Phi.   Peace, lady ! pause, or be more
  temperate :
It ill beseems this presence to cry aim
To these ill-tuned repetitions.
Some trumpet summon hither to the walls
These men of Angiers : let us hear them speak
Whose title they admit, Arthur's or John's.

Trumpet sounds. Enter certain Citizens *upon
  the walls.*

First Cit.   Who is it that hath warn'd us to
  the walls ?   201

K. Phi.   'Tis France, for England.

K. John.   England, for itself.
You men of Angiers, and my loving subjects,—

K. Phi.   You loving men of Angiers, Arthur's subjects,

Our trumpet call'd you to this gentle parle—

K. John.   For our advantage ; therefore
  hear us first.
These flags of France, that are advanced here
Before the eye and prospect of your town,

Have hither march'd to your endamagement :
The cannons have their bowels full of wrath,
And ready mounted are they to spit forth 211
Their iron indignation 'gainst your walls :
All preparation for a bloody siege
And merciless proceeding by these French
Confronts your city's eyes, your winking gates ;
And but for our approach those sleeping
  stones,
That as a waist doth girdle you about,
By the compulsion of their ordinance
By this time from their fixed beds of lime 219
Had been dishabited, and wide havoc made
For bloody power to rush upon your peace.
But on the sight of us your lawful king,
Who painfully with much expedient march
Have brought a countercheck before your
  gates,
To save unscratch'd your city's threatened
  cheeks,
Behold, the French amazed vouchsafe a parle ;
And now, instead of bullets wrapp'd in fire,
To make a shaking fever in your walls,
They shoot but calm words folded up in
  smoke,
To make a faithless error in your ears :   230
Which trust accordingly, kind citizens,
And let us in, your king, whose labor'd spirits,
Forwearied in this action of swift speed,
Crave harborage within your city walls.

K. Phi.   When I have said, make answer to
  us both.
Lo, in this right hand, whose protection
Is most divinely vow'd upon the right
Of him it holds, stands young Plantagenet,
Son to the elder brother of this man,   239
And king o'er him and all that he enjoys :
For this down-trodden equity, we tread
In warlike march these greens before your
  town,
Being no further enemy to you
Than the constraint of hospitable zeal
In the relief of this oppressed child
Religiously provokes. Be pleased then
To pay that duty which you truly owe
To him that owes it, namely this young
  prince :
And then our arms, like to a muzzled bear,
Save in aspect, hath all offence seal'd up ; 250
Our cannons' malice vainly shall be spent
Against the invulnerable clouds of heaven ;
And with a blessed and unvex'd retire,
With unhack'd swords and helmets all un-
  bruised,
We will bear home that lusty blood again
Which here we came to spout against your
  town,
And leave your children, wives and you in
  peace.
But if you fondly pass our proffer'd offer,
'Tis not the roundure of your old-faced walls
Can hide you from our messengers of war, 260
Though all these English and their discipline
Were harbor'd in their rude circumference.
Then tell us, shall your city call us lord,
In that behalf which we have challenged it ?
Or shall we give the signal to our rage
And stalk in blood to our possession ?

First Cit.   In brief, we are the king of England's subjects :
For him, and in his right, we hold this town.

K. John.   Acknowledge then the king, and
  let me in.

First Cit. That can we not; but he that
  proves the king,   270
To him will we prove loyal : till that time
Have we ramm'd up our gates against the
  world.
K. John. Doth not the crown of England
  prove the king ?
And if not that, I bring you witnesses,
Twice fifteen thousand hearts of England's
  breed,—
Bast. Bastards, and else.
K. John. To verify our title with their lives.
K. Phi. As many and as well-born bloods
  as those,—
Bast. Some bastards too.
K. Phi....Stand in his face to contradict his
  claim.   280
First Cit. Till you compound whose right
  is worthiest,
We for the worthiest hold the right from both.
K. John. Then God forgive the sin of all
  those souls
That to their everlasting residence,
Before the dew of evening fall, shall fleet,
In dreadful trial of our kingdom's king !
K. Phi. Amen, amen ! Mount, chevaliers !
  to arms !
Bast. Saint George, that swinged the
  dragon, and e'er since
Sits on his horseback at mine hostess' door,
Teach us some fence ! [*To Aust.*] Sirrah,
  were I at home,   290
At your den, sirrah, with your lioness,
I would set an ox-head to your lion's hide,
And make a monster of you.
Aust.   Peace ! no more.
Bast. O tremble, for you hear the lion
  roar.
K. John. Up higher to the plain ; where
  we'll set forth
In best appointment all our regiments.
Bast. Speed then, to take advantage of the
  field.
K. Phi. It shall be so ; and at the other hill
Command the rest to stand. God and our
  right !   [*Exeunt.*

Here after excursions, enter the Herald *of*
  France, *with trumpets, to the gates.*

F. Her. You men of Angiers, open wide
  your gates,   300
And let young Arthur, Duke of Bretagne, in,
Who by the hand of France this day hath
  made
Much work for tears in many an English
  mother,
Whose sons lie scattered on the bleeding
  ground ;
Many a widow's husband grovelling lies,
Coldly embracing the discolor'd earth ;
And victory, with little loss, doth play
Upon the dancing banners of the French,
Who are at hand, triumphantly display'd,
To enter conquerors and to proclaim   310
Arthur of Bretagne England's king and yours.

Enter English Herald, *with trumpet.*

E. Her. Rejoice, you men of Angiers, ring
  your bells :
King John, your king and England's doth approach,
Commander of this hot malicious day :

Their armors, that march'd hence so silver-
  bright,
Hither return all gilt with Frenchmen's blood ;
There stuck no plume in any English crest
That is removed by a staff of France ;
Our colors do return in those same hands
That did display them when we first march'd
  forth ;   320
And, like a jolly troop of huntsmen, come
Our lusty English, all with purpled hands,
Dyed in the dying slaughter of their foes :
Open your gates and give the victors way.
First Cit. Heralds, from off our towers we
  might behold,
From first to last, the onset and retire
Of both your armies ; whose equality
By our best eyes cannot be censured :
Blood hath bought blood and blows have an-
  swer'd blows ;
Strength match'd with strength, and power con-
  fronted power :   330
Both are alike ; and both alike we like.
One must prove greatest : while they weigh so
  even,
We hold our town for neither, yet for both.

Re-enter the two KINGS, *with their powers,
  severally.*

K. John. France, hast thou yet more blood
  to cast away ?
Say, shall the current of our right run on ?
Whose passage, vex'd with thy impediment,
Shall leave his native channel and o'erswell
With course disturb'd even thy confining
  shores,
Unless thou let his silver water keep
A peaceful progress to the ocean.   340
K. Phi. England, thou hast not saved one
  drop of blood,
In this hot trial, more than we of France ;
Rather, lost more. And by this hand I swear,
That sways the earth this climate overlooks,
Before we will lay down our just-borne arms,
We'll put thee down, 'gainst whom these arms
  we bear,
Or add a royal number to the dead,
Gracing the scroll that tells of this war's loss
With slaughter coupled to the name of kings.
Bast. Ha, majesty ! how high thy glory
  towers,   350
When the rich blood of kings is set on fire !
O, now doth Death line his dead chaps with
  steel ;
The swords of soldiers are his teeth, his fangs ;
And now he feasts, mousing the flesh of men,
In undetermined differences of kings.
Why stand these royal fronts amazed thus ?
Cry, ' havoc ! ' kings ; back to the stained field,
You equal potents, fiery kindled spirits !
Then let confusion of one part confirm
The other's peace : till then, blows, blood and
  death !   360
K. John. Whose party do the townsmen
  yet admit ?
K. Phi. Speak, citizens, for England ; who's
  your king ?
First Cit. The king of England ; when we
  know the king.
K. Phi. Know him in us, that here hold up
  his right.
K. John. In us, that are our own great
  deputy,
And bear possession of our person here,

Lord of our presence, Angiers, and of you.
  First Cit. A greater power than we denies
    all this;
And till it be undoubted, we do lock   369
Our former scruple in our strong-barr'd gates;
King'd of our fears, until our fears, resolved,
Be by some certain king purged and deposed.
  Bast. By heaven, these scroyles of Angiers
    flout you, kings,
And stand securely on their battlements,
As in a theatre, whence they gape and point
At your industrious scenes and acts of death.
Your royal presences be ruled by me:
Do like the mutines of Jerusalem,
Be friends awhile and both conjointly bend
Your sharpest deeds of malice on this town:
By east and west let France and England
    mount   381
Their battering cannon charged to the mouths,
Till their soul-fearing clamors have brawl'd
    down
The flinty ribs of this contemptuous city:
I'ld play incessantly upon these jades,
Even till unfenced desolation
Leave them as naked as the vulgar air.
That done, dissever your united strengths, 388
And part your mingled colors once again;
Turn face to face and bloody point to point;
Then, in a moment, Fortune shall cull forth
Out of one side her happy minion,
To whom in favor she shall give the day,
And kiss him with a glorious victory.
How like you this wild counsel, mighty states?
Smacks it not something of the policy?
  K. John. Now, by the sky that hangs above
    our heads,
I like it well. France, shall we knit our powers
And lay this Angiers even with the ground;
Then after fight who shall be king of it?   400
  Bast. An if thou hast the mettle of a king,
Being wronged as we are by this peevish town,
Turn thou the mouth of thy artillery,
As we will ours, against these saucy walls;
And when that we have dash'd them to the
    ground,
Why then defy each other and pell-mell
Make work upon ourselves, for heaven or hell.
  K. Phi. Let it be so. Say, where will you
    assault?
  K. John. We from the west will send de-
    struction
Into this city's bosom.   410
  Aust. I from the north.
  K. Phi.   Our thunder from the south
Shall rain their drift of bullets on this town.
  Bast. O prudent discipline! From north to
    south:
Austria and France shoot in each other's
    mouth:
I'll stir them to it. Come, away, away!
  First Cit. Hear us, great kings: vouchsafe
    awhile to stay,
And I shall show you peace and fair-faced
    league;
Win you this city without stroke or wound;
Rescue those breathing lives to die in beds,
That here come sacrifices for the field: 420
Persever not, but hear me, mighty kings.
  K. John. Speak on with favor; we are bent
    to hear.
  First Cit. That daughter there of Spain,
    the Lady Blanch,

Is niece to England: look upon the years
Of Lewis the Dauphin and that lovely maid:
If lusty love should go in quest of beauty,
Where should he find it fairer than in Blanch?
If zealous love should go in search of virtue,
Where should he find it purer than in Blanch?
If love ambitious sought a match of birth, 430
Whose veins bound richer blood than Lady
    Blanch?
Such as she is, in beauty, virtue, birth,
Is the young Dauphin every way complete:
If not complete of, say he is not she;
And she again wants nothing, to name want,
If want it be not that she is not he:
He is the half part of a blessed man,
Left to be finished by such as she;
And she a fair divided excellence,
Whose fulness of perfection lies in him.   440
O, two such silver currents, when they join,
Do glorify the banks that bound them in;
And two such shores to two such streams made
    one,
Two such controlling bounds shall you be,
    kings,
To these two princes, if you marry them.
This union shall do more than battery can
To our fast-closed gates; for at this match,
With swifter spleen than powder can enforce,
The mouth of passage shall we fling wide ope,
And give you entrance: but without this
    match,   450
The sea enraged is not half so deaf,
Lions more confident, mountains and rocks
More free from motion, no, not Death himself
In moral fury half so peremptory,
As we to keep this city.
  Bast.   Here's a stay
That shakes the rotten carcass of old Death
Out of his rags! Here's a large mouth, indeed,
That spits forth death and mountains, rocks
    and seas,
Talks as familiarly of roaring lions
As maids of thirteen do of puppy-dogs! 460
What cannoneer begot this lusty blood?
He speaks plain cannon fire, and smoke and
    bounce;
He gives the bastinado with his tongue:
Our ears are cudgell'd; not a word of his
But buffets better than a fist of France:
Zounds! I was never so bethump'd with words
Since I first call'd my brother's father dad.
  Eli. Son, list to this conjunction, make this
    match;
Give with our niece a dowry large enough:
For by this knot thou shalt so surely tie 470
Thy now unsured assurance to the crown,
That yon green boy shall have no sun to ripe
The bloom that promiseth a mighty fruit.
I see a yielding in the looks of France;
Mark, how they whisper: urge them while
    their souls
Are capable of this ambition,
Lest zeal, now melted by the windy breath
Of soft petitions, pity and remorse,
Cool and congeal again to what it was.
  First Cit. Why answer not the double maj-
    esties   480
This friendly treaty of our threaten'd town?
  K. Phi. Speak England first, that hath been
    forward first
To speak unto this city: what say you?

K. John. If that the Dauphin there, thy
    princely son,
Can in this book of beauty read 'I love,'
Her dowry shall weigh equal with a queen :
For Anjou and fair Touraine, Maine, Poictiers,
And all that we upon this side the sea,
Except this city now by us besieged,
Find liable to our crown and dignity,   490
Shall gild her bridal bed and make her rich
In titles, honors and promotions,
As she in beauty, education, blood,
Holds hand with any princess of the world.
    K. Phi. What say'st thou, boy ? look in the
    lady's face.
    Lew. I do, my lord ; and in her eye I find
A wonder, or a wondrous miracle,
The shadow of myself form'd in her eye :
Which being but the shadow of your son,
Becomes a sun and makes your son a shadow :
I do protest I never loved myself   501
Till now infixed I beheld myself
Drawn in the flattering table of her eye.
        [*Whispers with Blanch.*
    Bast. Drawn in the flattering table of her
    eye !
Hang'd in the frowning wrinkle of her brow !
And quarter'd in her heart ! he doth espy
    Himself love's traitor : this is pity now,
That hang'd and drawn and quarter'd, there
    should be
In such a love so vile a lout as he.
    Blanch. My uncle's will in this respect is
    mine :   510
If he see aught in you that makes him like,
That any thing he sees, which moves his liking,
I can with ease translate it to my will ;
Or if you will, to speak more properly,
I will enforce it easily to my love.
Further I will not flatter you, my lord,
That all I see in you is worthy love,
Than this ; that nothing do I see in you,
Though churlish thoughts themselves should be
    your judge,
That I can find should merit any hate.   520
    K. John. What say these young ones ?
    What say you, my niece ?
    Blanch. That she is bound in honor still to
    do
What you in wisdom still vouchsafe to say.
    K. John. Speak then, prince Dauphin ; can
    you love this lady ?
    Lew. Nay, ask me if I can refrain from
    love ;
For I do love her most unfeignedly.
    K. John. Then do I give Volquessen, Tou-
    raine, Maine,
Poictiers and Anjou, these five provinces,
With her to thee ; and this addition more,
Full thirty thousand marks of English coin.
Philip of France, if thou be pleased withal,
Command thy son and daughter to join hands.
    K. Phi. It likes us well ; young princes,
    close your hands.
    Aust. And your lips too ; for I am well
    assured
That I did so when I was first assured.
    K. Phi. Now, citizens of Angiers, ope your
    gates,
Let in that amity which you have made ;
For at Saint Mary's chapel presently
The rites of marriage shall be solemnized.
Is not the Lady Constance in this troop ? 540

I know she is not, for this match made up
Her presence would have interrupted much :
Where is she and her son ? tell me, who knows.
    Lew. She is sad and passionate at your
    highness' tent.
    K. Phi. And, by my faith, this league that
    we have made
Will give her sadness very little cure.
Brother of England, how may we content
This widow lady ? In her right we came ;
Which we, God knows, have turn'd another
    way,
To our own vantage.   549
    K. John.   We will heal up all ;
For we'll create young Arthur Duke of Bre-
    tagne
And Earl of Richmond ; and this rich fair town
We make him lord of. Call the Lady Con-
    stance ;
Some speedy messenger bid her repair
To our solemnity : I trust we shall,
If not fill up the measure of her will,
Yet in some measure satisfy her so
That we shall stop her exclamation.
Go we, as well as haste will suffer us,
To this unlook'd for, unprepared pomp.   560
        [*Exeunt all but the Bastard.*
    Bast. Mad world ! mad kings ! mad com-
    position !
John, to stop Arthur's title in the whole,
Hath willingly departed with a part,
And France, whose armor conscience buckled
    on,
Whom zeal and charity brought to the field
As God's own soldier, rounded in the ear
With that same purpose-changer, that sly devil,
That broker, that still breaks the pate of faith,
That daily break-vow, he that wins of all,
Of kings, of beggars, old men, young men,
    maids,   570
Who, having no external thing to lose
But the word 'maid,' cheats the poor maid of
    that,
That smooth-faced gentleman, tickling Com-
    modity,
Commodity, the bias of the world,
The world, who of itself is peised well,
Made to run even upon even ground,
Till this advantage, this vile-drawing bias,
This sway of motion, this Commodity,
Makes it take head from all indifferency,
From all direction, purpose, course, intent :
And this same bias, this Commodity,   581
This bawd, this broker, this all-changing word,
Clapp'd on the outward eye of fickle France,
Hath drawn him from his own determined aid,
From a resolved and honorable war,
To a most base and vile-concluded peace.
And why rail I on this Commodity ?
But for because he hath not woo'd me yet :
Not that I have the power to clutch my hand,
When his fair angels would salute my palm ;
But for my hand, as unattempted yet,   591
Like a poor beggar, raileth on the rich.
Well, whiles I am a beggar, I will rail
And say there is no sin but to be rich ;
And being rich, my virtue then shall be
To say there is no vice but beggary.
Since kings break faith upon commodity,
Gain, be my lord, for I will worship thee.
        [*Exit.*

ACT III.

SCENE I. *The French* KING'S *pavilion.*

Enter CONSTANCE, ARTHUR, *and* SALISBURY.

Const. Gone to be married ! gone to swear
    a peace !
False blood to false blood join'd ! gone to be
    friends !
Shall Lewis have Blanch, and Blanch those
    provinces ?
It is not so; thou hast misspoke, misheard :
Be well advised, tell o'er thy tale again :
It cannot be ; thou dost but say 'tis so :
I trust I may not trust thee ; for thy word
Is but the vain breath of a common man :
Believe me, I do not believe thee, man ;
I have a king's oath to the contrary.   10
Thou shalt be punish'd for thus frighting me,
For I am sick and capable of fears,
Oppress'd with wrongs and therefore full of
    fears,
A widow, husbandless, subject to fears,
A woman, naturally born to fears ;
And though thou now confess thou didst but
    jest,
With my vex'd spirits I cannot take a truce,
But they will quake and tremble all this day.
What dost thou mean by shaking of thy head ?
Why dost thou look so sadly on my son ?   20
What means that hand upon that breast of
    thine ?
Why holds thine eye that lamentable rheum,
Like a proud river peering o'er his bounds ?
Be these sad signs confirmers of thy words ?
Then speak again ; not all thy former tale,
But this one word, whether thy tale be true.
  Sal. As true as I believe you think them
    false
That give you cause to prove my saying true.
  Const. O, if thou teach me to believe this
    sorrow,
Teach thou this sorrow how to make me die,
And let belief and life encounter so   31
As doth the fury of two desperate men
Which in the very meeting fall and die.
Lewis marry Blanch ! O boy, then where art
    thou ?
France friend with England, what becomes of
    me ?
Fellow, be gone : I cannot brook thy sight :
This news hath made thee a most ugly man.
  Sal. What other harm have I, good lady,
    done,
But spoke the harm that is by others done ?
  Const. Which harm within itself so hei-
    nous is   40
As it makes harmful all that speak of it.
  Arth. I do beseech you, madam, be con-
    tent.
  Const. If thou, that bid'st me be content,
    wert grim,
Ugly and slanderous to thy mother's womb,
Full of unpleasing blots and sightless stains,
Lame, foolish, crooked, swart, prodigious,
Patch'd with foul moles and eye-offending
    marks,
I would not care, I then would be content,
For then I should not love thee, no, nor thou
Become thy great birth nor deserve a crown.
But thou art fair, and at thy birth, dear boy,

Nature and Fortune join'd to make thee great :
Of Nature's gifts thou mayst with lilies boast,
And with the half-blown rose. But Fortune, O,
She is corrupted, changed and won from thee ;
She adulterates hourly with thine uncle John,
And with her golden hand hath pluck'd on
    France
To tread down fair respect of sovereignty,
And made his majesty the bawd to theirs. 59
France is a bawd to Fortune and King John,
That strumpet Fortune, that usurping John !
Tell me, thou fellow, is not France forsworn ?
Envenom him with words, or get thee gone
And leave those woes alone which I alone
Am bound to under-bear.
  Sal.   Pardon me, madam,
I may not go without you to the kings.
  Const. Thou mayst, thou shalt ; I will not
    go with thee :
I will instruct my sorrows to be proud ;
For grief is proud and makes his owner stoop.
To me and to the state of my great grief   70
Let kings assemble ; for my grief's so great
That no supporter but the huge firm earth
Can hold it up : here I and sorrows sit ;
Here is my throne, bid kings come bow to it.
                [Seats herself on the ground.

Enter KING JOHN, KING PHILIP, LEWIS,
  BLANCH, ELINOR, *the* BASTARD, AUSTRIA,
  and Attendants.

  K. Phi. 'Tis true, fair daughter ; and this
    blessed day
Ever in France shall be kept festival :
To solemnize this day the glorious sun
Stays in his course and plays the alchemist,
Turning with splendor of his precious eye
The meagre cloddy earth to glittering gold : 80
The yearly course that brings this day about
Shall never see it but a holiday.
  Const. A wicked day, and not a holy day !
                          [Rising.
What hath this day deserved ? what hath it
    done,
That it in golden letters should be set
Among the high tides in the calendar ?
Nay, rather turn this day out of the week,
This day of shame, oppression, perjury.
Or, if it must stand still, let wives with child
Pray that their burthens may not fall this day,
Lest that their hopes prodigiously be cross'd :
But on this day let seamen fear no wreck ;
No bargains break that are not this day made :
This day, all things begun come to ill end,
Yea, faith itself to hollow falsehood change !
  K. Phi. By heaven, lady, you shall have
    no cause
To curse the fair proceedings of this day :
Have I not pawn'd to you my majesty ?
  Const. You have beguiled me with a
    counterfeit
Resembling majesty, which, being touch'd and
    tried,   100
Proves valueless : you are forsworn, forsworn ;
You came in arms to spill mine enemies' blood,
But now in arms you strengthen it with yours :
The grappling vigor and rough frown of war
Is cold in amity and painted peace,
And our oppression hath made up this league.
Arm, arm, you heavens, against these perjured
    kings !
A widow cries ; be husband to me, heavens !
Let not the hours of this ungodly day   109

Wear out the day in peace ; but, ere sunset,
Set armed discord 'twixt these perjured kings !
Hear me, O, hear me !
 Aust.   Lady Constance, peace !
 Const. War ! war ! no peace ! peace is to
  me a war
O Lymoges ! O Austria ! thou dost shame
That bloody spoil : thou slave, thou wretch,
  thou coward !
Thou little valiant, great in villany !
Thou ever strong upon the stronger side !
Thou Fortune's champion that dost never fight
But when her humorous ladyship is by
To teach thee safety ! thou art perjured too,
And soothest up greatness. What a fool art
  thou,   121
A ramping fool, to brag and stamp and swear
Upon my party ! Thou cold-blooded slave,
Hast thou not spoke like thunder on my side,
Been sworn my soldier, bidding me depend
Upon thy stars, thy fortune and thy strength,
And dost thou now fall over to my foes ?
Thou wear a lion's hide ! doff it for shame,
And hang a calf's-skin on those recreant limbs.
 Aust. O, that a man should speak those
  words to me !   130
 Bast. And hang a calf's-skin on those
  recreant limbs.
 Aust. Thou darest not say so, villain, for
  thy life.
 Bast. And hang a calf's-skin on those
  recreant limbs.
 K. John. We like not this ; thou dost for-
  get thyself.

    Enter PANDULPH.

 K. Phi. Here comes the holy legate of the
  pope.
 Pand. Hail, you anointed deputies of
  heaven !
To thee, King John, my holy errand is.
I Pandulph, of fair Milan cardinal,
And from Pope Innocent the legate here,
Do in his name religiously demand 140
Why thou against the church, our holy mother,
So wilfully dost spurn ; and force perforce
Keep Stephen Langton, chosen archbishop
Of Canterbury, from that holy see ?
This, in our foresaid holy father's name,
Pope Innocent, I do demand of thee.
 K. John. What earthy name to interroga-
  tories
Can task the free breath of a sacred king ?
Thou canst not, cardinal, devise a name
So slight, unworthy and ridiculous, 150
To charge me to an answer, as the pope.
Tell him this tale ; and from the mouth of
  England
Add thus much more, that no Italian priest
Shall tithe or toll in our dominions ;
But as we, under heaven, are supreme head,
So under Him that great supremacy,
Where we do reign, we will alone uphold,
Without the assistance of a mortal hand :
So tell the pope, all reverence set apart
To him and his usurp'd authority. 160
 K. Phi. Brother of England, you blaspheme
  in this.
 K. John. Though you and all the kings of
  Christendom
Are led so grossly by this meddling priest,
Dreading the curse that money may buy out ;
And by the merit of vile gold, dross, dust,

Purchase corrupted pardon of a man,
Who in that sale sells pardon from himself,
Though you and all the rest so grossly led
This juggling witchcraft with revenue cherish,
Yet I alone, alone do me oppose 170
Against the pope and count his friends my
  foes.
 Pand. Then, by the lawful power that I
  have,
Thou shalt stand cursed and excommunicate.
And blessed shall he be that doth revolt
From his allegiance to an heretic ;
And meritorious shall that hand be call'd,
Canonized and worshipped as a saint,
That takes away by any secret course
Thy hateful life.
 Const.   O, lawful let it be
That I have room with Rome to curse awhile !
Good father cardinal, cry thou amen 181
To my keen curses ; for without my wrong
There is no tongue hath power to curse him
  right.
 Pand. There's law and warrant, lady, for
  my curse.
 Const. And for mine too : when law can
  do no right,
Let it be lawful that law bar no wrong :
Law cannot give my child his kingdom here,
For he that holds his kingdom holds the law ;
Therefore, since law itself is perfect wrong,
How can the law forbid my tongue to curse ?
 Pand. Philip of France, on peril of a curse,
Let go the hand of that arch-heretic ;
And raise the power of France upon his head,
Unless he do submit himself to Rome.
 Eli. Look'st thou pale, France ? do not let
  go thy hand.
 Const. Look to that, devil ; lest that France
  repent,
And by disjoining hands, hell lose a soul.
 Aust. King Philip, listen to the cardinal.
 Bast. And hang a calf's-skin on his rec-
  reant limbs.
 Aust. Well, ruffian, I must pocket up these
  wrongs,   200
Because—
 Bast. Your breeches best may carry them.
 K. John. Philip, what say'st thou to the
  cardinal ?
 Const. What should he say, but as the
  cardinal ?
 Lew. Bethink you, father ; for the differ
  ence
Is purchase of a heavy curse from Rome,
Or the light loss of England for a friend :
Forego the easier.
 Blanch.   That's the curse of Rome.
 Const. O Lewis, stand fast ! the dev
  tempts thee here
In likeness of a new untrimmed bride.
 Blanch. The Lady Constance speaks no
  from her faith,   21
But from her need.
 Const.   O, if thou grant my need
Which only lives but by the death of faith,
That need must needs infer this principle,
That faith would live again by death of need
O then, tread down my need, and faith moun
  up ;
Keep my need up, and faith is trodden down
 K. John. The king is moved, and answe
  not to this.

Const. O, be removed from him, and an-
　　swer well !
Aust. Do so, King Philip ; hang no more
　　in doubt.
Bast. Hang nothing but a calf's-skin, most
　　sweet lout.　　　　　　　　　　220
K. Phi. I am perplex'd, and know not what
　　to say.
Pand. What canst thou say but will perplex
　　thee more,
If thou stand excommunicate and cursed ?
K. Phi. Good reverend father, make my
　　person yours,
And tell me how you would bestow yourself.
This royal hand and mine are newly knit,
And the conjunction of our inward souls
Married in league, coupled and linked together
With all religious strength of sacred vows ;
The latest breath that gave the sound of words
Was deep-sworn faith, peace, amity, true love
Between our kingdoms and our royal selves,
And even before this truce, but new before,
No longer than we well could wash our hands
To clap this royal bargain up of peace,
Heaven knows, they were besmear'd and over-
　　stain'd
With slaughter's pencil, where revenge did
　　paint
The fearful difference of incensed kings :
And shall these hands, so lately purged of
　　blood,
So newly join'd in love, so strong in both,　240
Unyoke this seizure and this kind regreet ?
Play fast and loose with faith ? so jest with
　　heaven,
Make such unconstant children of ourselves,
As now again to snatch our palm from palm,
Unswear faith sworn, and on the marriage-bed
Of smiling peace to march a bloody host,
And make a riot on the gentle brow
Of true sincerity ? O, holy sir,
My reverend father, let it not be so !
Out of your grace, devise, ordain, impose　250
Some gentle order ; and then we shall be blest
To do your pleasure and continue friends.
Pand. All form is formless, order orderless,
Save what is opposite to England's love.
Therefore to arms ! be champion of our
　　church,
Or let the church, our mother, breathe her
　　curse,
A mother's curse, on her revolting son.
France, thou mayst hold a serpent by the
　　tongue,
A chafed lion by the mortal paw,
A fasting tiger safer by the tooth,　　260
Than keep in peace that hand which thou dost
　　hold.
K. Phi. I may disjoin my hand, but not my
　　faith.
Pand. So makest thou faith an enemy to
　　faith ;
And like a civil war set'st oath to oath,
Thy tongue against thy tongue. O, let thy vow
First made to heaven, first be to heaven per-
　　form'd,
That is, to be the champion of our church !
What since thou sworest is sworn against thy-
　　self
And may not be performed by thyself,
Or that which thou hast sworn to do amiss
Not amiss when it is truly done,　　271
And being not done, where doing tends to ill,

The truth is then most done not doing it :
The better act of purposes mistook
Is to mistake again ; though indirect,
Yet indirection thereby grows direct,
And falsehood falsehood cures, as fire cools
　　fire
Within the scorched veins of one new-burn'd.
It is religion that doth make vows kept ;
But thou hast sworn against religion,　　280
By what thou swear'st against the thing thou
　　swear'st,
And makest an oath the surety for thy truth
Against an oath : the truth thou art unsure
To swear, swears only not to be forsworn ;
Else what a mockery should it be to swear !
But thou dost swear only to be forsworn ;
And most forsworn, to keep what thou dost
　　swear.
Therefore thy later vows against thy first
Is in thyself rebellion to thyself ;　　289
And better conquest never canst thou make
Than arm thy constant and thy nobler parts
Against these giddy loose suggestions :
Upon which better part our prayers come in,
If thou vouchsafe them. But if not, then know
The peril of our curses light on thee
So heavy as thou shalt not shake them off,
But in despair die under their black weight.
　Aust. Rebellion, flat rebellion !
　Bast.　　　　　　　　Will't not be ?
Will not a calf's-skin stop that mouth of
　　thine ?
　Lew. Father, to arms !
　Blanch.　　Upon thy wedding-day ?　300
Against the blood that thou hast married ?
What, shall our feast be kept with slaughter'd
　　men ?
Shall braying trumpets and loud churlish
　　drums,
Clamors of hell, be measures to our pomp ?
O husband, hear me ! ay, alack, how new
Is husband in my mouth ! even for that name,
Which till this time my tongue did ne'er pro-
　　nounce,
Upon my knee I beg, go not to arms
Against mine uncle.
　Const.　　　　O, upon my knee,　309
Made hard with kneeling, I do pray to thee,
Thou virtuous Dauphin, alter not the doom
Forethought by heaven !
　Blanch. Now shall I see thy love : what
　　motive may
Be stronger with thee than the name of wife ?
　Const. That which upholdeth him that thee
　　upholds,
His honor : O, thine honor, Lewis, thine
　　honor !
　Lew. I muse your majesty doth seem so
　　cold,
When such profound respects do pull you on.
　Pand. I will denounce a curse upon his
　　head.
　K. Phi. Thou shalt not need. England, I
　　will fall from thee.　　320
　Const. O fair return of banish'd majesty !
　Eli. O foul revolt of French inconstancy !
　K. John. France, thou shalt rue this hour
　　within this hour.
　Bast. Old Time the clock-setter, that bald
　　sexton Time,
Is it as he will ? well then, France shall rue.
　Blanch. The sun's o'ercast with blood : fair
　　day, adieu !

Which is the side that I must go withal ?
I am with both : each army hath a hand ;
And in their rage, I having hold of both,
They whirl asunder and dismember me.   330
Husband, I cannot pray that thou mayst win ;
Uncle, I needs must pray that thou mayst
    lose ;
Father, I may not wish the fortune thine ;
Grandam, I will not wish thy wishes thrive :
Whoever wins, on that side shall I lose ;
Assured loss before the match be play'd.
    Lew.   Lady, with me, with me thy fortune
    lies.
    Blanch.   There where my fortune lives,
    there my life dies.
    K. John.   Cousin, go draw our puissance
    together.   [*Exit Bastard.*
France, I am burn'd up with inflaming wrath ;
A rage whose heat hath this condition,   341
That nothing can allay, nothing but blood,
The blood, and dearest-valued blood, of
    France.
    K. Phi.   Thy rage shall burn thee up, and
    thou shalt turn
To ashes, ere our blood shall quench that fire :
Look to thyself, thou art in jeopardy.
    K. John.   No more than he that threats.
    To arms let's hie !   [*Exeunt.*

SCENE II.   *The same. Plains near Angiers.*

Alarums, excursions.   Enter the BASTARD, *with*
AUSTRIA'S *head.*

    Bast.   Now, by my life, this day grows won-
    drous hot ;
Some airy devil hovers in the sky
And pours down mischief. Austria's head lie
    there,
While Philip breathes.

Enter KING JOHN, ARTHUR, *and* HUBERT.

    K. John.   Hubert, keep this boy. Philip,
    make up :
My mother is assailed in our tent,
And ta'en, I fear.
    Bast.   My lord, I rescued her ;
Her highness is in safety, fear you not :
But on, my liege ; for very little pains
Will bring this labor to an happy end.
                           [*Exeunt.*

SCENE III.   *The same.*

Alarums, excursions, retreat. Enter KING
JOHN, ELINOR, ARTHUR, *the* BASTARD, HU-
BERT, *and* Lords.

    K. John.   [*To Elinor*] So shall it be ; your
    grace shall stay behind
So strongly guarded. [*To Arthur*] Cousin,
    look not sad :
Thy grandam loves thee ; and thy uncle will
As dear be to thee as thy father was.
    Arth.   O, this will make my mother die with
    grief !
    K. John.   [*To the Bastard*] Cousin, away
    for England ! haste before :
And, ere our coming, see thou shake the bags
Of hoarding abbots ; imprisoned angels
Set at liberty : the fat ribs of peace
Must by the hungry now be fed upon :   10
Use our commission in his utmost force.
    Bast.   Bell, book, and candle shall not drive
    me back,
When gold and silver becks me to come on.

I leave your highness. Grandam, I will pray,
If ever I remember to be holy,
For your fair safety ; so, I kiss your hand.
    Eli.   Farewell, gentle cousin.
    K. John.   Coz, farewell.   [*Exit Bastard.*
    Eli.   Come hither, little kinsman ; hark, a
    word.
    K. John.   Come hither, Hubert. O my gen-
    tle Hubert,
We owe thee much ! within this wall of flesh
There is a soul counts thee her creditor   21
And with advantage means to pay thy love :
And, my good friend, thy voluntary oath
Lives in this bosom, dearly cherished.
Give me thy hand. I had a thing to say,
But I will fit it with some better time.
By heaven, Hubert, I am almost ashamed
To say what good respect I have of thee.
    Hub.   I am much bounden to your majesty.
    K. John.   Good friend, thou hast no cause
    to say so yet,   30
But thou shalt have ; and creep time ne'er so
    slow,
Yet it shall come from me to do thee good.
I had a thing to say, but let it go :
The sun is in the heaven, and the proud day,
Attended with the pleasures of the world,
Is all too wanton and too full of gawds
To give me audience : if the midnight bell
Did, with his iron tongue and brazen mouth,
Sound on into the drowsy race of night ;   39
If this same were a churchyard where we
    stand,
And thou possessed with a thousand wrongs,
Or if that surly spirit, melancholy,
Had baked thy blood and made it heavy-thick,
Which else runs tickling up and down the
    veins,
Making that idiot, laughter, keep men's eyes
And strain their cheeks to idle merriment,
A passion hateful to my purposes,
Or if that thou couldst see me without eyes,
Hear me without thine ears, and make reply
Without a tongue, using conceit alone,   50
Without eyes, ears and harmful sound of
    words ;
Then, in despite of brooded watchful day,
I would into thy bosom pour my thoughts :
But, ah, I will not ! yet I love thee well ;
And, by my troth, I think thou lovest me well.
    Hub.   So well, that what you bid me under-
    take,
Though that my death were adjunct to my act,
By heaven, I would do it.
    K. John.   Do not I know thou wouldst ?
Good Hubert, Hubert, Hubert, throw thine eye
On yon young boy : I'll tell thee what, my
    friend,   60
He is a very serpent in my way ;
And whereso'er this foot of mine doth tread,
He lies before me : dost thou understand me ?
Thou art his keeper.
    Hub.   And I'll keep him so,
That he shall not offend your majesty.
    K. John.   Death
    Hub.   My lord ?
    K. John.   A grave.
    Hub.   He shall not live.
    K. John.   Enough
I could be merry now. Hubert, I love thee ;
Well, I'll not say what I intend for thee :
Remember. Madam, fare you well :
I'll send those powers o'er to your majesty.   7

Eli. My blessing go with thee !
K. John.   For England, cousin, go :
Hubert shall be your man, attend on you
With all true duty. On toward Calais, ho !
                                  [*Exeunt.*

Scene IV. *The same. The French* King's
                      tent.

Enter King Philip, Lewis, Pandulph, *and*
                  Attendants.

K. Phi. So, by a roaring tempest on the
     flood,
A whole armado of convicted sail
Is scatter'd and disjoin'd from fellowship.
Pand. Courage and comfort ! all shall yet
     go well.
K. Phi. What can go well, when we have
     run so ill ?
Are we not beaten ? Is not Angiers lost ?
Arthur ta'en prisoner ? divers dear friends
     slain ?
And bloody England into England gone,
O'erbearing interruption, spite of France ?
Lew. What he hath won, that hath he forti-
     fied :   10
So hot a speed with such advice disposed,
Such temperate order in so fierce a cause,
Doth want example : who hath read or heard
Of any kindred action like to this ?
K. Phi. Well could I bear that England
     had this praise,
So we could find some pattern of our shame.

          Enter Constance.

Look, who comes here ! a grave unto a soul ;
Holding the eternal spirit against her will,
In the vile prison of afflicted breath.
I prithee, lady, go away with me.   20
Const. Lo, now ! now see the issue of your
     peace.
K. Phi. Patience, good lady ! comfort, gen-
     tle Constance !
Const. No, I defy all counsel, all redress,
But that which ends all counsel, true redress,
Death, death ; O amiable lovely death !
Thou odoriferous stench ! sound rottenness !
Arise forth from the couch of lasting night,
Thou hate and terror to prosperity,
And I will kiss thy detestable bones
And put my eyeballs in thy vaulty brows   30
And ring these fingers with thy household
     worms
And stop this gap of breath with fulsome dust
And be a carrion monster like thyself :
Come, grin on me, and I will think thou
     smilest
And buss thee as thy wife. Misery's love,
O, come to me !
K. Phi. O fair affliction, peace !
Const. No, no, I will not, having breath to
     cry :
O, that my tongue were in the thunder's
     mouth !
Then with a passion would I shake the world ;
And rouse from sleep that fell anatomy   40
Which cannot hear a lady's feeble voice,
Which scorns a modern invocation.
Pand. Lady, you utter madness, and not
     sorrow.
Const. Thou art not holy to belie me so ;
I am not mad : this hair I tear is mine ;
My name is Constance ; I was Geffrey's wife ;
Young Arthur is my son, and he is lost :

I am not mad : I would to heaven I were !
For then, 'tis like I should forget myself :
O, if I could, what grief should I forget !   50
Preach some philosophy to make me mad,
And thou shalt be canonized, cardinal ;
For being not mad but sensible of grief,
My reasonable part produces reason
How I may be deliver'd of these woes,
And teaches me to kill or hang myself :
If I were mad, I should forget my son,
Or madly think a babe of clouts were he :
I am not mad ; too well, too well I feel
The different plague of each calamity.   60
K. Phi. Bind up those tresses. O, what love
     I note
In the fair multitude of those her hairs !
Where but by chance a silver drop hath fallen,
Even to that drop ten thousand wiry friends
Do glue themselves in sociable grief,
Like true, inseparable, faithful loves,
Sticking together in calamity.
Const. To England, if you will.
K. Phi.   Bind up your hairs.
Const. Yes, that I will ; and wherefore will
     I do it ?   69
I tore them from their bonds and cried aloud
' O that these hands could so redeem my son,
As they have given these hairs their liberty ! '
But now I envy at their liberty,
And will again commit them to their bonds,
Because my poor child is a prisoner.
And, father cardinal, I have heard you say
That we shall see and know our friends in
     heaven :
If that be true, I shall see my boy again ;
For since the birth of Cain, the first male
     child,
To him that did but yesterday suspire,   80
There was not such a gracious creature born.
But now will canker-sorrow eat my bud
And chase the native beauty from his cheek
And he will look as hollow as a ghost,
As dim and meagre as an ague's fit,
And so he'll die ; and, rising so again,
When I shall meet him in the court of heaven
I shall not know him : therefore never, never
Must I behold my pretty Arthur more.
Pand. You hold too heinous a respect of
     grief.   90
Const. He talks to me that never had a son.
K. Phi. You are as fond of grief as of your
     child.
Const. Grief fills the room up of my absent
     child,
Lies in his bed, walks up and down with me,
Puts on his pretty looks, repeats his words,
Remembers me of all his gracious parts,
Stuffs out his vacant garments with his form ;
Then, have I reason to be fond of grief ?
Fare you well : had you such a loss as I,
I could give better comfort than you do.   100
I will not keep this form upon my head,
When there is such disorder in my wit.
O Lord ! my boy, my Arthur, my fair son !
My life, my joy, my food, my all the world !
My widow-comfort, and my sorrows' cure !
                                    [*Exit.*
K. Phi. I fear some outrage, and I'll follow
     her.   [*Exit.*
Lew. There's nothing in this world can
     make me joy :
Life is as tedious as a twice-told tale
Vexing the dull ear of a drowsy man ;

And bitter shame hath spoil'd the sweet world's
   taste,   110
That it yields nought but shame and bitterness.
  Pand. Before the curing of a strong dis-
   ease,
Even in the instant of repair and health,
The fit is strongest ; evils that take leave,
On their departure most of all show evil :
What have you lost by losing of this day ?
  Lew. All days of glory, joy and happiness.
  Pand. If you had won it, certainly you had.
No, no ; when Fortune means to men most
   good,
She looks upon them with a threatening eye.
'Tis strange to think how much King John
   hath lost   121
In this which he accounts so clearly won :
Are not you grieved that Arthur is his pris-
   oner ?
  Lew. As heartily as he is glad he hath him.
  Pand. Your mind is all as youthful as your
   blood.
Now hear me speak with a prophetic spirit ;
For even the breath of what I mean to speak
Shall blow each dust, each straw, each little
   rub,
Out of the path which shall directly lead
Thy foot to England's throne ; and therefore
   mark.   130
John hath seized Arthur ; and it cannot be
That, whiles warm life plays in that infant's
   veins,
The misplaced John should entertain an hour,
One minute, nay, one quiet breath of rest.
A sceptre snatch'd with an unruly hand
Must be as boisterously maintain'd as gain'd ;
And he that stands upon a slippery place
Makes nice of no vile hold to stay him up :
That John may stand, then Arthur needs must
   fall ;
So be it, for it cannot be but so.   140
  Lew. But what shall I gain by young Ar-
   thur's fall ?
  Pand. You, in the right of Lady Blanch
   your wife,
May then make all the claim that Arthur did.
  Lew. And lose it, life and all, as Arthur
   did.
  Pand. How green you are and fresh in this
   old world !
John lays you plots ; the times conspire with
   you ;
For he that steeps his safety in true blood
Shall find but bloody safety and untrue.
This act so evilly born shall cool the hearts
Of all his people and freeze up their zeal,   150
That none so small advantage shall step forth
To check his reign, but they will cherish it ;
No natural exhalation in the sky,
No scope of nature, no distemper'd day,
No common wind, no customed event,
But they will pluck away his natural cause
And call them meteors, prodigies and signs,
Abortives, presages and tongues of heaven,
Plainly denouncing vengeance upon John.
  Lew. May be he will not touch young Ar-
   thur's life,   160
But hold himself safe in his prisonment.
  Pand. O, sir, when he shall hear of your
   approach,
If that young Arthur be not gone already,
Even at that news he dies ; and then the hearts
Of all his people shall revolt from him

And kiss the lips of unacquainted change
And pick strong matter of revolt and wrath
Out of the bloody fingers' ends of John.
Methinks I see this hurly all on foot :
And, O, what better matter breeds for you 170
Than I have named ! The bastard Faulcon-
   bridge
Is now in England, ransacking the church,
Offending charity : if but a dozen French
Were there in arms, they would be as a call
To train ten thousand English to their side,
Or as a little snow, tumbled about,
Anon becomes a mountain. O noble Dauphin,
Go with me to the king : 'tis wonderful
What may be wrought out of their discontent,
Now that their souls are topful of offence. 180
For England go : I will whet on the king.
  Lew. Strong reasons make strong actions :
   let us go :
If you say ay, the king will not say no.
                       [Exeunt.

ACT IV.

SCENE I. *A room in a castle.*

Enter HUBERT *and* Executioners.

  Hub. Heat me these irons hot ; and look
   thou stand
Within the arras : when I strike my foot
Upon the bosom of the ground, rush forth,
And bind the boy which you shall find with me
Fast to the chair : be heedful : hence, and
   watch.
  First Exec. I hope your warrant will bear
   out the deed.
  Hub. Uncleanly scruples ! fear not you :
   look to't.   *[Exeunt Executioners.*
Young lad, come forth ; I have to say with
   you.

Enter ARTHUR.

  Arth. Good morrow, Hubert.
  Hub.   Good morrow, little prince.
  Arth. As little prince, having so great a
   title   10
To be more prince, as may be. You are sad.
  Hub. Indeed, I have been merrier.
  Arth.   Mercy on me !
Methinks no body should be sad but I :
Yet, I remember, when I was in France,
Young gentlemen would be as sad as night,
Only for wantonness. By my christendom,
So I were out of prison and kept sheep,
I should be as merry as the day is long ;
And so I would be here, but that I doubt
My uncle practises more harm to me :   20
He is afraid of me and I of him :
Is it my fault that I was Geffrey's son ?
No, indeed, is't not ; and I would to heaven
I were your son, so you would love me, Hu-
   bert.
  Hub. [*Aside*] If I talk to him, with his in-
   nocent prate
He will awake my mercy which lies dead :
Therefore I will be sudden and dispatch.
  Arth. Are you sick, Hubert ? you look pale
   to-day :
In sooth, I would you were a little sick,
That I might sit all night and watch with you :
I warrant I love you more than you do me. 31
  Hub. [*Aside*] His words do take posses-
   sion of my bosom.

Read here, young Arthur.   [*Showing a paper.*
               [*Aside*] How now, foolish rheum !
Turning dispiteous torture out of door !
I must be brief, lest resolution drop
Out at mine eyes in tender womanish tears.
Can you not read it ? is it not fair writ ?
  Arth. Too fairly, Hubert, for so foul ef-
    fect :
Must you with hot irons burn out both mine
    eyes ?
  Hub. Young boy, I must.
  Arth.   And will you ?
  Hub.   And I will. 40
  Arth. Have you the heart ? When your
    head did but ache,
I knit my handercher about your brows,
The best I had, a princess wrought it me,
And I did never ask it you again ;
And with my hand at midnight held your head,
And like the watchful minutes to the hour,
Still and anon cheer'd up the heavy time,
Saying, ' What lack you ? ' and ' Where lies
    your grief ? '
Or ' What good love may I perform for you ? '
Many a poor man's son would have lien still 50
And ne'er have spoke a loving word to you ;
But you at your sick service had a prince.
Nay, you may think my love was crafty love
And call it cunning : do, an if you will :
If heaven is pleased that you must use me ill,
Why then you must. Will you put out mine
    eyes ?
These eyes that never did nor never shall
So much as frown on you.
  Hub.   I have sworn to do it ;
And with hot irons must I burn them out.
  Arth. Ah, none but in this iron age would
    do it !   60
The iron of itself, though heat red-hot,
Approaching near these eyes, would drink my
    tears
And quench his fiery indignation
Even in the matter of mine innocence ;
Nay, after that, consume away in rust
But for containing fire to harm mine eye.
Are you more stubborn-hard than hammer'd
    iron ?
An if an angel should have come to me
And told me Hubert should put out mine eyes,
I would not have believed him,—no tongue but
    Hubert's.   70
  Hub. Come forth.   [*Stamps.*

Re-enter Executioners, *with a cord, irons, &c.*
Do as I bid you do.
  Arth. O, save me, Hubert, save me ! my
    eyes are out
Even with the fierce looks of these bloody
    men.
  Hub. Give me the iron, I say, and bind
    him here.
  Arth. Alas, what need you be so boister-
    ous-rough ?
I will not struggle, I will stand stone-still.
For heaven sake, Hubert, let me not be
    bound !
Nay, hear me, Hubert, drive these men away,
And I will sit as quiet as a lamb ;   80
I will not stir, nor wince, nor speak a word,
Nor look upon the iron angerly :
Thrust but these men away, and I'll forgive
    you,
Whatever torment you do put me to.

  Hub. Go, stand within ; let me alone with
    him.
  First Exec. I am best pleased to be from
    such a deed.   [*Exeunt Executioners.*
  Arth. Alas, I then have chid away my
    friend !
He hath a stern look, but a gentle heart :
Let him come back, that his compassion may
Give life to yours.   89
  Hub.   Come, boy, prepare yourself.
  Arth. Is there no remedy ?
  Hub.   None, but to lose your eyes.
  Arth. O heaven, that there were but a mote
    in yours,
A grain, a dust, a gnat, a wandering hair,
Any annoyance in that precious sense !
Then feeling what small things are boisterous
    there,
Your vile intent must needs seem horrible.
  Hub. Is this your promise ? go to, hold
    your tongue.
  Arth. Hubert, the utterance of a brace of
    tongues
Must needs want pleading for a pair of eyes :
Let me not hold my tongue, let me not, Hu-
    bert ;   100
Or, Hubert, if you will, cut out my tongue,
So I may keep mine eyes : O, spare mine
    eyes.
Though to no use but still to look on you !
Lo, by my truth, the instrument is cold
And would not harm me.
  Hub.   I can heat it, boy.
  Arth. No, in good sooth : the fire is dead
    with grief,
Being create for comfort, to be used
In undeserved extremes : see else yourself ;
There is no malice in this burning coal ;
The breath of heaven has blown his spirit out
And strew'd repentent ashes on his head. 111
  Hub. But with my breath I can revive it,
    boy.
  Arth. An if you do, you will but make it
    blush
And glow with shame of your proceedings,
    Hubert :
Nay, it perchance will sparkle in your eyes ;
And like a dog that is compell'd to fight,
Snatch at his master that doth tarre him on.
All things that you should use to do me wrong
Deny their office : only you do lack
That mercy which fierce fire and iron extends,
Creatures of note for mercy-lacking uses. 121
  Hub. Well, see to live ; I will not touch
    thine eye
For all the treasure that thine uncle owes :
Yet am I sworn and I did purpose, boy,
With this same very iron to burn them out.
  Arth. O, now you look like Hubert ! all
    this while
You were disguised.
  Hub.   Peace ; no more. Adieu.
Your uncle must not know but you are dead ;
I'll fill these dogged spies with false reports :
And, pretty child, sleep doubtless and secure,
That Hubert, for the wealth of all the world,
Will not offend thee.   132
  Arth.   O heaven ! I thank you, Hubert.
  Hub. Silence ; no more : go closely in with
    me :
Much danger do I undergo for thee.
                           [*Exeunt.*

SCENE II. KING JOHN'S *palace.*

Enter KING JOHN, PEMBROKE, SALISBURY, *and other* Lords.

K. John. Here once again we sit, once
   again crown'd,
And looked upon, I hope, with cheerful eyes.
Pem. This 'once again,' but that your
   highness pleased,
Was once superfluous : you were crown'd be-
   fore,
And that high royalty was ne'er pluck'd off,
The faiths of men ne'er stained with revolt ;
Fresh expectation troubled not the land
With any long'd-for change or better state.
Sal. Therefore, to be possess'd with double
   pomp,
To guard a title that was rich before,   10
To gild refined gold, to paint the lily,
To throw a perfume on the violet,
To smooth the ice, or add another hue
Unto the rainbow, or with taper-light
To seek the beauteous eye of heaven to gar-
   nish,
Is wasteful and ridiculous excess.
Pem. But that your royal pleasure must be
   done,
This act is as an ancient tale new told,
And in the last repeating troublesome,
Being urged at a time unseasonable.   20
Sal. In this the antique and well noted
   face
Of plain old form is much disfigured ;
And, like a shifted wind unto a sail,
It makes the course of thoughts to fetch about,
Startles and frights consideration,
Makes sound opinion sick and truth suspected,
For putting on so new a fashion'd robe.
Pem. When workmen strive to do better
   than well,
They do confound their skill in covetousness ;
And oftentimes excusing of a fault   30
Doth make the fault the worse by the excuse,
As patches set upon a little breach
Discredit more in hiding of the fault
Than did the fault before it was so patch'd.
Sal. To this effect, before you were new
   crown'd,
We breathed our counsel : but it pleased your
   highness
To overbear it, and we are all well pleased,
Since all and every part of what we would
Doth make a stand at what your highness will.
K. John. Some reasons of this double
   coronation   40
I have possess'd you with and think them
   strong ;
And more, more strong, then lesser is my fear,
I shall indue you with : meantime but ask
What you would have reform'd that is not well,
And well shall you perceive how willingly
I will both hear and grant you your requests.
Pem. Then I, as one that am the tongue of
   these,
To sound the purposes of all their hearts,
Both for myself and them, but, chief of all,
Your safety, for the which myself and them
Bend their best studies, heartily request   51
The enfranchisement of Arthur ; whose re-
   straint
Doth move the murmuring lips of discontent
To break into this dangerous argument,—

If what in rest you have in right you hold,
Why then your fears, which, as they say, at-
   tend
The steps of wrong, should move you to mew
   up
Your tender kinsman and to choke his days
With barbarous ignorance and deny his youth
The rich advantage of good exercise ?   60
That the time's enemies may not have this
To grace occasions, let it be our suit
That you have bid us ask his liberty ;
Which for our goods we do no further ask
Than whereupon our weal, on you depending,
Counts it your weal he have his liberty.

Enter HUBERT.

K. John. Let it be so : I do commit his
   youth
To your direction. Hubert, what news with
   you ?   [*Taking him apart.*
Pem. This is the man should do the bloody
   deed ;
He show'd his warrant to a friend of mine :
The image of a wicked heinous fault   71
Lives in his eye ; that close aspect of his
Does show the mood of a much troubled
   breast ;
And I do fearfully believe 'tis done,
What we so fear'd he had a charge to do.
Sal. The color of the king doth come and
   go
Between his purpose and his conscience,
Like heralds 'twixt two dreadful battles set :
His passion is so ripe, it needs must break.
Pem. And when it breaks, I fear will issue
   thence   80
The foul corruption of a sweet child's death.
K. John. We cannot hold mortality's strong
   hand :
Good lords, although my will to give is living,
The suit which you demand is gone and dead :
He tells us Arthur is deceased to-night.
Sal. Indeed we fear'd his sickness was past
   cure.
Pem. Indeed we heard how near his death
   he was
Before the child himself felt he was sick :
This must be answer'd either here or hence.
K. John. Why do you bend such solemn
   brows on me ?   90
Think you I bear the shears of destiny ?
Have I commandment on the pulse of life ?
Sal. It is apparent foul play ; and 'tis
   shame
That greatness should so grossly offer it :
So thrive it in your game ! and so, farewell.
Pem. Stay yet, Lord Salisbury ; I'll go with
   thee,
And find the inheritance of this poor child,
His little kingdom of a forced grave.
That blood which owed the breadth of all this
   isle,
Three foot of it doth hold : bad world the
   while !   100
This must not be thus borne : this will break
   out
To all our sorrows, and ere long I doubt.
                              [*Exeunt Lords.*
K. John. They burn in indignation. I re-
   pent :
There is no sure foundation set on blood,
No certain life achieved by others' death.

Enter a Messenger.

A fearful eye thou hast : where is that blood
That I have seen inhabit in those cheeks ?
So foul a sky clears not without a storm :
Pour down thy weather : how goes all in
	France ?
	Mess.	From France to England. Never
	such a power	110
For any foreign preparation
Was levied in the body of a land.
The copy of your speed is learn'd by them ;
For when you should be told they do prepare,
The tidings comes that they are all arrived.
	K. John.	O, where hath our intelligence
	been drunk ?
Where hath it slept ? Where is my mother's
	care,
That such an army could be drawn in France,
And she not hear of it ?
	Mess.	My liege, her ear	119
Is stopp'd with dust ; the first of April died
Your noble mother : and, as I hear, my lord,
The Lady Constance in a frenzy died
Three days before : but this from rumor's
	tongue
I idly heard ; if true or false I know not.
	K. John.	Withhold thy speed, dreadful oc-
	casion !
O, make a league with me, till I have pleased
My discontented peers ! What ! mother dead !
How wildly then walks my estate in France !
Under whose conduct came those powers of
	France
That thou for truth givest out are landed here ?
	Mess.	Under the Dauphin.	130
	K. John.	Thou hast made me giddy
With these ill tidings.

Enter the BASTARD *and* PETER *of Pomfret.*

	Now, what says the world
To your proceedings ? do not seek to stuff
My head with more ill news, for it is full.
	Bast.	But if you be afeard to hear the
	worst,
Then let the worst unheard fall on your head.
	K. John.	Bear with me cousin, for I was
	amazed
Under the tide : but now I breathe again
Aloft the flood, and can give audience
To any tongue, speak it of what it will.	140
	Bast.	How I have sped among the clergy-
	men,
The sums I have collected shall express.
But as I travell'd hither through the land,
I find the people strangely fantasied ;
Possess'd with rumors, full of idle dreams,
Not knowing what they fear, but full of fear :
And here's a prophet, that I brought with me
From forth the streets of Pomfret, whom I
	found
With many hundreds treading on his heels ;
To whom he sung, in rude harsh-sounding
	rhymes,	150
That, ere the next Ascension-day at noon,
Your highness should deliver up your crown.
	K. John.	Thou idle dreamer, wherefore
	didst thou so ?
	Peter.	Foreknowing that the truth will fall
	out so.
	K. John.	Hubert, away with him ; imprison
	him ;
And on that day at noon whereon he says

I shall yield up my crown, let him be hang'd.
Deliver him to safety ; and return,
For I must use thee.
	[*Exeunt Hubert with Peter.*
	O my gentle cousin,
Hear'st thou the news abroad, who are ar-
	rived ?	160
	Bast.	The French, my lord ; men's mouths
	are full of it :
Besides, I met Lord Bigot and Lord Salisbury,
With eyes as red as new-enkindled fire,
And others more, going to seek the grave
Of Arthur, whom they say is kill'd to-night
On your suggestion.
	K. John.	Gentle kinsman, go,
And thrust thyself into their companies :
I have a way to win their loves again ;
Bring them before me.
	Bast.	I will seek them out.
	K. John.	Nay, but make haste ; the better
	foot before.	170
O, let me have no subject enemies,
When adverse foreigners affright my towns
With dreadful pomp of stout invasion !
Be Mercury, set feathers to thy heels,
And fly like thought from them to me again.
	Bast.	The spirit of the time shall teach me
	speed.	[*Exit.*
	K. John.	Spoke like a sprightful noble gen-
	tleman.
Go after him ; for he perhaps shall need
Some messenger betwixt me and the peers ;
And be thou he.
	Mess.	With all my heart, my liege.	180
	[*Exit.*

	K. John.	My mother dead !

Re-enter HUBERT.

	Hub.	My lord, they say five moons were
	seen to-night ;
Four fixed, and the fifth did whirl about
The other four in wondrous motion.
	K. John.	Five moons !
	Hub.	Old men and beldams in the streets
Do prophecy upon it dangerously :
Young Arthur's death is common in their
	mouths :
And when they talk of him, they shake their
	heads
And whisper one another in the ear ;
And he that speaks doth gripe the hearer's
	wrist,	190
Whilst he that hears makes fearful action,
With wrinkled brows, with nods, with rolling
	eyes.
I saw a smith stand with his hammer, thus,
The whilst his iron did on the anvil cool,
With open mouth swallowing a tailor's news ;
Who, with his shears and measure in his hand,
Standing on slippers, which his nimble haste
Had falsely thrust upon contrary feet,
Told of a many thousand warlike French
That were embattailed and rank'd in Kent :
Another lean unwash'd artificer	201
Cuts off his tale and talks of Arthur's death.
	K. John.	Why seek'st thou to possess me
	with these fears ?
Why urgest thou so oft young Arthur's death ?
Thy hand hath murder'd him : I had a mighty
	cause
To wish him dead, but thou hadst none to kill
	him.

Hub. No had, my lord! why, did you not
　provoke me?
K. John. It is the curse of kings to be at-
tended
By slaves that take their humors for a warrant
To break within the bloody house of life, 210
And on the winking of authority
To understand a law, to know the meaning
Of dangerous majesty, when perchance it
　frowns
More upon humor than advised respect.
Hub. Here is your hand and seal for what
　I did.
K. John. O, when the last account 'twixt
　heaven and earth
Is to be made, then shall this hand and seal
Witness against us to damnation!
How oft the sight of means to do ill deeds
Make deeds ill done! Hadst not thou been by,
A fellow by the hand of nature mark'd, 221
Quoted and sign'd to do a deed of shame,
This murder had not come into my mind:
But taking note of thy abhorr'd aspect,
Finding thee fit for bloody villany,
Apt, liable to be employ'd in danger,
I faintly broke with thee of Arthur's death;
And thou, to be endeared to a king,
Made it no conscience to destroy a prince.
Hub. My lord,— 230
K. John. Hadst thou but shook thy head
　or made a pause
When I spake darkly what I purposed,
Or turn'd an eye of doubt upon my face,
As bid me tell my tale in express words,
Deep shame had struck me dumb, made me
　break off,
And those thy fears might have wrought fears
　in me:
But thou didst understand me by my signs
And didst in signs again parley with sin;
Yea, without stop, didst let thy heart consent,
And consequently thy rude hand to act 240
The deed, which both our tongues held vile to
　name.
Out of my sight, and never see me more!
My nobles leave me; and my state is braved,
Even at my gates, with ranks of foreign
　powers:
Nay, in the body of this fleshly land,
This kingdom, this confine of blood and breath,
Hostility and civil tumult reigns
Between my conscience and my cousin's death.
Hub. Arm you against your other enemies,
I'll make a peace between your soul and you.
Young Arthur is alive: this hand of mine 251
Is yet a maiden and an innocent hand,
Not painted with the crimson spots of blood.
Within this bosom never enter'd yet
The dreadful motion of a murderous thought;
And you have slander'd nature in my form,
Which, howsoever rude exteriorly,
Is yet the cover of a fairer mind
Than to be butcher of an innocent child.
K. John. Doth Arthur live? O, haste thee
　to the peers, 260
Throw this report on their incensed rage,
And make them tame to their obedience!
Forgive the comment that my passion made
Upon thy feature; for my rage was blind,
And foul imaginary eyes of blood
Presented thee more hideous than thou art.
O, answer not, but to my closet bring
The angry lords with all expedient haste.

I conjure thee but slowly; run more fast.
　　　　　　　　　　　　　　[Exeunt.

SCENE III. *Before the castle.*

Enter ARTHUR, *on the walls.*

Arth. The wall is high, and yet will I leap
　down:
Good ground, be pitiful and hurt me not!
There's few or none do know me: if they did,
This ship-boy's semblance hath disguised me
　quite.
I am afraid; and yet I'll venture it.
If I get down, and do not break my limbs,
I'll find a thousand shifts to get away:
As good to die and go, as die and stay.
　　　　　　　　　　　　　[Leaps down.
O me! my uncle's spirit is in these stones:
Heaven take my soul, and England keep my
　bones!　　　　　　　　　　*[Dies.* 10

Enter PEMBROKE, SALISBURY, *and* BIGOT.

Sal. Lords, I will meet him at Saint Ed-
mundsbury:
It is our safety, and we must embrace
This gentle offer of the perilous time.
Pem. Who brought that letter from the
　cardinal?
Sal. The Count Melun, a noble lord of
　France;
Whose private with me of the Dauphin's love
Is much more general than these lines import.
Big. To-morrow morning let us meet him
　then.
Sal. Or rather then set forward; for 'twill
　be
Two long days' journey, lords, or ere we meet.

Enter the BASTARD.

Bast. Once more to-day well met, dis-
temper'd lords! 21
The king by me requests your presence straight.
Sal. The king hath dispossess'd himself of
　us:
We will not line his thin bestained cloak
With our pure honors, nor attend the foot
That leaves the print of blood where'er it
　walks.
Return and tell him so: we know the worst.
Bast. Whate'er you think, good words, I
　think, were best.
Sal. Our griefs, and not our manners, rea-
son now. 29
Bast. But there is little reason in your
　grief;
Therefore 'twere reason you had manners now.
Pem. Sir, sir, impatience hath his privilege.
Bast. 'Tis true, to hurt his master, no man
　else.
Sal. This is the prison. What is he lies
　here?　　　　　　　　　*[Seeing Arthur.*
Pem. O death, made proud with pure and
　princely beauty!
The earth had not a hole to hide this deed.
Sal. Murder, as hating what himself hath
　done,
Doth lay it open to urge on revenge.
Big. Or, when he doom'd this beauty to a
　grave,
Found it too precious-princely for a grave. 40
Sal. Sir Richard, what think you? have
　you beheld,
Or have you read or heard? or could you
　think?

Or do you almost think, although you see,
That you do see ? could thought, without this
  object,
Form such another ? This is the very top,
The height, the crest, or crest unto the crest,
Of murder's arms : this is the bloodiest shame,
The wildest savagery, the vilest stroke,
That ever wall-eyed wrath or staring rage
Presented to the tears of soft remorse.   50
  Pem. All murders past do stand excused
    in this :
And this, so sole and so unmatchable,
Shall give a holiness, a purity,
To the yet unbegotten sin of times ;
And prove a deadly bloodshed but a jest,
Exampled by this heinous spectacle.
  Bast. It is a damned and a bloody work ;
The graceless action of a heavy hand,
If that it be the work of any hand.
  Sal. If that it be the work of any hand ! 60
We had a kind of light what would ensue :
It is the shameful work of Hubert's hand ;
The practice and the purpose of the king :
From whose obedience I forbid my soul,
Kneeling before this ruin of sweet life,
And breathing to his breathless excellence
The incense of a vow, a holy vow,
Never to taste the pleasures of the world,
Never to be infected with delight,
Nor conversant with ease and idleness,   70
Till I have set a glory to this hand,
By giving it the worship of revenge.
  Pem. } Our souls religiously confirm thy
  Big. } words.

        Enter HUBERT.

  Hub. Lords, I am hot with haste in seeking
    you :
Arthur doth live ; the king hath sent for you.
  Sal. O, he is bold and blushes not at death.
Avaunt, thou hateful villain, get thee gone !
  Hub. I am no villain.
  Sal.   Must I rob the law ?
              [*Drawing his sword.*
  Bast. Your sword is bright, sir ; put it up
    again.
  Sal. Not till I sheathe it in a murderer's
    skin.   80
  Hub. Stand back, Lord Salisbury, stand
    back, I say ;
By heaven, I think my sword's as sharp as
    yours :
I would not have you, lord, forget yourself,
Nor tempt the danger of my true defence ;
Lest I, by marking of your rage, forget
Your worth, your greatness and nobility.
  Big. Out, dunghill ! darest thou brave a
    nobleman ?
  Hub. Not for my life : but yet I dare defend
My innocent life against an emperor.
  Sal. Thou art a murderer.
  Hub.   Do not prove me so ;   90
Yet I am none : whose tongue soe'er speaks
    false,
Not truly speaks ; who speaks not truly, lies.
  Pem. Cut him to pieces.
  Bast.   Keep the peace, I say.
  Sal. Stand by, or I shall gall you, Faulconbridge.
  Bast. Thou wert better gall the devil, Salisbury :
If thou but frown on me, or stir thy foot,

Or teach thy hasty spleen to do me shame,
I'll strike thee dead. Put up thy sword betime ;
Or I'll so maul you and your toasting-iron,
That you shall think the devil is come from
    hell.   100
  Big. What wilt thou do, renowned Faulconbridge ?
Second a villain and a murderer ?
  Hub. Lord Bigot, I am none.
  Big.   Who kill'd this prince ?
  Hub. 'Tis not an hour since I left him
    well :
I honor'd him, I loved him, and will weep
My date of life out for his sweet life's loss.
  Sal. Trust not those cunning waters of his
    eyes,
For villany is not without such rheum ;
And he, long traded in it, makes it seem
Like rivers of remorse and innocency.   110
Away with me, all you whose souls abhor
The uncleanly savors of a slaughter-house ;
For I am stifled with this smell of sin.
  Big. Away toward Bury, to the Dauphin
    there !
  Pem. There tell the king he may inquire us
    out.   [*Exeunt Lords.*
  Bast. Here's a good world ! Knew you of
    this fair work ?
Beyond the infinite and boundless reach
Of mercy, if thou didst this deed of death,
Art thou damn'd, Hubert.
  Hub.   Do but hear me, sir.
  Bast. Ha ! I'll tell thee what ;   120
Thou'rt damn'd as black—nay, nothing is so
    black ;
Thou art more deep damn'd than Prince Lucifer :
There is not yet so ugly a fiend of hell
As thou shalt be, if thou didst kill this child.
  Hub. Upon my soul—
  Bast.   If thou didst but consent
To this most cruel act, do but despair ;
And if thou want'st a cord, the smallest thread
That ever spider twisted from her womb
Will serve to strangle thee, a rush will be a
    beam
To hang thee on ; or wouldst thou drown thyself,   130
Put but a little water in a spoon,
And it shall be as all the ocean,
Enough to stifle such a villain up.
I do suspect thee very grievously.
  Hub. If I in act, consent, or sin of thought,
Be guilty of the stealing that sweet breath
Which was embounded in this beauteous clay,
Let hell want pains enough to torture me.
I left him well.
  Bast.   Go, bear him in thine arms.
I am amazed, methinks, and lose my way 140
Among the thorns and dangers of this world.
How easy dost thou take all England up !
From forth this morsel of dead royalty,
The life, the right and truth of all this realm
Is fled to heaven ; and England now is left
To tug and scamble and to part by the teeth
The unowed interest of proud-swelling state.
Now for the bare-pick'd bone of majesty
Doth dogged war bristle his angry crest
And snarleth in the gentle eyes of peace : 150
Now powers from home and discontents at
    home
Meet in one line ; and vast confusion waits,
As doth a raven on a sick-fall'n beast,

The imminent decay of wrested pomp.
Now happy he whose cloak and cincture can
Hold out this tempest. Bear away that child
And follow me with speed : I'll to the king :
A thousand businesses are brief in hand,
And heaven itself doth frown upon the land.
                                        [*Exeunt.*

ACT V.

SCENE I. KING JOHN'S *palace.*

Enter KING JOHN, PANDULPH, *and* Attendants.

K. John. Thus have I yielded up into your
        hand
The circle of my glory.   [*Giving the crown.*
Pand.   Take again
From this my hand, as holding of the pope
Your sovereign greatness and authority.
K. John. Now keep your holy word : go
        meet the French,
And from his holiness use all your power
To stop their marches 'fore we are inflamed.
Our discontented counties do revolt ;
Our people quarrel with obedience,   10
Swearing allegiance and the love of soul
To stranger blood, to foreign royalty.
This inundation of mistemper'd humor
Rests by you only to be qualified :
Then pause not ; for the present time's so sick,
That present medicine must be minister'd,
Or overthrow incurable ensues.
Pand. It was my breath that blew this
        tempest up,
Upon your stubborn usage of the pope ;
But since you are a gentle convertite,   19
My tongue shall hush again this storm of war
And make fair weather in your blustering land.
On this Ascension-day, remember well,
Upon your oath of service to the pope,
Go I to make the French lay down their arms.
                                        [*Exit.*
K. John. Is this Ascension-day ? Did not
        the prophet
Say that before Ascension-day at noon
My crown I should give off ? Even so I have :
I did suppose it should be on constraint :
But, heaven be thank'd, it is but voluntary.

Enter the BASTARD.

Bast. All Kent hath yielded ; nothing there
        holds out   30
But Dover castle : London hath received,
Like a kind host, the Dauphin and his powers :
Your nobles will not hear you, but are gone
To offer service to your enemy,
And wild amazement hurries up and down
The little number of your doubtful friends.
K. John. Would not my lords return to me
        again,
After they heard young Arthur was alive ?
Bast. They found him dead and cast into
        the streets,
An empty casket, where the jewel of life   40
By some damn'd hand was robb'd and ta'en
        away.
K. John. That villain Hubert told me he
        did live.
Bast. So, on my soul, he did, for aught he
        knew.
But wherefore do you droop ? why look you
        sad ?

Be great in act, as you have been in thought ;
Let not the world see fear and sad distrust
Govern the motion of a kingly eye :
Be stirring as the time ; be fire with fire ;
Threaten the threatener and outface the brow
Of bragging horror : so shall inferior eyes,   50
That borrow their behaviors from the great,
Grow great by your example and put on
The dauntless spirit of resolution.
Away, and glister like the god of war,
When he intendeth to become the field :
Show boldness and aspiring confidence.
What, shall they seek the lion in his den,
And fright him there ? and make him tremble
        there ?
O, let it not be said : forage, and run
To meet displeasure farther from the doors,   60
And grapple with him ere he comes so nigh.
K. John. The legate of the pope hath been
        with me,
And I have made a happy peace with him ;
And he hath promised to dismiss the powers
Led by the Dauphin.
Bast.   O inglorious league !
Shall we, upon the footing of our land,
Send fair-play orders and make compromise,
Insinuation, parley and base truce
To arms invasive ? shall a beardless boy,
A cocker'd silken wanton, brave our fields,   70
And flesh his spirit in a warlike soil,
Mocking the air with colors idly spread,
And find no check ? Let us, my liege, to arms :
Perchance the cardinal cannot make your
        peace ;
Or if he do, let it at least be said
They saw we had a purpose of defence.
K. John. Have thou the ordering of this
        present time.
Bast. Away, then, with good courage ! yet,
        I know,
Our party may well meet a prouder foe.
                                        [*Exeunt.*

SCENE II. *The* DAUPHIN'S *camp at St. Edmundsbury.*

Enter, in arms, LEWIS, SALISBURY, MELUN,
        PEMBROKE, BIGOT, *and* Soldiers.

Lew. My Lord Melun, let this be copied
        out,
And keep it safe for our remembrance :
Return the precedent to these lords again ;
That, having our fair order written down,
Both they and we, perusing o'er these notes,
May know wherefore we took the sacrament
And keep our faiths firm and inviolable.
Sal. Upon our sides it never shall be
        broken.
And, noble Dauphin, albeit we swear
A voluntary zeal and an unurged faith   10
To your proceedings ; yet believe me, prince,
I am not glad that such a sore of time
Should seek a plaster by contemn'd revolt,
And heal the inveterate canker of one wound
By making many. O, it grieves my soul,
That I must draw this metal from my side
To be a widow-maker ! O, and there
Where honorable rescue and defence
Cries out upon the name of Salisbury !
But such is the infection of the time,   20
That, for the health and physic of our right,
We cannot deal but with the very hand
Of stern injustice and confused wrong.
And is't not pity, O my grieved friends,

That we, the sons and children of this isle,
Were born to see so sad an hour as this ;
Wherein we step after a stranger march
Upon her gentle bosom, and fill up
Her enemies' ranks,—I must withdraw and
    weep
Upon the spot of this enforced cause,—   30
To grace the gentry of a land remote,
And follow unacquainted colors here ?
What, here ? O nation, that thou couldst re-
    move !
That Neptune's arms, who clippeth thee about,
Would bear thee from the knowledge of thy-
    self,
And grapple thee unto a pagan shore ;
Where these two Christian armies might com-
    bine
The blood of malice in a vein of league,
And not to spend it so unneighborly !
    Lew. A noble temper dost thou show in
        this ;   40
And great affections wrestling in thy bosom
Doth make an earthquake of nobility.
O, what a noble combat hast thou fought
Between compulsion and a brave respect !
Let me wipe off this honorable dew,
That silverly doth progress on thy cheeks :
My heart hath melted at a lady's tears,
Being an ordinary inundation ;
But this effusion of such manly drops,
This shower, blown up by tempest of the soul,
Startles mine eyes, and makes me more
    amazed   51
Than had I seen the vaulty top of heaven
Figured quite o'er with burning meteors.
Lift up thy brow, renowned Salisbury,
And with a great heart heave away the storm :
Commend these waters to those baby eyes
That never saw the giant world enraged ;
Nor met with fortune other than at feasts,
Full of warm blood, of mirth, of gossiping.
Come, come ; for thou shalt thrust thy hand
    as deep   60
Into the purse of rich prosperity
As Lewis himself : so, nobles, shall you all,
That knit your sinews to the strength of mine.
And even there, methinks, an angel spake :

Enter PANDULPH.

Look, where the holy legate comes apace,
To give us warrant from the hand of heaven
And on our actions set the name of right
With holy breath.
    Pand.   Hail, noble prince of France !
The next is this, King John hath reconciled
Himself to Rome ; his spirit is come in,   70
That so stood out against the holy church,
The great metropolis and see of Rome :
Therefore thy threatening colors now wind up ;
And tame the savage spirit of wild war,
That, like a lion foster'd up at hand,
It may lie gently at the foot of peace,
And be no further harmful than in show.
    Lew. Your grace shall pardon me, I will
        not back :
I am too high-born to be propertied,
To be a secondary at control,   80
Or useful serving-man and instrument,
To any sovereign state throughout the world.
Your breath first kindled the dead coal of wars
Between this chastised kingdom and myself,
And brought in matter that should feed this
    fire ;

And now 'tis far too huge to be blown out
With that same weak wind which enkindled it.
You taught me how to know the face of right,
Acquainted me with interest to this land,
Yea, thrust this enterprise into my heart ;   90
And come ye now to tell me John hath made
His peace with Rome ? What is that peace to
    me ?
I, by the honor of my marriage-bed,
After young Arthur, claim this land for mine ;
And, now it is half-conquer'd, must I back
Because that John hath made his peace with
    Rome ?
Am I Rome's slave ? What penny hath Rome
    borne,
What men provided, what munition sent,
To underprop this action ? Is't not I
That undergo this charge ? who else but I,   100
And such as to my claim are liable,
Sweat in this business and maintain this war ?
Have I not heard these islanders shout out
' Vive le roi ! ' as I have bank'd their towns ?
Have I not here the best cards for the game,
To win this easy match play'd for a crown ?
And shall I now give o'er the yielded set ?
No, no, on my soul, it never shall be said.
    Pand.   You look but on the outside of this
        work.
    Lew. Outside or inside, I will not return
Till my attempt so much be glorified   111
As to my ample hope was promised
Before I drew this gallant head of war,
And cull'd these fiery spirits from the world,
To outlook conquest and to win renown
Even in the jaws of danger and of death.
                        [*Trumpet sounds.*
What lusty trumpet thus doth summon us ?

Enter the BASTARD, *attended.*

    Bast. According to the fair play of the
        world,
Let me have audience ; I am sent to speak :
My holy lord of Milan, from the king   120
I come, to learn how you have dealt for him ;
And, as you answer, I do know the scope
And warrant limited unto my tongue.
    Pand. The Dauphin is too wilful-opposite,
And will not temporize with my entreaties ;
He flatly says he'll not lay down his arms.
    Bast. By all the blood that ever fury
        breathed,
The youth says well. Now hear our English
    king ;
For thus his royalty doth speak in me.
He is prepared, and reason too he should :   130
This apish and unmannerly approach,
This harness'd masque and unadvised revel,
This unhair'd sauciness and boyish troops,
The king doth smile at ; and is well prepared
To whip this dwarfish war, these pigmy arms,
From out the circle of his territories.
That hand which had the strength, even at
    your door,
To cudgel you and make you take the hatch,
To dive like buckets in concealed wells,
To crouch in litter of your stable planks,   140
To lie like pawns lock'd up in chests and
    trunks,
To hug with swine, to seek sweet safety out
In vaults and prisons, and to thrill and shake
Even at the crying of your nation's crow,
Thinking his voice an armed Englishman ;
Shall that victorious hand be feebled here,

That in your chambers gave you chastisement ?
No : know the gallant monarch is in arms
And like an eagle o'er his aery towers,
To souse annoyance that comes near his nest.
And you degenerate, you ingrate revolts, 151
You bloody Neroes, ripping up the womb
Of your dear mother England, blush for
    shame ;
For your own ladies and pale-visaged maids
Like Amazons come tripping after drums,
Their thimbles into armed gauntlets change,
Their needles to lances, and their gentle hearts
To fierce and bloody inclination.
  Lew. There end thy brave, and turn thy
    face in peace ;
We grant thou canst outscold us : fare thee
  well ; 160
We hold our time too precious to be spent
With such a brabbler.
  Pand.   Give me leave to speak.
  Bast. No, I will speak.
  Lew.   We will attend to neither.
Strike up the drums ; and let the tongue of war
Plead for our interest and our being here.
  Bast. Indeed your drums, being beaten, will
    cry out ;
And so shall you, being beaten : do but start
An echo with the clamor of thy drum,
And even at hand a drum is ready braced
That shall reverberate all as loud as thine ; 170
Sound but another, and another shall
As loud as thine rattle the welkin's ear
And mock the deep-mouth'd thunder : for at
    hand,
Not trusting to this halting legate here,
Whom he hath used rather for sport than need
Is warlike John ; and in his forehead sits
A bare-ribb'd death, whose office is this day
To feast upon whole thousands of the French.
  Lew. Strike up our drums, to find this dan-
    ger out.
  Bast. And thou shalt find it, Dauphin, do
    not doubt.   [*Exeunt.* 180

    Scene III. *The field of battle.*

  Alarums. Enter King John *and* Hubert.

  K. John. How goes the day with us ? O,
tell me, Hubert.
  Hub. Badly, I fear. How fares your majesty ?
  K. John. This fever, that hath troubled me
so long,
Lies heavy on me ; O, my heart is sick !

    Enter a Messenger.

  Mess. My lord, your valiant kinsman,
Faulconbridge,
Desires your majesty to leave the field
And send him word by me which way you go.
  K. John. Tell him, toward Swinstead, to
the abbey there.
  Mess. Be of good comfort ; for the great
supply
That was expected by the Dauphin here, 10
Are wreck'd three nights ago on Goodwin
Sands.
This news was brought to Richard but even
now :
The French fight coldly, and retire themselves.
  K. John. Ay me ! this tyrant fever burns
me up,
And will not let me welcome this good news.

Set on toward Swinstead : to my litter
  straight ;
Weakness possesseth me, and I am faint.
                  [*Exeunt.*

    Scene IV. *Another part of the field.*

  Enter Salisbury, Pembroke, *and* Bigot.

  Sal. I did not think the king so stored with
friends.
  Pem. Up once again ; put spirit in the
French :
If they miscarry, we miscarry too.
  Sal. That misbegotten devil, Faulcon-
bridge,
In spite of spite, alone upholds the day.
  Pem. They say King John sore sick hath
left the field.

    Enter Melun, *wounded.*

  Mel. Lead me to the revolts of England
here.
  Sal. When we were happy we had other
names.
  Pem. It is the Count Melun.
  Sal.   Wounded to death.
  Mel. Fly, noble English, you are bought
    and sold ; 10
Unthread the rude eye of rebellion
And welcome home again discarded faith.
Seek out King John and fall before his feet ;
For if the French be lords of this loud day,
He means to recompense the pains you take
By cutting off your heads : thus hath he sworn
And I with him, and many moe with me,
Upon the altar at Saint Edmundsbury ;
Even on that altar where we swore to you
Dear amity and everlasting love. 20
  Sal. May this be possible ? may this be
true ?
  Mel. Have I not hideous death within my
    view,
Retaining but a quantity of life,
Which bleeds away, even as a form of wax
Resolveth from his figure 'gainst the fire ?
What in the world should make me now de-
    ceive,
Since I must lose the use of all deceit ?
Why should I then be false, since it is true
That I must die here and live hence by truth ?
I say again, if Lewis do win the day, 30
He is forsworn, if e'er those eyes of yours
Behold another day break in the east :
But even this night, whose black contagious
    breath
Already smokes about the burning crest
Of the old, feeble and day-wearied sun,
Even this ill night, your breathing shall expire,
Paying the fine of rated treachery
Even with a treacherous fine of all your lives,
If Lewis by your assistance win the day.
Commend me to one Hubert with your king :
The love of him, and this respect besides, 41
For that my grandsire was an Englishman,
Awakes my conscience to confess all this.
In lieu whereof, I pray you, bear me hence
From forth the noise and rumor of the field,
Where I may think the remnant of my thoughts
In peace, and part this body and my soul
With contemplation and devout desires.
  Sal. We do believe thee : and beshrew my
soul
But I do love the favor and the form 50
Of this most fair occasion, by the which

We will untread the steps of damned flight,
And like a bated and retired flood,
Leaving our rankness and irregular course,
Stoop low within those bounds we have o'er-
　　look'd
And calmly run on in obedience
Even to our ocean, to our great King John.
My arm shall give thee help to bear thee
　　hence ;
For I do see the cruel pangs of death
Right in thine eye. Away, my friends ! New
　　flight ;　　　　　　　　　　　　　　　60
And happy newness, that intends old right.
　　　　　　　　[Exeunt, leading off Melun.

SCENE V. *The French camp.*

Enter LEWIS *and his train.*

Lew. The sun of heaven methought was
　　loath to set,
But stay'd and made the western welkin blush,
When English measure backward their own
　　ground
In faint retire. O, bravely came we off,
When with a volley of our needless shot,
After such bloody toil, we bid good night ;
And wound our tattering colors clearly up,
Last in the field, and almost lords of it !

Enter a Messenger.

Mess. Where is my prince, the Dauphin ?
Lew. 　　　　　Here : what news ?
Mess. The Count Melun is slain ; the Eng-
　　lish lords　　　　　　　　　　　　10
By his persuasion are again fall'n off,
And your supply, which you have wish'd so
　　long,
Are cast away and sunk on Goodwin Sands.
Lew. Ah, foul shrewd news ! beshrew thy
　　very heart !
I did not think to be so sad to-night
As this hath made me. Who was he that said
King John did fly an hour or two before
The stumbling night did part our weary pow-
　　ers ?
Mess. Whoever spoke it, it is true, my lord.
Lew. Well ; keep good quarter and good
　　care to-night :　　　　　　　　　　20
The day shall not be up so soon as I,
To try the fair adventure of to-morrow.
　　　　　　　　　　　　　　[Exeunt.

SCENE VI. *An open place in the neighbor-
　　hood of Swinstead Abbey.*

Enter the BASTARD *and* HUBERT, *severally.*

Hub. Who's there ? speak, ho ! speak
　　quickly, or I shoot.
Bast. A friend. What art thou ?
Hub. 　　　　Of the part of England.
Bast. Whither dost thou go ?
Hub. 　　What's that to thee ? why may not I
　　demand
Of thine affairs, as well as thou of mine ?
Bast. Hubert, I think ?
Hub. 　　　　Thou hast a perfect thought :
I will upon all hazards well believe
Thou art my friend, that know'st my tongue
　　so well.
Who art thou ?
Bast. Who thou wilt : and if thou please,
Thou mayst befriend me so much as to think
I come one way of the Plantagenets.　　11
Hub. Unkind remembrance ! thou and eye-
　　less night

Have done me shame : brave soldier, pardon
　　me,
That any accent breaking from thy tongue
Should 'scape the true acquaintance of mine
　　ear.
Bast. Come, come ; sans compliment, what
　　news abroad ?
Hub. Why, here walk I in the black brow
　　of night,
To find you out.
Bast. 　　　　Brief, then ; and what's the
　　news ?
Hub. O, my sweet sir, news fitting to the
　　night,
Black, fearful, comfortless and horrible.　　20
Bast. Show me the very wound of this ill
　　news :
I am no woman, I'll not swoon at it.
Hub. The king, I fear, is poison'd by a
　　monk :
I left him almost speechless ; and broke out
To acquaint you with this evil, that you might
The better arm you to the sudden time,
Than if you had at leisure known of this.
Bast. How did he take it ? who did taste to
　　him ?
Hub. A monk, I tell you ; a resolved vil-
　　lain,
Whose bowels suddenly burst out : the king
Yet speaks and peradventure may recover.　31
Bast. Who didst thou leave to tend his maj-
　　esty ?
Hub. Why, know you not ? the lords are
　　all come back,
And brought Prince Henry in their company ;
At whose request the king hath pardon'd them,
And they are all about his majesty.
Bast. Withhold thine indignation, mighty
　　heaven,
And tempt us not to bear above our power !
I'll tell thee, Hubert, half my power this night,
Passing these flats, are taken by the tide ;　40
These Lincoln Washes have devoured them ;
Myself, well mounted, hardly have escaped.
Away before : conduct me to the king ;
I doubt he will be dead or ere I come. [*Exeunt.*

SCENE VII. *The orchard in Swinstead Abbey.*

Enter PRINCE HENRY, SALISBURY, *and* BIGOT.

P. Hen. It is too late : the life of all his
　　blood
Is touch'd corruptibly, and his pure brain,
Which some suppose the soul's frail dwelling-
　　house,
Doth by the idle comments that it makes
Foretell the ending of mortality.

Enter PEMBROKE.

Pem. His highness yet doth speak, and
　　holds belief
That, being brought into the open air,
It would allay the burning quality
Of that fell poison which assaileth him.
P. Hen. Let him be brought into the or-
　　chard here.　　　　　　　　　　　10
Doth he still rage ?　　　　　　*[Exit Bigot.*
Pem. 　　　　He is more patient
Than when you left him ; even now he sung.
P. Hen. O vanity of sickness ! fierce ex-
　　tremes
In their continuance will not feel themselves.
Death, having prey'd upon the outward parts,
Leaves them invisible, and his siege is now

Against the mind, the which he pricks and
  wounds
With many legions of strange fantasies,
Which, in their throng and press to that last
  hold,
Confound themselves. 'Tis strange that death
  should sing.   20
I am the cygnet to this pale faint swan,
Who chants a doleful hymn to his own death,
And from the organ-pipe of frailty sings
His soul and body to their lasting rest.
  Sal. Be of good comfort, prince ; for you
  are born
To set a form upon that indigest
Which he hath left so shapeless and so rude.

Enter Attendants, *and* BIGOT, *carrying* KING
      JOHN *in a chair.*

  K. John. Ay, marry, now my soul hath el-
  bow-room ;
It would not out at windows nor at doors.
There is so hot a summer in my bosom,   30
That all my bowels crumble up to dust :
I am a scribbled form, drawn with a pen
Upon a parchment, and against this fire
Do I shrink up.
  P. Hen.   How fares your majesty ?
  K. John. Poison'd,—ill fare—dead, for-
  sook, cast off :
And none of you will bid the winter come
To thrust his icy fingers in my maw,
Nor let my kingdom's rivers take their course
Through my burn'd bosom, nor entreat the
  north
To make his bleak winds kiss my parched lips
And comfort me with cold. I do not ask you
  much,   41
I beg cold comfort ; and you are so strait
And so ingrateful, you deny me that.
  P. Hen. O that there were some virtue in
  my tears,
That might relieve you !
  K. John.   The salt in them is hot.
Within me is a hell ; and there the poison
Is as a fiend confined to tyrannize
On unreprievable condemned blood.

Enter the BASTARD.

  Bast. O, I am scalded with my violent mo-
  tion,
And spleen of speed to see your majesty !   50
  K. John. O cousin, thou art come to set
  mine eye :
The tackle of my heart is crack'd and burn'd,
And all the shrouds wherewith my life should
  sail
Are turned to one thread, one little hair :
My heart hath one poor string to stay it by,
Which holds but till thy news be uttered :
And then all this thou seest is but a clod
And module of confounded royalty.
  Bast. The Dauphin is preparing hither-
  ward,
Where heaven He knows how we shall answer
  him ;   60
For in a night the best part of my power,
As I upon advantage did remove,
Were in the Washes all unwarily
Devoured by the unexpected flood.
                              [*The king dies.*

  Sal. You breathe these dead news in as
  dead an ear.
My liege ! my lord ! but now a king, now thus.
  P. Hen. Even so must I run on, and even
  so stop.
What surety of the world, what hope, what
  stay,
When this was now a king, and now is clay ?
  Bast. Art thou gone so ? I do but stay be-
  hind   70
To do the office for thee of revenge,
And then my soul shall wait on thee to heaven,
As it on earth hath been thy servant still.
Now, now, you stars that move in your right
  spheres,
Where be your powers ? show now your
  mended faiths,
And instantly return with me again,
To push destruction and perpetual shame
Out of the weak door of our fainting land.
Straight let us seek, or straight we shall be
  sought ;
The Dauphin rages at our very heels.   80
  Sal. It seems you know not, then, so much
  as we :
The Cardinal Pandulph is within at rest,
Who half an hour since came from the
  Dauphin,
And brings from him such offers of our peace
As we with honor and respect may take,
With purpose presently to leave this war.
  Bast. He will the rather do it when he sees
Ourselves well sinewed to our defence.
  Sal. Nay, it is in a manner done already ;
For many carriages he hath dispatch'd   90
To the sea-side, and put his cause and quarrel
To the disposing of the cardinal :
With whom yourself, myself and other lords,
If you think meet, this afternoon will post
To consummate this business happily.
  Bast. Let it be so : and you, my noble
  prince,
With other princes that may best be spared,
Shall wait upon your father's funeral.
  P. Hen. At Worcester must his body be
  interr'd ;
For so he will'd it.
  Bast.   Thither shall it then :   100
And happily may your sweet self put on
The lineal state and glory of the land !
To whom, with all submission, on my knee
I do bequeath my faithful services
And true subjection everlastingly.
  Sal. And the like tender of our love we
  make,
To rest without a spot for evermore.
  P. Hen. I have a kind soul that would give
  you thanks
And knows not how to do it but with tears.
  Bast. O, let us pay the time but needful
  woe,
Since it hath been beforehand with our griefs.
This England never did, nor never shall,   112
Lie at the proud foot of a conqueror,
But when it first did help to wound itself.
Now these her princes are come home again,
Come the three corners of the world in arms,
And we shall shock them. Nought shall make
  us rue,
If England to itself do rest but true. [*Exeunt.*

THE MERCHANT OF VENICE.

(WRITTEN ABOUT 1596.)

INTRODUCTION.

This play takes a place by itself, midway between the group of Shakespeare's early comedies and that more brilliant group of comedies which clusters about the year 1600. With the early comedies it is allied by the frequent rhymes, the occasional doggerel verse, and the numerous classical allusions; with the later group it is connected by its centring the interest of the drama in the development of character, and by the variety, depth, and beauty of the characterization. No person depicted in any preceding comedy can compare in vigor of drawing and depth of color with Shylock; and Portia is the first of Shakespeare's women who unites in beautiful proportion, intellectual power, high and refined, with unrestrained ardor of the heart. The story of the caskets and the story of the pound of flesh had been told separately many times and in various countries. The former is first found in the mediæval Greek romance of *Barlaam and Josaphat*, by Joannes Damascenus (about A.D. 800); in another form it is told by the English poet Gower, and the Italian novelist Boccaccio. But points of resemblance are most striking between Shakespeare's version of the casket incident and that given in the collection of stories so popular in the Middle Ages, the *Gesta Romanorum*. The incident of the pound of flesh also appears in the *Gesta*; it is found in a long religious poem, written in the Northumbrian dialect about the end of the thirteenth century, the *Cursor Mundi*, in an old ballad, "showing the crueltie of Gernutus a Jew," and elsewhere; there are Persian and Egyptian versions of the tale, which itself perhaps originally came from the East. The form in which we have it in Shakespeare is most closely connected with the version found in a collection of tales, *Il Pecorone*, written by Ser Giovanni, a notary of Florence, about A.D., 1378. Here, and only here, the incident of the ring, which forms the subject of the fifth act of *The Merchant of Venice*, is given; and here the name Belmont appears. It is probable, however, that Shakespeare to become acquainted with these stories had not to go to *Il Pecorone* and the *Gesta Romanorum*. Stephen Gosson writing in 1579, in his *Schoole of Abuse*, about plays which were "tollerable at sometime," mentions "the Jew . . . showne at the Bull . . . representing the greedinesse of worldly chusers and bloody mindes of usurers." The greediness of worldly choosers seems to point to the casket incident, and the bloody minds of usurers to that of the pound of flesh; we therefore infer that a pre-Shakespearian play existed which combined these two incidents. And it is highly probable that Shakespeare's task in the case of *The Merchant of Venice*, as afterwards in that of *King Lear*, consisted in creating from old and worthless dramatic material found among the crude productions of the early English theatre those forms of beauty and of majesty with which we are familiar. Although the play is named after the merchant, Antonio, he is not the chief dramatic person; he forms, however, a centre around which the other characters are grouped: Bassanio, his friend; Shylock, his erring and would-be murderer; Portia, his savior. Antonio's part is rather a passive than an active one; he is to be an object of contention and a prize; much is to be done against him and on his behalf, but not much is to be done *by* him; and therefore, although his character is very firmly conceived and clearly indicated, his part is subdued and kept low, lest it might interfere with the exhibition of the two chief forces of the play—the cruel masculine force of Shylock, which holds the merchant in its relentless, vice-like grip; and the feminine force of Portia, which is as bright as sunlight, and as beneficent. Yet Shakespeare is careful to interest us in Antonio, and to show us that he was worth every exertion to save. The distinction of Portia among the women of Shakespeare is the union in her nature of high intellectual powers and decision of will with a heart full of ardor and susceptibility to romantic feelings. She has herself never known trouble or sorrow, but prosperity has left her generous and quick in sympathy. Her noble use of wealth and joyous life, surrounded with flowers and fountains and marble statues and music, stands in contrast over against the hard, sad, and contracted life of Shylock, one of a persecuted tribe, absorbed in one or two narrowing and intense passions— the love of money-bags he clutches and yet fails to keep, and his hatred of the man who had scorned his tribe, insulted his creed, and diminished his gains. Yet Shylock is not like Marlowe's Jew, Barabas, a preternatural monster. Wolf-like as his revenge shows him, we pity his joyless, solitary life; and when, ringed round in the trial scene with hostile force, he stands firm upon his foothold of law, there is something sublime in his tenacity of passion and resolve. But we feel that it is right that his evil strength should be utterly crushed and quelled, and when Shylock leaves the court a broken man, we know it is needful that this should be so. The date of the play is uncertain. Perhaps 1596 is as likely a date as we can fix upon; but the precise year matters little if it be remembered that the play occupies an intermediate place between the early and the middle group of comedies.

DRAMATIS PERSONÆ.

The DUKE OF VENICE.
The PRINCE OF MOROCCO, } suitors to Portia.
The PRINCE OF ARRAGON, }
ANTONIO, a merchant of Venice.
BASSANIO, his friend, suitor likewise to Portia.
SALANIO,
SALARINO, } friends to Antonio and Bas-
GRATIANO,   sanio.
SALERIO,
LORENZO, in love with Jessica.
SHYLOCK, a rich Jew.
TUBAL, a Jew, his friend.
LAUNCELOT GOBBO, the clown, servant to Shylock.

OLD GOBBO, father to Launcelot.
LEONARDO, servant to Bassanio.
BALTHASAR, } servants to Portia.
STEPHANO, }

PORTIA, a rich heiress.
NERISSA, her waiting-maid.
JESSICA, daughter to Shylock.

Magnificoes of Venice, Officers of the Court of Justice, Gaoler, Servants to Portia, and other Attendants.

SCENE: *Partly at Venice, and partly at Belmont, the seat of Portia, on the Continent.*

ACT I.

SCENE I. *Venice. A street.*

Enter ANTONIO, SALARINO, *and* SALANIO.

Ant. In sooth, I know not why I am so sad :
It wearies me ; you say it wearies you ;
But how I caught it, found it, or came by it,
What stuff 'tis made of, whereof it is born,
I am to learn ;
And such a want-wit sadness makes of me,
That I have much ado to know myself.
Salar. Your mind is tossing on the ocean ;
There, where your argosies with portly sail,
Like signiors and rich burghers on the flood,
Or, as it were, the pageants of the sea,   11
Do overpeer the petty traffickers,
That curtsy to them, do them reverence,
As they fly by them with their woven wings.
Salan. Believe me, sir, had I such venture forth,
The better part of my affections would
Be with my hopes abroad. I should be still
Plucking the grass, to know where sits the wind,
Peering in maps for ports and piers and roads ;
And every object that might make me fear   20
Misfortune to my ventures, out of doubt
Would make me sad.
Salar.   My wind cooling my broth
Would blow me to an ague, when I thought
What harm a wind too great at sea might do.
I should not see the sandy hour-glass run,
But I should think of shallows and of flats,
And see my wealthy Andrew dock'd in sand,
Vailing her high-top lower than her ribs
To kiss her burial. Should I go to church
And see the holy edifice of stone,   30
And not bethink me straight of dangerous rocks,
Which touching but my gentle vessel's side,
Would scatter all her spices on the stream,
Enrobe the roaring waters with my silks,
And, in a word, but even now worth this,
And now worth nothing ? Shall I have the thought
To think on this, and shall I lack the thought
That such a thing bechanced would make me sad ?
But tell not me ; I know, Antonio
Is sad to think upon his merchandise.   40

Ant. Believe me, no : I thank my fortune for it,
My ventures are not in one bottom trusted,
Nor to one place ; nor is my whole estate
Upon the fortune of this present year :
Therefore my merchandise makes me not sad.
Salar. Why, then you are in love.
Ant.   Fie, fie !
Salar. Not in love neither ? Then let us say you are sad,
Because you are not merry : and 'twere as easy
For you to laugh and leap and say you are merry,
Because you are not sad. Now, by two-headed Janus,   50
Nature hath framed strange fellows in her time :
Some that will evermore peep through their eyes
And laugh like parrots at a bag-piper,
And other of such vinegar aspect
That they'll not show their teeth in way of smile,
Though Nestor swear the jest be laughable.

Enter BASSANIO, LORENZO, *and* GRATIANO.

Salan. Here comes Bassanio, your most noble kinsman,
Gratiano and Lorenzo. Fare ye well :
We leave you now with better company.
Salar. I would have stay'd till I had made you merry,   60
If worthier friends had not prevented me.
Ant. Your worth is very dear in my regard.
I take it, your own business calls on you
And you embrace the occasion to depart.
Salar. Good morrow, my good lords.
Bass. Good signiors both, when shall we laugh ? say, when ?
You grow exceeding strange : must it be so ?
Salar. We'll make our leisures to attend on yours.
                [*Exeunt Salarino and Salanio.*
Lor. My Lord Bassanio, since you have found Antonio,   70
We two will leave you : but at dinner-time,
I pray you, have in mind where we must meet.
Bass. I will not fail you.
Gra. You look not well, Signior Antonio ;
You have too much respect upon the world :
They lose it that do buy it with much care :
Believe me, you are marvellously changed.

Ant. I hold the world but as the world,
Gratiano ;
A stage where every man must play a part,
And mine a sad one.
Gra.   Let me play the fool :
With mirth and laughter let old wrinkles come,
And let my liver rather heat with wine   81
Than my heart cool with mortifying groans.
Why should a man, whose blood is warm
within,
Sit like his grandsire cut in alabaster ?
Sleep when he wakes and creep into the
jaundice
By being peevish ? I tell thee what, Antonio—
I love thee, and it is my love that speaks—
There are a sort of men whose visages
Do cream and mantle like a standing pond,
And do a wilful stillness entertain,   90
With purpose to be dress'd in an opinion
Of wisdom, gravity, profound conceit,
As who should say 'I am Sir Oracle,
And when I ope my lips let no dog bark ! '
O my Antonio, I do know of these
That therefore only are reputed wise
For saying nothing ; when, I am very sure,
If they should speak, would almost damn those
ears,
Which, hearing them, would call their brothers
fools.
I'll tell thee more of this another time :   100
But fish not, with this melancholy bait,
For this fool gudgeon, this opinion.
Come, good Lorenzo. Fare ye well awhile :
I'll end my exhortation after dinner.
Lor. Well, we will leave you then till
dinner-time :
I must be one of these same dumb wise men,
For Gratiano never lets me speak.
Gra. Well, keep me company but two
years moe,
Thou shalt not know the sound of thine own
tongue.
Ant. Farewell : I'll grow a talker for this
gear.
Gra. Thanks, i' faith, for silence is only
commendable   110
In a neat's tongue dried and a maid not vend-
ible.   [*Exeunt Gratiano and Lorenzo.*
Ant. Is that any thing now ?
Bass. Gratiano speaks an infinite deal of
nothing, more than any man in all Venice.
His reasons are as two grains of wheat hid in
two bushels of chaff : you shall seek all day
ere you find them, and when you have them,
they are not worth the search.
Ant. Well, tell me now what lady is the
same
To whom you swore a secret pilgrimage,   120
That you to-day promised to tell me of ?
Bass. 'Tis not unknown to you, Antonio,
How much I have disabled mine estate,
By something showing a more swelling port
Than my faint means would grant continu-
ance :
Nor do I now make moan to be abridged
From such a noble rate ; but my chief care
Is to come fairly off from the great debts
Wherein my time something too prodigal
Hath left me gaged. To you, Antonio,   130
I owe the most, in money and in love,
And from your love I have a warranty
To unburden all my plots and purposes
How to get clear of all the debts I owe.

Ant. I pray you, good Bassanio, let me
know it ;
And if it stand, as you yourself still do,
Within the eye of honor, be assured,
My purse, my person, my extremest means,
Lie all unlock'd to your occasions.
Bass. In my school-days, when I had lost
one shaft,   140
I shot his fellow of the self-same flight
The self-same way with more advised watch,
To find the other forth, and by adventuring
both
I oft found both : I urge this childhood proof,
Because what follows is pure innocence.
I owe you much, and, like a wilful youth,
That which I owe is lost ; but if you please
To shoot another arrow that self way
Which you did shoot the first, I do not doubt,
As I will watch the aim, or to find both   150
Or bring your latter hazard back again
And thankfully rest debtor for the first.
Ant. You know me well, and herein spend
but time
To wind about my love with circumstance ;
And out of doubt you do me now more wrong
In making question of my uttermost
Than if you had made waste of all I have :
Then do but say to me what I should do
That in your knowledge may by me be done,
And I am prest unto it : therefore, speak.   160
Bass. In Belmont is a lady richly left ;
And she is fair, and, fairer than that word,
Of wondrous virtues : sometimes from her
eyes
I did receive fair speechless messages :
Her name is Portia, nothing undervalued
To Cato's daughter, Brutus' Portia :
Nor is the wide world ignorant of her worth,
For the four winds blow in from every coast
Renowned suitors, and her sunny locks
Hang on her temples like a golden fleece ;   170
Which makes her seat of Belmont Colchos'
strand,
And many Jasons come in quest of her.
O my Antonio, had I but the means
To hold a rival place with one of them,
I have a mind presages me such thrift,
That I should questionless be fortunate !
Ant. Thou know'st that all my fortunes are
at sea ;
Neither have I money nor commodity
To raise a present sum : therefore go forth ;
Try what my credit can in Venice do :   180
That shall be rack'd, even to the uttermost,
To furnish thee to Belmont, to fair Portia.
Go, presently inquire, and so will I,
Where money is, and I no question make
To have it of my trust or for my sake.
        [*Exeunt.*

SCENE II.   *Belmont.   A room in* PORTIA'S
house.

Enter PORTIA *and* NERISSA.

Por. By my troth, Nerissa, my little body
is aweary of this great world.
Ner. You would be, sweet madam, if your
miseries were in the same abundance as your
good fortunes are : and yet, for aught I see,
they are as sick that surfeit with too much as
they that starve with nothing. It is no mean
happiness therefore, to be seated in the mean :
superfluity comes sooner by white hairs, but
competency lives longer.   10

Por. Good sentences and well pronounced.

Ner. They would be better, if well followed.

Por. If to do were as easy as to know what were good to do, chapels had been churches and poor men's cottages princes' palaces. It is a good divine that follows his own instructions : I can easier teach twenty what were good to be done, than be one of the twenty to follow mine own teaching. The brain may devise laws for the blood, but a hot temper leaps o'er a cold decree : such a hare is madness the youth, to skip o'er the meshes of good counsel the cripple. But this reasoning is not in the fashion to choose me a husband. O me, the word ' choose ! ' I may neither choose whom I would nor refuse whom I dislike ; so is the will of a living daughter curbed by the will of a dead father. Is it not hard, Nerissa, that I cannot choose one nor refuse none ?   29

Ner. Your father was ever virtuous ; and holy men at their death have good inspirations : therefore the lottery, that he hath devised in these three chests of gold, silver and lead, whereof who chooses his meaning chooses you, will, no doubt, never be chosen by any rightly but one who shall rightly love. But what warmth is there in your affection towards any of these princely suitors that are already come ?

Por. I pray thee, over-name them ; and as thou namest them, I will describe them ; and, according to my description, level at my affection.

Ner. First, there is the Neapolitan prince.

Por. Ay, that's a colt indeed, for he doth nothing but talk of his horse ; and he makes it a great appropriation to his own good parts, that he can shoe him himself. I am much afeard my lady his mother played false with a smith.

Ner. Then there is the County Palatine.

Por. He doth nothing but frown, as who should say ' If you will not have me, choose : ' he hears merry tales and smiles not : I fear he will prove the weeping philosopher when he grows old, being so full of unmannerly sadness in his youth. I had rather be married to a death's-head with a bone in his mouth than to either of these. God defend me from these two !

Ner. How say you by the French lord, Monsieur Le Bon ?

Por. God made him, and therefore let him pass for a man. In truth, I know it is a sin to be a mocker : but, he ! why, he hath a horse better than the Neapolitan's, a better bad habit of frowning than the Count Palatine ; he is every man in no man ; if a throstle sing, he falls straight a capering : he will fence with his own shadow : if I should marry him, I should marry twenty husbands. If he would despise me I would forgive him, for if he love me to madness, I shall never requite him.   70

Ner. What say you, then, to Falconbridge, the young baron of England ?

Por. You know I say nothing to him, for he understands not me, nor I him : he hath neither Latin, French, nor Italian, and you will come into the court and swear that I have a poor pennyworth in the English. He is a proper man's picture, but, alas, who can converse with a dumb-show ? How oddly he is suited ! I think he bought his doublet in Italy, his round hose in France, his bonnet in Germany and his behavior every where.

Ner. What think you of the Scottish lord, his neighbor ?

Por. That he hath a neighborly charity in him, for he borrowed a box of the ear of the Englishman and swore he would pay him again when he was able : I think the Frenchman became his surety and sealed under for another.

Ner. How like you the young German, the Duke of Saxony's nephew ?   91

Por. Very vilely in the morning, when he is sober, and most vilely in the afternoon, when he is drunk : when he is best, he is a little worse than a man, and when he is worst, he is little better than a beast : and the worst fall that ever fell, I hope I shall make shift to go without him.

Ner. If he should offer to choose, and choose the right casket, you should refuse to perform your father's will, if you should refuse to accept him.

Por. Therefore, for fear of the worst, I pray thee, set a deep glass of rhenish wine on the contrary casket, for if the devil be within and that temptation without, I know he will choose it. I will do any thing, Nerissa, ere I'll be married to a sponge.

Ner. You need not fear, lady, the having any of these lords : they have acquainted me with their determinations ; which is, indeed, to return to their home and to trouble you with no more suit, unless you may be won by some other sort than your father's imposition depending on the caskets.

Por. If I live to be as old as Sibylla, I will die as chaste as Diana, unless I be obtained by the manner of my father's will. I am glad this parcel of wooers are so reasonable, for there is not one among them but I dote on his very absence, and I pray God grant them a fair departure.

Ner. Do you not remember, lady, in your father's time, a Venetian, a scholar and a soldier, that came hither in company of the Marquis of Montferrat ?

Por. Yes, yes, it was Bassanio ; as I think, he was so called.

Ner. True, madam : he, of all the men that ever my foolish eyes looked upon, was the best deserving a fair lady.   131

Por. I remember him well, and I remember him worthy of thy praise.

Enter a Serving-man.

How now ! what news ?

Serv. The four strangers seek for you, madam, to take their leave : and there is a forerunner come from a fifth, the Prince of Morocco, who brings word the prince his master will be here to-night.   139

Por. If I could bid the fifth welcome with so good a heart as I can bid the other four farewell, I should be glad of his approach : if he have the condition of a saint and the complexion of a devil, I had rather he should shrive me than wive me.

Come, Nerissa. Sirrah, go before.

Whiles we shut the gates upon one wooer, another knocks at the door.   [*Exeunt.*

SCENE III. *Venice. A public place.*

Enter BASSANIO *and* SHYLOCK.

Shy. Three thousand ducats ; well.

Bass. Ay, sir, for three months.

Shy. For three months ; well.

Bass. For the which, as I told you, Antonio shall be bound.

Shy. Antonio shall become bound ; well.

Bass. May you stead me ? will you pleasure me ? shall I know your answer ?

Shy. Three thousand ducats for three months and Antonio bound. 10

Bass. Your answer to that.

Shy. Antonio is a good man.

Bass. Have you heard any imputation to the contrary ?

Shy. Oh, no, no, no, no : my meaning in saying he is a good man is to have you understand me that he is sufficient. Yet his means are in supposition : he hath an argosy bound to Tripolis, another to the Indies ; I understand moreover, upon the Rialto, he hath a third at Mexico, a fourth for England, and other ventures he hath, squandered abroad. But ships are but boards, sailors but men : there be land-rats and water-rats, water-thieves and land-thieves, I mean pirates, and then there is the peril of waters, winds and rocks. The man is, notwithstanding, sufficient. Three thousand ducats ; I think I may take his bond.

Bass. Be assured you may.

Shy. I will be assured I may ; and, that I may be assured, I will bethink me. May I speak with Antonio ?

Bass. If it please you to dine with us.

Shy. Yes, to smell pork ; to eat of the habitation which your prophet the Nazarite conjured the devil into. I will buy with you, sell with you, talk with you, walk with you, and so following, but I will not eat with you, drink with you, nor pray with you. What news on the Rialto ? Who is he comes here ? 40

Enter ANTONIO.

Bass. This is Signior Antonio.

Shy. [*Aside*] How like a fawning publican he looks !

I hate him for he is a Christian,
But more for that in low simplicity
He lends out money gratis and brings down
The rate of usance here with us in Venice.
If I can catch him once upon the hip,
I will feed fat the ancient grudge I bear him.
He hates our sacred nation, and he rails,
Even there where merchants most do congregate, 50
On me, my bargains and my well-won thrift,
Which he calls interest. Cursed be my tribe,
If I forgive him !

Bass. Shylock, do you hear ?

Shy. I am debating of my present store,
And, by the near guess of my memory,
I cannot instantly raise up the gross
Of full three thousand ducats. What of that ?
Tubal, a wealthy Hebrew of my tribe,
Will furnish me. But soft ! how many months
Do you desire ? [*To Ant.*] Rest you fair, good signior ; 60
Your worship was the last man in our mouths.

Ant. Shylock, although I neither lend nor borrow
By taking nor by giving of excess,

Yet, to supply the ripe wants of my friend,
I'll break a custom. Is he yet possess'd
How much ye would ?

Shy. Ay, ay, three thousand ducats.

Ant. And for three months.

Shy. I had forgot ; three months ; you told me so.
Well then, your bond ; and let me see ; but hear you ;
Methought you said you neither lend nor borrow
Upon advantage. 70

Ant. I do never use it.

Shy. When Jacob grazed his uncle Laban's sheep—
This Jacob from our holy Abram was,
As his wise mother wrought in his behalf,
The third possessor ; ay, he was the third—

Ant. And what of him ? did he take interest ?

Shy. No, not take interest, not, as you would say,
Directly interest : mark what Jacob did.
When Laban and himself were compromised
That all the eanlings which were streak'd and pied 80
Should fall as Jacob's hire, the ewes, being rank,
In the end of autumn turned to the rams,
And, when the work of generation was
Between these woolly breeders in the act,
The skilful shepherd peel'd me certain wands,
And, in the doing of the deed of kind,
He stuck them up before the fulsome ewes,
Who then conceiving did in eaning time
Fall parti-color'd lambs, and those were Jacob's.
This was a way to thrive, and he was blest : 90
And thrift is blessing, if men steal it not.

Ant. This was a venture, sir, that Jacob served for ;
A thing not in his power to bring to pass,
But sway'd and fashion'd by the hand of heaven.
Was this inserted to make interest good ?
Or is your gold and silver ewes and rams ?

Shy. I cannot tell ; I make it breed as fast :
But note me, signior.

Ant. Mark you this, Bassanio,
The devil can cite Scripture for his purpose.
An evil soul producing holy witness 100
Is like a villain with a smiling cheek,
A goodly apple rotten at the heart :
O, what a goodly outside falsehood hath !

Shy. Three thousand ducats ; 'tis a good round sum.
Three months from twelve ; then, let me see ; the rate—

Ant. Well, Shylock, shall we be beholding to you ?

Shy. Signior Antonio, many a time and oft
In the Rialto you have rated me
About my moneys and my usances :
Still have I borne it with a patient shrug, 110
For sufferance is the badge of all our tribe.
You call me misbeliever, cut-throat dog,
And spit upon my Jewish gaberdine,
And all for use of that which is mine own.
Well then, it now appears you need my help :
Go to, then ; you come to me, and you say
' Shylock, we would have moneys : ' you say so ;
You, that did void your rheum upon my beard

And foot me as you spurn a stranger cur   119
Over your threshold ; moneys is your suit.
What should I say to you ? Should I not say
' Hath a dog money ? is it possible
A cur can lend three thousand ducats ? ' Or
Shall I bend low and in a bondman's key,
With bated breath and whispering humbleness,
Say this ;
' Fair sir, you spit on me on Wednesday last ;
You spurn'd me such a day ; another time
You call'd me dog ; and for these courtesies
I'll lend you thus much moneys ' ?   130
    Ant. I am as like to call thee so again,
To spit on thee again, to spurn thee too.
If thou wilt lend this money, lend it not
As to thy friends ; for when did friendship take
A breed for barren metal of his friend ?
But lend it rather to thine enemy,
Who, if he break, thou mayst with better face
Exact the penalty.
    Shy.   Why, look you, how you storm !
I would be friends with you and have your
    love,
Forget the shames that you have stain'd me
    with,   140
Supply your present wants and take no doit
Of usance for my moneys, and you'll not hear
    me :
This is kind I offer.
    Bass. This were kindness.
    Shy.   This kindness will I show.
Go with me to a notary, seal me there
Your single bond ; and, in a merry sport,
If you repay me not on such a day,
In such a place, such sum or sums as are
Express'd in the condition, let the forfeit
Be nominated for an equal pound   150
Of your fair flesh, to be cut off and taken
In what part of your body pleaseth me.
    Ant. Content, i' faith : I'll seal to such a
    bond
And say there is much kindness in the Jew.
    Bass. You shall not seal to such a bond for
    me :
I'll rather dwell in my necessity.
    Ant. Why, fear not, man ; I will not forfeit
    it :
Within these two months, that's a month be-
    fore
This bond expires, I do expect return   160
Of thrice three times the value of this bond.
    Shy. O father Abram, what these Chris-
    tians are,
Whose own hard dealings teaches them suspect
The thoughts of others ! Pray you, tell me this ;
If he should break his day, what should I gain
By the exaction of the forfeiture ?
A pound of man's flesh taken from a man
Is not so estimable, profitable neither,
As flesh of muttons, beefs, or goats. I say,
To buy his favor, I extend this friendship :
If he will take it, so ; if not, adieu ;   170
And, for my love, I pray you wrong me not.
    Ant. Yes, Shylock, I will seal unto this
    bond.
    Shy. Then meet me forthwith at the no-
    tary's ;
Give him direction for this merry bond,
And I will go and purse the ducats straight,
See to my house, left in the fearful guard
Of an unthrifty knave, and presently
I will be with you.
    Ant. Hie thee, gentle Jew. [*Exit Shylock.*

The Hebrew will turn Christian : he grows
    kind.   180
    Bass. I like not fair terms and a villain's
    mind.
    Ant. Come on : in this there can be no dis-
    may ;
My ships come home a month before the day.
          [*Exeunt.*

ACT II.

SCENE I. *Belmont.   A room in* PORTIA'S
          house.

Flourish of cornets.   Enter the PRINCE OF
    MOROCCO *and his train ;* PORTIA, NERISSA,
    and others attending.

    Mor. Mislike me not for my complexion,
The shadow'd livery of the burnish'd sun,
To whom I am a neighbor and near bred.
Bring me the fairest creature northward born,
Where Phœbus' fire scarce thaws the icicles,
And let us make incision for your love,
To prove whose blood is reddest, his or mine.
I tell thee, lady, this aspect of mine
Hath fear'd the valiant : by my love I swear
The best-regarded virgins of our clime   10
Have loved it too : I would not change this
    hue,
Except to steal your thoughts, my gentle queen.
    Por. In terms of choice I am not solely led
By nice direction of a maiden's eyes ;
Besides, the lottery of my destiny
Bars me the right of voluntary choosing :
But if my father had not scanted me
And hedged me by his wit, to yield myself
His wife who wins me by that means I told
    you,
Yourself, renowned prince, then stood as fair
As any comer I have look'd on yet   21
For my affection.
    Mor.   Even for that I thank you :
Therefore, I pray you, lead me to the caskets
To try my fortune. By this scimitar
That slew the Sophy and a Persian prince
That won three fields of Sultan Solyman,
I would outstare the sternest eyes that look,
Outbrave the heart most daring on the earth,
Pluck the young sucking cubs from the she-
    bear,
Yea, mock the lion when he roars for prey, 30
To win thee, lady. But, alas the while !
If Hercules and Lichas play at dice
Which is the better man, the greater throw
May turn by fortune from the weaker hand :
So is Alcides beaten by his page ;
And so may I, blind fortune leading me,
Miss that which one unworthier may attain,
And die with grieving.
    Por.   You must take your chance,
And either not attempt to choose at all
Or swear before you choose, if you choose
    wrong   40
Never to speak to lady afterward
In way of marriage : therefore be advised.
    Mor. Nor will not. Come, bring me unto
    my chance.
    Por. First, forward to the temple : after
    dinner
Your hazard shall be made.
    Mor.   Good fortune then !

To make me blest or cursed'st among men.
[*Cornets, and exeunt.*

SCENE II. *Venice. A street.*

Enter LAUNCELOT.

Laun. Certainly my conscience will serve me to run from this Jew my master. The fiend is at mine elbow and tempts me saying to me 'Gobbo, Launcelot Gobbo, good Launcelot,' or 'good Gobbo,' or good Launcelot Gobbo, use your legs, take the start, run away. My conscience says 'No; take heed,' honest Launcelot; take heed, honest Gobbo, or, as aforesaid, 'honest Launcelot Gobbo; do not run; scorn running with thy heels.' Well, the most courageous fiend bids me pack : 'Via!' says the fiend; 'away!' says the fiend; 'for the heavens, rouse up a brave mind,' says the fiend, 'and run.' Well, my conscience, hanging about the neck of my heart, says very wisely to me 'My honest friend Launcelot, being an honest man's son,' or rather an honest woman's son; for, indeed, my father did something smack, something grow to, he had a kind of taste; well, my conscience says 'Launcelot, budge not.' 'Budge,' says the fiend. 'Budge not,' says my conscience. 'Conscience,' say I, 'you counsel well;' 'Fiend,' say I, 'you counsel well :' to be ruled by my conscience, I should stay with the Jew my master, who, God bless the mark, is a kind of devil; and, to run away from the Jew, I should be ruled by the fiend, who, saving your reverence, is the devil himself. Certainly the Jew is the very devil incarnal; and, in my conscience, my conscience is but a kind of hard conscience, to offer to counsel me to stay with the Jew. The fiend gives the more friendly counsel : I will run, fiend; my heels are at your command; I will run.

Enter Old GOBBO, *with a basket.*

Gob. Master young man, you, I pray you, which is the way to master Jew's?

Laun. [*Aside*] O heavens, this is my true-begotten father! who, being more than sand-blind, high-gravel blind, knows me not : I will try confusions with him.

Gob. Master young gentleman, I pray you, which is the way to master Jew's?   41

Laun. Turn up on your right hand at the next turning, but, at the next turning of all, on your left; marry, at the very next turning, turn of no hand, but turn down indirectly to the Jew's house.

Gob. By God's sonties, 'twill be a hard way to hit. Can you tell me whether one Launcelot, that dwells with him, dwell with him or no?

Laun. Talk you of young Master Launcelot? [*Aside*] Mark me now; now will I raise the waters. Talk you of young Master Launcelot?

Gob. No master, sir, but a poor man's son : his father, though I say it, is an honest exceeding poor man and, God be thanked, well to live.

Laun. Well, let his father be what a' will, we talk of young Master Launcelot.

Gob. Your worship's friend and Launcelot, sir.

Laun. But I pray you, ergo, old man, ergo, I beseech you, talk you of young Master Launcelot?

Gob. Of Launcelot, an't please your mastership.

Laun. Ergo, Master Launcelot. Talk not of Master Launcelot, father; for the young gentleman, according to Fates and Destinies and such odd sayings, the Sisters Three and such branches of learning, is indeed deceased, or, as you would say in plain terms, gone to heaven.

Gob. Marry, God forbid! the boy was the very staff of my age, my very prop.   70

Laun. Do I look like a cudgel or a hovel-post, a staff or a prop? Do you know me, father?

Gob. Alack the day, I know you not, young gentleman : but, I pray you, tell me, is my boy, God rest his soul, alive or dead?

Laun. Do you not know me, father?

Gob. Alack, sir, I am sand-blind; I know you not.

Laun. Nay, indeed, if you had your eyes, you might fail of the knowing me : it is a wise father that knows his own child. Well, old man, I will tell you news of your son : give me your blessing : truth will come to light; murder cannot be hid long; a man's son may, but at the length truth will out.

Gob. Pray you, sir, stand up : I am sure you are not Launcelot, my boy.

Laun. Pray you, let's have no more fooling about it, but give me your blessing : I am Launcelot, your boy that was, your son that is, your child that shall be.   91

Gob. I cannot think you are my son.

Laun. I know not what I shall think of that : but I am Launcelot, the Jew's man, and I am sure Margery your wife is my mother.

Gob. Her name is Margery, indeed : I'll be sworn, if thou be Launcelot, thou art mine own flesh and blood. Lord worshipped might he be! what a beard hast thou got! thou hast got more hair on thy chin than Dobbin my fill-horse has on his tail.   101

Laun. It should seem, then, that Dobbin's tail grows backward : I am sure he had more hair of his tail than I have of my face when I last saw him.

Gob. Lord, how art thou changed! How dost thou and thy master agree? I have brought him a present. How 'gree you now?

Laun. Well, well : but, for mine own part, as I have set up my rest to run away, so I will not rest till I have run some ground. My master's a very Jew : give him a present! give him a halter : I am famished in his service; you may tell every finger I have with my ribs. Father, I am glad you are come : give me your present to one Master Bassanio, who, indeed, gives rare new liveries : if I serve not him, I will run as far as God has any ground. O rare fortune! here comes the man : to him, father; for I am a Jew, if I serve the Jew any longer.   120

Enter BASSANIO, *with* LEONARDO *and other followers.*

Bass. You may do so; but let it be so hasted that supper be ready at the farthest by five of the clock. See these letters delivered; put the liveries to making, and desire Gratiano to come anon to my lodging. [*Exit a Servant.*

Laun. To him, father.

Gob. God bless your worship!

Bass. Gramercy! wouldst thou aught with me?

Gob. Here's my son, sir, a poor boy,—

Laun. Not a poor boy, sir, but the rich Jew's man; that would, sir, as my father shall specify—

Gob. He hath a great infection, sir, as one would say, to serve,—

Laun. Indeed, the short and the long is, I serve the Jew, and have a desire, as my father shall specify—

Gob. His master and he, saving your worship's reverence, are scarce cater-cousins—

Laun. To be brief, the very truth is that the Jew, having done me wrong, doth cause me, as my father, being, I hope, an old man, shall frutify unto you—

Gob. I have here a dish of doves that I would bestow upon your worship, and my suit is—

Laun. In very brief, the suit is impertinent to myself, as your worship shall know by this honest old man; and, though I say it, though old man, yet poor man, my father.

Bass. One speak for both. What would you?   150

Laun. Serve you, sir.

Gob. That is the very defect of the matter, sir.

Bass. I know thee well; thou hast obtain'd thy suit:
Shylock thy master spoke with me this day,
And hath preferr'd thee, if it be preferment
To leave a rich Jew's service, to become
The follower of so poor a gentleman.

Laun. The old proverb is very well parted between my master Shylock and you, sir: you have the grace of God, sir, and he hath enough.

Bass. Thou speak'st it well. Go, father, with thy son.
Take leave of thy old master and inquire
My lodging out. Give him a livery
More guarded than his fellows': see it done.

Laun. Father, in. I cannot get a service, no; I have ne'er a tongue in my head. Well, if any man in Italy have a fairer table which doth offer to swear upon a book, I shall have good fortune. Go to, here's a simple line of life: here's a small trifle of wives: alas, fifteen wives is nothing! eleven widows and nine maids is a simple coming-in for one man: and then to 'scape drowning thrice, and to be in peril of my life with the edge of a feather-bed; here are simple scapes. Well, if Fortune be a woman, she's a good wench for this gear. Father, come; I'll take my leave of the Jew in the twinkling of an eye.

[Exeunt Launcelot and Old Gobbo.

Bass. I pray thee, good Leonardo, think on this:
These things being bought and orderly bestow'd,
Return in haste, for I do feast to-night   180
My best-esteem'd acquaintance: hie thee, go.

Leon. My best endeavors shall be done herein.

Enter GRATIANO.

Gra. Where is your master?

Leon.   Yonder, sir, he walks. [*Exit.*

Gra. Signior Bassanio!

Bass. Gratiano!

Gra. I have a suit to you.

Bass.   You have obtain'd it.

Gra. You must not deny me; I must go with you to Belmont.

Bass. Why then you must. But hear thee, Gratiano;
Thou art too wild, too rude and bold of voice;
Parts that become thee happily enough   191
And in such eyes as ours appear not faults;
But where thou art not known, why, there they show
Something too liberal. Pray thee, take pain
To allay with some cold drops of modesty
Thy skipping spirit, lest through thy wild behavior
I be misconstrued in the place I go to,
And lose my hopes.

Gra.   Signior Bassanio, hear me:
If I do not put on a sober habit,
Talk with respect and swear but now and then,
Wear prayer-books in my pocket, look demurely,   201
Nay more, while grace is saying, hood mine eyes
Thus with my hat, and sigh and say ' amen,'
Use all the observance of civility,
Like one well studied in a sad ostent
To please his grandam, never trust me more.

Bass. Well, we shall see your bearing.

Gra. Nay, but I bar to-night: you shall not gauge me
By what we do to-night.

Bass.   No, that were pity:
I would entreat you rather to put on   210
Your boldest suit of mirth, for we have friends
That purpose merriment. But fare you well:
I have some business.

Gra. And I must to Lorenzo and the rest:
But we will visit you at supper-time. [*Exeunt.*

SCENE III. *The same. A room in* SHYLOCK'S *house.*

Enter JESSICA *and* LAUNCELOT.

Jes. I am sorry thou wilt leave my father so:
Our house is hell, and thou, a merry devil,
Didst rob it of some taste of tediousness.
But fare thee well, there is a ducat for thee:
And, Launcelot, soon at supper shalt thou see
Lorenzo, who is thy new master's guest:
Give him this letter; do it secretly;
And so farewell: I would not have my father
See me in talk with thee.   9

Laun. Adieu! tears exhibit my tongue. Most beautiful pagan, most sweet Jew! if a Christian did not play the knave and get thee, I am much deceived. But, adieu: these foolish drops do something drown my manly spirit: adieu.

Jes. Farewell, good Launcelot.

[Exit Launcelot.

Alack, what heinous sin is it in me
To be ashamed to be my father's child!
But though I am a daughter to his blood,
I am not to his manners. O Lorenzo,
If thou keep promise, I shall end this strife,   20
Become a Christian and thy loving wife. [*Exit.*

SCENE IV. *The same. A street.*

Enter GRATIANO, LORENZO, SALARINO, *and* SALANIO.

Lor. Nay, we will slink away in supper-time,

Disguise us at my lodging and return,
All in an hour.
  Gra. We have not made good preparation.
  Salar. We have not spoke us yet of torch-
    bearers.
  Salan. 'Tis vile, unless it may be quaintly
    order'd,
And better in my mind not undertook.
  Lor. 'Tis now but four o'clock : we have
    two hours
To furnish us.

    Enter LAUNCELOT, *with a letter.*
      Friend Launcelot, what's the news ?
  Laun. An it shall please you to break up
this, it shall seem to signify.   11
  Lor. I know the hand : in faith, 'tis a fair
    hand ;
And whiter than the paper it writ on
Is the fair hand that writ.
  Gra.   Love-news, in faith.
  Laun. By your leave, sir.
  Lor. Whither goest thou ?
  Laun. Marry, sir, to bid my old master the
Jew to sup to-night with my new master the
Christian.
  Lor. Hold here, take this : tell gentle Jes-
    sica   20
I will not fail her ; speak it privately.
Go, gentlemen,   *[Exit Launcelot.*
Will you prepare you for this masque to-
night ?
I am provided of a torch-bearer.
  Salar. Ay, marry, I'll be gone about it
    straight.
  Salan. And so will I.
  Lor.   Meet me and Gratiano
At Gratiano's lodging some hour hence.
  Salar. 'Tis good we do so.
          [Exeunt Salar. and Salan.
  Gra. Was not that letter from fair Jessica ?
  Lor. I must needs tell thee all. She hath
    directed   30
How I shall take her from her father's house,
What gold and jewels she is furnish'd with,
What page's suit she hath in readiness.
If e'er the Jew her father come to heaven,
It will be for his gentle daughter's sake :
And never dare misfortune cross her foot,
Unless she do it under this excuse,
That she is issue to a faithless Jew.
Come, go with me ; peruse this as thou goest :
Fair Jessica shall be my torch-bearer.
            [Exeunt.

  SCENE V. *The same. Before* SHYLOCK'S
    house.

    Enter SHYLOCK *and* LAUNCELOT.

  Shy. Well, thou shalt see, thy eyes shall be
    thy judge,
The difference of old Shylock and Bassanio :—
What, Jessica !—thou shalt not gormandise,
As thou hast done with me :—What, Jes-
    sica !—
And sleep and snore, and rend apparel out ;—
Why, Jessica, I say !
  Laun.   Why, Jessica !
  Shy. Who bids thee call ? I do not bid
    thee call.
  Laun. Your worship was wont to tell me
    that
I could do nothing without bidding.

    Enter JESSICA.

  Jes. Call you ? what is your will ?   10
  Shy. I am bid forth to supper, Jessica :
There are my keys. But wherefore should I go ?
I am not bid for love ; they flatter me :
But yet I'll go in hate, to feed upon
The prodigal Christian. Jessica, my girl,
Look to my house. I am right loath to go :
There is some ill a-brewing towards my rest,
For I did dream of money-bags to-night.
  Laun. I beseech you, sir, go : my young
master doth expect your reproach.   20
  Shy. So do I his.
  Laun. An they have conspired together, I
will not say you shall see a masque ; but if you
do, then it was not for nothing that my nose
fell a-bleeding on Black-Monday last at six
o'clock i' the morning, falling out that year on
Ash-Wednesday was four year, in the after-
noon.
  Shy. What, are there masques ? Hear you
me, Jessica :
Lock up my doors ; and when you hear the
    drum
And the vile squealing of the wry-neck'd fife,
Clamber not you up to the casements then, 31
Nor thrust your head into the public street
To gaze on Christian fools with varnish'd faces,
But stop my house's ears, I mean my case-
    ments :
Let not the sound of shallow foppery enter
My sober house. By Jacob's staff, I swear,
I have no mind of feasting forth to-night :
But I will go. Go you before me, sirrah ;
Say I will come.
  Laun. I will go before, sir. Mistress, look
out at window, for all this ;   41
      There will come a Christian by,
      Will be worth a Jewess' eye.   *[Exit.*
  Shy. What says that fool of Hagar's off-
spring, ha ?
  Jes. His words were ' Farewell mistress ; '
nothing else.
  Shy. The patch is kind enough, but a huge
feeder ;
Snail-slow in profit, and he sleeps by day
More than the wild-cat : drones hive not with
me ;
Therefore I part with him, and part with him
To one that I would have him help to waste
His borrow'd purse. Well, Jessica, go in ; 51
Perhaps I will return immediately :
Do as I bid you ; shut doors after you :
Fast bind, fast find ;
A proverb never stale in thrifty mind. *[Exit.*
  Jes. Farewell ; and if my fortune be not
    crost,
I have a father, you a daughter, lost.   *[Exit.*

    SCENE VI. *The same.*

  Enter GRATIANO *and* SALARINO, *masqued.*

  Gra. This is the pent-house under which
    Lorenzo
Desired us to make stand.
  Salar.   His hour is almost past.
  Gra. And it is marvel he out-dwells his
    hour,
For lovers ever run before the clock.
  Salar. O, ten times faster Venus' pigeons
    fly
To seal love's bonds new-made, than they are
    wont

To keep obliged faith unforfeited !
  Gra. That ever holds : who riseth from a
    feast
With that keen appetite that he sits down ?
Where is the horse that doth untread again 10
His tedious measures with the unbated fire
That he did pace them first ? All things that
  are,
Are with more spirit chased than enjoy'd.
How like a younker or a prodigal
The scarfed bark puts from her native bay,
Hugg'd and embraced by the strumpet wind !
How like the prodigal doth she return,
With over-weather'd ribs and ragged sails,
Lean, rent and beggar'd by the strumpet wind !
  Salar. Here comes Lorenzo : more of this
    hereafter.   20

Enter LORENZO.

  Lor. Sweet friends, your patience for my
    long abode ;
Not I, but my affairs, have made you wait :
When you shall please to play the thieves for
  wives,
I'll watch as long for you then. Approach ;
Here dwells my father Jew. Ho ! who's within ?

Enter JESSICA, *above, in boy's clothes.*

  Jes. Who are you ? Tell me, for more cer-
    tainty,
Albeit I'll swear that I do know your tongue.
  Lor. Lorenzo, and thy love.
  Jes. Lorenzo, certain, and my love indeed,
For who love I so much ? And now who knows
But you, Lorenzo, whether I am yours ?   31
  Lor. Heaven and thy thoughts are witness
    that thou art.
  Jes. Here, catch this casket ; it is worth the
    pains.
I am glad 'tis night, you do not look on me,
For I am much ashamed of my exchange :
But love is blind and lovers cannot see
The pretty follies that themselves commit ;
For if they could, Cupid himself would blush
To see me thus transformed to a boy.
  Lor. Descend, for you must be my torch-
    bearer.   40
  Jes. What, must I hold a candle to my
    shames ?
They in themselves, good-sooth, are too too
  light.
Why, 'tis an office of discovery, love ;
And I should be obscured.
  Lor.   So are you, sweet,
Even in the lovely garnish of a boy.
But come at once ;
For the close night doth play the runaway,
And we are stay'd for at Bassanio's feast.
  Jes. I will make fast the doors, and gild
    myself
With some more ducats, and be with you
  straight.   [*Exit above.* 50
  Gra. Now, by my hood, a Gentile and no
    Jew.
  Lor. Beshrew me but I love her heartily ;
For she is wise, if I can judge of her,
And fair she is, if that mine eyes be true,
And true she is, as she hath proved herself,
And therefore, like herself, wise, fair and true,
Shall she be placed in my constant soul.

Enter JESSICA, *below.*

What, art thou come ? On, gentlemen ; away !

Our masquing mates by this time for us stay.
    [*Exit with Jessica and Salarino.*

Enter ANTONIO.

  Ant. Who's there ?   60
  Gra. Signior Antonio !
  Ant. Fie, fie, Gratiano ! where are all the
    rest ?
'Tis nine o'clock : our friends all stay for you.
No masque to-night : the wind is come about ;
Bassanio presently will go aboard :
I have sent twenty out to seek for you.
  Gra. I am glad on't : I desire no more de-
    light
Than to be under sail and gone to-night.
    [*Exeunt.*

SCENE VII.   *Belmont.   A room in* PORTIA'S
house.

Flourish of cornets. Enter PORTIA, *with the*
PRINCE OF MOROCCO, *and their trains.*

  Por. Go draw aside the curtains and dis-
    cover
The several caskets to this noble prince.
Now make your choice.
  Mor.   The first, of gold, who this inscrip-
    tion bears,
' Who chooseth me shall gain what many men
    desire ; '
The second, silver, which this promise carries,
' Who chooseth me shall get as much as he
    deserves ; '
This third, dull lead, with warning all as blunt,
' Who chooseth me must give and hazard all
    he hath.'
How shall I know if I do choose the right ? 10
  Por. The one of them contains my picture,
    prince :
If you choose that, then I am yours withal.
  Mor. Some god direct my judgment ! Let
    me see ;
I will survey the inscriptions back again.
What says this leaden casket ?
' Who chooseth me must give and hazard all
    he hath.'
Must give : for what ? for lead ? hazard for
    lead ?
This casket threatens. Men that hazard all
Do it in hope of fair advantages :   19
A golden mind stoops not to shows of dross ;
I'll then nor give nor hazard aught for lead.
What says the silver with her virgin hue ?
' Who chooseth me shall get as much as he de-
    serves.'
As much as he deserves ! Pause there, Mo-
    rocco,
And weigh thy value with an even hand :
If thou be'st rated by thy estimation,
Thou dost deserve enough ; and yet enough
May not extend so far as to the lady :
And yet to be afeard of my deserving
Were but a weak disabling of myself.   30
As much as I deserve ! Why, that's the lady :
I do in birth deserve her, and in fortunes,
In graces and in qualities of breeding ;
But more than these, in love I do deserve.
What if I stray'd no further, but chose here ?
Let's see once more this saying graved in gold ;
' Who chooseth me shall gain what many men
    desire.'
Why, that's the lady ; all the world desires her ;
From the four corners of the earth they come,

To kiss this shrine, this mortal-breathing
    saint :   40
The Hyrcanian deserts and the vasty wilds
Of wide Arabia are as throughfares now
For princes to come view fair Portia :
The watery kingdom, whose ambitious head
Spits in the face of heaven, is no bar
To stop the foreign spirits, but they come,
As o'er a brook, to see fair Portia.
One of these three contains her heavenly pic-
    ture.
Is't like that lead contains her ? 'Twere dam-
    nation
To think so base a thought : it were too gross
To rib her cerecloth in the obscure grave. 51
Or shall I think in silver she's immured,
Being ten times undervalued to tried gold ?
O sinful thought ! Never so rich a gem
Was set in worse than gold. They have in Eng-
    land
A coin that bears the figure of an angel
Stamped in gold, but that's insculp'd upon ;
But here an angel in a golden bed
Lies all within. Deliver me the key :
Here do I choose, and thrive I as I may ! 60
    Por. There, take it, prince ; and if my form
    lie there,
Then I am yours.
        [He unlocks the golden casket.
    Mor.   O hell ! what have we here ?
A carrion Death, within whose empty eye
There is a written scroll ! I'll read the writing.
[Reads] All that glisters is not gold ;
    Often have you heard that told :
    Many a man his life hath sold
    But my outside to behold :
    Gilded tombs do worms infold.
    Had you been as wise as bold, 70
    Young in limbs, in judgment old,
    Your answer had not been inscroll'd :
    Fare you well ; your suit is cold.
Cold, indeed ; and labor lost :
    Then, farewell, heat, and welcome, frost !
Portia, adieu. I have too grieved a heart
To take a tedious leave : thus losers part.
    [Exit with his train. Flourish of cornets.
    Por. A gentle riddance. Draw the curtains,
    go.
Let all of his complexion choose me so.
                      [Exeunt.

    SCENE VIII. *Venice. A street.*

    Enter SALARINO *and* SALANIO.

    Salar. Why, man, I saw Bassanio under
    sail :
With him is Gratiano gone along ;
And in their ship I am sure Lorenzo is not.
    Salan. The villain Jew with outcries raised
    the duke,
Who went with him to search Bassanio's ship.
    Salar. He came too late, the ship was un-
    der sail :
But there the duke was given to understand
That in a gondola were seen together
Lorenzo and his amorous Jessica :
Besides, Antonio certified the duke 10
They were not with Bassanio in his ship.
    Salan. I never heard a passion so confused,
So strange, outrageous, and so variable,
As the dog Jew did utter in the streets :
' My daughter ! O my ducats ! O my daughter !
Fled with a Christian ! O my Christian ducats !

Justice ! the law ! my ducats, and my daugh-
    ter !
A sealed bag, two sealed bags of ducats,
Of double ducats, stolen from me by my
    daughter !
And jewels, two stones, two rich and precious
    stones, 20
Stolen by my daughter ! Justice ! find the girl ;
She hath the stones upon her, and the ducats.'
    Salar. Why, all the boys in Venice follow
    him,
Crying, his stones, his daughter, and his
    ducats.
    Salan. Let good Antonio look he keep his
    day,
Or he shall pay for this.
    Salar.   Marry, well remember'd.
I reason'd with a Frenchman yesterday,
Who told me, in the narrow seas that part
The French and English, there miscarried
A vessel of our country richly fraught : 30
I thought upon Antonio when he told me ;
And wish'd in silence that it were not his.
    Salan. You were best to tell Antonio what
    you hear ;
Yet do not suddenly, for it may grieve him.
    Salar. A kinder gentleman treads not the
    earth.
I saw Bassanio and Antonio part :
Bassanio told him he would make some speed
Of his return : he answer'd, ' Do not so ;
Slubber not business for my sake, Bassanio,
But stay the very riping of the time ; 40
And for the Jew's bond which he hath of me,
Let it not enter in your mind of love :
Be merry, and employ your chiefest thoughts
To courtship and such fair ostents of love
As shall conveniently become you there : '
And even there, his eye being big with tears,
Turning his face, he put his hand behind him,
And with affection wondrous sensible
He wrung Bassanio's hand ; and so they parted.
    Salan. I think he only loves the world for
    him. 50
I pray thee, let us go and find him out
And quicken his embraced heaviness
With some delight or other.
    Salar.   Do we so. *[Exeunt.*

    SCENE IX. *Belmont. A room in* PORTIA'S
                house.

    Enter NERISSA *with a* Servitor.

    Ner. Quick, quick, I pray thee ; draw the
    curtain straight :
The Prince of Arragon hath ta'en his oath,
And comes to his election presently.

Flourish of cornets. Enter the PRINCE OF
  ARRAGON, PORTIA, *and their trains.*

    Por. Behold, there stand the caskets, noble
    prince :
If you choose that wherein I am contain'd,
Straight shall our nuptial rites be solemnized :
But if you fail, without more speech, my lord,
You must be gone from hence immediately.
    Ar. I am enjoin'd by oath to observe three
    things :
First, never to unfold to any one 10
Which casket 'twas I chose ; next, if I fail
Of the right casket, never in my life
To woo a maid in way of marriage :
Lastly,
If I do fail in fortune of my choice,

Immediately to leave you and be gone.

Por. To these injunctions every one doth
swear

That comes to hazard for my worthless self.

Ar. And so have I address'd me. Fortune
now

To my heart's hope ! Gold ; silver ; and base
lead.   20

' Who chooseth me must give and hazard all
he hath.'

You shall look fairer, ere I give or hazard.

What says the golden chest ? ha ! let me see :

' Who chooseth me shall gain what many men
desire.'

What many men desire ! that ' many ' may be
meant

By the fool multitude, that choose by show,

Not learning more than the fond eye doth
teach ;

Which pries not to the interior, but, like the
martlet,

Builds in the weather on the outward wall,

Even in the force and road of casualty.

I will not choose what many men desire,

Because I will not jump with common spirits

And rank me with the barbarous multitudes.

Why, then to thee, thou silver treasure-house ;

Tell me once more what title thou dost bear :

' Who chooseth me shall get as much as he deserves : '

And well said too ; for who shall go about

To cozen fortune and be honorable

Without the stamp of merit ? Let none presume

To wear an undeserved dignity.   40

O, that estates, degrees and offices

Were not derived corruptly, and that clear
honor

Were purchased by the merit of the wearer !

How many then should cover that stand bare !

How many be commanded that command !

How much low peasantry would then be
glean'd

From the true seed of honor ! and how much
honor

Pick'd from the chaff and ruin of the times

To be new-varnish'd ! Well, but to my choice :

' Who chooseth me shall get as much as he de-
serves.'   50

I will assume desert. Give me a key for this,

And instantly unlock my fortunes here.

[*He opens the silver casket.*

Por. Too long a pause for that which you
find there.

Ar. What's here ? the portrait of a blink-
ing idiot,

Presenting me a schedule ! I will read it.

How much unlike art thou to Portia !

How much unlike my hopes and my deservings !

' Who chooseth me shall have as much as he
deserves.'

Did I deserve no more than a fool's head ?

Is that my prize ? are my deserts no better ?

Por. To offend, and judge, are distinct of-
fices   61

And of opposed natures.

Ar.   What is here ?

[*Reads*] The fire seven times tried this :

Seven times tried that judgment is,

That did never choose amiss.

Some there be that shadows kiss ;

Such have but a shadow's bliss :

There be fools alive, I wis,

Silver'd o'er ; and so was this.

Take what wife you will to bed,   70

I will ever be your head :

So be gone : you are sped.

Still more fool I shall appear

By the time I linger here

With one fool's head I came to woo,

But I go away with two.

Sweet, adieu. I'll keep my oath,

Patiently to bear my wroth.

[*Exeunt Arragon and train.*

Por. Thus hath the candle singed the moth.

O, these deliberate fools ! when they do choose,

They have the wisdom by their wit to lose.   81

Ner. The ancient saying is no heresy,

Hanging and wiving goes by destiny.

Por. Come, draw the curtain, Nerissa.

Enter a Servant.

Serv. Where is my lady ?

Por.   Here : what would my lord ?

Serv. Madam, there is alighted at your gate

A young Venetian, one that comes before

To signify the approaching of his lord ;

From whom he bringeth sensible regreets,

To wit, besides commends and courteous
breath,   90

Gifts of rich value. Yet I have not seen

So likely an ambassador of love :

A day in April never came so sweet,

To show how costly summer was at hand,

As this fore-spurrer comes before his lord.

Por. No more, I pray thee : I am half
afeard

Thou wilt say anon he is some kin to thee,

Thou spend'st such high-day wit in praising
him.

Come, come, Nerissa ; for I long to see   99

Quick Cupid's post that comes so mannerly.

Ner. Bassanio, lord Love, if thy will it be !

[*Exeunt.*

ACT III.

Scene I. *Venice. A street.*

Enter Salanio *and* Salarino.

Salan. Now, what news on the Rialto ?

Salar. Why, yet it lives there unchecked
that Antonio hath a ship of rich lading
wrecked on the narrow seas ; the Goodwins,
I think they call the place ; a very dangerous
flat and fatal, where the carcases of many a
tall ship lie buried, as they say, if my gossip
Report be an honest woman of her word.

Salan. I would she were as lying a gossip in
that as ever knapped ginger or made her neighbors believe she wept for the death of a third
husband. But it is true, without any slips of
prolixity or crossing the plain highway of talk,
that the good Antonio, the honest Antonio,——
O that I had a title good enough to keep his
name company !—

Salar. Come, the full stop.

Salan. Ha ! what sayest thou ? Why, the
end is, he hath lost a ship.

Salar. I would it might prove the end of his
losses.   21

Salan. Let me say ' amen ' betimes, lest the
devil cross my prayer, for here he comes in
the likeness of a Jew.

Enter SHYLOCK.

How now, Shylock! what news among the merchants?

Shy. You know, none so well, none so well as you, of my daughter's flight.

Salar. That's certain: I, for my part, knew the tailor that made the wings she flew withal.   30

Salan. And Shylock, for his own part, knew the bird was fledged; and then it is the complexion of them all to leave the dam.

Shy. She is damned for it.

Salan. That's certain, if the devil may be her judge.

Shy. My own flesh and blood to rebel!

Salan. Out upon it, old carrion! rebels it at these years?

Shy. I say, my daughter is my flesh and blood.   40

Salar. There is more difference between thy flesh and hers than between jet and ivory; more between your bloods than there is between red wine and rhenish. But tell us, do you hear whether Antonio have had any loss at sea or no?

Shy. There I have another bad match: a bankrupt, a prodigal, who dare scarce show his head on the Rialto; a beggar, that was used to come so smug upon the mart; let him look to his bond: he was wont to call me usurer; let him look to his bond: he was wont to lend money for a Christian courtesy; let him look to his bond.

Salar. Why, I am sure, if he forfeit, thou wilt not take his flesh: what's that good for?

Shy. To bait fish withal: if it will feed nothing else, it will feed my revenge. He hath disgraced me, and hindered me half a million; laughed at my losses, mocked at my gains, scorned my nation, thwarted my bargains, cooled my friends, heated mine enemies; and what's his reason? I am a Jew. Hath not a Jew eyes? hath not a Jew hands, organs, dimensions, senses, affections, passions? fed with the same food, hurt with the same weapons, subject to the same diseases, healed by the same means, warmed and cooled by the same winter and summer, as a Christian is? If you prick us, do we not bleed? if you tickle us, do we not laugh? if you poison us, do we not die? and if you wrong us, shall we not revenge? If we are like you in the rest, we will resemble you in that. If a Jew wrong a Christian, what is his humility? Revenge. If a Christian wrong a Jew, what should his sufferance be by Christian example? Why, revenge. The villany you teach me, I will execute, and it shall go hard but I will better the instruction.

Enter a Servant.

Serv. Gentlemen, my master Antonio is at his house and desires to speak with you both.

Salar. We have been up and down to seek him.

Enter TUBAL.

Salan. Here comes another of the tribe: a third cannot be matched, unless the devil himself turn Jew.

[*Exeunt Salan., Salar., and Servant.*

Shy. How now, Tubal! what news from Genoa? hast thou found my daughter?

Tub. I often came where I did hear of her, but cannot find her.

Shy. Why, there, there, there, there! a diamond gone, cost me two thousand ducats in Frankfort! The curse never fell upon our nation till now; I never felt it till now: two thousand ducats in that; and other precious, precious jewels. I would my daughter were dead at my foot, and the jewels in her ear! would she were hearsed at my foot, and the ducats in her coffin! No news of them? Why, so: and I know not what's spent in the search: why, thou loss upon loss! the thief gone with so much, and so much to find the thief; and no satisfaction, no revenge: nor no ill luck stirring but what lights on my shoulders; no sighs but of my breathing; no tears but of my shedding.   101

Tub. Yes, other men have ill luck too: Antonio, as I heard in Genoa,—

Shy. What, what, what? ill luck, ill luck?

Tub. Hath an argosy cast away, coming from Tripolis.

Shy. I thank God, I thank God. Is't true, is't true?

Tub. I spoke with some of the sailors that escaped the wreck.   110

Shy. I thank thee, good Tubal: good news, good news! ha, ha! where? in Genoa?

Tub. Your daughter spent in Genoa, as I heard, in one night fourscore ducats.

Shy. Thou stickest a dagger in me: I shall never see my gold again: fourscore ducats at a sitting! fourscore ducats!

Tub. There came divers of Antonio's creditors in my company to Venice, that swear he cannot choose but break.   120

Shy. I am very glad of it: I'll plague him; I'll torture him: I am glad of it.

Tub. One of them showed me a ring that he had of your daughter for a monkey.

Shy. Out upon her! Thou torturest me, Tubal: it was my turquoise; I had it of Leah when I was a bachelor: I would not have given it for a wilderness of monkeys.

Tub. But Antonio is certainly undone.

Shy. Nay, that's true, that's very true. Go, Tubal, fee me an officer; bespeak him a fortnight before. I will have the heart of him, if he forfeit; for, were he out of Venice, I can make what merchandise I will. Go, go, Tubal, and meet me at our synagogue; go, good Tubal; at our synagogue, Tubal.   [*Exeunt.*

SCENE II.   *Belmont.   A room in* PORTIA'S
house.

Enter BASSANIO, PORTIA, GRATIANO, NERISSA,
and Attendants.

Por. I pray you, tarry: pause a day or two
Before you hazard; for, in choosing wrong,
I lose your company: therefore forbear
    awhile.
There's something tells me, but it is not love,
I would not lose you; and you know yourself,
Hate counsels not in such a quality.
But lest you should not understand me well,—
And yet a maiden hath no tongue but
    thought,—
I would detain you here some month or two
Before you venture for me. I could teach you
How to choose right, but I am then forsworn;
So will I never be: so may you miss me;
But if you do, you'll make me wish a sin,

That I had been forsworn. Beshrew your eyes,
They have o'erlook'd me and divided me ;
One half of me is yours, the other half yours,
Mine own, I would say ; but if mine, then
  yours,
And so all yours. O, these naughty times
Put bars between the owners and their rights !
And so, though yours, not yours. Prove it so,
Let fortune go to hell for it, not I.   21
I speak too long ; but 'tis to peize the time,
To eke it and to draw it out in length,
To stay you from election.
   Bass.   Let me choose ;
For as I am, I live upon the rack.
   Por. Upon the rack, Bassanio ! then confess
What treason there is mingled with your love.
   Bass. None but that ugly treason of mis-
    trust,
Which makes me fear the enjoying of my love :
There may as well be amity and life   30
'Tween snow and fire, as treason and my love.
   Por. Ay, but I fear you speak upon the
    rack,
Where men enforced do speak anything.
   Bass. Promise me life, and I'll confess the
    truth.
   Por. Well then, confess and live.
   Bass.   'Confess' and 'love'
Had been the very sum of my confession :
O happy torment, when my torturer
Doth teach me answers for deliverance !
But let me to my fortune and the caskets.
   Por. Away, then ! I am lock'd in one of
    them :   40
If you do love me, you will find me out.
Nerissa and the rest, stand all aloof.
Let music sound while he doth make his
    choice ;
Then, if he lose, he makes a swan-like end,
Fading in music : that the comparison
May stand more proper, my eye shall be the
    stream
And watery death-bed for him. He may win ;
And what is music then ? Then music is
Even as the flourish when true subjects bow
To a new-crowned monarch : such it is   50
As are those dulcet sounds in break of day
That creep into the dreaming bridegroom's ear,
And summon him to marriage. Now he goes,
With no less presence, but with much more
    love,
Than young Alcides, when he did redeem
The virgin tribute paid by howling Troy
To the sea-monster : I stand for sacrifice ;
The rest aloof are the Dardanian wives,
With bleared visages, come forth to view
The issue of the exploit. Go, Hercules !   60
Live thou, I live : with much, much more dis-
    may
I view the fight than thou that makest the fray.

Music, whilst BASSANIO *comments on the cas-*
    kets to himself.

          SONG.

  Tell me where is fancy bred,
  Or in the heart, or in the head ?
  How begot, how nourished ?
    Reply, reply.
  It is engender'd in the eyes,
  With gazing fed ; and fancy dies
  In the cradle where it lies.
    Let us all ring fancy's knell :   70
    I'll begin it,—Ding, dong, bell.

   All. Ding, dong, bell.
   Bass. So may the outward shows be least
    themselves :
The world is still deceived with ornament.
In law, what plea so tainted and corrupt,
But, being seasoned with a gracious voice,
Obscures the show of evil ? In religion,
What damned error, but some sober brow
Will bless it and approve it with a text,
Hiding the grossness with fair ornament ?   80
There is no vice so simple but assumes
Some mark of virtue on his outward parts :
How many cowards, whose hearts are all as
    false
As stairs of sand, wear yet upon their chins
The beards of Hercules and frowning Mars ;
Who, inward search'd, have livers white as
    milk ;
And these assume but valor's excrement
To render them redoubted ! Look on beauty,
And you shall see 'tis purchased by the weight ;
Which therein works a miracle in nature,   90
Making them lightest that wear most of it :
So are those crisped snaky golden locks
Which make such wanton gambols with the
    wind,
Upon supposed fairness, often known
To be the dowry of a second head,
The skull that bred them in the sepulchre.
Thus ornament is but the guiled shore
To a most dangerous sea ; the beauteous scarf
Veiling an Indian beauty ; in a word,
The seeming truth which cunning times put
    on   100
To entrap the wisest. Therefore, thou gaudy
    gold,
Hard food for Midas, I will none of thee ;
Nor none of thee, thou pale and common
    drudge
'Tween man and man : but thou, thou meagre
    lead,
Which rather threatenest than dost promise
    aught,
Thy paleness moves me more than eloquence ;
And here choose I ; joy be the consequence !
   Por. [*Aside*] How all the other passions
    fleet to air,
As doubtful thoughts, and rash-embraced de-
    spair,
And shuddering fear, and green-eyed jealousy !
O love,   111
Be moderate ; allay thy ecstasy,
In measure rein thy joy ; scant this excess.
I feel too much thy blessing : make it less,
For fear I surfeit.
   Bass.   What find I here ?
        [*Opening the leaden casket.*
Fair Portia's counterfeit ! What demi-god
Hath come so near creation ? Move these eyes ?
Or whether, riding on the balls of mine,
Seem they in motion ? Here are sever'd lips,
Parted with sugar breath : so sweet a bar
Should sunder such sweet friends. Here in her
    hairs   120
The painter plays the spider and hath woven
A golden mesh to entrap the hearts of men,
Faster than gnats in cobwebs ; but her eyes,—
How could he see to do them ? having made
    one,
Methinks it should have power to steal both
    his
And leave itself unfurnish'd. Yet look, how far

The substance of my praise doth wrong this
 shadow
In underprizing it, so far this shadow
Doth limp behind the substance. Here's the
 scroll, 130
The continent and summary of my fortune.
 [*Reads*] You that choose not by the view,
 Chance as fair and choose as true !
 Since this fortune falls to you,
 Be content and seek no new,
 If you be well pleased with this
 And hold your fortune for your bliss,
 Turn you where your lady is
 And claim her with a loving kiss.
A gentle scroll. Fair lady, by your leave ; 140
I come by note, to give and to receive.
Like one of two contending in a prize,
That thinks he hath done well in people's eyes,
Hearing applause and universal shout,
Giddy in spirit, still gazing in a doubt
Whether those pearls of praise be his or no ;
So, thrice fair lady, stand I, even so ;
As doubtful whether what I see be true,
Until confirm'd, sign'd, ratified by you.
 Por. You see me, Lord Bassanio, where I
 stand, 150
Such as I am : though for myself alone
I would not be ambitious in my wish,
To wish myself much better ; yet, for you
I would be trebled twenty times myself ;
A thousand times more fair, ten thousand
 times
More rich ;
That only to stand high in your account,
I might in virtue, beauties, livings, friends,
Exceed account ; but the full sum of me 159
Is sum of something, which, to term in gross,
Is an unlesson'd girl, unschool'd, unpractised ;
Happy in this, she is not yet so old
But she may learn ; happier than this,
She is not bred so dull but she can learn ;
Happiest of all is that her gentle spirit
Commits itself to yours to be directed,
As from her lord, her governor, her king.
Myself and what is mine to you and yours
Is now converted : but now I was the lord
Of this fair mansion, master of my servants,
Queen o'er myself : and even now, but now,
This house, these servants and this same myself
Are yours, my lord : I give them with this
 ring ;
Which when you part from, lose, or give away,
Let it presage the ruin of your love
And be my vantage to exclaim on you.
 Bass. Madam, you have bereft me of all
 words,
Only my blood speaks to you in my veins ;
And there is such confusion in my powers,
As after some oration fairly spoke 180
By a beloved prince, there doth appear
Among the buzzing pleased multitude ;
Where every something, being blent together,
Turns to a wild of nothing, save of joy,
Express'd and not express'd. But when this ring
Parts from this finger, then parts life from
 hence :
O, then be bold to say Bassanio's dead !
 Ner. My lord and lady, it is now our time,
That have stood by and seen our wishes
 prosper,
To cry, good joy : good joy, my lord and
 lady ! 190
 Gra. My lord Bassanio and my gentle lady,

I wish you all the joy that you can wish ;
For I am sure you can wish none from me :
And when your honors mean to solemnize
The bargain of your faith, I do beseech you,
Even at that time I may be married too.
 Bass. With all my heart, so thou canst get
 a wife.
 Gra. I thank your lordship, you have got
 me one.
My eyes, my lord, can look as swift as yours :
You saw the mistress, I beheld the maid ; 200
You loved, I loved for intermission.
No more pertains to me, my lord, than you.
Your fortune stood upon the casket there,
And so did mine too, as the matter falls ;
For wooing here until I sweat again,
And swearing till my very roof was dry
With oaths of love, at last, if promise last,
I got a promise of this fair one here
To have her love, provided that your fortune
Achieved her mistress.
 Por. Is this true, Nerissa ? 210
 Ner. Madam, it is, so you stand pleased
 withal.
 Bass. And do you, Gratiano, mean good
 faith ?
 Gra. Yes, faith, my lord.
 Bass. Our feast shall be much honor'd in
 your marriage.
 Gra. We'll play with them the first boy for
 a thousand ducats.
 Ner. What, and stake down ?
 Gra. No ; we shall ne'er win at that sport,
and stake down. 220
But who comes here ? Lorenzo and his infidel ?
What, and my old Venetian friend Salerio ?

Enter Lorenzo, Jessica, *and* Salerio, *a Messenger from Venice.*

 Bass. Lorenzo and Salerio, welcome hither ;
If that the youth of my new interest here
Have power to bid you welcome. By your
 leave,
I bid my very friends and countrymen,
Sweet Portia, welcome.
 Por. So do I, my lord :
They are entirely welcome.
 Lor. I thank your honor. For my part, my
 lord,
My purpose was not to have seen you here ;
But meeting with Salerio by the way, 231
He did entreat me, past all saying nay,
To come with him along.
 Saler. I did, my lord ;
And I have reason for it. Signior Antonio
Commends him to you.
     [*Gives Bassanio a letter.*
 Bass. Ere I ope his letter,
I pray you, tell me how my good friend doth.
 Saler. Not sick, my lord, unless it be in
 mind ;
Nor well, unless in mind : his letter there
Will show you his estate.
 Gra. Nerissa, cheer yon stranger ; bid her
 welcome. 240
Your hand, Salerio : what's the news from
 Venice ?
How doth that royal merchant, good Antonio ?
I know he will be glad of our success ;
We are the Jasons, we have won the fleece.
 Saler. I would you had won the fleece that
 he hath lost.

Por. There are some shrewd contents in
  yon same paper,
That steals the color from Bassanio's cheek :
Some dear friend dead ; else nothing in the
  world
Could turn so much the constitution   149
Of any constant man. What, worse and worse !
With leave, Bassanio : I am half yourself,
And I must freely have the half of anything
That this same paper brings you.
  Bass.   O sweet Portia,
Here are a few of the unpleasant'st words
That ever blotted paper ! Gentle lady,
When I did first impart my love to you,
I freely told you, all the wealth I had
Ran in my veins, I was a gentleman ;
And then I told you true : and yet, dear lady,
Rating myself at nothing, you shall see   260
How much I was a braggart. When I told you
My state was nothing, I should then have told
  you
That I was worse than nothing ; for, indeed,
I have engaged myself to a dear friend,
Engaged my friend to his mere enemy,
To feed my means. Here is a letter, lady ;
The paper as the body of my friend,
And every word in it a gaping wound,
Issuing life-blood. But is it true, Salerio ?
Have all his ventures fail'd ? What, not one
  hit ?   270
From Tripolis, from Mexico and England,
From Lisbon, Barbary and India ?
And not one vessel 'scape the dreadful touch
Of merchant-marring rocks ?
  Saler.   Not one, my lord.
Besides, it should appear, that if he had
The present money to discharge the Jew,
He would not take it. Never did I know
A creature, that did bear the shape of man,
So keen and greedy to confound a man :
He plies the duke at morning and at night,   279
And doth impeach the freedom of the state,
If they deny him justice : twenty merchants,
The duke himself, and the magnificoes
Of greatest port, have all persuaded with him ;
But none can drive him from the envious plea
Of forfeiture, of justice and his bond.
  Jes. When I was with him I have heard
  him swear
To Tubal and to Chus, his countrymen,
That he would rather have Antonio's flesh
Than twenty times the value of the sum
That he did owe him : and I know, my lord,
If law, authority and power deny not,   291
It will go hard with poor Antonio.
  Por. Is it your dear friend that is thus in
  trouble ?
  Bass. The dearest friend to me, the kindest
  man,
The best-condition'd and unwearied spirit
In doing courtesies, and one in whom
The ancient Roman honor more appears
Than any that draws breath in Italy.
  Por. What sum owes he the Jew ?
  Bass. For me three thousand ducats.
  Por.   What, no more ?   300
Pay him six thousand, and deface the bond ;
Double six thousand, and then treble that,
Before a friend of this description
Shall lose a hair through Bassanio's fault.
First go with me to church and call me wife,
And then away to Venice to your friend ;
For never shall you lie by Portia's side

With an unquiet soul. You shall have gold
To pay the petty debt twenty times over :
When it is paid, bring your true friend along.
My maid Nerissa and myself meantime   311
Will live as maids and widows. Come, away !
For you shall hence upon your wedding-day :
Bid your friends welcome, show a merry
  cheer :
Since you are dear bought, I will love you
  dear.
But let me hear the letter of your friend.   331
  Bass. [*Reads*] Sweet Bassanio, my ships
have all miscarried, my creditors grow cruel,
my estate is very low, my bond to the Jew is
forfeit ; and since in paying it, it is impossible
I should live, all debts are cleared between you
and I, if I might but see you at my death. Not-
withstanding, use your pleasure : if your love
do not persuade you to come, let not my letter.
  Por. O love, dispatch all business, and be
  gone !
  Bass. Since I have your good leave to go
  away,
I will make haste : but, till I come again,
No bed shall e'er be guilty of my stay,
No rest be interposer 'twixt us twain.
                                        [*Exeunt.*

SCENE III. *Venice. A street.*

Enter SHYLOCK, SALARINO, ANTONIO, *and*
  Gaoler.

  Shy. Gaoler, look to him : tell not me of
  mercy ;
This is the fool that lent out money gratis :
Gaoler, look to him.
  Ant.   Hear me yet, good Shylock.
  Shy. I'll have my bond ; speak not against
  my bond :
I have sworn an oath that I will have my bond.
Thou call'dst me dog before thou hadst a
  cause ;
But, since I am a dog, beware my fangs :
The duke shall grant me justice. I do wonder,
Thou naughty gaoler, that thou art so fond
To come abroad with him at his request.   10
  Ant. I pray thee, hear me speak.
  Shy. I'll have my bond ; I will not hear
  thee speak :
I'll have my bond ; and therefore speak no
  more.
I'll not be made a soft and dull-eyed fool,
To shake the head, relent, and sigh, and yield
To Christian intercessors. Follow not ;
I'll have no speaking : I will have my bond.
                                        [*Exit.*
  Salar. It is the most impenetrable cur
That ever kept with men.
  Ant.   Let him alone :
I'll follow him no more with bootless prayers.
He seeks my life ; his reason well I know :   21
I oft deliver'd from his forfeitures
Many that have at times made moan to me ;
Therefore he hates me.
  Salar.   I am sure the duke
Will never grant this forfeiture to hold.
  Ant. The duke cannot deny the course of
  law :
For the commodity that strangers have
With us in Venice, if it be denied,
Will much impeach the justice of his state ;
Since that the trade and profit of the city   30
Consisteth of all nations. Therefore, go :
These griefs and losses have so bated me,

That I shall hardly spare a pound of flesh
To-morrow to my bloody creditor.
Well, gaoler, on. Pray God, Bassanio come
To see me pay his debt, and then I care not !
            [*Exeunt.*

SCENE IV. *Belmont. A room in* PORTIA'S
            house.

Enter PORTIA, NERISSA, LORENZO, JESSICA, *and*
            BALTHASAR.

  Lor. Madam, although I speak it in your
        presence,
You have a noble and a true conceit
Of god-like amity ; which appears most
        strongly
In bearing thus the absence of your lord.
But if you knew to whom you show this honor,
How true a gentleman you send relief,
How dear a lover of my lord your husband,
I know you would be prouder of the work
Than customary bounty can enforce you.
  Por. I never did repent for doing good, 10
Nor shall not now : for in companions
That do converse and waste the time together,
Whose souls do bear an equal yoke of love,
There must be needs a like proportion
Of lineaments, of manners and of spirit ;
Which makes me think that this Antonio,
Being the bosom lover of my lord,
Must needs be like my lord. If it be so,
How little is the cost I have bestow'd
In purchasing the semblance of my soul 20
From out the state of hellish misery !
This comes too near the praising of myself ;
Therefore no more of it : hear other things.
Lorenzo, I commit into your hands
The husbandry and manage of my house
Until my lord's return : for mine own part,
I have toward heaven breathed a secret vow
To live in prayer and contemplation,
Only attended by Nerissa here,
Until her husband and my lord's return : 30
There is a monastery two miles off ;
And there will we abide. I do desire you
Not to deny this imposition ;
The which my love and some necessity
Now lays upon you.
  Lor.   Madam, with all my heart ;
I shall obey you in all fair commands.
  Por. My people do already know my mind,
And will acknowledge you and Jessica
In place of Lord Bassanio and myself.
And so farewell, till we shall meet again. 40
  Lor. Fair thoughts and happy hours attend
        on you !
  Jes. I wish your ladyship all heart's con-
        tent.
  Por. I thank you for your wish, and am
        well pleased
To wish it back on you : fare you well, Jessica.
            [*Exeunt Jessica and Lorenzo.*
Now, Balthasar,
As I have ever found thee honest-true,
So let me find thee still. Take this same letter,
And use thou all the endeavor of a man
In speed to Padua : see thou render this
Into my cousin's hand, Doctor Bellario ; 50
And, look, what notes and garments he doth
        give thee,
Bring them, I pray thee, with imagined speed
Unto the tranect, to the common ferry
Which trades to Venice. Waste no time in
        words,

But get thee gone : I shall be there before thee.
  Balth. Madam, I go with all convenient
        speed.   [*Exit.*
  Por. Come on, Nerissa ; I have work in
        hand
That you yet know not of : we'll see our hus-
        bands
Before they think of us.
  Ner.   Shall they see us ?
  Por. They shall, Nerissa ; but in such a
        habit,   60
That they shall think we are accomplished
With that we lack. I'll hold thee any wager,
When we are both accoutred like young men,
I'll prove the prettier fellow of the two,
And wear my dagger with the braver grace,
And speak between the change of man and boy
With a reed voice, and turn two mincing steps
Into a manly stride, and speak of frays
Like a fine bragging youth, and tell quaint lies,
How honorable ladies sought my love, 70
Which I denying, they fell sick and died ;
I could not do withal ; then I'll repent,
And wish, for all that, that I had not kill'd
        them ;
And twenty of these puny lies I'll tell,
That men shall swear I have discontinued
        school
Above a twelvemonth. I have within my mind
A thousand raw tricks of these bragging Jacks,
Which I will practise.
  Ner. Why, shall we turn to men ?
  Por. Fie, what a question's that,
If thou wert near a lewd interpreter ! 80
But come, I'll tell thee all my whole device
When I am in my coach, which stays for us
At the park gate ; and therefore haste away,
For we must measure twenty miles to-day.
            [*Exeunt.*

SCENE V. *The same. A garden.*

Enter LAUNCELOT *and* JESSICA.

  Laun. Yes, truly ; for, look you, the sins of
the father are to be laid upon the children :
therefore, I promise ye, I fear you. I was always plain with you, and so now I speak my
agitation of the matter : therefore be of good
cheer, for truly I think you are damned. There
is but one hope in it that can do you any
good ; and that is but a kind of bastard hope
neither.   9
  Jes. And what hope is that, I pray thee ?
  Laun. Marry, you may partly hope that
your father got you not, that you are not the
Jew's daughter.
  Jes. That were a kind of bastard hope, indeed : so the sins of my mother should be
visited upon me.
  Laun. Truly then I fear you are damned
both by father and mother : thus when I shun
Scylla, your father, I fall into Charybdis, your
mother : well, you are gone both ways. 20
  Jes. I shall be saved by my husband ; he
hath made me a Christian.
  Laun. Truly, the more to blame he : we
were Christians enow before ; e'en as many as
could well live, one by another. This making
of Christians will raise the price of hogs : if we
grow all to be pork-eaters, we shall not shortly
have a rasher on the coals for money.

Enter LORENZO.

  Jes. I'll tell my husband, Launcelot, what
you say : here he comes.   30

Lor. I shall grow jealous of you shortly, Launcelot, if you thus get my wife into corners.

Jes. Nay, you need not fear us, Lorenzo : Launcelot and I are out. He tells me flatly, there is no mercy for me in heaven, because I am a Jew's daughter : and he says, you are no good member of the commonwealth, for in converting Jews to Christians, you raise the price of pork. 39

Lor. I shall answer that better to the commonwealth than you can the getting up of the negro's belly : the Moor is with child by you, Launcelot.

Laun. It is much that the Moor should be more than reason : but if she be less than an honest woman, she is indeed more than I took her for.

Lor. How every fool can play upon the word ! I think the best grace of wit will shortly turn into silence, and discourse grow commendable in none only but parrots. Go in, sirrah ; bid them prepare for dinner. 52

Laun. That is done, sir ; they have all stomachs.

Lor. Goodly Lord, what a wit-snapper are you ! then bid them prepare dinner.

Laun. That is done too, sir ; only ' cover ' is the word.

Lor. Will you cover then, sir ?

Laun. Not so, sir, neither ; I know my duty. 59

Lor. Yet more quarrelling with occasion ! Wilt thou show the whole wealth of thy wit in an instant ? I pray thee, understand a plain man in his plain meaning : go to thy fellows ; bid them cover the table, serve in the meat, and we will come in to dinner.

Laun. For the table, sir, it shall be served in ; for the meat, sir, it shall be covered ; for your coming in to dinner, sir, why, let it be as humors and conceits shall govern.   [*Exit.*

Lor. O dear discretion, how his words are suited ! 70
The fool hath planted in his memory
An army of good words ; and I do know
A many fools, that stand in better place,
Garnish'd like him, that for a tricksy word
Defy the matter. How cheer'st thou, Jessica ?
And now, good sweet, say thy opinion,
How dost thou like the Lord Bassanio's wife ?

Jes. Past all expressing. It is very meet
The Lord Bassanio live an upright life ;
For, having such a blessing in his lady, 80
He finds the joys of heaven here on earth ;
And if on earth he do not mean it, then
In reason he should never come to heaven.
Why, if two gods should play some heavenly match
And on the wager lay two earthly women,
And Portia one, there must be something else
Pawn'd with the other, for the poor rude world
Hath not her fellow.

Lor.   Even such a husband
Hast thou of me as she is for a wife. 89

Jes. Nay, but ask my opinion too of that.

Lor. I will anon : first, let us go to dinner.

Jes. Nay, let me praise you while I have a stomach.

Lor. No, pray thee, let it serve for tabletalk ;
Then, howso'er thou speak'st, 'mong other things

I shall digest it.

Jes.   Well, I'll set you forth. [*Exeunt.*

ACT IV.

SCENE I. *Venice. A court of justice.*

Enter the DUKE, *the* Magnificoes, ANTONIO, BASSANIO, GRATIANO, SALERIO, *and others.*

Duke. What, is Antonio here ?

Ant. Ready, so please your grace.

Duke. I am sorry for thee : thou art come to answer
A stony adversary, an inhuman wretch
Uncapable of pity, void and empty
From any dram of mercy.

Ant.   I have heard
Your grace hath ta'en great pains to qualify
His rigorous course ; but since he stands obdurate
And that no lawful means can carry me
Out of his envy's reach, I do oppose 10
My patience to his fury, and am arm'd
To suffer, with a quietness of spirit,
The very tyranny and rage of his.

Duke. Go one, and call the Jew into the court.

Saler. He is ready at the door : he comes, my lord.

Enter SHYLOCK.

Duke. Make room, and let him stand before our face.
Shylock, the world thinks, and I think so too,
That thou but lead'st this fashion of thy malice
To the last hour of act ; and then 'tis thought
Thou'lt show thy mercy and remorse more strange 20
Than is thy strange apparent cruelty ;
And where thou now exact'st the penalty,
Which is a pound of this poor merchant's flesh,
Thou wilt not only loose the forfeiture,
But, touch'd with human gentleness and love,
Forgive a moiety of the principal ;
Glancing an eye of pity on his losses,
That have of late so huddled on his back,
Enow to press a royal merchant down
And pluck commiseration of his state 30
From brassy bosoms and rough hearts of flint,
From stubborn Turks and Tartars, never train'd
To offices of tender courtesy.
We all expect a gentle answer, Jew.

Shy. I have possess'd your grace of what I purpose ;
And by our holy Sabbath have I sworn
To have the due and forfeit of my bond :
If you deny it, let the danger light
Upon your charter and your city's freedom.
You'll ask me, why I rather choose to have 40
A weight of carrion flesh than to receive
Three thousand ducats : I'll not answer that :
But, say, it is my humor : is it answer'd ?
What if my house be troubled with a rat
And I be pleased to give ten thousand ducats
To have it baned ? What, are you answer'd yet ?
Some men there are love not a gaping pig ;
Some, that are mad if they behold a cat ;
And others, when the bagpipe sings i' the nose,
Cannot contain their urine : for affection, 50

Mistress of passion, sways it to the mood
Of what it likes or loathes. Now, for your
　　answer :
As there is no firm reason to be render'd,
Why he cannot abide a gaping pig ;
Why he, a harmless necessary cat ;
Why he, a woollen bagpipe ; but of force
Must yield to such inevitable shame
As to offend, himself being offended ;
So can I give no reason, nor I will not,
More than a lodged hate and a certain loathing
I bear Antonio, that I follow thus　　61
A losing suit against him. Are you answer'd ?
　　Bass. This is no answer, thou unfeeling
　　　　man,
To excuse the current of thy cruelty.
　　Shy. I am not bound to please thee with
　　　　my answers.
　　Bass. Do all men kill the things they do not
　　　　love ?
　　Shy. Hates any man the thing he would
　　　　not kill ?
　　Bass. Every offence is not a hate at first.
　　Shy. What, wouldst thou have a serpent
　　　　sting thee twice ?
　　Ant. I pray you, think you question with
　　　　the Jew :　　70
You may as well go stand upon the beach
And bid the main flood bate his usual height ;
You may as well use question with the wolf
Why he hath made the ewe bleat for the lamb ;
You may as well forbid the mountain pines
To wag their high tops and to make no noise,
When they are fretten with the gusts of
　　heaven ;
You may as well do anything most hard,
As seek to soften that—than which what's
　　harder ?—　　79
His Jewish heart : therefore, I do beseech you,
Make no more offers, use no farther means,
But with all brief and plain conveniency
Let me have judgment and the Jew his will.
　　Bass. For thy three thousand ducats here
　　　　is six.
　　Shy. What judgment shall I dread, doing
Were in six parts and every part a ducat,
I would not draw them ; I would have my
　　bond.
　　Duke. How shalt thou hope for mercy,
　　　　rendering none ?
　　Shy. What judgment shall I dread, doing
　　　　no wrong ?
You have among you many a purchased slave,
Which, like your asses and your dogs and
　　mules,　　91
You use in abject and in slavish parts,
Because you bought them : shall I say to you,
Let them be free, marry them to your heirs ?
Why sweat they under burthens ? let their beds
Be made as soft as yours and let their palates
Be season'd with such viands ? You will an-
　　swer
The slaves are ours : ' so do I answer you :
The pound of flesh, which I demand of him,
Is dearly bought ; 'tis mine and I will have it.
If you deny me, fie upon your law !　　101
There is no force in the decrees of Venice.
　　stand for judgment : answer ; shall I have
　　　　it ?
　　Duke. Upon my power I may dismiss this
　　　　court,
Unless Bellario, a learned doctor,
Whom I have sent for to determine this,

Come here to-day.
　　Saler.　　My lord, here stays without
A messenger with letters from the doctor,
New come from Padua.
　　Duke. Bring us the letter ; call the mes-
　　　　senger.　　110
　　Bass. Good cheer, Antonio ! What, man,
　　　　courage yet !
The Jew shall have my flesh, blood, bones and
　　all,
Ere thou shalt lose for me one drop of blood.
　　Ant. I am a tainted wether of the flock,
Meetest for death : the weakest kind of fruit
Drops earliest to the ground ; and so let me :
You cannot better be employ'd, Bassanio,
Than to live still and write mine epitaph.

Enter Nerissa, *dressed like a lawyer's clerk.*

　　Duke. Came you from Padua, from Bel-
　　　　lario ?
　　Ner. From both, my lord. Bellario greets
　　　　your grace. [*Presenting a letter.*　120
　　Bass. Why dost thou whet thy knife so
　　　　earnestly ?
　　Shy. To cut the forfeiture from that bank-
　　　　rupt there.
　　Gra. Not on thy sole, but on thy soul,
　　　　harsh Jew,
Thou makest thy knife keen ; but no metal
　　can,
No, not the hangman's axe, bear half the keen-
　　ness
Of thy sharp envy. Can no prayers pierce
　　thee ?
　　Shy. No, none that thou hast wit enough
　　　　to make.
　　Gra. O, be thou damn'd, inexecrable dog !
And for thy life let justice be accused.
Thou almost makest me waver in my faith 130
To hold opinion with Pythagoras,
That souls of animals infuse themselves
Into the trunks of men : thy currish spirit
Govern'd a wolf, who, hang'd for human
　　slaughter,
Even from the gallows did his fell soul fleet,
And, whilst thou lay'st in thy unhallow'd dam,
Infused itself in thee ; for thy desires
Are wolvish, bloody, starved and ravenous.
　　Shy. Till thou canst rail the seal from off
　　my bond,
Thou but offend'st thy lungs to speak so loud :
Repair thy wit, good youth, or it will fall　141
To cureless ruin. I stand here for law.
　　Duke. This letter from Bellario doth com-
　　　　mend
A young and learned doctor to our court.
Where is he ?
　　Ner.　　He attendeth here hard by,
To know your answer, whether you'll admit
　　him.
　　Duke. With all my heart. Some three or
　　　　four of you
Go give him courteous conduct to this place.
Meantime the court shall hear Bellario's letter.
　　Clerk. [*Reads*] Your grace shall understand that at the receipt of your letter I am
very sick : but in the instant that your messenger came, in loving visitation was with me
a young doctor of Rome ; his name is Balthasar. I acquainted him with the cause in
controversy between the Jew and Antonio the
merchant : we turned o'er many books together : he is furnished with my opinion ;

which, bettered with his own learning, the greatness whereof I cannot enough commend, comes with him, at my importunity, to fill up your grace's request in my stead. I beseech you, let his lack of years be no impediment to let him lack a reverend estimation; for I never knew so young a body with so old a head. I leave him to your gracious acceptance, whose trial shall better publish his commendation.

Duke. You hear the learn'd Bellario, what he writes:
And here, I take it, is the doctor come.

Enter PORTIA, *dressed like a doctor of laws.*

Give me your hand. Come you from old Bellario?
Por. I did, my lord.
Duke. You are welcome: take your place.
Are you acquainted with the difference   171
That holds this present question in the court?
Por. I am informed thoroughly of the cause.
Which is the merchant here, and which the Jew?
Duke. Antonio and old Shylock, both stand forth.
Por. Is your name Shylock?
Shy.   Shylock is my name.
Por. Of a strange nature is the suit you follow;
Yet in such rule that the Venetian law
Cannot impugn you as you do proceed.
You stand within his danger, do you not? 180
Ant. Ay, so he says.
Por.   Do you confess the bond?
Ant. I do.
Por.   Then must the Jew be merciful.
Shy. On what compulsion must I? tell me that.
Por. The quality of mercy is not strain'd,
It droppeth as the gentle rain from heaven
Upon the place beneath: it is twice blest;
It blesseth him that gives and him that takes:
'Tis mightiest in the mightiest: it becomes
The throned monarch better than his crown;
His sceptre shows the force of temporal power,
The attribute to awe and majesty,   191
Wherein doth sit the dread and fear of kings;
But mercy is above this sceptred sway;
It is enthroned in the hearts of kings,
It is an attribute to God himself;
And earthly power doth then show likest God's
When mercy seasons justice. Therefore, Jew,
Though justice be thy plea, consider this,
That, in the course of justice, none of us
Should see salvation: we do pray for mercy;
And that same prayer doth teach us all to render   201
The deeds of mercy. I have spoke thus much
To mitigate the justice of thy plea;
Which if thou follow, this strict court of Venice
Must needs give sentence 'gainst the merchant there.
Shy. My deeds upon my head! I crave the law,
The penalty and forfeit of my bond.
Por. Is he not able to discharge the money?
Bass. Yes, here I tender it for him in the court;
Yea, twice the sum: if that will not suffice,

I will be bound to pay it ten times o'er,   211
On forfeit of my hands, my head, my heart:
If this will not suffice, it must appear
That malice bears down truth. And I beseech you,
Wrest once the law to your authority:
To do a great right, do a little wrong,
And curb this cruel devil of his will.
Por. It must not be; there is no power in Venice
Can alter a decree established:
'Twill be recorded for a precedent,   220
And many an error by the same example
Will rush into the state: it cannot be.
Shy. A Daniel come to judgment! yea, a Daniel!
O wise young judge, how I do honor thee!
Por. I pray you, let me look upon the bond.
Shy. Here 'tis, most reverend doctor, here it is.
Por. Shylock, there's thrice thy money offer'd thee.
Shy. An oath, an oath, I have an oath in heaven:
Shall I lay perjury upon my soul?
No, not for Venice.
Por.   Why, this bond is forfeit; 230
And lawfully by this the Jew may claim
A pound of flesh, to be by him cut off
Nearest the merchant's heart. Be merciful:
Take thrice thy money; bid me tear the bond.
Shy. When it is paid according to the tenor.
It doth appear you are a worthy judge;
You know the law, your exposition
Hath been most sound: I charge you by the law,
Whereof you are a well-deserving pillar,
Proceed to judgment: by my soul I swear 240
There is no power in the tongue of man
To alter me: I stay here on my bond.
Ant. Most heartily I do beseech the court
To give the judgment.
Por.   Why then, thus it is:
You must prepare your bosom for his knife.
Shy. O noble judge! O excellent young man!
Por. For the intent and purpose of the law
Hath full relation to the penalty,
Which here appeareth due upon the bond.
Shy. 'Tis very true: O wise and upright judge!   250
How much more elder art thou than thy looks!
Por. Therefore lay bare your bosom.
Shy.   Ay, his breast:
So says the bond: doth it not, noble judge?
'Nearest his heart:' those are the very words.
Por. It is so. Are there balance here to weigh
The flesh?
Shy. I have them ready.
Por. Have by some surgeon, Shylock, on your charge,
To stop his wounds, lest he do bleed to death.
Shy. Is it so nominated in the bond?
Por. It is not so express'd: but what of that?
'Twere good you do so much for charity. 261
Shy. I cannot find it; 'tis not in the bond.
Por. You, merchant, have you any thing to say?

Ant. But little : I am arm'd and well pre-
pared.
Give me your hand, Bassanio : fare you well !
Grieve not that I am fallen to this for you ;
For herein Fortune shows herself more kind
Than is her custom : it is still her use
To let the wretched man outlive his wealth,
To view with hollow eye and wrinkled brow
An age of poverty ; from which lingering
     penance
Of such misery doth she cut me off.
Commend me to your honorable wife :
Tell her the process of Antonio's end ;
Say how I loved you, speak me fair in death ;
And, when the tale is told, bid her be judge
Whether Bassanio had not once a love.
Repent but you that you shall lose your friend,
And he repents not that he pays your debt ;
For if the Jew do cut but deep enough,   280
I'll pay it presently with all my heart.
Bass. Antonio, I am married to a wife
Which is as dear to me as life itself ;
But life itself, my wife, and all the world,
Are not with me esteem'd above thy life :
I would lose all, ay, sacrifice them all
Here to this devil, to deliver you.
Por. Your wife would give you little thanks
     for that,
If she were by, to hear you make the offer.
Gra. I have a wife, whom, I protest, I
     love :   290
I would she were in heaven, so she could
Entreat some power to change this currish
     Jew.
Ner. 'Tis well you offer it behind her
     back ;
The wish would make else an unquiet house.
Shy. These be the Christian husbands. I
     have a daughter ;
Would any of the stock of Barrabas
Had been her husband rather than a Chris-
     tian !   [*Aside.*
We trifle time : I pray thee, pursue sentence.
Por. A pound of that same merchant's
     flesh is thine :
The court awards it, and the law doth give it.
Shy. Most rightful judge !   301
Por. And you must cut this flesh from off
     his breast :
The law allows it, and the court awards it.
Shy. Most learned judge ! A sentence !
     Come, prepare !
Por. Tarry a little ; there is something else.
This bond doth give thee here no jot of blood;
The words expressly are ' a pound of flesh : '
Take then thy bond, take thou thy pound of
     flesh ;
But, in the cutting it, if thou dost shed
One drop of Christian blood, thy lands and
     goods   310
Are, by the laws of Venice, confiscate
Unto the state of Venice.
Gra. O upright judge ! Mark, Jew : O
     learned judge !
Shy. Is that the law ?
Por.   Thyself shalt see the act :
For, as thou urgest justice, be assured
Thou shalt have justice, more than thou
     desirest.
Gra. O learned judge ! Mark, Jew : a
     learned judge !
Shy. I take this offer, then ; pay the bond
     thrice

And let the Christian go.
Bass.   Here is the money.
Por. Soft !   320
The Jew shall have all justice ; soft ! no haste :
He shall have nothing but the penalty.
Gra. O Jew ! an upright judge, a learned
     judge !
Por. Therefore prepare thee to cut off the
     flesh.
Shed thou no blood, nor cut thou less nor more
But just a pound of flesh : if thou cut'st more
Or less than a just pound, be it but so much
As makes it light or heavy in the substance,
Or the division of the twentieth part
Of one poor scruple, nay, if the scale do turn
But in the estimation of a hair,   331
Thou diest and all thy goods are confiscate.
Gra. A second Daniel, a Daniel, Jew !
Now, infidel, I have you on the hip.
Por. Why doth the Jew pause ? take thy
     forfeiture.
Shy. Give me my principal, and let me go.
Bass. I have it ready for thee ; here it is.
Por. He hath refused it in the open court :
He shall have merely justice and his bond.
Gra. A Daniel, still say I, a second Daniel !
I thank thee, Jew, for teaching me that word.
Shy. Shall I not have barely my principal ?
Por. Thou shalt have nothing but the
     forfeiture,
To be so taken at thy peril, Jew.
Shy. Why, then the devil give him good
     of it !
I'll stay no longer question.
Por.   Tarry, Jew :
The law hath yet another hold on you.
It is enacted in the laws of Venice,
If it be proved against an alien
That by direct or indirect attempts   350
He seek the life of any citizen,
The party 'gainst the which he doth contrive
Shall seize one half his goods ; the other half
Comes to the privy coffer of the state ;
And the offender's life lies in the mercy
Of the duke only, 'gainst all other voice.
In which predicament, I say, thou stand'st ;
For it appears, by manifest proceeding,
That indirectly and directly too
Thou hast contrived against the very life   360
Of the defendant ; and thou hast incurr'd
The danger formerly by me rehearsed.
Down therefore and beg mercy of the duke.
Gra. Beg that thou mayst have leave to
     hang thyself :
And yet, thy wealth being forfeit to the state,
Thou hast not left the value of a cord ;
Therefore thou must be hang'd at the state's
     charge.
Duke. That thou shalt see the difference of
     our spirits,
I pardon thee thy life before thou ask it :
For half thy wealth, it is Antonio's ;   370
The other half comes to the general state,
Which humbleness may drive unto a fine.
Por. Ay, for the state, not for Antonio.
Shy. Nay, take my life and all ; pardon
     not that :
You take my house when you do take the
     prop
That doth sustain my house ; you take my
     life
When you do take the means whereby I live.

Por. What mercy can you render him,
Antonio?
Gra. A halter gratis; nothing else, for
God's sake.
Ant. So please my lord the duke and all
the court   380
To quit the fine for one half of his goods,
I am content; so he will let me have
The other half in use, to render it,
Upon his death, unto the gentleman
That lately stole his daughter:
Two things provided more, that, for this
favor,
He presently become a Christian;
The other, that he do record a gift,
Here in the court, of all he dies possess'd,
Unto his son Lorenzo and his daughter.   390
Duke. He shall do this, or else I do recant
The pardon that I late pronounced here.
Por. Art thou contented, Jew? what dost
thou say?
Shy. I am content.
Por.   Clerk, draw a deed of gift.
Shy. I pray you, give me leave to go from
hence;
I am not well: send the deed after me,
And I will sign it.
Duke.   Get thee gone, but do it.
Gra. In christening shalt thou have two
god-fathers:
Had I been judge, thou shouldst have had ten
more,
To bring thee to the gallows, not the font. 400
                            [*Exit Shylock.*
Duke. Sir, I entreat you home with me to
dinner.
Por. I humbly do desire your grace of
pardon:
I must away this night toward Padua,
And it is meet I presently set forth.
Duke. I am sorry that your leisure serves
you not.
Antonio, gratify this gentleman,
For, in my mind, you are much bound to him.
                   [*Exeunt Duke and his train.*
Bass. Most worthy gentleman, I and my
friend
Have by your wisdom been this day acquitted
Of grievous penalties; in lieu whereof,   410
Three thousand ducats, due unto the Jew,
We freely cope your courteous pains withal.
Ant. And stand indebted, over and above,
In love and service to you evermore.
Por. He is well paid that is well satisfied;
And I, delivering you, am satisfied
And therein do account myself well paid:
My mind was never yet more mercenary.
I pray you, know me when we meet again:
I wish you well, and so I take my leave.   420
Bass. Dear sir, of force I must attempt you
further:
Take some remembrance of us, as a tribute,
Not as a fee: grant me two things, I pray you,
Not to deny me, and to pardon me.
Por. You press me far, and therefore I will
yield.
[*To Ant.*] Give me your gloves, I'll wear them
for your sake;
[*To Bass.*] And, for your love, I'll take this
ring from you:
Do not draw back your hand; I'll take no
more;
And you in love shall not deny me this.

Bass. This ring, good sir, alas, it is a trifle!
I will not shame myself to give you this.   431
Por. I will have nothing else but only this;
And now methinks I have a mind to it.
Bass. There's more depends on this than
on the value.
The dearest ring in Venice will I give you,
And find it out by proclamation:
Only for this, I pray you, pardon me.
Por. I see, sir, you are liberal in offers:
You taught me first to beg; and now me-
thinks
You teach me how a beggar should be
answer'd.
Bass. Good sir, this ring was given me by
my wife;   441
And when she put it on, she made me vow
That I should neither sell nor give nor lose it.
Por. That 'scuse serves many men to save
their gifts.
An if your wife be not a mad-woman,
And know how well I have deserved the ring,
She would not hold out enemy for ever,
For giving it to me. Well, peace be with you!
                        [*Exeunt Portia and Nerissa.*
Ant. My Lord Bassanio, let him have the
ring:
Let his deservings and my love withal   450
Be valued 'gainst your wife's commandment.
Bass. Go, Gratiano, run and overtake him;
Give him the ring, and bring him, if thou
canst,
Unto Antonio's house: away! make haste.
                            [*Exit Gratiano.*
Come, you and I will thither presently;
And in the morning early will we both
Fly toward Belmont: come, Antonio. [*Exeunt.*

SCENE II. *The same. A street.*

Enter PORTIA *and* NERISSA.

Por. Inquire the Jew's house out, give him
this deed
And let him sign it: we'll away to-night
And be a day before our husbands home:
This deed will be well welcome to Lorenzo.

Enter GRATIANO.

Gra. Fair sir, you are well o'erta'en
My Lord Bassanio upon more advice
Hath sent you here this ring, and doth entreat
Your company at dinner.
Por.   That cannot be:
His ring I do accept most thankfully:
And so, I pray you, tell him: furthermore, 10
I pray you, show my youth old Shylock's
house.
Gra. That will I do.
Ner.   Sir, I would speak with you.
[*Aside to Por.*] I'll see if I can get my hus-
band's ring,
Which I did make him swear to keep for ever.
Por. [*Aside to Ner.*] Thou mayst, I war-
rant. We shall have old swearing
That they did give the rings away to men;
But we'll outface them, and outswear them
too.
[*Aloud*] Away! make haste: thou know'st
where I will tarry.
Ner. Come, good sir, will you show me to
this house?   [*Exeunt.*

ACT V.

SCENE I. *Belmont. Avenue to* PORTIA'S
house.

Enter LORENZO *and* JESSICA.

Lor. The moon shines bright : in such a
  night as this,
When the sweet wind did gently kiss the trees
And they did make no noise, in such a night
Troilus methinks mounted the Troyan walls
And sigh'd his soul toward the Grecian tents,
Where Cressid lay that night.
Jes.   In such a night
Did Thisbe fearfully o'ertrip the dew
And saw the lion's shadow ere himself
And ran dismay'd away.
Lor.   In such a night
Stood Dido with a willow in her hand 10
Upon the wild sea banks and waft her love
To come again to Carthage.
Jes.   In such a night
Medea gather'd the enchanted herbs
That did renew old Æson.
Lor.   In such a night
Did Jessica steal from the wealthy Jew
And with an unthrift love did run from Venice
As far as Belmont.
Jes.   In such a night
Did young Lorenzo swear he loved her well,
Stealing her soul with many vows of faith
And ne'er a true one.
Lor.   In such a night 20
Did pretty Jessica, like a little shrew,
Slander her love, and he forgave it her.
Jes. I would out-night you, did no body
  come ;
But, hark, I hear the footing of a man.

Enter STEPHANO.

Lor. Who comes so fast in silence of the
  night ?
Steph. A friend.
Lor. A friend ! what friend ? your name,
  I pray you, friend ?
Steph. Stephano is my name ; and I bring
  word
My mistress will before the break of day
Be here at Belmont ; she doth stray about 30
By holy crosses, where she kneels and prays
For happy wedlock hours.
Lor.   Who comes with her ?
Steph. None but a holy hermit and her
  maid.
I pray you, is my master yet return'd ?
Lor. He is not, nor we have not heard
  from him.
But go we in, I pray thee, Jessica,
And ceremoniously let us prepare
Some welcome for the mistress of the house.

Enter LAUNCELOT.

Laun. Sola, sola ! wo ha, ho ! sola, sola !
Lor. Who calls ? 40
Laun. Sola ! did you see Master Lorenzo ?
Master Lorenzo, sola, sola !
Lor. Leave holloaing, man : here.
Laun. Sola ! where ? where ?
Lor. Here.
Laun. Tell him there's a post come from
my master, with his horn full of good news :
my master will be here ere morning. [*Exit.*

Lor. Sweet soul, let's in, and there expect
  their coming.
And yet no matter : why should we go in ? 50
My friend Stephano, signify, I pray you,
Within the house, your mistress is at hand ;
And bring your music forth into the air.
        [*Exit Stephano.*
How sweet the moonlight sleeps upon this
  bank !
Here will we sit and let the sounds of music
Creep in our ears : soft stillness and the night
Become the touches of sweet harmony.
Sit, Jessica. Look how the floor of heaven
Is thick inlaid with patines of bright gold :
There's not the smallest orb which thou be-
  hold'st 60
But in his motion like an angel sings,
Still quiring to the young-eyed cherubins ;
Such harmony is in immortal souls ;
But whilst this muddy vesture of decay
Doth grossly close it in, we cannot hear it.

Enter Musicians.

Come, ho ! and wake Diana with a hymn !
With sweetest touches pierce your mistress'
  ear,
And draw her home with music. [*Music.*
Jes. I am never merry when I hear sweet
  music.
Lor. The reason is, your spirits are atten-
  tive : 70
For do but note a wild and wanton herd,
Or race of youthful and unhandled colts,
Fetching mad bounds, bellowing and neighing
  loud,
Which is the hot condition of their blood ;
If they but hear perchance a trumpet sound,
Or any air of music touch their ears,
You shall perceive them make a mutual stand,
Their savage eyes turn'd to a modest gaze
By the sweet power of music : therefore the
  poet
Did feign that Orpheus drew trees, stones and
  floods ; 80
Since nought so stockish, hard and full of
  rage,
But music for the time doth change his nature.
The man that hath no music in himself,
Nor is not moved with concord of sweet
  sounds,
Is fit for treasons, stratagems and spoils ;
The motions of his spirit are dull as night
And his affections dark as Erebus :
Let no such man be trusted. Mark the music.

Enter PORTIA *and* NERISSA.

Por. That light we see is burning in my
  hall.
How far that little candle throws his beams !
So shines a good deed in a naughty world. 91
Ner. When the moon shone, we did not see
  the candle.
Por. So doth the greater glory dim the
  less :
A substitute shines brightly as a king
Unto the king be by, and then his state
Empties itself, as doth an inland brook
Into the main of waters. Music ! hark !
Ner. It is your music, madam, of the house.
Por. Nothing is good, I see, without re-
  spect :
Methinks it sounds much sweeter than by day.

Ner. Silence bestows that virtue on it,
  madam.   101
Por. The crow doth sing as sweetly as the
  lark,
When neither is attended, and I think
The nightingale, if she should sing by day,
When every goose is cackling, would be
  thought
No better a musician than the wren.
How many things by season season'd are
To their right praise and true perfection!
Peace, ho! the moon sleeps with Endymion
And would not be awaked.   [*Music ceases.*
Lor.   That is the voice, 110
Or I am much deceived, of Portia.
Por. He knows me as the blind man knows
  the cuckoo,
By the bad voice.
Lor.   Dear lady, welcome home.
Por. We have been praying for our hus-
  bands' healths,
Which speed, we hope, the better for our
  words.
Are they return'd?
Lor.   Madam, they are not yet;
But there is come a messenger before,
To signify their coming.
Por.   Go in, Nerissa;
Give order to my servants that they take
No note at all of our being absent hence; 120
Nor you, Lorenzo; Jessica, nor you.
                [*A tucket sounds.*
Lor. Your husband is at hand; I hear his
  trumpet:
We are no tell-tales, madam; fear you not.
Por. This night methinks is but the day-
  light sick;
It looks a little paler: 'tis a day,
Such as the day is when the sun is hid.

Enter BASSANIO, ANTONIO, GRATIANO, *and
    their followers.*

Bass. We should hold day with the Antip-
  odes,
If you would walk in absence of the sun.
Por. Let me give light, but let me not be
  light;
For a light wife doth make a heavy husband,
And never be Bassanio so for me: 131
But God sort all! You are welcome home, my
  lord.
Bass. I thank you, madam. Give welcome
  to my friend.
This is the man, this is Antonio,
To whom I am so infinitely bound.
Por. You should in all sense be much
  bound to him,
For, as I hear, he was much bound for you.
Ant. No more than I am well acquitted of.
Por. Sir, you are very welcome to our
  house:
It must appear in other ways than words, 140
Therefore I scant this breathing courtesy.
Gra. [*To Ner.*] By yonder moon I swear
  you do me wrong;
In faith, I gave it to the judge's clerk:
Would he were gelt that had it, for my part,
Since you do take it, love, so much at heart.
Por. A quarrel, ho, already! what's the
  matter?
Gra. About a hoop of gold, a paltry ring
That she did give me, whose posy was
For all the world like cutler's poetry

Upon a knife, 'Love me, and leave me not.'
Ner. What talk you of the posy or the
  value?   151
You swore to me, when I did give it you,
That you would wear it till your hour of death
And that it should lie with you in your grave:
Though not for me, yet for your vehement
  oaths,
You should have been respective and have
  kept it.
Gave it a judge's clerk! no, God's my judge,
The clerk will ne'er wear hair on's face that
  had it.
Gra. He will, an if he live to be a man.
Ner. Ay, if a woman live to be a man. 160
Gra. Now, by this hand, I gave it to a
  youth,
A kind of boy, a little scrubbed boy,
No higher than thyself, the judge's clerk,
A prating boy, that begg'd it as a fee:
I could not for my heart deny it him.
Por. You were to blame, I must be plain
  with you,
To part so slightly with your wife's first gift:
A thing stuck on with oaths upon your finger
And so riveted with faith unto your flesh.
I gave my love a ring and made him swear 170
Never to part with it; and here he stands;
I dare be sworn for him he would not leave it
Nor pluck it from his finger, for the wealth
That the world masters. Now, in faith, Gra-
  tiano,
You give your wife too unkind a cause of
  grief:
An 'twere to me, I should be mad at it.
Bass. [*Aside*] Why, I were best to cut my
  left hand off
And swear I lost the ring defending it.
Gra. My Lord Bassanio gave his ring away
Unto the judge that begg'd it and indeed 180
Deserved it too; and then the boy, his clerk,
That took some pains in writing, he begg'd
  mine;
And neither man nor master would take aught
But the two rings.
Por.   What ring gave you, my lord?
Not that, I hope, which you received of me.
Bass. If I could add a lie unto a fault,
I would deny it; but you see my finger
Hath not the ring upon it; it is gone.
Por. Even so void is your false heart of
  truth.
By heaven, I will ne'er come in your bed 190
Until I see the ring.
Ner.   Nor I in yours
Till I again see mine.
Bass.   Sweet Portia,
If you did know to whom I gave the ring,
If you did know for whom I gave the ring
And would conceive for what I gave the ring
And how unwillingly I left the ring,
When nought would be accepted but the ring,
You would abate the strength of your dis-
  pleasure.
Por. If you had known the virtue of the
  ring,
Or half her worthiness that gave the ring, 200
Or your own honor to contain the ring,
You would not then have parted with the
  ring.
What man is there so much unreasonable,
If you had pleased to have defended it
With any terms of zeal, wanted the modesty

To urge the thing held as a ceremony?
Nerissa teaches me what to believe:
I'll die for't but some woman had the ring.
  Bass. No, by my honor, madam, by my
    soul,
No woman had it, but a civil doctor,   210
Which did refuse three thousand ducats of me
And begg'd the ring; the which I did deny
  him
And suffer'd him to go displeased away;
Even he that did uphold the very life
Of my dear friend. What should I say, sweet
  lady?
I was enforced to send it after him;
I was beset with shame and courtesy;
My honor would not let ingratitude
So much besmear it. Pardon me, good lady;
For, by these blessed candles of the night, 220
Had you been there, I think you would have
  begg'd
The ring of me to give the worthy doctor.
  Por. Let not that doctor e'er come near my
    house:
Since he hath got the jewel that I loved,
And that which you did swear to keep for me,
I will become as liberal as you;
I'll not deny him any thing I have,
No, not my body nor my husband's bed:
Know him I shall, I am well sure of it:
Lie not a night from home; watch me like
  Argus: 230
If you do not, if I be left alone,
Now, by mine honor, which is yet mine own,
I'll have that doctor for my bedfellow.
  Ner. And I his clerk; therefore be well
    advised
How you do leave me to mine own protection.
  Gra. Well, do you so; let not me take
    him, then;
For if I do, I'll mar the young clerk's pen.
  Ant. I am the unhappy subject of these
    quarrels.
  Por. Sir, grieve not you; you are welcome
    notwithstanding.
  Bass. Portia, forgive me this enforced
    wrong;   240
And, in the hearing of these many friends,
I swear to thee, even by thine own fair eyes,
Wherein I see myself—
  Por.   Mark you but that!
In both my eyes he doubly sees himself;
In each eye, one: swear by your double self,
And there's an oath of credit.
  Bass.   Nay, but hear me:
Pardon this fault, and by my soul I swear
I never more will break an oath with thee.
  Ant. I once did lend my body for his
    wealth;
Which, but for him that had your husband's
  ring,
Had quite miscarried: I dare be bound again,
My soul upon the forfeit, that your lord
Will never more break faith advisedly.
  Por. Then you shall be his surety. Give
    him this
And bid him keep it better than the other.
  Ant. Here, Lord Bassanio; swear to keep
    this ring.
  Bass. By heaven, it is the same I gave the
    doctor!

  Por. I had it of him: pardon me, Bassanio;
For, by this ring, the doctor lay with me. 259
  Ner. And pardon me, my gentle Gratiano;
For that same scrubbed boy, the doctor's
  clerk,
In lieu of this last night did lie with me.
  Gra. Why, this is like the mending of high-
    ways
In summer, where the ways are fair enough:
What, are we cuckolds ere we have deserved
  it?
  Por. Speak not so grossly. You are all
    amazed:
Here is a letter; read it at your leisure;
It comes from Padua, from Bellario:
There you shall find that Portia was the doc-
  tor,
Nerissa there her clerk: Lorenzo here   270
Shall witness I set forth as soon as you
And even but now return'd; I have not yet
Enter'd my house. Antonio, you are welcome;
And I have better news in store for you
Than you expect: unseal this letter soon;
There you shall find three of your argosies
Are richly come to harbor suddenly:
You shall not know by what strange accident
I chanced on this letter.
  Ant.   I am dumb.
  Bass. Were you the doctor and I knew
    you not?   280
  Gra. Were you the clerk that is to make
    me cuckold?
  Ner. Ay, but the clerk that never means
    to do it,
Unless he live until he be a man.
  Bass. Sweet doctor, you shall be my bed-
    fellow:
When I am absent, then lie with my wife.
  Ant. Sweet lady, you have given me life
    and living;
For here I read for certain that my ships
Are safely come to road.
  Por.   How now, Lorenzo!
My clerk hath some good comforts too for
  you.
  Ner. Ay, and I'll give them him without a
    fee.   290
There do I give to you and Jessica,
From the rich Jew, a special deed of gift,
After his death, of all he dies possess'd of.
  Lor. Fair ladies, you drop manna in the
    way
Of starved people.
  Por.   It is almost morning,
And yet I am sure you are not satisfied
Of these events at full. Let us go in;
And charge us there upon inter'gatories,
And we will answer all things faithfully.
  Gra. Let it be so: the first inter'gatory
That my Nerissa shall be sworn on is,   301
Whether till the next night she had rather
  stay,
Or go to bed now, being two hours to day:
But were the day come, I should wish it dark,
That I were couching with the doctor's clerk.
Well, while I live I'll fear no other thing
So sore as keeping safe Nerissa's ring.
                      [Exeunt.

KING HENRY IV. PART I.

(WRITTEN ABOUT 1597–98.)

INTRODUCTION.

The two parts of *King Henry IV.* may be considered as one play in ten acts. It is probable that Shakespeare went on with little or no delay from the first part to its continuation in the second. Both were written before the entry of the first in the Stationers' register, Feb. 25, 1597–98 ; for the entry shows that the name of the fat knight, who originally appeared in both parts under the name of Oldcastle, had been already altered to Falstaff. Meres makes mention of *Henry IV. ;* and Ben Jonson, in *Every Man Out of His Humour* (1599), alludes to Justice Silence, one of the characters of the Second Part of Shakespeare's play. The materials upon which Shakespeare worked in *Henry IV.* and *Henry V.* were obtained from Holinshed, and from an old play, full of vulgar mirth, and acted before 1588, *The Famous Victories of Henry V.* Both parts of *Henry IV.* consist of a comedy and a history fused together. The hero of the one is the royal Bolingbroke, the hero of the other is Falstaff, while Prince Henry passes to and fro between the history and the comedy, serving as the bond which unites the two. Henry IV. is the same Bolingbroke who had been so greatly conceived in *Richard II. ;* only he is no longer in the full force of his manhood. He is worn by care and toil, harassed by revolts and conspiracies, yet still resolved to hold firmly what he has forcibly attained. There is a pathetic power in the figure of this weary ambitious man, who can take no rest until the rest of death comes upon him. Hotspur, who, to bring him into contrast with the Prince, is made much younger than the Harry Percy of history, is as ardent in the pursuit of glory as the Prince seems to be indifferent to it. To his hot temper and quick sense of personal honor small matters are great ; he does not see things in their true proportions ; he lacks self-control, he has no easiness of nature. Yet he is gallant, chivalrous, not devoid of generosity nor of quick affections, though never in a high sense disinterested. Prince Hal, whom Shakespeare admires and loves more than any other person in English history, afterwards to become Shakespeare's ideal king of England, cares little for mere reputation. He does not think much of himself and of his own honor ; and while there is nothing to do, and his great father holds all power in his own right hand, he escapes from the cold proprieties of the court to the boisterous life and mirth of the tavern. He is, however, only waiting for a call to action, and Shakespeare declares that from the first he was conscious of his great destiny, and while seeming to scatter his force in frivolity, was holding his true self, well-guarded, in reserve. Falstaff is everything in little, or rather everything in *much* ; for is he not a tun of flesh ? English literature knows no humorous creation to set beside Falstaff ; and to find his equal—yet his opposite—we must turn to the gaunt figure of the romantic knight of La Mancha, in whose person Cervantes smiled away pathetically the chivalry of the Middle Ages from out our modern world. Falstaff exercises upon the reader of these plays much the same fascination which he exercised upon the Prince. We know him to be a gross-bodied, self-indulgent old sinner, devoid of moral sense and of self-respect, and yet we cannot part with him. We cannot live in this world without humor, and Falstaff is humor maintaining its mastery against all antagonisms. We admit, however, the necessity of his utter banishment from Henry, when Henry enters upon the grave responsibilities of kingship. Still we have a tender thought for Sir John in his exile from London taverns. And at the last, when he fumbles with the sheets and plays with flowers, when " a' went away, an it had been any christom child," we bid him adieu with a tear that does not forbid a smile. The historical period represented by 1 *Henry IV.* dates from the battle of Holmedon Hill, Sept. 14, 1402, to the battle of Shrewsbury, July 21, 1403. 2 *Henry IV.* continues the history to the king's death and the accession of Henry V., 1413.

DRAMATIS PERSONÆ.

KING HENRY the Fourth.
HENRY, Prince of Wales, ⎱ sons to the
JOHN of Lancaster, ⎰ King.
EARL OF WESTMORELAND.
SIR WALTER BLUNT.
THOMAS PERCY, Earl of Worcester.
HENRY PERCY, Earl of Northumberland.
HENRY PERCY, surnamed HOTSPUR, his son.
EDMUND MORTIMER, Earl of March.
RICHARD SCROOP, Archbishop of York.
ARCHIBALD, Earl of Douglas.

OWEN GLENDOWER.
SIR RICHARD VERNON.
SIR JOHN FALSTAFF.
SIR MICHAEL, a friend to the Archbishop of York.
POINS.
GADSHILL.
PETO.
BARDOLPH.

LADY PERCY, wife to Hotspur, and sister to Mortimer.

Lady Mortimer, daughter to Glendower, and wife to Mortimer.
Mistress Quickly, hostess of a tavern in Eastcheap.

Lords, Officers, Sheriff, Vintner, Chamberlain, Drawers, two Carriers, Travellers, and Attendants.

Scene: *England.*

ACT I.

Scene I. *London. The palace.*

Enter King Henry, Lord John of Lancaster, the Earl of Westmoreland, Sir Walter Blunt, *and others.*

King. So shaken as we are, so wan with care,
Find we a time for frighted peace to pant,
And breathe short-winded accents of new broils
To be commenced in strands afar remote.
No more the thirsty entrance of this soil
Shall daub her lips with her own children's blood ;
Nor more shall trenching war channel her fields,
Nor bruise her flowerets with the armed hoofs
Of hostile paces : those opposed eyes,
Which, like the meteors of a troubled heaven,
All of one nature, of one substance bred,   11
Did lately meet in the intestine shock
And furious close of civil butchery,
Shall now, in mutual well-beseeming ranks,
March all one way and be no more opposed
Against acquaintance, kindred and allies :
The edge of war, like an ill-sheathed knife,
No more shall cut his master. Therefore, friends,
As far as to the sepulchre of Christ,
Whose soldier now, under whose blessed cross
We are impressed and engaged to fight,   21
Forthwith a power of English shall we levy ;
Whose arms were moulded in their mothers' womb
To chase these pagans in those holy fields
Over whose acres walk'd those blessed feet
Which fourteen hundred years ago were nail'd
For our advantage on the bitter cross.
But this our purpose now is twelve month old,
And bootless 'tis to tell you we will go :
Therefore we meet not now. Then let me hear
Of you, my gentle cousin Westmoreland,   31
What yesternight our council did decree
In forwarding this dear expedience.
West. My liege, this haste was hot in question,
And many limits of the charge set down
But yesternight : when all athwart there came
A post from Wales loaden with heavy news ;
Whose worst was, that the noble Mortimer,
Leading the men of Herefordshire to fight
Against the irregular and wild Glendower,   40
Was by the rude hands of that Welshman taken,
A thousand of his people butchered ;
Upon whose dead corpse there was such misuse,
Such beastly shameless transformation,
By those Welshwomen done as may not be
Without much shame retold or spoken of.
King. It seems then that the tidings of this broil
Brake off our business for the Holy Land.

West. This match'd with other did, my gracious lord ;
For more uneven and unwelcome news   50
Came from the north and thus it did import :
On Holy-rood day, the gallant Hotspur there,
Young Harry Percy and brave Archibald,
That ever-valiant and approved Scot,
At Holmedon met,
Where they did spend a sad and bloody hour,
As by discharge of their artillery,
And shape of likelihood, the news was told ;
For he that brought them, in the very heat
And pride of their contention did take horse,
Uncertain of the issue any way.   61
King. Here is a dear, a true industrious friend,
Sir Walter Blunt, new lighted from his horse.
Stain'd with the variation of each soil
Betwixt that Holmedon and this seat of ours ;
And he hath brought us smooth and welcome news.
The Earl of Douglas is discomfited :
Ten thousand bold Scots, two and twenty knights,
Balk'd in their own blood did Sir Walter see
On Holmedon's plains. Of prisoners, Hotspur took   70
Mordake the Earl of Fife, and eldest son
To beaten Douglas ; and the Earl of Athol,
Of Murray, Angus, and Menteith :
And is not this an honorable spoil ?
A gallant prize ? ha, cousin, is it not ?
West. In faith,
It is a conquest for a prince to boast of.
King. Yea, there thou makest me sad and makest me sin
In envy that my Lord Northumberland
Should be the father to so blest a son,   80
A son who is the theme of honor's tongue ;
Amongst a grove, the very straightest plant ;
Who is sweet Fortune's minion and her pride :
Whilst I, by looking on the praise of him,
See riot and dishonor stain the brow
Of my young Harry. O that it could be proved
That some night-tripping fairy had exchanged
In cradle-clothes our children where they lay,
And call'd mine Percy, his Plantagenet !
Then would I have his Harry, and he mine.   90
But let him from my thoughts. What think you, coz,
Of this young Percy's pride ? the prisoners,
Which he in this adventure hath surprised,
To his own use he keeps ; and sends me word,
I shall have none but Mordake Earl of Fife.
West. This is his uncle's teaching ; this is Worcester,
Malevolent to you in all aspects ;
Which makes him prune himself, and bristle up
The crest of youth against your dignity.
King. But I have sent for him to answer this ;   100
And for this cause awhile we must neglect
Our holy purpose to Jerusalem.
Cousin, on Wednesday next our council we
Will hold at Windsor ; so inform the lords :

But come yourself with speed to us again;
For more is to be said and to be done
Than out of anger can be uttered.

West. I will, my liege. [*Exeunt.*

SCENE II. *London. An apartment of the Prince's.*

Enter the PRINCE OF WALES *and* FALSTAFF.

Fal. Now, Hal, what time of day is it, lad?

Prince. Thou art so fat-witted, with drinking of old sack and unbuttoning thee after supper and sleeping upon benches after noon, that thou hast forgotten to demand that truly which thou wouldst truly know. What a devil hast thou to do with the time of the day? Unless hours were cups of sack and minutes capons and clocks the tongues of bawds and dials the signs of leaping-houses and the blessed sun himself a fair hot wench in flame-colored taffeta, I see no reason why thou shouldst be so superfluous to demand the time of the day.

Fal. Indeed, you come near me now, Hal; for we that take purses go by the moon and the seven stars, and not by Phœbus, he, 'that wandering knight so fair.' And, I prithee, sweet wag, when thou art king, as, God save thy grace,—majesty I should say, for grace thou wilt have none,— 20

Prince. What, none?

Fal. No, by my troth, not so much as will serve to be prologue to an egg and butter.

Prince. Well, how then? come, roundly, roundly.

Fal. Marry, then, sweet wag, when thou art king, let not us that are squires of the night's body be called thieves of the day's beauty: let us be Diana's foresters, gentlemen of the shade, minions of the moon; and let men say we be men of good government, being governed, as the sea is, by our noble and chaste mistress the moon, under whose countenance we steal.

Prince. Thou sayest well, and it holds well too; for the fortune of us that are the moon's men doth ebb and flow like the sea, being governed, as the sea is, by the moon. As, for proof, now: a purse of gold most resolutely snatched on Monday night and most dissolutely spent on Tuesday morning; got with swearing 'Lay by' and spent with crying 'Bring in;' now in as low an ebb as the foot of the ladder and by and by in as high a flow as the ridge of the gallows.

Fal. By the Lord, thou sayest true, lad. And is not my hostess of the tavern a most sweet wench?

Prince. As the honey of Hybla, my old lad of the castle. And is not a buff jerkin a most sweet robe of durance? 49

Fal. How now, how now, mad wag! what, in thy quips and thy quiddities? what a plague have I to do with a buff jerkin?

Prince. Why, what a pox have I to do with my hostess of the tavern?

Fal. Well, thou hast called her to a reckoning many a time and oft.

Prince. Did I ever call for thee to pay thy part?

Fal. No; I'll give thee thy due, thou hast paid all there. 60

Prince. Yea, and elsewhere, so far as my coin would stretch; and where it would not, I have used my credit.

Fal. Yea, and so used it that, were it not here apparent that thou art heir apparent— But, I prithee, sweet wag, shall there be gallows standing in England when thou art king? and resolution thus fobbed as it is with the rusty curb of old father antic the law? Do not thou, when thou art king, hang a thief. 70

Prince. No; thou shalt.

Fal. Shall I? O rare! By the Lord, I'll be a brave judge.

Prince. Thou judgest false already: I mean, thou shalt have the hanging of the thieves and so become a rare hangman.

Fal. Well, Hal, well; and in some sort it jumps with my humor as well as waiting in the court, I can tell you.

Prince. For obtaining of suits? 80

Fal. Yea, for obtaining of suits, whereof the hangman hath no lean wardrobe. 'Sblood, I am as melancholy as a gib cat or a lugged bear.

Prince. Or an old lion, or a lover's lute.

Fal. Yea, or the drone of a Lincolnshire bagpipe.

Prince. What sayest thou to a hare, or the melancholy of Moor-ditch?

Fal. Thou hast the most unsavory similes and art indeed the most comparative, rascal-liest, sweet young prince. But, Hal, I prithee, trouble me no more with vanity. I would to God thou and I knew where a commodity of good names were to be bought. An old lord of the council rated me the other day in the street about you, sir, but I marked him not; and yet he talked very wisely, but I regarded him not; and yet he talked wisely, and in the street too.

Prince. Thou didst well; for wisdom cries out in the streets, and no man regards it. 100

Fal. O, thou hast damnable iteration and art indeed able to corrupt a saint. Thou hast done much harm upon me, Hal; God forgive thee for it! Before I knew thee, Hal, I knew nothing; and now am I, if a man should speak truly, little better than one of the wicked. I must give over this life, and I will give it over: by the Lord, and I do not, I am a villain: I'll be damned for never a king's son in Christendom.

Prince. Where shall we take a purse to-morrow, Jack? 111

Fal. 'Zounds, where thou wilt, lad; I'll make one; an I do not, call me villain and baffle me.

Prince. I see a good amendment of life in thee; from praying to purse-taking.

Fal. Why, Hal, 'tis my vocation, Hal; 'tis no sin for a man to labor in his vocation.

Enter POINS.

Poins! Now shall we know if Gadshill have set a match. O, if men were to be saved by merit, what hole in hell were hot enough for him? This is the most omnipotent villain that ever cried 'Stand' to a true man.

Prince. Good morrow, Ned.

Poins. Good morrow, sweet Hal. What says Monsieur Remorse? what says Sir John Sack and Sugar? Jack! how agrees the devil and thee about thy soul, that thou soldest him

on Good-Friday last for a cup of Madeira and
a cold capon's leg ?   129
Prince. Sir John stands to his word, the
devil shall have his bargain ; for he was never
yet a breaker of proverbs : he will give the
devil his due.
Poins. Then art thou damned for keeping
thy word with the devil.
Prince. Else he had been damned for cozening the devil.
Poins. But, my lads, my lads, to-morrow
morning, by four o'clock, early at Gadshill !
there are pilgrims going to Canterbury with
rich offerings, and traders riding to London
with fat purses : I have vizards for you all ;
you have horses for yourselves : Gadshill lies
to-night in Rochester : I have bespoke supper
to-morrow night in Eastcheap : we may do it
as secure as sleep. If you will go, I will stuff
your purses full of crowns ; if you will not,
tarry at home and be hanged.
Fal. Hear ye, Yedward ; if I tarry at home
and go not, I'll hang you for going.   150
Poins. You will, chops ?
Fal. Hal, wilt thou make one ?
Prince. Who, I rob ? I a thief ? not I, by
my faith.
Fal. There's neither honesty, manhood,
nor good fellowship in thee, nor thou camest
not of the blood royal, if thou darest not
stand for ten shillings.
Prince. Well then, once in my days I'll be
a madcap.   160
Fal. Why, that's well said.
Prince. Well, come what will, I'll tarry at
home.
Fal. By the Lord, I'll be a traitor then,
when thou art king.
Prince. I care not.
Poins. Sir John, I prithee, leave the prince
and me alone : I will lay him down such reasons for this adventure that he shall go.   169
Fal. Well, God give thee the spirit of persuasion and him the ears of profiting, that
what thou speakest may move and what he
hears may be believed, that the true prince
may, for recreation sake, prove a false thief ;
for the poor abuses of the time want countenance. Farewell : you shall find me in Eastcheap.
Prince. Farewell, thou latter spring ! farewell, All-hallown summer !   [*Exit Falstaff.*
Poins. Now, my good sweet honey lord,
ride with us to-morrow : I have a jest to execute that I cannot manage alone. Falstaff,
Bardolph, Peto and Gadshill shall rob those
men that we have already waylaid : yourself
and I will not be there ; and when they have
the booty, if you and I do not rob them, cut
this head off from my shoulders.
Prince. How shall we part with them in
setting forth ?
Poins. Why, we will set forth before or
after them, and appoint them a place of meeting, wherein it is at our pleasure to fail, and
then will they adventure upon the exploit
themselves ; which they shall have no sooner
achieved, but we'll set upon them.
Prince. Yea, but 'tis like that they will
know us by our horses, by our habits and by
every other appointment, to be ourselves.
Poins. Tut ! our horses they shall not see :
I'll tie them in the wood ; our vizards we will

change after we leave them : and, sirrah, I
have cases of buckram for the nonce, to im-
mask our noted outward garments.
Prince. Yea, but I doubt they will be too
hard for us.
Poins. Well, for two of them, I know them
to be as true-bred cowards as ever turned
back ; and for the third, if he fight longer
than he sees reason, I'll forswear arms. The
virtue of this jest will be, the incomprehensible
lies that this same fat rogue will tell us when
we meet at supper : how thirty, at least, he
fought with ; what wards, what blows, what extremities he endured ; and in the reproof of
this lies the jest.
Prince. Well, I'll go with thee : provide us
all things necessary and meet me to-morrow
night in Eastcheap ; there I'll sup. Farewell.
Poins. Farewell, my lord.   [*Exit.*
Prince. I know you all, and will awhile
uphold
The unyoked humor of your idleness :   220
Yet herein will I imitate the sun,
Who doth permit the base contagious clouds
To smother up his beauty from the world,
That, when he please again to be himself,
Being wanted, he may be more wonder'd at,
By breaking through the foul and ugly mists
Of vapors that did seem to strangle him.
If all the year were playing holidays,
To sport would be as tedious as to work ;
But when they seldom come, they wish'd for
come,   230
And nothing pleaseth but rare accidents.
So, when this loose behavior I throw off
And pay the debt I never promised,
By how much better than my word I am,
By so much shall I falsify men's hopes ;
And like bright metal on a sullen ground,
My reformation, glittering o'er my fault,
Shall show more goodly and attract more
eyes
Than that which hath no foil to set it off.
I'll so offend, to make offence a skill ;   240
Redeeming time when men think least I will.
[*Exit.*

SCENE III. *London. The palace.*

Enter the KING, NORTHUMBERLAND, WORCES-
TER, HOTSPUR, SIR WALTER BLUNT, *with
others.*

King. My blood hath been too cold and
temperate,
Unapt to stir at these indignities,
And you have found me ; for accordingly
You tread upon my patience : but be sure
I will from henceforth rather be myself,
Mighty and to be fear'd, than my condition ;
Which hath been smooth as oil, soft as young
down,
And therefore lost that title of respect
Which the proud soul ne'er pays but to the
proud.
Wor. Our house, my sovereign liege, little
deserves   10
The scourge of greatness to be used on it ;
And that same greatness too which our own
hands
Have holp to make so portly.
North. My lord.—
King. Worcester, get thee gone ; for I do
see
Danger and disobedience in thine eye :

O, sir, your presence is too bold and peremp-
tory,
And majesty might never yet endure
The moody frontier of a servant brow.
You have good leave to leave us : when we
        need   20
Your use and counsel, we shall send for you.
                                    [Exit Wor.
You were about to speak.   [To North.
    North.   Yea, my good lord.
Those prisoners in your highness' name de-
        manded,
Which Harry Percy here at Holmedon took,
Were, as he says, not with such strength de-
        nied
As is deliver'd to your majesty :
Either envy, therefore, or misprision
Is guilty of this fault and not my son.
    Hot. My liege, I did deny no prisoners.
But I remember, when the fight was done, 30
When I was dry with rage and extreme toil,
Breathless and faint, leaning upon my sword,
Came there a certain lord, neat, and trimly
        dress'd,
Fresh as a bridegroom ; and his chin new
        reap'd
Show'd like a stubble-land at harvest-home ;
He was perfumed like a milliner ;
And 'twixt his finger and his thumb he held
A pouncet-box, which ever and anon
He gave his nose and took't away again ;
Who therewith angry, when it next came
        there,   40
Took it in snuff ; and still he smiled and
        talk'd,
And as the soldiers bore dead bodies by,
He call'd them untaught knaves, unmannerly,
To bring a slovenly unhandsome corse
Betwixt the wind and his nobility.
With many holiday and lady terms
He question'd me ; amongst the rest, de-
        manded
My prisoners in your majesty's behalf.
I then, all smarting with my wounds being
        cold,
To be so pester'd with a popinjay,   50
Out of my grief and my impatience,
Answer'd neglectingly I know not what,
He should or he should not ; for he made me
        mad
To see him shine so brisk and smell so sweet
And talk so like a waiting-gentlewoman
Of guns and drums and wounds,—God save
        the mark !—
And telling me the sovereign'st thing on earth
Was parmaceti for an inward bruise ;
And that it was great pity, so it was,
This villanous salt-petre should be digg'd 60
Out of the bowels of the harmless earth,
Which many a good tall fellow had destroy'd
So cowardly ; and but for these vile guns,
He would himself have been a soldier.
This bald unjointed chat of his, my lord,
I answer'd indirectly, as I said ;
And I beseech you, let not his report
Come current for an accusation
Betwixt my love and your high majesty.
    Blunt. The circumstance consider'd, good
        my lord,   70
Whate'er Lord Harry Percy then had said
To such a person and in such a place,
At such a time, with all the rest retold,
May reasonably die and never rise

To do him wrong or any way impeach
What then he said, so he unsay it now.
    King. Why, yet he doth deny his prisoners,
But with proviso and exception,
That we at our own charge shall ransom
        straight
His brother-in-law, the foolish Mortimer ; 80
Who, on my soul, hath wilfully betray'd
The lives of those that he did lead to fight
Against that great magician, damn'd Glen-
        dower,
Whose daughter, as we hear, the Earl of
        March
Hath lately married. Shall our coffers, then,
Be emptied to redeem a traitor home ?
Shall we buy treason ? and indent with fears,
When they have lost and forfeited themselves ?
No, on the barren mountains let him starve ;
For I shall never hold that man my friend 90
Whose tongue shall ask me for one penny cost
To ransom home revolted Mortimer.
    Hot. Revolted Mortimer !
He never did fall off, my sovereign liege,
But by the chance of war ; to prove that true
Needs no more but one tongue for all those
        wounds,
Those mouthed wounds, which valiantly he
        took
When on the gentle Severn's sedgy bank,
In single opposition, hand to hand,
He did confound the best part of an hour 100
In changing hardiment with great Glendower :
Three times they breathed and three times did
        they drink,
Upon agreement, of swift Severn's flood ;
Who then, affrighted with their bloody looks,
Ran fearfully among the trembling reeds,
And hid his crisp head in the hollow bank
Bloodstained with these valiant combatants.
Never did base and rotten policy
Color her working with such deadly wounds ;
Nor never could the noble Mortimer   110
Receive so many, and all willingly :
Then let not him be slander'd with revolt.
    King. Thou dost belie him, Percy, thou
        dost belie him ;
He never did encounter with Glendower :
I tell thee,
He durst as well have met the devil alone
As Owen Glendower for an enemy.
Art thou not ashamed ? But, sirrah, hence-
        forth
Let me not hear you speak of Mortimer :
Send me your prisoners with the speediest
        means,   120
Or you shall hear in such a kind from me
As will displease you. My Lord Northumber-
        land,
We license your departure with your son.
Send us your prisoners, or you will hear of it.
        [Exeunt King Henry, Blunt, and train.
    Hot. An if the devil come and roar for
        them,
I will not send them : I will after straight
And tell him so ; for I will ease my heart,
Albeit I make a hazard of my head.
    North. What, drunk with choler ? stay and
        pause awhile :
Here comes your uncle.

                Re-enter WORCESTER.

    Hot.   Speak of Mortimer ! 130
'Zounds, I will speak of him ; and let my soul

Want mercy, if I do not join with him :
Yea, on his part I'll empty all these veins,
And shed my dear blood drop by drop in the
　　dust,
But I will lift the down-trod Mortimer
As high in the air as this unthankful king,
As this ingrate and canker'd Bolingbroke.
　　North. Brother, the king hath made your
　　nephew mad.
　　Wor. Who struck this heat up after I was
　　gone ?
　　Hot. He will, forsooth, have all my pris-
　　oners ;
And when I urged the ransom once again 141
Of my wife's brother, then his cheek look'd
　　pale,
And on my face he turn'd an eye of death,
Trembling even at the name of Mortimer.
　　Wor. I cannot blame him : was not he pro-
　　claim'd
By Richard that dead is the next of blood ?
　　North. He was ; I heard the proclama-
　　tion :
And then it was when the unhappy king,—
Whose wrongs in us God pardon !—did set
　　forth
Upon his Irish expedition ;　　　　　150
From whence he intercepted did return
To be deposed and shortly murdered.
　　Wor. And for whose death we in the
　　world's wide mouth
Live scandalized and foully spoken of.
　　Hot. But, soft, I pray you ; did King Rich-
　　ard then
Proclaim my brother Edmund Mortimer
Heir to the crown ?
　　North. 　　　　He did ; myself did hear it.
　　Hot. Nay, then I cannot blame his cousin
　　king,
That wished him on the barren mountains
　　starve.
But shall it be that you, that set the crown 160
Upon the head of this forgetful man
And for his sake wear the detested blot
Of murderous subornation, shall it be,
That you a world of curses undergo,
Being the agents, or base second means,
The cords, the ladder, or the hangman rather ?
O, pardon me that I descend so low,
To show the line and the predicament
Wherein you range under this subtle king ;
Shall it for shame be spoken in these days, 170
Or fill up chronicles in time to come,
That men of your nobility and power
Did gage them both in an unjust behalf,
As both of you—God pardon it !—have done,
To put down Richard, that sweet lovely rose,
And plant this thorn, this canker, Boling-
　　broke ?
And shall it in more shame be further spoken,
That you are fool'd, discarded and shook off
By him for whom these shames ye under-
　　went ?　　　　　　　　179
No ; yet time serves wherein you may redeem
Your banish'd honors and restore yourselves
Into the good thoughts of the world again,
Revenge the jeering and disdain'd contempt
Of this proud king, who studies day and night
To answer all the debt he owes to you
Even with the bloody payment of your deaths :
Therefore, I say,—
　　Wor. 　　　　Peace, cousin, say no more :
And now I will unclasp a secret book,

And to your quick-conceiving discontents
I'll read you matter deep and dangerous, 190
As full of peril and adventurous spirit
As to o'er-walk a current roaring loud
On the unsteadfast footing of a spear.
　　Hot. If he fall in, good night ! or sink or
　　swim :
Send danger from the east unto the west,
So honor cross it from the north to south,
And let them grapple : O, the blood more stirs
To rouse a lion than to start a hare !
　　North. Imagination of some great exploit
Drives him beyond the bounds of patience.
　　Hot. By heaven, methinks it were an easy
　　leap,　　　　　　　201
To pluck bright honor from the pale-faced
　　moon,
Or dive into the bottom of the deep,
Where fathom-line could never touch the
　　ground,
And pluck up drowned honor by the locks ;
So he that doth redeem her thence might
　　wear
Without corrival, all her dignities :
But out upon this half-faced fellowship !
　　Wor. He apprehends a world of figures
　　here,
But not the form of what he should attend.
Good cousin, give me audience for a while.
　　Hot. I cry you mercy.　　　　212
　　Wor. 　　　　Those same noble Scots
That are your prisoners,—
　　Hot. 　　　　I'll keep them all ;
By God, he shall not have a Scot of them ;
No, if a Scot would save his soul, he shall
　　not :
I'll keep them, by this hand.
　　Wor. 　　　　You start away
And lend no ear unto my purposes.
Those prisoners you shall keep.
　　Hot. 　　　　Nay, I will ; that's flat :
He said he would not ransom Mortimer ;
Forbad my tongue to speak of Mortimer ; 220
But I will find him when he lies asleep,
And in his ear I'll holla ' Mortimer ! '
Nay,
I'll have a starling shall be taught to speak
Nothing but ' Mortimer,' and give it him
To keep his anger still in motion.
　　Wor. Hear you, cousin ; a word.
　　Hot. All studies here I solemnly defy,
Save how to gall and pinch this Bolingbroke :
And that same sword-and-buckler Prince of
　　Wales,　　　　　　230
But that I think his father loves him not
And would be glad he met with some mis-
　　chance,
I would have him poison'd with a pot of ale.
　　Wor. Farewell, kinsman : I'll talk to you
When you are better temper'd to attend.
　　North. Why, what a wasp-stung and im-
　　patient fool
Art thou to break into this woman's mood,
Tying thine ear to no tongue but thine own !
　　Hot. Why, look you, I am whipp'd and
　　scourged with rods,
Nettled and stung with pismires, when I hear
Of this vile politician, Bolingbroke.　　241
In Richard's time,—what do you call the
　　place ?—
A plague upon it, it is in Gloucestershire ;
'Twas where the madcap duke his uncle kept,
His uncle York ; where I first bow'd my knee

Unto this king of smiles, this Bolingbroke,—
'Sblood !—
When you and he came back from Ravens-
    purgh.
North. At Berkley castle.
Hot. You say true :   250
Why, what a candy deal of courtesy
This fawning greyhound then did proffer me !
Look, ' when his infant fortune came to age,'
And ' gentle Harry Percy,' and ' kind cousin ; '
O, the devil take such cozeners ! God forgive
    me !
Good uncle, tell your tale ; I have done.
Wor. Nay, if you have not, to it again ;
We will stay your leisure.
Hot.   I have done, i' faith.
Wor. Then once more to your Scottish
    prisoners.   259
Deliver them up without their ransom straight,
And make the Douglas' son your only mean
For powers in Scotland ; which, for divers
    reasons
Which I shall send you written, be assured,
Will easily be granted. You, my lord,
              [*To Northumberland.*
Your son in Scotland being thus employ'd,
Shall secretly into the bosom creep
Of that same noble prelate, well beloved,
The archbishop.
Hot. Of York, is it not ?
Wor. True ; who bears hard   270
His brother's death at Bristol, the Lord
    Scroop.
I speak not this in estimation,
As what I think might be, but what I know
Is ruminated, plotted and set down,
And only stays but to behold the face
Of that occasion that shall bring it on.
Hot. I smell it : upon my life, it will do
    well.
North. Before the game is afoot, thou still
    let'st slip.
Hot. Why, it cannot choose but be a noble
    plot ;
And then the power of Scotland and of York,
To join with Mortimer, ha ?   281
Wor.   And so they shall.
Hot. In faith, it is exceedingly well aim'd.
Wor. And 'tis no little reason bids us
    speed,
To save our heads by raising of a head ;
For, bear ourselves as even as we can,
The king will always think him in our debt,
And think we think ourselves unsatisfied,
Till he hath found a time to pay us home :
And see already how he doth begin
To make us strangers to his looks of love.
Hot. He does, he does : we'll be revenged
    on him.   291
Wor. Cousin, farewell : no further go in
    this
Than I by letters shall direct your course.
When time is ripe, which will be suddenly,
I'll steal to Glendower and Lord Mortimer ;
Where you and Douglas and our powers at
    once,
As I will fashion it, shall happily meet,
To bear our fortunes in our own strong arms,
Which now we hold at much uncertainty.
North. Farewell, good brother : we shall
    thrive, I trust.   300
Hot. Uncle, Adieu : O, let the hours be
    short

Till fields and blows and groans applaud our
    sport !   [*Exeunt.*

ACT II.

SCENE I. *Rochester. An inn yard.*

Enter a Carrier *with a lantern in his hand.*

First Car. Heigh-ho ! an it be not four by
the day, I'll be hanged : Charles' wain is over
the new chimney, and yet our horse not
packed. What, ostler !
Ost. [*Within*] Anon, anon.
First Car. I prithee, Tom, beat Cut's saddle, put a few flocks in the point ; poor jade,
is wrung in the withers out of all cess.

Enter another Carrier.

Sec. Car. Peas and beans are as dank here
as a dog, and that is the next way to give poor
jades the bots : this house is turned upside
down since Robin Ostler died.
First Car. Poor fellow, never joyed since
the price of oats rose ; it was the death of
him.
Sec. Car. I think this be the most villanous
house in all London road for fleas : I am stung
like a tench.
First Car. Like a tench ! by the mass,
there is ne'er a king christen could be better
bit than I have been since the first cock.   20
Sec. Car. Why, they will allow us ne'er a
jordan, and then we leak in your chimney ;
and your chamber-lie breeds fleas like a loach.
First Car. What, ostler ! come away and
be hanged ! come away.
Sec. Car. I have a gammon of bacon and
two razes of ginger, to be delivered as far as
Charing-cross.
First Car. God's body ! the turkeys in my
pannier are quite starved. What, ostler ! A
plague on thee ! hast thou never an eye in thy
head ? canst not hear ? An 'twere not as
good deed as drink, to break the pate on thee,
I am a very villain. Come, and be hanged !
hast no faith in thee ?

Enter GADSHILL.

Gads. Good morrow, carriers. What's
o'clock ?
First Car. I think it be two o'clock.
Gads. I pray thee lend me thy lantern, to
see my gelding in the stable.
First Car. Nay, by God, soft ; I know a
trick worth two of that, i' faith.   41
Gads. I pray thee, lend me thine.
Sec. Car. Ay, when ? can'st tell ? Lend
me thy lantern, quoth he ? marry, I'll see thee
hanged first.
Gads. Sirrah carrier, what time do you
mean to come to London ?
Sec. Car. Time enough to go to bed with a
candle, I warrant thee. Come, neighbor Mugs,
we'll call up the gentlemen : they will along
with company, for they have great charge. 51
           [*Exeunt carriers.*
Gads. What, ho ! chamberlain !
Cham. [*Within*] At hand, quoth pick-
purse.
Gads. That's even as fair as—at hand,
quoth the chamberlain ; for thou variest no
more from picking of purses than giving di-

rection doth from laboring; thou layest the plot how.

Enter Chamberlain.

Cham. Good morrow, Master Gadshill. It holds current that I told you yesternight: there's a franklin in the wild of Kent hath brought three hundred marks with him in gold: I heard him tell it to one of his company last night at supper; a kind of auditor; one that hath abundance of charge too, God knows what. They are up already, and call for eggs and butter; they will away presently.

Gads. Sirrah, if they meet not with Saint Nicholas' clerks, I'll give thee this neck.

Cham. No, I'll none of it: I pray thee, keep that for the hangman; for I know thou worshippest St. Nicholas as truly as a man of falsehood may.

Gads. What talkest thou to me of the hangman? if I hang, I'll make a fat pair of gallows; for if I hang, old Sir John hangs with me, and thou knowest he is no starveling. Tut! there are other Trojans that thou dreamest not of, the which for sport sake are content to do the profession some grace; that would, if matters should be looked into, for their own credit sake, make all whole. I am joined with no foot-land rakers, no long-staff sixpenny strikers, none of these mad mustachio purple-hued malt-worms; but with nobility and tranquillity, burgomasters and great oneyers, such as can hold in, such as will strike sooner than speak, and speak sooner than drink, and drink sooner than pray: and yet, 'zounds, I lie; for they pray continually to their saint, the commonwealth; or rather, not pray to her, but prey on her, for they ride up and down on her and make her their boots.   91

Cham. What, the commonwealth their boots? will she hold out water in foul way?

Gads. She will, she will; justice hath liquored her. We steal as in a castle, cocksure; we have the receipt of fern-seed, we walk invisible.

Cham. Nay, by my faith, I think you are more beholding to the night than to fern-seed for your walking invisible.

Gads. Give me thy hand: thou shalt have a share in our purchase, as I am a true man.

Cham. Nay, rather let me have it, as you are a false thief.

Gads. Go to; 'homo' is a common name to all men. Bid the ostler bring my gelding out of the stable. Farewell, you muddy knave.

[*Exeunt.*

Scene II. *The highway, near Gadshill.*

Enter Prince Henry *and* Poins.

Poins. Come, shelter, shelter: I have removed Falstaff's horse, and he frets like a gummed velvet.

Prince. Stand close.

Enter Falstaff.

Fal. Poins! Poins, and be hanged! Poins!

Prince. Peace, ye fat-kidneyed rascal! what a brawling dost thou keep!

Fal. Where's Poins, Hal?

Prince. He is walked up to the top of the hill: I'll go seek him.   9

Fal. I am accursed to rob in that thief's company: the rascal hath removed my horse, and tied him I know not where. If I travel but four foot by the squier further afoot, I shall break my wind. Well, I doubt not but to die a fair death for all this, if I 'scape hanging for killing that rogue. I have forsworn his company hourly any time this two and twenty years, and yet I am bewitched with the rogue's company. If the rascal hath not given me medicines to make me love him, I'll be hanged; it could not be else; I have drunk medicines. Poins! Hal! a plague upon you both! Bardolph! Peto! I'll starve ere I'll rob a foot further. An 'twere not as good a deed as drink, to turn true man and to leave these rogues, I am the veriest varlet that ever chewed with a tooth. Eight yards of uneven ground is threescore and ten miles afoot with me; and the stony-hearted villains know it well enough: a plague upon it when thieves cannot be true one to another! [*They whistle.*] Whew! A plague upon you all! Give me my horse, you rogues; give me my horse, and be hanged!

Prince. Peace, ye fat-guts! lie down; lay thine ear close to the ground and list if thou canst hear the tread of travellers.

Fal. Have you any levers to lift me up again, being down? 'Sblood, I'll not bear mine own flesh so far afoot again for all the coin in thy father's exchequer. What a plague mean ye to colt me thus?   40

Prince. Thou liest; thou art not colted, thou art uncolted.

Fal. I prithee, good Prince Hal, help me to my horse, good king's son.

Prince. Out, ye rogue! shall I be your ostler?

Fal. Go, hang thyself in thine own heir-apparent garters! If I be ta'en, I'll peach for this. An I have not ballads made on you all and sung to filthy tunes, let a cup of sack be my poison: when a jest is so forward, and afoot too! I hate it.

Enter Gadshill, Bardolph *and* Peto *with him.*

Gads. Stand.

Fals. So I do, against my will.

Poins. O, 'tis our setter: I know his voice. Bardolph, what news?

Bard. Case ye, case ye; on with your vizards: there's money of the king's coming down the hill; 'tis going to the king's exchequer.

Fal. You lie, ye rogue; 'tis going to the king's tavern.

Gads. There's enough to make us all.   60

Fal. To be hanged.

Prince. Sirs, you four shall front them in the narrow lane; Ned Poins and I will walk lower: if they 'scape from your encounter, then they light on us.

Peto. How many be there of them?

Gads. Some eight or ten.

Fal. 'Zounds, will they not rob us?

Prince. What, a coward, Sir John Paunch?

Fal. Indeed, I am not John of Gaunt, your grandfather; but yet no coward, Hal.   71

Prince. Well, we leave that to the proof.

Poins. Sirrah Jack, thy horse stands behind the hedge: when thou needest him, there thou shalt find him. Farewell, and stand fast.

Fal. Now cannot I strike him, if I should be hanged.

Prince. Ned, where are our disguises?

Poins. Here, hard by: stand close.

[*Exeunt Prince and Poins.*

Fal. Now, my masters, happy man be his dole, say I : every man to his business.

Enter the Travellers.

First Trav. Come, neighbor: the boy shall lead our horses down the hill; we'll walk afoot awhile, and ease our legs.

Thieves. Stand!

Travellers. Jesus bless us!

Fal. Strike; down with them; cut the villains' throats: ah! whoreson caterpillars! bacon-fed knaves! they hate us youth: down with them: fleece them.   90

Travellers. O, we are undone, both we and ours for ever!

Fal. Hang ye, gorbellied knaves, are ye undone? No, ye fat chuffs; I would your store were here! On, bacons, on! What, ye knaves! young men must live. You are grand-jurors, are ye? we'll jure ye, 'faith.

[*Here they rob them and bind them. Exeunt.*

Re-enter PRINCE HENRY *and* POINS.

Prince. The thieves have bound the true men. Now could thou and I rob the thieves and go merrily to London, it would be argument for a week, laughter for a month and a good jest for ever.

Poins. Stand close; I hear them coming.

Enter the Thieves again.

Fal. Come, my masters, let us share, and then to horse before day. An the Prince and Poins be not two arrant cowards, there's no equity stirring: there's no more valor in that Poins than in a wild-duck.

Prince. Your money!

Poins. Villains!   110

[*As they are sharing, the Prince and Poins set upon them; they all run away; and Falstaff, after a blow or two, runs away too, leaving the booty behind them.*]

Prince. Got with much ease. Now merrily to horse:
The thieves are all scatter'd and possess'd with fear
So strongly that they dare not meet each other;
Each takes his fellow for an officer.
Away, good Ned. Falstaff sweats to death,
And lards the lean earth as he walks along:
Were 't not for laughing, I should pity him.

Poins. How the rogue roar'd!   [*Exeunt.*

SCENE III. *Warkworth castle.*

Enter HOTSPUR, *solus, reading a letter.*

Hot. 'But for mine own part, my lord, I could be well contented to be there, in respect of the love I bear your house.' He could be contented: why is he not, then? In respect of the love he bears our house: he shows in this, he loves his own barn better than he loves our house. Let me see some more. 'The purpose you undertake is dangerous;'—why, that's certain: 'tis dangerous to take a cold, to sleep, to drink; but I tell you, my lord fool, out of this nettle, danger, we pluck this flower, safety. 'The purpose you undertake is dangerous; the friends you have named uncertain; the time itself unsorted; and your whole plot too light for the counterpoise of so great an opposition.' Say you so, say you so? I say unto you again, you are a shallow cowardly hind, and you lie. What a lack-brain is this! By the Lord, our plot is a good plot as ever was laid; our friends true and constant: a good plot, good friends, and full of expectation; an excellent plot, very good friends. What a frosty-spirited rogue is this! Why, my lord of York commends the plot and the general course of the action. 'Zounds, an I were now by this rascal, I could brain him with his lady's fan. Is there not my father, my uncle and myself? lord Edmund Mortimer, my lord of York and Owen Glendower? is there not besides the Douglas? have I not all their letters to meet me in arms by the ninth of the next month? and are they not some of them set forward already? What a pagan rascal is this! an infidel! Ha! you shall see now in very sincerity of fear and cold heart, will he to the king and lay open all our proceedings. O, I could divide myself and go to buffets, for moving such a dish of skim milk with so honorable an action! Hang him! let him tell the king: we are prepared. I will set forward to-night.

Enter LADY PERCY.

How now, Kate! I must leave you within these two hours.

Lady. O, my good lord, why are you thus alone?   40
For what offence have I this fortnight been
A banish'd woman from my Harry's bed?
Tell me, sweet lord, what is't that takes from thee
Thy stomach, pleasure and thy golden sleep?
Why dost thou bend thine eyes upon the earth,
And start so often when thou sit'st alone?
Why hast thou lost the fresh blood in thy cheeks;
And given my treasures and my rights of thee
To thick-eyed musing and cursed melancholy?
In thy faint slumbers I by thee have watch'd,
And heard thee murmur tales of iron wars;
Speak terms of manage to thy bounding steed;
Cry 'Courage! to the field!' And thou hast talk'd
Of sallies and retires, of trenches, tents,
Of palisadoes, frontiers, parapets,
Of basilisks, of cannon, culverin,
Of prisoners' ransom and of soldiers slain,
And all the currents of a heady fight.
Thy spirit within thee hath been so at war 59
And thus hath so bestirr'd thee in thy sleep,
That beads of sweat have stood upon thy brow
Like bubbles in a late-disturbed stream;
And in thy face strange motions have appear'd,
Such as we see when men restrain their breath
On some great sudden hest. O, what portents are these?
Some heavy business hath my lord in hand,
And I must know it, else he loves me not.

Hot. What, ho!

Enter Servant.

Is Gilliams with the packet gone?

Serv. He is, my lord, an hour ago.

Hot. Hath Butler brought those horses
    from the sheriff ?   70
Serv. One horse, my lord, he brought even
    now.
Hot. What horse ? a roan, a crop-ear, is it
    not ?
Serv. It is, my lord.
Hot.   That roan shall by my throne.
Well, I will back him straight : O esperance !
Bid Butler lead him forth into the park.
                                        [*Exit Servant.*
Lady. But hear you, my lord.
Hot. What say'st thou, my lady ?
Lady. What is it carries you away ?
Hot. Why, my horse, my love, my horse.
Lady. Out, you mad-headed ape !   80
A weasel hath not such a deal of spleen
As you are toss'd with. In faith,
I'll know your business, Harry, that I will.
I fear my brother Mortimer doth stir
About his title, and hath sent for you
To line his enterprize : but if you go,—
Hot. So far afoot, I shall be weary, love.
Lady. Come, come, you paraquito, answer
    me
Directly unto this question that I ask :
In faith, I'll break thy little finger, Harry, 90
An if thou wilt not tell me all things true.
Hot. Away,
Away, you trifler ! Love ! I love thee not,
I care not for thee, Kate : this is no world
To play with mammets and to tilt with lips :
We must have bloody noses and crack'd
    crowns,
And pass them current too. God's me, my
    horse !
What say'st thou, Kate ? what would'st thou
    have with me ?
Lady. Do you not love me ? do you not,
    indeed ?   99
Well, do not then ; for since you love me not,
I will not love myself. Do you not love me ?
Nay, tell me if you speak in jest or no.
Hot. Come, wilt thou see me ride ?
And when I am o' horseback, I will swear
I love thee infinitely. But hark you, Kate ;
I must not have you henceforth question me
Whither I go, nor reason whereabout :
Whither I must, I must ; and, to conclude,
This evening must I leave you, gentle Kate.
I know you wise, but yet no farther wise   110
Than Harry Percy's wife : constant you are,
But yet a woman : and for secrecy,
No lady closer ; for I well believe
Thou wilt not utter what thou dost not know ;
And so far will I trust thee, gentle Kate.
Lady. How ! so far ?
Hot. Not an inch further. But hark you,
    Kate :
Whither I go, thither shall you go too ;
To-day will I set forth, to-morrow you.
Will this content you, Kate ?
Lady. It must of force.   [*Exeunt.* 120

SCENE IV. *The Boar's-Head Tavern,*
            Eastcheap.

Enter the PRINCE, *and* POINS.

Prince. Ned, prithee, come out of that fat
room, and lend me thy hand to laugh a little.
Poins. Where hast been, Hal ?
Prince. With three or four loggerheads
amongst three or four score hogsheads. I have
sounded the very base-string of humility.

Sirrah, I am sworn brother to a leash of drawers ; and can call them all by their christen
names, as Tom, Dick, and Francis. They take
it already upon their salvation, that though I
be but Prince of Wales, yet I am the king of
courtesy ; and tell me flatly I am no proud
Jack, like Falstaff, but a Corinthian, a lad of
mettle, a good boy, by the Lord, so they call
me, and when I am king of England, I shall
command all the good lads in Eastcheap. They
call drinking deep, dyeing scarlet ; and when
you breathe in your watering, they cry ' hem ! '
and bid you play it off. To conclude, I am so
good a proficient in one quarter of an hour,
that I can drink with any tinker in his own
language during my life. I tell thee, Ned,
thou hast lost much honor, that thou wert not
with me in this action. But, sweet Ned,—to
sweeten which name of Ned, I give thee this
pennyworth of sugar, clapped even now into
my hand by an under-skinker, one that never
spake other English in his life than ' Eight shillings and sixpence,' and ' You are welcome,'
with this shrill addition, ' Anon, anon, sir !
Score a pint of bastard in the Half-moon,' or
so. But, Ned, to drive away the time till Falstaff come, I prithee, do thou stand in some
by-room, while I question my puny drawer to
what end he gave me the sugar ; and do thou
never leave calling ' Francis,' that his tale to
me may be nothing but ' Anon.' Step aside,
and I'll show thee a precedent.
Poins. Francis !
Prince. Thou art perfect.
Poins. Francis !   [*Exit Poins.* 40

Enter FRANCIS.

Fran. Anon, anon, sir. Look down into the
Pomgarnet, Ralph.
Prince. Come hither, Francis.
Fran. My lord ?
Prince. How long hast thou to serve,
Francis ?
Fran. Forsooth, five years, and as much
as to—
Poins. [*Within*] Francis !
Fran. Anon, anon, sir.   49
Prince. Five year ! by'r lady, a long lease
for the clinking of pewter. But, Francis, darest
thou be so valiant as to play the coward with
thy indenture and show it a fair pair of heels
and run from it ?
Fran. O Lord, sir, I'll be sworn upon all
the books in England, I could find in my
heart.
Poins. [*Within*] Francis !
Fran. Anon, sir.
Prince. How old art thou, Francis ?
Fran. Let me see—about Michaelmas next
I shall be—   61
Poins. [*Within*] Francis !
Fran. Anon, sir. Pray stay a little, my lord.
Prince. Nay, but hark you, Francis : for
the sugar thou gavest me, 'twas a pennyworth,
wast not ?
Fran. O Lord, I would it had been two !
Prince. I will give thee for it a thousand
pound : ask me when thou wilt, and thou shalt
have it.   70
Poins. [*Within*] Francis !
Fran. Anon, anon.
Prince. Anon, Francis ? No, Francis ; but
to-morrow, Francis ; or, Francis, o' Thurs-

day ; or indeed, Francis, when thou wilt. But,
Francis !

Fran. My lord ?

Prince. Wilt thou rob this leathern jerkin,
crystal-button, not-pated, agate-ring, puke-
stocking, caddis-garter, smooth-tongue, Span-
ish-pouch,—   80

Fran. O Lord, sir, who do you mean ?

Prince. Why, then, your brown bastard is
your only drink ; for look you, Francis, your
white canvas doublet will sully : in Barbary,
sir, it cannot come to so much.

Fran. What, sir ?

Poins. [*Within*] Francis !

Prince. Away, you rogue ! dost thou not
hear them call ?

[*Here they both call him ; the drawer stands
      amazed, not knowing which way to go.*

Enter Vintner.

Vint. What, standest thou still, and hear-
est such a calling ? Look to the guests within.
[*Exit Francis.*] My lord, old Sir John, with
half-a-dozen more, are at the door : shall I
let them in ?

Prince. Let them alone awhile, and then
open the door. [*Exit Vintner.*] Poins !

Re-enter POINS.

Poins. Anon, anon, sir.

Prince. Sirrah, Falstaff and the rest of the
thieves are at the door : shall we be merry ?

Poins. As merry as crickets, my lad. But
hark ye ; what cunning match have you made
with this jest of the drawer ? come, what's the
issue ?

Prince. I am now of all humors that have
showed themselves humors since the old days
of goodman Adam to the pupil age of this
present twelve o'clock at midnight.

Re-enter FRANCIS.

What's o'clock, Francis ?

Fran. Anon, anon, sir.   [*Exit.* 109

Prince. That ever this fellow should have
fewer words than a parrot, and yet the son of
a woman ! His industry is up-stairs and down-
stairs ; his eloquence the parcel of a reckoning.
I am not yet of Percy's mind, the Hotspur of
the north ; he that kills me some six or seven
dozen of Scots at a breakfast, washes his
hands, and says to his wife ' Fie upon this
quiet life ! I want work.' ' O my sweet Harry,'
says she, ' how many hast thou killed to-day ? '
' Give my roan horse a drench,' says he ; and
answers ' Some fourteen,' an hour after ; ' a
trifle, a trifle.' I prithee, call in Falstaff : I'll
play Percy, and that damned brawn shall play
Dame Mortimer his wife. ' Rivo ! ' says the
drunkard. Call in ribs, call in tallow.

Enter FALSTAFF, GADSHILL, BARDOLPH, *and*
      PETO ; FRANCIS *following with wine.*

Poins. Welcome, Jack : where hast thou
been ?

Fal. A plague of all cowards, I say, and a
vengeance too ! marry, and amen ! Give me
a cup of sack, boy. Ere I lead this life long,
I'll sew nether stocks and mend them and foot
them too. A plague of all cowards ! Give me
a cup of sack, rogue. Is there no virtue extant ?
                                    [*He drinks.*

Prince. Didst thou never see Titan kiss a

dish of butter ? pitiful-hearted Titan, that
melted at the sweet tale of the sun's ! if thou
didst, then behold that compound.

Fal. You rogue, here's lime in this sack
too : there is nothing but roguery to be found
in villanous man : yet a coward is worse than
a cup of sack with lime in it. A villanous
coward ! Go thy ways, old Jack ; die when
thou wilt, if manhood, good manhood, be not
forgot upon the face of the earth, then am I
a shotten herring. There live not three good
men unhanged in England ; and one of them
is fat and grows old : God help the while ! a
bad world, I say. I would I were a weaver ;
I could sing psalms or any thing. A plague of
all cowards, I say still.

Prince. How now, wool-sack ! what mut-
ter you ?   149

Fal. A king's son ! If I do not beat thee
out of thy kingdom with a dagger of lath, and
drive all thy subjects afore thee like a flock of
wild-geese, I'll never wear hair on my face
more. You Prince of Wales !

Prince. Why, you whoreson round man,
what's the matter ?

Fal. Are not you a coward ? answer me to
that : and Poins there ?

Poins. 'Zounds, ye fat paunch, an ye call
me coward, by the Lord, I'll stab thee.   160

Fal. I call thee coward ! I'll see thee
damned ere I call thee coward : but I would
give a thousand pound I could run as fast as
thou canst. You are straight enough in the
shoulders, you care not who sees your back :
call you that backing of your friends ? A
plague upon such backing ! give me them that
will face me. Give me a cup of sack : I am a
rogue, if I drunk to-day.

Prince. O villain ! thy lips are scarce wiped
since thou drunkest last.   171

Fal. All's one for that. [*He drinks.*] A
plague of all cowards, still say I.

Prince. What's the matter ?

Fal. What's the matter ! there be four of
us here have ta'en a thousand pound this day
morning.

Prince. Where is it, Jack ? where is it ?

Fal. Where is it ! taken from us it is : a
hundred upon poor four of us.   180

Prince. What, a hundred, man ?

Fal. I am a rogue, if I were not at half-
sword with a dozen of them two hours together. I have 'scaped by miracle. I am eight
times thrust through the doublet, four through
the hose ; my buckler cut through and
through ; my sword hacked like a hand-saw—
ecce signum ! I never dealt better since I was
a man : all would not do. A plague of all
cowards ! Let them speak : if they speak more
or less than truth, they are villains and the
sons of darkness.   191

Prince. Speak, sirs ; how was it ?

Gads. We four set upon some dozen—

Fal. Sixteen at least, my lord.

Gads. And bound them.

Peto. No, no, they were not bound.

Fal. You rogue, they were bound, every
man of them ; or I am a Jew else, an Ebrew
Jew.

Gads. As we were sharing, some six or
seven fresh men set upon us—   200

Fal. And unbound the rest, and then come
in the other.

Prince. What, fought you with them all ?

Fal. All ! I know not what you call all ; but if I fought not with fifty of them, I am a bunch of radish : if there were not two or three and fifty upon poor old Jack, then am I no two-legged creature.

Prince. Pray God you have not murdered some of them. 210

Fal. Nay, that's past praying for : I have peppered two of them ; two I am sure I have paid, two rogues in buckram suits. I tell thee what, Hal, if I tell thee a lie, spit in my face, call me horse. Thou knowest my old ward ; here I lay, and thus I bore my point. Four rogues in buckram let drive at me—

Prince. What, four ? thou saidst but two even now.

Fal. Four, Hal ; I told thee four. 220

Poins. Ay, ay, he said four.

Fal. These four came all a-front, and mainly thrust at me. I made me no more ado but took all their seven points in my target, thus.

Prince. Seven ? why, there were but four even now.

Fal. In buckram ?

Poins. Ay, four, in buckram suits.

Fal. Seven, by these hilts, or I am a villain else. 230

Prince. Prithee, let him alone ; we shall have more anon.

Fal. Dost thou hear me, Hal ?

Prince. Ay, and mark thee too, Jack.

Fal. Do so, for it is worth the listening to. These nine in buckram that I told thee of—

Prince. So, two more already.

Fal. Their points being broken,—

Poins. Down fell their hose. 239

Fal. Began to give me ground : but I followed me close, came in foot and hand ; and with a thought seven of the eleven I paid.

Prince. O monstrous ! eleven buckram men grown out of two !

Fal. But, as the devil would have it, three misbegotten knaves in Kendal green came at my back and let drive at me ; for it was so dark, Hal, that thou couldst not see my hand.

Prince. These lies are like their father that begets them ; gross as a mountain, open, palpable. Why, thou clay-brained guts, thou knotty-pated fool, thou whoreson, obscene, greasy tallow-catch,—

Fal. What, art thou mad ? art thou mad ? is not the truth the truth ?

Prince. Why, how couldst thou know these men in Kendal green, when it was so dark thou couldst not see thy hand ? come, tell us your reason : what sayest thou to this ? 259

Poins. Come, your reason, Jack, your reason.

Fal. What, upon compulsion ? 'Zounds, an I were at the strappado, or all the racks in the world, I would not tell you on compulsion. Give you a reason on compulsion ! if reasons were as plentiful as blackberries, I would give no man a reason upon compulsion, I.

Prince. I'll be no longer guilty of this sin ; this sanguine coward, this bed-presser, this horseback-breaker, this huge hill of flesh,—

Fal. 'Sblood, you starveling, you elf-skin, you dried neat's tongue, you bull's pizzle, you stock-fish ! O for breath to utter what is like thee ! you tailor's-yard, you sheath, you bowcase, you vile standing-tuck,—

Prince. Well, breathe awhile, and then to it again : and when thou hast tired thyself in base comparisons, hear me speak but this.

Poins. Mark, Jack.

Prince. We two saw you four set on four and bound them, and were masters of their wealth. Mark now, how a plain tale shall put you down. Then did we two set on you four ; and, with a word, out-faced you from your prize, and have it ; yea, and can show it you here in the house : and, Falstaff, you carried your guts away as nimbly, with as quick dexterity, and roared for mercy and still run and roared, as ever I heard bull-calf. What a slave art thou, to hack thy sword as thou hast done, and then say it was in fight ! What trick, what device, what starting-hole, canst thou now find out to hide thee from this open and apparent shame ?

Poins. Come, let's hear, Jack ; what trick hast thou now ?

Fal. By the Lord, I knew ye as well as he that made ye. Why, hear you, my masters : was it for me to kill the heir-apparent ? should I turn upon the true prince ? why, thou knowest I am as valiant as Hercules : but beware instinct ; the lion will not touch the true prince. Instinct is a great matter ; I was now a coward on instinct. I shall think the better of myself and thee during my life ; I for a valiant lion, and thou for a true prince. But, by the Lord, lads, I am glad you have the money. Hostess, clap to the doors : watch tonight, pray to-morrow. Gallants, lads, boys, hearts of gold, all the titles of good fellowship come to you ! What, shall we be merry ? shall we have a play extempore ?

Prince. Content ; and the argument shall be thy running away. 311

Fal. Ah, no more of that, Hal, an thou lovest me !

Enter Hostess.

Host. O Jesu, my lord the prince !

Prince. How now, my lady the hostess ! what sayest thou to me ?

Host. Marry, my lord, there is a nobleman of the court at door would speak with you : he says he comes from your father. 319

Prince. Give him as much as will make him a royal man, and send him back again to my mother.

Fal. What manner of man is he ?

Host. An old man.

Fal. What doth gravity out of his bed at midnight ? Shall I give him his answer ?

Prince. Prithee, do, Jack.

Fal. 'Faith, and I'll send him packing.

[*Exit.*

Prince. Now, sirs : by'r lady, you fought fair ; so did you, Peto ; so did you, Bardolph : you are lions too, you ran away upon instinct, you will not touch the true prince ; no, fie !

Bard. 'Faith, I ran when I saw others run.

Prince. 'Faith, tell me now in earnest, how came Falstaff's sword so hacked ?

Peto. Why, he hacked it with his dagger, and said he would swear truth out of England but he would make you believe it was done in fight, and persuaded us to do the like. 339

Bard. Yea, and to tickle our noses with

spear-grass to make them bleed, and then to beslubber our garments with it and swear it was the blood of true men. I did that I did not this seven year before, I blushed to hear his monstrous devices.

Prince. O villain, thou stolest a cup of sack eighteen years ago, and wert taken with the manner, and ever since thou hast blushed extempore. Thou hadst fire and sword on thy side, and yet thou rannest away : what instinct hadst thou for it ?   350

Bard. My lord, do you see these meteors ? do you behold these exhalations ?

Prince. I do.

Bard. What think you they portend ?

Prince. Hot livers and cold purses.

Bard. Choler, my lord, if rightly taken.

Prince. No, if rightly taken, halter.

Re-enter FALSTAFF.

Here comes lean Jack, here comes bare-bone. How now, my sweet creature of bombast ! How long is't ago, Jack, since thou sawest thine own knee?   361

Fal. My own knee ! when I was about thy years, Hal, I was not an eagle's talon in the waist ; I could have crept into any alderman's thumb-ring : a plague of sighing and grief ! it blows a man up like a bladder. There's villanous news abroad ; there was Sir John Bracy from your father ; you must to the court in the morning. That same mad fellow of the north, Percy, and he of Wales, that gave Amamon the bastinado and made Lucifer cuckold and swore the devil his true liegeman upon the cross of a Welsh hook—what a plague call you him ?

Poins. O, Glendower.

Fal. Owen, Owen, the same ; and his son-in-law Mortimer, and old Northumberland, and that sprightly Scot of Scots, Douglas, that runs o' horseback up a hill perpendicular,—

Prince. He that rides at high speed and with his pistol kills a sparrow flying.   380

Fal. You have hit it.

Prince. So did he never the sparrow.

Fal. Well, that rascal hath good mettle in him ; he will not run.

Prince. Why, what a rascal art thou then, to praise him so for running !

Fal. O' horseback, ye cuckoo ; but afoot he will not budge a foot.

Prince. Yes, Jack, upon instinct.   389

Fal. I grant ye, upon instinct. Well, he is there too, and one Mordake, and a thousand blue-caps more : Worcester is stolen away to-night ; thy father's beard is turned white with the news : you may buy land now as cheap as stinking mackerel.

Prince. Why, then, it is like, if there come a hot June and this civil buffeting hold, we shall buy maidenheads as they buy hob-nails, by the hundreds.   399

Fal. By the mass, lad, thou sayest true ; it is like we shall have good trading that way. But tell me, Hal, art not thou horrible afeard ? thou being heir-apparent, could the world pick thee out three such enemies again as that fiend Douglas, that spirit Percy, and that devil Glendower ? Art thou not horribly afraid ? doth not thy blood thrill at it ?

Prince. Not a whit, i' faith ; I lack some of thy instinct.   409

Fal. Well, thou wilt be horribly chid to-morrow when thou comest to thy father : if thou love me, practise an answer.

Prince. Do thou stand for my father, and examine me upon the particulars of my life.

Fal. Shall I ? content : this chair shall be my state, this dagger my sceptre, and this cushion my crown.

Prince. Thy state is taken for a joined-stool, thy golden sceptre for a leaden dagger, and thy precious rich crown for a pitiful bald crown !   420

Fal. Well, an the fire of grace be not quite out of thee, now shalt thou be moved. Give me a cup of sack to make my eyes look red, that it may be thought I have wept ; for I must speak in passion, and I will do it in King Cambyses' vein.

Prince. Well, here is my leg.

Fal. And here is my speech. Stand aside, nobility.   429

Host. O Jesu, this is excellent sport, i' faith !

Fal. Weep not, sweet queen ; for trickling tears are vain.

Host. O, the father, how he holds his countenance !

Fal. For God's sake, lords, convey my tristful queen ;

For tears do stop the flood-gates of her eyes.

Host. O Jesu, he doth it as like one of these harlotry players as ever I see !

Fal. Peace, good pint-pot ; peace, good tickle-brain. Harry, I do not only marvel where thou spendest thy time, but also how thou art accompanied : for though the camo-mile, the more it is trodden on the faster it grows, yet youth, the more it is wasted the sooner it wears. That thou art my son, I have partly thy mother's word, partly my own opinion, but chiefly a villanous trick of thine eye and a foolish hanging of thy nether lip, that doth warrant me. If then thou be son to me, here lies the point ; why, being son to me, art thou so pointed at ? Shall the blessed sun of heaven prove a micher and eat black-berries ? a question not to be asked. Shall the sun of England prove a thief and take purses ? a question to be asked. There is a thing, Harry, which thou hast often heard of and it is known to many in our land by the name of pitch : this pitch, as ancient writers do report, doth defile ; so doth the company thou keepest : for, Harry, now I do not speak to thee in drink but in tears, not in pleasure but in passion, not in words only, but in woes also : and yet there is a virtuous man whom I have often noted in thy company, but I know not his name.   461

Prince. What manner of man, an it like your majesty ?

Fal. A goodly portly man, i' faith, and a corpulent ; of a cheerful look, a pleasing eye and a most noble carriage ; and, as I think, his age some fifty, or, by'r lady, inclining to three score ; and now I remember me, his name is Falstaff : if that man should be lewdly given, he deceiveth me ; for, Harry, I see virtue in his looks. If then the tree may be known by the fruit, as the fruit by the tree, then, peremptorily I speak it, there is virtue in that Falstaff : him keep with, the rest banish. And tell me now, thou naughty varlet, tell me, where hast thou been this month?

Prince. Dost thou speak like a king? Do thou stand for me, and I'll play my father.

Fal. Depose me? if thou dost it half so gravely, so majestically, both in word and matter, hang me up by the heels for a rabbit-sucker or a poulter's hare.   481

Prince. Well, here I am set.

Fal. And here I stand : judge, my masters.

Prince. Now, Harry, whence come you?

Fal. My noble lord, from Eastcheap.

Prince. The complaints I hear of thee are grievous.

Fal. 'Sblood, my lord, they are false : nay, I'll tickle ye for a young prince, i' faith.   489

Prince. Swearest thou, ungracious boy? henceforth ne'er look on me. Thou art violently carried away from grace : there is a devil haunts thee in the likeness of an old fat man ; a tun of man is thy companion. Why dost thou converse with that trunk of humors, that bolting-hutch of beastliness, that swollen parcel of dropsies, that huge bombard of sack, that stuffed cloak-bag of guts, that roasted Manningtree ox with the pudding in his belly, that reverend vice, that grey iniquity, that father ruffian, that vanity in years? Wherein is he good, but to taste sack and drink it? wherein neat and cleanly, but to carve a capon and eat it? wherein cunning, but in craft? wherein crafty, but in villany? wherein villanous, but in all things? wherein worthy, but in nothing?

Fal. I would your grace would take me with you : whom means your grace?

Prince. That villanous abominable misleader of youth, Falstaff, that old white-bearded Satan.

Fal. My lord, the man I know.   510

Prince. I know thou dost.

Fal. But to say I know more harm in him than in myself, were to say more than I know. That he is old, the more the pity, his white hairs do witness it ; but that he is, saving your reverence, a whoremaster, that I utterly deny. If sack and sugar be a fault, God help the wicked ! if to be old and merry be a sin, then many an old host that I know is damned : if to be fat be to be hated, then Pharaoh's lean kine are to be loved. No, my good lord ; banish Peto, banish Bardolph, banish Poins : but for sweet Jack Falstaff, kind Jack Falstaff, true Jack Falstaff, valiant Jack Falstaff, and therefore more valiant, being, as he is, old Jack Falstaff, banish not him thy Harry's company, banish not him thy Harry's company : banish plump Jack, and banish all the world.

Prince. I do, I will.   [*A knocking heard.*
[*Exeunt Hostess, Francis, and Bardolph.*

Re-enter Bardolph, *running.*

Bard. O, my lord, my lord ! the sheriff with a most monstrous watch is at the door.

Fal. Out, ye rogue ! Play out the play : I have much to say in the behalf of that Falstaff.

Re-enter the Hostess.

Host. O Jesu, my lord, my lord !

Prince. Heigh, heigh ! the devil rides upon a fiddlestick : what's the matter?

Host. The sheriff and all the watch are at

the door : they are come to search the house. Shall I let them in?

Fal. Dost thou hear, Hal? never call a true piece of gold a counterfeit : thou art essentially mad, without seeming so.   541

Prince. And thou a natural coward, without instinct.

Fal. I deny your major : if you will deny the sheriff, so ; if not, let him enter : if I become not a cart as well as another man, a plague on my bringing up ! I hope I shall as soon be strangled with a halter as another.

Prince. Go, hide thee behind the arras : the rest walk up above. Now, my masters, for a true face and good conscience.   551

Fal. Both which I have had : but their date is out, and therefore I'll hide me.

Prince. Call in the sheriff.
[*Exeunt all except the Prince and Peto.*

Enter Sheriff *and the* Carrier.

Now, master sheriff, what is your will with me?

Sher. First, pardon me, my lord. A hue and cry
Hath follow'd certain men unto this house.

Prince. What men?

Sher. One of them is well known, my gracious lord,
A gross fat man.

Car.   As fat as butter.   560

Prince. The man, I do assure you, is not here ;
For I myself at this time have employ'd him.
And, sheriff, I will engage my word to thee
That I will, by to-morrow dinner-time,
Send him to answer thee, or any man,
For any thing he shall be charged withal :
And so let me entreat you leave the house.

Sher. I will, my lord. There are two gentlemen
Have in this robbery lost three hundred marks.

Prince. It may be so : if he have robb'd these men,   570
He shall be answerable ; and so farewell.

Sher. Good night, my noble lord.

Prince. I think it is good morrow, is it not?

Sher. Indeed, my lord, I think it be two o'clock.   [*Exeunt Sheriff and Carrier.*

Prince. This oily rascal is known as well as Paul's. Go, call him forth.

Peto. Falstaff !—Fast asleep behind the arras, and snorting like a horse.

Prince. Hark, how hard he fetches breath. Search his pockets. [*He searcheth his pockets, and findeth certain papers.*] What hast thou found?

Peto. Nothing but papers, my lord.

Prince. Let's see what they be : read them.

Peto. [*Reads*] Item, A capon, . . 2s. 2d.
Item, Sauce, . . 4d.
Item, Sack, two gallons, 5s. 8d.
Item, Anchovies and sack
after supper, . 2s. 6d.
Item, Bread, . . ob.

Prince. O monstrous ! but one half-penny-worth of bread to this intolerable deal of sack ! What there is else, keep close ; we'll read it at more advantage : there let him sleep till day. I'll to the court in the morning. We must all to the wars, and thy place shall be honorable. I'll procure this fat rogue a charge

of foot; and I know his death will be a march
of twelve-score. The money shall be paid back
again with advantage. Be with me betimes in
the morning; and so, good morrow, Peto. 601
        [*Exeunt.*
Peto. Good morrow, good my lord.

ACT III.

SCENE I. *Bangor. The Archdeacon's house.*

Enter HOTSPUR, WORCESTER, MORTIMER, *and*
        GLENDOWER.

Mort. These promises are fair, the parties
        sure,
And our induction full of prosperous hope.
Hot. Lord Mortimer, and cousin Glen-
        dower,
Will you sit down?
And uncle Worcester: a plague upon it!
I have forgot the map.
Glend.   No, here it is.
Sit, cousin Percy; sit, good cousin Hotspur,
For by that name as oft as Lancaster
Doth speak of you, his cheek looks pale and
        with
A rising sigh he wisheth you in heaven.   10
Hot. And you in hell, as oft as he hears
Owen Glendower spoke of.
Glend. I cannot blame him: at my nativity
The front of heaven was full of fiery shapes,
Of burning cressets; and at my birth
The frame and huge foundation of the earth
Shaked like a coward.
Hot. Why, so it would have done at the
same season, if your mother's cat had but kit-
tened, though yourself had never been born.
Glend. I say the earth did shake when I
        was born.   21
Hot. And I say the earth was not of my
        mind,
If you suppose as fearing you it shook.
Glend. The heavens were all on fire, the
        earth did tremble.
Hot. O, then the earth shook to see the
        heavens on fire,
And not in fear of your nativity.
Diseased nature oftentimes breaks forth
In strange eruptions; oft the teeming earth
Is with a kind of colic pinch'd and vex'd
By the imprisoning of unruly wind   30
Within her womb; which, for enlargement
        striving,
Shakes the old beldam earth and topples down
Steeples and moss-grown towers. At your birth
Our grandam earth, having this distempera-
        ture,
In passion shook.
Glend.   Cousin, of many men
I do not bear these crossings. Give me leave
To tell you once again that at my birth
The front of heaven was full of fiery shapes,
The goats ran from the mountains, and the
        herds
Were strangely clamorous to the frighted
        fields.   40
These signs have mark'd me extraordinary;
And all the courses of my life do show
I am not in the roll of common men.
Where is he living, clipp'd in with the sea
That chides the banks of England, Scotland,
        Wales,

Which calls me pupil, or hath read to me?
And bring him out that is but woman's son
Can trace me in the tedious ways of art
And hold me pace in deep experiments.
Hot. I think there's no man speaks better
Welsh. I'll to dinner.   50
Mort. Peace, cousin Percy; you will make
        him mad.
Glend. I can call spirits from the vasty
        deep.
Hot. Why, so can I, or so can any man;
But will they come when you do call for
        them?
Glend. Why, I can teach you, cousin, to
        command
The devil.
Hot. And I can teach thee, coz, to shame
        the devil
By telling truth: tell truth and shame the
        devil.
If thou have power to raise him, bring him
        hither,   60
And I'll be sworn I have power to shame him
        hence.
O, while you live, tell truth and shame the
        devil!
Mort. Come, come, no more of this un-
        profitable chat.
Glend. Three times hath Henry Boling-
        broke made head
Against my power; thrice from the banks of
        Wye
And sandy-bottom'd Severn have I sent him
Bootless home and weather-beaten back.
Hot. Home without boots, and in foul
        weather too!
How 'scapes he agues, in the devil's name?
Glend. Come, here's the map: shall we di-
        vide our right   70
According to our threefold order ta'en?
Mort. The archdeacon hath divided it
Into three limits very equally:
England, from Trent and Severn hitherto,
By south and east is to my part assign'd:
All westward, Wales beyond the Severn shore,
And all the fertile land within that bound,
To Owen Glendower: and, dear coz, to you
The remnant northward, lying off from Trent.
And our indentures tripartite are drawn; 80
Which being sealed interchangeably,
A business that this night may execute,
To-morrow, cousin Percy, you and I
And my good Lord of Worcester will set forth
To meet your father and the Scottish power,
As is appointed us, at Shrewsbury.
My father Glendower is not ready yet,
Nor shall we need his help these fourteen days.
Within that space you may have drawn to-
        gether
Your tenants, friends and neighboring gentle-
        men.   90
Glend. A shorter time shall send me to
        you, lords:
And in my conduct shall your ladies come;
From whom you now must steal and take no
        leave,
For there will be a world of water shed
Upon the parting of your wives and you.
Hot. Methinks my moiety, north from Bur-
        ton here,
In quantity equals not one of yours:
See how this river comes me cranking in,
And cuts me from the best of all my land 99

A huge half-moon, a monstrous cantle out.
I'll have the current in this place damm'd up ;
And here the smug and silver Trent shall run
In a new channel, fair and evenly ;
It shall not wind with such a deep indent,
To rob me of so rich a bottom here.
 Glend. Not wind ? it shall, it must ; you
  see it doth.
 Mort. Yea, but
Mark how he bears his course, and runs me up
With like advantage on the other side ;
Gelding the opposed continent as much 110
As on the other side it takes from you.
 Wor. Yea, but a little charge will trench
  him here
And on this north side win this cape of land ;
And then he runs straight and even.
 Hot. I'll have it so : a little charge will do
  it.
 Glend. I'll not have it alter'd.
 Hot.   Will not you ?
 Glend. No, nor you shall not.
 Hot. Who shall say me nay ?
 Glend. Why, that will I.
 Hot. Let me not understand you, then ;
speak it in Welsh. 120
 Glend. I can speak English, lord, as well as
  you ;
For I was train'd up in the English court ;
Where, being but young, I framed to the harp
Many an English ditty lovely well
And gave the tongue a helpful ornament,
A virtue that was never seen in you.
 Hot. Marry,
And I am glad of it with all my heart :
I had rather be a kitten and cry mew 129
Than one of these same metre ballad-mongers ;
I had rather hear a brazen canstick turn'd,
Or a dry wheel grate on the axle-tree ;
And that would set my teeth nothing on edge,
Nothing so much as mincing poetry :
'Tis like the forced gait of a shuffling nag.
 Glend. Come, you shall have Trent turn'd.
 Hot. I do not care : I'll give thrice so
  much land
To any well-deserving friend ;
But in the way of bargain, mark ye me,
I'll cavil on the ninth part of a hair. 140
Are the indentures drawn ? shall we be gone ?
 Glend. The moon shines fair ; you may
  away by night :
I'll haste the writer and withal
Break with your wives of your departure
  hence :
I am afraid my daughter will run mad,
So much she doteth on her Mortimer. [*Exit.*
 Mort. Fie, cousin Percy ! how you cross my
  father !
 Hot. I cannot choose : sometime he angers
  me
With telling me of the moldwarp and the ant,
Of the dreamer Merlin and his prophecies,
And of a dragon and a finless fish, 151
A clip-wing'd griffin and a moulten raven,
A couching lion and a ramping cat,
And such a deal of skimble-skamble stuff
As puts me from my faith. I tell you what ;
He held me last night at least nine hours
In reckoning up the several devils' names
That were his lackeys : I cried 'hum,' and
'well, go to,'
But mark'd him not a word. O, he is as tedious
As a tired horse, a railing wife ; 160

Worse than a smoky house : I had rather live
With cheese and garlic in a windmill, far,
Than feed on cates and have him talk to me
In any summer-house in Christendom.
 Mort. In faith, he is a worthy gentleman,
Exceedingly well read, and profited
In strange concealments, valiant as a lion
And wondrous affable and as bountiful
As mines of India. Shall I tell you, cousin ?
He holds your temper in a high respect 170
And curbs himself even of his natural scope
When you come 'cross his humor ; faith, he
  does :
I warrant you, that man is not alive
Might so have tempted him as you have done,
Without the taste of danger and reproof :
But do not use it oft, let me entreat you.
 Wor. In faith, my lord, you are too wilful-
  blame ;
And since your coming hither have done
  enough
To put him quite beside his patience.
You must needs learn, lord, to amend this
  fault : 180
Though sometimes it show greatness, courage,
  blood,—
And that's the dearest grace it renders you,—
Yet oftentimes it doth present harsh rage,
Defect of manners, want of government,
Pride, haughtiness, opinion and disdain :
The least of which haunting a nobleman
Loseth men's hearts and leaves behind a stain
Upon the beauty of all parts besides,
Beguiling them of commendation.
 Hot. Well, I am school'd : good manners
  be your speed ! 190
Here come our wives, and let us take our
  leave.

  Re-enter Glendower *with the ladies.*

 Mort. This is the deadly spite that angers
  me ;
My wife can speak no English, I no Welsh.
 Glend. My daughter weeps : she will not
  part with you ;
She'll be a soldier too, she'll to the wars.
 Mort. Good father, tell her that she and
  my aunt Percy
Shall follow in your conduct speedily.
  [*Glendower speaks to her in Welsh, and she*
       answers him in the same.
 Glend. She is desperate here ; a peevish
self-will'd harlotry, one that no persuasion can
do good upon. [*The lady speaks in Welsh.*
 Mort. I understand thy looks : that pretty
  Welsh 201
Which thou pour'st down from these swelling
  heavens
I am too perfect in ; and, but for shame,
In such a parley should I answer thee.
  [*The lady speaks again in Welsh.*
I understand thy kisses and thou mine,
And that's a feeling disputation :
But I will never be a truant, love,
Till I have learned thy language ; for thy
  tongue
Makes Welsh as sweet as ditties highly penn'd,
Sung by a fair queen in a summer's bower, 210
With ravishing division, to her lute.
 Glend. Nay, if you melt, then will she run
  mad. [*The lady speaks again in Welsh.*
 Mort. O, I am ignorance itself in this !

Glend. She bids you on the wanton rushes
lay you down
And rest your gentle head upon her lap,
And she will sing the song that pleaseth you
And on your eyelids crown the god of sleep,
Charming your blood with pleasing heaviness,
Making such difference 'twixt wake and sleep
As is the difference betwixt day and night   220
The hour before the heavenly-harness'd team
Begins his golden progress in the east.
Mort. With all my heart I'll sit and hear
her sing :
By that time will our book, I think, be drawn.
Glend. Do so ;
And those musicians that shall play to you
Hang in the air a thousand leagues from
hence,
And straight they shall be here : sit, and at-
tend.
Hot. Come, Kate, thou art perfect in lying
down : come, quick, quick, that I may lay my
head in thy lap.   231
Lady P. Go, ye giddy goose.
[*The music plays.*
Hot. Now I perceive the devil understands
Welsh ;
And 'tis no marvel he is so humorous.
By'r lady, he is a good musician.
Lady P. Then should you be nothing but
musical for you are altogether governed by
humors. Lie still, ye thief, and hear the lady
sing in Welsh.
Hot. I had rather hear Lady, my brach,
howl in Irish.   241
Lady P. Wouldst thou have thy head
broken ?
Hot. No.
Lady P. Then be still.
Hot. Neither ; 'tis a woman's fault.
Lady P. Now God help thee !
Hot. To the Welsh lady's bed.
Lady P. What's that ?
Hot. Peace ! she sings.
[*Here the lady sings a Welsh song.*
Hot. Come, Kate, I'll have your song too.
Lady P. Not mine, in good sooth.   251
Hot. Not yours, in good sooth ! Heart !
you swear like a comfit-maker's wife. ' Not
you, in good sooth,' and ' as true as I live,' and
' as God shall mend me,' and ' as sure as day,'
And givest such sarcenet surety for thy oaths,
As if thou never walk'st further than Fins-
bury.
Swear me, Kate, like a lady as thou art,
A good mouth-filling oath, and leave ' in
sooth,'
And such protest of pepper-gingerbread,   260
To velvet-guards and Sunday-citizens.
Come, sing.
Lady P. I will not sing.
Hot. 'Tis the next way to turn tailor, or
be red-breast teacher. An the indentures be
drawn, I'll away within these two hours ; and
so, come in when ye will.   [*Exit.*
Glend. Come, come, Lord Mortimer ; you
are as slow
As hot Lord Percy is on fire to go.
By this our book is drawn ; we'll but seal,   270
And then to horse immediately.
Mort. With all my heart.   [*Exeunt.*

SCENE II. *London. The palace.*

Enter the KING, PRINCE OF WALES, *and others.*

King. Lords, give us leave ; the Prince of
Wales and I
Must have some private conference ; but be
near at hand,
For we shall presently have need of you.
[*Exeunt Lords.*
I know not whether God will have it so,
For some displeasing service I have done,
That, in his secret doom, out of my blood
He'll breed revengement and a scourge for
me ;
But thou dost in thy passages of life
Make me believe that thou art only mark'd
For the hot vengeance and the rod of heaven
To punish my mistreadings. Tell me else,   11
Could such inordinate and low desires,
Such poor, such bare, such lewd, such mean
attempts,
Such barren pleasures, rude society,
As thou art match'd withal and grafted to,
Accompany the greatness of thy blood
And hold their level with thy princely heart ?
Prince. So please your majesty, I would I
could
Quit all offences with as clear excuse
As well as I am doubtless I can purge   20
Myself of many I am charged withal :
Yet such extenuation let me beg,
As, in reproof of many tales devised,
Which oft the ear of greatness needs must
hear,
By smiling pick-thanks and base news-
mongers,
I may, for some things true, wherein my youth
Hath faulty wander'd and irregular,
Find pardon on my true submission.
King. God pardon thee ! yet let me won-
der, Harry,
At thy affections, which do hold a wing   30
Quite from the flight of all thy ancestors.
Thy place in council thou hast rudely lost,
Which by thy younger brother is supplied,
And art almost an alien to the hearts
Of all the court and princes of my blood :
The hope and expectation of thy time
Is ruin'd, and the soul of every man
Prophetically doth forethink thy fall.
Had I so lavish of my presence been,
So common-hackney'd in the eyes of men,   40
So stale and cheap to vulgar company,
Opinion, that did help me to the crown,
Had still kept loyal to possession
And left me in reputeless banishment,
A fellow of no mark nor likelihood.
By being seldom seen, I could not stir
But like a comet I was wonder'd at ;
That men would tell their children ' This is
he ; '
Others would say ' Where, which is Boling-
broke ? '
And then I stole all courtesy from heaven,   50
And dress'd myself in such humility
That I did pluck allegiance from men's hearts,
Loud shouts and salutations from their mouths,
Even in the presence of the crowned king.
Thus did I keep my person fresh and new ;
My presence, like a robe pontifical,
Ne'er seen but wonder'd at : and so my state,
Seldom but sumptuous, showed like a feast
And won by rareness such solemnity.

The skipping king, he ambled up and down 60
With shallow jesters and rash bavin wits,
Soon kindled and soon burnt; carded his
  state,
Mingled his royalty with capering fools,
Had his great name profaned with their scorns
And gave his countenance, against his name,
To laugh at gibing boys and stand the push
Of every beardless vain comparative,
Grew a companion to the common streets,
Enfeoff'd himself to popularity;
That, being daily swallow'd by men's eyes, 70
They surfeited with honey and began
To loathe the taste of sweetness, whereof a
  little
More than a little is by much too much.
So when he had occasion to be seen,
He was but as the cuckoo is in June,
Heard, not regarded; seen, but with such eyes
As, sick and blunted with community,
Afford no extraordinary gaze,
Such as is bent on sun-like majesty
When it shines seldom in admiring eyes; 80
But rather drowzed and hung their eyelids
  down,
Slept in his face and render'd such aspect
As cloudy men use to their adversaries,
Being with his presence glutted, gorged and
  full.
And in that very line, Harry, standest thou;
For thou hast lost thy princely privilege
With vile participation: not an eye
But is a-weary of thy common sight,
Save mine, which hath desired to see thee
  more;
Which now doth that I would not have it do,
Make blind itself with foolish tenderness. 91
  Prince. I shall hereafter, my thrice gracious
    lord,
Be more myself.
  King.   For all the world
As thou art to this hour was Richard then
When I from France set foot at Ravenspurgh,
And even as I was then is Percy now.
Now, by my sceptre and my soul to boot,
He hath more worthy interest to the state
Than thou the shadow of succession;
For of no right, nor color like to right, 100
He doth fill fields with harness in the realm,
Turns head against the lion's armed jaws,
And, being no more in debt to years than thou,
Leads ancient lords and reverend bishops on
To bloody battles and to bruising arms.
What never-dying honor hath he got
Against renowned Douglas! whose high deeds,
Whose hot incursions and great name in arms
Holds from all soldiers chief majority
And military title capital   110
Through all the kingdoms that acknowledge
    Christ:
Thrice hath this Hotspur, Mars in swathling
    clothes,
This infant warrior, in his enterprizes
Discomfited great Douglas, ta'en him once,
Enlarged him and made a friend of him,
To fill the mouth of deep defiance up
And shake the peace and safety of our throne.
And what say you to this? Percy, Northum-
    berland,
The Archbishop's grace of York, Douglas,
    Mortimer,
Capitulate against us and are up.   120
But wherefore do I tell these news to thee?

Why, Harry, do I tell thee of my foes,
Which art my near'st and dearest enemy?
Thou that art like enough, through vassal fear,
Base inclination and the start of spleen
To fight against me under Percy's pay,
To dog his heels and curtsy at his frowns,
To show how much thou art degenerate.
  Prince. Do not think so; you shall not find
    it so:
And God forgive them that so much have
    sway'd   130
Your majesty's good thoughts away from me!
I will redeem all this on Percy's head
And in the closing of some glorious day
Be bold to tell you that I am your son;
When I will wear a garment all of blood
And stain my favors in a bloody mask,
Which, wash'd away, shall scour my shame
    with it:
And that shall be the day, whene'er it lights,
That this same child of honor and renown,
This gallant Hotspur, this all-praised knight,
And your unthought-of Harry chance to meet.
For every honor sitting on his helm,
Would they were multitudes, and on my head
My shames redoubled! for the time will come,
That I shall make this northern youth ex-
    change
His glorious deeds for my indignities.
Percy is but my factor, good my lord,
To engross up glorious deeds on my behalf;
And I will call him to so strict account,
That he shall render every glory up,   150
Yea, even the slightest worship of his time,
Or I will tear the reckoning from his heart.
This, in the name of God, I promise here:
The which if He be pleased I shall perform,
I do beseech your majesty may salve
The long-grown wounds of my intemperance:
If not, the end of life cancels all bands;
And I will die a hundred thousand deaths
Ere break the smallest parcel of this vow.
  King. A hundred thousand rebels die in
    this: 160
Thou shalt have charge and sovereign trust
    herein.

Enter Blunt.

How now, good Blunt? thy looks are full of
    speed.
  Blunt. So hath the business that I come to
    speak of.
Lord Mortimer of Scotland hath sent word
That Douglas and the English rebels met
The eleventh of this month at Shrewsbury
A mighty and a fearful head they are,
If promises be kept on every hand,
As ever offer'd foul play in a state.
  King. The Earl of Westmoreland set forth
    to-day;   170
With him my son, Lord John of Lancaster;
For this advertisement is five days old:
On Wednesday next, Harry, you shall set for-
    ward;
On Thursday we ourselves will march: our
    meeting
Is Bridgenorth: and, Harry, you shall march
Through Gloucestershire; by which account,
Our business valued, some twelve days hence
Our general forces at Bridgenorth shall meet.
Our hands are full of business: let's away;
Advantage feeds him fat, while men delay. 180
                                    [*Exeunt.*

SCENE III. *Eastcheap. The Boar's-Head
Tavern*

Enter FALSTAFF *and* BARDOLPH.

Fal. Bardolph, am I not fallen away vilely
since this last action ? do I not bate ? do I not
dwindle ? Why, my skin hangs about me like
an old lady's loose gown ; I am withered like
an old apple-john. Well, I'll repent, and that
suddenly, while I am in some liking ; I shall
be out of heart shortly, and then I shall have
no strength to repent. An I have not forgotten
what the inside of a church is made of, I am
a peppercorn, a brewer's horse : the inside of
a church ! Company, villanous company, hath
been the spoil of me.

Bard. Sir John, you are so fretful, you
cannot live long.

Fal. Why, there is it : come sing me a
bawdy song ; make me merry. I was as virtuously given as a gentleman need to be ; virtuous enough ; swore little ; diced not above
seven times a week ; went to a bawdy-house
not above once in a quarter—of an hour ; paid
money that I borrowed, three or four times ;
lived well and in good compass : and now I
live out of all order, out of all compass.

Bard. Why, you are so fat, Sir John, that
you must needs be out of all compass, out of
all reasonable compass, Sir John.

Fal. Do thou amend thy face, and I'll
amend my life : thou art our admiral, thou
bearest the lantern in the poop, but 'tis in the
nose of thee ; thou art the Knight of the Burn-
ing Lamp.   30

Bard. Why, Sir John, my face does you no
harm.

Fal. No, I'll be sworn ; I make as good
use of it as many a man doth of a Death's-
head or a memento mori : I never see thy
face but I think upon hell-fire and Dives that
lived in purple ; for there he is in his robes,
burning, burning. If thou wert any way given
to virtue, I would swear by thy face ; my oath
should be ' By this fire, that's God's angel : '
but thou art altogether given over ; and wert
indeed, but for the light in thy face, the son of
utter darkness. When thou rannest up Gadshill in the night to catch my horse, if I did
not think thou hadst been an ignis fatuus or a
ball of wildfire, there's no purchase in money.
O, thou art a perpetual triumph, an everlasting
bonfire-light ! Thou hast saved me a thousand
marks in links and torches, walking with thee
in the night betwixt tavern and tavern : but
the sack that thou hast drunk me would have
bought me lights as good cheap at the dearest
chandler's in Europe. I have maintained that
salamander of yours with fire any time this
two and thirty years ; God reward me for it !

Bard. 'Sblood, I would my face were in
your belly !

Fal. God-a-mercy ! so should I be sure to
be heart-burned.

Enter Hostess.

How now, Dame Partlet the hen ! have you
inquired yet who picked my pocket ?   61

Host. Why, Sir John, what do you think,
Sir John ? do you think I keep thieves in my
house ? I have searched, I have inquired, so
has my husband, man by man, boy by boy,
servant by servant : the tithe of a hair was
never lost in my house before.

Fal. Ye lie, hostess : Bardolph was shaved
and lost many a hair ; and I'll be sworn my
pocket was picked. Go to, you are a woman,
go.

Host. Who, I ? no ; I defy thee : God's
light, I was never called so in mine own house
before.

Fal. Go to, I know you well enough.

Host. No, Sir John ; you do not know me,
Sir John. I know you, Sir John : you owe me
money, Sir John ; and now you pick a quarrel
to beguile me of it : I bought you a dozen of
shirts to your back.

Fal. Dowlas, filthy dowlas : I have given
them away to bakers' wives, and they have
made bolters of them.   81

Host. Now, as I am a true woman, holland of eight shillings an ell. You owe money
here besides, Sir John, for your diet and by-
drinkings, and money lent you, four and
twenty pound.

Fal. He had his part of it ; let him pay.

Host. He ? alas, he is poor ; he hath nothing.

Fal. How ! poor ? look upon his face ;
what call you rich ? let them coin his nose,
let them coin his cheeks : I'll not pay a denier.
What, will you make a younker of me ? shall
I not take mine ease in mine inn but I shall
have my pocket picked ? I have lost a seal-
ring of my grandfather's worth forty mark.

Host. O Jesu, I have heard the prince tell
him, I know not how oft, that that ring was
copper !

Fal. How ! the prince is a Jack, a sneak-
cup : 'sblood, an he were here, I would cudgel
him like a dog, if he would say so.   101

Enter the PRINCE *and* PETO, *marching, and*
FALSTAFF *meets them playing on his truncheon like a fife.*

How now, lad ! is the wind in that door, i'
faith ? must we all march ?

Bard. Yea, two and two, Newgate fashion.

Host. My lord, I pray you, hear me.

Prince. What sayest thou, Mistress
Quickly ? How doth thy husband ? I love him
well ; he is an honest man.

Host. Good my lord, hear me.

Fal. Prithee, let her alone, and list to me.

Prince. What sayest thou, Jack ?   111

Fal. The other night I fell asleep here behind the arras and had my pocket picked :
this house is turned bawdy-house ; they pick
pockets.

Prince. What didst thou lose, Jack ?

Fal. Wilt thou believe me, Hal ? three or
four bonds of forty pound a-piece, and a seal-
ring of my grandfather's.

Prince. A trifle, some eight-penny matter.

Host. So I told him, my lord ; and I said
I heard your grace say so : and, my lord, he
speaks most vilely of you, like a foul-mouthed
man as he is ; and said he would cudgel you.

Prince. What ! he did not ?

Host. There's neither faith, truth, nor
womanhood in me else.

Fal. There's no more faith in thee than in
a stewed prune ; nor no more truth in thee
than in a drawn fox ; and for womanhood,

Maid Marian may be the deputy's wife of the ward to thee. Go, you thing, go. 131

Host. Say, what thing ? what thing ?

Fal. What thing ! why, a thing to thank God on.

Host. I am no thing to thank God on, I would thou shouldst know it ; I am an honest man's wife : and, setting thy knighthood aside, thou art a knave to call me so.

Fal. Setting thy womanhood aside, thou art a beast to say otherwise. 140

Host. Say, what beast, thou knave, thou ?

Fal. What beast ! why, an otter.

Prince. An otter, Sir John ! why an otter ?

Fal. Why, she's neither fish nor flesh ; a man knows not where to have her.

Host. Thou art an unjust man in saying so : thou or any man knows where to have me, thou knave, thou !

Prince. Thou sayest true, hostess ; and he slanders thee most grossly. 150

Host. So he doth you, my lord ; and said this other day you ought him a thousand pound.

Prince. Sirrah, do I owe you a thousand pound ?

Fal. A thousand pound, Hal ! a million : thy love is worth a million : thou owest me thy love.

Host. Nay, my lord, he called you Jack, and said he would cudgel you.

Fal. Did I, Bardolph ? 160

Bard. Indeed, Sir John, you said so.

Fal. Yea, if he said my ring was copper.

Prince. I say 'tis copper : darest thou be as good as thy word now ?

Fal. Why, Hal, thou knowest, as thou art but man, I dare : but as thou art prince, I fear thee as I fear the roaring of the lion's whelp.

Prince. And why not as the lion ?

Fal. The king himself is to be feared as the lion : dost thou think I'll fear thee as I fear thy father ? nay, an I do, I pray Cod my girdle break.

Prince. O, if it should, how would thy guts fall about thy knees ! But, sirrah, there's no room for faith, truth, nor honesty in this bosom of thine ; it is all filled up with guts and midriff. Charge an honest woman with picking thy pocket ! why, thou whoreson, impudent, embossed rascal, if there were anything in thy pocket but tavern-reckonings, memorandums of bawdy-houses, and one poor pennyworth of sugar-candy to make thee longwinded, if thy pocket were enriched with any other injuries but these, I am a villain : and yet you will stand to it ; you will not pocket up wrong : art thou not ashamed ?

Fal. Dost thou hear, Hal ? thou knowest in the state of innocency Adam fell ; and what should poor Jack Falstaff do in the days of villany ? Thou seest I have more flesh than another man, and therefore more frailty. You confess then, you picked my pocket ? 190

Prince. It appears so by the story.

Fal. Hostess, I forgive thee : go, make ready breakfast ; love thy husband, look to thy servants, cherish thy guests : thou shalt find me tractable to any honest reason : thou seest I am pacified still. Nay, prithee, be gone. [*Exit Hostess.*] Now, Hal, to the news at ourt : for the robbery, lad, how is that answered ?

Prince. O, my sweet beef, I must still be good angel to thee : the money is paid back again. 200

Fal. O, I do not like that paying back ; 'tis a double labor.

Prince. I am good friends with my father and may do any thing.

Fal. Rob me the exchequer the first thing thou doest, and do it with unwashed hands too.

Bard. Do, my lord.

Prince. I have procured thee, Jack, a charge of foot. 209

Fal. I would it had been of horse. Where shall I find one that can steal well ? O for a fine thief, of the age of two and twenty or thereabouts ! I am heinously unprovided. Well, God be thanked for these rebels, they offend none but the virtuous : I laud them, I praise them.

Prince. Bardolph !

Bard. My lord ?

Prince. Go bear this letter to Lord John of Lancaster, to my brother John ; this to my Lord of Westmoreland. [*Exit Bardolph.*] Go, Peto, to horse, to horse ; for thou and I have thirty miles to ride yet ere dinner time. [*Exit Peto.*] Jack, meet me to-morrow in the temple hall at two o'clock in the afternoon. There shalt thou know thy charge ; and there receive

Money and order for their furniture.
The land is burning ; Percy stands on high ;
And either we or they must lower lie. [*Exit.*

Fal. Rare words ! brave world ! Hostess, my breakfast, come ! 229
O, I could wish this tavern were my drum ! [*Exit.*

ACT IV.

SCENE I. *The rebel camp near Shrewsbury.*

Enter HOTSPUR, WORCESTER, *and* DOUGLAS.

Hot. Well said, my noble Scot : if speaking truth
In this fine age were not thought flattery,
Such attribution should the Douglas have,
As not a soldier of this season's stamp
Should go so general current through the world.
By God, I cannot flatter ; I do defy
The tongues of soothers ; but a braver place
In my heart's love hath no man than yourself :
Nay, task me to my word ; approve me, lord.

Doug. Thou art the king of honor : 10
No man so potent breathes upon the ground
But I will beard him.

Hot.   Do so, and 'tis well.

Enter a Messenger *with letters.*

What letters hast thou there ?—I can but thank you.

Mess. These letters come from your father.

Hot. Letters from him ! why comes he not himself ?

Mess. He cannot come, my lord ; he is grievous sick.

Hot. 'Zounds ! how has he the leisure to be sick
In such a justling time ? Who leads his power ?
Under whose government come they along ?

Mess. His letters bear his mind, not I, my lord. 20

Wor. I prithee, tell me, doth he keep his bed ?

Mess. He did, my lord, four days ere I set forth ;
And at the time of my departure thence
He was much fear'd by his physicians.

Wor. I would the state of time had first been whole
Ere he by sickness had been visited :
His health was never better worth than now.

Hot. Sick now! droop now! this sickness doth infect
The very life-blood of our enterprise ;
'Tis catching hither, even to our camp. 30
He writes me here, that inward sickness—
And that his friends by deputation could not
So soon be drawn, nor did he think it meet
To lay so dangerous and dear a trust
On any soul removed but on his own.
Yet doth he give us bold advertisement,
That with our small conjunction we should on,
To see how fortune is disposed to us ;
For, as he writes, there is no quailing now,
Because the king is certainly possess'd 40
Of all our purposes. What say you to it ?

Wor. Your father's sickness is a maim to us.

Hot. A perilous gash, a very limb lopp'd off :
And yet, in faith, it is not ; his present want
Seems more than we shall find it : were it good
To set the exact wealth of all our states
All at one cast ? to set so rich a main
On the nice hazard of one doubtful hour ?
It were not good ; for therein should we read
The very bottom and the soul of hope, 50
The very list, the very utmost bound
Of all our fortunes.

Doug.   'Faith, and so we should ;
Where now remains a sweet reversion :
We may boldly spend upon the hope of what
Is to come in :
A comfort of retirement lives in this.

Hot. A rendezvous, a home to fly unto,
If that the devil and mischance look big
Upon the maidenhead of our affairs.

Wor. But yet I would your father had been here. 60
The quality and hair of our attempt
Brooks no division : it will be thought
By some, that know not why he is away,
That wisdom, loyalty and mere dislike
Of our proceedings kept the earl from hence :
And think how such an apprehension
May turn the tide of fearful faction
And breed a kind of question in our cause ;
For well you know we of the offering side
Must keep aloof from strict arbitrement, 70
And stop all sight-holes, every loop from whence
The eye of reason may pry in upon us :
This absence of your father's draws a curtain,
That shows the ignorant a kind of fear
Before not dreamt of.

Hot.   You strain too far.
I rather of his absence make this use :
It lends a lustre and more great opinion,
A larger dare to our great enterprise,
Than if the earl were here ; for men must think,

If we without his help can make a head 80
To push against a kingdom, with his help
We shall o'erturn it topsy-turvy down.
Yet all goes well, yet all our joints are whole.

Doug. As heart can think : there is not such a word
Spoke of in Scotland as this term of fear.

Enter SIR RICHARD VERNON.

Hot. My cousin Vernon, welcome, by my soul.

Ver. Pray God my news be worth a welcome, lord.
The Earl of Westmoreland, seven thousand strong,
Is marching hitherwards ; with him Prince John.

Hot. No harm : what more ?

Ver.   And further, I have learn'd, 90
The king himself in person is set forth,
Or hitherwards intended speedily,
With strong and mighty preparation.

Hot. He shall be welcome too. Where is his son,
The nimble-footed madcap Prince of Wales,
And his comrades, that daff'd the world aside,
And bid it pass ?

Ver.   All furnish'd, all in arms ;
All plumed like estridges that with the wind
Baited like eagles having lately bathed ;
Glittering in golden coats, like images ; 100
As full of spirit as the month of May,
And gorgeous as the sun at midsummer ;
Wanton as youthful goats, wild as young bulls.
I saw young Harry, with his beaver on,
His cuisses on his thighs, gallantly arm'd,
Rise from the ground like feather'd Mercury,
And vaulted with such ease into his seat,
As if an angel dropp'd down from the clouds,
To turn and wind a fiery Pegasus
And witch the world with noble horsemanship.

Hot. No more, no more : worse than the sun in March, 111
This praise doth nourish agues. Let them come ;
They come like sacrifices in their trim,
And to the fire-eyed maid of smoky war
All hot and bleeding will we offer them :
The mailed Mars shall on his altar sit
Up to the ears in blood. I am on fire
To hear this rich reprisal is so nigh
And yet not ours. Come, let me taste my horse,
Who is to bear me like a thunderbolt 120
Against the bosom of the Prince of Wales :
Harry to Harry shall, hot horse to horse,
Meet and ne'er part till one drop down a corse.
O that Glendower were come !

Ver.   There is more news :
I learn'd in Worcester, as I rode along,
He cannot draw his power this fourteen days.

Doug. That's the worst tidings that I hear of yet.

Wor. Ay, by my faith, that bears a frosty sound.

Hot. What may the king's whole battle reach unto ?

Ver. To thirty thousand.

Hot.   Forty let it be : 130
My father and Glendower being both away,
The powers of us may serve so great a day
Come, let us take a muster speedily :
Doomsday is near ; die all, die merrily.

Doug. Talk not of dying : I am out of fear
Of death or death's hand for this one-half
year.   [*Exeunt.*

SCENE II. *A public road near Coventry.*

Enter FALSTAFF *and* BARDOLPH.

Fal. Bardolph, get thee before to Coventry ; fill me a bottle of sack : our soldiers shall
march through ; we'll to Sutton Co'fil' to-
night.
Bard. Will you give me money, captain ?
Fal. Lay out, lay out.
Bard. This bottle makes an angel.
Fal. An if it do, take it for thy labor ; and
if it make twenty, take them all ; I'll answer
the coinage. Bid my lieutenant Peto meet me
at town's end.   10
Bard. I will, captain : farewell.   [*Exit.*
Fal. If I be not ashamed of my soldiers, I
am a soused gurnet. I have misused the king's
press damnably. I have got, in exchange of a
hundred and fifty soldiers, three hundred and
odd pounds. I press me none but good house-
holders, yeoman's sons ; inquire me out contracted bachelors, such as had been asked
twice on the banns ; such a commodity of
warm slaves, as had as lieve hear the devil as a
drum ; such as fear the report of a caliver
worse than a struck fowl or a hurt wild-duck.
I pressed me none but such toasts-and-butter,
with hearts in their bellies no bigger than pins'
heads, and they have bought out their services ; and now my whole charge consists of
ancients, corporals, lieutenants, gentlemen of
companies, slaves as ragged as Lazarus in the
painted cloth, where the glutton's dogs licked
his sores ; and such as indeed were never soldiers, but discarded unjust serving-men,
younger sons to younger brothers, revolted
tapsters and ostlers trade-fallen, the cankers
of a calm world and a long peace, ten times
more dishonorable ragged than an old faced
ancient : and such have I, to fill up the rooms
of them that have bought out their services,
that you would think that I had a hundred
and fifty tattered prodigals lately come from
wine-keeping, from eating draff and husks.
A mad fellow met me on the way and told me
I had unloaded all the gibbets and pressed the
dead bodies. No eye hath seen such scare-
crows. I'll not march through Coventry with
them, that's flat : nay, and the villains march
wide betwixt the legs, as if they had gyves
on ; for indeed I had the most of them out of
prison. There's but a shirt and a half in all
my company ; and the half shirt is two napkins tacked together and thrown over the
shoulders like an herald's coat without sleeves ;
and the shirt, to say the truth, stolen from
my host at Saint Alban's, or the red-nose
inkeeper of Daventry. But that's all one ;
they'll find linen enough on every hedge.

Enter the PRINCE *and* WESTMORELAND.

Prince. How now, blown Jack ! how now,
quilt !
Fal. What, Hal ! how now, mad wag !
what a devil dost thou in Warwickshire ? My
good Lord of Westmoreland, I cry you mercy :
I thought your honor had already been at
Shrewsbury.   59
West. Faith, Sir John, 'tis more than time
that I were there, and you too ; but my powers

are there already. The king, I can tell you,
looks for us all : we must away all night.
Fal. Tut, never fear me : I am as vigilant
as a cat to steal cream.
Prince. I think, to steal cream indeed, for
thy theft hath already made thee butter. But
tell me, Jack, whose fellows are these that
come after ?
Fal. Mine, Hal, mine.   69
Prince. I did never see such pitiful rascals.
Fal. Tut, tut ; good enough to toss ; food
for powder, food for powder ; they'll fill a pit
as well as better : tush, man, mortal men, mor-
tal men.
West. Ay, but, Sir John, methinks they are
exceeding poor and bare, too beggarly.
Fal. 'Faith, for their poverty, I know not
where they had that ; and for their bareness,
I am sure they never learned that of me.
Prince. No, I'll be sworn ; unless you call
three fingers on the ribs bare. But, sirrah,
make haste : Percy is already in the field.   81
Fal. What, is the king encamped ?
West. He is, Sir John : I fear we shall stay
too long.
Fal. Well,
To the latter end of a fray and the beginning
   of a feast   85
Fits a dull fighter and a keen guest.
                                         [*Exeunt.*

SCENE III. *The rebel camp near Shrewsbury.*

Enter HOTSPUR, WORCESTER, DOUGLAS, *and*
VERNON.

Hot. We'll fight with him to-night.
Wor.   It may not be.
Doug. You give him then advantage.
Ver.   Not a whit.
Hot. Why say you so ? looks he not for
   supply ?
Ver. So do we.
Hot.   His is certain, ours is doubtful.
Wor. Good cousin, be advised ; stir not to-
   night.
Ver. Do not, my lord.
Doug.   You do not counsel well :
You speak it out of fear and cold heart.
Ver. Do me no slander, Douglas : by my
   life,
And I dare well maintain it with my life,
If well-respected honor bid me on,   10
I hold as little counsel with weak fear
As you, my lord, or any Scot that this day
   lives :
Let it be seen to-morrow in the battle
Which of us fears.
Doug.   Yea, or to-night.
Ver.   Content.
Hot. To-night, say I.
Ver. Come, come, it may not be. I wonder
   much,
Being men of such great leading as you are,
That you foresee not what impediments
Drag back our expedition : certain horse
Of my cousin Vernon's are not yet come up :
Your uncle Worcester's horse came but to-
   day ;   21
And now their pride and mettle is asleep,
Their courage with hard labor tame and dull,
That not a horse is half the half of himself.
Hot. So are the horses of the enemy
In general, journey-bated and brought low :
The better part of ours are full of rest.

Wor. The number of the king exceedeth
ours :
For God's sake, cousin, stay till all come in.
          [*The trumpet sounds a parley.*

          Enter SIR WALTER BLUNT.

Blunt. I come with gracious offers from
          the king,   30
If you vouchsafe me hearing and respect.
Hot. Welcome, Sir Walter Blunt ; and
          would to God
You were of our determination !
Some of us love you well ; and even those
          some
Envy your great deservings and good name,
Because you are not of our quality,
But stand against us like an enemy.
    Blunt. And God defend but still I should
          stand so,
So long as out of limit and true rule
You stand against anointed majesty.   40
But to my charge. The king hath sent to know
The nature of your griefs, and whereupon
You conjure from the breast of civil peace
Such bold hostility, teaching his duteous land
Audacious cruelty. If that the king
Have any way your good deserts forgot,
Which he confesseth to be manifold,
He bids you name your griefs ; and with all
          speed
You shall have your desires with interest
And pardon absolute for yourself and these 50
Herein misled by your suggestion.
    Hot. The king is kind ; and well we know
          the king
Knows at what time to promise, when to pay.
My father and my uncle and myself
Did give him that same royalty he wears ;
And when he was not six and twenty strong,
Sick in the world's regard, wretched and low,
A poor unminded outlaw sneaking home,
My father gave him welcome to the shore ;
And when he heard him swear and vow to God
He came but to be Duke of Lancaster,   61
To sue his livery and beg his peace,
With tears of innocency and terms of zeal,
My father, in kind heart and pity moved,
Swore him assistance and perform'd it too.
Now when the lords and barons of the realm
Perceived Northumberland did lean to him,
The more and less came in with cap and
          knee ;
Met him in boroughs, cities, villages,
Attended him on bridges, stood in lanes,   70
Laid gifts before him, proffer'd him their
          oaths,
Gave him their heirs, as pages follow'd him
Even at the heels in golden multitudes.
He presently, as greatness knows itself,
Steps me a little higher than his vow
Made to my father, while his blood was poor,
Upon the naked shore at Ravenspurgh ;
And now, forsooth, takes on him to reform
Some certain edicts and some strait decrees
That lie too heavy on the commonwealth,   80
Cries out upon abuses, seems to weep
Over his country's wrongs ; and by this face,
This seeming brow of justice, did he win
The hearts of all that he did angle for ;
Proceeded further ; cut me off the heads
Of all the favorites that the absent king
In deputation left behind him here,
When he was personal in the Irish war.

Blunt. Tut, I came not to hear this.
Hot.   Then to the point.
In short time after, he deposed the king ;   90
Soon after that, deprived him of his life ;
And in the neck of that, task'd the whole state :
To make that worse, suffer'd his kinsman
          March,
Who is, if every owner were well placed,
Indeed his king, to be engaged in Wales,
There without ransom to lie forfeited ;
Disgraced me in my happy victories,
Sought to entrap me by intelligence ;
Rated mine uncle from the council-board ;
In rage dismiss'd my father from the court ;
Broke oath on oath, committed wrong on
          wrong,   101
And in conclusion drove us to seek out
This head of safety ; and withal to pry
Into his title, the which we find
Too indirect for long continuance.
    Blunt. Shall I return this answer to the
          king ?
Hot. Not so, Sir Walter : we'll withdraw
          awhile.
Go to the king ; and let there be impawn'd
Some surety for a safe return again,
And in the morning early shall my uncle   110
Bring him our purposes : and so farewell.
    Blunt. I would you would accept of grace
          and love.
Hot. And may be so we shall.
Blunt.   Pray God you do.
                                   [*Exeunt.*

SCENE IV. *York. The* ARCHBISHOP'S *palace.*
    Enter the ARCHBISHOP OF YORK *and* SIR
          MICHAEL.

Arch. Hie, good Sir Michael ; bear this
          sealed brief
With winged haste to the lord marshal ;
This to my cousin Scroop, and all the rest
To whom they are directed. If you knew
How much they do import, you would make
          haste.
Sir M. My good lord,
I guess their tenor.
Arch.   Like enough you do.
To-morrow, good Sir Michael, is a day
Wherein the fortune of ten thousand men
Must bide the touch ; for, sir, at Shrewsbury,
As I am truly given to understand,   11
The king with mighty and quick-raised power
Meets with Lord Harry : and, I fear, Sir
          Michael,
What with the sickness of Northumberland,
Whose power was in the first proportion,
And what with Owen Glendower's absence
          thence,
Who with them was a rated sinew too
And comes not in, o'er-ruled by prophecies,
I fear the power of Percy is too weak
To wage an instant trial with the king.   20
    Sir M. Why, my good lord, you need not
          fear ;
There is Douglas and Lord Mortimer.
    Arch. No, Mortimer is not there.
    Sir M. But there is Mordake, Vernon, Lord
          Harry Percy,
And there is my Lord of Worcester and a head
Of gallant warriors, noble gentlemen.
    Arch. And so there is : but yet the king
          hath drawn
The special head of all the land together :

The Prince of Wales, Lord John of Lancaster,
The noble Westmoreland and warlike Blunt;
And many moe corrivals and dear men   31
Of estimation and command in arms.
  Sir M. Doubt not, my lord, they shall be
    well opposed.
  Arch. I hope no less, yet needful 'tis to
    fear;
And, to prevent the worst, Sir Michael, speed:
For if Lord Percy thrive not, ere the king
Dismiss his power, he means to visit us,
For he hath heard of our confederacy,
And 'tis but wisdom to make strong against
    him:
Therefore make haste. I must go write again
To other friends; and so farewell, Sir Michael.
                            [Exeunt.

ACT V.

Scene I. *The* King's *camp near Shrewsbury.*

Enter the King, Prince of Wales, Lord
John of Lancaster, Earl of Westmoreland, Sir Walter Blunt, *and* Falstaff.

  King. How bloodily the sun begins to peer
Above yon busky hill! the day looks pale
At his distemperature.
  Prince.   The southern wind
Doth play the trumpet to his purposes,
And by his hollow whistling in the leaves
Foretells a tempest and a blustering day.
  King. Then with the losers let it sympa-
    thize,
For nothing can seem foul to those that win.
                [The trumpet sounds.

Enter Worcester *and* Vernon.

How now, my Lord of Worcester! 'tis not well
That you and I should meet upon such terms
As now we meet. You have deceived our trust,
And made us doff our easy robes of peace,
To crush our old limbs in ungentle steel:
This is not well, my lord, this is not well.
What say you to it? will you again unknit
This curlish knot of all-abhorred war?
And move in that obedient orb again
Where you did give a fair and natural light,
And be no more an exhaled meteor,
A prodigy of fear and a portent   20
Of broached mischief to the unborn times?
  Wor. Hear me, my liege:
For mine own part, I could be well content
To entertain the lag-end of my life
With quiet hours; for I do protest,
I have not sought the day of this dislike.
  King. You have not sought it! how comes
    it, then?
  Fal. Rebellion lay in his way, and he found
    it.
  Prince. Peace, chewet, peace!
  Wor. It pleased your majesty to turn your
    looks   30
Of favor from myself and all our house;
And yet I must remember you, my lord,
We were the first and dearest of your friends.
For you my staff of office did I break
In Richard's time; and posted day and night
To meet you on the way, and kiss your hand,
When yet you were in place and in account
Nothing so strong and fortunate as I.
It was myself, my brother and his son,

That brought you home and boldly did outdare
The dangers of the time. You swore to us, 41
And you did swear that oath at Doncaster,
That you did nothing purpose 'gainst the state;
Nor claim no further than your new-fall'n
    right,
The seat of Gaunt, dukedom of Lancaster:
To this we swore our aid. But in short space
It rain'd down fortune showering on your
    head;
And such a flood of greatness fell on you,
What with our help, what with the absent king,
What with the injuries of a wanton time,   50
The seeming sufferances that you had borne,
And the contrarious winds that held the king
So long in his unlucky Irish wars
That all in England did repute him dead:
And from this swarm of fair advantages
You took occasion to be quickly woo'd
To gripe the general sway into your hand;
Forgot your oath to us at Doncaster;
And being fed by us you used us so
As that ungentle gull, the cuckoo's bird,   60
Useth the sparrow; did oppress our nest;
Grew by our feeding to so great a bulk
That even our love durst not come near your
    sight
For fear of swallowing; but with nimble wing
We were enforced, for safety sake, to fly
Out of your sight and raise this present head;
Whereby we stand opposed by such means
As you yourself have forged against yourself
By unkind usage, dangerous countenance,
And violation of all faith and troth   70
Sworn to us in your younger enterprise.
  King. These things indeed you have artic-
    ulate,
Proclaim'd at market-crosses, read in churches,
To face the garment of rebellion
With some fine color that may please the eye
Of fickle changelings and poor discontents,
Which gape and rub the elbow at the news
Of hurlyburly innovation:
And never yet did insurrection want
Such water-colors to impaint his cause;   80
Nor moody beggars, starving for a time
Of pellmell havoc and confusion.
  Prince. In both your armies there is many
    a soul
Shall pay full dearly for this encounter,
If once they join in trial. Tell your nephew,
The Prince of Wales doth join with all the
    world
In praise of Henry Percy: by my hopes,
This present enterprise set off his head,
I do not think a braver gentleman,
More active-valiant or more valiant-young, 90
More daring or more bold, is now alive
To grace this latter age with noble deeds.
For my part, I may speak it to my shame,
I have a truant been to chivalry;
And so I hear he doth account me too;
Yet this before my father's majesty—
I am content that he shall take the odds
Of his great name and estimation,
And will, to save the blood on either side,
Try fortune with him in a single fight.   100
  King. And, Prince of Wales, so dare we
    venture thee,
Albeit considerations infinite
Do make against it. No, good Worcester, no,
We love our people well; even those we love
That are misled upon your cousin's part;

And, will they take the offer of our grace,
Both he and they and you, yea, every man
Shall be my friend again and I'll be his :
So tell your cousin, and bring me word
What he will do : but if he will not yield, 110
Rebuke and dread correction wait on us
And they shall do their office. So, be gone ;
We will not now be troubled with reply :
We offer fair ; take it advisedly.
    [Exeunt Worcester and Vernon.
  Prince. It will not be accepted, on my life :
The Douglas and the Hotspur both together
Are confident against the world in arms.
  King. Hence, therefore, every leader to his
    charge ;
For, on their answer, will we set on them :
And God befriend us, as our cause is just ! 120
    [Exeunt all but the Prince of Wales and
                  Falstaff.
  Fal. Hal, if thou see me down in the
battle and bestride me, so ; 'tis a point of
friendship.
  Prince. Nothing but a colossus can do thee
that friendship. Say thy prayers, and farewell.
  Fal. I would 'twere bed-time, Hal, and all
well.
  Prince. Why, thou owest God a death.
                            [Exit.
  Fal. 'Tis not due yet ; I would be loath to
pay him before his day. What need I be so
forward with him that calls not on me ? Well,
'tis no matter ; honor pricks me on. Yea, but
how if honor prick me off when I come on ?
how then ? Can honor set to a leg ? no : or an
arm ? no : or take away the grief of a wound ?
no. Honor hath no skill in surgery, then ? no.
What is honor ? a word. What is in that word
honor ? what is that honor ? air. A trim reckoning ! Who hath it ? he that died o' Wednesday. Doth he feel it ? no. Doth he hear it ?
no. 'Tis insensible, then. Yea, to the dead. But
will it not live with the living ? no. Why ? de-
traction will not suffer it. Therefore I'll none
of it. Honor is a mere scutcheon : and so
ends my catechism.   *[Exit.*

    SCENE II. *The rebel camp.*
    Enter WORCESTER *and* VERNON.
  Wor. O, no, my nephew must not know,
    Sir Richard,
The liberal and kind offer of the king.
  Ver. 'Twere best he did.
  Wor.   Then are we all undone.
It is not possible, it cannot be,
The king should keep his word in loving us ;
He will suspect us still and find a time
To punish this offence in other faults :
Suspicion all our lives shall be stuck full of
    eyes ;
For treason is but trusted like the fox,
Who, ne'er so tame, so cherish'd and lock'd
    up,   10
Will have a wild trick of his ancestors.
Look how we can, or sad or merrily,
Interpretation will misquote our looks,
And we shall feed like oxen at a stall,
The better cherish'd, still the nearer death.
My nephew's trespass may be well forgot ;
It hath the excuse of youth and heat of blood,
And an adopted name of privilege,
A hair-brain'd Hotspur, govern'd by a spleen :
All his offences live upon my head   20
And on his father's ; we did train him on,

And, his corruption being ta'en from us,
We, as the spring of all, shall pay for all.
Therefore, good cousin, let not Harry know,
In any case, the offer of the king.
  Ver. Deliver what you will ; I'll say 'tis so.
Here comes your cousin.

    Enter HOTSPUR *and* DOUGLAS.

  Hot. My uncle is return'd :
Deliver up my Lord of Westmoreland.
Uncle, what news ?   30
  Wor. The king will bid you battle pres-
ently.
  Doug. Defy him by the Lord of Westmore-
land.
  Hot. Lord Douglas, go you and tell him so.
  Doug. Marry, and shall, and very willingly.
                                [Exit.
  Wor. There is no seeming mercy in the
    king.
  Hot. Did you beg any ? God forbid !
  Wor. I told him gently of our grievances,
Of his oath-breaking ; which he mended thus,
By now forswearing that he is forsworn :
He calls us rebels, traitors ; and will scourge
With haughty arms this hateful name in us. 41

    Re-enter DOUGLAS.

  Doug. Arm, gentlemen ; to arms ! for I
    have thrown
A brave defiance in King Henry's teeth,
And Westmoreland, that was engaged, did
    bear it ;
Which cannot choose but bring him quickly
    on.
  Wor. The Prince of Wales stepp'd forth
    before the king,
And, nephew, challenged you to single fight.
  Hot. O, would the quarrel lay upon our
    heads,
And that no man might draw short breath to-
    day
But I and Harry Monmouth ! Tell me, tell
    me,   50
How show'd his tasking ? seem'd it in con-
    tempt ?
  Ver. No, by my soul ; I never in my life
Did hear a challenge urged more modestly,
Unless a brother should a brother dare
To gentle exercise and proof of arms.
He gave you all the duties of a man ;
Trimm'd up your praises with a princely
    tongue,
Spoke your deservings like a chronicle,
Making you ever better than his praise
By still dispraising praise valued with you ; 60
And, which became him like a prince indeed,
He made a blushing cital of himself ;
And chid his truant youth with such a grace
As if he master'd there a double spirit
Of teaching and of learning instantly.
There did he pause : but let me tell the world,
If he outlive the envy of this day,
England did never owe so sweet a hope,
So much misconstrued in his wantonness.
  Hot. Cousin, I think thou art enamored 70
On his follies : never did I hear
Of any prince so wild a libertine.
But be he as he will, yet once ere night
I will embrace him with a soldier's arm,
That he shall shrink under my courtesy.
Arm, arm with speed : and, fellows, soldiers,
    friends,

Better consider what you have to do
Than I, that have not well the gift of tongue,
Can lift your blood up with persuasion.

Enter a Messenger.

Mess. My lord, here are letters for you. 80
Hot. I cannot read them now.
O gentlemen, the time of life is short !
To spend that shortness basely were too long,
If life did ride upon a dial's point,
Still ending at the arrival of an hour.
An if we live, we live to tread on kings ;
If die, brave death, when princes die with us !
Now, for our consciences, the arms are fair,
When the intent of bearing them is just.

Enter another Messenger.

Mess. My lord, prepare ; the king comes
    on apace.   90
Hot. I thank him, that he cuts me from my
    tale,
For I profess not talking ; only this—
Let each man do his best : and here draw I
A sword, whose temper I intend to stain
With the best blood that I can meet withal
In the adventure of this perilous day.
Now, Esperance ! Percy ! and set on.
Sound all the lofty instruments of war,
And by that music let us all embrace ;
For, heaven to earth, some of us never shall
A second time do such a courtesy.   101
    [*The trumpets sound. They embrace, and
                                        exeunt.*

SCENE III. *Plain between the camps.*

The KING *enters with his power. Alarum to
    the battle. Then enter* DOUGLAS *and* SIR
    WALTER BLUNT.

Blunt. What is thy name, that in the battle
    thus
Thou crossest me ? what honor dost thou seek
Upon my head ?
Doug. Know then, my name is Douglas ;
And I do haunt thee in the battle thus
Because some tell me that thou art a king.
Blunt. They tell thee true.
Doug. The Lord of Stafford dear to-day
    hath bought
Thy likeness, for instead of thee, King Harry,
This sword hath ended him : so shall it thee,
Unless thou yield thee as my prisoner.   10
Blunt. I was not born a yielder, thou
    proud Scot ;
And thou shalt find a king that will revenge
Lord Stafford's death.
    [*They fight. Douglas kills Blunt.*

Enter HOTSPUR.

Hot. O Douglas, hadst thou fought at
    Holmedon thus,
I never had triumph'd upon a Scot.
Doug. All's done, all's won ; here breath-
    less lies the king.
Hot. Where ?
Doug. Here.
Hot. This, Douglas ? no : I know this face
    full well :
A gallant knight he was, his name was Blunt ;
Semblably furnish'd like the king himself. 21
Doug. A fool go with thy soul, whither it
    goes !
A borrow'd title hast thou bought too dear :
Why didst thou tell me that thou wert a king ?

Hot. The king hath many marching in his
    coats.
Doug. Now, by my sword, I will kill all his
    coats ;
I'll murder all his wardrobe, piece by piece,
Until I meet the king.
Hot.   Up, and away !
Our soldiers stand full fairly for the day.   29
                                        [*Exeunt.*

Alarum. Enter FALSTAFF, *solus.*

Fal. Though I could 'scape shot-free at
London, I fear the shot here ; here's no scor-
ing but upon the pate. Soft ! who are you ? Sir
Walter Blunt : there's honor for you ! here's
no vanity ! I am as hot as molten lead, and as
heavy too : God keep lead out of me ! I need
no more weight than mine own bowels. I have
led my ragamuffins where they are peppered :
there's not three of my hundred and fifty left
alive ; and they are for the town's end, to beg
during life. But who comes here ?   40

Enter the PRINCE.

Prince. What, stand'st thou idle here ? lend
me thy sword !
Many a nobleman lies stark and stiff
Under the hoofs of vaunting enemies,
Whose deaths are yet unrevenged : I prithee,
    lend me thy sword.
Fal. O Hal, I prithee, give me leave to
breathe awhile. Turk Gregory never did such
deeds in arms as I have done this day. I have
paid Percy, I have made him sure.
Prince. He is, indeed ; and living to kill
thee. I prithee, lend me thy sword.   50
Fal. Nay, before God, Hal, if Percy be
alive, thou get'st not my sword ; but take my
pistol, if thou wilt.
Prince. Give it me : what, is it in the case ?
Fal. Ay, Hal ; 'tis hot, 'tis hot ; there's
that will sack a city. [*The Prince draws it out,
        and finds it to be a bottle of sack.*
Prince. What, is it a time to jest and dally
now ?   [*He throws the bottle at him. Exit.*
Fal. Well, if Percy be alive, I'll pierce him.
If he do come in my way, so : if he do not, if
I come in his willingly, let him make a car-
bonado of me. I like not such grinning honor
as Sir Walter hath : give me life : which if I
can save, so ; if not, honor comes unlooked
for, and there's an end.   [*Exit.*

SCENE IV. *Another part of the field.*

Alarum. Excursions. Enter the KING, *the*
PRINCE, LORD JOHN OF LANCASTER, *and*
EARL OF WESTMORELAND.

King. I prithee,
Harry, withdraw thyself ; thou bleed'st too
    much.
Lord John of Lancaster, go you with him.
Lan. Not I, my lord, unless I did bleed too.
Prince. I beseech your majesty, make up,
Lest your retirement do amaze your friends.
King. I will do so.
My Lord of Westmoreland, lead him to his
    tent.
West. Come, my lord, I'll lead you to your
    tent.
Prince. Lead me, my lord ? I do not need
    your help :   10
And God forbid a shallow scratch should drive
The Prince of Wales from such a field as this,

Where stain'd nobility lies trodden on,
And rebels' arms triumph in massacres !
　Lan. We breathe too long : come, cousin
　　Westmoreland,
Our duty this way lies ; for God's sake come.
　　　[*Exeunt Prince John and Westmoreland.*
　Prince. By God, thou hast deceived me,
　　Lancaster ;
I did not think thee lord of such a spirit :
Before, I loved thee as a brother, John ;
But now, I do respect thee as my soul.　20
　King. I saw him hold Lord Percy at the
　　point
With lustier maintenance than I did look for
Of such an ungrown warrior.
　Prince.　　　　　　　O, this boy
Lends mettle to us all !　　　　[*Exit.*

　　　Enter DOUGLAS.

　Doug. Another king ! they grow like Hy-
　　dra's heads :
I am the Douglas, fatal to all those
That wear those colors on them : what art
　thou,
That counterfeit'st the person of a king ?
　King. The king himself ; who, Douglas,
　　grieves at heart
So many of his shadows thou hast met　30
And not the very king. I have two boys
Seek Percy and thyself about the field :
But, seeing thou fall'st on me so luckily,
I will assay thee : so, defend thyself.
　Doug. I fear thou art another counterfeit ;
And yet, in faith, thou bear'st thee like a king :
But mine I am sure thou art, whoe'er thou be,
And thus I win thee. [*They fight ; the King
　being in danger, re-enter Prince of Wales.*
　Prince. Hold up thy head, vile Scot, or
　　thou art like
Never to hold it up again ! the spirits　40
Of valiant Shirley, Stafford, Blunt, are in my
　arms :
It is the Prince of Wales that threatens thee ;
Who never promiseth but he means to pay.
　　　　　　[*They fight : Douglas flies.*
Cheerly, my lord : how fares your grace ?
Sir Nicholas Gawsey hath for succor sent,
And so hath Clifton : I'll to Clifton straight.
　King. Stay, and breathe awhile :
Thou hast redeem'd thy lost opinion,
And show'd thou makest some tender of my
　life,
In this fair rescue thou hast brought to me. 50
　Prince. O God ! they did me too much in-
　　jury
That ever said I hearken'd for your death.
If it were so, I might have let alone
The insulting hand of Douglas over you,
Which would have been as speedy in your end
As all the poisonous potions in the world
And saved the treacherous labor of your son.
　King. Make up to Clifton : I'll to Sir
　　Nicholas Gawsey.　　　　　　[*Exit.*

　　　Enter HOTSPUR.

　Hot. If I mistake not, thou art Harry
　　Monmouth.
　Prince. Thou speak'st as if I would deny
　　my name.　　　　　　　　　　　60
　Hot. My name is Harry Percy.
　Prince.　　　　　　Why, then I see
A very valiant rebel of the name.

I am the Prince of Wales ; and think not,
　Percy,
To share with me in glory any more :
Two stars keep not their motion in one sphere ;
Nor can one England brook a double reign,
Of Harry Percy and the Prince of Wales.
　Hot. Nor shall it, Harry ; for the hour is
　　come
To end the one of us ; and would to God
Thy name in arms were now as great as mine !
　Prince. I'll make it greater ere I part from
　　thee ;　　　　　　　　　　　　71
And all the budding honors on thy crest
I'll crop, to make a garland for my head.
　Hot. I can no longer brook thy vanities.
　　　　　　　　　　　　　[*They fight.*

　　　Enter FALSTAFF.

　Fal. Well said, Hal ! to it, Hal ! Nay, you
shall find no boy's play here, I can tell you.

Re-enter DOUGLAS ; *he fights with* FALSTAFF,
　who falls down as if he were dead, and exit
　DOUGLAS. HOTSPUR *is wounded, and falls.*
　Hot. O, Harry, thou hast robb'd me of my
　　youth !
I better brook the loss of brittle life
Than those proud titles thou hast won of me ;
They wound my thoughts worse than thy
　sword my flesh :　　　　　　　　80
But thought's the slave of life, and life time's
　fool ;
And time, that takes survey of all the world,
Must have a stop. O, I could prophesy,
But that the earthy and cold hand of death
Lies on my tongue : no, Percy, thou art dust.
And food for—　　　　　　　[*Dies.*
　Prince. For worms, brave Percy : fare thee
　　well, great heart !
Ill-weaved ambition, how much art thou
　shrunk !
When that this body did contain a spirit,
A kingdom for it was too small a bound ;　90
But now two paces of the vilest earth
Is room enough : this earth that bears thee
　dead
Bears not alive so stout a gentleman.
If thou wert sensible of courtesy,
I should not make so dear a show of zeal :
But let my favors hide thy mangled face ;
And, even in thy behalf, I'll thank myself
For doing these fair rites of tenderness.
Adieu, and take thy praise with thee to
　heaven !
Thy ignominy sleep with thee in the grave, 100
But not remember'd in thy epitaph !
　　　[*He spieth Falstaff on the ground.*
What, old acquaintance ! could not all this
　flesh
Keep in a little life ? Poor Jack, farewell !
I could have better spared a better man :
O, I should have a heavy miss of thee,
If I were much in love with vanity !
Death hath not struck so fat a deer to-day,
Though many dearer, in this bloody fray.
Embowell'd will I see thee by and by :　109
Till then in blood by noble Percy lie.　[*Exit.*
　Fal. [*Rising up*] Embowelled ! if thou em-
bowel me to-day, I'll give you leave to powder
me and eat me too to-morrow. 'Sblood, 'twas
time to counterfeit, or that hot termagant Scot
had paid me scot and lot too. Counterfeit ? I
lie, I am no counterfeit : to die, is to be a

counterfeit; for he is but the counterfeit of a
man who hath not the life of a man: but to
counterfeit dying, when a man thereby liveth,
is to be no counterfeit, but the true and perfect
image of life indeed. The better part of valor
is discretion; in the which better part I have
saved my life. 'Zounds, I am afraid of this
gunpowder Percy, though he be dead: how,
if he should counterfeit too and rise? by my
faith, I am afraid he would prove the better
counterfeit. Therefore I'll make him sure;
yea, and I'll swear I killed him. Why may
not he rise as well as I? Nothing confutes me
but eyes, and nobody sees me. Therefore,
sirrah [*stabbing him*], with a new wound in
your thigh, come you along with me.

[*Takes up Hotspur on his back.*

Re-enter the PRINCE OF WALES *and* LORD
JOHN OF LANCASTER.

Prince. Come, brother John; full bravely
    hast thou flesh'd
Thy maiden sword.
    Lan.   But, soft! whom have we here?
Did you not tell me this fat man was dead?
    Prince. I did; I saw him dead,
Breathless and bleeding on the ground. Art
    thou alive?
Or is it fantasy that plays upon our eyesight?
I prithee, speak; we will not trust our eyes   139
Without our ears: thou art not what thou
    seem'st.
    Fal. No, that's certain; I am not a double
man: but if I be not Jack Falstaff, then am I
a Jack. There is Percy [*throwing the body
down*]: if your father will do me any honor,
so; if not, let him kill the next Percy himself.
I look to be either earl or duke, I can assure
you.
    Prince. Why, Percy I killed myself and
    saw thee dead.
    Fal. Didst thou? Lord, Lord, how this
world is given to lying! I grant you I was
down and out of breath; and so was he: but
we rose both at an instant and fought a long
hour by Shrewsbury clock. If I may be believed, so; if not, let them that should reward
valor bear the sin upon their own heads. I'll
take it upon my death, I gave him this wound
in the thigh: if the man were alive and would
deny it, 'zounds, I would make him eat a piece
of my sword.
    Lan. This is the strangest tale that ever I
    heard.
    Prince. This is the strangest fellow, brother
    John.   159
Come, bring your luggage nobly on your back:
For my part, if a lie may do thee grace,
I'll gild it with the happiest terms I have.

[*A retreat is sounded.*
The trumpet sounds retreat; the day is ours.
Come, brother, let us to the highest of the
    field,
To see what friends are living, who are dead.

[*Exeunt Prince of Wales and Lancaster.*
    Fal. I'll follow, as they say, for reward.
He that rewards me, God reward him! If I

do grow great, I'll grow less; for I'll purge,
and leave sack, and live cleanly as a nobleman
should do.   [*Exit.*

SCENE V.   *Another part of the field.*

The trumpets sound. Enter the KING, PRINCE
    OF WALES, LORD JOHN OF LANCASTER,
    EARL OF WESTMORELAND, *with* WORCES-
    TER *and* VERNON *prisoners.*

King. Thus ever did rebellion find rebuke.
Ill-spirited Worcester! did not we send grace,
Pardon and terms of love to all of you?
And wouldst thou turn our offers contrary?
Misuse the tenor of thy kinsman's trust?
Three knights upon our party slain to-day,
A noble earl and many a creature else
Had been alive this hour,
If like a Christian thou hadst truly borne
Betwixt our armies true intelligence.   10
    Wor. What I have done my safety urged
    me to;
And I embrace this fortune patiently,
Since not to be avoided it falls on me.
    King. Bear Worcester to the death and
    Vernon too:
Other offenders we will pause upon.
    [*Exeunt Worcester and Vernon, guarded.*
How goes the field?
    Prince. The noble Scot, Lord Douglas,
    when he saw
The fortune of the day quite turn'd from him,
The noble Percy slain, and all his men
Upon the foot of fear, fled with the rest;   20
And falling from a hill, he was so bruised
That the pursuers took him. At my tent
The Douglas is; and I beseech your grace
I may dispose of him.
    King.   With all my heart.
    Prince. Then, brother John of Lancaster,
    to you
This honorable bounty shall belong:
Go to the Douglas, and deliver him
Up to his pleasure, ransomless and free:
His valor shown upon our crests to-day
Hath taught us how to cherish such high
    deeds   30
Even in the bosom of our adversaries.
    Lan. I thank your grace for this high cour-
    tesy,
Which I shall give away immediately.
    King. Then this remains, that we divide
    our power.
You, son John, and my cousin Westmoreland
Towards York shall bend you with your dear-
    est speed,
To meet Northumberland and the prelate
    Scroop,
Who, as we hear, are busily in arms:
Myself and you, son Harry, will towards
    Wales,
To fight with Glendower and the Earl of
    March.   40
Rebellion in this land shall lose his sway,
Meeting the check of such another day:
And since this business so fair is done,
Let us not leave till all our own be won.

[*Exeunt.*

KING HENRY IV. PART II.

(WRITTEN ABOUT 1597–98.)

INTRODUCTION.

[See Introduction to Part I.]

DRAMATIS PERSONÆ.

RUMOUR, the Presenter.
KING HENRY the Fourth.
HENRY, PRINCE OF WALES, afterwards King Henry V.,
THOMAS, DUKE OF CLARENCE,
PRINCE JOHN OF LANCASTER,
PRINCE HUMPHREY OF GLOUCESTER, } his sons.
EARL OF WARWICK.
EARL OF WESTMORELAND.
EARL OF SURREY.
GOWER.
HARCOURT.
BLUNT.
Lord Chief-Justice of the King's Bench.
A Servant of the Chief-Justice.
EARL OF NORTHUMBERLAND.
SCROOP, Archbishop of York.
LORD MOWBRAY.
LORD HASTINGS.
LORD BARDOLPH.
SIR JOHN COLEVILE.
TRAVERS and MORTON, retainers of Northumberland.

SIR JOHN FALSTAFF.
His Page.
BARDOLPH.
PISTOL.
POINS.
PETO.
SHALLOW,
SILENCE, } country justices.
DAVY, Servant to Shallow.
MOULDY, SHADOW, WART, FEEBLE, and BULLCALF, recruits.
FANG and SNARE, sheriff's officers.

LADY NORTHUMBERLAND.
LADY PERCY.
MISTRESS QUICKLY, hostess of a tavern in Eastcheap.
DOLL TEARSHEET.

Lords and Attendants ; Porter, Drawers, Beadles, Grooms, &c.

A Dancer, speaker of the epilogue.

SCENE : *England*.

INDUCTION.

Warkworth. Before the castle.

Enter RUMOUR, *painted full of tongues.*

Rum. Open your ears ; for which of you will stop
The vent of hearing when loud Rumour speaks ?
I, from the orient to the drooping west,
Making the wind my post-horse, still unfold
The acts commenced on this ball of earth :
Upon my tongues continual slanders ride,
The which in every language I pronounce,
Stuffing the ears of men with false reports.
I speak of peace, while covert enmity
Under the smile of safety wounds the world :
And who but Rumour, who but only I,   11
Make fearful musters and prepared defence,
Whiles the big year, swoln with some other grief,
Is thought with child by the stern tyrant war,
And no such matter ? Rumour is a pipe
Blown by surmises, jealousies, conjectures,
And of so easy and so plain a stop
That the blunt monster with uncounted heads,
The still-discordant wavering multitude,

Can play upon it. But what need I thus   20
My well-known body to anatomize
Among my household ? Why is Rumour here ?
I run before King Harry's victory ;
Who in a bloody field by Shrewsbury
Hath beaten down young Hotspur and his troops,
Quenching the flame of bold rebellion
Even with the rebel's blood. But what mean I
To speak so true at first ? my office is
To noise abroad that Harry Monmouth fell
Under the wrath of noble Hotspur's sword, 30
And that the king before the Douglas' rage
Stoop'd his anointed head as low as death.
This have I rumor'd through the peasant towns
Between that royal field of Shrewsbury
And this worm-eaten hold of ragged stone,
Where Hotspur's father, old Northumberland,
Lies crafty-sick : the posts come tiring on,
And not a man of them brings other news
Than they have learn'd me : from Rumour's tongues
They bring smooth comforts false, worse than true wrongs.   [*Exit.* 40

ACT I.

SCENE I. *The same.*

Enter LORD BARDOLPH.

L. Bard. Who keeps the gate here, ho ?

The Porter *opens the gate.*

Where is the earl ?
Port. What shall I say you are ?
L. Bard. Tell thou the earl
That the Lord Bardolph doth attend him here.
Port. His lordship is walk'd forth into the
orchard ;
Please it your honor, knock but at the gate,
And he himself will answer.

Enter NORTHUMBERLAND.

L. Bard. Here comes the earl.
[*Exit Porter.*
North. What news, Lord Bardolph ? every
minute now
Should be the father of some stratagem :
The times are wild ; contention, like a horse
Full of high feeding, madly hath broke loose
And bears down all before him.   11
L. Bard. Noble earl,
I bring you certain news from Shrewsbury.
North. Good, an God will !
L. Bard.   As good as heart can wish :
The king is almost wounded to the death ;
And, in the fortune of my lord your son,
Prince Harry slain outright ; and both the
Blunts
Kill'd by the hand of Douglas ; young Prince
John
And Westmoreland and Stafford fled the field ;
And Harry Monmouth's brawn, the hulk Sir
John,
Is prisoner to your son : O, such a day,   20
So fought, so follow'd and so fairly won,
Came not till now to dignify the times,
Since Cæsar's fortunes !
North.   How is this derived ?
Saw you the field ? came you from Shrews-
bury ?
L. Bard. I spake with one, my lord, that
came from thence,
A gentleman well bred and of good name,
That freely render'd me these news for true.
North. Here comes my servant Travers,
whom I sent
On Tuesday last to listen after news.

Enter TRAVERS.

L. Bard. My lord, I over-rode him on the
way ;   30
And he is furnish'd with no certainties
More than he haply may retail from me.
North. Now, Travers, what good tidings
comes with you ?
Tra. My lord, Sir John Umfrevile turn'd
me back
With joyful tidings ; and, being better horsed,
Out-rode me. After him came spurring hard
A gentleman, almost forspent with speed,
That stopp'd by me to breathe his bloodied
horse.
He ask'd the way to Chester ; and of him
I did demand what news from Shrewsbury : 40
He told me that rebellion had bad luck
And that young Harry Percy's spur was cold.
With that, he gave his able horse the head,
And bending forward struck his armed heels
Against the panting sides of his poor jade
Up to the rowel-head, and starting so
He seem'd in running to devour the way,
Staying no longer question.
North.   Ha ! Again :
Said he young Harry Percy's spur was cold ?
Of Hotspur Coldspur ? that rebellion   50
Had met ill luck ?
L. Bard.   My lord, I'll tell you what ;
If my young lord your son have not the day,
Upon mine honor, for a silken point
I'll give my barony : never talk of it.
North. Why should that gentleman that
rode by Travers
Give then such instances of loss ?
L. Bard.   Who, he ?
He was some hilding fellow that had stolen
The horse he rode on, and, upon my life,
Spoke at a venture. Look, here comes more
news.

Enter MORTON.

North. Yea, this man's brow, like to a title-
leaf,   60
Foretells the nature of a tragic volume :
So looks the strand whereon the imperious
flood
Hath left a witness'd usurpation.
Say, Morton, didst thou come from Shrews-
bury ?
Mor. I ran from Shrewsbury, my noble
lord ;
Where hateful death put on his ugliest mask
To fright our party.
North. How doth my son and brother ?
Thou tremblest ; and the whiteness in thy
cheek
Is apter than thy tongue to tell thy errand.
Even such a man, so faint, so spiritless,   70
So dull, so dead in look, so woe-begone,
Drew Priam's curtain in the dead of night,
And would have told him half his Troy was
burnt ;
But Priam found the fire ere he his tongue,
And I my Percy's death ere thou report'st it.
This thou wouldst say, ' Your son did thus and
thus ;
Your brother thus : so fought the noble
Douglas : '
Stopping my greedy ear with their bold deeds:
But in the end, to stop my ear indeed,
Thou hast a sigh to blow away this praise, 80
Ending with ' Brother, son, and all are dead.'
Mor. Douglas is living, and your brother,
yet ;
But, for my lord your son,—
North.   Why, he is dead.
See what a ready tongue suspicion hath !
He that but fears the thing he would not know
Hath by instinct knowledge from others' eyes
That what he fear'd is chanced. Yet speak,
Morton,
Tell thou an earl his divination lies,
And I will take it as a sweet disgrace
And make thee rich for doing me such wrong.
Mor. You are too great to be by me gain-
said :   91
Your spirit is too true, your fears too certain.
North. Yet, for all this, say not that Percy's
dead.
I see a strange confession in thine eye :
Thou shakest thy head and hold'st it fear or sin

To speak a truth. If he be slain, say so;
The tongue offends not that reports his death :
And he doth sin that doth belie the dead,
Not he which says the dead is not alive.
Yet the first bringer of unwelcome news   100
Hath but a losing office, and his tongue
Sounds ever after as a sullen bell,
Remember'd tolling a departing friend.
    L. Bard. I cannot think, my lord, your son
        is dead.
    Mor. I am sorry I should force you to be-
        lieve
That which I would to God I had not seen ;
But these mine eyes saw him in bloody state,
Rendering faint quittance, wearied and out-
        breathed,
To Harry Monmouth ; whose swift wrath beat
        down
The never-daunted Percy to the earth,   110
From whence with life he never more sprung
        up.
In few, his death, whose spirit lent a fire
Even to the dullest peasant in his camp,
Being bruited once, took fire and heat away
From the best temper'd courage in his troops ;
For from his metal was his party steel'd ;
Which once in him abated, all the rest
Turn'd on themselves, like dull and heavy
        lead :
And as the thing that's heavy in itself,
Upon enforcement flies with greatest speed,
So did our men, heavy in Hotspur's loss,   121
Lend to this weight such lightness with their
        fear
That arrows fled not swifter toward their aim
Than did our soldiers, aiming at their safety,
Fly from the field. Then was the noble
        Worcester
Too soon ta'en prisoner ; and that furious
        Scot,
The bloody Douglas, whose well-laboring
        sword
Had three times slain the appearance of the
        king,
'Gan vail his stomach and did grace the
        shame
Of those that turn'd their backs, and in his
        flight,   130
Stumbling in fear, was took. The sum of all
Is that the king hath won, and hath sent out
A speedy power to encounter you, my lord,
Under the conduct of young Lancaster
And Westmoreland. This is the news at full.
    North. For this I shall have time enough
        to mourn.
In poison there is physic ; and these news,
Having been well, that would have made me
        sick,
Being sick, have in some measure made me
        well :
And as the wretch, whose fever-weaken'd
        joints,   140
Like strengthless hinges, buckle under life,
Impatient of his fit, breaks like a fire
Out of his keeper's arms, even so my limbs,
Weaken'd with grief, being now enraged with
        grief,
Are thrice themselves. Hence, therefore, thou
        nice crutch !
A scaly gauntlet now with joints of steel
Must glove this hand : and hence, thou sickly
        quoif !
Thou art a guard too wanton for the head

Which princes, flesh'd with conquest, aim to
        hit.
Now bind my brows with iron ; and approach
The ragged'st hour that time and spite dare
        bring   151
To frown upon the enraged Northumberland !
Let heaven kiss earth ! now let not Nature's
        hand
Keep the wild flood confined ! let order die !
And let this world no longer be a stage
To feed contention in a lingering act ;
But let one spirit of the first-born Cain
Reign in all bosoms, that, each heart being
        set
On bloody courses, the rude scene may end,
And darkness be the burier of the dead !   160
    Tra. This strained passion doth you wrong,
        my lord.
    L. Bard. Sweet earl, divorce not wisdom
        from your honor.
    Mor. The lives of all your loving complices
Lean on your health ; the which, if you give
        o'er
To stormy passion, must perforce decay.
You cast the event of war, my noble lord,
And summ'd the account of chance, before
        you said
' Let us make head.' It was your presurmise,
That, in the dole of blows, your son might
        drop :
You knew he walk'd o'er perils, on an edge,
More likely to fall in than to get o'er ;   171
You were advised his flesh was capable
Of wounds and scars and that his forward
        spirit
Would lift him where most trade of danger
        ranged :
Yet did you say ' Go forth ; ' and none of this,
Though strongly apprehended, could restrain
The stiff-borne action : what hath then be-
        fallen,
Or what hath this bold enterprise brought
        forth,
More than that being which was like to be ?
    L. Bard. We all that are engaged to this
        loss   180
Knew that we ventured on such dangerous seas
That if we wrought our life 'twas ten to one ;
And yet we ventured, for the gain proposed
Choked the respect of likely peril fear'd ;
And since we are o'erset, venture again.
Come, we will all put forth, body and goods.
    Mor. 'Tis more than time : and, my most
        noble lord,
I hear for certain, and do speak the truth,
The gentle Archbishop of York is up
With well-appointed powers : he is a man   190
Who with a double surety binds his followers.
My lord your son had only but the corpse,
But shadows and the shows of men, to fight ;
For that same word, rebellion, did divide
The action of their bodies from their souls ;
And they did fight with queasiness, constrain'd,
As men drink potions, that their weapons only
Seem'd on our side ; but, for their spirits and
        souls,
This word, rebellion, it had froze them up,
As fish are in a pond. But now the bishop   200
Turns insurrection to religion :
Supposed sincere and holy in his thoughts,
He's followed both with body and with mind ;
And doth enlarge his rising with the blood

Of fair King Richard, scraped from Pomfret
    stones ;
Derives from heaven his quarrel and his
    cause ;
Tells them he doth bestride a bleeding land,
Gasping for life under great Bolingbroke ;
And more and less do flock to follow him.
  North. I knew of this before ; but, to speak
    truth,   210
This present grief had wiped it from my mind.
Go in with me ; and counsel every man
The aptest way for safety and revenge :
Get posts and letters, and make friends with
    speed :
Never so few, and never yet more need.
                      [Exeunt.

Scene II. London. A street.

Enter Falstaff, *with his* Page *bearing his
sword and buckler.*

  Fal. Sirrah, you giant, what says the doctor to my water ?
  Page. He said, sir, the water itself was a
good healthy water ; but, for the party that
owed it, he might have more diseases than he
knew for.
  Fal. Men of all sorts take a pride to gird
at me : the brain of this foolish-compounded
clay, man, is not able to invent anything that
tends to laughter, more than I invent or is invented on me : I am not only witty in myself,
but the cause that wit is in other men. I do
here walk before thee like a sow that hath
overwhelmed all her litter but one. If the
prince put thee into my service for any other
reason than to set me off, why then I have no
judgment. Thou whoreson mandrake, thou art
fitter to be worn in my cap than to wait at my
heels. I was never manned with an agate till
now : but I will inset you neither in gold nor
silver, but in vile apparel, and send you back
again to your master, for a jewel,—the juvenal,
the prince your master, whose chin is not yet
fledged. I will sooner have a beard grow in the
palm of my hand than he shall get one on his
cheek ; and yet he will not stick to say his face
is a face-royal : God may finish it when he
will, 'tis not a hair amiss yet : he may keep it
still at a face-royal, for a barber shall never
earn sixpence out of it ; and yet he'll be crow-
ing as if he had writ man ever since his father
was a bachelor. He may keep his own grace,
but he's almost out of mine, I can assure him.
What said Master Dombledon about the satin
for my short cloak and my slops ?
  Page. He said, sir, you should procure him
better assurance than Bardolph : he would not
take his band and yours ; he liked not the security.
  Fal. Let him be damned, like the glutton !
pray God his tongue be hotter ! A whoreson
Achitophel ! a rascally yea-forsooth knave ! to
bear a gentleman in hand, and then stand
upon security ! The whoreson smooth-pates do
now wear nothing but high shoes, and bunches
of keys at their girdles ; and if a man is
through with them in honest taking up, then
they must stand upon security. I had as lief
they would put ratsbane in my mouth as offer
to stop it with security. I looked a' should have
sent me two and twenty yards of satin, as I am
a true knight, and he sends me security. Well,
he may sleep in security ; for he hath the horn

of abundance, and the lightness of his wife
shines through it : and yet cannot he see,
though he have his own lanthorn to light him.
Where's Bardolph ?
  Page. He's gone into Smithfield to buy your
worship a horse.
  Fal. I bought him in Paul's, and he'll buy
me a horse in Smithfield : an I could get me
but a wife in the stews, I were manned, horsed,
and wived.   61

Enter the Lord Chief-Justice *and* Servant.

  Page. Sir, here comes the nobleman that
committed the prince for striking him about
Bardolph.
  Fal. Wait, close ; I will not see him.
  Ch. Just. What's he that goes there ?
  Serv. Falstaff, an't please your lordship.
  Ch. Just. He that was in question for the
robbery ?   69
  Serv. He, my lord : but he hath since done
good service at Shrewsbury ; and, as I hear, is
now going with some charge to the Lord John
of Lancaster.
  Ch. Just. What, to York ? Call him back
again.
  Serv. Sir John Falstaff !
  Fal. Boy, tell him I am deaf.
  Page. You must speak louder ; my master
is deaf.   79
  Ch. Just. I am sure he is, to the hearing of
any thing good. Go, pluck him by the elbow ;
I must speak with him.
  Serv. Sir John !
  Fal. What ! a young knave, and begging !
Is there not wars ? is there not employment ?
doth not the king lack subjects ? do not the
rebels need soldiers ? Though it be a shame to
be on any side but one, it is worse shame to
beg than to be on the worst side, were it worse
than the name of rebellion can tell how to
make it.   90
  Serv. You mistake me, sir.
  Fal. Why, sir, did I say you were an honest
man ? setting my knighthood and my soldiership aside, I had lied in my throat, if I had
said so.
  Serv. I pray you, sir, then set your knighthood and your soldiership aside ; and give me
leave to tell you, you lie in your throat, if you
say I am any other than an honest man.
  Fal. I give thee leave to tell me so ! I lay
aside that which grows to me ! If thou gettest
any leave of me, hang me ; if thou takest leave,
thou wert better be hanged. You hunt counter : hence ! avaunt !
  Serv. Sir, my lord would speak with you.
  Ch. Just. Sir John Falstaff, a word with
you.
  Fal. My good lord ! God give your lordship good time of day. I am glad to see your
lordship abroad : I heard say your lordship
was sick : I hope your lordship goes abroad by
advice. Your lordship, though not clean past
your youth, hath yet some smack of age in
you, some relish of the saltness of time ; and I
must humbly beseech your lordship to have
a reverent care of your health.
  Ch. Just. Sir John, I sent for you before
your expedition to Shrewsbury.
  Fal. An't please your lordship, I hear his
majesty is returned with some discomfort from
Wales.

Ch. Just. I talk not of his majesty : you would not come when I sent for you.   121

Fal. And I hear, moreover, his highness is fallen into this same whoreson apoplexy.

Ch. Just. Well, God mend him ! I pray you, let me speak with you.

Fal. This apoplexy is, as I take it, a kind of lethargy, an't please your lordship ; a kind of sleeping in the blood, a whoreson tingling.

Ch. Just. What tell you me of it ? be it as it is.   130

Fal. It hath its original from much grief, from study and perturbation of the brain : I have read the cause of his effects in Galen : it is a kind of deafness.

Ch. Just. I think you are fallen into the disease ; for you hear not what I say to you.

Fal. Very well, my lord, very well : rather, an't please you, it is the disease of not listening, the malady of not marking, that I am troubled withal.   140

Ch. Just. To punish you by the heels would amend the attention of your ears ; and I care not if I do become your physician.

Fal. I am as poor as Job, my lord, but not so patient : your lordship may minister the potion of imprisonment to me in respect of poverty ; but how should I be your patient to follow your prescriptions, the wise may make some dram of a scruple, or indeed a scruple itself.

Ch. Just. I sent for you, when there were matters against you for your life, to come speak with me.

Fal. As I was then advised by my learned counsel in the laws of this land-service, I did not come.

Ch. Just. Well, the truth is, Sir John, you live in great infamy.

Fal. He that buckles him in my belt cannot live in less.

Ch. Just. Your means are very slender, and your waste is great.   160

Fal. I would it were otherwise ; I would my means were greater, and my waist slenderer.

Ch. Just. You have misled the youthful prince.

Fal. The young prince hath misled me : I am the fellow with the great belly, and he my dog.

Ch. Just. Well, I am loath to gall a new-healed wound : your day's service at Shrewsbury hath a little gilded over your night's exploit on Gad's-hill : you may thank the unquiet time for your quiet o'er-posting that action.   171

Fal. My lord ?

Ch. Just. But since all is well, keep it so : wake not a sleeping wolf.

Fal. To wake a wolf is as bad as to smell a fox.

Ch. Just. What ! you are as a candle, the better part burnt out.

Fal. A wassail candle, my lord, all tallow : if I did say of wax, my growth would approve the truth.   181

Ch. Just. There is not a white hair on your face but should have his effect of gravity.

Fal. His effect of gravy, gravy, gravy.

Ch. Just. You follow the young prince up and down, like his ill angel.

Fal. Not so, my lord ; your ill angel is

light ; but I hope he that looks upon me will take me without weighing : and yet, in some respects, I grant, I cannot go : I cannot tell. Virtue is of so little regard in these costermonger times that true valor is turned bearherd : pregnancy is made a tapster, and hath his quick wit wasted in giving reckonings : all the other gifts appertinent to man, as the malice of this age shapes them, are not worth a gooseberry. You that are old consider not the capacities of us that are young ; you do measure the heat of our livers with the bitterness of your galls : and we that are in the vaward of our youth, I must confess, are wags too.   200

Ch. Just. Do you set down your name in the scroll of youth, that are written down old with all the characters of age ? Have you not a moist eye ? a dry hand ? a yellow cheek ? a white beard ? a decreasing leg ? an increasing belly ? is not your voice broken ? your wind short ? your chin double ? your wit single ? and every part about you blasted with antiquity ? and will you yet call yourself young ? Fie, fie, fie, Sir John !

Fal. My lord, I was born about three of the clock in the afternoon, with a white head and something a round belly. For my voice, I have lost it with halloing and singing of anthems. To approve my youth further, I will not : the truth is, I am only old in judgment and understanding ; and he that will caper with me for a thousand marks, let him lend me the money, and have at him ! For the box of the ear that the prince gave you, he gave it like a rude prince, and you took it like a sensible lord. I have checked him for it, and the young lion repents ; marry, not in ashes and sack-cloth, but in new silk and old sack.

Ch. Just. Well, God send the prince a better companion !

Fal. God send the companion a better prince ! I cannot rid my hands of him.

Ch. Just. Well, the king hath severed you and Prince Harry : I hear you are going with Lord John of Lancaster against the Archbishop and the Earl of Northumberland.   230

Fal. Yea ; I thank your pretty sweet wit for it. But look you pray, all you that kiss my lady Peace at home, that our armies join not in a hot day ; for, by the Lord, I take but two shirts out with me, and I mean not to sweat extraordinarily : if it be a hot day, and I brandish any thing but a bottle, I would I might never spit white again. There is not a dangerous action can peep out his head but I am thrust upon it : well, I cannot last ever : but it was alway yet the trick of our English nation, if they have a good thing, to make it too common. If ye will needs say I am an old man, you should give me rest. I would to God my name were not so terrible to the enemy as it is : I were better to be eaten to death with a rust than to be scoured to nothing with perpetual motion.

Ch. Just. Well, be honest, be honest ; and God bless your expedition !

Fal. Will your lordship lend me a thousand pound to furnish me forth ?   251

Ch. Just. Not a penny, not a penny ; you are too impatient to bear crosses. Fare you well : commend me to my cousin Westmoreland.   [*Exeunt Chief-Justice and Servant.*

Fal. If I do, fillip me with a three-man beetle. A man can no more separate age and covetousness than a' can part young limbs and lechery : but the gout galls the one, and the pox pinches the other ; and so both the degrees prevent my curses. Boy !   260
Page. Sir ?
Fal. What money is in my purse ?
Page. Seven groats and two pence.
Fal. I can get no remedy against this consumption of the purse : borrowing only lingers and lingers it out, but the disease is incurable. Go bear this letter to my Lord of Lancaster ; this to the prince; this to the Earl of Westmoreland ; and this to old Mistress Ursula, whom I have weekly sworn to marry since I perceived the first white hair on my chin. About it : you know where to find me. [*Exit Page.*] A pox of this gout ! or, a gout of this pox ! for the one or the other plays the rogue with my great toe. 'Tis no matter if I do halt ; I have the wars for my color, and my pension shall seem the more reasonable. A good wit will make use of any thing : I will turn diseases to commodity.   [*Exit.*

SCENE III. *York. The* ARCHBISHOP'S *palace.*

Enter the ARCHBISHOP, *the* LORDS HASTINGS, MOWBRAY, *and* BARDOLPH.

Arch. Thus have you heard our cause and known our means ;
And, my most noble friends, I pray you all,
Speak plainly your opinions of our hopes :
And first, lord marshal, what say you to it ?
Mowb. I well allow the occasion of our arms ;
But gladly would be better satisfied
How in our means we should advance ourselves
To look with forehead bold and big enough
Upon the power and puissance of the king.
Hast. Our present musters grow upon the file   10
To five and twenty thousand men of choice ;
And our supplies live largely in the hope
Of great Northumberland, whose bosom burns
With an incensed fire of injuries.
L. Bard. The question then, Lord Hastings, standeth thus ;
Whether our present five and twenty thousand
May hold up head without Northumberland ?
Hast. With him, we may.
L. Bard.   Yea, marry, there's the point :
But if without him we be thought too feeble,
My judgment is, we should not step too far
Till we had his assistance by the hand ;   21
For in a theme so bloody-faced as this
Conjecture, expectation, and surmise
Of aids incertain should not be admitted.
Arch. 'Tis very true, Lord Bardolph ; for indeed
It was young Hotspur's case at Shrewsbury.
L. Bard. It was, my lord ; who lined himself with hope,
Eating the air on promise of supply,
Flattering himself in project of a power
Much smaller than the smallest of his thoughts :   30
And so, with great imagination
Proper to madmen, led his powers to death
And winking leap'd into destruction.
Hast. But, by your leave, it never yet did hurt

To lay down likelihoods and forms of hope.
L. Bard. Yes, if this present quality of war,
Indeed the instant action : a cause on foot
Lives so in hope as in an early spring
We see the appearing buds ; which to prove fruit,
Hope gives not so much warrant as despair 40
That frosts will bite them. When we mean to build,
We first survey the plot, then draw the model ;
And when we see the figure of the house,
Then must we rate the cost of the erection ;
Which if we find outweighs ability,
What do we then but draw anew the model
In fewer offices, or at last desist
To build at all ? Much more, in this great work,
Which is almost to pluck a kingdom down
And set another up, should we survey   50
The plot of situation and the model,
Consent upon a sure foundation,
Question surveyors, know our own estate,
How able such a work to undergo,
To weigh against his opposite ; or else
We fortify in paper and in figures,
Using the names of men instead of men :
Like one that draws the model of a house
Beyond his power to build it ; who, half through,
Gives o'er and leaves his part-created cost   60
A naked subject to the weeping clouds
And waste for churlish winter's tyranny.
Hast. Grant that our hopes, yet likely of fair birth,
Should be still-born, and that we now possess'd
The utmost man of expectation,
I think we are a body strong enough,
Even as we are, to equal with the king.
L. Bard. What, is the king but five and twenty thousand ?
Hast. To us no more ; nay, not so much, Lord Bardolph.
For his divisions, as the times do brawl,   70
Are in three heads : one power against the French,
And one against Glendower ; perforce a third
Must take up us : so is the unfirm king
In three divided ; and his coffers sound
With hollow poverty and emptiness.
Arch. That he should draw his several strengths together
And come against us in full puissance,
Need not be dreaded.
Hast.   If he should do so,
He leaves his back unarm'd, the French and Welsh
Baying him at the heels : never fear that.   80
L. Bard. Who is it like should lead his forces hither ?
Hast. The Duke of Lancaster and Westmoreland ;
Against the Welsh, himself and Harry Monmouth :
But who is substituted 'gainst the French,
I have no certain notice.
Arch.   Let us on,
And publish the occasion of our arms.
The commonwealth is sick of their own choice ;
Their over-greedy love hath surfeited :
An habitation giddy and unsure
Hath he that buildeth on the vulgar heart.   90

O thou fond many, with what loud applause
Didst thou beat heaven with blessing Boling-
broke,
Before he was what thou wouldst have him be !
And being now trimm'd in thine own desires,
Thou, beastly feeder, art so full of him,
That thou provokest thyself to cast him up.
So, so, thou common dog, didst thou disgorge
Thy glutton bosom of the royal Richard ;
And now thou wouldst eat thy dead vomit up,
And howl'st to find it. What trust is in these
      times ?   100
They that, when Richard lived, would have
      him die,
Are now become enamor'd on his grave :
Thou, that threw'st dust upon his goodly head
When through proud London he came sighing
      on
After the admired heels of Bolingbroke,
Criest now ' O earth, yield us that king again,
And take thou this ! ' O thoughts of men ac-
cursed !
Past and to come seems best ; things present
      worst.
    Mowb. Shall we go draw our numbers and
      set on ?
    Hast. We are time's subjects, and time bids
      be gone.   [*Exeunt.*

ACT II.

SCENE I. *London. A street.*

Enter Hostess, FANG *and his* Boy *with her,
and* SNARE *following.*

    Host. Master Fang, have you entered the
action ?
    Fang. It is entered.
    Host. Where's your yeoman ? Is't a lusty
yeoman ? will a' stand to 't ?
    Fang. Sirrah, where's Snare ?
    Host. O Lord, ay ! good Master Snare.
    Snare. Here, here.
    Fang. Snare, we must arrest Sir John Fal-
staff.   10
    Host. Yea, good Master Snare ; I have en-
tered him and all.
    Snare. It may chance cost some of us our
lives, for he will stab.
    Host. Alas the day ! take heed of him ; he
stabbed me in mine own house, and that most
beastly : in good faith, he cares not what mischief he does, if his weapon be out : he will
foin like any devil ; he will spare neither man,
woman, nor child.   20
    Fang. If I can close with him, I care not
for his thrust.
    Host. No, nor I neither : I'll be at your
elbow.
    Fang. An I but fist him once ; an a' come
but within my vice,—
    Host. I am undone by his going ; I warrant
you, he's an infinitive thing upon my score.
Good Master Fang, hold him sure : good Master Snare, let him not 'scape. A' comes contin-
uantly to Pie-corner—saving your manhoods
—to buy a saddle ; and he is indited to dinner
to the Lubber's-head in Lumbert street, to
Master Smooth's the silkman : I pray ye, since
my exion is entered and my case so openly
known to the world, let him be brought in to
his answer. A hundred mark is a long one for

a poor lone woman to bear : and I have borne,
and borne, and borne, and have been fubbed
off, and fubbed off, and fubbed off, from this
day to that day, that it is a shame to be
thought on. There is no honesty in such dealing ; unless a woman should be made an ass
and a beast, to bear every knave's wrong.
Yonder he comes ; and that arrant malmsey-
nose knave, Bardolph, with him. Do your offices, do your offices : Master Fang and Master
Snare, do me, do me, do me your offices.

Enter FALSTAFF, Page, *and* BARDOLPH.

    Fal. How now ! whose mare's dead ?
what's the matter ?
    Fang. Sir John, I arrest you at the suit of
Mistress Quickly.   49
    Fal. Away, varlets ! Draw, Bardolph : cut
me off the villain's head : throw the quean in
the channel.
    Host. Throw me in the channel ! I'll throw
thee in the channel. Wilt thou ? wilt thou ?
thou bastardly rogue ! Murder, murder ! Ah,
thou honey-suckle villain ! wilt thou kill God's
officers and the king's ? Ah, thou honey-seed
rogue ! thou art a honey-seed, a man-queller,
and a woman-queller.
    Fal. Keep them off, Bardolph.   60
    Fang. A rescue ! a rescue !
    Host. Good people, bring a rescue or two.
Thou wo't, wo't thou ? thou wo't, wo't ta ? do,
do, thou rogue ! do, thou hemp-seed !
    Fal. Away, you scullion ! you rampallion !
you fustilarian ! I'll tickle your catastrophe.

Enter the Lord Chief-Justice, *and his men.*

    Ch. Just. What is the matter ? keep the
peace here, ho !
    Host. Good my lord, be good to me. I be-
seech you, stand to me.   70
    Ch. Just. How now, Sir John ! what are
you brawling here ?
Doth this become your place, your time and
      business ?
You should have been well on your way to
      York.
Stand from him, fellow : wherefore hang'st
      upon him ?
    Host. O most worshipful lord, an't please
your grace, I am a poor widow of Eastcheap,
and he is arrested at my suit.
    Ch. Just. For what sum ?
    Host. It is more than for some, my lord ; it
is for all, all I have. He hath eaten me out of
house and home ; he hath put all my substance
into that fat belly of his : but I will have some
of it out again, or I will ride thee o' nights like
the mare.
    Fal. I think I am as like to ride the mare,
if I have any vantage of ground to get up.
    Ch. Just. How comes this, Sir John ? Fie !
what man of good temper would endure this
tempest of exclamation ? Are you not ashamed
to enforce a poor widow to so rough a course
to come by her own ?   90
    Fal. What is the gross sum that I owe
thee ?
    Host. Marry, if thou wert an honest man,
thyself and the money too. Thou didst swear to
me upon a parcel-gilt goblet, sitting in my
Dolphin-chamber, at the round table, by a sea-
coal fire, upon Wednesday in Wheeson week,
when the prince broke thy head for liking his

father to a singing-man of Windsor, thou didst swear to me then, as I was washing thy wound, to marry me and make me my lady thy wife. Canst thou deny it ? Did not goodwife Keech, the butcher's wife, come in then and call me gossip Quickly ? coming in to borrow a mess of vinegar ; telling us she had a good dish of prawns ; whereby thou didst desire to eat some ; whereby I told thee they were ill for a green wound ? And didst thou not, when she was gone down stairs, desire me to be no more so familiarity with such poor people ; saying that ere long they should call me madam ? And didst thou not kiss me and bid me fetch thee thirty shillings ? I put the now to thy book-oath : deny it, if thou canst.

Fal. My lord, this is a poor mad soul ; and she says up and down the town that the eldest son is like you : she hath been in good case, and the truth is, poverty hath distracted her. But for these foolish officers, I beseech you I may have redress against them.

Ch. Just. Sir John, Sir John, I am well acquainted with your manner of wrenching the true cause the false way. It is not a confident brow, nor the throng of words that come with such more than impudent sauciness from you, can thrust me from a level consideration : you have, as it appears to me, practised upon the easy-yielding spirit of this woman, and made her serve your uses both in purse and in person.

Host. Yea, in truth, my lord.

Ch. Just. Pray thee, peace. Pay her the debt you owe her, and unpay the villany you have done her : the one you may do with sterling money, and the other with current repentance.

Fal. My lord, I will not undergo this sneap without reply. You call honorable boldness impudent sauciness : if a man will make courtesy and say nothing, he is virtuous : no, my lord, my humble duty remembered, I will not be your suitor. I say to you, I do desire deliverance from these officers, being upon hasty employment in the king's affairs. 140

Ch. Just. You speak as having power to do wrong : but answer in the effect of your reputation, and satisfy the poor woman.

Fal. Come hither, hostess.

Enter Gower.

Ch. Just. Now, Master Gower, what news ?

Gow. The king, my lord, and Harry Prince of Wales
Are near at hand : the rest the paper tells.

Fal. As I am a gentleman.

Host. Faith, you said so before.

Fal. As I am a gentleman. Come, no more words of it. 151

Host. By this heavenly ground I tread on, I must be fain to pawn both my plate and the tapestry of my dining-chambers.

Fal. Glasses, glasses is the only drinking : and for thy walls, a pretty slight drollery, or the story of the Prodigal, or the German hunting in water-work, is worth a thousand of these bed-hangings and these fly-bitten tapestries. Let it be ten pound, if thou canst. Come, an 'twere not for thy humors, there's not a better wench in England. Go, wash thy face, and draw the action. Come, thou must not be in this humor with me ; dost not know me ? come, come, I know thou wast set on to this.

Host. Pray thee, Sir John, let it be but twenty nobles : i' faith, I am loath to pawn my plate, so God save me, la !

Fal. Let it alone ; I'll make other shift : you'll be a fool still. 170

Host. Well, you shall have it, though I pawn my gown. I hope you'll come to supper. You'll pay me all together ?

Fal. Will I live ? [*To Bardolph*] Go, with her, with her ; hook on, hook on.

Host. Will you have Doll Tearsheet meet you at supper ?

Fal. No more words ; let's have her.

[*Exeunt Hostess, Bardolph, Officers and Boy.*

Ch. Just. I have heard better news.

Fal. What's the news, my lord ? 180

Ch. Just. Where lay the king last night ?

Gow. At Basingstoke, my lord.

Fal. I hope, my lord, all's well : what is the news, my lord ?

Ch. Just. Come all his forces back ?

Gow. No ; fifteen hundred foot, five hundred horse,
Are marched up to my lord of Lancaster,
Against Northumberland and the Archbishop.

Fal. Comes the king back from Wales, my noble lord ?

Ch. Just. You shall have letters of me presently : 190
Come, go along with me, good Master Gower.

Fal. My lord !

Ch. Just. What's the matter ?

Fal. Master Gower, shall I entreat you with me to dinner ?

Gow. I must wait upon my good lord here ; I thank you, good Sir John.

Ch. Just. Sir John, you loiter here too long, being you are to take soldiers up in counties as you go. 200

Fal. Will you sup with me, Master Gower ?

Ch. Just. What foolish master taught you these manners, Sir John ?

Fal. Master Gower, if they become me not, he was a fool that taught them me. This is the right fencing grace, my lord ; tap for tap, and so part fair.

Ch. Just. Now the Lord lighten thee ! thou art a great fool. [*Exeunt.*

Scene II. *London. Another street.*

Enter Prince Henry *and* Poins.

Prince. Before God, I am exceeding weary.

Poins. Is't come to that ? I had thought weariness durst not have attached one of so high blood.

Prince. Faith, it does me ; though it discolors the complexion of my greatness to acknowledge it. Doth it not show vilely in me to desire small beer ?

Poins. Why, a prince should not be so loosely studied as to remember so weak a composition.

Prince. Belike then my appetite was not princely got ; for, by my troth, I do now remember the poor creature, small beer. But, indeed, these humble considerations make me out of love with my greatness. What a disgrace is it to me to remember thy name ! or to know thy face to-morrow ! or to take note how many pair of silk stockings thou hast, viz. these, and those that were thy peach-colored ones ! or to bear the inventory of thy shirts, as, one for superfluity, and another for use ! But that the tennis-court-keeper knows better than I ; for it is a low ebb of linen with thee when thou keepest not racket there ; as thou hast not done a great while, because the rest of thy low countries have made a shift to eat up thy holland : and God knows, whether those that bawl out the ruins of thy linen shall inherit his kingdom : but the midwives say the children are not in the fault ; whereupon the world increases, and kindreds are mightily strengthened.

Poins. How ill it follows, after you have labored so hard, you should talk so idly ! Tell me, how many good young princes would do so, their fathers being so sick as yours at this time is ?

Prince. Shall I tell thee one thing, Poins ?

Poins. Yes, faith ; and let it be an excellent good thing.

Prince. It shall serve among wits of no higher breeding than thine.

Poins. Go to ; I stand the push of your one thing that you will tell. 41

Prince. Marry, I tell thee, it is not meet that I should be sad, now my father is sick : albeit I could tell thee, as to one it pleases me, for fault of a better, to call my friend, I could be sad, and sad indeed too.

Poins. Very hardly upon such a subject.

Prince. By this hand, thou thinkest me as far in the devil's book as thou and Falstaff for obduracy and persistency : let the end try the man. But I tell thee, my heart bleeds inwardly that my father is so sick : and keeping such vile company as thou art hath in reason taken from me all ostentation of sorrow.

Poins. The reason ?

Prince. What wouldst thou think of me, if I should weep ?

Poins. I would think thee a most princely hypocrite. 59

Prince. It would be every man's thought ; and thou art a blessed fellow to think as every man thinks : never a man's thought in the world keeps the road-way better than thine : every man would think me an hypocrite indeed. And what accites your most worshipful thought to think so ?

Poins. Why, because you have been so lewd and so much engraffed to Falstaff.

Prince. And to thee.

Poins. By this light, I am well spoke on ; I can hear it with my own ears : the worst that they can say of me is that I am a second brother and that I am a proper fellow of my hands ; and those two things, I confess, I cannot help. By the mass, here comes Bardolph.

Enter BARDOLPH *and* Page.

Prince. And the boy that I gave Falstaff : a' had him from me Christian ; and look, if the fat villain have not transformed him ape.

Bard. God save your grace !

Prince. And yours, most noble Bardolph !

Bard. Come, you virtuous ass, you bashful fool, must you be blushing ? wherefore blush you now ? What a maidenly man-at-arms are you become ! Is't such a matter to get a pottle-pot's maidenhead ?

Page. A' calls me e'en now, my lord, through a red lattice, and I could discern no part of his face from the window : at last I spied his eyes, and methought he had made two holes in the ale-wife's new petticoat and so peeped through.

Prince. Has not the boy profited ? 90

Bard. Away, you whoreson upright rabbit, away !

Page. Away, you rascally Althæa's dream, away !

Prince. Instruct us, boy ; what dream, boy ?

Page. Marry, my lord, Althæa dreamed she was delivered of a fire-brand ; and therefore I call him her dream.

Prince. A crown's worth of good interpretation : there 'tis, boy. 100

Poins. O, that this good blossom could be kept from cankers ! Well, there is sixpence to preserve thee.

Bard. An you do not make him hanged among you, the gallows shall have wrong.

Prince. And how doth thy master, Bardolph ?

Bard. Well, my lord. He heard of your grace's coming to town : there's a letter for you.

Poins. Delivered with good respect. And how doth the martlemas, your master ? 110

Bard. In bodily health, sir.

Poins. Marry, the immortal part needs a physician ; but that moves not him : though that be sick, it dies not.

Prince. I do allow this wen to be as familiar with me as my dog ; and he holds his place ; for look you how he writes.

Poins. [*Reads*] 'John Falstaff, knight,'— every man must know that, as oft as he has occasion to name himself : even like those that are kin to the king ; for they never prick their finger but they say, 'There's some of the king's blood spilt.' 'How comes that ?' says he, that takes upon him not to conceive. The answer is as ready as a borrower's cap, 'I am the king's poor cousin, sir.'

Prince. Nay, they will be kin to us, or they will fetch it from Japhet. But to the letter.

Poins. [*Reads*] 'Sir John Falstaff, knight, to the son of the king, nearest his father, Harry Prince of Wales, greeting.' Why, this is a certificate.

Prince. Peace !

Poins. [*Reads*] 'I will imitate the honorable Romans in brevity : ' he sure means brevity in breath, short-winded. 'I commend me to thee, I commend thee, and I leave thee. Be not too familiar with Poins ; for he misuses thy favors so much, that he swears thou art to marry his sister Nell. Repent at idle times as thou mayest ; and so, farewell. 141
'Thine, by yea and no, which is as much as to say, as thou usest him, JACK FALSTAFF with my familiars, JOHN with my brothers and sisters, and SIR JOHN with all Europe.'

My lord, I'll steep this letter in sack and make him eat it.

Prince. That's to make him eat twenty of his words. But do you use me thus, Ned ? must I marry your sister ? 151

Poins. God send the wench no worse fortune ! But I never said so.

Prince. Well, thus we play the fools with the time, and the spirits of the wise sit in the

clouds and mock us. Is your master here in
London ?

Bard.　Yea, my lord.

Prince.　Where sups he ? doth the old boar
feed in the old frank ?　　　　　　　　160

Bard.　At the old place, my lord, in Eastcheap.

Prince.　What company ?

Page.　Ephesians, my lord, of the old
church.

Prince.　Sup any women with him ?

Page.　None, my lord, but old Mistress
Quickly and Mistress Doll Tearsheet.

Prince.　What pagan may that be ?

Page.　A proper gentlewoman, sir, and a
kinswoman of my master's.　　　　　170

Prince.　Even such kin as the parish heifers
are to the town bull. Shall we steal upon them,
Ned, at supper ?

Poins.　I am your shadow, my lord ; I'll
follow you.

Prince.　Sirrah, you boy, and Bardolph, no
word to your master that I am yet come to
town : there's for your silence.

Bard.　I have no tongue, sir.　　　　179

Page.　And for mine, sir, I will govern it.

Prince.　Fare you well ; go. [*Exeunt Bardolph and Page.*] This Doll Tearsheet should
be some road.

Poins.　I warrant you, as common as the
way between Saint Alban's and London.

Prince.　How might we see Falstaff bestow
himself to-night in his true colors, and not ourselves be seen ?

Poins.　Put on two leathern jerkins and
aprons, and wait upon him at his table as
drawers.　　　　　　　　　　　　191

Prince.　From a God to a bull ? a heavy
decension ! it was Jove's case. From a prince
to a prentice ? a low transformation ! that
shall be mine ; for in every thing the purpose
must weigh with the folly. Follow me, Ned.

　　　　　　　　　　　　　[*Exeunt.*

SCENE III.　*Warkworth. Before the castle.*

Enter NORTHUMBERLAND, LADY NORTHUMBER-
　　LAND, *and* LADY PERCY.

North.　I pray thee, loving wife, and gentle
　daughter,
Give even way unto my rough affairs :
Put not you on the visage of the times
And be like them to Percy troublesome.

Lady N.　I have given over, I will speak no
　more :
Do what you will ; your wisdom be your
　guide.

North.　Alas, sweet wife, my honor is at
　pawn ;
And, but my going, nothing can redeem it.

Lady P.　O yet, for God's sake, go not to
　these wars !
The time was, father, that you broke your
　word,　　　　　　　　　　　　　10
When you were more endeared to it than now ;
When your own Percy, when my heart's dear
　Harry,
Threw many a northward look to see his father
Bring up his powers ; but he did long in vain.
Who then persuaded you to stay at home ?
There were two honors lost, yours and your
　son's.
For yours, the God of heaven brighten it !
For his, it stuck upon him as the sun

In the grey vault of heaven, and by his light
Did all the chivalry of England move　　20
To do brave acts : he was indeed the glass
Wherein the noble youth did dress themselves :
He had no legs that practised not his gait ;
And speaking thick, which nature made his
　blemish,
Became the accents of the valiant ;
For those that could speak low and tardily
Would turn their own perfection to abuse,
To seem like him : so that in speech, in gait,
In diet, in affections of delight,
In military rules, humors of blood,　　30
He was the mark and glass, copy and book,
That fashion'd others. And him, O wondrous
　him !
O miracle of men ! him did you leave,
Second to none, unseconded by you,
To look upon the hideous god of war
In disadvantage ; to abide a field
Where nothing but the sound of Hotspur's
　name
Did seem defensible : so you left him.
Never, O never, do his ghost the wrong
To hold your honor more precise and nice　40
With others than with him ! let them alone :
The marshal and the archbishop are strong :
Had my sweet Harry had but half their num-
　bers,
To-day might I, hanging on Hotspur's neck,
Have talk'd of Monmouth's grave.

North.　　　　　　　Beshrew your heart,
Fair daughter, you do draw my spirits from
　me
With new lamenting ancient oversights.
But I must go and meet with danger there,
Or it will seek me in another place
And find me worse provided.

Lady N.　　　　　O, fly to Scotland,　50
Till that the nobles and the armed commons
Have of their puissance made a little taste.

Lady P.　If they get ground and vantage of
　the king,
Then join you with them, like a rib of steel,
To make strength stronger ; but, for all our
　loves,
First let them try themselves. So did your son ;
He was so suffer'd : so came I a widow ;
And never shall have length of life enough
To rain upon remembrance with mine eyes,
That it may grow and sprout as high as
　heaven,　　　　　　　　　　　　60
For recordation to my noble husband.

North.　Come, come, go in with me. 'Tis
　with my mind
As with the tide swell'd up unto his height,
That makes a still-stand, running neither way :
Fain would I go to meet the archbishop,
But many thousand reasons hold me back.
I will resolve for Scotland : there am I,
Till time and vantage crave my company.

　　　　　　　　　　　　　[*Exeunt.*

SCENE IV.　*London.　The Boar's-head Tavern
in Eastcheap.*

Enter two Drawers.

First Draw.　What the devil hast thou
brought there ? apple-johns ? thou knowest
Sir John cannot endure an apple-john.

Sec. Draw.　Mass, thou sayest true. The
prince once set a dish of apple-johns before
him, and told him there were five more Sir
Johns, and, putting off his hat, said ' I will now

take my leave of these six dry, round, old,
withered knights.' It angered him to the
heart : but he hath forgot that.   10
First Draw. Why, then, cover, and set them
down : and see if thou canst find out Sneak's
noise ; Mistress Tearsheet would fain hear
some music. Dispatch : the room where they
supped is too hot ; they'll come in straight.
Sec. Draw. Sirrah, here will be the prince
and Master Poins anon ; and they will put on
two of our jerkins and aprons ; and Sir John
must not know of it : Bardolph hath brought
word.   20
First Draw. By the mass, here will be old
Utis : it will be an excellent stratagem.
Sec. Draw. I'll see if I can find out Sneak.
          [*Exit.*

Enter HOSTESS *and* DOLL TEARSHEET.

Host. I' faith, sweetheart, methinks now
you are in an excellent good temperality : your
pulsidge beats as extraordinarily as heart
would desire ; and your color, I warrant you,
is as red as any rose, in good truth, la ! But,
i' faith, you have drunk too much canaries ;
and that's a marvellous searching wine, and it
perfumes the blood ere one can say ' What's
this ?' How do you now ?
Dol. Better than I was : hem !
Host. Why, that's well said ; a good heart's
worth gold. Lo, here comes Sir John.

Enter FALSTAFF.

Fal. [*Singing*] ' When Arthur first in
court,'
—Empty the jordan. [*Exit First Drawer.*]—
[*Singing*] ' And was a worthy king.' How
now, Mistress Doll !
Host. Sick of a calm ; yea, good faith. 40
Fal. So is all her sect ; an they be once in
a calm, they are sick.
Dol. You muddy rascal, is that all the
comfort you give me ?
Fal. You make fat rascals, Mistress Doll.
Dol. I make them ! gluttony and diseases
make them ; I make them not.
Fal. If the cook help to make the gluttony,
you help to make the diseases, Doll : we catch
of you, Doll, we catch of you ; grant that, my
poor virtue, grant that.   51
Dol. Yea, joy, our chains and our jewels.
Fal. ' Your brooches, pearls, and ouches : '
for to serve bravely is to come halting off, you
know : to come off the breach with his pike
bent bravely, and to surgery bravely ; to venture upon the charged chambers bravely,—
Dol. Hang yourself, you muddy conger,
hang yourself !   59
Host. By my troth, this is the old fashion ;
you two never meet but you fall to some discord : you are both, i' good truth, as rheumatic as two dry toasts ; you cannot one bear
with another's confirmities. What the good-
year ! one must bear, and that must be you :
you are the weaker vessel, as they say, the
emptier vessel.
Dol. Can a weak empty vessel bear such a
huge full hogshead ? there's a whole merchant's venture of Bourdeaux stuff in him ;
you have not seen a hulk better stuffed in the
hold. Come, I'll be friends with thee, Jack :
thou art going to the wars ; and whether I

shall ever see thee again or no, there is nobody
cares.

Re-enter First Drawer.

First Draw. Sir, Ancient Pistol's below,
and would speak with you.
Dol. Hang him, swaggering rascal ! let
him not come hither : it is the foul-mouthed'st
rogue in England.
Host. If he swagger, let him not come
here : no, by my faith ; I must live among my
neighbors ; I'll no swaggerers : I am in good
name and fame with the very best : shut the
door ; there comes no swaggerers here : I have
not lived all this while, to have swaggering
now : shut the door, I pray you.
Fal. Dost thou hear, hostess ?
Host. Pray ye, pacify yourself, Sir John :
there comes no swaggerers here.
Fal. Dost thou hear ? it is mine ancient.
Host. Tilly-fally, Sir John, ne'er tell me :
your ancient swaggerer comes not in my doors.
I was before Master Tisick, the debuty, t'other
day ; and, as he said to me, 'twas no longer
ago than Wednesday last, ' I' good faith,
neighbor Quickly,' says he ; Master Dumbe,
our minister, was by then ; ' neighbor Quickly,'
says he, ' receive those that are civil ; for,'
said he, ' you are in an ill name : ' now a' said
so, I can tell whereupon ; ' for,' says he, ' you
are an honest woman, and well thought on ;
therefore take heed what guests you receive :
receive,' says he, ' no swaggering companions.' There comes none here : you would
bless you to hear what he said : no, I'll no
swaggerers.
Fal. He's no swaggerer, hostess ; a tame
cheater, i' faith ; you may stroke him as
gently as a puppy greyhound : he'll not swagger with a Barbary hen, if her feathers turn
back in any show of resistance. Call him up,
drawer.   [*Exit First Drawer.*
Host. Cheater, call you him ? I will bar
no honest man my house, nor no cheater : but
I do not love swaggering, by my troth ; I am
the worse, when one says swagger : feel, masters, how I shake ; look you, I warrant you.
Dol. So you do, hostess.
Host. Do I ? yea, in very truth, do I, an
'twere an aspen leaf : I cannot abide swaggerers.

Enter PISTOL, BARDOLPH, *and* PAGE.

Pist. God save you, Sir John !   119
Fal. Welcome, Ancient Pistol. Here, Pistol,
I charge you with a cup of sack : do you discharge upon mine hostess.
Pist. I will discharge upon her, Sir John,
with two bullets.
Fal. She is pistol-proof, sir ; you shall
hardly offend her.
Host. Come, I'll drink no proofs nor no
bullets : I'll drink no more than will do me
good, for no man's pleasure, I.
Pist. Then to you, Mistress Dorothy ; I
will charge you.   131
Dol. Charge me ! I scorn you, scurvy companion. What ! you poor, base, rascally, cheat-
ing, lack-linen mate ! Away, you mouldy
rogue, away ! I am meat for your master.
Pist. I know you, Mistress Dorothy.
Dol. Away, you cut-purse rascal ! you
filthy bung, away ! by this wine, I'll thrust

my knife in your mouldy chaps, an you play
the saucy cuttle with me. Away, you bottle-
ale rascal ! you basket-hilt stale juggler, you !
Since when, I pray you, sir ? God's light, with
two points on your shoulder ? much !

Pist. God let me not live, but I will murder
your ruff for this.

Fal. No more, Pistol ; I would not have
you go off here : discharge yourself of our
company, Pistol.

Host. No, Good Captain Pistol ; not here,
sweet captain. 150

Dol. Captain ! thou abominable damned
cheater, art thou not ashamed to be called
captain ? An captains were of my mind, they
would truncheon you out, for taking their
names upon you before you have earned them.
You a captain ! you slave, for what ? for
tearing a poor whore's ruff in a bawdy-house ?
He a captain ! hang him, rogue ! he lives
upon mouldy stewed prunes and dried cakes.
A captain ! God's light, these villains will
make the word as odious as the word ' oc-
cupy ; ' which was an excellent good word before it was ill sorted : therefore captains had
need look to 't.

Bard. Pray thee, go down, good ancient.

Fal. Hark thee hither, Mistress Doll.

Pist. Not I : I tell thee what, Corporal
Bardolph, I could tear her : I'll be revenged
of her.

Page. Pray thee, go down.

Pist. I'll see her damned first ; to Pluto's
damned lake, by this hand, to the infernal
deep, with Erebus and tortures vile also. Hold
hook and line, say I. Down, down, dogs !
down, faitors ! Have we not Hiren here ?

Host. Good Captain Peesel, be quiet ; 'tis
very late, i' faith : I beseek you now, aggravate your choler.

Pist. These be good humors, indeed ! Shall
　　　pack-horses
And hollow pamper'd jades of Asia,
Which cannot go but thirty mile a-day,
Compare with Cæsars, and with Cannibals,
And Trojan Greeks ? nay, rather damn them
　　　with 181
King Cerberus ; and let the welkin roar.
Shall we fall foul for toys ?

Host. By my troth, captain, these are very
bitter words.

Bard. Be gone, good ancient : this will
grow to a brawl anon.

Pist. Die men like dogs ! give crowns like
pins ! Have we not Heren here ? 189

Host. O' my word, captain, there's none
such here. What the good-year ! do you think
I would deny her ? For God's sake, be quiet.

Pist. Then feed, and be fat, my fair Calip-
olis.

Come, give's some sack.
' Si fortune me tormente, sperato me con-
　　　tento.'
Fear we broadsides ? no, let the fiend give
　　　fire :
Give me some sack : and, sweetheart, lie thou
　　　there.　　　[*Laying down his sword.*
Come we to full points here ; and are etceteras
nothing ?

Fal. Pistol, I would be quiet.

Pist. Sweet knight, I kiss thy neif : what !
we have seen the seven stars. 201

Dol. For God's sake, thrust him down

stairs : I cannot endure such a fustian rascal.

Pist. Thrust him down stairs ! know we
not Galloway nags ?

Fal. Quoit him down, Bardolph, like a
shove-groat shilling : nay, an a' do nothing
but speak nothing, a' shall be nothing here.

Bard. Come, get you down stairs. 209

Pist. What ! shall we have incision ? shall
we imbrue ? [*Snatching up his sword.*
Then death rock me asleep, abridge my dole-
　　　ful days !
Why, then, let grievous, ghastly, gaping
　　　wounds
Untwine the Sisters Three ! Come, Atropos, I
say !

Host. Here's goodly stuff toward !

Fal. Give me my rapier, boy.

Dol. I pray thee, Jack, I pray thee, do not
draw.

Fal. Get you down stairs.
　　　[*Drawing, and driving Pistol out.*

Host. Here's a goodly tumult ! I'll forswear keeping house, afore I'll be in these
tirrits and frights. So ; murder, I warrant
now. Alas, alas! put up your naked weapons,
put up your naked weapons.
　　　[*Exeunt Pistol and Bardolph.*

Dol. I pray thee, Jack, be quiet ; the
rascal's gone. Ah, you whoreson little valiant
villain, you !

Host. Are you not hurt i' the groin ? methought a' made a shrewd thrust at your belly.

Re-enter BARDOLPH.

Fal. Have you turned him out o' doors ?

Bard. Yea, sir. The rascal's drunk : you
have hurt him, sir, i' the shoulder. 231

Fal. A rascal ! to brave me !

Dol. Ah, you sweet little rogue, you ! alas,
poor ape, how thou sweatest ! come, let me
wipe thy face ; come on, you whoreson chops :
ah, rogue ! i' faith, I love thee : thou art as
valorous as Hector of Troy, worth five of
Agamemnon, and ten times better than the
Nine Worthies : ah, villain !

Fal. A rascally slave ! I will toss the rogue
in a blanket. 241

Dol. Do, an thou darest for thy heart : an
thou dost, I'll canvass thee between a pair of
sheets.

Enter Music.

Page. The music is come, sir.

Fal. Let them play. Play, sirs. Sit on my
knee, Doll. A rascal bragging slave ! the rogue
fled from me like quicksilver.

Dol. I' faith, and thou followedst him like
a church. Thou whoreson little tidy Bartholomew boar-pig, when wilt thou leave fighting o' days and foining o' nights, and begin to
patch up thine old body for heaven ?

Enter, behind, PRINCE HENRY *and* POINS, *dis-*
　　　guised.

Fal. Peace, good Doll ! do not speak like
a death's-head ; do not bid me remember mine
end.

Dol. Sirrah, what humor's the prince of ?

Fal. A good shallow young fellow : a'
would have made a good pantler, a' would
ha' chipped bread well.

Dol. They say Poins has a good wit. 260

Fal. He a good wit ? hang him, baboon !

his wit's as thick as Tewksbury mustard; there's no more conceit in him than is in a mallet.

Dol. Why does the prince love him so, then?

Fal. Because their legs are both of a bigness, and a' plays at quoits well, and eats conger and fennel, and drinks off candles' ends for flap-dragons, and rides the wild-mare with the boys, and jumps upon joined-stools, and swears with a good grace, and wears his boots very smooth, like unto the sign of the leg, and breeds no bate with telling of discreet stories; and such other gambol faculties a' has, that show a weak mind and an able body, for the which the prince admits him: for the prince himself is such another; the weight of a hair will turn the scales between their avoirdupois.

Prince. Would not this nave of a wheel have his ears cut off? 279

Poins. Let's beat him before his whore.

Prince. Look, whether the withered elder hath not his poll clawed like a parrot. 281

Poins. Is it not strange that desire should so many years outlive performance?

Fal. Kiss me, Doll.

Prince. Saturn and Venus this year in conjunction! what says the almanac to that?

Poins. And look, whether the fiery Trigon, his man, be not lisping to his master's old tables, his note-book, his counsel-keeper. 290

Fal. Thou dost give me flattering busses.

Dol. By my troth, I kiss thee with a most constant heart.

Fal. I am old, I am old.

Dol. I love thee better than I love e'er a scurvy young boy of them all.

Fal. What stuff wilt have a kirtle of? I shall receive money o' Thursday: shalt have a cap to-morrow. A merry song, come: it grows late; we'll to bed. Thou'lt forget me when I am gone.

Dol. By my troth, thou'lt set me a-weeping, an thou sayest so: prove that ever I dress myself handsome till thy return: well, harken at the end.

Fal. Some sack, Francis.

Prince. } Anon, anon, sir.
Poins. }   [*Coming forward.*

Fal. Ha! a bastard son of the king's? And art not thou Poins his brother?

Prince. Why, thou globe of sinful continents, what a life dost thou lead! 310

Fal. A better than thou: I am a gentleman; thou art a drawer.

Prince. Very true, sir; and I come to draw you out by the ears.

Host. O, the Lord preserve thy good grace! by my troth, welcome to London. Now, the Lord bless that sweet face of thine! O Jesu, are you come from Wales?

Fal. Thou whoreson mad compound of majesty, by this light flesh and corrupt blood, thou art welcome. 321

Dol. How, you fat fool! I scorn you.

Poins. My lord, he will drive you out of your revenge and turn all to a merriment, if you take not the heat.

Prince. You whoreson candle-mine, you, how vilely did you speak of me even now before this honest, virtuous, civil gentlewoman!

Host. God's blessing of your good heart!

and so she is, by my troth.   330

Fal. Didst thou hear me?

Prince. Yea, and you knew me, as you did when you ran away by Gad's-hill: you knew I was at your back, and spoke it on purpose to try my patience.

Fal. No, no, no; not so; I did not think thou wast within hearing.

Prince. I shall drive you then to confess the wilful abuse; and then I know how to handle you.

Fal. No abuse, Hal, o' mine honor, no abuse.

Prince. Not to dispraise me, and call me pantler and bread-chipper and I know not what?

Fal. No abuse, Hal.

Poins. No abuse?

Fal. No abuse, Ned, i' the world; honest Ned, none. I dispraised him before the wicked, that the wicked might not fall in love with him; in which doing, I have done the part of a careful friend and a true subject, and thy father is to give me thanks for it. No abuse, Hal: none, Ned, none: no, faith, boys, none.

Prince. See now, whether pure fear and entire cowardice doth not make thee wrong this virtuous gentlewoman to close with us? is she of the wicked? is thine hostess here of the wicked? or is thy boy of the wicked? or honest Bardolph, whose zeal burns in his nose, of the wicked?

Poins. Answer, thou dead elm, answer.

Fal. The fiend hath pricked down Bardolph irrecoverable; and his face is Lucifer's privy-kitchen, where he doth nothing but roast malt-worms. For the boy, there is a good angel about him; but the devil outbids him too.

Prince. For the women?

Fal. For one of them, she is in hell already, and burns poor souls. For the other, I owe her money; and whether she be damned for that, I know not.

Host. No, I warrant you.   369

Fal. No, I think thou art not; I think thou art quit for that. Marry, there is another indictment upon thee, for suffering flesh to be eaten in thy house, contrary to the law; for the which I think thou wilt howl.

Host. All victuallers do so; what's a joint of mutton or two in a whole Lent?

Prince. You, gentlewoman,—

Dol. What says your grace?

Fal. His grace says that which his flesh rebels against.   [*Knocking within.* 380

Host. Who knocks so loud at door? Look to the door there, Francis.

Enter PETO.

Prince. Peto, how now! what news?

Peto. The king your father is at Westminster:
And there are twenty weak and wearied posts
Come from the north: and, as I came along,
I met and overtook a dozen captains,
Bare-headed, sweating, knocking at the taverns,
And asking every one for Sir John Falstaff.

Prince. By heaven, Poins, I feel me much to blame,   390
So idly to profane the precious time,
When tempest of commotion, like the south

Borne with black vapor, doth begin to melt
And drop upon our bare unarmed heads.
Give me my sword and cloak. Falstaff, good
    night.   [*Exeunt Prince Henry, Poins,*
                        Peto and Bardolph.
    Fal. Now comes in the sweetest morsel of
the night, and we must hence and leave it un-
picked. [*Knocking within.*] More knocking
at the door!

                Re-enter BARDOLPH.

How now! what's the matter?   400
    Bard. You must away to court, sir, pres-
    ently;
A dozen captains stay at door for you.
    Fal. [*To the Page*] Pay the musicians,
sirrah. Farewell, hostess; farewell, Doll. You
see, my good wenches, how men of merit are
sought after: the undeserver may sleep, when
the man of action is called on. Farewell, good
wenches: if I be not sent away post, I will
see you again ere I go.
    Dol. I cannot speak; if my heart be not
ready to burst,—well, sweet Jack, have a care
of thyself.
    Fal. Farewell, farewell.
              [*Exeunt Falstaff and Bardolph.*
    Host. Well, fare thee well: I have known
thee these twenty-nine years, come peascod-
time; but an honester and truer-hearted man,
—well, fare thee well.
    Bard. [*Within*] Mistress Tearsheet!
    Host. What's the matter?
    Bard. [*Within*] Good Mistress Tearsheet
come to my master.   419
    Host. O, run, Doll, run; run, good Doll:
come. [*She comes blubbered.*] Yea, will you
come, Doll?   [*Exeunt.*

ACT III.

SCENE I. *Westminster. The palace.*

Enter the KING *in his nightgown, with a* Page.

    King. Go call the Earls of Surrey and of
        Warwick;
But, ere they come, bid them o'er-read these
        letters,
And well consider of them; make good speed.
                        [*Exit Page.*
How many thousand of my poorest subjects
Are at this hour asleep! O sleep, O gentle
        sleep,
Nature's soft nurse, how have I frighted thee,
That thou no more wilt weigh my eyelids down
And steep my senses in forgetfulness?
Why rather, sleep, liest thou in smoky cribs,
Upon uneasy pallets stretching thee   10
And hush'd with buzzing night-flies to thy
        slumber,
Than in the perfumed chambers of the great,
Under the canopies of costly state,
And lull'd with sound of sweetest melody?
O thou dull god, why liest thou with the vile
In loathsome beds, and leavest the kingly couch
A watch-case or a common 'larum-bell?
Wilt thou upon the high and giddy mast
Seal up the ship-boy's eyes, and rock his brains
In cradle of the rude imperious surge   20
And in the visitation of the winds,
Who take the ruffian billows by the top,

Curling their monstrous heads and hanging
        them
With deafening clamor in the slippery clouds,
That, with the hurly, death itself awakes?
Canst thou, O partial sleep, give thy repose
To the wet sea-boy in an hour so rude,
And in the calmest and most stillest night,
With all appliances and means to boot,
Deny it to a king? Then happy low, lie down!
Uneasy lies the head that wears a crown.   31

                Enter WARWICK *and* SURREY.

    War. Many good morrows to your maj-
        esty!
    King. Is it good morrow, lords?
    War. 'Tis one o'clock, and past.
    King. Why, then, good morrow to you all,
        my lords.
Have you read o'er the letters that I sent you?
    War. We have, my liege.
    King.   Then you perceive the body of our
        kingdom
How foul it is; what rank diseases grow
And with what danger, near the heart of it. 40
    War. It is but as a body yet distemper'd;
Which to his former strength may be restored
With good advice and little medicine:
My Lord Northumberland will soon be cool'd.
    King. O God! that one might read the
        book of fate,
And see the revolution of the times
Make mountains level, and the continent,
Weary of solid firmness, melt itself
Into the sea! and, other times, to see
The beachy girdle of the ocean   50
Too wide for Neptune's hips; how chances
        mock,
And changes fill the cup of alteration
With divers liquors! O, if this were seen,
The happiest youth, viewing his progress
        through,
What perils past, what crosses to ensue,
Would shut the book, and sit him down and
        die.
'Tis not ten years gone
Since Richard and Northumberland, great
        friends,
Did feast together, and in two years after
Were they at wars: it is but eight years since
This Percy was the man nearest my soul,   61
Who like a brother toil'd in my affairs
And laid his love and life under my foot,
Yea, for my sake, even to the eyes of Richard
Gave him defiance. But which of you was by—
You, cousin Nevil, as I may remember—
                        [*To Warwick.*
When Richard, with his eye brimful of tears,
Then check'd and rated by Northumberland,
Did speak these words, now proved a proph-
        ecy?   69
'Northumberland, thou ladder by the which
My cousin Bolingbroke ascends my throne;'
Though then, God knows, I had no such
        intent,
But that necessity so bow'd the state
That I and greatness were compell'd to kiss:
'The time shall come,' thus did he follow it,
'The time will come, that foul sin, gathering
        head,
Shall break into corruption:' so went on,
Foretelling this same time's condition
And the division of our amity.
    War. There is a history in all men's lives,

Figuring the nature of the times deceased; 81
The which observed, a man may prophesy,
With a near aim, of the main chance of things
As yet not come to life, which in their seeds
And weak beginnings lie intreasured.
Such things become the hatch and brood of
     time ;
And by the necessary form of this
King Richard might create a perfect guess
That great Northumberland, then false to him,
Would of that seed grow to a greater false-
     ness ;
Which should not find a ground to root upon,
Unless on you.
     King. Are these things then necessities ?
Then let us meet them like necessities :
And that same word even now cries out on us :
They say the bishop and Northumberland
Are fifty thousand strong.
     War.   It cannot be, my lord ;
Rumor doth double, like the voice and echo,
The numbers of the fear'd. Please it your grace
To go to bed. Upon my soul, my lord,
The powers that you already have sent forth
Shall bring this prize in very easily.   101
To comfort you the more, I have received
A certain instance that Glendower is dead.
Your majesty hath been this fortnight ill,
And these unseason'd hours perforce must
     add
Unto your sickness.
     King.   I will take your counsel :
And were these inward wars once out of hand,
We would, dear lords, unto the Holy Land.
     [*Exeunt.*

SCENE II.   *Gloucestershire. Before* JUSTICE
     SHALLOW'S *house.*

Enter SHALLOW *and* SILENCE, *meeting ;*
MOULDY, SHADOW, WART, FEEBLE, BULL-
CALF, *a* Servant *or two with them.*

     Shal. Come on, come on, come on, sir ;
give me your hand, sir, give me your hand,
sir : an early stirrer, by the rood ! And how
doth my good cousin Silence ?
     Sil. Good morrow, good cousin Shallow.
     Shal. And how doth my cousin, your bed-
fellow ? and your fairest daughter and mine,
my god-daughter Ellen ?
     Sil. Alas, a black ousel, cousin Shallow ! 9
     Shal. By yea and nay, sir, I dare say my
cousin William is become a good scholar : he
is at Oxford still, is he not ?
     Sil. Indeed, sir, to my cost.
     Shal. A' must, then, to the inns o' court
shortly. I was once of Clement's Inn, where I
think they will talk of mad Shallow yet.
     Sil. You were called ' lusty Shallow ' then,
cousin.
     Shal. By the mass, I was called any thing ;
and I would have done any thing indeed too,
and roundly too. There was I, and little John
Doit of Staffordshire, and black George
Barnes, and Francis Pickbone, and Will
Squele, a Cotswold man ; you had not four
such swinge-bucklers in all the inns o' court
again : and I may say to you, we knew where
the bona-robas were and had the best of them
all at commandment. Then was Jack Falstaff,
now Sir John, a boy, and page to Thomas
Mowbray, Duke of Norfolk.
     Sil. This Sir John, cousin, that comes
hither anon about soldiers ?   31

     Shal. The same Sir John, the very same. I
see him break Skogan's head at the court-gate,
when a' was a crack not thus high : and the
very same day did I fight with one Sampson
Stockfish, a fruiterer, behind Gray's Inn.
Jesu, Jesu, the mad days that I have spent !
and to see how many of my old acquaintance
are dead !
     Sil. We shall all follow, cousin.   39
     Shal. Certain, 'tis certain ; very sure, very
sure : death, as the Psalmist saith, is certain
to all ; all shall die. How a good yoke of bullocks at Stamford fair ?
     Sil. By my troth, I was not there.
     Shal. Death is certain. Is old Double of
your town living yet ?
     Sil. Dead, sir.
     Shal. Jesu, Jesu, dead ! a' drew a good
bow ; and dead ! a' shot a fine shoot : John a
Gaunt loved him well, and betted much money
on his head. Dead ! a' would have clapped
i' the clout at twelve score ; and carried you a
forehand shaft a fourteen and fourteen and a
half, that it would have done a man's heart
good to see. How a score of ewes now ?
     Sil. Thereafter as they be : a score of good
ewes may be worth ten pounds.
     Shal. And is old Double dead ?
     Sil. Here come two of Sir John Falstaff's
men, as I think.   60

     Enter BARDOLPH *and one with him.*

     Bard. Good morrow, honest gentlemen : I
beseech you, which is Justice Shallow ?
     Shal. I am Robert Shallow, sir ; a poor es-
quire of this county, and one of the king's justices of the peace : what is your good pleasure
with me ?
     Bard. My captain, sir, commends him to
you ; my captain, Sir John Falstaff, a tall
gentleman, by heaven, and a most gallant
leader.
     Shal. He greets me well, sir. I knew him a
good backsword man. How doth the good
knight ? may I ask how my lady his wife
doth ?   71
     Bard. Sir, pardon ; a soldier is better ac-
commodated than with a wife.
     Shal. It is well said, in faith, sir ; and it is
well said indeed too. Better accommodated !
it is good ; yea, indeed, is it : good phrases
are surely, and ever were, very commendable.
Accommodated ! it comes of ' accommodo :'
very good ; a good phrase.   79
     Bard. Pardon me, sir ; I have heard the
word. Phrase call you it ? by this good day,
I know not the phrase ; but I will maintain
the word with my sword to be a soldier-like
word, and a word of exceeding good command, by heaven. Accommodated ; that is,
when a man is, as they say, accommodated ; or
when a man is, being, whereby a' may be
thought to be accommodated ; which is an
excellent thing.
     Shal. It is very just.   89

     Enter FALSTAFF.

Look, here comes good Sir John. Give me
your good hand, give me your worship's good
hand : by my troth, you like well and bear
your years very well : welcome, good Sir
John.
     Fal. I am glad to see you well, good Mas-

ter Robert Shallow : Master Surecard, as I think ?

Shal. No, Sir John ; it is my cousin Silence, in commission with me.

Fal. Good Master Silence, it well befits you should be of the peace.

Sil. Your good worship is welcome.   100

Fal. Fie ! this is hot weather, gentlemen. Have you provided me here half a dozen sufficient men ?

Shal. Marry, have we, sir. Will you sit ?

Fal. Let me see them, I beseech you.

Shal. Where's the roll ? where's the roll ? where's the roll ? Let me see, let me see, let me see. So, so, so, so, so, so, so : yea, marry, sir : Ralph Mouldy ! Let them appear as I call ; let them do so, let them do so. Let me see ; where is Mouldy ?   111

Moul. Here, an't please you.

Shal. What think you, Sir John ? a good-limbed fellow ; young, strong, and of good friends.

Fal. Is thy name Mouldy ?

Moul. Yea, an't please you.

Fal. 'Tis the more time thou wert used.

Shal. Ha, ha, ha ! most excellent, i' faith ! things that are mouldy lack use : very singular good ! in faith, well said, Sir John, very well said.   120

Fal. Prick him.

Moul. I was pricked well enough before, an you could have let me alone : my old dame will be undone now for one to do her husbandry and her drudgery : you need not to have pricked me ; there are other men fitter to go out than I.

Fal. Go to : peace, Mouldy ; you shall go. Mouldy, it is time you were spent.

Moul. Spent !   129

Shal. Peace, fellow, peace ; stand aside : know you where you are ? For the other, Sir John : let me see : Simon Shadow !

Fal. Yea, marry, let me have him to sit under : he's like to be a cold soldier.

Shal. Where's Shadow ?

Shad. Here, sir.

Fal. Shadow, whose son art thou ?

Shad. My mother's son, sir.

Fal. Thy mother's son ! like enough, and thy father's shadow : so the son of the female is the shadow of the male : it is often so, indeed ; but much of the father's substance !

Shal. Do you like him, Sir John ?

Fal. Shadow will serve for summer ; prick him, for we have a number of shadows to fill up the muster-book.

Shal. Thomas Wart !

Fal. Where's he ?

Wart. Here, sir.

Fal. Is thy name Wart ?   150

Wart. Yea, sir.

Fal. Thou art a very ragged wart.

Shal. Shall I prick him down, Sir John ?

Fal. It were superfluous ; for his apparel is built upon his back and the whole frame stands upon pins : prick him no more.

Shal. Ha, ha, ha ! you can do it, sir ; you can do it : I commend you well. Francis Feeble !

Fee. Here, sir.

Fal. What trade art thou, Feeble ?   160

Fee. A woman's tailor, sir.

Shal. Shall I prick him, sir ?

Fal. You may : but if he had been a man's tailor, he'ld ha' pricked you. Wilt thou make as many holes in an enemy's battle as thou hast done in a woman's petticoat ?

Fee. I will do my good will, sir ; you can have no more.

Fal. Well said, good woman's tailor ! well said, courageous Feeble ! thou wilt be as valiant as the wrathful dove or most magnanimous mouse. Prick the woman's tailor : well, Master Shallow ; deep, Master Shallow.

Fee. I would Wart might have gone, sir.

Fal. I would thou wert a man's tailor, that thou mightst mend him and make him fit to go. I cannot put him to a private soldier that is the leader of so many thousands : let that suffice, most forcible Feeble.

Fee. It shall suffice, sir.   180

Fal. I am bound to thee, reverend Feeble. Who is next ?

Shal. Peter Bullcalf o' the green !

Fal. Yea, marry, let's see Bullcalf.

Bull. Here, sir.

Fal. 'Fore God, a likely fellow ! Come, prick me Bullcalf till he roar again.

Bull. O Lord ! good my lord captain,—

Fal. What, dost thou roar before thou art pricked ?   190

Bull. O Lord, sir ! I am a diseased man.

Fal. What disease hast thou ?

Bull. A whoreson cold, sir, a cough, sir, which I caught with ringing in the king's affairs upon his coronation-day, sir.

Fal. Come, thou shalt go to the wars in a gown ; we will have away thy cold ; and I will take such order that my friends shall ring for thee. Is here all ?   199

Shal. Here is two more called than your number ; you must have but four here, sir : and so, I pray you, go in with me to dinner.

Fal. Come, I will go drink with you, but I cannot tarry dinner. I am glad to see you, by my troth, Master Shallow.

Shal. O, Sir John, do you remember since we lay all night in the windmill in Saint George's field ?

Fal. No more of that, good Master Shallow, no more of that.

Shal. Ha ! 'twas a merry night. And is Jane Nightwork alive ?   211

Fal. She lives, Master Shallow.

Shal. She never could away with me.

Fal. Never, never ; she would always say she could not abide Master Shallow.

Shal. By the mass, I could anger her to the heart. She was then a bona-roba. Doth she hold her own well ?

Fal. Old, old, Master Shallow.   219

Shal. Nay, she must be old ; she cannot choose but be old ; certain she's old ; and had Robin Nightwork by old Nightwork before I came to Clement's Inn.

Sil. That's fifty-five year ago.

Shal. Ha, cousin Silence, that thou hadst seen that that this knight and I have seen ! Ha, Sir John, said I well ?

Fal. We have heard the chimes at midnight, Master Shallow.   229

Shal. That we have, that we have, that we have ; in faith, Sir John, we have : our watchword was 'Hem boys ! ' Come, let's to dinner ;

come, let's to dinner : Jesus, the days that we
have seen ! Come, come.

[*Exeunt Falstaff and the Justices.*

Bull. Good Master Corporate Bardolph,
stand my friend ; and here's four Harry ten
shillings in French crowns for you. In very
truth, sir, I had as lief be hanged, sir, as go :
and yet, for mine own part, sir, I do not care ;
but rather, because I am unwilling, and, for
mine own part, have a desire to stay with my
friends ; else, sir, I did not care, for mine own
part, so much.

Bard. Go to ; stand aside.

Moul. And, good master corporal captain,
for my old dame's sake, stand my friend : she
has nobody to do any thing about her when I
am gone ; and she is old, and cannot help herself : you shall have forty, sir.

Bard. Go to ; stand aside.　　　　　249

Fee. By my troth, I care not ; a man can
die but once : we owe God a death : I'll ne'er
bear a base mind : an't be my destiny, so ;
an't be not, so : no man is too good to serve's
prince ; and let it go which way it will, he
that dies this year is quit for the next.

Bard. Well said ; thou'rt a good fellow.

Fee. Faith, I'll bear no base mind.

Re-enter FALSTAFF *and the* Justices.

Fal. Come, sir, which men shall I have ?

Shal. Four of which you please.

Bard. Sir, a word with you : I have three
pound to free Mouldy and Bullcalf.　　　　　261

Fal. Go to ; well.

Shal. Come, Sir John, which four will you
have ?

Fal. Do you choose for me.

Shal. Marry, then, Mouldy, Bullcalf,
Feeble and Shadow.

Fal. Mouldy and Bullcalf : for you,
Mouldy, stay at home till you are past service : and for your part, Bullcalf, grow till you
come unto it : I will none of you.　　　　　271

Shal. Sir John, Sir John, do not yourself
wrong : they are your likeliest men, and I
would have you served with the best.

Fal. Will you tell me, Master Shallow, how
to choose a man ? Care I for the limb, the
thewes, the stature, bulk, and big assemblance
of a man ! Give me the spirit, Master Shallow.
Here's Wart ; you see what a ragged appearance it is ; a' shall charge you and discharge
you with the motion of a pewterer's hammer,
come off and on swifter than he that gibbets
on the brewer's bucket. And this same half-
faced fellow, Shadow ; give me this man : he
presents no mark to the enemy ; the foeman
may with as great aim level at the edge of a
penknife. And for a retreat ; how swiftly will
this Feeble the woman's tailor run off ! O, give
me the spare men, and spare me the great
ones. Put me a caliver into Wart's hand, Bardolph.　　　　　290

Bard. Hold, Wart, traverse ; thus, thus,
thus.

Fal. Come, manage me your caliver. So :
very well : go to : very good, exceeding good.
O, give me always a little, lean, old, chapt,
bald shot. Well said, i' faith, Wart ; thou'rt a
good scab : hold, there's a tester for thee.

Shal. He is not his craft's master ; he doth
not do it right. I remember at Mile-end Green,
when I lay at Clement's Inn,—I was then Sir

Dagonet in Arthur's show,—there was a little
quiver fellow, and a' would manage you his
piece thus; and a' would about and about, and
come you in and come you in : ' rah, tah, tah,'
would a' say ; ' bounce ' would a' say ; and
away again would a' go, and again would a'
come : I shall ne'er see such a fellow.

Fal. These fellows will do well, Master
Shallow. God keep you, Master Silence : I will
not use many words with you. Fare you well,
gentlemen both : I thank you : I must a
dozen mile to-night. Bardolph, give the soldiers
coats.　　　　　311

Shal. Sir John, the Lord bless you ! God
prosper your affairs ! God send us peace ! At
your return visit our house ; let our old acquaintance be renewed ; peradventure I will
with ye to the court.

Fal. 'Fore God, I would you would, Master Shallow.

Shal. Go to ; I have spoke at a word. God
keep you.　　　　　320

Fal. Fare you well, gentle gentlemen.
[*Exeunt Justices.*] On, Bardolph ; lead the men
away. [*Exeunt Bardolph, Recruits, &c.*] As
I return, I will fetch off these justices : I do
see the bottom of Justice Shallow. Lord, Lord,
how subject we old men are to this vice of lying ! This same starved justice hath done nothing but prate to me of the wildness of his
youth, and the feats he hath done about Turn-
bull Street : and every third word a lie, duer
paid to the hearer than the Turk's tribute. I do
remember him at Clement's Inn like a man
made after supper of a cheese-paring : when a'
was naked, he was, for all the world, like a
forked radish, with a head fantastically carved
upon it with a knife : a' was so forlorn, that
his dimensions to any thick sight were invincible : a' was the very genius of famine ; yet
lecherous as a monkey, and the whores called
him mandrake : a' came ever in the rearward
of the fashion, and sung those tunes to the
overscutched huswives that he heard the car-
men whistle, and swear they were his fancies or
his good-nights. And now is this Vice's dagger
become a squire, and talks as familiarly of
John a Gaunt as if he had been sworn brother
to him ; and I'll be sworn a' ne'er saw him but
once in the Tilt-yard ; and then he burst his
head for crowding among the marshal's men.
I saw it, and told John a Gaunt he beat his
own name ; for you might have thrust him
and all his apparel into an eel-skin ; the case
of a treble hautboy was a mansion for him, a
court : and now has he land and beefs. Well,
I'll be acquainted with him, if I return ; and it
shall go hard but I will make him a philosopher's two stones to me : if the young dace be
a bait for the old pike, I see no reason in the
law of nature but I may snap at him. Let time
shape, and there an end.　　　　　[*Exit.*

ACT IV.

SCENE I. *Yorkshire. Gaultree Forest.*

Enter the ARCHBISHOP OF YORK, MOWBRAY,
HASTINGS, *and others.*

Arch. What is this forest call'd ?

Hast. 'Tis Gaultree Forest, an't shall please
your grace.

Arch. Here stand, my lords ; and send dis-
coverers forth
To know the numbers of our enemies.
Hast. We have sent forth already.
Arch.   'Tis well done.
My friends and brethren in these great affairs,
I must acquaint you that I have received
New-dated letters from Northumberland ;
Their cold intent, tenor and substance, thus :
Here doth he wish his person, with such pow-
ers
As might hold sortance with his quality,   11
The which he could not levy ; whereupon
He is retired, to ripe his growing fortunes,
To Scotland : and concludes in hearty prayers
That your attempts may overlive the hazard
And fearful meeting of their opposite.
Mowb. Thus do the hopes we have in him
touch ground
And dash themselves to pieces.

Enter a Messenger.

Hast.   Now, what news ?
Mess. West of this forest, scarcely off a
mile,
In goodly form comes on the enemy ;   20
And, by the ground they hide, I judge their
number
Upon or near the rate of thirty thousand.
Mowb. The just proportion that we gave
them out.
Let us sway on and face them in the field.
Arch. What well-appointed leader fronts
us here ?

Enter WESTMORELAND.

Mowb. I think it is my Lord of Westmore-
land.
West. Health and fair greeting from our
general,
The prince, Lord John and Duke of Lancaster.
Arch. Say on, my Lord of Westmoreland,
in peace :
What doth concern your coming ?
West.   Then, my lord, 30
Unto your grace do I in chief address
The substance of my speech. If that rebellion
Came like itself, in base and abject routs,
Led on by bloody youth, guarded with rags,
And countenanced by boys and beggary,
I say, if damn'd commotion so appear'd,
In his true, native and most proper shape,
You, reverend father, and these noble lords
Had not been here, to dress the ugly form
Of base and bloody insurrection   40
With your fair honors. You, lord archbishop,
Whose see is by a civil peace maintain'd,
Whose beard the silver hand of peace hath
touch'd,
Whose learning and good letters peace hath
tutor'd,
Whose white investments figure innocence,
The dove and very blessed spirit of peace,
Wherefore do you so ill translate yourself
Out of the speech of peace that bears such
grace,
Into the harsh and boisterous tongue of war ;
Turning your books to graves, your ink to
blood,   50
Your pens to lances and your tongue divine
To a loud trumpet and a point of war ?
Arch. Wherefore do I this ? so the ques-
tion stands.

Briefly to this end : we are all diseased,
And with our surfeiting and wanton hours
Have brought ourselves into a burning fever,
And we must bleed for it ; of which disease
Our late king, Richard, being infected, died.
But, my most noble Lord of Westmoreland,
I take not on me here as a physician,   60
Nor do I as an enemy to peace
Troop in the throngs of military men ;
But rather show awhile like fearful war,
To diet rank minds sick of happiness
And purge the obstructions which begin to
stop
Our very veins of life. Hear me more plainly.
I have in equal balance justly weigh'd
What wrongs our arms may do, what wrongs
we suffer,
And find our griefs heavier than our offences.
We see which way the stream of time doth run,
And are enforced from our most quiet there 71
By the rough torrent of occasion ;
And have the summary of all our griefs,
When time shall serve, to show in articles ;
Which long ere this we offer'd to the king,
And might by no suit gain our audience :
When we are wrong'd and would unfold our
griefs,
We are denied access unto his person
Even by those men that most have done us
wrong.
The dangers of the days but newly gone,   80
Whose memory is written on the earth
With yet appearing blood, and the examples
Of every minute's instance, present now,
Hath put us in these ill-beseeming arms,
Not to break peace or any branch of it,
But to establish here a peace indeed,
Concurring both in name and quality.
West. When ever yet was your appeal de-
nied ?
Wherein have you been galled by the king ?
What peer hath been suborn'd to grate on you,
That you should seal this lawless bloody book
Of forged rebellion with a seal divine
And consecrate commotion's bitter edge ?
Arch. My brother general, the common-
wealth,
To brother born an household cruelty,
I make my quarrel in particular.
West. There is no need of any such re-
dress ;
Or if there were, it not belongs to you.
Mowb. Why not to him in part, and to us
all
That feel the bruises of the days before,   100
And suffer the condition of these times
To lay a heavy and unequal hand
Upon our honors ?
West.   O, my good Lord Mowbray,
Construe the times to their necessities,
And you shall say indeed, it is the time,
And not the king, that doth you injuries.
Yet for your part, it not appears to me
Either from the king or in the present time
That you should have an inch of any ground
To build a grief on : were you not restored
To all the Duke of Norfolk's signories,   111
Your noble and right well remember'd fa-
ther's ?
Mowb. What thing, in honor, had my fa-
ther lost,
That need to be revived and breathed in me ?

The king that loved him, as the state stood
then,
Was force perforce compell'd to banish him :
And then that Harry Bolingbroke and he,
Being mounted and both roused in their seats,
Their neighing coursers daring of the spur,
Their armed staves in charge, their beavers
down,　　　　　　　　　　　　　　　120
Their eyes of fire sparkling through sights of
steel
And the loud trumpet blowing them together,
Then, then, when there was nothing could have
stay'd
My father from the breast of Bolingbroke,
O, when the king did throw his warder down,
His own life hung upon the staff he threw ;
Then threw he down himself and all their lives
That by indictment and by dint of sword
Have since miscarried under Bolingbroke.
　　West. You speak, Lord Mowbray, now you
　　　know not what.　　　　　　　130
The Earl of Hereford was reputed then
In England the most valiant gentlemen :
Who knows on whom fortune would then have
smiled ?
But if your father had been victor there,
He ne'er had borne it out of Coventry :
For all the country in a general voice
Cried hate upon him ; and all their prayers
and love
Were set on Hereford, whom they doted on
And bless'd and graced indeed, more than the
king.
But this is mere digression from my purpose.
Here come I from our princely general　141
To know your griefs ; to tell you from his
grace
That he will give you audience ; and wherein
It shall appear that your demands are just,
You shall enjoy them, every thing set off
That might so much as think you enemies.
　　Mowb. But he hath forced us to compel
　　　this offer ;
And it proceeds from policy, not love.
　　West. Mowbray, you overween to take it
　　　so ;
This offer comes from mercy, not from fear :
For, lo ! within a ken our army lies,　151
Upon mine honor, all too confident
To give admittance to a thought of fear.
Our battle is more full of names than yours,
Our men more perfect in the use of arms,
Our armor all as strong, our cause the best ;
Then reason will our heart should be as good :
Say you not then our offer is compell'd.
　　Mowb. Well, by my will we shall admit no
　　　parley.
　　West. That argues but the shame of your
　　　offence :　　　　　　　　160
A rotten case abides no handling.
　　Hast. Hath the Prince John a full commis-
　　　sion,
In very ample virtue of his father,
To hear and absolutely to determine
Of what conditions we shall stand upon ?
　　West. That is intended in the general's
　　　name :
I muse you make so slight a question.
　　Arch. Then take, my Lord of Westmore-
　　　land, this schedule,
For this contains our general grievances :
Each several article herein redress'd,　170

All members of our cause, both here and
hence,
That are insinew'd to this action,
Acquitted by a true substantial form
And present execution of our wills
To us and to our purposes confined,
We come within our awful banks again
And knit our powers to the arm of peace.
　　West. This will I show the general. Please
　　　you, lords,
In sight of both our battles we may meet ; 179
And either end in peace, which God so frame !
Or to the place of difference call the swords
Which must decide it.
　　Arch. 　　　My lord, we will do so. [*Exit West.*
　　Mowb. There is a thing within my bosom
　　　tells me
That no conditions of our peace can stand.
　　Hast. Fear you not that : if we can make
　　　our peace
Upon such large terms and so absolute
As our conditions shall consist upon,
Our peace shall stand as firm as rocky moun-
tains.
　　Mowb. Yea, but our valuation shall be
　　　such
That every slight and false-derived cause,　190
Yea, every idle, nice and wanton reason
Shall to the king taste of this action ;
That, were our royal faiths martyrs in love,
We shall be winnow'd with so rough a wind
That even our corn shall seem as light as chaff
And good from bad find no partition.
　　Arch. No, no, my lord. Note this ; the
　　　king is weary
Of dainty and such picking grievances :
For he hath found to end one doubt by death
Revives two greater in the heirs of life,　200
And therefore will he wipe his tables clean
And keep no tell-tale to his memory
That may repeat and history his loss
To new remembrance ; for full well he knows
He cannot so precisely weed this land
As his misdoubts present occasion :
His foes are so enrooted with his friends
That, plucking to unfix an enemy,
He doth unfasten so and shake a friend :
So that this land, like an offensive wife　210
That hath enraged him on to offer strokes,
As he is striking, holds his infant up
And hangs resolved correction in the arm
That was uprear'd to execution.
　　Hast. Besides, the king hath wasted all his
　　　rods
On late offenders, that he now doth lack
The very instruments of chastisement :
So that his power, like to a fangless lion,
May offer, but not hold.
　　Arch. 　　　　　　'Tis very true :
And therefore be assured, my good lord mar-
shal,　　　　　　　　　　　　220
If we do now make our atonement well,
Our peace will, like a broken limb united,
Grow stronger for the breaking.
　　Mowb. 　　　　　　Be it so.
Here is return'd my Lord of Westmoreland.

　　　　　　Re-enter WESTMORELAND.

　　West. The prince is here at hand : pleaseth
　　　your lordship
To meet his grace just distance 'tween our
armies.

Mowb. Your grace of York, in God's
name, then, set forward.
Arch. Before, and greet his grace : my
lord, we come.   [*Exeunt.*

Scene II. *Another part of the forest.*

Enter, from one side, Mowbray, *attended ;
afterwards the* Archbishop, Hastings, *and
others : from the other side,* Prince John
of Lancaster, *and* Westmoreland ; Officers, *and others with them.*

Lan. You are well encounter'd here, my
cousin Mowbray :
Good day to you, gentle lord archbishop ;
And so to you, Lord Hastings, and to all.
My Lord of York, it better show'd with you
When that your flock, assembled by the bell,
Encircled you to hear with reverence
Your exposition on the holy text
Than now to see you here an iron man,   9
Cheering a rout of rebels with your drum,
Turning the word to sword and life to death.
That man that sits within a monarch's heart,
And ripens in the sunshine of his favor,
Would he abuse the countenance of the king,
Alack, what mischiefs might he set abrooch
In shadow of such greatness ! With you, lord
bishop,
It is even so. Who hath not heard it spoken
How deep you were within the books of God ?
To us the speaker in his parliament ;
To us the imagined voice of God himself ;
The very opener and intelligencer   20
Between the grace, the sanctities of heaven
And our dull workings. O, who shall believe
But you misuse the reverence of your place,
Employ the countenance and grace of heaven,
As a false favorite doth his prince's name,
In deeds dishonorable ? You have ta'en up,
Under the counterfeited zeal of God,
The subjects of his substitute, my father,
And both against the peace of heaven and him
Have here up-swarm'd them.
Arch.   Good my Lord of Lancaster, 30
I am not here against your father's peace ;
But, as I told my lord of Westmoreland,
The time misorder'd doth, in common sense,
Crowd us and crush us to this monstrous form,
To hold our safety up. I sent your grace
The parcels and particulars of our grief,
The which hath been with scorn shoved from
the court,
Whereon this Hydra son of war is born ;
Whose dangerous eyes may well be charm'd
asleep
With grant of our most just and right desires,
And true obedience, of this madness cured,
Stoop tamely to the foot of majesty.
Mowb. If not, we ready are to try our for-
tunes
To the last man.
Hast.   And though we here fall down,
We have supplies to second our attempt :
If they miscarry, theirs shall second them ;
And so success of mischief shall be born
And heir from heir shall hold this quarrel up
Whiles England shall have generation.
Lan. You are too shallow, Hastings, much
too shallow,   50
To sound the bottom of the after-times.
West. Pleaseth your grace to answer them
directly
How far forth you do like their articles.

Lan. I like them all, and do allow them
well,
And swear here, by the honor of my blood,
My father's purposes have been mistook,
And some about him have too lavishly
Wrested his meaning and authority.
My lord, these griefs shall be with speed re-
dress'd ;
Upon my soul, they shall. If this may please
you,   60
Discharge your powers unto their several
counties,
As we will ours : and here between the armies
Let's drink together friendly and embrace,
That all their eyes may bear those tokens
home
Of our restored love and amity.
Arch. I take your princely word for these
redresses.
Lan. I give it you, and will maintain my
word :
And thereupon I drink unto your grace.
Hast. Go, captain, and deliver to the army
This news of peace : let them have pay, and
part :   70
I know it will well please them. Hie thee,
captain.   [*Exit Officer.*
Arch. To you, my noble Lord of West-
moreland.
West. I pledge your grace ; and, if you
knew what pains
I have bestow'd to breed this present peace,
You would drink freely : but my love to ye
Shall show itself more openly hereafter.
Arch. I do not doubt you.
West.   I am glad of it.
Health to my lord and gentle cousin, Mow-
bray.
Mowb. You wish me health in very happy
season ;
For I am, on the sudden, something ill.   80
Arch. Against ill chances men are ever
merry ;
But heaviness foreruns the good event.
West. Therefore be merry, coz ; since sud-
den sorrow
Serves to say thus, ' some good thing comes
to-morrow.'
Arch. Believe me, I am passing light in
spirit.
Mowb. So much the worse, if your own
rule be true.   [*Shouts within.*
Lan. The word of peace is render'd : hark,
how they shout !
Mowb. This had been cheerful after vic-
tory.
Arch. A peace is of the nature of a con-
quest ;
For then both parties nobly are subdued,   90
And neither party loser.
Lan.   Go, my lord,
And let our army be discharged too.
                    [*Exit Westmoreland.*
And, good my lord, so please you, let our
trains
March by us, that we may peruse the men
We should have coped withal.
Arch.   Go, good Lord Hastings,
And, ere they be dismiss'd, let them march by.
                    [*Exit Hastings.*
Lan. I trust, lords, we shall lie to-night to-
gether.

Re-enter WESTMORELAND.

Now, cousin, wherefore stands our army still ?
  West. The leaders, having charge from you
      to stand,
Will not go off until they hear you speak.   100
  Lan. They know their duties.

Re-enter HASTINGS.

  Hast. My lord, our army is dispersed al-
      ready ;
Like youthful steers unyoked, they take their
      courses
East, west, north, south ; or, like a school
      broke up,
Each hurries toward his home and sporting-
      place.
  West. Good tidings, my Lord Hastings ;
      for the which
I do arrest thee, traitor, of high treason :
And you, lord archbishop, and you, Lord
      Mowbray,
Of capital treason I attach you both.
  Mowb. Is this proceeding just and honor-
      able ?   110
  West. Is your assembly so ?
  Arch. Will you thus break your faith ?
  Lan.   I pawn'd thee none :
I promised you redress of these same griev-
      ances
Whereof you did complain ; which, by mine
      honor,
I will perform with a most Christian care.
But for you, rebels, look to taste the due
Meet for rebellion and such acts as yours.
Most shallowly did you these arms commence,
Fondly brought here and foolishly sent hence.
Strike up our drums, pursue the scatter'd
      stray :   120
God, and not we, hath safely fought to-day.
Some guard these traitors to the block of
      death,
Treason's true bed and yielder up of breath.
                                        [*Exeunt.*

SCENE III. *Another part of the forest.*

Alarum. Excursions. Enter FALSTAFF *and*
      COLEVILE, *meeting.*

  Fal. What's your name, sir ? of what condition are you, and of what place, I pray ?
  Cole. I am a knight, sir, and my name is
Colevile of the dale.
  Fal. Well, then, Colevile is your name, a
knight is your degree, and your place the dale :
Colevile shall be still your name, a traitor your
degree, and the dungeon your place, a place
deep enough ; so shall you be still Colevile of
the dale.   10
  Cole. Are not you Sir John Falstaff ?
  Fal. As good a man as he, sir, whoe'er I
am. Do ye yield, sir ? or shall I sweat for
you ? If I do sweat, they are the drops of thy
lovers, and they weep for thy death : therefore
rouse up fear and trembling, and do observance to my mercy.
  Cole. I think you are Sir John Falstaff, and
in that thought yield me.   19
  Fal. I have a whole school of tongues in
this belly of mine, and not a tongue of them
all speaks any other word but my name. An I
had but a belly of any indifference, I were
simply the most active fellow in Europe : my

womb, my womb, my womb, undoes me. Here
comes our general.

Enter PRINCE JOHN OF LANCASTER, WEST-
      MORELAND, BLUNT, *and others.*

  Lan. The heat is past ; follow no further
      now :
Call in the powers, good cousin Westmoreland.
                        [*Exit Westmoreland.*
Now, Falstaff, where have you been all this
      while ?
When every thing is ended, then you come : 30
These tardy tricks of yours will, on my life,
One time or other break some gallows' back.
  Fal. I would be sorry, my lord, but it
should be thus : I never knew yet but rebuke
and check was the reward of valor. Do you
think me a swallow, an arrow, or a bullet ?
have I, in my poor and old motion, the expedition of thought ? I have speeded hither with
the very extremest inch of possibility ; I have
foundered nine score and odd posts : and here,
travel-tainted as I am, have, in my pure and
immaculate valor, taken Sir John Colevile of
the dale, a most furious knight and valorous
enemy. But what of that ? he saw me, and
yielded ; that I may justly say, with the hook-
nosed fellow of Rome, ' I came, saw, and overcame.'
  Lan. It was more of his courtesy than your
deserving.
  Fal. I know not : here he is, and here I
yield him : and I beseech your grace, let it be
booked with the rest of this day's deeds ; or,
by the Lord, I will have it in a particular ballad else, with mine own picture on the top on't,
Colevile kissing my foot : to the which course
if I be enforced, if you do not all show like gilt
twopences to me, and I in the clear sky of
fame o'ershine you as much as the full moon
doth the cinders of the element, which show
like pins' heads to her, believe not the word of
the noble : therefore let me have right, and let
desert mount.   61
  Lan. Thine's too heavy to mount.
  Fal. Let it shine, then.
  Lan. Thine's too thick to shine.
  Fal. Let it do something, my good lord,
that may do me good, and call it what you
will.
  Lan. Is thy name Colevile ?
  Cole. It is, my lord.
  Lan. A famous rebel art thou, Colevile. 69
  Fal. And a famous true subject took him.
  Cole. I am, my lord, but as my betters are
That led me hither : had they been ruled by
      me,
You should have won them dearer than you
      have.
  Fal. I know not how they sold themselves :
but thou, like a kind fellow, gavest thyself
away gratis ; and I thank thee for thee.

Re-enter WESTMORELAND.

  Lan. Now, have you left pursuit ?
  West. Retreat is made and execution
      stay'd.
  Lan. Send Colevile with his confederates
To York, to present execution :   80
Blunt, lead him hence ; and see you guard him
      sure.
            [*Exeunt Blunt and others with Colevile*
And now dispatch we toward the court, my
      lords :

I hear the king my father is sore sick :
Our news shall go before us to his majesty,
Which, cousin, you shall bear to comfort him,
And we with sober speed will follow you.
  Fal. My lord, I beseech you, give me leave
    to go
Through Gloucestershire : and, when you
    come to court,
Stand my good lord, pray, in your good report.
  Lan. Fare you well, Falstaff : I, in my con-
    dition,   90
Shall better speak of you than you deserve.
              [*Exeunt all but Falstaff.*
  Fal. I would you had but the wit : 'twere
better than your dukedom. Good faith, this
same young sober-blooded boy doth not love
me ; nor a man cannot make him laugh ; but
that's no marvel, he drinks no wine. There's
never none of these demure boys come to any
proof ; for thin drink doth so over-cool their
blood, and making many fish-meals, that they
fall into a kind of male green-sickness ; and
then, when they marry, they get wenches : they
are generally fools and cowards ; which some
of us should be too, but for inflammation. A
good sherris sack hath a two-fold operation
in it. It ascends me into the brain ; dries me
there all the foolish and dull and curdy vapors
which environ it ; makes it apprehensive,
quick, forgetive, full of nimble fiery and delectable shapes ; which, delivered o'er to the
voice, the tongue, which is the birth, becomes
excellent wit. The second property of your excellent sherris is, the warming of the blood ;
which, before cold and settled, left the liver
white and pale, which is the badge of pusil-
lanimity and cowardice ; but the sherris warms
it and makes it course from the inwards to
the parts extreme : it illumineth the face,
which as a beacon gives warning to all the
rest of this little kingdom, man, to arm ; and
then the vital commoners and inland petty
spirits muster me all to their captain, the
heart, who, great and puffed up with this ret-
inue, doth any deed of courage ; and this valor
comes of sherris. So that skill in the weapon is
nothing without sack, for that sets it a-work ;
and learning a mere hoard of gold kept by a
devil, till sack commences it and sets it in act
and use. Hereof comes it that Prince Harry
is valiant ; for the cold blood he did naturally
inherit of his father, he hath, like lean, sterile
and bare land, manured, husbanded and tilled
with excellent endeavor of drinking good and
good store of fertile sherris, that he is become
very hot and valiant. If I had a thousand sons,
the first humane principle I would teach them
should be, to forswear thin potations and to
addict themselves to sack.

              Enter BARDOLPH.

How now Bardolph ?
  Bard. The army is discharged all and gone.
  Fal. Let them go. I'll through Gloucestershire ; and there will I visit Master Robert
Shallow, esquire : I have him already tempering between my finger and my thumb, and
shortly will I seal with him. Come away.
                                      [*Exeunt.*

  SCENE IV. *Westminster. The Jerusalem
                    Chamber.*

Enter the KING, *the* PRINCES THOMAS OF

CLARENCE *and* HUMPHREY OF GLOUCESTER,
WARWICK, *and others.*

  King. Now, lords, if God doth give suc-
    cessful end
To this debate that bleedeth at our doors,
We will our youth lead on to higher fields
And draw no swords but what are sanctified.
Our navy is address'd, our power collected,
Our substitutes in absence well invested,
And every thing lies level to our wish :
Only, we want a little personal strength ;
And pause us, till these rebels, now afoot,
Come underneath the yoke of government. 10
  War. Both which we doubt not but your
    majesty
Shall soon enjoy.
  King. Humphrey, my son of Gloucester,
Where is the prince your brother ?
  Glou. I think he's gone to hunt, my lord,
    at Windsor.
  King. And how accompanied ?
  Glou.   I do not know, my lord.
  King. Is not his brother, Thomas of Clar-
    ence, with him ?
  Glou. No, my good lord ; he is in presence
    here.
  Clar. What would my lord and father ?
  King. Nothing but well to thee, Thomas of
    Clarence.
How chance thou art not with the prince thy
    brother ?   20
He loves thee, and thou dost neglect him,
    Thomas ;
Thou hast a better place in his affection
Than all thy brothers : cherish it, my boy,
And noble offices thou mayst effect
Of mediation, after I am dead,
Between his greatness and thy other brethren :
Therefore omit him not ; blunt not his love,
Nor lose the good advantage of his grace
By seeming cold or careless of his will ;
For he is gracious, if he be observed :   30
He hath a tear for pity and a hand
Open as day for melting charity :
Yet notwithstanding, being incensed, he's flint,
As humorous as winter and as sudden
As flaws congealed in the spring of day.
His temper, therefore, must be well observed :
Chide him for faults, and do it reverently,
When you perceive his blood inclined to
    mirth ;
But, being moody, give him line and scope,
Till that his passions, like a whale on ground,
Confound themselves with working. Learn this,
    Thomas,   41
And thou shalt prove a shelter to thy friends,
A hoop of gold to bind thy brothers in,
That the united vessel of their blood,
Mingled with venom of suggestion—
As, force perforce, the age will pour it in—
Shall never leak, though it do work as strong
As aconitum or rash gunpowder.
  Clar. I shall observe him with all care and
    love.
  King. Why art thou not at Windsor with
    him, Thomas ?   50
  Clar. He is not there to-day ; he dines in
    London.
  King. And how accompanied ? canst thou
    tell that ?
  Clar. With Poins, and other his continual
    followers.

King. Most subject is the fattest soil to
   weeds;
And he, the noble image of my youth,
Is overspread with them: therefore my grief
Stretches itself beyond the hour of death:
The blood weeps from my heart when I do
   shape
In forms imaginary the unguided days
And rotten times that you shall look upon 60
When I am sleeping with my ancestors.
For when his headstrong riot hath no curb,
When rage and hot blood are his counsellors,
When means and lavish manners meet to-
   gether,
O, with what wings shall his affections fly
Towards fronting peril and opposed decay!
   War. My gracious lord, you look beyond
   him quite:
The prince but studies his companions
Like a strange tongue, wherein, to gain the
   language,
'Tis needful that the most immodest word 70
Be look'd upon and learn'd; which once at-
   tain'd,
Your highness knows, comes to no further use
But to be known and hated. So, like gross
   terms,
The prince will in the perfectness of time
Cast off his followers; and their memory
Shall as a pattern or a measure live,
By which his grace must mete the lives of
   others,
Turning past evils to advantages.
   King. 'Tis seldom when the bee doth leave
   her comb
In the dead carrion.

     Enter WESTMORELAND.

       Who's here? Westmoreland? 80
   West. Health to my sovereign, and new
   happiness
Added to that that I am to deliver!
Prince John your son doth kiss your grace's
   hand:
Mowbray, the Bishop Scroop, Hastings and all
Are brought to the correction of your law;
There is not now a rebel's sword unsheath'd
But peace puts forth her olive every where.
The manner how this action hath been borne
Here at more leisure may your highness read,
With every course in his particular. 90
   King. O Westmoreland, thou art a summer
   bird,
Which ever in the haunch of winter sings
The lifting up of day.

     Enter HARCOURT.

       Look, here's more news.
   Har. From enemies heaven keep your maj-
   esty;
And, when they stand against you, may they
   fall
As those that I am come to tell you of!
The Earl Northumberland and the Lord Bar-
   dolph,
With a great power of English and of Scots,
Are by the sheriff of Yorkshire overthrown:
The manner and true order of the fight 100
This packet, please it you, contains at large.
   King. And wherefore should these good
   news make me sick?
Will fortune never come with both hands full,
But write her fair words still in foulest letters?

She either gives a stomach and no food;
Such are the poor, in health; or else a feast
And takes away the stomach; such are the
   rich,
That have abundance and enjoy it not.
I should rejoice now at this happy news; 109
And now my sight fails, and my brain is
   giddy:
O me! come near me; now I am much ill.
   Glou. Comfort, your majesty!
   Clar.   O my royal father!
   West. My sovereign lord, cheer up your-
   self, look up.
   War. Be patient, princes; you do know,
   these fits
Are with his highness very ordinary.
Stand from him, give him air; he'll straight
   be well.
   Clar. No, no, he cannot long hold out
   these pangs:
The incessant care and labor of his mind
Hath wrought the mure that should confine it
   in
So thin that life looks through and will break
   out.
   Glou. The people fear me; for they do
   observe
Unfather'd heirs and loathly births of nature:
The seasons change their manners, as the year
Had found some months asleep and leap'd
   them over.
   Clar. The river hath thrice flow'd, no ebb
   between;
And the old folk, time's doting chronicles,
Say it did so a little time before
That our great-grandsire, Edward, sick'd and
   died.
   War. Speak lower, princes, for the king
   recovers.
   Glou. This apoplexy will certain be his end.
   King. I pray you, take me up, and bear
   me hence 131
Into some other chamber: softly, pray.

     SCENE V. *Another chamber.*

The KING *lying on a bed:* CLARENCE,
  GLOUCESTER, WARWICK, *and others in at-*
  tendance.

   King. Let there be no noise made, my
   gentle friends;
Unless some dull and favorable hand
Will whisper music to my weary spirit.
   War. Call for the music in the other room.
   King. Set me the crown upon my pillow
   here.
   Clar. His eye is hollow, and he changes
   much.
   War. Less noise, less noise!

     Enter PRINCE HENRY.

   Prince.   Who saw the Duke of Clarence?
   Clar. I am here, brother, full of heaviness.
   Prince. How now! rain within doors, and
   none abroad!
How doth the king? 10
   Glou. Exceeding ill.
   Prince.   Heard he the good news yet?
Tell it him.
   Glou. He alter'd much upon the hearing it.
   Prince. If he be sick with joy, he'll re-
   cover without physic.
   War. Not so much noise, my lords: sweet
   prince, speak low;

The king your father is disposed to sleep.
  Clar. Let us withdraw into the other room.
  War. Will't please your grace to go along
    with us ?   19
  Prince. No ; I will sit and watch here by
    the king.   [*Exeunt all but the Prince.*
Why doth the crown lie there upon his pillow,
Being so troublesome a bedfellow ?
O polish'd perturbation ! golden care !
That keep'st the ports of slumber open wide
To many a watchful night ! sleep with it now !
Yet not so sound and half so deeply sweet
As he whose brow with homely biggen bound
Snores out the watch of night. O majesty !
When thou dost pinch thy bearer, thou dost
  sit
Like a rich armor worn in heat of day,   30
That scalds with safety. By his gates of breath
There lies a downy feather which stirs not :
Did he suspire, that light and weightless down
Perforce must move. My gracious lord ! my
  father !
This sleep is sound indeed ; this is a sleep
That from this golden rigol hath divorced
So many English kings. Thy due from me
Is tears and heavy sorrows of the blood,
Which nature, love, and filial tenderness,
Shall, O dear father, pay thee plenteously : 40
My due from thee is this imperial crown,
Which, as immediate from thy place and
  blood,
Derives itself to me. Lo, here it sits,
Which God shall guard : and put the world's
  whole strength
Into one giant arm, it shall not force
This lineal honor from me : this from thee
Will I to mine leave, as 'tis left to me. [*Exit.*
  King. Warwick ! Gloucester ! Clarence !

Re-enter WARWICK, GLOUCESTER, CLARENCE,
    and the rest.

  Clar. Doth the king call ?
  War. What would your majesty ? How
    fares your grace ?   50
  King. Why did you leave me here alone,
    my lords ?
  Clar. We left the prince my brother here,
    my liege,
Who undertook to sit and watch by you.
  King. The Prince of Wales ! Where is
    he ? let me see him :
He is not here.
  War. This door is open ; he is gone this
    way.
  Glou. He came not through the chamber
    where we stay'd.
  King. Where is the crown ? who took it
    from my pillow ?
  War. When we withdrew, my liege, we
    left it here.
  King. The prince hath ta'en it hence : go,
    seek him out.   60
Is he so hasty that he doth suppose
My sleep my death ?
Find him, my Lord of Warwick ; chide him
  hither.   [*Exit Warwick.*
This part of his conjoins with my disease,
And helps to end me. See, sons, what things
  you are !
How quickly nature falls into revolt
When gold becomes her object !
For this the foolish over-careful fathers

Have broke their sleep with thoughts, their
  brains with care,
Their bones with industry ;   70
For this they have engrossed and piled up
The canker'd heaps of strange-achieved gold ;
For this they have been thoughtful to invest
Their sons with arts and martial exercises :
When, like the bee, culling from every flower
The virtuous sweets,
Our thighs pack'd with wax, our mouths with
  honey,
We bring it to the hive, and, like the bees,
Are murdered for our pains. This bitter taste
Yield his engrossments to the ending father.

        Re-enter WARWICK.

Now, where is he that will not stay so long
Till his friend sickness hath determined me ?
  War. My lord, I found the prince in the
    next room,
Washing with kindly tears his gentle cheeks,
With such a deep demeanor in great sorrow
That tyranny, which never quaff'd but blood,
Would, by beholding him, have wash'd his
  knife
With gentle eye-drops. He is coming hither.
  King. But wherefore did he take away
    the crown ?

      Re-enter PRINCE HENRY.

Lo, where he comes. Come hither to me,
  Harry.
Depart the chamber, leave us here alone.   91
        [*Exeunt Warwick and the rest.*
  Prince. I never thought to hear you speak
    again.
  King. Thy wish was father, Harry, to that
    thought :
I stay too long by thee, I weary thee.
Dost thou so hunger for mine empty chair
That thou wilt needs invest thee with my
  honors
Before thy hour be ripe ? O foolish youth !
Thou seek'st the greatness that will overwhelm
  thee.
Stay but a little ; for my cloud of dignity
Is held from falling with so weak a wind 100
That it will quickly drop : my day is dim.
Thou hast stolen that which after some few
  hours
Were thine without offence ; and at my death
Thou hast seal'd up my expectation :
Thy life did manifest thou lovedst me not,
And thou wilt have me die assured of it.
Thou hidest a thousand daggers in thy
  thoughts,
Which thou hast whetted on thy stony heart,
To stab at half an hour of my life.
What ! canst thou not forbear me half an
  hour ?   110
Then get thee gone and dig my grave thyself,
And bid the merry bells ring to thine ear
That thou art crowned, not that I am dead.
Let all the tears that should bedew my hearse
Be drops of balm to sanctify thy head :
Only compound me with forgotten dust ;
Give that which gave thee life unto the
  worms.
Pluck down my officers, break my decrees ;
For now a time is come to mock at form :
Harry the Fifth is crown'd : up, vanity ! 120
Down, royal state ! all you sage counsellors,
  hence !

And to the English court assemble now,
From every region, apes of idleness!
Now, neighbor confines, purge you of your
    scum:
Have you a ruffian that will swear, drink,
    dance,
Revel the night, rob, murder, and commit
The oldest sins the newest kind of ways?
Be happy, he will trouble you no more;
England shall double gild his treble guilt, 129
England shall give him office, honor, might;
For the fifth Harry from curb'd license plucks
The muzzle of restraint, and the wild dog
Shall flesh his tooth on every innocent.
O my poor kingdom, sick with civil blows!
When that my care could not withhold thy
    riots,
What wilt thou do when riot is thy care?
O, thou wilt be a wilderness again,
Peopled with wolves, thy old inhabitants!
  Prince. O, pardon me, my liege! but for
    my tears,
The moist impediments unto my speech, 140
I had forestall'd this dear and deep rebuke
Ere you with grief had spoke and I had heard
The course of it so far. There is your crown;
And He that wears the crown immortally
Long guard it yours! If I affect it more
Than as your honor and as your renown,
Let me no more from this obedience rise,
Which my most inward true and duteous spirit
Teacheth, this prostrate and exterior bending.
God witness with me, when I here came in,
And found no course of breath within your
    majesty,   151
How cold it struck my heart! If I do feign,
O, let me in my present wildness die
And never live to show the incredulous world
The noble change that I have purposed!
Coming to look on you, thinking you dead,
And dead almost, my liege, to think you were,
I spake unto this crown as having sense,
And thus upbraided it: ' The care on thee de-
    pending
Hath fed upon the body of my father;   160
Therefore, thou best of gold art worst of gold:
Other, less fine in carat, is more precious,
Preserving life in medicine potable;
But thou, most fine, most honor'd, most re-
    nown'd,
Hast eat thy bearer up.' Thus, my most royal
    liege,
Accusing it, I put it on my head,
To try with it, as with an enemy
That had before my face murder'd my father,
The quarrel of a true inheritor.
But if it did infect my blood with joy,   170
Or swell my thoughts to any strain of pride;
If any rebel or vain spirit of mine
Did with the least affection of a welcome
Give entertainment to the might of it,
Let God for ever keep it from my head
And make me as the poorest vassal is
That doth with awe and terror kneel to it!
  King. O my son,
God put it in thy mind to take it hence,
That thou mightst win the more thy father's
    love,   180
Pleading so wisely in excuse of it!
Come hither, Harry, sit thou by my bed;
And hear, I think, the very latest counsel
That ever I shall breathe. God knows, my son,
By what by-paths and indirect crook'd ways

I met this crown; and I myself know well
How troublesome it sat upon my head.
To thee it shall descend with better quiet,
Better opinion, better confirmation;
For all the soil of the achievement goes   190
With me into the earth. It seem'd in me
But as an honor snatch'd with boisterous
    hand,
And I had many living to upbraid
My gain of it by their assistances;
Which daily grew to quarrel and to bloodshed,
Wounding supposed peace: all these bold
    fears
Thou see'st with peril I have answered;
For all my reign hath been but as a scene
Acting that argument: and now my death
Changes the mode; for what in me was pur-
    chased,   200
Falls upon thee in a more fairer sort;
So thou the garland wear'st successively.
Yet, though thou stand'st more sure than I
    could do,
Thou art not firm enough, since griefs are
    green;
And all my friends, which thou must make
    thy friends,
Have but their stings and teeth newly ta'en
    out;
By whose fell working I was first advanced
And by whose power I well might lodge a fear
To be again displaced: which to avoid,
I cut them off; and had a purpose now   210
To lead out many to the Holy Land,
Lest rest and lying still might make them look
Too near unto my state. Therefore, my Harry,
Be it thy course to busy giddy minds
With foreign quarrels; that action, hence
    borne out,
May waste the memory of the former days.
More would I, but my lungs are wasted so
That strength of speech is utterly denied me.
How I came by the crown, O God forgive;
And grant it may with thee in true peace live!
  Prince. My gracious liege,   221
You won it, wore it, kept it, gave it me;
Then plain and right must my possession be:
Which I with more than with a common pain
'Gainst all the world will rightfully maintain.

      Enter LORD JOHN OF LANCASTER.

  King. Look, look, here comes my John of
    Lancaster.
  Lan. Health, peace, and happiness to my
    royal father!
  King. Thou bring'st me happiness and
    peace, son John;
But health, alack, with youthful wings is flown
From this bare wither'd trunk: upon thy sight
My worldly business makes a period.   231
Where is my Lord of Warwick?
  Prince.   My Lord of Warwick!

      Enter WARWICK, *and others.*

  King. Doth any name particular belong
Unto the lodging where I first did swoon?
  War. 'Tis call'd Jerusalem, my noble lord.
  King. Laud be to God! even there my life
    must end.
It hath been prophesied to me many years,
I should not die but in Jerusalem;
Which vainly I supposed the Holy Land: 239
But bear me to that chamber; there I'll lie;
In that Jerusalem shall Harry die.   [*Exeunt*

ACT V.

Scene I. *Gloucestershire.* Shallow's *house.*

Enter Shallow, Falstaff, Bardolph, *and*
Page.

Shal. By cock and pie, sir, you shall not
away to-night. What, Davy, I say!

Fal. You must excuse me, Master Robert
Shallow.

Shal. I will not excuse you; you shall not
be excused; excuses shall not be admitted;
there is no excuse shall serve; you shall not
be excused. Why, Davy!

Enter Davy.

Davy. Here, sir.   9

Shal. Davy, Davy, Davy, Davy, let me see,
Davy; let me see, Davy; let me see: yea,
marry, William cook, bid him come hither.
Sir John, you shall not be excused.

Davy. Marry, sir, thus; those precepts cannot be served: and, again, sir, shall we sow
the headland with wheat?

Shal. With red wheat, Davy. But for William cook: are there no young pigeons?

Davy. Yes, sir. Here is now the smith's
note for shoeing and plough-irons.   20

Shal. Let it be cast and paid. Sir John,
you shall not be excused.

Davy. Now, sir, a new link to the bucket
must need be had: and, sir, do you mean to
stop any of William's wages, about the sack he
lost the other day at Hinckley fair?

Shal. A' shall answer it. Some pigeons,
Davy, a couple of short-legged hens, a joint of
mutton, and any pretty little tiny kickshaws,
tell William cook.   30

Davy. Doth the man of war stay all night,
sir?

Shal. Yea, Davy. I will use him well: a
friend i' the court is better than a penny in
purse. Use his men well, Davy; for they are
arrant knaves, and will backbite.

Davy. No worse than they are backbitten,
sir; for they have marvellous foul linen.

Shal. Well conceited, Davy: about thy
business, Davy.   40

Davy. I beseech you, sir, to countenance
William Visor of Woncot against Clement
Perkes of the hill.

Shal. There is many complaints, Davy,
against that Visor: that Visor is an arrant
knave, on my knowledge.

Davy. I grant your worship that he is a
knave, sir; but yet, God forbid, sir, but a
knave should have some countenance at his
friend's request. An honest man, sir, is able to
speak for himself, when a knave is not. I have
served your worship truly, sir, this eight years;
and if I cannot once or twice in a quarter
bear out a knave against an honest man, I
have but a very little credit with your worship.
The knave is mine honest friend, sir; therefore, I beseech your worship, let him be
countenanced.

Shal. Go to; I say he shall have no wrong.
Look about, Davy. [*Exit Davy.*] Where are
you, Sir John? Come, come, come, off with
your boots. Give me your hand, Master Bardolph.

Bard. I am glad to see your worship.

Shal. I thank thee with all my heart, kind
Master Bardolph: and welcome, my tall fellow
[*to the Page*]. Come, Sir John.

Fal. I'll follow you, good Master Robert
Shallow. [*Exit Shallow.*] Bardolph, look to
our horses. [*Exeunt Bardolph and Page.*] If
I were sawed into quantities, I should make
four dozen of such bearded hermits' staves as
Master Shallow. It is a wonderful thing to see
the semblable coherence of his men's spirits
and his: they, by observing of him, do bear
themselves like foolish justices; he, by conversing with them, is turned into a justice-
like serving-man: their spirits are so married
in conjunction with the participation of society
that they flock together in consent, like so
many wild-geese. If I had a suit to Master
Shallow, I would humor his men with the
imputation of being near their master: if to
his men, I would curry with Master Shallow
that no man could better command his servants. It is certain that either wise bearing or
ignorant carriage is caught, as men take diseases, one of another: therefore let men take
heed of their company. I will devise matter
enough out of this Shallow to keep Prince
Harry in continual laughter the wearing out
of six fashions, which is four terms, or two
actions, and a' shall laugh without interval-
lums. O, it is much that a lie with a slight oath
and a jest with a sad brow will do with a fellow
that never had the ache in his shoulders! O,
you shall see him laugh till his face be like a
wet cloak ill laid up!

Shal. [*Within*] Sir John!

Fal. I come, Master Shallow; I come,
Master Shallow.   [*Exit.*

Scene II. *Westminster. The palace.*

Enter Warwick *and the* Lord Chief-Justice,
meeting.

War. How now, my lord chief-justice!
whither away?

Ch. Just. How doth the king?

War. Exceeding well; his cares are now
all ended.

Ch. Just. I hope, not dead.

War. He's walk'd the way of nature;
And to our purposes he lives no more.

Ch. Just. I would his majesty had call'd
me with him:
The service that I truly did his life
Hath left me open to all injuries.

War. Indeed I think the young king loves
you not.

Ch. Just. I know he doth not, and do arm
myself   10
To welcome the condition of the time,
Which cannot look more hideously upon me
Than I have drawn it in my fantasy.

Enter Lancaster, Clarence, Gloucester,
Westmoreland, *and others.*

War. Here come the heavy issue of dead
Harry:
O that the living Harry had the temper
Of him, the worst of these three gentlemen!
How many nobles then should hold their
places
That must strike sail to spirits of vile sort!

Ch. Just. O God, I fear all will be over-
turn'd!

Lan. Good morrow, cousin Warwick, good
   morrow.   20
Glou. }
Clar. } Good morrow, cousin.
Lan. We meet like men that had forgot to
   speak.
War. We do remember ; but our argument
Is all too heavy to admit much talk.
  Lan. Well, peace be with him that hath
   made us heavy !
  Ch. Just. Peace be with us, lest we be
   heavier !
  Glou. O, good my lord, you have lost a
   friend indeed ;
And I dare swear you borrow not that face
Of seeming sorrow, it is sure your own.
  Lan. Though no man be assured what
   grace to find,   30
You stand in coldest expectation :
I am the sorrier ; would 'twere otherwise.
  Clar. Well, you must now speak Sir John
   Falstaff fair ;
Which swims against your stream of quality.
  Ch. Just. Sweet princes, what I did, I did
   in honor,
Led by the impartial conduct of my soul :
And never shall you see that I will beg
A ragged and forestall'd remission.
If truth and upright innocency fail me,
I'll to the king my master that is dead,   40
And tell him who hath sent me after him.
  War. Here comes the prince.

    Enter KING HENRY *the Fifth, attended.*

  Ch. Just. Good morrow ; and God save
   your majesty !
  King. This new and gorgeous garment,
   majesty,
Sits not so easy on me as you think.
Brothers, you mix your sadness with some
   fear :
This is the English, not the Turkish court ;
Not Amurath an Amurath succeeds,
But Harry Harry. Yet be sad, good brothers,
For, by my faith, it very well becomes you :
Sorrow so royally in you appears   51
That I will deeply put the fashion on
And wear it in my heart : why then, be sad ;
But entertain no more of it, good brothers,
Than a joint burden laid upon us all.
For me, by heaven, I bid you be assured,
I'll be your father and your brother too ;
Let me but bear your love, I'll bear your
   cares :
Yet weep that Harry's dead ; and so will I ;
But Harry lives, that shall convert those tears
By number into hours of happiness.   61
  Princes. We hope no other from your
   majesty.
  King. You all look strangely on me : and
   you most ;
You are, I think, assured I love you not.
  Ch. Just. I am assured, if I be measured
   rightly,
Your majesty hath no just cause to hate me.
  King. No !
How might a prince of my great hopes forget
So great indignities you laid upon me ?
What ! rate, rebuke, and roughly send to
   prison
The immediate heir of England ! Was this
   easy ?
May this be wash'd in Lethe, and forgotten ?

  Ch. Just. I then did use the person of your
   father ;
The image of his power lay then in me :
And, in the administration of his law,
Whiles I was busy for the commonwealth,
Your highness pleased to forget my place,
The majesty and power of law and justice,
The image of the king whom I presented,
And struck me in my very seat of judgment ;
Whereon, as an offender to your father,   81
I gave bold way to my authority
And did commit you. If the deed were ill,
Be you contented, wearing now the garland,
To have a son set your decrees at nought,
To pluck down justice from your awful bench,
To trip the course of law and blunt the sword
That guards the peace and safety of your per-
   son ;
Nay, more, to spurn at your most royal image
And mock your workings in a second body.
Question your royal thoughts, make the case
   yours ;   91
Be now the father and propose a son,
Hear your own dignity so much profaned,
See your most dreadful laws so loosely
   slighted,
Behold yourself so by a son disdain'd ;
And then imagine me taking your part
And in your power soft silencing your son :
After this cold considerance, sentence me ;
And, as you are a king, speak in your state
What I have done that misbecame my place,
My person, or my liege's sovereignty.   101
  King. You are right, justice, and you
   weigh this well ;
Therefore still bear the balance and the
   sword :
And I do wish your honors may increase,
Till you do live to see a son of mine
Offend you and obey you, as I did.
So shall I live to speak my father's words :
' Happy am I, that have a man so bold,
That dares do justice on my proper son ;
And not less happy, having such a son,   110
That would deliver up his greatness so
Into the hands of justice.' You did commit
   me :
For which, I do commit into your hand
The unstained sword that you have used to
   bear ;
With this remembrance, that you use the
   same
With the like bold, just and impartial spirit
As you have done 'gainst me. There is my
   hand.
You shall be as a father to my youth :
My voice shall sound as you do prompt mine
   ear,
And I will stoop and humble my intents   120
To your well-practised wise directions.
And, princes all, believe me, I beseech you ;
My father is gone wild into his grave,
For in his tomb lie my affections ;
And with his spirit sadly I survive,
To mock the expectation of the world,
To frustrate prophecies and to raze out
Rotten opinion, who hath writ me down
After my seeming. The tide of blood in me
Hath proudly flow'd in vanity till now :   130
Now doth it turn and ebb back to the sea
Where it shall mingle with the state of flood
And flow henceforth in formal majesty.
Now call we our high court of parliament :

And let us choose such limbs of noble coun-
sel,
That the great body of our state may go
In equal rank with the best govern'd nation ;
That war, or peace, or both at once, may be
As things acquainted and familiar to us ;
In which you, father, shall have foremost
hand.   140
Our coronation done, we will accite,
As I before remember'd, all our state :
And, God consigning to my good intents,
No prince nor peer shall have just cause to
say,
God shorten Harry's happy life one day !
    [*Exeunt.*

SCENE III. *Gloucestershire.* SHALLOW'S
orchard.

Enter FALSTAFF, SHALLOW, SILENCE, DAVY,
BARDOLPH, *and the* Page.

Shal. Nay, you shall see my orchard,
where, in an arbor, we will eat a last year's
pippin of my own graffing, with a dish of
caraways, and so forth : come, cousin Silence :
and then to bed.
Fal. 'Fore God, you have here a goodly
dwelling and a rich.
Shal. Barren, barren, barren ; beggars all,
beggars all, Sir John : marry, good air.
Spread, Davy ; spread, Davy ; well said,
Davy.   10
Fal. This Davy serves you for good uses;
he is your serving-man and your husband.
Shal. A good varlet, a good varlet, a very
good varlet, Sir John : by the mass, I have
drunk too much sack at supper : a good var-
let. Now sit down, now sit down : come,
cousin.
Sil. Ah, sirrah ! quoth-a, we shall
    Do nothing but eat, and make good cheer,
        [*Singing.*
    And praise God for the merry year ;
    When flesh is cheap and females dear, 20
    And lusty lads roam here and there
        So merrily,
    And ever among so merrily.
Fal. There's a merry heart ! Good Master
Silence, I'll give you a health for that anon.
Shal. Give Master Bardolph some wine,
Davy.
Davy. Sweet sir, sit ; I'll be with you anon ;
most sweet sir, sit. Master page, good master
page, sit. Proface ! What you want in meat,
we'll have in drink : but you must bear ; the
heart's all.   [*Exit.*
Shal. Be merry, Master Bardolph ; and,
my little soldier there, be merry.
Sil. Be merry, be merry, my wife has all ;
        [*Singing.*
    For women are shrews, both short and
      tall :
    'Tis merry in hall when beards wag all,
      And welcome merry Shrove-tide.
    Be merry, be merry.
Fal. I did not think Master Silence had
been a man of this mettle.   41
Sil. Who, I ? I have been merry twice and
once ere now.

Re-enter DAVY.

Davy. There's a dish of leather-coats for
you.   [*To Bardolph.*
Shal. Davy !

Davy. Your worship ! I'll be with you
straight [*to Bardolph*]. A cup of wine, sir ?
Sil. A cup of wine that's brisk and fine,
        [*Singing.*
    And drink unto the leman mine ;
      And a merry heart lives long-a. 50
Fal. Well said, Master Silence.
Sil. An we shall be merry, now comes in
the sweet o' the night.
Fal. Health and long life to you, Master
Silence.
Sil. Fill the cup, and let it come ; [*Singing.*
    I'll pledge you a mile to the bottom.
Shal. Honest Bardolph, welcome : if thou
wantest any thing, and wilt not call, beshrew
thy heart. Welcome, my little tiny thief [*to
the Page*], and welcome indeed too. I'll drink
to Master Bardolph, and to all the cavaleros
about London.
Davy. I hope to see London once ere I die.
Bard. An I might see you there, Davy,—
Shal. By the mass, you'll crack a quart to-
gether, ha ! will you not, Master Bardolph ?
Bard. Yea, sir, in a pottle-pot.
Shal. By God's liggens, I thank thee : the
knave will stick by thee, I can assure thee
that. A' will not out ; he is true bred.   71
Bard. And I'll stick by him, sir.
Shal. Why, there spoke a king. Lack noth-
ing : be merry. [*Knocking within.*] Look
who's at door there, ho ! who knocks ?
        [*Exit Davy.*
Fal. Why, now you have done me right.
[*To Silence, seeing him take off a bumper.*
Sil.   Do me right,   [*Singing.*
    And dub me knight :
      Samingo.
Is't not so ?   80
Fal. 'Tis so.
Sil. Is't so ? Why then, say an old man
can do somewhat.

Re-enter DAVY.

Davy. An't please your worship, there's
one Pistol come from the court with news.
Fal. From the court ! let him come in.

Enter PISTOL.

How now, Pistol !
Pist. Sir John, God save you !
Fal. What wind blew you hither, Pistol ?
Pist. Not the ill wind which blows no man
to good. Sweet knight, thou art now one of
the greatest men in this realm.
Sil. By'r lady, I think a' be, but goodman
Puff of Barson.
Pist. Puff !
Puff in thy teeth, most recreant coward base !
Sir John, I am thy Pistol and thy friend,
And helter-skelter have I rode to thee,
And tidings do I bring and lucky joys
And golden times and happy news of price.
Fal. I pray thee now, deliver them like a
man of this world.   101
Pist. A foutre for the world and worldlings
    base !
I speak of Africa and golden joys.
Fal. O base Assyrian knight, what is thy
    news ?
Let King Cophetua know the truth thereof.
Sil. And Robin Hood, Scarlet, and John.
        [*Singing.*

Pist. Shall dunghill curs confront the Helicons?
And shall good news be baffled?
Then, Pistol, lay thy head in Furies' lap. 110
Sil. Honest gentleman, I know not your breeding.
Pist. Why then, lament therefore.
Shal. Give me pardon, sir : if, sir, you come with news from the court, I take it there's but two ways, either to utter them, or to conceal them. I am, sir, under the king, in some authority.
Pist. Under which king, Besonian? speak, or die.
Shal. Under King Harry.
Pist.   Harry the Fourth? or Fifth?
Shal. Harry the Fourth.
Pist.   A foutre for thine office! 120
Sir John, thy tender lambkin now is king;
Harry the Fifth's the man. I speak the truth :
When Pistol lies, do this; and fig me, like
The bragging Spaniard.
Fal. What, is the old king dead?
Pist. As nail in door : the things I speak are just.
Fal. Away, Bardolph! saddle my horse.
Master Robert Shallow, choose what office thou wilt in the land, 'tis thine. Pistol, I will double-charge thee with dignities.   130
Bard. O joyful day!
I would not take a knighthood for my fortune.
Pist. What! I do bring good news.
Fal. Carry Master Silence to bed. Master Shallow, my Lord Shallow,—be what thou wilt; I am fortune's steward—get on thy boots : we'll ride all night. O sweet Pistol! Away, Bardolph! [*Exit Bard.*] Come, Pistol, utter more to me; and withal devise something to do thyself good. Boot, boot, Master Shallow : I know the young king is sick for me. Let us take any man's horses; the laws of England are at my commandment. Blessed are they that have been my friends; and woe to my lord chief-justice!
Pist. Let vultures vile seize on his lungs also!
' Where is the life that late I led?' say they :
Why, here it is; welcome these pleasant days!   [*Exeunt.*

SCENE IV. *London. A street.*

Enter Beadles, *dragging in* HOSTESS QUICKLY *and* DOLL TEARSHEET.

Host. No, thou arrant knave; I would to God that I might die, that I might have thee hanged : thou hast drawn my shoulder out of joint.
First Bead. The constables have delivered her over to me; and she shall have whipping-cheer enough, I warrant her : there hath been a man or two lately killed about her.
Dol. Nut-hook, nut-hook, you lie. Come on; I'll tell thee what, thou damned tripe-visaged rascal, an the child I now go with do miscarry, thou wert better thou hadst struck thy mother, thou paper-faced villain.
Host. O the Lord, that Sir John were come! he would make this a bloody day to somebody. But I pray God the fruit of her womb miscarry!
First Bead. If it do, you shall have a dozen of cushions again; you have but eleven now.

Come, I charge you both go with me; for the man is dead that you and Pistol beat amongst you.
Dol. I'll tell you what, you thin man in a censer, I will have you as soundly swinged for this,—you blue-bottle rogue, you filthy famished correctioner, if you be not swinged, I'll forswear half-kirtles.
First Bead. Come, come, you she knight-errant, come.
Host. O God, that right should thus overcome might! Well, of sufferance comes ease.
Dol. Come, you rogue, come; bring me to a justice.   30
Host. Ay, come, you starved blood-hound.
Dol. Goodman death, goodman bones!
Host. Thou atomy, thou!
Dol. Come, you thin thing; come you rascal.
First Bead. Very well.   [*Exeunt.*

SCENE V. *A public place near Westminster Abbey.*

Enter two Grooms, *strewing rushes.*

First Groom. More rushes, more rushes.
Sec. Groom. The trumpets have sounded twice.
First Groom. 'Twill be two o'clock ere they come from the coronation : dispatch, dispatch.
          [*Exeunt.*

Enter FALSTAFF, SHALLOW, PISTOL, BARDOLPH, *and* Page.

Fal. Stand here by me, Master Robert Shallow; I will make the king do you grace : I will leer upon him as a' comes by; and do but mark the countenance that he will give me.
Pist. God bless thy lungs, good knight. 9
Fal. Come here, Pistol; stand behind me. O, if I had had time to have made new liveries, I would have bestowed the thousand pound I borrowed of you. But 'tis no matter; this poor show doth better : this doth infer the zeal I had to see him.
Shal. It doth so.
Fal. It shows my earnestness of affection,—
Shal. It doth so.
Fal. My devotion,—
Shal. It doth, it doth, it doth.   20
Fal. As it were, to ride day and night; and not to deliberate, not to remember, not to have patience to shift me,—
Shal. It is best, certain.
Fal. But to stand stained with travel, and sweating with desire to see him; thinking of nothing else, putting all affairs else in oblivion, as if there were nothing else to be done but to see him.   29
Pist. 'Tis ' semper idem,' for ' obsque hoc nihil est : ' 'tis all in every part.
Shal. 'Tis so, indeed.
Pist. My knight, I will inflame thy noble liver,
And make thee rage.
Thy Doll, and Helen of thy noble thoughts,
Is in base durance and contagious prison
Haled thither
By most mechanical and dirty hand :
Rouse up revenge from ebon den with fell
          Alecto's snake,   3
For Doll is in. Pistol speaks nought but truth

Fal. I will deliver her.
[*Shouts within, and the trumpets sound.*
Pist. There roar'd the sea, and trumpet-clangor sounds.

Enter the King *and his train, the* Lord Chief-Justice *among them.*

Fal. God save thy grace, King Hal! my royal Hal!
Pist. The heavens thee guard and keep, most royal imp of fame!
Fal. God save thee, my sweet boy!
King. My lord chief-justice, speak to that vain man.
Ch. Just. Have you your wits? know you what 'tis to speak?
Fal. My king! my Jove! I speak to thee, my heart!   50
King. I know thee not, old man: fall to thy prayers;
How ill white hairs become a fool and jester!
I have long dream'd of such a kind of man,
So surfeit-swell'd, so old and so profane;
But, being awaked, I do despise my dream.
Make less thy body hence, and more thy grace;
Leave gormandizing; know the grave doth gape
For thee thrice wider than for other men.
Reply not to me with a fool-born jest:
Presume not that I am the thing I was;   60
For God doth know, so shall the world perceive,
That I have turn'd away my former self;
So will I those that kept me company.
When thou dost hear I am as I have been,
Approach me, and thou shalt be as thou wast,
The tutor and the feeder of my riots:
Till then, I banish thee, on pain of death,
As I have done the rest of my misleaders,
Not to come near our person by ten mile.
For competence of life I will allow you,   70
That lack of means enforce you not to evil:
And, as we hear you do reform yourselves,
We will, according to your strengths and qualities,
Give you advancement. Be it your charge, my lord,
To see perform'd the tenor of our word.
Set on.   [*Exeunt King, &c.*
Fal. Master Shallow, I owe you a thousand pound.
Shal. Yea, marry, Sir John; which I beseech you to let me have home with me.   80
Fal. That can hardly be, Master Shallow.
Do not you grieve at this; I shall be sent for in private to him: look you, he must seem thus to the world: fear not your advancements; I will be the man yet that shall make you great.
Shal. I cannot well perceive how, unless you should give me your doublet and stuff me out with straw. I beseech you, good Sir John, let me have five hundred of my thousand.
Fal. Sir, I will be as good as my word: this that you heard was but a color.   91
Shal. A color that I fear you will die in, Sir John.
Fal. Fear no colors: go with me to dinner: come, Lieutenant Pistol; come, Bardolph: I shall be sent for soon at night.

Re-enter Prince John, *the* Lord Chief-Justice; Officers *with them.*

Ch. Just. Go, carry Sir John Falstaff to the Fleet:
Take all his company along with him.
Fal. My lord, my lord,—
Ch. Just. I cannot now speak: I will hear you soon.   100
Take them away.
Pist. Si fortuna me tormenta, spero contenta.
[*Exeunt all but Prince John and the Chief-Justice.*
Lan. I like this fair proceeding of the king's:
He hath intent his wonted followers
Shall all be very well provided for;
But all are banish'd till their conversations
Appear more wise and modest to the world.
Ch. Just. And so they are.
Lan. The king hath call'd his parliament, my lord.
Ch. Just. He hath.   110
Lan. I will lay odds that, ere this year expire,
We bear our civil swords and native fire
As far as France: I heard a bird so sing,
Whose music, to my thinking, pleased the king.
Come, will you hence?   [*Exeunt.*

EPILOGUE.

Spoken by a Dancer.

First my fear; then my courtesy; last my speech. My fear is, your displeasure; my courtesy, my duty; and my speech, to beg your pardons. If you look for a good speech now, you undo me: for what I have to say is of mine own making; and what indeed I should say will, I doubt, prove mine own marring. But to the purpose, and so to the venture. Be it known to you, as it is very well, I was lately here in the end of a displeasing play, to pray your patience for it and to promise you a better. I meant indeed to pay you with this; which, if like an ill venture it come unluckily home, I break, and you, my gentle creditors, lose. Here I promised you I would be and here I commit my body to your mercies: bate me some and I will pay you some and, as most debtors do, promise you infinitely.

If my tongue cannot entreat you to acquit me, will you command me to use my legs? and yet that were but light payment, to dance out of your debt. But a good conscience will make any possible satisfaction, and so would I. All the gentlewomen here have forgiven me: if the gentlemen will not, then the gentlemen do not agree with the gentlewomen, which was never seen before in such an assembly.

One word more, I beseech you. If you be not too much cloyed with fat meat, our humble author will continue the story, with Sir John in it, and make you merry with fair Katharine of France: where, for any thing I know, Falstaff shall die of a sweat, unless already a' be killed with your hard opinions; for Oldcastle died a martyr, and this is not the man. My tongue is weary; when my legs are too, I will bid you good night: and so kneel down before you; but, indeed, to pray for the queen.

KING HENRY V.

(WRITTEN ABOUT 1599.)

INTRODUCTION.

This play is not mentioned by Meres, and the reference in the chorus of Act V. to Essex in Ireland, and in the Prologue to "this wooden O," *i.e.* the Globe Theatre, built in 1599, make it probable that 1599 was the date of its production. A pirated imperfect quarto appeared in the following year. In this play Shakespeare bade farewell in trumpet tones to the history of England. It was a fitting climax to the great series of works which told of the sorrow and the glory of his country, embodying as it did the purest patriotism of the days of Elizabeth. And as the noblest glories of England are presented in this play, so it presents Shakespeare's ideal of active, practical, heroic manhood. If Hamlet exhibits the dangers and weakness of the contemplative nature, and Prospero, its calm and its conquest, Henry exhibits the utmost greatness which the active nature can attain. He is not an astute politician like his father; having put every thing upon a sound substantial basis he need not strain anxious eyes of foresight to discern and provide for contingencies arising out of doubtful deeds; for all that naturally comes within its range he has an unerring eye. A devotion to great objects outside of self fills him with a force of glorious enthusiasm. Hence his religious spirit and his humility or modesty—he feels that the strength he wields comes not from any clever disposition of forces due to his own prudence, but streams into him and through him from his people, his country, his cause, his God. He can be terrible to traitors, and his sternness is without a touch of personal revenge. In the midst of danger he can feel so free from petty heart-eating cares as to enjoy a piece of honest, soldierly mirth. His wooing is as plain, frank, and true as are his acts of piety. He unites around himself in loyal service, the jarring nationalities of his father's time—Englishmen, Scotchmen, Welshmen, Irishmen, all are at Henry's side at Agincourt. Having presented his ideal of English kinghood, Shakespeare could turn aside from history. In this play no character except Henry greatly interested Shakespeare, unless it be the Welsh Fluellen, whom he loves (as Scott loved the Baron of Bradwardine) for his real simplicity underlying his apparatus of learning, and his touching faith in the theory of warfare.

DRAMATIS PERSONÆ.

KING HENRY the Fifth.
DUKE OF GLOUCESTER, } brothers to the
DUKE OF BEDFORD, } King.
DUKE OF EXETER, uncle to the King.
DUKE OF YORK, cousin to the King.
EARLS OF SALISBURY, WESTMORELAND, and WARWICK.
ARCHBISHOP OF CANTERBURY.
BISHOP OF ELY.
EARL OF CAMBRIDGE.
LORD SCROOP.
SIR THOMAS GREY.
SIR THOMAS ERPINGHAM, GOWER, FLUELLEN, MACMORRIS, JAMY, officers in King Henry's army.
BATES, COURT, WILLIAMS, soldiers in the same.
PISTOL, NYM, BARDOLPH.
Boy.
A Herald.

CHARLES the Sixth, King of France.
LEWIS, the Dauphin.
DUKES OF BURGUNDY, ORLEANS, and BOURBON.
The Constable of France.
RAMBURES and GRANDPRE, French Lords.
Governor of Harfleur.
MONTJOY, a French Herald.
Ambassadors to the King of England.

ISABEL, Queen of France.
KATHARINE, daughter to Charles and Isabel.
ALICE, a lady attending on her.
Hostess of a tavern in Eastcheap, formerly Mistress Quickly, and now married to Pistol.

Lords, Ladies, Officers, Soldiers, Citizens, Messengers, and Attendants.
Chorus.

SCENE : *England ; afterwards France.*

PROLOGUE.

Enter Chorus.

Chor. O for a Muse of fire, that would as-
    cend
The brightest heaven of invention,
A kingdom for a stage, princes to act
And monarchs to behold the swelling scene!
Then should the warlike Harry, like himself,
Assume the port of Mars; and at his heels,
Leash'd in like hounds, should famine, sword
    and fire
Crouch for employment. But pardon, gentles
    all,
The flat unraised spirits that have dared
On this unworthy scaffold to bring forth   10
So great an object: can this cockpit hold
The vasty fields of France? or may we cram
Within this wooden O the very casques
That did affright the air at Agincourt?
O, pardon! since a crooked figure may
Attest in little place a million;
And let us, ciphers to this great accompt,
On your imaginary forces work.
Suppose within the girdle of these walls
Are now confined two mighty monarchies,   20
Whose high upreared and abutting fronts
The perilous narrow ocean parts asunder:
Piece out our imperfections with your
    thoughts;
Into a thousand parts divide one man,
And make imaginary puissance;
Think when we talk of horses, that you see
    them
Printing their proud hoofs i' the receiving
    earth;
For 'tis your thoughts that now must deck our
    kings,
Carry them here and there; jumping o'er
    times,
Turning the accomplishment of many years 30
Into an hour-glass: for the which supply,
Admit me Chorus to this history;
Who prologue-like your humble patience pray,
Gently to hear, kindly to judge, our play.
                                      [*Exit.*

ACT I.

SCENE I. *London. An ante-chamber in the*
    KING'S *palace.*

Enter the ARCHBISHOP OF CANTERBURY, *and*
    the BISHOP OF ELY.

Cant. My lord, I'll tell you; that self bill
    is urged,
Which in the eleventh year of the last king's
    reign
Was like, and had indeed against us pass'd,
But that the scambling and unquiet time
Did push it out of farther question.
Ely. But how, my lord, shall we resist it
    now?
Cant. It must be thought on. If it pass
    against us,
We lose the better half of our possession:
For all the temporal lands which men devout
By testament have given to the church   10
Would they strip from us; being valued thus:
As much as would maintain, to the king's
    honor,

Full fifteen earls and fifteen hundred knights,
Six thousand and two hundred good esquires;
And, to relief of lazars and weak age,
Of indigent faint souls past corporal toil,
A hundred almshouses right well supplied;
And to the coffers of the king beside,
A thousand pounds by the year: thus runs
    the bill.
Ely. This would drink deep.
Cant.   'Twould drink the cup and all. 20
Ely. But what prevention?
Cant. The king is full of grace and fair re-
    gard.
Ely. And a true lover of the holy church.
Cant. The courses of his youth promised it
    not.
The breath no sooner left his father's body,
But that his wildness, mortified in him,
Seem'd to die too; yea, at that very moment
Consideration, like an angel, came
And whipp'd the offending Adam out of him,
Leaving his body as a paradise,   30
To envelop and contain celestial spirits.
Never was such a sudden scholar made;
Never came reformation in a flood,
With such a heady currance, scouring faults
Nor never Hydra-headed wilfulness
So soon did lose his seat and all at once
As in this king.
Ely.   We are blessed in the change.
Cant. Hear him but reason in divinity,
And all-admiring with an inward wish
You would desire the king were made a
    prelate: 40
Hear him debate of commonwealth affairs,
You would say it hath been all in all his
    study:
List his discourse of war, and you shall hear
A fearful battle render'd you in music:
Turn him to any cause of policy,
The Gordian knot of it he will unloose,
Familiar as his garter: that, when he speaks,
The air, a charter'd libertine, is still,
And the mute wonder lurketh in men's ears,
To steal his sweet and honey'd sentences;   50
So that the art and practic part of life
Must be the mistress to this theoric:
Which is a wonder how his grace should
    glean it,
Since his addiction was to courses vain,
His companies unletter'd, rude and shallow,
His hours fill'd up with riots, banquets, sports,
And never noted in him any study,
Any retirement, any sequestration
From open haunts and popularity.
Ely. The strawberry grows underneath the
    nettle   60
And wholesome berries thrive and ripen best
Neighbor'd by fruit of baser quality:
And so the prince obscured his contemplation
Under the veil of wildness; which, no doubt,
Grew like the summer grass, fastest by night,
Unseen, yet crescive in his faculty.
Cant. It must be so; for miracles are
    ceased;
And therefore we must needs admit the means
How things are perfected.
Ely.   But, my good lord,
How now for mitigation of this bill   70
Urged by the commons? Doth his majesty
Incline to it, or no?
Cant.   He seems indifferent,

Or rather swaying more upon our part
Than cherishing the exhibiters against us ;
For I have made an offer to his majesty
Upon our spiritual convocation
And in regard of causes now in hand,
Which I have open'd to his grace at large,
As touching France, to give a greater sum
Than ever at one time the clergy yet   80
Did to his predecessors part withal.

   Ely. How did this offer seem received, my
      lord ?

   Cant. With good acceptance of his maj-
      esty ;
Save that there was not time enough to hear,
As I perceived his grace would fain have done,
The severals and unhidden passages
Of his true titles to some certain dukedoms
And generally to the crown and seat of France
Derived from Edward, his great-grandfather.

   Ely. What was the impediment that broke
      this off ?   90

   Cant. The French ambassador upon that
      instant
Craved audience ; and the hour, I think, is
      come
To give him hearing : is it four o'clock ?

   Ely. It is.

   Cant. Then go we in, to know his em-
      bassy ;
Which I could with a ready guess declare,
Before the Frenchman speak a word of it.

   Ely. I'll wait upon you, and I long to hear
      it.   [*Exeunt.*

SCENE II.   *The same. The Presence chamber.*

Enter KING HENRY, GLOUCESTER, BEDFORD,
   EXETER, WARWICK, WESTMORELAND, *and*
   Attendants.

   K. Hen. Where is my gracious Lord of
      Canterbury ?

   Exe. Not here in presence.

   K. Hen.   Send for him, good uncle.

   West. Shall we call in the ambassador, my
      liege ?

   K. Hen. Not yet, my cousin : we would be
      resolved,
Before we hear him, of some things of weight
That task our thoughts, concerning us and
      France.

Enter the ARCHBISHOP OF CANTERBURY, *and
   the* BISHOP OF ELY.

   Cant. God and his angels guard your sa-
      cred throne
And make you long become it !

   K. Hen.   Sure, we thank you.
My learned lord, we pray you to proceed
And justly and religiously unfold   10
Why the law Salique that they have in France
Or should, or should not, bar us in our claim :
And God forbid, my dear and faithful lord,
That you should fashion, wrest, or bow your
      reading,
Or nicely charge your understanding soul
With opening titles miscreate, whose right
Suits not in native colors with the truth
For God doth know how many now in health
Shall drop their blood in approbation
Of what your reverence shall incite us to.   20
Therefore take heed how you impawn our per-
      son,
How you awake our sleeping sword of war :

We charge you, in the name of God, take heed ;
For never two such kingdoms did contend
Without much fall of blood ; whose guiltless
      drops
Are every one a woe, a sore complaint
'Gainst him whose wrong gives edge unto the
      swords
That make such waste in brief mortality.
Under this conjuration, speak, my lord ;
For we will hear, note and believe in heart
That what you speak is in your conscience
      wash'd   31
As pure as sin with baptism.

   Cant. Then hear me, gracious sovereign,
      and you peers,
That owe yourselves, your lives and services
To this imperial throne. There is no bar
To make against your highness' claim to
      France
But this, which they produce from Pharamond,
' In terram Salicam mulieres ne succedant : '
' No woman shall succeed in Salique land : '
Which Salique land the French unjustly gloze
To be the realm of France, and Pharamond
The founder of this law and female bar.   42
Yet their own authors faithfully affirm
That the land Salique is in Germany,
Between the floods of Sala and of Elbe ;
Where Charles the Great, having subdued the
      Saxons,
There left behind and settled certain French ;
Who, holding in disdain the German women
For some dishonest manners of their life,
Establish'd then this law ; to wit, no female 50
Should be inheritrix in Salique land :
Which Salique, as I said, 'twixt Elbe and Sala,
Is at this day in Germany call'd Meisen.
Then doth it well appear that Salique law
Was not devised for the realm of France :
Nor did the French possess the Salique land
Until four hundred one and twenty years
After defunction of King Pharamond,
Idly supposed the founder of this law ;
Who died within the year of our redemption
Four hundred twenty-six ; and Charles the
      Great   61
Subdued the Saxons, and did seat the French
Beyond the river Sala, in the year
Eight hundred five. Besides, their writers say,
King Pepin, which deposed Childeric,
Did, as heir general, being descended
Of Blithild, which was daughter to King Clo-
      thair,
Make claim and title to the crown of France.
Hugh Capet also, who usurped the crown
Of Charles the duke of Lorraine, sole heir
      male   70
Of the true line and stock of Charles the
      Great,
To find his title with some shows of truth,
Though, in pure truth, it was corrupt and
      naught,
Convey'd himself as heir to the Lady Lingare
Daughter to Charlemain, who was the son
To Lewis the emperor, and Lewis the son
Of Charles the Great. Also King Lewis the
      Tenth,
Who was sole heir to the usurper Capet,
Could not keep quiet in his conscience,
Wearing the crown of France, till satisfied   80
That fair Queen Isabel, his grandmother,
Was lineal of the Lady Ermengare,

Daughter to Charles the foresaid duke of Lorraine :
By the which marriage the line of Charles the Great
Was re-united to the crown of France.
So that, as clear as is the summer's sun,
King Pepin's title and Hugh Capet's claim,
King Lewis his satisfaction, all appear
To hold in right and title of the female :
So do the kings of France unto this day ;   90
Howbeit they would hold up this Salique law
To bar your highness claiming from the female,
And rather choose to hide them in a net
Than amply to imbar their crooked titles
Usurp'd from you and your progenitors.
  K. Hen. May I with right and conscience make this claim ?
  Cant. The sin upon my head, dread sovereign !
For in the book of Numbers is it writ,
When the man dies, let the inheritance   99
Descend unto the daughter. Gracious lord,
Stand for your own ; unwind your bloody flag ;
Look back into your mighty ancestors :
Go, my dread lord, to your great-grandsire's tomb,
From whom you claim ; invoke his warlike spirit,
And your great-uncle's, Edward the Black Prince,
Who on the French ground play'd a tragedy,
Making defeat on the full power of France,
Whiles his most mighty father on a hill
Stood smiling to behold his lion's whelp
Forage in blood of French nobility.   110
O noble English, that could entertain
With half their forces the full pride of France
And let another half stand laughing by,
All out of work and cold for action !
  Ely. Awake remembrance of these valiant dead
And with your puissant arm renew their feats :
You are their heir ; you sit upon their throne ;
The blood and courage that renowned them
Runs in your veins ; and my thrice-puissant liege
Is in the very May-morn of his youth,   120
Ripe for exploits and mighty enterprises.
  Exe. Your brother kings and monarchs of the earth
Do all expect that you should rouse yourself,
As did the former lions of your blood.
  West. They know your grace hath cause and means and might ;
So hath your highness ; never king of England
Had nobles richer and more loyal subjects,
Whose hearts have left their bodies here in England
And lie pavilion'd in the fields of France.
  Cant. O, let their bodies follow, my dear liege,   130
With blood and sword and fire to win your right ;
In aid whereof we of the spirituality
Will raise your highness such a mighty sum
As never did the clergy at one time
Bring in to any of your ancestors.
  K. Hen. We must not only arm to invade the French,
But lay down our proportions to defend

Against the Scot, who will make road upon us
With all advantages.
  Cant. They of those marches, gracious sovereign,   140
Shall be a wall sufficient to defend
Our inland from the pilfering borderers.
  K. Hen. We do not mean the coursing snatchers only,
But fear the main intendment of the Scot,
Who hath been still a giddy neighbor to us ;
For you shall read that my great-grandfather
Never went with his forces into France
But that the Scot on his unfurnish'd kingdom
Came pouring, like the tide into a breach,
With ample and brim fulness of his force, 150
Galling the gleaned land with hot assays,
Girding with grievous siege castles and towns ;
That England, being empty of defence,
Hath shook and trembled at the ill neighborhood.
  Cant. She hath been then more fear'd than harm'd, my liege ;
For hear her but exampled by herself :
When all her chivalry hath been in France
And she a mourning widow of her nobles,
She hath herself not only well defended
But taken and impounded as a stray   160
The King of Scots ; whom she did send to France,
To fill King Edward's fame with prisoner kings
And make thy chronicle as rich with praise
As is the ooze and bottom of the sea
With sunken wreck and sunless treasuries.
  West. But there's a saying very old and true,
   ' If that you will France win,
    Then with Scotland first begin : '
For once the eagle England being in prey,
To her unguarded nest the weasel Scot   170
Comes sneaking and so sucks her princely eggs,
Playing the mouse in absence of the cat,
To tear and havoc more than she can eat.
  Exe. It follows then the cat must stay at home :
Yet that is but a crush'd necessity,
Since we have locks to safeguard necessaries,
And pretty traps to catch the petty thieves.
While that the armed hand doth fight abroad,
The advised head defends itself at home ;
For government, though high and low and lower,   180
Put into parts, doth keep in one consent,
Congreeing in a full and natural close,
Like music.
  Cant. Therefore doth heaven divide
The state of man in divers functions,
Setting endeavor in continual motion ;
To which is fixed, as an aim or butt,
Obedience : for so work the honey-bees,
Creatures that by a rule in nature teach
The act of order to a peopled kingdom.
They have a king and officers of sorts ;   190
Where some, like magistrates, correct at home,
Others, like merchants, venture trade abroad,
Others, like soldiers, armed in their stings,
Make boot upon the summer's velvet buds,
Which pillage they with merry march bring home
To the tent-royal of their emperor ;
Who, busied in his majesty, surveys
The singing masons building roofs of gold,
The civil citizens kneading up the honey,

The poor mechanic porters crowding in   200
Their heavy burdens at his narrow gate,
The sad-eyed justice, with his surly hum,
Delivering o'er to executors pale
The lazy yawning drone. I this infer,
That many things, having full reference
To one consent, may work contrariously :
As many arrows, loosed several ways,
Come to one mark ; as many ways meet in
    one town ;
As many fresh streams meet in one salt sea ;
As many lines close in the dial's centre ;   210
So may a thousand actions, once afoot,
End in one purpose, and be all well borne
Without defeat. Therefore to France, my liege.
Divide your happy England into four ;
Whereof take you one quarter into France,
And you withal shall make all Gallia shake.
If we, with thrice such powers left at home,
Cannot defend our own doors from the dog,
Let us be worried and our nation lose
The name of hardiness and policy.   220
    K. Hen. Call in the messengers sent from
        the Dauphin. [*Exeunt some Attendants.*
Now are we well resolved ; and, by God's help,
And yours, the noble sinews of our power,
France being ours, we'll bend it to our awe,
Or break it all to pieces : or there we'll sit,
Ruling in large and ample empery
O'er France and all her almost kingly duke-
    doms,
Or lay these bones in an unworthy urn,
Tombless, with no remembrance over them :   230
Either our history shall with full mouth
Speak freely of our acts, or else our grave,
Like Turkish mute, shall have a tongueless
    mouth,
Not worshipp'd with a waxen epitaph.

    Enter Ambassadors *of France.*

Now are we well prepared to know the pleas-
    ure
Of our fair cousin Dauphin ; for we hear
Your greeting is from him, not from the king.
    First Amb. May't please your majesty to
        give us leave
Freely to render what we have in charge ;
Or shall we sparingly show you far off
The Dauphin's meaning and our embassy ?
    K. Hen. We are no tyrant, but a Christian
        king ;   241
Unto whose grace our passion is as subject
As are our wretches fetter'd in our prisons :
Therefore with frank and with uncurbed plain-
    ness
Tell us the Dauphin's mind.
    First Amb.   Thus, then, in few.
Your highness, lately sending into France,
Did claim some certain dukedoms, in the right
Of your great predecessor, King Edward the
    Third.
In answer of which claim, the prince our mas-
    ter
Says that you savor too much of your youth,
And bids you be advised there's nought in
    France   251
That can be with a nimble galliard won ;
You cannot revel into dukedoms there.
He therefore sends you, meeter for your spirit,
This tun of treasure ; and, in lieu of this,
Desires you let the dukedoms that you claim
Hear no more of you. This the Dauphin
speaks.

    K. Hen. What treasure, uncle ?
    Exe.   Tennis-balls, my liege.
    K. Hen. We are glad the Dauphin is so
        pleasant with us ;
His present and your pains we thank you for :
When we have march'd our rackets to these
    balls,   261
We will, in France, by God's grace, play a set
Shall strike his father's crown into the hazard.
Tell him he hath made a match with such a
    wrangler
That all the courts of France will be disturb'd
With chaces. And we understand him well,
How he comes o'er us with our wilder days,
Not measuring what use we made of them.
We never valued this poor seat of England ;
And therefore, living hence, did give ourself
To barbarous license ; as 'tis ever common
That men are merriest when they are from
    home.
But tell the Dauphin I will keep my state,
Be like a king and show my sail of greatness
When I do rouse me in my throne of France :
For that I have laid by my majesty
And plodded like a man for working-days,
But I will rise there with so full a glory
That I will dazzle all the eyes of France,   279
Yea, strike the Dauphin blind to look on us.
And tell the pleasant prince this mock of his
Hath turn'd his balls to gun-stones ; and his
    soul
Shall stand sore charged for the wasteful
    vengeance
That shall fly with them : for many a thousand
    widows
Shall this his mock mock out of their dear
    husbands ;
Mock mothers from their sons, mock castles
    down ;
And some are yet ungotten and unborn
That shall have cause to curse the Dauphin's
    scorn.
But this lies all within the will of God,
To whom I do appeal ; and in whose name
Tell you the Dauphin I am coming on,
To venge me as I may and to put forth
My rightful hand in a well-hallow'd cause.
So get you hence in peace ; and tell the
    Dauphin
His jest will savor but of shallow wit,
When thousands weep more than did laugh at
    it.
Convey them with safe conduct. Fare you well.
                    [*Exeunt Ambassadors.*
    Exe. This was a merry message.
    K. Hen. We hope to make the sender blush
        at it.
Therefore, my lords, omit no happy hour   300
That may give furtherance to our expedition ;
For we have now no thought in us but France,
Save those to God, that run before our busi-
    ness.
Therefore let our proportions for these wars
Be soon collected and all things thought upon
That may with reasonable swiftness add
More feathers to our wings ; for, God before,
We'll chide this Dauphin at his father's door.
Therefore let every man now task his thought
That this fair action may on foot be brought
                    [*Exeunt. Flourish*

ACT II.

PROLOGUE.

Enter Chorus.

Chor. Now all the youth of England are
　　on fire,
And silken dalliance in the wardrobe lies :
Now thrive the armorers, and honor's thought
Reigns solely in the breast of every man :
They sell the pasture now to buy the horse,
Following the mirror of all Christian kings,
With winged heels, as English Mercuries.
For now sits Expectation in the air,
And hides a sword from hilts unto the point
With crowns imperial, crowns and coronets,
Promised to Harry and his followers.　　11
The French, advised by good intelligence
Of this most dreadful preparation,
Shake in their fear and with pale policy
Seek to divert the English purposes.
O England ! model to thy inward greatness,
Like little body with a mighty heart,
What mightst thou do, that honor would thee
　　do,
Were all thy children kind and natural !
But see thy fault ! France hath in thee found
　　out　　20
A nest of hollow bosoms, which he fills
With treacherous crowns ; and three corrupted
　　men,
One, Richard Earl of Cambridge, and the sec-
　　ond,
Henry Lord Scroop of Masham, and the third,
Sir Thomas Grey, knight, of Northumberland,
Have, for the gilt of France,—O guilt indeed !
Confirm'd conspiracy with fearful France ;
And by their hands this grace of kings must
　　die,
If hell and treason hold their promises,
Ere he take ship for France, and in South-
　　ampton.　　30
Linger your patience on ; and we'll digest
The abuse of distance ; force a play :
The sum is paid ; the traitors are agreed ;
The king is set from London ; and the scene
Is now transported, gentles, to Southampton.
There is the playhouse now, there must you
　　sit :
And thence to France shall we convey you
　　safe,
And bring you back, charming the narrow
　　seas
To give you gentle pass ; for, if we may,　　39
We'll not offend one stomach with our play.
But, till the king come forth, and not till then,
Unto Southampton do we shift our scene.
　　　　　　　　　　　　　　　　[*Exit.*

Scene I. *London. A street.*

Enter Corporal Nym *and* Lieutenant
Bardolph.

Bard. Well met, Corporal Nym.

Nym. Good morrow, Lieutenant Bardolph.

Bard. What, are Ancient Pistol and you
friends yet ?

Nym. For my part, I care not : I say little ; but when time shall serve, there shall be
smiles ; but that shall be as it may. I dare not
fight ; but I will wink and hold out mine iron :
it is a simple one ; but what though ? it will
toast cheese, and it will endure cold as another
man's sword will : and there's an end.　　11

Bard. I will bestow a breakfast to make
you friends ; and we'll be all three sworn
brothers to France : let it be so, good Corporal Nym.

Nym. Faith, I will live so long as I may,
that's the certain of it ; and when I cannot
live any longer, I will do as I may : that is my
rest, that is the rendezvous of it.

Bard. It is certain, corporal, that he is
married to Nell Quickly : and certainly she
did you wrong ; for you were troth-plight to
her.　　21

Nym. I cannot tell : things must be as they
may : men may sleep, and they may have their
throats about them at that time ; and some
say knives have edges. It must be as it may :
though patience be a tired mare, yet she will
plod. There must be conclusions. Well, I cannot tell.

Enter Pistol *and* Hostess.

Bard. Here comes Ancient Pistol and his
wife : good corporal, be patient here. How
now, mine host Pistol !　　30

Pist. Base tike, call'st thou me host ?
Now, by this hand, I swear, I scorn the term ;
Nor shall my Nell keep lodgers.

Host. No, by my troth, not long ; for we
cannot lodge and board a dozen or fourteen
gentlewomen that live honestly by the prick
of their needles, but it will be thought we keep
a bawdy house straight. [*Nym and Pistol
draw.*] O well a day, Lady, if he be not
drawn now ! we shall see wilful adultery and
murder committed.　　40

Bard. Good lieutenant ! good corporal !
offer nothing here.

Nym. Pish !

Pist. Pish for thee, Iceland dog ! thou
　　prick-ear'd cur of Iceland !

Host. Good Corporal Nym, show thy
valor, and put up your sword.

Nym. Will you shog off ? I would have
you solus.

Pist. 'Solus,' egregious dog ? O viper vile !
The 'solus' in thy most mervailous face ;　　50
The 'solus' in thy teeth, and in thy throat,
And in thy hateful lungs, yea, in thy maw,
　　perdy,
And, which is worse, within thy nasty mouth !
I do retort the 'solus' in thy bowels ;
For I can take, and Pistol's cock is up,
And flashing fire will follow.

Nym. I am not Barbason ; you cannot
conjure me. I have an humor to knock you
indifferently well. If you grow foul with me,
Pistol, I will scour you with my rapier, as I
may, in fair terms : if you would walk off, I
would prick your guts a little, in good terms,
as I may : and that's the humor of it.

Pist. O braggart vile and damned furious
wight !
The grave doth gape, and doting death is
　　near ;
Therefore exhale.

Bard. Hear me, hear me what I say : he
that strikes the first stroke, I'll run him up
to the hilts, as I am a soldier.　　[*Draws.*

Pist. An oath of mickle might ; and fury
shall abate.　　70
Give me thy fist, thy fore-foot to me give :
Thy spirits are most tall.

Nym. I will cut thy throat, one time or other, in fair terms ; that is the humor of it.

Pist. ' Couple a gorge ! '
That is the word. I thee defy again.
O hound of Crete, think'st thou my spouse to get ?
No ; to the spital go,
And from the powdering tub of infamy
Fetch forth the lazar kite of Cressid's kind, 80
Doll Tearsheet she by name, and her espouse :
I have, and I will hold, the quondam Quickly
For the only she ; and—pauca, there's enough.
Go to.

Enter the Boy.

Boy. Mine host Pistol, you must come to my master, and you, hostess : he is very sick, and would to bed. Good Bardolph, put thy face between his sheets, and do the office of a warming-pan. Faith, he's very ill.

Bard. Away, you rogue !   90

Host. By my troth, he'll yield the crow a pudding one of these days. The king has killed his heart. Good husband, come home presently.   [*Exeunt Hostess and Boy.*

Bard. Come, shall I make you two friends ? We must to France together : why the devil should we keep knives to cut one another's throats ?

Pist. Let floods o'erswell, and fiends for food howl on !

Nym. You'll pay me the eight shillings I won of you at betting ?

Pist. Base is the slave that pays.   100

Nym. That now I will have : that's the humor of it.

Pist. As manhood shall compound : push home.   [*They draw.*

Bard. By this sword, he that makes the first thrust, I'll kill him ; by this sword, I will.

Pist. Sword is an oath, and oaths must have their course.

Bard. Corporal Nym, an thou wilt be friends, be friends : an thou wilt not, why, then, be enemies with me too. Prithee, put up.

Nym. I shall have my eight shillings I won of you at betting ?   111

Pist. A noble shalt thou have, and present pay ;
And liquor likewise will I give to thee,
And friendship shall combine, and brotherhood :
I'll live by Nym, and Nym shall live by me ;
Is not this just ? for I shall sutler be
Unto the camp, and profits will accrue.
Give me thy hand.

Nym. I shall have my noble ?

Pist. In cash most justly paid.   120

Nym. Well, then, that's the humor of't.

Re-enter Hostess.

Host. As ever you came of women, come in quickly to Sir John. Ah, poor heart ! he is so shaked of a burning quotidian tertian, that it is most lamentable to behold. Sweet men, come to him.

Nym. The king hath run bad humors on the knight ; that's the even of it.

Pist. Nym, thou hast spoke the right ; His heart is fracted and corroborate.   130

Nym. The king is a good king : but it must be as it may ; he passes some humors and careers.

Pist. Let us condole the knight ; for, lambkins we will live.

SCENE II. *Southampton. A council-chamber.*

Enter EXETER, BEDFORD, *and* WESTMORELAND.

Bed. 'Fore God, his grace is bold, to trust these traitors.

Exe. They shall be apprehended by and by.

West. How smooth and even they do bear themselves !
As if allegiance in their bosoms sat,
Crowned with faith and constant loyalty.

Bed. The king hath note of all that they intend,
By interception which they dream not of.

Exe. Nay, but the man that was his bedfellow,
Whom he hath dull'd and cloy'd with gracious favors,
That he should, for a foreign purse, so sell 10
His sovereign's life to death and treachery.

Trumpets sound. Enter KING HENRY, SCROOP, CAMBRIDGE, GREY, *and* Attendants.

K. Hen. Now sits the wind fair, and we will aboard.
My Lord of Cambridge, and my kind Lord of Masham,
And you, my gentle knight, give me your thoughts :
Think you not that the powers we bear with us
Will cut their passage through the force of France,
Doing the execution and the act
For which we have in head assembled them ?

Scroop. No doubt, my liege, if each man do his best.

K. Hen. I doubt not that ; since we are well persuaded   20
We carry not a heart with us from hence
That grows not in a fair consent with ours,
Nor leave not one behind that doth not wish
Success and conquest to attend on us.

Cam. Never was monarch better fear'd and loved
Than is your majesty : there's not, I think, a subject
That sits in heart-grief and uneasiness
Under the sweet shade of your government.

Grey. True : those that were your father's enemies
Have steep'd their galls in honey and do serve you   30
With hearts create of duty and of zeal.

K. Hen. We therefore have great cause of thankfulness ;
And shall forget the office of our hand,
Sooner than quittance of desert and merit
According to the weight and worthiness.

Scroop. So service shall with steeled sinews toil,
And labor shall refresh itself with hope,
To do your grace incessant services.

K. Hen. We judge no less. Uncle of Exeter,
Enlarge the man committed yesterday,   40
That rail'd against our person : we consider
It was excess of wine that set him on ;
And on his more advice we pardon him.

Scroop. That's mercy, but too much security :

Let him be punish'd, sovereign, lest example
Breed, by his sufferance, more of such a kind.
  K. Hen. O, let us yet be merciful.
  Cam. So may your highness, and yet pun-
    ish too.
  Grey. Sir,
You show great mercy, if you give him life, 50
After the taste of much correction.
  K. Hen. Alas, your too much love and
    care of me
Are heavy orisons 'gainst this poor wretch !
If little faults, proceeding on distemper,
Shall not be wink'd at, how shall we stretch
    our eye
When capital crimes, chew'd, swallow'd and
    digested,
Appear before us ? We'll yet enlarge that man,
Though Cambridge, Scroop and Grey, in their
    dear care
And tender preservation of our person,
Would have him punished. And now to our
    French causes :   60
Who are the late commissioners ?
  Cam. I one, my lord :
Your highness bade me ask for it to-day.
  Scroop. So did you me, my liege.
  Grey. And I, my royal sovereign.
  K. Hen. Then, Richard Earl of Cambridge,
    there is yours ;
There yours, Lord Scroop of Masham ; and,
    sir knight,
Grey of Northumberland, this same is yours :
Read them ; and know, I know your worthi-
    ness.
My Lord of Westmoreland, and uncle Exeter,
We will aboard to night. Why, how now, gen-
    tlemen !   71
What see you in those papers that you lose
So much complexion ? Look ye, how they
    change !
Their cheeks are paper. Why, what read you
    there
That hath so cowarded and chased your blood
Out of appearance ?
  Cam.   I do confess my fault ;
And do submit me to your highness' mercy.
  Grey. } To which we all appeal.
  Scroop.
  K. Hen. The mercy that was quick in us
    but late,   79
By your own counsel is suppress'd and kill'd :
You must not dare, for shame, to talk of
    mercy ;
For your own reasons turn into your bosoms,
As dogs upon their masters, worrying you.
See you, my princes, and my noble peers,
These English monsters ! My Lord of Cam-
    bridge here,
You know how apt our love was to accord
To furnish him with all appertinents
Belonging to his honor ; and this man
Hath, for a few light crowns, lightly conspired,
And sworn unto the practices of France,   90
To kill us here in Hampton : to the which
This knight, no less for bounty bound to us
Than Cambridge is, hath likewise sworn.
    But, O,
What shall I say to thee, Lord Scroop ? thou
    cruel,
Ingrateful, savage and inhuman creature !
Thou that didst bear the key of all my coun-
    sels,
That knew'st the very bottom of my soul,

That almost mightst have coin'd me into gold,
Wouldst thou have practised on me for thy
    use,
May it be possible, that foreign hire   100
Could out of thee extract one spark of evil
That might annoy my finger ? 'tis so strange,
That, though the truth of it stands off as gross
As black and white, my eye will scarcely see it.
Treason and murder ever kept together,
As two yoke-devils sworn to either's purpose,
Working so grossly in a natural cause,
That admiration did not whoop at them :
But thou, 'gainst all proportion, didst bring in
Wonder to wait on treason and on murder :
And whatsoever cunning fiend it was   111
That wrought upon thee so preposterously
Hath got the voice in hell for excellence :
All other devils that suggest by treasons
Do botch and bungle up damnation
With patches, colors, and with forms being
    fetch'd
From glistering semblances of piety ;
But he that temper'd thee bade thee stand up,
Gave thee no instance why thou shouldst do
    treason,   119
Unless to dub thee with the name of traitor.
If that same demon that hath gull'd thee thus
Should with his lion gait walk the whole
    world,
He might return to vasty Tartar back,
And tell the legions ' I can never win
A soul so easy as that Englishman's.'
O, how hast thou with jealousy infected
The sweetness of affiance ! Show men dutiful ?
Why, so didst thou : seem they grave and
    learned ?
Why, so didst thou : come they of noble fam-
    ily ?
Why, so didst thou : seem they religious ? 130
Why, so didst thou : or are they spare in diet,
Free from gross passion or of mirth or anger,
Constant in spirit, not swerving with the blood,
Garnish'd and deck'd in modest complement,
Not working with the eye without the ear,
And but in purged judgment trusting neither ?
Such and so finely bolted didst thou seem :
And thus thy fall hath left a kind of blot,
To mark the full-fraught man and best imbued
With some suspicion. I will weep for thee ; 140
For this revolt of thine, methinks, is like
Another fall of man. Their faults are open :
Arrest them to the answer of the law ;
And God acquit them of their practices !
  Exe. I arrest thee of high treason, by the
name of Richard Earl of Cambridge.
  I arrest thee of high treason, by the name of
Henry Lord Scroop of Masham.
  I arrest thee of high treason, by the name of
Thomas Grey, knight, of Northumberland. 150
  Scroop. Our purposes God justly hath dis-
    cover'd ;
And I repent my fault more than my death ;
Which I beseech your highness to forgive,
Although my body pay the price of it.
  Cam. For me, the gold of France did not
    seduce ;
Although I did admit it as a motive
The sooner to effect what I intended :
But God be thanked for prevention ;
Which I in sufferance heartily will rejoice,
Beseeching God and you to pardon me.   160
  Grey. Never did faithful subject more re-
    joice

At the discovery of most dangerous treason
Than I do at this hour joy o'er myself.
Prevented from a damned enterprise :
My fault, but not my body, pardon, sovereign.
  K. Hen. God quit you in his mercy ! Hear
    your sentence.
You have conspired against our royal person,
Join'd with an enemy proclaim'd and from his
    coffers
Received the golden earnest of our death ;
Wherein you would have sold your king to
    slaughter,   170
His princes and his peers to servitude,
His subjects to oppression and contempt
And his whole kingdom into desolation.
Touching our person seek we no revenge ;
But we our kingdom's safety must so tender,
Whose ruin you have sought, that to her laws
We do deliver you. Get you therefore hence,
Poor miserable wretches, to your death :
The taste whereof, God of his mercy give 179
You patience to endure, and true repentance
Of all your dear offences ! Bear them hence.
    [*Exeunt Cambridge, Scroop and Grey,
                                guarded.*
Now, lords, for France ; the enterprise
    whereof
Shall be to you, as us, like glorious.
We doubt not of a fair and lucky war,
Since God so graciously hath brought to light
This dangerous treason lurking in our way
To hinder our beginnings. We doubt not now
But every rub is smoothed on our way.
Then forth, dear countrymen : let us deliver
Our puissance into the hand of God,   190
Putting it straight in expedition.
Cheerly to sea ; the signs of war advance :
No king of England, if not king of France.
                                        [*Exeunt.*

SCENE III. *London. Before a tavern.*

Enter PISTOL, Hostess, NYM, BARDOLPH, *and*
    Boy.

  Host. Prithee, honey-sweet husband, let me
bring thee to Staines.
  Pist. No ; for my manly heart doth yearn.
Bardolph, be blithe : Nym, rouse thy vaunt-
    ing veins :
Boy, bristle thy courage up ; for Falstaff he is
    dead,
And we must yearn therefore.
  Bard. Would I were with him, where-
some'er he is, either in heaven or in hell !
  Host. Nay, sure, he's not in hell : he's in
Arthur's bosom, if ever man went to Arthur's
bosom. A' made a finer end and went away
an it had been any christom child ; a' parted
even just between twelve and one, even at the
turning o' the tide : for after I saw him fumble
with the sheets and play with flowers and smile
upon his fingers' ends, I knew there was but
one way ; for his nose was as sharp as a pen,
and a' babbled of green fields. ' How now, sir
John ! ' quoth I : ' what, man ! be o' good
cheer.' So a' cried out ' God, God, God ! '
three or four times. Now I, to comfort him,
bid him a' should not think of God ; I hoped
there was no need to trouble himself with any
such thoughts yet. So a' bade me lay more
clothes on his feet : I put my hand into the
bed and felt them, and they were as cold as
any stone ; then I felt to his knees, and they
were as cold as any stone, and so upward and

upward, and all was as cold as any stone.
  Nym. They say he cried out of sack.
  Host. Ay, that a' did.   30
  Bard. And of women.
  Host. Nay, that a' did not.
  Boy. Yes, that a' did ; and said they were
devils incarnate.
  Host. A' could never abide carnation ;
'twas a color he never liked.
  Boy. A' said once, the devil would have
him about women.
  Host. A' did in some sort, indeed, handle
women ; but then he was rheumatic, and
talked of the whore of Babylon.   41
  Boy. Do you not remember, a' saw a flea
stick upon Bardolph's nose, and a' said it was
a black soul burning in hell-fire ?
  Bard. Well, the fuel is gone that main-
tained that fire : that's all the riches I got in
his service.
  Nym. Shall we shog ? the king will be gone
from Southampton.
  Pist. Come, let's away. My love, give me
thy lips.
Look to my chattels and my movables :   50
Let senses rule ; the word is ' Pitch and Pay : '
Trust none ;
For oaths are straws, men's faiths are wafer-
    cakes,
And hold-fast is the only dog, my duck :
Therefore, Caveto be thy counsellor.
Go, clear thy crystals. Yoke-fellows in arms,
Let us to France ; like horse-leeches, my boys,
To suck, to suck, the very blood to suck !
  Boy. And that's but unwholesome food
they say.   60
  Pist. Touch her soft mouth, and march.
  Bard. Farewell, hostess.   [*Kissing her.*
  Nym. I cannot kiss, that is the humor of
it ; but, adieu.
  Pist. Let housewifery appear : keep close,
    I thee command.
  Host. Farewell ; adieu.   [*Exeunt.*

SCENE IV. *France. The* KING'S *palace.*

Flourish. Enter the FRENCH KING, *the* DAU-
PHIN, *the* DUKES OF BERRI *and* BRETAGNE,
the CONSTABLE, *and others.*

  Fr. King. Thus comes the English with full
    power upon us ;
And more than carefully it us concerns
To answer royally in our defences.
Therefore the Dukes of Berri and of Bretagne,
Of Brabant and of Orleans, shall make forth,
And you, Prince Dauphin, with all swift dis-
    patch,
To line and new repair our towns of war
With men of courage and with means defend-
    ant ;
For England his approaches makes as fierce
As waters to the sucking of a gulf.   10
It fits us then to be as provident
As fear may teach us out of late examples
Left by the fatal and neglected English
Upon our fields.
  Dau.   My most redoubted father,
It is most meet we arm us 'gainst the foe ;
For peace itself should not so dull a kingdom,
Though war nor no known quarrel were in
    question,
But that defences, musters, preparations,
Should be maintain'd, assembled and collected,
As were a war in expectation.   20

Therefore, I say 'tis meet we all go forth
To view the sick and feeble parts of France :
And let us do it with no show of fear ;
No, with no more than if we heard that Eng-
    land
Were busied with a Whitsun morris-dance :
For, my good liege, she is so idly king'd,
Her sceptre so fantastically borne
By a vain, giddy, shallow, humorous youth,
That fear attends her not.
   Con.   O peace, Prince Dauphin !
You are too much mistaken in this king :   30
Question your grace the late ambassadors,
With what great state he heard their embassy,
How well supplied with noble counsellors,
How modest in exception, and withal
How terrible in constant resolution,
And you shall find his vanities forespent
Were but the outside of the Roman Brutus,
Covering discretion with a coat of folly ;
As gardeners do with ordure hide those roots
That shall first spring and be most delicate. 40
   Dau. Well, 'tis not so, my lord high con-
    stable ;
But though we think it so, it is no matter :
In cases of defence 'tis best to weigh
The enemy more mighty than he seems :
So the proportions of defence are fill'd ;
Which of a weak or niggardly projection
Doth, like a miser, spoil his coat with scant-
    ing
A little cloth.
   Fr. King. Think we King Harry strong ;
And, princes, look you strongly arm to meet
    him.
The kindred of him hath been flesh'd upon us ;
And he is bred out of that bloody strain   51
That haunted us in our familiar paths :
Witness our too much memorable shame
When Cressy battle fatally was struck,
And all our princes captived by the hand
Of that black name, Edward, Black Prince of
    Wales ;
Whiles that his mountain sire, on mountain
    standing,
Up in the air, crown'd with the golden sun,
Saw his heroical seed, and smiled to see him,
Mangle the work of nature and deface   60
The patterns that by God and by French
    fathers
Had twenty years been made. This is a stem
Of that victorious stock ; and let us fear
The native mightiness and fate of him.

          Enter a Messenger.

   Mess. Ambassadors from Harry King of
    England
Do crave admittance to your majesty.
   Fr. King. We'll give them present audience.
    Go, and bring them.
        [*Exeunt Messenger and certain Lords.*
You see this chase is hotly follow'd, friends.
   Dau. Turn head, and stop pursuit ; for
    coward dogs
Most spend their mouths when what they
    seem to threaten   70
Runs far before them. Good my sovereign,
Take up the English short, and let them know
Of what a monarchy you are the head :
Self-love, my liege, is not so vile a sin
As self-neglecting.

   Re-enter Lords, *with* Exeter *and train.*

   Fr. King.   From our brother England ?
   Exe. From him ; and thus he greets your
    majesty.
He wills you, in the name of God Almighty,
That you divest yourself, and lay apart
The borrow'd glories that by gift of heaven,
By law of nature and of nations, 'long   80
To him and to his heirs ; namely, the crown
And all wide-stretched honors that pertain
By custom and the ordinance of times
Unto the crown of France. That you may
    know
'Tis no sinister nor no awkward claim,
Pick'd from the worm-holes of long-vanish'd
    days,
Nor from the dust of old oblivion raked,
He sends you this most memorable line,
In every branch truly demonstrative ;
Willing you overlook this pedigree :   90
And when you find him evenly derived
From his most famed of famous ancestors,
Edward the Third, he bids you then resign
Your crown and kingdom, indirectly held
From him the native and true challenger.
   Fr. King. Or else what follows ?
   Exe. Bloody constraint ; for if you hide
    the crown
Even in your hearts, there will he rake for it :
Therefore in fierce tempest is he coming,
In thunder and in earthquake, like a Jove, 100
That, if requiring fail, he will compel ;
And bids you, in the bowels of the Lord,
Deliver up the crown, and to take mercy
On the poor souls for whom this hungry war
Opens his vasty jaws ; and on your head
Turning the widows' tears, the orphans' cries
The dead men's blood, the pining maidens
    groans,
For husbands, fathers and betrothed lovers,
That shall be swallow'd in this controversy.
This is his claim, his threatening and my mes-
    sage ;   110
Unless the Dauphin be in presence here,
To whom expressly I bring greeting too.
   Fr. King. For us, we will consider of this
    further :
To-morrow shall you bear our full intent
Back to our brother England.
   Dau.   For the Dauphin,
I stand here for him : what to him from Eng-
    land ?
   Exe. Scorn and defiance ; slight regard,
    contempt,
And any thing that may not misbecome
The mighty sender, doth he prize you at.
Thus says my king ; an' if your father's high-
    ness   120
Do not, in grant of all demands at large,
Sweeten the bitter mock you sent his majesty,
He'll call you to so hot an answer of it,
That caves and womby vaultages of France
Shall chide your trespass and return your
    mock
In second accent of his ordnance.
   Dau. Say, if my father render fair return,
It is against my will ; for I desire
Nothing but odds with England : to that end,
As matching to his youth and vanity,   130
I did present him with the Paris balls.
   Exe. He'll make your Paris Louvre shake
    for it,
Were it the mistress-court of mighty Europe :
And, be assured, you'll find a difference,

As we his subjects have in wonder found,
Between the promise of his greener days
And these he masters now : now he weighs
    time
Even to the utmost grain : that you shall read
In your own losses, if he stay in France.
    Fr. King. To-morrow shall you know our
        mind at full.   140
    Exe. Dispatch us with all speed, lest that
        our king
Come here himself to question our delay ;
For he is footed in this land already.
    Fr. King. You shall be soon dispatch'd
        with fair conditions :
A night is but small breath and little pause
To answer matters of this consequence.
                              [*Flourish. Exeunt.*

ACT III.

PROLOGUE.

Enter Chorus.

Chor. Thus with imagined wing our swift
        scene flies
In motion of no less celerity
Than that of thought. Suppose that you have
        seen
The well-appointed king at Hampton pier
Embark his royalty ; and his brave fleet
With silken streamers the young Phœbus fan-
        ning :
Play with your fancies, and in them behold
Upon the hempen tackle ship-boys climbing ;
Hear the shrill whistle which doth order give
To sounds confused ; behold the threaden
        sails,   10
Borne with the invisible and creeping wind,
Draw the huge bottoms through the furrow'd
        sea,
Breasting the lofty surge : O, do but think
You stand upon the rivage and behold
A city on the inconstant billows dancing ;
For so appears this fleet majestical,
Holding due course to Harfleur. Follow, fol-
        low :
Grapple your minds to sternage of this navy,
And leave your England, as dead midnight
        still,
Guarded with grandsires, babies and old
        women,
Either past or not arrived to pith and puis-
        sance ;
For who is he, whose chin is but enrich'd
With one appearing hair, that will not follow
These cull'd and choice-drawn cavaliers to
        France ?
Work, work your thoughts, and therein see a
        siege ;
Behold the ordnance on their carriages,
With fatal mouths gaping on girded Harfleur.
Suppose the ambassador from the French
        comes back ;
Tells Harry that the king doth offer him
Katharine his daughter, and with her, to
        dowry,   30
Some petty and unprofitable dukedoms.
The offer likes not : and the nimble gunner
With linstock now the devilish cannon
        touches, [*Alarum, and chambers go off.*

And down goes all before them. Still be kind,
And eke out our performance with your mind.
                                      [*Exit.*

SCENE I. *France. Before Harfleur.*

Alarum. Enter KING HENRY, EXETER, BED-
FORD, GLOUCESTER, *and* Soldiers, *with
scaling-ladders.*

    K. Hen. Once more unto the breach, dear
        friends, once more ;
Or close the wall up with our English dead.
In peace there's nothing so becomes a man
As modest stillness and humility :
But when the blast of war blows in our ears,
Then imitate the action of the tiger ;
Stiffen the sinews, summon up the blood,
Disguise fair nature with hard-favor'd rage ;
Then lend the eye a terrible aspect ;
Let it pry through the portage of the head   10
Like the brass cannon ; let the brow o'erwhelm
        it
As fearfully as doth a galled rock
O'erhang and jutty his confounded base,
Swill'd with the wild and wasteful ocean.
Now set the teeth and stretch the nostril wide,
Hold hard the breath and bend up every spirit
To his full height. On, on, you noblest Eng-
        lish,
Whose blood is fet from fathers of war-proof !
Fathers that, like so many Alexanders,
Have in these parts from morn till even fought
And sheathed their swords for lack of argu-
        ment :   21
Dishonor not your mothers ; now attest
That those whom you call'd fathers did beget
        you.
Be copy now to men of grosser blood,
And teach them how to war. And you, good
        yeomen,
Whose limbs were made in England, show us
        here
The mettle of your pasture ; let us swear
That you are worth your breeding ; which I
        doubt not ;
For there is none of you so mean and base,
That hath not noble lustre in your eyes.   30
I see you stand like greyhounds in the slips,
Straining upon the start. The game's afoot :
Follow your spirit, and upon this charge
Cry 'God for Harry, England, and Saint
        George ! '
            [*Exeunt. Alarum, and chambers go off.*

SCENE II. *The same.*

Enter NYM, BARDOLPH, PISTOL, *and* BOY.

    Bard. On, on, on, on, on ! to the breach, to
the breach !
    Nym. Pray thee, corporal, stay : the knocks
are too hot ; and, for mine own part, I have
not a case of lives : the humor of it is too hot,
that is the very plain-song of it.
    Pist. The plain-song is most just : for hu-
mors do abound :
Knocks go and come ; God's vassals drop and
        die ;
        And sword and shield,
          In bloody field,   10
Doth win immortal fame.
    Boy. Would I were in an alehouse in Lon-
don ! I would give all my fame for a pot of
ale and safety.

Pist. And I :
    If wishes would prevail with me,
    My purpose should not fail with me,
    But thither would I hie.
Boy. As duly, but not as truly,
    As bird doth sing on bough. 20

Enter FLUELLEN.

Flu. Up to the breach, you dogs! avaunt,
you cullions!   [*Driving them forward.*
Pist. Be merciful, great duke, to men of
    mould.
Abate thy rage, abate thy manly rage,
Abate thy rage, great duke !
Good bawcock, bate thy rage ; use lenity,
    sweet chuck !
Nym. These be good humors ! your honor
wins bad humors.   [*Exeunt all but Boy.*
Boy. As young as I am, I have observed
these three swashers. I am boy to them all
three : but all they three, though they would
serve me, could not be man to me ; for indeed
three such antics do not amount to a man.
For Bardolph, he is white-livered and red-
faced ; by the means whereof a' faces it out,
but fights not. For Pistol, he hath a killing
tongue and a quiet sword ; by the means
whereof a' breaks words, and keeps whole
weapons. For Nym, he hath heard that men
of few words are the best men ; and therefore
he scorns to say his prayers, lest a' should be
thought a coward : but his few bad words are
matched with as few good deeds ; for a' never
broke any man's head but his own, and that
was against a post when he was drunk. They
will steal any thing, and call it purchase.
Bardolph stole a lute-case, bore it twelve
leagues, and sold it for three half pence. Nym
and Bardolph are sworn brothers in filching,
and in Calais they stole a fire-shovel : I knew
by that piece of service the men would carry
coals. They would have me as familiar with
men's pockets as their gloves or their hand-
kerchers : which makes much against my
manhood, if I should take from another's
pocket to put into mine ; for it is plain pock-
eting up of wrongs. I must leave them, and
seek some better service : their villany goes
against my weak stomach, and therefore I
must cast it up.   [*Exit.*

Re-enter FLUELLEN, GOWER *following.*

Gow. Captain Fluellen, you must come
presently to the mines ; the Duke of Gloucester would speak with you. 60
Flu. To the mines I tell you the duke, it is
not so good to come to the mines ; for, look
you, the mines is not according to the disciplines of the war : the concavities of it is not
sufficient ; for, look you, th' athversary, you
may discuss unto the duke, look you, is digt
himself four yard under the countermines : by
Cheshu, I think a' will plow up all, if there is
not better directions.
Gow. The Duke of Gloucester, to whom
the order of the siege is given, is altogether
directed by an Irishman, a very valiant gentleman, i' faith.
Flu. It is Captain Macmorris, is it not ?
Gow. I think it be.
Flu. By Cheshu, he is an ass, as in the
world : I will verify as much in his beard : he
has no more directions in the true disciplines

of the wars, look you, of the Roman disciplines, than is a puppy-dog.

Enter MACMORRIS *and* Captain JAMY.

Gow. Here a' comes ; and the Scots captain, Captain Jamy, with him. 80
Flu. Captain Jamy is a marvellous falorous
gentleman, that is certain ; and of great expedition and knowledge in th' aunchient wars,
upon my particular knowledge of his directions : by Cheshu, he will maintain his argument as well as any military man in the
world, in the disciplines of the pristine wars
of the Romans.
Jamy. I say gud-day, Captain Fluellen.
Flu. God-den to your worship, good Captain James. 90
Gow. How now, Captain Macmorris ! have
you quit the mines ? have the pioneers given
o'er ?
Mac. By Chrish, la ! tish ill done : the
work ish give over, the trumpet sound the retreat. By my hand, I swear, and my father's
soul, the work ish ill done ; it ish give over :
I would have blowed up the town, so Chrish
save me, la ! in an hour : O, tish ill done,
tish ill done ; by my hand, tish ill done ! 99
Flu. Captain Macmorris, I beseech you
now, will you voutsafe me, look you, a few
disputations with you, as partly touching or
concerning the disciplines of the war, in the Roman wars, in the way of argument, look you,
and friendly communication ; partly to satisfy my opinion, and partly for the satisfaction, look you, of my mind, as touching the
direction of the military discipline ; that is the
point.
Jamy. It sall be vary gud, gud feith, gud
captains bath : and I sall quit you with gud
leve, as I may pick occasion ; that sall I,
marry. 111
Mac. It is no time to discourse, so Chrish
save me : the day is hot, and the weather,
and the wars, and the king, and the dukes :
it is no time to discourse. The town is be-
seeched, and the trumpet call us to the
breach ; and we talk, and, be Chrish, do nothing : 'tis shame for us all : so God sa' me, 'tis
shame to stand still ; it is shame, by my
hand : and there is throats to be cut, and
works to be done; and there ish nothing done,
so Chrish sa' me, la ! 121
Jamy. By the mess, ere theise eyes of mine
take themselves to slomber, ay'll de gud service, or ay'll lig i' the grund for it ; ay, or go
to death ; and ay'll pay 't as valorously as I
may, that sall I suerly do, that is the breff
and the long. Marry, I wad full fain hear some
question 'tween you tway.
Flu. Captain Macmorris, I think, look
you, under your correction, there is not many
of your nation— 131
Mac. Of my nation ! What ish my nation ?
Ish a villain, and a bastard, and a knave, and
a rascal. What ish my nation ? Who talks of
my nation ?
Flu. Look you, if you take the matter
otherwise than is meant, Captain Macmorris,
peradventure I shall think you do not use me
with that affability as in discretion you ought
to use me, look you : being as good a man as
yourself, both in the disciplines of war, and

in the derivation of my birth, and in other particularities.

Mac. I do not know you so good a man as myself : so Chrish save me, I will cut off your head.

Gow. Gentlemen both, you will mistake each other.

Jamy. A ! that's a foul fault.

[*A parley sounded.*

Gow. The town sounds a parley.　149

Flu. Captain Macmorris, when there is more better opportunity to be required, look you, I will be so bold as to tell you I know the disciplines of war ; and there is an end.

[*Exeunt.*

SCENE III. *The same. Before the gates.*

The Governor *and some* Citizens *on the walls ; the* English *forces below. Enter* KING HENRY *and his train.*

K. Hen. How yet resolves the governor of the town ?
This is the latest parle we will admit ;
Therefore to our best mercy give yourselves ;
Or like to men proud of destruction
Defy us to our worst : for, as I am a soldier,
A name that in my thoughts becomes me best,
If I begin the battery once again,
I will not leave the half-achieved Harfleur
Till in her ashes she lie buried.
The gates of mercy shall be all shut up,　10
And the flesh'd soldier, rough and hard of heart,
In liberty of bloody hand shall range
With conscience wide as hell, mowing like grass
Your fresh-fair virgins and your flowering infants.
What is it then to me, if impious war,
Array'd in flames like to the prince of fiends,
Do, with his smirch'd complexion, all fell feats
Enlink'd to waste and desolation ?
What is't to me, when you yourselves are cause,
If your pure maidens fall into the hand　20
Of hot and forcing violation ?
What rein can hold licentious wickedness
When down the hill he holds his fierce career ?
We may as bootless spend our vain command
Upon the enraged soldiers in their spoil
As send precepts to the leviathan
To come ashore. Therefore, you men of Harfleur,
Take pity of your town and of your people,
Whiles yet my soldiers are in my command ;
Whiles yet the cool and temperate wind of grace　30
O'erblows the filthy and contagious clouds
Of heady murder, spoil and villany.
If not, why, in a moment look to see
The blind and bloody soldier with foul hand
Defile the locks of your shrill-shrieking daughters ;
Your fathers taken by the silver beards,
And their most reverend heads dash'd to the walls,
Your naked infants spitted upon pikes,
Whiles the mad mothers with their howls confused
Do break the clouds, as did the wives of Jewry　40

At Herod's bloody-hunting slaughtermen.
What say you ? will you yield, and this avoid,
Or, guilty in defence, be thus destroy'd ?

Gov. Our expectation hath this day an end :
The Dauphin, whom of succors we entreated,
Returns us that his powers are yet not ready
To raise so great a siege. Therefore, great king,
We yield our town and lives to thy soft mercy.
Enter our gates ; dispose of us and ours ;
For we no longer are defensible.　50

K. Hen. Open your gates. Come, uncle Exeter,
Go you and enter Harfleur ; there remain,
And fortify it strongly 'gainst the French :
Use mercy to them all. For us, dear uncle,
The winter coming on and sickness growing
Upon our soldiers, we will retire to Calais.
To-night in Harfleur we will be your guest ;
To-morrow for the march are we addrest.

[*Flourish. The King and his train enter the town.*

SCENE IV. *The* FRENCH KING'S *palace.*

Enter KATHARINE *and* ALICE.

Kath. Alice, tu as été en Angleterre, et tu parles bien le langage.

Alice. Un peu, madame.

Kath. Je te prie, m'enseignez : il faut que j'apprenne à parler. Comment appelez-vous la main en Anglois ?

Alice. La main ? elle est appelée de hand.

Kath. De hand. Et les doigts ?

Alice. Les doigts ? ma foi, j'oublie les doigts ; mais je me souviendrai. Les doigts ? je pense qu'ils sont appelés de fingres ; oui, de fingres.　11

Kath. La main, de hand ; les doigts, de fingres. Je pense que je suis le bon écolier ; j'ai gagné deux mots d'Anglois vîtement. Comment appelez-vous les ongles ?

Alice. Les ongles ? nous les appelons de nails.

Kath. De nails. Ecoutez ; dites-moi, si je parle bien : de hand, de fingres, et de nails.

Alice. C'est bien dit, madame ; il est fort bon Anglois.　20

Kath. Dites-moi l'Anglois pour le bras.

Alice. De arm, madame.

Kath. Et le coude ?

Alice. De elbow.

Kath. De elbow. Je m'en fais la répétition de tous les mots que vous m'avez appris dès à présent.

Alice. Il est trop difficile, madame, comme je pense.

Kath. Excusez-moi, Alice ; écoutez : de hand, de fingres, de nails, de arma, de bilbow.　31

Alice. De elbow, madame.

Kath. O Seigneur Dieu, je m'en oublie ! de elbow. Comment appelez-vous le col ?

Alice. De neck, madame.

Kath. De nick. Et le menton ?

Alice. De chin.

Kath. De sin. Le col, de nick ; de menton, de sin.　39

Alice. Oui. Sauf votre honneur, en vérité, vous prononcez les mots aussi droit que les natifs d' Angleterre.

Kath. Je ne doute point d'apprendre, par
la grace de Dieu, et en peu de temps.

Alice. N'avez vous pas déjà oublié ce que
je vous ai enseigné ?

Kath. Non, je reciterai à vous prompte-
ment : de hand, de fingres, de mails,—

Alice. De nails, madame.

Kath. De nails, de arm, de ilbow.　50

Alice. Sauf votre honneur, de elbow.

Kath. Ainsi dis-je ; de elbow, de nick, et
de sin. Comment appelez-vous le pied et la
robe ?

Alice. De foot, madame ; et de coun.

Kath. De foot et de coun ! O Seigneur
Dieu ! ce sont mots de son mauvais, corrupti-
ble, gros, et impudique, et non pour les dames
d'honneur d'user : je ne voudrais prononcer
ces mots devant les seigneurs de France pour
tout le monde. Foh ! le foot et le coun !
Néanmoins, je reciterai une autre fois ma
leçon ensemble : de hand, de fingres, de nails,
de arm, de elbow, de nick, de sin, de foot, de
coun.

Alice. Excellent, madame !

Kath. C'est assez pour une fois : allons-
nous à dîner.　[*Exeunt.*

SCENE V. *The same.*

Enter the KING OF FRANCE, *the* DAUPHIN, *the*
DUKE OF BOURBON, *the* CONSTABLE OF
FRANCE, *and others.*

Fr. King. 'Tis certain he hath pass'd the
river Somme.

Con. And if he be not fought withal, my
lord,
Let us not live in France ; let us quit all
And give our vineyards to a barbarous people.

Dau. O Dieu vivant ! shall a few sprays of
us,
The emptying of our fathers' luxury,
Our scions, put in wild and savage stock,
Spirt up so suddenly into the clouds,
And overlook their grafters ?

Bour. Normans, but bastard Normans,
Norman bastards !　10
Mort de ma vie ! if they march along
Unfought withal, but I will sell my dukedom,
To buy a slobbery and a dirty farm
In that nook-shotten isle of Albion.

Con. Dieu de batailles ! where have they
this mettle ?
Is not their climate foggy, raw and dull,
On whom, as in despite, the sun looks pale,
Killing their fruit with frowns ? Can sodden
water,
A drench for sur-rein'd jades, their barley-
broth,　19
Decoct their cold blood to such valiant heat ?
And shall our quick blood, spirited with wine,
Seem frosty ? O, for honor of our land,
Let us not hang like roping icicles
Upon our houses' thatch, whiles a more frosty
people
Sweat drops of gallant youth in our rich fields !
Poor we may call them in their native lords.

Dau. By faith and honor,
Our madams mock at us, and plainly say
Our mettle is bred out and they will give
Their bodies to the lust of English youth　30
To new-store France with bastard warriors.

Bour. They bid us to the English dancing-
schools,

And teach lavoltas high and swift corantos ;
Saying our grace is only in our heels,
And that we are most lofty runaways.

Fr. King. Where is Montjoy the herald ?
speed him hence :
Let him greet England with our sharp defiance.
Up, princes ! and, with spirit of honor edged
More sharper than your swords, hie to the
field :　39
Charles Delabreth, high constable of France ;
You Dukes of Orleans, Bourbon, and of
Berri,
Alençon, Brabant, Bar, and Burgundy ;
Jaques Chatillon, Rambures, Vaudemont,
Beaumont, Grandpré, Roussi, and Faucon-
berg,
Foix, Lestrale, Bouciqualt, and Charolois ;
High dukes, great princes, barons, lords and
knights,
For your great seats now quit you of great
shames.
Bar Harry England, that sweeps through our
land
With pennons painted in the blood of Har-
fleur :
Rush on his host, as doth the melted snow　50
Upon the valleys, whose low vassal seat
The Alps doth spit and void his rheum upon :
Go down upon him, you have power enough,
And in a captive chariot into Rouen
Bring him our prisoner.

Con.　This becomes the great.
Sorry am I his numbers are so few,
His soldiers sick and famish'd in their march,
For I am sure, when he shall see our army,
He'll drop his heart into the sink of fear
And for achievement offer us his ransom.　60

Fr. King. Therefore, lord constable, haste
on Montjoy,
And let him say to England that we send
To know what willing ransom he will give.
Prince Dauphin, you shall stay with us in
Rouen.

Dau. Not so, I do beseech your majesty.

Fr. King. Be patient, for you shall remain
with us.
Now forth, lord constable and princes all,
And quickly bring us word of England's fall.
[*Exeunt.*

SCENE VI. *The English camp in Picardy.*

Enter GOWER *and* FLUELLEN, *meeting.*

Gow. How now, Captain Fluellen ! come
you from the bridge ?

Flu. I assure you, there is very excellent
services committed at the bridge.

Gow. Is the Duke of Exeter safe ?

Flu. The Duke of Exeter is as magnanimous as Agamemnon ; and a man that I love
and honor with my soul, and my heart, and
my duty, and my life, and my living, and my
uttermost power : he is not—God be praised
and blessed !—any hurt in the world ; but keeps
the bridge most valiantly, with excellent discipline. There is an aunchient lieutenant there
at the pridge, I think in my very conscience he
is as valiant a man as Mark Antony ; and he
is a man of no estimation in the world ; but
I did see him do as gallant service.

Gow. What do you call him ?

Flu. He is called Aunchient Pistol.

Gow. I know him not.　20

Enter PISTOL.

Flu. Here is the man.

Pist. Captain, I thee beseech to do me favors :
The Duke of Exeter doth love thee well.

Flu. Ay, I praise God ; and I have merited
some love at his hands.

Pist. Bardolph, a soldier, firm and sound
of heart,
And of buxom valor, hath, by cruel fate,
And giddy Fortune's furious fickle wheel,
That goddess blind,   30
That stands upon the rolling restless stone—

Flu. By your patience, Aunchient Pistol.
Fortune is painted blind, with a muffler afore
her eyes, to signify to you that Fortune is
blind ; and she is painted also with a wheel,
to signify to you, which is the moral of it, that
she is turning, and inconstant, and mutability,
and variation : and her foot, look you, is fixed
upon a spherical stone, which rolls, and rolls,
and rolls : in good truth, the poet makes a
most excellent description of it : Fortune is
an excellent moral.   40

Pist. Fortune is Bardolph's foe, and frowns
on him ;
For he hath stolen a pax, and hanged must a'
be :
A damned death !
Let gallows gape for dog ; let man go free
And let not hemp his wind-pipe suffocate :
But Exeter hath given the doom of death
For pax of little price.
Therefore, go speak : the duke will hear thy
voice :
And let not Bardolph's vital thread be cut
With edge of penny cord and vile reproach :
Speak, captain, for his life, and I will thee
requite.   51

Flu. Aunchient Pistol, I do partly understand your meaning.

Pist. Why then, rejoice therefore.

Flu. Certainly, aunchient, it is not a thing
to rejoice at : for if, look you, he were my
brother, I would desire the duke to use his
good pleasure, and put him to execution ; for
discipline ought to be used.

Pist. Die and be damn'd ! and figo for thy
friendship !   60

Flu. It is well.

Pist. The fig of Spain !   [*Exit.*

Flu. Very good.

Gow. Why, this is an arrant counterfeit
rascal ; I remember him now ; a bawd, a cut-
purse.

Flu. I'll assure you, a' uttered as brave
words at the bridge as you shall see in a summer's day. But it is very well ; what he has
spoke to me, that is well, I warrant you, when
time is serve.   69

Gow. Why, 'tis a gull, a fool, a rogue, that
now and then goes to the wars, to grace himself at his return into London under the form
of a soldier. And such fellows are perfect in
the great commanders' names : and they will
learn you by rote where services were done ;
at such and such a sconce, at such a breach, at
such a convoy ; who came off bravely, who
was shot, who disgraced, what terms the
enemy stood on ; and this they con perfectly
in the phrase of war, which they trick up with
new-tuned oaths : and what a beard of the

general's cut and a horrid suit of the camp
will do among foaming bottles and ale-washed
wits, is wonderful to be thought on. But you
must learn to know such slanders of the age,
or else you may be marvellously mistook.

Flu. I tell you what, Captain Gower ; I do
perceive he is not the man that he would gladly
make show to the world he is : if I find a hole
in his coat, I will tell him my mind. [*Drum
heard.*] Hark you, the king is coming, and I
must speak with him from the pridge.   91

Drum and colors. Enter KING HENRY,
GLOUCESTER, *and* Soldiers.

God pless your majesty !

K. Hen. How now, Fluellen ! camest thou
from the bridge ?

Flu. Ay, so please your majesty. The Duke
of Exeter has very gallantly maintained the
pridge : the French is gone off, look you ; and
there is gallant and most prave passages ;
marry, th' athversary was have possession of
the pridge ; but he is enforced to retire, and
the Duke of Exeter is master of the pridge : I
can tell your majesty, the duke is a prave
man.   101

K. Hen. What men have you lost, Fluellen ?

Flu. The perdition of th' athversary hath
been very great, reasonable great : marry, for
my part, I think the duke hath lost never a
man, but one that is like to be executed for
robbing a church, one Bardolph, if your majesty know the man : his face is all bubukles,
and whelks, and knobs, and flames o' fire :
and his lips blows at his nose, and it is like a
coal of fire, sometimes plue and sometimes
red ; but his nose is executed and his fire's out.

K. Hen. We would have all such offenders
so cut off : and we give express charge, that
in our marches through the country, there be
nothing compelled from the villages, nothing
taken but paid for, none of the French upbraided or abused in disdainful language ; for
when lenity and cruelty play for a kingdom,
the gentler gamester is the soonest winner. 120

Tucket. Enter MONTJOY.

Mont. You know me by my habit.

K. Hen. Well then I know thee : what
shall I know of thee ?

Mont. My master's mind.

K. Hen. Unfold it.

Mont. Thus says my king : Say thou to
Harry of England : Though we seemed dead,
we did but sleep : advantage is a better soldier
than rashness. Tell him we could have re-
buked him at Harfleur, but that we thought
not good to bruise an injury till it were full
ripe : now we speak upon our cue, and our
voice is imperial : England shall repent his
folly, see his weakness, and admire our sufferance. Bid him therefore consider of his
ransom ; which must proportion the losses we
have borne, the subjects we have lost, the disgrace we have digested ; which in weight to
re-answer, his pettiness would bow under. For
our losses, his exchequer is too poor ; for the
effusion of our blood, the muster of his kingdom too faint a number ; and for our disgrace,
his own person, kneeling at our feet, but a
weak and worthless satisfaction. To this add
defiance : and tell him, for conclusion, he hath

betrayed his followers, whose condemnation is
pronounced. So far my king and master; so
much my office.

K. Hen. What is thy name? I know thy
quality.

Mont. Montjoy.

K. Hen. Thou dost thy office fairly. Turn
thee back,
And tell thy king I do not seek him now;
But could be willing to march on to Calais 150
Without impeachment: for, to say the sooth,
Though 'tis no wisdom to confess so much
Unto an enemy of craft and vantage,
My people are with sickness much enfeebled,
My numbers lessened, and those few I have
Almost no better than so many French;
Who when they were in health, I tell thee,
herald,
I thought upon one pair of English legs
Did march three Frenchmen. Yet, forgive me,
God, 159
That I do brag thus! This your air of France
Hath blown that vice in me; I must repent.
Go therefore, tell thy master here I am;
My ransom is this frail and worthless trunk,
My army but a weak and sickly guard;
Yet, God before, tell him we will come on,
Though France himself and such another
neighbor
Stand in our way. There's for thy labor,
Montjoy.
Go, bid thy master well advise himself:
If we may pass, we will; if we be hinder'd,
We shall your tawny ground with your red
blood 170
Discolor: and so, Montjoy, fare you well.
The sum of all our answer is but this:
We would not seek a battle, as we are;
Nor, as we are, we say we will not shun it:
So tell your master.

Mont. I shall deliver so. Thanks to your
highness. [*Exit.*

Glou. I hope they will not come upon us
now.

K. Hen. We are in God's hand, brother,
not in theirs.
March to the bridge; it now draws toward
night:
Beyond the river we'll encamp ourselves, 180
And on to-morrow, bid them march away.
[*Exeunt.*

Scene VII. *The French camp, near Agincourt.*

Enter the Constable of France, *the* Lord
Rambures, Orleans, Dauphin, *with others.*

Con. Tut! I have the best armor of the
world. Would it were day!

Orl. You have an excellent armor; but let
my horse have his due.

Con. It is the best horse of Europe.

Orl. Will it never be morning?

Dau. My lord of Orleans, and my lord high
constable, you talk of horse and armor?

Orl. You are as well provided of both as
any prince in the world. 10

Dau. What a long night is this! I will
not change my horse with any that treads but
on four pasterns. Ca, ha! he bounds from
the earth, as if his entrails were hairs; le
cheval volant, the Pegasus, chez les narines
de feu! When I bestride him, I soar, I am a
hawk: he trots the air; the earth sings when

he touches it; the basest horn of his hoof is
more musical than the pipe of Hermes.

Orl. He's of the color of the nutmeg. 20

Dau. And of the heat of the ginger. It is a
beast for Perseus: he is pure air and fire; and
the dull elements of earth and water never
appear in him, but only in patient stillness
while his rider mounts him: he is indeed a
horse; and all other jades you may call beasts.

Con. Indeed, my lord, it is a most absolute
and excellent horse.

Dau. It is the prince of palfreys; his
neigh is like the bidding of a monarch and
his countenance enforces homage. 31

Orl. No more, cousin.

Dau. Nay, the man hath no wit that cannot, from the rising of the lark to the lodging
of the lamb, vary deserved praise on my palfrey: it is a theme as fluent as the sea: turn
the sands into eloquent tongues, and my horse
is argument for them all: 'tis a subject for a
sovereign to reason on, and for a sovereign's
sovereign to ride on; and for the world, familiar to us and unknown to lay apart their
particular functions and wonder at him. I once
writ a sonnet in his praise and began thus:
'Wonder of nature,'—

Orl. I have heard a sonnet begin so to
one's mistress.

Dau. Then did they imitate that which I
composed to my courser, for my horse is my
mistress.

Orl. Your mistress bears well.

Dau. Me well; which is the prescript
praise and perfection of a good and particular
mistress.

Con. Nay, for methought yesterday your
mistress shrewdly shook your back.

Dau. So perhaps did yours.

Con. Mine was not bridled.

Dau. O then belike she was old and gentle;
and you rode, like a kern of Ireland, your
French hose off, and in your straight strossers.

Con. You have good judgment in horsemanship. 59

Dau. Be warned by me, then: they that
ride so and ride not warily, fall into foul bogs.
I had rather have my horse to my mistress.

Con. I had as lief have my mistress a jade.

Dau. I tell thee, constable, my mistress
wears his own hair.

Con. I could make as true a boast as that,
if I had a sow to my mistress.

Dau. 'Le chien est retourné à son propre
vomissement, et la truie lavée au bourbier;'
thou makest use of any thing. 70

Con. Yet do I not use my horse for my
mistress, or any such proverb so little kin to
the purpose.

Ram. My lord constable, the armor that I
saw in your tent to-night, are those stars or
suns upon it?

Con. Stars, my lord.

Dau. Some of them will fall to-morrow, I
hope.

Con. And yet my sky shall not want.

Dau. That may be, for you bear a many
superfluously, and 'twere more honor some
were away. 81

Con. Even as your horse bears your
praises; who would trot as well, were some
of your brags dismounted.

Dau. Would I were able to load him with

his desert! Will it never be day? I will trot to-morrow a mile, and my way shall be paved with English faces.

Con. I will not say so, for fear I should be faced out of my way: but I would it were morning; for I would fain be about the ears of the English.

Ram. Who will go to hazard with me for twenty prisoners?

Con. You must first go yourself to hazard, ere you have them.

Dau. 'Tis midnight; I'll go arm myself.
                                             [*Exit.*

Orl. The Dauphin longs for morning.

Ram. He longs to eat the English.

Con. I think he will eat all he kills.   100

Orl. By the white hand of my lady, he's a gallant prince.

Con. Swear by her foot, that she may tread out the oath.

Orl. He is simply the most active gentleman of France.

Con. Doing is activity; and he will still be doing.

Orl. He never did harm, that I heard of.

Con. Nor will do none to-morrow: he will keep that good name still.   111

Orl. I know him to be valiant.

Con. I was told that by one that knows him better than you.

Orl. What's he?

Con. Marry, he told me so himself; and he said he cared not who knew it.

Orl. He needs not; it is no hidden virtue in him.   119

Con. By my faith, sir, but it is; never any body saw it but his lackey: 'tis a hooded valor; and when it appears, it will bate.

Orl. Ill will never said well.

Con. I will cap that proverb with 'There is flattery in friendship.'

Orl. And I will take up that with 'Give the devil his due.'

Con. Well placed: there stands your friend for the devil: have at the very eye of that proverb with 'A pox of the devil.'   130

Orl. You are the better at proverbs, by how much 'A fool's bolt is soon shot.'

Con. You have shot over.

Orl. 'Tis not the first time you were over-shot.

Enter a Messenger.

Mess. My lord high constable, the English lie within fifteen hundred paces of your tents.

Con. Who hath measured the ground?

Mess. The Lord Grandpré.

Con. A valiant and most expert gentleman. Would it were day! Alas, poor Harry of England! he longs not for the dawning as we do.   141

Orl. What a wretched and peevish fellow is this king of England, to mope with his fat-brained followers so far out of his knowledge!

Con. If the English had any apprehension, they would run away.

Orl. That they lack; for if their heads had any intellectual armor, they could never wear such heavy head-pieces.   149

Ram. That island of England breeds very valiant creatures; their mastiffs are of un-matchable courage.

Orl. Foolish curs, that run winking into the mouth of a Russian bear and have their heads crushed like rotten apples! You may as well say, that's a valiant flea that dare eat his breakfast on the lip of a lion.

Con. Just, just; and the men do sympa-thize with the mastiffs in robustious and rough coming on, leaving their wits with their wives: and then give them great meals of beef and iron and steel, they will eat like wolves and fight like devils.

Orl. Ay, but these English are shrewdly out of beef.

Con. Then shall we find to-morrow they have only stomachs to eat and none to fight. Now is it time to arm: come, shall we about it?

Orl. It is now two o'clock: but, let me see, by ten
We shall have each a hundred Englishmen.
                                          [*Exeunt.*

ACT IV.

PROLOGUE.

Enter Chorus.

Chor. Now entertain conjecture of a time
When creeping murmur and the poring dark
Fills the wide vessel of the universe.
From camp to camp through the foul womb
    of night
The hum of either army stilly sounds,
That the fixed sentinels almost receive
The secret whispers of each other's watch:
Fire answers fire, and through their paly flames
Each battle sees the other's umber'd face;
Steed threatens steed, in high and boastful
    neighs   10
Piercing the night's dull ear, and from the tents
The armorers, accomplishing the knights,
With busy hammers closing rivets up,
Give dreadful note of preparation:
The country cocks do crow, the clocks do toll,
And the third hour of drowsy morning name.
Proud of their numbers and secure in soul,
The confident and over-lusty French
Do the low-rated English play at dice;
And chide the cripple tardy-gaited night   20
Who, like a foul and ugly witch, doth limp
So tediously away. The poor condemned Eng-
    lish,
Like sacrifices, by their watchful fires
Sit patiently and inly ruminate
The morning's danger, and their gesture sad
Investing lank-lean cheeks and war-worn coats
Presenteth them unto the gazing moon
So many horrid ghosts. O now, who will be-
    hold
The royal captain of this ruin'd band
Walking from watch to watch, from tent to
    tent,   30
Let him cry 'Praise and glory on his head!'
For forth he goes and visits all his host.
Bids them good morrow with a modest smile
And calls them brothers, friends and country-
    men.
Upon his royal face there is no note
How dread an army hath enrounded him;
Nor doth he dedicate one jot of color
Unto the weary and all-watched night,
But freshly looks and over-bears attaint
With cheerful semblance and sweet majesty;

That every wretch, pining and pale before,   41
Beholding him, plucks comfort from his looks :
A largess universal like the sun
His liberal eye doth give to every one,
Thawing cold fear, that mean and gentle all,
Behold, as may unworthiness define,
A little touch of Harry in the night.
And so our scene must to the battle fly ;
Where—O for pity !—we shall much disgrace
With four or five most vile and ragged foils,
Right ill-disposed in brawl ridiculous,   51
The name of Agincourt. Yet sit and see,
Minding true things by what their mockeries
    be.   [*Exit.*

SCENE I. *The English camp at Agincourt.*
   Enter KING HENRY, BEDFORD, *and*
          GLOUCESTER.

  K. Hen. Gloucester, 'tis true that we are in
    great danger ;
The greater therefore should our courage be.
Good morrow, brother Bedford. God Al-
    mighty !
There is some soul of goodness in things evil,
Would men observingly distil it out.
For our bad neighbor makes us early stirrers,
Which is both healthful and good husbandry :
Besides, they are our outward consciences,
And preachers to us all, admonishing
That we should dress us fairly for our end. 10
Thus may we gather honey from the weed,
And make a moral of the devil himself.

        Enter ERPINGHAM.

Good morrow, old Sir Thomas Erpingham :
A good soft pillow for that good white head
Were better than a churlish turf of France.
  Erp. Not so, my liege : this lodging likes
    me better,
Since I may say ' Now lie I like a king.'
  K. Hen. 'Tis good for men to love their
    present pains
Upon example ; so the spirit is eased :   19
And when the mind is quicken'd, out of doubt,
The organs, though defunct and dead before,
Break up their drowsy grave and newly move,
With casted slough and fresh legerity.
Lend me thy cloak, Sir Thomas. Brothers both,
Commend me to the princes in our camp ;
Do my good morrow to them, and anon
Desire them all to my pavilion.
  Glou. We shall, my liege.
  Erp. Shall I attend your grace ?
  K. Hen.   No, my good knight ;
Go with my brothers to my lords of England :
I and my bosom must debate awhile,   31
An.l then I would no other company.
  Erp. The Lord in heaven bless thee, noble
    Harry !   [*Exeunt all but King.*
  K. Hen. God-a-mercy, old heart ! thou
    speak'st cheerfully.

        Enter PISTOL.

  Pist. Qui va là ?
  K. Hen. A friend.
  Pist. Discuss unto me ; art thou officer ?
Or art thou base, common and popular ?
  K. Hen. I am a gentleman of a company.
  Pist. Trail'st thou the puissant pike ?   40
  K. Hen. Even so. What art you ?
  Pist. As good a gentleman as the emperor.
  K. Hen. Then you are a better than the
king.

  Pist. The king's a bawcock, and a heart of
    gold,
A lad of life, an imp of fame ;
Of parents good, of fist most valiant.
I kiss his dirty shoe, and from heart-string
I love the lovely bully. What is thy name ?
  K. Hen. Harry le Roy.
  Pist. Le Roy ! a Cornish name : art thou of
    Cornish crew ?   50
  K. Hen. No, I am a Welshman.
  Pist. Know'st thou Fluellen ?
  K. Hen. Yes.
  Pist. Tell him, I'll knock his leek about his
    pate
Upon Saint Davy's day.
  K. Hen. Do not you wear your dagger in
your cap that day, lest he knock that about
yours.
  Pist. Art thou his friend ?
  K. Hen. And his kinsman too.
  Pist. The figo for thee, then !   60
  K. Hen. I thank you : God be with you !
  Pist. My name is Pistol call'd.   [*Exit.*
  K. Hen. It sorts well with your fierceness.

     Enter FLUELLEN *and* GOWER.

  Gow. Captain Fluellen !
  Flu. So ! in the name of Jesu Christ, speak
lower. It is the greatest admiration of the universal world, when the true and aunchient
prerogatifes and laws of the wars is not kept :
if you would take the pains but to examine the
wars of Pompey the Great, you shall find, I
warrant you, that there is no tiddle taddle nor
pibble pabble in Pompey's camp ; I warrant
you, you shall find the ceremonies of the wars,
and the cares of it, and the forms of it, and
the sobriety of it, and the modesty of it, to be
otherwise.
  Gow. Why, the enemy is loud ; you hear
him all night.
  Flu. If the enemy is an ass and a fool and a
prating coxcomb, is it meet, think you, that we
should also, look you, be an ass and a fool and
a prating coxcomb ? in your own conscience,
now ?
  Gow. I will speak lower.
  Flu. I pray you and beseech you that you
will.   [*Exeunt Gower and Fluellen.*
  K. Hen. Though it appear a little out of
    fashion,
There is much care and valor in this Welsh-
    man.

Enter three soldiers, JOHN BATES, ALEXANDER
   COURT, *and* MICHAEL WILLIAMS.

  Court. Brother John Bates, is not that the
morning which breaks yonder ?
  Bates. I think it be : but we have no great
cause to desire the approach of day.   90
  Will. We see yonder the beginning of the
day, but I think we shall never see the end of
it. Who goes there ?
  K. Hen. A friend.
  Will. Under what captain serve you ?
  K. Hen. Under Sir Thomas Erpingham.
  Will. A good old commander and a most
kind gentleman : I pray you, what thinks he
of our estate ?
  K. Hen. Even as men wrecked upon a sand,
that look to be washed off the next tide.   101
  Bates. He hath not told his thought to the
king ?

K. Hen. No ; nor it is not meet he should. For, though I speak it to you, I think the king is but a man, as I am : the violet smells to him as it doth to me : the element shows to him as it doth to me ; all his senses have but human conditions : his ceremonies laid by, in his nakedness he appears but a man ; and though his affections are higher mounted than ours, yet, when they stoop, they stoop with the like wing. Therefore when he sees reason of fears, as we do, his fears, out of doubt, be of the same relish as ours are : yet, in reason, no man should possess him with any appearance of fear, lest he, by showing it, should dishearten his army.

Bates. He may show what outward courage he will ; but I believe, as cold a night as 'tis, he could wish himself in Thames up to the neck ; and so I would he were, and I by him, at all adventures, so we were quit here.

K. Hen. By my troth, I will speak my conscience of the king : I think he would not wish himself any where but where he is.

Bates. Then I would he were here alone ; so should he be sure to be ransomed, and a many poor men's lives saved.

K. Hen. I dare say you love him not so ill, to wish him here alone, howsoever you speak this to feel other men's minds : methinks I could not die any where so contented as in the king's company ; his cause being just and his quarrel honorable.

Will. That's more than we know.

Bates. Ay, or more than we should seek after ; for we know enough, if we know we are the king's subjects : if his cause be wrong, our obedience to the king wipes the crime of it out of us.

Will. But if the cause be not good, the king himself hath a heavy reckoning to make, when all those legs and arms and heads, chopped off in battle, shall join together at the latter day and cry all ' We died at such a place ; ' some swearing, some crying for a surgeon, some upon their wives left poor behind them, some upon the debts they owe, some upon their children rawly left. I am afeard there are few die well that die in a battle ; for how can they charitably dispose of any thing, when blood is their argument ? Now, if these men do not die well, it will be a black matter for the king that led them to it ; whom to disobey were against all proportion of subjection.

K. Hen. So, if a son that is by his father sent about merchandise do sinfully miscarry upon the sea, the imputation of his wickedness by your rule, should be imposed upon his father that sent him : or if a servant, under his master's command transporting a sum of money, be assailed by robbers and die in many irreconciled iniquities, you may call the business of the master the author of the servant's damnation : but this is not so : the king is not bound to answer the particular endings of his soldiers, the father of his son, nor the master of his servant ; for they purpose not their death, when they purpose their services. Besides, there is no king, be his cause never so spotless, if it come to the arbitrement of swords, can try it out with all unspotted soldiers : some peradventure have on them the guilt of premeditated and contrived murder ; some, of beguiling virgins with the broken seals of perjury ; some, making the wars their bulwark, that have before gored the gentle bosom of peace with pillage and robbery. Now, if these men have defeated the law and outrun native punishment, though they can outstrip men, they have no wings to fly from God : war is his beadle, war is his vengeance ; so that here men are punished for before-breach of the king's laws in now the king's quarrel : where they feared the death, they have borne life away ; and where they would be safe, they perish : then if they die unprovided, no more is the king guilty of their damnation than he was before guilty of those impieties for the which they are now visited. Every subject's duty is the king's ; but every subject's soul is his own. Therefore should every soldier in the wars do as every sick man in his bed, wash every mote out of his conscience : and dying so, death is to him advantage ; or not dying, the time was blessedly lost wherein such preparation was gained : and in him that escapes, it were not sin to think that, making God so free an offer, He let him outlive that day to see His greatness and to teach others how they should prepare.

Will. 'Tis certain, every man that dies ill, the ill upon his own head, the king is not to answer it.   199

Bates. But I do not desire he should answer for me ; and yet I determine to fight lustily for him.

K. Hen. I myself heard the king say he would not be ransomed.

Will. Ay, he said so, to make us fight cheerfully : but when our throats are cut, he may be ransomed, and we ne'er the wiser.

K. Hen. If I live to see it, I will never trust his word after.

Will. You pay him then. That's a perilous shot out of an elder-gun, that a poor and private displeasure can do against a monarch ! you may as well go about to turn the sun to ice with fanning in his face with a peacock's feather. You'll never trust his word after ! come, 'tis a foolish saying.

K. Hen. Your reproof is something too round : I should be angry with you, if the time were convenient.

Will. Let it be a quarrel between us, if you live.   220

K. Hen. I embrace it.

Will. How shall I know thee again ?

K. Hen. Give me any gage of thine, and I will wear it in my bonnet : then, if ever thou darest acknowledge it, I will make it my quarrel.

Will. Here's my glove : give me another of thine.

K. Hen. There.

Will. This will I also wear in my cap : if ever thou come to me and say, after to-morrow, ' This is my glove,' by this hand, I will take thee a box on the ear.

K. Hen. If ever I live to see it, I will challenge it.

Will. Thou darest as well be hanged.

K. Hen. Well, I will do it, though I take thee in the king's company.

Will. Keep thy word : fare thee well.

Bates. Be friends, you English fools, be friends : we have French quarrels enow, if you could tell how to reckon.   241

K. Hen. Indeed, the French may lay twenty
French crowns to one, they will beat us; for
they bear them on their shoulders: but it is no
English treason to cut French crowns, and to-
morrow the king himself will be a clipper.
                              [*Exeunt soldiers.*
Upon the king! let us our lives, our souls,
Our debts, our careful wives,
Our children and our sins lay on the king!
We must bear all. O hard condition,   250
Twin-born with greatness, subject to the breath
Of every fool, whose sense no more can feel
But his own wringing! What infinite heart's-
    ease
Must kings neglect, that private men enjoy!
And what have kings, that privates have not
    too,
Save ceremony, save general ceremony?
And what art thou, thou idle ceremony?
What kind of god art thou, that suffer'st more
Of mortal griefs than do thy worshippers?
What are thy rents? what are thy comings in?
O ceremony, show me but thy worth!   261
What is thy soul of adoration?
Art thou aught else but place, degree and form,
Creating awe and fear in other men?
Wherein thou art less happy being fear'd
Than they in fearing.
What drink'st thou oft, instead of homage
    sweet,
But poison'd flattery? O, be sick, great great-
    ness,
And bid thy ceremony give thee cure!
Think'st thou the fiery fever will go out   270
With titles blown from adulation?
Will it give place to flexure and low bending?
Canst thou, when thou command'st the beg-
    gar's knee,
Command the health of it? No, thou proud
    dream,
That play'st so subtly with a king's repose;
I am a king that find thee, and I know
'Tis not the balm, the sceptre and the ball,
The sword, the mace, the crown imperial,
The intertissued robe of gold and pearl,
The farced title running 'fore the king,   280
The throne he sits on, nor the tide of pomp
That beats upon the high shore of this world,
No, not all these, thrice-gorgeous ceremony,
Not all these, laid in bed majestical,
Can sleep so soundly as the wretched slave,
Who with a body fill'd and vacant mind
Gets him to rest, cramm'd with distressful
    bread;
Never sees horrid night, the child of hell,
But, like a lackey, from the rise to set
Sweats in the eye of Phœbus and all night   290
Sleeps in Elysium; next day after dawn,
Doth rise and help Hyperion to his horse,
And follows so the ever-running year,
With profitable labor, to his grave:
And, but for ceremony, such a wretch,
Winding up days with toil and nights with
    sleep,
Had the fore-hand and vantage of a king.
The slave, a member of the country's peace,
Enjoys it; but in gross brain little wots
What watch the king keeps to maintain the
    peace,   300
Whose hours the peasant best advantages.

Enter Erpingham.

Erp. My lord, your nobles, jealous of your
    absence,
Seek through your camp to find you.
    K. Hen.   Good old knight,
Collect them all together at my tent:
I'll be before thee.
    Erp.   I shall do't, my lord. [*Exit.*
    K. Hen. O God of battles! steel my sol-
        diers' hearts;
Possess them not with fear; take from them
    now
The sense of reckoning, if the opposed numbers
Pluck their hearts from them. Not to-day, O
    Lord,
O, not to-day, think not upon the fault   310
My father made in compassing the crown!
I Richard's body have interred anew;
And on it have bestow'd more contrite tears
Than from it issued forced drops of blood:
Five hundred poor I have in yearly pay,
Who twice a-day their wither'd hands hold up
Toward heaven, to pardon blood; and I have
    built
Two chantries, where the sad and solemn
    priests
Sing still for Richard's soul. More will I do;
Though all that I can do is nothing worth,   320
Since that my penitence comes after all,
Imploring pardon.

Enter Gloucester.

    Glou. My liege!
    K. Hen. My brother Gloucester's voice?
        Ay;
I know thy errand, I will go with thee:
The day, my friends and all things stay for me.
                              [*Exeunt.*

Scene II. *The French camp.*

Enter the Dauphin, Orleans, Rambures, *and
    others.*

    Orl. The sun doth gild our armor; up, my
        lords!
    Dau. Montez à cheval! My horse! varlet!
        laquais! ha!
    Orl. O brave spirit!
    Dau. Via! les eaux et la terre.
    Orl. Rien puis? l'air et la feu.
    Dau. Ciel, cousin Orleans.

Enter Constable.

Now, my lord constable!
    Con. Hark, how our steeds for present
        service neigh!
    Dau. Mount them, and make incision in
        their hides,   9
That their hot blood may spin in English eyes,
And dout them with superfluous courage, ha!
    Ram. What, will you have them weep our
        horses' blood?
How shall we, then, behold their natural tears?

Enter Messenger.

    Mess. The English are embattled, you
        French peers.
    Con. To horse, you gallant princes!
        straight to horse!
Do but behold yon poor and starved band,
And your fair show shall suck away their souls,
Leaving them but the shales and husks of men.
There is not work enough for all our hands;
Scarce blood enough in all their sickly veins 20
To give each naked curtle-axe a stain,

That our French gallants shall to-day draw
  out,
And sheathe for lack of sport : let us but blow
  on them,
The vapor of our valor will o'erturn them.
'Tis positive 'gainst all exceptions, lords,
That our superfluous lackeys and our peasants,
Who in unnecessary action swarm
About our squares of battle, were enow
To purge this field of such a hilding foe,
Though we upon this mountain's basis by   30
Took stand for idle speculation :
But that our honors must not. What's to say ?
A very little little let us do.
And all is done. Then let the trumpets sound
The tucket sonance and the note to mount ;
For our approach shall so much dare the field
That England shall couch down in fear and
  yield.

Enter GRANDPRE.

Grand. Why do you stay so long, my lords
  of France ?
Yon island carrions, desperate of their bones,
Ill-favoredly become the morning field :   40
Their ragged curtains poorly are let loose,
And our air shakes them passing scornfully :
Big Mars seems bankrupt in their beggar'd
  host
And faintly through a rusty beaver peeps :
The horsemen sit like fixed candlesticks,
With torch-staves in their hand ; and their
  poor jades
Lob down their heads, dropping the hides and
  hips,
The gum down-roping from their pale-dead
  eyes
And in their pale dull mouths the gimmal bit
Lies foul with chew'd grass, still and motion-
  less ;   50
And their executors, the knavish crows,
Fly o'er them, all impatient for their hour.
Description cannot suit itself in words
To demonstrate the life of such a battle
In life so lifeless as it shows itself.
Con. They have said their prayers, and
  they stay for death.
Dau. Shall we go send them dinners and
  fresh suits
And give their fasting horses provender,
And after fight with them ?
Con. I stay but for my guidon : to the
  field !   60
I will the banner from a trumpet take,
And use it for my haste. Come, come, away !
The sun is high, and we outwear the day.
                       [*Exeunt.*

SCENE III. *The English camp.*

Enter GLOUCESTER, BEDFORD, EXETER, ERPING-
HAM, *with all his host :* SALISBURY *and*
WESTMORELAND.

Glou. Where is the king ?
Bed. The king himself is rode to view their
  battle.
West. Of fighting men they have full three
  score thousand.
Exe. There's five to one ; besides, they all
  are fresh.
Sal. God's arm strike with us ! 'tis a fearful
  odds.
God be wi' you, princes all ; I'll to my charge :
If we no more meet till we meet in heaven,

Then, joyfully, my noble Lord of Bedford,
My dear Lord Gloucester, and my good Lord
  Exeter,
And my kind kinsman, warriors all, adieu ! 10
Bed. Farewell, good Salisbury ; and good
  luck go with thee !
Exe. Farewell, kind lord ; fight valiantly
  to-day :
And yet I do thee wrong to mind thee of it,
For thou art framed of the firm truth of valor.
                    [*Exit Salisbury.*
Bed. He is full of valor as of kindness ;
Princely in both.

Enter the KING.

West.   O that we now had here
But one ten thousand of those men in Eng-
  land
That do no work to-day !
K. Hen.   What's he that wishes so ?
My cousin Westmoreland ? No, my fair
  cousin :
If we are mark'd to die, we are enow   20
To do our country loss ; and if to live,
The fewer men, the greater share of honor.
God's will ! I pray thee, wish not one man
  more.
By Jove, I am not covetous for gold,
Nor care I who doth feed upon my cost ;
It yearns me not if men my garments wear ;
Such outward things dwell not in my desires :
But if it be a sin to covet honor,
I am the most offending soul alive.
No, faith, my coz, wish not a man from Eng-
  land :   30
God's peace ! I would not lose so great an
  honor
As one man more, methinks, would share from
  me
For the best hope I have. O, do not wish one
  more !
Rather proclaim it, Westmoreland, through my
  host,
That he which hath no stomach to this fight,
Let him depart ; his passport shall be made
And crowns for convoy put into his purse :
We would not die in that man's company
That fears his fellowship to die with us.
This day is called the feast of Crispian : 40
He that outlives this day, and comes safe
  home,
Will stand a tip-toe when the day is named,
And rouse him at the name of Crispian.
He that shall live this day, and see old age,
Will yearly on the vigil feast his neighbors,
And say 'To-morrow is Saint Crispian :'
Then will he strip his sleeve and show his
  scars.
And say 'These wounds I had on Crispin's
  day.'
Old men forget : yet all shall be forgot,
But he'll remember with advantages   50
What feats he did that day : then shall our
  names,
Familiar in his mouth as household words
Harry the king, Bedford and Exeter,
Warwick and Talbot, Salisbury and Gloucester,
Be in their flowing cups freshly remember'd.
This story shall the good man teach his son ;
And Crispin Crispian shall ne'er go by,
From this day to the ending of the world,
But we in it shall be remember'd ;
We few, we happy few, we band of brothers ;

For he to-day that sheds his blood with me
Shall be my brother; be he ne'er so vile,
This day shall gentle his condition:
And gentlemen in England now a-bed
Shall think themselves accursed they were not
    here,
And hold their manhoods cheap whiles any
    speaks
That fought with us upon Saint Crispin's day.

         Re-enter SALISBURY.

  Sal. My sovereign lord, bestow yourself
    with speed:
The French are bravely in their battles set,
And will with all expedience charge on us.   70
  K. Hen. All things are ready, if our minds
    be so.
  West. Perish the man whose mind is back-
    ward now!
  K. Hen. Thou dost not wish more help
    from England, coz?
  West. God's will! my liege, would you and
    I alone,
Without more help, could fight this royal
    battle!
  K. Hen. Why, now thou hast unwish'd five
    thousand men;
Which likes me better than to wish us one.
You know your places: God be with you all!

     Tucket. Enter MONTJOY.

  Mont. Once more I come to know of thee,
    King Harry,
If for thy ransom thou wilt now compound, 80
Before thy most assured overthrow:
For certainly thou art so near the gulf,
Thou needs must be englutted. Besides, in
    mercy,
The constable desires thee thou wilt mind
Thy followers of repentance; that their souls
May make a peaceful and a sweet retire
From off these fields, where, wretches, their
    poor bodies
Must lie and fester.
  K. Hen.   Who hath sent thee now?
  Mont. The Constable of France.
  K. Hen. I pray thee, bear my former an-
    swer back: 90
Bid them achieve me and then sell my bones.
Good God! why should they mock poor fel-
    lows thus?
The man that once did sell the lion's skin
While the beast lived, was killed with hunting
    him.
A many of our bodies shall no doubt
Find native graves; upon the which, I trust,
Shall witness live in brass of this day's work:
And those that leave their valiant bones in
    France,
Dying like men, though buried in your dung-
    hills,
They shall be famed; for there the sun shall
    greet them,   100
And draw their honors reeking up to heaven;
Leaving their earthly parts to choke your
    clime,
The smell whereof shall breed a plague in
    France.
Mark then abounding valor in our English,
That being dead, like to the bullet's grazing,
Break out into a second course of mischief,
Killing in relapse of mortality.
Let me speak proudly: tell the constable

We are but warriors for the working-day;
Our gayness and our gilt are all besmirch'd
With rainy marching in the painful field; 111
There's not a piece of feather in our host—
Good argument, I hope, we will not fly—
And time hath worn us into slovenry:
But, by the mass, our hearts are in the trim;
And my poor soldiers tell me, yet ere night
They'll be in fresher robes, or they will pluck
The gay new coats o'er the French soldiers'
    heads
And turn them out of service. If they do this,—
As, if God please, they shall,—my ransom then
Will soon be levied. Herald, save thou thy
    labor;   121
Come thou no more for ransom, gentle herald:
They shall have none, I swear, but these my
    joints;
Which if they have as I will leave 'em them,
Shall yield them little, tell the constable.
  Mont. I shall, King Harry. And so fare
    thee well:
Thou never shalt hear herald any more. [*Exit.*
  K. Hen. I fear thou 'lt once more come
    again for ransom.

           Enter YORK.

  York. My lord, most humbly on my knee I
    beg
The leading of the vaward.   130
  K. Hen. Take it, brave York. Now, sol-
    diers, march away:
And how thou pleasest, God, dispose the day!
                         [*Exeunt.*

    SCENE IV. *The field of battle.*

Alarum. Excursions. Enter PISTOL, French
    Soldier, *and* Boy.

  Pist. Yield, cur!
  Fr. Sol. Je pense que vous êtes gentilhomme
de bonne qualité.
  Pist. Qualtitie calmie custure me! Art thou
a gentleman? what is thy name? discuss.
  Fr. Sol. O Seigneur Dieu!
  Pist. O, Signieur Dew should be a gentle-
man:
Perpend my words, O Signieur Dew, and
    mark;
O Signieur Dew, thou diest on point of fox,
Except, O signieur, thou do give to me   10
Egregious ransom.
  Fr. Sol. O, prenez miséricorde! ayez pitié
de moi!
  Pist. Moy shall not serve; I will have forty
    moys;
Or I will fetch thy rim out at thy throat
In drops of crimson blood.
  Fr. Sol. Est-il impossible d'échapper la
force de ton bras?
  Pist. Brass, cur!
Thou damned and luxurious mountain goat, 20
Offer'st me brass?
  Fr. Sol. O pardonnez moi!
  Pist. Say'st thou me so? is that a ton of
    moys?
Come hither, boy: ask me this slave in French
What is his name.
  Boy. Ecoutez: comment êtes-vous appelé?
  Fr. Sol. Monsieur le Fer.
  Boy. He says his name is Master Fer.
  Pist. Master Fer! I'll fer him, and firk
him, and ferret him: discuss the same in
French unto him.   31

Boy. I do not know the French for fer, and ferret, and firk.

Pist. Bid him prepare; for I will cut his throat.

Fr. Sol. Que dit-il, monsieur?

Boy. Il me commande de vous dire que vous faites vous prêt; car ce soldat ici est disposé tout à cette heure de couper votre gorge.

Pist. Owy, cuppele gorge, permafoy, Peasant, unless thou give me crowns, brave crowns;   40
Or mangled shalt thou be by this my sword.

Fr. Sol. O, je vous supplie, pour l'amour de Dieu, me pardonner! Je suis gentilhomme de bonne maison: gardez ma vie, et je vous donnerai deux cents écus.

Pist. What are his words?

Boy. He prays you to save his life: he is a gentleman of a good house; and for his ransom he will give you two hundred crowns.

Pist. Tell him my fury shall abate, and I The crowns will take.   51

Fr. Sol. Petit monsieur, que dit-il?

Boy. Encore qu'il est contre son jurement de pardonner aucun prisonnier, néanmoins, pour les écus que vous l'avez promis, il est content de vous donner la liberté, le franchisement.

Fr. Sol. Sur mes genoux je vous donne mille remercîmens; et je m'estime heureux que je suis tombé entre les mains d'un chevalier, je pense, le plus brave, vaillant, et très distingué seigneur d'Angleterre.   61

Pist. Expound unto me, boy.

Boy. He gives you, upon his knees, a thousand thanks; and he esteems himself happy that he hath fallen into the hands of one, as he thinks, the most brave, valorous, and thrice-worthy signieur of England.

Pist. As I suck blood, I will some mercy show.
Follow me!   69

Boy. Suivez-vous le grand capitaine.
[*Exeunt Pistol, and French Soldier.*] I did never know so full a voice issue from so empty a heart: but the saying is true, 'The empty vessel makes the greatest sound.' Bardolph and Nym had ten times more valor than this roaring devil i' the old play, that every one may pare his nails with a wooden dagger; and they are both hanged; and so would this be, if he durst steal any thing adventurously. I must stay with the lackeys, with the luggage of our camp: the French might have a good prey of us, if he knew of it; for there is none to guard it but boys.   [*Exit.*

SCENE V. *Another part of the field.*

Enter CONSTABLE, ORLEANS, BOURBON, DAUPHIN, *and* RAMBURES.

Con. O diable!

Orl. O seigneur! le jour est perdu, tout est perdu!

Dau. Mort de ma vie! all is confounded, all!
Reproach and everlasting shame
Sits mocking in our plumes. O méchante fortune!
Do not run away.   [*A short alarum.*

Con. Why, all our ranks are broke.

Dau. O perdurable shame! let's stab ourselves.

Be these the wretches that we play'd at dice for?

Orl. Is this the king we sent to for his ransom?

Bour. Shame and eternal shame, nothing but shame!   10
Let us die in honor: once more back again;
And he that will not follow Bourbon now,
Let him go hence, and with his cap in hand,
Like a base pander, hold the chamber-door
Whilst by a slave, no gentler than my dog,
His fairest daughter is contaminated.

Con. Disorder, that hath spoil'd us, friend us now!
Let us on heaps go offer up our lives.

Orl. We are enow yet living in the field
To smother up the English in our throngs,   20
If any order might be thought upon.

Bour. The devil take order now! I'll to the throng:
Let life be short; else shame will be too long.
[*Exeunt.*

SCENE VI. *Another part of the field.*

Alarums. Enter KING HENRY *and forces,* EXETER, *and others.*

K. Hen. Well have we done, thrice valiant countrymen:
But all's not done; yet keep the French the field.

Exe. The Duke of York commends him to your majesty.

K. Hen. Lives he, good uncle? thrice within this hour
I saw him down; thrice up again and fighting;
From helmet to the spur all blood he was.

Exe. In which array, brave soldier, doth he lie,
Larding the plain; and by his bloody side,
Yoke-fellow to his honor-owing wounds,
The noble Earl of Suffolk also lies.   10
Suffolk first died: and York, all haggled over,
Comes to him, where in gore he lay insteep'd,
And takes him by the beard; kisses the gashes
That bloodily did yawn upon his face;
And cries aloud 'Tarry, dear cousin Suffolk!
My soul shall thine keep company to heaven;
Tarry, sweet soul, for mine, then fly abreast,
As in this glorious and well-foughten field
We kept together in our chivalry!'   19
Upon these words I came and cheer'd him up:
He smiled me in the face, raught me his hand,
And, with a feeble gripe, says 'Dear my lord,
Commend my service to my sovereign.'
So did he turn and over Suffolk's neck
He throws his wounded arm and kiss'd his lips;
And so espoused to death, with blood he seal'd
A testament of noble-ending love.
The pretty and sweet manner of it forced
Those waters from me which I would have stopp'd;
But I had not so much of man in me,   30
And all my mother came into mine eyes
And gave me up to tears.

K. Hen.   I blame you not;
For, hearing this, I must perforce compound
With mistful eyes, or they will issue too.
[*Alarum.*
But, hark! what new alarum is this same?
The French have reinforced their scatter'd men:
Then every soldier kill his prisoners:
Give the word through.   [*Exeunt.*

SCENE VII. *Another part of the field.*
Enter FLUELLEN *and* GOWER.

Flu. Kill the poys and the luggage ! 'tis expressly against the law of arms : 'tis as arrant
a piece of knavery, mark you now, as can be
offer't ; in your conscience, now, is it not ?

Gow. 'Tis certain there's not a boy left
alive ; and the cowardly rascals that ran from
the battle ha' done this slaughter : besides, they
have burned and carried away all that was in
the king's tent ; wherefore the king, most
worthily, hath caused every soldier to cut his
prisoner's throat. O, 'tis a gallant king ! 11

Flu. Ay, he was porn at Monmouth, Captain Gower. What call you the town's name
where Alexander the Pig was born !

Gow. Alexander the Great.

Flu. Why, I pray you, is not pig great ? the
pig, or the great, or the mighty, or the huge, or
the magnanimous, are all one reckonings, save
the phrase is a little variations. 19

Gow. I think Alexander the Great was
born in Macedon ; his father was called Philip
of Macedon, as I take it.

Flu. I think it is in Macedon where Alexander is porn. I tell you, captain, if you look in
the maps of the 'orld, I warrant you sall find,
in the comparisons between Macedon and
Monmouth, that the situations, look you, is
both alike. There is a river in Macedon ; and
there is also moreover a river at Monmouth :
it is called Wye at Monmouth ; but it is out of
my prains what is the name of the other river ;
but 'tis all one, 'tis alike as my fingers is to my
fingers, and there is salmons in both. If you
mark Alexander's life well, Harry of Monmouth's life is come after it indifferent well ;
for there is figures in all things. Alexander,
God knows, and you know, in his rages, and
his furies, and his wraths, and his cholers, and
his moods, and his displeasures, and his indig-
nations, and also being a little intoxicates in
his prains, did, in his ales and his angers, look
you, kill his best friend, Cleitus. 41

Gow. Our king is not like him in that : he
never killed any of his friends.

Flu. It is not well done, mark you now, to
take the tales out of my mouth, ere it is made
and finished. I speak but in the figures and
comparisons of it : as Alexander killed his
friend Cleitus, being in his ales and his cups ;
so also Harry Monmouth, being in his right
wits and his good judgments, turned away the
fat knight with the great belly-doublet : he was
full of jests, and gipes, and knaveries, and
mocks ; I have forgot his name.

Gow. Sir John Falstaff.

Flu. That is he : I'll tell you there is good
men porn at Monmouth.

Gow. Here comes his majesty.

Alarum. Enter KING HENRY, *and forces ;*
WARWICK, GLOUCESTER, EXETER, *and others.*

K. Hen. I was not angry since I came to
France
Until this instant. Take a trumpet, herald ;
Ride thou unto the horsemen on yon hill : 60
If they will fight with us, bid them come down,
Or void the field ; they do offend our sight :
If they'll do neither, we will come to them,
And make them skirr away, as swift as stones

Enforced from the old Assyrian slings :
Besides, we'll cut the throats of those we have,
And not a man of them that we shall take
Shall taste our mercy. Go and tell them so.

Enter MONTJOY.

Exe. Here comes the herald of the French,
my liege.

Glo. His eyes are humbler than they used
to be. 70

K. Hen. How now ! what means this, herald ? know'st thou not
That I have fined these bones of mine for ransom ?
Comest thou again for ransom ?

Mont. No, great king :
I come to thee for charitable license,
That we may wander o'er this bloody field
To look our dead, and then to bury them ;
To sort our nobles from our common men.
For many of our princes—woe the while !—
Lie drown'd and soak'd in mercenary blood ;
So do our vulgar drench their peasant limbs 80
In blood of princes ; and their wounded steeds
Fret fetlock deep in gore and with wild rage
Yerk out their armed heels at their dead mas-
ters,
Killing them twice. O, give us leave, great king,
To view the field in safety and dispose
Of their dead bodies !

K. Hen. I tell thee truly, herald,
I know not if the day be ours or no ;
For yet a many of your horsemen peer
And gallop o'er the field.

Mont. The day is yours.

K. Hen. Praised be God, and not our
strength, for it ! 90
What is this castle call'd that stands hard by ?

Mont. They call it Agincourt.

K. Hen. Then call we this the field of
Agincourt,
Fought on the day of Crispin Crispianus.

Flu. Your grandfather of famous memory,
an't please your majesty, and your great-uncle
Edward the Plack Prince of Wales, as I have
read in the chronicles, fought a most prave
pattle here in France.

K. Hen. They did, Fluellen. 100

Flu. Your majesty says very true : if your
majesties is remembered of it, the Welshmen
did good service in a garden where leeks did
grow, wearing leeks in their Monmouth caps ;
which, your majesty know, to this hour is an
honorable badge of the service ; and I do believe your majesty takes no scorn to wear the
leek upon Saint Tavy's day.

K. Hen. I wear it for a memorable honor ;
For I am Welsh, you know, good countryman.

Flu. All the water in Wye cannot wash
your majesty's Welsh plood out of your pody,
I can tell you that : God pless it and preserve
it, as long as it pleases his grace, and his majesty too !

K. Hen. Thanks, good my countryman.

Flu. By Jeshu, I am your majesty's countryman, I care not who know it ; I will confess it to all the 'orld : I need not to be
ashamed of your majesty, praised be God, so
long as your majesty is an honest man. 120

K. Hen. God keep me so ! Our heralds go
with him :
Bring me just notice of the numbers dead

On both our parts. Call yonder fellow hither.
[*Points to Williams. Exeunt Heralds
with Montjoy.*
Exe. Soldier, you must come to the king.
K. Hen. Soldier, why wearest thou that
glove in thy cap ?
Will. An't please your majesty, 'tis the
gage of one that I should fight withal, if he be
alive.
K. Hen. An Englishman ?   129
Will. An't please your majesty, a rascal
that swaggered with me last night ; who, if
alive and ever dare to challenge this glove, I
have sworn to take him a box o' th' ear : or if
I can see my glove in his cap, which he swore,
as he was a soldier, he would wear if alive, I
will strike it out soundly.
K. Hen. What think you, Captain Fluellen ?
is it fit this soldier keep his oath ?
Flu. He is a craven and a villain else, an't
please your majesty, in my conscience.   140
K. Hen. It may be his enemy is a gentleman of great sort, quite from the answer of his
degree.
Flu. Though he be as good a gentleman as
the devil is, as Lucifer and Belzebub himself,
it is necessary, look your grace, that he keep
his vow and his oath : if he be perjured, see
you now, his reputation is as arrant a villain
and a Jacksauce, as ever his black shoe trod
upon God's ground and his earth, in my conscience, la !   150
K. Hen. Then keep thy vow, sirrah, when
thou meetest the fellow.
Will. So I will, my liege, as I live.
K. Hen. Who servest thou under ?
Will. Under Captain Gower, my liege.
Flu. Gower is a good captain, and is good
knowledge and literatured in the wars.
K. Hen. Call him hither to me, soldier.
Will. I will, my liege.   [*Exit.*
K. Hen. Here, Fluellen ; wear thou this
favor for me and stick it in thy cap : when
Alençon and myself were down together, I
plucked this glove from his helm : if any man
challenge this, he is a friend to Alençon, and
an enemy to our person ; if thou encounter
any such, apprehend him, an thou dost me
love.
Flu. Your grace doo's me as great honors
as can be desired in the hearts of his subjects :
I would fain see the man, that has but two
legs, that shall find himself aggrieved at this
glove ; that is all ; but I would fain see it
once, an please God of his grace that I might
see.
K. Hen. Knowest thou Gower ?
Flu. He is my dear friend, an please you.
K. Hen. Pray thee, go seek him, and bring
him to my tent.
Flu. I will fetch him.   [*Exit.*
K. Hen. My Lord of Warwick, and my
brother Gloucester,
Follow Fluellen closely at the heels :
The glove which I have given him for a favor
May haply purchase him a box o' th' ear ; 181
It is the soldier's ; I by bargain should
Wear it myself. Follow, good cousin War-
wick :
If that the soldier strike him, as I judge
By his blunt bearing he will keep his word,
Some sudden mischief may arise of it ;
For I do know Fluellen valiant

And, touched with choler, hot as gunpowder,
And quickly will return an injury :
Follow, and see there be no harm between
them.   190
Go you with me, uncle of Exeter.   [*Exeunt.*

SCENE VIII. *Before* KING HENRY'S *pavilion.*

Enter GOWER *and* WILLIAMS.

Will. I warrant it is to knight you, captain.

Enter FLUELLEN.

Flu. God's will and his pleasure, captain,
I beseech you now, come apace to the king :
there is more good toward you peradventure
than is in your knowledge to dream of.
Will. Sir, know you this glove ?
Flu. Know the glove ! I know the glove is
a glove.
Will. I know this ; and thus I challenge it.
                    [*Strikes him.*
Flu. 'Sblood ! an arrant traitor as any is
in the universal world, or in France, or in
England !   11
Gow. How now, sir ! you villain !
Will. Do you think I'll be forsworn ?
Flu. Stand away, Captain Gower ; I will
give treason his payment into plows, I warrant
you.
Will. I am no traitor.
Flu. That's a lie in thy throat. I charge
you in his majesty's name, apprehend him :
he's a friend of the Duke Alençon's.   19

Enter WARWICK *and* GLOUCESTER.

War. How now, how now ! what's the
matter ?
Flu. My Lord of Warwick, here is—
praised be God for it !—a most contagious
treason come to light, look you, as you shall
desire in a summer's day. Here is his majesty.

Enter KING HENRY *and* EXETER.

K. Hen. How now ! what's the matter ?
Flu. My liege, here is a villain and a traitor, that, look your grace, has struck the glove
which your majesty is take out of the helmet
of Alençon.
Will. My liege, this was my glove ; here is
the fellow of it ; and he that I gave it to in
change promised to wear it in his cap : I
promised to strike him, if he did : I met this
man with my glove in his cap, and I have been
as good as my word.
Flu. Your majesty hear now, saving your
majesty's manhood, what an arrant, rascally,
beggarly, lousy knave it is : I hope your majesty is pear me testimony and witness, and
will avouchment, that this is the glove of
Alençon, that your majesty is give me ; in
your conscience, now ?   40
K. Hen. Give me thy glove, soldier : look,
here is the fellow of it.
'Twas I, indeed, thou promised'st to strike ;
And thou hast given me most bitter terms.
Flu. An please your majesty, let his neck
answer for it, if there is any martial law in the
world.
K. Hen. How canst thou make me satisfaction ?
Will. All offences, my lord, come from the
heart : never came any from mine that might
offend your majesty.   51
K. Hen. It was ourself thou didst abuse.

Will. Your majesty came not like yourself :
you appeared to me but as a common man ;
witness the night, your garments, your lowliness ; and what your highness suffered under
that shape, I beseech you take it for your own
fault and not mine : for had you been as I
took you for, I made no offence ; therefore, I
beseech your highness, pardon me.   60
K. Hen. Here, uncle Exeter, fill this glove
      with crowns,
And give it to this fellow. Keep it, fellow ;
And wear it for an honor in thy cap
Till I do challenge it. Give him the crowns :
And, captain, you must needs be friends with
      him.
Flu. By this day and this light, the fellow
has mettle enough in his belly. Hold, there
is twelve pence for you ; and I pray you to
serve Got, and keep you out of prawls, and
prabbles, and quarrels, and dissensions, and, I
warrant you, it is the better for you.   71
Will. I will none of your money.
Flu. It is with a good will ; I can tell you,
it will serve you to mend your shoes : come,
wherefore should you be so pashful ? your
shoes is not so good : 'tis a good silling, I warrant you, or I will change it.

      Enter an English Herald.

K. Hen. Now, herald, are the dead num-
      ber'd ?
Her. Here is the number of the slaughter'd
      French.
K. Hen. What prisoners of good sort are
      taken, uncle ?   80
Exe. Charles Duke of Orleans, nephew to
      the king ;
John Duke of Bourbon, and Lord Bouciqualt :
Of other lords and barons, knights and squires,
Full fifteen hundred, besides common men.
K. Hen. This note doth tell me of ten thou-
      sand French
That in the field lie slain : of princes, in this
      number,
And nobles bearing banners, there lie dead
One hundred twenty six : added to these,
Of knights, esquires, and gallant gentlemen, 89
Eight thousand and four hundred ; of the
      which,
Five hundred were but yesterday dubb'd
      knights :
So that, in these ten thousand they have lost,
There are but sixteen hundred mercenaries ;
The rest are princes, barons, lords, knights,
      squires,
And gentlemen of blood and quality.
The names of those their nobles that lie dead :
Charles Delabreth, high constable of France ;
Jaques of Chatillon, admiral of France;
The master of the cross-bows, Lord Rambures ;
Great Master of France, the brave Sir Gui-
      chard Dolphin,   100
John Duke of Alençon, Anthony Duke of Bra-
      bant,
The brother of the Duke of Burgundy,
And Edward Duke of Bar : of lusty earls,
Grandpré and Roussi, Fauconberg and Foix,
Beaumont and Marle, Vaudemont and Les-
      trale.
Here was a royal fellowship of death !
Where is the number of our English dead ?
      [*Herald shews him another paper.*
Edward the Duke of York, the Earl of Suffolk,

Sir Richard Ketly, Davy Gam, esquire :
None else of name ; and of all other men 110
But five and twenty. O God, thy arm was
      here ;
And not to us, but to thy arm alone,
Ascribe we all ! When, without stratagem,
But in plain shock and even play of battle,
Was ever known so great and little loss
On one part and on the other ? Take it, God,
For it is none but thine !
Exe.   'Tis wonderful !
K. Hen. Come, go we in procession to the
      village.
And be it death proclaimed through our host
To boast of this or take the praise from God
Which is his only.   121
Flu. Is it not lawful, an please your maj-
      esty, to tell how many is killed ?
K. Hen. Yes, captain ; but with this ac-
      knowledgment,
That God fought for us.
Flu. Yes, my conscience, he did us great
      good.
K. Hen. Do we all holy rites ;
Let there be sung 'Non nobis' and 'Te
      Deum ; '
The dead with charity enclosed in clay :
And then to Calais ; and to England then : 130
Where ne'er from France arrived more happy
      men.   [*Exeunt.*

      _____

      ACT V.

      PROLOGUE.

      Enter Chorus.

Chor. Vouchsafe to those that have not
      read the story,
That I may prompt them : and of such as
      have,
I humbly pray them to admit the excuse
Of time, of numbers and due course of things,
Which cannot in their huge and proper life
Be here presented. Now we bear the king
Toward Calais : grant him there ; there seen,
Heave him away upon your winged thoughts
Athwart the sea. Behold, the English beach
Pales in the flood with men, with wives and
      boys,   10
Whose shouts and claps out-voice the deep-
      mouth'd sea,
Which like a mighty whiffler 'fore the king
Seems to prepare his way : so let him land,
And solemnly see him set on to London.
So swift a pace hath thought that even now
You may imagine him upon Blackheath ;
Where that his lords desire him to have borne
His bruised helmet and his bended sword
Before him through the city : he forbids it, 19
Being free from vainness and self-glorious
      pride ;
Giving full trophy, signal and ostent
Quite from himself to God. But now behold,
In the quick forge and working-house of
      thought,
How London doth pour out her citizens !
The mayor and all his brethren in best sort,
Like to the senators of the antique Rome,
With the plebeians swarming at their heels,
Go forth and fetch their conquering Cæsar in :
As, by a lower but loving likelihood,   29
Were now the general of our gracious empress,

As in good time he may, from Ireland coming,
Bringing rebellion broached on his sword,
How many would the peaceful city quit,
To welcome him ! much more, and much more
    cause,
Did they this Harry. Now in London place
    him ;
As yet the lamentation of the French
Invites the King of England's stay at home ;
The emperor's coming in behalf of France,
To order peace between them ; and omit
All the occurrences, whatever chanced,   40
Till Harry's back-return again to France :
There must we bring him ; and myself have
    play'd
The interim, by remembering you 'tis past.
Then brook abridgment, and your eyes ad-
    vance,
After your thoughts, straight back again to
    France.   [Exit.

SCENE I. France. The English camp.

Enter FLUELLEN and GOWER.

Gow. Nay, that's right ; but why wear you
your leek to-day ? Saint Davy's day is past.
    Flu. There is occasions and causes why and
wherefore in all things : I will tell you, asse
my friend, Captain Gower : the rascally, scald,
beggarly, lousy, pragging knave, Pistol, which
you and yourself and all the world know to be
no petter than a fellow, look you now, of no
merits, he is come to me and prings me pread
and salt yesterday, look you, and bid me eat
my leek : it was in a place where I could not
breed no contention with him ; but I will be
so bold as to wear it in my cap till I see him
once again, and then I will tell him a little
piece of my desires.

Enter PISTOL.

Gow. Why, here he comes, swelling like a
turkey-cock.
    Flu. 'Tis no matter for his swellings nor
his turkey-cocks. God pless you, Aunchient
Pistol ! you scurvy, lousy knave, God pless
you !
    Pist. Ha ! art thou bedlam ? dost thou   20
thirst, base Trojan,
To have me fold up Parca's fatal web ?
Hence ! I am qualmish at the smell of leek.
    Flu. I peseech you heartily, scurvy, lousy
knave, at my desires, and my requests, and my
petitions, to eat, look you, this leek : because,
look you, you do not love it, nor your affections and your appetites and your digestions
doo's not agree with it, I would desire you to
eat it.
    Pist. Not for Cadwallader and all his
    goats.
    Flu. There is one goat for you.   30
                            [Strikes him.]
Will you be so good, scauld knave, as eat it ?
    Pist. Base Trojan, thou shalt die.
    Flu. You say very true, scauld knave, when
God's will is : I will desire you to live in the
mean time, and eat your victuals : come, there
is sauce for it. [Strikes him.] You called
me yesterday mountain-squire ; but I will make
you to-day a squire of low degree. I pray you,
fall to : if you can mock a leek, you can eat a
leek.
    Gow. Enough, captain : you have aston-
ished him.   41

    Flu. I say, I will make him eat some part
of my leek, or I will peat his pate four days.
Bite, I pray you ; it is good for your green
wound and your ploody coxcomb.
    Pist. Must I bite ?
    Flu. Yes, certainly, and out of doubt and
out of question too, and ambiguities.
    Pist. By this leek, I will most horribly re-
venge : I eat and eat, I swear—   50
    Flu. Eat, I pray you : will you have some
more sauce to your leek ? there is not enough
leek to swear by.
    Pist. Quiet thy cudgel ; thou dost see I eat.
    Flu. Much good do you, scauld knave,
heartily. Nay, pray you, throw none away ;
the skin is good for your broken coxcomb.
When you take occasions to see leeks hereafter, I pray you, mock at 'em ; that is all.
    Pist. Good.   60
    Flu. Ay, leeks is good : hold you, there is
a groat to heal your pate.
    Pist. Me a groat !
    Flu. Yes, verily and in truth, you shall
take it ; or I have another leek in my pocket,
which you shall eat.
    Pist. I take thy groat in earnest of revenge.
    Flu. If I owe you any thing, I will pay you
in cudgels : you shall be a woodmonger, and
buy nothing of me but cudgels. God b' wi'
you, and keep you, and heal your pate.   71
                                        [Exit.
    Pist. All hell shall stir for this.
    Gow. Go, go ; you are a counterfeit cow-
ardly knave. Will you mock at an ancient
tradition, begun upon an honorable respect,
and worn as a memorable trophy of prede-
ceased valor and dare not avouch in your
deeds any of your words ? I have seen you
gleeking and galling at this gentleman twice or
thrice. You thought, because he could not
speak English in the native garb, he could not
therefore handle an English cudgel : you find
it otherwise ; and henceforth let a Welsh correction teach you a good English condition.
Fare ye well.   [Exit.
    Pist. Doth Fortune play the huswife with
        me now ?
News have I, that my Nell is dead i' the spital
Of malady of France ;
And there my rendezvous is quite cut off.
Old I do wax ; and from my weary limbs
Honor is cudgelled. Well, bawd I'll turn,   90
And something lean to cutpurse of quick hand.
To England will I steal, and there I'll steal :
And patches will I get unto these cudgell'd
        scars,
And swear I got them in the Gallia wars. [Exit.

SCENE II. France. A royal palace.

Enter, at one door, KING HENRY, EXETER,
    BEDFORD, GLOUCESTER, WARWICK, WEST-
    MORELAND, and other Lords ; at another, the
    FRENCH KING, QUEEN ISABEL, the PRINCESS
    KATHARINE, ALICE and other Ladies ; the
    DUKE OF BURGUNDY, and his train.

    K. Hen. Peace to this meeting, wherefore
        we are met !
Unto our brother France, and to our sister,
Health and fair time of day ; joy and good
        wishes
To our most fair and princely cousin Kath-
        arine ;
And, as a branch and member of this royalty,

By whom this great assembly is contrived,
We do salute you, Duke of Burgundy;
And, princes French, and peers, health to you
   all!
  Fr. King. Right joyous are we to behold
   your face,
Most worthy brother England; fairly met: 10
So are you, princes English, every one.
  Q. Isa. So happy be the issue, brother Eng-
   land,
Of this good day and of this gracious meeting,
As we are now glad to behold your eyes;
Your eyes, which hitherto have borne in them
Against the French, that met them in their
   bent,
The fatal balls of murdering basilisks:
The venom of such looks, we fairly hope,
Have lost their quality, and that this day
Shall change all griefs and quarrels into love.
  K. Hen. To cry amen to that, thus we ap-
   pear.   21
  Q. Isa. You English princes all, I do salute
   you.
  Bur. My duty to you both, on equal love,
Great Kings of France and England! That I
   have labor'd,
With all my wits, my pains and strong en-
   deavors,
To bring your most imperial majesties
Unto this bar and royal interview,
Your mightiness on both parts best can wit-
   ness.
Since then my office hath so far prevail'd
That, face to face and royal eye to eye, 30
You have congreeted, let it not disgrace me,
If I demand, before this royal view,
What rub or what impediment there is,
Why that the naked, poor and mangled
   Peace,
Dear nurse of arts, plenties and joyful births,
Should not in this best garden of the world
Our fertile France, put up her lovely visage?
Alas, she hath from France too long been
   chased,
And all her husbandry doth lie on heaps,
Corrupting in its own fertility.   40
Her vine, the merry cheerer of the heart,
Unpruned dies; her hedges even-pleach'd,
Like prisoners wildly overgrown with hair,
Put forth disorder'd twigs; her fallow leas
The darnel, hemlock and rank fumitory
Doth root upon, while that the coulter rusts
That should deracinate such savagery;
The even mead, that erst brought sweetly
   forth
The freckled cowslip, burnet and green clover,
Wanting the scythe, all uncorrected, rank, 50
Conceives by idleness and nothing teems
But hateful docks, rough thistles, kecksies,
   burs,
Losing both beauty and utility.
And as our vineyards, fallows, meads and
   hedges,
Defective in their natures, grow to wildness,
Even so our houses and ourselves and children
Have lost, or do not learn for want of time,
The sciences that should become our country;
But grow like savages,—as soldiers will
That nothing do but meditate on blood,— 60
To swearing and stern looks, diffused attire
And every thing that seems unnatural.
Which to reduce into our former favor
You are assembled: and my speech entreats

That I may know the let, why gentle Peace
Should not expel these inconveniences
And bless us with her former qualities.
  K. Hen. If, Duke of Burgundy, you would
   the peace,
Whose want gives growth to the imperfec-
   tions
Which you have cited, you must buy that
   peace   70
With full accord to all our just demands;
Whose tenors and particular effects
You have enscheduled briefly in your hands.
  Bur. The king hath heard them; to the
   which as yet
There is no answer made.
  K. Hen.   Well then the peace,
Which you before so urged, lies in his an-
   swer.
  Fr. King. I have but with a cursorary eye
O'erglanced the articles: pleaseth your grace
To appoint some of your council presently
To sit with us once more, with better heed 80
To re-survey them, we will suddenly
Pass our accept and peremptory answer.
  K. Hen. Brother, we shall. Go, uncle Ex-
   eter,
And brother Clarence, and you, brother
   Gloucester,
Warwick and Huntingdon, go with the king;
And take with you free power to ratify,
Augment, or alter, as your wisdoms best
Shall see advantageable for our dignity,
Any thing in or out of our demands,
And we'll consign thereto. Will you, fair
   sister,   90
Go with the princes, or stay here with us?
  Q. Isa. Our gracious brother, I will go with
   them:
Haply a woman's voice may do some good,
When articles too nicely urged be stood on.
  K. Hen. Yet leave our cousin Katharine
   here with us:
She is our capital demand, comprised
Within the fore-rank of our articles.
  Q. Isa. She hath good leave.
       [Exeunt all except Henry, Katharine,
                      and Alice.
  K. Hen.   Fair Katharine, and most fair,
Will you vouchsafe to teach a soldier terms
Such as will enter at a lady's ear   100
And plead his love-suit to her gentle heart?
  Kath. Your majesty shall mock at me; I
cannot speak your England.
  K. Hen. O fair Katharine, if you will love
me soundly with your French heart, I will be
glad to hear you confess it brokenly with your
English tongue. Do you like me, Kate?
  Kath. Pardonnez-moi, I cannot tell vat is
'like me.'
  K. Hen. An angel is like you, Kate, and
you are like an angel.   111
  Kath. Que dit-il? que je suis semblable à
les anges?
  Alice. Oui, vraiment, sauf votre grace,
ainsi dit-il.
  K. Hen. I said so, dear Katharine; and I
must not blush to affirm it.
  Kath. O bon Dieu! les langues des hommes
sont pleines de tromperies.
  K. Hen. What says she, fair one? that the
tongues of men are full of deceits?   121
  Alice. Oui, dat de tongues of de mans is be
full of deceits: dat is de princess.

K. Hen. The princess is the better English-woman. I' faith, Kate, my wooing is fit for thy understanding : I am glad thou canst speak no better English ; for, if thou couldst, thou wouldst find me such a plain king that thou wouldst think I had sold my farm to buy my crown. I know no ways to mince it in love, but directly to say 'I love you : ' then if you urge me farther than to say ' do you in faith ? ' I wear out my suit. Give me your answer ; i' faith, do : and so clap hands and a bargain : how say you, lady ?

Kath. Sauf votre honneur, me understand vell.

K. Hen. Marry, if you would put me to verses or to dance for your sake, Kate, why you undid me : for the one, I have neither words nor measure, and for the other, I have no strength in measure, yet a reasonable measure in strength. If I could win a lady at leap-frog, or by vaulting into my saddle with my armor on my back, under the correction of bragging be it spoken, I should quickly leap into a wife. Or if I might buffet for my love, or bound my horse for her favors, I could lay on like a butcher and sit like a jack-an-apes, never off. But, before God, Kate, I cannot look greenly nor gasp out my elo-quence, nor I have no cunning in protesta-tion ; only downright oaths, which I never use till urged, nor never break for urging. If thou canst love a fellow of this temper, Kate, whose face is not worth sun-burning, that never looks in his glass for love of any thing he sees there, let thine eye be thy cook. I speak to thee plain soldier : if thou canst love me for this, take me ; if not, to say to thee that I shall die, is true ; but for thy love, by the Lord, no ; yet I love thee too. And while thou livest, dear Kate, take a fellow of plain and uncoined constancy ; for he perforce must do thee right, because he hath not the gift to woo in other places : for these fellows of infinite tongue, that can rhyme themselves into ladies' favors, they do always reason them-selves out again. What ! a speaker is but a prater ; a rhyme is but a ballad. A good leg will fall ; a straight back will stoop ; a black beard will turn white ; a curled pate will grow bald ; a fair face will wither ; a full eye will wax hollow : but a good heart, Kate, is the sun and the moon ; or, rather, the sun, and not the moon ; for it shines bright and never changes, but keeps his course truly. If thou would have such a one, take me ; and take me, take a soldier ; take a soldier, take a king. And what sayest thou then to my love ? speak, my fair, and fairly, I pray thee.

Kath. Is it possible dat I sould love de enemy of France ?   179

K. Hen. No ; it is not possible you should love the enemy of France, Kate : but, in lov-ing me, you should love the friend of France ; for I love France so well that I will not part with a village of it ; I will have it all mine : and, Kate, when France is mine and I am yours, then yours is France and you are mine.

Kath. I cannot tell vat is dat.

K. Hen. No, Kate ? I will tell thee in French ; which I am sure will hang upon my tongue like a new-married wife about her hus-band's neck, hardly to be shook off. Je quand sur le possession de France, et quand vous

avez le possession de moi,—let me see, what then ? Saint Denis be my speed !—donc votre est France et vous êtes mienne. It is as easy for me, Kate, to conquer the kingdom as to speak so much more French : I shall never move thee in French, unless it be to laugh at me.

Kath. Sauf votre honneur, le François que vous parlez, il est meilleur que l'Anglois le-quel je parle.   301

K. Hen. No, faith, is't not, Kate : but thy speaking of my tongue, and I thine, most truly-falsely, must needs be granted to be much at one. But, Kate, dost thou understand thus much English, canst thou love me ?

Kath. I cannot tell.

K. Hen. Can any of your neighbors tell, Kate ? I'll ask them. Come, I know thou lovest me : and at night, when you come into your closet, you'll question this gentlewoman about me ; and I know, Kate, you will to her dispraise those parts in me that you love with your heart : but, good Kate, mock me merci-fully ; the rather, gentle princess, because I love thee cruelly. If ever thou beest mine, Kate, as I have a saving faith within me tells me thou shalt, I get thee with scambling, and thou must therefore needs prove a good sol-dier-breeder : shall not thou and I, between Saint Denis and Saint George, compound a boy, half French, half English, that shall go to Constantinople and take the Turk by the beard ? shall we not ? what sayest thou, my fair flower-de-luce?

Kath. I do not know dat.

K. Hen. No ; 'tis hereafter to know, but now to promise : do but now promise, Kate, you will endeavor for your French part of such a boy ; and for my English moiety take the word of a king and a bachelor. How an-swer you, la plus belle Katharine du monde, mon très cher et devin déesse ?

Kath. Your majestee ave fausse French enough to deceive de most sage demoiselle dat is en France.

K. Hen. Now, fie upon my false French ! By mine honor, in true English, I love thee, Kate : by which honor I dare not swear thou lovest me ; yet my blood begins to flatter me that thou dost, notwithstanding the poor and untempering effect of my visage. Now, be-shrew my father's ambition ! he was thinking of civil wars when he got me : therefore was I created with a stubborn outside, with an aspect of iron, that, when I come to woo ladies, I fright them. But, in faith, Kate, the elder I wax, the better I shall appear : my comfort is, that old age, that ill layer up of beauty, can do no more spoil upon my face : thou hast me, if thou hast me, at the worst ; and thou shalt wear me, if thou wear me, bet-ter and better : and therefore tell me, most fair Katharine, will you have me ? Put off your maiden blushes ; avouch the thoughts of your heart with the looks of an empress ; take me by the hand, and say 'Harry of England, I am thine : ' which word thou shalt no sooner bless mine ear withal, but I will tell thee aloud ' England is thine, Ireland is thine, France is thine, and Harry Plantagenet is thine ; ' who, though I speak it before his face, if he be not fellow with the best king, thou shalt find the best king of good fellows. Come, your answer in broken music; for thy voice is music and thy English broken; therefore, queen of all, Katharine, break thy mind to me in broken English; wilt thou have me?

Kath. Dat is as it sall please de roi mon père.

K. Hen. Nay, it will please him well, Kate; it shall please him, Kate.

Kath. Den it sall also content me.   370

K. Hen. Upon that I kiss your hand, and I call you my queen.

Kath. Laissez, mon seigneur, laissez, laissez: ma foi, je ne veux point que vous abaissiez votre grandeur en baisant la main d'une de votre seigneurie indigne serviteur; excusez-moi, je vous supplie, mon très-puissant seigneur.

K. Hen. Then I will kiss your lips, Kate.

Kath. Les dames et demoiselles pour être baisées devant leur noces, il n'est pas la coutume de France.   381

K. Hen. Madam my interpreter, what says she?

Alice. Dat it is not be de fashion pour les ladies of France,—I cannot tell vat is baiser en Anglish.

K. Hen. To kiss.

Alice. Your majesty entendre bettre que moi.

K. Hen. It is not a fashion for the maids in France to kiss before they are married, would she say?

Alice. Oui, vraiment.

K. Hen. O Kate, nice customs curtsy to great kings. Dear Kate, you and I cannot be confined within the weak list of a country's fashion: we are the makers of manners, Kate; and the liberty that follows our places stops the mouth of all find-faults; as I will do yours, for upholding the nice fashion of your country in denying me a kiss: therefore, patiently and yielding. [*Kissing her.*] You have witchcraft in your lips, Kate: there is more eloquence in a sugar touch of them than in the tongues of the French council; and they should sooner persuade Harry of England than a general petition of monarchs. Here comes your father.

Re-enter the French King *and his* Queen, Burgundy, *and other* Lords.

Bur. God save your majesty! my royal cousin, teach you our princess English?

K. Hen. I would have her learn, my fair cousin, how perfectly I love her; and that is good English.

Bur. Is she not apt?

K. Hen. Our tongue is rough, coz, and my condition is not smooth; so that, having neither the voice nor the heart of flattery about me, I cannot so conjure up the spirit of love in her, that he will appear in his true likeness.

Bur. Pardon the frankness of my mirth, if I answer you for that. If you would conjure in her, you must make a circle; if conjure up love in her in his true likeness, he must appear naked and blind. Can you blame her then, being a maid yet rosed over with the virgin crimson of modesty, if she deny the appearance of a naked blind boy in her naked seeing self? It were, my lord, a hard condition for a maid to consign to.

K. Hen. Yet they do wink and yield, as love is blind and enforces.

Bur. They are then excused, my lord, when they see not what they do.   430

K. Hen. Then, good my lord, teach your cousin to consent winking.

Bur. I will wink on her to consent, my lord, if you will teach her to know my meaning: for maids, well summered and warm kept, are like flies at Bartholomew-tide, blind, though they have their eyes; and then they will endure handling, which before would not abide looking on.

K. Hen. This moral ties me over to time and a hot summer; and so I shall catch the fly, your cousin, in the latter end and she must be blind too.

Bur. As love is, my lord, before it loves.

K. Hen. It is so: and you may, some of you, thank love for my blindness, who cannot see many a fair French city for one fair French maid that stands in my way.

Fr. King. Yes, my lord, you see them perspectively, the cities turned into a maid; for they are all girdled with maiden walls that war hath never entered.   450

K. Hen. Shall Kate be my wife?

Fr. King. So please you.

K. Hen. I am content; so the maiden cities you talk of may wait on her: so the maid that stood in the way for my wish shall show me the way to my will.

Fr. King. We have consented to all terms of reason.

K. Hen. Is't so, my lords of England?

West. The king hath granted every article: His daughter first, and then in sequel all,   461 According to their firm proposed natures.

Exe. Only he hath not yet subscribed this: Where your majesty demands, that the King of France, having any occasion to write for matter of grant, shall name your highness in this form and with this addition in French, *Notre trèscher fils Henri, Roi d'Angleterre, Héritier de France*; and thus in Latin, *Præclarissimus filius noster Henricus, Rex Angliæ, et Hæres Franciæ.*

Fr. King. Nor this I have not, brother, so denied,
But your request shall make me let it pass.

K. Hen. I pray you then, in love and dear alliance,
Let that one article rank with the rest;
And thereupon give me your daughter.

Fr. King. Take her, fair son, and from her blood raise up
Issue to me; that the contending kingdoms
Of France and England, whose very shores look pale
With envy of each other's happiness,
May cease their hatred, and this dear conjunction   480
Plant neighborhood and Christian-like accord
In their sweet bosoms, that never war advance
His bleeding sword 'twixt England and fair France.

All. Amen!

K. Hen. Now, welcome, Kate: and bear me witness all,
That here I kiss her as my sovereign queen.
[*Flourish.*

Q. Isa. God, the best maker of all mar-
    riages,
Combine your hearts in one, your realms in
    one !
As man and wife, being two, are one in love,
So be there 'twixt your kingdoms such a
    spousal,
That never may ill office, or fell jealousy,
Which troubles oft the bed of blessed mar-
    riage,
Thrust in between the paction of these king-
    doms,
To make divorce of their incorporate league ;
That English may as French, French English-
    men,
Receive each other. God speak this Amen !
    All. Amen !
    K. Hen. Prepare we for our marriage—on
    which day,   498
My Lord of Burgundy, we'll take your oath,
And all the peers', for surety of our leagues.
Then shall I swear to Kate, and you to me ;
And may our oaths well kept and prosperous
    be !   [*Sennet. Exeunt.*

EPILOGUE.

Enter Chorus.

Chor. Thus far, with rough and all-unable
    pen,
Our bending author hath pursued the story,
In little room confining mighty men,
    Mangling by starts the full course of their
    glory.
Small time, but in that small most greatly
    lived
    This star of England : Fortune made his
    sword ;
By which the world's best garden he achieved,
    And of it left his son imperial lord.
Henry the Sixth, in infant bands crown'd King
    Of France and England, did this king suc-
    ceed ;   10
Whose state so many had the managing,
    That they lost France and made his England
    bleed :
Which oft our stage hath shown ; and, for
    their sake,
In your fair minds let this acceptance take.
                                          [*Exit.*

THE TAMING OF THE SHREW.

(WRITTEN ABOUT 1597.)

INTRODUCTION.

This comedy first appeared in the folio of 1623, but it is in some way closely connected with a play published in 1594, and bearing the almost identical title, *The Taming of A Shrew*. Pope was of the opinion that Shakespeare wrote both plays, but this is hardly plausible. The play in the folio is certainly an enlargement and alteration of the earlier play, and it only remains to ask, was Shakespeare the sole reviser and adapter, or did his task consist of adding and altering certain scenes, so as to render yet more amusing and successful an enlarged version of the play of 1594, already made by some unknown hand? The last seems upon the whole the opinion best supported by the internal evidence. In *The Taming of the Shrew* three parts may be distinguished: (1) The humorous Induction, in which Sly, the drunken tinker, is the chief person; (2) A comedy of character, the Shrew and her tamer, Petruchio, being the hero and heroine; (3) A comedy of intrigue—the story of Bianca and her rival lovers. Now the old play of *A* Shrew contains, in a rude form, the scenes of the Induction and the chief scenes in which Petruchio and Katharina (named by the original writer Ferando and Kate) appear; but nothing in the old play corresponds with the intrigues of Bianca's disguised lovers. It is, however, in the scenes concerned with these intrigues that Shakespeare's hand is least apparent. It may be said that Shakespeare's genius goes in and out with the person of Katharina. We would therefore conjecturally assign the intrigue-comedy to the adapter of the old play, reserving for Shakespeare a title to those scenes—in the main enlarged from the play of *A* Shrew—in which Katharina, Petruchio, and Grumio are speakers. Turning this statement into figures we find that Shakespeare's part in *The Taming of the Shrew* is comprised in the following portions: Induction; Act II., Sc. I., L. 169–326; Act III., Sc. II., L. 1–125, and 151–241; Act IV., Sc. I. II. and III.; Act V., Sc. II., L. 1–180. Such a division, it must be borne in mind, is no more than a conjecture, but it seems to be suggested and fairly indicated by the style of the several parts of the comedy. However this may be, it is clear that Shakespeare cared little for the other characters in comparison with Sly, Katharina, and Petruchio. The play is full of energy and bustling movement; and the characters of Katharina and Petruchio in particular, are firmly and finely drawn, the scenes in which they appear, though infinitely amusing, never quite passing into downright farce. Widely separated dates have been assigned for *The Taming of the Shrew*, from 1594 to 1606. The best portions are in the manner of Shakespeare's comedies of the second period; and attributing the Bianca intrigue-comedy to a writer intermediate between the author of the play of *A* Shrew and Shakespeare, there is no difficulty in supposing that the Shakespeare scenes were written about 1597. Fletcher wrote a humorous continuation of Shakespeare's play, entitled *The Woman's Prize, or the Tamer Tamed*, in which Petruchio reappears.

DRAMATIS PERSONÆ.

A Lord.
CHRISTOPHER SLY, a tinker. }
Hostess, Page, Players, Huntsmen, and Servants. } Persons in the Induction.

BAPTISTA, a rich gentleman of Padua.
VINCENTIO, an old gentleman of Pisa.
LUCENTIO, son to Vincentio, in love with Bianca.
PETRUCHIO, a gentleman of Verona, a suitor to Katharina.
GREMIO, }
HORTENSIO, } suitors to Bianca.

TRANIO, }
BIONDELLO, } servants to Lucentio.
GRUMIO, }
CURTIS, } servants to Petruchio.
A Pedant.

KATHARINA, the shrew, } daughters to Baptista.
BIANCA, }
Widow.

Tailor, Haberdasher, and Servants attending on Baptista and Petruchio.

SCENE : *Padua, and Petruchio's country house.*

INDUCTION.

SCENE I. *Before an alehouse on a heath.*

Enter HOSTESS *and* SLY.

Sly. I'll pheeze you, in faith.

Host. A pair of stocks, you rogue!

Sly. Ye are a baggage: the Slys are no
rogues; look in the chronicles; we came in
with Richard Conqueror. Therefore paucas
pallabris; let the world slide: sessa!

Host. You will not pay for the glasses you
have burst?

Sly. No, not a denier. Go by, Jeronimy:
go to thy cold bed, and warm thee.   10

Host. I know my remedy; I must go fetch
the third-borough.   [*Exit.*

Sly. Third, or fourth, or fifth borough, I'll
answer him by law: I'll not budge an inch,
boy: let him come, and kindly.   [*Falls asleep.*

Horns winded. Enter a Lord *from hunting,
with his train.*

Lord. Huntsman, I charge thee, tender well
my hounds:
Brach Merriman, the poor cur is emboss'd;
And couple Clowder with the deep-mouth'd
brach.
Saw'st thou not, boy, how Silver made it good
At the hedge-corner, in the coldest fault?   20
I would not lose the dog for twenty pound.

First Hun. Why, Belman is as good as he,
my lord;
He cried upon it at the merest loss
And twice to-day pick'd out the dullest scent:
Trust me, I take him for the better dog.

Lord. Thou art a fool: if Echo were as
fleet,
I would esteem him worth a dozen such.
But sup them well and look unto them all:
To-morrow I intend to hunt again.

First Hun. I will, my lord.   30

Lord. What's here? one dead, or drunk?
See, doth he breathe?

Sec. Hun. He breathes, my lord. Were he
not warm'd with ale,
This were a bed but cold to sleep so soundly.

Lord. O monstrous beast! how like a swine
he lies!
Grim death, how foul and loathsome is thine
image!
Sirs, I will practice on this drunken man.
What think you, if he were convey'd to bed,
Wrapp'd in sweet clothes, rings put upon his
fingers,
A most delicious banquet by his bed,   39
And brave attendants near him when he wakes,
Would not the beggar then forget himself?

First Hun. Believe me, lord, I think he
cannot choose.

Sec. Hun. It would seem strange unto him
when he waked.

Lord. Even as a flattering dream or worth-
less fancy.
Then take him up and manage well the jest:
Carry him gently to my fairest chamber
And hang it round with all my wanton pic-
tures:
Balm his foul head in warm distilled waters
And burn sweet wood to make the lodging
sweet:
Procure me music ready when he wakes,   50

To make a dulcet and a heavenly sound;
And if he chance to speak, be ready straight
And with a low submissive reverence
Say 'What is it your honor will command?'
Let one attend him with a silver basin
Full of rose-water and bestrew'd with flowers,
Another bear the ewer, the third a diaper,
And say 'Will't please your lordship cool your
hands?'
Some one be ready with a costly suit
And ask him what apparel he will wear;   60
Another tell him of his hounds and horse,
And that his lady mourns at his disease:
Persuade him that he hath been lunatic;
And when he says he is, say that he dreams,
For he is nothing but a mighty lord.
This do and do it kindly, gentle sirs:
It will be pastime passing excellent,
If it be husbanded with modesty.

First Hun. My lord, I warrant you we will
play our part,
As he shall think by our true diligence   70
He is no less than what we say he is.

Lord. Take him up gently and to bed with
him;
And each one to his office when he wakes.
[*Some bear out Sly. A trumpet sounds.*
Sirrah, go see what trumpet 'tis that sounds:
[*Exit Servingman.*
Belike, some noble gentleman that means,
Travelling some journey, to repose him here.

Re-enter Servingman.

How now! who is it?

Serv. An't please your honor, players
That offer service to your lordship.

Lord. Bid them come near.

Enter Players.

Now, fellows, you are welcome.

Players. We thank your honor.   80

Lord. Do you intend to stay with me to-
night?

A Player. So please your lordship to accept our duty.

Lord. With all my heart. This fellow I re-
member,
Since once he play'd a farmer's eldest son:
'Twas where you woo'd the gentlewoman so
well:
I have forgot your name; but, sure, that part
Was aptly fitted and naturally perform'd.

A Player. I think 'twas Soto that your
honor means.

Lord. 'Tis very true: thou didst it excel-
lent.
Well, you are come to me in happy time;   90
The rather for I have some sport in hand
Wherein your cunning can assist me much.
There is a lord will hear you play to-night:
But I am doubtful of your modesties;
Lest over-eyeing of his odd behavior,—
For yet his honor never heard a play—
You break into some merry passion
And so offend him; for I tell you, sirs,
If you should smile he grows impatient.

A Player. Fear not, my lord: we can contain ourselves,   100
Were he the veriest antic in the world.

Lord. Go, sirrah, take them to the buttery,
And give them friendly welcome every one:
Let them want nothing that my house affords.
[*Exit one with the Players.*

Sirrah, go you to Barthol'mew my page,
And see him dress'd in all suits like a lady :
That done, conduct him to the drunkard's
　　chamber ;
And call him 'madam,' do him obeisance.
Tell him from me, as he will win my love,
He bear himself with honorable action,　　110
Such as he hath observed in noble ladies
Unto their lords, by them accomplished :
Such duty to the drunkard let him do
With soft low tongue and lowly courtesy,
And say ' What is't your honor will command,
Wherein your lady and your humble wife
May show her duty and make known her
　　love ? '
And then with kind embracements, tempting
　　kisses,
And with declining head into his bosom,
Bid him shed tears, as being overjoy'd　　120
To see her noble lord restored to health,
Who for this seven years hath esteem'd him
No better than a poor and loathsome beggar :
And if the boy have not a woman's gift
To rain a shower of commanded tears,
An onion will do well for such a shift,
Which in a napkin being close convey'd
Shall in despite enforce a watery eye.
See this dispatch'd with all the haste thou
　　canst :
Anon I'll give thee more instructions.　　130
　　　　　　　[*Exit a Servingman.*
I know the boy will well usurp the grace,
Voice, gait and action of a gentlewoman :
I long to hear him call the drunkard husband,
And how my men will stay themselves from
　　laughter
When they do homage to this simple peasant.
I'll in to counsel them ; haply my presence
May well abate the over-merry spleen
Which otherwise would grow into extremes.
　　　　　　　[*Exeunt.*

SCENE II.　*A bedchamber in the* Lord's *house.*

Enter aloft SLY, *with* Attendants ; *some with
apparel, others with basin and ewer and
other appurtenances ; and* Lord.

Sly.　For God's sake, a pot of small ale.
First Serv.　Will't please your lordship
　　drink a cup of sack ?
Sec. Serv.　Will't please your honor taste of
　　these conserves ?
Third Serv.　What raiment will your honor
　　wear to-day ?
Sly.　I am Christophero Sly ; call not me
' honor ' nor ' lordship : ' I ne'er drank sack in
my life ; and if you give me any conserves,
give me conserves of beef : ne'er ask me what
raiment I'll wear ; for I have no more doublets
than backs, no more stockings than legs, nor
no more shoes than feet ; nay, sometimes more
feet than shoes, or such shoes as my toes look
through the over-leather.
Lord.　Heaven cease this idle humor in your
　　honor !
O, that a mighty man of such descent,
Of such possessions and so high esteem,
Should be infused with so foul a spirit !
Sly.　What, would you make me mad ? Am
not I Christopher Sly, old Sly's son of Burton-
heath, by birth a pedlar, by education a card-
maker, by transmutation a bear-herd, and now
by present profession a tinker ? Ask Marian
Hacket, the fat ale-wife of Wincot, if she know

me not : if she say I am not fourteen pence on
the score for sheer ale, score me up for the
lyingest knave in Christendom. What ! I am
not bestraught : here's—
Third Serv.　O, this it is that makes your
　　lady mourn !
Sec. Serv.　O, this is it that makes your serv-
　　ants droop !
Lord.　Hence comes it that your kindred
　　shuns your house,　　30
As beaten hence by your strange lunacy.
O noble lord, bethink thee of thy birth,
Call home thy ancient thoughts from banish-
　　ment
And banish hence these abject lowly dreams.
Look how thy servants do attend on thee,
Each in his office ready at thy beck.
Wilt thou have music ? hark ! Apollo plays,
　　　　　　　[*Music.*
And twenty caged nightingales do sing :
Or wilt thou sleep ? we'll have thee to a couch
Softer and sweeter than the lustful bed　　40
On purpose trimm'd up for Semiramis.
Say thou wilt walk ; we will bestrew the
　　ground :
Or wilt thou ride ? thy horses shall be trapp'd,
Their harness studded all with gold and pearl.
Dost thou love hawking ? thou hast hawks will
　　soar
Above the morning lark : or wilt thou hunt ?
Thy hounds shall make the welkin answer them
And fetch shrill echoes from the hollow earth.
First Serv.　Say thou wilt course ; thy grey-
　　hounds are as swift
As breathed stags, ay, fleeter than the roe.　　50
Sec. Serv.　Dost thou love pictures ? we will
　　fetch thee straight
Adonis painted by a running brook,
And Cytherea all in sedges hid,
Which seem to move and wanton with her
　　breath,
Even as the waving sedges play with wind.
Lord.　We'll show thee Io as she was a
　　maid,
And how she was beguiled and surprised,
As lively painted as the deed was done.
Third Serv.　Or Daphne roaming through a
　　thorny wood,
Scratching her legs that one shall swear she
　　bleeds,　　60
And at that sight shall sad Apollo weep,
So workmanly the blood and tears are drawn.
Lord.　Thou art a lord, and nothing but a
　　lord :
Thou hast a lady far more beautiful
Than any woman in this waning age.
First Serv.　And till the tears that she hath
　　shed for thee
Like envious floods o'er-run her lovely face,
She was the fairest creature in the world ;
And yet she is inferior to none.　　69
Sly.　Am I a lord ? and have I such a lady ?
Or do I dream ? or have I dream'd till now ?
I do not sleep : I see, I hear, I speak ;
I smell sweet savors and I feel soft things :
Upon my life, I am a lord indeed
And not a tinker nor Christophero Sly.
Well, bring our lady hither to our sight ;
And once again, a pot o' the smallest ale.
Sec. Serv.　Will't please your mightiness to
　　wash your hands ?
O, how we joy to see your wit restored !

O, that once more you knew but what you
    are !   80
These fifteen years you have been in a dream ;
Or when you waked, so waked as if you slept.
  Sly. These fifteen years ! by my fay, a
    goodly nap.
But did I never speak of all that time ?
  First Serv. O, yes, my lord, but very idle
    words :
For though you lay here in this goodly cham-
    ber,
Yet would you say ye were beaten out of door ;
And rail upon the hostess of the house ;
And say you would present her at the leet,
Because she brought stone jugs and no seal'd
    quarts :   90
Sometimes you would call out for Cicely
    Hacket.
  Sly. Ay, the woman's maid of the house.
  Third Serv. Why, sir, you know no house
    nor no such maid,
Nor no such men as you have reckon'd up,
As Stephen Sly and old John Naps of Greece
And Peter Turph and Henry Pimpernell
And twenty more such names and men as
    these
Which never were nor no man ever saw.
  Sly. Now Lord be thanked for my good
    amends !   100
  All. Amen.
  Sly. I thank thee : thou shalt not lose by it.

Enter the Page *as a lady, with attendants.*

  Page. How fares my noble lord ?
  Sly. Marry, I fare well ; for here is cheer
    enough.
Where is my wife ?
  Page. Here, noble lord : what is thy will
    with her ?
  Sly. Are you my wife and will not call me
    husband ?
My men should call me ' lord : ' I am your
    goodman.
  Page. My husband and my lord, my lord
    and husband ;
I am your wife in all obedience.
  Sly. I know it well. What must I call her ?
  Lord. Madam.   111
  Sly. Al'ce madam, or Joan madam ?
  Lord. ' Madam,' and nothing else : so lords
    call ladies.
  Sly. Madam wife, they say that I have
    dream'd
And slept above some fifteen year or more.
  Page. Ay, and the time seems thirty unto
    me,
Being all this time abandon'd from your bed.
  Sly. 'Tis much. Servants, leave me and her
    alone.
Madam, undress you and come now to bed.
  Page. Thrice noble lord, let me entreat of
    you   120
To pardon me yet for a night or two,
Or, if not so, until the sun be set :
For your physicians have expressly charged,
In peril to incur your former malady,
That I should yet absent me from your bed :
I hope this reason stands for my excuse.
  Sly. Ay, it stands so that I may hardly
tarry so long. But I would be loath to fall into
my dreams again : I will therefore tarry in de-
spite of the flesh and the blood.   130

Enter a Messenger.

  Mess. Your honor's players, hearing your
    amendment,
Are come to play a pleasant comedy ;
For so your doctors hold it very meet,
Seeing too much sadness hath congeal'd your
    blood,
And melancholy is the nurse of frenzy :
Therefore they thought it good you hear a play
And frame your mind to mirth and merriment,
Which bars a thousand harms and lengthens
    life.
  Sly. Marry, I will, let them play it. Is not a
comonty a Christmas gambold or a tumbling-
trick ?   141
  Page. No, my good lord ; it is more pleas-
    ing stuff.
  Sly. What, household stuff ?
  Page. It is a kind of history.
  Sly. Well, we'll see't. Come, madam wife,
sit by my side and let the world slip : we shall
ne'er be younger.

Flourish.

ACT I.

SCENE I. *Padua. A public place.*

Enter LUCENTIO *and his man* TRANIO.

  Luc. Tranio, since for the great desire I
    had
To see fair Padua, nursery of arts,
I am arrived for fruitful Lombardy,
The pleasant garden of great Italy ;
And by my father's love and leave am arm'd
With his good will and thy good company,
My trusty servant, well approved in all,
Here let us breathe and haply institute
A course of learning and ingenious studies.
Pisa renown'd for grave citizens   10
Gave me my being and my father first,
A merchant of great traffic through the world,
Vincentio, come of the Bentivolii.
Vincentio's son brought up in Florence
It shall become to serve all hopes conceived,
To deck his fortune with his virtuous deeds :
And therefore, Tranio, for the time I study,
Virtue and that part of philosophy
Will I apply that treats of happiness
By virtue specially to be achieved.   20
Tell me thy mind ; for I have Pisa left
And am to Padua come, as he that leaves
A shallow plash to plunge him in the deep
And with satiety seeks to quench his thirst.
  Tra. Mi perdonato, gentle master mine,
I am in all affected as yourself ;
Glad that you thus continue your resolve
To suck the sweets of sweet philosophy.
Only, good master, while we do admire
This virtue and this moral discipline,   30
Let's be no stoics nor no stocks, I pray ;
Or so devote to Aristotle's checks
As Ovid be an outcast quite abjured :
Balk logic with acquaintance that you have
And practise rhetoric in your common talk ;
Music and poesy use to quicken you ;
The mathematics and the metaphysics,
Fall to them as you find your stomach serves
    you ;
No profit grows where is no pleasure ta'en :
In brief, sir, study what you most affect.   40

Luc. Gramercies, Tranio, well dost thou
advise.
If, Biondello, thou wert come ashore,
We could at once put us in readiness,
And take a lodging fit to entertain
Such friends as time in Padua shall beget.
But stay a while : what company is this ?
Tra. Master, some show to welcome us to
town.

Enter BAPTISTA, KATHARINA, BIANCA, GREMIO,
and HORTENSIO. LUCENTIO *and* TRANIO
stand by.

Bap. Gentlemen, importune me no farther,
For how I firmly am resolved you know ;
That is, not to bestow my youngest daughter
Before I have a husband for the elder :   51
If either of you both love Katharina,
Because I know you well and love you well,
Leave shall you have to court her at your
pleasure.
Gre. [*Aside*] To cart her rather : she's too
rough for me.
There, there, Hortensio, will you any wife ?
Kath. I pray you, sir, is it your will
To make a stale of me amongst these mates ?
Hor. Mates, maid ! how mean you that ? no
mates for you,
Unless you were of gentler, milder mould.   60
Kath. I'faith, sir, you shall never need to
fear :
I wis it is not half way to her heart ;
But if it were, doubt not her care should be
To comb your noddle with a three-legg'd stool
And paint your face and use you like a fool.
Hor. From all such devils, good Lord de-
liver us !
Gre. And me too, good Lord !
Tra. Hush, master ! here's some good pas-
time toward :
That wench is stark mad or wonderful fro-
ward.
Luc. But in the other's silence do I see   70
Maid's mild behavior and sobriety.
Peace, Tranio !
Tra. Well said, master ; mum ! and gaze
your fill.
Bap. Gentlemen, that I may soon make
good
What I have said, Bianca, get you in :
And let it not displease thee, good Bianca,
For I will love thee ne'er the less, my girl.
Kath. A pretty peat ! it is best
Put finger in the eye, an she knew why.
Bian. Sister, content you in my discontent.
Sir, to your pleasure humbly I subscribe :   81
My books and instruments shall be my com-
pany,
On them to look and practise by myself.
Luc. Hark, Tranio ! thou may'st hear Mi-
nerva speak.
Hor. Signior Baptista, will you be so
strange ?
Sorry am I that our good will effects
Bianca's grief.
Gre. Why will you mew her up,
Signior Baptista, for this fiend of hell,
And make her bear the penance of her
tongue ?
Bap. Gentlemen, content ye ; I am re-
solved :   90
Go in, Bianca :   [*Exit Bianca.*
And for I know she taketh most delight

In music, instruments and poetry,
Schoolmasters will I keep within my house,
Fit to instruct her youth. If you, Hortensio,
Or Signior Gremio, you, know any such,
Prefer them hither ; for to cunning men
I will be very kind, and liberal
To mine own children in good bringing up :
And so farewell. Katharina, you may stay ;
For I have more to commune with Bianca. 101
                                             [*Exit.*
Kath. Why, and I trust I may go too, may
I not ? What, shall I be appointed hours ; as
though, belike, I knew not what to take, and
what to leave, ha ?   [*Exit.*
Gre. You may go to the devil's dam : your
gifts are so good, here's none will hold you.
Their love is not so great, Hortensio, but we
may blow our nails together, and fast it fairly
out : our cake's dough on both sides. Farewell : yet, for the love I bear my sweet Bianca,
if I can by any means light on a fit man to
teach her that wherein she delights, I will wish
him to her father.
Hor. So will I, Signior Gremio : but a
word, I pray. Though the nature of our quarrel yet never brooked parle, know now, upon
advice, it toucheth us both, that we may yet
again have access to our fair mistress and be
happy rivals in Bianca's love, to labor and
effect one thing specially.   121
Gre. What's that, I pray ?
Hor. Marry, sir, to get a husband for her
sister.
Gre. A husband ! a devil.
Hor. I say, a husband.
Gre. I say, a devil. Thinkest thou, Hortensio, though her father be very rich, any man
is so very a fool to be married to hell ?
Hor. Tush, Gremio, though it pass your
patience and mine to endure her loud alarums,
why, man, there be good fellows in the world,
an a man could light on them, would take her
with all faults, and money enough.
Gre. I cannot tell ; but I had as lief take
her dowry with this condition, to be whipped
at the high cross every morning.
Hor. Faith, as you say, there's small choice
in rotten apples. But come ; since this bar in
law makes us friends, it shall be so far forth
friendly maintained till by helping Baptista's
eldest daughter to a husband we set his youngest free for a husband, and then have to't
afresh. Sweet Bianca ! Happy man be his dole !
He that runs fastest gets the ring. How say you,
Signior Gremio ?
Gre. I am agreed ; and would I had given
him the best horse in Padua to begin his woo-
ing that would thoroughly woo her, wed her
and bed her and rid the house of her ! Come
on.   [*Exeunt Gremio and Hortensio.* 150
Tra. I pray, sir, tell me, is it possible
That love should of a sudden take such hold ?
Luc. O Tranio, till I found it to be true,
I never thought it possible or likely ;
But see, while idly I stood looking on,
I found the effect of love in idleness :
And now in plainness do confess to thee,
That art to me as secret and as dear
As Anna to the queen of Carthage was,
Tranio, I burn, I pine, I perish, Tranio,   160
If I achieve not this young modest girl.
Counsel me, Tranio, for I know thou canst ;
Assist me, Tranio, for I know thou wilt.

Tra. Master, it is no time to chide you now;
Affection is not rated from the heart;
If love have touch'd you, nought remains but so,
' Redime te captum quam queas minimo.'
Luc. Gramercies, lad, go forward; this contents :
The rest will comfort, for thy counsel's sound.
Tra. Master, you look'd so longly on the maid,   170
Perhaps you mark'd not what's the pith of all.
Luc. O yes, I saw sweet beauty in her face,
Such as the daughter of Agenor had,
That made great Jove to humble him to her hand,
When with his knees he kiss'd the Cretan strand.
Tra. Saw you no more ? mark'd you not how her sister
Began to scold and raise up such a storm
That mortal ears might hardly endure the din ?
Luc. Tranio, I saw her coral lips to move
And with her breath she did perfume the air :
Sacred and sweet was all I saw in her.   181
Tra. Nay, then, 'tis time to stir him from his trance.
I pray, awake, sir : if you love the maid,
Bend thoughts and wits to achieve her. Thus it stands :
Her eldest sister is so curst and shrewd
That till the father rid his hands of her,
Master, your love must live a maid at home ;
And therefore has he closely mew'd her up,
Because she will not be annoy'd with suitors.
Luc. Ah, Tranio, what a cruel father's he !
But art thou not advised, he took some care
To get her cunning schoolmasters to instruct her ?
Tra. Ay, marry, am I, sir ; and now 'tis plotted.
Luc. I have it, Tranio.
Tra.   Master, for my hand,
Both our inventions meet and jump in one.
Luc. Tell me thine first.
Tra.   You will be schoolmaster
And undertake the teaching of the maid :
That's your device.
Luc.   It is : may it be done ?
Tra. Not possible ; for who shall bear your part,
And be in Padua here Vincentio's son,   200
Keep house and ply his book, welcome his friends,
Visit his countrymen and banquet them ?
Luc. Basta ; content thee, for I have it full.
We have not yet been seen in any house,
Nor can we be distinguish'd by our faces
For man or master ; then it follows thus ;
Thou shalt be master, Tranio, in my stead,
Keep house and port and servants, as I should :
I will some other be, some Florentine,
Some Neapolitan, or meaner man of Pisa. 210
'Tis hatch'd and shall be so : Tranio, at once
Uncase thee ; take my color'd hat and cloak :
When Biondello comes, he waits on thee;
But I will charm him first to keep his tongue.
Tra. So had you need.
In brief, sir, sith it your pleasure is,
And I am tied to be obedient ;
For so your father charged me at our parting,
' Be serviceable to my son,' quoth he,

Although I think 'twas in another sense ;   220
I am content to be Lucentio,
Because so well I love Lucentio.
Luc. Tranio, be so, because Lucentio loves :
And let me be a slave, to achieve that maid
Whose sudden sight hath thrall'd my wounded eye.
Here comes the rogue.

Enter BIONDELLO.

                Sirrah, where have you been ?
Bion. Where have I been ! Nay, how now ! where are you ? Master, has my fellow Tranio stolen your clothes ? Or you stolen his ? or both ? pray, what's the news ?   230
Luc. Sirrah, come hither : 'tis no time to jest,
And therefore frame your manners to the time.
Your fellow Tranio here, to save my life,
Puts my apparel and my countenance on,
And I for my escape have put on his ;
For in a quarrel since I came ashore
I kill'd a man and fear I was descried :
Wait you on him, I charge you, as becomes,
While I make way from hence to save my life :
You understand me ?
Bion.   I, sir ! ne'er a whit.   240
Luc. And not a jot of Tranio in your mouth :
Tranio is changed into Lucentio.
Bion. The better for him : would I were so too !
Tra. So could I, faith, boy, to have the next wish after,
That Lucentio indeed had Baptista's youngest daughter.
But, sirrah, not for my sake, but your master's, I advise
You use your manners discreetly in all kind of companies :
When I am alone, why, then I am Tranio ;
But in all places else your master Lucentio.
Luc. Tranio, let's go : one thing more rests, that thyself execute, to make one among these wooers : if thou ask me why, sufficeth, my reasons are both good and weighty.
                        [*Exeunt.*

The presenters above speak.

First Serv. My lord, you nod ; you do not mind the play.
Sly. Yes, by Saint Anne, do I. A good matter, surely : comes there any more of it ?
Page. My lord, 'tis but begun.
Sly. 'Tis a very excellent piece of work, madam lady : would 'twere done !   259
                        [*They sit and mark.*

SCENE II. *Padua. Before* HORTENSIO'S *house.*
Enter PETRUCHIO *and his man* GRUMIO.

Pet. Verona, for a while I take my leave,
To see my friends in Padua, but of all
My best beloved and approved friend,
Hortensio ; and I trow this is his house.
Here, sirrah Grumio ; knock, I say.
Gru. Knock, sir ! whom should I knock ?
is there any man has rebused your worship ?
Pet. Villain, I say, knock me here soundly.
Gru. Knock you here, sir ! why, sir, what am I, sir, that I should knock you here, sir ?
Pet. Villain, I say, knock me at this gate

And rap me well, or I'll knock your knave's
    pate.
Gru. My master is grown quarrelsome. I
    should knock you first,
And then I know after who comes by the
    worst.
Pet. Will it not be?
Faith, sirrah, an you'll not knock, I'll ring it;
I'll try how you can sol, fa, and sing it.
        [*He wrings him by the ears.*
Gru. Help, masters, help! my master is
    mad.
Pet. Now, knock when I bid you, sirrah
    villain!

        Enter HORTENSIO.

Hor. How now! what's the matter? My
old friend Grumio! and my good friend
Petruchio!
How do you all at Verona?
Pet. Signior Hortensio, come you to part
    the fray?
' Con tutto il cuore, ben trovato,' may I say.
Hor. ' Alla nostra casa ben venuto, molto
honorato signor mio Petruchio.'
Rise, Grumio, rise: we will compound this
    quarrel.
Gru. Nay, 'tis no matter, sir, what he 'leges
in Latin. If this be not a lawful cause for me
to leave his service, look you, sir, he bid me
knock him and rap him soundly, sir: well, was
it fit for a servant to use his master so, being
perhaps, for aught I see, two and thirty, a pip
out?
Whom would to God I had well knock'd at
    first,
Then had not Grumio come by the worst.
Pet. A senseless villain! Good Hortensio,
I bade the rascal knock upon your gate
And could not get him for my heart to do it.
Gru. Knock at the gate! O heavens!
Spake you not these words plain, ' Sirrah,
knock me here, rap me here, knock me well,
and knock me soundly'? And come you now
with, ' knocking at the gate'?
Pet. Sirrah, be gone, or talk not, I advise
    you.
Hor. Petruchio, patience; I am Grumio's
    pledge:
Why, this's a heavy chance 'twixt him and you,
Your ancient, trusty, pleasant servant Grumio.
And tell me now, sweet friend, what happy gale
Blows you to Padua here from old Verona?
Pet. Such wind as scatters young men
    through the world,   50
To seek their fortunes farther than at home
Where small experience grows. But in a few,
Signior Hortensio, thus it stands with me:
Antonio, my father, is deceased;
And I have thrust myself into this maze,
Haply to wive and thrive as best I may:
Crowns in my purse I have and goods at home,
And so am come abroad to see the world.
Hor. Petruchio, shall I then come roundly
    to thee   59
And wish thee to a shrewd ill-favor'd wife?
Thou'ldst thank me but a little for my coun-
    sel:
And yet I'll promise thee she shall be rich
And very rich: but thou'rt too much my
    friend,
And I'll not wish thee to her.

Pet. Signior Hortensio, 'twixt such friends
    as we
Few words suffice; and therefore, if thou know
One rich enough to be Petruchio's wife,
As wealth is burden of my wooing dance,
Be she as foul as was Florentius' love,
As old as Sibyl and as curst and shrewd   70
As Socrates' Xanthippe, or a worse,
She moves me not, or not removes, at least,
Affection's edge in me, were she as rough
As are the swelling Adriatic seas:
I come to wive it wealthily in Padua;
If wealthily, then happily in Padua.
Gru. Nay, look you, sir, he tells you flatly
what his mind is: why, give him gold enough
and marry him to a puppet or an aglet-baby;
or an old trot with ne'er a tooth in her head,
though she have as many diseases as two and
fifty horses: why, nothing comes amiss, so
money comes withal.
Hor. Petruchio, since we are stepp'd thus
    far in,
I will continue that I broach'd in jest.
I can, Petruchio, help thee to a wife
With wealth enough and young and beauteous,
Brought up as best becomes a gentlewoman:
Her only fault, and that is faults enough,
Is that she is intolerable curst
And shrewd and froward, so beyond all meas-
    ure
That, were my state far worser than it is,   91
I would not wed her for a mine of gold.
Pet. Hortensio, peace! thou know'st not
    gold's effect:
Tell me her father's name and 'tis enough;
For I will board her, though she chide as loud
As thunder when the clouds in autumn crack.
Hor. Her father is Baptista Minola,
An affable and courteous gentleman:
Her name is Katharina Minola,
Renown'd in Padua for her scolding tongue.
Pet. I know her father, though I know not
    her;   101
And he knew my deceased father well.
I will not sleep, Hortensio, till I see her;
And therefore let me be thus bold with you
To give you over at this first encounter,
Unless you will accompany me thither.
Gru. I pray you, sir, let him go while the
humor lasts. O' my word, an she knew him as
well as I do, she would think scolding would
do little good upon him: she may perhaps call
him half a score knaves or so: why, that's
nothing; an he begin once, he'll rail in his
rope-tricks. I'll tell you what, sir, an she stand
him but a little, he will throw a figure in her
face and so disfigure her with it that she shall
have no more eyes to see withal than a cat.
You know him not, sir.
Hor. Tarry, Petruchio, I must go with thee,
For in Baptista's keep my treasure is:
He hath the jewel of my life in hold,
His youngest daughter, beautiful Bianca,   120
And her withholds from me and other more,
Suitors to her and rivals in my love,
Supposing it a thing impossible,
For those defects I have before rehearsed,
That ever Katharina will be woo'd;
Therefore this order hath Baptista ta'en,
That none shall have access unto Bianca
Till Katharine the curst have got a husband.
Gru. Katharine the curst!
A title for a maid of all titles the worst.   130

Hor. Now shall my friend Petruchio do me
  grace,
And offer me disguised in sober robes
To old Baptista as a schoolmaster
Well seen in music, to instruct Bianca;
That so I may, by this device, at least
Have leave and leisure to make love to her
And unsuspected court her by herself.
  Gru. Here's no knavery! See, to beguile
the old folks, how the young folks lay their
heads together!   140

Enter GREMIO, *and* LUCENTIO *disguised.*

Master, master, look about you: who goes
  there, ha?
  Hor. Peace, Grumio! it is the rival of my
  love.
Petruchio, stand by a while.
  Gru. A proper stripling and an amorous!
  Gre. O, very well; I have perused the note.
Hark you, sir: I'll have them very fairly
  bound:
All books of love, see that at any hand;
And see you read no other lectures to her:
You understand me: over and beside
Signior Baptista's liberality,   150
I'll mend it with a largess. Take your paper
  too,
And let me have them very well perfumed:
For she is sweeter than perfume itself
To whom they go to. What will you read to
  her?
  Luc. Whate'er I read to her, I'll plead for
  you
As for my patron, stand you so assured,
As firmly as yourself were still in place:
Yea, and perhaps with more successful words
Than you, unless you were a scholar, sir.
  Gre. O this learning, what a thing it is!
  Gru. O this woodcock, what an ass it is!
  Pet. Peace, sirrah!   162
  Hor. Grumio, mum! God save you, Si-
  gnior Gremio.
  Gre. And you are well met, Signior Hor-
  tensio.
Trow you whither I am going? To Baptista
  Minola.
I promised to inquire carefully
About a schoolmaster for the fair Bianca:
And by good fortune I have lighted well
On this young man, for learning and behavior
Fit for her turn, well read in poetry   170
And other books, good ones, I warrant ye.
  Hor. 'Tis well; and I have met a gentle-
  man
Hath promised me to help me to another,
A fine musician to instruct our mistress;
So shall I no whit be behind in duty
To fair Bianca, so beloved of me.
  Gre. Beloved of me; and that my deeds
    shall prove.
  Gru. And that his bags shall prove.
  Hor. Gremio, 'tis now no time to vent our
    love:
Listen to me, and if you speak me fair,   180
I'll tell you news indifferent good for either.
Here is a gentleman whom by chance I met,
Upon agreement from us to his liking,
Will undertake to woo curst Katharine,
Yea, and to marry her, if her dowry please.
  Gre. So said, so done, is well.
Hortensio, have you told him all her faults?

  Pet. I know she is an irksome brawling
    scold:
If that be all, masters, I hear no harm.
  Gre. No, say'st me so, friend? What coun-
    tryman?   190
  Pet. Born in Verona, old Antonio's son:
My father dead, my fortune lives for me;
And I do hope good days and long to see.
  Gre. O sir, such a life, with such a wife,
    were strange!
But if you have a stomach, to't i' God's name:
You shall have me assisting you in all.
But will you woo this wild-cat?
  Pet.   Will I live?
  Gru. Will he woo her? ay, or I'll hang her.
  Pet. Why came I hither but to that intent?
Think you a little din can daunt mine ears?
Have I not in my time heard lions roar?   201
Have I not heard the sea puff'd up with winds
Rage like an angry boar chafed with sweat?
Have I not heard great ordnance in the field,
And heaven's artillery thunder in the skies?
Have I not in a pitched battle heard
Loud 'larums, neighing steeds, and trumpets'
    clang?
And do you tell me of a woman's tongue,
That gives not half so great a blow to hear
As will a chestnut in a farmer's fire?   210
Tush, tush! fear boys with bugs.
  Gru.   For he fears none.
  Gre. Hortensio, hark:
This gentleman is happily arrived,
My mind presumes, for his own good and ours.
  Hor. I promised we would be contributors
And bear his charge of wooing, whatsoe'er.
  Gre. And so we will, provided that he
    win her.
  Gru. I would I were as sure of a good
    dinner.

Enter TRANIO *brave, and* BIONDELLO.

  Tra. Gentlemen, God save you. If I may
    be bold,
Tell me, I beseech you, which is the readiest
    way
To the house of Signior Baptista Minola?   221
  Bion. He that has the two fair daughters:
    is't he you mean?
  Tra. Even he, Biondello.
  Gre. Hark you, sir; you mean not her to—
  Tra. Perhaps, him and her, sir: what have
    you to do?
  Pet. Not her that chides, sir, at any hand,
    I pray.
  Tra. I love no chiders, sir. Biondello, let's
    away.
  Luc. Well begun, Tranio.
  Hor.   Sir, a word ere you go;
Are you a suitor to the maid you talk of, yea
    or no?   230
  Tra. And if I be, sir, is it any offence?
  Gre. No; if without more words you will
    get you hence.
  Tra. Why, sir, I pray, are not the streets
    as free
For me as for you?
  Gre.   But so is not she.
  Tra. For what reason, I beseech you?
  Gre.   For this reason, if you'll know,
That she's the choice love of Signior Gremio.
  Hor. That she's the chosen of Signior Hor-
    tensio.

Tra. Softly, my masters! if you be gentle-
    men,
Do me this right; hear me with patience.
Baptista is a noble gentleman,   240
To whom my father is not all unknown;
And were his daughter fairer than she is,
She may more suitors have and me for one.
Fair Leda's daughter had a thousand wooers;
Then well one more may fair Bianca have:
And so she shall; Lucentio shall make one,
Though Paris came in hope to speed alone.
  Gre. What! this gentleman will out-talk us
    all.
  Luc. Sir, give him head: I know he'll
    prove a jade.
  Pet. Hortensio, to what end are all these
    words?   250
  Hor. Sir, let me be so bold as ask you,
Did you yet ever see Baptista's daughter?
  Tra. No, sir; but hear I do that he hath
    two,
The one as famous for a scolding tongue
As is the other for beauteous modesty.
  Pet. Sir, sir, the first's for me; let her go
    by.
  Gre. Yea, leave that labor to great Her-
    cules;
And let it be more than Alcides' twelve.
  Pet. Sir, understand you this of me in
    sooth:
The youngest daughter whom you hearken for
Her father keeps from all access of suitors,
And will not promise her to any man   262
Until the elder sister first be wed:
The younger then is free and not before.
  Tra. If it be so, sir, that you are the man
Must stead us all and me amongst the rest,
And if you break the ice and do this feat,
Achieve the elder, set the younger free
For our access, whose hap shall be to have her
Will not so graceless be to be ingrate.   270
  Hor. Sir, you say well and well you do
    conceive;
And since you do profess to be a suitor,
You must, as we do, gratify this gentleman,
To whom we all rest generally beholding.
  Tra. Sir, I shall not be slack: in sign
    whereof,
Please ye we may contrive this afternoon,
And quaff carouses to our mistress' health,
And do as adversaries do in law,
Strive mightily, but eat and drink as friends.
  Gru. Bion. O excellent motion! Fellows,
    let's be gone.   280
  Hor. The motion's good indeed and be it
    so,
Petruchio, I shall be your ben venuto.
                              [Exeunt.

ACT II.

Scene I. *Padua. A room in* Baptista's
    house.

Enter Katharina *and* Bianca.

  Bian. Good sister, wrong me not, nor
    wrong yourself,
To make a bondmaid and a slave of me;
That I disdain: but for these other gawds,
Unbind my hands, I'll pull them off myself,
Yea, all my raiment, to my petticoat,
Or what you will command me will I do,

So well I know my duty to my elders.
  Kath. Of all thy suitors, here I charge thee,
    tell
Whom thou lovest best: see thou dissemble
    not.
  Bian. Believe me, sister, of all the men
    alive   10
I never yet beheld that special face
Which I could fancy more than any other.
  Kath. Minion, thou liest. Is't not Hor-
    tensio?
  Bian. If you affect him, sister, here I swear
I'll plead for you myself, but you shall have
    him.
  Kath. O then, belike, you fancy riches
    more:
You will have Gremio to keep you fair.
  Bian. Is it for him you do envy me so?
Nay then you jest, and now I well perceive
You have but jested with me all this while: 20
I prithee, sister Kate, untie my hands.
  Kath. If that be jest, then all the rest was
    so.   *[Strikes her.*

Enter Baptista.

  Bap. Why, how now, dame! whence grows
    this insolence?
Bianca, stand aside. Poor girl! she weeps.
Go ply thy needle; meddle not with her.
For shame, thou hilding of a devilish spirit,
Why dost thou wrong her that did ne'er wrong
    thee?
When did she cross thee with a bitter word?
  Kath. Her silence flouts me, and I'll be re-
    venged.   *[Flies after Bianca.*
  Bap. What, in my sight? Bianca, get thee
    in.   *[Exit Bianca.*   30
  Kath. What, will you not suffer me? Nay,
    now I see
She is your treasure, she must have a husband;
I must dance bare-foot on her wedding day
And for your love to her lead apes in hell.
Talk not to me: I will go sit and weep
Till I can find occasion of revenge.   *[Exit.*
  Bap. Was ever gentleman thus grieved as
    I?
But who comes here?

Enter Gremio, Lucentio *in the habit of a
    mean man;* Petruchio, *with* Hortensio *as
    a musician; and* Tranio, *with* Biondello
    bearing a lute and books.*

  Gre. Good morrow, neighbor Baptista.
  Bap. Good morrow, neighbor Gremio.
God save you, gentlemen!   41
  Pet. And you, good sir! Pray, have you
    not a daughter
Call'd Katharina, fair and virtuous?
  Bap. I have a daughter, sir, called Katha-
    rina.
  Gre. You are too blunt: go to it orderly.
  Pet. You wrong me, Signior Gremio: give
    me leave.
I am a gentleman of Verona, sir,
That, hearing of her beauty and her wit,
Her affability and bashful modesty,
Her wondrous qualities and mild behavior, 50
Am bold to show myself a forward guest
Within your house, to make mine eye the wit-
    ness
Of that report which I so oft have heard.
And, for an entrance to my entertainment,

I do present you with a man of mine,
                 [*Presenting Hortensio.*
Cunning in music and the mathematics,
To instruct her fully in those sciences,
Whereof I know she is not ignorant:
Accept of him, or else you do me wrong:
His name is Licio, born in Mantua.   60
  Bap. You're welcome, sir; and he, for
    your good sake.
But for my daughter Katharine, this I know,
She is not for your turn, the more my grief.
  Pet. I see you do not mean to part with
    her,
Or else you like not of my company.
  Bap. Mistake me not; I speak but as I
    find.
Whence are you, sir? what may I call your
    name?
  Pet. Petruchio is my name; Antonio's son,
A man well known throughout all Italy.
  Bap. I know him well: you are welcome
    for his sake.   70
  Gre. Saving your tale, Petruchio, I pray,
Let us, that are poor petitioners, speak too:
Baccare! you are marvellous forward.
  Pet. O, pardon me, Signior Gremio; I
    would fain be doing.
  Gre. I doubt it not, sir; but you will curse
    your wooing.
Neighbor, this is a gift very grateful, I am
sure of it. To express the like kindness, myself,
that have been more kindly beholding to you
than any, freely give unto you this young
scholar [*presenting Lucentio*], that hath been
long studying at Rheims; as cunning in Greek,
Latin, and other languages, as the other in
music and mathematics: his name is Cambio;
pray, accept his service.
  Bap. A thousand thanks, Signior Gremio.
Welcome, good Cambio. [*To Tranio*] But,
gentle sir, methinks you walk like a stranger:
may I be so bold to know the cause of your
coming?
  Tra. Pardon me, sir, the boldness is mine
    own,
That, being a stranger in this city here,   90
Do make myself a suitor to your daughter,
Unto Bianca, fair and virtuous.
Nor is your firm resolve unknown to me,
In the preferment of the eldest sister.
This liberty is all that I request,
That, upon knowledge of my parentage,
I may have welcome 'mongst the rest that woo
And free access and favor as the rest:
And, toward the education of your daughters,
I here bestow a simple instrument,   100
And this small packet of Greek and Latin
    books:
If you accept them, then their worth is great.
  Bap. Lucentio is your name; of whence, I
    pray?
  Tra. Of Pisa, sir; son to Vincentio.
  Bap. A mighty man of Pisa; by report
I know him well: you are very welcome, sir,
Take you the lute, and you the set of books;
You shall go see your pupils presently.
Holla, within!

        Enter a Servant.
        Sirrah, lead these gentlemen
To my daughters; and tell them both,   110
These are their tutors: bid them use them well.

      [*Exit Servant, with Lucentio and Hortensio,
                  Biondello following.*
We will go walk a little in the orchard,
And then to dinner. You are passing welcome,
And so I pray you all to think yourselves.
  Pet. Signior Baptista, my business asketh
    haste,
And every day I cannot come to woo.
You knew my father well, and in him me,
Left solely heir to all his lands and goods,
Which I have better'd rather than decreased:
Then tell me, if I get your daughter's love, 120
What dowry shall I have with her to wife?
  Bap. After my death the one half of my
    lands,
And in possession twenty thousand crowns.
  Pet. And, for that dowry, I'll assure her of
Her widowhood, be it that she survive me,
In all my lands and leases whatsoever:
Let specialties be therefore drawn between us,
That covenants may be kept on either hand.
  Bap. Ay, when the special thing is well ob-
    tain'd,
That is, her love; for that is all in all.   130
  Pet. Why, that is nothing: for I tell you,
    father,
I am as peremptory as she proud-minded;
And where two raging fires meet together
They do consume the thing that feeds their
    fury:
Though little fire grows great with little wind,
Yet extreme gusts will blow out fire and all:
So I to her and so she yields to me;
For I am rough and woo not like a babe.
  Bap. Well mayst thou woo, and happy be
    thy speed!
But be thou arm'd for some unhappy words.
  Pet. Ay, to the proof; as mountains are
    for winds,   141
That shake not, though they blow perpetually.

Re-enter HORTENSIO, *with his head broke.*
  Bap. How now, my friend! why dost thou
    look so pale?
  Hor. For fear, I promise you, if I look
    pale.
  Bap. What, will my daughter prove a good
    musician?
  Hor. I think she'll sooner prove a soldier:
Iron may hold with her, but never lutes.
  Bap. Why, then thou canst not break her
    to the lute?
  Hor. Why, no; for she hath broke the lute
    to me.
I did but tell her she mistook her frets,   150
And bow'd her hand to teach her fingering;
When, with a most impatient devilish spirit,
'Frets, call you these?' quoth she; 'I'll fume
    with them:'
And, with that word, she struck me on the
    head,
And through the instrument my pate made
    way;
And there I stood amazed for a while,
As on a pillory, looking through the lute;
While she did call me rascal fiddler
And twangling Jack; with twenty such vile
    terms,
As had she studied to misuse me so.   160
  Pet. Now, by the world, it is a lusty
    wench!
I love her ten times more than e'er I did:
O, how I long to have some chat with her!

Bap. Well, go with me and be not so dis-
comfited :
Proceed in practice with my younger daughter ;
She's apt to learn and thankful for good turns.
Signior Petruchio, will you go with us,
Or shall I send my daughter Kate to you ?
Pet. I pray you do. [*Exeunt all but Petru-*
chio.] I will attend her here,   169
And woo her with some spirit when she comes.
Say that she rail ; why then I'll tell her plain
She sings as sweetly as a nightingale :
Say that she frown ; I'll say she looks as clear
As morning roses newly wash'd with dew :
Say she be mute and will not speak a word ;
Then I'll commend her volubility,
And say she uttereth piercing eloquence :
If she do bid me pack, I'll give her thanks,
As though she bid me stay by her a week :
If she deny to wed, I'll crave the day   180
When I shall ask the banns and when be mar-
ried.
But here she comes ; and now, Petruchio,
speak.

Enter KATHARINA.

Good morrow, Kate ; for that's your name, I
hear.
  Kath. Well have you heard, but something
hard of hearing :
They call me Katharine that do talk of me.
  Pet. You lie, in faith ; for you are call'd
plain Kate,
And bonny Kate and sometimes Kate the
curst ;
But Kate, the prettiest Kate in Christendom
Kate of Kate Hall, my super-dainty Kate,
For dainties are all Kates, and therefore, Kate,
Take this of me, Kate of my consolation ; 191
Hearing thy mildness praised in every town,
Thy virtues spoke of, and thy beauty sounded,
Yet not so deeply as to thee belongs,
Myself am moved to woo thee for my wife.
  Kath. Moved ! in good time : let him that
moved you hither
Remove you hence : I knew you at the first
You were a moveable.
  Pet.   Why, what's a moveable ?
  Kath. A join'd-stool.
  Pet.   Thou hast hit it : come, sit on me.
  Kath. Asses are made to bear, and so are
you.
  Pet. Women are made to bear, and so are
you.
  Kath. No such jade as you, if me you
mean.
  Pet. Alas ! good Kate, I will not burden
thee ;
For, knowing thee to be but young and light—
  Kath. Too light for such a swain as you to
catch ;
And yet as heavy as my weight should be.
  Pet. Should be ! should—buzz !
  Kath.   Well ta'en, and like a buzzard.
  Pet. O slow-wing'd turtle ! shall a buzzard
take thee ?
  Kath. Ay, for a turtle, as he takes a buz-
zard.
  Pet. Come, come, you wasp ; i' faith, you
are too angry.   210
  Kath. If I be waspish, best beware my
sting.
  Pet. My remedy is then, to pluck it out.

  Kath. Ay, if the fool could find it where
it lies.
  Pet. Who knows not where a wasp does
wear his sting ? In his tail.
  Kath. In his tongue.
  Pet. Whose tongue ?
  Kath. Yours, if you talk of tails : and so
farewell.
  Pet. What, with my tongue in your tail ?
nay, come again,
Good Kate ; I am a gentleman.
  Kath. That I'll try. [*She strikes him.* 220
  Pet. I swear I'll cuff you, if you strike
again.
  Kath. So may you lose your arms :
If you strike me, you are no gentleman ;
And if no gentleman, why then no arms.
  Pet. A herald, Kate ? O, put me in thy
books !
  Kath. What is your crest ? a coxcomb ?
  Pet. A combless cock, so Kate will be my
hen.
  Kath. No cock of mine ; you crow too like
a craven.
  Pet. Nay, come, Kate, come ; you must not
look so sour.
  Kath. It is my fashion, when I see a crab.
  Pet. Why, here's no crab ; and therefore
look not sour.   231
  Kath. There is, there is.
  Pet. Then show it me.
  Kath. Had I a glass, I would.
  Pet. What, you mean my face ?
  Kath. Well aim'd of such a young one.
  Pet. Now, by Saint George, I am too young
for you.
  Kath. Yet you are wither'd.
  Pet. 'Tis with cares.   240
  Kath. I care not.
  Pet. Nay, hear you, Kate : in sooth you
scape not so.
  Kath. I chafe you, if I tarry : let me go.
  Pet. No, not a whit : I find you passing
gentle.
'Twas told me you were rough and coy and
sullen,
And now I find report a very liar ;
For thou are pleasant, gamesome, passing
courteous,
But slow in speech, yet sweet as spring-time
flowers :
Thou canst not frown, thou canst not look
askance,
Nor bite the lip, as angry wenches will,   250
Nor hast thou pleasure to be cross in talk,
But thou with mildness entertain'st thy wooers,
With gentle conference, soft and affable,
Why does the world report that Kate doth
limp ?
O slanderous world ! Kate like the hazel-twig
Is straight and slender and as brown in hue
As hazel nuts and sweeter than the kernels.
O, let me see thee walk : thou dost not halt.
  Kath. Go, fool, and whom thou keep'st
command.
  Pet. Did ever Dian so become a grove 260
As Kate this chamber with her princely gait ?
O, be thou Dian, and let her be Kate ;
And then let Kate be chaste and Dian sport-
ful !
  Kath. Where did you study all this goodly
speech ?
  Pet. It is extempore, from my mother-wit.

Kath. A witty mother ! witless else her son.
Pet. Am I not wise ?
Kath. Yes ; keep you warm.
Pet. Marry, so I mean, sweet Katharine, in thy bed :
And therefore, setting all this chat aside, 270
Thus in plain terms : your father hath consented
That you shall be my wife ; your dowry 'greed on ;
And, will you, nill you, I will marry you.
Now, Kate, I am a husband for your turn ;
For, by this light, whereby I see thy beauty,
Thy beauty, that doth make me like thee well,
Thou must be married to no man but me ;
For I am he am born to tame you Kate,
And bring you from a wild Kate to a Kate
Conformable as other household Kates.   280
Here comes your father : never make denial ;
I must and will have Katharine to my wife.

Re-enter BAPTISTA, GREMIO, *and* TRANIO.

Bap. Now, Signior Petruchio, how speed you with my daughter ?
Pet. How but well, sir ? how but well ?
It were impossible I should speed amiss.
Bap. Why, how now, daughter Katharine ! in your dumps ?
Kath. Call you me daughter ? now, I promise you
You have show'd a tender fatherly regard,
To wish me wed to one half lunatic ;
A mad-cup ruffian and a swearing Jack,   290
That thinks with oaths to face the matter out.
Pet. Father, 'tis thus : yourself and all the world,
That talk'd of her, have talk'd amiss of her :
If she be curst, it is for policy,
For she's not froward, but modest as the dove ;
She is not hot, but temperate as the morn ;
For patience she will prove a second Grissel,
And Roman Lucrece for her chastity :
And to conclude, we have 'greed so well together,
That upon Sunday is the wedding-day.   300
Kath. I'll see thee hang'd on Sunday first.
Gre. Hark, Petruchio ; she says she'll see thee hang'd first.
Tra. Is this your speeding ? nay, then, good night our part !
Pet. Be patient, gentlemen ; I choose her for myself :
If she and I be pleased, what's that to you ?
'Tis bargain'd 'twixt us twain, being alone,
That she shall still be curst in company.
I tell you, 'tis incredible to believe
How much she loves me : O, the kindest Kate !
She hung about my neck ; and kiss on kiss
She vied so fast, protesting oath on oath,   311
That in a twink she won me to her love.
O, you are novices ! 'tis a world to see,
How tame, when men and women are alone,
A meacock wretch can make the curstest shrew.
Give me thy hand, Kate : I will unto Venice,
To buy apparel 'gainst the wedding-day.
Provide the feast, father, and bid the guests ;
I will be sure my Katharine shall be fine.
Bap. I know not what to say : but give me your hands ;   320
God send you joy, Petruchio ! 'tis a match.
Gre. Tra. Amen, say we : we will be witnesses.

Pet. Father, and wife, and gentlemen, adieu ;
I will to Venice ; Sunday comes apace :
We will have rings and things and fine array ;
And kiss me, Kate, we will be married o'Sunday.

[*Exeunt Petruchio and Katharina severally.*
Gre. Was ever match clapp'd up so suddenly ?
Bap. Faith, gentlemen, now I play a merchant's part,
And venture madly on a desperate mart.
Tra. 'Twas a commodity lay fretting by you :   330
'Twill bring you gain, or perish on the seas.
Bap. The gain I seek is, quiet in the match.
Gre. No doubt but he hath got a quiet catch.
But now, Baptista, to your younger daughter :
Now is the day we long have looked for :
I am your neighbor, and was suitor first.
Tra. And I am one that love Bianca more
Than words can witness, or your thoughts can guess.
Gre. Youngling, thou canst not love so dear as I.
Tra. Greybeard, thy love doth freeze.
Gre.   But thine doth fry.   340
Skipper, stand back : 'tis age that nourisheth.
Tra. But youth in ladies' eyes that flourisheth.
Bap. Content you, gentlemen : I will compound this strife :
'Tis deeds must win the prize ; and he of both
That can assure my daughter greatest dower
Shall have my Bianca's love.
Say, Signior Gremio, what can you assure her ?
Gre. First, as you know, my house within the city
Is richly furnished with plate and gold ;
Basins and ewers to lave her dainty hands ;
My hangings all of Tyrian tapestry ;   351
In ivory coffers I have stuff'd my crowns ;
In cypress chests my arras counterpoints,
Costly apparel, tents, and canopies,
Fine linen, Turkey cushions boss'd with pearl,
Valance of Venice gold in needlework,
Pewter and brass and all things that belong
To house or housekeeping : then, at my farm
I have a hundred milch-kine to the pail,
Sixscore fat oxen standing in my stalls,   360
And all things answerable to this portion.
Myself am struck in years, I must confess ;
And if I die to-morrow, this is hers,
If whilst I live she will be only mine.
Tra. That ' only ' came well in. Sir, list to me :
I am my father's heir and only son :
If I may have your daughter to my wife,
I'll leave her houses three or four as good,
Within rich Pisa walls, as any one
Old Signior Gremio has in Padua ;   370
Besides two thousand ducats by the year
Of fruitful land, all which shall be her jointure.
What, have I pinch'd you, Signior Gremio ?
Gre. Two thousand ducats by the year of land !
My land amounts not to so much in all :
That she shall have ; besides an argosy
That now is lying in Marseilles' road.
What, have I choked you with an argosy ?

Tra. Gremio, 'tis known my father hath
no less
Than three great argosies; besides two gal-
liases,   380
And twelve tight galleys : these I will assure
her,
And twice as much, whate'er thou offer'st
next.
Gre. Nay, I have offer'd all, I have no
more ;
And she can have no more than all I have :
If you like me, she shall have me and mine.
Tra. Why, then the maid is mine from all
the world,
By your firm promise : Gremio is out-vied.
Bap. I must confess your offer is the best ;
And, let your father make her the assurance,
She is your own ; else, you must pardon me,
If you should die before him, where's her
dower ?   391
Tra. That's but a cavil : he is old, I young.
Gre. And may not young men die, as well
as old ?
Bap. Well, gentlemen,
I am thus resolved : on Sunday next you know
My daughter Katharine is to be married :
Now, on the Sunday following, shall Bianca
Be bride to you, if you make this assurance ;
If not, to Signior Gremio :
And so, I take my leave, and thank you both.
Gre. Adieu, good neighbor.   400
                            [*Exit Baptista.*
                Now I fear thee not :
Sirrah young gamester, your father were a fool
To give thee all, and in his waning age
Set foot under thy table : tut, a toy !
An old Italian fox is not so kind, my boy.
                                          [*Exit.*
Tra. A vengeance on your crafty wither'd
hide !
Yet I have faced it with a card of ten.
'Tis in my head to do my master good :
I see no reason but supposed Lucentio
Must get a father, call'd 'supposed Vincen-
tio ; '
And that's a wonder : fathers commonly   411
Do get their children ; but in this case of woo-
ing,
A child shall get a sire, if I fail not of my cun-
ning.   [*Exit.*

ACT III.

SCENE I. *Padua.* BAPTISTA'S *house.*

Enter LUCENTIO, HORTENSIO, *and* BIANCA.

Luc. Fiddler, forbear ; you grow too for-
ward, sir :
Have you so soon forgot the entertainment
Her sister Katharine welcomed you withal ?
Hor. But, wrangling pedant, this is
The patroness of heavenly harmony :
Then give me leave to have prerogative ;
And when in music we have spent an hour,
Your lecture shall have leisure for as much.
Luc. Preposterous ass, that never read so
far
To know the cause why music was ordain'd !
Was it not to refresh the mind of man   11
After his studies or his usual pain ?
Then give me leave to read philosophy,
And while I pause, serve in your harmony.

Hor. Sirrah, I will not bear these braves
of thine.
Bian. Why, gentlemen, you do me double
wrong,
To strive for that which resteth in my choice :
I am no breeching scholar in the schools ;
I'll not be tied to hours nor 'pointed times,
But learn my lessons as I please myself.   20
And, to cut off all strife, here sit we down :
Take you your instrument, play you the
whiles ;
His lecture will be done ere you have tuned.
Hor. You'll leave his lecture when I am in
tune ?
Luc. That will be never : tune your instru-
ment.
Bian. Where left we last ?
Luc. Here, madam :
' Hic ibat Simois ; hic est Sigeia tellus ;
Hic steterat Priami regia celsa senis.'
Bian. Construe them.   30
Luc. ' Hic ibat,' as I told you before, ' Si-
mois,' I am Lucentio, ' hic est,' son unto Vin-
centio of Pisa, ' Sigeia tellus,' disguised thus
to get your love ; ' Hic steterat,' and that
Lucentio that comes a-wooing, ' Priami,' is my
man Tranio, ' regia,' bearing my port, ' celsa
senis,' that we might beguile the old panta-
loon.
Hor. Madam, my instrument's in tune.
Bian. Let's hear. O fie ! the treble jars.
Luc. Spit in the hole, man, and tune again.
Bian. Now let me see if I can construe it :
' Hic ibat Simois,' I know you not, ' hic est
Sigeia tellus,' I trust you not ; ' Hic steterat
Priami,' take heed he hear us not, ' regia,'
presume not, ' celsa senis,' despair not.
Hor. Madam, 'tis now in tune.
Luc.   All but the base.
Hor. The base is right ; 'tis the base knave
that jars.
[*Aside*] How fiery and forward our pedant
is !
Now, for my life, the knave doth court my
love :
Pedascule, I'll watch you better yet.   50
Bian. In time I may believe, yet I mistrust.
Luc. Mistrust it not : for, sure, Æacides
Was Ajax, call'd so from his grandfather.
Bian. I must believe my master ; else, I
promise you,
I should be arguing still upon that doubt :
But let it rest. Now, Licio, to you :
Good masters, take it not unkindly, pray,
That I have been thus pleasant with you both.
Hor. You may go walk, and give me leave
a while :
My lessons make no music in three parts.   60
Luc. Are you so formal, sir ? well, I must
wait,
[*Aside*] And watch withal ; for, but I be de-
ceived,
Our fine musician groweth amorous.
Hor. Madam, before you touch the instru-
ment,
To learn the order of my fingering,
I must begin with rudiments of art ;
To teach you gamut in a briefer sort,
More pleasant, pithy and effectual,
Than hath been taught by any of my trade :
And there it is in writing, fairly drawn.   70
Bian. Why, I am past my gamut long ago.
Hor. Yet read the gamut of Hortensio.

Bian. [*Reads*] " ' Gamut ' I am, the ground
of all accord,
' A re,' to plead Hortensio's passion ;
' B mi,' Bianca, take him for thy lord,
' C fa ut,' that loves with all affection :
' D sol re,' one clef, two notes have I :
' E la mi,' show pity, or I die."
Call you this gamut ? tut, I like it not :
Old fashions please me best ; I am not so nice,
To change true rules for old inventions. 81

Enter a Servant.

Serv. Mistress, your father prays you leave
your books
And help to dress your sister's chamber up :
You know to-morrow is the wedding-day.
Bian. Farewell, sweet masters both ; I must
be gone. [*Exeunt Bianca and Servant.*
Luc. Faith, mistress, then I have no cause
to stay. [*Exit.*
Hor. But I have cause to pry into this ped-
ant :
Methinks he looks as though he were in love :
Yet if thy thoughts, Bianca, be so humble
To cast thy wandering eyes on every stale, 90
Seize thee that list : if once I find thee rang-
ing,
Hortensio will be quit with thee by changing.
[*Exit.*

SCENE II. *Padua. Before* BAPTISTA'S *house.*
Enter BAPTISTA, GREMIO, TRANIO, KATHARINA,
BIANCA, LUCENTIO, *and* others, attendants.

Bap. [*To Tranio*] Signior Lucentio, this is
the 'pointed day.
That Katharine and Petruchio should be mar-
ried,
And yet we hear not of our son-in-law.
What will be said ? what mockery will it be,
To want the bridegroom when the priest at-
tends
To speak the ceremonial rites of marriage !
What says Lucentio to this shame of ours ?
Kath. No shame but mine : I must, for-
sooth, be forced
To give my hand opposed against my heart
Unto a mad-brain rudesby full of spleen ; 10
Who woo'd in haste and means to wed at lei-
sure.
I told you, I, he was a frantic fool,
Hiding his bitter jests in blunt behavior :
And, to be noted for a merry man,
He'll woo a thousand, 'point the day of mar-
riage,
Make feasts, invite friends, and proclaim the
banns ;
Yet never means to wed where he hath woo'd.
Now must the world point at poor Katharine,
And say, ' Lo, there is mad Petruchio's wife,
If it would please him come and marry her ! '
Tra. Patience, good Katharine, and Bap-
tista too. 21
Upon my life, Petruchio means but well,
Whatever fortune stays him from his word :
Though he be blunt, I know him passing wise ;
Though he be merry, yet withal he's honest.
Kath. Would Katharine had never seen
him though !
[*Exit weeping, followed by Bianca and others.*
Bap. Go, girl ; I cannot blame thee now to
weep ;
For such an injury would vex a very saint,
Much more a shrew of thy impatient humor.

Enter BIONDELLO.

Bion. Master, master ! news, old news, and
such news as you never heard of ! 31
Bap. Is it new and old too ? how may that
be ?
Bion. Why, is it not news, to hear of Pe-
truchio's coming ?
Bap. Is he come ?
Bion. Why, no, sir.
Bap. What then ?
Bion. He is coming.
Bap. When will he be here ?
Bion. When he stands where I am and sees
you there. 41
Tra. But say, what to thine old news ?
Bion. Why, Petruchio is coming in a new
hat and an old jerkin, a pair of old breeches
thrice turned, a pair of boots that have been
candle-cases, one buckled, another laced, an
old rusty sword ta'en out of the town-armory,
with a broken hilt, and chapeless ; with two
broken points : his horse hipped with an old
mothy saddle and stirrups of no kindred ; besides, possessed with the glanders and like to
mose in the chine ; troubled with the lampass,
infected with the fashions, full of windgalls,
sped with spavins, rayed with the yellows, past
cure of the fives, stark spoiled with the staggers, begnawn with the bots, swayed in the
back and shoulder-shotten ; near-legged before
and with a half-checked bit and a head-stall
of sheep's leather which, being restrained to
keep him from stumbling, hath been often
burst and now repaired with knots ; one girth
six times pieced and a woman's crupper of
velure, which hath two letters for her name
fairly set down in studs, and here and there
pieced with packthread.
Bap. Who comes with him ?
Bion. O, sir, his lackey, for all the world
caparisoned like the horse ; with a linen stock
on one leg and a kersey boot-hose on the
other, gartered with a red and blue list ; an old
hat and ' the humor of forty fancies ' pricked
in't for a feather : a monster, a very monster
in apparel, and not like a Christian footboy or
a gentleman's lackey.
Tra. 'Tis some odd humor pricks him to
this fashion ;
Yet oftentimes he goes but mean-apparell'd.
Bap. I am glad he's come, howsoe'er he
comes.
Bion. Why, sir, he comes not.
Bap. Didst thou not say he comes ?
Bion. Who ? that Petruchio came ?
Bap. Ay, that Petruchio came. 80
Bion. No, sir ; I say his horse comes, with
him on his back.
Bap. Why, that's all one.
Bion. Nay, by Saint Jamy,
I hold you a penny,
A horse and a man
Is more than one,
And yet not many.

Enter PETRUCHIO *and* GRUMIO.

Pet. Come, where be these gallants ? who's
at home ?
Bap. You are welcome, sir.
Pet. And yet I come not well. 90
Bap. And yet you halt not.
Tra. Not so well apparell'd
As I wish you were.

Pet. Were it better, I should rush in thus.
But where is Kate ? where is my lovely bride ?
How does my father ? Gentles, methinks you
    frown :
And wherefore gaze this goodly company,
As if they saw some wondrous monument,
Some comet or unusual prodigy ?
    Bap. Why, sir, you know this is your wed-
        ding-day :
First were we sad, fearing you would not
    come ;   100
Now sadder, that you come so unprovided.
Fie, doff this habit, shame to your estate,
An eye-sore to our solemn festival !
    Tra. And tells us, what occasion of import
Hath all so long detain'd you from your wife,
And sent you hither so unlike yourself ?
    Pet. Tedious it were to tell, and harsh to
        hear :
Sufficeth, I am come to keep my word,
Though in some part enforced to digress ;
Which, at more leisure, I will so excuse   110
As you shall well be satisfied withal.
But where is Kate ? I stay too long from her :
The morning wears, 'tis time we were at
    church.
    Tra. See not your bride in these unreverent
        robes :
Go to my chamber ; put on clothes of mine.
    Pet. Not I, believe me : thus I'll visit her.
    Bap. But thus, I trust, you will not marry
        her.
    Pet. Good sooth, even thus ; therefore ha'
        done with words :
To me she's married, not unto my clothes :
Could I repair what she will wear in me,   120
As I can change these poor accoutrements,
'Twere well for Kate and better for myself.
But what a fool am I to chat with you,
When I should bid good morrow to my bride,
And seal the title with a lovely kiss !
            [*Exeunt Petruchio and Grumio.*
    Tra. He hath some meaning in his mad
        attire :
We will persuade him, be it possible,
To put on better ere he go to church.
    Bap. I'll after him, and see the event of
        this.
        [*Exeunt Baptista, Gremio, and attendants.*
    Tra. But to her love concerneth us to add
Her father's liking : which to bring to pass,
As I before imparted to your worship,
I am to get a man,—whate'er he be,
It skills not much, we'll fit him to our turn,—
And he shall be Vincentio of Pisa ;
And make assurance here in Padua
Of greater sums than I have promised.
So shall you quietly enjoy your hope,
And marry sweet Bianca with consent.
    Luc. Were it not that my fellow-school-
        master   140
Doth watch Bianca's steps so narrowly,
'Twere good, methinks, to steal our marriage ;
Which once perform'd, let all the world say
    no,
I'll keep mine own, despite of all the world.
    Tra. That by degrees we mean to look
        into,
And watch our vantage in this business :
We'll over-reach the greybeard, Gremio,
The narrow-prying father, Minola,
The quaint musician, amorous Licio ;
All for my master's sake, Lucentio.   150

Re-enter GREMIO.

Signior Gremio, came you from the church ?
    Gre. As willingly as e'er I came from
        school.
    Tra. And is the bride and bridegroom
        coming home ?
    Gre. A bridegroom say you ? 'tis a groom
        indeed,
A grumbling groom, and that the girl shall
    find.
    Tra. Curster than she ? why, 'tis impos-
        sible.
    Gre. Why, he's a devil, a devil, a very
        fiend.
    Tra. Why, she's a devil, a devil, the devil's
        dam.
    Gre. Tut, she's a lamb, a dove, a fool to
        him !
I'll tell you, Sir Lucentio : when the priest 160
Should ask, if Katharine should be his wife,
' Ay, by gogs-wouns,' quoth he ; and swore so
    loud,
That, all-amazed, the priest let fall the book ;
And, as he stoop'd again to take it up,
The mad-brain'd bridegroom took him such a
    cuff
That down fell priest and book and book and
    priest :
' Now take them up,' quoth he, ' if any list.'
    Tra. What said the wench when he rose
        again ?
    Gre. Trembled and shook ; for why, he
        stamp'd and swore,
As if the vicar meant to cozen him.   170
But after many ceremonies done,
He calls for wine : ' A health ! ' quoth he, as
    if
He had been aboard, carousing to his mates
After a storm ; quaff'd off the muscadel
And threw the sops all in the sexton's face ;
Having no other reason
But that his beard grew thin and hungerly
And seem'd to ask him sops as he was drink-
    ing.
This done, he took the bride about the neck
And kiss'd her lips with such a clamorous
    smack   180
That at the parting all the church did echo :
And I seeing this came thence for very shame ;
And after me, I know, the rout is coming.
Such a mad marriage never was before :
Hark, hark ! I hear the minstrels play.
                                        [*Music.*

Re-enter PETRUCHIO, KATHARINA, BIANCA,
BAPTISTA, HORTENSIO, GRUMIO, *and* Train.

    Pet. Gentlemen and friends, I thank you
        for your pains :
I know you think to dine with me to-day,
And have prepared great store of wedding
    cheer ;
But so it is, my haste doth call me hence,   189
And therefore here I mean to take my leave.
    Bap. Is't possible you will away to-night ?
    Pet. I must away to-day, before night
        come :
Make it no wonder ; if you knew my business,
You would entreat me rather go than stay.
And, honest company, I thank you all,
That have beheld me give away myself
To this most patient, sweet and virtuous wife :
Dine with my father, drink a health to me ;

For I must hence; and farewell to you all.
  Tra. Let us entreat you stay till after din-
    ner.
  Pet. It may not be.
  Gre.   Let me entreat you.
  Pet. It cannot be.
  Kath.   Let me entreat you. 201
  Pet. I am content.
  Kath.   Are you content to stay?
  Pet. I am content you shall entreat me
    stay;
But yet not stay, entreat me how you can.
  Kath. Now, if you love me, stay.
  Pet.   Grumio, my horse.
  Gru. Ay, sir, they be ready: the oats have
eaten the horses.
  Kath. Nay, then,
Do what thou canst, I will not go to-day; 210
No, nor to-morrow, not till I please myself.
The door is open, sir; there lies your way;
You may be jogging whiles your boots are
  green;
For me, I'll not be gone till I please myself:
'Tis like you'll prove a jolly surly groom,
That take it on you at the first so roundly.
  Pet. O Kate, content thee; prithee, be not
    angry.
  Kath. I will be angry: what hast thou to
    do?
Father, be quiet; he shall stay my leisure. 219
  Gre. Ay, marry, sir, now it begins to work.
  Kath. Gentlemen, forward to the bridal
    dinner:
I see a woman may be made a fool,
If she had not a spirit to resist.
  Pet. They shall go forward, Kate, at thy
    command.
Obey the bride, you that attend on her;
Go to the feast, revel and domineer,
Carouse full measure to her maidenhead,
Be mad and merry, or go hang yourselves:
But for my bonny Kate, she must with me.
Nay, look not big, nor stamp, nor stare, nor
  fret;   230
I will be master of what is mine own:
She is my goods, my chattels; she is my house,
My household stuff, my field, my barn,
My horse, my ox, my ass, my any thing;
And here she stands, touch her whoever dare;
I'll bring mine action on the proudest he
That stops my way in Padua. Grumio,
Draw forth thy weapon, we are beset with
  thieves;
Rescue thy mistress, if thou be a man.
Fear not, sweet wench, they shall not touch
  thee, Kate: 240
I'll buckler thee against a million.
  [*Exeunt Petruchio, Katharina, and Grumio.*
  Bap. Nay, let them go, a couple of quiet
    ones.
  Gre. Went they not quickly, I should die
    with laughing.
  Tra. Of all mad matches never was the
    like.
  Luc. Mistress, what's your opinion of your
    sister?
  Bian. That, being mad herself, she's madly
    mated.
  Gre. I warrant him, Petruchio is Kated.
  Bap. Neighbors and friends, though bride
    and bridegroom wants
For to supply the places at the table,
You know there wants no junkets at the feast.

Lucentio, you shall supply the bridegroom's
  place: 251
And let Bianca take her sister's room.
  Tra. Shall sweet Bianca practise how to
    bride it?
  Bap. She shall, Lucentio. Come, gentlemen,
    let's go.   [*Exeunt.*

ACT IV.

SCENE I. PETRUCHIO'S *country house.*

Enter GRUMIO.

  Gru. Fie, fie on all tired jades, on all mad
masters, and all foul ways! Was ever man so
beaten? was ever man so rayed? was ever
man so weary? I am sent before to make a
fire, and they are coming after to warm them.
Now, were not I a little pot and soon hot, my
very lips might freeze to my teeth, my tongue
to the roof of my mouth, my heart in my belly,
ere I should come by a fire to thaw me: but
I, with blowing the fire, shall warm myself;
for, considering the weather, a taller man than
I will take cold. Holla, ho! Curtis.

Enter CURTIS.

  Curt. Who is that calls so coldly?
  Gru. A piece of ice: if thou doubt it, thou
mayst slide from my shoulder to my heel with
no greater a run but my head and my neck. A
fire, good Curtis.
  Curt. Is my master and his wife coming,
Grumio?
  Gru. O, ay, Curtis, ay: and therefore fire,
fire; cast on no water.   21
  Curt. Is she so hot a shrew as she's reported?
  Gru. She was, good Curtis, before this
frost: but, thou knowest, winter tames man,
woman and beast; for it hath tamed my old
master and my new mistress and myself, fellow Curtis.
  Curt. Away, you three-inch fool! I am no
beast.
  Gru. Am I but three inches? why, thy
horn is a foot; and so long am I at the least.
But wilt thou make a fire, or shall I complain
on thee to our mistress, whose hand, she being
now at hand, thou shalt soon feel, to thy cold
comfort, for being slow in thy hot office?
  Curt. I prithee, good Grumio, tell me, how
goes the world?
  Gru. A cold world, Curtis, in every office
but thine; and therefore fire: do thy duty,
and have thy duty; for my master and mistress
are almost frozen to death.   40
  Curt. There's fire ready; and therefore,
good Grumio, the news.
  Gru. Why, 'Jack, boy! ho! boy!' and as
much news as will thaw.
  Curt. Come, you are so full of cony-catching!
  Gru. Why, therefore fire; for I have
caught extreme cold. Where's the cook? is
supper ready, the house trimmed, rushes
strewed, cobwebs swept; the serving-men in
their new fustian, their white stockings, and
every officer his wedding-garment on? Be the
jacks fair within, the jills fair without, the car-
pets laid, and every thing in order?

Curt. All ready ; and therefore, I pray thee, news.

Gru. First, know, my horse is tired ; my master and mistress fallen out.

Curt. How ?

Gru. Out of their saddles into the dirt ; and thereby hangs a tale.   60

Curt. Let's ha't, good Grumio.

Gru. Lend thine ear.

Curt. Here.

Gru. There.   [*Strikes him.*

Curt. This is to feel a tale, not to hear a tale.

Gru. And therefore 'tis called a sensible tale : and this cuff was but to knock at your ear, and beseech listening. Now I begin : Imprimis, we came down a foul hill, my master riding behind my mistress,—   70

Curt. Both of one horse ?

Gru. What's that to thee ?

Curt. Why, a horse.

Gru. Tell thou the tale : but hadst thou not crossed me, thou shouldst have heard how her horse fell and she under her horse ; thou shouldst have heard in how miry a place, how she was bemoiled, how he left her with the horse upon her, how he beat me because her horse stumbled, how she waded through the dirt to pluck him off me, how he swore, how she prayed, that never prayed before, how I cried, how the horses ran away, how her bridle was burst, how I lost my crupper, with many things of worthy memory, which now shall die in oblivion and thou return unexperienced to thy grave.

Curt. By this reckoning he is more shrew than she.

Gru. Ay ; and that thou and the proudest of you all shall find when he comes home. But what talk I of this ? Call forth Nathaniel, Joseph, Nicholas, Philip, Walter, Sugarsop and the rest : let their heads be sleekly combed, their blue coats brushed and their garters of an indifferent knit : let them curtsy with their left legs and not presume to touch a hair of my master's horse-tail till they kiss their hands. Are they all ready ?

Curt. They are.

Gru. Call them forth.

Curt. Do you hear, ho ? you must meet my master to countenance my mistress.   101

Gru. Why, she hath a face of her own.

Curt. Who knows not that ?

Gru. Thou, it seems, that calls for company to countenance her.

Curt. I call them forth to credit her.

Gru. Why, she comes to borrow nothing of them.

Enter four or five Serving-men.

Nath. Welcome home, Grumio !

Phil. How now, Grumio !   110

Jos. What, Grumio !

Nich. Fellow Grumio !

Nath. How now, old lad ?

Gru. Welcome, you ;—how now, you ;— what, you ;—fellow, you ;—and thus much for greeting. Now, my spruce companions, is all ready, and all things neat ?

Nath. All things is ready. How near is our master ?   119

Gru. E'en at hand, alighted by this ; and therefore be not—Cock's passion, silence ! I hear my master.

Enter PETRUCHIO *and* KATHARINA.

Pet. Where be these knaves ? What, no man at door To hold my stirrup nor to take my horse ! Where is Nathaniel, Gregory, Philip ?

All Serv. Here, here, sir ; here, sir.

Pet. Here, sir ! here, sir ! here, sir ! here, sir !

You logger-headed and unpolish'd grooms ! What, no attendance ? no regard ? no duty ? Where is the foolish knave I sent before ?   130

Gru. Here, sir ; as foolish as I was before.

Pet. You peasant swain ! you whoreson malt-horse drudge ! Did I not bid thee meet me in the park, And bring along these rascal knaves with thee ?

Gru. Nathaniel's coat, sir, was not fully made, And Gabriel's pumps were all unpink'd i' the heel ; There was no link to color Peter's hat, And Walter's dagger was not come from sheathing : There were none fine but Adam, Ralph, and Gregory ; The rest were ragged, old, and beggarly ;   140 Yet, as they are, here are they come to meet you.

Pet. Go, rascals, go, and fetch my supper in.   [*Exeunt Servants.*

[*Singing*] Where is the life that late I led—

Where are those—Sit down, Kate, and welcome.—

Soud, soud, soud, soud !

Re-enter Servants with supper.

Why, when, I say ? Nay, good sweet Kate, be merry.

Off with my boots, you rogues ! you villains, when ?

[*Sings*] It was the friar of orders grey, As he forth walked on his way :—

Out, you rogue ! you pluck my foot awry :   150 Take that, and mend the plucking off the other.   [*Strikes him.*

Be merry, Kate. Some water, here ; what, ho ! Where's my spaniel Troilus ? Sirrah, get you hence, And bid my cousin Ferdinand come hither : One, Kate, that you must kiss, and be acquainted with.

Where are my slippers ? Shall I have some water ?

Enter one with water.

Come, Kate, and wash, and welcome heartily. You whoreson villain ! will you let it fall ?   [*Strikes him.*

Kath. Patience, I pray you ; 'twas a fault unwilling.

Pet. A whoreson beetle-headed, flap-ear'd knave !   160

Come, Kate, sit down ; I know you have a stomach.

Will you give thanks, sweet Kate ; or else shall I ?

What's this ? mutton ?

First Serv.   Ay.

Pet.   Who brought it ?

Peter.   I.
Pet. 'Tis burnt; and so is all the meat.
What dogs are these ! Where is the rascal
    cook ?
How durst you, villains, bring it from the
    dresser,
And serve it thus to me that love it not ?
There, take it to you, trenchers, cups, and all ;
    [*Throws the meat, &c. about the stage.*
You heedless joltheads and unmanner'd
    slaves !
What, do you grumble ? I'll be with you
    straight.   170
    Kath. I pray you, husband, be not so dis-
    quiet :
The meat was well, if you were so contented.
    Pet. I tell thee, Kate, 'twas burnt and dried
    away ;
And I expressly am forbid to touch it,
For it engenders choler, planteth anger ;
And better 'twere that both of us did fast,
Since, of ourselves, ourselves are choleric,
Than feed it with such over-roasted flesh.
Be patient ; to-morrow 't shall be mended, 179
And, for this night, we'll fast for company :
Come, I will bring thee to thy bridal chamber.
                        [*Exeunt.*

    Re-enter Servants *severally.*

    Nath. Peter, didst ever see the like ?
    Peter. He kills her in her own humor.

    Re-enter CURTIS.

    Gru. Where is he ?
    Curt. In her chamber, making a sermon
of continency to her ;
And rails, and swears, and rates, that she, poor
    soul,
Knows not which way to stand, to look, to
    speak,
And sits as one new-risen from a dream.
Away, away ! for he is coming hither.   200
                        [*Exeunt.*

    Re-enter PETRUCHIO.

    Pet. Thus have I politicly begun my reign,
And 'tis my hope to end successfully.
My falcon now is sharp and passing empty ;
And till she stoop she must not be full-gorged,
For then she never looks upon her lure.
Another way I have to man my haggard,
To make her come and know her keeper's
    call,
That is, to watch her, as we watch these kites
That bate and beat and will not be obedient.
She eat no meat to-day, nor none shall eat ;
Last night she slept not, nor to-night she shall
    not ;
As with the meat, some undeserved fault
I'll find about the making of the bed ;
And here I'll fling the pillow, there the bolster,
This way the coverlet, another way the sheets :
Ay, and amid this hurly I intend
That all is done in reverend care of her ;
And in conclusion she shall watch all night :
And if she chance to nod I'll rail and brawl
And with the clamor keep her still awake. 220
This is a way to kill a wife with kindness ;
And thus I'll curb her mad and headstrong
    humor.
He that knows better how to tame a shrew,
Now let him speak : 'tis charity to show.
                        [*Exit.*

SCENE II. *Padua. Before* BAPTISTA'S *house.*
    Enter TRANIO *and* HORTENSIO.

    Tra. Is't possible, friend Licio, that Mis
tress Bianca
Doth fancy any other but Lucentio ?
I tell you, sir, she bears me fair in hand.
    Hor. Sir, to satisfy you in what I have said,
Stand by and mark the manner of his teaching.

    Enter BIANCA *and* LUCENTIO.

    Luc. Now, mistress, profit you in what you
read ?
    Bian. What, master, read you ? first re-
solve me that.
    Luc. I read that I profess, the Art to Love.
    Bian. And may you prove, sir, master of
your art !
    Luc. While you, sweet dear, prove mistress
of my heart !   10
    Hor. Quick proceeders, marry ! Now, tell
me, I pray,
You that durst swear that your mistress Bianca
Loved none in the world so well as Lucentio.
    Tra. O despiteful love ! unconstant woman-
kind !
I tell thee, Licio, this is wonderful.
    Hor. Mistake no more : I am not Licio,
Nor a musician, as I seem to be ;
But one that scorn to live in this disguise,
For such a one as leaves a gentleman,
And makes a god of such a cullion :   20
Know, sir, that I am call'd Hortensio.
    Tra. Signior Hortensio, I have often heard
Of your entire affection to Bianca ;
And since mine eyes are witness of her light-
ness,
I will with you, if you be so contented,
Forswear Bianca and her love for ever.
    Hor. See, how they kiss and court ! Signior
Lucentio,
Here is my hand, and here I firmly vow
Never to woo her more, but do forswear her,
As one unworthy all the former favors   30
That I have fondly flatter'd her withal.
    Tra. And here I take the like unfeigned
oath,
Never to marry with her though she would en-
treat :
Fie on her ! see, how beastly she doth court
him !
    Hor. Would all the world but he had quite
forsworn !
For me, that I may surely keep mine oath,
I will be married to a wealthy widow,
Ere three days pass, which hath as long loved
me
As I have loved this proud disdainful haggard.
And so farewell, Signior Lucentio.   40
Kindness in women, not their beauteous looks,
Shall win my love : and so I take my leave,
In resolution as I swore before.   [*Exit.*
    Tra. Mistress Bianca, bless you with such
grace
As 'longeth to a lover's blessed case !
Nay, I have ta'en you napping, gentle love,
And have forsworn you with Hortensio.
    Bian. Tranio, you jest : but have you both
forsworn me ?
    Tra. Mistress, we have.
    Luc.   Then we are rid of Licio.
    Tra. I' faith, he'll have a lusty widow now,
That shall be woo'd and wedded in a day. 51

Bian. God give him joy !
Tra. Ay, and he'll tame her.
Bian.   He says so, Tranio.
Tra. Faith, he is gone unto the taming-
school.
Bian. The taming-school ! what, is there
such a place ?
Tra. Ay, mistress, and Petruchio is the
master ;
That teacheth tricks eleven and twenty long,
To tame a shrew and charm her chattering
tongue.

Enter BIONDELLO.

Bion. O master, master, I have watch'd so
long
That I am dog-weary : but at last I spied   60
An ancient angel coming down the hill,
Will serve the turn.
Tra.   What is he, Biondello ?
Bion. Master, a mercatante, or a pedant,
I know not what ; but formal in apparel,
In gait and countenance surely like a father.
Luc. And what of him, Tranio ?
Tra. If he be credulous and trust my tale,
I'll make him glad to seem Vincentio,
And give assurance to Baptista Minola,
As if he were the right Vincentio   70
Take in your love, and then let me alone.
                    [*Exeunt Lucentio and Bianca.*

Enter a Pedant.

Ped. God save you, sir !
Tra.   And you, sir ! you are welcome.
Travel you far on, or are you at the farthest ?
Ped. Sir, at the farthest for a week or two :
But then up farther, and as far as Rome ;
And so to Tripoli, if God lend me life.
Tra. What countryman, I pray ?
Ped.   Of Mantua.
Tra. Of Mantua, sir ? marry, God forbid !
And come to Padua, careless of your life ?
Ped. My life, sir ! how, I pray ? for that
goes hard.   80
Tra. 'Tis death for any one in Mantua
To come to Padua. Know you not the cause ?
Your ships are stay'd at Venice, and the duke,
For private quarrel 'twixt your duke and him,
Hath publish'd and proclaim'd it openly :
'Tis marvel, but that you are but newly come,
You might have heard it else proclaim'd about.
Ped. Alas ! sir, it is worse for me than so ;
For I have bills for money by exchange
From Florence and must here deliver them.
Tra. Well, sir, to do you courtesy,   91
This will I do, and this I will advise you :
First, tell me, have you ever been at Pisa ?
Ped. Ay, sir, in Pisa have I often been,
Pisa renowned for grave citizens.
Tra. Among them know you one Vin-
centio ?
Ped. I know him not, but I have heard of
him ;
A merchant of incomparable wealth.
Tra. He is my father, sir ; and, sooth to
say,   99
In countenance somewhat doth resemble you.
Bion. [*Aside*] As much as an apple doth
an oyster, and all one.
Tra. To save your life in this extremity,
This favor will I do you for his sake ;
And think it not the worst of all your fortunes
That you are like to Sir Vincentio.

His name and credit shall you undertake,
And in my house you shall be friendly lodged :
Look that you take upon you as you should ;
You understand me, sir : so shall you stay
Till you have done your business in the city :
If this be courtesy, sir, accept of it.   111
Ped. O sir, I do ; and will repute you ever
The patron of my life and liberty.
Tra. Then go with me to make the matter
good.
This, by the way, I let you understand ;
My father is here look'd for every day,
To pass assurance of a dower in marriage
'Twixt me and one Baptista's daughter here :
In all these circumstances I'll instruct you :
Go with me to clothe you as becomes you. 120
                                    [*Exeunt.*

SCENE III. *A room in* PETRUCHIO'S *house.*
Enter KATHARINA *and* GRUMIO.

Gru. No, no, forsooth ; I dare not for my
life.
Kath. The more my wrong, the more his
spite appears :
What, did he marry me to famish me ?
Beggars, that come unto my father's door,
Upon entreaty have a present alms ;
If not, elsewhere they meet with charity :
But I, who never knew how to entreat,
Nor never needed that I should entreat,
Am starved for meat, giddy for lack of sleep,
With oaths kept waking and with brawling
fed :   10
And that which spites me more than all these
wants,
He does it under name of perfect love ;
As who should say, if I should sleep or eat,
'Twere deadly sickness or else present death.
I prithee go and get me some repast ;
I care not what, so it be wholesome food.
Gru. What say you to a neat's foot ?
Kath. 'Tis passing good : I prithee let me
have it.
Gru. I fear it is too choleric a meat.
How say you to a fat tripe finely broil'd ? 20
Kath. I like it well : good Grumio, fetch it
me.
Gru. I cannot tell ; I fear 'tis choleric.
What say you to a piece of beef and mustard ?
Kath. A dish that I do love to feed upon.
Gru. Ay, but the mustard is too hot a little.
Kath. Why then, the beef, and let the mus-
tard rest.
Gru. Nay then, I will not : you shall have
the mustard,
Or else you get no beef of Grumio.
Kath. Then both, or one, or any thing thou
wilt.
Gru. Why then, the mustard without the
beef.   30
Kath. Go, get thee gone, thou false delud-
ing slave,   [*Beats him.*
That feed'st me with the very name of meat :
Sorrow on thee and all the pack of you,
That triumph thus upon my misery !
Go, get thee gone, I say.

Enter PETRUCHIO *and* HORTENSIO *with meat.*

Pet. How fares my Kate ? What, sweeting,
all amort ?
Hor. Mistress, what cheer ?
Kath.   Faith, as cold as can be.

Pet. Pluck up thy spirits ; look cheerfully
    upon me.
Here, love ; thou see'st how diligent I am   39
To dress thy meat myself and bring it thee :
I am sure, sweet Kate, this kindness merits
    thanks.
What, not a word ? Nay, then thou lovest it
    not ;
And all my pains is sorted to no proof.
Here, take away this dish.
    Kath.   I pray you, let it stand.
    Pet. The poorest service is repaid with
    thanks ;
And so shall mine, before you touch the meat.
    Kath. I thank you, sir.
    Hor. Signior Petruchio, fie ! you are to
blame.
Come, Mistress Kate, I'll bear you company.
    Pet. [*Aside*] Eat it up all, Hortensio, if thou
    lovest me.   50
Much good do it unto thy gentle heart !
Kate, eat apace : and now, my honey love,
Will we return unto thy father's house
And revel it as bravely as the best,
With silken coats and caps and golden rings,
With ruffs and cuffs and fardingales and
    things ;
With scarfs and fans and double change of
    bravery,
With amber bracelets, beads and all this
    knavery.
What, hast thou dined ? The tailor stays thy
    leisure,   59
To deck thy body with his ruffling treasure.

            Enter Tailor.

Come, tailor, let us see these ornaments ;
Lay forth the gown.

          Enter Haberdasher.

             What news with you, sir ?
    Hab. Here is the cap your worship did
bespeak.
    Pet. Why, this was moulded on a porrin-
    ger ;
A velvet dish : fie, fie ! 'tis lewd and filthy :
Why, 'tis a cockle or a walnut-shell,
A knack, a toy, a trick, a baby's cap :
Away with it ! come, let me have a bigger.
    Kath. I'll have no bigger : this doth fit the
    time,
And gentlewomen wear such caps as these. 70
    Pet. When you are gentle, you shall have
    one too,
And not till then.
    Hor. [*Aside*] That will not be in haste.
    Kath. Why, sir, I trust I may have leave to
    speak ;
And speak I will ; I am no child, no babe :
Your betters have endured me say my mind,
And if you cannot, best you stop your ears.
My tongue will tell the anger of my heart,
Or else my heart concealing it will break,
And rather than it shall, I will be free
Even to the uttermost, as I please, in words.
    Pet. Why, thou say'st true ; it is a paltry
    cap,   81
A custard-coffin, a bauble, a silken pie :
I love thee well, in that thou likest it not.
    Kath. Love me or love me not, I like the
    cap ;
And it I will have, or I will have none.
                [*Exit Haberdasher.*

    Pet. Thy gown ? why, ay : come, tailor, let
    us see't.
O mercy, God ! what masquing stuff is here ?
What's this ? a sleeve ? 'tis like a demi-
    cannon :
What, up and down, carved like an apple-
    tart ?
Here's snip and nip and cut and slish and
    slash,   90
Like to a censer in a barber's shop :
Why, what, i' devil's name, tailor, call'st thou
    this ?
    Hor. [*Aside*] I see she's like to have nei-
    ther cap nor gown.
    Tai. You bid me make it orderly and well,
According to the fashion and the time.
    Pet. Marry, and did ; but if you be remem-
    ber'd,
I did not bid you mar it to the time.
Go, hop me over every kennel home,
For you shall hop without my custom, sir :   99
I'll none of it : hence ! make your best of it.
    Kath. I never saw a better-fashion'd gown,
More quaint, more pleasing, nor more com-
    mendable :
Belike you mean to make a puppet of me.
    Pet. Why, true ; he means to make a pup-
    pet of thee.
    Tai. She says your worship means to make
a puppet of her.
    Pet. O monstrous arrogance ! Thou liest,
    thou thread, thou thimble,
Thou yard, three-quarters, half-yard, quarter,
    nail !
Thou flea, thou nit, thou winter-cricket thou !
Braved in mine own house with a skein of
    thread ?
Away, thou rag, thou quantity, thou remnant,
Or I shall so be-mete thee with thy yard
As thou shalt think on prating whilst thou
    livest !
I tell thee, I, that thou hast marr'd her gown.
    Tai. Your worship is deceived ; the gown is
    made
Just as my master had direction :
Grumio gave order how it should be done.
    Gru. I gave him no order ; I gave him the
    stuff.
    Tai. But how did you desire it should be
    made ?   120
    Gru. Marry, sir, with needle and thread.
    Tai. But did you not request to have it
    cut ?
    Gru. Thou hast faced many things.
    Tai. I have.
    Gru. Face not me : thou hast braved many
men ; brave not me ; I will neither be faced
nor braved. I say unto thee, I bid thy master
cut out the gown ; but I did not bid him cut it
to pieces : ergo, thou liest.
    Tai. Why, here is the note of the fashion to
testify.   131
    Pet. Read it.
    Gru. The note lies in's throat, if he say I
said so.
    Tai. [*Reads*] ' Imprimis, a loose-bodied
gown : '
    Gru. Master, if ever I said loose-bodied
gown, sew me in the skirts of it, and beat me
to death with a bottom of brown thread : I
said a gown.
    Pet. Proceed.

Tai. [*Reads*] 'With a small compassed cape : '   140
Gru. I confess the cape.
Tai. [*Reads*] 'With a trunk sleeve : '
Gru. I confess two sleeves.
Tai. [*Reads*] 'The sleeves curiously cut.'
Pet. Ay, there's the villany.
Gru. Error i' the bill, sir ; error i' the bill.
I commanded the sleeves should be cut out and
sewed up again ; and that I'll prove upon thee,
though thy little finger be armed in a thimble.
Tai. This is true that I say : an I had thee
in place where, thou shouldst know it.   151
Gru. I am for thee straight : take thou the
bill, give me thy mete-yard, and spare not me.
Hor. God-a-mercy, Grumio ! then he shall
have no odds.
Pet. Well, sir, in brief, the gown is not for
me.
Gru. You are i' the right, sir : 'tis for my
mistress.
Pet. Go, take it up unto thy master's use.
Gru. Villain, not for thy life : take up my
mistress' gown for thy master's use !   161
Pet. Why, sir, what's your conceit in that ?
Gru. O, sir, the conceit is deeper than you
     think for :
Take up my mistress' gown to his master's use !
O, fie, fie, fie !
Pet. [*Aside*] Hortensio, say thou wilt see
     the tailor paid.
Go take it hence ; be gone, and say no more.
Hor. Tailor, I'll pay thee for thy gown to-
     morrow :
Take no unkindness of his hasty words :
Away ! I say ; commend me to thy master. 170
                                        [*Exit Tailor.*
Pet. Well, come, my Kate ; we will unto
     your father's
Even in these honest mean habiliments :
Our purses shall be proud, our garments poor ;
For 'tis the mind that makes the body rich ;
And as the sun breaks through the darkest
     clouds,
So honor peereth in the meanest habit.
What is the jay more precious than the lark,
Because his feathers are more beautiful ?
Or is the adder better than the eel,
Because his painted skin contents the eye ? 180
O, no, good Kate ; neither art thou the worse
For this poor furniture and mean array.
If thou account'st it shame, lay it on me ;
And therefore frolic : we will hence forthwith,
To feast and sport us at thy father's house.
Go, call my men, and let us straight to him ;
And bring our horses unto Long-lane end ;
There will we mount, and thither walk on foot
Let's see ; I think 'tis now some seven o'clock,
And well we may come there by dinner-time.
Kath. I dare assure you, sir, 'tis almost
     two ;
And 'twill be supper-time ere you come there.
Pet. It shall be seven ere I go to horse :
Look, what I speak, or do, or think to do,
You are still crossing it. Sirs, let's alone :
I will not go to-day ; and ere I do,
It shall be what o'clock I say it is.
Hor. [*Aside*] Why, so this gallant will
     command the sun.   [*Exeunt.*

SCENE IV. *Padua. Before* BAPTISTA'S *house.*
Enter TRANIO, *and the* Pedant *dressed like*
                  VINCENTIO.

Tra. Sir, this is the house : please it you
     that I call ?
Ped. Ay, what else ? and but I be deceived
Signior Baptista may remember me,
Near twenty years ago, in Genoa,
Where we were lodgers at the Pegasus.
Tra. 'Tis well ; and hold your own, in any
     case,
With such austerity as 'longeth to a father.
Ped. I warrant you.

                Enter BIONDELLO.

                       But, sir, here comes your boy ;
'Twere good he were school'd.
Tra. Fear you not him. Sirrah Biondello,
Now do your duty throughly, I advise you : 11
Imagine 'twere the right Vincentio.
Bion. Tut, fear not me.
Tra. But hast thou done thy errand to
     Baptista ?
Bion. I told him that your father was at
     Venice,
And that you look'd for him this day in Padua.
Tra. Thou'rt a tall fellow : hold thee that
     to drink.
Here comes Baptista : set your countenance,
     sir.

        Enter BAPTISTA *and* LUCENTIO.

Signior Baptista, you are happily met.
[*To the Pedant*] Sir, this is the gentleman I
     told you of :   20
I pray you, stand good father to me now,
Give me Bianca for my patrimony.
Ped. Soft, son !
Sir, by your leave : having come to Padua
To gather in some debts, my son Lucentio
Made me acquainted with a weighty cause
Of love between your daughter and himself :
And, for the good report I hear of you
And for the love he beareth to your daughter
And she to him, to stay him not too long, 30
I am content, in a good father's care,
To have him match'd ; and if you please to like
No worse than I, upon some agreement
Me shall you find ready and willing
With one consent to have her so bestow'd ;
For curious I cannot be with you,
Signior Baptista, of whom I hear so well.
Bap. Sir, pardon me in what I have to
     say :
Your plainness and your shortness please me
     well.
Right true it is, your son Lucentio here   40
Doth love my daughter and she loveth him,
Or both dissemble deeply their affections :
And therefore, if you say no more than this,
That like a father you will deal with him
And pass my daughter a sufficient dower,
The match is made, and all is done :
Your son shall have my daughter with con-
     sent.
Tra. I thank you, sir. Where then do you
     know best
We be affied and such assurance ta'en
As shall with either part's agreement stand ?
Bap. Not in my house, Lucentio ; for, you
     know,   51
Pitchers have ears, and I have many servants :
Besides, old Gremio is hearkening still ;
And happily we might be interrupted.
Tra. Then at my lodging, an it like you :
There doth my father lie ; and there, this night,

We'll pass the business privately and well.
Send for your daughter by your servant here :
My boy shall fetch the scrivener presently.
The worst is this, that, at so slender warning,
You are like to have a thin and slender pit-
    tance.   61
    Bap. It likes me well. Biondello, hie you
        home,
And bid Bianca make her ready straight ;
And, if you will, tell what hath happened,
Lucentio's father is arrived in Padua,
And how she's like to be Lucentio's wife.
    Bion. I pray the gods she may with all my
        heart !
    Tra. Dally not with the gods, but get thee
        gone.   [*Exit Bion.*
Signior Baptista, shall I lead the way ?
Welcome ! one mess is like to be your cheer :
Come, sir ; we will better it in Pisa.   71
    Bap. I follow you.
        [*Exeunt Tranio, Pedant, and Baptista.*

Re-enter BIONDELLO.

    Bion. Cambio !
    Luc. What sayest thou, Biondello ?
    Bion. You saw my master wink and laugh
upon you ?
    Luc. Biondello, what of that ?
    Bion. Faith, nothing ; but has left me here
behind, to expound the meaning or moral of
his signs and tokens.   80
    Luc. I pray thee, moralize them.
    Bion. Then thus. Baptista is safe, talking
with the deceiving father of a deceitful son.
    Luc. And what of him ?
    Bion. His daughter is to be brought by you
to the supper.
    Luc. And then ?
    Bion. The old priest of Saint Luke's church
is at your command at all hours.
    Luc. And what of all this ?   90
    Bion. I cannot tell ; expect they are busied
about a counterfeit assurance : take you assurance of her, ' cum privilegio ad imprimen-
dum solum : ' to the church ; take the priest,
clerk, and some sufficient honest witnesses :
If this be not that you look for, I have no
        more to say,
But bid Bianca farewell for ever and a day.
    Luc. Hearest thou, Biondello ?
    Bion. I cannot tarry : I knew a wench
married in an afternoon as she went to the garden for parsley to stuff a rabbit ; and so may
you, sir : and so, adieu, sir. My master hath
appointed me to go to Saint Luke's, to bid the
priest be ready to come against you come with
your appendix.   [*Exit.*
    Luc. I may, and will, if she be so con-
        tented :
She will be pleased ; then wherefore should I
        doubt ?
Hap what hap may, I'll roundly go about her :
It shall go hard if Cambio go without her.
                                    [*Exit.*

SCENE V. *A public road.*

Enter PETRUCHIO, KATHARINA, HORTENSIO, *and*
        Servants.

    Pet. Come on, i' God's name ; once more
        toward our father's.
Good Lord, how bright and goodly shines the
        moon !

    Kath. The moon ! the sun : it is not moon-
        light now.
    Pet. I say it is the moon that shines so
        bright.
    Kath. I know it is the sun that shines so
        bright.
    Pet. Now, by my mother's son, and that's
        myself,
It shall be moon, or star, or what I list,
Or ere I journey to your father's house.
Go on, and fetch our horses back again.
Evermore cross'd and cross'd ; nothing but
        cross'd !   10
    Hor. Say as he says, or we shall never go.
    Kath. Forward, I pray, since we have
        come so far,
And be it moon, or sun, or what you please :
An if you please to call it a rush-candle,
Henceforth I vow it shall be so for me.
    Pet. I say it is the moon.
    Kath.   I know it is the moon.
    Pet. Nay, then you lie : it is the blessed
        sun.
    Kath. Then, God be bless'd, it is the
        blessed sun :
But sun it is not, when you say it is not ;
And the moon changes even as your mind. 20
What you will have it named, even that it is ;
And so it shall be so for Katharine.
    Hor. Petruchio, go thy ways ; the field is
        won.
    Pet. Well, forward, forward ! thus the bowl
        should run,
And not unluckily against the bias.
But, soft ! company is coming here.

Enter VINCENTIO.

[*To Vincentio.*] Good morrow, gentle mis-
        tress : where away ?
Tell me, sweet Kate, and tell me truly too,
Hast thou beheld a fresher gentlewoman ?
Such war of white and red within her cheeks !
What stars do spangle heaven with such
        beauty,   31
As those two eyes become that heavenly face ?
Fair lovely maid, once more good day to thee.
Sweet Kate, embrace her for her beauty's sake.
    Hor. A' will make the man mad, to make
a woman of him.
    Kath. Young budding virgin, fair and fresh
        and sweet,
Whither away, or where is thy abode ?
Happy the parents of so fair a child ;
Happier the man, whom favorable stars   40
Allot thee for his lovely bed-fellow !
    Pet. Why, how now, Kate ! I hope thou art
        not mad :
This is a man, old, wrinkled, faded, wither'd,
And not a maiden, as thou say'st he is.
    Kath. Pardon, old father, my mistaking
        eyes,
That have been so bedazzled with the sun
That everything I look on seemeth green :
Now I perceive thou art a reverend father ;
Pardon, I pray thee, for my mad mistaking.
    Pet. Do, good old grandsire ; and withal
        make known   50
Which way thou travellest : if along with us,
We shall be joyful of thy company.
    Vin. Fair sir, and you my merry mistress,
That with your strange encounter much
        amazed me,

My name is call'd Vincentio ; my dwelling
    Pisa ;
And bound I am to Padua ; there to visit
A son of mine, which long I have not seen.
Pet. What is his name ?
Vin.   Lucentio, gentle sir.
Pet. Happily met ; the happier for thy son.
And now by law, as well as reverend age,   60
I may entitle thee my loving father :
The sister to my wife, this gentlewoman,
Thy son by this hath married. Wonder not,
Nor be griev'd : she is of good esteem,
Her dowry wealthy, and of worthy birth ;
Beside, so qualified as may beseem
The spouse of any noble gentleman.
Let me embrace with old Vincentio,
And wander we to see thy honest son,
Who will of thy arrival be full joyous.   70
Vin. But is this true ? or is it else your
    pleasure,
Like pleasant travellers, to break a jest
Upon the company you overtake ?
Hor. I do assure thee, father, so it is.
Pet. Come, go along, and see the truth
    hereof ;
For our first merriment hath made thee jeal-
    ous.   *[Exeunt all but Hortensio.*
Hor. Well, Petruchio, this has put me in
    heart.
Have to my widow ! and if she be froward,
Then hast thou taught Hortensio to be un-
    toward.   *[Exit.*

ACT V.

Scene I. *Padua. Before* Lucentio's *house.*

Gremio *discovered. Enter behind* Biondello,
    Lucentio, *and* Bianca.

Bion. Softly and swiftly, sir ; for the priest
is ready.
Luc. I fly, Biondello : but they may chance
to need thee at home ; therefore leave us.
Bion. Nay, faith, I'll see the church o' your
back ; and then come back to my master's as
soon as I can.
    [Exeunt Lucentio, Bianca, and Biondello.
Gre. I marvel Cambio comes not all this
while.

Enter Petruchio, Katharina, Vincentio,
    Grumio, *with* Attendants.

Pet. Sir, here's the door, this is Lucentio's
house :
My father's bears more toward the market-
    place ;   10
Thither must I, and here I leave you, sir.
Vin. You shall not choose but drink before
    you go :
I think I shall command your welcome here,
And, by all likelihood, some cheer is toward.
                        [Knocks.
Gre. They're busy within ; you were best
knock louder.

Pedant *looks out of the window.*

Ped. What's he that knocks as he would
beat down the gate ?
Vin. Is Signior Lucentio within, sir ?
Ped. He's within, sir, but not to be spoken
withal.
Vin. What if a man bring him a hundred
pound or two, to make merry withal ?

Ped. Keep your hundred pounds to your-
self : he shall need none, so long as I live.
Pet. Nay, I told you your son was well beloved in Padua. Do you hear, sir ? To leave
frivolous circumstances, I pray you, tell Signior Lucentio that his father is come from
Pisa, and is here at the door to speak with
him.   30
Ped. Thou liest : his father is come from
Padua and here looking out at the window.
Vin. Art thou his father ?
Ped. Ay, sir ; so his mother says, if I may
believe her.
Pet. [*To Vincentio*] Why, how now, gentleman ! why, this is flat knavery, to take upon
you another man's name.
Ped. Lay hands on the villain : I believe a'
means to cozen somebody in this city under
my countenance.   41

Re-enter Biondello.

Bion. I have seen them in the church together : God send 'em good shipping ! But who
is here ? mine old master Vincentio ! now we
are undone and brought to nothing.
Vin. [*Seeing Biondello*] Come hither,
crack-hemp.
Bion. I hope I may choose, sir.
Vin. Come hither, you rogue. What, have
you forgot me ?   50
Bion. Forgot you ! no, sir : I could not forget you, for I never saw you before in all my
life.
Vin. What, you notorious villain, didst
thou never see thy master's father, Vincentio ?
Bion. What, my old worshipful old master ? yes, marry, sir : see where he looks out of
the window.
Vin. Is't so, indeed. [*Beats Biondello.* 60
Bion. Help, help, help ! here's a madman
will murder me.   *[Exit.*
Ped. Help, son ! help, Signior Baptista !
                      [Exit from above.
Pet. Prithee, Kate, let's stand aside and see
the end of this controversy.   *[They retire.*

Re-enter Pedant *below ;* Tranio, Baptista, *and*
    Servants.

Tra. Sir, what are you that offer to beat
my servant ?
Vin. What am I, sir ! nay, what are you,
sir ? O immortal gods ! O fine villain ! A silken
doublet ! a velvet hose ! a scarlet cloak ! and a
copatain hat ! O, I am undone ! I am undone !
while I play the good husband at home, my
son and my servant spend all at the university.
Tra. How now ! what's the matter ?
Bap. What, is the man lunatic ?
Tra. Sir, you seem a sober ancient gentle-
man by your habit, but your words show you
a madman. Why, sir, what 'cerns it you if I
wear pearl and gold ? I thank my good father,
I am able to maintain it.   79
Vin. Thy father ! O villain ! he is a sail-
maker in Bergamo.
Bap. You mistake, sir, you mistake, sir.
Pray, what do you think is his name ?
Vin. His name ! as if I knew not his name :
I have brought him up ever since he was three
years old, and his name is Tranio.
Ped. Away, away, mad ass ! his name is
Lucentio ; and he is mine only son, and heir to
the lands of me, Signior Vincentio.   89

Vin. Lucentio! O, he hath murdered his master! Lay hold on him, I charge you, in the duke's name. O, my son, my son! Tell me, thou villain, where is my son Lucentio?
Tra. Call forth an officer.

Enter one with an Officer.

Carry this mad knave to the gaol. Father Baptista, I charge you see that he be forthcoming.
Vin. Carry me to the gaol!
Gre. Stay, officer: he shall not go to prison.
Bap. Talk not, Signior Gremio: I say he shall go to prison.   100
Gre. Take heed, Signior Baptista, lest you be cony-catched in this business: I dare swear this is the right Vincentio.
Ped. Swear, if thou darest.
Gre. Nay, I dare not swear it.
Tra. Then thou wert best say that I am not Lucentio.
Gre. Yes, I know thee to be Signior Lucentio.
Bap. Away with the dotard! to the gaol with him!   110
Vin. Thus strangers may be hailed and abused: O monstrous villain!

Re-enter BIONDELLO, *with* LUCENTIO *and* BIANCA.

Bion. O! we are spoiled and—yonder he is: deny him, forswear him, or else we are all undone.
Luc. [*Kneeling*] Pardon, sweet father.
Vin.   Lives my sweet son?
[*Exeunt Biondello, Tranio, and Pedant, as fast as may be.*
Bian. Pardon, dear father.
Bap.   How hast thou offended?
Where is Lucentio?
Luc.   Here's Lucentio,
Right son to the right Vincentio;
That have by marriage made thy daughter mine,
While counterfeit supposes blear'd thine eyne.
Gre. Here's packing, with a witness to deceive us all!
Vin. Where is that damned villain Tranio,
That faced and braved me in this matter so?
Bap. Why, tell me, is not this my Cambio?
Bian. Cambio is changed into Lucentio.
Luc. Love wrought these miracles. Bianca's love
Made me exchange my state with Tranio,
While he did bear my countenance in the town;
And happily I have arrived at the last   130
Unto the wished haven of my bliss.
What Tranio did, myself enforced him to;
Then pardon him, sweet father, for my sake.
Vin. I'll slit the villain's nose, that would have sent me to the gaol.
Bap. But do you hear, sir? have you married my daughter without asking my good will?
Vin. Fear not, Baptista; we will content you, go to: but I will in, to be revenged for this villany.   [*Exit.* 140
Bap. And I, to sound the depth of this knavery.   [*Exit.*
Luc. Look not pale, Bianca; thy father will not frown. [*Exeunt Lucentio and Bianca.*

Gre. My cake is dough; but I'll in among the rest,
Out of hope of all, but my share of the feast.
                                          [*Exit.*
Kath. Husband, let's follow, to see the end of this ado.
Pet. First kiss me, Kate, and we will.
Kath. What, in the midst of the street?
Pet. What, art thou ashamed of me?   150
Kath. No, sir, God forbid; but ashamed to kiss.
Pet. Why, then let's home again. Come, sirrah, let's away.
Kath. Nay, I will give thee a kiss: now pray thee, love, stay.
Pet. Is not this well? Come, my sweet Kate:
Better once than never, for never too late.
                                         [*Exeunt.*

SCENE II. *Padua.* LUCENTIO's *house.*

Enter BAPTISTA, VINCENTIO, GREMIO, *the* Pedant, LUCENTIO, BIANCA, PETRUCHIO, KATHARINA, HORTENSIO, *and* Widow, TRANIO, BIONDELLO, *and* GRUMIO: *the Serving-men with Tranio bringing in a banquet.*

Luc. At last, though long, our jarring notes agree:
And time it is, when raging war is done,
To smile at scapes and perils overblown.
My fair Bianca, bid my father welcome,
While I with self-same kindness welcome thine.
Brother Petruchio, sister Katharina,
And thou, Hortensio, with thy loving widow,
Feast with the best, and welcome to my house:
My banquet is to close our stomachs up,
After our great good cheer. Pray you, sit down;   10
For now we sit to chat as well as eat.
Pet. Nothing but sit and sit, and eat and eat!
Bap. Padua affords this kindness, son Petruchio.
Pet. Padua affords nothing but what is kind.
Hor. For both our sakes, I would that word were true.
Pet. Now, for my life, Hortensio fears his widow.
Wid. Then never trust me, if I be afeard.
Pet. You are very sensible, and yet you miss my sense:
I mean, Hortensio is afeard of you.
Wid. He that is giddy thinks the world turns round.   20
Pet. Roundly replied.
Kath.   Mistress, how mean you that?
Wid. Thus I conceive by him.
Pet. Conceives by me! How likes Hortensio that?
Hor. My widow says, thus she conceives her tale.
Pet. Very well mended. Kiss him for that, good widow.
Kath. 'He that is giddy thinks the world turns round:'
I pray you, tell me what you meant by that.
Wid. Your husband, being troubled with a shrew,
Measures my husband's sorrow by his woe:
And now you know my meaning.   30
Kath. A very mean meaning.
Wid.   Right, I mean you.

Kath. And I am mean indeed, respecting you.
Pet. To her, Kate!
Hor. To her, widow!
Pet. A hundred marks, my Kate does put her down.
Hor. That's my office.
Pet. Spoke like an officer; ha' to thee, lad!
                                    [*Drinks to Hortensio.*
Bap. How likes Gremio these quick-witted folks?
Gre. Believe me, sir, they butt together well.
Bian. Head, and butt! an hasty-witted body
Would say your head and butt were head and horn.
Vin. Ay, mistress bride, hath that awaken'd you?
Bian. Ay, but not frighted me; therefore I'll sleep again.
Pet. Nay, that you shall not: since you have begun,
Have at you for a bitter jest or two!
Bian. Am I your bird? I mean to shift my bush;
And then pursue me as you draw your bow.
You are welcome all.
                [*Exeunt Bianca, Katharina, and Widow.*
Pet. She hath prevented me. Here, Signior Tranio.
This bird you aim'd at, though you hit her not;   50
Therefore a health to all that shot and miss'd.
Tra. O, sir, Lucentio slipp'd me like his greyhound,
Which runs himself and catches for his master.
Pet. A good swift simile, but something currish.
Tra. 'Tis well, sir, that you hunted for yourself:
'Tis thought your deer does hold you at a bay.
Bap. O ho, Petruchio! Tranio hits you now.
Luc. I thank thee for that gird, good Tranio.
Hor. Confess, confess, hath he not hit you here?
Pet. A' has a little gall'd me, I confess;   60
And, as the jest did glance away from me,
'Tis ten to one it maim'd you two outright.
Bap. Now, in good sadness, son Petruchio,
I think thou hast the veriest shrew of all.
Pet. Well, I say no: and therefore for assurance
Let's each one send unto his wife;
And he whose wife is most obedient
To come at first when he doth send for her,
Shall win the wager which we will propose.
Hor. Content. What is the wager?
Luc.   Twenty crowns.   70
Pet. Twenty crowns!
I'll venture so much of my hawk or hound,
But twenty times so much upon my wife.
Luc. A hundred then.
Hor.   Content.
Pet.   A match! 'tis done.
Hor. Who shall begin?
Luc.   That will I.
Go, Biondello, bid your mistress come to me.
Bion. I go.   [*Exit.*

Bap. Son, I'll be your half, Bianca comes.
Luc. I'll have no halves; I'll bear it all myself.

                Re-enter BIONDELLO.

How now! what news?
Bion.   Sir, my mistress sends you word
That she is busy and she cannot come.
Pet. How! she is busy and she cannot come!
Is that an answer?
Gre.   Ay, and a kind one too:
Pray God, sir, your wife send you not a worse.
Pet. I hope, better.
Hor. Sirrah Biondello, go and entreat my wife
To come to me forthwith.   [*Exit Bion.*
Pet.   O, ho! entreat her!
Nay, then she must needs come.
Hor.   I am afraid, sir,
Do what you can, yours will not be entreated.

                Re-enter BIONDELLO.

Now, where's my wife?   90
Bion. She says you have some goodly jest in hand;
She will not come: she bids you come to her.
Pet. Worse and worse; she will not come!
O vile,
Intolerable, not to be endured!
Sirrah Grumio, go to your mistress;
Say, I command her to come to me.
                                    [*Exit Grumio.*
Hor. I know her answer.
Pet.   What?
Hor.   She will not.
Pet. The fouler fortune mine, and there an end.
Bap. Now, by my holidame, here comes Katharina!

                Re-enter KATHARINA.

Kath. What is your will, sir, that you send for me?   100
Pet. Where is your sister, and Hortensio's wife?
Kath. They sit conferring by the parlor fire.
Pet. Go fetch them hither: if they deny to come.
Swinge me them soundly forth unto their husbands:
Away, I say, and bring them hither straight.
                                    [*Exit Katharina.*
Luc. Here is a wonder, if you talk of a wonder.
Hor. And so it is: I wonder what it bodes.
Pet. Marry, peace it bodes, and love and quiet life,
And awful rule and right supremacy;
And, to be short, what not, that's sweet and happy?   110
Bap. Now, fair befal thee, good Petruchio!
The wager thou hast won; and I will add
Unto their losses twenty thousand crowns;
Another dowry to another daughter,
For she is changed, as she had never been.
Pet. Nay, I will win my wager better yet
And show more sign of her obedience,
Her new-built virtue and obedience.
See where she comes and brings your froward wives
As prisoners to her womanly persuasion. 120

Re-enter KATHARINA, *with* BIANCA *and* Widow.

Katharina, that cap of yours becomes you
    not :
Off with that bauble, throw it under-foot.
    Wid. Lord, let me never have a cause to
        sigh,
Till I be brought to such a silly pass !
    Bian. Fie ! what a foolish duty call you
        this ?
    Luc. I would your duty were as foolish
        too :
The wisdom of your duty, fair Bianca,
Hath cost me an hundred crowns since supper-
    time.
    Bian. The more fool you, for laying on my
        duty.
    Pet. Katharine, I charge thee, tell these
        headstrong women   130
What duty they do owe their lords and hus-
    bands.
    Wid. Come, come, you're mocking : we
        will have no telling.
    Pet. Come on, I say ; and first begin with
        her.
    Wid. She shall not.
    Pet. I say she shall : and first begin with
        her.
    Kath. Fie, fie ! unknit that threatening un-
        kind brow,
And dart not scornful glances from those eyes,
To wound thy lord, thy king, thy governor :
It blots thy beauty as frosts do bite the meads,
Confounds thy fame as whirlwinds shake fair
    buds,   140
And in no sense is meet or amiable.
A woman moved is like a fountain troubled,
Muddy, ill-seeming, thick, bereft of beauty ;
And while it is so, none so dry or thirsty
Will deign to sip or touch one drop of it.
Thy husband is thy lord, thy life, thy keeper,
Thy head, thy sovereign ; one that cares for
    thee,
And for thy maintenance commits his body
To painful labor both by sea and land,
To watch the night in storms, the day in cold,
Whilst thou liest warm at home, secure and
    safe ;   151
And craves no other tribute at thy hands
But love, fair looks and true obedience ;

Too little payment for so great a debt.
Such duty as the subject owes the prince
Even such a woman oweth to her husband ;
And when she is froward, peevish, sullen, sour,
And not obedient to his honest will,
What is she but a foul contending rebel
And graceless traitor to her loving lord ?   160
I am ashamed that women are so simple
To offer war where they should kneel for
    peace ;
Or seek for rule, supremacy and sway,
When they are bound to serve, love and obey.
Why are our bodies soft and weak and smooth,
Unapt to toil and trouble in the world,
But that our soft conditions and our hearts
Should well agree with our external parts ?
Come, come, you froward and unable worms !
My mind hath been as big as one of yours, 170
My heart as great, my reason haply more,
To bandy word for word and frown for
    frown ;
But now I see our lances are but straws,
Our strength as weak, our weakness past com-
    pare,
That seeming to be most which we indeed least
    are.
Then vail your stomachs, for it is no boot,
And place your hands below your husband's
    foot :
In token of which duty, if he please,
My hand is ready ; may it do him ease.
    Pet. Why, there's a wench ! Come on, and
        kiss me, Kate.   180
    Luc. Well, go thy ways, old lad ; for thou
        shalt ha't.
    Vin. 'Tis a good hearing when children are
        toward.
    Luc. But a harsh hearing when women are
        froward.
    Pet. Come, Kate, we'll to bed.
We three are married, but you two are sped.
[*To Luc.*] 'Twas I won the wager, though
        you hit the white ;
And, being a winner, God give you good
        night !
            [*Exeunt Petruchio and Katharina.*
    Hor. Now, go thy ways ; thou hast tamed
        a curst shrew.
    Luc. 'Tis a wonder, by your leave, she will
        be tamed so.   [*Exeunt.*

THE
MERRY WIVES OF WINDSOR.

(WRITTEN ABOUT 1598.)

INTRODUCTION.

This is an offshoot from the comedy of *King Henry IV.*, while *King Henry V.* is the direct continuation of the history. Dennis, in 1702, reports a tradition that this play was written in fourteen days, by order of the Queen; and Rowe adds: "She was so well pleased with that admirable character of Falstaff, in the two parts of *Henry IV.*, that she commanded him to continue it for one play more, and to show him in love." This may have been the cause why Shakespeare does not fulfill the promise made in the Epilogue of Henry IV., that Falstaff should re-appear with Henry V. in France; but, indeed, among the great deeds of the victor of Agincourt there would be small room for a Falstaff. The choice of Windsor as the scene, and the compliments to the owner of Windsor Castle, and to the wearers of the Order of the Garter, suggest that the play was meant especially for Elizabeth and her courtiers. An early sketch of *The Merry Wives* was published in quarto, 1602; some touches in the play, as given in the folio, were evidently made after the accession of James I. (1603); the word " council " is altered to "king" (Act I., Sc. I., L. 113); "these knights will hack," exclaims Mrs. Page (Act II., Sc. I., L. 52), and the allusion to James's too liberal creation of knights in 1604 was probably appreciated. Some critics have held that the first sketch of *The Merry Wives* was written as early as 1592. A German duke is spoken of by Bardolph as about to visit Windsor, and his gentlemen ride off with mine host of the Garter's horses unpaid for. In the early sketch (Act IV., Sc. v., of the revised play), instead of "cousin-germans," where Evans puns upon the words *cozen* and *German,* occurs the strange "cosen garmombles." Now, Count Frederick of Mömpelgard had visited England and accompanied the Queen to Windsor, Aug. 1592; and in the passport which he received for his journey back to the Continent, we read that he shall be furnished with post-horses, and shall pay nothing for the same. Next year the Count became Duke of Wirtemberg, and in 1595 he craved that, in accordance with a promise given, Elizabeth would confer upon him the Order of the Garter, which Elizabeth, on various pretexts, declined. "Garmombles" obviously reverses the true name "Mömpelgard; " but the inference that the date of the play is 1592, because it refers to the visit of the Germans, is unwarrantable, for such an event would be remembered, and the more so because of the Duke's subsequent unavailing attempt to obtain the honor of the Garter. If we try to make out exact relations between the characters of *The Merry Wives* and the same characters as they appear in the historical plays, we shall fail. The comedy has a certain independence of the histories, and cannot be pieced on to them in any way: the persons are the same and not the same. Mrs. Quickly, servant of Dr. Caius, has a different history from the Mrs. Quickly of the Boar's Head Tavern. Nor is Falstaff conceived in quite the same manner as the Falstaff of *Henry IV.* Here the knight is fatuous, his genius deserts him; the never-defeated hangs his head before two country dames; the buck-basket, the drench of Thames water, the blows of Ford's cudgel, are reprisals too coarse upon the most inimitable of jesters. Yet the play is indeed a merry one, with well-contrived incidents and abundance of broad mirth. A country air breathes over the whole; nowhere else has Shakespeare represented English middle-class life in the country, and he has here done it with a vigorous, healthy pleasure. It is not, however, a poetical play, unless comely English maidenhood, in the person of pretty Anne Page, lend it something of poetry. There is a propriety in the fact that this comedy is written almost wholly in prose. The merry wives are a delightful pair, with "their sly laughing looks, their apple-red cheeks, their brows the lines whereon look more like the work of mirth than of years; " and Slender, most brainless of youths, most incapable of lovers, is dear for sake of the laugh at him which pretty Anne Page must have when alone. Altogether, if we can accept Falstaff's discomfitures, it is a merry play to laugh at if not to love.

DRAMATIS PERSONÆ.

SIR JOHN FALSTAFF.
FENTON, a gentleman.
SHALLOW, a country justice.
SLENDER, cousin to Shallow.
FORD, } two gentlemen dwelling at Windsor.
PAGE, }
WILLIAM PAGE, a boy, son to Page.
SIR HUGH EVANS, a Welsh parson.
DOCTOR CAIUS, a French physician.
Host of the Garter Inn.
BARDOLPH, ⎫
PISTOL,   ⎬ sharpers attending on Falstaff.
NYM,   ⎭

ROBIN, page to Falstaff.
SIMPLE, servant to Slender.
RUGBY, servant to Doctor Caius.

MISTRESS FORD.
MISTRESS PAGE.
ANNE PAGE, her daughter.
MISTRESS QUICKLY, servant to Doctor Caius.

Servants to Page, Ford, &c.

SCENE :   *Windsor, and the neighborhood.*

ACT I.

SCENE I. *Windsor. Before* PAGE'S *house.*

Enter JUSTICE SHALLOW, SLENDER, *and* SIR
         HUGH EVANS.

Shal. Sir Hugh, persuade me not; I will make a Star-chamber matter of it : if he were twenty Sir John Falstaffs, he shall not abuse Robert Shallow, esquire.

Slen. In the county of Gloucester, justice of peace and ' Coram.'

Shal. Ay, cousin Slender, and ' Custa-lorum.'

Slen. Ay, and ' Rato-lorum ' too ; and a gentleman born, master parson ; who writes himself ' Armigero,' in any bill, warrant, quittance, or obligation, ' Armigero.'   11

Shal. Ay, that I do ; and have done any time these three hundred years.

Slen. All his successors gone before him hath done't ; and all his ancestors that come after him may : they may give the dozen white luces in their coat.

Shal. It is an old coat.

Evans. The dozen white louses do become an old coat well ; it agrees well, passant ; it is a familiar beast to man, and signifies love.   21

Shal. The luce is the fresh fish ; the salt fish is an old coat.

Slen. I may quarter, coz.

Shal. You may, by marrying.

Evans. It is marring indeed, if he quarter it.

Shal. Not a whit.

Evans. Yes, py'r lady ; if he has a quarter of your coat, there is but three skirts for yourself, in my simple conjectures : but that is all one. If Sir John Falstaff have committed disparagements unto you, I am of the church, and will be glad to do my benevolence to make atonements and compromises between you.

Shal. The council shall hear it ; it is a riot.

Evans. It is not meet the council hear a riot ; there is no fear of Got in a riot : the council, look you, shall desire to hear the fear of Got, and not to hear a riot ; take your vizaments in that.

Shal. Ha ! o' my life, if I were young again, the sword should end it.   41

Evans. It is petter that friends is the sword, and end it : and there is also another device

in my prain, which peradventure prings goot discretions with it : there is Anne Page, which is daughter to Master Thomas Page, which is pretty virginity.

Slen. Mistress Anne Page ? She has brown hair, and speaks small like a woman.

Evans. It is that fery person for all the orld, as just as you will desire ; and seven hundred pounds of moneys, and gold and silver, is her grandsire upon his death's-bed—Got deliver to a joyful resurrections !—give, when she is able to overtake seventeen years old : it were a goot motion if we leave our pribbles and prabbles, and desire a marriage between Master Abraham and Mistress Anne Page.

Slen. Did her grandsire leave her seven hundred pound ?   60

Evans. Ay, and her father is make her a petter penny.

Slen. I know the young gentlewoman ; she has good gifts.

Evans. Seven hundred pounds and possibilities is goot gifts.

Shal. Well, let us see honest Master Page. Is Falstaff there ?

Evans. Shall I tell you a lie ? I do despise a liar as I do despise one that is false, or as I despise one that is not true. The knight, Sir John, is there ; and, I beseech you, be ruled by your well-willers. I will peat the door for Master Page. [*Knocks.*] What, hoa ! Got pless your house here !

Page. [*Within*] Who's there ?

Enter PAGE.

Evans. Here is Got's plessing, and your friend, and Justice Shallow ; and here young Master Slender, that peradventures shall tell you another tale, if matters grow to your likings.

Page. I am glad to see your worships well. I thank you for my venison, Master Shallow.

Shal. Master Page, I am glad to see you : much good do it your good heart ! I wished your venison better ; it was ill killed. How doth good Mistress Page ?—and I thank you always with my heart, la ! with my heart.

Page. Sir, I thank you.

Shal. Sir, I thank you ; by yea and no, I do.

Page. I am glad to see you, good Master Slender.   90

Slen. How does your fallow greyhound, sir ? I heard say he was outrun on Cotsall.

Page. It could not be judged, sir.

Slen. You'll not confess, you'll not confess.

Shal. That he will not. 'Tis your fault, 'tis your fault ; 'tis a good dog.

Page. A cur, sir.

Shal. Sir, he's a good dog, and a fair dog : can there be more said ? he is good and fair. Is Sir John Falstaff here ?   100

Page. Sir, he is within ; and I would I could do a good office between you.

Evans. It is spoke as a Christians ought to speak.

Shal. He hath wronged me, Master Page.

Page. Sir, he doth in some sort confess it.

Shal. If it be confessed, it is not redress'd : is not that so, Master Page ? He hath wronged me ; indeed he hath, at a word, he hath, believe me : Robert Shallow, esquire, saith, he is wronged.   110

Page. Here comes Sir John.

Enter Sir John Falstaff, Bardolph, Nym, *and* Pistol.

Fal. Now, Master Shallow, you'll complain of me to the king ?

Shal. Knight, you have beaten my men, killed my deer, and broke open my lodge.

Fal. But not kissed your keeper's daughter ?

Shal. Tut, a pin ! this shall be answered.

Fal. I will answer it straight ; I have done all this. That is now answered.

Shal. The council shall know this.   120

Fal. 'Twere better for you if it were known in counsel : you'll be laughed at.

Evans. Pauca verba, Sir John ; goot worts.

Fal. Good worts ! good cabbage. Slender, I broke your head : what matter have you against me ?

Slen. Marry, sir, I have matter in my head against you ; and against your cony-catching rascals, Bardolph, Nym, and Pistol.

Bard. You Banbury cheese !   130

Slen. Ay, it is no matter.

Pist. How now, Mephostophilus !

Slen. Ay, it is no matter.

Nym. Slice, I say ! pauca, pauca : slice ! that's my humor.

Slen. Where's Simple, my man ? Can you tell, cousin ?

Evans. Peace, I pray you. Now let us understand. There is three umpires in this matter, as I understand ; that is, Master Page, fidelicet Master Page ; and there is myself, fidelicet myself ; and the three party is, lastly and finally, mine host of the Garter.

Page. We three, to hear it and end it between them.

Evans. Fery goot : I will make a prief of it in my note-book ; and we will afterwards ork upon the cause with as great discreetly as we can.

Fal. Pistol !

Pist. He hears with ears.   150

Evans. The tevil and his tam ! what phrase is this, 'He hears with ear' ? why, it is affectations.

Fal. Pistol, did you pick Master Slender's purse ?

Slen. Ay, by these gloves, did he, or I

would I might never come in mine own great chamber again else, of seven groats in mill-sixpences, and two Edward shovel-boards, that cost me two shilling and two pence a-piece of Yead Miller, by these gloves.   161

Fal. Is this true, Pistol ?

Evans. No ; it is false, if it is a pick-purse.

Pist. Ha, thou mountain-foreigner ! Sir John and Master mine, I combat challenge of this latten bilbo. Word of denial in thy labras here ! Word of denial : froth and scum, thou liest !

Slen. By these gloves, then, 'twas he.

Nym. Be avised, sir, and pass good humors : I will say 'marry trap' with you, if you run the nuthook's humor on me ; that is the very note of it.

Slen. By this hat, then, he in the red face had it ; for though I cannot remember what I did when you made me drunk, yet I am not altogether an ass.

Fal. What say you, Scarlet and John ?

Bard. Why, sir, for my part, I say the gentleman had drunk himself out of his five sentences.   180

Evans. It is his five senses : fie, what the ignorance is !

Bard. And being fap, sir, was, as they say, cashiered ; and so conclusions passed the careires.

Slen. Ay, you spake in Latin then too ; but 'tis no matter : I'll ne'er be drunk whilst I live again, but in honest, civil, godly company, for this trick : if I be drunk, I'll be drunk with those that have the fear of God, and not with drunken knaves.   190

Evans. So Got udge me, that is a virtuous mind.

Fal. You hear all these matters denied, gentlemen ; you hear it.

Enter Anne Page, *with wine ;* Mistress Ford *and* Mistress Page, *following.*

Page. Nay, daughter, carry the wine in ; we'll drink within.   [*Exit Anne Page.*

Slen. O heaven ! this is Mistress Anne Page.

Page. How now, Mistress Ford !

Fal. Mistress Ford, by my troth, you are very well met : by your leave, good mistress.
                                     [*Kisses her.* 200

Page. Wife, bid these gentlemen welcome. Come, we have a hot venison pasty to dinner ; come, gentlemen, I hope we shall drink down all unkindness.

  [*Exeunt all except Shal., Slen., and Evans.*

Slen. I had rather than forty shillings I had my Book of Songs and Sonnets here.

Enter Simple.

How now, Simple ! where have you been ? I must wait on myself, must I ? You have not the Book of Riddles about you, have you ?

Sim. Book of Riddles ! why, did you not lend it to Alice Shortcake upon All-hallowmas last, a fortnight afore Michaelmas ?

Shal. Come, coz ; come, coz ; we stay for you. A word with you, coz ; marry, this, coz : there is, as 'twere, a tender, a kind of tender, made afar off by Sir Hugh here. Do you understand me ?

Slen. Ay, sir, you shall find me reasonable ; if it be so, I shall do that that is reason.

Shal. Nay, but understand me.

Slen. So I do, sir.   220

Evans. Give ear to his motions, Master Slender : I will description the matter to you, if you be capacity of it.

Slen. Nay, I will do as my cousin Shallow says : I pray you, pardon me ; he's a justice of peace in his country, simple though I stand here.

Evans. But that is not the question : the question is concerning your marriage.

Shal. Ay, there's the point, sir.

Evans. Marry, is it ; the very point of it ; to Mistress Anne Page.   231

Slen. Why, if it be so, I will marry her upon any reasonable demands.

Evans. But can you affection the 'oman ? Let us command to know that of your mouth or of your lips ; for divers philosophers hold that the lips is parcel of the mouth. Therefore, precisely, can you carry your good will to the maid ?

Shal. Cousin Abraham Slender, can you love her ?   240

Slen. I hope, sir, I will do as it shall become one that would do reason.

Evans. Nay, Got's lords and his ladies ! you must speak possitable, if you can carry her your desires towards her.

Shal. That you must. Will you, upon good dowry, marry her ?

Slen. I will do a greater thing than that, upon your request, cousin, in any reason.

Shal. Nay, conceive me, conceive me, sweet coz : what I do is to pleasure you, coz. Can you love the maid ?

Slen. I will marry her, sir, at your request : but if there be no great love in the beginning, yet heaven may decrease it upon better acquaintance, when we are married and have more occasion to know one another ; I hope, upon familiarity will grow more contempt : but if you say, ' Marry her,' I will marry her ; that I am freely dissolved, and dissolutely. 260

Evans. It is a fery discretion answer ; save the fall is in the ort ' dissolutely : ' the ort is, according to our meaning, ' resolutely : ' his meaning is good.

Shal. Ay, I think my cousin meant well.

Slen. Ay, or else I would I might be hanged, la !

Shal. Here comes fair Mistress Anne.

Re-enter ANNE PAGE.

Would I were young for your sake, Mistress Anne !

Anne. The dinner is on the table ; my father desires your worships' company.   271

Shal. I will wait on him, fair Mistress Anne.

Evans. Od's plessed will ! I will not be absence at the grace.

               [*Exeunt Shallow and Evans.*

Anne. Will't please your worship to come in, sir ?

Slen. No, I thank you, forsooth, heartily ; I am very well.

Anne. The dinner attends you, sir.

Slen. I am not a-hungry, I thank you, forsooth. Go, sirrah, for all you are my man, go wait upon my cousin Shallow. [*Exit Simple.*] A justice of peace sometimes may be beholding to his friend for a man. I keep but three men and a boy yet, till my mother be dead : but what though ? yet I live like a poor gentleman born.

Anne. I may not go in without your worship : they will not sit till you come.

Slen. I' faith, I'll eat nothing ; I thank you as much as though I did.   291

Anne. I pray you, sir, walk in.

Slen. I had rather walk here, I thank you. I bruised my shin th' other day with playing at sword and dagger with a master of fence ; three veneys for a dish of stewed prunes ; and, by my troth, I cannot abide the smell of hot meat since. Why do your dogs bark so ? be there bears i' the town ?

Anne. I think there are, sir ; I heard them talked of.   301

Slen. I love the sport well ; but I shall as soon quarrel at it as any man in England. You are afraid, if you see the bear loose, are you not ?

Anne. Ay, indeed, sir.

Slen. That's meat and drink to me, now. I have seen Sackerson loose twenty times, and have taken him by the chain ; but, I warrant you, the women have so cried and shrieked at it, that it passed : but women, indeed, cannot abide 'em ; they are very ill-favored rough things.

Re-enter PAGE.

Page. Come, gentle Master Slender, come ; we stay for you.

Slen. I'll eat nothing, I thank you, sir.

Page. By cock and pie, you shall not choose, sir ! come, come.

Slen. Nay, pray you, lead the way.

Page. Come on, sir.

Slen. Mistress Anne, yourself shall go first.

Anne. Not I, sir ; pray you, keep on. 321

Slen. Truly, I will not go first ; truly, la ! I will not do you that wrong.

Anne. I pray you, sir.

Slen. I'll rather be unmannerly than troublesome. You do yourself wrong, indeed, la !

                         [*Exeunt.*

SCENE II. *The same.*

Enter SIR HUGH EVANS *and* SIMPLE.

Evans. Go your ways, and ask of Doctor Caius' house which is the way : and there dwells one Mistress Quickly, which is in the manner of his nurse, or his dry nurse, or his cook, or his laundry, his washer, and his wringer.

Sim. Well, sir.

Evans. Nay, it is petter yet. Give her this letter ; for it is a 'oman that altogether's acquaintance with Mistress Anne Page : and the letter is, to desire and require her to solicit your master's desires to Mistress Anne Page. I pray you, be gone : I will make an end of my dinner ; there's pippins and cheese to come.   [*Exeunt.*

SCENE III. *A room in the Garter Inn.*

Enter FALSTAFF, HOST, BARDOLPH, NYM, PISTOL, *and* ROBIN.

Fal. Mine host of the Garter !

Host. What says my bully-rook ? speak scholarly and wisely.

Fal. Truly, mine host, I must turn away some of my followers.

Host. Discard, bully Hercules ; cashier :
let them wag ; trot, trot.

Fal. I sit at ten pounds a week.

Host. Thou'rt an emperor, Cæsar, Keisar,
and Pheezar. I will entertain Bardolph ; he
shall draw, he shall tap : said I well, bully
Hector ?

Fal. Do so, good mine host.

Host. I have spoke ; let him follow. [*To
Bard.*] Let me see thee froth and lime : I am
at a word ; follow.   [*Exit.*

Fal. Bardolph, follow him. A tapster is a
good trade : an old cloak makes a new jerkin ;
a withered serving-man a fresh tapster. Go ;
adieu.   20

Bard. It is a life that I have desired : I will
thrive.

Pist. O base Hungarian wight ! wilt thou
the spigot wield ?   [*Exit Bardolph.*

Nym. He was gotten in drink : is not the
humor conceited ?

Fal. I am glad I am so acquit of this tin-
derbox : his thefts were too open ; his filching
was like an unskilful singer ; he kept not time.

Nym. The good humor is to steal at a
minute's rest.   31

Pist. 'Convey,' the wise it call. 'Steal !'
foh ! a fico for the phrase !

Fal. Well, sirs, I am almost out at heels.

Pist. Why, then, let kibes ensue.

Fal. There is no remedy ; I must cony-
catch ; I must shift.

Pist. Young ravens must have food.

Fal. Which of you know Ford of this
town ?

Pist. I ken the wight : he is of substance
good.   41

Fal. My honest lads, I will tell you what I
am about.

Pist. Two yards, and more.

Fal. No quips now, Pistol ! Indeed, I am
in the waist two yards about ; but I am now
about no waste ; I am about thrift. Briefly, I
do mean to make love to Ford's wife : I spy
entertainment in her ; she discourses, she
carves, she gives the leer of invitation : I can
construe the action of her familiar style ; and
the hardest voice of her behavior, to be Eng-
lished rightly, is, ' I am Sir John Falstaff's.'

Pist. He hath studied her will, and translated her will, out of honesty into English.

Nym. The anchor is deep : will that humor pass ?

Fal. Now, the report goes she has all the
rule of her husband's purse : he hath a legion
of angels.   60

Pist. As many devils entertain ; and ' To
her, boy,' say I.

Nym. The humor rises ; it is good : humor me the angels.

Fal. I have writ me here a letter to her :
and here another to Page's wife, who even now
gave me good eyes too, examined my parts
with most judicious œillades ; sometimes the
beam of her view gilded my foot, sometimes
my portly belly.

Pist. Then did the sun on dunghill shine.

Nym. I thank thee for that humor.   71

Fal. O, she did so course o'er my exteriors
with such a greedy intention, that the appetite
of her eye did seem to scorch me up like a
burning-glass ! Here's another letter to her :
she bears the purse too ; she is a region in

Guiana, all gold and bounty. I will be cheater
to them both, and they shall be exchequers to
me ; they shall be my East and West Indies,
and I will trade to them both. Go bear thou
this letter to Mistress Page ; and thou this to
Mistress Ford : we will thrive, lads, we will
thrive.

Pist. Shall I Sir Pandarus of Troy become,
And by my side wear steel ? then, Lucifer
    take all !

Nym. I will run no base humor : here,
take the humor-letter : I will keep the havior
of reputation.

Fal. [*To Robin*] Hold, sirrah, bear you
these letters tightly ;
Sail like my pinnace to these golden shores.
Rogues, hence, avaunt ! vanish like hailstones,
    go ;
Trudge, plod away o' the hoof ; seek shelter,
    pack !
Falstaff will learn the humor of the age,
French thrift, you rogues ; myself and skirted
    page.   [*Exeunt Falstaff and Robin.*

Pist. Let vultures gripe thy guts ! for gourd
    and fullam holds,
And high and low beguiles the rich and poor :
Tester I'll have in pouch when thou shalt lack,
Base Phrygian Turk !

Nym. I have operations which be humors
of revenge.

Pist. Wilt thou revenge ?   100

Nym. By welkin and her star !

Pist. With wit or steel ?

Nym. With both the humors, I :
I will discuss the humor of this love to Page.

Pist. And I to Ford shall eke unfold
        How Falstaff, varlet vile,
His dove will prove, his gold will hold,
        And his soft couch defile.

Nym. My humor shall not cool : I will incense Page to deal with poison ; I will possess
him with yellowness, for the revolt of mine
is dangerous : that is my true humor.

Pist. Thou art the Mars of malecontents :
I second thee ; troop on.   [*Exeunt.*

SCENE IV.   *A room in* DOCTOR CAIUS'S *house.*

Enter MISTRESS QUICKLY, SIMPLE, *and*
RUGBY.

Quick. What, John Rugby ! I pray thee,
go to the casement, and see if you can see my
master, Master Doctor Caius, coming. If he
do, i' faith, and find any body in the house,
here will be an old abusing of God's patience
and the king's English.

Rug. I'll go watch.

Quick. Go ; and we'll have a posset for't
soon at night, in faith, at the latter end of a
sea-coal fire. [*Exit Rugby.*] An honest, willing, kind fellow, as ever servant shall come
in house withal, and, I warrant you, no tell-
tale nor no breed-bate : his worst fault is, that
he is given to prayer ; he is something peevish
that way : but nobody but has his fault ; but
let that pass. Peter Simple, you say your name
is ?

Sim. Ay, for fault of a better.

Quick. And Master Slender's your master ?

Sim. Ay, forsooth.

Quick. Does he not wear a great round
beard, like a glover's paring-knife ?   21

Sim. No, forsooth : he hath but a little wee

face, with a little yellow beard, a Cain-colored beard.

Quick. A softly-sprighted man, is he not?

Sim. Ay, forsooth : but he is as tall a man of his hands as any is between this and his head ; he hath fought with a warrener.

Quick. How say you ? O, I should remember him : does he not hold up his head, as it were, and strut in his gait ?   31

Sim. Yes, indeed, does he.

Quick. Well, heaven send Anne Page no worse fortune ! Tell Master Parson Evans I will do what I can for your master : Anne is a good girl, and I wish—

Re-enter RUGBY.

Rug. Out, alas ! here comes my master.

Quick. We shall all be shent. Run in here, good young man ; go into this closet : he will not stay long. [*Shuts Simple in the closet.*] What, John Rugby ! John ! what, John, I say ! Go, John, go inquire for my master ; I doubt he be not well, that he comes not home.   43
[*Singing*] And down, down, adown-a, &c.

Enter DOCTOR CAIUS.

Caius. Vat is you sing ? I do not like des toys. Pray you, go and vetch me in my closet un boitier vert, a box, a green-a box : do intend vat I speak ? a green-a box.

Quick. Ay, forsooth ; I'll fetch it you. [*Aside*] I am glad he went not in himself : if he had found the young man, he would have been horn-mad.   52

Caius. Fe, fe, fe, fe ! ma foi, il fait fort chaud. Je m'en vais a la cour—la grande affaire.

Quick. Is it this, sir ?

Caius. Oui ; mette le au mon pocket : depeche, quickly. Vere is dat knave Rugby ?

Quick. What, John Rugby ! John !

Rug. Here, sir !

Caius. You are John Rugby, and you are Jack Rugby. Come, take-a your rapier, and come after my heel to the court.   62

Rug. 'Tis ready, sir, here in the porch.

Caius. By my trot, I tarry too long. Od's me ! Qu'ai-j'oublie ! dere is some simples in my closet, dat I vill not for the varld I shall leave behind.

Quick. Ay me, he'll find the young man there, and be mad !

Caius. O diable, diable ! vat is in my closet ? Villain ! larron ! [*Pulling Simple out.*] Rugby, my rapier !   72

Quick. Good master, be content.

Caius. Wherefore shall I be content-a ?

Quick. The young man is an honest man.

Caius. What shall de honest man do in my closet ? dere is no honest man dat shall come in my closet.

Quick. I beseech you, be not so phlegmatic. Hear the truth of it : he came of an errand to me from Parson Hugh.   81

Caius. Vell.

Sim. Ay, forsooth ; to desire her to—

Quick. Peace, I pray you.

Caius. Peace-a your tongue. Speak-a your tale.

Sim. To desire this honest gentlewoman, your maid, to speak a good word to Mistress Anne Page for my master in the way of marriage.

Quick. This is all, indeed, la ! but I'll ne'er put my finger in the fire, and need not.   91

Caius. Sir Hugh send-a you ? Rugby, baille me some paper. Tarry you a little-a while.
[*Writes.*

Quick. [*Aside to Simple.*] I am glad he is so quiet : if he had been thoroughly moved, you should have heard him so loud and so melancholy. But notwithstanding, man, I'll do you your master what good I can : and the very yea and the no is, the French doctor, my master,—I may call him my master, look you, for I keep his house ; and I wash, wring, brew, bake, scour, dress meat and drink, make the beds, and do all myself,—

Sim. [*Aside to Quickly*] 'Tis a great charge to come under one body's hand.

Quick. [*Aside to Simple*] Are you avised o' that ? you shall find it a great charge : and to be up early and down late ; but notwithstanding,—to tell you in your ear ; I would have no words of it,—my master himself is in love with Mistress Anne Page : but notwithstanding that, I know Anne's mind,—that's neither here nor there.

Caius. You jack'nape, give-a this letter to Sir Hugh ; by gar, it is a shallenge : I will cut his troat in dee park ; and I will teach a scurvy jack-a-nape priest to meddle or make. You may be gone ; it is not good you tarry here. By gar, I will cut all his two stones ; by gar, he shall not have a stone to throw at his dog.
[*Exit Simple.*

Quick. Alas, he speaks but for his friend.

Caius. It is no matter-a ver dat : do not you tell-a me dat I shall have Anne Page for myself ? By gar, I vill kill de Jack priest ; and I have appointed mine host of de Jarteer to measure our weapon. By gar, I will myself have Anne Page.

Quick. Sir, the maid loves you, and all shall be well. We must give folks leave to prate : what, the good-jer !

Caius. Rugby, come to the court with me. By gar, if I have not Anne Page, I shall turn your head out of my door. Follow my heels, Rugby.   [*Exeunt Caius and Rugby.*

Quick. You shall have An fool's-head of your own. No, I know Anne's mind for that : never a woman in Windsor knows more of Anne's mind than I do ; nor can do more than I do with her, I thank heaven.

Fent. [*Within*] Who's within there ? ho !

Quick. Who's there, I trow ! Come near the house, I pray you.   141

Enter FENTON.

Fent. How now, good woman ! how dost thou ?

Quick. The better that it pleases your good worship to ask.

Fent. What news ? how does pretty Mistress Anne ?

Quick. In truth, sir, and she is pretty, and honest, and gentle ; and one that is your friend, I can tell you that by the way ; I praise heaven for it.   151

Fent. Shall I do any good, thinkest thou ? shall I not lose my suit ?

Quick. Troth, sir, all is in his hands above : but notwithstanding, Master Fenton, I'll be sworn on a book, she loves you. Have not your worship a wart above your eye ?

Fent. Yes, marry, have I ; what of that ?

Quick. Well, thereby hangs a tale : good faith, it is such another Nan ; but, I detest, an honest maid as ever broke bread : we had an hour's talk of that wart. I shall never laugh but in that maid's company ! But indeed she is given too much to allicholy and musing : but for you—well, go to.

Fent. Well, I shall see her to-day. Hold, there's money for thee ; let me have thy voice in my behalf : if thou seest her before me, commend me.

Quick. Will I ? i' faith, that we will ; and I will tell your worship more of the wart the next time we have confidence ; and of other wooers.

Fent. Well, farewell ; I am in great haste now.

Quick. Farewell to your worship. [*Exit Fenton.*] Truly, an honest gentleman : but Anne loves him not ; for I know Anne's mind as well as another does. Out upon't ! what have I forgot ?   [*Exit.* 180

ACT II.

Scene I. *Before* Page's *house.*

Enter Mistress Page, *with a letter.*

Mrs. Page. What, have I scaped love-letters in the holiday-time of my beauty, and am I now a subject for them ? Let me see.
                                        [*Reads.*
' Ask me no reason why I love you ; for though Love use Reason for his physician, he admits him not for his counsellor. You are not young, no more am I ; go to then, there's sympathy : you are merry, so am I ; ha, ha ! then there's more sympathy : you love sack, and so do I ; would you desire better sympathy ? Let it suffice thee, Mistress Page,—at the least, if the love of soldier can suffice,— that I love thee. I will not say, pity me ; 'tis not a soldier-like phrase : but I say, love me. By me,

          Thine own true knight,
          By day or night,
          Or any kind of light,
          With all his might
          For thee to fight, John Falstaff.'
What a Herod of Jewry is this ! O wicked, wicked world ! One that is well-nigh worn to pieces with age to show himself a young gallant ! What an unweighed behavior hath this Flemish drunkard picked—with the devil's name !—out of my conversation, that he dares in this manner assay me ? Why, he hath not been thrice in my company ! What should I say to him ? I was then frugal of my mirth : Heaven forgive me ! Why, I'll exhibit a bill in the parliament for the putting down of men. How shall I be revenged on him ? for revenged I will be, as sure as his guts are made of puddings.

Enter Mistress Ford.

Mrs. Ford. Mistress Page ! trust me, I was going to your house.

Mrs. Page. And, trust me, I was coming to you. You look very ill.

Mrs. Ford. Nay, I'll ne'er believe that ; I have to show to the contrary.

Mrs. Page. Faith, but you do, in my mind.

Mrs. Ford. Well, I do then ; yet I say I could show you to the contrary. O Mistress Page, give me some counsel !

Mrs. Page. What's the matter, woman ?

Mrs. Ford. O woman, if it were not for one trifling respect, I could come to such honor !

Mrs. Page. Hang the trifle, woman ! take the honor. What is it ? dispense with trifles ; what is it ?

Mrs. Ford. If I would but go to hell for an eternal moment or so, I could be knighted. 50

Mrs. Page. What ? thou liest ! Sir Alice Ford ! These knights will hack ; and so thou shouldst not alter the article of thy gentry.

Mrs. Ford. We burn daylight : here, read, read ; perceive how I might be knighted. I shall think the worse of fat men, as long as I have an eye to make difference of men's liking : and yet he would not swear ; praised women's modesty ; and gave such orderly and well-behaved reproof to all uncomeliness, that I would have sworn his disposition would have gone to the truth of his words ; but they do no more adhere and keep place together than the Hundredth Psalm to the tune of ' Green Sleeves.' What tempest, I trow, threw this whale, with so many tuns of oil in his belly, ashore at Windsor ? How shall I be revenged on him ? I think the best way were to entertain him with hope, till the wicked fire of lust have melted him in his own grease. Did you ever hear the like ?   70

Mrs. Page. Letter for letter, but that the name of Page and Ford differs ! To thy great comfort in this mystery of ill opinions, here's the twin-brother of thy letter : but let thine inherit first ; for, I protest, mine never shall. I warrant he hath a thousand of these letters, writ with blank space for different names,— sure, more,—and these are of the second edition : he will print them, out of doubt ; for he cares not what he puts into the press, when he would put us two. I had rather be a giantess, and lie under Mount Pelion. Well, I will find you twenty lascivious turtles ere one chaste man.

Mrs. Ford. Why, this is the very same ; the very hand, the very words. What doth he think of us ?

Mrs. Page. Nay, I know not : it makes me almost ready to wrangle with mine own honesty. I'll entertain myself like one that I am not acquainted withal ; for, sure, unless he know some strain in me, that I know not myself, he would never have boarded me in this fury.

Mrs. Ford. ' Boarding,' call you it ? I'll be sure to keep him above deck.

Mrs. Page. So will I : if he come under my hatches, I'll never to sea again. Let's be revenged on him : let's appoint him a meeting ; give him a show of comfort in his suit and lead him on with a fine-baited delay, till he hath pawned his horses to mine host of the Garter.   100

Mrs. Ford. Nay, I will consent to act any villany against him, that may not sully the chariness of our honesty. O, that my husband saw this letter ! it would give eternal food to his jealousy.

Mrs. Page. Why, look where he comes; and my good man too : he's as far from jealousy as I am from giving him cause; and that I hope is an unmeasurable distance.   109

Mrs. Ford. You are the happier woman.

Mrs. Page. Let's consult together against this greasy knight. Come hither.   [*They retire.*

Enter FORD *with* PISTOL, *and* PAGE *with* NYM.

Ford. Well, I hope it be not so.

Pist. Hope is a curtal dog in some affairs : Sir John affects thy wife.

Ford. Why, sir, my wife is not young.

Pist. He wooes both high and low, both rich and poor,

Both young and old, one with another, Ford;

He loves the gallimaufry : Ford, perpend.

Ford. Love my wife !   120

Pist. With liver burning hot. Prevent, or go thou,

Like Sir Actæon he, with Ringwood at thy heels :

O, odious is the name !

Ford. What name, sir ?

Pist. The horn, I say. Farewell.

Take heed, have open eye, for thieves do foot by night :

Take heed, ere summer comes or cuckoo-birds do sing.

Away, Sir Corporal Nym !

Believe it, Page ; he speaks sense.   [*Exit.*

Ford. [*Aside*] I will be patient; I will find out this.   131

Nym. [*To Page*] And this is true ; I like not the humor of lying. He hath wronged me in some humors : I should have borne the humored letter to her ; but I have a sword and it shall bite upon my necessity. He loves your wife ; there's the short and the long. My name is Corporal Nym ; I speak and I avouch ; 'tis true : my name is Nym and Falstaff loves your wife. Adieu. I love not the humor of bread and cheese, and there's the humor of it. Adieu.   [*Exit.* 141

Page. 'The humor of it,' quoth a' ! here's a fellow frights English out of his wits.

Ford. I will seek out Falstaff.

Page. I never heard such a drawling, affecting rogue.

Ford. If I do find it : well.

Page. I will not believe such a Cataian, though the priest o' the town commended him for a true man.   150

Ford. 'Twas a good sensible fellow : well.

Page. How now, Meg !

[*Mrs. Page and Mrs. Ford come forward.*

Mrs. Page. Whither go you, George ? Hark you.

Mrs. Ford. How now, sweet Frank ! why art thou melancholy ?

Ford. I melancholy ! I am not melancholy. Get you home, go.

Mrs. Ford. Faith, thou hast some crotchets in thy head. Now, will you go, Mistress Page ?

Mrs. Page. Have with you. You'll come to dinner, George. [*Aside to Mrs. Ford*] Look who comes yonder : she shall be our messenger to this paltry knight.

Mrs. Ford. [*Aside to Mrs. Page*] Trust me, I thought on her : she'll fit it.

Enter MISTRESS QUICKLY.

Mrs. Page. You are come to see my daughter Anne ?

Quick. Ay, forsooth ; and, I pray, how does good Mistress Anne ?   170

Mrs. Page. Go in with us and see : we have an hour's talk with you.

[*Exeunt Mrs. Page, Mrs. Ford, and Mrs. Quickly.*

Page. How now, Master Ford !

Ford. You heard what this knave told me, did you not ?

Page. Yes : and you heard what the other told me ?

Ford. Do you think there is truth in them ?

Page. Hang 'em, slaves ! I do not think the knight would offer it : but these that accuse him in his intent towards our wives are a yoke of his discarded men ; very rogues, now they be out of service.

Ford. Were they his men ?

Page. Marry, were they.

Ford. I like it never the better for that. Does he lie at the Garter ?

Page. Ay, marry, does he. If he should intend this voyage towards my wife, I would turn her loose to him ; and what he gets more of her than sharp words, let it lie on my head.

Ford. I do not misdoubt my wife ; but I would be loath to turn them together. A man may be too confident : I would have nothing lie on my head : I cannot be thus satisfied.

Page. Look where my ranting host of the Garter comes : there is either liquor in his pate or money in his purse when he looks so merrily.

Enter HOST.

How now, mine host !

Host. How now, bully-rook ! thou'rt a gentleman. Cavaleiro-justice, I say !   201

Enter SHALLOW.

Shal. I follow, mine host, I follow. Good even and twenty, good Master Page ! Master Page, will you go with us ? we have sport in hand.

Host. Tell him, cavaleiro-justice ; tell him, bully-rook.

Shal. Sir, there is a fray to be fought between Sir Hugh the Welsh priest and Caius the French doctor.   210

Ford. Good mine host o' the Garter, a word with you.   [*Drawing him aside.*

Host. What sayest thou, my bully-rook ?

Shal. [*To Page*] Will you go with us to behold it ? My merry host hath had the measuring of their weapons ; and, I think, hath appointed them contrary places ; for, believe me, I hear the parson is no jester. Hark, I will tell you what our sport shall be.

[*They converse apart.*

Host. Hast thou no suit against my knight, my guest-cavaleire ?   221

Ford. None, I protest : but I'll give you a pottle of burnt sack to give me recourse to him and tell him my name is Brook ; only for a jest.

Host. My hand, bully ; thou shalt have egress and regress ;—said I well ?—and thy name shall be Brook. It is a merry knight. Will you go, An-heires ?

Shal. Have with you, mine host.

Page. I have heard the Frenchman hath good skill in his rapier.   231

Shal. Tut, sir, I could have told you more. In these times you stand on distance, your passes, stoccadoes, and I know not what : 'tis the heart, Master Page ; 'tis here, 'tis here. I have seen the time, with my long sword I would have made you four tall fellows skip like rats.

Host. Here, boys, here, here ! shall we wag ?

Page. Have with you. I would rather hear them scold than fight.   240

[*Exeunt Host, Shal., and Page.*

Ford. Though Page be a secure fool, an stands so firmly on his wife's frailty, yet I cannot put off my opinion so easily : she was in his company at Page's house ; and what they made there, I know not. Well, I will look further into't : and I have a disguise to sound Falstaff. If I find her honest, I lose not my labor ; if she be otherwise, 'tis labor well bestowed.   [*Exit.*

SCENE II.   *A room in the Garter Inn.*

Enter FALSTAFF and PISTOL.

Fal. I will not lend thee a penny.

Pist. Why, then the world's mine oyster. Which I with sword will open.

Fal. Not a penny. I have been content, sir, you should lay my countenance to pawn ; I have grated upon my good friends for three reprieves for you and your coach-fellow Nym ; or else you had looked through the grate, like a geminy of baboons. I am damned in hell for swearing to gentlemen my friends, you were good soldiers and tall fellows ; and when Mistress Bridget lost the handle of her fan, I took't upon mine honor thou hadst it not.

Pist. Didst not thou share ? hadst thou not fifteen pence ?

Fal. Reason, you rogue, reason : thinkest thou I'll endanger my soul gratis ? At a word, hang no more about me, I am no gibbet for you. Go. A short knife and a throng ! To your manor of Pickt-hatch ! Go. You'll not bear a letter for me, you rogue ! you stand upon your honor ! Why, thou unconfinable baseness, it is as much as I can do to keep the terms of my honor precise : I, I, I myself sometimes, leaving the fear of God on the left hand and hiding mine honor in my necessity, am fain to shuffle, to hedge and to lurch ; and yet you, rogue, will ensconce your rags, your cat-a-mountain looks, your red-lattice phrases, and your bold-beating oaths, under the shelter of your honor ! You will not do it, you !   30

Pist. I do relent : what would thou more of man ?

Enter ROBIN.

Rob. Sir, here's a woman would speak with you.

Fal. Let her approach.

Enter MISTRESS QUICKLY.

Quick. Give your worship good morrow.

Fal. Good morrow, good wife.

Quick. Not so, an't please your worship.

Fal. Good maid, then.

Quick. I'll be sworn, As my mother was, the first hour I was born.

Fal. I do believe the swearer. What with me ?

Quick. Shall I vouchsafe your worship a word or two ?

Fal. Two thousand, fair woman : and I'll vouchsafe thee the hearing.

Quick. There is one Mistress Ford, sir :— I pray, come a little nearer this ways :—I myself dwell with master Doctor Caius,—

Fal. Well, on : Mistress Ford, you say,—

Quick. Your worship says very true : I pray your worship, come a little nearer this ways.

Fal. I warrant thee, nobody hears ; mine own people, mine own people.   51

Quick. Are they so ? God bless them and make them his servants !

Fal. Well, Mistress Ford ; what of her ?

Quick. Why, sir, she's a good creature. Lord, Lord ! your worship's a wanton ! Well, heaven forgive you and all of us, I pray !

Fal. Mistress Ford ; come, Mistress Ford,—

Quick. Marry, this is the short and the long of it ; you have brought her into such a canaries as 'tis wonderful. The best courtier of them all, when the court lay at Windsor, could never have brought her to such a canary. Yet there has been knights, and lords, and gentlemen, with their coaches, I warrant you, coach after coach, letter after letter, gift after gift ; smelling so sweetly, all musk, and so rushling, I warrant you, in silk and gold ; and in such alligant terms ; and in such wine and sugar of the best and the fairest, that would have won any woman's heart ; and, I warrant you, they could never get an eye-wink of her : I had myself twenty angels given me this morning ; but I defy all angels, in any such sort, as they say, but in the way of honesty : and, I warrant you, they could never get her so much as sip on a cup with the proudest of them all : and yet there has been earls, nay, which is more, pensioners ; but, I warrant you, all is one with her.   80

Fal. But what says she to me ? be brief, my good she-Mercury.

Quick. Marry, she hath received your letter, for the which she thanks you a thousand times ; and she gives you to notify that her husband will be absence from his house between ten and eleven.

Fal. Ten and eleven ?

Quick. Ay, forsooth ; and then you may come and see the picture, she says, that you wot of : Master Ford, her husband, will be from home. Alas ! the sweet woman leads an ill life with him : he's a very jealousy man : she leads a very frampold life with him, good heart.

Fal. Ten and eleven. Woman, commend me to her ; I will not fail her.

Quick. Why, you say well. But I have another messenger to your worship. Mistress Page hath her hearty commendations to you too : and let me tell you in your ear, she's as fartuous a civil modest wife, and one, I tell you, that will not miss you morning nor evening prayer, as any is in Windsor, whoe'er be the other : and she bade me tell your worship that her husband is seldom from home ; but she hopes there will come a time. I never knew a woman so dote upon a man : surely

I think you have charms, la ; yes, in truth.

Fal. Not I, I assure thee : setting the attractions of my good parts aside I have no other charms. 111

Quick. Blessing on your heart for't !

Fal. But, I pray thee, tell me this : has Ford's wife and Page's wife acquainted each other how they love me ?

Quick. That were a jest indeed ! they have not so little grace, I hope : that were a trick indeed ! but Mistress Page would desire you to send her your little page, of all loves : her husband has a marvellous infection to the little page ; and truly Master Page is an honest man. Never a wife in Windsor leads a better life than she does : do what she will, say what she will, take all, pay all, go to bed when she list, rise when she list, all is as she will : and truly she deserves it ; for if there be a kind woman in Windsor, she is one. You must send her your page ; no remedy.

Fal. Why, I will.

Quick. Nay, but do so, then : and, look you, he may come and go between you both ; and in any case have a nay-word, that you may know one another's mind, and the boy never need to understand any thing ; for 'tis not good that children should know any wickedness : old folks, you know, have discretion, as they say, and know the world.

Fal. Fare thee well : commend me to them both : there's my purse ; I am yet thy debtor. Boy, go along with this woman. [*Exeunt Mistress Quickly and Robin.*] This news distracts me !

Pist. This punk is one of Cupid's carriers : Clap on more sails ; pursue ; up with your fights :
Give fire : she is my prize, or ocean whelm them all !   [*Exit.*

Fal. Sayest thou so, old Jack ? go thy ways ; I'll make more of thy old body than I have done. Will they yet look after thee ? Wilt thou, after the expense of so much money, be now a gainer ? Good body, I thank thee. Let them say 'tis grossly done ; so it be fairly done, no matter.

Enter BARDOLPH.

Bard. Sir John, there's one Master Brook below would fain speak with you, and be acquainted with you ; and hath sent your worship a morning's draught of sack.

Fal. Brook is his name ?

Bard. Ay, sir.

Fal. Call him in. [*Exit Bardolph.*] Such Brooks are welcome to me, that o'erflow such liquor. Ah, ha ! Mistress Ford and Mistress Page have I encompassed you ? go to ; via !

Re-enter BARDOLPH, *with* FORD *disguised.*

Ford. Bless you, sir !   160

Fal. And you, sir ! Would you speak with me ?

Ford. I make bold to press with so little preparation upon you.

Fal. You're welcome. What's your will ? Give us leave, drawer.   [*Exit Bardolph.*

Ford. Sir, I am a gentleman that have spent much ; my name is Brook.

Fal. Good Master Brook, I desire more acquaintance of you.

Ford. Good Sir John, I sue for yours : not to charge you ; for I must let you understand I think myself in better plight for a lender than you are : the which hath something emboldened me to this unseasoned intrusion ; for they say, if money go before, all ways do lie open.

Fal. Money is a good soldier, sir, and will on.

Ford. Troth, and I have a bag of money here troubles me : if you will help to bear it, Sir John, take all, or half, for easing me of the carriage.

Fal. Sir, I know not how I may deserve to be your porter.   181

Ford. I will tell you, sir, if you will give me the hearing.

Fal. Speak, good Master Brook : I shall be glad to be your servant.

Ford. Sir, I hear you are a scholar,—I will be brief with you,—and you have been a man long known to me, though I had never so good means, as desire, to make myself acquainted with you. I shall discover a thing to you, wherein I must very much lay open mine own imperfection : but, good Sir John, as you have one eye upon my follies, as you hear them unfolded, turn another into the register of your own ; that I may pass with a reproof the easier, sith you yourself know how easy it is to be such an offender.

Fal. Very well, sir ; proceed.

Ford. There is a gentlewoman in this town ; her husband's name is Ford.

Fal. Well, sir.   200

Ford. I have long loved her, and, I protest to you, bestowed much on her ; followed her with a doting observance ; engrossed opportunities to meet her ; fee'd every slight occasion that could but niggardly give me sight of her ; not only bought many presents to give her, but have given largely to many to know what she would have given ; briefly, I have pursued her as love hath pursued me ; which hath been on the wing of all occasions. But whatsoever I have merited, either in my mind or in my means, meed, I am sure, I have received none ; unless experience be a jewel that I have purchased at an infinite rate, and that hath taught me to say this :
' Love like a shadow flies when substance love pursues ;
Pursuing that that flies, and flying what pursues.'

Fal. Have you received no promise of satisfaction at her hands ?

Ford. Never.

Fal. Have you importuned her to such a purpose ?   221

Ford. Never.

Fal. Of what quality was your love, then ?

Ford. Like a fair house built on another man's ground ; so that I have lost my edifice by mistaking the place where I erected it.

Fal. To what purpose have you unfolded this to me ?

Ford. When I have told you that, I have told you all. Some say, that though she appear honest to me, yet in other places she enlargeth her mirth so far that there is shrewd construction made of her. Now, Sir John, here is the heart of my purpose : you are a gentleman of excellent breeding, admirable discourse, of great admittance, authentic in your

place and person, generally allowed for your
many war-like, court-like, and learned preparations.

Fal. O, sir!

Ford. Believe it, for you know it. There
is money; spend it, spend it; spend more;
spend all I have; only give me so much of
your time in exchange of it, as to lay an amiable siege to the honesty of this Ford's wife:
use your art of wooing; win her to consent
to you: if any man may, you may as soon
as any.

Fal. Would it apply well to the vehemency
of your affection, that I should win what you
would enjoy? Methinks you prescribe to yourself very preposterously.   250

Ford. O, understand my drift. She dwells
so securely on the excellency of her honor,
that the folly of my soul dares not present itself: she is too bright to be looked against.
Now, could I come to her with any detection
in my hand, my desires had instance and argument to commend themselves: I could drive
her then from the ward of her purity, her reputation, her marriage-vow, and a thousand
other her defences, which now are too too
strongly embattled against me. What say you
to't, Sir John?   261

Fal. Master Brook, I will first make bold
with your money; next, give me your hand;
and last, as I am a gentleman, you shall, if
you will, enjoy Ford's wife.

Ford. O good sir!

Fal. I say you shall.

Ford. Want no money, Sir John; you shall
want none.

Fal. Want no Mistress Ford, Master
Brook; you shall want none. I shall be with
her, I may tell you, by her own appointment;
even as you came in to me, her assistant or
go-between parted from me: I say I shall be
with her between ten and eleven; for at that
time the jealous rascally knave her husband
will be forth. Come you to me at night; you
shall know how I speed.

Ford. I am blest in your acquaintance. Do
you know Ford, sir?   280

Fal. Hang him, poor cuckoldly knave! I
know him not: yet I wrong him to call him
poor; they say the jealous wittolly knave hath
masses of money; for the which his wife seems
to me well-favored. I will use her as the key
of the cuckoldly rogue's coffer; and there's
my harvest-home.

Ford. I would you knew Ford, sir, that
you might avoid him if you saw him.

Fal. Hang him, mechanical salt-butter
rogue! I will stare him out of his wits; I will
awe him with my cudgel: it shall hang like a
meteor o'er the cuckold's horns. Master
Brook, thou shalt know I will predominate
over the peasant, and thou shalt lie with his
wife. Come to me soon at night. Ford's a
knave, and I will aggravate his style; thou,
Master Brook, shalt know him for knave and
cuckold. Come to me soon at night.   [*Exit.*

Ford. What a damned Epicurean rascal is
this! My heart is ready to crack with impatience. Who says this is improvident jealousy? my wife hath sent to him; the hour is
fixed; the match is made. Would any man
have thought this? See the hell of having a
false woman! My bed shall be abused, my

coffers ransacked, my reputation gnawn at;
and I shall not only receive this villanous
wrong, but stand under the adoption of abominable terms, and by him that does me this
wrong. Terms! names! Amaimon sounds
well; Lucifer, well; Barbason, well; yet they
are devils' additions, the names of fiends: but
Cuckold! Wittol!—Cuckold! the devil himself hath not such a name. Page is an ass, a
secure ass: he will trust his wife; he will not
be jealous. I will rather trust a Fleming with
my butter, Parson Hugh the Welshman with
my cheese, an Irishman with my aqua-vitæ
bottle, or a thief to walk my ambling gelding,
than my wife with herself; then she plots,
then she ruminates, then she devises; and
what they think in their hearts they may effect, they will break their hearts but they will
effect. God be praised for my jealousy!
Eleven o'clock the hour. I will prevent this,
detect my wife, be revenged on Falstaff, and
laugh at Page. I will about it; better three
hours too soon than a minute too late. Fie, fie,
fie! cuckold! cuckold! cuckold!   [*Exit.*

SCENE III. *A field near Windsor.*

Enter CAIUS *and* RUGBY.

Caius. Jack Rugby!

Rug. Sir?

Caius. Vat is de clock, Jack?

Rug. 'Tis past the hour, sir, that Sir Hugh
promised to meet.

Caius. By gar, he has save his soul, dat he
is no come; he has pray his Pible well, dat he
is no come: by gar, Jack Rugby, he is dead
already, if he be come.

Rug. He is wise, sir; he knew your wor-
ship would kill him, if he came.   11

Caius. By gar, de herring is no dead so as
I vill kill him. Take your rapier, Jack; I vill
tell you how I vill kill him.

Rug. Alas, sir, I cannot fence.

Caius. Villany, take your rapier.

Rug. Forbear; here's company.

Enter HOST, SHALLOW, SLENDER, *and* PAGE.

Host. Bless thee, bully doctor!

Shal. Save you, Master Doctor Caius!

Page. Now, good master doctor!   20

Slen. Give you good morrow, sir.

Caius. Vat be all you, one, two, tree, four,
come for?

Host. To see thee fight, to see thee foin, to
see thee traverse; to see thee here, to see thee
there; to see thee pass thy punto, thy stock,
thy reverse, thy distance, thy montant. Is he
dead, my Ethiopian? is he dead, my Fran-
cisco? ha, bully! What says my Æsculapius?
my Galen? my heart of elder? ha! is he dead,
bully stale? is he dead?   31

Caius. By gar, he is de coward Jack priest
of de vorld; he is not show his face.

Host. Thou art a Castalion-King-Urinal.
Hector of Greece, my boy!

Caius. I pray you, bear vitness that me
have stay six or seven, two, tree hours for him,
and he is no come.

Shal. He is the wiser man, master doctor:
he is a curer of souls, and you a curer of
bodies; if you should fight, you go against the
hair of your professions. Is it not true, Master
Page?

Page. Master Shallow, you have yourself

been a great fighter, though now a man of peace.

Shal. Bodykins, Master Page, though I now be old and of the peace, if I see a sword out, my finger itches to make one. Though we are justices and doctors and churchmen, Master Page, we have some salt of our youth in us ; we are the sons of women, Master Page.   51

Page. 'Tis true, Master Shallow.

Shal. It will be found so, Master Page. Master Doctor Caius, I am come to fetch you home. I am sworn of the peace : you have showed yourself a wise physician, and Sir Hugh hath shown himself a wise and patient churchman. You must go with me, master doctor.

Host. Pardon, guest-justice. A word, Mounseur Mockwater.   60

Caius. Mock-vater ! vat is dat ?

Host. Mock-water, in our English tongue, is valor, bully.

Caius. By gar, den, I have as mush mock-vater as de Englishman. Scurvy jack-dog priest ! by gar, me vill cut his ears.

Host. He will clapper-claw thee tightly, bully.

Caius. Clapper-de-claw ! vat is dat ?

Host. That is, he will make thee amends.70

Caius. By gar, me do look he shall clapper-de-claw me ; for, by gar, me vill have it.

Host. And I will provoke him to't, or let him wag.

Caius. Me tank you for dat.

Host. And, moreover, bully,—but first, master guest, and Master Page, and eke Cavaleiro Slender, go you through the town to Frogmore.   [*Aside to them.*

Page. Sir Hugh is there, is he ?

Host. He is there : see what humor he is in ; and I will bring the doctor about by the fields. Will it do well ?

Shal. We will do it.

Page, Shal., and Slen. Adieu, good master doctor.   [*Exeunt Page, Shal., and Slen.*

Caius. By gar, me vill kill de priest ; for he speak for a jack-an-ape to Anne Page.

Host. Let him die : sheathe thy impatience, throw cold water on thy choler : go about the fields with me through Frogmore : I will bring thee where Mistress Anne Page is, at a farmhouse a-feasting ; and thou shalt woo her. Cried I aim ? said I well ?

Caius. By gar, me dank you for dat : by gar, I love you ; and I shall procure-a you de good guest, de earl, de knight, de lords, de gentlemen, my patients.

Host. For the which I will be thy adversary toward Anne Page. Said I well ?

Caius. By gar, 'tis good ; vell said.   100

Host. Let us wag, then.

Caius. Come at my heels, Jack Rugby.   [*Exeunt.*

ACT III.

SCENE I.   *A field near Frogmore.*

Enter SIR HUGH EVANS *and* SIMPLE.

Evans. I pray you now, good Master Slender's serving-man, and friend Simple by your name, which way have you looked for Master

Caius, that calls himself doctor of physic ?

Sim. Marry, sir, the pittie-ward, the park-ward, every way ; old Windsor way, and every way but the town way.

Evans. I most fehemently desire you you will also look that way.

Sim. I will, sir.   [*Exit.* 10

Evans. 'Pless my soul, how full of chollors I am, and trempling of mind ! I shall be glad if he have deceived me. How melancholies I am ! I will knog his urinals about his knave's costard when I have good opportunities for the ork. 'Pless my soul !   [*Sings.*

To shallow rivers, to whose falls
  Melodious birds sings madrigals ;
There will we make our peds of roses,
  And a thousand fragrant posies.   20
To shallow—

Mercy on me ! I have a great dispositions to cry.   [*Sings.*

Melodious birds sing madrigals—
When as I sat in Pabylon—
And a thousand vagram posies.
To shallow &c.

Re-enter SIMPLE.

Sim. Yonder he is coming, this way, Sir Hugh.

Evans. He's welcome.   [*Sings.*

To shallow rivers, to whose falls—
Heaven prosper the right ! What weapons is he ?

Sim. No weapons, sir. There comes my master, Master Shallow, and another gentleman, from Frogmore, over the stile, this way.

Evans. Pray you, give me my gown ; or else keep it in your arms.

Enter PAGE, SHALLOW, *and* SLENDER.

Shal. How now, master Parson ! Good morrow, good Sir Hugh. Keep a gamester from the dice, and a good student from his book, and it is wonderful.

Slen. [*Aside*] Ah, sweet Anne Page !   40

Page. 'Save you, good Sir Hugh !

Evans. 'Pless you from his mercy sake, all of you !

Shal. What, the sword and the word ! do you study them both, master parson ?

Page. And youthful still ! in your doublet and hose this raw rheumatic day !

Evans. There is reasons and causes for it.

Page. We are come to you to do a good office, master parson.   50

Evans. Fery well : what is it ?

Page. Yonder is a most reverend gentleman, who, belike having received wrong by some person, is at most odds with his own gravity and patience that ever you saw.

Shal. I have lived fourscore years and upward ; I never heard a man of his place, gravity and learning, so wide of his own respect.

Evans. What is he ?

Page. I think you know him ; Master Doctor Caius, the renowned French physician.

Evans. Got's will, and his passion of my heart ! I had as lief you would tell me of a mess of porridge.

Page. Why ?

Evans. He has no more knowledge in Hibocrates and Galen,—and he is a knave besides ; a cowardly knave as you would desires to be acquainted withal.

Page. I warrant you, he's the man should fight with him.   71
Slen. [*Aside*] O sweet Anne Page!
Shal. It appears so by his weapons. Keep them asunder : here comes Doctor Caius.

Enter HOST, CAIUS, *and* RUGBY.

Page. Nay, good master parson, keep in your weapon.
Shal. So do you, good master doctor.
Host. Disarm them, and let them question : let them keep their limbs whole and hack our English.   80
Caius. I pray you, let-a me speak a word with your ear. Vherefore vill you not meet-a me ?
Evans. [*Aside to Caius*] Pray you, use your patience : in good time.
Caius. By gar, you are de coward, de Jack dog, John ape.
Evans. [*Aside to Caius*] Pray you, let us not be laughing-stocks to other men's humors ; I desire you in friendship, and I will one way or other make you amends. [*Aloud*] I will knog your urinals about your knave's cogscomb for missing your meetings and appointments.   92
Caius. Diable ! Jack Rugby,—mine host de Jarteer,—have I not stay for him to kill him ? have I not, at de place I did appoint ?
Evans. As I am a Christians soul now, look you, this is the place appointed : I'll be judgement by mine host of the Garter.
Host. Peace, I say, Gallia and Gaul, French and Welsh, soul-curer and body-curer !
Caius. Ay, dat is very good ; excellent. 101
Host. Peace, I say ! hear mine host of the Garter. Am I politic ? am I subtle ? am I a Machiavel ? Shall I lose my doctor ? no ; he gives me the potions and the motions. Shall I lose my parson, my priest, my Sir Hugh ? no ; he gives me the proverbs and the no-verbs. Give me thy hand, terrestrial ; so. Give me thy hand, celestial ; so. Boys of art, I have deceived you both ; I have directed you to wrong places : your hearts are mighty, your skins are whole, and let burnt sack be the issue. Come, lay their swords to pawn. Follow me, lads of peace ; follow, follow, follow.
Shal. Trust me, a mad host. Follow, gentlemen, follow.
Slen. [*Aside*] O sweet Anne Page !
[*Exeunt Shal., Slen., Page, and Host.*
Caius. Ha, do I perceive dat ? have you make-a de sot of us, ha, ha ?
Evans. This is well ; he has made us his vlouting-stog. I desire you that we may be friends ; and let us knog our prains together to be revenge on this same scall, scurvy, cogging companion, the host of the Garter.
Caius. By gar, with all my heart. He promise to bring me where is Anne Page ; by gar, he deceive me too.
Evans. Well, I will smite his noddles. Pray you, follow.   [*Exeunt.*

SCENE II. *A street.*

Enter MISTRESS PAGE *and* ROBIN.

Mrs. Page. Nay, keep your way, little gallant ; you were wont to be a follower, but now you are a leader. Whether had you rather lead mine eyes, or eye your master's heels ?

Rob. I had rather, forsooth, go before you like a man than follow him like a dwarf.
Mrs. Page. O, you are a flattering boy : now I see you'll be a courtier.

Enter FORD.

Ford. Well met, Mistress Page. Whither go you ?   10
Mrs. Page. Truly, sir, to see your wife. Is she at home ?
Ford. Ay ; and as idle as she may hang together, for want of company. I think, if your husbands were dead, you two would marry.
Mrs. Page. Be sure of that,—two other husbands.
Ford. Where had you this pretty weathercock ?
Mrs. Page. I cannot tell what the dickens his name is my husband had him of. What do you call your knight's name, sirrah ?   21
Rob. Sir John Falstaff.
Ford. Sir John Falstaff !
Mrs. Page. He, he ; I can never hit on's name. There is such a league between my good man and he ! Is your wife at home indeed ?
Ford. Indeed she is.
Mrs. Page. By your leave, sir : I am sick till I see her. [*Exeunt Mrs. Page and Robin.*
Ford. Has Page any brains ? hath he any eyes ? hath he any thinking ? Sure, they sleep ; he hath no use of them. Why, this boy will carry a letter twenty mile, as easy as a cannon will shoot point-blank twelve score. He pieces out his wife's inclination ; he gives her folly motion and advantage : and now she's going to my wife, and Falstaff's boy with her. A man may hear this shower sing in the wind. And Falstaff's boy with her ! Good plots, they are laid ; and our revolted wives share damnation together. Well ; I will take him, then torture my wife, pluck the borrowed veil of modesty from the so seeming Mistress Page, divulge Page himself for a secure and wilful Actæon ; and to these violent proceedings all my neighbors shall cry aim. [*Clock heard.*] The clock gives me my cue, and my assurance bids me search : there I shall find Falstaff : I shall be rather praised for this than mocked ; for it is as positive as the earth is firm that Falstaff is there : I will go.   50

Enter PAGE, SHALLOW, SLENDER, HOST, SIR HUGH EVANS, CAIUS, *and* RUGBY.

Shal., Page, &c. Well met, Master Ford.
Ford. Trust me, a good knot : I have good cheer at home ; and I pray you all go with me.
Shal. I must excuse myself, Master Ford.
Slen. And so must I, sir : we have appointed to dine with Mistress Anne, and I would not break with her for more money than I'll speak of.
Shal. We have lingered about a match between Anne Page and my cousin Slender, and this day we shall have our answer.   60
Slen. I hope I have your good will, father Page.
Page. You have, Master Slender ; I stand wholly for you : but my wife, master doctor, is for you altogether.
Caius. Ay, be-gar ; and de maid is love-a me : my nursh-a Quickly tell me so mush.
Host. What say you to young Master Fenton ? he capers, he dances, he has eyes of

youth, he writes verses, he speaks holiday, he smells April and May : he will carry't, he will carry't ; 'tis in his buttons ; he will carry't. 71

Page. Not by my consent, I promise you. The gentleman is of no having : he kept company with the wild prince and Poins ; he is of too high a region ; he knows too much. No, he shall not knit a knot in his fortunes with the finger of my substance : if he take her, let him take her simply ; the wealth I have waits on my consent, and my consent goes not that way.

Ford. I beseech you heartily, some of you go home with me to dinner : besides your cheer, you shall have sport ; I will show you a monster. Master doctor, you shall go ; so shall you, Master Page ; and you, Sir Hugh.

Shal. Well, fare you well : we shall have the freer wooing at Master Page's.
[*Exeunt Shal. and Slen.*

Caius. Go home, John Rugby ; I come anon. [*Exit Rugby.*

Host. Farewell, my hearts : I will to my honest knight Falstaff, and drink canary with him. [*Exit.*

Ford. [*Aside*] I think I shall drink in pipe wine first with him ; I'll make him dance. Will you go, gentles ?

All. Have with you to see this monster.
[*Exeunt.*

SCENE III. *A room in* FORD'S *house.*

Enter MISTRESS FORD *and* MISTRESS PAGE.

Mrs. Ford. What, John ! What, Robert !

Mrs. Page. Quickly, quickly ! is the buck-basket—

Mrs. Ford. I warrant. What, Robin, I say !

Enter Servants *with a basket.*

Mrs. Page. Come, come, come.

Mrs. Ford. Here, set it down.

Mrs. Page. Give your men the charge ; we must be brief.

Mrs. Ford. Marry, as I told you before, John and Robert, be ready here hard by in the brew-house : and when I suddenly call you, come forth, and without any pause or staggering take this basket on your shoulders : that done, trudge with it in all haste, and carry it among the whitsters in Datchet-mead, and there empty it in the muddy ditch close by the Thames side.

Mrs. Page. You will do it ?

Mrs. Ford. I ha' told them over and over ; they lack no direction. Be gone, and come when you are called. [*Exeunt Servants.* 20

Mrs. Page. Here comes little Robin.

Enter ROBIN.

Mrs. Ford. How now, my eyas-musket ! what news with you ?

Rob. My master, Sir John, is come in at your back-door, Mistress Ford, and requests your company.

Mrs. Page. You little Jack-a-Lent, have you been true to us ?

Rob. Ay, I'll be sworn. My master knows not of your being here and hath threatened to put me into everlasting liberty if I tell you of it ; for he swears he'll turn me away.

Mrs. Page. Thou'rt a good boy : this secrecy of thine shall be a tailor to thee and shall make thee a new doublet and hose. I'll go hide me.

Mrs. Ford. Do so. Go tell thy master I am alone. [*Exit Robin.*] Mistress Page, remember you your cue.

Mrs. Page. I warrant thee ; if I do not act it, hiss me. [*Exit.* 41

Mrs. Ford. Go to, then : we'll use this unwholesome humidity, this gross watery pumpion ; we'll teach him to know turtles from jays.

Enter FALSTAFF.

Fal. Have I caught thee, my heavenly jewel ? Why, now let me die, for I have lived long enough : this is the period of my ambition : O this blessed hour !

Mrs. Ford. O sweet Sir John !

Fal. Mistress Ford, I cannot cog, I cannot prate, Mistress Ford. Now shall I sin in my wish : I would thy husband were dead : I'll speak it before the best lord ; I would make thee my lady.

Mrs. Ford. I your lady, Sir John ! alas, I should be a pitiful lady !

Fal. Let the court of France show me such another. I see how thine eye would emulate the diamond : thou hast the right arched beauty of the brow that becomes the ship-tire, the tire-valiant, or any tire of Venetian admittance. 61

Mrs. Ford. A plain kerchief, Sir John : my brows become nothing else ; nor that well neither.

Fal. By the Lord, thou art a traitor to say so : thou wouldst make an absolute courtier ; and the firm fixture of thy foot would give an excellent motion to thy gait in a semi-circled farthingale. I see what thou wert, if Fortune thy foe were not, Nature thy friend. Come, thou canst not hide it. 71

Mrs. Ford. Believe me, there is no such thing in me.

Fal. What made me love thee ? let that persuade thee there's something extraordinary in thee. Come, I cannot cog and say thou art this and that, like a many of these lisping hawthorn-buds, that come like women in men's apparel, and smell like Bucklersbury in simple time ; I cannot : but I love thee ; none but thee ; and thou deservest it. 81

Mrs. Ford. Do not betray me, sir. I fear you love Mistress Page.

Fal. Thou mightst as well say I love to walk by the Counter-gate, which is as hateful to me as the reek of a lime-kiln.

Mrs. Ford. Well, heaven knows how I love you ; and you shall one day find it.

Fal. Keep in that mind ; I'll deserve it.

Mrs. Ford. Nay, I must tell you, so you do ; or else I could not be in that mind. 91

Rob. [*Within*] Mistress Ford, Mistress Ford ! here's Mistress Page at the door, sweating and blowing and looking wildly, and would needs speak with you presently.

Fal. She shall not see me : I will ensconce me behind the arras.

Mrs. Ford. Pray you, do so : she's a very tattling woman. [*Falstaff hides himself.*

Re-enter MISTRESS PAGE *and* ROBIN.

What's the matter ? how now ! 100

Mrs. Page. O Mistress Ford, what have you done ? You're shamed, you're overthrown, you're undone for ever !

Mrs. Ford. What's the matter, good Mistress Page ?

Mrs. Page. O well-a-day, Mistress Ford ! having an honest man to your husband, to give him such cause of suspicion !

Mrs. Ford. What cause of suspicion ?

Mrs. Page. What cause of suspicion ! Out pon you ! how am I mistook in you !   111

Mrs. Ford. Why, alas, what's the matter ?

Mrs. Page. Your husband's coming hither, woman, with all the officers in Windsor, to search for a gentleman that he says is here now in the house by your consent, to take an ill advantage of his absence : you are undone.

Mrs. Ford. 'Tis not so, I hope.

Mrs. Page. Pray heaven it be not so, that you have such a man here ! but 'tis most certain your husband's coming, with half Windsor at his heels, to search for such a one. I come before to tell you. If you know yourself clear, why, I am glad of it ; but if you have a friend here, convey, convey him out. Be not amazed ; call all your senses to you ; defend your reputation, or bid farewell to your good life for ever.

Mrs. Ford. What shall I do ? There is a gentleman my dear friend ; and I fear not mine own shame so much as his peril : I had rather than a thousand pound he were out of the house.

Mrs. Page. For shame ! never stand ' you had rather ' and ' you had rather : ' your husband's here at hand, bethink you of some conveyance : in the house you cannot hide him. O, how have you deceived me ! Look, here is a basket : if he be of any reasonable stature, he may creep in here ; and throw foul linen upon him, as if it were going to bucking : or—it is whiting-time—send him by your two men to Datchet-mead.   141

Mrs. Ford. He's too big to go in there. What shall I do ?

Fal. [*Coming forward*] Let me see't, let me see't, O, let me see't ! I'll in, I'll in. Follow your friend's counsel. I'll in.

Mrs. Page. What, Sir John Falstaff ! Are these your letters, knight ?

Fal. I love thee. Help me away. Let me creep in here. I'll never—   150
[*Gets into the basket ; they cover him with foul linen.*

Mrs. Page. Help to cover your master, boy. Call your men, Mistress Ford. You dissembling knight !

Mrs. Ford. What, John ! Robert ! John !
[*Exit Robin.*

Re-enter Servants.

Go take up these clothes here quickly. Where's the cowl-staff ? look, how you drumble ! Carry them to the laundress in Datchet-meat ; quickly, come.

Enter FORD, PAGE, CAIUS, *and* SIR HUGH EVANS.

Ford. Pray you, come near : if I suspect without cause, why then make sport at me ; then let me be your jest ; I deserve it. How now ! whither bear you this ?

Serv. To the laundress, forsooth.

Mrs. Ford. Why, what have you to do whither they bear it ? You were best meddle with buck-washing.

Ford. Buck ! I would I could wash myself of the buck ! Buck, buck, buck ! Ay, buck ; I warrant you, buck ; and of the season too, it shall appear. [*Exeunt servants with the basket.*] Gentlemen, I have dreamed to-night ; I'll tell you my dream. Here, here, here be my keys : ascend my chambers ; search, seek, find out : I'll warrant we'll unkennel the fox. Let me stop this way first. [*Locking the door.*] So, now uncape.

Page. Good Master Ford, be contented : you wrong yourself too much.

Ford. True, Master Page. Up, gentlemen : you shall see sport anon : follow me, gentlemen.   [*Exit.*   180

Evans. This is fery fantastical humors and jealousies.

Caius. By gar, 'tis no the fashion of France ; it is not jealous in France.

Page. Nay, follow him, gentlemen ; see the issue of his search.
[*Exeunt Page, Caius, and Evans.*

Mrs. Page. Is there not a double excellency in this ?

Mrs. Ford. I know not which pleases me better, that my husband is deceived, or Sir John.

Mrs. Page. What a taking was he in when your husband asked who was in the basket !

Mrs. Ford. I am half afraid he will have need of washing ; so throwing him into the water will do him a benefit.

Mrs. Page. Hang him, dishonest rascal ! I would all of the same strain were in the same distress.

Mrs. Ford. I think my husband hath some special suspicion of Falstaff's being here ; for I never saw him so gross in his jealousy till now.

Mrs. Page. I will lay a plot to try that ; and we will yet have more tricks with Falstaff : his dissolute disease will scarce obey this medicine.

Mrs. Ford. Shall we send that foolish carrion, Mistress Quickly, to him, and excuse his throwing into the water ; and give him another hope, to betray him to another punishment ?

Mrs. Page. We will do it : let him be sent for to-morrow, eight o'clock, to have amends.

Re-enter FORD, PAGE, CAIUS, *and* SIR HUGH EVANS.

Ford. I cannot find him : may be the knave bragged of that he could not compass.

Mrs. Page. [*Aside to Mrs. Ford*] Heard you that ?

Mrs. Ford. You use me well, Master Ford, do you ?

Ford. Ay, I do so.

Mrs. Ford. Heaven make you better than your thoughts !

Ford. Amen !   220

Mrs. Page. You do yourself mighty wrong, Master Ford.

Ford. Ay, ay ; I must bear it.

Evans. If there be any pody in the house, and in the chambers, and in the coffers, and in the presses, and in the coffers, and in the presses, heaven forgive my sins at the day of judgment !

Caius. By gar, nor I too : there is no bodies.

Page. Fie, fie, Master Ford ! are you not ashamed ? What spirit, what devil suggests this imagination ? I would not ha' your distemper in this kind for the wealth of Windsor Castle.

Ford. 'Tis my fault, Master Page : I suffer for it.

Evans. You suffer for a pad conscience : your wife is as honest a 'omans as I will desires among five thousand, and five hundred too.

Caius. By gar, I see 'tis an honest woman.

Ford. Well, I promised you a dinner. Come, come, walk in the Park : I pray you, pardon me ; I will hereafter make known to you why I have done this. Come, wife ; come, Mistress Page. I pray you, pardon me ; pray heartily, pardon me.

Page. Let's go in, gentlemen ; but, trust me, we'll mock him. I do invite you to-morrow morning to my house to breakfast : after, we'll a-birding together ; I have a fine hawk for the bush. Shall it be so ?

Ford. Any thing.

Evans. If there is one, I shall make two in the company. 251

Caius. If dere be one or two, I shall make-a the turd.

Ford. Pray you, go, Master Page.

Evans. I pray you now, remembrance to-morrow on the lousy knave, mine host.

Caius. Dat is good ; by gar, with all my heart !

Evans. A lousy knave, to have his gibes and his mockeries ! [*Exeunt.* 260

SCENE IV. *A room in* PAGE's *house.*

Enter FENTON *and* ANNE PAGE.

Fent. I see I cannot get thy father's love ; Therefore no more turn me to him, sweet Nan.

Anne. Alas, how then ?

Fent.　　　　　Why, thou must be thyself. He doth object I am too great of birth ; And that, my state being gall'd with my expense, I seek to heal it only by his wealth : Besides these, other bars he lays before me, My riots past, my wild societies ; And tells me 'tis a thing impossible I should love thee but as a property. 10

Anne. May be he tells you true.

Fent. No, heaven so speed me in my time to come ! Albeit I will confess thy father's wealth Was the first motive that I woo'd thee, Anne : Yet, wooing thee, I found thee of more value Than stamps in gold or sums in sealed bags ; And 'tis the very riches of thyself That now I aim at.

Anne.　　　　　Gentle Master Fenton, Yet seek my father's love ; still seek it, sir : If opportunity and humblest suit 20 Cannot attain it, why, then,—hark you hither ! [*They converse apart.*

Enter SHALLOW, SLENDER, *and* MISTRESS QUICKLY.

Shal. Break their talk, Mistress Quickly : my kinsman shall speak for himself.

Slen. I'll make a shaft or a bolt on't : 'slid, 'tis but venturing.

Shal. Be not dismayed.

Slen. No, she shall not dismay me : I care not for that, but that I am afeard.

Quick. Hark ye ; Master Slender would speak a word with you. 30

Anne. I come to him. [*Aside*] This is my father's choice. O, what a world of vile ill-favor'd faults Looks handsome in three hundred pounds a-year !

Quick. And how does good Master Fenton ? Pray you, a word with you.

Shal. She's coming ; to her, coz. O boy, thou hadst a father !

Slen. I had a father, Mistress Anne ; my uncle can tell you good jests of him. Pray you, uncle, tell Mistress Anne the jest, how my father stole two geese out of a pen, good uncle. 41

Shal. Mistress Anne, my cousin loves you.

Slen. Ay, that I do ; as well as I love any woman in Gloucestershire.

Shal. He will maintain you like a gentle-woman.

Slen. Ay, that I will, come cut and long-tail, under the degree of a squire.

Shal. He will make you a hundred and fifty pounds jointure. 50

Anne. Good Master Shallow, let him woo for himself.

Shal. Marry, I thank you for it ; I thank you for that good comfort. She calls you, coz : I'll leave you.

Anne. Now, Master Slender,—

Slen. Now, good Mistress Anne,—

Anne. What is your will ?

Slen. My will ! 'od's heartlings, that's a pretty jest indeed ! I ne'er made my will yet, I thank heaven ; I am not such a sickly creature, I give heaven praise. 62

Anne. I mean, Master Slender, what would you with me ?

Slen. Truly, for mine own part, I would little or nothing with you. Your father and my uncle hath made motions : if it be my luck, so ; if not, happy man be his dole ! They can tell you how things go better than I can : you may ask your father ; here he comes. 70

Enter PAGE *and* MISTRESS PAGE.

Page. Now, Master Slender : love him, daughter Anne. Why, how now ! what does Master Fenton here ? You wrong me, sir, thus still to haunt my house : I told you, sir, my daughter is disposed of.

Fent. Nay, Master Page, be not impatient.

Mrs. Page. Good Master Fenton, come not to my child.

Page. She is no match for you.

Fent. Sir, will you hear me ?

Page.　　　　　No, good Master Fenton. Come, Master Shallow ; come, son Slender, in. Knowing my mind, you wrong me, Master Fenton. [*Exeunt Page, Shal., and Slen.*

Quick. Speak to Mistress Page.

Fent. Good Mistress Page, for that I love your daughter In such a righteous fashion as I do, Perforce, against all checks, rebukes and manners, I must advance the colors of my love And not retire : let me have your good will.

Anne. Good mother, do not marry me to yond fool.

Mrs. Page. I mean it not ; I seek you a better husband.

Quick. That's my master, master doctor.

Anne. Alas, I had rather be set quick i' the
earth   90
And bowl'd to death with turnips !

Mrs. Page. Come, trouble not yourself.
Good Master Fenton,
I will not be your friend nor enemy :
My daughter will I question how she loves you,
And as I find her, so am I affected.
Till then farewell, sir : she must needs go in ;
Her father will be angry.

Fent. Farewell, gentle mistress : farewell,
Nan.   [*Exeunt Mrs. Page and Anne.*

Quick. This is my doing, now : ' Nay,' said
I, ' will you cast away your child on a fool,
and a physician ? Look on Master Fenton : '
this is my doing.

Fent. I thank thee ; and I pray thee, once
to-night
Give my sweet Nan this ring : there's for thy
pains.

Quick. Now heaven send thee good fortune ! [*Exit Fenton.*] A kind heart he hath :
a woman would run through fire and water
for such a kind heart. But yet I would my
master had Mistress Anne ; or I would Master
Slender had her ; or, in sooth, I would Master
Fenton had her : I will do what I can for them
all three ; for so I have promised, and I'll be
as good as my word ; but speciously for Master Fenton. Well, I must of another errand to
Sir John Falstaff from my two mistresses :
what a beast am I to slack it !   [*Exit.*

Scene V. *A room in the Garter Inn.*

Enter FALSTAFF *and* BARDOLPH.

Fal. Bardolph, I say,—

Bard. Here, sir.

Fal. Go fetch me a quart of sack ; put a
toast in't. [*Exit Bard.*] Have I lived to be
carried in a basket, like a barrow of butcher's
offal, and to be thrown in the Thames ? Well,
if I be served such another trick, I'll have my
brains ta'en out and buttered, and give them to
a dog for a new-year's gift. The rogues slighted
me into the river with as little remorse as they
would have drowned a blind bitch's puppies,
fifteen i' the litter : and you may know by my
size that I have a kind of alacrity in sinking ;
if the bottom were as deep as hell, I should
down. I had been drowned, but that the shore
was shelvy and shallow,—a death that I abhor ; for the water swells a man ; and what a
thing should I have been when I had been
swelled ! I should have been a mountain of
mummy.

Re-enter BARDOLPH *with sack.*

Bard. Here's Mistress Quickly, sir, to speak
with you.   21

Fal. Come, let me pour in some sack to the
Thames water ; for my belly's as cold as if I
had swallowed snowballs for pills to cool the
reins. Call her in.

Bard. Come in, woman !

Enter MISTRESS QUICKLY.

Quick. By your leave ; I cry you mercy :
give your worship good morrow.

Fal. Take away these chalices. Go brew me
a pottle of sack finely.   30

Bard. With eggs, sir ?

Fal. Simple of itself ; I'll no pullet-sperm

in my brewage. [*Exit Bardolph.*] How now !

Quick. Marry, sir, I come to your worship
from Mistress Ford.

Fal. Mistress Ford ! I have had ford
enough ; I was thrown into the ford ; I have
my belly full of ford.

Quick. Alas the day ! good heart, that was
not her fault : she does so take on with her
men ; they mistook their erection.   41

Fal. So did I mine, to build upon a foolish
woman's promise.

Quick. Well, she laments, sir, for it, that it
would yearn your heart to see it. Her husband
goes this morning a-birding ; she desires you
once more to come to her between eight and
nine : I must carry her word quickly : she'll
make you amends, I warrant you.

Fal. Well, I will visit her : tell her so ; and
bid her think what a man is : let her consider
his frailty, and then judge of my merit.   52

Quick. I will tell her.

Fal. Do so. Between nine and ten, sayest
thou ?

Quick. Eight and nine, sir.

Fal. Well, be gone : I will not miss her.

Quick. Peace be with you, sir.   [*Exit.*

Fal. I marvel I hear not of Master Brook ;
he sent me word to stay within : I like his
money well. O, here he comes.   60

Enter FORD.

Ford. Bless you, sir !

Fal. Now, master Brook, you come to know
what hath passed between me and Ford's wife ?

Ford. That, indeed, Sir John, is my business.

Fal. Master Brook, I will not lie to you : I
was at her house the hour she appointed me.

Ford. And sped you, sir ?

Fal. Very ill-favoredly, Master Brook.

Ford. How so, sir ? Did she change her determination ?   70

Fal. No, Master Brook ; but the peaking
Cornuto her husband, Master Brook, dwelling
in a continual 'larum of jealousy, comes me in
the instant of our encounter, after we had embraced, kissed, protested, and, as it were, spoke
the prologue of our comedy ; and at his heels
a rabble of his companions, thither provoked
and instigated by his distemper, and, forsooth,
to search his house for his wife's love.

Ford. What, while you were there ?   80

Fal. While I was there.

Ford. And did he search for you, and
could not find you ?

Fal. You shall hear. As good luck would
have it, comes in one Mistress Page ; gives intelligence of Ford's approach ; and, in her invention and Ford's wife's distraction, they conveyed me into a buck-basket.

Ford. A buck-basket !

Fal. By the Lord, a buck-basket ! rammed
me in with foul shirts and smocks, socks, foul
stockings, greasy napkins ; that, Master Brook,
there was the rankest compound of villanous
smell that ever offended nostril.

Ford. And how long lay you there ?

Fal. Nay, you shall hear, Master Brook,
what I have suffered to bring this woman to
evil for your good. Being thus crammed in
the basket, a couple of Ford's knaves, his
hinds, were called forth by their mistress to
carry me in the name of foul clothes to

Datchet-lane : they took me on their shoulders ; met the jealous knave their master in the door, who asked them once or twice what they had in their basket : I quaked for fear, lest the lunatic knave would have searched it ; but fate, ordaining he should be a cuckold, held his hand. Well : on went he for a search, and away went I for foul clothes. But mark the sequel, Master Brook : I suffered the pangs of three several deaths ; first, an intolerable fright, to be detected with a jealous rotten bell-wether ; next, to be compassed, like a good bilbo, in the circumference of a peck, hilt to point, heel to head ; and then, to be stopped in, like a strong distillation, with stinking clothes that fretted in their own grease : think of that, — a man of my kidney,—think of that, —that am as subject to heat as butter ; a man of continual dissolution and thaw : it was a miracle to scape suffocation. And in the height of this bath, when I was more than half stewed in grease, like a Dutch dish, to be thrown into the Thames, and cooled, glowing hot, in that surge, like a horse-shoe ; think of that,—hissing hot,—think of that, Master Brook.

Ford. In good sadness, sir, I am sorry that for my sake you have suffered all this. My suit then is desperate ; you'll undertake her no more ?

Fal. Master Brook, I will be thrown into Etna, as I have been into Thames, ere I will leave her thus. Her husband is this morning gone a-birding : I have received from her another embassy of meeting ; 'twixt eight and nine is the hour, Master Brook.

Ford. 'Tis past eight already, sir.

Fal. Is it ? I will then address me to my appointment. Come to me at your convenient leisure, and you shall know how I speed ; and the conclusion shall be crowned with your enjoying her. Adieu. You shall have her, Master Brook ; Master Brook, you shall cuckold Ford.
                                                    [*Exit.*

Ford. Hum ! ha ! is this a vision ? is this a dream ? do I sleep ? Master Ford, awake ! awake, Master Ford ! there's a hole made in your best coat, Master Ford. This 'tis to be married ! this 'tis to have linen and buck-baskets ! Well, I will proclaim myself what I am : I will now take the lecher ; he is at my house ; he cannot 'scape me ; 'tis impossible he should ; he cannot creep into a halfpenny purse, nor into a pepper-box : but, lest the devil that guides him should aid him, I will search impossible places. Though what I am I cannot avoid, yet to be what I would not shall not make me tame : if I have horns to make one mad, let the proverb go with me : I'll be horn-mad.   [*Exit.*

ACT IV.

SCENE I. *A street.*

Enter MISTRESS PAGE, MISTRESS QUICKLY, *and* WILLIAM.

Mrs. Page. Is he at Master Ford's already, think'st thou ?

Quick. Sure he is by this, or will be presently : but, truly, he is very courageous mad about his throwing into the water. Mistress Ford desires you to come suddenly.

Mrs. Page. I'll be with her by and by ; I'll but bring my young man here to school. Look, where his master comes ; 'tis a playing-day, I see.

Enter SIR HUGH EVANS.

How now, Sir Hugh ! no school to-day ?   10

Evans. No ; Master Slender is let the boys leave to play.

Quick. Blessing of his heart !

Mrs. Page. Sir Hugh, my husband says my son profits nothing in the world at his book. I pray you, ask him some questions in his accidence.

Evans. Come hither, William ; hold up your head ; come.

Mrs. Page. Come on, sirrah ; hold up your head ; answer your master, be not afraid.   20

Evans. William, how many numbers is in nouns ?

Will. Two.

Quick. Truly, I thought there had been one number more, because they say, ' 'Od's nouns.'

Evans. Peace your tattlings ! What is ' fair,' William ?

Will. Pulcher.

Quick. Polecats ! there are fairer things than polecats, sure.   30

Evans. You are a very simplicity 'oman : I pray you, peace. What is ' lapis,' William ?

Will. A stone.

Evans. And what is ' a stone,' William ?

Will. A pebble.

Evans. No, it is ' lapis : ' I pray you, remember in your prain.

Will. Lapis.

Evans. That is a good William. What is he, William, that does lend articles ?   40

Will. Articles are borrowed of the pronoun, and be thus declined, Singulariter, nominativo, hic, hæc, hoc.

Evans. Nominativo, hig, hag, hog ; pray you, mark : genitivo, hujus. Well, what is your accusative case ?

Will. Accusativo, hinc.

Evans. I pray you, have your remembrance, child ; accusativo, hung, hang, hog.

Quick. ' Hang-hog ' is Latin for bacon, I warrant you.   51

Evans. Leave your prabbles, 'oman. What is the focative case, William ?

Will. O,—vocativo, O.

Evans. Remember, William ; focative is caret.

Quick. And that's a good root.

Evans. 'Oman, forbear.

Mrs. Page. Peace !

Evans. What is your genitive case plural, William ?   60

Will. Genitive case !

Evans. Ay.

Will. Genitive,—horum, harum, horum.

Quick. Vengeance of Jenny's case ! fie on her ! never name her, child, if she be a whore.

Evans. For shame, 'oman.

Quick. You do ill to teach the child such words : he teaches him to hick and to hack, which they'll do fast enough of themselves, and to call ' horum : ' fie upon you !   70

Evans. 'Oman, art thou lunatics ? hast thou no understandings for thy cases and the numbers of the genders ? Thou art as foolish Christian creatures as I would desires.

Mrs. Page. Prithee, hold thy peace.

Evans. Show me now, William, some declensions of your pronouns.

Will. Forsooth, I have forgot.

Evans. It is qui, quæ, quod : if you forget your ' quies,' your ' quæs,' and your ' quods,' you must be preeches. Go your ways, and play ; go.

Mrs. Page. He is a better scholar than I thought he was.

Evans. He is a good sprag memory. Farewell, Mistress Page.

Mrs. Page. Adieu, good Sir Hugh. [*Exit Sir Hugh.*] Get you home, boy. Come, we stay too long. [*Exeunt.*

SCENE II. *A room in* FORD'S *house.*

Enter FALSTAFF *and* MISTRESS FORD.

Fal. Mistress Ford, your sorrow hath eaten up my sufferance. I see you are obsequious in your love, and I profess requital to a hair's breadth ; not only, Mistress Ford, in the simple office of love, but in all the accoutrement, complement and ceremony of it. But are you sure of your husband now ?

Mrs. Ford. He's a-birding, sweet Sir John.

Mrs. Page. [*Within*] What, ho, gossip Ford ! what, ho ! 10

Mrs. Ford. Step into the chamber, Sir John. [*Exit Falstaff.*

Enter MISTRESS PAGE.

Mrs. Page. How now, sweetheart ! who's at home besides yourself ?

Mrs. Ford. Why, none but mine own people.

Mrs. Page. Indeed !

Mrs. Ford. No, certainly. [*Aside to her*] Speak louder.

Mrs. Page. Truly, I am so glad you have nobody here.

Mrs. Ford. Why ? 20

Mrs. Page. Why, woman, your husband is in his old lunes again : he so takes on yonder with my husband ; so rails against all married mankind ; so curses all Eve's daughters, of what complexion soever ; and so buffets himself on the forehead, crying, ' Peer out, peer out !' that any madness I ever yet beheld seemed but tameness, civility and patience, to this his distemper he is in now : I am glad the fat knight is not here.

Mrs. Ford. Why, does he talk of him ? 30

Mrs. Page. Of none but him ; and swears he was carried out, the last time he searched for him, in a basket ; protests to my husband he is now here, and hath drawn him and the rest of their company from their sport, to make another experiment of his suspicion : but I am glad the knight is not here ; now he shall see his own foolery.

Mrs. Ford. How near is he, Mistress Page ?

Mrs. Page. Hard by ; at street end ; he will be here anon. 41

Mrs. Ford. I am undone ! The knight is here.

Mrs. Page. Why then you are utterly shamed, and he's but a dead man. What a woman are you !—Away with him, away with him ! better shame than murder.

Mrs. Ford. Which way should he go ? how

should I bestow him ? Shall I put him into the basket again ?

Re-enter FALSTAFF.

Fal. No, I'll come no more i' the basket. May I not go out ere he come ? 51

Mrs. Page. Alas, three of Master Ford's brothers watch the door with pistols, that none shall issue out ; otherwise you might slip away ere he came. But what make you here ?

Fal. What shall I do ? I'll creep up into the chimney.

Mrs. Ford. There they always use to discharge their birding-pieces. Creep into the kiln-hole.

Fal. Where is it ? 60

Mrs. Ford. He will seek there, on my word. Neither press, coffer, chest, trunk, well, vault, but he hath an abstract for the remembrance of such places, and goes to them by his note : there is no hiding you in the house.

Fal. I'll go out then.

Mrs. Page. If you go out in your own semblance, you die, Sir John. Unless you go out disguised— 69

Mrs. Ford. How might we disguise him ?

Mrs. Page. Alas the day, I know not ! There is no woman's gown big enough for him ; otherwise he might put on a hat, a muffler and a kerchief, and so escape.

Fal. Good hearts, devise something : any extremity rather than a mischief.

Mrs. Ford. My maid's aunt, the fat woman of Brentford, has a gown above.

Mrs. Page. On my word, it will serve him ; she's as big as he is : and there's her thrummed hat and her muffler too. Run up, Sir John.

Mrs. Ford. Go, go, sweet Sir John : Mistress Page and I will look some linen for your head.

Mrs. Page. Quick, quick ! we'll come dress you straight : put on the gown the while. 81 [*Exit Falstaff.*

Mrs. Ford. I would my husband would meet him in this shape : he cannot abide the old woman of Brentford ; he swears she's a witch ; forbade her my house and hath threatened to beat her.

Mrs. Page. Heaven guide him to thy husband's cudgel, and the devil guide his cudgel afterwards !

Mrs. Ford. But is my husband coming ?

Mrs. Page. Ah, in good sadness, is he ; and talks of the basket too, howsoever he hath had intelligence.

Mrs. Ford. We'll try that ; for I'll appoint my men to carry the basket again, to meet him at the door with it, as they did last time.

Mrs. Page. Nay, but he'll be here presently : let's go dress him like the witch of Brentford.

Mrs. Ford. I'll first direct my men what they shall do with the basket. Go up ; I'll bring linen for him straight. [*Exit.*

Mrs. Page. Hang him, dishonest varlet ! we cannot misuse him enough.

We'll leave a proof, by that which we will do,

Wives may be merry, and yet honest too :

We do not act that often jest and laugh ;

'Tis old, but true, Still swine eat all the draff. [*Exit.*

Re-enter MISTRESS FORD *with two* Servants.

Mrs. Ford. Go, sirs, take the basket again on your shoulders : your master is hard at door ; if he bid you set it down, obey him : quickly, dispatch.   [*Exit.*

First Serv. Come, come, take it up.

Sec. Serv. Pray heaven it be not full of knight again.

First Serv. I hope not ; I had as lief bear so much lead.

Enter FORD, PAGE, SHALLOW, CAIUS, *and* SIR HUGH EVANS.

Ford. Ay, but if it prove true, Master Page, have you any way then to unfool me again ? Set down the basket, villain ! Somebody call my wife. Youth in a basket ! O you panderly rascals ! there's a knot, a ging, a pack, a conspiracy against me : now shall the devil be shamed. What, wife, I say ! Come, come forth ! Behold what honest clothes you send forth to bleaching !

Page. Why, this passes, Master Ford ; you are not to go loose any longer ; you must be pinioned.

Evans. Why, this is lunatics ! this is mad as a mad dog !   131

Shal. Indeed, Master Ford, this is not well, indeed.

Ford. So say I too, sir.

Re-enter MISTRESS FORD.

Come hither, Mistress Ford ; Mistress Ford, the honest woman, the modest wife, the virtuous creature, that hath the jealous fool to her husband ! I suspect without cause, mistress, do I ?

Mrs. Ford. Heaven be my witness you do, if you suspect me in any dishonesty.   140

Ford. Well said, brazen-face ! hold it out. Come forth, sirrah !

          [*Pulling clothes out of the basket.*

Page. This passes !

Mrs. Ford. Are you not ashamed ? let the clothes alone.

Ford. I shall find you anon.

Evans. 'Tis unreasonable ! Will you take up your wife's clothes ? Come away.

Ford. Empty the basket, I say !

Mrs. Ford. Why, man, why ?   150

Ford. Master Page, as I am a man, there was one conveyed out of my house yesterday in this basket : why may not he be there again ? In my house I am sure he is : my intelligence is true ; my jealousy is reasonable. Pluck me out all the linen.

Mrs. Ford. If you find a man there, he shall die a flea's death.

Page. Here's no man.

Shal. By my fidelity, this is not well, Master Ford ; this wrongs you.   161

Evans. Master Ford, you must pray, and not follow the imaginations of your own heart : this is jealousies.

Ford. Well, he's not here I seek for.

Page. No, nor nowhere else but in your brain.

Ford. Help to search my house this one time. If I find not what I seek, show no color for my extremity ; let me for ever be your table-sport ; let them say of me, ' As jealous as Ford, that searched a hollow walnut for his wife's leman.' Satisfy me once more ; once more search with me.

Mrs. Ford. What, ho, Mistress Page ! come you and the old woman down ; my husband will come into the chamber.

Ford. Old woman ! what old woman's that ?

Mrs. Ford. Why, it is my maid's aunt of Brentford.

Ford. A witch, a quean, an old cozening quean ! Have I not forbid her my house ? She comes of errands, does she ? We are simple men ; we do not know what's brought to pass under the profession of fortune-telling. She works by charms, by spells, by the figure, and such daubery as this is, beyond our element : we know nothing. Come down, you witch, you hag, you ; come down, I say !

Mrs. Ford. Nay, good, sweet husband ! Good gentlemen, let him not strike the old woman.   190

Re-enter FALSTAFF *in woman's clothes, and* MISTRESS PAGE.

Mrs. Page. Come, Mother Prat ; come, give me your hand.

Ford. I'll prat her. [*Beating him*] Out of my door, you witch, you hag, you baggage, you polecat, you ronyon ! out, out ! I'll conjure you, I'll fortune-tell you.   [*Exit Falstaff.*

Mrs. Page. Are you not ashamed ? I think you have killed the poor woman.

Mrs. Ford. Nay, he will do it. 'Tis a goodly credit for you.   200

Ford. Hang her, witch !

Evans. By yea and no, I think the 'oman is a witch indeed : I like not when a 'oman has a great peard ; I spy a great peard under his muffler.

Ford. Will you follow, gentlemen ? I beseech you, follow ; see but the issue of my jealousy : if I cry out thus upon no trail, never trust me when I open again.

Page. Let's obey his humor a little further : come, gentlemen.   211

[*Exeunt Ford, Page, Shal., Caius, and Evans.*

Mrs. Page. Trust me, he beat him most pitifully.

Mrs. Ford. Nay, by the mass, that he did not ; he beat him most unpitifully, methought.

Mrs. Page. I'll have the cudgel hallowed and hung o'er the altar ; it hath done meritorious service.

Mrs. Ford. What think you ? may we, with the warrant of womanhood and the witness of a good conscience, pursue him with any further revenge ?   222

Mrs. Page. The spirit of wantonness is, sure, scared out of him : if the devil have him not in fee-simple, with fine and recovery, he will never, I think, in the way of waste, attempt us again.

Mrs. Ford. Shall we tell our husbands how we have served him ?

Mrs. Page. Yes, by all means ; if it be but to scrape the figures out of your husband's brains. If they can find in their hearts the poor unvirtuous fat knight shall be any further afflicted, we two will still be the ministers.

Mrs. Ford. I'll warrant they'll have him publicly shamed : and methinks there would be no period to the jest, should he not be publicly shamed.

Mrs. Page. Come, to the forge with it then; shape it: I would not have things cool.
[*Exeunt.*

Scene III. *A room in the Garter Inn.*
Enter Host *and* Bardolph.

Bard. Sir, the Germans desire to have three of your horses: the duke himself will be to-morrow at court, and they are going to meet him.
Host. What duke should that be comes so secretly? I hear not of him in the court. Let me speak with the gentlemen: they speak English?
Bard. Ay, sir; I'll call them to you.
Host. They shall have my horses; but I'll make them pay; I'll sauce them: they have had my house a week at command; I have turned away my other guests: they must come off; I'll sauce them. Come.   [*Exeunt.*

Scene IV. *A room in* Ford's *house.*
Enter Page, Ford, Mistress Page, Mistress Ford, *and* Sir Hugh Evans.

Evans. 'Tis one of the best discretions of a 'oman as ever I did look upon.
Page. And did he send you both these letters at an instant?
Mrs. Page. Within a quarter of an hour.
Ford. Pardon me, wife. Henceforth do what thou wilt;
I rather will suspect the sun with cold
Than thee with wantonness: now doth thy honor stand,
In him that was of late an heretic,
As firm as faith.
Page.   'Tis well, 'tis well; no more: 10
Be not as extreme in submission
As in offence.
But let our plot go forward: let our wives
Yet once again, to make us public sport,
Appoint a meeting with this old fat fellow,
Where we may take him and disgrace him for it.
Ford. There is no better way than that they spoke of.
Page. How? to send him word they'll meet him in the park at midnight? Fie, fie! he'll never come.
Evans. You say he has been thrown in the rivers and has been grievously peaten as an old 'oman: methinks there should be terrors in him that he should not come; methinks his flesh is punished, he shall have no desires.
Page. So think I too.
Mrs. Ford. Devise but how you'll use him when he comes,
And let us two devise to bring him thither.
Mrs. Page. There is an old tale goes that Herne the hunter,
Sometime a keeper here in Windsor forest,
Doth all the winter-time, at still midnight, 30
Walk round about an oak, with great ragg'd horns;
And there he blasts the tree and takes the cattle
And makes milch-kine yield blood and shakes a chain
In a most hideous and dreadful manner:
You have heard of such a spirit, and well you know
The superstitious idle-headed eld

Received and did deliver to our age
This tale of Herne the hunter for a truth.
Page. Why, yet there want not many that do fear
In deep of night to walk by this Herne's oak:
But what of this?   41
Mrs. Ford.   Marry, this is our device;
That Falstaff at that oak shall meet with us.
Page. Well, let it not be doubted but he'll come:
And in this shape when you have brought him thither,
What shall be done with him? what is your plot?
Mrs. Page. That likewise have we thought upon, and thus:
Nan Page my daughter and my little son
And three or four more of their growth we'll dress
Like urchins, ouphes and fairies, green and white,   49
With rounds of waxen tapers on their heads,
And rattles in their hands: upon a sudden,
As Falstaff, she and I, are newly met,
Let them from forth a sawpit rush at once
With some diffused song: upon their sight,
We two in great amazedness will fly:
Then let them all encircle him about
And, fairy-like, to-pinch the unclean knight,
And ask him why, that hour of fairy revel,
In their so sacred paths he dares to tread
In shape profane.
Mrs. Ford.   And till he tell the truth, 60
Let the supposed fairies pinch him sound
And burn him with their tapers.
Mrs. Page.   The truth being known,
We'll all present ourselves, dis-horn the spirit,
And mock him home to Windsor.
Ford.   The children must
Be practiced well to this, or they'll ne'er do't.
Evans. I will teach the children their behaviors; and I will be like a jack-an-apes also, to burn the knight with my taber.
Ford. That will be excellent. I'll go and buy them vizards.   70
Mrs. Page. My Nan shall be the queen of all the fairies,
Finely attired in a robe of white.
Page. That silk will I go buy. [*Aside*]
And in that time
Shall Master Slender steal my Nan away
And marry her at Eton. Go send to Falstaff straight.
Ford. Nay, I'll to him again in name of Brook:
He'll tell me all his purpose: sure, he'll come.
Mrs. Page. Fear not you that. Go get us properties
And tricking for our fairies.
Evans. Let us about it: it is admirable pleasures and fery honest knaveries.   81
[*Exeunt Page, Ford, and Evans.*
Mrs. Page. Go, Mistress Ford,
Send quickly to Sir John, to know his mind.
[*Exit Mrs. Ford.*
I'll to the doctor: he hath my good will,
And none but he, to marry with Nan Page.
That Slender, though well landed, is an idiot;
And he my husband best of all affects.
The doctor is well money'd, and his friends
Potent at court: he, none but he, shall have her,

Though twenty thousand worthier come to
crave her. [*Exit.* 90

SCENE V. *A room in the Garter Inn.*

Enter HOST *and* SIMPLE.

Host. What wouldst thou have, boor?
what, thick-skin? speak, breathe, discuss;
brief, short, quick, snap.

Sim. Marry, sir, I come to speak with Sir
John Falstaff from Master Slender.

Host. There's his chamber, his house, his
castle, his standing-bed and truckle-bed; 'tis
painted about with the story of the Prodigal,
fresh and new. Go knock and call; he'll speak
like an Anthropophaginian unto thee: knock,
I say. 11

Sim. There's an old woman, a fat woman,
gone up into his chamber: I'll be so bold as
stay, sir, till she come down; I come to speak
with her, indeed.

Host. Ha! a fat woman! the knight may
be robbed: I'll call. Bully knight! bully Sir
John! speak from thy lungs military: art thou
there? it is thine host, thine Ephesian, calls.

Fal. [*Above*] How now, mine host! 20

Host. Here's a Bohemian-Tartar tarries the
coming down of thy fat woman. Let her descend, bully, let her descend; my chambers
are honorable: fie! privacy? fie!

Enter FALSTAFF.

Fal. There was, mine host, an old fat
woman even now with me; but she's gone.

Sim. Pray you, sir, was't not the wise
woman of Brentford?

Fal. Ay, marry, was it, mussel-shell: what
would you with her? 30

Sim. My master, sir, Master Slender, sent
to her, seeing her go through the streets, to
know, sir, whether one Nym, sir, that beguiled
him of a chain, had the chain or no.

Fal. I spake with the old woman about it.

Sim. And what says she, I pray, sir?

Fal. Marry, she says that the very same
man that beguiled Master Slender of his chain
cozened him of it.

Sim. I would I could have spoken with the
woman herself; I had other things to have
spoken with her too from him. 42

Fal. What are they? let us know.

Sim. I may not conceal them, sir.

Host. Conceal them, or thou diest.

Sim. Why, sir, they were nothing but about
Mistress Anne Page; to know if it were my
master's fortune to have her or no.

Fal. 'Tis, 'tis his fortune. 50

Sim. What, sir?

Fal. To have her, or no. Go; say the
woman told me so.

Sim. May I be bold to say so, sir?

Fal. Ay, sir; like who more bold.

Sim. I thank your worship: I shall make
my master glad with these tidings. [*Exit.*

Host. Thou art clerkly, thou art clerkly,
Sir John. Was there a wise woman with thee?

Fal. Ay, that there was, mine host; one
that hath taught me more wit than ever I
learned before in my life; and I paid nothing
for it neither, but was paid for my learning.

Enter BARDOLPH.

Bard. Out, alas, sir! cozenage, mere cozenage!

Host. Where be my horses? speak well of
them, varletto.

Bard. Run away with the cozeners; for so
soon as I came beyond Eton, they threw me off
from behind one of them, in a slough of mire;
and set spurs and away, like three German
devils, three Doctor Faustuses. 71

Host. They are gone but to meet the duke,
villain: do not say they be fled; Germans are
honest men.

Enter SIR HUGH EVANS.

Evans. Where is mine host?

Host. What is the matter, sir?

Evans. Have a care of your entertain-
ments: there is a friend of mine come to
town, tells me there is three cozen-germans
that has cozened all the hosts of Readins, of
Maidenhead, of Colebrook, of horses and
money. I tell you for good will, look you: you
are wise and full of gibes and vlouting-stocks,
and 'tis not convenient you should be cozened.
Fare you well. [*Exit.*

Enter DOCTOR CAIUS.

Caius. Vere is mine host de Jarteer?

Host. Here, master doctor, in perplexity
and doubtful dilemma.

Caius. I cannot tell vat is dat: but it is
tell-a me dat you make grand preparation for
a duke de Jamany: by my trot, dere is no
duke dat the court is know to come. I tell you
for good vill: adieu. [*Exit.* 91

Host. Hue and cry, villain, go! Assist me,
knight. I am undone! Fly, run, hue and cry,
villain! I am undone!

[*Exeunt Host and Bard.*

Fal. I would all the world might be cozened; for I have been cozened and beaten too.
If it should come to the ear of the court, how
I have been transformed and how my transformation hath been washed and cudgelled,
they would melt me out of my fat drop by
drop and liquor fishermen's boots with me; I
warrant they would whip me with their fine
wits till I were as crest-fallen as a dried pear.
I never prospered since I forswore myself at
primero. Well, if my wind were but long
enough to say my prayers, I would repent.

Enter MISTRESS QUICKLY.

Now, whence come you?

Quick. From the two parties, forsooth.

Fal. The devil take one party and his dam
the other! and so they shall be both bestowed.
I have suffered more for their sakes, more
than the villanous inconstancy of man's disposition is able to bear.

Quick. And have not they suffered? Yes,
I warrant; speciously one of them; Mistress
Ford, good heart, is beaten black and blue,
that you cannot see a white spot about her.

Fal. What tellest thou me of black and
blue? I was beaten myself into all the colors
of the rainbow; and I was like to be apprehended for the witch of Brentford: but that
my admirable dexterity of wit, my counterfeiting the action of an old woman, delivered
me, the knave constable had set me i' the
stocks, i' the common stocks, for a witch.

Quick. Sir, let me speak with you in your chamber : you shall hear how things go ; and, I warrant, to your content. Here is a letter will say somewhat. Good hearts, what ado here is to bring you together ! Sure, one of you does not serve heaven well, that you are so crossed.

Fal. Come up into my chamber. 131
[*Exeunt.*

SCENE VI. *Another room in the Garter Inn.*
Enter FENTON *and* HOST.

Host. Master Fenton, talk not to me ; my mind is heavy : I will give over all.

Fent. Yet hear me speak. Assist me in my purpose,
And, as I am a gentleman, I'll give thee
A hundred pound in gold more than your loss.

Host. I will hear you, Master Fenton ; and I will at the least keep your counsel.

Fent. From time to time I have acquainted you
With the dear love I bear to fair Anne Page ;
Who mutually hath answer'd my affection, 10
So far forth as herself might be her chooser,
Even to my wish : I have a letter from her
Of such contents as you will wonder at ;
The mirth whereof so larded with my matter,
That neither singly can be manifested,
Without the show of both ; fat Falstaff
Hath a great scene : the image of the jest
I'll show you here at large. Hark, good mine host.
To-night at Herne's oak, just 'twixt twelve and one, 19
Must my sweet Nan present the Fairy Queen ;
The purpose why, is here : in which disguise,
While other jests are something rank on foot,
Her father hath commanded her to slip
Away with Slender and with him at Eton
Immediately to marry : she hath consented :
Now, sir,
Her mother, ever strong against that match
And firm for Doctor Caius, hath appointed
That he shall likewise shuffle her away, 29
While other sports are tasking of their minds,
And at the deanery, where a priest attends,
Straight marry her : to this her mother's plot
She seemingly obedient likewise hath
Made promise to the doctor. Now, thus it rests :
Her father means she shall be all in white,
And in that habit, when Slender sees his time
To take her by the hand and bid her go,
She shall go with him : her mother hath intended,
The better to denote her to the doctor,
For they must all be mask'd and vizarded, 40
That quaint in green she shall be loose enrobed,
With ribands pendent, flaring 'bout her head ;
And when the doctor spies his vantage ripe,
To pinch her by the hand, and, on that token,
The maid hath given consent to go with him.

Host. Which means she to deceive, father or mother ?

Fent. Both, my good host, to go along with me :
And here it rests, that you'll procure the vicar
To stay for me at church 'twixt twelve and one,
And, in the lawful name of marrying, 50

To give our hearts united ceremony.

Host. Well, husband your device ; I'll to the vicar :
Bring you the maid, you shall not lack a priest.

Fent. So shall I evermore be bound to thee ;
Besides, I'll make a present recompense.
[*Exeunt.*

ACT V.

SCENE I. *A room in the Garter Inn.*

Enter FALSTAFF *and* MISTRESS QUICKLY.

Fal. Prithee, no more prattling ; go. I'll hold. This is the third time ; I hope good luck lies in odd numbers. Away ! go. They say there is divinity in odd numbers, either in nativity, chance, or death. Away !

Quick. I'll provide you a chain ; and I'll do what I can to get you a pair of horns.

Fal. Away, I say ; time wears : hold up your head, and mince. [*Exit Mrs. Quickly.*

Enter FORD.

How now, Master Brook ! Master Brook, the matter will be known to-night, or never. Be you in the Park about midnight, at Herne's oak, and you shall see wonders.

Ford. Went you not to her yesterday, sir, as you told me you had appointed ?

Fal. I went to her, Master Brook, as you see, like a poor old man : but I came from her, Master Brook, like a poor old woman. That same knave Ford, her husband, hath the finest mad devil of jealousy in him, Master Brook, that ever governed frenzy. I will tell you : he beat me grievously, in the shape of a woman ; for in the shape of man, Master Brook, I fear not Goliath with a weaver's beam ; because I know also life is a shuttle. I am in haste ; go along with me : I'll tell you all, Master Brook. Since I plucked geese, played truant and whipped top, I knew not what 'twas to be beaten till lately. Follow me : I'll tell you strange things of this knave Ford, on whom to-night I will be revenged, and I will deliver his wife into your hand. Follow. Strange things in hand, Master Brook ! Follow.
[*Exeunt.*

SCENE II. *Windsor Park.*

Enter PAGE, SHALLOW, *and* SLENDER.

Page. Come, come ; we'll couch i' the castle-ditch till we see the light of our fairies. Remember, son Slender, my daughter.

Slen. Ay, forsooth ; I have spoke with her and we have a nay-word how to know one another : I come to her in white, and cry ' mum ; ' she cries ' budget ; ' and by that we know one another.

Shal. That's good too : but what needs either your ' mum ' or her ' budget ? ' the white will decipher her well enough. It hath struck ten o'clock.

Page. The night is dark ; light and spirits will become it well. Heaven prosper our sport ! No man means evil but the devil, and we shall know him by his horns. Let's away ; follow me. [*Exeunt.*

SCENE III. *A street leading to the Park.*
Enter MISTRESS PAGE, MISTRESS FORD, *and*
DOCTOR CAIUS.

Mrs. Page. Master doctor, my daughter is
in green : when you see your time, take her
by the hand, away with her to the deanery,
and dispatch it quickly. Go before into the
Park : we two must go together.
Caius. I know vat I have to do. Adieu.
Mrs. Page. Fare you well, sir. [*Exit Caius.*]
My husband will not rejoice so much at the
abuse of Falstaff as he will chafe at the doctor's marrying my daughter : but 'tis no matter ; better a little chiding than a great deal
of heart-break.   11
Mrs. Ford. Where is Nan now and her
troop of fairies, and the Welsh devil Hugh ?
Mrs. Page. They are all couched in a pit
hard by Herne's oak, with obscured lights ;
which, at the very instant of Falstaff's and
our meeting, they will at once display to the
night.
Mrs. Ford. That cannot choose but amaze
him.
Mrs. Page. If he be not amazed, he will be
mocked ; if he be amazed, he will every way
be mocked.   21
Mrs. Ford. We'll betray him finely.
Mrs. Page. Against such lewdsters and
their lechery
Those that betray them do no treachery.
Mrs. Ford. The hour draws on. To the
oak, to the oak !   [*Exeunt.*

SCENE IV. *Windsor Park.*
Enter SIR HUGH EVANS, *disguised, with others
as Fairies.*

Evans. Trib, trib, fairies ; come ; and remember your parts : be pold, I pray you ;
follow me into the pit ; and when I give the
watch-'ords, do as I pid you : come, come ;
trib, trib.   [*Exeunt.*

SCENE V. *Another part of the Park.*
Enter FALSTAFF *disguised as Herne.*

Fal. The Windsor bell hath struck twelve ;
the minute draws on. Now, the hot-blooded
gods assist me ! Remember, Jove, thou wast a
bull for thy Europa ; love set on thy horns.
O powerful love ! that, in some respects, makes
a beast a man, in some other, a man a beast.
You were also, Jupiter, a swan for the love of
Leda. O omnipotent Love ! how near the god
drew to the complexion of a goose ! A fault
done first in the form of a beast. O Jove,
a beastly fault ! And then another fault in the
semblance of a fowl ; think on 't, Jove ; a foul
fault ! When gods have hot backs, what shall
poor men do ? For me, I am here a Windsor
stag ; and the fattest, I think, i' the forest. Send
me a cool rut-time, Jove, or who can blame
me to piss my tallow ? Who comes here ? my
doe ?

Enter MISTRESS FORD *and* MISTRESS PAGE.

Mrs. Ford. Sir John ! art thou there, my
deer ? my male deer ?
Fal. My doe with the black scut ! Let the
sky rain potatoes ; let it thunder to the tune
of Green Sleeves, hail kissing-comfits and
snow eringoes ; let there come a tempest of
provocation, I will shelter me here.
Mrs. Ford. Mistress Page is come with me,
sweetheart.
Fal. Divide me like a bribe buck, each a
haunch : I will keep my sides to myself, my
shoulders for the fellow of this walk, and my
horns I bequeath your husbands. Am I a
woodman, ha ? Speak I like Herne the
hunter ? Why, now is Cupid a child of conscience ; he makes restitution. As I am a true
spirit, welcome !   [*Noise within.*
Mrs. Page. Alas, what noise ?
Mrs. Ford. Heaven forgive our sins !
Fal. What should this be ?
Mrs. Ford. } Away, away ! [*They run off.*
Mrs. Page. }
Fal. I think the devil will not have me
damned, lest the oil that's in me should set
hell on fire ; he would never else cross me
thus.   40

Enter SIR HUGH EVANS, *disguised as before ;*
PISTOL, *as Hobgoblin ;* MISTRESS QUICKLY,
ANNE PAGE, *and others, as Fairies, with
tapers.*

Quick. Fairies, black, grey, green, and
white,
You moonshine revellers and shades of night,
You orphan heirs of fixed destiny,
Attend your office and your quality.
Crier Hobgoblin, make the fairy oyes.
Pist. Elves, list your names ; silence, you
airy toys.
Cricket, to Windsor chimneys shalt thou leap :
Where fires thou find'st unraked and hearths
unswept,
There pinch the maids as blue as bilberry :
Our radiant queen hates sluts and sluttery. 50
Fal. They are fairies ; he that speaks to
them shall die :
I'll wink and couch : no man their works must
eye.   [*Lies down upon his face.*
Evans. Where's Bede ? Go you, and where
you find a maid
That, ere she sleep, has thrice her prayers
said,
Raise up the organs of her fantasy ;
Sleep she as sound as careless infancy :
But those as sleep and think not on their sins,
Pinch them, arms, legs, backs, shoulders, sides
and shins.
Quick. About, about :
Search Windsor Castle, elves, within and out :
Strew good luck, ouphes, on every sacred
room :   61
That it may stand till the perpetual doom,
In state as wholesome as in state 'tis fit,
Worthy the owner, and the owner it.
The several chairs of order look you scour
With juice of balm and every precious flower :
Each fair instalment, coat, and several crest,
With loyal blazon, evermore be blest !
And nightly, meadow-fairies, look you sing,
Like to the Garter's compass, in a ring : 70
The expressure that it bears, green let it be,
More fertile-fresh than all the field to see ;
And ' Honi soit qui mal y pense ' write
In emerald tufts, flowers purple, blue and
white ;
Let sapphire, pearl and rich embroidery,
Buckled below fair knighthood's bending
knee :

Fairies use flowers for their charactery.
Away; disperse : but till 'tis one o'clock,
Our dance of custom round about the oak
Of Herne the hunter, let us not forget.   80
   Evans. Pray you, lock hand in hand ; your-
     selves in order set ;
And twenty glow-worms shall our lanterns be,
To guide our measure round about the tree.
But, stay ; I smell a man of middle-earth.
   Fal. Heavens defend me from that Welsh
fairy, lest he transform me to a piece of
cheese !
   Pist. Vile worm, thou wast o'erlook'd even
     in thy birth.
   Quick. With trial-fire touch me his finger-
     end :
If he be chaste, the flame will back descend
And turn him to no pain ; but if he start,   90
It is the flesh of a corrupted heart.
   Pist. A trial, come.
   Evans.   Come, will this wood take fire ?
     [*They burn him with their tapers.*
   Fal. Oh, Oh, Oh !
   Quick. Corrupt, corrupt, and tainted in
     desire !
About him, fairies ; sing a scornful rhyme ;
And, as you trip, still pinch him to your time.
            SONG.
Fie on sinful fantasy !
Fie on lust and luxury !
Lust is but a bloody fire,
Kindled with unchaste desire,   100
   Fed in heart, whose flames aspire
As thoughts do blow them, higher and
     higher.
Pinch him, fairies, mutually ;
Pinch him for his villany ;
Pinch him, and burn him, and turn him about,
Till candles and starlight and moonshine be
   out.

During this song they pinch FALSTAFF. DOC-
   TOR CAIUS *comes one way, and steals away*
   a boy in green ; SLENDER *another way, and*
   takes off a boy in white ; and FENTON *comes*
   and steals away MISTRESS ANNE PAGE. *A*
   noise of hunting is heard within. All the
   Fairies run away. FALSTAFF *pulls off his*
   buck's head, and rises.

Enter PAGE, FORD, MISTRESS PAGE, *and* MIS-
        TRESS FORD.

   Page. Nay, do not fly ; I think we have
watch'd you now :
Will none but Herne the hunter serve your
   turn ?
   Mrs. Page. I pray you, come, hold up the
jest no higher
Now, good Sir John, how like you Windsor
wives ?
See you these, husband ? do not these fair
   yokes
Become the forest better than the town ?
   Ford. Now, sir, who's a cuckold now ?
Master Brook, Falstaff's a knave, a cuckoldly
knave ; here are his horns, Master Brook :
and, Master Brook, he hath enjoyed nothing
of Ford's but his buck-basket, his cudgel, and
twenty pounds of money, which must be paid
to Master Brook ; his horses are arrested for
it, Master Brook.
   Mrs. Ford. Sir John, we have had ill luck ;
we could never meet. I will never take you for

my love again ; but I will always count you my
deer.
   Fal. I do begin to perceive that I am
made an ass.
   Ford. Ay, and an ox too : both the proofs
are extant.
   Fal. And these are not fairies ? I was three
or four times in the thought they were not
fairies : and yet the guiltiness of my mind,
the sudden surprise of my powers, drove the
grossness of the foppery into a received belief,
in despite of the teeth of all rhyme and reason,
that they were fairies. See now how wit may
be made a Jack-a-Lent, when 'tis upon ill employment !
   Evans. Sir John Falstaff, serve Got, and
leave your desires, and fairies will not pinse
you.
   Ford. Well said, fairy Hugh.
   Evans. And leave your jealousies too, I
pray you.   140
   Ford. I will never mistrust my wife again,
till thou art able to woo her in good English.
   Fal. Have I laid my brain in the sun and
dried it, that it wants matter to prevent so
gross o'erreaching as this ? Am I ridden with
a Welsh goat too ? shall I have a coxcomb of
frize ? 'Tis time I were choked with a piece of
toasted cheese.
   Evans. Seese is not good to give putter ;
your belly is all putter.
   Fal. ' Seese ' and ' putter ' ! have I lived
to stand at the taunt of one that makes fritters
of English ? This is enough to be the decay of
lust and late-walking through the realm.
   Mrs. Page. Why, Sir John, do you think,
though we would have thrust virtue out of our
hearts by the head and shoulders and have
given ourselves without scruple to hell, that
ever the devil could have made you our delight ?
   Ford. What, a hodge-pudding ? a bag of
flax ?
   Mrs. Page. A puffed man ?   160
   Page. Old, cold, withered and of intolerable entrails ?
   Ford. And one that is as slanderous as
Satan ?
   Page. And as poor as Job ?
   Ford. And as wicked as his wife ?
   Evans. And given to fornications, and to
taverns and sack and wine and metheglins,
and to drinkings and swearings and starings,
pribbles and prabbles ?
   Fal. Well, I am your theme : you have
the start of me ; I am dejected ; I am not able
to answer the Welsh flannel ; ignorance itself
is a plummet o'er me : use me as you will.
   Ford. Marry, sir, we'll bring you to Windsor, to one Master Brook, that you have cozened of money, to whom you should have
been a pander : over and above that you have
suffered, I think to repay that money will be a
biting affliction.
   Page. Yet be cheerful, knight : thou shalt
eat a posset to-night at my house ; where I will
desire thee to laugh at my wife, that now
laughs at thee : tell her Master Slender hath
married her daughter.
   Mrs. Page. [*Aside*] Doctors doubt that : if
Anne Page be my daughter, she is, by this,
Doctor Caius' wife.

Enter SLENDER.

Slen. Whoa, ho ! ho, father Page !

Page. Son, how now ! how now, son ! have you dispatched ?

Slen. Dispatched ! I'll make the best in Gloucestershire know on't ; would I were hanged, la, else.

Page. Of what, son ?

Slen. I came yonder at Eton to marry Mistress Anne Page, and she's a great lubberly boy. If it had not been i' the church, I would have swinged him, or he should have swinged me. If I did not think it had been Anne Page, would I might never stir !—and 'tis a postmaster's boy.

Page. Upon my life, then, you took the wrong.   201

Slen. What need you tell me that ? I think so, when I took a boy for a girl. If I had been married to him, for all he was in woman's apparel, I would not have had him.

Page. Why, this is your own folly. Did not I tell you how you should know my daughter by her garments ?

Slen. I went to her in white, and cried ' mum,' and she cried ' budget,' as Anne and I had appointed ; and yet it was not Anne, but a postmaster's boy.

Mrs. Page. Good George, be not angry : I knew of your purpose ; turned my daughter into green ; and, indeed, she is now with the doctor at the deanery, and there married.

Enter CAIUS.

Caius. Vere is Mistress Page ? By gar, I am cozened : I ha' married un garçon, a boy ; un paysan, by gar, a boy ; it is not Anne Page : by gar, I am cozened.   220

Mrs. Page. Why, did you take her in green ?

Caius. Ay, by gar, and 'tis a boy : by gar, I'll raise all Windsor.   [*Exit.*

Ford. This is strange. Who hath got the right Anne ?

Page. My heart misgives me : here comes Master Fenton.

Enter FENTON *and* ANNE PAGE.

How now, Master Fenton !

Anne. Pardon, good father ! good my mother, pardon !

Page. Now, mistress, how chance you went not with Master Slender ?   231

Mrs. Page. Why went you not with master doctor, maid ?

Fent. You do amaze her : hear the truth of it.
You would have married her most shamefully,
Where there was no proportion held in love.
Tho truth is, she and I, long since contracted,
Are now so sure that nothing can dissolve us.
The offence is holy that she hath committed ;
And this deceit loses the name of craft,
Of disobedience, or unduteous title,   240
Since therein she doth evitate and shun
A thousand irreligious cursed hours,
Which forced marriage would have brought upon her.

Ford. Stand not amazed ; here is no remedy :
In love the heavens themselves do guide the state ;
Money buys lands, and wives are sold by fate.

Fal. I am glad, though you have ta'en a special stand to strike at me, that your arrow hath glanced.

Page. Well, what remedy ? Fenton, heaven give thee joy !   250
What cannot be eschew'd must be embraced.

Fal. When night-dogs run, all sorts of deer are chased.

Mrs. Page. Well, I will muse no further. Master Fenton,
Heaven give you many, many merry days !
Good husband, let us every one go home,
And laugh this sport o'er by a country fire ;
Sir John and all.

Ford.   Let it be so. Sir John,
To Master Brook you yet shall hold your word ;
For he to-night shall lie with Mistress Ford.
                                              [*Exeunt.*

MUCH ADO ABOUT NOTHING.

(WRITTEN ABOUT 1598.)

INTRODUCTION.

Much Ado About Nothing was entered on the Stationer's register, August 23, 1600, and a well-printed quarto edition appeared in the same year. The play is not mentioned by Meres, who wrote in 1598, and it is probable therefore that it was written at some time in the interval between 1598 and 1600. For the graver portion of the play—the Claudio and Hero story—Shakespeare had an original, perhaps Belleforest's translation in his *Histoires Tragiques* of Bandello's 22nd Novella. The story of Ariodante and Genevra in Ariosto's *Orlando Furioso* (canto v.) is substantially the same. This episode had been translated twice into English before Harrington's complete translation of the *Orlando Furioso* appeared in 1591; and it had formed the subject of a play acted before the Queen in 1582–83; the story was also told, in a somewhat altered form, by Spenser (*Faerie Queen*, II., 4). No original has been found for the merrier portion of the play, and Benedick and Beatrice were probably creations of Shakespeare. *Much Ado About Nothing* was popular on the stage in Shakespeare's day, and has sustained its reputation. Its variety, ranging from almost burlesque to almost tragedy, and from the euphemistic speech of courtiers to the blundering verbosity of clowns, has contributed to the success of the play. The chief persons, Hero and Claudio, Beatrice and Benedick, are contrasted pairs. Hero's character is kept subdued and quiet in tone, to throw out the force and color of the character of Beatrice; she is gentle, affectionate, tender, and if playful, playful in a gentle way. If our interest in Hero were made very strong, the pain of her unmerited shame and suffering would be too keen. And Claudio is far from being a lover like Romeo; his wooing is done by proxy, and he does not sink under the anguish of Hero's disgrace and supposed death. Don John, the villain of the piece, is a melancholy egoist, who looks sourly on all the world, and has a special grudge against his brother's young favorite Claudio. The chief force of Shakespeare in the play comes out in the characters of Benedick and Beatrice. They have not a touch of misanthropy, nor of sentimentality, but are thoroughly healthy and hearty human creatures; at first a little too much self-pleased, but framed by-and-by to be entirely pleased with one another. The thoughts of each from the first are pre-occupied with the other, but neither will put self-esteem to the hazard of a rebuke of making the first advances in love; it only needs, however, that this danger should be removed for the pair to admit the fact that nature has made them over against one another—as their significant names suggest—for man and wife. Dogberry and Verges, as well as Beatrice and Benedick, are creations of Shakespeare. The blundering watchmen of the time are a source of fun with several Elizabethan playwrights; but Dogberry and goodman Verges are the princes of blundering and incapable officials. It is a charming incongruity to find, while Leonato rages and Benedick offers his challenge, that the solemn ass Dogberry is the one to unravel the tangled threads of their fate.

DRAMATIS PERSONÆ.

DON PEDRO, prince of Arragon.
DON JOHN, his bastard brother.
CLAUDIO, a young lord of Florence.
BENEDICK, a young lord of Padua.
LEONATO, governor of Messina.
ANTONIO, his brother.
BALTHASAR, attendant on Don Pedro.
CONRADE, } followers of Don John.
BORACHIO, }
FRIAR FRANCIS.
DOGBERRY, a constable.

VERGES, a headborough.
A Sexton.
A Boy.

HERO, daughter to Leonato.
BEATRICE, niece to Leonato.
MARGARET, } gentlewomen attending on
URSULA, } Hero.

Messengers, Watch, Attendants, &c.

SCENE : *Messina.*

ACT I.

SCENE I. *Before* LEONATO'S *house.*

Enter LEONATO, HERO, *and* BEATRICE, *with a* Messenger.

Leon. I learn in this letter that Don Peter of Arragon comes this night to Messina.

Mess. He is very near by this : he was not three leagues off when I left him.

Leon. How many gentlemen have you lost in this action ?

Mess. But few of any sort, and none of name.

Leon. A victory is twice itself when the achiever brings home full numbers. I find here that Don Peter hath bestowed much honor on a young Florentine called Claudio.

Mess. Much deserved on his part and equally remembered by Don Pedro : he hath borne himself beyond the promise of his age, doing, in the figure of a lamb, the feats of a lion : he hath indeed better bettered expectation than you must expect of me to tell you how.

Leon. He hath an uncle here in Messina will be very much glad of it.

Mess. I have already delivered him letters, and there appears much joy in him ; even so much that joy could not show itself modest enough without a badge of bitterness.

Leon. Did he break out into tears ?

Mess. In great measure.

Leon. A kind overflow of kindness : there are no faces truer than those that are so washed. How much better is it to weep at joy than to joy at weeping !

Beat. I pray you, is Signior Mountanto returned from the wars or no ? 31

Mess. I know none of that name, lady : there was none such in the army of any sort.

Leon. What is he that you ask for, niece ?

Hero. My cousin means Signior Benedick of Padua.

Mess. O, he's returned ; and as pleasant as ever he was.

Beat. He set up his bills here in Messina and challenged Cupid at the flight ; and my uncle's fool, reading the challenge, subscribed for Cupid, and challenged him at the birdbolt. I pray you, how many hath he killed and eaten in these wars ? But how many hath he killed ? for indeed I promised to eat all of his killing.

Leon. Faith, niece, you tax Signior Benedick too much ; but he'll be meet with you, I doubt it not.

Mess. He hath done good service, lady, in these wars.

Beat. You had musty victual, and he hath holp to eat it : he is a very valiant trencherman ; he hath an excellent stomach.

Mess. And a good soldier too, lady.

Beat. And a good soldier to a lady : but what is he to a lord ?

Mess. A lord to a lord, a man to a man ; stuffed with all honorable virtues.

Beat. It is so, indeed ; he is no less than a stuffed man : but for the stuffing,—well, we are all mortal. 60

Leon. You must not, sir, mistake my niece. There is a kind of merry war betwixt Signior Benedick and her : they never meet but there's a skirmish of wit between them.

Beat. Alas ! he gets nothing by that. In our last conflict four of his five wits went halting off, and now is the whole man governed with one : so that if he have wit enough to keep himself warm, let him bear it for a difference between himself and his horse ; for it is all the wealth that he hath left, to be known a reasonable creature. Who is his companion now ? He hath every month a new sworn brother.

Mess. Is't possible ?

Beat. Very easily possible : he wears his faith but as the fashion of his hat ; it ever changes with the next block.

Mess. I see, lady, the gentleman is not in your books.

Beat. No ; an he were, I would burn my study. But, I pray you, who is his companion ? Is there no young squarer now that will make a voyage with him to the devil ?

Mess. He is most in the company of the right noble Claudio.

Beat. O Lord, he will hang upon him like a disease : he is sooner caught than the pestilence, and the taker runs presently mad. God help the noble Claudio ! if he have caught the Benedick, it will cost him a thousand pound ere a' be cured. 90

Mess. I will hold friends with you, lady.

Beat. Do, good friend.

Leon. You will never run mad, niece.

Beat. No, not till a hot January.

Mess. Don Pedro is approached.

Enter DON PEDRO, DON JOHN, CLAUDIO, BENEDICK, *and* BALTHASAR.

D. Pedro. Good Signior Leonato, you are come to meet your trouble : the fashion of the world is to avoid cost, and you encounter it.

Leon. Never came trouble to my house in the likeness of your grace : for trouble being gone, comfort should remain ; but when you depart from me, sorrow abides and happiness takes his leave.

D. Pedro. You embrace your charge too willingly. I think this is your daughter.

Leon. Her mother hath many times told me so.

Bene. Were you in doubt, sir, that you asked her ?

Leon. Signior Benedick, no ; for then were you a child.

D. Pedro. You have it full, Benedick : we may guess by this what you are, being a man. Truly, the lady fathers herself. Be happy, lady ; for you are like an honorable father.

Bene. If Signior Leonato be her father, she would not have his head on her shoulders for all Messina, as like him as she is.

Beat. I wonder that you will still be talking, Signior Benedick : nobody marks you.

Bene. What, my dear Lady Disdain ! are you yet living ? 120

Beat. Is it possible disdain should die while she hath such meet food to feed it as Signior Benedick ? Courtesy itself must convert to disdain, if you come in her presence.

Bene. Then is courtesy a turncoat. But it is certain I am loved of all ladies, only you excepted : and I would I could find in my heart that I had not a hard heart ; for, truly, I love none.

Beat. A dear happiness to women : they would else have been troubled with a pernicious suitor. I thank God and my cold blood, I am of your humor for that : I had rather hear my dog bark at a crow than a man swear he loves me.

Bene. God keep your ladyship still in that mind ! so some gentleman or other shall 'scape a predestinate scratched face.

Beat. Scratching could not make it worse, an 'twere such a face as yours were.

Bene. Well, you are a rare parrot-teacher.

Beat. A bird of my tongue is better than a beast of yours.   141

Bene. I would my horse had the speed of your tongue, and so good a continuer. But keep your way, i' God's name ; I have done.

Beat. You always end with a jade's trick : I know you of old.

D. Pedro. That is the sum of all, Leonato. Signior Claudio and Signior Benedick, my dear friend Leonato hath invited you all. I tell him we shall stay here at the least a month ; and he heartily prays some occasion may detain us longer. I dare swear he is no hypocrite, but prays from his heart.

Leon. If you swear, my lord, you shall not be forsworn. [*To Don John*] Let me bid you welcome, my lord : being reconciled to the prince your brother, I owe you all duty.

D. John. I thank you : I am not of many words, but I thank you.

Leon. Please it your grace lead on ?   160

D. Pedro. Your hand, Leonato ; we will go together.

[*Exeunt all except Benedick and Claudio.*

Claud. Benedick, didst thou note the daughter of Signior Leonato ?

Bene. I noted her not ; but I looked on her.

Claud. Is she not a modest young lady ?

Bene. Do you question me, as an honest man should do, for my simple true judgment ; or would you have me speak after my custom, as being a professed tyrant to their sex ?   170

Claud. No ; I pray thee speak in sober judgment.

Bene. Why, i' faith, methinks she's too low for a high praise, too brown for a fair praise and too little for a great praise : only this commendation I can afford her, that were she other than she is, she were unhandsome ; and being no other but as she is, I do not like her.

Claud. Thou thinkest I am in sport : I pray thee tell me truly how thou likest her.

Bene. Would you buy her, that you inquire after her ?   181

Claud. Can the world buy such a jewel ?

Bene. Yea, and a case to put it into. But speak you this with a sad brow ? or do you play the flouting Jack, to tell us Cupid is a good hare-finder and Vulcan a rare carpenter ? Come, in what key shall a man take you, to go in the song ?

Claud. In mine eye she is the sweetest lady that ever I looked on.   190

Bene. I can see yet without spectacles and I see no such matter : there's her cousin, an she were not possessed with a fury, exceeds her as much in beauty as the first of May doth the last of December. But I hope you have no intent to turn husband, have you ?

Claud. I would scarce trust myself, though I had sworn the contrary, if Hero would be my wife.

Bene. Is't come to this ? In faith, hath not the world one man but he will wear his cap with suspicion ? Shall I never see a bachelor of three-score again ? Go to, i' faith ; an thou wilt needs thrust thy neck into a yoke, wear the print of it and sigh away Sundays. Look ; Don Pedro is returned to seek you.

Re-enter DON PEDRO.

D. Pedro. What secret hath held you here, that you followed not to Leonato's ?

Bene. I would your grace would constrain me to tell.

D. Pedro. I charge thee on thy allegiance.

Bene. You hear, Count Claudio : I can be secret as a dumb man ; I would have you think so ; but, on my allegiance, mark you this, on my allegiance. He is in love. With who ? now that is your grace's part. Mark how short his answer is ;—With Hero, Leonato's short daughter.

Claud. If this were so, so were it uttered.

Bene. Like the old tale, my lord : 'it is not so, nor 'twas not so, but, indeed, God forbid it should be so.'   220

Claud. If my passion change not shortly, God forbid it should be otherwise.

D. Pedro. Amen, if you love her ; for the lady is very well worthy.

Claud. You speak this to fetch me in, my lord.

D. Pedro. By my troth, I speak my thought.

Claud. And, in faith, my lord, I spoke mine.

Bene. And, by my two faiths and troths, my lord, I spoke mine.

Claud. That I love her, I feel.   230

D. Pedro. That she is worthy, I know.

Bene. That I neither feel how she should be loved nor know how she should be worthy, is the opinion that fire cannot melt out of me : I will die in it at the stake.

D. Pedro. Thou wast ever an obstinate heretic in the despite of beauty.

Claud. And never could maintain his part but in the force of his will.

Bene. That a woman conceived me, I thank her ; that she brought me up, I likewise give her most humble thanks : but that I will have a recheat winded in my forehead, or hang my bugle in an invisible baldrick, all women shall pardon me. Because I will not do them the wrong to mistrust any, I will do myself the right to trust none ; and the fine is, for the which I may go the finer, I will live a bachelor.

D. Pedro. I shall see thee, ere I die, look pale with love.   250

Bene. With anger, with sickness, or with hunger, my lord, not with love : prove that ever I lose more blood with love than I will get again with drinking, pick out mine eyes with a ballad-maker's pen and hang me up at the door of a brothel-house for the sign of blind Cupid.

D. Pedro. Well, if ever thou dost fall from this faith, thou wilt prove a notable argument.

Bene. If I do, hang me in a bottle like a cat and shoot at me ; and he that hits me, let him be clapped on the shoulder, and called Adam.   261

D. Pedro. Well, as time shall try :
' In time the savage bull doth bear the yoke.'

Bene. The savage bull may ; but if ever the sensible Benedick bear it, pluck off the bull's horns and set them in my forehead : and let me be vilely painted, and in such great letters as they write ' Here is good horse to hire,' let them signify under my sign ' Here you may see Bendick the married man.'   270

Claud. If this should ever happen, thou wouldst be horn-mad.

D. Pedro. Nay, if Cupid have not spent all his quiver in Venice, thou wilt quake for this shortly.

Bene. I look for an earthquake too, then.

D. Pedro. Well, you will temporize with the hours. In the meantime, good Signior Bendick, repair to Leonato's : commend me to him and tell him I will not fail him at supper ; for indeed he hath made great preparation.   280

Bene. I have almost matter enough in me for such an embassage ; and so I commit you—

Claud. To the tuition of God : From my house, if I had it,—

D. Pedro. The sixth of July : Your loving friend, Benedick.

Bene. Nay, mock not, mock not. The body of your discourse is sometime guarded with fragments, and the guards are but slightly basted on neither : ere you flout old ends any further, examine your conscience : and so I leave you.   [*Exit.* 291

Claud. My liege, your highness now may do me good.

D. Pedro. My love is thine to teach : teach it but how,
And thou shalt see how apt it is to learn
Any hard lesson that may do thee good.

Claud. Hath Leonato any son, my lord ?

D. Pedro. No child but Hero ; she's his only heir.
Dost thou affect her, Claudio ?

Claud.   O, my lord,
When you went onward on this ended action,
I look'd upon her with a soldier's eye,   300
That liked, but had a rougher task in hand
Than to drive liking to the name of love :
But now I am return'd and that war-thoughts
Have left their places vacant, in their rooms
Come thronging soft and delicate desires,
All prompting me how fair young Hero is,
Saying, I liked her ere I went to wars.

D. Pedro. Thou wilt be like a lover presently
And tire the hearer with a book of words.
If thou dost love fair Hero, cherish it,   310
And I will break with her and with her father,
And thou shalt have her. Was't not to this end
That thou began'st to twist so fine a story ?

Claud. How sweetly you do minister to love,
That know love's grief by his complexion !
But lest my liking might too sudden seem,
I would have salved it with a longer treatise.

D. Pedro. What need the bridge much broader than the flood ?
The fairest grant is the necessity.
Look, what will serve is fit : 'tis once, thou lovest,   320
And I will fit thee with the remedy.
I know we shall have revelling to-night :
I will assume thy part in some disguise
And tell fair Hero I am Claudio,
And in her bosom I'll unclasp my heart
And take her hearing prisoner with the force
And strong encounter of my amorous tale :
Then after to her father will I break ;
And the conclusion is, she shall be thine.
In practice let us put it presently.   330
                                        [*Exeunt.*

SCENE II. *A room in* LEONATO'S *house.*

Enter LEONATO *and* ANTONIO, *meeting.*

Leon. How now, brother ! Where is my cousin, your son ? hath he provided this music ?

Ant. He is very busy about it. But, brother, I can tell you strange news that you yet dreamt not of.

Leon. Are they good ?

Ant. As the event stamps them : but they have a good cover ; they show well outward. The prince and Count Claudio, walking in a thick-pleached alley in mine orchard, were thus much overheard by a man of mine : the prince discovered to Claudio that he loved my niece your daughter and meant to acknowledge it this night in a dance : and if he found her accordant, he meant to take the present time by the top and instantly break with you of it.

Leon. Hath the fellow any wit that told you this ?

Ant. A good sharp fellow : I will send for him ; and question him yourself.   20

Leon. No, no ; we will hold it as a dream till it appear itself : but I will acquaint my daughter withal, that she may be the better prepared for an answer, if peradventure this be true. Go you and tell her of it. [*Enter attendants.*] Cousins, you know what you have to do. O, I cry you mercy, friend ; go you with me, and I will use your skill. Good cousin, have a care this busy time.   [*Exeunt.*

SCENE III. *The same.*

Enter DON JOHN *and* CONRADE.

Con. What the good-year, my lord ! why are you thus out of measure sad ?

D. John. There is no measure in the occasion that breeds ; therefore the sadness is without limit.

Con. You should hear reason.

D. John. And when I have heard it, what blessing brings it ?

Con. If not a present remedy, at least a patient sufferance.   10

D. John. I wonder that thou, being, as thou sayest thou art, born under Saturn, goest about to apply a moral medicine to a mortifying mischief. I cannot hide what I am : I must be sad when I have cause and smile at no man's jests, eat when I have stomach and wait for no man's leisure, sleep when I am drowsy and tend on no man's business, laugh when I am merry and claw no man in his humor.

Con. Yea, but you must not make the full show of this till you may do it without controlment. You have of late stood out against your brother, and he hath ta'en you newly into his grace; where it is impossible you should take true root but by the fair weather that you make yourself: it is needful that you frame the season for your own harvest.

D. John. I had rather be a canker in a hedge than a rose in his grace, and it better fits my blood to be disdained of all than to fashion a carriage to rob love from any: in this, though I cannot be said to be a flattering honest man, it must not be denied but I am a plain-dealing villain. I am trusted with a muzzle and enfranchised with a clog; therefore I have decreed not to sing in my cage. If I had my mouth, I would bite; if I had my liberty, I would do my liking: in the meantime let me be that I am and seek not to alter me.

Con. Can you make no use of your discontent?   40

D. John. I make all use of it, for I use it only.

Who comes here?

Enter BORACHIO.

What news, Borachio?

Bora. I came yonder from a great supper: the prince your brother is royally entertained by Leonato: and I can give you intelligence of an intended marriage.

D. John. Will it serve for any model to build mischief on? What is he for a fool that betroths himself to unquietness?   50

Bora. Marry, it is your brother's right hand.

D. John. Who? the most exquisite Claudio?

Bora. Even he.

D. John. A proper squire! And who, and who? which way looks he?

Bora. Marry, on Hero, the daughter and heir of Leonato.

D. John. A very forward March-chick! How came you to this?

Bora. Being entertained for a perfumer, as I was smoking a musty room, comes me the prince and Claudio, hand in hand, in sad conference: I whipt me behind the arras, and there heard it agreed upon that the prince should woo Hero for himself, and having obtained her, give her to Count Claudio.

D. John. Come, come, let us thither: this may prove food to my displeasure. That young start-up hath all the glory of my overthrow: if I can cross him any way, I bless myself every way. You are both sure, and will assist me?   71

Con. To the death, my lord.

D. John. Let us to the great supper: their cheer is the greater that I am subdued. Would the cook were of my mind! Shall we go prove what's to be done?

Bora. We'll wait upon your lordship.

[*Exeunt.*

ACT II.

SCENE I. *A hall in* LEONATO'S *house.*

Enter LEONATO, ANTONIO, HERO, BEATRICE, *and others.*

Leon. Was not Count John here at supper?

Ant. I saw him not.

Beat. How tartly that gentleman looks! I never can see him but I am heart-burned an hour after.

Hero. He is of a very melancholy disposition.

Beat. He were an excellent man that were made just in the midway between him and Benedick: the one is too like an image and says nothing, and the other too like my lady's eldest son, evermore tattling.   11

Leon. Then half Signior Benedick's tongue in Count John's mouth, and half Count John's melancholy in Signior Benedick's face,—

Beat. With a good leg and a good foot, uncle, and money enough in his purse, such a man would win any woman in the world, if a' could get her good-will.

Leon. By my troth, niece, thou wilt never get thee a husband, if thou be so shrewd of thy tongue.   21

Ant. In faith, she's too curst.

Beat. Too curst is more than curst: I shall lessen God's sending that way; for it is said, 'God sends a curst cow short horns;' but to a cow too curst he sends none.

Leon. So, by being too curst, God will send you no horns.

Beat. Just, if he send me no husband; for the which blessing I am at him upon my knees every morning and evening. Lord, I could not endure a husband with a beard on his face: I had rather lie in the woollen.

Leon. You may light on a husband that hath no beard.

Beat. What should I do with him? dress him in my apparel and make him my waiting-gentlewoman? He that hath a beard is more than a youth, and he that hath no beard is less than a man: and he that is more than a youth is not for me, and he that is less than a man, I am not for him: therefore, I will even take sixpence in earnest of the bear-ward, and lead his apes into hell.

Leon. Well, then, go you into hell?

Beat. No, but to the gate; and there will the devil meet me, like an old cuckold, with horns on his head, and say 'Get you to heaven, Beatrice, get you to heaven; here's no place for you maids:' so deliver I up my apes, and away to Saint Peter for the heavens; he shows me where the bachelors sit, and there live we as merry as the day is long.

Ant. [*To Hero*] Well, niece, I trust you will be ruled by your father.

Beat. Yes, faith; it is my cousin's duty to make curtsy and say 'Father, as it please you.' But yet for all that, cousin, let him be a handsome fellow, or else make another curtsy and say 'Father, as it please me.'

Leon. Well, niece, I hope to see you one day fitted with a husband.   61

Beat. Not till God make men of some other metal than earth. Would it not grieve a woman to be overmastered with a piece of valiant dust? to make an account of her life to a clod of wayward marl? No, uncle, I'll none: Adam's sons are my brethren; and, truly, I hold it a sin to match in my kindred.

Leon. Daughter, remember what I told you: if the prince do solicit you in that kind, you know your answer.   71

Beat. The fault will be in the music, cousin, if you be not wooed in good time: if the prince be too important, tell him there is measure in every thing and so dance out the answer. For, hear me, Hero : wooing, wedding, and repenting, is as a Scotch jig, a measure, and a cinque pace : the first suit is hot and hasty, like a Scotch jig, and full as fantastical ; the wedding, mannerly-modest, as a measure, full of state and ancientry ; and then comes repentance and, with his bad legs, falls into the cinque pace faster and faster, till he sink into his grave.

Leon. Cousin, you apprehend passing shrewdly.

Beat. I have a good eye, uncle ; I can see a church by daylight.

Leon. The revellers are entering, brother : make good room.   [*All put on their masks.*

Enter DON PEDRO, CLAUDIO, BENEDICK, BALTHASAR, DON JOHN, BORACHIO, MARGARET, URSULA, *and others, masked.*

D. Pedro. Lady, will you walk about with your friend ?   90

Hero. So you walk softly and look sweetly and say nothing, I am yours for the walk ; and especially when I walk away.

D. Pedro. With me in your company ?

Hero. I may say so, when I please.

D. Pedro. And when please you to say so ?

Hero. When I like your favor ; for God defend the lute should be like the case !

D. Pedro. My visor is Philemon's roof ; within the house is Jove.   100

Hero. Why, then, your visor should be thatched.

D. Pedro. Speak low, if you speak love.
          [*Drawing her aside.*

Balth. Well, I would you did like me.

Marg. So would not I, for your own sake ; for I have many ill-qualities.

Balth. Which is one ?

Marg. I say my prayers aloud.

Balth. I love you the better : the hearers may cry, Amen.   110

Marg. God match me with a good dancer !

Balth. Amen.

Marg. And God keep him out of my sight when the dance is done ! Answer, clerk.

Balth. No more words : the clerk is answered.

Urs. I know you well enough ; you are Signior Antonio.

Ant. At a word, I am not.

Urs. I know you by the waggling of your head.   120

Ant. To tell you true, I counterfeit him.

Urs. You could never do him so ill-well, unless you were the very man. Here's his dry hand up and down : you are he, you are he.

Ant. At a word, I am not.

Urs. Come, come, do you think I do not know you by your excellent wit ? can virtue hide itself ? Go to, mum, you are he : graces will appear, and there's an end.

Beat. Will you not tell me who told you so ?

Bene. No, you shall pardon me.   131

Beat. Nor will you not tell me who you are ?

Bene. Not now.

Beat. That I was disdainful, and that I had my good wit out of the 'Hundred Merry

Tales : '—well this was Signior Benedick that said so.

Bene. What's he ?

Beat. I am sure you know him well enough.

Bene. Not I, believe me.

Beat. Did he never make you laugh ?   140

Bene. I pray you, what is he ?

Beat. Why, he is the prince's jester : a very dull fool ; only his gift is in devising impossible slanders : none but libertines delight in him ; and the commendation is not in his wit, but in his villany ; for he both pleases men and angers them, and then they laugh at him and beat him. I am sure he is in the fleet : I would he had boarded me.

Bene. When I know the gentleman, I'll tell him what you say.   151

Beat. Do, do : he'll but break a comparison or two on me ; which, peradventure not marked or not laughed at, strikes him into melancholy ; and then there's a partridge wing saved, for the fool will eat no supper that night. [*Music.*] We must follow the leaders.

Bene. In every good thing.

Beat. Nay, if they lead to any ill, I will leave them at the next turning.   160

          [*Dance. Then exeunt all except Don John, Borachio, and Claudio.*

D. John. Sure my brother is amorous on Hero and hath withdrawn her father to break with him about it. The ladies follow her and but one visor remains.

Bora. And that is Claudio : I know him by his bearing.

D. John. Are not you Signior Benedick ?

Claud. You know me well ; I am he.

D. John. Signior, you are very near my brother in his love : he is enamored on Hero ; I pray you, dissuade him from her : she is no equal for his birth : you may do the part of an honest man in it.

Claud. How know you he loves her ?

D. John. I heard him swear his affection.

Bora. So did I too ; and he swore he would marry her to-night.

D. John. Come, let us to the banquet.
          [*Exeunt Don John and Borachio.*

Claud. Thus answer I in the name of Benedick,
But hear these ill news with the ears of
          Claudio.   180
'Tis certain so ; the prince wooes for himself.
Friendship is constant in all other things
Save in the office and affairs of love :
Therefore, all hearts in love use their own
          tongues ;
Let every eye negotiate for itself
And trust no agent ; for beauty is a witch
Against whose charms faith melteth into
          blood.
This is an accident of hourly proof,
Which I mistrusted not. Farewell, therefore,
          Hero !

Re-enter BENEDICK.

Bene. Count Claudio ?   190

Claud. Yea, the same.

Bene. Come, will you go with me ?

Claud. Whither ?

Bene. Even to the next willow, about your own business, county. What fashion will you wear the garland of ? about your neck, like an usurer's chain ? or under your arm, like a lieutenant's scarf ? You must wear it one way, for the prince hath got your Hero.

Claud. I wish him joy of her.   200

Bene. Why, that's spoken like an honest drovier : so they sell bullocks. But did you think the prince would have served you thus ?

Claud. I pray you, leave me.

Bene. Ho ! now you strike like the blind man : 'twas the boy that stole your meat, and you'll beat the post.

Claud. If it will not be, I'll leave you.
                                    [*Exit.*

Bene. Alas, poor hurt fowl ! now will he creep into sedges. But that my Lady Beatrice should know me, and not know me ! The prince's fool ! Ha ? It may be I go under that title because I am merry. Yea, but so I am apt to do myself wrong ; I am not so reputed : it is the base, though bitter, disposition of Beatrice that puts the world into her person, and so gives me out. Well, I'll be revenged as I may.

Re-enter DON PEDRO.

D. Pedro. Now, signior, where's the count ? did you see him ?

Bene. Troth, my lord, I have played the part of Lady Fame. I found him here as melancholy as a lodge in a warren : I told him, and I think I told him true, that your grace had got the good will of this young lady ; and I offered him my company to a willow-tree, either to make him a garland, as being forsaken, or to bind him up a rod, as being worthy to be whipped.

D. Pedro. To be whipped ! What's his fault ?

Bene. The flat transgression of a schoolboy, who, being overjoyed with finding a birds' nest, shows it his companion, and he steals it.

D. Pedro. Wilt thou make a trust a transgression ? The transgression is in the stealer.

Bene. Yet it had not been amiss the rod had been made, and the garland too ; for the garland he might have worn himself, and the rod he might have bestowed on you, who, as I take it, have stolen his birds' nest.

D. Pedro. I will but teach them to sing, and restore them to the owner.   240

Bene. If their singing answer your saying, by my faith, you say honestly.

D. Pedro. The Lady Beatrice hath a quarrel to you : the gentleman that danced with her told her she is much wronged by you.

Bene. O, she misused me past the endurance of a block ! an oak but with one green leaf on it would have answered her ; my very visor began to assume life and scold with her. She told me, not thinking I had been myself, that I was the prince's jester, that I was duller than a great thaw ; huddling jest upon jest with such impossible conveyance upon me that I stood like a man at a mark, with a whole army shooting at me. She speaks poniards, and every word stabs : if her breath were as terrible as her terminations, there were no living near her ; she would infect to the north star. I would not marry her, though she were endowed with all that Adam had left him before he transgressed : she would have made Hercules have turned spit, yea, and have cleft his club to make the fire too. Come, talk not of her : you shall find her the infernal

Ate in good apparel. I would to God some scholar would conjure her ; for certainly, while she is here, a man may live as quiet in hell as in a sanctuary ; and people sin upon purpose, because they would go thither ; so, indeed, all disquiet, horror and perturbation follows her.

D. Pedro. Look, here she comes.   270

Enter CLAUDIO, BEATRICE, HERO, *and*
LEONATO.

Bene. Will your grace command me any service to the world's end ? I will go on the slightest errand now to the Antipodes that you can devise to send me on ; I will fetch you a tooth-picker now from the furthest inch of Asia, bring you the length of Prester John's foot, fetch you a hair off the great Cham's beard, do you any embassage to the Pigmies, rather than hold three words' conference with this harpy. You have no employment for me ?

D. Pedro. None, but to desire your good company.

Bene. O God, sir, here's a dish I love not : I cannot endure my Lady Tongue.   [*Exit.*

D. Pedro. Come, lady, come ; you have lost the heart of Signior Benedick.

Beat. Indeed, my lord, he lent it me awhile ; and I gave him use for it, a double heart for his single one : marry, once before he won it of me with false dice, therefore your grace may well say I have lost it.   291

D. Pedro. You have put him down, lady, you have put him down.

Beat. So I would not he should do me, my lord, lest I should prove the mother of fools. I have brought Count Claudio, whom you sent me to seek.

D. Pedro. Why, how now, count ! wherefore are you sad ?

Claud. Not sad, my lord.   300

D. Pedro. How then ? sick ?

Claud. Neither, my lord.

Beat. The count is neither sad, nor sick, nor merry, nor well ; but civil count, civil as an orange, and something of that jealous complexion.

D. Pedro. I' faith, lady, I think your blazon to be true ; though, I'll be sworn, if he be so, his conceit is false. Here, Claudio, I have wooed in thy name, and fair Hero is won : I have broke with her father, and his good will obtained : name the day of marriage, and God give thee joy !

Leon. Count, take of me my daughter, and with her my fortunes : his grace hath made the match, and all grace say Amen to it.

Beat. Speak, count, 'tis your cue.

Claud. Silence is the perfectest herald of joy : I were but little happy, if I could say how much. Lady, as you are mine, I am yours : I give away myself for you and dote upon the exchange.   320

Beat. Speak, cousin ; or, if you cannot, stop his mouth with a kiss, and let not him speak neither.

D. Pedro. In faith, lady, you have a merry heart.

Beat. Yea, my lord ; I thank it, poor fool, it keeps on the windy side of care. My cousin tells him in his ear he is in her heart.

Claud. And so she doth, cousin.

Beat. Good Lord, for alliance ! Thus goes every one to the world but I, and I am sunburnt; I may sit in a corner and cry heigh-ho for a husband!

D. Pedro. Lady Beatrice, I will get you one.

Beat. I would rather have one of your father's getting. Hath your grace ne'er a brother like you? Your father got excellent husbands, if a maid could come by them.

D. Pedro. Will you have me, lady?

Beat. No, my lord, unless I might have another for working-days: your grace is too costly to wear every day. But, I beseech your grace, pardon me: I was born to speak all mirth and no matter.

D. Pedro. Your silence most offends me, and to be merry best becomes you; for, out of question, you were born in a merry hour.

Beat. No, sure, my lord, my mother cried; but then there was a star danced, and under that was I born. Cousins, God give you joy!

Leon. Niece, will you look to those things I told you of?

Beat. I cry you mercy, uncle. By your grace's pardon.   [*Exit.*

D. Pedro. By my troth, a pleasant-spirited lady.

Leon. There's little of the melancholy element in her, my lord: she is never sad but when she sleeps, and not ever sad then; for I have heard my daughter say, she hath often dreamed of unhappiness and waked herself with laughing.

D. Pedro. She cannot endure to hear tell of a husband.

Leon. O, by no means: she mocks all her wooers out of suit.

D. Pedro. She were an excellent wife for Benedick.

Leon. O Lord, my lord, if they were but a week married, they would talk themselves mad.

D. Pedro. County Claudio, when mean you to go to church?   371

Claud. To-morrow, my lord: time goes on crutches till love have all his rites.

Leon. Not till Monday, my dear son, which is hence a just seven-night; and a time too brief, too, to have all things answer my mind.

D. Pedro. Come, you shake the head at so long a breathing: but, I warrant thee, Claudio, the time shall not go dully by us. I will in the interim undertake one of Hercules' labors; which is, to bring Signior Benedick and the Lady Beatrice into a mountain of affection the one with the other. I would fain have it a match, and I doubt not but to fashion it, if you three will but minister such assistance as I shall give you direction.

Leon. My lord, I am for you, though it cost me ten nights' watchings.

Claud. And I, my lord.

D. Pedro. And you too, gentle Hero?

Hero. I will do any modest office, my lord, to help my cousin to a good husband.   391

D. Pedro. And Benedick is not the unhopefullest husband that I know. Thus far can I praise him; he is of a noble strain, of approved valor and confirmed honesty. I will teach you how to humor your cousin, that she shall fall in love with Benedick; and I, with your two helps, will so practice on Benedick that, in despite of his quick wit and his queasy stomach, he shall fall in love with Beatrice. If we can do this, Cupid is no longer an archer: his glory shall be ours, for we are the only love-gods. Go in with me, and I will tell you my drift.   [*Exeunt.*

SCENE II. *The same.*

Enter DON JOHN *and* BORACHIO

D. John. It is so; the Count Claudio shall marry the daughter of Leonato.

Bora. Yea, my lord; but I can cross it.

D. John. Any bar, any cross, any impediment will be medicinable to me: I am sick in displeasure to him, and whatsoever comes athwart his affection ranges evenly with mine. How canst thou cross this marriage?

Bora. Not honestly, my lord; but so covertly that no dishonesty shall appear in me.

D. John. Show me briefly how.   11

Bora. I think I told your lordship a year since, how much I am in the favor of Margaret, the waiting gentlewoman to Hero.

D. John. I remember.

Bora. I can, at any unseasonable instant of the night, appoint her to look out at her lady's chamber window.

D. John. What life is in that, to be the death of this marriage?   20

Bora. The poison of that lies in you to temper. Go you to the prince your brother; spare not to tell him that he hath wronged his honor in marrying the renowned Claudio—whose estimation do you mightily hold up—to a contaminated stale, such a one as Hero.

D. John. What proof shall I make of that?

Bora. Proof enough to misuse the prince, to vex Claudio, to undo Hero and kill Leonato. Look you for any other issue?   30

D. John. Only to despite them, I will endeavor any thing.

Bora. Go, then; find me a meet hour to draw Don Pedro and the Count Claudio alone: tell them that you know that Hero loves me; intend a kind of zeal both to the prince and Claudio, as,—in love of your brother's honor, who hath made this match, and his friend's reputation, who is thus like to be cozened with the semblance of a maid,—that you have discovered thus. They will scarcely believe this without trial: offer them instances; which shall bear no less likelihood than to see me at her chamber-window, hear me call Margaret Hero, hear Margaret term me Claudio; and bring them to see this the very night before the intended wedding,—for in the meantime I will so fashion the matter that Hero shall be absent,—and there shall appear such seeming truth of Hero's disloyalty that jealousy shall be called assurance and all the preparation overthrown.   51

D. John. Grow this to what adverse issue it can, I will put it in practice. Be cunning in the working this, and thy fee is a thousand ducats.

Bora. Be you constant in the accusation, and my cunning shall not shame me.

D. John. I will presently go learn their day of marriage.   [*Exeunt.*

SCENE III. LEONATO'S *orchard.*

Enter BENEDICK.

Bene. Boy!

Enter Boy.

Boy. Signior?

Bene. In my chamber-window lies a book : bring it hither to me in the orchard.

Boy. I am here already, sir.

Bene. I know that ; but I would have thee hence, and here again. [*Exit Boy.*] I do much wonder that one man, seeing how much another man is a fool when he dedicates his behaviors to love, will, after he hath laughed at such shallow follies in others, become the argument of his own scorn by falling in love : and such a man is Claudio. I have known when there was no music with him but the drum and the fife ; and now had he rather hear the tabor and the pipe : I have known when he would have walked ten mile a-foot to see a good armor ; and now will he lie ten nights awake, carving the fashion of a new doublet. He was wont to speak plain and to the purpose, like an honest man and a soldier ; and now is he turned orthography ; his words are a very fantastical banquet, just so many strange dishes. May I be so converted and see with these eyes ? I cannot tell ; I think not : I will not be sworn but love may transform me to an oyster ; but I'll take my oath on it, till he have made an oyster of me, he shall never make me such a fool. One woman is fair, yet I am well ; another is wise, yet I am well ; another virtuous, yet I am well ; but till all graces be in one woman, one woman shall not come in my grace. Rich she shall be, that's certain ; wise, or I'll none ; virtuous, or I'll never cheapen her ; fair, or I'll never look on her ; mild, or come not near me ; noble, or not I for an angel ; of good discourse, an excellent musician, and her hair shall be of what color it please God. Ha ! the prince and Monsieur Love ! I will hide me in the arbor.

[*Withdraws.*

Enter Don Pedro, Claudio, *and* Leonato.

D. Pedro. Come, shall we hear this music ?

Claud. Yea, my good lord. How still the evening is,   40
As hush'd on purpose to grace harmony !

D. Pedro. See you where Benedick hath hid himself ?

Claud. O, very well, my lord : the music ended,
We'll fit the kid-fox with a pennyworth.

Enter Balthasar *with Music.*

D. Pedro. Come, Balthasar, we'll hear that song again.

Balth. O, good my lord, tax not so bad a voice
To slander music any more than once.

D. Pedro. It is the witness still of excellency
To put a strange face on his own perfection.
I pray thee, sing, and let me woo no more. 50

Balth. Because you talk of wooing, I will sing ;
Since many a wooer doth commence his suit
To her he thinks not worthy, yet he wooes,
Yet will he swear he loves.

D. Pedro.   Now, pray thee, come ;
Or, if thou wilt hold longer argument,
Do it in notes.

Balth.   Note this before my notes ;
There's not a note of mine that's worth the noting.

D. Pedro. Why, these are very crotchets that he speaks ;
Note, notes, forsooth, and nothing. [*Air.*

Bene. Now, divine air ! now is his soul ravished ! Is it not strange that sheeps' guts should hale souls out of men's bodies ? Well, a horn for my money, when all's done.

The Song.

Balth. Sigh no more, ladies, sigh no more,
        Men were deceivers ever,
    One foot in sea and one on shore,
        To one thing constant never :
    Then sigh not so, but let them go,
        And be you blithe and bonny,
    Converting all your sounds of woe   70
        Into Hey nonny, nonny.

    Sing no more ditties, sing no moe,
        Of dumps so dull and heavy ;
    The fraud of men was ever so,
        Since summer first was leafy :
        Then sigh not so, &c.

D. Pedro. By my troth, a good song.

Balth. And an ill singer, my lord.

D. Pedro. Ha, no, no, faith ; thou singest well enough for a shift.   80

Bene. An he had been a dog that should have howled thus, they would have hanged him : and I pray God his bad voice bode no mischief. I had as lief have heard the night-raven, come what plague could have come after it.

D. Pedro. Yea, marry, dost thou hear, Balthasar ? I pray thee, get us some excellent music ; for to-morrow night we would have it at the Lady Hero's chamber-window.

Balth. The best I can, my lord.   90

D. Pedro. Do so : farewell. [*Exit Balthasar.*] Come hither, Leonato. What was it you told me of to-day, that your niece Beatrice was in love with Signior Benedick ?

Claud. O, ay : stalk on, stalk on ; the fowl sits. I did never think that lady would have loved any man.

Leon. No, nor I neither ; but most wonderful that she should so dote on Signior Benedick, whom she hath in all outward behaviors seemed ever to abhor.   101

Bene. Is't possible ? Sits the wind in that corner ?

Leon. By my troth, my lord, I cannot tell what to think of it but that she loves him with an enraged affection : it is past the infinite of thought.

D. Pedro. May be she doth but counterfeit.

Claud. Faith, like enough.

Leon. O God, counterfeit ! There was never counterfeit of passion came so near the life of passion as she discovers it.   111

D. Pedro. Why, what effects of passion shows she ?

Claud. Bait the hook well ; this fish will bite.

Leon. What effects, my lord ? She will sit you, you heard my daughter tell you how.

Claud. She did, indeed.

D. Pedro. How, how, I pray you ? You amaze me : I would have thought her spirit had been invincible against all assaults of affection.   120

Leon. I would have sworn it had, my lord ; especially against Benedick.

Bene. I should think this a gull, but that the white-bearded fellow speaks it : knavery cannot, sure, hide himself in such reverence.

Claud. He hath ta'en the infection : hold it up.

D. Pedro. Hath she made her affection known to Benedick ?

Leon. No ; and swears she never will : that's her torment.   130

Claud. 'Tis true, indeed ; so your daughter says : ' Shall I,' says she, ' that have so oft encountered him with scorn, write to him that I love him ? '

Leon. This says she now when she is beginning to write to him ; for she'll be up twenty times a night, and there will she sit in her smock till she have writ a sheet of paper : my daughter tells us all.

Claud. Now you talk of a sheet of paper, I remember a pretty jest your daughter told us of.

Leon. O, when she had writ it and was reading it over, she found Benedick and Beatrice between the sheet ?

Claud. That.

Leon. O, she tore the letter into a thousand halfpence ; railed at herself, that she should be so immodest to write to one that she knew would flout her ; ' I measure him,' says she, ' by my own spirit ; for I should flout him, if he writ to me ; yea, though I love him, I should.'   151

Claud. Then down upon her knees she falls, weeps, sobs, beats her heart, tears her hair, prays, curses ; ' O sweet Benedick ! God give me patience ! '

Leon. She doth indeed ; my daughter says so : and the ecstasy hath so much overborne her that my daughter is sometime afeared she will do a desperate outrage to herself : it is very true.

D. Pedro. It were good that Benedick knew of it by some other, if she will not discover it.

Claud. To what end ? He would make but a sport of it and torment the poor lady worse.

D. Pedro. An he should, it were an alms to hang him. She's an excellent sweet lady ; and, out of all suspicion, she is virtuous.

Claud. And she is exceeding wise.

D. Pedro. In every thing but in loving Benedick.

Leon. O, my lord, wisdom and blood combating in so tender a body, we have ten proofs to one that blood hath the victory. I am sorry for her, as I have just cause, being her uncle and her guardian.

D. Pedro. I would she had bestowed this dotage on me : I would have daffed all other respects and made her half myself. I pray you, tell Benedick of it, and hear what a' will say.

Leon. Were it good, think you ?

Claud. Hero thinks surely she will die ; for she says she will die, if he love her not, and she will die, ere she make her love known, and she will die, if he woo her, rather than she will bate one breath of her accustomed crossness.

D. Pedro. She doth well : if she should make tender of her love, 'tis very possible he'll scorn it ; for the man, as you know all, hath a contemptible spirit.

Claud. He is a very proper man.

D. Pedro. He hath indeed a good outward happiness.   191

Claud. Before God ! and, in my mind, very wise.

D. Pedro. He doth indeed show some sparks that are like wit.

Claud. And I take him to be valiant.

D. Pedro. As Hector, I assure you : and in the managing of quarrels you may say he is wise ; for either he avoids them with great discretion, or undertakes them with a most Christian-like fear.   200

Leon. If he do fear God, a' must necessarily keep peace : if he break the peace, he ought to enter into a quarrel with fear and trembling.

D. Pedro. And so will he do ; for the man doth fear God, howsoever it seems not in him by some large jests he will make. Well, I am sorry for your niece. Shall we go seek Benedick, and tell him of her love ?

Claud. Never tell him, my lord : let her wear it out with good counsel.

Leon. Nay, that's impossible : she may wear her heart out first.   210

D. Pedro. Well, we will hear further of it by your daughter : let it cool the while. I love Benedick well ; and I could wish he would modestly examine himself, to see how much he is unworthy so good a lady.

Leon. My lord, will you walk ? dinner is ready.

Claud. If he do not dote on her upon this, I will never trust my expectation.   220

D. Pedro. Let there be the same net spread for her ; and that must your daughter and her gentlewomen carry. The sport will be, when they hold one an opinion of another's dotage, and no such matter : that's the scene that I would see, which will be merely a dumb-show. Let us send her to call him in to dinner.

[*Exeunt Don Pedro, Claudio, and Leonato.*

Bene. [*Coming forward*] This can be no trick : the conference was sadly borne. They have the truth of this from Hero. They seem to pity the lady : it seems her affections have their full bent. Love me ! why, it must be requited. I hear how I am censured : they say I will bear myself proudly, if I perceive the love come from her ; they say too that she will rather die than give any sign of affection. I did never think to marry : I must not seem proud : happy are they that hear their detractions and can put them to mending. They say the lady is fair ; 'tis a truth, I can bear them witness ; and virtuous ; 'tis so, I cannot reprove it ; and wise, but for loving me ; by my troth, it is no addition to her wit, nor no great argument of her folly, for I will be horribly in love with her. I may chance have some odd quirks and remnants of wit broken on me, because I have railed so long against marriage : but doth not the appetite alter ? a man loves the meat in his youth that he cannot endure in his age. Shall quips and sentences and these paper bullets of the brain awe a man from the career of his humor ? No, the world must be peopled. When I said I would die a bachelor, I did not think I should live till I were married. Here comes Beatrice. By this day ! she's a fair lady : I do spy some marks of love in her.

Enter BEATRICE.

Beat. Against my will I am sent to bid you come in to dinner.

Bene. Fair Beatrice, I thank you for your pains.

Beat. I took no more pains for those thanks than you take pains to thank me : if it had been painful, I would not have come.   261

Bene. You take pleasure then in the message ?

Beat. Yea, just so much as you may take upon a knife's point and choke a daw withal. You have no stomach, signior : fare you well. [*Exit.*

Bene. Ha ! ' Against my will I am sent to bid you come in to dinner ; ' there's a double meaning in that. ' I took no more pains for those thanks than you took pains to thank me.' that's as much as to say, Any pains that I take for you is as easy as thanks. If I do not take pity of her, I am a villain ; if I do not love her, I am a Jew. I will go get her picture.   [*Exit.*

ACT III.

SCENE I. LEONATO'S *garden.*

Enter HERO, MARGARET, *and* URSULA.

Hero. Good Margaret, run thee to the parlor ;
There shalt thou find my cousin Beatrice
Proposing with the prince and Claudio :
Whisper her ear and tell her, I and Ursula
Walk in the orchard and our whole discourse
Is all of her ; say that thou overheard'st us ;
And bid her steal into the pleached bower,
Where honeysuckles, ripen'd by the sun,
Forbid the sun to enter, like favorites,
Made proud by princes, that advance their
     pride   10
Against that power that bred it : there will she
     hide her,
To listen our purpose. This is thy office ;
Bear thee well in it and leave us alone.

Marg. I'll make her come, I warrant you,
     presently.   [*Exit.*

Hero. Now, Ursula, when Beatrice doth
     come,
As we do trace this alley up and down,
Our talk must only be of Benedick.
When I do name him, let it be thy part
To praise him more than ever man did merit :
My talk to thee must be how Benedick   20
Is sick in love with Beatrice. Of this matter
Is little Cupid's crafty arrow made,
That only wounds by hearsay.

Enter BEATRICE, *behind.*

                         Now begin ;
For look where Beatrice, like a lapwing, runs
Close by the ground, to hear our conference.

Urs. The pleasant'st angling is to see the
     fish
Cut with her golden oars the silver stream,
And greedily devour the treacherous bait :
So angle we for Beatrice ; who even now
Is couched in the woodbine coverture.   30
Fear you not my part of the dialogue.

Hero. Then go we near her, that her ear
     lose nothing

Of the false sweet bait that we lay for it.
                    [*Approaching the bower.*
No, truly, Ursula, she is too disdainful ;
I know her spirits are as coy and wild
As haggerds of the rock.

Urs.   But are you sure
That Benedick loves Beatrice so entirely ?

Hero. So says the prince and my new-
     trothed lord.

Urs. And did they bid you tell her of it,
     madam ?

Hero. They did entreat me to acquaint her
     of it ;   40
But I persuaded them, if they loved Benedick,
To wish him wrestle with affection,
And never to let Beatrice know of it.

Urs. Why did you so ? Doth not the gentleman
Deserve as full as fortunate a bed
As ever Beatrice shall couch upon ?

Hero. O god of love ! I know he doth deserve
As much as may be yielded to a man :
But Nature never framed a woman's heart
Of prouder stuff than that of Beatrice ; 50
Disdain and scorn ride sparkling in her eyes,
Misprising what they look on, and her wit
Values itself so highly that to her
All matter else seems weak : she cannot love,
Nor take no shape nor project of affecton,
She is so self-endeared.

Urs.   Sure, I think so ;
And therefore certainly it were not good
She knew his love, lest she make sport at it.

Hero. Why, you speak truth. I never yet
     saw man,
How wise, how noble, young, how rarely featured,   60
But she would spell him backward : if fairfaced,
She would swear the gentleman should be her
     sister ;
If black, why, Nature, drawing of an antique,
Made a foul blot ; if tall, a lance ill-headed ;
If low, an agate very vilely cut ;
If speaking, why, a vane blown with all winds ;
If silent, why, a block moved with none.
So turns she every man the wrong side out
And never gives to truth and virtue that
Which simpleness and merit purchaseth.   70

Urs. Sure, sure, such carping is not commendable.

Hero. No, not to be so odd and from all
     fashions
As Beatrice is, cannot be commendable :
But who dare tell her so ? If I should speak,
She would mock me into air ; O, she would
     laugh me
Out of myself, press me to death with wit.
Therefore let Benedick, like cover'd fire,
Consume away in sighs, waste inwardly :
It were a better death than die with mocks,
Which is as bad as die with tickling.   80

Urs. Yet tell her of it : hear what she will
     say.

Hero. No ; rather I will go to Benedick
And counsel him to fight against his passion.
And, truly, I'll devise some honest slanders
To stain my cousin with : one doth not know
How much an ill word may empoison liking.

Urs. O, do not do your cousin such a
     wrong.

She cannot be so much without true judg-
     ment—
Having so swift and excellent a wit
As she is prized to have—as to refuse   90
So rare a gentleman as Signior Benedick.
Hero. He is the only man of Italy,
Always excepted my dear Claudio.
Urs. I pray you, be not angry with me,
     madam,
Speaking my fancy : Signior Benedick,
For shape, for bearing, argument and valor,
Goes foremost in report through Italy.
Hero. Indeed, he hath an excellent good
     name.
Urs. His excellence did earn it, ere he had
     it.
When are you married, madam ?   100
Hero. Why, every day, to-morrow. Come,
     go in :
I'll show thee some attires, and have thy
     counsel
Which is the best to furnish me to-morrow.
Urs. She's limed, I warrant you : we have
     caught her, madam.
Hero. If it proves so, then loving goes by
     haps :
Some Cupid kills with arrows, some with traps.
          [*Exeunt Hero and Ursula.*
Beat. [*Coming forward*] What fire is in
     mine ears ? Can this be true ?
     Stand I condemn'd for pride and scorn so
          much ?
Contempt, farewell ! and maiden pride, adieu !
     No glory lives behind the back of such.
And, Benedick, love on ; I will requite thee,
     Taming my wild heart to thy loving hand :
If thou dost love, my kindness shall incite thee
     To bind our loves up in a holy band ;
For others say thou dost deserve, and I
Believe it better than reportingly.   [*Exit.*

SCENE II. *A room in* LEONATO'S *house.*

Enter DON PEDRO, CLAUDIO, BENEDICK, *and*
     LEONATO.

D. Pedro. I do but stay till your marriage
be consummate, and then go I toward Arragon.
Claud. I'll bring you thither, my lord, if
you'll vouchsafe me.
D. Pedro. Nay, that would be as great a
soil in the new gloss of your marriage as to
show a child his new coat and forbid him to
wear it. I will only be bold with Benedick for
his company ; for, from the crown of his head
to the sole of his foot, he is all mirth : he hath
twice or thrice cut Cupid's bow-string and the
little hangman dare not shoot at him ; he hath
a heart as sound as a bell and his tongue is
the clapper, for what his heart thinks his tongue
speaks.
Bene. Gallants, I am not as I have been.
Leon. So say I : methinks you are sadder.
Claud. I hope he be in love.
D. Pedro. Hang him, truant ! there's no
true drop of blood in him, to be truly touched
with love : if he be sad, he wants money.   20
Bene. I have the toothache.
D. Pedro. Draw it.
Bene. Hang it !
Claud. You must hang it first, and draw it
afterwards.
D. Pedro. What ! sigh for the toothache ?
Leon. Where is but a humor or a worm.

Bene. Well, every one can master a grief
but he that has it.
Claud. Yet say I, he is in love.   30
D. Pedro. There is no appearance of fancy
in him, unless it be a fancy that he hath to
strange disguises ; as, to be a Dutchman to-
day, a Frenchman to-morrow, or in the shape
of two countries at once, as, a German from
the waist downward, all slops, and a Spaniard
from the hip upward, no doublet. Unless he
have a fancy to this foolery, as it appears he
hath, he is no fool for fancy, as you would
have it appear he is.
Claud. If he be not in love with some
woman, there is no believing old signs : a'
brushes his hat o' mornings ; what should that
bode ?   42
D. Pedro. Hath any man seen him at the
barber's ?
Claud. No, but the barber's man hath been
seen with him, and the old ornament of his
cheek hath already stuffed tennis-balls.
Leon. Indeed, he looks younger than he
did, by the loss of a beard.
D. Pedro. Nay, a' rubs himself with civet :
can you smell him out by that ?   51
Claud. That's as much as to say, the sweet
youth's in love.
D. Pedro. The greatest note of it is his
melancholy.
Claud. And when was he wont to wash his
face ?
D. Pedro. Yea, or to paint himself ? for the
which, I hear what they say of him.
Claud. Nay, but his jesting spirit ; which is
now crept into a lute-string and now governed
by stops.
D. Pedro. Indeed, that tells a heavy tale
for him : conclude, conclude he is in love.
Claud. Nay, but I know who loves him.
D. Pedro. That would I know too : I warrant, one that knows him not.
Claud. Yes, and his ill conditions ; and, in
despite of all, dies for him.
D. Pedro. She shall be buried with her face
upwards.   71
Bene. Yet is this no charm for the toothache. Old signior, walk aside with me : I have
studied eight or nine wise words to speak to
you, which these hobby-horses must not hear.
          [*Exeunt Benedick and Leonato.*
D. Pedro. For my life, to break with him
about Beatrice.
Claud. 'Tis even so. Hero and Margaret
have by this played their parts with Beatrice ;
and then the two bears will not bite one another when they meet.   81

Enter DON JOHN.

D. John. My lord and brother, God save
you !
D. Pedro. Good den, brother.
D. John. If your leisure served, I would
speak with you.
D. Pedro. In private ?
D. John. If it please you : yet Count
Claudio may hear ; for what I would speak of
concerns him.
D. Pedro. What's the matter ?   90
D. John. [*To Claudio*] Means your lord-
ship to be married to-morrow ?
D. Pedro. You know he does.

D. John. I know not that, when he knows what I know.

Claud. If there be any impediment, I pray you discover it.

D. John. You may think I love you not: let that appear hereafter, and aim better at me by that I now will manifest. For my brother, I think he holds you well, and in dearness of heart hath holp to effect your ensuing marriage;—surely suit ill spent and labor ill bestowed.

D. Pedro. Why, what's the matter?

D. John. I came hither to tell you; and, circumstances shortened, for she has been too long a talking of, the lady is disloyal.

Claud. Who, Hero?

D. Pedro. Even she; Leonato's Hero, your Hero, every man's Hero.   110

Claud. Disloyal?

D. John. The word is too good to paint out her wickedness; I could say she were worse: think you of a worse title, and I will fit her to it. Wonder not till further warrant: go but with me to-night, you shall see her chamberwindow entered, even the night before her wedding-day: if you love her then, to-morrow wed her; but it would better fit your honor to change your mind.

Claud. May this be so?   120

D. Pedro. I will not think it.

D. John. If you dare not trust that you see, confess not that you know: if you will follow me, I will show you enough; and when you have seen more and heard more, proceed accordingly.

Claud. If I see any thing to-night why I should not marry her to-morrow, in the congregation, where I should wed, there will I shame her.

D. Pedro. And, as I wooed for thee to obtain her, I will join with thee to disgrace her.

D. John. I will disparage her no farther till you are my witnesses: bear it coldly but till midnight, and let the issue show itself.

D. Pedro. O day untowardly turned!

Claud. O mischief strangely thwarting!

D. John. O plague right well prevented! so will you say when you have seen the sequel.

                                        [*Exeunt.*

SCENE III. *A street.*

Enter DOGBERRY *and* VERGES *with the Watch.*

Dog. Are you good men and true?

Verg. Yea, or else it were pity but they should suffer salvation, body and soul.

Dog. Nay, that were a punishment too good for them, if they should have any allegiance in them, being chosen for the prince's watch.

Verg. Well, give them their charge, neighbor Dogberry.

Dog. First, who think you the most desartless man to be constable?   10

First Watch. Hugh Otecake, sir, or George Seacole; for they can write and read.

Dog. Come hither, neighbor Seacole. God hath blessed you with a good name: to be a well-favored man is the gift of fortune; but to write and read comes by nature.

Sec. Watch. Both which, master constable,—

Dog. You have: I knew it would be your answer. Well, for your favor, sir, why, give

God thanks, and make no boast of it; and for your writing and reading, let that appear when there is no need of such vanity. You are thought here to be the most senseless and fit man for the constable of the watch; therefore bear you the lantern. This is your charge: you shall comprehend all vagrom men; you are to bid any man stand, in the prince's name.

Sec. Watch. How if a' will not stand?

Dog. Why, then, take no note of him, but let him go; and presently call the rest of the watch together and thank God you are rid of a knave.

Verg. If he will not stand when he is bidden, he is none of the prince's subjects.

Dog. True, and they are to meddle with none but the prince's subjects. You shall also make no noise in the streets; for, for the watch to babble and to talk is most tolerable and not to be endured.

Watch. We will rather sleep than talk: we know what belongs to a watch.   40

Dog. Why, you speak like an ancient and most quiet watchman; for I cannot see how sleeping should offend: only, have a care that your bills be not stolen. Well, you are to call at all the ale-houses, and bid those that are drunk get them to bed.

Watch. How if they will not?

Dog. Why, then, let them alone till they are sober: if they make you not then the better answer, you may say they are not the men you took them for.   51

Watch. Well, sir.

Dog. If you meet a thief, you may suspect him, by virtue of your office, to be no true man; and, for such kind of men, the less you meddle or make with them, why the more is for your honesty.

Watch. If we know him to be a thief, shall we not lay hands on him?

Dog. Truly, by your office, you may; but I think they that touch pitch will be defiled: the most peaceable way for you, if you do take a thief, is to let him show himself what he is and steal out of your company.

Verg. You have been always called a merciful man, partner.

Dog. Truly, I would not hang a dog by my will, much more a man who hath any honesty in him.

Verg. If you hear a child cry in the night, you must call to the nurse and bid her still it.

Watch. How if the nurse be asleep and will not hear us?   71

Dog. Why, then, depart in peace, and let the child wake her with crying; for the ewe that will not hear her lamb when it baes will never answer a calf when he bleats.

Verg. 'Tis very true.

Dog. This is the end of the charge:—you, constable, are to present the prince's own person: if you meet the prince in the night, you may stay him.   81

Verg. Nay, by'r our lady, that I think a' cannot.

Dog. Five shillings to one on't, with any man that knows the statutes, he may stay him: marry, not without the prince be willing; for, indeed, the watch ought to offend no man; and it is an offence to stay a man against his will.

Verg. By'r lady, I think it be so.

Dog. Ha, ha, ha! Well, masters, good

night : an there be any matter of weight chances, call up me : keep your fellows' counsels and your own ; and good night. Come, neighbor.

Watch. Well, masters, we hear our charge : let us go sit here upon the church-bench till two, and then all to bed.

Dog. One word more, honest neighbors. I pray you watch about Signior Leonato's door ; for the wedding being there to-morrow, there is a great coil to-night. Adieu : be vigitant, I beseech you.   100

        [*Exeunt Dogberry and Verges.*

        Enter BORACHIO *and* CONRADE.

Bora. What Conrade !

Watch. [*Aside*] Peace ! stir not.

Bora. Conrade, I say !

Con. Here, man ; I am at thy elbow.

Bora. Mass, and my elbow itched ; I thought there would a scab follow.

Con. I will owe thee an answer for that : and now forward with thy tale.

Bora. Stand thee close, then, under this pent-house, for it drizzles rain ; and I will, like a true drunkard, utter all to thee.

Watch. [*Aside*] Some treason, masters : yet stand close.

Bora. Therefore know I have earned of Don John a thousand ducats.

Con. Is it possible that any villany should be so dear ?

Bora. Thou shouldst rather ask if it were possible any villany should be so rich ; for when rich villains have need of poor ones, poor ones may make what price they will.

Con. I wonder at it.

Bora. That shows thou art unconfirmed. Thou knowest that the fashion of a doublet, or a hat, or a cloak, is nothing to a man.

Con. Yes, it is apparel.

Bora. I mean, the fashion.

Con. Yes, the fashion is the fashion.

Bora. Tush ! I may as well say the fool's the fool. But seest thou not what a deformed thief this fashion is ?

Watch. [*Aside*] I know that Deformed ; a' has been a vile thief this seven year ; a' goes up and down like a gentleman : I remember his name.

Bora. Didst thou not hear somebody ?

Con. No ; 'twas the vane on the house.

Bora. Seest thou not, I say, what a deformed thief this fashion is ? how giddily a' turns about all the hot bloods between fourteen and five-and-thirty ? sometimes fashioning them like Pharaoh's soldiers in the reeky painting, sometime like god Bel's priests in the old church-window, sometime like the shaven Hercules in the smirched worm-eaten tapestry, where his codpiece seems as massy as his club ?

Con. All this I see ; and I see that the fashion wears out more apparel than the man. But art not thou thyself giddy with the fashion too, that thou hast shifted out of thy tale into telling me of the fashion ?

Bora. Not so, neither : but know that I have to-night wooed Margaret, the Lady Hero's gentlewoman, by the name of Hero : she leans me out at her mistress' chamber-window, bids me a thousand times good night, —I tell this tale vilely :—I should first tell thee how the prince, Claudio and my master,

planted and placed and possessed by my master Don John, saw afar off in the orchard this amiable encounter.   161

Con. And thought they Margaret was Hero ?

Bora. Two of them did, the prince and Claudio ; but the devil my master knew she was Margaret ; and partly by his oaths, which first possessed them, partly by the dark night, which did deceive them, but chiefly by my villany, which did confirm any slander that Don John had made, away went Claudio enraged ; swore he would meet her, as he was appointed, next morning at the temple, and there, before the whole congregation, shame her with what he saw o'er night and send her home again without a husband.

First Watch. We charge you, in the prince's name, stand !

Sec. Watch. Call up the right master constable. We have here recovered the most dangerous piece of lechery that ever was known in the commonwealth.   181

First Watch. And one Deformed is one of them : I know him ; a' wears a lock.

Con. Masters, masters,—

Sec. Watch. You'll be made bring Deformed forth, I warrant you.

Con. Masters,—

First Watch. Never speak : we charge you let us obey you to go with us.

Bora. We are like to prove a goodly commodity, being taken up of these men's bills.

Con. A commodity in question, I warrant you. Come, we'll obey you.   [*Exeunt.*

        SCENE IV. HERO'S *apartment.*

        Enter HERO, MARGARET, *and* URSULA.

Hero. Good Ursula, wake my cousin Beatrice, and desire her to rise.

Urs. I will, lady.

Hero. And bid her come hither.

Urs. Well.   [*Exit.*

Marg. Troth, I think your other rabato were better.

Hero. No, pray thee, good Meg, I'll wear this.

Marg. By my troth, 's not so good ; and I warrant your cousin will say so.   10

Hero. My cousin's a fool, and thou art another : I'll wear none but this.

Marg. I like the new tire within excellently, if the hair were a thought browner ; and your gown's a most rare fashion, i' faith. I saw the Duchess of Milan's gown that they praise so.

Hero. O, that exceeds, they say.

Marg. By my troth, 's but a night-gown in respect of yours : cloth o' gold, and cuts, and laced with silver, set with pearls, down sleeves, side sleeves, and skirts, round underborne with a bluish tinsel : but for a fine, quaint, graceful and excellent fashion, yours is worth ten on 't.

Hero. God give me joy to wear it ! for my heart is exceeding heavy.

Marg. 'Twill be heavier soon by the weight of a man.

Hero. Fie upon thee ! art not ashamed ?

Marg. Of what, lady ? of speaking honorably ? Is not marriage honorable in a beggar ? Is not your lord honorable without marriage ? I think you would have me say, ' saving your reverence, a husband : ' and bad thinking do not wrest true speaking, I'll offend nobody : is

there any harm in ' the heavier for a husband ' ? None, I think, and it be the right husband and the right wife ; otherwise 'tis light,
and not heavy : ask my Lady Beatrice else ;
here she comes.

Enter Beatrice.

Hero. Good morrow, coz.

Beat. Good morrow, sweet Hero.   40

Hero. Why, how now ? do you speak in the
sick tune ?

Beat. I am out of all other tune, methinks.

Marg. Clap's into ' Light o' love ; ' that
goes without a burden : do you sing it, and I'll
dance it.

Beat. Ye light o' love, with your heels !
then, if your husband have stables enough,
you'll see he shall lack no barns.

Marg. O illegitimate construction ! I scorn
that with my heels.   51

Beat. 'Tis almost five o'clock, cousin ; 'tis
time you were ready. By my troth, I am exceeding ill : heigh-ho !

Marg. For a hawk, a horse, or a husband ?

Beat. For the letter that begins them all, H.

Marg. Well, and you be not turned Turk,
there's no more sailing by the star.

Beat. What means the fool, trow ?

Marg. Nothing I ; but God send every one
their heart's desire !   61

Hero. These gloves the count sent me ;
they are an excellent perfume.

Beat. I am stuffed, cousin ; I cannot smell.

Marg. A maid, and stuffed ! there's goodly
catching of cold.

Beat. O, God help me ! God help me ! how
long have you professed apprehension ?

Marg. Even since you left it. Doth not my
wit become me rarely ?   70

Beat. It is not seen enough, you should
wear it in your cap. By my troth, I am sick.

Marg. Get you some of this distilled Car-
duus Benedictus, and lay it to your heart : it
is the only thing for a qualm.

Hero. There thou prickest her with a
thistle.

Beat. Benedictus ! why Benedictus ? you
have some moral in this Benedictus.

Marg. Moral ! no, by my troth, I have no
moral meaning ; I meant, plain holy-thistle.
You may think perchance that I think you are
in love : nay, by'r lady, I am not such a fool to
think what I list, nor I list not to think what I
can, nor indeed I cannot think, if I would
think my heart out of thinking, that you are in
love or that you will be in love or that you can
be in love. Yet Benedick was such another,
and now is he become a man : he swore he
would never marry, and yet now, in despite of
his heart, he eats his meat without grudging :
and how you may be converted I know not, but
methinks you look with your eyes as other
women do.

Beat. What pace is this that thy tongue
keeps ?

Marg. Not a false gallop.

Re-enter Ursula.

Urs. Madam, withdraw : the prince, the
count, Signior Benedick, Don John, and all the
gallants of the town, are come to fetch you to
church.

Hero. Help to dress me, good coz, good
Meg, good Ursula.   [*Exeunt.*

Scene V.   *Another room in* Leonato's
house.

Enter Leonato, *with* Dogberry *and* Verges.

Leon. What would you with me, honest
neighbor ?

Dog. Marry, sir, I would have some confidence with you that decerns you nearly.

Leon. Brief, I pray you ; for you see it is a
busy time with me.

Dog. Marry, this it is, sir.

Verg. Yes, in truth it is, sir.

Leon. What is it, my good friends ?

Dog. Goodman Verges, sir, speaks a little
off the matter : an old man, sir, and his wits
are not so blunt as, God help, I would desire
they were ; but, in faith, honest as the skin between his brows.

Verg. Yes, I thank God I am as honest as
any man living that is an old man and no
honester than I.

Dog. Comparisons are odorous : palabras,
neighbor Verges.

Leon. Neighbors, you are tedious.   20

Dog. It pleases your worship to say so, but
we are the poor duke's officers ; but truly, for
mine own part, if I were as tedious as a king,
I could find it in my heart to bestow it all of
your worship.

Leon. All thy tediousness on me, ah ?

Dog. Yea, an 'twere a thousand pound
more than 'tis ; for I hear as good exclamation
on your worship as of any man in the city ;
and though I be but a poor man, I am glad to
hear it.   30

Verg. And so am I.

Leon. I would fain know what you have to
say.

Verg. Marry, sir, our watch to-night, excepting your worship's presence, ha' ta'en a
couple of as arrant knaves as any in Messina.

Dog. A good old man, sir ; he will be talking : as they say, When the age is in, the wit is
out : God help us ! it is a world to see. Well
said, i' faith, neighbor Verges : well, God's a
good man ; an two men ride of a horse, one
must ride behind. An honest soul, i' faith, sir ;
by my troth he is, as ever broke bread ; but
God is to be worshipped ; all men are not
alike ; alas, good neighbor !

Leon. Indeed, neighbor, he comes too short
of you.

Dog. Gifts that God gives.

Leon. I must leave you.

Dog. One word, sir : our watch, sir, have
indeed comprehended two aspicious persons,
and we would have them this morning examined before your worship.

Leon. Take their examination yourself and
bring it me : I am now in great haste, as it
may appear unto you.

Dog. It shall be suffigance.

Leon. Drink some wine ere you go : fare
you well.

Enter a Messenger.

Mess. My lord, they stay for you to give
your daughter to her husband.   60

Leon. I'll wait upon them : I am ready.
        [*Exeunt Leonato and Messenger.*

Dog. Go, good partner, go, get you to

Francis Seacole ; bid him bring his pen and inkhorn to the gaol : we are now to examination these men.

Verg. And we must do it wisely.

Dog. We will spare for no wit, I warrant you ; here's that shall drive some of them to a non-come : only get the learned writer to set down our excommunication and meet me at the gaol.   [*Exeunt.*

ACT IV.

SCENE I. *A church.*

Enter DON PEDRO, DON JOHN, LEONATO, FRIAR FRANCIS, CLAUDIO, BENEDICK, HERO, BEATRICE, *and attendants.*

Leon. Come, Friar Francis, be brief ; only to the plain form of marriage, and you shall recount their particular duties afterwards.

Friar. You come hither, my lord, to marry this lady.

Claud. No.

Leon. To be married to her : friar, you come to marry her.

Friar. Lady, you come hither to be married to this count.   10

Hero. I do.

Friar. If either of you know any inward impediment why you should not be conjoined, I charge you, on your souls, to utter it.

Claud. Know you any, Hero ?

Hero. None, my lord.

Friar. Know you any, count ?

Leon. I dare make his answer, none.

Claud. O, what men dare do ! what men may do ! what men daily do, not knowing what they do !   21

Bene. How now ! interjections ? Why, then, some be of laughing, as, ah, ha, he !

Claud. Stand thee by, friar. Father, by your leave :
Will you with free and unconstrained soul
Give me this maid, your daughter ?

Leon. As freely, son, as God did give her me.

Claud. And what have I to give you back, whose worth
May counterpoise this rich and precious gift ?

D. Pedro. Nothing, unless you render her again.   30

Claud. Sweet prince, you learn me noble thankfulness.
There, Leonato, take her back again :
Give not this rotten orange to your friend ;
She's but the sign and semblance of her honor.
Behold how like a maid she blushes here !
O, what authority and show of truth
Can cunning sin cover itself withal !
Comes not that blood as modest evidence
To witness simple virtue ? Would you not swear,
All you that see her, that she were a maid,   40
By these exterior shows ? But she is none :
She knows the heat of a luxurious bed ;
Her blush is guiltiness, not modesty.

Leon. What do you mean, my lord ?

Claud.   Not to be married,
Not to knit my soul to an approved wanton.

Leon. Dear my lord, if you, in your own proof,

Have vanquish'd the resistance of her youth,
And made defeat of her virginity,—

Claud. I know what you would say : if I have known her,
You will say she did embrace me as a husband,
And so extenuate the 'forehand sin :   51
No, Leonato,
I never tempted her with word too large ;
But, as a brother to his sister, show'd
Bashful sincerity and comely love.

Hero. And seem'd I ever otherwise to you ?

Claud. Out on thee ! Seeming ! I will write against it :
You seem to me as Dian in her orb,
As chaste as is the bud ere it be blown ;
But you are more intemperate in your blood
Than Venus, or those pamper'd animals   61
That rage in savage sensuality.

Hero. Is my lord well, that he doth speak so wide ?

Leon. Sweet prince, why speak not you ?

D. Pedro.   What should I speak ?
I stand dishonor'd, that have gone about
To link my dear friend to a common stale.

Leon. Are these things spoken, or do I but dream ?

D. John. Sir, they are spoken, and these things are true.

Bene. This looks not like a nuptial.

Hero.   True ! O God !

Claud. Leonato, stand I here ?   70
Is this the prince ? is this the prince's brother ?
Is this face Hero's ? are our eyes our own ?

Leon. All this is so : but what of this, my lord ?

Claud. Let me but move one question to your daughter ;
And, by that fatherly and kindly power
That you have in her, bid her answer truly.

Leon. I charge thee do so, as thou art my child.

Hero. O, God defend me ! how am I beset !
What kind of catechising call you this ?

Claud. To make you answer truly to your name.   80

Hero. Is it not Hero ? Who can blot that name
With any just reproach ?

Claud.   Marry, that can Hero ;
Hero itself can blot out Hero's virtue.
What man was he talk'd with you yesternight
Out at your window betwixt twelve and one ?
Now, if you are a maid, answer to this.

Hero. I talk'd with no man at that hour, my lord.

D. Pedro. Why, then are you no maiden.
Leonato,
I am sorry you must hear : upon mine honor,
Myself, my brother and this grieved count   90
Did see her, hear her, at that hour last night
Talk with a ruffian at her chamber-window
Who hath indeed, most like a liberal villain,
Confess'd the vile encounters they have had
A thousand times in secret.

D. John. Fie, fie ! they are not to be named, my lord,
Not to be spoke of ;
There is not chastity enough in language
Without offence to utter them. Thus, pretty lady,
I am sorry for thy much misgovernment.   100

Claud. O Hero, what a Hero hadst thou been,
If half thy outward graces had been placed
About thy thoughts and counsels of thy heart!
But fare thee well, most foul, most fair! fare-well,
Thou pure impiety and impious purity!
For thee I'll lock up all the gates of love,
And on my eyelids shall conjecture hang,
To turn all beauty into thoughts of harm,
And never shall it more be gracious.
   Leon. Hath no man's dagger here a point
     for me?   [*Hero swoons.* 110
   Beat. Why, how now, cousin! wherefore
     sink you down?
   D. John. Come, let us go. These things, come thus to light,
Smother her spirits up.
   [*Exeunt Don Pedro, Don John, and Claudio.*
   Bene. How doth the lady?
   Beat.   Dead, I think. Help, uncle!
Hero! why, Hero! Uncle! Signior Benedick!
   Friar!
   Leon. O Fate! take not away thy heavy hand.
Death is the fairest cover for her shame
That may be wish'd for.
   Beat.   How now, cousin Hero!
   Friar. Have comfort, lady.
   Leon. Dost thou look up?   120
   Friar. Yea, wherefore should she not?
   Leon. Wherefore! Why, doth not every earthly thing
Cry shame upon her? Could she here deny
The story that is printed in her blood?
Do not live, Hero; do not ope thine eyes:
For, did I think thou wouldst not quickly die,
Thought I thy spirits were stronger than thy shames,
Myself would, on the rearward of reproaches,
Strike at thy life. Grieved I, I had but one?
Chid I for that at frugal nature's frame? 130
O, one too much by thee! Why had I one?
Why ever wast thou lovely in my eyes?
Why had I not with charitable hand
Took up a beggar's issue at my gates,
Who smirch'd thus and mired with infamy,
I might have said 'No part of it is mine;
This shame derives itself from unknown loins'?
But mine and mine I loved and mine I praised
And mine that I was proud on, mine so much
That I myself was to myself not mine, 140
Valuing of her,—why, she, O, she is fallen
Into a pit of ink, that the wide sea
Hath drops too few to wash her clean again
And salt too little which may season give
To her foul-tainted flesh!
   Bene.   Sir, sir, be patient.
For my part, I am so attired in wonder,
I know not what to say.
   Beat. O, on my soul, my cousin is belied!
   Bene. Lady, were you her bedfellow last
     night?
   Beat. No, truly not; although, until last
     night,   150
I have this twelvemonth been her bedfellow.
   Leon. Confirm'd, confirm'd! O, that is
     stronger made
Which was before barr'd up with ribs of iron!
Would the two princes lie, and Claudio lie,
Who loved her so, that, speaking of her foulness,

Wash'd it with tears? Hence from her! let her die.
   Friar. Hear me a little; for I have only been
Silent so long and given way unto
This course of fortune. . . .
By noting of the lady I have mark'd 160
A thousand blushing apparitions
To start into her face, a thousand innocent shames
In angel whiteness beat away those blushes;
And in her eye there hath appear'd a fire,
To burn the errors that these princes hold
Against her maiden truth. Call me a fool;
Trust not my reading nor my observations,
Which with experimental seal doth warrant
The tenor of my book; trust not my age, 170
My reverence, calling, nor divinity,
If this sweet lady lie not guiltless here
Under some biting error.
   Leon.   Friar, it cannot be.
Thou seest that all the grace that she hath left
Is that she will not add to her damnation
A sin of perjury; she not denies it:
Why seek'st thou then to cover with excuse
That which appears in proper nakedness?
   Friar. Lady, what man is he you are ac-
     cused of?
   Hero. They know that do accuse me; I
     know none:
If I know more of any man alive 180
Than that which maiden modesty doth war-
     rant,
Let all my sins lack mercy! O my father,
Prove you that any man with me conversed
At hours unmeet, or that I yesternight
Maintain'd the change of words with any crea-
     ture,
Refuse me, hate me, torture me to death!
   Friar. There is some strange misprision in
     the princes.
   Bene. Two of them have the very bent of
     honor;
And if their wisdoms be misled in this,
The practice of it lives in John the bastard, 190
Whose spirits toil in frame of villanies.
   Leon. I know not. If they speak but truth
     of her,
These hands shall tear her; if they wrong her honor,
The proudest of them shall well hear of it.
Time hath not yet so dried this blood of mine,
Nor age so eat up my invention,
Nor fortune made such havoc of my means,
Nor my bad life reft me so much of friends,
But they shall find, awaked in such a kind,
Both strength of limb and policy of mind, 200
Ability in means and choice of friends,
To quit me of them throughly.
   Friar.   Pause awhile,
And let my counsel sway you in this case.
Your daughter here the princes left for dead:
Let her awhile be secretly kept in,
And publish it that she is dead indeed;
Maintain a mourning ostentation
And on your family's old monument
Hang mournful epitaphs and do all rites
That appertain unto a burial. 210
   Leon. What shall become of this? what
     will this do?
   Friar. Marry, this well carried shall on her
     behalf

Change slander to remorse; that is some
       good:
But not for that dream I on this strange
       course,
But on this travail look for greater birth.
She dying, as it must so be maintain'd,
Upon the instant that she was accused,
Shall be lamented, pitied and excused
Of every hearer: for it so falls out   219
That what we have we prize not to the worth
Whiles we enjoy it, but being lack'd and lost,
Why, then we rack the value, then we find
The virtue that possession would not show us
Whiles it was ours. So will it fare with
       Claudio:
When he shall hear she died upon his words,
The idea of her life shall sweetly creep
Into his study of imagination,
And every lovely organ of her life
Shall come apparell'd in more precious habit,
More moving-delicate and full of life,   230
Into the eye and prospect of his soul,
Than when she lived indeed; then shall he
       mourn,
If ever love had interest in his liver,
And wish he had not so accused her,
No, though he thought his accusation true.
Let this be so, and doubt not but success
Will fashion the event in better shape
Than I can lay it down in likelihood.
But if all aim but this be levell'd false,
The supposition of the lady's death   240
Will quench the wonder of her infamy:
And if it sort not well, you may conceal her,
As best befits her wounded reputation,
In some reclusive and religious life,
Out of all eyes, tongues, minds and injuries.
       Bene. Signior Leonato, let the friar advise
       you:
And though you know my inwardness and love
Is very much unto the prince and Claudio,
Yet, by mine honor, I will deal in this
As secretly and justly as your soul   250
Should with your body.
       Leon.   Being that I flow in grief,
The smallest twine may lead me.
       Friar. 'Tis well consented: presently away;
For to strange sores strangely they strain the
       cure.
Come, lady, die to live: this wedding-day
       Perhaps is but prolong'd: have patience and
       endure.
       [*Exeunt all but Benedick and Beatrice.*
       Bene. Lady Beatrice, have you wept all this
       while?
       Beat. Yea, and I will weep a while longer.
       Bene. I will not desire that.
       Beat. You have no reason; I do it freely.
       Bene. Surely I do believe your fair cousin
is wronged.   261
       Beat. Ah, how much might the man de-
serve of me that would right her!
       Bene. Is there any way to show such friend-
ship?
       Beat. A very even way, but no such friend.
       Bene. May a man do it?
       Beat. It is a man's office, but not yours.
       Bene. I do love nothing in the world so
well as you: is not that strange?   270
       Beat. As strange as the thing I know not. It
were as possible for me to say I loved nothing
so well as you: but believe me not; and yet I

lie not; I confess nothing, nor I deny nothing.
I am sorry for my cousin.
       Bene. By my sword, Beatrice, thou lovest
me.
       Beat. Do not swear, and eat it.
       Bene. I will swear by it that you love me;
and I will make him eat it that says I love not
you.
       Beat. Will you not eat your word?   280
       Bene. With no sauce that can be devised to
it. I protest I love thee.
       Beat. Why, then, God forgive me!
       Bene. What offence, sweet Beatrice?
       Beat. You have stayed me in a happy
hour: I was about to protest I loved you.
       Bene. And do it with all thy heart.
       Beat. I love you with so much of my heart
that none is left to protest.
       Bene. Come, bid me do any thing for thee.
       Beat. Kill Claudio.   291
       Bene. Ha! not for the wide world.
       Beat. You kill me to deny it. Farewell.
       Bene. Tarry, sweet Beatrice.
       Beat. I am gone, though I am here: there
is no love in you: nay, I pray you, let me go.
       Bene. Beatrice,—
       Beat. In faith, I will go.
       Bene. We'll be friends first.
       Beat. You dare easier be friends with me
than fight with mine enemy.   301
       Bene. Is Claudio thine enemy?
       Beat. Is he not approved in the height a
villain, that hath slandered, scorned, dishonored my kinswoman? O that I were a man!
What, bear her in hand until they come to take
hands; and then, with public accusation, un-
covered slander, unmitigated rancor,—O God,
that I were a man! I would eat his heart in the
market-place.
       Bene. Hear me, Beatrice,—   310
       Beat. Talk with a man out at a window! A
proper saying!
       Bene. Nay, but, Beatrice,—
       Beat. Sweet Hero! She is wronged, she is
slandered, she is undone.
       Bene. Beat—
       Beat. Princes and counties! Surely, a
princely testimony, a goodly count, Count
Comfect; a sweet gallant, surely! O that I
were a man for his sake! or that I had any
friend would be a man for my sake! But manhood is melted into courtesies, valor into compliment, and men are only turned into tongue,
and trim ones too: he is now as valiant as
Hercules that only tells a lie and swears it. I
cannot be a man with wishing, therefore I will
die a woman with grieving.
       Bene. Tarry, good Beatrice. By this hand.
I love thee.
       Beat. Use it for my love some other way
than swearing by it.   330
       Bene. Think you in your soul the Count
Claudio hath wronged Hero?
       Beat. Yea, as sure as I have a thought or a
soul.
       Bene. Enough, I am engaged; I will chal-
lenge him. I will kiss your hand, and so I
leave you. By this hand, Claudio shall render
me a dear account. As you hear of me, so
think of me. Go, comfort your cousin: I must
say she is dead: and so, farewell.   [*Exeunt.*

SCENE II. *A prison.*

Enter DOGBERRY, VERGES, *and* Sexton, *in gowns; and the* Watch, *with* CONRADE *and* BORACHIO.

Dog. Is our whole dissembly appeared ?

Verg. O, a stool and a cushion for the sexton.

Sex. Which be the malefactors ?

Dog. Marry, that am I and my partner.

Verg. Nay, that's certain ; we have the exhibition to examine.

Sex. But which are the offenders that are to be examined ? let them come before master constable.

Dog. Yea, marry, let them come before me. What is your name, friend ?   11

Bora. Borachio.

Dog. Pray, write down, Borachio. Yours, sirrah ?

Con. I am a gentleman, sir, and my name is Conrade.

Dog. Write down, master gentleman Conrade. Masters, do you serve God ?

Con. } Yea, sir, we hope.
Bora. }

Dog. Write down, that they hope they serve God : and write God first ; for God defend but God should go before such villains ! Masters, it is proved already that you are little better than false knaves ; and it will go near to be thought so shortly. How answer you for yourselves ?

Con. Marry, sir, we say we are none.

Dog. A marvellous witty fellow, I assure you : but I will go about with him. Come you hither, sirrah ; a word in your ear : sir, I say to you, it is thought you are false knaves.

Bora. Sir, I say to you we are none.

Dog. Well, stand aside. 'Fore God, they are both in a tale. Have you writ down, that they are none ?

Sex. Master constable, you go not the way to examine : you must call forth the watch that are their accusers.

Dog. Yea, marry, that's the eftest way. Let the watch come forth. Masters, I charge you, in the prince's name, accuse these men.   40

First Watch. This man said, sir, that Don John, the prince's brother, was a villain.

Dog. Write down Prince John a villain. Why, this is flat perjury, to call a prince's brother villain.

Bora. Master constable,—

Dog. Pray thee, fellow, peace : I do not like thy look, I promise thee.

Sex. What heard you him say else ?

Sec. Watch. Marry, that he had received a thousand ducats of Don John for accusing the Lady Hero wrongfully.   51

Dog. Flat burglary as ever was committed.

Verg. Yea, by mass, that it is.

Sex. What else, fellow ?

First Watch. And that Count Claudio did mean, upon his words, to disgrace Hero before the whole assembly, and not marry her.

Dog. O villain ! thou wilt be condemned into everlasting redemption for this.

Sex. What else ?   60

Watch. This is all.

Sex. And this is more, masters, than you can deny. Prince John is this morning secretly stolen away ; Hero was in this manner accused, in this very manner refused, and upon the grief of this suddenly died. Master constable, let these men be bound, and brought to Leonato's : I will go before and show him their examination.   [*Exit.*

Dog. Come, let them be opinioned.

Verg. Let them be in the hands—   70

Con. Off, coxcomb !

Dog. God's my life, where's the sexton ? let him write down the prince's officer coxcomb. Come, bind them. Thou naughty varlet !

Con. Away ! you are an ass, you are an ass.

Dog. Dost thou not suspect my place ? dost thou not suspect my years ? O that he were here to write me down an ass ! But, masters, remember that I am an ass ; though it be not written down, yet forget not that I am an ass. No, thou villain, thou art full of piety, as shall be proved upon thee by good witness. I am a wise fellow, and, which is more, an officer, and, which is more, a householder, and, which is more, as pretty a piece of flesh as any is in Messina, and one that knows the law, go to ; and a rich fellow enough, go to ; and a fellow that hath had losses, and one that hath two gowns and every thing handsome about him. Bring him away. O that I had been writ down an ass !   [*Exeunt.* 90

ACT V.

SCENE I. *Before* LEONATO'S *house.*

Enter LEONATO *and* ANTONIO.

Ant. If you go on thus, you will kill yourself :
And 'tis not wisdom thus to second grief
Against yourself.

Leon.   I pray thee, cease thy counsel,
Which falls into mine ears as profitless
As water in a sieve : give not me counsel ;
Nor let no comforter delight mine ear
But such a one whose wrongs do suit with mine.
Bring me a father that so loved his child,
Whose joy of her is overwhelm'd like mine,
And bid him speak of patience ;   10
Measure his woe the length and breadth of mine
And let it answer every strain for strain,
As thus for thus and such a grief for such,
In every lineament, branch, shape, and form :
If such a one will smile and stroke his beard,
Bid sorrow wag, cry ' hem ! ' when he should groan,
Patch grief with proverbs, make misfortune drunk
With candle-wasters ; bring him yet to me,
And I of him will gather patience.   19
But there is no such man : for, brother, men
Can counsel and speak comfort to that grief
Which they themselves not feel ; but, tasting it,
Their counsel turns to passion, which before
Would give preceptial medicine to rage,
Fetter strong madness in a silken thread,
Charm ache with air and agony with words :
No, no ; 'tis all men's office to speak patience
To those that wring under the load of sorrow,
But no man's virtue nor sufficiency
To be so moral when he shall endure   30

The like himself. Therefore give me no coun-
    sel :
My griefs cry louder than advertisement.
    Ant.   Therein do men from children noth-
    ing differ.
    Leon.   I pray thee, peace. I will be flesh and
    blood ;
For there was never yet philosopher
That could endure the toothache patiently,
However they have writ the style of gods
And made a push at chance and sufferance.
    Ant.   Yet bend not all the harm upon your-
    self ;
Make those that do offend you suffer too.   40
    Leon.   There thou speak'st reason : nay, I
    will do so.
My soul doth tell me Hero is belied ;
And that shall Claudio know ; so shall the
    prince
And all of them that thus dishonor her.
    Ant.   Here comes the prince and Claudio
    hastily.

    Enter DON PEDRO *and* CLAUDIO.

    D. Pedro.   Good den, good den.
    Claud.   Good day to both of you.
    Leon.   Hear you, my lords,—
    D. Pedro.   We have some haste, Leonato.
    Leon.   Some haste, my lord ! well, fare you
    well, my lord :
Are you so hasty now ? well, all is one.
    D. Pedro.   Nay, do not quarrel with us,
    good old man.   50
    Ant.   If he could right himself with quar-
    reling,
Some of us would lie low.
    Claud.   Who wrongs him ?
    Leon.   Marry, thou dost wrong me ; thou
    dissembler, thou :—
Nay, never lay thy hand upon thy sword ;
I fear thee not.
    Claud.   Marry, beshrew my hand,
If it should give your age such cause of fear :
In faith, my hand meant nothing to my sword.
    Leon.   Tush, tush, man ; never fleer and
    jest at me :
I speak not like a dotard nor a fool,
As under privilege of age to brag   60
What I have done being young, or what would
    do
Were I not old. Know, Claudio, to thy head,
Thou hast so wrong'd mine innocent child and
    me
That I am forced to lay my reverence by
And, with grey hairs and bruise of many days,
Do challenge thee to trial of a man.
I say thou hast belied mine innocent child ;
Thy slander hath gone through and through
    her heart,
And she lies buried with her ancestors ;
O, in a tomb where never scandal slept,   70
Save this of hers, framed by thy villany !
    Claud.   My villany ?
    Leon.   Thine, Claudio ; thine, I say.
    D. Pedro.   You say not right, old man.
    Leon.   My lord, my lord,
I'll prove it on his body, if he dare,
Despite his nice fence and his active practice,
His May of youth and bloom of lustihood.
    Claud.   Away ! I will not have to do with
    you.
    Leon.   Canst thou so daff me ? Thou hast
    kill'd my child :

If thou kill'st me, boy, thou shalt kill a man.
    Ant.   He shall kill two of us, and men in-
    deed :   80
But that's no matter ; let him kill one first ;
Win me and wear me ; let him answer me.
Come, follow me, boy ; come, sir boy, come,
    follow me :
Sir boy, I'll whip you from your foining fence ;
Nay, as I am a gentleman, I will.
    Leon.   Brother,—
    Ant.   Content yourself. God knows I loved
    my niece ;
And she is dead, slander'd to death by villains,
That dare as well answer a man indeed
As I dare take a serpent by the tongue :   90
Boys, apes, braggarts, Jacks, milksops !
    Leon.   Brother Antony,—
    Ant.   Hold you content. What, man ! I
    know them, yea,
And what they weigh, even to the utmost
    scruple,—
Scrambling, out-facing, fashion-monging boys,
That lie and cog and flout, deprave and slan-
    der,
Go anticly, show outward hideousness,
And speak off half a dozen dangerous words,
How they might hurt their enemies, if they
    durst ;
And this is all.
    Leon.   But, brother Antony,—
    Ant.   Come, 'tis no matter :   100
Do not you meddle ; let me deal in this.
    D. Pedro.   Gentlemen both, we will not
    wake your patience.
My heart is sorry for your daughter's death :
But, on my honor, she was charged with noth-
    ing
But what was true and very full of proof.
    Leon.   My lord, my lord,—
    D. Pedro.   I will not hear you.
    Leon.   No ? Come, brother ; away ! I will be
    heard.
    Ant.   And shall, or some of us will smart
    for it.
            [*Exeunt Leonato and Antonio.*
    D. Pedro.   See, see ; here comes the man
    we went to seek.   110

    Enter BENEDICK.

    Claud.   Now, signior, what news ?
    Bene.   Good day, my lord.
    D. Pedro.   Welcome, signior : you are al-
most come to part almost a fray.
    Claud.   We had like to have had our two
noses snapped off with two old men without
teeth.
    D. Pedro.   Leonato and his brother. What
thinkest thou ? Had we fought, I doubt we
should have been too young for them.
    Bene.   In a false quarrel there is no true
valor. I came to seek you both.   121
    Claud.   We have been up and down to seek
thee ; for we are high-proof melancholy and
would fain have it beaten away. Wilt thou
use thy wit ?
    Bene.   It is in my scabbard : shall I draw
it ?
    D. Pedro.   Dost thou wear thy wit by thy
side ?
    Claud.   Never any did so, though very many
have been beside their wit. I will bid thee draw,
as we do the minstrels ; draw, to pleasure us.
    D. Pedro.   As I am an honest man, he looks

pale. Art thou sick, or angry ?   131

Claud. What, courage, man ! What though care killed a cat, thou hast mettle enough in thee to kill care.

Bene. Sir, I shall meet your wit in the career, and you charge it against me. I pray you choose another subject.

Claud. Nay, then, give him another staff : this last was broke cross.

D. Pedro. By this light, he changes more and more : I think he be angry indeed.   141

Claud. If he be, he knows how to turn his girdle.

Bene. Shall I speak a word in your ear ?

Claud. God bless me from a challenge !

Bene. [*Aside to Claudio.*] You are a villain ; I jest not : I will make it good how you dare, with what you dare, and when you dare. Do me right, or I will protest your cowardice. You have killed a sweet lady, and her death shall fall heavy on you. Let me hear from you.   151

Claud. Well, I will meet you, so I may have good cheer.

D. Pedro. What, a feast, a feast ?

Claud. I' faith, I thank him ; he hath bid me to a calf's head and a capon ; the which if I do not carve most curiously, say my knife's naught. Shall I not find a woodcock too ?

Bene. Sir, your wit ambles well ; it goes easily.

D. Pedro. I'll tell thee how Beatrice praised thy wit the other day. I said, thou hadst a fine wit : ' True,' said she, ' a fine little one.' ' No,' said I, ' a great wit : ' ' Right,' says she, ' a great gross one.' ' Nay,' said I, ' a good wit : ' ' Just,' said she, ' it hurts nobody.' ' Nay,' said I, ' the gentleman is wise : ' ' Certain,' said she, ' a wise gentleman.' ' Nay,' said I, ' he hath the tongues : ' ' That I believe,' said she, ' for he swore a thing to me on Monday night, which he forswore on Tuesday morning ; there's a double tongue ; there's two tongues.' Thus did she, an hour together, transshape thy particular virtues : yet at last she concluded with a sigh, thou wast the properest man in Italy.

Claud. For the which she wept heartily and said she cared not.

D. Pedro. Yea, that she did : but yet, for all that, an if she did not hate him deadly, she would love him dearly : the old man's daughter told us all.   180

Claud. All, all ; and, moreover, God saw him when he was hid in the garden.

D. Pedro. But when shall we set the savage bull's horns on the sensible Benedick's head ?

Claud. Yea, and text underneath, ' Here dwells Benedick the married man ' ?

Bene. Fare you well, boy : you know my mind. I will leave you now to your gossiplike humor : you break jests as braggarts do their blades, which God be thanked, hurt not. My lord, for your many courtesies I thank you : I must discontinue your company : your brother the bastard is fled from Messina : you have among you killed a sweet and innocent lady. For my Lord Lackbeard there, he and I shall meet : and, till then, peace be with him.

                      [*Exit.*

D. Pedro. He is in earnest.

Claud. In most profound earnest ; and, I'll warrant you, for the love of Beatrice.

D. Pedro. And hath challenged thee.   200

Claud. Most sincerely.

D. Pedro. What a pretty thing man is when he goes in his doublet and hose and leaves off his wit !

Claud. He is then a giant to an ape ; but then is an ape a doctor to such a man.

D. Pedro. But, soft you, let me be : pluck up, my heart, and be sad. Did he not say, my brother was fled ?

Enter DOGBERRY, VERGES, *and the* Watch, *with* CONRADE *and* BORACHIO.

Dog. Come you, sir : if justice cannot tame you, she shall ne'er weigh more reasons in her balance : nay, an you be a cursing hypocrite once, you must be looked to.

D. Pedro. How now ? two of my brother's men bound ! Borachio one !

Claud. Hearken after their offence, my lord.

D. Pedro. Officers, what offence have these men done ?

Dog. Marry, sir, they have committed false report ; moreover, they have spoken untruths ; secondarily, they are slanders ; sixth and lastly, they have belied a lady ; thirdly, they have verified unjust things ; and, to conclude, they are lying knaves.

D. Pedro. First, I ask thee what they have done ; thirdly, I ask thee what's their offence ; sixth and lastly, why they are committed ; and, to conclude, what you lay to their charge.

Claud. Rightly reasoned, and in his own division : and, by my troth, there's one meaning well suited.   231

D. Pedro. Who have you offended, masters, that you are thus bound to your answer ? this learned constable is too cunning to be understood : what's your offence ?

Bora. Sweet prince, let me go no farther to mine answer : do you hear me, and let this count kill me. I have deceived even your very eyes : what your wisdoms could not discover, these shallow fools have brought to light : who in the night overheard me confessing to this man how Don John your brother incensed me to slander the Lady Hero, how you were brought into the orchard and saw me court Margaret in Hero's garments, how you disgraced her, when you should marry her : my villany they have upon record ; which I had rather seal with my death than repeat over to my shame. The lady is dead upon mine and my master's false accusation ; and, briefly, I desire nothing but the reward of a villain.

D. Pedro. Runs not this speech like iron through your blood ?

Claud. I have drunk poison whiles he utter'd it.

D. Pedro. But did my brother set thee on to this ?

Bora. Yea, and paid me richly for the practice of it.

D. Pedro. He is composed and framed of treachery :

And fled he is upon this villany.

Claud. Sweet Hero ! now thy image doth appear

In the rare semblance that I loved it first. 260

Dog. Come, bring away the plaintiffs : by this time our sexton hath reformed Signior Leonato of the matter : and, masters, do not forget to specify, when time and place shall serve, that I am an ass.

Verg. Here, here comes master Signior Leonato, and the Sexton too.

Re-enter LEONATO *and* ANTONIO, *with the* Sexton.

Leon. Which is the villain ? let me see his eyes,
That, when I note another man like him, 270
I may avoid him : which of these is he ?

Bora. If you would know your wronger, look on me.

Leon. Art thou the slave that with thy breath hast kill'd
Mine innocent child ?

Bora.   Yea, even I alone.

Leon. No, not so, villain ; thou beliest thyself :
Here stand a pair of honorable men ;
A third is fled, that had a hand in it.
I thank you, princes, for my daughter's death :
Record it with your high and worthy deeds :
'Twas bravely done, if you bethink you of it.

Claud. I know not how to pray your patience ;
Yet I must speak. Choose your revenge yourself ;
Impose me to what penance your invention
Can lay upon my sin : yet sinn'd I not
But in mistaking.

D. Pedro.   By my soul, nor I :
And yet, to satisfy this good old man,
I would bend under any heavy weight
That he'll enjoin me to.

Leon. I cannot bid you bid my daughter live ;
That were impossible : but, I pray you both,
Possess the people in Messina here   290
How innocent she died ; and if your love
Can labor ought in sad invention,
Hang her an epitaph upon her tomb
And sing it to her bones, sing it to-night :
To-morrow morning come you to my house,
And since you could not be my son-in-law,
Be yet my nephew : my brother hath a daughter,
Almost the copy of my child that's dead,
And she alone is heir to both of us :
Give her the right you should have given her cousin,   300
And so dies my revenge.

Claud.   O noble sir,
Your over-kindness doth wring tears from me !
I do embrace your offer ; and dispose
For henceforth of poor Claudio.

Leon. To-morrow then I will expect your coming ;
To-night I take my leave. This naughty man
Shall face to face be brought to Margaret,
Who I believe was pack'd in all this wrong,
Hired to it by your brother.

Bora.   No, by my soul, she was not,
Nor knew not what she did when she spoke to me,   310
But always hath been just and virtuous
In any thing that I do know by her.

Dog. Moreover, sir, which indeed is not under white and black, this plaintiff here, the offender, did call me ass : I beseech you, let it be remembered in his punishment. And also, the watch heard them talk of one Deformed : they say he wears a key in his ear and a lock

hanging by it, and borrows money in God's name, the which he hath used so long and never paid that now men grow hard-hearted and will lend nothing for God's sake : pray you, examine him upon that point.

Leon. I thank thee for thy care and honest pains.

Dog. Your worship speaks like a most thankful and reverend youth ; and I praise God for you.

Leon. There's for thy pains.

Dog. God save the foundation !

Leon. Go, I discharge thee of thy prisoner, and I thank thee.

Dog. I leave an arrant knave with your worship ; which I beseech your worship to correct yourself, for the example of others. God keep your worship ! I wish your worship well ; God restore you to health ! I humbly give you leave to depart ; and if a merry meeting may be wished, God prohibit it ! Come, neighbor.   [*Exeunt Dogberry and Verges.*

Leon. Until to-morrow morning, lords, farewell.

Ant. Farewell, my lords : we look for you to-morrow.

D. Pedro. We will not fail.

Claud.   To-night I'll mourn with Hero.

Leon. [*To the Watch*] Bring you these fellows on. We'll talk with Margaret,
How her acquaintance grew with this lewd fellow.   [*Exeunt, severally.*

SCENE II. LEONATO'S *garden.*

Enter BENEDICK *and* MARGARET, *meeting.*

Bene. Pray thee, sweet Mistress Margaret, deserve well at my hands by helping me to the speech of Beatrice.

Marg. Will you then write me a sonnet in praise of my beauty ?

Bene. In so high a style, Margaret, that no man living shall come over it ; for, in most comely truth, thou deservest it.

Marg. To have no man come over me ! why, shall I always keep below stairs ?   10

Bene. Thy wit is as quick as the greyhound's mouth ; it catches.

Marg. And yours as blunt as the fencer's foils, which hit, but hurt not.

Bene. A most manly wit, Margaret ; it will not hurt a woman : and so, I pray thee, call Beatrice : I give thee the bucklers.

Marg. Give us the swords ; we have bucklers of our own.

Bene. If you use them, Margaret, you must put in the pikes with a vice ; and they are dangerous weapons for maids.

Marg. Well, I will call Beatrice to you, who I think hath legs.

Bene. And therefore will come.

[*Exit Margaret.*

[*Sings*]   The god of love,
                That sits above,
        And knows me, and knows me,
                How pitiful I deserve,—

I mean in singing ; but in loving, Leander the good swimmer, Troilus the first employer of panders, and a whole bookful of these quondam carpet-mongers, whose names yet run smoothly in the even road of a blank verse, why, they were never so truly turned over and over as my poor self in love. Marry, I cannot

show it in rhyme ; I have tried : I can find out
no rhyme to 'lady' but 'baby,' an innocent
rhyme ; for 'scorn,' 'horn,' a hard rhyme ;
for, 'school,' 'fool,' a babbling rhyme ; very
ominous endings : no, I was not born under a
rhyming planet, nor I cannot woo in festival
terms.   41

Enter BEATRICE.

Sweet Beatrice, wouldst thou come when I
called thee ?

Beat. Yea, signior, and depart when you
bid me.

Bene. O, stay but till then !

Beat. 'Then' is spoken ; fare you well
now : and yet, ere I go, let me go with that I
came ; which is, with knowing what hath
passed between you and Claudio.

Bene. Only foul words ; and thereupon I
will kiss thee.   51

Beat. Foul words is but foul wind, and foul
wind is but foul breath, and foul breath is
noisome ; therefore I will depart unkissed.

Bene. Thou hast frighted the word out of
his right sense, so forcible is thy wit. But I
must tell thee plainly, Claudio undergoes my
challenge ; and either I must shortly hear from
him, or I will subscribe him a coward. And, I
pray thee now, tell me for which of my bad
parts didst thou first fall in love with me ? 61

Beat. For them all together ; which maintained so politic a state of evil that they will
not admit any good part to intermingle with
them. But for which of my good parts did
you first suffer love for me ?

Bene. Suffer love ! a good epithet ! I do
suffer love indeed, for I love thee against my
will.

Beat. In spite of your heart, I think ; alas,
poor heart ! If you spite it for my sake, I will
spite it for yours ; for I will never love that
which my friend hates.

Bene. Thou and I are too wise to woo
peaceably.

Beat. It appears not in this confession :
there's not one wise man among twenty that
will praise himself.

Bene. An old, an old instance, Beatrice,
that lived in the time of good neighbors. If a
man do not erect in this age his own tomb ere
he dies, he shall live no longer in monument
than the bell rings and the widow weeps.

Beat. And how long is that, think you ?

Bene. Question : why, an hour in clamor
and a quarter in rheum : therefore is it most
expedient for the wise, if Don Worm, his conscience, find no impediment to the contrary, to
be the trumpet of his own virtues, as I am to
myself. So much for praising myself, who, I
myself will bear witness, is praiseworthy : and
now tell me, how doth your cousin ? 91

Beat. Very ill.

Bene. And how do you ?

Beat. Very ill too.

Bene. Serve God, love me and mend. There
will I leave you too, for here comes one in
haste.

Enter URSULA.

Urs. Madam, you must come to your uncle. Yonder's old coil at home : it is proved
my Lady Hero hath been falsely accused, the
prince and Claudio mightily abused ; and Don

John is the author of all, who is fled and gone.
Will you come presently ?

Beat. Will you go hear this news, signior ?

Bene. I will live in thy heart, die in thy
lap and be buried in thy eyes ; and moreover
I will go with thee to thy uncle's. [*Exeunt.*

SCENE III. *A church.*

Enter DON PEDRO, CLAUDIO, *and three or four
with tapers.*

Claud. Is this the monument of Leonato ?

A Lord. It is, my lord.

Claud. [*Reading out of a scroll*]

  Done to death by slanderous tongues
    Was the Hero that here lies :
  Death, in guerdon of her wrongs,
    Gives her fame which never dies.
  So the life that died with shame
  Lives in death with glorious fame.
Hang thou there upon the tomb,
  Praising her when I am dumb. 10
Now, music, sound, and sing your solemn
  hymn.

SONG.

  Pardon, goddess of the night,
  Those that slew thy virgin knight ;
  For the which, with songs of woe,
  Round about her tomb they go.
    Midnight, assist our moan ;
    Help us to sigh and groan,
      Heavily, heavily :
    Graves, yawn and yield your dead,
    Till death be uttered, 20
      Heavily, heavily.

Claud. Now, unto thy bones good night !
  Yearly will I do this rite.

D. Pedro. Good morrow, masters ; put
  your torches out :
The wolves have prey'd ; and look, the gen-
  tle day,
Before the wheels of Phœbus, round about
Dapples the drowsy east with spots of grey.
Thanks to you all, and leave us : fare you well.

Claud. Good morrow, masters : each his
  several way.

D. Pedro. Come, let us hence, and put on
  other weeds ; 30
And then to Leonato's we will go.

Claud. And Hymen now with luckier issue
  speed's
Than this for whom we render'd up this woe.
                   [*Exeunt.*

SCENE IV. *A room in* LEONATO'S *house.*

Enter LEONATO, ANTONIO, BENEDICK, BEA-
TRICE, MARGARET, URSULA, FRIAR FRANCIS,
and HERO.

Friar. Did I not tell you she was innocent ?

Leon. So are the prince and Claudio, who
  accused her
Upon the error that you heard debated :
But Margaret was in some fault for this,
Although against her will, as it appears
In the true course of all the question.

Ant. Well, I am glad that all things sort so
  well.

Bene. And so am I, being else by faith enforced
To call young Claudio to a reckoning for it.

Leon. Well, daughter, and you gentlewomen all, 10
Withdraw into a chamber by yourselves,

And when I send for you, come hither mask'd.
[*Exeunt Ladies.*
The prince and Claudio promised by this hour
To visit me. You know your office, brother :
You must be father to your brother's daughter,
And give her to young Claudio.
Ant.   Which I will do with confirm'd countenance.
Bene.   Friar, I must entreat your pains, I think.
Friar.   To do what, signior ?
Bene.   To bind me, or undo me ; one of them.   20
Signior Leonato, truth it is, good signior,
Your niece regards me with an eye of favor.
Leon.   That eye my daughter lent her : 'tis most true.
Bene.   And I do with an eye of love requite her.
Leon.   The sight whereof I think you had from me,
From Claudio and the prince : but what's your will ?
Bene.   Your answer, sir, is enigmatical :
But, for my will, my will is your good will
May stand with ours, this day to be conjoin'd
In the state of honorable marriage :   30
In which, good friar, I shall desire your help.
Leon.   My heart is with your liking.
Friar.   And my help.
Here comes the prince and Claudio.

Enter DON PEDRO *and* CLAUDIO, *and two or three others.*

D. Pedro.   Good morrow to this fair assembly.
Leon.   Good morrow, prince ; good morrow, Claudio :
We here attend you. Are you yet determined
To-day to marry with my brother's daughter ?
Claud.   I'll hold my mind, were she an Ethiope.
Leon.   Call her forth, brother ; here's the friar ready.   [*Exit Antonio.*
D. Pedro.   Good morrow, Benedick. Why, what's the matter,   40
That you have such a February face,
So full of frost, of storm and cloudiness ?
Claud.   I think he thinks upon the savage bull.
Tush, fear not, man ; we'll tip thy horns with gold
And all Europa shall rejoice at thee,
As once Europa did at lusty Jove,
When he would play the noble beast in love.
Bene.   Bull Jove, sir, had an amiable low ;
And some such strange bull leap'd your father's cow,
And got a calf in that same noble feat   50
Much like to you, for you have just his bleat.
Claud.   For this I owe you : here comes other reckonings.

Re-enter ANTONIO, *with the* Ladies *masked.*
Which is the lady I must seize upon ?
Ant.   This same is she, and I do give you her.
Claud.   Why, then she's mine. Sweet, let me see your face.
Leon.   No, that you shall not, till you take her hand
Before this friar and swear to marry her.

Claud.   Give me your hand : before this holy friar,
I am your husband, if you like of me.
Hero.   And when I lived, I was your other wife :   60
[*Unmasking.*
And when you loved, you were my other husband.
Claud.   Another Hero !
Hero.   Nothing certainer :
One Hero died defiled, but I do live,
And surely as I live, I am a maid.
D. Pedro.   The former Hero ! Hero that is dead !
Leon.   She died, my lord, but whiles her slander lived.
Friar.   All this amazement can I qualify ;
When after that the holy rites are ended,
I'll tell you largely of fair Hero's death :
Meantime let wonder seem familiar,   70
And to the chapel let us presently.
Bene.   Soft and fair, friar. Which is Beatrice ?
Beat.   [*Unmasking*] I answer to that name. What is your will ?
Bene.   Do not you love me ?
Beat.   Why, no ; no more than reason.
Bene.   Why, then your uncle and the prince and Claudio
Have been deceived ; they swore you did.
Beat.   Do not you love me ?
Bene.   Troth, no ; no more than reason.
Beat.   Why, then my cousin Margaret and Ursula
Are much deceived ; for they did swear you did.
Bene.   They swore that you were almost sick for me.   80
Beat.   They swore that you were well-nigh dead for me.
Bene.   'Tis no such matter. Then you do not love me ?
Beat.   No, truly, but in friendly recompense.
Leon.   Come, cousin, I am sure you love the gentleman.
Claud.   And I'll be sworn upon't that he loves her ;
For here's a paper written in his hand,
A halting sonnet of his own pure brain,
Fashion'd to Beatrice.
Hero.   And here's another
Writ in my cousin's hand, stolen from her pocket,
Containing her affection unto Benedick.   90
Bene.   A miracle ! here's our own hands against our hearts. Come, I will have thee ; but, by this light, I take thee for pity.
Beat.   I would not deny you ; but, by this good day, I yield upon great persuasion ; and partly to save your life, for I was told you were in a consumption.
Bene.   Peace ! I will stop your mouth.
[*Kissing her.*
D. Pedro.   How dost thou, Benedick, the married man ?   100
Bene.   I'll tell thee what, prince ; a college of wit-crackers cannot flout me out of my humor. Dost thou think I care for a satire or an epigram ? No : if a man will be beaten with brains, a' shall wear nothing handsome about him. In brief, since I do purpose to marry, I will think nothing to any purpose that the world can say against it ; and there-

fore never flout at me for what I have said against it; for man is a giddy thing, and this is my conclusion. For thy part, Claudio, I did think to have beaten thee; but in that thou art like to be my kinsman, live unbruised and love my cousin.

Claud. I had well hoped thou wouldst have denied Beatrice, that I might have cudgelled thee out of thy single life, to make thee a double-dealer; which, out of question, 'thou wilt be, if my cousin do not look exceedingly narrowly to thee.

Bene. Come, come, we are friends: let's have a dance ere we are married, that we may lighten our own hearts and our wives' heels.

Leon. We'll have dancing afterward.

Bene. First, of my word; therefore play, music. Prince, thou art sad; get thee a wife, get thee a wife: there is no staff more reverend than one tipped with horn.

Enter a Messenger.

Mess. My lord, your brother John is ta'en in flight,
And brought with armed men back to Messina.

Bene. Think not on him till to-morrow: I'll devise thee brave punishments for him. Strike up, pipers. [*Dance.* 131
  [*Exeunt.*

AS YOU LIKE IT.

(WRITTEN ABOUT 1599.)

INTRODUCTION.

As You Like It was entered on the Stationers' register together with *Henry V., Much Ado About Nothing*, and Jonson's *Every Man in His Humour*, " to be staied," *i.e.* not printed ; the date is August 4, but the year is not mentioned. The previous entry is dated May 27, 1600, and as the other plays were printed in 1600 and 1601, we infer that the August was that of the year 1600. The comedy is not mentioned by Meres. A line, " Who ever loved that loved not at first sight ? " is quoted (Act III., Sc. v., L. 82 from Marlowe's *Hero and Leander*, which was published in 1598. We may set down the following year, 1599, as the probable date of the creation of this charming comedy. The story is taken from Thomas Lodge's prose tale, *Rosalynde, Euphues Golden Legacie*, first printed in 1590, and a passage in Lodge's dedication probably suggested to Shakespeare the name of his play. Lodge, who wrote this tale on his voyage to the Canaries, founded it in part on the Cook's Tale of Gamelyn, wrongly ascribed to Chaucer, and inserted in some editions as one of the *Canterbury Tales*. In parts of his work the dramatist follows the story-teller closely, but there are some important differences. The heroic names Orlando, Oliver, and Sir Rowland are due to Shakespeare. It was a thought of Shakespeare to make the rightful and usurping dukes, as in *The Tempest*, brothers. In Lodge's novel the girl-friends pass in the forest for lady and page, in Shakespeare for brother and sister. Shakespeare omits the incident of Aliena's rescue from robbers by her future husband ; love at first sight was natural in Arden, but a band of robbers would have marred the tranquillity of the scene. To Shakespeare we owe the creation of the characters of Jacques, Touchstone, and Audrey. Written perhaps immediately after *Henry V.*, the play presents a striking contrast with that high-pitched historical drama. It is as if Shakespeare's imagination craved repose and refreshment after the life of courts and camps. We are still on French soil, but instead of the sound of the shock of battle at Agincourt, we, hear the waving forest boughs, and the forest streams of Arden, where " they fleet the time carelessly as they did in the Golden World." There is an open-air feeling about this play, as there is about *The Merry Wives of Windsor*; but in *The Merry Wives* all the surroundings are English and real, here they belong to a land of romance. For the Renaissance, that age of vast energy, national enterprise, religious strife, and court intrigue, pastoral or idyllic poetry possessed a peculiar charm ; the quiet and innocence of a poetical Arcadia was a solace to a life of highly-wrought ambition and aspiration. " Sweet are the uses of adversity," moralizes the banished Duke, and external, material adversity has come to him, to Rosalind, and to Orlando ; but if fortune is harsh, nature—both external nature and human character—is sound and sweet, and of real suffering there is none in the play. All that is evil remains in the society which the denizens of the forest have left behind ; and both seriously, in the characters of the usurping Duke and Oliver, and playfully, through Touchstone's mockery of court follies, a criticism on what is evil and artificial in society is suggested in contrast with the woodland life. Yet Shakespeare never falls into the conventional, pastoral manner. Orlando is an ideal of youthful strength, beauty, and noble innocence of heart ; and Rosalind's bright, tender womanhood seems but to grow more exquisitely feminine in the male attire which she has assumed in self-defence. Her feelings are almost as quick and fine as those of Imogen (she has not, like Imogen, known fear and sorrow), and she uses her wit and bright play of intellect as a protection against her own eager and vivid emotions. Possessed of a delighted consciousness of power to confer happiness, she can dally with disguises, and make what is most serious to her at the same time possess the charm of an exquisite frolic. The melancholy Jacques is a sentimentalist and in some degree a superficial cynic, but he is not a bad-hearted egoist, like Don John ; he is a perfectly idle seeker for new sensations and an observer of his own feelings; he is weary of all he has found, and especially professes to despise the artificial society, which yet he never really escapes from as the others do. His wisdom is half foolery, as Touchstone's foolery is half wisdom. Touchstone is the daintiest fool of the comedies, and in comparing him with the clowns of *The Comedy of Errors* or *The Two Gentlemen of Verona*, we perceive how Shakespeare's humor has grown in refinement.

DRAMATIS PERSONÆ.

DUKE, living in banishment.
FREDERICK, his brother, an usurper of his dominions.
AMIENS, } lords attending on the banished
JAQUES, } duke.

LE BEAU, a courtier attending upon Frederick.
CHARLES, wrestler to Frederick.
OLIVER,
JAQUES, } sons of Sir Rowland de Boys.
ORLANDO,

ADAM, } servants to Oliver.
DENNIS, }
TOUCHSTONE, a clown.
SIR OLIVER MARTEXT, a vicar.
CORIN, } shepherds.
SILVIUS, }
WILLIAM, a country fellow in love with Audrey.

A person representing Hymen.
ROSALIND, daughter to the banished duke.
CELIA, daughter to Frederick.
PHEBE, a shepherdess.
AUDREY, a country wench.
　　Lords, pages, and attendants, &c.
SCENE : *Oliver's house; Duke Frederick's court; and the Forest of Arden.*

ACT I.

SCENE I. *Orchard of* OLIVER'S *house.*

Enter ORLANDO *and* ADAM.

Orl. As I remember, Adam, it was upon this fashion bequeathed me by will but poor a thousand crowns, and, as thou sayest, charged my brother, on his blessing, to breed me well : and there begins my sadness. My brother Jaques he keeps at school, and report speaks goldenly of his profit : for my part, he keeps me rustically at home, or, to speak more properly, stays me here at home unkept; for call you that keeping for a gentleman of my birth, that differs not from the stalling of an ox ? His horses are bred better; for, besides that they are fair with their feeding, they are taught their manage, and to that end riders dearly hired : but I, his brother, gain nothing under him but growth; for the which his animals on his dunghills are as much bound to him as I. Besides this nothing that he so plentifully gives me, the something that nature gave me his countenance seems to take from me : he lets me feed with his hinds, bars me the place of a brother, and, as much as in him lies, mines my gentility with my education. This is it, Adam, that grieves me; and the spirit of my father, which I think is within me, begins to mutiny against this servitude : I will no longer endure it, though yet I know no wise remedy how to avoid it.

Adam. Yonder comes my master, your brother.

Orl. Go apart, Adam, and thou shalt hear how he will shake me up. 30

Enter OLIVER.

Oli. Now, sir ! what make you here ?

Orl. Nothing : I am not taught to make any thing.

Oli. What mar you then, sir ?

Orl. Marry, sir, I am helping you to mar that which God made, a poor unworthy brother of yours, with idleness.

Oli. Marry, sir, be better employed, and be naught awhile. 39

Orl. Shall I keep your hogs and eat husks with them ? What prodigal portion have I spent, that I should come to such penury ?

Oli. Know you where your are, sir ?

Orl. O, sir, very well; here in your orchard.

Oli. Know you before whom, sir ?

Orl. Ay, better than him I am before knows me. I know you are my eldest brother; and, in the gentle condition of blood, you should so know me. The courtesy of nations allows you my better, in that you are the first-born : but the same tradition takes not away my blood, were there twenty brothers betwixt us : I have as much of my father in me as you; albeit, I confess, your coming before me is nearer to his reverence.

Oli. What, boy !

Orl. Come, come, elder brother, you are too young in this.

Oli. Wilt thou lay hands on me, villain ?

Orl. I am no villain; I am the youngest son of Sir Rowland de Boys; he was my father, and he is thrice a villain that says such a father begot villains. Wert thou not my brother, I would not take this hand from thy throat till this other had pulled out thy tongue for saying so : thou hast railed on thyself.

Adam. Sweet masters, be patient : for your father's remembrance, be at accord.

Oli. Let me go, I say.

Orl. I will not, till I please : you shall hear me. My father charged you in his will to give me good education : you have trained me like a peasant, obscuring and hiding from me all gentleman-like qualities. The spirit of my father grows strong in me, and I will no longer endure it : therefore allow me such exercises as may become a gentleman, or give me the poor allottery my father left me by testament ; with that I will go buy my fortunes.

Oli. And what wilt thou do ? beg, when that is spent ? Well, sir, get you in : I will not long be troubled with you; you shall have some part of your will : I pray you, leave me.

Orl. I will no further offend you than becomes me for my good.

Oli. Get you with him, you old dog.

Adam. Is 'old dog' my reward ? Most true, I have lost my teeth in your service. God be with my old master ! he would not have spoke such a word.

　　[Exeunt Orlando and Adam.

Oli. Is it even so ? begin you to grow upon me ? I will physic your rankness, and yet give no thousand crowns neither. Holla, Dennis !

Enter DENNIS.

Den. Calls your worship ?

Oli. Was not Charles, the duke's wrestler, here to speak with me ?

Den. So please you, he is here at the door and importunes access to you.

Oli. Call him in. [*Exit Dennis.*] 'Twill be a good way; and to-morrow the wrestling is.

Enter CHARLES.

Cha. Good morrow to your worship. 100

Oli. Good Monsieur Charles, what's the new news at the new court ?

Cha. There's no news at the court, sir, but the old news : that is, the old duke is banished by his younger brother the new duke; and three or four loving lords have put themselves into voluntary exile with him, whose lands and revenues enrich the new duke; therefore he gives them good leave to wander.

Oli. Can you tell if Rosalind, the duke's daughter, be banished with her father ? 111

Cha. O, no ; for the duke's daughter, her cousin, so loves her, being ever from their cradles bred together, that she would have followed her exile, or have died to stay behind her. She is at the court, and no less beloved of her uncle than his own daughter ; and never two ladies loved as they do.

Oli. Where will the old duke live ?

Cha. They say he is already in the forest of Arden, and a many merry men with him ; and there they live like the old Robin Hood of England : they say many young gentlemen flock to him every day, and fleet the time carelessly, as they did in the golden world.

Oli. What, you wrestle to-morrow before the new duke ?

Cha. Marry, do I, sir ; and I came to acquaint you with a matter. I am given, sir, secretly to understand that your younger brother Orlando hath a disposition to come in disguised against me to try a fall. To-morrow, sir, I wrestle for my credit ; and he that escapes me without some broken limb shall acquit him well. Your brother is but young and tender ; and, for your love, I would be loath to foil him, as I must, for my own honor, if he come in : therefore, out of my love to you, I came hither to acquaint you withal, that either you might stay him from his intendment or brook such disgrace well as he shall run into, in that it is a thing of his own search and altogether against my will.

Oli. Charles, I thank thee for thy love to me, which thou shalt find I will most kindly requite. I had myself notice of my brother's purpose herein and have by underhand means labored to dissuade him from it, but he is resolute. I'll tell thee, Charles : it is the stubbornest young fellow of France, full of ambition, an envious emulator of every man's good parts, a secret and villanous contriver against me his natural brother : therefore use thy discretion ; I had as lief thou didst break his neck as his finger. And thou wert best look to't ; for if thou dost him any slight disgrace or if he do not mightily grace himself on thee, he will practice against thee by poison, entrap thee by some treacherous device and never leave thee till he hath ta'en thy life by some indirect means or other ; for, I assure thee, and almost with tears I speak it, there is not one so young and so villanous this day living. I speak but brotherly of him ; but should I anatomize him to thee as he is, I must blush and weep and thou must look pale and wonder.

Cha. I am heartily glad I came hither to you. If he come to-morrow, I'll give him his payment : if ever he go alone again, I'll never wrestle for prize more : and so God keep your worship !

Oli. Farewell, good Charles. [*Exit Charles.*] Now will I stir this gamester : I hope I shall see an end of him ; for my soul, yet I know not why, hates nothing more than him. Yet he's gentle, never schooled and yet learned, full of noble device, of all sorts enchantingly beloved, and indeed so much in the heart of the world, and especially of my own people, who best know him, that I am altogether misprised : but it shall not be so long ; this wrestler shall clear all : nothing remains but that I kindle the boy thither ; which now I'll go about. 180

[*Exit.*

SCENE II. *Lawn before the* DUKE'S *palace.*

Enter CELIA *and* ROSALIND.

Cel. I pray thee, Rosalind, sweet my coz, be merry.

Ros. Dear Celia, I show more mirth than I am mistress of ; and would you yet I were merrier ? Unless you could teach me to forget a banished father, you must not learn me how to remember any extraordinary pleasure.

Cel. Herein I see thou lovest me not with the full weight that I love thee. If my uncle, thy banished father, had banished thy uncle, the duke my father, so thou hadst been still with me, I could have taught my love to take thy father for mine : so wouldst thou, if the truth of thy love to me were so righteously tempered as mine is to thee.

Ros. Well, I will forget the condition of my estate, to rejoice in yours.

Cel. You know my father hath no child but I, nor none is like to have : and, truly, when he dies, thou shalt be his heir, for what he hath taken away from thy father perforce, I will render thee again in affection ; by mine honor, I will ; and when I break that oath, let me turn monster : therefore, my sweet Rose, my dear Rose, be merry.

Ros. From henceforth I will, coz, and devise sports. Let me see ; what think you of falling in love ?

Cel. Marry, I prithee, do, to make sport withal : but love no man in good earnest ; nor no further in sport neither than with safety of a pure blush thou mayst in honor come off again.

Ros. What shall be our sport, then ?

Cel. Let us sit and mock the good housewife Fortune from her wheel, that her gifts may henceforth be bestowed equally.

Ros. I would we could do so, for her benefits are mightily misplaced, and the bountiful blind woman doth most mistake in her gifts to women.

Cel. 'Tis true ; for those that she makes fair she scarce makes honest, and those that she makes honest she makes very ill-favoredly.

Ros. Nay, now thou goest from Fortune's office to Nature's : Fortune reigns in gifts of the world, not in the lineaments of Nature.

Enter TOUCHSTONE.

Cel. No ? when Nature hath made a fair creature, may she not by Fortune fall into the fire ? Though Nature hath given us wit to flout at Fortune, hath not Fortune sent in this fool to cut off the argument ? 50

Ros. Indeed, there is Fortune too hard for Nature, when Fortune makes Nature's natural the cutter-off of Nature's wit.

Cel. Peradventure this is not Fortune's work neither, but Nature's ; who perceiveth our natural wits too dull to reason of such goddesses and hath sent this natural for our whetstone ; for always the dulness of the fool is the whetstone of the wits. How now, wit ! whither wander you ?

Touch. Mistress, you must come away to your father. 61

Cel. Were you made the messenger ?

Touch. No, by mine honor, but I was bid to come for you.

Ros. Where learned you that oath, fool?

Touch. Of a certain knight that swore by his honor they were good pancakes and swore by his honor the mustard was naught: now I'll stand to it, the pancakes were naught and the mustard was good, and yet was not the knight forsworn. 71

Cel. How prove you that, in the great heap of your knowledge?

Ros. Ay, marry, now unmuzzle your wisdom.

Touch. Stand you both forth now: stroke your chins, and swear by your beards that I am a knave.

Cel. By our beards, if we had them, thou art.

Touch. By my knavery, if I had it, then I were; but if you swear by that that is not, you are not forsworn: no more was this knight, swearing by his honor, for he never had any; or if he had, he had sworn it away before ever he saw those pancakes or that mustard.

Cel. Prithee, who is't that thou meanest?

Touch. One that old Frederick, your father, loves.

Cel. My father's love is enough to honor him: enough! speak no more of him; you'll be whipped for taxation one of these days. 91

Touch. The more pity, that fools may not speak wisely what wise men do foolishly.

Cel. By my troth, thou sayest true; for since the little wit that fools have was silenced, the little foolery that wise men have makes a great show. Here comes Monsieur Le Beau.

Ros. With his mouth full of news.

Cel. Which he will put on us, as pigeons feed their young. 100

Ros. Then shall we be news-crammed.

Cel. All the better; we shall be the more marketable.

Enter Le Beau.

Bon jour, Monsieur Le Beau: what's the news?

Le Beau. Fair princess, you have lost much good sport.

Cel. Sport! of what color?

Le Beau. What color, madam! how shall I answer you?

Ros. As wit and fortune will. 110

Touch. Or as the Destinies decree.

Cel. Well said: that was laid on with a trowel.

Touch. Nay, if I keep not my rank,—

Ros. Thou losest thy old smell.

Le Beau. You amaze me, ladies: I would have told you of good wrestling, which you have lost the sight of.

Ros. You tell us the manner of the wrestling.

Le Beau. I will tell you the beginning; and, if it please your ladyships, you may see the end; for the best is yet to do; and here, where you are, they are coming to perform it.

Cel. Well, the beginning, that is dead and buried.

Le Beau. There comes an old man and his three sons,—

Cel. I could match this beginning with an old tale.

Le Beau. Three proper young men, of excellent growth and presence. 130

Ros. With bills on their necks, 'Be it known unto all men by these presents.'

Le Beau. The eldest of the three wrestled with Charles, the duke's wrestler; which Charles in a moment threw him and broke three of his ribs, that there is little hope of life in him: so he served the second, and so the third. Yonder they lie; the poor old man, their father, making such pitiful dole over them that all the beholders take his part with weeping. 140

Ros. Alas!

Touch. But what is the sport, monsieur, that the ladies have lost?

Le Beau. Why, this that I speak of.

Touch. Thus men may grow wiser every day: it is the first time that ever I heard breaking of ribs was sport for ladies.

Cel. Or I, I promise thee.

Ros. But is there any else longs to see this broken music in his sides? is there yet another dotes upon rib-breaking? Shall we see this wrestling, cousin?

Le Beau. You must, if you stay here; for here is the place appointed for the wrestling, and they are ready to perform it.

Cel. Yonder, sure, they are coming: let us now stay and see it.

Flourish. Enter Duke Frederick, Lords, Orlando, Charles, *and* Attendants.

Duke F. Come on: since the youth will not be entreated, his own peril on his forwardness.

Ros. Is yonder the man? 160

Le Beau. Even he, madam.

Cel. Alas, he is too young! yet he looks successfully.

Duke F. How now, daughter and cousin! are you crept hither to see the wrestling?

Ros. Ay, my liege, so please you give us leave.

Duke F. You will take little delight in it, I can tell you; there is such odds in the man. In pity of the challenger's youth I would fain dissuade him, but he will not be entreated. Speak to him, ladies; see if you can move him.

Cel. Call him hither, good Monsieur Le Beau.

Duke F. Do so: I'll not be by.

Le Beau. Monsieur the challenger, the princesses call for you.

Orl. I attend them with all respect and duty.

Ros. Young man, have you challenged Charles the wrestler? 179

Orl. No, fair princess; he is the general challenger: I come but in, as others do, to try with him the strength of my youth.

Cel. Young gentleman, your spirits are too bold for your years. You have seen cruel proof of this man's strength: if you saw yourself with your eyes or knew yourself with your judgment, the fear of your adventure would counsel you to a more equal enterprise. We pray you, for your own sake, to embrace your own safety and give over this attempt. 190

Ros. Do, young sir; your reputation shall not therefore be misprised: we will make it our suit to the duke that the wrestling might not go forward.

Orl. I beseech you, punish me not with your hard thoughts; wherein I confess me much guilty, to deny so fair and excellent ladies any thing. But let your fair eyes and gentle wishes go with me to my trial : wherein if I be foiled, there is but one shamed that was never gracious; if killed, but one dead that was willing to be so : I shall do my friends no wrong, for I have none to lament me, the world no injury, for in it I have nothing ; only in the world I fill up a place, which may be better supplied when I have made it empty.

Ros. The little strength that I have, I would it were with you.

Cel. And mine, to eke out hers.

Ros. Fare you well : pray heaven I be deceived in you !   210

Cel. Your heart's desires be with you !

Cha. Come, where is this young gallant that is so desirous to lie with his mother earth ?

Orl. Ready, sir ; but his will hath in it a more modest working.

Duke F. You shall try but one fall.

Cha. No, I warrant your grace, you shall not entreat him to a second, that have so mightily persuaded him from a first.   219

Orl. An you mean to mock me after, you should not have mocked me before : but come your ways.

Ros. Now Hercules be thy speed, young man !

Cel. I would I were invisible, to catch the strong fellow by the leg.   [*They wrestle.*

Ros. O excellent young man !

Cel. If I had a thunderbolt in mine eye, I can tell who should down.

                                [*Shout. Charles is thrown.*

Duke F. No more, no more.

Orl. Yes, I beseech your grace : I am not yet well breathed.   230

Duke F. How dost thou, Charles ?

Le Beau. He cannot speak, my lord.

Duke F. Bear him away. What is thy name, young man ?

Orl. Orlando, my liege ; the youngest son of Sir Rowland de Boys.

Duke F. I would thou hadst been son to some man else :

The world esteem'd thy father honorable,
But I did find him still mine enemy :
Thou shouldst have better pleased me with this deed,   240
Hadst thou descended from another house.
But fare thee well ; thou art a gallant youth :
I would thou hadst told me of another father.
                [*Exeunt Duke Fred., train, and Le Beau.*

Cel. Were I my father, coz, would I do this ?

Orl. I am more proud to be Sir Rowland's son,
His youngest son ; and would not change that calling,
To be adopted heir to Frederick.

Ros. My father loved Sir Rowland as his soul,
And all the world was of my father's mind :
Had I before known this young man his son,
I should have given him tears unto entreaties,
Ere he should thus have ventured.   251

Cel.   Gentle cousin,
Let us go thank him and encourage him :
My father's rough and envious disposition

Sticks me at heart. Sir, you have well deserved :
If you do keep your promises in love
But justly, as you have exceeded all promise,
Your mistress shall be happy.

Ros.   Gentleman,
                [*Giving him a chain from her neck.*
Wear this for me, one out of suits with fortune,
That could give more, but that her hand lacks means.
Shall we go, coz ?

Cel.   Ay. Fare you well, fair gentleman.

Orl. Can I not say, I thank you ? My better parts   261
Are all thrown down, and that which here stands up
Is but a quintain, a mere lifeless block.

Ros. He calls us back : my pride fell with my fortunes ;
I'll ask him what he would. Did you call, sir ?
Sir, you have wrestled well and overthrown
More than your enemies.

Cel.   Will you go, coz ?

Ros. Have with you. Fare you well.
                [*Exeunt Rosalind and Celia.*

Orl. What passion hangs these weights upon my tongue ?
I cannot speak to her, yet she urged conference.
O poor Orlando, thou art overthrown !   271
Or Charles or something weaker masters thee.

Re-enter LE BEAU.

Le Beau. Good sir, I do in friendship counsel you
To leave this place. Albeit you have deserved
High commendation, true applause and love,
Yet such is now the duke's condition
That he misconstrues all that you have done.
The duke is humorous ; what he is indeed,
More suits you to conceive than I to speak of.

Orl. I thank you, sir : and, pray you, tell me this ;   280
Which of the two was daughter of the duke
That here was at the wrestling ?

Le Beau. Neither his daughter, if we judge by manners ;
But yet indeed the lesser is his daughter :
The other is daughter to the banish'd duke,
And here detain'd by her usurping uncle,
To keep his daughter company ; whose loves
Are dearer than the natural bond of sisters.
But I can tell you that of late this duke
Hath ta'en displeasure 'gainst his gentle niece,
Grounded upon no other argument   291
But that the people praise her for her virtues
And pity her for her good father's sake ;
And, on my life, his malice 'gainst the lady
Will suddenly break forth. Sir, fare you well :
Hereafter, in a better world than this,
I shall desire more love and knowledge of you.

Orl. I rest much bounden to you : fare you well.   [*Exit Le Beau.*
Thus must I from the smoke into the smother ;
From tyrant duke unto a tyrant brother : 300
But heavenly Rosalind !   [*Exit.*

SCENE III. *A room in the palace.*

Enter CELIA *and* ROSALIND.

Cel. Why, cousin ! why, Rosalind ! Cupid have mercy ! not a word ?

Ros. Not one to throw at a dog.

Cel. No, thy words are too precious to be cast away upon curs; throw some of them at me; come, lame me with reasons.

Ros. Then there were two cousins laid up; when the one should be lamed with reasons and the other mad without any.

Cel. But is all this for your father? 10

Ros. No, some of it is for my child's father. O, how full of briers is this working-day world!

Cel. They are but burs, cousin, thrown upon thee in holiday foolery: if we walk not in the trodden paths, our very petticoats will catch them.

Ros. I could shake them off my coat: these burs are in my heart.

Cel. Hem them away.

Ros. I would try, if I could cry 'hem' and have him. 20

Cel. Come, come, wrestle with thy affections.

Ros. O, they take the part of a better wrestler than myself!

Cel. O, a good wish upon you! you will try in time, in despite of a fall. But, turning these jests out of service, let us talk in good earnest: is it possible, on such a sudden, you should fall into so strong a liking with old Sir Rowland's youngest son?

Ros. The duke my father loved his father dearly. 31

Cel. Doth it therefore ensue that you should love his son dearly? By this kind of chase, I should hate him, for my father hated his father dearly; yet I hate not Orlando.

Ros. No, faith, hate him not, for my sake.

Cel. Why should I not? doth he not deserve well?

Ros. Let me love him for that, and do you love him because I do. Look, here comes the duke. 41

Cel. With his eyes full of anger.

Enter DUKE FREDERICK, *with* Lords.

Duke F. Mistress, dispatch you with your safest haste

And get you from our court.

Ros.   Me, uncle?

Duke F.   You, cousin:

Within these ten days if that thou be'st found So near our public court as twenty miles, Thou diest for it.

Ros.   I do beseech your grace, Let me the knowledge of my fault bear with me:

If with myself I hold intelligence Or have acquaintance with mine own desires, If that I do not dream or be not frantic,— 51 As I do trust I am not—then, dear uncle, Never so much as in a thought unborn Did I offend your highness.

Duke F.   Thus do all traitors: If their purgation did consist in words, They are as innocent as grace itself: Let it suffice thee that I trust thee not.

Ros. Yet your mistrust cannot make me a traitor: Tell me whereon the likelihood depends.

Duke F. Thou art thy father's daughter; there's enough. 60

Ros. So was I when your highness took his dukedom;

So was I when your highness banish'd him: Treason is not inherited, my lord; Or, if we did derive it from our friends, What's that to me? my father was no traitor: Then, good my liege, mistake me not so much To think my poverty is treacherous.

Cel. Dear sovereign, hear me speak.

Duke F. Ay, Celia; we stay'd her for your sake, Else had she with her father ranged along. 70

Cel. I did not then entreat to have her stay; It was your pleasure and your own remorse: I was too young that time to value her; But now I know her: if she be a traitor, Why so am I; we still have slept together, Rose at an instant, learn'd, play'd, eat together, And wheresoe'er we went, like Juno's swans, Still we went coupled and inseparable.

Duke F. She is too subtle for thee; and her smoothness, Her very silence and her patience 80 Speak to the people, and they pity her. Thou art a fool: she robs thee of thy name; And thou wilt show more bright and seem more virtuous When she is gone. Then open not thy lips: Firm and irrevocable is my doom Which I have pass'd upon her; she is banish'd.

Cel. Pronounce that sentence then on me, my liege: I cannot live out of her company.

Duke F. You are a fool. You, niece, provide yourself: If you outstay the time, upon mine honor, 90 And in the greatness of my word, you die.

                    [*Exeunt Duke Frederick and Lords.*

Cel. O my poor Rosalind, whither wilt thou go? Wilt thou change fathers? I will give thee mine. I charge thee, be not thou more grieved than I am.

Ros. I have more cause.

Cel.   Thou hast not, cousin; Prithee, be cheerful: know'st thou not, the duke Hath banish'd me, his daughter?

Ros.   That he hath not.

Cel. No, hath not? Rosalind lacks then the love Which teacheth thee that thou and I am one: Shall we be sunder'd? shall we part, sweet girl? 100 No: let my father seek another heir. Therefore devise with me how we may fly, Whither to go and what to bear with us; And do not seek to take your change upon you, To bear your griefs yourself and leave me out; For, by this heaven, now at our sorrows pale, Say what thou canst, I'll go along with thee.

Ros. Why, whither shall we go?

Cel. To seek my uncle in the forest of Arden. 109

Ros. Alas, what danger will it be to us, Maids as we are, to travel forth so far! Beauty provoketh thieves sooner than gold.

Cel. I'll put myself in poor and mean attire And with a kind of umber smirch my face;

The like do you : so shall we pass along
And never stir assailants.
 Ros.   Were it not better,
Because that I am more than common tall,
That I did suit me all points like a man ?
A gallant curtle-axe upon my thigh,
A boar-spear in my hand ; and—in my heart
Lie there what hidden woman's fear there
 will—   121
We'll have a swashing and a martial outside,
As many other mannish cowards have
That do outface it with their semblances.
 Cel. What shall I call thee when thou art
  a man ?
 Ros. I'll have no worse a name than Jove's
  own page ;
And therefore look you call me Ganymede.
But what will you be call'd ?
 Cel. Something that hath a reference to my
  state
No longer Celia, but Aliena.   130
 Ros. But, cousin, what if we assay'd to
  steal
The clownish fool out of your father's court ?
Would he not be a comfort to our travel ?
 Cel. He'll go along o'er the wide world
  with me ;
Leave me alone to woo him. Let's away,
And get our jewels and our wealth together,
Devise the fittest time and safest way
To hide us from pursuit that will be made
After my flight. Now go we in content
To liberty and not to banishment. 140
           [*Exeunt.*

ACT II.

SCENE I. *The Forest of Arden.*

Enter DUKE senior, AMIENS, *and two or
 three* Lords, *like foresters.*

 Duke S. Now, my co-mates and brothers
  in exile,
Hath not old custom made this life more sweet
Than that of painted pomp ? Are not these
 woods
More free from peril than the envious court ?
Here feel we but the penalty of Adam,
The seasons' difference, as the icy fang
And churlish chiding of the winter's wind,
Which, when it bites and blows upon my body,
Even till I shrink with cold, I smile and say
' This is no flattery : these are counsellors 10
That feelingly persuade me what I am.'
Sweet are the uses of adversity,
Which, like the toad, ugly and venomous,
Wears yet a precious jewel in his head ;
And this our life exempt from public haunt
Finds tongues in trees, books in the running
 brooks,
Sermons in stones and good in every thing.
I would not change it.
 Ami.   Happy is your grace,
That can translate the stubbornness of fortune
Into so quiet and so sweet a style. 20
 Duke S. Come, shall we go and kill us
  venison ?
And yet it irks me the poor dappled fools,
Being native burghers of this desert city,
Should in their own confines with forked heads
Have their round haunches gored.
 First Lord.   Indeed, my lord,

The melancholy Jaques grieves at that,
And, in that kind, swears you do more usurp
Than doth your brother that hath banish'd
 you.
To-day my Lord of Amiens and myself
Did steal behind him as he lay along 30
Under an oak whose antique root peeps out
Upon the brook that brawls along this wood :
To the which place a poor sequester'd stag,
That from the hunter's aim had ta'en a hurt,
Did come to languish, and indeed, my lord,
The wretched animal heaved forth such groans
That their discharge did stretch his leathern
 coat
Almost to bursting, and the big round tears
Coursed one another down his innocent nose
In piteous chase ; and thus the hairy fool, 40
Much marked of the melancholy Jaques,
Stood on the extremest verge of the swift
 brook,
Augmenting it with tears.
 Duke S.   But what said Jaques ?
Did he not moralize this spectacle ?
 First Lord. O, yes, into a thousand similes.
First, for his weeping into the needless stream ;
' Poor deer,' quoth he, ' thou makest a testa-
 ment
As worldlings do, giving thy sum of more
To that which had too much : ' then, being
 there alone,
Left and abandon'd of his velvet friends, 50
' 'Tis right : ' quoth he ; ' thus misery doth part
The flux of company : ' anon a careless herd,
Full of the pasture, jumps along by him
And never stays to greet him ; ' Ay,' quoth
 Jaques,
' Sweep on, you fat and greasy citizens ;
'Tis just the fashion : wherefore do you look
Upon that poor and broken bankrupt there ?'
Thus most invectively he pierceth through
The body of the country, city, court,
Yea, and of this our life, swearing that we 60
Are mere usurpers, tyrants and what's worse,
To fright the animals and to kill them up
In their assign'd and native dwelling-place.
 Duke S. And did you leave him in this
  contemplation ?
 Sec. Lord. We did, my lord, weeping and
  commenting
Upon the sobbing deer.
 Duke S.   Show me the place :
I love to cope him in these sullen fits,
For then he's full of matter.
 First Lord. I'll bring you to him straight.
          [*Exeunt.*

SCENE II. *A room in the palace.*

Enter DUKE FREDERICK, *with* Lords.

 Duke F. Can it be possible that no man
  saw them ?
It cannot be : some villains of my court
Are of consent and sufferance in this.
 First Lord. I cannot hear of any that did
  see her.
The ladies, her attendants of her chamber,
Saw her a-bed, and in the morning early
They found the bed untreasured of their mis-
 tress.
 Sec. Lord. My lord, the roynish clown, at
  whom so oft
Your grace was wont to laugh, is also missing.
Hisperia, the princess' gentlewoman, 10
Confesses that she secretly o'erheard

Your daughter and her cousin much commend
The parts and graces of the wrestler
That did but lately foil the sinewy Charles;
And she believes, wherever they are gone,
That youth is surely in their company.
  Duke F. Send to his brother; fetch that
    gallant hither;
If he be absent, bring his brother to me;
I'll make him find him: do this suddenly,
And let not search and inquisition quail   20
To bring again these foolish runaways.
                          [Exeunt.

     SCENE III. *Before* OLIVER'S *house.*
    Enter ORLANDO *and* ADAM, *meeting.*

  Orl. Who's there?
  Adam. What, my young master? O my
  gentle master!
O my sweet master! O you memory
Of old Sir Rowland! why, what make you
  here?
Why are you virtuous? why do people love
  you?
And wherefore are you gentle, strong and val-
  iant?
Why would you be so fond to overcome
The bonny priser of the humorous duke?
Your praise is come too swiftly home before
  you.
Know you not, master, to some kind of men
Their graces serve them but as enemies?   11
No more do yours: your virtues, gentle mas-
  ter,
Are sanctified and holy traitors to you.
O, what a world is this, when what is comely
Envenoms him that bears it!
  Orl. Why, what's the matter?
  Adam. O unhappy youth!
Come not within these doors; within this roof
The enemy of all your graces lives:
Your brother—no, no brother; yet the son—
Yet not the son, I will not call him son   20
Of him I was about to call his father—
Hath heard your praises, and this night he
  means
To burn the lodging where you use to lie
And you within it: if he fail of that,
He will have other means to cut you off.
I overheard him and his practices.
This is no place; this house is but a butchery:
Abhor it, fear it, do not enter it.
  Orl. Why, whither, Adam, wouldst thou
  have me go?
  Adam. No matter whither, so you come
  not here.   30
  Orl. What, wouldst thou have me go and
  beg my food?
Or with a base and boisterous sword enforce
A thievish living on the common road?
This I must do, or know not what to do:
Yet this I will not do, do how I can;
I rather will subject me to the malice
Of a diverted blood and bloody brother.
  Adam. But do not so. I have five hundred
  crowns,
The thrifty hire I saved under your father,
Which I did store to be my foster-nurse   40
When service should in my old limbs lie lame
And unregarded age in corners thrown:
Take that, and He that doth the ravens feed,
Yea, providently caters for the sparrow,
Be comfort to my age! Here is the gold;

And all this I give you. Let me be your serv-
  ant:
Though I look old, yet I am strong and lusty;
For in my youth I never did apply
Hot and rebellious liquors in my blood,
Nor did not with unbashful forehead woo 50
The means of weakness and debility;
Therefore my age is as a lusty winter,
Frosty, but kindly: let me go with you;
I'll do the service of a younger man
In all your business and necessities.
  Orl. O good old man, how well in thee
  appears
The constant service of the antique world,
When service sweat for duty, not for meed!
Thou art not for the fashion of these times,
Where none will sweat but for promotion, 60
And having that, do choke their service up
Even with the having: it is not so with thee.
But, poor old man, thou prunest a rotten tree,
That cannot so much as a blossom yield
In lieu of all thy pains and husbandry
But come thy ways; we'll go along together,
And ere we have thy youthful wages spent,
We'll light upon some settled low content.
  Adam. Master, go on, and I will follow
  thee,
To the last gasp, with truth and loyalty.   70
From seventeen years till now almost four-
  score
Here lived I, but now live here no more.
At seventeen years many their fortunes seek;
But at fourscore it is too late a week:
Yet fortune cannot recompense me better
Than to die well and not my master's debtor.
                          [Exeunt.

     SCENE IV. *The Forest of Arden.*
  Enter ROSALIND *for* GANYMEDE, CELIA *for*
     ALIENA, *and* TOUCHSTONE.

  Ros. O Jupiter, how weary are my spirits!
  Touch. I care not for my spirits, if my legs
were not weary.
  Ros. I could find in my heart to disgrace
my man's apparel and to cry like a woman;
but I must comfort the weaker vessel, as
doublet and hose ought to show itself courageous to petticoat: therefore courage, good
Aliena!
  Cel. I pray you, bear with me; I cannot
go no further.   10
  Touch. For my part, I had rather bear
with you than bear you; yet I should bear no
cross if I did bear you, for I think you have
no money in your purse.
  Ros. Well, this is the forest of Arden.
  Touch. Ay, now am I in Arden; the more
fool I; when I was at home, I was in a better
place: but travellers must be content.
  Ros. Ay, be so, good Touchstone.

     Enter CORIN *and* SILVIUS.

Look you, who comes here; a young man and
an old in solemn talk.   21
  Cor. That is the way to make her scorn
  you still.
  Sil. O Corin, that thou knew'st how I do
  love her!
  Cor. I partly guess; for I have loved ere
  now.
  Sil. No, Corin, being old, thou canst not
  guess,
Though in thy youth thou wast as true a lover

As ever sigh'd upon a midnight pillow :
But if thy love were ever like to mine—
As sure I think did never man love so—
How many actions most ridiculous   30
Hast thou been drawn to by thy fantasy ?
  Cor. Into a thousand that I have forgotten.
  Sil. O, thou didst then ne'er love so
    heartily !
If thou remember'st not the slightest folly
That ever love did make thee run into,
Thou hast not loved :
Or if thou hast not sat as I do now,
Wearying thy hearer in thy mistress' praise,
Thou hast not loved :
Or if thou hast not broke from company   40
Abruptly, as my passion now makes me,
Thou hast not loved.
O Phebe, Phebe, Phebe !   [*Exit.*
  Ros. Alas, poor shepherd ! searching of
    thy wound,
I have by hard adventure found mine own.
  Touch. And I mine. I remember, when I
was in love I broke my sword upon a stone
and bid him take that for coming a-night to
Jane Smile ; and I remember the kissing of
her batlet and the cow's dugs that her pretty
chopt hands had milked ; and I remember the
wooing of a peascod instead of her, from
whom I took two cods and, giving her them
again, said with weeping tears ' Wear these for
my sake.' We that are true lovers run into
strange capers ; but as all is mortal in nature,
so is all nature in love mortal in folly.
  Ros. Thou speakest wiser than thou art
    ware of.
  Touch. Nay, I shall ne'er be ware of mine
own wit till I break my shins against it.   60
  Ros. Jove, Jove ! this shepherd's passion
    Is much upon my fashion.
  Touch. And mine ; but it grows something
    stale with me.
  Cel. I pray you, one of you question yond
    man
If he for gold will give us any food :
I faint almost to death.
  Touch.   Holla, you clown !
  Ros. Peace, fool : he's not thy kinsman.
  Cor.   Who calls ?
  Touch. Your betters, sir.
  Cor.   Else are they very wretched.
  Ros. Peace, I say. Good even to you,
    friend.
  Cor. And to you, gentle sir, and to you all.
  Ros. I prithee, shepherd, if that love or
    gold
Can in this desert place buy entertainment,
Bring us where we may rest ourselves and
    feed :
Here's a young maid with travel much op-
    press'd
And faints for succor.
  Cor.   Fair sir, I pity her
And wish, for her sake more than for mine
    own,
My fortunes were more able to relieve her ;
But I am shepherd to another man
And do not shear the fleeces that I graze :
My master is of churlish disposition   80
And little recks to find the way to heaven
By doing deeds of hospitality :
Besides, his cote, his flocks and bounds of feed
Are now on sale, and at our sheepcote now,
By reason of his absence, there is nothing

That you will feed on ; but what is, come see,
And in my voice most welcome shall you be.
  Ros. What is he that shall buy his flock
    and pasture ?
  Cor. That young swain that you saw here
    but erewhile,
That little cares for buying any thing.   90
  Ros. I pray thee, if it stand with honesty,
Buy thou the cottage, pasture and the flock,
And thou shalt have to pay for it of us.
  Cel. And we will mend thy wages. I like
    this place,
And willingly could waste my time in it.
  Cor. Assuredly the thing is to be sold :
Go with me : if you like upon report
The soil, the profit and this kind of life,
I will your very faithful feeder be
And buy it with your gold right suddenly. 100
                              [*Exeunt.*

SCENE V. *The Forest.*

Enter AMIENS, JAQUES, *and others.*

SONG.

  Ami.   Under the greenwood tree
          Who loves to lie with me,
          And turn his merry note
          Unto the sweet bird's throat,
      Come hither, come hither, come hither :
              Here shall he see
              No enemy
      But winter and rough weather.
  Jaq. More, more, I prithee, more.
  Ami. It will make you melancholy, Monsieur Jaques.
  Jaq. I thank it. More, I prithee, more. I
can suck melancholy out of a song, as a weasel
sucks eggs. More, I prithee, more.
  Ami. My voice is ragged : I know I cannot
please you.
  Jaq. I do not desire you to please me ; I
do desire you to sing. Come, more ; another
stanzo : call you 'em stanzos ?
  Ami. What you will, Monsieur Jaques.   20
  Jaq. Nay, I care not for their names ; they
owe me nothing. Will you sing ?
  Ami. More at your request than to please
myself.
  Jaq. Well then, if ever I thank any man,
I'll thank you ; but that they call compliment
is like the encounter of two dog-apes, and
when a man thanks me heartily, methinks I
have given him a penny and he renders me
the beggarly thanks. Come, sing ; and you that
will not, hold your tongues.
  Ami. Well, I'll end the song. Sirs, cover
the while ; the duke will drink under this tree.
He hath been all this day to look you.
  Jaq. And I have been all this day to avoid
him. He is too disputable for my company :
I think of as many matters as he, but I give
heaven thanks and make no boast of them.
Come, warble, come.

SONG.

      Who doth ambition shun   40
                      [*All together here.*
          And loves to live i' the sun,
          Seeking the food he eats
          And pleased with what he gets,
      Come hither, come hither, come hither :
              Here shall he see
              No enemy
      But winter and rough weather.

Jaq. I'll give you a verse to this note that I made yesterday in despite of my invention.
Ami. And I'll sing it.   50
Jaq. Thus it goes :—

If it do come to pass
That any man turn ass,
Leaving his wealth and ease,
A stubborn will to please,
Ducdame, ducdame, ducdame :
　Here shall he see
　Gross fools as he,
An if he will come to me.

Ami. What's that ' ducdame ' ?   60
Jaq. 'Tis a Greek invocation, to call fools into a circle. I'll go sleep, if I can ; if I cannot, I'll rail against all the first-born of Egypt.
Ami. And I'll go seek the duke : his banquet is prepared.   [*Exeunt severally.*

SCENE VI. *The forest.*
Enter ORLANDO and ADAM.

Adam. Dear master, I can go no further : O, I die for food ! Here lie I down, and measure out my grave. Farewell, kind master.
Orl. Why, how now, Adam ! no greater heart in thee ? Live a little ; comfort a little ; cheer thyself a little. If this uncouth forest yield any thing savage, I will either be food for it or bring it for food to thee. Thy conceit is nearer death than thy powers. For my sake be comfortable ; hold death awhile at the arm's end : I will here be with thee presently ; and if I bring thee not something to eat, I will give thee leave to die : but if thou diest before I come, thou art a mocker of my labor. Well said ! thou lookest cheerly, and I'll be with thee quickly. Yet thou liest in the bleak air : come, I will bear thee to some shelter ; and thou shalt not die for lack of a dinner, if there live any thing in this desert. Cheerly, good Adam !   [*Exeunt.*

SCENE VII. *The forest.*
A table set out. Enter DUKE senior, AMIENS, *and* Lords *like* outlaws.

Duke S. I think he be transform'd into a beast ;
For I can no where find him like a man.
First Lord. My lord, he is but even now gone hence :
Here was he merry, hearing of a song.
Duke S. If he, compact of jars, grow musical,
We shall have shortly discord in the spheres.
Go, seek him : tell him I would speak with him.

Enter JAQUES.

First Lord. He saves my labor by his own approach.
Duke S. Why, how now, monsieur ! what a life is this,
That your poor friends must woo your company ?   10
What, you look merrily !
Jaq. A fool, a fool ! I met a fool i' the forest,
A motley fool ; a miserable world !
As I do live by food, I met a fool ;
Who laid him down and bask'd him in the sun,
And rail'd on Lady Fortune in good terms,
In good set terms and yet a motley fool.

' Good morrow, fool,' quoth I. ' No, sir,' quoth he,
' Call me not fool till heaven hath sent me fortune : '
And then he drew a dial from his poke,   20
And, looking on it with lack-lustre eye,
Says very wisely, ' It is ten o'clock :
Thus we may see,' quoth he, ' how the world wags :
'Tis but an hour ago since it was nine,
And after one hour more 'twill be eleven ;
And so, from hour to hour, we ripe and ripe,
And then, from hour to hour, we rot and rot ;
And thereby hangs a tale.' When I did hear
The motley fool thus moral on the time,
My lungs began to crow like chanticleer,   30
That fools should be so deep-contemplative,
And I did laugh sans intermission
An hour by his dial. O noble fool !
A worthy fool ! Motley's the only wear.
Duke S. What fool is this ?
Jaq. O worthy fool ! One that hath been a courtier,
And says, if ladies be but young and fair,
They have the gift to know it : and in his brain,
Which is as dry as the remainder biscuit
After a voyage, he hath strange places cramm'd   40
With observation, the which he vents
In mangled forms. O that I were a fool !
I am ambitious for a motley coat.
Duke S. Thou shalt have one.
Jaq. 　　　　　　It is my only suit ;
Provided that you weed your better judgments
Of all opinion that grows rank in them
That I am wise. I must have liberty
Withal, as large a charter as the wind,
To blow on whom I please ; for so fools have ;
And they that are most galled with my folly,
They most must laugh. And why, sir, must they so ?   51
The ' why ' is plain as way to parish church :
He that a fool doth very wisely hit
Doth very foolishly, although he smart,
Not to seem senseless of the bob : if not,
The wise man's folly is anatomized
Even by the squandering glances of the fool.
Invest me in my motley ; give me leave
To speak my mind, and I will through and through
Cleanse the foul body of the infected world,
If they will patiently receive my medicine.   61
Duke S. Fie on thee ! I can tell what thou wouldst do.
Jaq. What, for a counter, would I do but good ?
Duke S. Most mischievous foul sin, in chiding sin :
For thou thyself hast been a libertine,
As sensual as the brutish sting itself ;
And all the embossed sores and headed evils,
That thou with license of free foot hast caught,
Wouldst thou disgorge into the general world.
Jaq. Why, who cries out on pride,   70
That can therein tax any private party ?
Doth it not flow as hugely as the sea,
Till that the weary very means do ebb ?
What woman in the city do I name,
When that I say the city-woman bears
The cost of princes on unworthy shoulders ?
Who can come in and say that I mean her,
When such a one as she such is her neighbor ?

Or what is he of basest function
That says his bravery is not of my cost,   80
Thinking that I mean him, but therein suits
His folly to the mettle of my speech?
There then; how then? what then? Let me
        see wherein
My tongue hath wrong'd him: if it do him
        right,
Then he hath wrong'd himself; if he be free,
Why then my taxing like a wild-goose flies,
Unclaim'd of any man. But who comes here?

Enter ORLANDO, *with his sword drawn.*

Orl. Forbear, and eat no more.
Jaq.   Why, I have eat none yet.
Orl. Nor shalt not, till necessity be served.
Jaq. Of what kind should this cock come
        of?   90
Duke S. Art thou thus bolden'd, man, by
        thy distress,
Or else a rude despiser of good manners,
That in civility thou seem'st so empty?
Orl. You touch'd my vein at first: the
        thorny point
Of bare distress hath ta'en from me the show
Of smooth civility: yet am I inland bred
And know some nurture. But forbear, I say:
He dies that touches any of this fruit
Till I and my affairs are answered.
Jaq. An you will not be answered with
reason, I must die.   101
Duke S. What would you have? Your
        gentleness shall force
More than your force move us to gentleness.
Orl. I almost die for food; and let me
        have it.
Duke. S. Sit down and feed, and welcome
        to our table.
Orl. Speak you so gently? Pardon me, I
        pray you:
I thought that all things had been savage
        here;
And therefore put I on the countenance
Of stern commandment. But whate'er you are
That in this desert inaccessible,   110
Under the shade of melancholy boughs,
Lose and neglect the creeping hours of time;
If ever you have look'd on better days,
If ever been where bells have knoll'd to
        church,
If ever sat at any good man's feast,
If ever from your eyelids wiped a tear
And know what 'tis to pity and be pitied,
Let gentleness my strong enforcement be:
In the which hope I blush, and hide my
        sword.
Duke S. True is it that we have seen
        better days,   120
And have with holy bell been knoll'd to
        church
And sat at good men's feasts and wiped our
        eyes
Of drops that sacred pity hath engender'd:
And therefore sit you down in gentleness
And take upon command what help we have
That to your wanting may be minister'd.
Orl. Then but forbear your food a little
        while,
Whiles, like a doe, I go to find my fawn
And give it food. There is an old poor man,
Who after me hath many a weary step   130
Limp'd in pure love: till he be first sufficed,

Oppress'd with two weak evils, age and
        hunger,
I will not touch a bit.
Duke S.   Go find him out,
And we will nothing waste till you return.
Orl. I thank ye; and be blest for your
        good comfort!   [*Exit.*
Duke S. Thou seest we are not all alone
        unhappy:
This wide and universal theatre
Presents more woeful pageants than the scene
Wherein we play in.
Jaq.   All the world's a stage,
And all the men and women merely players:
They have their exits and their entrances;
And one man in his time plays many parts,
His acts being seven ages. At first the infant,
Mewling and puking in the nurse's arms.
And then the whining school-boy, with his
        satchel
And shining morning face, creeping like snail
Unwillingly to school. And then the lover,
Sighing like furnace, with a woeful ballad
Made to his mistress' eyebrow. Then a soldier,
Full of strange oaths and bearded like the
        pard,   150
Jealous in honor, sudden and quick in quarrel,
Seeking the bubble reputation
Even in the cannon's mouth. And then the
        justice,
In fair round belly with good capon lined,
With eyes severe and beard of formal cut,
Full of wise saws and modern instances;
And so he plays his part. The sixth age shifts
Into the lean and slipper'd pantaloon,
With spectacles on nose and pouch on side,
His youthful hose, well saved, a world too
        wide   160
For his shrunk shank; and his big manly
        voice,
Turning again toward childish treble, pipes
And whistles in his sound. Last scene of all,
That ends this strange eventful history,
Is second childishness and mere oblivion,
Sans teeth, sans eyes, sans taste, sans every
        thing.

Re-enter ORLANDO, *with* ADAM.

Duke S. Welcome. Set down your vener-
        able burthen,
And let him feed.
Orl. I thank you most for him.
Adam.   So had you need:
I scarce can speak to thank you for myself.
Duke S. Welcome; fall to: I will not
        trouble you   171
As yet, to question you about your fortunes.
Give us some music; and, good cousin, sing.

        SONG.

Ami. Blow, blow, thou winter wind.
        Thou art not so unkind
                As man's ingratitude;
        Thy tooth is not so keen,
        Because thou art not seen,
                Although thy breath be rude.
Heigh-ho! sing, heigh-ho! unto the green
        holly: 180
Most friendship is feigning, most loving mere
        folly:
        Then, heigh-ho, the holly!
                This life is most jolly.
        Freeze, freeze, thou bitter sky,
        That dost not bite so nigh

As benefits forgot :
        Though thou the waters warp,
        Thy sting is not so sharp
            As friend remember'd not.
Heigh-ho ! sing, &c.   190
    Duke S. If that you were the good Sir
        Rowland's son,
As you have whisper'd faithfully you were,
And as mine eye doth his effigies witness
Most truly limn'd and living in your face,
Be truly welcome hither : I am the duke
That loved your father : the residue of your
        fortune,
Go to my cave and tell me. Good old man,
Thou art right welcome as thy master is.
Support him by the arm. Give me your hand,
And let me all your fortunes understand.
                                        [*Exeunt.*

ACT III.

SCENE I. *A room in the palace.*

Enter DUKE FREDERICK, Lords, *and* OLIVER.

    Duke F. Not see him since ? Sir, sir, that
        cannot be :
But were I not the better part made mercy,
I should not seek an absent argument
Of my revenge, thou present. But look to it :
Find out thy brother, wheresoe'er he is ;
Seek him with candle ; bring him dead or
        living
Within this twelvemonth, or turn thou no
        more
To seek a living in our territory.
Thy lands and all things that thou dost call
        thine
Worth seizure do we seize into our hands, 10
Till thou canst quit thee by thy brother's
        mouth
Of what we think against thee.
    Oli. O that your highness knew my heart
        in this !
I never loved my brother in my life.
    Duke F. More villain thou. Well, push
        him out of doors ;
And let my officers of such a nature
Make an extent upon his house and lands :
Do this expediently and turn him going.
                                        [*Exeunt.*

SCENE II. *The forest.*

Enter ORLANDO, *with a paper.*

    Orl. Hang there, my verse, in witness of
        my love :
    And thou, thrice-crowned queen of night,
        survey
    With thy chaste eye, from thy pale sphere
        above,
        Thy huntress' name that my full life doth
        sway.
    O Rosalind ! these trees shall be my books
    And in their barks my thoughts I'll charac-
        ter ;
That every eye which in this forest looks
Shall see thy virtue witness'd every where.
Run, run, Orlando ; carve on every tree
The fair, the chaste and unexpressive she.
                                          [*Exit.*

Enter CORIN *and* TOUCHSTONE.

    Cor. And how like you this shepherd's life,
Master Touchstone ?

    Touch. Truly, shepherd, in respect of it-
self, it is a good life ; but in respect that it is
a shepherd's life, it is naught. In respect that
it is solitary, I like it very well ; but in respect that it is private, it is a very vile life.
Now, in respect it is in the fields, it pleaseth
me well ; but in respect it is not in the court,
it is tedious. As it is a spare life, look you, it
fits my humor well ; but as there is no more
plenty in it, it goes much against my stomach.
Hast any philosophy in thee, shepherd ?
    Cor. No more but that I know the more
one sickens the worse at ease he is ; and that
he that wants money, means and content is
without three good friends ; that the property
of rain is to wet and fire to burn ; that good
pasture makes fat sheep, and that a great
cause of the night is lack of the sun ; that he
that hath learned no wit by nature nor art
may complain of good breeding or comes of a
very dull kindred.
    Touch. Such a one is a natural philoso-
pher. Wast ever in court, shepherd ?
    Cor. No, truly.
    Touch. Then thou art damned.
    Cor. Nay, I hope.
    Touch. Truly, thou art damned like an ill-
roasted egg, all on one side.   39
    Cor. For not being at court ? Your reason.
    Touch. Why, if thou never wast at court,
thou never sawest good manners ; if thou never
sawest good manners, then thy manners must
be wicked ; and wickedness is sin, and sin is
damnation. Thou art in a parlous state, shepherd.
    Cor. Not a whit, Touchstone : those that
are good manners at the court are as ridiculous in the country as the behavior of the
country is most mockable at the court. You
told me you salute not at the court, but you
kiss your hands : that courtesy would be uncleanly, if courtiers were shepherds.
    Touch. Instance, briefly ; come, instance.
    Cor. Why, we are still handling our ewes,
and their fells, you know, are greasy.
    Touch. Why, do not your courtier's hands
sweat ? and is not the grease of a mutton as
wholesome as the sweat of a man ? Shallow,
shallow. A better instance, I say ; come.
    Cor. Besides, our hands are hard.   60
    Touch. Your lips will feel them the sooner.
Shallow again. A more sounder instance,
come.
    Cor. And they are often tarred over with
the surgery of our sheep : and would you have
us kiss tar ? The courtier's hands are perfumed with civet.
    Touch. Most shallow man ! thou worms-
meat, in respect of a good piece of flesh indeed ! Learn of the wise, and perpend : civet
is of a baser birth than tar, the very uncleanly
flux of a cat. Mend the instance, shepherd.
    Cor. You have too courtly a wit for me :
I'll rest.
    Touch. Wilt thou rest damned ? God help
thee, shallow man ! God make incision in
thee ! thou art raw.
    Cor. Sir, I am a true laborer : I earn that
I eat, get that I wear, owe no man hate, envy
no man's happiness, glad of other men's good,
content with my harm, and the greatest of
my pride is to see my ewes graze and my
lambs suck.

Touch. That is another simple sin in you, to bring the ewes and the rams together and to offer to get your living by the copulation of cattle; to be bawd to a bell-wether, and to betray a she-lamb of a twelvemonth to a crooked-pated, old, cuckoldly ram, out of all reasonable match. If thou beest not damned for this, the devil himself will have no shepherds; I cannot see else how thou shouldst 'scape.   90

Cor. Here comes young Master Ganymede, my new mistress's brother.

Enter ROSALIND, *with a paper, reading.*

Ros. From the east to western Ind,
        No jewel is like Rosalind.
        Her worth, being mounted on the wind,
        Through all the world bears Rosalind.
        All the pictures fairest lined
        Are but black to Rosalind.
        Let no fair be kept in mind
        But the fair of Rosalind.   100

Touch. I'll rhyme you so eight years together, dinners and suppers and sleeping-hours excepted: it is the right butter-women's rank to market.

Ros. Out, fool!

Touch. For a taste:
        If a hart do lack a hind,
        Let him seek out Rosalind.
        If the cat will after kind,
        So be sure will Rosalind.   110
        Winter garments must be lined,
        So must slender Rosalind.
        They that reap must sheaf and bind;
        Then to cart with Rosalind.
        Sweetest nut hath sourest rind,
        Such a nut is Rosalind.
        He that sweetest rose will find
        Must find love's prick and Rosalind.
This is the very false gallop of verses: why do you infect yourself with them?   120

Ros. Peace, you dull fool! I found them on a tree.

Touch. Truly, the tree yields bad fruit.

Ros. I'll graff it with you, and then I shall graff it with a medlar: then it will be the earliest fruit i' the country; for you'll be rotten ere you be half ripe, and that's the right virtue of the medlar.

Touch. You have said; but whether wisely or no, let the forest judge.   130

Enter CELIA, *with a writing.*

Ros. Peace!
Here comes my sister, reading: stand aside.

Cel. [*Reads*]
        Why should this a desert be?
        For it is unpeopled? No:
        Tongues I'll hang on every tree,
        That shall civil sayings show:
        Some, how brief the life of man
        Runs his erring pilgrimage,
        That the stretching of a span
        Buckles in his sum of age;   140
        Some, of violated vows
        'Twixt the souls of friend and friend:
        But upon the fairest boughs,
        Or at every sentence end,
        Will I Rosalinda write,
        Teaching all that read to know
        The quintessence of every sprite

        Heaven would in little show.
        Therefore Heaven Nature charged
        That one body should be fill'd   150
        With all graces wide-enlarged:
        Nature presently distill'd
        Helen's cheek, but not her heart,
        Cleopatra's majesty,
        Atalanta's better part,
        Sad Lucretia's modesty.
        Thus Rosalind of many parts
        By heavenly synod was devised,
        Of many faces, eyes and hearts,
        To have the touches dearest prized.
        Heaven would that she these gifts should have,   161
        And I to live and die her slave.

Ros. O most gentle pulpiter! what tedious homily of love have you wearied your parishioners withal, and never cried 'Have patience, good people!'

Cel. How now! back, friends! Shepherd, go off a little. Go with him, sirrah.

Touch. Come, shepherd, let us make an honorable retreat; though not with bag and baggage, yet with scrip and scrippage.   171
[*Exeunt Corin and Touchstone.*

Cel. Didst thou hear these verses?

Ros. O, yes, I heard them all, and more too; for some of them had in them more feet than the verses would bear.

Cel. That's no matter: the feet might bear the verses.

Ros. Ay, but the feet were lame and could not bear themselves without the verse and therefore stood lamely in the verse.   180

Cel. But didst thou hear without wondering how thy name should be hanged and carved upon these trees?

Ros. I was seven of the nine days out of the wonder before you came; for look here what I found on a palm-tree. I was never so be-rhymed since Pythagoras' time, that I was an Irish rat, which I can hardly remember.

Cel. Trow you who hath done this?

Ros. Is it a man?   190

Cel. And a chain, that you once wore, about his neck. Change you color?

Ros. I prithee, who?

Cel. O Lord, Lord! it is a hard matter for friends to meet; but mountains may be removed with earthquakes and so encounter.

Ros. Nay, but who is it?

Cel. Is it possible?

Ros. Nay, I prithee now with most petitionary vehemence, tell me who it is.   200

Cel. O wonderful, wonderful, and most wonderful wonderful! and yet again wonderful, and after that, out of all hooping!

Ros. Good my complexion! dost thou think, though I am caparisoned like a man, I have a doublet and hose in my disposition? One inch of delay more is a South-sea of discovery; I prithee, tell me who is it quickly, and speak apace. I would thou couldst stammer, that thou mightst pour this concealed man out of thy mouth, as wine comes out of a narrow-mouthed bottle, either too much at once, or none at all. I prithee, take the cork out of thy mouth that I may drink thy tidings.

Cel. So you may put a man in your belly.

Ros. Is he of God's making? What manner of man? Is his head worth a hat, or his chin worth a beard?

Cel. Nay, he hath but a little beard.

Ros. Why, God will send more, if the man will be thankful : let me stay the growth of his beard, if thou delay me not the knowledge of his chin.

Cel. It is young Orlando, that tripped up the wrestler's heels and your heart both in an instant.

Ros. Nay, but the devil take mocking : speak, sad brow and true maid.

Cel. I' faith, coz, 'tis he.

Ros. Orlando ?

Cel. Orlando.   230

Ros. Alas the day ! what shall I do with my doublet and hose ? What did he when thou sawest him ? What said he ? How looked he ? Wherein went he ? What makes him here ? Did he ask for me ? Where remains he ? How parted he with thee ? and when shalt thou see him again ? Answer me in one word.

Cel. You must borrow me Gargantua's mouth first : 'tis a word too great for any mouth of this age's size. To say ay and no to these particulars is more than to answer in a catechism.   241

Ros. But doth he know that I am in this forest and in man's apparel ? Looks he as freshly as he did the day he wrestled ?

Cel. It is as easy to count atomies as to resolve the propositions of a lover ; but take a taste of my finding him, and relish it with good observance. I found him under a tree, like a dropped acorn.

Ros. It may well be called Jove's tree, when it drops forth such fruit.   250

Cel. Give me audience, good madam.

Ros. Proceed.

Cel. There lay he, stretched along, like a wounded knight.

Ros. Though it be pity to see such a sight, it well becomes the ground.

Cel. Cry ' holla ' to thy tongue, I prithee ; it curvets unseasonably. He was furnished like a hunter.   259

Ros. O, ominous ! he comes to kill my heart.

Cel. I would sing my song without a burden : thou bringest me out of tune.

Ros. Do you not know I am a woman ? when I think, I must speak. Sweet, say on.

Cel. You bring me out. Soft ! comes he not here ?

Enter ORLANDO *and* JAQUES.

Ros. 'Tis he : slink by, and note him.

Jaq. I thank you for your company ; but, good faith, I had as lief have been myself alone.   270

Orl. And so had I ; but yet, for fashion sake, I thank you too for your society.

Jaq. God be wi' you : let's meet as little as we can.

Orl. I do desire we may be better strangers.

Jaq. I pray you, mar no more trees with writing love-songs in their barks.

Orl. I pray you, mar no more of my verses with reading them ill-favoredly.

Jaq. Rosalind is your love's name ? 280

Orl. Yes, just.

Jaq. I do not like her name.

Orl. There was no thought of pleasing you when she was christened.

Jaq. What stature is she of ?

Orl. Just as high as my heart.

Jaq. You are full of pretty answers. Have you not been acquainted with goldsmiths' wives, and conned them out of rings ? 289

Orl. Not so ; but I answer you right painted cloth, from whence you have studied your questions.

Jaq. You have a nimble wit : I think 'twas made of Atalanta's heels. Will you sit down with me ? and we two will rail against our mistress the world and all our misery.

Orl. I will chide no breather in the world but myself, against whom I know most faults.

Jaq. The worst fault you have is to be in love.   300

Orl. 'Tis a fault I will not change for your best virtue. I am weary of you.

Jaq. By my troth, I was seeking for a fool when I found you.

Orl. He is drowned in the brook : look but in, and you shall see him.

Jaq. There I shall see mine own figure.

Orl. Which I take to be either a fool or a cipher.

Jaq. I'll tarry no longer with you : farewell, good Signior Love.   310

Orl. I am glad of your departure : adieu, good Monsieur Melancholy. [*Exit Jaques.*

Ros. [*Aside to Celia*] I will speak to him, like a saucy lackey and under that habit play the knave with him. Do you hear, forester ?

Orl. Very well : what would you ?

Ros. I pray you, what is't o'clock ?

Orl. You should ask me what time o' day : there's no clock in the forest.   319

Ros. Then there is no true lover in the forest ; else sighing every minute and groaning every hour would detect the lazy foot of Time as well as a clock.

Orl. And why not the swift foot of Time ? had not that been as proper ?

Ros. By no means, sir : Time travels in divers paces with divers persons. I'll tell you who Time ambles withal, who Time trots withal, who Time gallops withal and who he stands still withal.

Orl. I prithee, who doth he trot withal ?

Ros. Marry, he trots hard with a young maid between the contract of her marriage and the day it is solemnized : if the interim be but a se'nnight, Time's pace is so hard that it seems the length of seven year.

Orl. Who ambles Time withal ?

Ros. With a priest that lacks Latin and a rich man that hath not the gout, for the one sleeps easily because he cannot study, and the other lives merrily because he feels no pain, the one lacking the burden of lean and wasteful learning, the other knowing no burden of heavy tedious penury ; these Time ambles withal.

Orl. Who doth he gallop withal ?

Ros. With a thief to the gallows, for though he go as softly as foot can fall, he thinks himself too soon there.

Orl. Who stays it still withal ?

Ros. With lawyers in the vacation, for they sleep between term and term and then they perceive not how Time moves. 351

Orl. Where dwell you, pretty youth ?

Ros. With this shepherdess, my sister ;

here in the skirts of the forest, like fringe upon a petticoat.

Orl. Are you native of this place?

Ros. As the cony that you see dwell where she is kindled. 359

Orl. Your accent is something finer than you could purchase in so removed a dwelling.

Ros. I have been told so of many: but indeed an old religious uncle of mine taught me to speak, who was in his youth an inland man; one that knew courtship too well, for there he fell in love. I have heard him read many lectures against it, and I thank God I am not a woman, to be touched with so many giddy offences as he hath generally taxed their whole sex withal.

Orl. Can you remember any of the principal evils that he laid to the charge of women? 370

Ros. There were none principal; they were all like one another as half-pence are, every one fault seeming monstrous till his fellow fault came to match it.

Orl. I prithee, recount some of them.

Ros. No, I will not cast away my physic but on those that are sick. There is a man haunts the forest, that abuses our young plants with carving 'Rosalind' on their barks; hangs odes upon hawthorns and elegies on brambles, all, forsooth, deifying the name of Rosalind: if I could meet that fancy-monger, I would give him some good counsel, for he seems to have the quotidian of love upon him.

Orl. I am he that is so love-shaked: I pray you tell me your remedy.

Ros. There is none of my uncle's marks upon you: he taught me how to know a man in love; in which cage of rushes I am sure you are not prisoner. 390

Orl. What were his marks?

Ros. A lean cheek, which you have not, a blue eye and sunken, which you have not, an unquestionable spirit, which you have not, a beard neglected, which you have not; but I pardon you for that, for simply your having in beard is a younger brother's revenue: then your hose should be ungartered, your bonnet unbanded, your sleeve unbuttoned, your shoe untied and every thing about you demonstrating a careless desolation; but you are no such man; you are rather point-device in your accoutrements as loving yourself than seeming the lover of any other.

Orl. Fair youth, I would I could make thee believe I love.

Ros. Me believe it! you may as soon make her that you love believe it; which, I warrant, she is apter to do than to confess she does: that is one of the points in the which women still give the lie to their consciences. But, in good sooth, are you he that hangs the verses on the trees, wherein Rosalind is so admired?

Orl. I swear to thee, youth, by the white hand of Rosalind, I am that he, that unfortunate he.

Ros. But are you so much in love as your rhymes speak?

Orl. Neither rhyme nor reason can express how much. 419

Ros. Love is merely a madness, and, I tell you, deserves as well a dark house and a whip as madmen do: and the reason why they are not so punished and cured is, that the lunacy is so ordinary that the whippers are in love too. Yet I profess curing it by counsel.

Orl. Did you ever cure any so?

Ros. Yes, one, and in this manner. He was to imagine me his love, his mistress; and I set him every day to woo me: at which time would I, being but a moonish youth, grieve, be effeminate, changeable, longing and liking, proud, fantastical, apish, shallow, inconstant, full of tears, full of smiles, for every passion something and for no passion truly any thing, as boys and women are for the most part cattle of this color; would now like him, now loathe him; then entertain him, then forswear him; now weep for him, then spit at him; that I drave my suitor from his mad humor of love to a living humor of madness; which was, to forswear the full stream of the world, and to live in a nook merely monastic. And thus I cured him; and this way will I take upon me to wash your liver as clean as a sound sheep's heart, that there shall not be one spot of love in't.

Orl. I would not be cured, youth.

Ros. I would cure you, if you would but call me Rosalind and come every day to my cote and woo me.

Orl. Now, by the faith of my love, I will: tell me where it is. 450

Ros. Go with me to it and I'll show it you: and by the way you shall tell me where in the forest you live. Will you go?

Orl. With all my heart, good youth.

Ros. Nay, you must call me Rosalind. Come, sister, will you go? [*Exeunt.*

SCENE III. *The forest.*

Enter TOUCHSTONE *and* AUDREY; JAQUES *behind.*

Touch. Come apace, good Audrey: I will fetch up your goats, Audrey. And how, Audrey? am I the man yet? doth my simple feature content you?

Aud. Your features! Lord warrant us! what features!

Touch. I am here with thee and thy goats, as the most capricious poet, honest Ovid, was among the Goths.

Jaq. [*Aside*] O knowledge ill-inhabited, worse than Jove in a thatched house! 11

Touch. When a man's verses cannot be understood, nor a man's good wit seconded with the forward child Understanding, it strikes a man more dead than a great reckoning in a little room. Truly, I would the gods had made thee poetical.

Aud. I do not know what 'poetical' is: is it honest in deed and word? is it a true thing?

Touch. No, truly; for the truest poetry is the most feigning; and lovers are given to poetry, and what they swear in poetry may be said as lovers they do feign.

Aud. Do you wish then that the gods had made me poetical?

Touch. I do, truly; for thou swearest to me thou art honest: now, if thou wert a poet, I might have some hope thou didst feign.

Aud. Would you not have me honest?

Touch. No, truly, unless thou wert hard-favored; for honesty coupled to beauty is to have honey a sauce to sugar. 31

Jaq. [*Aside*] A material fool!

Aud. Well, I am not fair; and therefore I pray the gods make me honest.

Touch. Truly, and to cast away honesty upon a foul slut were to put good meat into an unclean dish.

Aud. I am not a slut, though I thank the gods I am foul. 39

Touch. Well, praised be the gods for thy foulness! sluttishness may come hereafter. But be it as it may be, I will marry thee, and to that end I have been with Sir Oliver Martext, the vicar of the next village, who hath promised to meet me in this place of the forest and to couple us.

Jaq. [*Aside*] I would fain see this meeting.

Aud. Well, the gods give us joy!

Touch. Amen. A man may, if he were of a fearful heart, stagger in this attempt; for here we have no temple but the wood, no assembly but horn-beasts. But what though? Courage! As horns are odious, they are necessary. It is said, 'many a man knows no end of his goods:' right; many a man has good horns, and knows no end of them. Well, that is the dowry of his wife; 'tis none of his own getting. Horns? Even so. Poor men alone? No, no; the noblest deer hath them as huge as the rascal. Is the single man therefore blessed? No: as a walled town is more worthier than a village, so is the forehead of a married man more honorable than the bare brow of a bachelor; and by how much defence is better than no skill, by so much is a horn more precious than to want. Here comes Sir Oliver.

Enter SIR OLIVER MARTEXT.

Sir Oliver Martext, you are well met: will you dispatch us here under this tree, or shall we go with you to your chapel?

Sir Oli. Is there none here to give the woman?

Touch. I will not take her on gift of any man.

Sir Oli. Truly, she must be given, or the marriage is not lawful. 71

Jaq. [*Advancing*] Proceed, proceed: I'll give her.

Touch. Good even, good Master What-ye-call't: how do you, sir? You are very well met: God 'ild you for your last company: I am very glad to see you: even a toy in hand here, sir: nay, pray be covered.

Jaq. Will you be married, motley? 79

Touch. As the ox hath his bow, sir, the horse his curb and the falcon her bells, so man hath his desires; and as pigeons bill, so wedlock would be nibbling.

Jaq. And will you, being a man of your breeding, be married under a bush like a beggar? Get you to church, and have a good priest that can tell you what marriage is: this fellow will but join you together as they join wainscot; then one of you will prove a shrunk panel and, like green timber, warp, warp. 90

Touch. [*Aside*] I am not in the mind but I were better to be married of him than of another: for he is not like to marry me well; and not being well married, it will be a good excuse for me hereafter to leave my wife.

Jaq. Go thou with me, and let me counsel thee.

Touch. Come, sweet Audrey:
We must be married, or we must live in bawdry.
Farewell, good Master Oliver: not,— 100
　　　O sweet Oliver,
　　　O brave Oliver,
Leave me not behind thee:
but,—

　　　Wind away,
　　　Begone, I say,
I will not to wedding with thee.
[*Exeunt Jaques, Touchstone and Audrey.*
Sir Oli. 'Tis no matter: ne'er a fantastical knave of them all shall flout me out of my calling. [*Exit.* 109

SCENE IV. *The forest.*

Enter ROSALIND *and* CELIA.

Ros. Never talk to me; I will weep.

Cel. Do, I prithee; but yet have the grace to consider that tears do not become a man.

Ros. But have I not cause to weep?

Cel. As good cause as one would desire; therefore weep.

Ros. His very hair is of the dissembling color.

Cel. Something browner than Judas's: marry, his kisses are Judas's own children. 10

Ros. I' faith, his hair is of a good color.

Cel. An excellent color: your chestnut was ever the only color.

Ros. And his kissing is as full of sanctity as the touch of holy bread.

Cel. He hath bought a pair of cast lips of Diana: a nun of winter's sisterhood kisses not more religiously; the very ice of chastity is in them.

Ros. But why did he swear he would come this morning, and comes not? 21

Cel. Nay, certainly, there is no truth in him.

Ros. Do you think so?

Cel. Yes; I think he is not a pick-purse nor a horse-stealer, but for his verity in love, I do think him as concave as a covered goblet or a worm-eaten nut.

Ros. Not true in love?

Cel. Yes, when he is in; but I think he is not in. 30

Ros. You have heard him swear downright he was.

Cel. 'Was' is not 'is:' besides, the oath of a lover is no stronger than the word of a tapster; they are both the confirmer of false reckonings. He attends here in the forest on the duke your father.

Ros. I met the duke yesterday and had much question with him: he asked me of what parentage I was; I told him, of as good as he; so he laughed and let me go. But what talk we of fathers, when there is such a man as Orlando?

Cel. O, that's a brave man! he writes brave verses, speaks brave words, swears brave oaths and breaks them bravely, quite traverse, athwart the heart of his lover; as a puisny tilter, that spurs his horse but on one side, breaks his staff like a noble goose: but all's brave that youth mounts and folly guides. Who comes here?

Enter CORIN.

Cor.   Mistress and master, you have oft in-
     quired   50
After the shepherd that complain'd of love,
Who you saw sitting by me on the turf,
Praising the proud disdainful shepherdess
That was his mistress.
     Cel.   Well, and what of him ?
     Cor.   If you will see a pageant truly play'd,
Between the pale complexion of true love
And the red glow of scorn and proud disdain,
Go hence a little and I shall conduct you,
If you will mark it.
     Ros.   O, come, let us remove !
The sight of lovers feedeth those in love.   60
Bring us to this sight, and you shall say
I'll prove a busy actor in their play.
                                   [*Exeunt.*

SCENE V.   *Another part of the forest.*
        Enter SILVIUS *and* PHEBE.

Sil.   Sweet Phebe, do not scorn me ; do not,
     Phebe ;
Say that you love me not, but say not so
In bitterness. The common executioner,
Whose heart the accustom'd sight of death
     makes hard,
Falls not the axe upon the humbled neck
But first begs pardon : will you sterner be
Than he that dies and lives by bloody drops ?

Enter ROSALIND, CELIA, *and* CORIN, *behind.*

     Phe.   I would not be thy executioner :
I fly thee, for I would not injure thee.
Thou tell'st me there is murder in mine eye :
'Tis pretty, sure, and very probable,
That eyes, that are the frail'st and softest
     things,
Who shut their coward gates on atomies,
Should be call'd tyrants, butchers, murderers !
Now I do frown on thee with all my heart ;
And if mine eyes can wound, now let them
     kill thee :
Now counterfeit to swoon ; why now fall
     down ;
Or if thou canst not, O, for shame, for shame,
Lie not, to say mine eyes are murderers !
Now show the wound mine eye hath made in
     thee :   20
Scratch thee but with a pin, and there remains
Some scar of it ; lean but upon a rush,
The cicatrice and capable impressure
Thy palm some moment keeps ; but now mine
     eyes,
Which I have darted at thee, hurt thee not,
Nor, I am sure, there is no force in eyes
That can do hurt.
     Sil.   O dear Phebe,
If ever,—as that ever may be near,—
You meet in some fresh cheek the power of
     fancy,
Then shall you know the wounds invisible   30
That love's keen arrows make.
     Phe.   But till that time
Come not thou near me : and when that time
     comes,
Afflict me with thy mocks, pity me not ;
As till that time I shall not pity thee.
     Ros.   And why, I pray you ? Who might
     be your mother,
That you insult, exult, and all at once,
Over the wretched ? What though you have
     no beauty,—

As, by my faith, I see no more in you
Than without candle may go dark to bed—
Must you be therefore proud and pitiless ? 40
Why, what means this ? Why do you look on
     me ?
I see no more in you than in the ordinary
Of nature's sale-work. 'Od's my little life,
I think she means to tangle my eyes too !
No, faith, proud mistress, hope not after it :
'Tis not your inky brows, your black silk hair,
Your bugle eyeballs, nor your cheek of cream,
That can entame my spirits to your worship.
You foolish shepherd, wherefore do you
     follow her,
Like foggy south puffing with wind and rain ?
You are a thousand times a properer man
Than she a woman : 'tis such fools as you
That makes the world full of ill-favor'd chil-
     dren :
'Tis not her glass, but you, that flatters her ;
And out of you she sees herself more proper
Than any of her lineaments can show her.
But, mistress, know yourself : down on your
     knees,
And thank heaven, fasting, for a good man's
     love :
For I must tell you friendly in your ear,
Sell when you can : you are not for all
     markets :
Cry the man mercy ; love him ; take his offer :
Foul is most foul, being foul to be a scoffer.
So take her to thee, shepherd : fare you well.
     Phe.   Sweet youth, I pray you, chide a year
     together !
I had rather hear you chide than this man woo.
     Ros.   He's fallen in love with your foulness
and she'll fall in love with my anger. If it be
so, as fast as she answers thee with frowning
looks, I'll sauce her with bitter words. Why
look you so upon me ?   70
     Phe.   For no ill will I bear you.
     Ros.   I pray you, do not fall in love with
     me,
For I am falser than vows made in wine :
Besides, I like you not. If you will know my
     house,
'Tis at the tuft of olives here hard by.
Will you go, sister ? Shepherd, ply her hard.
Come, sister. Shepherdess, look on him better,
And be not proud : though all the world could
     see,
None could be so abused in sight as he.   80
Come, to our flock.
         [*Exeunt Rosalind, Celia and Corin.*
     Phe.   Dead Shepherd, now I find thy saw of
     might,
' Who ever loved that loved not at first sight ? '
     Sil.   Sweet Phebe,—
     Phe.   Ha, what say'st thou, Silvius ?
     Sil.   Sweet Phebe, pity me.
     Phe.   Why, I am sorry for thee, gentle Sil-
     vius.
     Sil.   Wherever sorrow is, relief would be :
If you do sorrow at my grief in love,
By giving love your sorrow and my grief
Were both extermined.
     Phe.   Thou hast my love : is not that
     neighborly ?   90
     Sil.   I would have you.
     Phe.   Why, that were covetousness.
Silvius, the time was that I hated thee,
And yet it is not that I bear thee love ;
But since that thou canst talk of love so well,

Thy company, which erst was irksome to me,
I will endure, and I'll employ thee too :
But do not look for further recompense
Than thine own gladness that thou art em-
    ploy'd.
  Sil. So holy and so perfect is my love,
And I in such a poverty of grace,   100
That I shall think it a most plenteous crop
To glean the broken ears after the man
That the main harvest reaps : loose now and
    then
A scatter'd smile, and that I'll live upon.
  Phe. Know'st now the youth that spoke to
    me erewhile ?
  Sil. Not very well, but I have met him
    oft ;
And he hath bought the cottage and the
    bounds
That the old carlot once was master of.
  Phe. Think not I love him, though I ask
    for him ;
'Tis but a peevish boy ; yet he talks well ; 110
But what care I for words ? yet words do well
When he that speaks them pleases those that
    hear.
It is a pretty youth : not very pretty :
But, sure, he's proud, and yet his pride be-
    comes him :
He'll make a proper man : the best thing in
    him
Is his complexion ; and faster than his tongue
Did make offence his eye did heal it up.
He is not very tall ; yet for his years he's tall :
His leg is but so so ; and yet 'tis well :
There was a pretty redness in his lip,   120
A little riper and more lusty red
Than that mix'd in his cheek ; 'twas just the
    difference
Between the constant red and mingled damask.
There be some women, Silvius, had they
    mark'd him
In parcels as I did, would have gone near
To fall in love with him ; but, for my part,
I love him not nor hate him not ; and yet
I have more cause to hate him than to love
    him :
For what had he to do to chide at me ?
He said mine eyes were black and my hair
    black :   130
And, now I am remember'd, scorn'd at me :
I marvel why I answer'd not again :
But that's all one ; omittance is no quittance.
I'll write to him a very taunting letter,
And thou shalt bear it : wilt thou, Silvius ?
  Sil. Phebe, with all my heart.
  Phe.   I'll write it straight ;
The matter's in my head and in my heart :
I will be bitter with him and passing short.
Go with me, Silvius.   [*Exeunt.*

ACT IV.

Scene I. *The forest.*

Enter Rosalind, Celia, *and* Jaques.

  Jaq. I prithee, pretty youth, let me be better acquainted with thee.
  Ros. They say you are a melancholy fellow.
  Jaq. I am so ; I do love it better than
laughing.
  Ros. Those that are in extremity of either

are abominable fellows and betray themselves
to every modern censure worse than drunk-
ards.
  Jaq. Why, 'tis good to be sad and say
nothing.
  Ros. Why then, 'tis good to be a post.   9
  Jaq. I have neither the scholar's melancholy, which is emulation, nor the musician's,
which is fantastical, nor the courtier's, which
is proud, nor the soldier's, which is ambitious,
nor the lawyer's, which is politic, nor the
lady's, which is nice, nor the lover's, which is
all these : but it is a melancholy of mine own,
compounded of many simples, extracted from
many objects, and indeed the sundry's contemplation of my travels, in which my often
rumination wraps me in a most humorous sadness.   20
  Ros. A traveller ! By my faith, you have
great reason to be sad : I fear you have sold
your own lands to see other men's ; then, to
have seen much and to have nothing, is to
have rich eyes and poor hands.
  Jaq. Yes, I have gained my experience.
  Ros. And your experience makes you sad :
I had rather have a fool to make me merry
than experience to make me sad ; and to
travel for it too !

Enter Orlando.

  Orl. Good day and happiness, dear Rosalind !
  Jaq. Nay, then, God be wi' you, an you
talk in blank verse.   [*Exit.*
  Ros. Farewell, Monsieur Traveller : look
you lisp and wear strange suits, disable all the
benefits of your own country, be out of love
with your nativity and almost chide God for
making you that countenance you are, or I
will scarce think you have swam in a gondola.
Why, how now, Orlando ! where have you
been all this while ? You a lover ! An you
serve me such another trick, never come in
my sight more.   41
  Orl. My fair Rosalind, I come within an
hour of my promise.
  Ros. Break an hour's promise in love ! He
that will divide a minute into a thousand parts
and break but a part of the thousandth part of
a minute in the affairs of love, it may be said
of him that Cupid hath clapped him o' the
shoulder, but I'll warrant him heart-whole.
  Orl. Pardon me, dear Rosalind.   50
  Ros. Nay, an you be so tardy, come no
more in my sight : I had as lief be wooed of
a snail.
  Orl. Of a snail ?
  Ros. Ay, of a snail ; for though he comes
slowly, he carries his house on his head ; a
better jointure, I think, than you make a
woman : besides he brings his destiny with
him.
  Orl. What's that ?
  Ros. Why, horns, which such as you are
fain to be beholding to your wives for : but
he comes armed in his fortune and prevents
the slander of his wife.
  Orl. Virtue is no horn-maker ; and my
Rosalind is virtuous.
  Ros. And I am your Rosalind.
  Cel. It pleases him to call you so ; but he
hath a Rosalind of a better leer than you.
  Ros. Come, woo me, woo me, for now I

am in a holiday humor and like enough to
consent. What would you say to me now, an
I were your very very Rosalind ?　　　　71
　Orl. I would kiss before I spoke.
　Ros. Nay, you were better speak first, and
when you were gravelled for lack of matter,
you might take occasion to kiss. Very good
orators, when they are out, they will spit ; and
for lovers lacking—God warn us !—matter,
the cleanliest shift is to kiss.
　Orl. How if the kiss be denied ?
　Ros. Then she puts you to entreaty, and
there begins new matter.　　　　　　81
　Orl. Who could be out, being before his
beloved mistress ?
　Ros. Marry, that should you, if I were
your mistress, or I should think my honesty
ranker than my wit.
　Orl. What, of my suit ?
　Ros. Not out of your apparel, and yet out
of your suit. Am not I your Rosalind ?
　Orl. I take some joy to say you are, because I would be talking of her.　　　91
　Ros. Well in her person I say I will not
have you.
　Orl. Then in mine own person I die.
　Ros. No, faith, die by attorney. The poor
world is almost six thousand years old, and in
all this time there was not any man died in his
own person, videlicit, in a love-cause. Troilus
had his brains dashed out with a Grecian
club ; yet he did what he could to die before,
and he is one of the patterns of love. Leander,
he would have lived many a fair year, though
Hero had turned nun, if it had not been for a
hot midsummer night ; for, good youth, he
went but forth to wash him in the Hellespont
and being taken with the cramp was drowned :
and the foolish coroners of that age found it
was 'Hero of Sestos.' But these are all lies :
men have died from time to time and worms
have eaten them, but not for love.
　Orl. I would not have my right Rosalind
of this mind, for, I protest, her frown might
kill me.
　Ros. By this hand, it will not kill a fly.
But come, now I will be your Rosalind in a
more coming-on disposition, and ask me what
you will, I will grant it.
　Orl. Then love me, Rosalind.
　Ros. Yes, faith, will I, Fridays and Satur-
days and all.
　Orl. And wilt thou have me ?
　Ros. Ay, and twenty such.
　Orl. What sayest thou ?　　　　120
　Ros. Are you not good ?
　Orl. I hope so.
　Ros. Why then, can one desire too much
of a good thing ? Come, sister, you shall be
the priest and marry us. Give me your hand,
Orlando. What do you say, sister ?
　Orl. Pray thee, marry us.
　Cel. I cannot say the words.
　Ros. You must begin, 'Will you, Or-
lando—'
　Cel. Go to. Will you, Orlando, have to
wife this Rosalind ?　　　　　　131
　Orl. I will.
　Ros. Ay, but when ?
　Orl. Why now ; as fast as she can marry
us.
　Ros. Then you must say 'I take thee,
Rosalind, for wife.'

　Orl. I take thee, Rosalind, for wife.
　Ros. I might ask you for your commission ; but I do take thee, Orlando, for my
husband : there's a girl goes before the priest ;
and certainly a woman's thought runs before
her actions.　　　　　　141
　Orl. So do all thoughts ; they are winged.
　Ros. Now tell me how long you would
have her after you have possessed her.
　Orl. For ever and a day.
　Ros. Say 'a day,' without the 'ever.' No,
no, Orlando ; men are April when they woo,
December when they wed : maids are May
when they are maids, but the sky changes
when they are wives. I will be more jealous
of thee than a Barbary cock-pigeon over his
hen, more clamorous than a parrot against
rain, more new-fangled than an ape, more
giddy in my desires than a monkey : I will
weep for nothing, like Diana in the fountain,
and I will do that when you are disposed to
be merry ; I will laugh like a hyen, and that
when thou art inclined to sleep.
　Orl. But will my Rosalind do so ?
　Ros. By my life, she will do as I do.
　Orl. O, but she is wise.　　　　160
　Ros. Or else she could not have the wit to
do this : the wiser, the waywarder : make the
doors upon a woman's wit and it will out at
the casement ; shut that and 'twill out at the
key-hole ; stop that, 'twill fly with the smoke
out at the chimney.
　Orl. A man that had a wife with such a
wit, he might say 'Wit, whither wilt ?'
　Ros. Nay, you might keep that check for
it till you met your wife's wit going to your
neighbor's bed.　　　　　　171
　Orl. And what wit could wit have to excuse that ?
　Ros. Marry, to say she came to seek you
there. You shall never take her without her
answer, unless you take her without her
tongue. O, that woman that cannot make her
fault her husband's occasion, let her never
nurse her child herself, for she will breed it
like a fool !
　Orl. For these two hours, Rosalind, I will
leave thee.　　　　　　181
　Ros. Alas ! dear love, I cannot lack thee
two hours.
　Orl. I must attend the duke at dinner : by
two o'clock I will be with thee again.
　Ros. Ay, go your ways, go your ways ; I
knew what you would prove : my friends told
me as much, and I thought no less : that flattering tongue of yours won me : 'tis but one
cast away, and so, come, death ! Two o'clock
is your hour ?　　　　　　190
　Orl. Ay, sweet Rosalind.
　Ros. By my troth, and in good earnest,
and so God mend me, and by all pretty oaths
that are not dangerous, if you break one jot
of your promise or come one minute behind
your hour, I will think you the most pathetical
break-promise and the most hollow lover and
the most unworthy of her you call Rosalind
that may be chosen out of the gross band of
the unfaithful : therefore beware my censure
and keep your promise.　　　　200
　Orl. With no less religion than if thou wert
indeed my Rosalind : so adieu.
　Ros. Well, Time is the old justice that ex-

amines all such offenders, and let Time try : adieu.   [*Exit Orlando.*

Cel. You have simply misused our sex in your love-prate : we must have your doublet and hose plucked over your head, and show the world what the bird hath done to her own nest.

Ros. O coz, coz, coz, my pretty little coz, that thou didst know how many fathom deep I am in love ! But it cannot be sounded : my affection hath an unknown bottom, like the bay of Portugal.

Cel. Or rather, bottomless, that as fast as you pour affection in, it runs out.

Ros. No, that same wicked bastard of Venus that was begot of thought, conceived of spleen and born of madness, that blind rascally boy that abuses every one's eyes because his own are out, let him be judge how deep I am in love. I'll tell thee, Aliena, I cannot be out of the sight ere Orlando : I'll go find a shadow and sigh till he come.

Cel. And I'll sleep.   [*Exeunt.*

SCENE II. *The forest.*

Enter JAQUES, Lords, *and* Foresters.

Jaq. Which is he that killed the deer ?

A Lord. Sir, it was I.

Jaq. Let's present him to the duke, like a Roman conqueror ; and it would do well to set the deer's horns upon his head, for a branch of victory. Have you no song, forester, for this purpose ?

For. Yes, sir.

Jaq. Sing it : 'tis no matter how it be in tune, so it make noise enough.   10

SONG.

For. What shall he have that kill'd the deer ?
His leather skin and horns to wear.
Then sing him home ;
[*The rest shall bear this burden.*
Take thou no scorn to wear the horn ;
It was a crest ere thou wast born :
Thy father's father wore it,
And thy father bore it :
The horn, the horn, the lusty horn
Is not a thing to laugh to scorn.
[*Exeunt.*

SCENE III. *The forest.*

Enter ROSALIND *and* CELIA.

Ros. How say you now ? Is it not past two o'clock ? and here much Orlando !

Cel. I warrant you, with pure love and troubled brain, he hath ta'en his bow and arrows and is gone forth to sleep. Look, who comes here.

Enter SILVIUS.

Sil. My errand is to you, fair youth ;
My gentle Phebe bid me give you this :
I know not the contents ; but, as I guess
By the stern brow and waspish action
Which she did use as she was writing of it,   10
It bears an angry tenor : pardon me :
I am but as a guiltless messenger.

Ros. Patience herself would startle at this letter
And play the swaggerer ; bear this, bear all :
She says I am not fair, that I lack manners ;
She calls me proud, and that she could not love me,
Were man as rare as phœnix. 'Od's my will !
Her love is not the hare that I do hunt :
Why writes she so to me ? Well, shepherd, well,
This is a letter of your own device.   20

Sil. No, I protest, I know not the contents :
Phebe did write it.

Ros.   Come, come, you are a fool
And turn'd into the extremity of love.
I saw her hand : she has a leathern hand,
A freestone-color'd hand ; I verily did think
That her old gloves were on, but 'twas her hands :
She has a huswife's hand ; but that's no matter :
I say she never did invent this letter ;
This is a man's invention and his hand.

Sil. Sure, it is hers.   30

Ros. Why, 'tis a boisterous and a cruel style,
A style for challengers ; why, she defies me,
Like Turk to Christian : women's gentle brain
Could not drop forth such giant-rude invention,
Such Ethiope words, blacker in their effect
Than in their countenance. Will you hear the letter ?

Sil. So please you, for I never heard it yet ;
Yet heard too much of Phebe's cruelty.

Ros. She Phebes me : mark how the tyrant writes.   [*Reads.*
Art thou god to shepherd turn'd,   40
That a maiden's heart hath burn'd ?
Can a woman rail thus ?

Sil. Call you this railing ?

Ros. [*Reads*]
Why, thy godhead laid apart,
Warr'st thou with a woman's heart ?
Did you ever hear such railing ?
Whiles the eye of man did woo me,
That could do no vengeance to me.
Meaning me a beast.
If the scorn of your bright eyne   50
Have power to raise such love in mine,
Alack, in me what strange effect
Would they work in mild aspect !
Whiles you chid me, I did love ;
How then might your prayers move !
He that brings this love to thee
Little knows this love in me :
And by him seal up thy mind ;
Whether that thy youth and kind
Will the faithful offer take   60
Of me and all that I can make ;
Or else by him my love deny,
And then I'll study how to die.

Sil. Call you this chiding ?

Cel. Alas, poor shepherd !

Ros. Do you pity him ? no, he deserves no pity. Wilt thou love such a woman ? What, to make thee an instrument and play false strains upon thee ! not to be endured ! Well, go your way to her, for I see love hath made thee a tame snake, and say this to her : that if she love me, I charge her to love thee ; if she will not, I will never have her unless thou entreat for her. If you be a true lover, hence, and not a word ; for here comes more company.   [*Exit Silvius.*

Enter OLIVER.

Oli. Good morrow, fair ones : pray you, if
you know,
Where in the purlieus of this forest stands
A sheep-cote fenced about with olive trees ?
Cel. West of this place, down in the neigh-
bor bottom :
The rank of osiers by the murmuring stream
Left on your right hand brings you to the
place.   81
But at this hour the house doth keep itself ;
There's none within.
Oli. If that an eye may profit by a tongue,
Then should I know you by description ;
Such garments and such years : ' The boy is
fair,
Of female favor, and bestows himself
Like a ripe sister : the woman low
And browner than her brother.' Are not you
The owner of the house I did inquire for ?   90
Cel. It is no boast, being ask'd, to say we
are.
Oli. Orlando doth commend him to you
both,
And to that youth he calls his Rosalind
He sends this bloody napkin. Are you he ?
Ros. I am : what must we understand by
this ?
Oli. Some of my shame ; if you will know
of me
What man I am, and how, and why, and where
This handkercher was stain'd.
Cel.   I pray you, tell it.
Oli. When last the young Orlando parted
from you
He left a promise to return again   100
Within an hour, and pacing through the
forest,
Chewing the food of sweet and bitter fancy,
Lo, what befel ! he threw his eye aside,
And mark what object did present itself :
Under an oak, whose boughs were moss'd with
age
And high top bald with dry antiquity,
A wretched ragged man, o'ergrown with hair,
Lay sleeping on his back : about his neck
A green and gilded snake had wreathed it-
self,
Who with her head nimble in threats ap-
proach'd   110
The opening of his mouth ; but suddenly,
Seeing Orlando, it unlink'd itself,
And with indented glides did slip away
Into a bush : under which bush's shade
A lioness, with udders all drawn dry,
Lay couching, head on ground, with catlike
watch,
When that the sleeping man should stir ; for
'tis
The royal disposition of that beast
To prey on nothing that doth seem as dead :
This seen, Orlando did approach the man 120
And found it was his brother, his elder
brother.
Cel. O, I have heard him speak of that
same brother ;
And he did render him the most unnatural
That lived amongst men.
Oli.   And well he might so do,
For well I know he was unnatural.
Ros. But, to Orlando : did he leave him
there,

Food to the suck'd and hungry lioness ?
Oli. Twice did he turn his back and pur-
posed so ;
But kindness, nobler ever than revenge,
And nature, stronger than his just occasion,
Made him give battle to the lioness,   131
Who quickly fell before him : in which hur-
tling
From miserable slumber I awaked.
Cel. Are you his brother ?
Ros.   Was't you he rescued ?
Cel. Was't you that did so oft contrive to
kill him ?
Oli. 'Twas I ; but 'tis not I : I do not
shame
To tell you what I was, since my conversion
So sweetly tastes, being the thing I am.
Ros. But, for the bloody napkin ?
Oli.   By and by.
When from the first to last betwixt us two 140
Tears our recountments had most kindly
bathed,
As how I came into that desert place :—
In brief, he led me to the gentle duke,—
Who gave me fresh array and entertainment,
Committing me unto my brother's love ;
Who led me instantly unto his cave,
There stripp'd himself, and here upon his arm
The lioness had torn some flesh away,
Which all this while had bled ; and now he
fainted
And cried, in fainting, upon Rosalind.   150
Brief, I recover'd him, bound up his wound ;
And, after some small space, being strong at
heart,
He sent me hither, stranger as I am,
To tell this story, that you might excuse
His broken promise, and to give this napkin
Dyed in his blood unto the shepherd youth
That he in sport doth call his Rosalind.
                              [*Rosalind swoons.*
Cel. Why, how now, Ganymede ! sweet
Ganymede !
Oli. Many will swoon when they do look
on blood.
Cel. There is more in it. Cousin Gany-
mede !   160
Oli. Look, he recovers.
Ros. I would I were at home.
Cel.   We'll lead you thither.
I pray you, will you take him by the arm ?
Oli. Be of good cheer, youth : you a man !
you lack a man's heart.
Ros. I do so, I confess it. Ah, sirrah, a
body would think this was well counterfeited !
I pray you, tell your brother how well I coun-
terfeited. Heigh-ho !   169
Oli. This was not counterfeit : there is too
great testimony in your complexion that it was
a passion of earnest.
Ros. Counterfeit, I assure you.
Oli. Well then, take a good heart and
counterfeit to be a man.
Ros. So I do : but, i' faith, I should have
been a woman by right.
Cel. Come, you look paler and paler ;
pray you, draw homewards. Good sir, go with
us.
Oli. That will I, for I must bear answer
back   180
How you excuse my brother, Rosalind.
Ros. I shall devise something : but, I pray

you, commend my counterfeiting to him. Will you go? [*Exeunt.*

ACT V.

SCENE I. *The forest.*

Enter TOUCHSTONE *and* AUDREY.

Touch. We shall find a time, Audrey; patience, gentle Audrey.

Aud. Faith, the priest was good enough, for all the old gentleman's saying.

Touch. A most wicked Sir Oliver, Audrey, a most vile Martext. But, Audrey, there is a youth here in the forest lays claim to you.

Aud. Ay, I know who 'tis; he hath no interest in me in the world: here comes the man you mean. 10

Touch. It is meat and drink to me to see a clown: by my troth, we that have good wits have much to answer for; we shall be flouting; we cannot hold.

Enter WILLIAM.

Will. Good even, Audrey.

Aud. God ye good even, William.

Will. And good even to you, sir.

Touch. Good even, gentle friend. Cover thy head, cover thy head; nay, prithee, be covered. How old are you, friend? 20

Will. Five and twenty, sir.

Touch. A ripe age. Is thy name William?

Will. William, sir.

Touch. A fair name. Wast born i' the forest here?

Will. Ay, sir, I thank God.

Touch. 'Thank God;' a good answer. Art rich?

Will. Faith, sir, so so.

Touch. 'So so' is good, very good, very excellent good; and yet it is not; it is but so so. Art thou wise? 31

Will. Ay, sir, I have a pretty wit.

Touch. Why, thou sayest well. I do now remember a saying, 'The fool doth think he is wise, but the wise man knows himself to be a fool.' The heathen philosopher, when he had a desire to eat a grape, would open his lips when he put it into his mouth; meaning thereby that grapes were made to eat and lips to open. You do love this maid? 40

Will. I do, sir.

Touch. Give me your hand. Art thou learned?

Will. No, sir.

Touch. Then learn this of me: to have, is to have; for it is a figure in rhetoric that drink, being poured out of a cup into a glass, by filling the one doth empty the other; for all your writers do consent that ipse is he: now, you are not ipse, for I am he.

Will. Which he, sir? 50

Touch. He, sir, that must marry this woman. Therefore, you clown, abandon,—which is in the vulgar leave,—the society,—which in the boorish is company,—of this female,—which in the common is woman; which together is, abandon the society of this female, or, clown, thou perishest; or, to thy better understanding, diest; or, to wit, I kill thee, make thee away, translate thy life into death, thy liberty into bondage: I will deal in poison with thee, or in bastinado, or in steel; I will

bandy with thee in faction; I will o'errun thee with policy; I will kill thee a hundred and fifty ways: therefore tremble, and depart.

Aud. Do, good William.

Will. God rest you merry, sir. [*Exit.*

Enter CORIN.

Cor. Our master and mistress seeks you; come, away, away!

Touch. Trip, Audrey! trip, Audrey! I attend, I attend. [*Exeunt.*

SCENE II. *The forest.*

Enter ORLANDO *and* OLIVER.

Orl. Is't possible that on so little acquaintance you should like her? that but seeing you should love her? and loving woo? and, wooing, she should grant? and will you persever to enjoy her?

Oli. Neither call the giddiness of it in question, the poverty of her, the small acquaintance, my sudden wooing, nor her sudden consenting; but say with me, I love Aliena; say with her that she loves me; consent with both that we may enjoy each other: it shall be to your good; for my father's house and all the revenue that was old Sir Rowland's will I estate upon you, and here live and die a shepherd.

Orl. You have my consent. Let your wedding be to-morrow: thither will I invite the duke and all's contented followers. Go you and prepare Aliena; for look you, here comes my Rosalind.

Enter ROSALIND.

Ros. God save you, brother. 20

Oli. And you, fair sister. [*Exit.*

Ros. O, my dear Orlando, how it grieves me to see thee wear thy heart in a scarf!

Orl. It is my arm.

Ros. I thought thy heart had been wounded with the claws of a lion.

Orl. Wounded it is, but with the eyes of a lady.

Ros. Did your brother tell you how I counterfeited to swoon when he showed me your handkercher? 30

Orl. Ay, and greater wonders than that.

Ros. O, I know where you are: nay, 'tis true: there was never any thing so sudden but the fight of two rams and Cæsar's thrasonical brag of 'I came, saw, and overcame:' for your brother and my sister no sooner met but they looked, no sooner looked but they loved, no sooner loved but they sighed, no sooner sighed but they asked one another the reason, no sooner knew the reason but they sought the remedy; and in these degrees have they made a pair of stairs to marriage which they will climb incontinent, or else be incontinent before marriage: they are in the very wrath of love and they will together; clubs cannot part them.

Orl. They shall be married to-morrow, and I will bid the duke to the nuptial. But, O, how bitter a thing it is to look into happiness through another man's eyes! By so much the more shall I to-morrow be at the height of heart-heaviness, by how much I shall think my brother happy in having what he wishes for.

Ros. Why then, to-morrow I cannot serve your turn for Rosalind?

Orl. I can live no longer by thinking.

Ros. I will weary you then no longer with idle talking. Know of me then, for now I speak to some purpose, that I know you are a gentleman of good conceit : I speak not this that you should bear a good opinion of my knowledge, insomuch I say I know you are ; neither do I labor for a greater esteem than may in some little measure draw a belief from you, to do yourself good and not to grace me. Believe then, if you please, that I can do strange things : I have, since I was three year old, conversed with a magician, most profound in his art and yet not damnable. If you do love Rosalind so near the heart as your gesture cries it out, when your brother marries Aliena, shall you marry her : I know into what straits of fortune she is driven ; and it is not impossible to me, if it appear not inconvenient to you, to set her before your eyes to-morrow human as she is and without any danger.

Orl. Speakest thou in sober meanings ?

Ros. By my life, I do ; which I tender dearly, though I say I am a magician. Therefore, put you in your best array : bid your friends ; for if you will be married to-morrow, you shall, and to Rosalind, if you will.   81

Enter SILVIUS *and* PHEBE.

Look, here comes a lover of mine and a lover of hers.

Phe. Youth, you have done me much ungentleness,
To show the letter that I writ to you.

Ros. I care not if I have : it is my study
To seem despiteful and ungentle to you :
You are there followed by a faithful shepherd ;
Look upon him, love him ; he worships you.

Phe. Good shepherd, tell this youth what 'tis to love.

Sil. It is to be all made of sighs and tears ;
And so am I for Phebe.   91

Phe. And I for Ganymede.

Orl. And I for Rosalind.

Ros. And I for no woman.

Sil. It is to be all made of faith and service ;
And so am I for Phebe.

Phe. And I for Ganymede.

Orl. And I for Rosalind.

Ros. And I for no woman.

Sil. It is to be all made of fantasy,   100
All made of passion and all made of wishes,
All adoration, duty, and observance,
All humbleness, all patience and impatience,
All purity, all trial, all observance ;
And so am I for Phebe.

Phe. And so am I for Ganymede.

Orl. And so am I for Rosalind.

Ros. And so am I for no woman.

Phe. If this be so, why blame you me to love you ?   110

Sil. If this be so, why blame you me to love you ?

Orl. If this be so, why blame you me to love you ?

Ros. Who do you speak to, ' Why blame you me to love you ?'

Orl. To her that is not here, nor doth not hear.

Ros. Pray you, no more of this ; 'tis like the howling of Irish wolves against the moon. [*To Sil.*] I will help you, if I can : [*To Phe.*] I would love you, if I could. To-morrow meet me all together. [*To Phe.*] I will marry you, if ever I marry woman, and I'll be married to-morrow ; [*To Orl.*] I will satisfy you, if ever I satisfied man, and you shall be married to-morrow : [*To Sil.*] I will content you, if what pleases you contents you, and you shall be married to-morrow. [*To Orl.*] As you love Rosalind, meet : [*To Sil.*] as you love Phebe, meet : and as I love no woman, I'll meet. So fare you well : I have left you commands.   131

Sil. I'll not fail, if I live.

Phe. Nor I.

Orl. Nor I.   [*Exeunt.*

SCENE III. *The forest.*

Enter TOUCHSTONE *and* AUDREY.

Touch. To-morrow is the joyful day, Audrey ; to-morrow will we be married.

Aud. I do desire it with all my heart ; and I hope it is no dishonest desire to desire to be a woman of the world. Here comes two of the banished duke's pages.

Enter two Pages.

First Page. Well met, honest gentleman.

Touch. By my troth, well met. Come, sit, sit, and a song.   9

Sec. Page. We are for you : sit i' the middle.

First Page. Shall we clap into't roundly, without hawking or spitting or saying we are hoarse, which are the only prologues to a bad voice ?

Sec. Page. I'faith, i'faith ; and both in a tune, like two gipsies on a horse.

SONG.

It was a lover and his lass,
    With a hey, and a ho, and a hey nonino,
That o'er the green corn-field did pass
    In the spring time, the only pretty ring time,
When birds do sing, hey ding a ding, ding :   21
    Sweet lovers love the spring.

Between the acres of the rye,
    With a hey, and a ho, and a hey nonino
These pretty country folks would lie,
    In spring time, &c.

This carol they began that hour,
    With a hey, and a ho, and a hey nonino,
How that a life was but a flower
    In spring time, &c.   30

And therefore take the present time,
    With a hey, and a ho, and a hey nonino ;
For love is crowned with the prime
    In spring time, &c.

Touch. Truly, young gentlemen, though there was no great matter in the ditty, yet the note was very untuneable.

First Page. You are deceived, sir : we kept time, we lost not our time.

Touch. By my troth, yes ; I count it but time lost to hear such a foolish song. God be wi' you ; and God mend your voices ! Come, Audrey.   [*Exeunt.*

SCENE IV. *The forest.*

Enter DUKE senior, AMIENS, JAQUES, ORLANDO, OLIVER, *and* CELIA.

Duke S. Dost thou believe, Orlando, that the boy
Can do all this that he hath promised ?

Orl. I sometimes do believe, and sometimes
   do not;
As those that fear they hope, and know they
   fear.

    Enter ROSALIND, SILVIUS, *and* PHEBE.

Ros. Patience once more, whiles our com-
   pact is urged:
You say, if I bring in your Rosalind,
You will bestow her on Orlando here?
Duke S. That would I, had I kingdoms to
   give with her.
Ros. And you say, you will have her, when
   I bring her?
Orl. That would I, were I of all kingdoms
   king. 10
Ros. You say, you'll marry me, if I be will-
   ing?
Phe. That will I, should I die the hour
   after.
Ros. But if you do refuse to marry me,
You'll give yourself to this most faithful shep-
   herd?
Phe. So is the bargain.
Ros. You say, that you'll have Phebe, if
   she will?
Sil. Though to have her and death were
   both one thing.
Ros. I have promised to make all this mat-
   ter even.
Keep you your word, O duke, to give your
   daughter; 19
You yours, Orlando, to receive his daughter:
Keep your word, Phebe, that you'll marry me,
Or else refusing me, to wed this shepherd:
Keep your word, Silvius, that you'll marry her,
If she refuse me: and from hence I go,
To make these doubts all even.
          [*Exeunt Rosalind and Celia.*
Duke S. I do remember in this shepherd
   boy
Some lively touches of my daughter's favor.
Orl. My lord, the first time that I ever saw
   him
Methought he was a brother to your daughter:
But, my good lord, this boy is forest-born, 30
And hath been tutor'd in the rudiments
Of many desperate studies by his uncle,
Whom he reports to be a great magician,
Obscured in the circle of this forest.

    Enter TOUCHSTONE *and* AUDREY.

Jaq. There is, sure, another flood toward,
and these couples are coming to the ark. Here
comes a pair of very strange beasts, which in
all tongues are called fools.
Touch. Salutation and greeting to you all!
Jaq. Good my lord, bid him welcome: this
is the motley-minded gentleman that I have so
often met in the forest: he hath been a courtier, he swears.
Touch. If any man doubt that, let him put
me to my purgation. I have trod a measure; I
have flattered a lady; I have been politic with
my friend, smooth with mine enemy; I have
undone three tailors; I have had four quarrels, and like to have fought one.
Jaq. And how was that ta'en up? 50
Touch. Faith, we met, and found the quarrel was upon the seventh cause.
Jaq. How seventh cause? Good my lord,
like this fellow.
Duke S. I like him very well.

Touch. God 'ild you, sir; I desire you of
the like. I press in here, sir, amongst the rest
of the country copulatives, to swear and to
forswear: according as marriage binds and
blood breaks: a poor virgin, sir, an ill-favored
thing, sir, but mine own; a poor humor of
mine, sir, to take that that no man else will:
rich honesty dwells like a miser, sir, in a poor
house; as your pearl in your foul oyster.
Duke S. By my faith, he is very swift and
sententious.
Touch. According to the fool's bolt, sir,
and such dulcet diseases.
Jaq. But, for the seventh cause; how did
you find the quarrel on the seventh cause? 70
Touch. Upon a lie seven times removed:
—bear your body more seeming, Audrey:—as
thus, sir. I did dislike the cut of a certain
courtier's beard: he sent me word, if I said his
beard was not cut well, he was in the mind it
was: this is called the Retort Courteous. If I
sent him word again 'it was not well cut,' he
would send me word, he cut it to please himself: this is called the Quip Modest. If again
'it was not well cut,' he disabled my judgment:
this is called the Reply Churlish. If again 'it
was not well cut,' he would answer, I spake
not true: this is called the Reproof Valiant.
If again 'it was not well cut,' he would say, I
lied: this is called the Counter-check Quarrelsome: and so to the Lie Circumstantial and
the Lie Direct.
Jaq. And how oft did you say his beard
was not well cut?
Touch. I durst go no further than the Lie
Circumstantial, nor he durst not give me the
Lie Direct; and so we measured swords and
parted.
Jaq. Can you nominate in order now the
degrees of the lie?
Touch. O sir, we quarrel in print, by the
book; as you have books for good manners:
I will name you the degrees. The first, the Retort Courteous; the second, the Quip Modest;
the third, the Reply Churlish; the fourth, the
Reproof Valiant; the fifth, the Countercheck
Quarrelsome; the sixth, the Lie with Circumstance; the seventh, the Lie Direct. All these
you may avoid but the Lie Direct; and you
may avoid that too, with an If. I knew when
seven justices could not take up a quarrel, but
when the parties were met themselves, one of
them thought but of an If, as, 'If you said so,
then I said so;' and they shook hands and
swore brothers. Your If is the only peace-
maker; much virtue in If.
Jaq. Is not this a rare fellow, my lord? he's
as good at any thing and yet a fool. 110
Duke S. He uses his folly like a stalking-
horse and under the presentation of that he
shoots his wit.

    Enter HYMEN, ROSALIND, *and* CELIA.
        Still Music.

Hym. Then is there mirth in heaven,
   When earthly things made even
      Atone together.
   Good duke, receive thy daughter:
   Hymen from heaven brought her,
      Yea, brought her hither,
   That thou mightst join her hand
      with his 120
   Whose heart within his bosom is.

Ros. [*To duke*] To you I give myself, for
   I am yours.
[*To Orl.*] To you I give myself, for I am
   yours.
Duke S. If there be truth in sight, you are
   my daughter.
Orl. If there be truth in sight, you are my
   Rosalind.
Phe. If sight and shape be true,
Why then, my love adieu!
Ros. I'll have no father, if you be not he :
I'll have no husband, if you be not he :
Nor ne'er wed woman, if you be not she.   130
Hym. Peace, ho ! I bar confusion :
   'Tis I must make conclusion
      Of these most strange events :
      Here's eight that must take hands
      To join in Hymen's bands,
      If truth holds true contents.
   You and you no cross shall part :
   You and you are heart in heart :
   You to his love must accord,
   Or have a woman to your lord :   140
   You and you are sure together,
   As the winter to foul weather.
   Whiles a wedlock-hymn we sing,
   Feed yourselves with questioning ;
   That reason wonder may diminish,
   How thus we met, and these things finish.

SONG.

Wedding is great Juno's crown :
   O blessed bond of board and bed !
'Tis Hymen peoples every town ;
   High wedlock then be honored :   150
Honor, high honor and renown,
To Hymen, god of every town !

Duke S. O my dear niece, welcome thou
   art to me !
Even daughter, welcome, in no less degree.
Phe. I will not eat my word, now thou art
   mine ;
Thy faith my fancy to thee doth combine.

Enter JAQUES DE BOYS.

Jaq. de B. Let me have audience for a
   word or two :
I am the second son of old Sir Rowland,
That bring these tidings to this fair assembly.
Duke Frederick, hearing how that every day
Men of great worth resorted to this forest,
Address'd a mighty power ; which were on
   foot,
In his own conduct, purposely to take
His brother here and put him to the sword :
And to the skirts of this wild wood he came ;
Where meeting with an old religious man,
After some question with him, was converted
Both from his enterprise and from the world,
His crown bequeathing to his banish'd brother,
And all their lands restored to them again   170
That were with him exiled. This to be true,
I do engage my life.
Duke S.   Welcome, young man ;
Thou offer'st fairly to thy brothers' wedding :
To one his lands withheld, and to the other
A land itself at large, a potent dukedom.
First, in this forest let us do those ends
That here were well begun and well begot :
And after, every of this happy number

That have endured shrewd days and nights
   with us
Shall share the good of our returned fortune,
According to the measure of their states.   181
Meantime, forget this new-fall'n dignity
And fall into our rustic revelry.
Play, music ! And you, brides and bride-
   grooms all,
With measure heap'd in joy, to the measures
   fall.
Jaq. Sir, by your patience. If I heard you
   rightly,
The duke hath put on a religious life
And thrown into neglect the pompous court ?
Jaq. de B. He hath.
Jaq. To him will I : out of these convert-
   ites   190
There is much matter to be heard and learn'd.
[*To duke*] You to your former honor I be-
   queath ;
Your patience and your virtue well deserves
   it :
[*To Orl.*] You to a love that your true faith
   doth merit :
[*To Oli.*] You to your land and love and
   great allies :
[*To Sil.*] You to a long and well-deserved
   bed :
[*To Touch.*] And you to wrangling ; for
   thy loving voyage
Is but for two months victuall'd. So, to your
   pleasures :
I am for other than for dancing measures.
Duke S. Stay, Jaques, stay.   200
Jaq. To see no pastime I : what you would
   have
I'll stay to know at your abandon'd cave.
                        [*Exit.*
Duke S. Proceed, proceed : we will begin
   these rites,
As we do trust they'll end, in true delights.
                   [*A dance.*

EPILOGUE.

Ros. It is not the fashion to see the lady
the epilogue ; but it is no more unhandsome
than to see the lord the prologue. If it be true
that good wine needs no bush, 'tis true that a
good play needs no epilogue ; yet to good
wine they do use good bushes, and good plays
prove the better by the help of good epilogues.
What a case am I in then, that am neither a
good epilogue nor cannot insinuate with you in
the behalf of a good play ! I am not furnished
like a beggar, therefore to beg will not become
me : my way is to conjure you ; and I'll begin
with the women. I charge you, O women, for
the love you bear to men, to like as much of
this play as please you : and I charge you,
O men, for the love you bear to women—as
I perceive by your simpering, none of you
hates them—that between you and the women
the play may please. If I were a woman I
would kiss as many of you as had beards that
pleased me, complexions that liked me and
breaths that I defied not : and, I am sure, as
many as have good beards or good faces or
sweet breaths will, for my kind offer, when I
make curtsy, bid me farewell.   [*Exeunt.*

TWELFTH NIGHT.

(WRITTEN ABOUT 1600–1601.)

INTRODUCTION.

We learn from Manningham's *Diary* that *Twelfth Night* was acted at the Middle Temple, February 2, 1601–1602. Its date is probably 1600–1601. Manningham writes of the play : " Much like *The Comedy of Errors* or *Menechmi* in Plautus, but most like and neere to that in Italian called *Inganni.* " There are two Italian plays of an earlier date than *Twelfth Night*, entitled *Gl' Inganni* (*The Cheats*), containing incidents in some degree resembling those of Shakespeare's comedy, and in that by Gonzaga, the sister who assumes male attire, producing thereby confusion of identity with her brother, is named Cesare (Shakespeare's Cesario). But a third Italian play, *Gl' Ingannati*, presents a still closer resemblance to *Twelfth Night,* and in its poetical induction, *Il Sacrificio*, occurs the name Malevolti (Malvolio). The story is told in Bandello's novel (ii. 36), and was translated by Belleforest into French, in *Histoires Tragiques.* Whether Shakespeare consulted any Italian source or not, he had doubtless before him the version of the story (from Cinthio's *Hecatomithi*) by Barnabe Rich—the *Historie of Apolonius and Silla* in *Riche His Farewell to Militarie Profession* (1581)—and this, in the main, he followed. The characters of Malvolio, Sir Toby Belch, Sir Andrew Aguecheek, Fabian, the clown Feste, and Maria, with the part they play in the comedy, are creations of Shakespeare. No comedy of Shakespeare's unites such abounding mirth and fine satire, with the charm of a poetical romance. It is the summing up of the several admirable qualities which appear in the joyous comedies, of which it forms the last. An edge is put on the roystering humor of Sir Toby by the sharp waiting-maid wit of Maria, which saves it from becoming an aimless rollicking. Sir Andrew is a Slender grown adult in brainlessness, and who has forgotten that he is not as richly endowed by nature as by fortune. Feste, the clown, is less quaint than Touchstone, but more versatile, less a contemplative fool, and more actively a lover of jest and waggery. Among this abandoned crew of topers and drolls stalks the solemn " yellow-legged stork " Malvolio. His sense of self-importance has diffused itself over all the details of his life, so that the whole of human existence, as he would have it, must become as pompous and as exemplary as the manners of my lady's steward. The cruelty of his deception and disillusion is in proportion to the greatness of his distempered self-esteem. The Duke Orsino is infected with the lover's melancholy, which is fantastical and nice. He nurses his love and dallies with it, and tries to yield up all his consciousness to it, as to a delicious sensation : and therefore his love is not quite earnest or deep. Olivia has not the love-languor of the Duke, but her resolved sorrow for her lost brother, so soon forgotten in a stronger feeling, shows a little of the same unreality of self-conscious emotion which we perceive in the Duke's love ; she is of a nature harmonious and refined, but is too much a child of wealth and ease to win away our chief interest from the heroine of the play. Viola is like a heightened portrait of the Julia of *The Two Gentlemen of Verona*, enriched with lovely color and placed among more poetical surroundings. She has not the pretty sauciness of Rosalind in her disguise, but owns a heart as tender, sweet-natured, and sound-natured as even Rosalind's.

DRAMATIS PERSONÆ.

ORSINO, Duke of Illyria.
SEBASTIAN, brother to Viola.
ANTONIO, a sea captain, friend to Sebastian.
A Sea Captain, friend to Viola.
VALENTINE, } gentlemen attending on the
CURIO, } Duke.
SIR TOBY BELCH, uncle to Olivia.
SIR ANDREW AGUECHEEK.
MALVOLIO, steward to Olivia.

FABIAN, }
FESTE, a Clown, } servants to Olivia.
OLIVIA.
VIOLA.
MARIA, Olivia's woman.
Lords, Priests, Sailors, Officers, Musicians, and other Attendants.

SCENE : *A city in Illyria, and the sea-coast near it.*

ACT I.

Scene I. *The* Duke's *palace*.

Enter Duke, Curio, *and other* Lords; Musicians *attending*.

Duke. If music be the food of love, play on ;
Give me excess of it, that, surfeiting,
The appetite may sicken, and so die.
That strain again ! it had a dying fall :
O, it came o'er my ear like the sweet sound,
That breathes upon a bank of violets,
Stealing and giving odor ! Enough ; no more :
'Tis not so sweet now as it was before.
O spirit of love ! how quick and fresh art thou,
That, notwithstanding thy capacity   10
Receiveth as the sea, nought enters there,
Of what validity and pitch soe'er,
But falls into abatement and low price,
Even in a minute : so full of shapes is fancy
That it alone is high fantastical.

Cur. Will you go hunt, my lord ?

Duke.   What, Curio ?

Cur. The hart.

Duke. Why, so I do, the noblest that I have :
O, when mine eyes did see Olivia first,
Methought she purged the air of pestilence !
That instant was I turn'd into a hart ;   21
And my desires, like fell and cruel hounds,
E'er since pursue me.

Enter Valentine.

                 How now ! what news from her ?

Val. So please my lord, I might not be admitted ;
But from her handmaid do return this answer :
The element itself, till seven years' heat,
Shall not behold her face at ample view ;
But, like a cloistress, she will veiled walk
And water once a day her chamber round
With eye-offending brine : all this to season
A brother's dead love, which she would keep fresh   31
And lasting in her sad remembrance.

Duke. O, she that hath a heart of that fine frame
To pay this debt of love but to a brother,
How will she love, when the rich golden shaft
Hath kill'd the flock of all affections else
That live in her ; when liver, brain and heart,
These sovereign thrones, are all supplied, and fill'd
Her sweet perfections with one self king !
Away before me to sweet beds of flowers :   40
Love-thoughts lie rich when canopied with bowers.   [*Exeunt.*

Scene II. *The sea-coast.*

Enter Viola, *a* Captain, *and* Sailors.

Vio. What country, friends, is this ?

Cap. This is Illyria, lady.

Vio. And what should I do in Illyria ?
My brother he is in Elysium.
Perchance he is not drown'd : what think you, sailors ?

Cap. It is perchance that you yourself were saved.

Vio. O my poor brother ! and so perchance may he be.

Cap. True, madam : and, to comfort you with chance,
Assure yourself, after our ship did split,
When you and those poor number saved with you   10
Hung on our driving boat, I saw your brother,
Most provident in peril, bind himself,
Courage and hope both teaching him the practice,
To a strong mast that lived upon the sea ;
Where, like Arion on the dolphin's back,
I saw him hold acquaintance with the waves
So long as I could see.

Vio. For saying so, there's gold :
Mine own escape unfoldeth to my hope,
Whereto thy speech serves for authority,   20
The like of him. Know'st thou this country ?

Cap. Ay, madam, well ; for I was bred and born
Not three hours' travel from this very place.

Vio. Who governs here ?

Cap. A noble duke, in nature as in name.

Vio. What is the name ?

Cap. Orsino.

Vio. Orsino ! I have heard my father name him :
He was a bachelor then.

Cap. And so is now, or was so very late ;
For but a month ago I went from hence,   31
And then 'twas fresh in murmur,—as, you know,
What great ones do the less will prattle of,—
That he did seek the love of fair Olivia.

Vio. What's she ?

Cap. A virtuous maid, the daughter of a count
That died some twelvemonth since, then leaving her
In the protection of his son, her brother,
Who shortly also died : for whose dear love,
They say, she hath abjured the company   40
And sight of men.

Vio.   O that I served that lady
And might not be delivered to the world,
Till I had made mine own occasion mellow,
What my estate is !

Cap.   That were hard to compass ;
Because she will admit no kind of suit,
No, not the duke's.

Vio. There is a fair behavior in thee, captain ;
And though that nature with a beauteous wall
Doth oft close in pollution, yet of thee
I will believe thou hast a mind that suits   50
With this thy fair and outward character.
I prithee, and I'll pay thee bounteously,
Conceal me what I am, and be my aid
For such disguise as haply shall become
The form of my intent. I'll serve this duke :
Thou shall present me as an eunuch to him :
It may be worth thy pains ; for I can sing
And speak to him in many sorts of music
That will allow me very worth his service.
What else may hap to time I will commit ;   60
Only shape thou thy silence to my wit.

Cap. Be you his eunuch, and your mute I'll be :
When my tongue blabs, then let mine eyes not see.

Vio. I thank thee : lead me on.   [*Exeunt.*

SCENE III. OLIVIA'S *house.*

Enter SIR TOBY BELCH *and* MARIA.

Sir To. What a plague means my niece, to take the death of her brother thus ? I am sure care's an enemy to life.

Mar. By my troth, Sir Toby, you must come in earlier o' nights : your cousin, my lady, takes great exceptions to your ill hours.

Sir To. Why, let her except, before excepted.

Mar. Ay, but you must confine yourself within the modest limits of order.　9

Sir To. Confine ! I'll confine myself no finer than I am : these clothes are good enough to drink in ; and so be these boots too : an they be not, let them hang themselves in their own straps.

Mar. That quaffing and drinking will undo you : I heard my lady talk of it yesterday ; and of a foolish knight that you brought in one night here to be her wooer.

Sir To. Who, Sir Andrew Aguecheek ?

Mar. Ay, he.

Sir To. He's as tall a man as any's in Illyria.　20

Mar. What's that to the purpose ?

Sir To. Why, he has three thousand ducats a year.

Mar. Ay, but he'll have but a year in all these ducats : he's a very fool and a prodigal.

Sir To. Fie, that you'll say so ! he plays o' the viol-de-gamboys, and speaks three or four languages word for word without book, and hath all the good gifts of nature.　29

Mar. He hath indeed, almost natural : for besides that he's a fool, he's a great quarreller : and but that he hath the gift of a coward to allay the gust he hath in quarrelling, 'tis thought among the prudent he would quickly have the gift of a grave.

Sir To. By this hand, they are scoundrels and subtractors that say so of him. Who are they ?

Mar. They that add, moreover, he's drunk nightly in your company.　39

Sir To. With drinking healths to my niece : I'll drink to her as long as there is a passage in my throat and drink in Illyria : he's a coward and a coystrill that will not drink to my niece till his brains turn o' the toe like a parish-top. What, wench ! Castiliano vulgo ! for here comes Sir Andrew Agueface.

Enter SIR ANDREW AGUECHEEK.

Sir And. Sir Toby Belch ! how now, Sir Toby Belch !

Sir To. Sweet Sir Andrew !

Sir And. Bless you, fair shrew.　50

Mar. And you too, sir.

Sir To. Accost, Sir Andrew, accost.

Sir And. What's that ?

Sir To. My niece's chambermaid.

Sir And. Good Mistress Accost, I desire better acquaintance.

Mar. My name is Mary, sir.

Sir And. Good Mistress Mary Accost,—

Sir To. You mistake, knight ; 'accost' is front her, board her, woo her, assail her.　60

Sir And. By my troth, I would not undertake her in this company. Is that the meaning of 'accost' ?

Mar. Fare you well, gentlemen.

Sir To. An thou let part so, Sir Andrew, would thou mightst never draw sword again.

Sir And. An you part so, mistress, I would I might never draw sword again. Fair lady, do you think you have fools in hand ?

Mar. Sir, I have not you by the hand.　70

Sir And. Marry, but you shall have ; and here's my hand.

Mar. Now, sir, 'thought is free : ' I pray you, bring your hand to the buttery-bar and let it drink.

Sir And. Wherefore, sweet-heart ? what's your metaphor ?

Mar. It's dry, sir.

Sir And. Why, I think so : I am not such an ass but I can keep my hand dry. But what's your jest ?　80

Mar. A dry jest, sir.

Sir And. Are you full of them ?

Mar. Ay, sir, I have them at my fingers' ends : marry, now I let go your hand, I am barren.　*[Exit.*

Sir To. O knight thou lackest a cup of canary : when did I see thee so put down ?

Sir And. Never in your life, I think ; unless you see canary put me down. Methinks sometimes I have no more wit than a Christian or an ordinary man has : but I am a great eater of beef and I believe that does harm to my wit.　91

Sir To. No question.

Sir And. An I thought that, I'ld forswear it. I'll ride home to-morrow, Sir Toby.

Sir To. Pourquoi, my dear knight ?

Sir And. What is 'pourquoi' ? do or not do ? I would I had bestowed that time in the tongues that I have in fencing, dancing and bear-baiting : O, had I but followed the arts !

Sir To. Then hadst thou had an excellent head of hair.　101

Sir And. Why, would that have mended my hair ?

Sir To. Past question ; for thou seest it will not curl by nature.

Sir And. But it becomes me well enough, does't not ?

Sir To. Excellent ; it hangs like flax on a distaff ; and I hope to see a housewife take thee between her legs and spin it off.　110

Sir And. Faith, I'll home to-morrow, Sir Toby : your niece will not be seen ; or if she be, it's four to one she'll none of me : the count himself here hard by woos her.

Sir To. She'll none o' the count : she'll not match above her degree, neither in estate, years, nor wit ; I have heard her swear't. Tut, there's life in't, man.

Sir And. I'll stay a month longer. I am a fellow o' the strangest mind i' the world ; I delight in masques and revels sometimes altogether.　121

Sir To. Art thou good at these kickshawses, knight ?

Sir And. As any man in Illyria, whatsoever he be, under the degree of my betters ; and yet I will not compare with an old man.

Sir To. What is thy excellence in a galliard, knight ?

Sir And. Faith, I can cut a caper.

Sir To. And I can cut the mutton to't.　130

Sir And. And I think I have the back-trick simply as strong as any man in Illyria.

Sir To. Wherefore are these things hid ?

wherefore have these gifts a curtain before
'em ? are they like to take dust, like Mistress
Mall's picture ? why dost thou not go to
church in a galliard and come home in a co-
ranto ? My very walk should be a jig ; I would
not so much as make water but in a sink-a-
pace. What dost thou mean ? Is it a world to
hide virtues in ? I did think, by the excellent
constitution of thy leg, it was formed under
the star of a galliard.

Sir And. Ay, 'tis strong, and it does indifferent well in a flame-colored stock. Shall we
set about some revels ?

Sir To. What shall we do else ? were we
not born under Taurus ?

Sir And. Taurus ! That's sides and heart.

Sir To. No, sir ; it is legs and thighs. Let
me see the caper ; ha ! higher : ha, ha ! excellent !   [*Exeunt.* 151

SCENE IV. *The* DUKE'S *palace.*

Enter VALENTINE *and* VIOLA *in man's attire.*

Val. If the duke continue these favors towards you, Cesario, you are like to be much
advanced : he hath known you but three days,
and already you are no stranger.

Vio. You either fear his humor or my negligence, that you call in question the continuance of his love : is he inconstant, sir, in his
favors ?

Val. No, believe me.

Vio. I thank you. Here comes the count.

Enter DUKE, CURIO, *and* Attendants.

Duke. Who saw Cesario, ho ?   10

Vio. On your attendance, my lord ; here.

Duke. Stand you a while aloof, Cesario,
Thou know'st no less but all ; I have unclasp'd
To thee the book even of my secret soul :
Therefore, good youth, address thy gait unto
     her ;
Be not denied access, stand at her doors,
And tell them, there thy fixed foot shall grow
Till thou have audience.

Vio.   Sure, my noble lord,
If she be so abandon'd to her sorrow
As it is spoke, she never will admit me.   20

Duke. Be clamorous and leap all civil
     bounds
Rather than make unprofited return.

Vio. Say I do speak with her, my lord,
     what then ?

Duke. O, then unfold the passion of my
     love,
Surprise her with discourse of my dear faith :
It shall become thee well to act my woes ;
She will attend it better in thy youth
Than in a nuncio's of more grave aspect.

Vio. I think not so, my lord.

Duke.   Dear lad, believe it ;
For they shall yet belie thy happy years,   30
That say thou art a man : Diana's lip
Is not more smooth and rubious ; thy small
     pipe
Is as the maiden's organ, shrill and sound,
And all is semblative a woman's part.
I know thy constellation is right apt
For this affair. Some four or five attend him ;
All, if you will ; for I myself am best
When least in company. Prosper well in this,
And thou shalt live as freely as thy lord,
To call his fortunes thine.

Vio.   I'll do my best   40
To woo your lady : [*Aside*] yet, a barful
     strife !
Whoe'er I woo, myself would be his wife.
          [*Exeunt.*

SCENE V. OLIVIA'S *house.*

Enter MARIA *and* CLOWN.

Mar. Nay, either tell me where thou hast
been, or I will not open my lips so wide as a
bristle may enter in way of thy excuse : my
lady will hang thee for thy absence.

Clo. Let her hang me : he that is well
hanged in this world needs to fear no colors.

Mar. Make that good.

Clo. He shall see none to fear.

Mar. A good lenten answer : I can tell
thee where that saying was born, of ' I fear no
colors.'   10

Clo. Where, good Mistress Mary ?

Mar. In the wars ; and that may you be
bold to say in your foolery.

Clo. Well, God give them wisdom that
have it ; and those that are fools, let them use
their talents.

Mar. Yet you will be hanged for being so
long absent ; or, to be turned away, is not that
as good as a hanging to you ?   19

Clo. Many a good hanging prevents a bad
marriage ; and, for turning away, let summer
bear it out.

Mar. You are resolute, then ?

Clo. Not so, neither ; but I am resolved on
two points.

Mar. That if one break, the other will
hold ; or, if both break, your gaskins fall.

Clo. Apt, in good faith ; very apt. Well,
go thy way ; if Sir Toby would leave drinking,
thou wert as witty a piece of Eve's flesh as
any in Illyria.   31

Mar. Peace, you rogue, no more o' that.
Here comes my lady : make your excuse
wisely, you were best.   [*Exit.*

Clo. Wit, an't be thy will, put me into
good fooling ! Those wits, that think they have
thee, do very oft prove fools ; and I, that am
sure I lack thee, may pass for a wise man : for
what says Quinapalus ? ' Better a witty fool,
than a foolish wit.'   40

Enter Lady OLIVIA *with* MALVOLIO.

God bless thee, lady !

Oli. Take the fool away.

Clo. Do you not hear, fellows ? Take away
the lady.

Oli. Go to, you're a dry fool ; I'll no more
of you : besides, you grow dishonest.

Clo. Two faults, madonna, that drink and
good counsel will amend : for give the dry fool
drink, then is the fool not dry : bid the dishonest man mend himself ; if he mend, he is
no longer dishonest ; if he cannot, let the
botcher mend him. Any thing that's mended
is but patched : virtue that transgresses is but
patched with sin ; and sin that amends is but
patched with virtue. If that this simple syl-
logism will serve, so ; if it will not, what remedy ? As there is no true cuckold but calamity, so beauty's a flower. The lady bade take
away the fool ; therefore, I say again, take her
away.

Oli. Sir, I bade them take away you.   60

Clo. Misprision in the highest degree !

Lady, cucullus non facit monachum ; that's as much to say as I wear not motley in my brain. Good madonna, give me leave to prove you a fool.

Oli. Can you do it ?

Clo. Dexterously, good madonna.

Oli. Make your proof.

Clo. I must catechize you for it, madonna : good my mouse of virtue, answer me.

Oli. Well, sir, for want of other idleness, I'll bide your proof. 71

Clo. Good madonna, why mournest thou ?

Oli. Good fool, for my brother's death.

Clo. I think his soul is in hell, madonna.

Oli. I know his soul is in heaven, fool.

Clo. The more fool, madonna, to mourn for your brother's soul being in heaven. Take away the fool, gentlemen.

Oli. What think you of this fool, Malvolio ? doth he not mend ? 80

Mal. Yes, and shall do till the pangs of death shake him : infirmity, that decays the wise, doth ever make the better fool.

Clo. God send you, sir, a speedy infirmity, for the better increasing your folly ! Sir Toby will be sworn that I am no fox ; but he will not pass his word for two pence that you are no fool.

Oli. How say you to that, Malvolio ?

Mal. I marvel your ladyship takes delight in such a barren rascal : I saw him put down the other day with an ordinary fool that has no more brain than a stone. Look you now, he's out of his guard already ; unless you laugh and minister occasion to him, he is gagged. I protest, I take these wise men, that crow so at these set kind of fools, no better than the fools' zanies.

Oli. Oh, you are sick of self-love, Malvolio, and taste with a distempered appetite. To be generous, guiltless and of free disposition, is to take those things for bird-bolts that you deem cannon-bullets : there is no slander in an allowed fool, though he do nothing but rail ; nor no railing in a known discreet man, though he do nothing but reprove.

Clo. Now Mercury endue thee with leasing, for thou speakest well of fools !

Re-enter MARIA.

Mar. Madam, there is at the gate a young gentleman much desires to speak with you.

Oli. From the Count Orsino, is it ?

Mar. I know not, madam : 'tis a fair young man, and well attended. 111

Oli. Who of my people hold him in delay ?

Mar. Sir Toby, madam, your kinsman.

Oli. Fetch him off, I pray you ; he speaks nothing but madman : fie on him ! [*Exit Maria.*] Go you, Malvolio : if it be a suit from the count, I am sick, or not at home ; what you will, to dismiss it. [*Exit Malvolio.*] Now you see, sir, how your fooling grows old, and people dislike it.

Clo. Thou hast spoke for us, madonna, as if thy eldest son should be a fool ; whose skull Jove cram with brains ! for,—here he comes, —one of thy kin has a most weak pia mater.

Enter SIR TOBY.

Oli. By mine honor, half drunk. What is he at the gate, cousin ?

Sir To. A gentleman.

Oli. A gentleman ! what gentleman ?

Sir To. 'Tis a gentleman here—a plague o' these pickle-herring ! How now, sot !

Clo. Good Sir Toby ! 130

Oli. Cousin, cousin, how have you come so early by this lethargy ?

Sir To. Lechery ! I defy lechery. There's one at the gate.

Oli. Ay, marry, what is he ?

Sir To. Let him be the devil, an he will, I care not : give me faith, say I. Well, it's all one. [*Exit.*

Oli. What's a drunken man like, fool ?

Clo. Like a drowned man, a fool and a mad man : one draught above heat makes him a fool ; the second mads him ; and a third drowns him.

Oli. Go thou and seek the crowner, and let him sit o' my coz ; for he's in the third degree of drink, he's drowned : go, look after him.

Clo. He is but mad yet, madonna ; and the fool shall look to the madman. [*Exit.*

Re-enter MALVOLIO.

Mal. Madam, yond young fellow swears he will speak with you. I told him you were sick ; he takes on him to understand so much, and therefore comes to speak with you. I told him you were asleep ; he seems to have a foreknowledge of that too, and therefore comes to speak with you. What is to be said to him, lady ? he's fortified against any denial.

Oli. Tell him he shall not speak with me.

Mal. Has been told so ; and he says, he'll stand at your door like a sheriff's post, and be the supporter to a bench, but he'll speak with you.

Oli. What kind o' man is he ?

Mal. Why, of mankind. 160

Oli. What manner of man ?

Mal. Of very ill manner ; he'll speak with you, will you or no.

Oli. Of what personage and years is he ?

Mal. Not yet old enough for a man, nor young enough for a boy ; as a squash is before 'tis a peascod, or a codling when 'tis almost an apple : 'tis with him in standing water, between boy and man. He is very well-favored and he speaks very shrewishly ; one would think his mother's milk were scarce out of him. 171

Oli. Let him approach : call in my gentlewoman.

Mal. Gentlewoman, my lady calls. [*Exit.*

Re-enter MARIA.

Oli. Give me my veil : come, throw it o'er my face.

We'll once more hear Orsino's embassy.

Enter VIOLA, *and* Attendants.

Vio. The honorable lady of the house, which is she ?

Oli. Speak to me ; I shall answer for her. Your will ? 180

Vio. Most radiant, exquisite and unmatchable beauty,—I pray you, tell me if this be the lady of the house, for I never saw her : I would be loath to cast away my speech, for besides that it is excellently well penned, I have taken great pains to con it. Good beauties, let me sustain no scorn; I am very comptible, even to the least sinister usage.

Oli. Whence came you, sir?   189

Vio. I can say little more than I have studied, and that question's out of my part. Good gentle one, give me modest assurance if you be the lady of the house, that I may proceed in my speech.

Oli. Are you a comedian?

Vio. No, my profound heart: and yet, by the very fangs of malice I swear, I am not that I play. Are you the lady of the house?

Oli. If I do not usurp myself, I am.

Vio. Most certain, if you are she, you do usurp yourself; for what is yours to bestow is not yours to reserve. But this is from my commission: I will on with my speech in your praise, and then show you the heart of my message.

Oli. Come to what is important in't: I forgive you the praise.

Vio. Alas, I took great pains to study it, and 'tis poetical.

Oli. It is the more like to be feigned: I pray you, keep it in. I heard you were saucy at my gates, and allowed your approach rather to wonder at you than to hear you. If you be not mad, be gone; if you have reason, be brief: 'tis not that time of moon with me to make one in so skipping a dialogue.

Mar. Will you hoist sail, sir? here lies your way.

Vio. No, good swabber; I am to hull here a little longer. Some mollification for your giant, sweet lady. Tell me your mind: I am a messenger.   220

Oli. Sure, you have some hideous matter to deliver, when the courtesy of it is so fearful. Speak your office.

Vio. It alone concerns your ear. I bring no overture of war, no taxation of homage: I hold the olive in my hand; my words are as full of peace as matter.

Oli. Yet you began rudely. What are you? what would you?   229

Vio. The rudeness that hath appeared in me have I learned from my entertainment. What I am, and what I would, are as secret as maidenhead; to your ears, divinity, to any other's, profanation.

Oli. Give us the place alone: we will hear this divinity. [*Exeunt Maria and Attendants.*] Now, sir, what is your text?

Vio. Most sweet lady,—

Oli. A comfortable doctrine, and much may be said of it. Where lies your text?   240

Vio. In Orsino's bosom.

Oli. In his bosom! In what chapter of his bosom?

Vio. To answer by the method, in the first of his heart.

Oli. O, I have read it: it is heresy. Have you no more to say?

Vio. Good madam, let me see your face.

Oli. Have you any commission from your lord to negotiate with my face? You are now out of your text: but we will draw the curtain and show you the picture. Look you, sir, such a one I was this present: is't not well done? [*Unveiling.*

Vio. Excellently done, if God did all.

Oli. 'Tis in grain, sir; 'twill endure wind and weather.

Vio. 'Tis beauty truly blent, whose red and white Nature's own sweet and cunning hand laid on: Lady, you are the cruell'st she alive, If you will lead these graces to the grave   260 And leave the world no copy.

Oli. O, sir, I will not be so hard-hearted; I will give out divers schedules of my beauty: it shall be inventoried, and every particle and utensil labelled to my will: as, item, two lips, indifferent red; item, two grey eyes, with lids to them; item, one neck, one chin, and so forth. Were you sent hither to praise me?

Vio. I see you what you are, you are too proud; But, if you were the devil, you are fair.   270 My lord and master loves you: O, such love Could be but recompensed, though you were crown'd The nonpareil of beauty!

Oli.   How does he love me?

Vio. With adorations, fertile tears, With groans that thunder love, with sighs of fire.

Oli. Your lord does know my mind; I cannot love him: Yet I suppose him virtuous, know him noble, Of great estate, of fresh and stainless youth; In voices well divulged, free, learn'd and valiant; And in dimension and the shape of nature 280 A gracious person: but yet I cannot love him; He might have took his answer long ago.

Vio. If I did love you in my master's flame, With such a suffering, such a deadly life, In your denial I would find no sense; I would not understand it.

Oli.   Why, what would you?

Vio. Make me a willow cabin at your gate, And call upon my soul within the house; Write loyal cantons of contemned love And sing them loud even in the dead of night; Halloo your name to the reverberate hills 291 And make the babbling gossip of the air Cry out 'Olivia!' O, you should not rest Between the elements of air and earth, But you should pity me!

Oli.   You might do much. What is your parentage?

Vio. Above my fortunes, yet my state is well: I am a gentleman.

Oli.   Get you to your lord; I cannot love him: let him send no more; Unless, perchance, you come to me again, 300 To tell me how he takes it. Fare you well: I thank you for your pains: spend this for me.

Vio. I am no fee'd post, lady; keep your purse: My master, not myself, lacks recompense. Love make his heart of flint that you shall love; And let your fervor, like my master's, be Placed in contempt! Farewell, fair cruelty. [*Exit.*

Oli. 'What is your parentage?' 'Above my fortunes, yet my state is well: I am a gentleman.' I'll be sworn thou art; 310 Thy tongue, thy face, thy limbs, actions and spirit, Do give thee five-fold blazon: not too fast: soft, soft!

Unless the master were the man. How now!
Even so quickly may one catch the plague?
Methinks I feel this youth's perfections
With an invisible and subtle stealth
To creep in at mine eyes. Well, let it be.
What ho, Malvolio!

Re-enter MALVOLIO.

Mal. Here, madam, at your service.
Oli. Run after that same peevish mes-
senger,
The county's man: he left this ring behind
him,
Would I or not: tell him I'll none of it. 321
Desire him not to flatter with his lord,
Nor hold him up with hopes; I am not for
him:
If that the youth will come this way to-mor-
row,
I'll give him reasons for't: hie thee, Malvolio.
Mal. Madam, I will. [*Exit.*
Oli. I do I know not what, and fear to find
Mine eye too great a flatterer for my mind.
Fate, show thy force: ourselves we do not
owe;
What is decreed must be, and be this so.
[*Exit.*

ACT II.

SCENE I. *The sea-coast.*

Enter ANTONIO *and* SEBASTIAN.

Ant. Will you stay no longer? nor will you
not that I go with you?
Seb. By your patience, no. My stars shine
darkly over me: the malignancy of my fate
might perhaps distemper yours; therefore I
shall crave of you your leave that I may bear
my evils alone: it were a bad recompense for
your love, to lay any of them on you.
Ant. Let me yet know of you whither you
are bound. 10
Seb. No, sooth, sir: my determinate voyage is mere extravagancy. But I perceive in
you so excellent a touch of modesty, that you
will not extort from me what I am willing to
keep in; therefore it charges me in manners
the rather to express myself. You must know
of me then, Antonio, my name is Sebastian,
which I called Roderigo. My father was that
Sebastian of Messaline, whom I know you
have heard of. He left behind him myself and
a sister, both born in an hour: if the heavens
had been pleased, would we had so ended!
but you, sir, altered that; for some hour before you took me from the breach of the sea
was my sister drowned.
Ant. Alas the day!
Seb. A lady, sir, though it was said she
much resembled me, was yet of many accounted beautiful: but, though I could not
with such estimable wonder overfar believe
that, yet thus far I will boldly publish her; she
bore a mind that envy could not but call fair.
She is drowned already, sir, with salt water,
though I seem to drown her remembrance
again with more.
Ant. Pardon me, sir, your bad entertainment.
Seb. O good Antonio, forgive me your
trouble.

Ant. If you will not murder me for my
love, let me be your servant.
Seb. If you will not undo what you have
done, that is, kill him whom you have recovered, desire it not. Fare ye well at once: my
bosom is full of kindness, and I am yet so
near the manners of my mother, that upon the
least occasion more mine eyes will tell tales of
me. I am bound to the Count Orsino's court:
farewell. [*Exit.*
Ant. The gentleness of all the gods go with
thee!
I have many enemies in Orsino's court,
Else would I very shortly see thee there.
But, come what may, I do adore thee so,
That danger shall seem sport, and I will go. 49
[*Exit.*

SCENE II. *A street.*

Enter VIOLA, MALVOLIO *following.*

Mal. Were not you even now with the
Countess Olivia?
Vio. Even now, sir; on a moderate pace I
have since arrived but hither.
Mal. She returns this ring to you, sir: you
might have saved me my pains, to have taken
it away yourself. She adds, moreover, that you
should put your lord into a desperate assurance she will none of him: and one thing
more, that you be never so hardy to come
again in his affairs, unless it be to report your
lord's taking of this. Receive it so.
Vio. She took the ring of me: I'll none of
it.
Mal. Come, sir, you peevishly threw it to
her; and her will is, it should be so returned:
if it be worth stooping for, there it lies in your
eye; if not, be it his that finds it. [*Exit.*
Vio. I left no ring with her: what means
this lady?
Fortune forbid my outside have not charm'd
her!
She made good view of me; indeed, so much,
That sure methought her eyes had lost her
tongue,
For she did speak in starts distractedly.
She loves me, sure; the cunning of her passion
Invites me in this churlish messenger.
None of my lord's ring! why, he sent her
none.
I am the man: if it be so, as 'tis,
Poor lady, she were better love a dream.
Disguise, I see, thou art a wickedness,
Wherein the pregnant enemy does much.
How easy is it for the proper-false 30
In women's waxen hearts to set their forms!
Alas, our frailty is the cause, not we!
For such as we are made of, such we be.
How will this fadge? my master loves her
dearly;
And I, poor monster, fond as much on him;
And she, mistaken, seems to dote on me.
What will become of this? As I am man,
My state is desperate for my master's love;
As I am woman,—now alas the day!—
What thriftless sighs shall poor Olivia breathe!
O time! thou must untangle this, not I; 41
It is too hard a knot for me to untie! [*Exit.*

SCENE III. OLIVIA'S *house.*

Enter SIR TOBY *and* SIR ANDREW.

Sir To. Approach, Sir Andrew: not to be

abed after midnight is to be up betimes ; and
' diluculo surgere,' thou know'st,—
Sir And. Nay, my troth, I know not : but
I know, to be up late is to be up late.
Sir To. A false conclusion : I hate it as an
unfilled can. To be up after midnight and to
go to bed then, is early : so that to go to bed
after midnight is to go to bed betimes. Does
not our life consist of the four elements ?   10
Sir And. Faith, so they say ; but I think it
rather consists of eating and drinking.
Sir To. Thou'rt a scholar ; let us therefore
eat and drink. Marian, I say ! a stoup of wine !

Enter CLOWN.

Sir And. Here comes the fool, i' faith.
Clo. How now, my hearts ! did you never
see the picture of ' we three ' ?
Sir To. Welcome, ass. Now let's have a
catch.
Sir And. By my troth, the fool has an excellent breast. I had rather than forty shillings I had such a leg, and so sweet a breath
to sing, as the fool has. In sooth, thou wast in
very gracious fooling last night, when thou
spokest of Pigrogromitus, of the Vapians passing the equinoctial of Queubus : 'twas very
good, i' faith. I sent thee sixpence for thy
leman : hadst it ?
Clo. I did impeticos thy gratillity ; for
Malvolio's nose is no whipstock : my lady has
a white hand, and the Myrmidons are no bot-
tle-ale houses.
Sir And. Excellent ! why, this is the best
fooling, when all is done. Now, a song.   31
Sir To. Come on ; there is sixpence for
you : let's have a song.
Sir And. There's a testril of me too : if one
knight give a—
Clo. Would you have a love-song, or a
song of good life ?
Sir To. A love-song, a love-song.
Sir And. Ay, ay : I care not for good life.
Clo. [Sings.]   39

O mistress mine, where are you roaming ?
O, stay and hear ; your true love's coming,
    That can sing both high and low :
Trip no further, pretty sweeting ;
Journeys end in lovers meeting,
    Every wise man's son doth know.
Sir And. Excellent good, i' faith.
Sir To. Good, good.
Clo. [Sings.]

What is love ? 'tis not hereafter ;
Present mirth hath present laughter ;
    What's to come is still unsure :   50
In delay there lies no plenty ;
Then come kiss me, sweet and twenty,
    Youth's a stuff will not endure.
Sir And. A mellifluous voice, as I am true
knight.
Sir To. A contagious breath.
Sir And. Very sweet and contagious, i'
faith.
Sir To. To hear by the nose, it is dulcet in
contagion. But shall we make the welkin dance
indeed ? shall we rouse the night-owl in a
catch that will draw three souls out of one
weaver ? shall we do that ?
Sir And. An you love me, let's do't : I am
dog at a catch.
Clo. By'r lady, sir, and some dogs will
    catch well.

Sir And. Most certain. Let our catch be,
' Thou knave.'
Clo. ' Hold thy peace, thou knave,' knight ?
I shall be constrained in't to call thee knave,
knight.   70
Sir And. 'Tis not the first time I have con-
strained one to call me knave. Begin, fool : it
begins ' Hold thy peace.'
Clo. I shall never begin if I hold my peace.
Sir And. Good, i' faith. Come, begin.
                                        [Catch sung.

Enter MARIA.

Mar. What a caterwauling do you keep
here ! If my lady have not called up her steward Malvolio and bid him turn you out of
doors, never trust me.   79
Sir To. My lady's a Cataian, we are politi-
cians, Malvolio's a Peg-a-Ramsey, and ' Three
merry men be we.' Am not I consanguineous ?
am I not of her blood ? Tillyvally. Lady !
                                           [Sings.]
' There dwelt a man in Babylon, lady, lady ! '
Clo. Beshrew me, the knight's in admirable
fooling.
Sir And. Ay, he does well enough if he be
disposed, and so do I too : he does it with a
better grace, but I do it more natural.
Sir To. [Sings] ' O, the twelfth day of
December,'—   91
Mar. For the love o' God, peace !

Enter MALVOLIO.

Mal. My masters, are you mad ? or what
are you ? Have ye no wit, manners, nor honesty, but to gabble like tinkers at this time of
night ? Do ye make an alehouse of my lady's
house, that ye squeak out your coziers' catches
without any mitigation or remorse of voice ?
Is there no respect of place, persons, nor time
in you ?
Sir To. We did keep time, sir, in our
catches. Sneck up !   101
Mal. Sir Toby, I must be round with you.
My lady bade me tell you, that, though she
harbors you as her kinsman, she's nothing
allied to your disorders. If you can separate
yourself and your misdemeanors, you are wel-
come to the house ; if not, an it would please
you to take leave of her, she is very willing to
bid you farewell.
Sir To. ' Farewell, dear heart, since I must
needs be gone.'   110
Mar. Nay, good Sir Toby.
Clo. ' His eyes do show his days are al-
most done.'
Mal. Is't even so ?
Sir To. ' But I will never die.'
Clo. Sir Toby, there you lie.
Mal. This is much credit to you.
Sir To. ' Shall I bid him go ? '
Clo. ' What an if you do ? '
Sir To. ' Shall I bid him go, and spare
not ? '
Clo. ' O no, no, no, no, you dare not.'   121
Sir To. Out o' tune, sir : ye lie. Art any
more than a steward ? Dost thou think, be-
cause thou art virtuous, there shall be no more
cakes and ale ?
Clo. Yes, by Saint Anne, and ginger shall
be hot i' the mouth too.
Sir To. Thou'rt i' the right. Go, sir, rub

your chain with crumbs. A stoup of wine,
Maria !

Mal. Mistress Mary, if you prized my
lady's favor at any thing more than contempt,
you would not give means for this uncivil
rule : she shall know of it, by this hand. [*Exit.*

Mar. Go shake your ears.

Sir And. 'Twere as good a deed as to drink
when a man's a-hungry, to challenge him the
field, and then to break promise with him and
make a fool of him.

Sir To. Do't, knight : I'll write thee a challenge : or I'll deliver thy indignation to him
by word of mouth.　　　141

Mar. Sweet Sir Toby, be patient for to-
night : since the youth of the count's was to-
day with my lady, she is much out of quiet.
For Monsieur Malvolio, let me alone with
him : if I do not gull him into a nayword,
and make him a common recreation, do not
think I have wit enough to lie straight in my
bed : I know I can do it.

Sir To. Possess us, possess us ; tell us
something of him.　　　150

Mar. Marry, sir, sometimes he is a kind of
puritan.

Sir And. O, if I thought that I'ld beat him
like a dog !

Sir To. What, for being a puritan ? thy exquisite reason, dear knight ?

Sir And. I have no exquisite reason for't,
but I have reason good enough.

Mar. The devil a puritan that he is, or any
thing constantly, but a time-pleaser ; an affec-
tioned ass, that cons state without book and
utters it by great swarths : the best persuaded
of himself, so crammed, as he thinks, with ex-
cellencies, that it is his grounds of faith that
all that look on him love him ; and on that
vice in him will my revenge find notable cause
to work.

Sir To. What wilt thou do ?

Mar. I will drop in his way some obscure
epistles of love ; wherein, by the color of his
beard, the shape of his leg, the manner of his
gait, the expressure of his eye, forehead, and
complexion, he shall find himself most feelingly personated. I can write very like my lady
your niece : on a forgotten matter we can
hardly make distinction of our hands.

Sir To. Excellent ! I smell a device.

Sir And. I have't in my nose too.

Sir To. He shall think, by the letters that
thou wilt drop, that they come from my niece,
and that she's in love with him.　　　180

Mar. My purpose is, indeed, a horse of
that color.

Sir And. And your horse now would make
him an ass.

Mar. Ass, I doubt not.

Sir And. O, 'twill be admirable !

Mar. Sport royal, I warrant you : I know
my physic will work with him. I will plant you
two, and let the fool make a third, where he
shall find the letter : observe his construction
of it. For this night, to bed, and dream on
the event. Farewell.　　　[*Exit.*

Sir To. Good night, Penthesilea.

Sir And. Before me, she's a good wench.

Sir To. She's a beagle, true-bred, and one
that adores me : what o' that ?

Sir And. I was adored once too.

Sir To. Let's to bed, knight. Thou hadst
need send for more money.

Sir And. If I cannot recover your niece, I
am a foul way out.　　　201

Sir To. Send for money, knight : if thou
hast her not i' the end, call me cut.

Sir And. If I do not, never trust me, take
it how you will.

Sir To. Come, come, I'll go burn some
sack ; 'tis too late to go to bed now : come,
knight ; come, knight.　　　[*Exeunt.*

SCENE IV. *The* DUKE'S *palace.*

Enter DUKE, VIOLA, CURIO, *and others.*

Duke. Give me some music. Now, good
morrow, friends.
Now, good Cesario, but that piece of song,
That old and antique song we heard last night :
Methought it did relieve my passion much,
More than light airs and recollected terms
Of these most brisk and giddy-paced times :
Come, but one verse.

Cur. He is not here, so please your lordship that should sing it.

Duke. Who was it ?　　　10

Cur. Feste, the jester, my lord ; a fool that
the lady Olivia's father took much delight in.
He is about the house.

Duke. Seek him out, and play the tune the
while.　　　[*Exit Curio. Music plays.*
Come hither, boy : if ever thou shalt love,
In the sweet pangs of it remember me ;
For such as I am all true lovers are,
Unstaid and skittish in all motions else,
Save in the constant image of the creature
That is beloved. How dost thou like this tune ?

Vio. It gives a very echo to the seat　　　21
Where Love is throned.

Duke. Thou dost speak masterly :
My life upon't, young though thou art, thine
　　　eye
Hath stay'd upon some favor that it loves :
Hath it not, boy ?

Vio. A little, by your favor.

Duke. What kind of woman is't ?

Vio. Of your complexion.

Duke. She is not worth thee, then. What
years, i' faith ?

Vio. About your years, my lord.

Duke. Too old, by heaven : let still the
　　　woman take　　　30
An elder than herself : so wears she to him,
So sways she level in her husband's heart :
For, boy, however we do praise ourselves,
Our fancies are more giddy and unfirm,
More longing, wavering, sooner lost and worn,
Than women's are.

Vio. I think it well, my lord.

Duke. Then let thy love be younger than
　　　thyself,
Or thy affection cannot hold the bent ;
For women are as roses, whose fair flower　　　39
Being once display'd, doth fall that very hour.

Vio. And so they are : alas, that they are
　　　so ;
To die, even when they to perfection grow !

Re-enter CURIO *and* CLOWN.

Duke. O, fellow, come, the song we had
　　　last night.
Mark it, Cesario, it is old and plain ;
The spinsters and the knitters in the sun

And the free maids that weave their thread
   with bones
Do use to chant it : it is silly sooth,
And dallies with the innocence of love,
Like the old age.
  Clo.   Are you ready, sir ?   50
  Duke.   Ay; prithee, sing.   [*Music.*

           SONG.

  Clo.   Come away, come away, death,
       And in sad cypress let me be laid ;
    Fly away, fly away, breath ;
       I am slain by a fair cruel maid.
    My shroud of white, stuck all with
       yew,
       O, prepare it !
    My part of death, no one so true
       Did share it.

    Not a flower, not a flower sweet, 60
       On my black coffin let there be
       strown ;
    Not a friend, not a friend greet
    My poor corpse, where my bones
       shall be thrown :
    A thousand thousand sighs to save,
       Lay me, O, where
    Sad true lover never find my grave,
       To weep there !
  Duke.   There's for thy pains.
  Clo.   No pains, sir : I take pleasure in
singing, sir.   70
  Duke.   I'll pay thy pleasure then.
  Clo.   Truly, sir, and pleasure will be paid,
one time or another.
  Duke.   Give me now leave to leave thee.
  Clo.   Now, the melancholy god protect
thee ; and the tailor make thy doublet of
changeable taffeta, for thy mind is a very opal.
I would have men of such constancy put to
sea, that their business might be every thing
and their intent every where ; for that's it that
always makes a good voyage of nothing. Fare-
well.   [*Exit.*   81
  Duke.   Let all the rest give place.
        [*Curio and Attendants retire.*
            Once more, Cesario,
Get thee to yond same sovereign cruelty :
Tell her, my love, more noble than the world,
Prizes not quantity of dirty lands ;
The parts that fortune hath bestow'd upon her,
Tell her, I hold as giddily as fortune ;
But 'tis that miracle and queen of gems
That nature pranks her in attracts my soul.
  Vio.   But if she cannot love you, sir ?   90
  Duke.   I cannot be so answer'd.
  Vio.   Sooth, but you must.
Say that some lady, as perhaps there is,
Hath for your love as great a pang of heart
As you have for Olivia : you cannot love her ;
You tell her so ; must she not then be an-
   swer'd ?
  Duke.   There is no woman's sides
Can bide the beating of so strong a passion
As love doth give my heart ; no woman's heart
So big, to hold so much ; they lack retention
Alas, their love may be call'd appetite,   100
No motion of the liver, but the palate,
That suffer surfeit, cloyment and revolt ;
But mine is all as hungry as the sea,
And can digest as much : make no compare
Between that love a woman can bear me
And that I owe Olivia.
  Vio.   Ay, but I know—

  Duke.   What dost thou know ?
  Vio.   Too well what love women to men
   may owe :
In faith, they are as true of heart as we.
My father had a daughter loved a man,   110
As it might be, perhaps, were I a woman,
I should your lordship.
  Duke.   And what's her history ?
  Vio.   A blank, my lord. She never told her
   love,
But let concealment, like a worm i' the bud,
Feed on her damask cheek : she pined in
   thought,
And with a green and yellow melancholy
She sat like patience on a monument,
Smiling at grief. Was not this love indeed ?
We men may say more, swear more : but in-
   deed
Our shows are more than will ; for still we
   prove   120
Much in our vows, but little in our love.
  Duke.   But died thy sister of her love, my
   boy ?
  Vio.   I am all the daughters of my father's
   house,
And all the brothers too : and yet I know not.
Sir, shall I to this lady ?
  Duke.   Ay, that's the theme.
To her in haste ; give her this jewel ; say,
My love can give no place, bide no denay.
                     [*Exeunt.*

    SCENE V.   OLIVIA'S *garden.*

   Enter SIR TOBY, SIR ANDREW, *and* FABIAN.

  Sir To.   Come thy ways, Signior Fabian.
  Fab.   Nay, I'll come : if I lose a scruple of
this sport, let me be boiled to death with melancholy.
  Sir To.   Wouldst thou not be glad to have
the niggardly rascally sheep-biter come by
some notable shame ?
  Fab.   I would exult, man : you know, he
brought me out o' favor with my lady about
a bear-baiting here.   10
  Sir To.   To anger him we'll have the bear
again ; and we will fool him black and blue :
shall we not, Sir Andrew ?
  Sir And.   An we do not, it is pity of our
lives.
  Sir To.   Here comes the little villain.

          Enter MARIA.

How now, my metal of India !
  Mar.   Get ye all three into the box-tree :
Malvolio's coming down this walk : he has
been yonder i' the sun practising behavior to
his own shadow this half hour : observe him,
for the love of mockery ; for I know this letter will make a contemplative idiot of him.
Close, in the name of jesting ! Lie thou there
[*throws down a letter*], for here comes the
trout that must be caught with tickling.
                     [*Exit.*

        Enter MALVOLIO.

  Mal.   'Tis but fortune ; all is fortune.
Maria once told me she did affect me : and I
have heard herself come thus near, that,
should she fancy, it should be one of my complexion. Besides, she uses me with a more exalted respect than any one else that follows
her. What should I think on't ?
  Sir To.   Here's an overweening rogue !

Fab. O, peace! Contemplation makes a rare turkey-cock of him: how he jets under his advanced plumes!

Sir And. 'Slight, I could so beat the rogue!

Sir To. Peace, I say.

Mal. To be Count Malvolio!	40

Sir To. Ah, rogue!

Sir And. Pistol him, pistol him.

Sir To. Peace, peace!

Mal. There is example for't; the lady of the Strachy married the yeoman of the wardrobe.

Sir And. Fie on him, Jezebel!

Fab. O, peace! now he's deeply in: look how imagination blows him.

Mal. Having been three months married to her, sitting in my state,—	50

Sir To. O, for a stone-bow, to hit him in the eye!

Mal. Calling my officers about me, in my branched velvet gown; having come from a day-bed, where I have left Olivia sleeping,—

Sir To. Fire and brimstone!

Fab. O, peace, peace!

Mal. And then to have the humor of state; and after a demure travel of regard, telling them I know my place as I would they should do theirs, to ask for my kinsman Toby,—	61

Sir To. Bolts and shackles!

Fab. O peace, peace, peace! now, now.

Mal. Seven of my people, with an obedient start, make out for him: I frown the while; and perchance wind up my watch, or play with my—some rich jewel. Toby approaches; courtesies there to me,—

Sir To. Shall this fellow live?

Fab. Though our silence be drawn from us with cars, yet peace.	71

Mal. I extend my hand to him thus, quenching my familiar smile with an austere regard of control,—

Sir To. And does not Toby take you a blow o' the lips then?

Mal. Saying, 'Cousin Toby, my fortunes having cast me on your niece give me this prerogative of speech,'—

Sir To. What, what?	80

Mal. 'You must amend your drunkenness.'

Sir To. Out, scab!

Fab. Nay, patience, or we break the sinews of our plot.

Mal. 'Besides, you waste the treasure of your time with a foolish knight,'—

Sir And. That's me, I warrant you.

Mal. 'One Sir Andrew,'—

Sir And. I knew 'twas I; for many do call me fool.	90

Mal. What employment have we here?
[*Taking up the letter.*

Fab. Now is the woodcock near the gin.

Sir To. O, peace! and the spirit of humors intimate reading aloud to him!

Mal. By my life, this is my lady's hand: these be her very C's, her U's and her T's; and thus makes she her great P's. It is, in contempt of question, her hand.

Sir And. Her C's, her U's and her T's: why that?	100

Mal. [*Reads*] 'To the unknown beloved, this, and my good wishes:'—her very phrases! By your leave, wax. Soft! and the impressure her Lucrece, with which she uses to seal:

'tis my lady. To whom should this be?

Fab. This wins him, liver and all.

Mal. [*Reads*]
   Jove knows I love:
      But who?
   Lips, do not move;
      No man must know.	110

'No man must know.' What follows? the numbers altered! 'No man must know:' if this should be thee, Malvolio?

Sir To. Marry, hang thee, brock!

Mal. [*Reads*]
   I may command where I adore;
      But silence, like a Lucrece knife,
   With bloodless stroke my heart doth gore:
      M, O, A, I, doth sway my life.

Fab. A fustian riddle!

Sir To. Excellent wench, say I.	120

Mal. 'M, O, A, I, doth sway my life.' Nay, but first, let me see, let me see, let me see.

Fab. What dish o' poison has she dressed him!

Sir To. And with what wing the staniel checks at it!

Mal. 'I may command where I adore.' Why, she may command me: I serve her; she is my lady. Why, this is evident to any formal capacity; there is no obstruction in this: and the end,—what should that alphabetical position portend? If I could make that resemble something in me,—Softly! M, O, A, I,—

Sir To. O, ay, make up that: he is now at a cold scent.

Fab. Sowter will cry upon't for all this, though it be as rank as a fox.

Mal. M,—Malvolio; M,—why, that begins my name.

Fab. Did not I say he would work it out? the cur is excellent at faults.	140

Mal. M,—but then there is no consonancy in the sequel; that suffers under probation: A should follow, but O does.

Fab. And O shall end, I hope.

Sir To. Ay, or I'll cudgel him, and make him cry O!

Mal. And then I comes behind.

Fab. Ay, an you had any eye behind you, you might see more detraction at your heels than fortunes before you.	150

Mal. M, O, A, I; this simulation is not as the former: and yet, to crush this a little, it would bow to me, for every one of these letters are in my name. Soft! here follows prose.

[*Reads*] 'If this fall into thy hand, revolve. In my stars I am above thee; but be not afraid of greatness: some are born great, some achieve greatness, and some have greatness thrust upon 'em. Thy Fates open their hands; let thy blood and spirit embrace them; and, to inure thyself to what thou art like to be, cast thy humble slough and appear fresh. Be opposite with a kinsman, surly with servants; let thy tongue tang arguments of state; put thyself into the trick of singularity: she thus advises thee that sighs for thee. Remember who commended thy yellow stockings, and wished to see thee ever cross-gartered: I say, remember. Go to, thou art made, if thou desirest to be so; if not, let me see thee a steward still, the fellow of servants, and not worthy to touch Fortune's fingers. Farewell. She that would alter services with thee,

THE FORTUNATE-UNHAPPY.'

Daylight and champain discovers not more : this is open. I will be proud, I will read politic authors, I will baffle Sir Toby, I will wash off gross acquaintance, I will be point-devise the very man. I do not now fool myself, to let imagination jade me ; for every reason excites to this, that my lady loves me. She did commend my yellow stockings of late, she did praise my leg being cross-gartered ; and in this she manifests herself to my love, and with a kind of injunction drives me to these habits of her liking. I thank my stars I am happy. I will be strange, stout, in yellow stockings, and cross-gartered, even with the swiftness of putting on. Jove and my stars be praised ! Here is yet a postscript.

[*Reads*] ' Thou canst not choose but know who I am. If thou entertainest my love, let it appear in thy smiling ; thy smiles become thee well ; therefore in my presence still smile, dear my sweet, I prithee.'

Jove, I thank thee : I will smile ; I will do everything that thou wilt have me. [*Exit.*

Fab. I will not give my part of this sport for a pension of thousands to be paid from the Sophy.

Sir To. I could marry this wench for this device.

Sir And. So could I too. 200

Sir To. And ask no other dowry with her but such another jest.

Sir And. Nor I neither.

Fab. Here comes my noble gull-catcher.

Re-enter MARIA.

Sir To. Wilt thou set thy foot o' my neck ?

Sir And. Or o' mine either ?

Sir To. Shall I play my freedom at tray-trip, and become thy bond-slave ?

Sir And. I' faith, or I either ? 209

Sir To. Why, thou hast put him in such a dream, that when the image of it leaves him he must run mad.

Mar. Nay, but say true ; does it work upon him ?

Sir To. Like aqua-vitæ with a midwife.

Mar. If you will then see the fruits of the sport, mark his first approach before my lady : he will come to her in yellow stockings, and 'tis a color she abhors, and cross-gartered, a fashion she detests ; and he will smile upon her, which will now be so unsuitable to her disposition, being addicted to a melancholy as she is, that it cannot but turn him into a notable contempt. If you will see it, follow me.

Sir To. To the gates of Tartar, thou most excellent devil of wit !

Sir And. I'll make one too. [*Exeunt.*

ACT III.

SCENE I. OLIVIA'S *garden.*

Enter VIOLA, *and* CLOWN *with a tabor.*

Vio. Save thee, friend, and thy music : dost thou live by thy tabor ?

Clo. No, sir, I live by the church.

Vio. Art thou a churchman ?

Clo. No such matter, sir : I do live by the

church ; for I do live at my house, and my house doth stand by the church.

Vio. So thou mayst say, the king lies by a beggar, if a beggar dwell near him ; or, the church stands by thy tabor, if thy tabor stand by the church. 11

Clo. You have said, sir. To see this age ! A sentence is but a cheveril glove to a good wit : how quickly the wrong side may be turned outward !

Vio. Nay, that's certain ; they that dally nicely with words may quickly make them wanton.

Clo. I would, therefore, my sister had had no name, sir. 20

Vio. Why, man ?

Clo. Why, sir, her name's a word ; and to dally with that word might make my sister wanton. But indeed words are very rascals since bonds disgraced them.

Vio. Thy reason, man ?

Clo. Troth, sir, I can yield you none without words ; and words are grown so false, I am loath to prove reason with them.

Vio. I warrant thou art a merry fellow and carest for nothing. 31

Clo. Not so, sir, I do care for something ; but in my conscience, sir, I do not care for you : if that be to care for nothing, sir, I would it would make you invisible.

Vio. Art not thou the Lady Olivia's fool ?

Clo. No, indeed, sir ; the Lady Olivia has no folly : she will keep no fool, sir, till she be married ; and fools are as like husbands as pilchards are to herrings ; the husband's the bigger : I am indeed not her fool, but her corrupter of words.

Vio. I saw thee late at the Count Orsino's.

Clo. Foolery, sir, does walk about the orb like the sun, it shines every where. I would be sorry, sir, but the fool should be as oft with your master as with my mistress : I think I saw your wisdom there.

Vio. Nay, an thou pass upon me, I'll no more with thee. Hold, there's expenses for thee.

Clo. Now Jove, in his next commodity of hair, send thee a beard ! 51

Vio. By my troth, I'll tell thee, I am almost sick for one ; [*Aside*] though I would not have it grow on my chin. Is thy lady within ?

Clo. Would not a pair of these have bred, sir ?

Vio. Yes, being kept together and put to use.

Clo. I would play Lord Pandarus of Phrygia, sir, to bring a Cressida to this Troilus.

Vio. I understand you, sir ; 'tis well begged.

Clo. The matter, I hope, is not great, sir, begging but a beggar : Cressida was a beggar. My lady is within, sir. I will construe to them whence you come ; who you are and what you would are out of my welkin, I might say ' element,' but the word is over-worn. [*Exit.*

Vio. This fellow is wise enough to play the fool ;

And to do that well craves a kind of wit : He must observe their mood on whom he jests, The quality of persons, and the time, 70 And, like the haggard, check at every feather That comes before his eye. This is a practice

As full of labor as a wise man's art :
For folly that he wisely shows is fit ;
But wise men, folly-fall'n, quite taint their wit.

Enter Sir Toby, *and* Sir Andrew.

Sir To. Save you, gentleman.
Vio. And you, sir.
Sir And. Dieu vous garde, monsieur.
Vio. Et vous aussi ; votre serviteur.
Sir And. I hope, sir, you are ; and I am yours.　　　81
Sir To. Will you encounter the house ? my niece is desirous you should enter, if your trade be to her.
Vio. I am bound to your niece, sir ; I mean, she is the list of my voyage.
Sir To. Taste your legs, sir ; put them to motion.
Vio. My legs do better understand me, sir, than I understand what you mean by bidding me taste my legs.　　　91
Sir To. I mean, to go, sir, to enter.
Vio. I will answer you with gait and entrance. But we are prevented.

Enter Olivia *and* Maria.

Most excellent accomplished lady, the heavens rain odors on you !
Sir And. That youth's a rare courtier : 'Rain odors ; ' well.
Vio. My matter hath no voice, lady, but to your own most pregnant and vouchsafed ear.
Sir And. 'Odors,' 'pregnant' and 'vouchsafed : ' I'll get 'em all three all ready.
Oli. Let the garden door be shut, and leave me to my hearing. [*Exeunt Sir Toby, Sir Andrew, and Maria.*] Give me your hand, sir.
Vio. My duty, madam, and most humble service.
Oli. What is your name ?
Vio. Cesario is your servant's name, fair princess.
Oli. My servant, sir ! 'Twas never merry world
Since lowly feigning was call'd compliment :
You're servant to the Count Orsino, youth.
Vio. And he is yours, and his must needs be yours :
Your servant's servant is your servant, madam.
Oli. For him, I think not on him : for his thoughts,
Would they were blanks, rather than fill'd with me !
Vio. Madam, I come to whet your gentle thoughts
On his behalf.
Oli.　　　O, by your leave, I pray you,
I bade you never speak again of him :
But, would you undertake another suit,
I had rather hear you to solicit that　　　120
Than music from the spheres.
Vio.　　　Dear lady,—
Oli. Give me leave, beseech you. I did send,
After the last enchantment you did here,
A ring in chase of you : so did I abuse
Myself, my servant, and, I fear me, you :
Under your hard construction must I sit,
To force that on you, in a shameful cunning,
Which you knew none of yours : what might you think ?
Have you not set mine honor at the stake

And baited it with all the unmuzzled thoughts
That tyrannous heart can think ? To one of your receiving　　　131
Enough is shown : a cypress, not a bosom,
Hideth my heart. So, let me hear you speak.
Vio. I pity you.
Oli.　　　That's a degree to love.
Vio. No, not a grize ; for 'tis a vulgar proof,
That very oft we pity enemies.
Oli. Why, then, methinks 'tis time to smile again.
O world, how apt the poor are to be proud !
If one should be a prey, how much the better
To fall before the lion than the wolf !　　　140
　　　　　　　　　　[*Clock strikes.*
The clock upbraids me with the waste of time.
Be not afraid, good youth, I will not have you :
And yet, when wit and youth is come to harvest,
Your wife is alike to reap a proper man :
There lies your way, due west.
Vio.　　　Then westward-ho ! Grace and good disposition
Attend your ladyship !
You'll nothing, madam, to my lord by me ?
Oli. Stay :
I prithee, tell me what thou thinkest of me.
Vio. That you do think you are not what you are.
Oli. If I think so, I think the same of you.
Vio. Then think you right : I am not what I am.
Oli. I would you were as I would have you be !
Vio. Would it be better, madam, than I am ?
I wish it might, for now I am your fool.
Oli. O, what a deal of scorn looks beautiful
In the contempt and anger of his lip !
A murderous guilt shows not itself more soon
Than love that would seem hid : love's night is noon.　　　160
Cesario, by the roses of the spring,
By maidhood, honor, truth and every thing,
I love thee so, that, maugre all thy pride,
Nor wit nor reason can my passion hide.
Do not extort thy reasons from this clause,
For that I woo, thou therefore hast no cause,
But rather reason thus with reason fetter,
Love sought is good, but given unsought is better.
Vio. By innocence I swear, and by my youth,
I have one heart, one bosom and one truth,
And that no woman has ; nor never none　　　171
Shall mistress be of it, save I alone.
And so adieu, good madam : never more
Will I my master's tears to you deplore.
Oli. Yet come again ; for thou perhaps mayst move
That heart, which now abhors, to like his love.
　　　　　　　　　　[*Exeunt.*

SCENE II. Olivia's *house.*

Enter Sir Toby, Sir Andrew, *and* Fabian.

Sir And. No, faith, I'll not stay a jot longer.
Sir To. Thy reason, dear venom, give thy reason.
Fab. You must needs yield your reason, Sir Andrew.

Sir And. Marry, I saw your niece do more favors to the count's serving-man than ever she bestowed upon me ; I saw't i' the orchard.

Sir To. Did she see thee the while, old boy ? tell me that.　　　　　　　　　　10

Sir And. As plain as I see you now.

Fab. This was a great argument of love in her toward you.

Sir And. 'Slight, will you make an ass o' me ?

Fab. I will prove it legitimate, sir, upon the oaths of judgment and reason.

Sir To. And they have been grand-jury-men since before Noah was a sailor.

Fab. She did show favor to the youth in your sight only to exasperate you, to awake your dormouse valor, to put fire in your heart, and brimstone in your liver. You should then have accosted her ; and with some excellent jests, fire-new from the mint, you should have banged the youth into dumbness. This was looked for at your hand, and this was balked : the double gilt of this opportunity you let time wash off, and you are now sailed into the north of my lady's opinion ; where you will hang like an icicle on a Dutchman's beard, unless you do redeem it by some laudable attempt either of valor or policy. 31

Sir And. An't be any way, it must be with valor ; for policy I hate : I had as lief be a Brownist as a politician.

Sir To. Why, then, build me thy fortunes upon the basis of valor. Challenge me the count's youth to fight with him ; hurt him in eleven places : my niece shall take note of it ; and assure thyself, there is no love-broker in the world can more prevail in man's commendation with woman than report of valor.　　41

Fab. There is no way but this, Sir Andrew.

Sir And. Will either of you bear me a challenge to him ?

Sir To. Go, write it in a martial hand ; be curst and brief ; it is no matter how witty, so it be eloquent and full of invention : taunt him with the license of ink : if thou thou'st him some thrice, it shall not be amiss ; and as many lies as will lie in thy sheet of paper, although the sheet were big enough for the bed of Ware in England, set 'em down : go, about it. Let there be gall enough in thy ink, though thou write with a goose-pen, no matter : about it.

Sir And. Where shall I find you ?

Sir To. We'll call thee at the cubiculo : go.　　　　　　　　　　[*Exit Sir Andrew.*

Fab. This is a dear manakin to you, Sir Toby.

Sir To. I have been dear to him, lad, some two thousand strong, or so.

Fab. We shall have a rare letter from him : but you'll not deliver't ?　　　　　　　61

Sir To. Never trust me, then ; and by all means stir on the youth to an answer. I think oxen and wainropes cannot hale them together. For Andrew, if he were opened, and you find so much blood in his liver as will clog the foot of a flea, I'll eat the rest of the anatomy.

Fab. And his opposite, the youth, bears in his visage no great presage of cruelty.

Enter MARIA.

Sir To. Look, where the youngest wren of nine comes.　　　　　　　　　　71

Mar. If you desire the spleen, and will laugh yourself into stitches, follow me. Yond gull Malvolio is turned heathen, a very renegado ; for there is no Christian, that means to be saved by believing rightly, can ever believe such impossible passages of grossness. He's in yellow stockings.

Sir To. And cross-gartered ?　　　　79

Mar. Most villanously ; like a pedant that keeps a school i' the church. I have dogged him, like his murderer. He does obey every point of the letter that I dropped to betray him : he does smile his face into more lines than is in the new map with the augmentation of the Indies : you have not seen such a thing as 'tis. I can hardly forbear hurling things at him. I know my lady will strike him : if she do, he'll smile and take't for a great favor.

Sir To. Come, bring us, bring us where he is.　　　　　　　　　　[*Exeunt.* 90

SCENE III. *A street.*

Enter SEBASTIAN *and* ANTONIO.

Seb. I would not by my will have troubled you ;

But, since you make your pleasure of your pains,

I will no further chide you.

Ant.　　I could not stay behind you : my desire,

More sharp than filed steel, did spur me forth ;

And not all love to see you, though so much

As might have drawn one to a longer voyage,

But jealousy what might befall your travel,

Being skilless in these parts ; which to a stranger,

Unguided and unfriended, often prove　　10

Rough and unhospitable : my willing love,

The rather by these arguments of fear,

Set forth in your pursuit.

Seb.　　　　My kind Antonio,

I can no other answer make but thanks,

And thanks ; and ever. . . . oft good turns

Are shuffled off with such uncurrent pay :

But, were my worth as is my conscience firm,

You should find better dealing. What's to do ?

Shall we go see the reliques of this town ?

Ant. To-morrow, sir : best first go see your lodging.　　　　　　　　　　20

Seb. I am not weary, and 'tis long to night :

I pray you, let us satisfy our eyes

With the memorials and the things of fame

That do renown this city.

Ant.　　　　Would you'ld pardon me ;

I do not without danger walk these streets :

Once, in a sea-fight, 'gainst the count his galleys

I did some service ; of such note indeed,

That were I ta'en here it would scarce be answer'd.

Seb. Belike you slew great number of his people.

Ant. The offence is not of such a bloody nature ;　　　　　　　　　　30

Albeit the quality of the time and quarrel

Might well have given us bloody argument.

It might have since been answer'd in repaying

What we took from them ; which, for traffic's sake,

Most of our city did : only myself stood out ;
For which, if I be lapsed in this place,
I shall pay dear.
Seb.   Do not then walk too open.
Ant. It doth not fit me. Hold, sir, here's
  my purse.
In the south suburbs, at the Elephant,
Is best to lodge : I will bespeak our diet,   40
Whiles you beguile the time and feed your
    knowlcdge
With viewing of the town : there shall you
    have me.
Seb. Why I your purse ?
Ant. Haply your eye shall light upon some
    toy
You have desire to purchase ; and your store,
I think, is not for idle markets, sir.
Seb. I'll be your purse-bearer and leave
    you
For an hour.
Ant. To the Elephant.
Seb.   I do remember. [*Exeunt.*

Scene IV. Olivia's *garden.*

Enter Olivia *and* Maria.

Oli. I have sent after him : he says he'll
    come ;
How shall I feast him ? what bestow of him ?
For youth is bought more oft than begg'd or
    borrow'd.
I speak too loud.
Where is Malvolio ? he is sad and civil,
And suits well for a servant with my fortunes :
Where is Malvolio ?
Mar. He's coming, madam ; but in very
strange manner. He is, sure, possessed,
madam.
Oli. Why, what's the matter ? does he
rave ?
Mar. No, madam, he does nothing but
smile : your ladyship were best to have some
guard about you, if he come ; for, sure, the
man is tainted in's wits.
Oli. Go call him hither. [*Exit Maria.*] I
am as mad as he,
If sad and merry madness equal be.

Re-enter Maria, *with* Malvolio.

How now, Malvolio !
Mal. Sweet lady, ho, ho.
Oli. Smilest thou ?
I sent for thee upon a sad occasion.   20
Mal. Sad, lady ! I could be sad : this does
make some obstruction in the blood, this cross-
gartering ; but what of that ? if it please the
eye of one, it is with me as the very true son-
net is, 'Please one, and please all.'
Oli. Why, how dost thou, man ? what is
the matter with thee ?
Mal. Not black in my mind, though yellow
in my legs. It did come to his hands, and commands shall be executed : I think we do know
the sweet Roman hand.   31
Oli. Wilt thou go to bed, Malvolio ?
Mal. To bed ! ay, sweet-heart, and I'll
come to thee.
Oli. God comfort thee ! Why dost thou
smile so and kiss thy hand so oft ?
Mar. How do you, Malvolio ?
Mal. At your request ! yes ; nightingales
answer daws.
Mar. Why appear you with this ridiculous
boldness before my lady ?   41

Mal. 'Be not afraid of greatness : ' 'twas
well writ.
Oli. What meanest thou by that, Mal-
volio ?
Mal. 'Some are born great,'—
Oli. Ha !
Mal. 'Some achieve greatness,'—
Oli. What sayest thou ?
Mal. 'And some have greatness thrust
upon them.'   50
Oli. Heaven restore thee !
Mal. 'Remember who commended thy yel-
low stockings,'—
Oli. Thy yellow stockings !
Mal. 'And wished to see thee cross-gar-
tered.'
Oli. Cross-gartered !
Mal. 'Go to, thou art made, if thou de-
sirest to be so ; '—
Oli. Am I made ?
Mal. 'If not, let me see thee a servant
still.'   60
Oli. Why, this is very midsummer mad-
ness.

Enter Servant.

Ser. Madam, the young gentleman of the
Count Orsino's is returned : I could hardly
entreat him back : he attends your ladyship's
pleasure.
Oli. I'll come to him. [*Exit Servant.*] Good
Maria, let this fellow be looked to. Where's my
cousin Toby ? Let some of my people have a
special care of him : I would not have him
miscarry for the half of my dowry.   70
          [*Exeunt Olivia and Maria.*
Mal. O, ho ! do you come near me now ?
no worse man than Sir Toby to look to me !
This concurs directly with the letter : she sends
him on purpose, that I may appear stubborn
to him ; for she incites me to that in the letter.
'Cast thy humble slough,' says she ; 'be opposite with a kinsman, surly with servants ; let
thy tongue tang with arguments of state ; put
thyself into the trick of singularity ; ' and consequently sets down the manner how ; as, a sad
face, a reverend carriage, a slow tongue, in
the habit of some sir of note, and so forth. I
have limed her ; but it is Jove's doing, and
Jove make me thankful ! And when she went
away now, 'Let this fellow be looked to : '
fellow ! not Malvolio, nor after my degree,
but fellow. Why, every thing adheres together,
that no dram of a scruple, no scruple of a
scruple, no obstacle, no incredulous or unsafe
circumstance—What can be said ? Nothing
that can be can come between me and the full
prospect of my hopes. Well, Jove, not I, is the
doer of this, and he is to be thanked.

Re-enter Maria, *with* Sir Toby *and* Fabian.

Sir To. Which way is he, in the name of
sanctity ? If all the devils of hell be drawn in
little, and Legion himself possessed him, yet
I'll speak to him.
Fab. Here he is, here he is. How is't with
you, sir ? how is't with you, man ?
Mal. Go off ; I discard you : let me enjoy
my private : go off.   100
Mar. Lo, how hollow the fiend speaks
within him ! did not I tell you ? Sir Toby, my
lady prays you to have a care of him.
Mal. Ah, ha ! does she so ?

Sir To. Go to, go to; peace, peace; we must deal gently with him : let me alone. How do you, Malvolio ? how is't with you ? What, man ! defy the devil : consider, he's an enemy to mankind.

Mal. Do you know what you say ?   110

Mar. La you, an you speak ill of the devil, how he takes it at heart ! Pray God, he be not bewitched !

Fab. Carry his water to the wise woman.

Mar. Marry, and it shall be done to-morrow morning, if I live. My lady would not lose him for more than I'll say.

Mal. How now, mistress !

Mar. O Lord !

Sir To. Prithee, hold thy peace ; this is not the way : do you not see you move him ? let me alone with him.   122

Fab. No way but gentleness ; gently, gently : the fiend is rough, and will not be roughly used.

Sir To. Why, how now, my bawcock ! how dost thou, chuck ?

Mal. Sir !

Sir To. Ay, Biddy, come with me. What, man ! 'tis not for gravity to play at cherry-pit with Satan : hang him, foul collier !   130

Mar. Get him to say his prayers, good Sir Toby, get him to pray.

Mal. My prayers, minx !

Mar. No, I warrant you, he will not hear of godliness.

Mal. Go, hang yourselves all! you are idle shallow things : I am not of your element : you shall know more hereafter.   [*Exit.*

Sir To. Is't possible !

Fab. If this were played upon a stage now, I could condemn it as an improbable fiction.

Sir To. His very genius hath taken the infection of the device, man.

Mar. Nay, pursue him now, lest the device take air and taint.

Fab. Why, we shall make him mad indeed.

Mar. The house will be the quieter.

Sir To. Come, we'll have him in a dark room and bound. My niece is already in the belief that he's mad : we may carry it thus, for our pleasure and his penance, till our very pastime, tired out of breath, prompt us to have mercy on him : at which time we will bring the device to the bar and crown thee for a finder of madmen. But see, but see.

Enter SIR ANDREW.

Fab. More matter for a May morning.

Sir And. Here's the challenge, read it : I warrant there's vinegar and pepper in't.

Fab. Is't so saucy ?

Sir And. Ay, is't, I warrant him : do but read.   161

Sir To. Give me. [*Reads*] ' Youth, whatsoever thou art, thou art but a scurvy fellow.'

Fab. Good, and valiant.

Sir To. [*Reads*] ' Wonder not, nor admire not in thy mind, why I do call thee so, for I will show thee no reason for't.'

Fab. A good note ; that keeps you from the blow of the law.   169

Sir To. [*Reads*] ' Thou comest to the lady Olivia, and in my sight she uses thee kindly : but thou liest in thy throat ; that is not the matter I challenge thee for.'

Fab. Very brief, and to exceeding good sense—less

Sir To. [*Reads*] ' I will waylay thee going home ; where if it be thy chance to kill me,'—

Fab. Good.

Sir To. [*Reads*] ' Thou killest me like a rogue and a villain.'   180

Fab. Still you keep o' the windy side of the law : good.

Sir To. [*Reads*] ' Fare thee well ; and God have mercy upon one of our souls ! He may have mercy upon mine ; but my hope is better, and so look to thyself. Thy friend, as thou usest him, and thy sworn enemy,

ANDREW AGUECHEEK.

If this letter move him not, his legs cannot : I'll give't him.

Mar. You may have very fit occasion for't : he is now in some commerce with my lady, and will by and by depart.

Sir To. Go, Sir Andrew : scout me for him at the corner of the orchard like a bum-baily : so soon as ever thou seest him, draw ; and, as thou drawest, swear horrible ; for it comes to pass oft that a terrible oath, with a swaggering accent sharply twanged off, gives manhood more approbation than ever proof itself would have earned him. Away !   200

Sir And. Nay, let me alone for swearing.

[*Exit.*

Sir To. Now will not I deliver his letter : for the behavior of the young gentleman gives him out to be of good capacity and breeding ; his employment between his lord and my niece confirms no less : therefore this letter, being so excellently ignorant, will breed no terror in the youth : he will find it comes from a clodpole. But, sir, I will deliver his challenge by word of mouth ; set upon Aguecheek a notable report of valor ; and drive the gentleman, as I know his youth will aptly receive it, into a most hideous opinion of his rage, skill, fury and impetuosity. This will so fright them both that they will kill one another by the look, like cockatrices.

Re-enter OLIVIA, *with* VIOLA.

Fab. Here he comes with your niece : give them way till he take leave, and presently after him.

Sir To. I will meditate the while upon some horrid message for a challenge.   220

[*Exeunt Sir Toby, Fabian, and Maria.*

Oli. I have said too much unto a heart of stone

And laid mine honor too unchary out :

There's something in me that reproves my fault ;

But such a headstrong potent fault it is,

That it but mocks reproof.

Vio. With the same 'havior that your passion bears

Goes on my master's grief.

Oli. Here, wear this jewel for me, 'tis my picture ;

Refuse it not ; it hath no tongue to vex you ;

And I beseech you come again to-morrow. 230

What shall you ask of me that I'll deny,

That honor saved may upon asking give ?

Vio. Nothing but this ; your true love for my master.

Oli. How with mine honor may I give him that

Which I have given to you?
Vio.　　　　　　　I will acquit you.
Oli. Well, come again to-morrow : fare thee well :
A fiend like thee might bear my soul to hell.
　　　　　　　　　　　　　　　　　[*Exit.*

Re-enter Sir Toby *and* Fabian.

Sir To. Gentleman, God save thee.
Vio. And you, sir.　　　　　　　239
Sir To. That defence thou hast, betake thee to't : of what nature the wrongs are thou hast done him, I know not ; but thy intercepter, full of despite, bloody as the hunter, attends thee at the orchard-end : dismount thy tuck, be yare in thy preparation, for thy assailant is quick, skilful and deadly.
Vio. You mistake, sir ; I am sure no man hath any quarrel to me : my remembrance is very free and clear from any image of offence done to any man.　　　　　　　250
Sir To. You'll find it otherwise, I assure you : therefore, if you hold your life at any price, betake you to your guard ; for your opposite hath in him what youth, strength, skill and wrath can furnish man withal.
Vio. I pray you, sir, what is he ?
Sir To. He is knight, dubbed with unhatched rapier and on carpet consideration ; but he is a devil in private brawl : souls and bodies hath he divorced three ; and his incensement at this moment is so implacable, that satisfaction can be none but by pangs of death and sepulchre. Hob, nob, is his word ; give't or take't.
Vio. I will return again into the house and desire some conduct of the lady. I am no fighter. I have heard of some kind of men that put quarrels purposely on others, to taste their valor : belike this is a man of that quirk.
Sir To. Sir, no ; his indignation derives itself out of a very competent injury : therefore, get you on and give him his desire. Back you shall not to the house, unless you undertake that with me which with as much safety you might answer him : therefore, on, or strip your sword stark naked ; for meddle you must, that's certain, or forswear to wear iron about you.
Vio. This is as uncivil as strange. I beseech you, do me this courteous office, as to know of the knight what my offence to him is : it is something of my negligence, nothing of my purpose.
Sir To. I will do so. Signior Fabian, stay you by this gentleman till my return.　[*Exit.*
Vio. Pray you, sir, do you know of this matter ?
Fab. I know the knight is incensed against you, even to a mortal arbitrement ; but nothing of the circumstance more.
Vio. I beseech you, what manner of man is he ?　　　　　　　289
Fab. Nothing of that wonderful promise, to read him by his form, as you are like to find him in the proof of his valor. He is, indeed, sir, the most skilful, bloody and fatal opposite that you could possibly have found in any part of Illyria. Will you walk towards him ? I will make your peace with him if I can.
Vio. I shall be much bound to you for't : I am one that had rather go with sir priest than sir knight : I care not who knows so much of my mettle.　　　[*Exeunt.* 300

Re-enter Sir Toby, *with* Sir Andrew.

Sir To. Why, man, he's a very devil ; I have not seen such a firago. I had a pass with him, rapier, scabbard and all, and he gives me the stuck in with such a mortal motion, that it is inevitable ; and on the answer, he pays you as surely as your feet hit the ground they step on. They say he has been fencer to the Sophy.
Sir And. Pox on't, I'll not meddle with him.
Sir To. Ay, but he will not now be pacified : Fabian can scarce hold him yonder. 310
Sir And. Plague on't, an I thought he had been valiant and so cunning in fence, I'ld have seen him damned ere I'ld have challenged him. Let him let the matter slip, and I'll give him my horse, grey Capilet.
Sir To. I'll make the motion : stand here, make a good show on't : this shall end without the perdition of souls. [*Aside*] Marry, I'll ride your horse as well as I ride you.　319

Re-enter Fabian *and* Viola.

[*To Fab.*] I have his horse to take up the quarrel : I have persuaded him the youth's a devil.
Fab. He is as horribly conceited of him ; and pants and looks pale, as if a bear were at his heels.
Sir To. [*To Vio.*] There's no remedy, sir ; he will fight with you for's oath sake : marry, he hath better bethought him of his quarrel, and he finds that now scarce to be worth talking of : therefore draw, for the supportance of his vow ; he protests he will not hurt you. 330
Vio. [*Aside*] Pray God defend me ! A little thing would make me tell them how much I lack of a man.
Fab. Give ground, if you see him furious.
Sir To. Come, Sir Andrew, there's no remedy ; the gentleman will, for his honor's sake, have one bout with you ; he cannot by the duello avoid it : but he has promised me, as he is a gentleman and a soldier, he will not hurt you. Come on ; to't.　　　340
Sir And. Pray God, he keep his oath !
Vio. I do assure you, 'tis against my will.
　　　　　　　　　　　　　　　[*They draw.*

Enter Antonio.

Ant. Put up your sword. If this young gentleman
Have done offence, I take the fault on me :
If you offend him, I for him defy you.
Sir To. You, sir ! why, what are you ?
Ant. One, sir, that for his love dares yet do more
Than you have heard him brag to you he will.
Sir To. Nay, if you be an undertaker, I am for you.　　　　　　[*They draw.* 350

Enter Officers.

Fab. O good Sir Toby, hold ! here come the officers.
Sir To. I'll be with you anon.
Vio. Pray, sir, put your sword up, if you please.
Sir And. Marry, will I, sir ; and, for that I promised you, I'll be as good as my word : he will bear you easily and reins well.

First Off. This is the man ; do thy office.
Sec. Off. Antonio, I arrest thee at the suit
of Count Orsino.   361
Ant. You do mistake me, sir.
First Off. No, sir, no jot ; I know your favor well,
Though now you have no sea-cap on your head.
Take him away : he knows I know him well.
Ant. I must obey. [*To Vio.*] This comes with seeking you :
But there's no remedy ; I shall answer it.
What will you do, now my necessity
Makes me to ask you for my purse ? It grieves me
Much more for what I cannot do for you 370
Than what befalls myself. You stand amazed;
But be of comfort.
Sec. Off. Come, sir, away.
Ant. I must entreat of you some of that money.
Vio. What money, sir ?
For the fair kindness you have show'd me here,
And, part, being prompted by your present trouble,
Out of my lean and low ability
I'll lend you something : my having is not much ;
I'll make division of my present with you :
Hold, there's half my coffer.   381
Ant.   Will you deny me now ?
Is't possible that my deserts to you
Can lack persuasion ? Do not tempt my misery,
Lest that it make me so unsound a man
As to upbraid you with those kindnesses
That I have done for you.
Vio.   I know of none ;
Nor know I you by voice or any feature :
I hate ingratitude more in a man
Than lying, vainness, babbling, drunkenness,
Or any taint of vice whose strong corruption
Inhabits our frail blood.   391
Ant.   O heavens themselves !
Sec. Off. Come, sir, I pray you, go.
Ant. Let me speak a little. This youth that you see here
I snatch'd one half out of the jaws of death,
Relieved him with such sanctity of love,
And to his image, which methought did promise
Most venerable worth, did I devotion.
First Off. What's that to us ? The time goes by : away !
Ant. But O how vile an idol proves this god
Thou hast, Sebastian, done good feature shame.   400
In nature there's no blemish but the mind ;
None can be call'd deform'd but the unkind :
Virtue is beauty, but the beauteous evil
Are empty trunks o'erflourish'd by the devil.
First Off. The man grows mad : away with him ! Come, come, sir.
Ant. Lead me on.   [*Exit with Officers.*
Vio. Methinks his words do from such passion fly,
That he believes himself : so do not I.
Prove true, imagination, O, prove true, 409
That I, dear brother, be now ta'en for you !
Sir To. Come hither, knight ; come hither, Fabian : we'll whisper o'er a couplet or two of most sage saws.

Vio. He named Sebastian : I my brother know
Yet living in my glass ; even such and 30
In favor was my brother, and he went
Still in this fashion, color, ornament,
For him I imitate : O, if it prove,
Tempests are kind and salt waves fresh in love.
                              [*Exit.*
Sir To. A very dishonest paltry boy, and more a coward than a hare : his dishonesty appears in leaving his friend here in necessity and denying him ; and for his cowardship, ask Fabian.
Fab. A coward, a most devout coward, religious in it.
Sir And. 'Slid, I'll after him again and beat him.
Sir To. Do ; cuff him soundly, but never draw thy sword.
Sir And. An I do not,—   [*Exit.* 430
Fab. Come, let's see the event.
Sir To. I dare lay any money 'twill be nothing yet.   [*Exeunt.*

ACT IV.

SCENE I. *Before* OLIVIA'S *house.*

Enter SEBASTIAN *and* CLOWN.

Clo. Will you make me believe that I am not sent for you ?
Seb. Go to, go to, thou art a foolish fellow :
Let me be clear of thee.
Clo. Well held out, i' faith ! No, I do not know you ; nor I am not sent to you by my lady, to bid you come speak with her ; nor your name is not Master Cesario ; nor this is not my nose neither. Nothing that is so is so.
Seb. I prithee, vent thy folly somewhere else :   11
Thou know'st not me.
Clo. Vent my folly ! he has heard that word of some great man and now applies it to a fool. Vent my folly ! I am afraid this great lubber, the world, will prove a cockney. I prithee now, ungird thy strangeness and tell me what I shall vent to my lady : shall I vent to her that thou art coming ?
Seb. I prithee, foolish Greek, depart from me :
There's money for thee : if you tarry longer, I shall give worse payment.   21
Clo. By my troth, thou hast an open hand. These wise men that give fools money get themselves a good report—after fourteen years' purchase.

Enter SIR ANDREW, SIR TOBY, *and* FABIAN.

Sir And. Now, sir, have I met you again ? there's for you.
Seb. Why, there's for thee, and there, and there.
Are all the people mad ?
Sir To. Hold, sir, or I'll throw your dagger o'er the house.   31
Clo. This will I tell my lady straight : I would not be in some of your coats for two pence.   [*Exit.*
Sir To. Come on, sir ; hold.
Sir And. Nay, let him alone : I'll go another way to work with him ; I'll have an ac-

tion of battery against him, if there be any law in Illyria : though I struck him first, yet it's no matter for that.

Seb. Let go thy hand.   40
Sir To. Come, sir, I will not let you go. Come, my young soldier, put up your iron : you are well fleshed ; come on.
Seb. I will be free from thee. What wouldst thou now ?
If thou darest tempt me further, draw thy sword.
Sir To. What, what ? Nay, then I must have an ounce or two of this malapert blood from you.

Enter OLIVIA.

Oli. Hold, Toby; on thy life I charge thee, hold !
Sir To. Madam !   50
Oli. Will it be ever thus ? Ungracious wretch,
Fit for the mountains and the barbarous caves,
Where manners ne'er were preach'd ! out of my sight !
Be not offended, dear Cesario.
Rudesby, be gone !
  [*Exeunt Sir Toby, Sir Andrew, and Fabian.*
        I prithee, gentle friend,
Let thy fair wisdom, not thy passion, sway
In this uncivil and unjust extent
Against thy peace. Go with me to my house,
And hear thou there how many fruitless pranks
This ruffian hath botch'd up, that thou thereby
Mayst smile at this : thou shalt not choose but go :   61
Do not deny. Beshrew his soul for me,
He started one poor heart of mine in thee.
Seb. What relish is in this ? how runs the stream ?
Or I am mad, or else this is a dream :
Let fancy still my sense in Lethe steep ;
If it be thus to dream, still let me sleep !
Oli. Nay, come, I prithee ; would thou 'ldst be ruled by me !
Seb. Madam, I will.
Oli. O, say so, and so be ! [*Exeunt.*

SCENE II. OLIVIA's *house.*

Enter MARIA *and* CLOWN.

Mar. Nay, I prithee, put on this gown and this beard ; make him believe thou art Sir Topas the curate : do it quickly ; I'll call Sir Toby the whilst.   [*Exit.*
Clo. Well, I'll put it on, and I will dissemble myself in't ; and I would I were the first that ever dissembled in such a gown. I am not tall enough to become the function well, nor lean enough to be thought a good student ; but to be said an honest man and a good housekeeper goes as fairly as to say a careful man and a great scholar. The competitors enter.

Enter SIR TOBY *and* MARIA.

Sir To. Jove bless thee, master Parson.
Clo. Bonos dies, Sir Toby : for, as the old hermit of Prague, that never saw pen and ink, very wittily said to a niece of King Gorboduc, 'That that is is ; ' so I, being Master Parson, am Master Parson ; for, what is 'that' but 'that,' and 'is' but 'is' ?
Sir To. To him, Sir Topas.   20
Clo. What, ho, I say ! peace in this prison !

Sir To. The knave counterfeits well ; a good knave.
Mal. [*Within*] Who calls there ?
Clo. Sir Topas the curate, who comes to visit Malvolio the lunatic.
Mal. Sir Topas, Sir Topas, good Sir Topas, go to my lady.
Clo. Out, hyperbolical fiend ! how vexest thou this man ! talkest thou nothing but of ladies ?   30
Sir To. Well said, Master Parson.
Mal. Sir Topas, never was man thus wronged : good Sir Topas, do not think I am mad : they have laid me here in hideous darkness.
Clo. Fie, thou dishonest Satan ! I call thee by the most modest terms ; for I am one of those gentle ones that will use the devil himself with courtesy : sayest thou that house is dark ?
Mal. As hell, Sir Topas.   39
Clo. Why it hath bay windows transparent as barricadoes, and the clearstores toward the south north are as lustrous as ebony ; and yet complainest thou of obstruction ?
Mal. I am not mad, Sir Topas : I say to you, this house is dark.
Clo. Madman, thou errest : I say, there is no darkness but ignorance ; in which thou art more puzzled than the Egyptians in their fog.
Mal. I say, this house is as dark as ignorance, though ignorance were as dark as hell ; and I say, there was never man thus abused. I am no more mad than you are : make the trial of it in any constant question.
Clo. What is the opinion of Pythagoras concerning wild fowl ?
Mal. That the soul of our grandam might haply inhabit a bird.
Clo. What thinkest thou of his opinion ?
Mal. I think nobly of the soul, and no way approve his opinion.   60
Clo. Fare thee well. Remain thou still in darkness : thou shalt hold the opinion of Pythagoras ere I will allow of thy wits, and fear to kill a woodcock, lest thou dispossess the soul of thy grandam. Fare thee well.
Mal. Sir Topas, Sir Topas !
Sir To. My most exquisite Sir Topas !
Clo. Nay, I am for all waters.
Mar. Thou mightst have done this without thy beard and gown : he sees thee not.   70
Sir To. To him in thine own voice, and bring me word how thou findest him : I would we were well rid of this knavery. If he may be conveniently delivered, I would he were, for I am now so far in offence with my niece that I cannot pursue with any safety this sport to the upshot. Come by and by to my chamber.
  [*Exeunt Sir Toby and Maria.*
Clo. [*Singing*] ' Hey, Robin, jolly Robin,
        Tell me how thy lady does.'
Mal. Fool !   80
Clo. ' My lady is unkind, perdy.'
Mal. Fool !
Clo. ' Alas, why is she so ? '
Mal. Fool, I say !
Clo. ' She loves another '—Who calls, ha ?
Mal. Good fool, as ever thou wilt deserve well at my hand, help me to a candle, and pen, ink and paper : as I am a gentleman, I will live to be thankful to thee for't.
Clo. Master Malvolio ?   90
Mal. Ay, good fool.

Clo. Alas, sir, how fell you besides your five wits ?

Mal. Fool, there was never a man so notoriously abused : I am as well in my wits, fool, as thou art.

Clo. But as well ? then you are mad indeed, if you be no better in your wits than a fool.

Mal. They have here propertied me ; keep me in darkness, send ministers to me, asses, and do all they can to face me out of my wits.

Clo. Advise you what you say ; the minister is here. Malvolio, Malvolio, thy wits the heavens restore ! endeavor thyself to sleep, and leave thy vain bibble babble.

Mal. Sir Topas !

Clo. Maintain no words with him, good fellow. Who, I, sir ? not I, sir. God be wi' you, good Sir Topas. Marry, amen. I will, sir, I will.

Mal. Fool, fool, fool, I say ! 110

Clo. Alas, sir, be patient. What say you sir ? I am shent for speaking to you.

Mal. Good fool, help me to some light and some paper : I tell thee, I am as well in my wits as any man in Illyria.

Clo. Well-a-day that you were, sir !

Mal. By this hand, I am. Good fool, some ink, paper and light ; and convey what I will set down to my lady : it shall advantage thee more than ever the bearing of letter did. 120

Clo. I will help you to't. But tell me true, are you not mad indeed ? or do you but counterfeit ?

Mal. Believe me, I am not ; I tell thee true.

Clo. Nay, I'll ne'er believe a madman till I see his brains. I will fetch you light and paper and ink.

Mal. Fool, I'll requite it in the highest degree : I prithee, be gone.

Clo. [*Singing*] I am gone, sir, 130
  And anon, sir,
  I'll be with you again,
    In a trice,
    Like to the old Vice,
  Your need to sustain ;
  Who, with dagger of lath,
  In his rage and his wrath,
    Cries, ah, ha ! to the devil :
    Like a mad lad,
  Pare thy nails, dad ; 140
  Adieu, good man devil. [*Exit.*

SCENE III. *Olivia's garden.*

Enter SEBASTIAN.

Seb. This is the air ; that is the glorious sun ;
This pearl she gave me, I do feel't and see't ;
And though 'tis wonder that enwraps me thus,
Yet 'tis not madness. Where's Antonio, then ?
I could not find him at the Elephant :
Yet there he was ; and there I found this credit,
That he did range the town to seek me out.
His counsel now might do me golden service ;
For though my soul disputes well with my sense,
That this may be some error, but no madness,
Yet doth this accident and flood of fortune
So far exceed all instance, all discourse,
That I am ready to distrust mine eyes
And wrangle with my reason that persuades me
To any other trust but that I am mad
Or else the lady's mad ; yet, if 'twere so,

She could not sway her house, command her followers,
Take and give back affairs and their dispatch
With such a smooth, discreet and stable bearing 19
As I perceive she does : there's something in 't
That is deceiveable. But here the lady comes.

Enter OLIVIA *and* Priest.

Oli. Blame not this haste of mine. If you mean well,
Now go with me and with this holy man
Into the chantry by : there, before him,
And underneath that consecrated roof,
Plight me the full assurance of your faith ;
That my most jealous and too doubtful soul
May live at peace. He shall conceal it
Whiles you are willing it shall come to note,
What time we will our celebration keep 30
According to my birth. What do you say ?

Seb. I'll follow this good man, and go with you ;
And, having sworn truth, ever will be true.

Oli. Then lead the way, good father ; and heavens so shine,
That they may fairly note this act of mine !
[*Exeunt.*

ACT V.

SCENE I. *Before* OLIVIA'S *house.*

Enter CLOWN *and* FABIAN.

Fab. Now, as thou lovest me, let me see his letter.

Clo. Good Master Fabian, grant me another request.

Fab. Any thing.

Clo. Do not desire to see this letter.

Fab. This is, to give a dog, and in recompense desire my dog again.

Enter DUKE, VIOLA, CURIO, *and* Lords.

Duke. Belong you to the Lady Olivia, friends ?

Clo. Ay, sir ; we are some of her trappings.

Duke. I know thee well ; how dost thou, my good fellow ? 11

Clo. Truly, sir, the better for my foes and the worse for my friends.

Duke. Just the contrary ; the better for thy friends.

Clo. No, sir, the worse.

Duke. How can that be ?

Clo. Marry, sir, they praise me and make an ass of me ; now my foes tell me plainly I am an ass : so that by my foes, sir, I profit in the knowledge of myself, and by my friends I am abused : so that, conclusions to be as kisses, if your four negatives make your two affirmatives, why then, the worse for my friends and the better for my foes.

Duke. Why, this is excellent.

Clo. By my troth, sir, no ; though it please you to be one of my friends.

Duke. Thou shalt not be the worse for me : there's gold. 31

Clo. But that it would be double-dealing, sir, I would you could make it another.

Duke. O, you give me ill counsel.

Clo. Put your grace in your pocket, sir, for this once, and let your flesh and blood obey it.

Duke. Well, I will be so much a sinner, to be a double-dealer : there's another.

Clo. Primo, secundo, tertio, is a good play ; and the old saying is, the third pays for all ; the triplex, sir, is a good tripping measure ; or the bells of Saint Bennet, sir, may put you in mind ; one, two, three.

Duke. You can fool no more money out of me at this throw : if you will let your lady know I am here to speak with her, and bring her along with you, it may awake my bounty further.

Clo. Marry, sir, lullaby to your bounty till I come again. I go, sir ; but I would not have you to think that my desire of having is the sin of covetousness : but, as you say, sir, let your bounty take a nap, I will awake it anon.
                                                        [*Exit.*

Vio. Here comes the man, sir, that did rescue me.

Enter Antonio *and* Officers.

Duke. That face of his I do remember well ;
Yet, when I saw it last, it was besmear'd
As black as Vulcan in the smoke of war :
A bawbling vessel was he captain of,
For shallow draught and bulk unprizable ;
With which such scathful grapple did he make
With the most noble bottom of our fleet,   60
That very envy and the tongue of loss
Cried fame and honor on him. What's the matter ?

First Off. Orsino, this is that Antonio
That took the Phœnix and her fraught from Candy ;
And this is he that did the Tiger board,
When your young nephew Titus lost his leg :
Here in the streets, desperate of shame and state,
In private brabble did we apprehend him.

Vio. He did me kindness, sir, drew on my side ;
But in conclusion put strange speech upon me :
I know not what 'twas but distraction.   71

Duke. Notable pirate ! thou salt-water thief !
What foolish boldness brought thee to their mercies,
Whom thou, in terms so bloody and so dear,
Hast made thine enemies ?

Ant.   Orsino, noble sir,
Be pleased that I shake off these names you give me :
Antonio never yet was thief or pirate,
Though I confess, on base and ground enough,
Orsino's enemy. A witchcraft drew me hither :
That most ingrateful boy there by your side,
From the rude sea's enraged and foamy mouth
Did I redeem ; a wreck past hope he was :
His life I gave him and did thereto add
My love, without retention or restraint,
All his in dedication ; for his sake
Did I expose myself, pure for his love,
Into the danger of this adverse town ;
Drew to defend him when he was beset :
Where being apprehended, his false cunning,
Not meaning to partake with me in danger,   90
Taught him to face me out of his acquaintance,
And grew a twenty years removed thing

While one would wink ; denied me mine own purse,
Which I had recommended to his use
Not half an hour before.

Vio.   How can this be ?

Duke. When came he to this town ?

Ant. To-day, my lord ; and for three months before,
No interim, not a minute's vacancy,
Both day and night did we keep company.

Enter Olivia *and* Attendants.

Duke. Here comes the countess : now heaven walks on earth.   100
But for thee, fellow ; fellow, thy words are madness :
Three months this youth hath tended upon me ;
But more of that anon. Take him aside.

Oli. What would my lord, but that he may not have,
Wherein Olivia may seem serviceable ?
Cesario, you do not keep promise with me.

Vio. Madam !

Duke. Gracious Olivia,—

Oli. What do you say, Cesario ? Good my lord,—

Vio. My lord would speak ; my duty hushes me.   110

Oli. If it be aught to the old tune, my lord,
It is as fat and fulsome to mine ear
As howling after music.

Duke.   Still so cruel ?

Oli. Still so constant, lord.

Duke. What, to perverseness ? you uncivil lady,
To whose ingrate and unauspicious altars
My soul the faithfull'st offerings hath breathed out
That e'er devotion tender'd ! What shall I do ?

Oli. Even what it please my lord, that shall become him.

Duke. Why should I not, had I the heart to do it,   120
Like to the Egyptian thief at point of death,
Kill what I love ?—a savage jealousy
That sometimes savors nobly. But hear me this :
Since you to non-regardance cast my faith,
And that I partly know the instrument
That screws me from my true place in your favor,
Live you the marble-breasted tyrant still ;
But this your minion, whom I know you love,
And whom, by heaven I swear, I tender dearly,
Him will I tear out of that cruel eye,   130
Where he sits crowned in his master's spite.
Come, boy, with me ; my thoughts are ripe in mischief :
I'll sacrifice the lamb that I do love,
To spite a raven's heart within a dove.

Vio. And I, most jocund, apt and willingly,
To do you rest, a thousand deaths would die.

Oli. Where goes Cesario ?

Vio.   After him I love
More than I love these eyes, more than my life,
More, by all mores, than e'er I shall love wife.
If I do feign, you witnesses above   140
Punish my life for tainting of my love !

Oli. Ay me, detested ! how am I beguiled !

Vio. Who does beguile you ? who does do you wrong ?

Oli. Hast thou forgot thyself ? is it so
  long ?
Call forth the holy father.
Duke. Come, away !
Oli. Whither, my lord ? Cesario, husband,
  stay.
Duke. Husband !
Oli. Ay, husband : can he that deny ?
Duke. Her husband, sirrah !
Vio. No, my lord, not I.
Oli. Alas, it is the baseness of thy fear
That makes thee strangle thy propriety :   150
Fear not, Cesario ; take thy fortunes up ;
Be that thou know'st thou art, and then thou
  art
As great as that thou fear'st.

Enter Priest.

    O, welcome, father !
Father, I charge thee, by thy reverence,
Here to unfold, though lately we intended
To keep in darkness what occasion now
Reveals before 'tis ripe, what thou dost know
Hath newly pass'd between this youth and me.
Priest. A contract of eternal bond of love,
Confirm'd by mutual joinder of your hands,
Attested by the holy close of lips,   161
Strengthen'd by interchangement of your
  rings ;
And all the ceremony of this compact
Seal'd in my function, by my testimony :
Since when, my watch hath told me, toward
  my grave
I have travell'd but two hours.
Duke. O thou dissembling cub ! what wilt
  thou be
When time hath sow'd a grizzle on thy case ?
Or will not else thy craft so quickly grow, 169
That thine own trip shall be thine overthrow ?
Farewell, and take her ; but direct thy feet
Where thou and I henceforth may never meet.
Vio. My lord, I do protest—
Oli. O, do not swear !
Hold little faith, though thou hast too much
  fear.

Enter SIR ANDREW.

Sir And. For the love of God, a surgeon !
Send one presently to Sir Toby.
Oli. What's the matter ?
Sir And. He has broke my head across and
has given Sir Toby a bloody coxcomb too : for
the love of God, your help ! I had rather than
forty pound I were at home.   181
Oli. Who has done this, Sir Andrew ?
Sir And. The count's gentleman, one Ce-
sario : we took him for a coward, but he's the
very devil incardinate.
Duke. My gentleman, Cesario ?
Sir And. 'Od's lifelings, here he is ! You
broke my head for nothing ; and that that I
did, I was set on to do't by Sir Toby.
Vio. Why do you speak to me ? I never
  hurt you :   190
You drew your sword upon me without cause ;
But I bespake you fair, and hurt you not.
Sir And. If a bloody coxcomb be a hurt,
you have hurt me : I think you set nothing by
a bloody coxcomb.

Enter SIR TOBY *and* CLOWN.

Here comes Sir Toby halting ; you shall hear
more : but if he had not been in drink, he
would have tickled you othergates than he did.
Duke. How now, gentleman ! how is't with
you ?   200
Sir. To. That's all one : has hurt me, and
there's the end on't. Sot, didst see Dick surgeon, sot ?
Clo. O, he's drunk, Sir Toby, an hour
agone ; his eyes were set at eight i' the morning.
Sir To. Then he's a rogue, and a passy
measures panyn : I hate a drunken rogue.
Oli. Away with him ! Who hath made this
havoc with them ?
Sir And. I'll help you, Sir Toby, because
we'll be dressed together.   211
Sir To. Will you help ? an ass-head and a
coxcomb and a knave, a thin-faced knave, a
gull !
Oli. Get him to bed, and let his hurt be
look'd to. [*Exeunt Clown, Fabian, Sir Toby,
     and Sir Andrew.*

Enter SEBASTIAN.

Seb. I am sorry, madam, I have hurt your
  kinsman ;
But, had it been the brother of my blood,
I must have done no less with wit and safety.
You throw a strange regard upon me, and by
  that
I do perceive it hath offended you :   220
Pardon me, sweet one, even for the vows
We made each other but so late ago.
Duke. One face, one voice, one habit, and
  two persons,
A natural perspective, that is and is not !
Seb. Antonio, O my dear Antonio !
How have the hours rack'd and tortured me,
Since I have lost thee !
Ant. Sebastian are you ?
Seb. Fear'st thou that, Antonio ?
Ant. How have you made division of your-
  self ?
An apple, cleft in two, is not more twin   230
Than these two creatures. Which is Sebastian ?
Oli. Most wonderful !
Seb. Do I stand there ? I never had a
  brother ;
Nor can there be that deity in my nature,
Of here and every where. I had a sister,
Whom the blind waves and surges have de-
  vour'd.
Of charity, what kin are you to me ?
What countryman ? what name ? what parent-
  age ?
Vio. Of Messaline : Sebastian was my fa-
  ther ;
Such a Sebastian was my brother too,   240
So went he suited to his watery tomb :
If spirits can assume both form and suit
You come to fright us.
Seb. A spirit I am indeed ;
But am in that dimension grossly clad
Which from the womb I did participate.
Were you a woman, as the rest goes even,
I should my tears let fall upon your cheek,
And say ' Thrice-welcome, drowned Viola ! '
Vio. My father had a mole upon his brow.
Seb. And so had mine.
Vio. And died that day when Viola from
  her birth   250
Had number'd thirteen years.
Seb. O, that record is lively in my soul !
He finished indeed his mortal act

That day that made my sister thirteen years.
Vio. If nothing lets to make us happy both
But this my masculine usurp'd attire,
Do not embrace me till each circumstance
Of place, time, fortune, do cohere and jump
That I am Viola : which to confirm,   260
I'll bring you to a captain in this town,
Where lie my maiden weeds ; by whose gentle
    help
I was preserved to serve this noble count.
All the occurrence of my fortune since
Hath been between this lady and this lord.
    Seb. [*To Olivia*] So comes it, lady, you
     have been mistook :
But nature to her bias drew in that.
You would have been contracted to a maid ;
Nor are you therein, by my life, deceived, 269
You are betroth'd both to a maid and man.
    Duke. Be not amazed ; right noble is his
     blood.
If this be so, as yet the glass seems true,
I shall have share in this most happy wreck.
[*To Viola*] Boy, thou hast said to me a thou-
     sand times
Thou never shouldst love woman like to me.
    Vio. And all those sayings will I over-
     swear ;
And all those swearings keep as true in soul
As doth that orbed continent the fire
That severs day from night.
    Duke.   Give me thy hand ;
And let me see thee in thy woman's weeds.
    Vio. The captain that did bring me first on
     shore
Hath my maid's garments : he upon some ac-
     tion
Is now in durance, at Malvolio's suit,
A gentleman, and follower of my lady's.
    Oli. He shall enlarge him : fetch Malvolio
     hither :
And yet, alas, now I remember me,
They say, poor gentleman, he's much distract.

Re-enter CLOWN *with a letter, and* FABIAN.
A most extracting frenzy of mine own
From my remembrance clearly banish'd his.
How does he, sirrah ?   290
    Clo. Truly, madam, he holds Belzebub at
the staves's end as well as a man in his case
may do : has here writ a letter to you ; I
should have given 't you to-day morning, but
as a madman's epistles are no gospels, so it
skills not much when they are delivered.
    Oli. Open 't, and read it.
    Clo. Look then to be well edified when the
fool delivers the madman. [*Reads*] ' By the
Lord, madam,'—   300
    Oli. How now ! art thou mad ?
    Clo. No, madam, I do but read madness :
an your ladyship will have it as it ought to be,
you must allow Vox.
    Oli. Prithee, read i' thy right wits.
    Clo. So I do, madonna ; but to read his
right wits is to read thus : therefore perpend,
my princess, and give ear.
    Oli. Read it you, sirrah.   [*To Fabian.*
    Fab. [*Reads*] ' By the Lord, madam, you
wrong me, and the world shall know it :
though you have put me into darkness and
given your drunken cousin rule over me, yet
have I the benefit of my senses as well as your
ladyship. I have your own letter that induced
me to the semblance I put on ; with the which

I doubt not but to do myself much right, or
you much shame. Think of me as you please.
I leave my duty a little unthought of and speak
out of my injury.
         THE MADLY-USED MALVOLIO.'
    Oli. Did he write this ?   320
    Clo. Ay, madam.
    Duke. This savors not much of distraction.
    Oli. See him deliver'd, Fabian ; bring him
     hither.   [*Exit Fabian.*
My lord, so please you, these things further
     thought on,
To think me as well a sister as a wife,
One day shall crown the alliance on't, so
     please you,
Here at my house and at my proper cost.
    Duke. Madam, I am most apt to embrace
     your offer.
[*To Viola*] Your master quits you ; and for
     your service done him,
So much against the mettle of your sex,   330
So far beneath your soft and tender breeding,
And since you call'd me master for so long,
Here is my hand : you shall from this time be
Your master's mistress.
    Oli.   A sister ! you are she.

     Re-enter FABIAN, *with* MALVOLIO.
    Duke. Is this the madman ?
    Oli.   Ay, my lord, this same.
How now, Malvolio !
    Mal.   Madam, you have done me wrong,
Notorious wrong.
    Oli.   Have I, Malvolio ? no.
    Mal. Lady, you have. Pray you, peruse
     that letter.
You must not now deny it is your hand :   339
Write from it, if you can, in hand or phrase ;
Or say 'tis not your seal, nor your invention :
You can say none of this : well, grant it then
And tell me, in the modesty of honor,
Why you have given me such clear lights of
     favor,
Bade me come smiling and cross-garter'd to
     you,
To put on yellow stockings and to frown
Upon Sir Toby and the lighter people ;
And, acting this in an obedient hope,
Why have you suffer'd me to be imprison'd,
Kept in a dark house, visited by the priest, 350
And made the most notorious geck and gull
That e'er invention play'd on ? tell me why.
    Oli. Alas, Malvolio, this is not my writing,
Though, I confess, much like the character :
But out of question 'tis Maria's hand.
And now I do bethink me, it was she
First told me thou wast mad ; then camest in
     smiling,
And in such forms which here were presup-
     posed
Upon thee in the letter. Prithee, be content :
This practice hath most shrewdly pass'd upon
     thee ;   360
But when we know the grounds and authors
     of it,
Thou shalt be both the plaintiff and the judge
Of thine own cause.
    Fab.   Good madam, hear me speak,
And let no quarrel nor no brawl to come
Taint the condition of this present hour,
Which I have wonder'd at. In hope it shall not,
Most freely I confess, myself and Toby
Set this device against Malvolio here,

Upon some stubborn and uncourteous parts
We had conceived against him : Maria writ
The letter at Sir Toby's great importance ; 371
In recompense whereof he hath married her.
How with a sportful malice it was follow'd,
May rather pluck on laughter than revenge ;
If that the injuries be justly weigh'd
That have on both sides pass'd.

Oli. Alas, poor fool, how have they baffled
thee !

Clo. Why, ' some are born great, some
achieve greatness, and some have greatness
thrown upon them.' I was one, sir, in this interlude ; one Sir Topas, sir ; but that's all one.
' By the Lord, fool, I am not mad.' But do you
remember ? ' Madam, why laugh you at such a
barren rascal ? an you smile not, he's gagged : '
and thus the whirligig of time brings in his re-
venges.

Mal. I'll be revenged on the whole pack of
you.　　　　　　　　　　　　　　*[Exit.*

Oli. He hath been most notoriously
abused.

Duke. Pursue him, and entreat him to a
peace :
He hath not told us of the captain yet :　390
When that is known and golden time convents,
A solemn combination shall be made
Of our dear souls. Meantime, sweet sister,
We will not part from hence. Cesario, come ;

For so you shall be, while you are a man ;
But when in other habits you are seen,
Orsino's mistress and his fancy's queen.
　　　　　　[Exeunt all, except Clown.

Clo. [*Sings*]
When that I was and a little tiny boy,
　With hey, ho, the wind and the rain,
A foolish thing was but a toy,　　　400
　For the rain it raineth every day.

But when I came to man's estate,
　With hey, ho, &c.
'Gainst knaves and thieves men shut their
　gate,
　For the rain, &c.

But when I came, alas ! to wive,
　With hey, ho, &c.
By swaggering could I never thrive,
　For the rain, &c.

But when I came unto my beds,　　410
　With hey, ho, &c.
With toss-pots still had drunken heads,
　For the rain, &c.

A great while ago the world begun,
　With hey, ho, &c.
But that's all one, our play is done,
　And we'll strive to please you every day.
　　　　　　　　　　　　　　[Exit.